# EDITION 28

## THE BEST OF NEWSPAPER DESIGN™

*The 2006 Creative Competition of the Society for News Design*

**SOCIETY FOR NEWS DESIGN**

| | |
|---|---|
| Marshall Matlock | Competition Committee Director |
| Kris Kinkade | 28th Edition Coordinator |
| Shamus Walker | 28th Edition Audit & Entry Director |
| Elise Burroughs | SND Executive Director |
| Susan Santoro | SND Membership Manager |
| Ron Johnson | The Best of Newspaper Design™ Editor |

*Judging takes place at the S.I. Newhouse School of Public Communications, Syracuse University (N.Y.)*

The mission of the Society for News Design
is to enhance communication around the world
through excellence in visual journalism.

To that end, the Society will —

Promote the highest ethical standards in all of our crafts.
Champion visual journalism as an integral discipline.
Educate journalists on a continuing basis.
Celebrate excellence in all aspects of journalism.
Encourage innovation throughout our industry.
Provide a forum for critical review and discussion of issues.
Value our unique and diverse international and multicultural character.



First printed in the USA by Rockport Publishers Inc., Gloucester, Mass.



Retina and Whitney typefaces by Hoefler & Frere-Jones, exclusively available at www.typography.com.

"Smoky River, 1919" published with permission of the Birger Sandzén Memorial Gallery, Lindsborg, Kan., www.birgersandzen.org.

**SOCIETY FOR NEWS DESIGN**
1130 Ten Rod Road, D202
North Kingstown, RI 02852-4180 USA
(401) 294-5233
(401) 294-5238 fax
snd@snd.org
www.snd.org

Other distribution by Rockport Publishers, www.rockpub.com.

ISBN: 1-878107-20-8
ISBN: 1-59253-376-0

# Contents

# Through chaos, beauty

2006 was a tough year in the newspaper business. Publications shrunk to smaller formats as corporate ownership evolved and staffs downsized.

But if you need a record of newspaper innovation, energy and beauty, despite such a year, you've found it. The Best of Newspaper Design 28™ is a testament to the vitality of newspapers, as they cover the world from the vantage of their communities.

Beyond the inspiration of competition, however, you'll see thriving publications that use visual journalism to inform, entertain, observe and incite — on deadline, with the brevity and depth that only newspapers can provide.

# Del caos, la belleza

El año 2006 fue duro para la industria de los periódicos. Las diarios pasaron a tener un formato más compacto mientras cambió la propiedad corporativa y se redujeron los equipos de trabajo.

Pese a lo duro del año, se logró todo un récord en la innovación, la energía y la belleza en los periódicos. La 28ª versión de Lo Mejor del Diseño de Periódicos™ es un testamento de la vitalidad de los periódicos a medida de que cubrían el mundo a través de la posición ventajosa de sus comunidades.

Sin embargo, más allá de la inspiración de la competencia, se puede observar periódicos florecientes que se valen del periodismo visual para informar, entretener, observar e incitar, todo esto bajo la presión de la hora de cierre, con la brevedad y la profundidad que sólo los periódicos pueden entregar.

Courtesy of the Birger Sandzén Memorial Gallery, www.birgersandzen.org

**"SMOKY RIVER," 1921**

Our book cover for SND members shows the broad brush strokes of Kansas artist Birger Sandzén, 1871-1954. Stand before one of his large oil paintings, and you'll lose yourself in the details. Step backward a dozen yards, and you're mesmerized with its precision.

A native Swede who studied with Post Impressionists in Paris, Sandzén immigrated to the United States in 1894. He devoted 52 years to teaching art at Bethany College, in the central-Kansas community of Lindsborg. He contributed numerous paintings to Kansas schools and public spaces.

**"SMOKY RIVER" (RÍO HUMEANTE), 1921**

Nuestra tapa o portada muestra los gruesos pincelazos del artista Birger Sandzén (1871-1954), del estado norteamericano de Kansas. Cuando uno se queda de pie frente a una de sus grandes óleos, se pierde en los detalles. Si uno retrocede una docena de metros, se queda cautivado por su precisión.

Originario de Suecia, Sandzén estudió con los post impresionistas en París. En 1894 emigró a Estados Unidos y dedicó 52 años de su vida a la enseñanza de arte en Bethany Collage, de la localidad de Lindsborg, en el centro de Kansas. Contribuyó muchas pinturas a las escuelas y los espacios públicos de ese estado.

# Introduction

Competition committee director & judging director
**MARSHALL MATLOCK**
Syracuse University (N.Y.)

After 28 years of promoting strong newspaper design and content, we continue to be surprised at each year's Society for News Design competition.

Judges gave no Gold Medals for the previous edition. But the 28th Edition was a surprise, with judges selecting a record 1,748 winners.

Thus the Society provides one of the largest books ever produced after any international design competition. What you are holding is, without question, the largest and most complex book produced in the Society's history. It took 384 pages to tell the world's story in news design for calendar year 2006.

You are in for a visual treat.

You'll see the painstaking effort, energy and creativity of thousands of designers and other staff members who help readers understand the day's news.

Why are there so many more winners in 2006? It's impossible to say for sure, but many think 2006 was a very good year for publication design. The winners in this book go far in supporting that theory.

In February 2007, four World's Best-Designed™ newspapers from 2006 were named in the first week of judging, and eight Gold Medals were given in the second week. For a Gold Medal, all five judges on a team must agree an entry deserves the honor. These winners must embody state of the art and push the limits of creativity.

The Silver Medal, awarded to 82 entries, was granted for work that exceeds excellence. The Silvers embody technical proficiency and expand the limits of the medium. These entries shine.

The Award of Excellence, for truly exceptional work, went to a record 1,647 entries that surpassed mere technical or aesthetic competency. The award appropriately honors outstanding entries for being daring or innovative, even if they are not perfect in every respect. Judges were told to "be tough, but fair." Unless otherwise noted, all winners in the book are Awards of Excellence.

Judges gave seven Judges' Special Recognition awards. This high honor is bestowed by some or all judges for work that is outstanding in one aspect but not necessarily designated for another award. The JSR does not replace an Award of Excellence, Silver or Gold.

Judges had to make tough calls. Yet because of their efforts, we can view one book of the best publication designs in 2006.

We hope our winners inspire, motivate and revitalize your creativity to excel.

# Introducción

Luego de 28 años de promoción de un contenido y un diseño de periódico potente, seguimos sorprendiéndonos en la competencia de la Sociedad de Diseño de Noticias de cada año.

Los jueces no otorgaron medallas de oro en la versión anterior de la competencia. Pero la 28ª, en la que los jueces eligieron un récord de 1.748 ganadores, dio toda una sorpresa.

De esta forma, la SND provee uno de los libros más grandes que se haya producido tras una competencia internacional de diseño. Lo que tiene en sus manos es, sin lugar a duda, el libro más grande y complejo que se ha producido en la historia de la SND. Tomó 384 páginas para dar cuenta de la reserva mundial de diseño de noticias en el año calendario del 2006.

Tiene por delante un placer visual.

Verá el resultado del esmerado esfuerzo, la energía y la creatividad de miles de diseñadores y otros integrantes del equipo periodístico que ayudan a los lectores a entender las noticias del día.

¿Por qué hay tantos ganadores más en el 2006? Es imposible asegurarlo, pero muchos creen que el año pasado fue un buen año para el diseño de periódicos. Los ganadores de este libro van lejos para sustentar esa teoría.

En febrero de 2007, en la primera semana de evaluación de la competencia, cuatro periódicos del 2006 fueron llamados los "Mejor diseñados del mundo" ™, y ocho medallas de oro fueron entregadas en la segunda semana. Para dar una medalla de oro, los cinco jueces de un equipo deben estar de acuerdo en otorgar ese reconocimiento. Estos ganadores deben personificar el estado de las artes y llevar los límites de la creatividad aun más lejos.

La medalla de plata, entregada a 82 piezas competidoras, significa que los trabajos van más allá de la excelencia. Las de plata personifican el dominio técnico y expanden los límites del medio. Estas piezas relucen.

El "Premio a la excelencia", a trabajos realmente excepcionales, fue entregado a un récord de 1.647 piezas que superaron la aptitud sólo técnica o estética. En efecto, el premio honra las piezas sobresalientes por ser arriesgadas o innovadoras, incluso si no son perfectas en cada ámbito. Se pidió a los jueces que fueran "duros, pero justos". A no ser de que se haga la salvedad, todos los ganadores en este libro son "Premios a la excelencia".

Los jueces entregaron siete premios de "Reconocimiento especial de los jueces". Algunos o todos los jueces entregan este alto honor a trabajos que son sobresalientes en algún aspecto, pero que no necesariamente reciben otro premio. El reconocimiento (JSR en sus siglas en inglés) no reemplaza el "Premio a la excelencia" o las medallas de oro o plata.

Los jueces deben tomar decisiones difíciles. Sin embargo, debido a sus esfuerzos, tenemos un libro con los mejores diseños de periódicos del 2006.

Esperamos que nuestros ganadores inspiren, motiven y revitalicen su creatividad para sobresalir.

# How the competition works

Each year's SND competition begins with a Call for Entries, with its guidelines and deadlines for arrival at Syracuse University (N.Y.).

You've toiled to assemble your entries. Now the fun begins.

### AUDITING THE ENTRIES

Each entry is reviewed, and then thousands of individual pages are sorted into categories in preparation for the two judgings — first for the World's Best category and then for remaining categories.

### WORLD'S BEST-DESIGNED™ JUDGING

Five judges meet for four long days for this category.

The judges spend most of their time at workstations, reviewing five issues of each publication. They look at overall design, as well as writing, visual storytelling, execution, photography, headlines and use of resources.

### CATEGORY JUDGING: CUPPING ROUND

More than two dozen judges work for three days to judge thousands of entries in the remaining categories.

It begins with a cupping round for categories with too many entries to display at once. Judges make a preliminary cut by placing cups on pages they'd like to see reviewed. It takes only one cup to remain in the competition at this point.

### CHIPPING ROUND

Each of the five judges uses a color chip to cast a "yes" or "no" vote for each entry.

Judges are encouraged to vote their conscience, so this gives them a touch of anonymity.

Once a given category is judged, facilitators uncup each page. Three "yes" votes merit an Award of Excellence. More than three votes qualify the entry for medal consideration.

### MEDAL DISCUSSIONS

For entries with three or more "yes" votes, a medal is not automatic. But at the end of discussions, three "yes" votes earn it an Award of Excellence.

A show of hands determines a medal — four for Silver and a unanimous five for Gold.

### BEST OF SHOW

At the conclusion of judging, all five judging teams, plus the two conflict judges, review all Gold Medal winners. Judges can offer one or several nominations for Best of Show.

To grant Best of Show, it takes a unanimous vote of all judges with no conflicts of interest with the entry.

### PUBLISHING THE RESULTS

Results are posted as soon as possible, with as few errors as possible — first at *www.snd.org*, with additional commentary at *www.snd28.blogspot.com*. Even more analysis appears in the Update newsletter and Design Journal. Finally, this book of winners arrives for members at SND's Annual Workshop in the fall.

### SO EXACTLY WHAT'S A MEDAL WORTH, ANYWAY?

## AWARD OF EXCELLENCE

Given to truly exceptional work, this award goes beyond mere technical or aesthetic competency. To win this, an entry must be near perfect.

All winners in the book are Awards of Excellence, unless otherwise designated.

## SILVER MEDAL

These winners exceed excellence. They stretch the limits of the medium.

## GOLD MEDAL

These winners define state of the art. All five judges agree on the designation for a winner that pushes the limits of creativity.

## JUDGES' SPECIAL RECOGNITION

A team of judges or all judges may award this distinction for outstanding work in any aspect. It does not replace another award. It complements it.

## BEST OF SHOW

At the end of the competition, judges convene to review Gold and Silver medalists.

No Best of Show was awarded this year. The last award honored information graphics in The New York Times in the 23rd Edition, for 2001.

### OUR CIRCULATION CATEGORIES

Captions for our winners include their circulations, as well as their categories.

175,000+
50,000-174,999
49,999 and below

Small-newspaper winners are presented in Chapter Seven, page 303.

**JUST HOW BIG WAS THE 28TH COMPETITION?**

13,862
Entries received

7,628
Slides shot for the 28th Edition photo shoot

6,490
Certificates issued

1,907
Estimated number of images shot for this book

1,748
Awards in news design

1,647
Awards of Excellence

1,012
Awards won by publications in the United States

351
Entries for the category World's Best-Designed Newspapers™

157
Total awards won by publications in Canada

107
The highest number of awards received by one publication, the Los Angeles Times and its magazine

103
Matching total awards won by publications both in Mexico and in Spain

# Tale of the tape

**ON THE EXCELSIOR REDESIGN —**

"The issues before the redesign were horrific. The photojournalism was awful, the content was terrible, the fonts were ridiculous, and the nameplate was bit-mapped. The redesigned issues show one of the best-designed newspapers in the competition. To make that leap in the span of a redesign is mind blowing." PAGES 34-37

---

**GULF NEWS: 'SORRY WE ARE OFF TODAY' —**

"The execution of this page is technically perfect." PAGE 97

---

**ON THE L.A. TIMES' WEST MAGAZINE —**

"These pages create art using ordinary objects that appear almost animated in how they are photographed, edited and cropped. It's like a piece from the Museum of Modern Art; every photo is something to frame on a wall." PAGE 58

**ON THE SUNDAY HERALD'S 'Z' AND LOGO PAGES —**

"These pages show a great designer at work. They offer simplicity and restraint, but also power and energy." PAGE 339

**ON THE NEW TYPOGRAPHY OF POLITIKEN —**

"The publication introduces readers to its new typography by transforming the letter 'g' into a friendly face. It gives them something to relate to while giving personality to the type." PAGE 241

**ON THE NEW YORK TIMES' 1-COLUMN "PERIOD" CHART —**

"No special computer skills were needed. It's just a very clever, clean, simple, instant read. This is a brilliant graphic. Period."

PAGE 30

**ON THE ARIZONA DAILY STAR'S SILVER-WINNING PHOTO STORY —**

"We can't imagine the moment when the photographer was there. When we saw it, we hurt." PAGE 44

---

**ON THE VIRGINIAN-PILOT'S '911+5' FRONT PAGE —**

"This commemorative front page marking the fifth anniversary of 9/11 lets you feel your own emotions. It simply remembers." PAGE 81

**ON THE GUARDIAN'S ELECTION GRAPHIC —**

This graphic "builds like a beautifully layered painting. We love its openness and the colors tied to geographic locations." PAGE 285

---

**ON THE SAN FRANCISCO CHRONICLE'S 'DA VINCI CODE' DATEBOOK —**

"We've seen 'Mona Lisa' over and over again with the release of the movie 'The Da Vinci Code.' This page plays on that familiarity by creating a playful paint-by-the-numbers illustration that invites the reader to participate." PAGE 73

**ON EL UNIVERSAL'S 'CHAIN OF CONFLICT' ILLUSTRATIONS —**

"We love how bold these illustrations are. They excel with volume and texture. Each illustration implies that it's a photograph from a different angle." PAGE 347

82
Silver Medal winners

35
Countries winning awards

31
Judges

19
Judgings at the S.I. Newhouse School of Public Communications, Syracuse University (N.Y.), since the 10th Edition.

13
Years that SND has named World's Best-Designed Newspapers™

8
Gold Medal winners

8
Page ironers to prepare winning pages for photo shoot. (Yes, pages are ironed before photographing.)

7
Judges' Special Recognitions

6
Entry auditors to check and process entries as they arrive.

4
World's Best-Designed Newspapers™

0
Best of Show winners

# Judging teams' overall observations

*There were five teams of five judges reviewing everything besides the World's Best-Designed™ category. Here's what they thought of the entries they reviewed.*

**FEATURES TEAM**
Nathalie Baylaucq
Mauricio Gutiérrez
Sarah Harbershon
Stephanie Grace Lim
Pilar Ostale

**WANTED:** Features design judging team in search of the perfect page

Communication skills are a must. Needs firm concepts and a great sense of type. A flair for delivering the unexpected. Rock-hard photo usage. A good sense of humor and an ability to be serious when required. We want brains behind beauty. If this is you, then you're all we ever dreamed of. Page us!

*Equipo de reportajes*

**SE BUSCA:** Equipo de jueces de diseño de reportajes en búsqueda de la página perfecta

Las destrezas comunicativas son claves. Se requiere tener conceptos sólidos y un alto dominio tipográfico. También una facilidad para producir lo inesperado, un uso de la fotografía a toda prueba, un buen sentido del humor y una habilidad para ser serio cuando sea necesario. Se necesitan sesos detrás de la belleza. Si usted cumple con todo eso, entonces es nuestro candidato soñado. ¡Contáctese con nosotros!

**GENERALIST JUDGES**
Resolve conflicts of interest
Joe Hutchinson
Jamila Robinson

**GRAPHICS TEAM**
Charles Apple
Carrie Cockburn
Karl Gude
Vivian Kent
Léo Tavejnhansky

God is in the details.

We saw brilliant work. We saw enormous talent and effort. We saw great storytelling and fabulous attention to detail.

What we wish for is to see more of a marriage of ambition and effort — a more effective channeling of resources and storytelling into a cohesive visual narrative. All too often execution wasn't on par with intent. And ambition for ambition's sake — without adequate attention to detail of rendering and presentation — is simply an empty grab for eyeballs.

Content. Detail. Execution. Innovation. That's what the award winners were all about.

*Equipo de gráficos*

Dios está en los detalles.

Vimos trabajos excelentes. Vimos un enorme talento y un gran esfuerzo. Vimos una excelente narración y una fabulosa dedicación a los detalles.

Lo que nos gustaría ver es una mejor unión entre ambición y esfuerzo; una dedicación de recursos y una narración de relatos con más efectividad para crear una narración visual cohesiva. A menudo, el resultado no estaba a la altura del intento. Y la ambición sin razón, sin prestar una atención adecuada a los detalles de la entrega y la presentación, es simplemente algo sin sentido a la vista.

Contenido. Detalle. Ejecución. Innovación. En eso consisten los trabajos ganadores.

**SMALL NEWSPAPERS & PHOTOGRAPHY**
Tim Broekema
Ariel Freaner
Lena Lilliehorn
Harry Walker
Paul Wallen

We hoped to see entries that were innovative and cutting edge, but maintained a strong sense of content and idea development. We challenged ourselves to set a high standard. Technological developments have closed the gap, and small papers are capable of providing good design as well as the larger papers. We wanted to send a message that ideas and talent are all that separate publications. All it takes is newsroom staff and management committed to solid journalism and proper display of the content.

The amount and quality of photojournalism in the photography categories was lacking. Several major publications were not represented in any of these categories. It is important for newspapers to encourage entries in this competition as far as use of photojournalism — both in the design and photo categories. A competition that uses published pages as its judging platform is the best way to understand how the readers ultimately see and respond to a newspaper's decision and the work it does. This competition reveals the power of teamwork within a news organization.

In the small-newspaper design categories, we were disappointed in the quality of the news-page designs. But in the feature categories, the quality made a marked improvement.

In years to come, we would encourage more entries from Latin American and European papers. We viewed virtually no newspapers from the Asian and Australian markets. In the photo categories, nearly all entries submitted were from the United States. The non-mainstream categories also had a low amount of entries.

We think an organic approach to news design is better than technological tricks. Intelligent, simple design and a powerful idea all have more weight in a successful entry. We wanted to see more innovation and fun, interactive ideas. We are dealing with a changing audience, and today's newspaper design needs to reflect this direction.

Learn more about the jury
**JUDGE BIOGRAPHIES** P.370>

Esperábamos ver piezas competidoras que fueran innovadoras y de avanzada, pero que mantuvieran un potente sentido de contenido y desarrollo de concepto. Nos impusimos el desafío de aspirar a un alto estándar. Los avances tecnológicos han cerrado la brecha y hoy los diarios de baja circulación son capaces de entregar un diseño tan bueno como el de los grandes diarios. Quisimos hacer notar que lo único que diferencia los periódicos son las ideas y el talento. Lo único que importa es que la planta laboral del diario y la gerencia se dediquen al periodismo sólido y la correcta exhibición del contenido.

Faltó cantidad y calidad fotoperiodística en las categorías de fotografía de la competencia. Varios de los grandes periódicos no estuvieron representados en ninguna de estas categorías. Es importante que los periódicos alienten las piezas en esta competición en lo que respecta al uso del fotoperiodismo, tanto en las categorías de diseño como de fotografía. Una competencia que usa páginas publicadas como formato de evaluación es la mejor forma de comprender la forma en que los lectores ven y responden en realidad ante las decisiones que toman los periódicos y el trabajo que realizan. Esta competición da cuenta del poder del equipo de trabajo dentro de una organización periodística.

En las categorías de diseño de diarios pequeños, nos desilucionó la calidad del diseño de las páginas de noticias. En cambio, en las categorías de reportaje, la calidad fue notoriamente superior.

En los años venideros, nos gustaría alentar la participación de más piezas de periódicos latinoamericanos y europeos. No se presentó prácticamente ningún diario de los mercados del Asia-Pacífico. En las categorías de foto, casi todas las piezas enviadas fue de Estados Unidos. Las categorías no masivas también tuvieron un bajo número de piezas.

Creemos que un enfoque orgánico del diseño de noticias es mejor que los trucos tecnológicos. La inteligencia, el diseño simple y una idea potente pesan mucho más en una pieza exitosa. Quisimos ver más innovación, diversión e ideas interactivas. Nuestra audiencia es cambiante y el actual diseño de periódicos debe reflejar esta tendencia.

**▮ NEWS TEAM**

Eddie Álvarez
Kathy Bogan
Steve Cavendish
Jay Judge
Susan McDonough

**THE CHALLENGE**

"They" keep saying we are in "challenging times" — challenges to newspapers, challenges to our futures.

We looked at a lot of your work, and we've got a few challenges of our own for the profession.

We challenge you and your paper to find an identity. Be true to it, and do not just mimic someone else's.

We challenge you to collaborate. The greatest work we saw was the function of designers, photographers, artists and editors serving their readership.

We challenge you to be an integral part of the journalism in your newspaper. We have a responsibility to do more than just process others' work. We must be editors.

We challenge you and your newspaper to make bold choices about the future. The best entries we saw not only covered our neighborhoods, countries and world, but they evoked change.

**EL DESAFÍO**

"Ellos" nos siguen diciendo que estamos pasando por un "momento difícil"; dificultades para los periódicos, desafíos para nuestro futuro.

Revisamos mucho del trabajo que ustedes han hecho, y tenemos algunos desafíos propios que plantear a la profesión.

Te desafiamos a ti y a tu periódico a encontrar una identidad. Sé fiel a ella y no imites la de otro.

Te desafiamos a colaborar. El mejor trabajo que vimos fue resultado del desempeño de diseñadores, fotógrafos, artistas y editores que sirven a sus lectores.

Te desafiamos a ser parte integral del periodismo que hace tu periódico. Tenemos la responsabilidad de hacer más que simplemente procesar el trabajo de otros. Debemos ser editores.

Te desafiamos a ti y a tu periódico a tomar decisiones audaces respecto del futuro. Las mejores piezas que vimos no sólo cubrían los barrios, los países y el mundo en que vivimos, sino que también provocaban el cambio.

**▮ LONG-FORM TEAM**

Beth Broadwater
Anita Hagin
Peter Ong
Kim Parson
Eric White

We have to engage our readers page after page, story after story, day after day. That means presenting well-edited, informative and entertaining content in an organized way that elicits emotion.

As readers we look for —

▮ Presentation that begs you to read the story.

▮ Design that communicates the thrust of the story before readers dive into the small type.

▮ Conversational headlines that tell what the story is about.

▮ Layers of information — long narratives with big photos don't always cut it. Provide context with lists, by-the-numbers rails and graphics that explain part of the story.

▮ Graphics that make the subject easier to understand — not harder.

▮ Alternative story forms.

▮ Smartly packaged content throughout the entire section, not just the cover.

Our industry is capable of producing great journalism. Our challenge is to forge a connection between the paper and the reader that will endure with every turn of the page.

Tenemos que captar la atención de nuestros lectores página tras página, artículo tras artículo, día tras día. Eso significa presentar contenidos bien editados, informativos y entretenidos de una forma organizada que provoque emoción.

Como lectores, buscamos lo siguiente:

▮ Una presentación informativa que ruegue la lectura del artículo.

▮ Un diseño que comunique el empuje del relato antes de que los lectores se sumerjan en el texto.

▮ Títulos conversacionales que cuentan de qué se trata el relato.

▮ Niveles de información; los relatos largos con grandes fotos no siempre sirven.

▮ Entregar contexto por medio de listas, barras de cifras y gráficos que explican parte del relato.

▮ Gráficos que hacen más fácil de entender el tema, y no más difícil.

▮ Formas de relato alternativas.

▮ Un contenido empaquetado de forma inteligente en toda la sección y no solamente en la portada.

Nuestra industria es capaz de producir periodismo de excelencia. Nuestro desafío es establecer una conexión entre el diario y el lector que se sostenga con cada vuelta de página.

# What the judges saw

**The 2006 World's Best-Designed™ judges**

Pål A. Berg

Nuri J. Ducassi

Bonnie Jo Mount

Ally Palmer

351 papers, four days, four judges. One mission: to find publications that set a standard of excellence, not just by the masterful execution of their pages, but by their ability to speak with a voice. We sought innovation and surprise, more than perfection.

In recent years, our industry has been plagued with many ailments: declining readerships and revenues, a lack of resources, the continuing exodus of talent from our newsrooms and even self-inflicted wounds. This cannot be ignored.

In an imperfect world, some surrender to their circumstances, while others find the energy and the enthusiasm to make the most of the situation. This became evident through the numerous pages that we reviewed.

We saw a lot of great individual pages; the challenge was to find excellence from cover to cover. We learned that a significant percentage — even among high circulation dailies — neglected basic typography. That is a real concern.

In the end, we chose four very different newspapers that excelled above all others. We found elegance, visual virtuosity, raw energy, grit and innovation. ▮

**Comentarios generales sobre los Mejores Diseñados del Mundo™**

Un total de 351 periódicos, cuatro días, cuatro jueces y una sola misión: Encontrar los periódicos que imponen una marca de excelencia no sólo por la realización maestra de sus páginas, sino también por su habilidad para tener una voz propia. Más que perfección, buscamos innovación y sorpresa.

En años recientes, nuestra industria ha estado afectada por muchos males: lectoría e  ingresos en baja, falta de recursos, el continuo éxodo del talento de nuestras salas de noticias, e incluso heridas autoinferidas. Es algo que no podemos ignorar.

En un mundo imperfecto, algunos se rinden ante sus circunstancias mientras que otros encuentran la energía y el entusiasmo para sobrellevar esta situación de la mejor forma posible. Esto se hizo evidente a través de la gran cantidad de páginas que revisamos.

Vimos muchas páginas individuales y el desafío fue descubrir la excelencia desde la portada hasta la última pagina. Nos dimos cuenta de que un porcentaje significativo de diarios, incluso de alta circulación, cometían errores básicos de tipografía. Esto nos preocupa mucho.

Al final, escogimos cuatro periódicos muy diferentes que sobresalieron de entre todos los demás. Encontramos elegancia, virtuosismo visual, energía pura, carácter e innovación. ▮

Chapter One

# WORLD'S BEST-DESIGNED™

Lo mejor diseñado del mundo

**ÄRIPÄEV**

**EL ECONOMISTA**

**FRANKFURTER ALLGEMEINE SONNTAGSZEITUNG**

**POLITIKEN**

8 TEATER

KONTSERT 9

Marilyn Monroe elustub Ugala laval

Jazz Dee Dee Bridgewater laulab prantsuse kaunimaid armastuslaule

Sädelev džässileedi Tallinnas

Jõulujazzil kuuleb kordumatuid hääli

Advendiaja algus Suurprojektina tuleb ettekandele Bruchi piiblioratoorium

"Mooses" esmakordselt Eestis

14

PORTREE Äp2

Urve Palo

Ehitusplatsi esileedi

4 UUDIS

UUDIS 5

Teenuste liikumine jätab leigeks

Euroopa direktiiv mõeldud eelkõige vanadele liikmetele

K-kohukese kohtuotsust ei tulnud

Veel üks Weroli juht kuriteokahtluse all

ERAA piiraks kolonnis sõitmist

BONDID PÄEVAD

KRISTIINE

Nädalavahetus Äp2

17.–19. november 2006 | nr 211 (3226) | 19 kr

Reportaaž ▶16–17 Mis tegelikult juhtus presidendi Ida-Virumaa tuuril

Urve Palo ▶14–15 Tegelikult polegi ju vahet, kas müüa kingi või ehitusmaterjale.

Auto ▶27 Mida teha, kui asfaldiaauk lõhub auto

Minu raha ▶25 Pensionikindlustus on tulusaim mängumaa 50selt liitujale

Pühkepäev

Täna kinno jõudev 007: kirglikum kui kunagi varem

Aleksandr Moissejev

Narva kuberner

Ühe mehe võim. Avalikkusele tundmatu Narva linnavolinik Aleksandr Moissejev on linna mõjuvõimsaim mees. ▶10–13, 34

Vaba teenusteturu vastu kasin huvi

10

11

LUUBI ALL Äp2

Mul on kaks püstolit, need on registreeritud

Narva võimuklubi

Piirilinna salapärane kuberner

Narvas on poliitiline ja majanduslik võim koondunud ühe seltskonna kätte, kelle liidrirollis troonib Eesti laiema avalikkuse jaoks tundmatu mees – Aleksandr Moissejev.

| USD ▼ 12,14 EEK | SEK ▲ 1,72 EEK | Euribor ▼ 3,736 | ÄP indeks 1,04% ▲ 2145,03 |
|---|---|---|---|

## Veokifirmad sarjavad uut piirangut

Maanteeamet plaanib piirata raskeveokite liiklust Tallinna–Tartu–Võru–Luhamaa maanteel. Transpordifirmade hinnangul see õnnetuste arvu ei vähenda, kuid toob neile lisakulutusi. "Toimunud avariid pole veoautode süü," ütleb ASi Lajos omanik **Einar Vallbaum.** ▸6

| **Esmaspäev 13. november 2006** | nr 207 (3222) | 19 kr |

# Keskerakond trügib abiturientide pähe

Keskerakondlikud Tallinna linnajuhid eesotsas **Jüri Ratasega** ajavad mälupulgakampaaniaga abituriente propagandat kuulama ▸4–5

▸ Tallinna linnapea Jüri Ratas.

Foto: Veiko Tõkman

ÄP NUMBER

**ca 5000**

▸ Tallinna gümnaasiumide abiturienti on sunnitud kuulama keskerakondlike linnajuhtide esinemist, mida õpilased peavad valimispropagandaks.

ARVAMUS

"Ettevõtja peab loobuma tootmisest, mida kasvavate kulude korral ei saa teha kasumlikult.

**Maris Lauri**, Hansapanga analüütik

▸35

BÖRS

**2,2**

**korda kasvas Olympic Casino kolmanda kvartali kasum. Analüütikud ootavad täna aktsiahinna tõusu, ehkki ootused võivad tänaseks juba hinna sees olla.**
▸10–11

LISAKS

KINNISVARA ▸16
Möbleeritud korter meelitab ostjat.

KOOLITUS ▸27
Haigekassale saab uuest aastast andmeid saata ka ilma ID-kaardita.

TÖÖSTUS ▸31
Hoolas määrimine pikendab reduktori kasutusaega.

### Rüütli meeskonnal uue töö leidmine kerge

President Arnold Rüütli endised nõuandjad on tööjõuturul kuum kaup. Nõunikud Jüri Kaljuvee ja Ester Šank läksid Tallinna volikokku, endise avalike suhete juhi Eero Rauna sai endale Estonia teater. ▸7

### Rakvere LK omanik laieneb Rootsi

Rakvere Lihakombinaadi ja Talleggi omanik HK Ruokatalo teatas, et ostab Rootsi Swedish Meatsi. Analüütiku hinnangul maksid soomlased raskustes Rootsi firma eest liiga kõrget hinda. ▸8

### Kaks Olerexi omanikku loobus

Kütuseärimehed Toomas Vaarmann ja Martin Reinik müüsid oma osaluse pidevalt kahjumiga võitlevas tanklaketis Olerex. Soome firma GT Oil tahab ostuga siseneda kütuse jaemüügiturule. ▸9

## Tallinki juhtide poolik vabandus

Ehkki Silja Line'i juhid edastasid laevaperele, et Silja Symphonyl purjutanud Tallinki juhid tulevad isiklikult vabandust paluma, Enn Pant, Andres Hunt ja Keijo Mehtonen seda siiski ei teinud, vabandus saadeti e-posti teel. ▸3

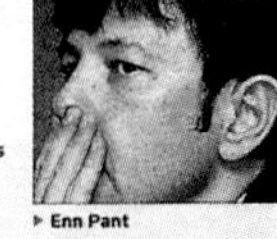

▸ Enn Pant

aripaev.ee | Milliseid ärikontakte lõid Eesti firmad Hiinas? ▸loe täna kell 12.00

# Aripäev

**TALLÍN, ESTONIA**
Circulation: 25,600
Daily

This paper is everything but business as usual. Dynamic, playful and full of energy, Äripäev feels much more open and spacious than its physical size. Typographic layering and a full range of scaling — all from one family of fonts — provides interest, movement and vitality. Double-page spreads dominate. So does a subtle palette of blues, grays and olive greens. We loved the use of "pink" space and the sense of volume and pacing throughout. This paper has rhythm. Play on.

Aripaev es todo lo opuesto a un diario común y corriente. Es dinámico, juguetón y lleno de energía. Aripaev se siente mucho más abierto y espacioso que el tamaño físico que tiene. El uso de capas y toda una gama de escalas de una sola familia tipográfica crea interés, movimiento y vitalidad. Dominan los artículos a doble página y también una sutil paleta de azules, grises y verdes oliva. Nos encantó el uso del espacio "rosado" y el sentido de volumen y compás a lo largo de las páginas. Este diario

MINU RAHA BÖRS 25

NUMBER

1,11

AKTSIAMÄNG

TOOMASE MILJON

# Kolmas sammas võimaldab edukalt makse optimeerida

Parimad võimalused pensionikindlustuses

30

ARVAMUS

| toimetuse seisukoht | kommentaarid |



50 aasta pärast, mister Bush!

# Mustkunstnik Priit Vilba trikid

NOORED

| õpingud | raha | karjäär |

TSITAAT

TENi regio-naalsessioo-nid on kõik erilised.

KUUPÄEV

23.11.

KUUPÄEV

25.11.

LOE VEEBIST

ÄP noorterubriik on üleval ka veebis. Loe ja kommenteeri. Ligipääs vaba!

Prestiižse tööga kaasnevad stress ja ületunnid

# Humoorikas äriidee: WC-värav

Kaardiga parkima

Omanäolised äriideed

Vabatahtlik töö välismaal annab parima kogemuse

Tuuli ei raiska raha tühjale-tähjale



BÖRS

PÄEVA TEGIJA

Volkswagen

+3,5%

NUMBER

61,34



# Euroopa aktsiad tõusnud taevasse

Euroopa aktsiaturud kerkivad USA tuules

361

58% 32% 31% 31% 28%

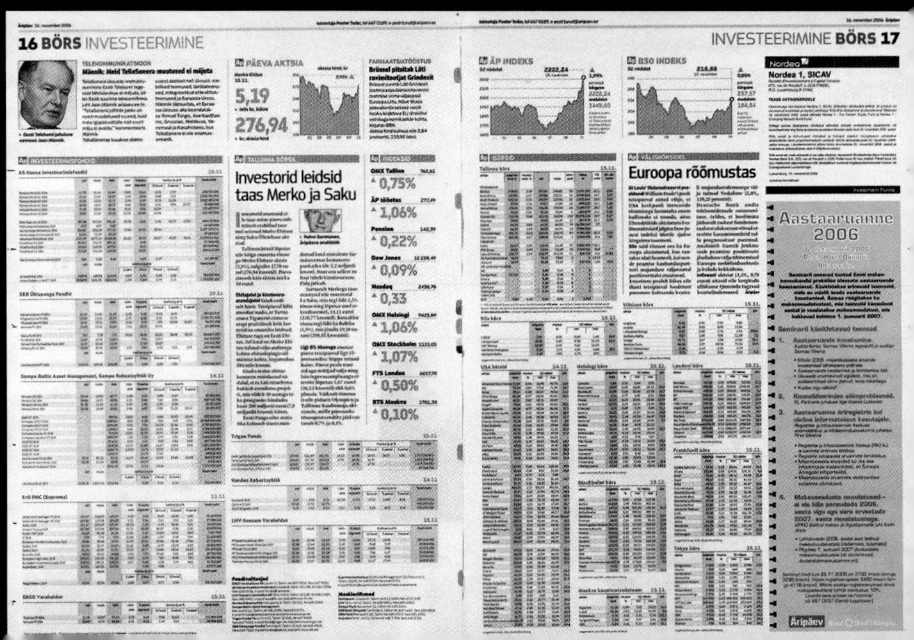

PÄEVA AKTSIA

5,19

276,94

ÄP INDEKS

B30 INDEKS



Investorid leidsid taas Merko ja Saku

0,75%

1,06%

0,22%

0,09%

0,33

1,06%

1,07%

0,50%

0,10%

Euroopa rõõmustas

Äripäev 16. november 2006 — toimetaja Meelis Mandel, tel 667 0128, e-post meelis.mandel@aripaev.ee — 16. november 2006 Äripäev

4 UUDIS — UUDIS 5

**TSITAAT**

Kuuldavasti tuli Tallinna Neste laev bensiiniga, mis aitab bensiinikriisi lahendada.

Alvo Pärn, AS Go Oil juhatuse liige ja Wostok Oili omanik

**NUMBER**

# 3000

▸ tonni bensiini 95E saabub täna-homme Leedust Eestisse. See on Eesti kütuseturu kolme päeva tarbimine. Bensiini 98E tarbitakse üle kümne korra vähem.

**TURG**

Lõõgi all 300miljonine turg

väiketanklad 300 mln kr aastas

suured ketid, 5700 mln kr aastas (Statoil, Neste, Olerex, Jetoil jt)

# Leedu põleng näitas Eesti bensiiniituru haavatavust

## Väikesed tanklad otsivad bensiini

Väinu Rozental

Sel ja eelmisel nädalal ripuatsid paljud Eesti väiketanklad välja sildi, mida pole nähtud kroonaja algusest – "bensiini pole".

## Neste Eesti juht: meil on kütust piisavalt

## Väiketankla ostis bensiini Neste tanklast

▸ Bensiinikriis Eesti moodi – Favora kütuseauto tankimas esmaspäeva õhtul Neste automaattanklas.

**TAUST**

**NUMBER**

# 15 000

▸ tonni naftat päevas suudab Mažeikiai naftatehas töödelda pärast põlengut.



Äripäev 1. detsember 2006

10

PORTREE Äp2

Hans H. Luik

# Ajakirjanikust ärimees

toimetaja Kristina Traks, tel 667 0095, e-post kristina.traks@aripaev.ee — 17. november 2006 Äripäev

15

## Maailma suurima ehitusmaterjalitootja Saint-Gobaini Eesti-poolse perenaise Urve Palo naeratus on sama päikeseline ja särav nagu tema kabineti kollane sein.

Mejl kontoris kostab sageli siit-seält naerupahvakaid. See on hea märk – kõik on korras.

Urve Palo

**Ester Eomois:** Urve ei hädalda kunagi

▸ Ester Eomois, Tamro Eesti OÜ turundus- ja müügidirektor, sõbranna

**Ingrid Tähismaa:** Tema peale võib alati loota

▸ Ingrid Tähismaa, ajakirja Kroonika peatoimetaja, sõbranna

**Hellart Kala:** Ei saagi aru, et ta ülemus on

▸ Hellart Kala, Saint-Gobain Ehitustooted Eesti AS turundusdirektor

**Meelis Loo:** Vaatasin, et kena asjalik tibi askeldab

▸ ASi Sarkop juhataja, sõber

**ELULUGU**

**Urve Palo**

▸ sündinud 10.07.1972 Tallinnas

**Haridus**

▸ 1990 Värska Keskkool
▸ 1994 Tartu Ülikooli turunduse-kaubanduse eriala
▸ 2001. aastast EBSi ärijuhtimise magistrant

**Ametid**

▸ 1995–1999 Saint Gobain Isover Eesti AS, eri ametikohad
▸ 1999–2006 Saint-Gobain Isover Eesti ASi juhataja
▸ al sept 2006 ühendfirma Saint-Gobain Eesti Ehitustooted ASi juhataja

▸ Huvid: sõbrad, reisimine, juhtimis- ja eneseareandamisalane kirjandus
▸ abielus, tütar

## Naisena meeste mängumaal: kõrged kontsad aitavad edasi

Recursos Humanos Ascensos laborales

# 'TREPAR', EL DEPORTE MÁS VIEJO EN LAS EMPRESAS SIGUE AL ALZA

Los expertos señalan que es la propia cultura de la empresa la que invita a sus trabajadores a hacerlo

Por lo general, un empleado trepador ha sido un buen profesional con anterioridad



# ISRAEL: UNA HERIDA ABIERTA HACE 2.000 AÑOS

CARLOS SALAS

Jerusalem
ISRAEL

SÁBADO Y DOMINGO, 4 Y 5 DE NOVIEMBRE DE 2006 LA REALIDAD A TRAVÉS DE LA ECONOMÍA www.eleconomista.es
elEconomista

TODOS CORTEJAN A RAM BHAVNANI
RECHAZA VENDER SU 12% EN BANKINTER

SEPA TODO SOBRE LA LEY DE OPAS

Carrefour arrasa en su estreno como operador móvil

Gana 1.200 clientes diarios a la competencia

Caja Madrid 'ayuda' a E.ON para financiar la opa a Endesa

Duro golpe a las librerías: el precio del libro de texto será libre

Sumario

Normas y Tributos

Mercados

# Espírito Santo arremete contra Garzón: el registro fue "desproporcionado"

Interior señala a Cahispa, origen de un fraude de 1.800 millones

¡¡NO SE RESISTAN!!
¡¡QUEDA INTERVENIDA SU "HUCHITA"!!

## El retraso del frío amenaza a Zara, que factura el 60% en invierno

Los beneficios pueden flaquear si las temperaturas no bajan





## Reportaje

Las grandes rutas económicas (III) Las calzadas romanas

TOÑO BENAVIDES

# Todos los caminos llevan riqueza a Roma

Nacidas como vías para movilizar con rapidez a las legiones romanas, las calzadas pronto se convirtieron en una intensa red comercial gracias a la cual el Imperio pudo florecer. **Por Andrea Casalegno**

En la época de su máxima extensión, en el siglo III después de Cristo, el Imperio controlaba todos los territorios que rodeaban el Mediterráneo y se extendía por el norte hasta el mar Báltico y la muralla levantada por Antonino Pío entre los estuarios del Clyde y del Forth, en Escocia; al este, limitaba con las estepas ucranianas y Persia. Al sur, el Sahara.

Unos centenares de soldados y de navíos de guerra defendían 4.800 kilómetros de costas y 9.000 kilómetros de fronteras terrestres, garantizando la paz y el orden a numerosas ciudades, que elegían a sus propios magistrados. Un resultado espectacular que se obtuvo con costes muy bajos, a pesar de la presión constante de las tribus *bárbaras*. Una de las claves era la rapidez con se abastecían los puestos fronterizos, que a su vez potenciaban un comercio que enriquecía las ciudades. Los negocios se desarrollaban en un foro porticado; la práctica religiosa, en majestuosos templos; las intrigas, en las termas.

Las autoridades municipales (*curatores viarum*) y por el fisco imperial mantenían en buen estado una tupida red de caminos; de 100.000 a 140.000 kilómetros, según las estimaciones. A lo largo de esas vías, nacidas por exigencias militares y construidas por las legiones, discurría un río perenne de mercancías.

**Del buen estado de las calzadas se ocupaban los 'curatores viarium' y el fisco imperial**

El flujo comercial también se efectuaba por mar. Desde que Pompeyo, en el 167 a. C., lo liberó en sólo tres meses de los piratas de la Cilicia, el Mediterráneo fue un lago romano hasta la conquista islámica en el siglo VII. Las flotas mercantes partían del Atlántico, del antiguo puerto de Gades (Cádiz), para vender sus productos y embarcar pescado y ámbar a lo largo de las costas bálticas.

Desde el mar Rojo, donde se concentraban las caravanas que se dirigían a Antioquía, Alejandría, Petra y Palmira, las naves alcanzaban los puertos de Oriente. Especias hindúes y setas chinas eran de uso común entre las clases altas, y al delta del Mekong llegaban los *aurei* de Antonio Pío. La moneda de oro imperial, apreciada incluso en China, era la de los grandes comerciantes, mientras el denario de plata –la relación entre ambas era de 10 a 1– lo utilizaban la pequeña burguesía y los legionarios.

### Barcos amarrados

De Ostia y Puteoli (Puzzuoli), principales puertos italianos, a Massilia (Marsella) se tardaba entre 4 y 10 días. Una nave ligera llegaba en dos días a Cartago (Túnez), en cinco a Tarraco (Tarragona). Pero el Mediterráneo no era siempre practicable. La navegación cesaba de noviembre a marzo e, incluso en verano, las borrascas dejaban amarradas a las naves en los puertos durante días.

### La calzada de la plata entre Roma y Cádiz

2.900 kilómetros separaban ambas ciudades, unidas por una calzada que bordeaba la costa hasta Cartagena.

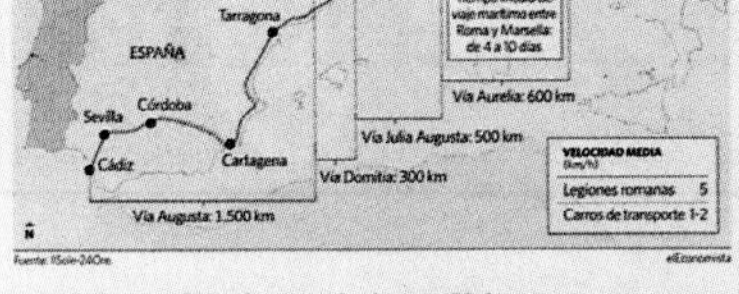
Calzada
FRANCIA
Vado Ligure
Génova
Arles
Narbona
Marsella
ITALIA
Roma
Tiempo medio de viaje marítimo entre Roma y Marsella: de 4 a 10 días
Tarragona
ESPAÑA
Vía Aurelia: 600 km
Sevilla
Córdoba
Cádiz
Cartagena
Vía Julia Augusta: 500 km
Vía Domitia: 300 km
Vía Augusta: 1.500 km
VELOCIDAD MEDIA (km/h)
Legiones romanas 5
Carros de transporte 1-2
N

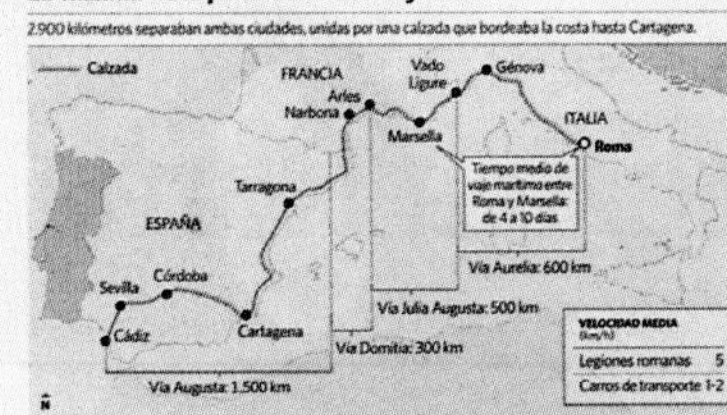

Fuente: Il Sole-24Ore. elEconomista

Las calzadas, en cambio, estaban abiertas en invierno y verano. A intervalos regulares había posadas, dotadas de rudimentarios mapas pintados en las paredes, y estaciones para el cambio de los caballos postales. Los funcionarios y los viajeros ilustres (juristas, científicos, literatos o profesores de las grandes escuelas de retórica) viajaban a cargo del Fisco. Los legionarios, con 30 kilos a la espalda, entre armas, instrumentos de trabajo y equipaje personal, recorrían 5 kilómetros por hora. Los pesados carros de transporte, sólo uno o dos.

La primera calzada, la Appia, toma el nombre del censor Appio Claudio, que en el 312 a. C. (Alejandro Magno había muerto diez años antes) la hizo trazar lo más recta posible de Roma a Capua. Empedrada en el 296, prolongada en el 281 hasta Tarento y, en el 267, hasta Brindisi, permitía controlar los territorios de la Magna Grecia, al sur de Italia, que acababan de ser sometidos. Paralelamente, se convierte en una gran vía comercial.

Iniciada en el 240 a. C., inmediatamente después de la victoria en la primera guerra púnica (264-241), la calzada Aurelia, tras cruzar el Tíber por el puente Aemilius, construido para la ocasión, seguía el trazado que todavía hoy lleva su nombre hasta la colonia romana de Cosa (Ansedonia) y las importantísimas minas de hierro del río Elba, en territorio germano. En el siglo siguiente se prolongó hasta Pisa y Luni, en la desembocadura del Magra. Augusto, el fundador del Principado (31 a. C.-14 d. C.), la continuó, con el nombre de vía Julia Augusta, hasta la colonia de Arelate (Arles), en la Galia, conectándola con la vía Domitia, que llegaba hasta los Pirineos, y con la antigua calzada que, desde finales del siglo II a. C., se había construido a lo largo de la costa mediterránea de Hispania.

**De la antigua Cádiz llegaba la plata con que se acuñaban los denarios que circulaban por el Imperio**

Rebautizada con el nombre de Augusta, esta vía llegaba al puerto de Gades, fundado por los fenicios en el 1100 antes de Cristo. El recorrido de Roma a Gades, casi 3.000 kilómetros, discurría a lo largo de la costa. Sólo a la altura de Nova Cartago (Cartagena), se adentraba en el interior, pasando por Corduba (Córdoba), Italica (la primera colonia romana en España), e Hispalis (Sevilla).

### Minas de plata

Con la segunda guerra púnica (218-202 a. C.), Roma se adueña de los territorios españoles controlados por los cartagineses, importantes sobre todo por las productivas minas de plata: con ese metal, la Urbe acuñará los denarios hasta el final del Imperio. En el siglo II a. C., los romanos someten a las poblaciones ibéricas, desde los celtas y los celtíberos hasta los fieros lusitanos de Viriato. Pero sólo Julio César alcanza el extremo occidental de Gallecia (Galicia), antes de iniciar sus campañas en la Galia.

España le dará a Roma no sólo oro, plata, cobre y productos agrícolas, sino también grandes personajes, como Columella, el máximo experto en agricultura de la antigüedad; Séneca, consejero de los emperadores y, después, víctima de Nerón; el príncipe de la Retórica Quintiliano, y dos geniales emperadores como Trajano (98-117) y Adriano (117-138), ambos nacidos en Italica.

Del 58 al 50 a. C., César conquistó las Galias, que Augusto dividió en tres provincias: Narbonense, Aquitania y Bélgica. Del 26 al 24 a. C., reside en Tarraco y la enriquece con dos espléndidos monumentos: el Arelate y el Augustus Nemausus. Sometidos los pueblos alpinos (sobre Mónaco domina todavía el Trofeo de los Alpes erigido en su nombre), Augusto restaura, por cuenta de su propio bolsillo, todo el recorrido desde Gades hasta los mercados romanos, que absorben tejidos, metales, ámbar del Báltico o el célebre *garum* de Gades, una salsa a base de pescado que estaba considerada como una ambrosía. El vino y el aceite hispano compiten a fondo con los productos itálicos. En Roma, los trozos de los millones de ánforas procedentes de Gades que se rompen en añicos se convierten en el monte Testaccio. Al final, toda la riqueza del Imperio se conduce a su capital.

© Il Sole

**El próximo sábado** las grandes rutas de la economía suben al **Transiberiano**

## Las calzadas siguen los pasos de los generales

La inauguración de una nueva vía constituía todo un honor para los mandatarios romanos, que crearon un sistema viario impecable.

### 312 a. C.

**Appia, la primera calzada**
Por decisión del censor Appio Claudio, las legiones construyen la calzada entre Roma y Capua (198 kilómetros). Empedrada en el 296 a. C. y prolongada en el 281 a. C. hasta Tarento, se convertirá desde el inicio en una gran arteria comercial.

### 240 a. C.

**La Aurelia alcanza la costa**
A lo largo de un trazado que aún hoy lleva su nombre, la calzada llega a la colonia de Cosa (Ansedonia). Luego prosigue hacia Pisa y en el 186 a. C. acaba en VadaSabatia, proxima a la actual frontera con Francia.

### 210-206 a. C.

**Escipión conquista España**
La antiquísima Gades (Cádiz), fundada por los fenicios en el 1100 a.C., es donde se reúne la plata que financia las campañas de Aníbal. En la segunda guerra púnica, la España cartaginesa es conquistada por Publio Cornelio Escipión.

### 26-24 a. C.

**Augusto indica el camina**
El fundador del Principado reside durante tres años en Tarragona y, con su inmenso patrimonio personal, hace restaurar todo el recorrido de las calzadas desde Roma hasta Cádiz.

### 98-180 a. C.

**El siglo de la seguridad**
El periodo de los Antoninos –Trajano (98-117), Adriano (117-138), Antonino Pío (138-161) y Marco Aurelio (161-180)– es el de máxima expansión y prosperidad del Imperio. Los dos primeros nacen en Italica, cerca de Córdoba.

# el Economista

**MADRID, SPAIN**

Circulation: 20,000
Daily

El Economista is a beauty. A real gem. This publication should appeal to everyone — not just business junkies. This very visual paper is well printed, well crafted, crisp and clean. Graphics and illustrations are a distinctive strength — from section fronts to inside pages. Typography is modern, with a classical feel. Color accentuates rather than dominates. There's plenty of variety within the format and a remarkable attention to detail that creates a distinctive fusion of freshness and formality.

El Economista es una belleza. Una verdadera joya. Este periódico interesaría a cualquiera, no sólo a los fanáticos de los negocios. Este diario es muy visual, fresco y limpio, y está bien realizado e impreso. Los gráficos y las ilustraciones son una fortaleza evidente, desde las tapas de sección hasta las páginas interiores. La tipografía es moderna, con un toque clásico. El color pone acentos sin imponerse. Hay una gran variedad dentro del formato y se ha puesto una atención sobresaliente a los detalles, lo que crea una fusión única de frescura y formalidad.

**MIÉRCOLES**, 8 DE NOVIEMBRE DE 2006 — UN NUEVO CONCEPTO DE PERIODISMO ECONÓMICO — www.eleconomista.es **Precio: 1€**

**SHARAPOVA S.A.: EL OTRO GOLPE DE LA RUSA**
TENISTA Y MODELO, FACTURA 18,2 MILLONES P12 Y 13

MATÍAS PRATS, EL MÁS CREÍBLE P32

AÑO I. **Nº 214** SEGUNDA EDICIÓN

OPINIÓN **P2** · EMPRESAS & FINANZAS **P5** · BOLSA & INVERSIÓN **P18** · ECONOMÍA **P26** · GESTIÓN EMPRESARIAL **P34** · TELEVISIÓN **P38** · BIENESTAR **P39**

**Sumario**

EMPRESAS & FINANZAS

**Autogrill, obligada a salir al rescate de su filial española**
Los 346 millones que desembolsó por Aldeasa llevaron a la empresa al borde de la disolución **P9**

**Expediente de Bruselas a Roma por el veto a Abertis**
La Comisión anuncia que actuará en breve contra el proteccionismo del Gobierno italiano **P11**

**Telefónica cambia sus planes en el mercado chino**
Estudia entrar en una firma de Hong Kong y sumarla a la alianza con Netcom para *Pekín 2008* **P10**

BOLSA & INVERSIÓN

**Cómo ganar dinero con Vocento en los primeros días**
El valor se estrena hoy a 15 euros, un 10,7% por debajo del precio orientativo **P21**

ECONOMÍA

**La mayor película de terror jamás contada**
El documental de Al Gore en torno al cambio climático arranca un serial sobre sus efectos **P28**

GESTIÓN EMPRESARIAL

**De recoger algas en la playa a exportar a siete países**
Japón, Alemania o Italia se las quitan de las manos a un emprendedor gallego **P37**

**Mercados**

| | | | |
|---|---|---|---|
| ▲ | **Ibex 35** | 14.058,30 | 0,64% |
| ▲ | **IGBM** | 1.529,97 | 0,54% |
| ▲ | **EuroStoxx 50** | 4.072,86 | 0,68% |
| ▲ | **Dow Jones** | 12.156,77 | 0,42% |
| ▲ | **Nasdaq 100** | 1.741,53 | 0,54% |

**Eco10** ▲ **145,62** CIERRE
STOXX **0,68%** CAMBIO DIARIO

BOLSA & INVERSIÓN **P23, 24 y 25**

# La bolsa, a velocidad de vértigo

## Sube mil puntos en sólo 24 sesiones

El Ibex está superando todas las plusmarcas. Y lo mejor es que cada vez lo hace en menos tiempo. Si, por ejemplo, tardó 106 sesiones en pasar de los 10.000 a los 11.000 puntos, apenas ha necesitado 24 para saltar de los 13.000 a los 14.000. Ayer subió un 0,64 por ciento, suficiente para cerrar en 14.058,3 puntos. Esta evolución ha propiciado que hoy tan sólo 17 valores ofrezcan un potencial alcista superior al 10 por ciento, cuando hace apenas cinco meses había más de 60 en esa situación.
BOLSA & INVERSIÓN **P18 a 20**

**El Ibex ha mejorado un...**
8,28% en apenas 24 sesiones

**Los que más han subido desde el 13.000**

| | |
|---|---|
| Metrovacesa | +23,71% |
| Acerinox | +21,49% |
| Acciona | +20,00% |
| Repsol YPF | +19,50% |
| Ferrovial | +17,07% |

# La mitad de los trenes del AVE estará en vía muerta en 2010

La red viaria no podrá acoger las 190 unidades

Problemas para Fomento. El Ministerio teme que más de la mitad de los AVE se queden aparcados en 2010. Y es que en esa fecha el parque de alta velocidad de Renfe será excesivo: 190 trenes para una red viaria de 2.200 kilómetros. Dicho de otro modo, los ferrocarriles adquiridos y los contratos en curso no se corresponden ni con las necesidades de los pasajeros ni con el desarrollo de las infraestructuras ferroviarias. El operador público tiene previsto gastarse un total de 1.146 millones de euros en nuevos pedidos entre 2005 y 2009.
EMPRESAS **P5**

Imagen del AVE.

Entrevista

## Joseph E. Stiglitz: "EEUU pide prestados 3.000 millones al día"

El Premio Nobel de Economía, en 2001, cree que, aunque los republicanos retengan la mayoría en el Congreso, eso no será un respaldo a Bush. "El presidente ha llevado a cabo unos abusos de poder que no se habían visto nunca", asegura.
ECONOMÍA **P26 y 27**

# Libros

Márketing

## Cómo crear conexiones emocionales

**SISOMO**
K. Roberts
Empresa Activa
170 páginas
22 euros

Quédese con esta palabra: pantalla. El futuro del márketing y comunicación van por esa línea

Juan Cardona

Detrás de la magia que provocan los escaparates en los consumidores o de la reproducción de imágenes en un *Ipod* hay una verdad que no deja de cumplirse: a todo el mundo le gusta mirar. ¿Será curiosidad? Es mucho más que eso. Las imágenes proyectadas tienen una enorme capacidad producir en el cerebro una conexión neuronal repleta de significados emocionales. Por eso, una imagen vale por mil palabras.

Esto no es nuevo. Hace años que se conoce la fuerza de la televisión para fabricar un mercado o derrocar a un Gobierno. Lo que es nuevo es el acceso a las imágenes desde una multitud de pantallas cada vez más variadas.

Hay miles de ejemplos. Hoy podemos ver vídeos musicales por teléfono, jugar con un portátil en la playa y admirar a estrellas del deporte en las pantallas de los estadios. Están empezando a arrasar las vallas de anuncios con vídeo (no las estáticas). La pasada semana participé en un congreso de los registradores españoles retransmitido en directo por Internet. No debe faltar mucho para que el mundo de los "contenidos" desembarque en los receptores GPS de los coches. Conozco a ejecutivos de una gran empresa que se intercambian videoclips corporativos a través de un reproductor MP3...

Y eso no es más que el principio. Quédese con esta palabra: pantalla. Es el futuro del márketing y de la comunicación, según vaticina el presidente mundial de Saatchi & Saatchi, Kevin Roberts en su último libro, *Sisomo*. El título es una mezcla de *sight* (visión), *sound* (sonido) y *motion* (movimiento) una poderosa combinación capaz de crear algunas de las conexiones emocionales más fuertes.

Además, está la cuestión instrumental. "Llegar a los consumidores de hoy es un reto similar a viajar a Marte", advierte Roberts. *Sisomo* es la nueva forma de atraer a la gente y una la oportunidad creativa fundamental para las empresas.

Roberts ya revolucionó el mundo del marketing con *Lovemarks*, un libro de éxito traducido a quince idiomas, que arrasó en todo el mundo e introdujo un nuevo concepto en la gestión de las marcas. En sus páginas, Roberts defiende que las marcas se han *desinflado* y la solución pasa por crear productos y experiencias que sean capaces de construir vínculos emocionales de larga duración con sus consumidores. *Lovemarks* contiene casos y experiencias de empresas de los cinco continentes, y ha sido traducido a quince lenguas. El libro demuestra que no son sólo los gurús de los negocios, sino una nueva clase de consumidores los que moldean la economía.

A los nuevos consumidores les gusta el sonido, la imagen y el movimiento. Y a medida que las pantallas se multiplican y aportan a *Sisomo* nuevas oportunidades, se transformarán las industrias del marketing y del entretenimiento, de la informática y de las telecomunicaciones. Pero lo importante nunca será la técnica. Roberts propugna que esta renovación digital se haga con inspiración y emoción y no sólo con tecnología.

Entre líneas

### Ahora vivimos en la edad de las pantallas

**"A la gente siempre le ha encantado mirar una pantalla. Todos hemos sentido esa atracción. Durante los primeros años de la teleivisión, antes de que tuviésemos un televisor propio, recuerdo la fascinación que se sentía por los televisores expuestos en los escaparates de las tiendas. Al igual que los demás, podía quedarme en la calle observando fijamente la magia de las imágenes en movimiento y sentir que el futuro había llegado.**

**Ahora vivimos en ese futuro. La edad de las pantallas. Pantallas para informar, entretener, cïomunicar, conectar, hacer transacciones, controlar. Pantallas para todas las necesidades y para todos los fines. Y a medida que estas pantallas se extienden por todos los rincones de nuestras vidas, se hace patente que utilizarlas con destreza y creatividad es la solución para los retos fundamentales de las comunicaciones y el marketing de nuestros tiempos".**

JORGE ARÉVALO

Recomendamos

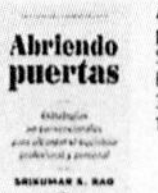

**Abriendo puertas**
Spikumar Rao
Empresa Activa
320 páginas
15,25 euros

### Cómo lograr el equilibrio personal y profesional

Este libro parte de una premisa sorprendente: todos podemos transformar el mundo en que vivimos, si estamos dispuestos a intentarlo. La realidad, tal y como la conocemos, viene determinada por una batería de hábitos arraigados en la mente. La buena noticia es que se cambiar el sentido que le damos a las cosas.

**El cuadro de mando personal**
Hubert K. Rampersad
Deusto
218 páginas
27,95 euros

### El conocimiento propio es la base del desarrollo

El cuadro de mando implica la búsqueda del conocimiento propio. El resultado es más felicidad, crecimiento personal y libertad, ya que permite a quienes lo utilizan ampliar sus horizontes, tener dominio de sí y adquirir una mayor comprensión de la responsabilidad. En el trabajo, ayuda a crear un ambiente de estimulante y de confianza.

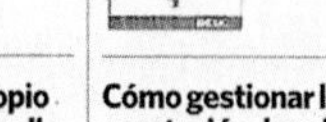

**Innovar con éxito**
J.Mª Sáinz de Vicuña
Ed. Esic
297 páginas
15 euros

### Cómo gestionar la aportación de valor

La innovación es una actitud organizacional, una capacidad que debe impregnar a las empresas en su cultura, sus empleados, su estructura y todas las interacciones internas y con el cliente y el mercado. Esta obra ofrece una visión clara, amena, rigurosa y práctica de lo que es la innovación así como del valor que aporta a la empresa.

**Equipos de alta implicación**
Varios autores
Ed. ESIC
161 páginas
12,50 euros

### Cómo montar equipos cohesionados y eficaces

Con la historia de una orquesta sinfónica, que cambia con un nuevo director, se aborda la creación de equipos de alto rendimiento, tanto desde la parte de recursos humanos, como de la formación de equipo, selección de las personas o tratamiento de los conflictos, entre otros temas, así como el enfoque al cliente de la propia organización.

**China, mil millones de consumidores**
James McGregor
Robinbook
304 páginas
23 euros

### Una biblia sobre cómo hacer negocios en China

Con 1.300 millones de habitantes, el mercado chino no tardará en superar al norteamericano y europeo juntos. Empresas de todo el mundo quieren estar presentes para comprar, vender, fabricar y crear nuevos productos. Este libro ofrece las claves para navegar por las aguas a menudo imprevisibles de las negociaciones con los chinos.

---

Séptimo arte Sus mejores días pasan a la historia

## ¿NAVIDADES DE CINE? LAS SALAS, MÁS VACÍAS CADA AÑO

Cae el número de espectadores en el mes de diciembre, uno de los más exitosos

8.000

'Pelis' para los pequeños

---



**Valor naranja** Ferrovial se convierte en el título destacado del Eco10 tras vender su división inmobiliaria P8

**Fondos** Para tener suerte en el parqué en 2007, no olvide comer uva europea P13

**Motor** Las carreras de Scalextric se llenan de público en España P17

**Viajar** Desde Extremadura a Salamanca, seguimos la ruta del jamón de Guijuelo P18

# elEspecial

2007

CARTERA DE CONSENSO

---



Inversión Cambio fiscal

## Llega la hora de afinar con la cirugía fiscal

¡Dése prisa! Le quedan menos de dos meses para ajustar la factura con Hacienda. Es más necesario que nunca porque las cosas cambian mucho en 2007. Por Bruno Pérez y Cristina Triana

Si entró en renta variable hace unos pocos meses le conviene esperar a enero para vender

### Llene la hucha de su plan de pensiones

Un tipo único

18

### Gana la bolsa, pierde el seguro

El nuevo IRPF convierte la renta variable en la opción más atractiva para los ahorradores

"A partir de 2007, los planes de pensiones y los seguros únicamente tendrán ventajas en el pago, no en el cobro"

---

LA COLUMNA INFILTRADA FERNANDO PASTOR

EN MANOS DE LA "NO REFORMA FISCAL"

## E.ON o Gas Natural: que gane el mejor, pero con juego limpio

Con salsa y picante

APUNTES

Amistad y negocios

La publicidad de E.ON

El Abbey despega

'Grandeur' francesa

SÁBADO Y DOMINGO, 30 Y 31 DE DICIEMBRE DE 2006 — LA REALIDAD A TRAVÉS DE LA ECONOMÍA

# elEconomista

elEspecial

Si quiere escoger los mejores fondos de inversión en 2007 piense en Europa

Homenaje al padre de Tintín

La mejor selección de puros para recibir el año

Sumario

"Caldera quiere quitarse a Air Madrid de encima"

Las tasadoras de viviendas no son independientes

Un investigador español, entre los mejores del mundo

elEconomista les desea Feliz Año Nuevo

LOS DESAFÍOS DE 2007

Los constructoras salen a la conquista

Las doce campanadas de la bolsa española

## BBVA, Mapfre, Inditex y Gamesa son los valores estrella para el nuevo año

Nueva cartera de consenso de 49 analistas para 'elEconomista'

La mejor cosecha del Ibex 35 desde 1998

Último 14.146,50

En el año +31,79%

## Zapatero choca con Montilla por el plazo de la financiación autonómica

No admite condiciones por el Estatut

La ley para invertir en sellos llega seis meses tarde

Los 25 negocios más ingeniosos

¿Por qué demanda a los Del Pino?

Inversión Bolsa

## ¿Viene para quedarse el 12.000?

Esta semana han vuelto los deseados 12.000 puntos al Ibex 35, en máximos anuales y a sólo un 6% de la cota histórica más alta. A la tercera puede ir la vencida. Joaquín Gómez

El principal índice de la bolsa está más barato ahora que en el 12.000 de mayo

Muchos valores en máximos

Cuando el Ibex alcanzó los 12.000 puntos en 2000 estaba un 70% más caro que en el momento actual

En dos meses, el índice de 'elEconomista' y Dow Jones sube más del 10%





Inversión Bolsa

En qué invertir en 2007 Quién entra y quién sale del índice de 'elEconomista'

# BBVA, Gamesa, Inditex y Mapfre entran en el Eco10

La revisión trimestral del Eco10, el índice de diez títulos que trata de batir al Ibex a través de la selección de valores de calidad, incluye para arrancar el año a estas cuatro nuevas compañías

El Eco10, el índice elaborado por este periódico y calculado por Stoxx, ha logrado en seis meses y medio de vida mejorar el comportamiento del Ibex 35, el índice más representativo de bolsa española, en siete puntos porcentuales. Desde el día en que vio la luz el Eco10 se anota un 36,4 por ciento, frente al 29 por ciento del principal índice español.

La clave de este mejor comportamiento se encuentra en la selección de valores de calidad. ¿Pero cómo se eligen las ideas de inversión más acertadas cada trimestre? El secreto de esta ventaja se esconde en el proceso de composición del índice. El Eco10 no se forma atendiendo sólo a una serie de requisitos técnicos estadísticos, como el Ibex 35 –volumen de negocio, liquidez y capitalización–, sino que se fundamenta en las estrategias que confeccionan 49 firmas de análisis para batir al mercado en un trimestre –ver páginas 4 y 5–. Pero como lo importante es concretar estas ideas de inversión, las empresas que conforman el Eco10 son las que logran mayor ponderación dentro de la cartera conjunta de los analistas.

## Los valores para batir al mercado

Composición del Eco10 para el comienzo del año. En negrita, las empresas que entran en el índice.

| | RENTABILIDAD 2006 (%) | ÚLTIMO PRECIO (€) | MÁXIMO DOCE MESES (€) | MÍNIMO DOCE MESES (€) | CAPITALIZACIÓN EN BOLSA (miles de euros) | PER 2007* (veces) | PAY OUT** |
|---|---|---|---|---|---|---|---|
| **BBVA** | **20,96** | **18,24** | **20,26** | **14,78** | **64.788** | **11,79** | **47,30** |
| Banco Popular | 33,30 | 13,73 | 13,83 | 9,99 | 16.688 | 13,68 | 50,36 |
| Ferrovial | 26,41 | 73,95 | 78,35 | 51,20 | 10.373 | 23,86 | 30,37 |
| **Gamesa** | **68,69** | **20,85** | **21,21** | **12,13** | **5.073** | **20,26** | **22,01** |
| Indra | 12,72 | 18,61 | 19,19 | 13,92 | 2.715 | 20,12 | 54,26 |
| **Inditex** | **48,13** | **40,81** | **42,70** | **26,55** | **25.438** | **22,02** | **52,00** |
| **Mapfre** | **22,58** | **3,42** | **3,71** | **2,76** | **4.085** | **12,30** | **30,60** |
| Repsol | 6,20 | 26,20 | 28,55 | 20,00 | 31.987 | 10,30 | 11,73 |
| Santander | 26,82 | 14,14 | 14,43 | 10,44 | 88.436 | 11,66 | 41,79 |
| Telefónica | 26,83 | 16,12 | 16,50 | 11,88 | 79.329 | 13,45 | 24,36 |

(*) Número de veces que el beneficio está contenido en el precio del título. (**) Porcentaje de los beneficios que se destinan a dividendos.

Fuente: Bloomberg. elEconomista

Hasta final de año, el indicador ha estado compuesto por Acerinox, Altadis, Banco Popular, Cintra, Ferrovial, Indra, Prisa, Repsol YPF, Santander y Telefónica. Pero tras la última revisión se caen de la lista Cintra, Altadis, Prisa y Acerinox, que serán sustituidas por BBVA, Mapfre, Gamesa e Inditex. Esta será la tercera revisión que se realiza del Eco10 y la más abultada, ya que en las dos anteriores se alternaron en las salidas Endesa y BBVA con Altadis y Prisa –ver gráfico–.

Pero que haya cambios demuestra la dinámica de este índice, cuyo objetivo es sacar a la luz ideas de inversión. Entre las que surgen hasta la próxima revisión recuperamos a BBVA. El banco vasco se cayó en septiembre del Eco10 porque había aprovechado en demasía durante el tercer trimestre de 2006 los rumores que le convertían en candidato a recibir una opa. Sin embargo, penalizado frente a Santander en el último mes por la ampliación de capital que llevó a cabo para mejorar su ratio de capital, ha entrado con fuerza dentro de la cartera para este trimestre, convirtiéndose en la quinta opción más votada. Aunque BBVA no logra tanto peso como Santander, el banco azul gana adeptos. Y es que la entidad sabe qué ritmo bursátil conviene bailar en cada momento. Si hasta hace unos meses los inversores se decantaban por las presas, hoy las firmas de inversión creen que son mucho más atractivos los bancos compradores. Una renovación de imagen que favorece a BBVA, pero veremos cómo lo interpreta un mercado que estaba dispuesto a pagar un sobreprecio por si llegaba una oferta.

### Los cambios de Mapfre

Otro valor que entra en el Eco10 es Mapfre. La aseguradora está completando una nueva estructura con la integración dentro de la antigua Corporación del negocio de automóviles entre otras actividades. La conversión de los mutualistas en accionistas de la nueva Mapfre –toda persona que tenga contratado su seguro de coche con la compañía en los tres últimos años– transformará a esta aseguradora en la empresa que más número de inversores tenga en España, por delante de los 2,24 millones de Santander; los 1,57 millones de Telefónica; o los 0,92 millones de BBVA.

Hasta ahora, Mapfre Mutualidad, que principalmente ofrece seguros de automóviles en España, estaba fuera de la bolsa y con esta operación pasa a estar dentro. De este modo, en el nuevo escenario la Fundación se queda con el 71 por ciento de las acciones en el mercado, frente al 45 por ciento actual. Pero lo que realmente valoran los expertos es que el accionista de Mapfre está comprando el negocio de automóviles a un precio muy reducido, entre 11 y 12 veces el beneficio previsto para 2006. Domingo Sugranyes, vicepresidente ejecutivo de la Corporación Mapfre, lo explicó a *elEconomista* en julio: "Si se comprase en España algo similar, que no lo hay, saldría mucho más caro porque habría que pagar una prima de control. Generali adquirió Toro a un PER (número de veces que el beneficio está recogido en la acción) de 17 veces".

También entra dentro de la cartera para el próximo trimestre el fabricante de aerogeneradores Gamesa. Ésta es una de las apuestas más arriesgadas de los 49 jefes de análisis que participan con las *Carteras de Consenso de elEconomista*. A pesar de que ha sobrepasado en cerca de un 15 por ciento su precio objetivo recogido por JCF, los expertos consideran que el componente especulativo le podría impulsar en 2007. Dos factores son claves para ello: la progresiva salida de BBVA de su accionariado, vendiendo porcentajes de su participación de Corporación IBV, en la que va a medias con Iberdrola, y el afianzamiento de ésta última en su capital hacen presagiar más movimientos dentro de Gamesa.

Precisamente, que Iberdrola vaya a comprar Scottish Power se interpreta como un primer paso de otra gran adquisición, lo que convierte a la participación de Gamesa como una futura fuente de financiación. Además, la compañía de energías renovables es una *perita en dulce* para el capital riesgo.

### Los resultados, en forma

Los factores que impulsan a los analistas a recomendar los títulos de Gamesa son bien diferentes de los que les llevan a aconsejar Inditex. La compañía textil sobrepasó su precio objetivo de consenso hace unas semanas, días antes de presentar sus resultados de los nueve primeros meses de 2006. Pero sus cuentas convencieron tanto al mercado como a los expertos, cuando el sentimiento general hacia la firma textil era de escepticismo por las dificultades atravesadas por la colección de otoño debido al calor. Ahora, su valoración ronda los 44 euros, casi un 8 por ciento más que a cierre de ayer.

### Las que salen

**Cintra**
■ Después de subir un 20 por ciento en el último trimestre, Cintra ocupa el puesto undécimo dentro de las predilecciones de los analistas.

**Altadis**
■ Las subidas que ha vivido ligadas a la oferta de Japan Tobacco sobre Gallaher han hecho que los analistas se muestren cautos con Altadis.

**Prisa**
■ La compañía de medios de comunicación cae al puesto decimocuarto de la *Cartera de Consenso*.

**Acerinox**
■ Según los analistas, la compañía siderúrgica española ha agotado su potencial de revalorización en el parqué debido a los rumores corporativos.

## Un nacimiento brillante

Cotización en base 100.

CLAVE: — Eco10 — Ibex 35

**16 DE JUNIO: NACIMIENTO**
Nace el índice de elEconomista, calculado por Stoxx. Debuta en **110,74** puntos. En el primer trimestre estaba integrado por Acerinox, Altadis, Cintra, Ferrovial, Indra, Popular, Prisa, Repsol, Santander y Telefónica.

**30 DE JUNIO: 1ª REVISIÓN TRIMESTRAL** BBVA Endesa
Endesa y BBVA se incorporan al Eco10, sustituyendo a Prisa y Altadis.

**30 DE SEPTIEMBRE: 2ª REVISIÓN TRIMESTRAL** Altadis
Las 48 firmas de análisis dejan de apoyar a Endesa y BBVA, que salen del Eco10. Las sustituyen Prisa y Altadis, que son la nueva apuesta de los expertos del mercado por su potencial de revalorización. Los cambios entraron en vigor el 2 de ocubre.

**30 DE NOVIEMBRE** ferrovial
El Eco10 se desmarca del Ibex. Esa semana Ferrovial impulsa al indicador con una subida del **9,14%**. Desde entonces, el Eco10 ha superado en rentabilidad, día a día, al índice de referencia de la bolsa española.

**7 DE DICIEMBRE: RÉCORD**
El Eco10 supera los **150** puntos, que no ha vuelto a perder, y marca un nuevo récord histórico.

Rentabilidad: **+36,42** % Cierre: **151,08** puntos

Rentabilidad: **+29,04** % Cierre: **14.146,50** puntos

30 20 10 0

Junio Julio Agosto Septiembre Octubre Noviembre Diciembre

2006

Fuente: Bloomberg y elaboración propia. elEconomista

# Acerinox ya resopla... mucha carga alcista

La empresa se despide del índice después de subir un 51,5% en los últimos tres meses

Imagínese que por una vez la vida le da la oportunidad de dar marcha atrás en el tiempo y aunque cuando vuelve en sí no se acuerda de qué es lo que había vivido, nota que tiene la capacidad de leer señales. Con ese nuevo talento seguro que no se le hubiera pasado que Acerinox tenía muchas cartas para convertirse en el valor revelación del trimestre.

Los títulos de la acerera han ganado entre octubre, noviembre y diciembre un 51,5 por ciento. Han sido las mejores del índice Eco10 y del Ibex 35. Pero es que, además, su subida ha sido paulatina, continuada, con lo que ha dado muchas oportunidades a los inversores para subirse al carro. La suya ha sido una trayectoria clave para que el índice de *elEconomista* en sus primeros seis meses de vida –nació el 16 de junio– haya conseguido sacar siete puntos porcentuales de rentabilidad al Ibex 35.

El índice ya no contará ahora con su ayuda, puesto que los analistas piensan que casi todo lo bueno que se puede obtener con ella se ha acabado. Aunque pertenece a un sector envuelto en movimientos corporativos, sus principales accionistas siguen comprando acciones y hacen imposible una opa hostil. El consenso de analistas que elabora JCF establece que el precio justo de Acerinox son 20,50 euros y ya cotiza casi tres euros por encima. Una evolución que provoca que muchas de las firmas de inversión que creían que podía batir al mercado, ahora consideren que ha perdido esa capacidad.

### La cifra

**87,55**

**POR CIENTO.** Es lo que han ganado este ejercicio las acciones de Acerinox, que se han colado en el grupo de las tres más alcistas del índice. Sólo la han superado dos compañías del sector del ladrillo, Metrovacesa y Sacyr-Vallehermoso, cuyas acciones han más que doblado su precio en bolsa en 2006. La primera –el mejor valor del índice– ha ganado un 150%.

### De la noticia al rumor...

... y otra vez a la noticia. De esta forma se podría resumir la trayectoria envolvente que ha llevado a Acerinox a vivir un ejercicio bursátil tan extraordinario. Empezando por el final, el último empujón a su cotización vino de la mano de la Familia Del Pino. Los propietarios de Ferrovial decidieron comprarse un cinco por ciento de la compañía hace pocas sesiones, una iniciativa que le dio un empujón final en el mercado.

Movimientos corporativos y cambios de capital que ya comenzaron hace bastante meses. La Familia March –principal accionista de Acerinox a través de Corporacion Financiera Alba– se dedicó durante meses a adquirir acciones de la compañía. Según consta en los registros de la CNMV (Comisión Nacional del Mercado de Valores), en este momento controla más de un 20 por ciento.

Antes, habían sido las buenas expectativas para su negocio –se esperaban subidas de los precios del acero inoxidable–, pero, sobre todo, el proceso de concentración en el sector del acero.

Tras la opa (oferta pública de adquisición) de Mittal Steel sobre Arcelor, dos acereras afincadas en países emergentes, la india Tata Steel y la brasileña CSN, se pelearon por el control de la británica Corus. En esas están. Las dos pueden mejorar hasta el 30 de enero las ofertas que ya han puesto sobre la mesa. Acerinox se ha beneficiado de este contexto.

Frankfurter Allgemeine
SONNTAGSZEITUNG
SONNTAG, 3. SEPTEMBER 2006 · SEITE B1

# Was der Welt den Atem nahm

Fünf Jahre danach: Die Erschütterungen des 11. September 2001 sind noch immer spürbar

Es ist die Art von Ereignis, bei der man einander viele Jahre später fragt: Wo warst du? Wo hast du gesehen, wie die Türme fielen? Ein Blick auf Überlebende und Täter, Rätsel und Theorien, Kriege und Kosten – und darauf, wie wir umgehen mit der Angst, die uns begleitet seit „9/11".

2. JULI 2006, NR. 26 · FRANKFURTER ALLGEMEINE SONNTAGSZEITUNG · SEITE 47

# Geld & Mehr

## Die Konzerne gieren nach Größe

Die Unternehmen sind in einem beispiellosen Übernahmerausch. Auch Deutschland mischt mit. Denn die Gewinne sprudeln. Die Anleger verdienen kräftig.

VON CATHERINE HOFFMANN

MÖGLICHE ÜBERNAHMEKANDIDATEN

MAN · Stada · TUI

TOPS & FLOPS

Daimler-Chrysler

Exxon Mobil

Vossloh

Klöco

### Keine Praxisgebühr mehr

Neun Prozent der Krankenversicherten sind befreit

WAS DEN MARKT BEWEGT

*Zinserhöhungen*

TEURES PLASTIK
Kreditkarten mit extra Versicherung sind überflüssig, *Seite 51*

TEURES PFLASTER
Der Finanzplatz London zieht mehr und mehr Investoren an, *Seite 49*

TEURES PAPIER
Comics können viele tausend Dollar kosten, *Seite 53*

Frankfurter Allgemeine
SONNTAGSZEITUNG
2,50 Euro · 2.7.2006

Jens Lehmann
Zupacken für Deutschland
SPORT, S. 15

Comics
Superman macht reich
GELD & MEHR, S. 53

Im Doping-Sumpf
Die Tour de Farce
SPORT, S. 21 · 22

Josef Ackermann
Weiter auf Einkaufskurs
WIRTSCHAFT, S. 35

# Gesundheit ohne Steuererhöhung

Merkel legt sich vor heutigem Koalitionsgespräch fest

MIT RHEIN-MAIN-SEITEN

## Frankreich entzaubert Brasilien

**Aus für den Weltmeister:** *Brasilien ist die Fußball-WM in Deutschland beendet. Der große Favorit unterlag am Samstag ...*

## „Köhler im Regen"

Westerwelle: Kanzlerin muß Präsidenten verteidigen

## Totengedenken

Das ist doch das Schöne an den Toten:
Da ist so gut wie alles erlaubt und nichts verboten.

Du kannst sie verhöhnen, du kannst sie beleidigen –
Sie werden sich nicht dagegen verteidigen.

Du kannst sie belästigen, du kannst sie verlassen –
Sie werden dich nicht dafür hassen.

Du kannst ihnen vorwerfen, sie übertrieben –
Sie werden dich deshalb nicht weniger lieben.

Du kannst sie foltern, du kannst sie quälen –
Sie werden es niemandem weitererzählen.

Du kannst sie verehren, du kannst sie verlachen –
Sie werden deshalb kein Aufhebens machen.

Du kannst sie salben, du kannst sie bespeien –
Sie werden dir weiterhin alles verzeihen.

Du kannst sie nach Strich und Faden betrügen –
Sie werden sich jeder Missetat fügen.

Du kannst sie erinnern, du kannst sie vergessen –
Sie werden an anderen Ellen gemessen.

Du kannst sie vergessen, du kannst sie erinnern –
Bei diesen Gewinnern bleibst du der Verlierer.

**Robert Gernhardt** ist vor zwei Tagen gestorben. Bis kurz vor seinem Tod hat er noch geschrieben. Dieses Gedicht war eines seiner letzten.

## Gefechte in Gaza

Israel lehnt Bedingungen für Geiselfreigabe ab

## „Discovery" noch am Boden

## Mehr als 60 Tote

Anschlag in Bagdad nach Botschaft Bin Ladins

## Ging Staatsräson vor?

Fall al Masri: FDP kritisiert Bundesregierung

Lizenz zum Panschen
EU-Reformvorschläge verunsichern Winzer. *Gesellschaft, Seite 62*

Mission erfüllt
Wie die Zentrale Intelligenz Agentur den Literaturbetrieb unterwandert. *Feuilleton, Seite 23*

Kurze Hosen, ganze Kerle
Was die Mailänder Modedesigner für den Sommer 2007 vorschlagen. *Gesellschaft, Seite 63*

CHRONIK

# Kriege und Allianzen

Was hat der 11. September geopolitisch verändert? Fünf zentrale Antworten. *Von Klaus-Dieter Frankenberger*

## „Fühlen, was jetzt sein muß"

Gerhard Schröders Reise nach New York an der Zeitenwende. *Von Eckart Lohse*

# Frankfurter Allgemeine

## SONNTAGSZEITUNG

NR. 35 R — HERAUSGEGEBEN VON WERNER D'INKA, BERTHOLD KOHLER, GÜNTHER NONNENMACHER, FRANK SCHIRRMACHER, HOLGER STELTZNER — 2,60 Euro D3499C — 3.9.2006

### Der Tag, der nicht vergeht

Beilage: Fünf Jahre nach „9/11"

**Überlebende** Traurige, Prediger und Trotzige
**Täter** Martin Amis über Muhammad Atta
**Hintermänner** Das Rätsel Usama Bin Ladin
**Konsequenzen** Kriege und neue Allianzen
**Strategien** Wie wir mit der Angst leben

Acht herausnehmbare Sonderseiten im Politik-Teil

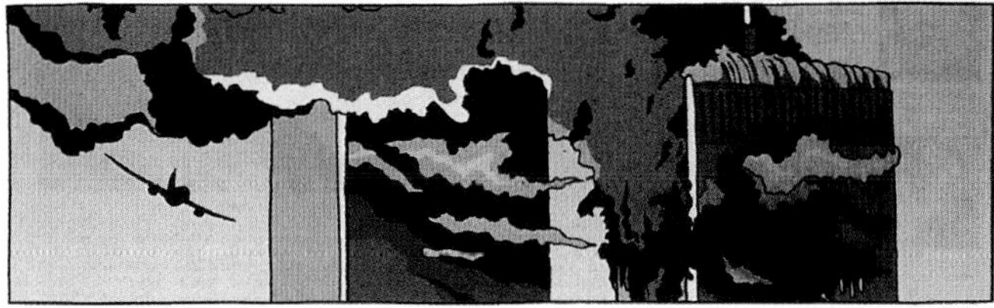

## Krach ums Fleisch

Seehofer-Ministerium wirft Bayern Versagen im Gammel-Skandal vor

## Kündigungsschutz wird bleiben

Union und SPD wollen ihre Koalitionsvereinbarung nicht umsetzen

### Deutsche Elf siegt 1:0

### Rasterfahndung ist nicht geplant

„Kofferbomber" reagierten auf Karikaturenstreit

### SPD kritisiert Minister Jung

**Geduld:** *Kofi Annan und Irans Außenminister Mottaki am Samstag*

### Annan will Iran überzeugen

EU setzt im Atomstreit weiter auf Verhandlungen

Barbies neue Welt

### Hartz IV für Ken

MIT RHEIN-MAIN-SEITEN

„Unterrichtsgarantie plus": Nagelprobe für Hessens Landesregierung

*10 Seiten Berichte aus der Region*

**Das Ende der Nacht**
Charlotte Gainsbourgs neues Album „5.55" ist eine kleine Ode an die Schlaflosigkeit. *Feuilleton, Seite 21*

**Die ersten Flatrates**
Telefon, Internet und Handy – endlich gibt es einen Tarif für alles zusammen. *Geld & Mehr, Seite 41*

**Der nächste Kaiser**
Japan hofft auf Prinzessin Kiko: Wird endlich ein Thronfolger geboren? *Gesellschaft, Seite 60*

WORLD'S BEST-DESIGNED™

# Frankfurter Allgemeine Sonntagszeitung

**FRANKFURT, GERMANY**
Circulation: 315,000
Weekly

From classically formed fonts to page-dominating visuals, Frankfurter Allgemeine exudes beauty, overwhelming beauty. This is a masterfully designed, visually intelligent publication. Turning the pages of this paper — with its great expanses of white — is like walking through a gallery that's filled with sophisticated photography, sensuous illustrations, and damn-near-perfect typography.

There are surprises and special treats, too, like graphic novel treatments and illustrations on the TV page.

Clearly aimed for an educated audience, this paper is filled with nuance. It doesn't shout — it illuminates.

Desde las tipografías de origen clásico hasta los elementos visuales dominantes de la página, el Frankfurter Allgemeine derrocha belleza, una belleza sobrecogedora. Este periódico está diseñado con maestría e inteligencia visual. Hojear este diario, con sus amplios blancos,

32 FERNSEHEN

FRANKFURTER ALLGEMEINE SONNTAGSZEITUNG, 2. JULI 2006, NR. 26

TELESPIELE

## Emotionen

ARD | ZDF | RTL | Sat.1 | Pro Sieben | Vox | 3sat

Arte | Ki.Ka | Kabel 1 | RTL 2 | Tele 5 | Super RTL | RBB | NDR | WDR | MDR | SWR | HR | BR | Phoenix | XXP | n-tv | N 24 | DSF | Eurosport

**Kids, Vox 22 Uhr** *Es gibt Leute, die den Fotografen und Regisseur Larry Clark für einen schmutzigen alten Mann halten, und wenn man ihm zusieht, wie er in diesem Film von 1995, in dem Sex und Drogen und Parties und Aids eine große Rolle spielen, den New Yorker Mittelschulschick zusieht, kann man sich seine Voreingenommenheiten bestätigen lassen – man kann aber auch das Drama darin finden und die Empathie, die sich in dieser Welt ohne Mitleid verbergen.*

TELEDIALOG

## Euphorismus

Wirtschaft

## Es kann nur aufwärtsgehen

Feuilleton

## Der Herbst kann kommen

POLITIK 3

## Sohn

## Gehorsam verweigert

Fielmann: Topmodische Brille für € 10,–. Gläser von Zeiss. Drei Jahre Garantie.

64 WISSENSCHAFT

# ZEIT, TOD UND SCHMUTZIGES GESCHIRR

## Tödliche Ordnung, produktiver Zerfall

Entropie und Information

Entropie und das Universum

8 POLITIK

## Wie war Ihr Jahr?

Alarm im Hühnerstall: Bodenhaltung bedeutet noch lange nicht, daß das Geflügel auch artgerecht lebt.

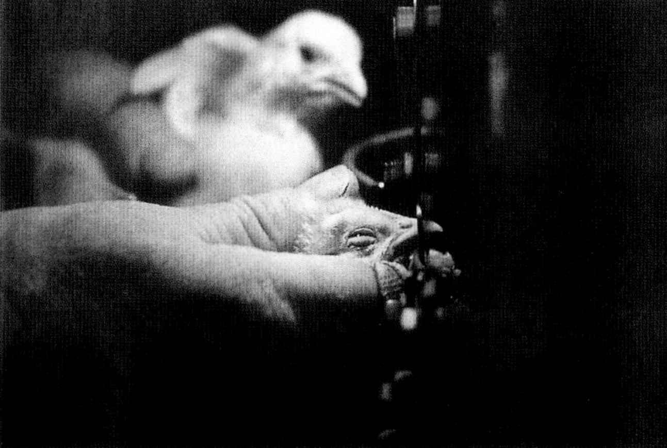

Immer noch gängige Praxis: Das schmerzhafte Stutzen der Schnäbel ist nach dem Tierschutzgesetz eigentlich verboten. Wenn die Tiere allerdings aufeinander losgehen, wird es in der Regel doch gestattet.

# Da kreischen selbst die Hühner

Seuchenzüge unter Nutztieren kommen nicht aus dem Nichts. Sie sind eine zwangsläufige Folge der modernen Massenhaltung.

VON JÖRG ALBRECHT, FOTOS JAN VAN IJKEN

Wer in diesen Tagen, von Bad Vilbel kommend, die Büdinger Straße Richtung Gronau fährt, dem bietet sich ein Bild mit Seltenheitswert. Linkerhand auf dem Dottenfelder Hof picken trotz der winterlichen Kälte an die siebenhundert Hühner im Freien, bewacht von einem guten Dutzend stolzer Hähne. Dem Federvieh geht es bestens: Will es zurück in den mobilen Stall, findet es dort ausreichend Stroh und Dinkelspelzen. Täglich bekommt jedes Tier hundert Gramm Weizen und Legeschrot. Dazu gibt es Muschelschrot, Quarkmolke, Küchenabfälle, im Winter auch gekochte Möhren, Kohl sowie Runkelrüben. Man könnte sagen: Der Dottenfelder Hof – ein anthroposophischer Vorzeigebetrieb – kommt dem Hühnerparadies recht nahe.

Leben Hühner unter Streß, fallen sie regelrecht übereinander her und picken sich gegenseitig blutig

Kontrolle ist besser: Defekte Küken werden per Hand aussortiert.

Serienimpfung: Puten sind vor alle Hühnervögel anfällig für jede Art von Erregern.

Achtzehn Monate: So lange währt das Leben einer Henne, dann ist sie reif für den Kochtopf.

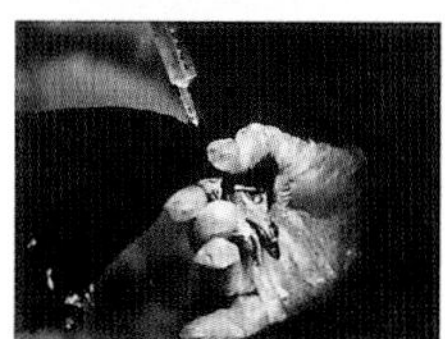

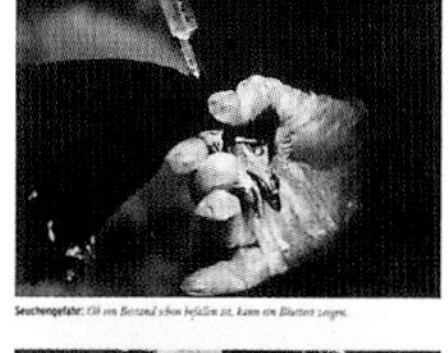

Alternative: Puten wird die Schnabelspitze versengt. Sie fällt dann später ab.

## Was ist mit meinem Kanarienvogel?

Zehn Fragen und Antworten zum besseren Verständnis der Vogelgrippe

Georg Rüschemeyer





Frankfurter Allgemeine SONNTAGSZEITUNG

Politik

Sport

Feuilleton

Wirtschaft

Geld & Mehr

Gesellschaft

Wissenschaft

Rhein-Main

Reise

Motor/Immobilien

## Rußland, der schwache Riese

Verwandte Seelen: Deutsche und Russen fühlen sich seit je voneinander angezogen und bedroht

Rußlands Revolution hat die Deutschen fasziniert – und sie mit der Angst vor dem Osten infiziert.

## Angela Merkels



Gestern kam die Bundeskanzlerin aus Washington zurück – morgen fliegt sie nach Moskau. Diese Choreographie des Reisens mag gut durchdacht sein. Deutschland soll unter Angela Merkel das Verhältnis zu Amerika wie zu Rußland verändern: mehr Nähe zum einen, mehr Distanz zum anderen Staat. Und gegenüber beiden: viel mehr Nüchternheit.

## Amerika, der rätselhafte Riese

Sie wecken unser Mißtrauen: Dollarjäger und Kirchgänger, die auch noch fest daran glauben, eine Mission in dieser Welt zu haben

Merkel hier, Bush da: Europa und Amerika wurden nur zufällig zu einer Einheit

## winziges Stolpern im East Room

## Ein Glücksspiel für Anleger mit starken Nerven

Lotto und Sportwetten finden immer mehr Anhänger. Das müßte den Aktien der Glücksspielbranche gut tun – würde der Staat nicht ständig eingreifen. Ein Risiko für Anleger.

Tipp 24

Bwin

William Hill

Fluxx

## Jagd auf harmlose Spieler

POLITIKEN Fredag

Tæskehold skal vogte sygehuse



Søndagsåbent 10. december 10-17

Fyr billigt med OK

POLITIKEN Onsdag

24/7/365

Los Estados Unidos de América

Far er død og har efterladt sig en suttekultur

Berlin 199,-

POLITIKEN | KULTUR | NAVNE | SPORT
Søndag 5. november 2006 www.politiken.dk
2



# Havet forvandlede drenge til mænd og kvinder til enker

Kommentatoren, essayisten og skarpretteren Carsten Jensen voksede op i skipperbyen Marstal. Nu har han skrevet 700 sider om søfartens dramatiske og farverige skæbner i et samfund, der tog forskud på moderniteten og fungerede uden faderfigurer. Som barn så forfatteren stort set intet til sin egen far, men det var en rejse på faderens skib, der gav ham den første idé til den nye roman. Det var en sætning, der lå og spirede i 36 år.

INTERVIEW

CARSTEN ANDERSEN

I efteråret 2002 sidder to forfattere i et lille lejet skipperhus i Marstal.

En dansk og en engelsk.

Lågene på deres bærbare computere rører næsten ved hinanden.

På den ene side af bordet sidder Carsten Jensen.

Hans kæreste Liz Jensen sidder på den anden.

Hun arbejder støt og godt. Hun har den ro, det giver, når ens bøger bliver solgt verden over, som det er sket med romanen 'Louis Drax' niende liv'. En bog, der er på vej som hollywoodfilm.

Carsten Jensen går rundt som løve i et bur. Gennem et år eller to har han jævnlig været i Marstal, fordi han vil skrive en bog om byen, søfolkene og deres liv i Marstal og på de syv have.

Søfartsmuseets arkiv har vist sig at være en guldgrube af historier, men Carsten Jensen kan ikke få hold på stoffet. Forfatteren, som ellers er kendt for velskrevne rejsebøger og skarptskårne essays og kommentarer, kan for en gangs skyld ikke få ordene til at makke ret.

Han kan se, der er enorme muligheder i stedets personhistorier, men de hænger ikke sammen. Igen og igen må han tilbage til søfartsmuseet for at lede efter nøglen til en samlet fortælling.

Sådan har det efterhånden været længe. Notaterne hober sig op. Det samme gør Carsten Jensens frustrationer.

Og det smitter åbenbart, for på et tidspunkt ser Liz Jensen på ham og siger:

»Nu er jeg simpelthen så træt af at se dig gå rundt og ævle om den research. Sæt dig for helvede ned og skriv«.

Carsten Jensen kunne mærke, hvordan han på et øjeblik blev fuldstændig stiv af aggression.

»Derefter satte vi os over for hinanden. Hun sad og skrev på en bog, der skulle sælges til 25 lande, og jeg sad og skumlede over, om jeg nu også kunne skrive en roman. Jeg gjorde det i fuldstændig barnlig trods, og for at jeg to timer senere kunne rejse mig og sige: Der kan du selv se. Det kan ikke lade sig gøre«.

Sådan gik det ikke.

Carsten Jensen rejste sig først fire år senere.

I mellemtiden har han været så meget i Marstal, at han har købt skipperhuset, og 10. november får han udgivet sin beretning. En 700 sider lang roman, 'Vi, de druknede'.

### Tæsk af tyskerne

Meget populært sagt fortæller romanen historien om Marstals storhed og fald. Sejlskibenes sidste store æra og senere endeligt. En historie, der begynder, da nogle af de lokale mænd er med til at få et ordentligt lag tæsk af tyskerne i søslaget ved Eckernförde i 1848. Den slutter fire generationer senere, da nye søfolk efter endt konvojsejlads for de allierede vender hjem til havnen på Ærø 4. maj 1945.

I romanen er der masser af digt, hvor forfatteren lader den ene skæbne gribe ind i den næste, men det meste af stoffet har han fundet inspiration til i det virkelige liv. I dagbøger, erindringsskitser og båndoptagelser, som hidtil kun har været udnyttet af lokalhistorikere og amatørslægtsforskere.

»Søfartsmuseet er et rent klondike af gode historier, men det er, som om folk tror, at eftertiden ikke ville være interesseret i deres almindelige liv, så de fortæller en masse om usædvanlige begivenheder – voldsomme, dramatiske eller pudsige – og næsten ikke andet. Den slags kan man ikke få til at hænge sammen, og derfor fandt jeg også ud af – med en vis skræk – at jeg var nødt til at tage skridtet ud i fiktionen. Specielt, hvis jeg ikke kun skulle skrive endnu en lokalhistorie, der blev solgt fra den lokale boghandel«, siger Carsten Jensen.

Igen og igen har han set, hvordan folk har rynket panden og set undrende på ham, når han har fortalt om sit projekt. Og han har fået tøvende, nærmest ængstelige bemærkninger fra folk, der har spurgt, om han nu også tror, bogen vil interessere nogen uden for Ærø.

Hvis tvivlen på et tidspunkt var til stede hos ham, er den i hvert fald forsvundet i dag. Allerede før udgivelsen i Danmark er bogen solgt til udgivelse i seks lande, heriblandt England og USA.

»Jeg var fra starten i tvivl om genren, og om, hvor jeg skulle begynde og slutte. På en måde er bogen bygget op om en række usædvanlige begivenheder. Den er vokset frem af syv-otte forskellige frø. Det første frø er historien fra 1848 om Laurits Madsen, som slår en saltomortale på et eksploderende krigsskib og lander på fødderne igen. I live. Han beskriver selv, at han har været oppe ved Himmerigs port, hvor Sankt Peter viste ham sin røv. Det er faktisk en virkelig begivenhed, jeg fandt i et erindringsstykke af Marstals måske eneste rigtige intellektuelle, som hed Erik Kromann. Han skrev havnens, hvilket vil sige byens historie gennem 100 år. I en bog taler han med en gammel lods, som deltog i slaget ved Eckernförde. Han oplevede det ikke selv, men han hørte om denne mand, som stod på dækket og vendte i luften, da skibet 'Chr. VIII' eksploderede. Da jeg læste det, tænkte jeg, at her har jeg min hovedperson. Senere fandt jeg også en historie om, hvordan der i 1848 blev slået falsk alarm, så alle troede tyskerne kom sejlende mod Marstal. De to historier har jeg koblet sammen i Laurits Madsen, og derefter gik digteriet i gang«, forklarer Carsten Jensen.

### Kollektiv fortæller

Strukturen for fortællingen om søfolkene og deres mange eventyr faldt dog først for alvor på plads, da han fandt ud af, hvem fortælleren skulle være. Den store historie bliver – noget usædvanligt – fortalt af et kollektiv, et vi. Af mændene i Marstal. Indimellem træder en enkelt fortællerstemme frem, men det er dybest set mændenes samlede historie, der bliver fortalt.

»Fra starten havde jeg ingen plan. Jeg vidste bare, at jeg havde lyst til at vende den vedtagne danmarkshistorie på hovedet. Normalt er det historien om puslingelandet, der hygger sig, og mens de store storme går over Europa, ligger vi i Læ. Selv om vi bliver besat, oplever vi ikke det samme drama, som de gør i andre besatte lande«.

»Men i Marstal har man en by, som på en måde altid er i en krigszone. Den er i fare på grund af naturen, men også fordi sømænd aldrig er neutrale i krig. Første Verdenskrig ramte Marstal meget hårdt, og byen kunne lige så godt have ligget i et land, der var med i alle Europas krige. Det er meget bevidst, at min roman starter og slutter med en krig«, siger Carsten Jensen.

Han har forsøgt at sætte proportioner på byens dramatiske liv ved at se på antallet af faldne i Anden Verdenskrig. 84 mænd fra Marstal døde, og det ville svare til 20.000 faldne i København eller 100.000 på landsplan.

Søfolkenes dramatiske liv sætter da også et kraftigt fingeraftryk på hans nye roman, som groft sagt er én lang kæde af spektakulære optrin og farverige skæbnefortællinger. Laurits Madsens lufttur er én historie, men man kunne også tage Marstalknægten Hermann, der kyler sin plejefar over bord på åbent hav og kommer tilbage som ene mand på båden. Eller Laurits' søn Albert, der finder skrumpehovedet efter Kaptajn Cook og i øvrigt senere finder en stenrig kinesisk elskerinde i Antwerpen. Eller enkefruen Klara Friis, der arver Alberts rederi og formue og ihærdigt forsøger at slå Marstal ihjel som søfartsby, fordi hun er så træt af, at havet tager alle mændene. Eller Klaras søn Knud Erik, der forelsker sig i en pige, som han først møder mange år senere under dramatiske omstændigheder – under vandet. Eller den sindssyge styrmand O'Connor, der slår en italiensk kok ihjel til søs. Eller skoledrengene, der forsøger at tage livet af deres sadistiske lærer, men må nøjes med hans hund.

*Tror du, folk nu vil sige, at Carsten Jensen har skrevet sådan en slags Peder Most-roman?*

»Jeg ved det ikke, men jeg har tænkt på, hvordan det kan være, at de voldsomme og dramatiske historier efterhånden skal være nogen, der skubbes ud i krimi- eller thrillergenren. Hvorfor er det blevet en kommerciel genre for sig? Sådan er det ikke, hvis du går tilbage i litteraturen, hvor mange af de blåstemplede værker er fulde af dramaer. Jeg havde på en måde lyst til at generobre dramaet for romanen. Jeg havde det lidt sådan, at læserne efter endt læsning skulle opleve, at de havde gået 15 runder med Muhammad Ali«.

*For nogle år siden sagde du i et interview, at du ville skrive dig helt ud?*

»Sagde jeg det? Gad nok vide, hvad jeg mente med det«.

*Og dø stående, tilføjede du?*

»Der har jeg nok mere tænkt på, at jeg ikke havde lyst til en forfatterkarriere, hvor det hele løber ud i filigranarbejde, broderier og nostalgiske erindringsskitser. Jeg har det sådan, at jeg bliver mere og mere ambitiøs med alderen, og jeg føler helt bestemt, at jeg har livsværket foran mig. Ser jeg tilbage, kan jeg se en del bøger, som ligner tilløb og forsøg. Jeg har skrevet to romaner tidligere, og 'Kannibalernes nadver' (1988) er jeg bestemt ikke tilfreds med. 'Jorden i munden' (1991) oplever jeg i dag som en halv roman. Hvis jeg dengang havde haft mere mod og ambition, var noget af historien blevet stående, hvor jeg så til gengæld skulle have givet den meget mere«.

*Det var faktisk noget af det, Poul Borum skrev*

Fortsættes side 3

**KULING.** Carsten Jensen besluttede sig for at skrive en roman om Marstal i 2000. Da var der inden for tre uger sket to dramatiske omvæltninger i hans liv. Hans far døde, og han blev selv skilt. Han tog tilbage til Marstal og genopdagede i barndommens havneby en ro, han nærmest havde glemt.
Foto: Jan Grarup

»Alt kan ændre sig, hvis jeg ikke vinder«

Målet er at blive anerkendt som verdens bedste bokser. Midlet er tæv til træning og salgsarbejde i USA. Modstanderen er først Markus Beyer, som Mikkel Kessler møder i Parken 14. oktober. Dernæst at finde boksere, der tør stille op mod verdensmesteren.

KRITIK

Når moderne kvinder maler

Livet er fedt, men vi lever for lidt

**WORLD'S BEST-DESIGNED™**

# Politiken

**COPENHAGEN, DENMARK**

Circulation: 130,000-170,000
Daily

This is not a paper of record. It has an agenda and something to say. Visually visceral, Politiken communicates with a variety of voices. Sometimes raspy, occasionally delicate; always strong. There's a mood and intention throughout — from the elegant opinion pages, and evocative, full width documentary photographs to the pure red navigational tools and heavy black, poster-like nameplate. There's nothing timid about this paper. We like it that way.

Politiken no es un diario notario de la actualidad; tiene una agenda y algo que decir. Visualmente visceral, Politiken comunica a través de una variedad de voces. A veces son rasposas, otras veces delicadas, pero siempre fuertes. Un ánimo y una intención son evidentes en todo el diario, desde las elegantes páginas de opinión y las evocativas fotografías documentales a todo ancho de la página, hasta las herramientas de navegación de rojo puro y el logo tipo afiche de negro intenso. No hay nada de timidez en este diario y nos gusta que sea así.

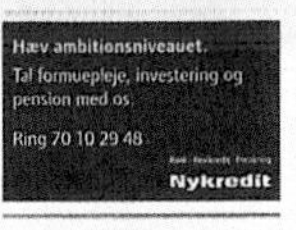


**VEJRET** Lidt eller nogen sol, efterhånden skyer fra vest. 5-10 grader. Svag til let vind fra skiftende retninger.

KULTUR

**Nyt dansk værk om Vestens idéhistorie**

Anmelder Steffen Heiberg byder velkommen om bord på Danmarks nye 2.468 sider lange tankegodstog, 'Tankens magt'. Lokomotivet, der trækker de tre tykke bind, drives frem af et forfatterkollegium på 60 spidskompetente tankekræfter underlagt effektiv og kompetent tekstredaktion. 'Tankens magt' er ypperlig oplysning for alle åbne sind og et kommende standardværk, vurderer Steffen Heiberg.

2 Side 1

2 Side 3

NAVNE

**Spionen, der blev tilbage i kulden, er død**

Hans arbejdsgivere gav ham kælenavnet 'Misja' for at understrege, at det egentlige hovedkvarter for hans efterretningstjeneste lå solidt placeret i Moskva. Markus Wolf var den onde skygge i John le Carrés filmatiserede roman om 'Spionen, der kom ind fra kulden'. Han var general på den kolde krigs koldeste front, i DDR-diktaturet. Blandt hans ofre var Vesttysklands Willy Brandt. Men han slap godt fra det hele.

2 Side 11

**POLITIKEN** Fredag

10. nov. 2006
Årgang 123. Nr. 41
Pris 19.50
Abonnement Service 70 15 01 01
1. udgave
www.politiken.dk

## Connie H. er parat til at gå af

Hvis de politiske resultater bliver for små, er miljøministeren parat til at stoppe efter næste valg.

RASMUS EMBORG OG LINE AARSLAND

Miljøminister Connie Hedegaard (K) er parat til at stoppe som minister efter næste valg, hvis hun ikke kan få opfyldt sine politiske mål. Det afslører hun i en ny bog, hvor hun kritiserer finansminister Thor Pedersen (V) for at mangle visioner på miljøområdet.

I interviewbogen 'Borgens dronninger', der er skrevet af journalist Gunilla Roijer, fortæller Connie Hedegaard, at hun er parat til at forlade sit politiske topjob. På spørgsmålet om hun vil fortsætte som minister, hvis VK-regeringen fortsætter efter næste valg, svarer hun:

»Det ved jeg ikke. Det kommer fuldstændig an på, om jeg synes, jeg kan gøre tilstrækkelig forskel og synes, at jeg kan flytte nogle dagsordener«.

Connie Hedegaard har taget en række interne slagsmål i regeringen, og hun har et anstrengt forhold til Dansk Folkeparti. I weekenden lagde hun sig ud med både regeringstoppen og DF, da hun under weekendens finanslovsforhandlinger beskyldte støttepartiet for politisk drilleri.

I boginterviewet, der blev gennemført i sommer og som miljøministeren har haft til gennemlæsning, langer hun ud efter Thor Pedersen.

»Altså, vi har en finansminister i Danmark, som dybest set ikke mener, at der i Danmark er nogen miljøproblemer. Det gør, at ALT inden for mit område skal der slås for«, siger Connie Hedegaard, der også indirekte kritiserer sin partiformand, økonomiminister Bendt Bendtsen:

»Opgaven for os som parti er at turde markere, at vi er forskellige fra Venstre«.

Connie Hedegaard ønskede i går ikke svare på spørgsmål. Via sin presserådgiver udtaler hun, at »interviewet bør læses i sammenhæng frem for løsrevne sætninger«, og at bemærkningen om finansministeren er sagt med »et glimt i øjet«.

»Selvfølgelig anerkender finansministeren, at der er miljøproblemer. Det viser regeringens politik også, og i øvrigt har dagsordenen flyttet sig markant, siden interviewet blev givet for snart mange måneder siden«, udtaler hun nu.

Bogcitaterne gav i går anledning til stor forbavselse i en række ministerier. Men hverken statsminister Anders Fogh Rasmussen (V) eller Thor Pedersen havde kommentarer til sagen. Fra økonomiminister Bendt Bendtsen lyder det:

»Jeg vil ikke kommentere brudstykker fra en bog, jeg har ikke set«.

Statsministerens tidligere pressechef, kommunikationsrådgiver Michael Kristiansen, karakteriserer Connie Hedegaard som et vigtigt kort for regeringen:

»Hun appellerer til en række vælgere, som resten af regeringen har svært ved at få i tale, men projektet Connie Hedegaard kan blive så stort, at det bliver et problem for regeringen. En række Venstreministre er allerede trætte af hende, men hendes interne status afhænger i sidste ende af Bendt Bendtsen«, siger han, og tilføjer: »Det er et kendt fænomen i politik, at man ikke skal true med at gå af«.

1. sektion side 4

## Stress giver sygdom

Mange FOA-medlemmer bliver langtidssyge af stress

SOLVEIG GRAM JENSEN

Hjemmehjælper Jette Jakobsen ville ikke indse, at hun ikke kunne klare mosten. Indtil hun ikke kunne huske noget længere:

»Lige pludselig begyndte jeg at glemme. Der gik kludder i det hele. Jeg kunne ikke huske, hvor jeg skulle hen, eller hvad jeg skulle. Jeg syntes også, alle de ældre var besværlige«.

Hjemmehjælpere og buschauffører er hårdt ramt af stress. En rundspørge blandt medlemmer af Fag og Arbejde (FOA) viser, at fem procent har været syge i over en måned i løbet af det seneste år, fordi de havde stress. Hvert fjerde medlem føler sig i høj grad stresset.

Jette Jakobsen sad til sidst grædende hos lægen og blev sygemeldt. Det var 26. september - siden har hun låst sig inde i hjemmet, og hun aner ikke, hvornår hun kan arbejde igen.

solveig.gram@pol.dk

1. sektion side 15

## 140 dokumentarfilm på 10 dage

CPH:DOX. Nordens største festival for dokumentarfilm. Læs tillægget inde i iBYEN.

POLITIKEN MENER

## Et fravalg

DR-udrensning bekræfter et mønster

DR og TV 2 ejes af staten. Det gør, at regeringen må påtage sig et særligt ansvar. Enhver tendens til misbrug af den statslige dominans er et alvorligt faresignal, som ikke mindst en borgerlig-liberal regering burde være yderst opmærksom på. DR's fravalg af Lisbeth Knudsen som nyheds- og mediedirektør er i det lys en meget dårlig nyhed, der bekræfter, at regeringen på medieområdet efterhånden tager meget afslappet på den fundamentale norm om, at der ingen politisk indblanding må finde sted.

Hvorfor nu det? Er Lisbeth Knudsens afgang ikke bare udtryk for den nye generaldirektørs saglige skøn? Gid det var så vel.

Det er usædvanligt at kunne foretage så klar en bedømmelse af et personvalg udefra. Men enhver, der kender til Lisbeth Knudsens karriere og indsats, vil vide, at hun er en af de i særklasse mest professionelle mediechefer i Danmark. Og de, der i stedet har fået pladserne i DR's direktion? Rutinerede folk, men ingen af dem er i nærheden af at have Lisbeth Knudsens dokumenterede ledelseserfaring og store journalistiske pondus.

OG HVAD har regeringen så med det at gøre? Jo, Lisbeth Knudsen er i en periode blevet udskreget som socialdemokrat og gjort ansvarlig for påståede »røde udskejelser« i DR. Men sandheden er, at Lisbeth Knudsen har været både erhvervsredaktør og politisk redaktør på Berlingske Tidende, før hun blev chef for Aktuelt. Og nok så afgørende: Der er aldrig nogen, der har taget hende i at opføre sig andet end afbalanceret og professionelt i de mange konflikter, der følger med et topjob i DR.

Til gengæld er det velkendt, at der i og omkring regeringen er mange, der har ønsket hendes hoved på et fad. Hvis den nye generaldirektør i den situation ville have nogen til at tro på, at Lisbeth Knudsen ikke er ofret for de herskende politiske vinde, kunne han i det mindste have sørget for, at hendes faglige kvalifikationer bare i et eller andet omfang var repræsenteret i den nye direktion. I stedet må man undre sig over, at hendes afgang ikke opvejes af nogen form for talenttilførsel.

I mangel af en bedre forklaring er der føjet endnu et kapitel til regeringens berlusconificering af det danske medielandskab. Først fyres topcheferne i både TV 2 og DR. Så bliver regeringspartiets politiske ordfører radiodirektør. Og nu dette. Man skal være blind og døv for ikke at kunne få øje på en tendens, der for længst burde have fået alle alarmklokker til at ringe. *ts*

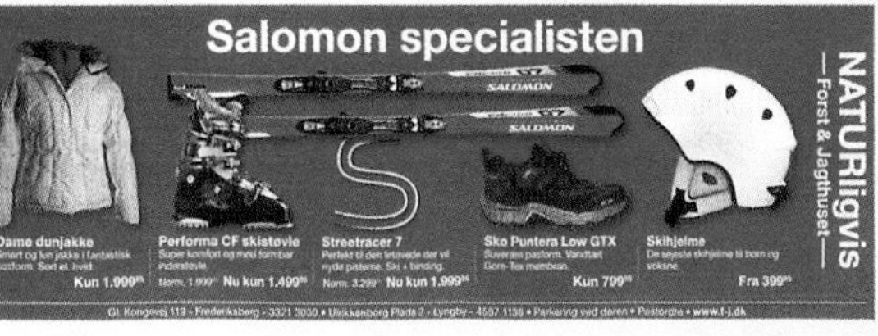

POLITIKEN Søndag 5. november 2006

# PS

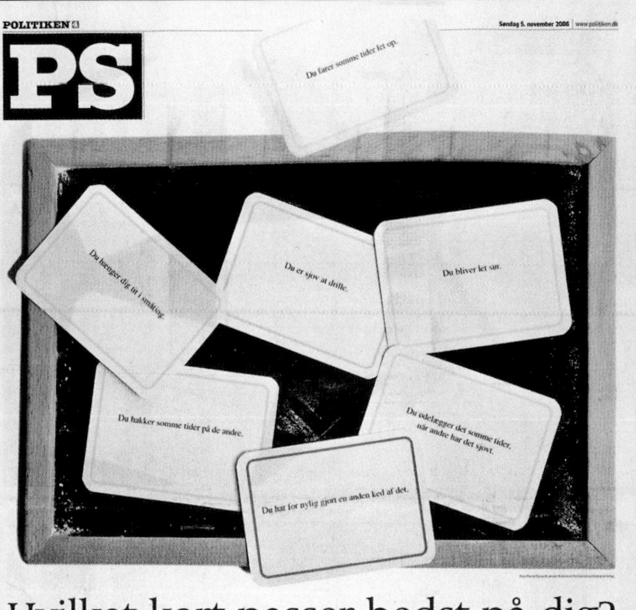


## Hvilket kort passer bedst på dig?

Metoder, der er kendt fra psykoterapien, er rykket ind i den danske folkeskole. Det er en farlig udvikling, mener kritikerne. Tilhængerne siger: Velkommen til 2006.

Med kortene giver man skyld og ansvar til den enkelte i stedet for at gøre det til et fælles ansvar. Helle Rabøl Hansen

POLITIKEN Søndag 5. november 2006

# VIDENSKAB & DEBAT

Respekt! Slå ikke på embedsmændene. Debat bagsiden

## Professoren og hans fantastiske får

Danmark har haft besøg af forskeren bag det klonede får Dolly. For ti år siden var dyret en sensation, men det gik ikke som forventet.

## »Vi regnede med, at det ville blive kontroversielt«

Skaberen af det klonede får Dolly forsker nu i kloning af menneskelige fosterceller. Professor Ian Wilmut ser det ikke som en glidebane – fordelene er store, og fostrene har ingen bevidsthed, siger han.

Men hvad angår ideen om at tage celler fra fostre, der vil jeg sige, at jeg er skuffet, når jeg tænker på, at forskningen kan bruges til at kurere uhelbredelige sygdomme.

SØNDAG 5. NOVEMBER 2006 POLITIKEN

# OPINION

POLITIKEN KOMMENTAR

## Afrikanske Dyremoser

Statsledere bør afløses, ikke belønnes

## Hovedet i busken

Den globale George W. Bush. Tegning: Per Marquard Otzen

## Global. Resten af verden eksisterer ikke længere

Huntington hænger fast i en forældet forestilling om, hvad 'kultur' er

## Hvad er meningen? »Finsk mand bider svensk hund«

NORDISKE VÆRDIER. Per Unckel, generalsekretær for Nordisk Ministerråd.

SØNDAG 5. NOVEMBER 2006 OPINION 5

Tøger Seidenfaden og Anita Bay Bundegaard blogger om bladets linje på politiken.dk/lederpladsen

LÆSERNE MENER

DAGENS CITAT

Det er med politikere som med bleer. De skal jævnligt udskiftes – og af samme grund

## Almene boliger i skruestik

## Stjerner straffer pæne piger

## Venstre, BUPL og den slemme solidaritet

KRONIKEN 5. november 2006

## Skiderikker og stortabere

GRETELISE HOLM

Mænd kan ikke diskvalificere sig til ledende og indflydelsesrige stillinger i medierne.

OPINION

POLITIKENS KOMMENTAR

Narkoauktion

Lugten i bageriet

Exit. USA går baglæns mod døren i Irak

Hvad er meningen? »Jeg opponerer imod bedraget som metode«

# søndagsliv

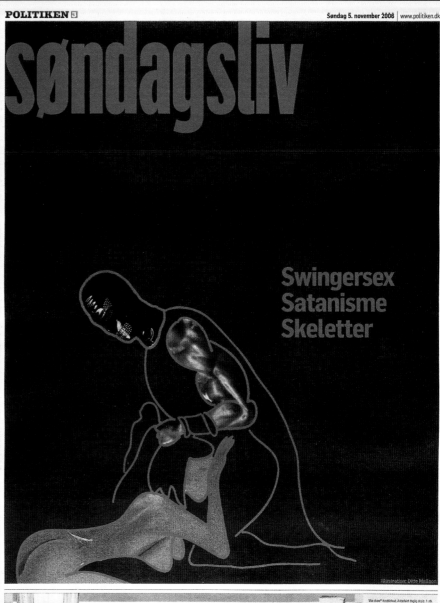

Swingersex
Satanisme
Skeletter

Illustration: Ditte Mailson

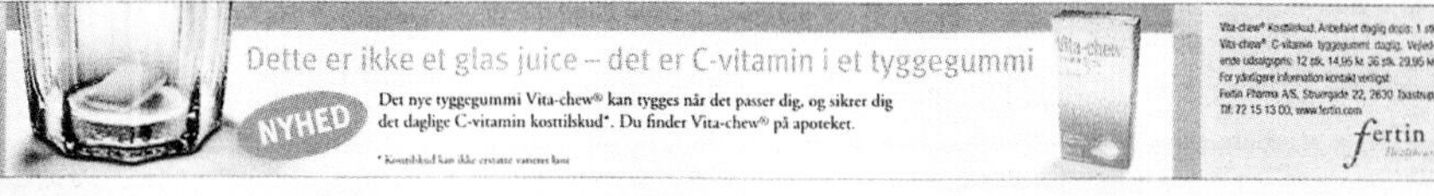


UDLAND

POLITIKEN.DK I DAG

Roms borgmester: Det er en tragedie

Saddam skriver brev til irakerne

Eritrea truer fredsaftale

3.000 koalitionssoldater dræbt

EU'S FORMAND

## »Russerne siger selv, de har demokrati - men det er ikke som vores demokrati«

Europa og Rusland er afhængige af hinanden - men det skal ikke forhindre kritik af manglende pressefrihed og andre demokratiske problemer, siger Finlands statsminister. Politiken møder EU-formand Matti Vanhanen to dage før, han skal være vært for et topmøde med Vladimir Putin, som kommer på et anspændt tidspunkt.

INTERVIEW

JUDGES' SPECIAL RECOGNITION
INFORMATION GRAPHICS

**THE NEW YORK TIMES**
Amanda Cox
**Silver:** Charting, 175,000+

# *From Scum, Perhaps the Tiniest Form of Life*

**By WILLIAM J. BROAD**

The smallest form of life known to science just got smaller.

Four million of a newly discovered microbe — assuming the discovery, reported yesterday in the journal Science, is confirmed — could fit into the period at the end of this sentence.

Scientists found the microbes living in a remarkably inhospitable environment, drainage water as caustic as battery acid from a mine in Northern California. The microbes, members of an ancient family of organisms known as archaea, formed a pink scum on green pools of hot mine water laden with toxic metals, including arsenic.

"It was amazing," said Jillian F. Banfield of the University of California, Berkeley, a member of the discovery team. "These were totally new." In their paper, the scientists call the microbes "smaller than any other known cellular life form."

Scientists say the discovery could bear on estimates of the pervasiveness of exotic microbial life, which some experts suspect forms a hidden biosphere extending down miles whose total mass may exceed that of all surface life.

It may also influence the search for microscopic life forms elsewhere in the solar system, a discovery that would prove that life in the universe is not unique to Earth but an inherent property of matter.

The tiny microbes came from an abandoned mine at Iron Mountain in Shasta County, Calif., which produced gold, silver, iron and copper before closing in 1963.

Today, rain and surface water run over exposed minerals, producing sulfuric acid. The mine is one of the largest Superfund cleanup sites.

Starting in 2002, the scientists obtained drops of the acidic slime and searched for genetic signs of novel microbes. "We were essentially looking for new stuff," one of the scientists, Brett J. Baker, said in statement from Berkeley, "and we found it."

The microbes are about 200 nanometers wide — the size of large viruses, which scientists consider lifeless because they cannot reproduce on their own. Bacteria average about five times that size.

The scientists must do further tests to confirm that the organisms are the smallest ever found, and that they can reproduce. If those analyses hold up, they said in their Science paper, "it may be necessary to reconsider existing paradigms for the minimum requirements for life."

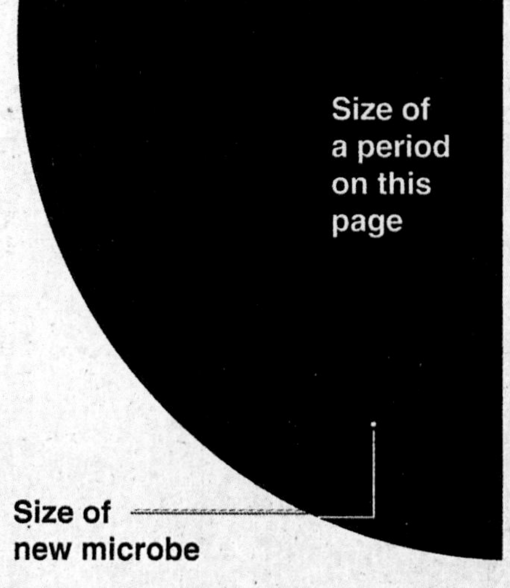


*Source: Jillian F. Banfield, University of California, Berkeley*

The New York Times

This graphic captures the essence of the story — the tiniest form of life. It's not a topic that might interest everyone, but the cool graphic tempts you. It takes you back to common knowledge, and then it introduces something new. It's not that big of a story, so the size is appropriate. No special computer skills were needed. It's just a very clever, clean, simple, instant read. This is a brilliant graphic. Period.

Este gráfico capta lo central del relato; la forma de vida más pequeña. No se trata de un tema que pueda interesar a todos, pero el genial gráfico es tentador. Recuerda el conocimiento general, y luego presenta algo nuevo. La noticia no es tan extensa, por lo que el tamaño es apropiado. No fueron necesarias habilidades computacionales especiales. Simplemente, es una forma de lectura muy inteligente, limpia, sencilla e instantánea. Éste es un gráfico brillante y punto.

Chapter Two

# JUDGES' SPECIAL RECOGNITION

Reconocimiento especial de los jueces

The New York Times Magazine / AUGUST 27, 2006
CHILDREN OF THE STORM
WHERE HURRICANE KATRINA, AND WE, HAVE LEFT THE KIDS.
A PHOTO ESSAY BY BRENDA ANN KENNEALLY
I. Kenisha's Return


## JUDGES' SPECIAL RECOGNITION: USE OF PHOTOGRAPHY

**THE NEW YORK TIMES**

Michele McNally, Meaghan Looram, Aviva Mikhaelov, Tom Bodkin

**Gold:** Staff photo
**Award of Excellence:** Special coverage, section, with ads

**THE NEW YORK TIMES MAGAZINE**

Janet Froelich, Arem Duplessis, Jeff Docherty, Kathy Ryan, Brenda Ann Kenneally, Cathy Gilmore-Barnes, Inez van Lamsweerde, Vinoodh Matadin

**Silver:** Photo series
**Award of Excellence:** Photo series

This powerful documentary photography of children affected by Hurricane Katrina has so much feeling, emotion and heart. The series offers intimacy in different ways — between a mother and child, between the children and the destruction, and among the children themselves. You can sense their despair, but you also see their resilience. The work is tightly edited, with smart presentation and pacing.

La potente fotografía documental de los niños afectados por el huracán Katrina exhibe mucho sentimiento, emoción y corazón. La serie ofrece intimidad de muchas maneras; entre una madre y su hijo, entre los niños y la destrucción, y entre los mismos niños. Se puede sentir su desesperanza, pero también su adaptabilidad. El trabajo está muy bien editado, con una presentación y un compás inteligente.

The Winds Shift in Washington

United, Divided, Embattled

In Iraq, Grief Without End

The New York Times

MONDAY, DECEMBER 25, 2006

2006: THE YEAR IN PICTURES

For a body of work, for one year, for a news organization — this rises above excellence. It's a shark in a big pond. It's comprehensive, with different avenues of the year's photos, on politics, war, sports, foreign strife and technology. There are so many pictures — 45 total — and the presentation doesn't drop anywhere. The image sizes complement each other for specific reasons. This work has effect, variety and depth.

Para un conjunto de trabajos, de todo un año, de sólo un medio periodístico, éste supera la excelencia. Es algo enorme en un medio pequeño. Es completo, con diferentes tipos de las fotos del año, sobre política, guerra, deportes, conflicto externo y tecnología. Hay tantas fotos -45 en total-, y la presentación no se cae en ninguna parte. Los tamaños de las imágenes se complementan entre sí por razones particulares. Este trabajo tiene efecto, variedad y profundidad.

Ordenó Fox Aplicar la ley en el Caso Bribiesca: Romero Ramos

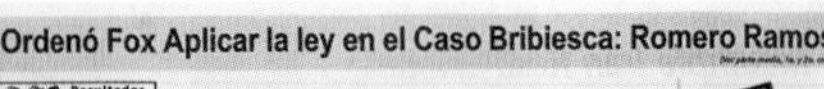

EXCELSIOR

EL PERIODICO DE LA VIDA NACIONAL

Jueves 2 de Febrero de 2006

# Extraditables Agotarán Todos los Recursos Legales

Niega Calderón Sentirse "Comprometido o Afectado"

"Firme Intención" de Modificar la Ley de Radio y TV: Senadores

Suspende SRE a ex Cónsul en Texas por Escándalo

Abascal Responde a Monsiváis

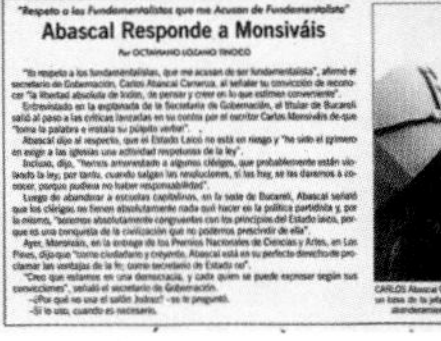

*Before the redesign*

## JUDGES' SPECIAL RECOGNITION: NEWS DESIGN

**EXCELSIOR,** México City

Abraham Solís, Marco Gonsen, Gunther Sahagún, Luzma Díaz de León Reyes, Marco A. Román, Alexandro Medrano, Gerardo Galarza, Pascal Beltrán del Río, Ernesto Rivera, Ricardo Peña, Ángeles Barajas, Mildred Ramo, Héctor Rendón, Juan Carlos Gutiérrez Alvarez, Paris Martínez, Óscar Cedillo, Ma. Luisa Díaz de León, Deneb Jacome, Ernesto Muñiz, María Luisa López, Daniel González Hernández, Erik Meza, Ana Maria Prado, Nancy Araiza, Carlos Meraz, Cecilia Estrada Medina, Olegario Vázquez Aldir, Eduardo Danilo Ruiz, Víctor Sánchez, Gustavo Belman, Perla Olmeda, Guadalupe Arrese

**Gold**
Redesign, overall newspaper

**Silvers**
News, A-Section page, broadsheet, 50,000-174,999
Business page, broadsheet, 50,000-174,999
News, local page, broadsheet, 50,000-174,999, two awards
Other news page, broadsheet, 50,000-174,999, three awards

EXCELSIOR

EL PERIÓDICO DE LA VIDA NACIONAL

Año XC-Tomo IV, Número 32,444 • México, D.F. • 92 páginas — $10.00 — MARTES 4 de julio de 2006

www.nuevoexcelsior.com.mx

REMEMBER FLORIDA
LA PRENSA INTERNACIONAL DESTACÓ LA INCERTIDUMBRE EN TORNO A LA ELECCIÓN Y LA CAÍDA DEL PRI. > TEMA DEL DÍA

HORA DE REFLEXIONAR
INTELECTUALES Y CREADORES OPTARON POR LA CAUTELA Y SUGIRIERON ESPERAR A QUE EL IFE HAGA SU LABOR. > COMUNIDAD

UN CONGRESO TODAVÍA MÁS PLURAL
ANALISTAS CONSIDERAN QUE EL PRI SERÁ FUNDAMENTAL PARA CONFORMAR MAYORÍAS EN EL NUEVO CONGRESO. > POLÍTICA

EL PREP NO FUE SUFICIENTE

# A esperar

POR ÉRICA MORA, LETICIA ROBLES DE LA ROSA Y JUAN MANUEL ANGUIANO

Mudos testigos de una jornada excepcional.

Repunte bursátil 4.77% — Cede el dólar 11.23

## Euforia en los mercados

POR PATRICIA ORTEGA Y ENGGE CHAVARRÍA

"En la democracia se gana o se pierde con un voto y esto lo asumo plenamente en la responsabilidad que me toca como candidato del partido que he concluido mi tarea."
ROBERTO MADRAZO, CANDIDATO DEL PRI

OTRO ARBITRO A PRUEBA

El silbante mexicano Armando Archundia no deberá influir en el resultado del duelo de hoy entre Alemania e Italia para aspirar a pitar la final.

Secretario general de la OCDE

## Gurría: a desempolvar las reformas que faltan

POR CARMEN ÁLVAREZ

3 MINUTOS

CÓDIGO: Intentaron recluir a Echeverría — Pág. 14

GLOBAL: Descarrila el Metro en Valencia, España — Pág. 4

COMUNIDAD: Amparo en el caso Remedios Varo — Pág. 1

GLOBAL: Ultimátum a Israel — Pág. 7

| COLUMNAS | | OPINIÓN | |
|---|---|---|---|
| Jorge Fernández Menéndez | 8 | Mario Moya Palencia | 10 |
| Denise Maerker | 9 | Marcelino Perelló | 10 |
| Francisco Garfias | 12 | Xavier Escalada S. J. | 11 |
| Leo Zuckermann | 14 | Axel Didriksson | 11 |
| David Páramo | DINERO 4 | Alejandro Anaya M. | GLOBAL 5 |

*After the redesign*

The issues before the redesign were horrific. The photojournalism was awful, the content was terrible, the fonts were ridiculous, and the nameplate was bit-mapped. The redesigned issues show one of the best-designed newspapers in the competition. To make that leap in the span of a redesign is mind blowing. Incredible resources must have been applied, and the commitment to storytelling is unrivaled. You want to read every page.

Los números antes del rediseño eran horribles. El fotoperiodismo era malo, el contenido era terrible, las tipografías eran ridículas y el logotipo del diario estaba pixelado. Los números rediseñados exhiben uno de los diarios mejor diseñados de la competencia. Dar tal salto a lo largo del rediseño es impresionante. Se deben haber empleado increíbles recursos y el compromiso con la narración no tiene rival. Es imprescindible leer cada página.

EXCELSIOR
MARTES 10 DE OCTUBRE DE 2006

# DINERO

dinero@nuevo.excelsior.com.mx

GABRIEL ZALZMAN, DIRECTOR GENERAL DE MATTEL MÉXICO

# MERCADO MADURO

EN MÉXICO VALE ALREDEDOR DE MIL MILLONES DE DÓLARES AL AÑO Y NO PARA DE CRECER: 30 MILLONES DE NIÑOS LO MANTIENEN EN MOVIMIENTO >06

Foto: Salomón Ramírez

## MIRILLA

**OPEP**
El organismo analiza recortar la producción en un millón de barriles diarios. Actualmente, ésta es de 28.5 millones. -Pág. 05

**CALZADO**
Las empresas de este sector prevén un aumento de 5% en el presente año. Denunciaron que el contrabando pone en riesgo esta actividad. -Pág. 07

**MEXICHEM**
Analistas anticipan que registrará un crecimiento en ventas, gracias a la ampliación de la capacidad instalada de las plantas. -Pág. 03

**PELIGRA EL OBJETIVO DE CONTROL DE PRECIOS**
La inflación de septiembre rebasó el límite permitido de Banco de México, 4.09% anual. Y la expectativa de los analistas es que el crecimiento de precios siga repuntando.



Fuente: Banco de México

## INFLACIÓN EN EU

PERSISTEN LAS VOCES QUE ALERTAN DE POSIBLES BACHES ECONÓMICOS EN ESE PAÍS, LUEGO DE LAS ELECCIONES DEL PRÓXIMO 7 DE NOVIEMBRE >08

## HOY EN LAS COLUMNAS

CONSEJERÍA: **Pedro Alonso** comenta que el terrorismo y los conflictos deben tomarse en cuenta en el análisis económico, como la prueba nuclear subterránea de Corea del Norte. -Pág. 02

ACTIVO EMPRESARIAL: **José Yuste** indica que la historia entre Telemundo y TV Azteca tomó un giro inesperado, ya que la primera sí demandó a la segunda. -Pág. 03

PERSONAJES DE RENOMBRE: **David Páramo** señala que los bancos no tienen interés en proteger a sus clientes de los fraudes a través de internet. -Pág. 04

ESTRATEGIA DE NEGOCIOS: **Marielena Vega** escribe que la iniciativa del precio único en los libros aún se encuentra en una ardua lucha, ya que podría abordarse hasta el 2007. -Pág. 09

VERNADA: **Carlos Velázquez** dice que Ernesto Cordero, asesor económico del Presidente electo, trabaja en los temas presupuestales para una reestructuración del sector turismo. -Pág. 09

GANAN LOS USUARIOS



COFETEL

# Posponen "el que llama paga nacional"

**Se llevan a cabo negociaciones entre proveedores, para la interconexión**

POR CELINA YAMASHIRO
celina.yamashiro@nuevoexcelsior.com.mx

La Comisión Federal de Telecomunicaciones (Cofetel) informó que no entrará en vigor el sistema "El que llama paga nacional", en el primer minuto de este miércoles, debido a que Temex y las compañías de celulares se encuentran negociando un convenio de interconexión.

José Luis Peralta, comisionado de la Cofetel, dijo a **Excélsior** que el 11 de octubre no era una fecha fatal para que comenzara a operar el esquema, ya que la resolución indica que los concesionarios tendrían que estar en condiciones de ofrecer el servicio y para ello requieren el convenio mencionado.

Detalló que si los concesionarios no se ponen de acuerdo tendrán que manifestarlo a la Cofetel y ésta terminará resolviendo el problema; sin embargo, confió en que haya un acuerdo en las próximas horas o en esta semana, con lo que el esquema podría comenzar a aplicarse en un plazo de uno o dos meses.

"De lo contrario, si no no hay un convenio, la Cofetel tiene 60 días hábiles para tomar una decisión al respecto, pues quieran o no los concesionarios El que llama paga nacional sí entrará en vigor".

Las negociaciones sobre el convenio de interconexión tienen que ver con los tiempos de pago, el nivel de la tarifa, tráficos internacionales, entre otros aspectos, que los concesionarios buscan ajustar.

Con este programa, las personas que reciban llamadas de larga distancia ya no cubrirán el costo, sino quienes llaman desde otra ciudad o del extranjero, tal y como sucede con El que llama paga local.

Sin embargo, los cargos por llamadas de larga distancia a celulares se realizarán sólo a los clientes de Telmex, las cuales se suman a otros conceptos de pago como servicio medido y larga distancia. Los usuarios receptores sólo tendrán que pagar el roaming.

Lo anterior, debido a que las telefónicas como Avantel, Axtel, Alestra y Maxcom interpusieron un juicio de nulidad, en donde el juez les otorgó una suspensión provisional.

SLIM, EN CAMPECHE

**PEMEX PUEDE EXPLORAR SIN ALIANZAS**
Carlos Slim Helú afirmó que la paraestatal puede hacer exploración en aguas profundas sin necesidad de alianzas con empresas extranjeras. "Sí, puede hacerlo solo y obviamente hay mucha tecnología en todo el mundo". -Reuters -Pág. 07

Foto: Carmen Infante Peck

ACUERDO COMERCIAL

# México y Brasil van por petroquímicos

POR ALICIA VALVERDE
alicia.valverde@nuevoexcelsior.com.mx

México ha iniciado un acercamiento con Brasil para ampliar el Acuerdo de Complementación Económica (ACE 56), para impulsar la venta de productos químicos y petroquímicos, informó el Consejo Empresarial Mexicano de Comercio Exterior (Comce).

El director técnico del organismo, Fernando Ruiz Huarte, comentó que no se van a negociar tarifas completas, ya que lo que quiere Brasil son productos sensibles para México y viceversa. Dicho acuerdo se daría dentro del marco de Asociación Latinoamericana de Integración (Aladi).

Comentó que es muy probable que el país carioca decida negociarlo en el marco del Mercosur por pertenecer a él.

El especialista auguró que la misma historia se puede repetir en la negociación con el ACE que se busca con Corea, al precisar que en general hay acuerdos sectoriales de que se firme.

Los principales productos que quiere vender Corea a México son los que no quieren que estén en el acuerdo y por lo tanto, no habría productos para pagarles las concesiones que les den. Las industrias que se oponen son acero, química, automotriz, que son precisamente donde los coreanos se sienten más competitivos. -Pág. 07

*After the redesign*

COMPUTACION

EXCELSIOR

# Financiera

# Crecimiento, una Quimera en 30 Años

CRECE 2.4% PRODUCCION MANUFACTURERA EN OCTUBRE: INEGI

Renueva Aeroméxico su Flota

Urge Cambiar el Marco Legal en Pemex: SE

Pobre Capacitación Laboral

*Before the redesign*

# adrenalina

Y la fiesta no para> España está de cabeza luego de la victoria que Alonso consiguió en Japón >9

JOSÉ ABRAMO LIRA · MAURICIO MORALES · ARMANDO ARCHUNDIA · HUGO LEÓN GUAJARDO

LA CRISIS NO TERMINA

# ARBITRAJE EN JAQUE

La jornada 12 los dejó en evidencia. Los silbantes se siguen equivocando y sus errores cambian resultados. Aarón Padilla, nuevo titular de la Comisión, hace frente a las fallas> 5

BEISBOL
**Oakland y Detroit inician su duelo**

APERTURA 2006
**Mizrahi y Romano, frente a frente**

DEPORTE ORGANIZADO

GOLF
**El día después del festejo**

VERACRUZ
**Arzuaga, figura del fin de semana**

COLUMNAS · LA MEMORIA DEL FUTBOL: Ricardo Salazar y la anatomía de un técnico · LA AUTOPSIA: André Marín adelanta el futuro de Alberto de la Torre · PASIONES Y GLORIA: David Faitelson, contento por Esteban Loaiza

*After the redesign*

# Repudian su presencia, no así su dinero

# Los indocumentados burlan grilletes en EU

ENBA

*After the redesign*

Hoy en agenda: La presidenta de Chile, Michelle Bachelet, anunciará nuevas medidas anticorrupción con las que enfrentará las irregularidades en las instituciones del Estado.

EXCELSIOR

GLOBAL

VUELTA AL MUNDO

Encierra a su mamá en el balcón

REALIZAN HOY EL FUNERAL

LUTO EN LÍBANO

MIGRANTES

Engañan a ilegales en iglesias de NY

500 MIL inmigrantes ilegales hay en en Nueva York, según datos de las autoridades locales

LE PERDONAN LA VIDA

Bloquean reforma agraria de E

OPINIÓN GUADALUPE GONZÁLEZ

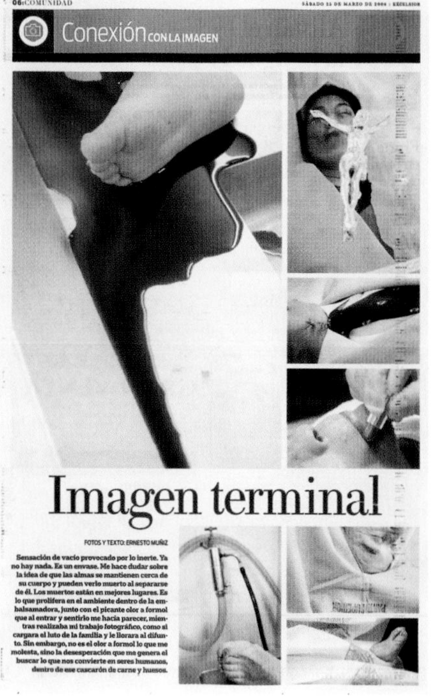

06 COMUNIDAD — SÁBADO 25 DE MARZO DE 2006 | EXCELSIOR

Conexión CON LA IMAGEN

Imagen terminal

FOTOS Y TEXTO: ERNESTO MUÑIZ

**Sensación de vacío provocado por lo inerte. Ya no hay nada. Es un envase. Me hace dudar sobre la idea de que las almas se mantienen cerca de su cuerpo y pueden verlo muerto al separarse de él. Los muertos están en mejores lugares. Es lo que prolifera en el ambiente dentro de la embalsamadora, junto con el picante olor a formol que al entrar y sentirlo me hacia parecer, mientras realizaba mi trabajo fotográfico, como si cargara el luto de la familia y le llorara al difunto. Sin embargo, no es el olor a formol lo que me molesta, sino la desesperación que me genera el buscar lo que nos convierte en seres humanos, dentro de ese cascarón de carne y huesos.**

**BATAS Y MICROSCOPIOS** Conozca junto con Cristina Aguayo los detalles de la nueva aventura genética del Reino Unido: el desarrollo de embriones humanos en la matriz de las vacas > 06

EXCELSIOR
LUNES 13 DE NOVIEMBRE DE 2006

# COMUNIDAD

comunidad@nuevoexcelsior.com.mx

# La *zona* dejó de ser rosa

Actos de violencia, extorsión, acoso y descriminación enrarecen el ambiente de fiesta y diversidad, incluso en los centros de reunión de la comunidad homosexual

> 03

Fotografía: Juan Carlos Gutiérrez

postal

## NO COMPRE CARO

En Xochimilco, donde se produce 50 por ciento de las flores *cuetlaxóchitl* del DF, inició la rehabilitación del corredor comercial de la calle Nuevo León, que abrirá el próximo viernes, cuando sea inaugurada la Expo Nochebuena 2006.

Foto: Cuartoscuro

## Centros artísticos del gobierno federal quedan inconclusos

*Este mes, se inaugurará el que aún se construye en Zamora, pero dos más permanecen a medias*

POR VIRGINIA BAUTISTA
*virginia.bautista@nuevoexcelsior.com.mx*

Al concluir el sexenio del presidente Vicente Fox Quesada, los mexicanos no tendrán los siete centros regionales de las artes que el mandatario se comprometió a construir al principio de su administración: los planteles de San Luis Potosí y Sinaloa aún no están terminados y, de hecho, la conclusión de las obra tardará hasta un año más.

Las autoridades culturales a nivel federal concluyen su periodo de gobierno dejando cuatro complejos funcionando, además de que el Centro Regional de las Artes de Michoacán –que ha motivado constantes protestas de las asociaciones civiles y los pobladores de Zamora, por la premura en su edificación– será el último que se inaugure, tentátivamente el 23 de noviembre.

Considerado uno de los ejes centrales del foxismo en materia cultural, este programa arrancó con bombo y platillo el 17 de noviembre de 2002, cuando el titular del Ejecutivo federal y los reyes de España cortaron el listón del Centro de las Artes de Guanajuato, en Salamanca.

A este plantel, erigido en el estado natal del presidente, le siguieron el Centro Veracruzano de las Artes (mayo de 2004), el Centro Estatal de las Artes de Baja California, en Mexicali (enero de 2005), y el Centro de las Artes de San Agustín, en Oaxaca (marzo de 2006).

EXPRESIONES > PÁG. 4

Foto: Vicente Guijosa

Con un conglomerado cultural en su natal Guanajuato, Fox inició la gestión que está por cerrar con la apertura de un centro más, en tierra de su esposa.

## Trazan mapas del arte en el Centro Histórico

POR VIRGINIA BAUTISTA
*virginia.bautista@nuevoexcelsior.com.mx*

El Instituto Nacional de Bellas Artes recupera la memoria de las obras literarias y los murales creados al abrigo del Centro Histórico de la ciudad y la trayectoria de sus autores, en dos guías con las que los capitalinos podrán acercarse a "la metrópoli originaria, al epicentro cultural, artístico, económico y político del país".

Las guías, patrocinadas por la empresa Telmex, poseen un tiraje de 50 mil ejemplares en español, inglés y francés que se distribuirán gratis en diversos restaurantes y comercios; así como en los recorridos literarios que organiza el instituto.

La *Guía literaria* ofrece un mapa de 27 casas de escritores, nueve cafés literarios y 33 sitios de interés; y la *Guía de murales* integra en siete recorridos a 95 obras de 38 pintores plasmadas en 22 recintos de esta demarcación.

> PÁG. 6

Foto: Cortesía INBA

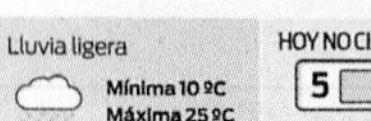

## Crecen edificios verdes

Foto: Cortesía Habitae

POR THELMA GÓMEZ DURÁN
*thelma.gomez@nuevoexcelsior.com.mx*

En la Ciudad de México comienzan a comercializarse condominios que presumen de ser "ecológicos", porque cuentan con sistemas de recolección y uso de agua de lluvias, calentadores solares de agua, ventanas que aíslan el ruido de la calle y conservar una temperatura agradable.

No obstante, debido a su alto costo, el mercado es muy escaso en el DF, acepta el arquitecto Pablo García del Gállego, subdirector de Habitae, de las pocas inmobiliarias en el Distrito Federal que se lanzó a crear un edificio amigable con el ambiente.

En Nueva York, Buenos Aires o Madrid, ya funcionan despachos especializados en las construcciones sustentables y ecológicas. En México, sin embargo, "todavía estamos lejos", asegura el arquitecto García.

> PÁG. 2

cultura de la tolerancia

## EJEMPLAR DEL HORROR

Ayer fue instalado en la Plaza Juárez uno de los vagones que usó el régimen nazi para trasladar judíos a campos de exterminio, y que formará parte del acervo del Museo Memoria y Tolerancia, todavía por construirse. EXPRESIONES > PÁG. 4

Foto: Ernesto Muñiz

# EXCELSIOR

EL PERIÓDICO DE LA VIDA NACIONAL

Año XC-Tomo VI, Número 32,604 • México, D.F. • 72 páginas

LUNES 11 de diciembre de 2006

$10.00

www.nuevoexcelsior.com.mx

AUGUSTO PINOCHET

## Murió impune

El artífice del sangriento golpe militar de 1973 y hombre fuerte de Chile durante 17 años no recibirá funerales de jefe de Estado ni se decretará duelo.

EL ICONO

DIGNO CAMPEÓN

En un gran segundo tiempo, Chivas venció a Toluca y conquistó su undécimo título.

adrenalina

CÁMARA DE DIPUTADOS

## Legislarán la transparencia

EL KNOW HOW DEL ÉXITO

3 MINUTOS

COLUMNAS

OPINIÓN

---

**Se rebelan en la red** Los fans de *Rebelde* abarrotaron la página de internet donde transmitieron finales alternativos >2

---

GLOBAL HOY

**JUSTICIA:** La policía tiene identificados a los 26 principales líderes de Atenco, cuyo común denominador, según perfiles oficiales, son la radicalidad y la violencia. > 2

EXCELSIOR

JUEVES 25 DE MAYO DE 2006

# CÓDIGO

*Información a fondo de México y el mundo*

*I'll be back...*

El ex jefe de gobierno italiano, Silvio Berlusconi, escribió una carta de despedida a su "amigo" y colega José Luis Rodríguez Zapatero, presidente del gobierno de España, en la que asegura que volverá al poder en poco tiempo. > 5

TAMAÑO, COMPOSICIÓN Y DINÁMICA DE LA POBLACIÓN

## YA SOMOS EN MÉXICO...

# 103,263,388

**Datos del II Conteo de Población y Vivienda revelan que el número de ancianos subió de 7.1% a 8.1%, y el analfabetismo bajó de 9.5% a 8.4%**

**48.7** millones son hombres

**51.3** millones son mujeres

**1.6%** de la población mundial representa a los mexicanos

JUNTOS, PERO NO REVUELTOS

DISTRIBUCIÓN TERRITORIAL DE LA POBLACIÓN

---

EXCELSIOR

VIERNES 1 DE DICIEMBRE DE 2006

# DINERO

## ECONOMÍA CALIBRADA

FOX DIO AL CLAVO CON EL CONTROL DE LA INFLACIÓN, TASAS DE INTERÉS A LA BAJA, TIPO DE CAMBIO ESTABLE, MÁXIMOS HISTÓRICOS EN EL ÍNDICE DE PRECIOS Y COTIZACIONES Y LA RESERVA INTERNACIONAL DEL BANCO DE MÉXICO. ASÍ, EL RIESGO-PAÍS SE MANTUVO AL MÍNIMO. ESTOS INSTRUMENTOS DE TRABAJO AHORA ESTÁN EN MANOS DEL GOBIERNO DE FELIPE CALDERÓN.

PIB · INFLACIÓN · RIESGO-PAÍS · DEUDA EXTERNA · RESERVAS INTERNACIONALES · TIPO DE CAMBIO · TASAS DE INTERÉS · BOLSA · TASA DE DESEMPLEO ABIERTO · SALARIO MÍNIMO · PETRÓLEO · INVERSIÓN EXTRANJERA DIRECTA · BALANCE PÚBLICO · BALANZA COMERCIAL

TREMENDOOOOS

BRIN Y PAGE, LOS CREADORES DE GOOGLE, TIENEN POCO TIEMPO PARA CAVILAR EN SU ÉXITO. ¿QUÉ MÁS DA: NO HAN LLEGADO A LOS 40 Y EL MUNDO ES SUYO >10

Microsoft celebró sin la presencia de Bill Gates

**VENTANAS AL VUELO**

Steve Ballmer, al centro, director general de Microsoft Corp., celebra luego de tocar la campana de apertura en las oficinas del índice NASDAQ, en Nueva York, durante la presentación de Windows Vista, así como Office y Exchange versiones 2007. Ballmer dijo que la demanda hacia estos productos será mayor a la que estiman los analistas. >11

HERNANDO DE SOTO

## Es urgente el paquete reestructural

En el nuevo sexenio deben lograrse mejoras a las políticas fiscal, energética y laboral si se desea el crecimiento económico

POR ENGGE CHAVARRÍA

El primer paso para abatir la economía informal en el país es aprobar las reformas estructurales, en especial la fiscal, energética y laboral, así como bajar los costos de operación, señaló Hernando de Soto, presidente del Instituto Libertad y Democracia (ILD).

Entrevistado en el marco de la XXXIV Convención Nacional del Instituto Mexicano de Ejecutivos de Finanzas (IMEF), el analista peruano llamó al gobierno a no olvidar que los empresarios son quienes generan el grueso del empleo, por lo que urgió a ejecutar acciones pertinentes, porque el crecimiento de la economía informal conlleva a bajos niveles competitivos y eso rezagaría más el crecimiento económico del país.

**Escenarios para 2007**

En su último día a cargo de la Secretaría de Hacienda, Francisco Gil sostuvo que Vicente Fox deja a Felipe Calderón una economía fuerte, mercados estables y un millón de empleos generados. Pese a la estabilidad, los analistas manifiestan incertidumbre. En la proyección económica más probable, las reformas estructurales seguirán retrasándose, pero la economía de Estados Unidos crecerá y los precios del petróleo se mantendrán altos, anotó Francisco Gutiérrez, director de análisis económico y planeación estratégica de Scotiabank México.

LOGRÓ AJUSTE EN EL PRECIO

### *Vientos huracanados para Aeroméxico*

OPINIÓN: Pedro Alonso · José Yuste · David Páramo · Marielena Vega · Carlos Velázquez

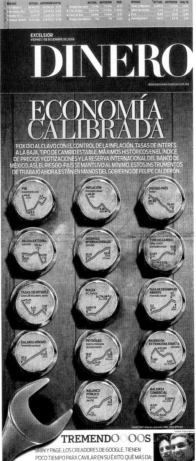

A CONTAR

Aplausos sí, pero nada de porras

ARRASA EL PRD EN ELECCIÓN LOCAL

En resultados parciales, el IEDF contabiliza más del 47 por ciento de la votación en favor de Marcelo Ebrard, y aun cuando asegura que la jornada transcurrió en calma, hubo varias irregularidades

12,194

JUDGES' SPECIAL RECOGNITION:
SPECIAL COVERAGE

**EXCELSIOR,** México City

Ángeles Barajas, Alejandro Gómez, Marco Gonsen, Luzma Díaz de León Reyes, Marco A. Román, Alexandro Medrano, Gerardo Galarza, Pascal Beltrán del Río, Ernesto Rivera, Héctor López, Staff

**Awards of Excellence**

A-Section page, broadsheet, 50,000-174,999
News, A-Section page, broadsheet, 50,000-174,999
Special coverage, section, with ads, two awards

# EXCELSIOR

EL PERIÓDICO DE LA VIDA NACIONAL

Año XC-Tomo IV, Número 32,443 • México, D.F. • 100 páginas

$10.00
LUNES 3 de julio de 2006

www.nuevoexcelsior.com.mx

# ¿Quién?

LÓPEZ OBRADOR:
**GANÉ Y ES IRREVERSIBLE**

Aunque ofreció respetar el resultado, así pierda por un voto, aseguró que su ventaja es de 500 mil sufragios

México amaneció hoy sin un ganador de los comicios presidenciales declarado por la autoridad electoral, y con sus dos candidatos más fuertes autoproclamados como triunfadores.

Una vez que Luis Carlos Ugalde, consejero presidente del Instituto Federal Electoral, informó a las 23:00 horas de anoche que las cifras de su conteo rápido no le permitían anunciar a un ganador, y de que inmediatamente después el presidente Vicente Fox exhortó a los aspirantes a respetar los tiempos marcados por el árbitro de los comicios para anunciar los resultados –por lo menos a partir del miércoles–, el perredista Andrés Manuel López Obrador emitió un mensaje en el que se declaró ganador con una ventaja de 500 mil votos.

Pese a que ofreció acatar el resultado de la elección aun cuando pierda por un voto, el tabasqueño exigió que se respete la ventaja que, aseguró, es "irreversible", anunció que buscará un pacto nacional y, en un mensaje posterior frente a simpatizantes en el Zócalo capitalino, advirtió que estará al pendiente del conteo "acta por acta".

Por quién, cómo y dónde votaron
Página 10

CALDERÓN:
**GANÉ Y NO CABE DUDA**

El festejo quedó para otro día.

Foto: Héctor López

El panista proclamó su triunfo, basado en las encuestas de salida y las cifras que hasta anoche ofreció el PREP

Felipe Calderón Hinojosa se dirigió a sus seguidores apenas unos minutos después de que Andrés Manuel López Obrador hiciera lo propio; sonriente, ofreció también respetar el resultado oficial, e inmediatamente después se dijo vencedor.

Para sustentar su dicho, se basó en tendencias de encuestas de salida difundidas por diversas empresas y en la ventaja que hasta ese momento le daba el Programa de Resultados Electorales Preliminares (PREP) del IFE.

"Con estos datos a nosotros no nos cabe la menor duda de que hemos ganado las elecciones y que los mismos serán corroborados por el IFE", proclamó Calderón, quien también dijo que se respetará la decisión de la autoridad "defendiendo cada uno de los millones de votos emitidos por los mexicanos".

El PRI –cuyo candidato Roberto Madrazo tuvo una votación, según el PREP, de alrededor de 20%– aseguró, en voz de su líder nacional Mariano Palacios, que es "el más importante factor de estabilidad, de gobernabilidad y de conducción política para México"

Un país prácticamente partido en dos
Página 4

GDF, Asamblea y 13 delegaciones, al PRD

## La capital seguirá pintada de amarillo

El Partido de la Revolución Democrática arrasó en la elección local del Distrito Federal

El triunfo de Marcelo Ebrard en los comicios para la jefatura de gobierno fue contundente, al igual que el de su partido en la mayoría de las diputaciones locales y jefaturas delegacionales en disputa.

Al cierre de esta edición, de acuerdo con los resultados parciales del Instituto Electoral local, el 47.24% de los capitalinos favorecieron con su voto al candidato de la coalición Por el Bien de Todos, PRD-PT-Convergencia, mientras que los aspirantes del PAN, Demetrio Sodi, y Beatriz Paredes, de la alianza PRI-PVEM, obtuvieron 27.57% y 21.85%, respectivamente.

En la Asamblea Legislativa, el partido gobernante llevaba ventaja en 35 distritos por cinco de Acción Nacional.

Tres jefaturas delegacionales –Benito Juárez, Miguel Hidalgo y Cuajimalpa– quedaron al margen de la ola amarilla y serán gobernadas por el PAN.

Páginas 12 y 13

## 3 MINUTOS

JALISCO: Acción Nacional da la vuelta
Pese a la desventaja con la que llegó, según las encuestas, iba anoche cuatro puntos adelante del PRI en la gubernatura.
—Pág. 16

MORELOS: Adame, ligeramente superior
El panista supera a su rival del PRD, que va arriba en las curules.
—Pág. 17

GUANAJUATO: Carro completo azul
El PAN retiene holgadamente la gubernatura y el Congreso local.
—Pág. 16



This work shows a sense of excitement on every page — you're part of the election process instead of being a witness to it. It connects with what is important to readers. How often do we elicit that emotion, especially in elections? On every page there's something different. Editors took the various pieces of information they wanted to communicate and chose the right format for each one. Maybe more people would vote if more election coverage were like this.

Este trabajo muestra un sentido de excitación en cada página; uno es parte del proceso eleccionario en vez de sólo un testigo. Conecta con lo que es importante para los lectores. ¿Cuán seguido se instiga, se provoca esa emoción, especialmente en las elecciones? Hay algo diferente en cada página. Los editores tomaron las variadas informaciones que querían comunicar y eligieron el formato correcto para cada una. Tal vez más gente votaría si hubiera más coberturas sobre elecciones como ésta.

# EXCELSIOR

EL PERIÓDICO DE LA VIDA NACIONAL

Año XC-Tomo IV, Número 32,442 • México, D.F. • 100 páginas

$12.00
DOMINGO 2 de julio de 2006

www.nuevoexcelsior.com.mx

EL ELENCO
Compiten cinco por la presidencia; tres gubernaturas y el GDF se renuevan.

LAS CIFRAS
A las 8 de la noche, las tendencias en **nuevoexcelsior.com.mx**. Las televisoras difundirán encuestas de salida. El mensaje presidencial será cerca de la medianoche.

LOS FESTEJOS
El PRD espera celebrar en el Zócalo. El PAN quiere congregarse en el Ángel de la Independencia y el PRI, en su sede nacional.

# DECIDE

## TÚ GOBIERNAS EL PAÍS

Más de 71 millones de mexicanos estamos hoy convocados a las urnas para la elección presidencial de mayor competencia en la historia.

El IFE difundirá a las 11 de la noche las tendencias y se conocerá el nombre del ganador. La apuesta de todos: un 3 de julio en paz.

Fotoarte: Ángeles Barajas y Alejandro Gómez

¡ZÍ... ZOU!
De Alemania emergerá un nuevo campeón, gracias a la magistral actuación de ayer de Zidane. El futbol también seguirá hablando portugués gracias al arquero lusitano Ricardo, que detuvo tres penalties a los ingleses.

Foto: AP

2 DE OCTUBRE

## LEA, encerrado en su casa; declara el lunes

POR RICARDO ZAMORA

El ex presidente Luis Echeverría Álvarez no ha rendido su declaración preparatoria por el presunto delito de genocidio ocurrido el 2 de octubre de 1968, y por el cual está bajo arresto domiciliario.

Juan Velásquez, abogado de Echeverría, explicó ayer que la notificación de que ya se cumplió la orden de arresto para su cliente no ha llegado al Juzgado 15 de Distrito del Reclusorio Preventivo Sur, que preside el impartidor de justicia Ranulfo Castillo Mendoza.

El litigante confió en que en una semana se resolverá la situación legal de Echeverría y que el juez 15 decretará su libertad.

Desde la madrugada de ayer, elementos de la Agencia Federal de Investigación (AFI) se apostaron en los dos accesos del domicilio de Echeverría y tienen la orden de evitar que éste salga, pues violaría el arresto domiciliario ordenado por el magistrado del Segundo Tribunal Unitario en materia penal, José Ángel Mattar Oliva.

En entrevista, Salvador Martínez della Roca "El Pino", dirigente estudiantil en 1968, felicitó al magistrado que ordenó aprehender a Echeverría y pidió que llegue hasta las últimas consecuencias.

## 3 MINUTOS

GLOBAL: Atentado en Irak; 66 muertos
Estalla un coche bomba en un barrio chiita de Bagdad, un día después de las amenazas de Osama Bin Laden.
—Pág. 8

ADRENALINA: La leyenda dice adiós a Wimbledon
Andre Agassi fue superado por el español Rafael Nadal; su despedida representó también la ruptura de una tradición.
—Pág. 1

COMUNIDAD: El arte de vivir en el DF
Creadores expresan su sentir de lo que es habitar en la metrópoli.
—Pág. 1

DECIDE
TÚ GOBIERNAS
ELECCIONES 2006

JACQUELINE BRACAMONTES > MODELO Y ACTRIZ

MOISÉS HERNÁNDEZ > OPERADOR DE TRÁILER

ILANA SOD
CASI DIEZ

*Tres no somos todos*

EN ESTA ESQUINA... LOS PRIMERIZOS

Nerviosos, le han preguntado a quienes ya lo hicieron: "¿Qué se siente?" Sus padres les han dicho que piensen bien el paso que darán, pues les marcará la vida: es su primera vez... en las urnas

ABRAHAM QUINTANA > MÚSICO

SARA MARTÍNEZ > PRODUCTORA DE DULCES TÍPICOS

ANASTASIO FLORES > FOTÓGRAFO

EN ESTA OTRA... LOS QUE *PASAN*

Mientras algunos jóvenes jalan para un lado, hay otros que tiran para el opuesto y afirman que no ejercerán su derecho. Prefieren abstenerse que elegir propuestas "que nunca serán cumplidas"

ANTÍDOTO PARA EL ABSTENCIONISMO

OLALLO RUBIO

*El verdadero voto del miedo*

## JUDGES' SPECIAL RECOGNITION: SPECIAL NEWS TOPICS

**LA PRESSE,** Montréal

Francis Leveillee, Benoit Giguere, Genevieve Dinel, Marie-Claude Mongrain, Caroline Touzin, Michele Ouimet, Silvia Galipeau, Mario Girard, Sylvie St-Jacques, Catherine Bernard, Alain-Pierre Hovasse, Marie-Claude Lortie, Marie-Claude Malboeuf

**Awards of Excellence**
Special news topics, local, three awards

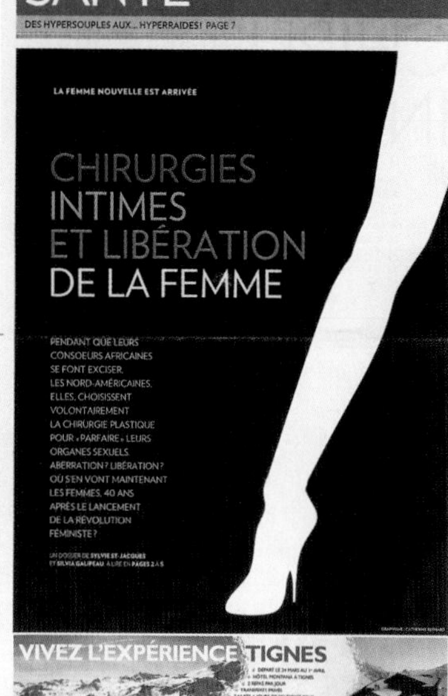

LA PRESSE MONTRÉAL DIMANCHE 26 FÉVRIER 2006

ACTUEL SANTÉ

LES SECRETS DU POIVRE PAGE 6

DES HYPERSOUPLES AUX... HYPERRAIDES! PAGE 7

LA FEMME NOUVELLE EST ARRIVÉE

CHIRURGIES INTIMES ET LIBÉRATION DE LA FEMME

PENDANT QUE LEURS CONSOEURS AFRICAINES SE FONT EXCISER, LES NORD-AMÉRICAINES, ELLES, CHOISISSENT VOLONTAIREMENT LA CHIRURGIE PLASTIQUE POUR « PARFAIRE » LEURS ORGANES SEXUELS. ABERRATION? LIBÉRATION? OÙ S'EN VONT MAINTENANT LES FEMMES, 40 ANS APRÈS LE LANCEMENT DE LA RÉVOLUTION FÉMINISTE?

UN DOSSIER DE SYLVIE ST-JACQUES ET SILVIA GALIPEAU À LIRE EN PAGES 2 À 5

LA PRESSE MONTRÉAL DIMANCHE 22 OCTOBRE 2006

PLUS /// DIMANCHE

ALIMENTATION VOYAGE AU PAYS DU SLOW-FOOD PAGES 4 ET 5

DU VENT DANS LES VOILES LA CHRONIQUE D'AGNÈS GRUDA PAGE 6

SÉRIE /// FILLES DE GANG

S'EN SORTIR?

UNE ENFANCE ROCK'N'ROLL. LE GRAND AMOUR AVEC UN MEMBRE DES ROUGES. COGNAC À FLOTS. PROSTITUTION. ON A ASSISTÉ HIER À LA DESCENTE AUX ENFERS DE JULIE, UNE JEUNE MONTRÉALAISE HAPPÉE PAR LES GANGS DE RUE. ON LA RETROUVE AUJOURD'HUI FRAUDEUSE EN ONTARIO, DANSEUSE AU NOUVEAU-BRUNSWICK ET, SURTOUT, MÈRE DE 25 ANS QUI TENTE DE RÉCUPÉRER SON FILS ET DE REFAIRE SA VIE. UN DÉFI.

› SUITE ET FIN DE NOTRE DOSSIER SUR LES FILLES DE GANG EN PAGES 2 ET 3

2 ACTUEL — LA PRESSE MONTRÉAL SAMEDI 8 AVRIL 2006

DOSSIER / EN BAS DE LA CEINTURE

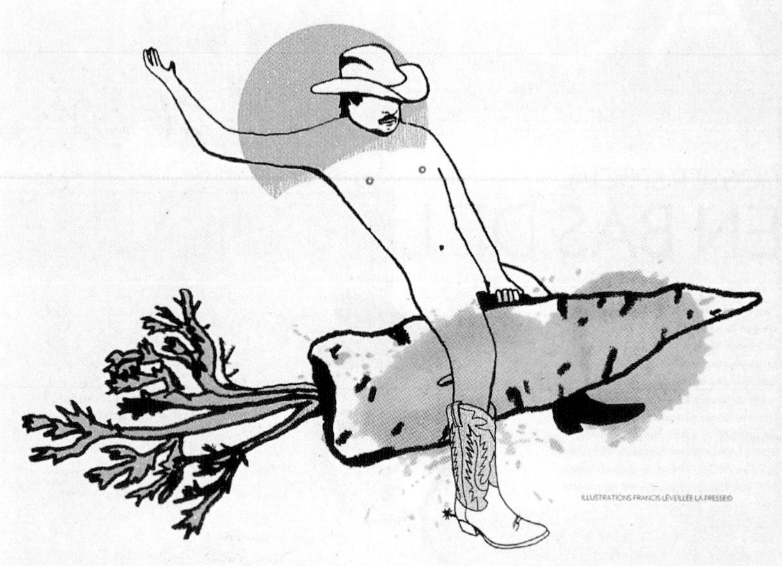

ILLUSTRATIONS FRANCIS LÉVEILLÉE LA PRESSE©

# La folie du sexe allongé

MARIO GIRARD

Pilules, pompes, programmes d'exercices, appareils à traction, poudres de perlimpinpin, une gigantesque industrie s'est créée au cours des dernières années. Son but? Procurer quelques centimètres de plus au sexe des hommes et, tant qu'à y être, le rendre plus performant, plus durable, plus efficace et plus agile.

L'arrivée d'Internet a donné à ce marché un essor incomparable. Avec des noms aussi édifiants que Penisexpert.com, Grand-penis.com, Quelpenis.com et Gros-penis.com, des sites nous bombardent de publicités constituant un impressionnant lot de pourriels sur Internet. À elles seules, les pilules soi-disant capables d'allonger et d'épaissir le pénis rapportent annuellement 100 millions de dollars en Amérique du Nord.

« Je trouve que la tactique de ces fabricants ressemble à celle des marques de maquillage, dit le psychologue François St-Père. On crée des complexes pour vendre. On dit: vous avez besoin de notre produit pour être *normal*. »

Effectivement, certains annonceurs n'hésitent pas à faire du « terrorisme publicitaire » pour promouvoir leurs produits. « Soixante-sept pour cent des femmes se disent déçues de la taille du pénis de leur conjoint », clame la publicité d'un élixir bidon offert à 69,95 $ et censé procurer 14 cm (4 pouces) supplémentaires au sexe.

« On est dans une période de superficialité, ajoute François St-Père. Ça nous permet de contourner les choses essentielles. Ce marketing s'inscrit dans cette vague. »

Et puis, avouons-le, il y a en ce moment une démocratisation du pénis. Tout le monde s'intéresse à cet organe qui fait maintenant la une des magazines branchés et l'objet de quelques spectacles d'humour.

Normal donc qu'une industrie se soit créée autour. Et au centre de cette industrie qui vise l'amélioration du pénis, se trouve une technique chirurgicale de pénoplastie qui permet au pénis de gagner instantanément quelques centimètres. Une poignée de médecins pratiquent cette intervention dans le monde, dont le plasticien torontois Robert Stubbs.

### Surtout les Québécois

« L'idée est de couper partiellement le ligament suspenseur de la verge, cette membrane qui relie le pénis à l'os du pubis, explique-t-il. Ainsi « décroché », le pénis gagne en moyenne de un à trois centimètres. »

Robert Stubbs a pratiqué cette intervention (qui coûte 6000 $) sur des centaines d'hommes. « Je fais beaucoup plus de phalloplastie, c'est-à-dire d'épaississement de la verge », dit-il. Dans ce cas-ci, des greffons graisseux, prélevés sur le corps du patient, sont injectés entre la peau de la verge et les corps caverneux.

Sur 300 patients rencontrés consécutivement sur une période de deux ans par le Dr Stubbs, seulement 12 avaient au départ un problème congénital. Les 288 autres désiraient un allongement pour des raisons esthétiques. La moyenne d'âge était de 37 ans et 95 % d'entre eux étaient hétérosexuels.

Le plasticien pense que l'obsession du gros pénis est plus forte chez les Québécois que dans le reste du Canada. « Ils sont plus ouverts là-dessus et ont été les premiers à en parler. Les Canadiens hésitent encore à utiliser ce mot. »

L'urologue François Besnard rencontre beaucoup d'hommes qui désirent un allongement du pénis. « Je les réfère à un sexologue ou un psychologue, dit ce médecin du CHUM. Le problème, il est dans la tête. »

François Besnard pense que seuls les cas de micropénis (huit à neuf centimètres en érection) méritent une attention particulière. « Il faut savoir que c'est très rare », dit-il.

François Besnard a récemment pris connaissance d'une étude portant sur des hommes désireux d'avoir un plus gros sexe. Or, la majorité des sujets avaient un pénis nettement plus imposant que la moyenne. « Quand on leur a parlé des normes, ils étaient surpris », dit l'urologue.

### C'est quoi, normal?

Mais au fait. Qu'est-ce qu'un pénis « normal »? Les spécialistes s'entendent pour dire que la taille moyenne du pénis est de 7 cm à 11 cm au repos et de 10 cm à 20cm en érection, la moyenne mondiale étant de 14 cm.

En se faisant allonger le pénis, les hommes s'achètent une part de virilité, pense la sexologue Michelle Laurette. « Mais à la différence des femmes qui se font faire une augmentation mammaire, cette transformation n'est pas apparente, explique-t-elle. Ce n'est donc pas pour le paraître mais pour la performance. »

Même dans un cabinet de psychologue ou de sexologue, la question de la taille du sexe n'est pas courante. Seulement un quart des hommes abordent ce sujet. « Ils parlent davantage de leurs craintes de ne pas être à la hauteur ou de ne pas savoir comment satisfaire leur partenaire », dit Mme Laurette.

Cette sexologue est désespérée de voir qu'on emprunte des chemins aussi faciles pour contourner un problème plus profond. « C'est comme pour le Viagra. Il est plus facile de prendre une pilule que de se demander pourquoi on éprouve moins de désir pour sa partenaire. »

« C'EST COMME POUR LE VIAGRA. IL EST PLUS FACILE DE PRENDRE UNE PILULE QUE DE SE DEMANDER POURQUOI ON ÉPROUVE MOINS DE DÉSIR POUR SA PARTENAIRE. »

## La zigounette en chiffres

**14** centimètres → la longueur moyenne mondiale d'un pénis en érection.

**1,9 milliard de dollars** → le chiffre d'affaires de Pfizer, fabricant de Viagra, en 2003.

**20** → le nombre de chirurgiens spécialisés dans l'allongement du pénis au monde.

**24** centimètres → la longueur du sexe de la star de la porno Rocco Siffredi.

**40** kilomètres/heure → la vitesse moyenne d'un éjaculat.

**10 000** → le nombre de partenaires de l'acteur porno John Holmes, qui avait un sexe de 45 centimètres.

**9,95$** → le prix d'une boîte de 12 préservatifs Durex Performax. Grâce à leur lubrifiant spécial, ils désensibilisent le pénis et retardent l'éjaculation

**3 à 10** → le nombre de jets de sperme par éjaculation.

**50 000** → le nombre moyen de courriels publicitaires envoyés chaque jour par un cybercom commerçant de produits érectiles.

These three entries explore a woman overtaken by her street environment, feminism in the time of cosmetic surgery and overt sexuality, and menstruation and the "male machine" as a health-education story. The illustrations demonstrate unblushing coverage of sensitive, serious topics that are tastefully executed and very inviting. The illustrations are consistent, reflecting the tone of each topic. There's a sense of humor to some, and yet they also can be very dark. Right away you get the feel — and you know the story through the illustrations. It's easy for newspapers to delve into sex in a titillating way, but, rather, these are very smart.

Estas tres piezas exploran el caso de una mujer sobrepasada por el ambiente de su calle, el feminismo en la era de la cirugía estética, y la sexualidad manifiesta, la menstruación y la máquina machista como un relato de educación sobre la salud. Las ilustraciones exhiben una cobertura sin tapujos de temas sensibles y serios que están realizados con gusto y que invitan al lector. Las ilustraciones son consistentes y reflejan el tono de cada tema. Algunos están tratados con cierto sentido del humor, aunque también pueden estar tratados con bastante seriedad. Esto se siente de inmediato, y el tema se revela por medio de las ilustraciones. Es fácil que los periódicos traten el sexo de forma excitante, pero, en cambio, estas piezas lo hacen de forma ingeniosa.

## JUDGES' SPECIAL RECOGNITION: COMBINATION PORTFOLIO

**HERALDO DE SORIA** (Spain)

Lola Gómez

**Silver:** Combination page design portfolio

dedomingo

HERALDO DE SORIA

9 de abril de 2006

Las instalaciones solares comienzan a usarse como medida eficaz de ahorro energético

¡SORPRENDENTE!

Una muestra en el Museo Arqueológico de Madrid nos descubre Ambrona y Torralba

Wow. This entry is different from anything we've seen in the small-circulation categories. It simply stopped us. The stripped-down design in black and white balances ample white space with bold typography to create energy. This designer is like a sprinter who runs the same race but always wins. These pages show that the strength of an idea can carry a page. It sets a benchmark for small-paper design.

Impresionante. Esta pieza es diferente de todo las demás que vimos en las categorías de baja circulación. Simplemente nos sorprendió. El diseño puro en blanco y negro equilibra amplios espacios blancos con tipografía audaz para generar energía. Este diseñador es como un velocista que correa la misma carrera pero que siempre gana. Estas páginas demuestran que la fortaleza de una idea puede sostener una página. Alza la vara del diseño de diarios pequeños.

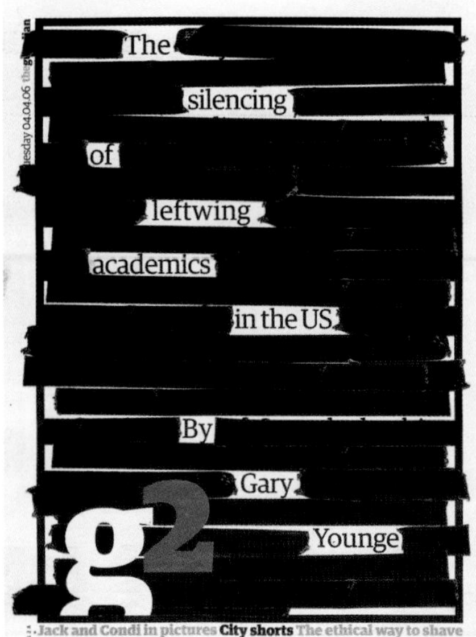

## JUDGES' SPECIAL RECOGNITION: FEATURE DESIGN

**THE GUARDIAN,** London

Richard Turley, Izabella Bielawska

**Awards of Excellence**
Other feature page, tabloid, 175,000+, five awards
Special coverage, section, with ads

These covers are creative and versatile. They show how this publication adapts the cover to the subject matter five days a week. They present a consistently high level of conceptual work each day.

Estas portadas son creativas y versátiles. Muestran la forma en que este periódico adapta la portada al tema cinco días a la semana. Cada día exhiben un consistente alto nivel de trabajo conceptual.

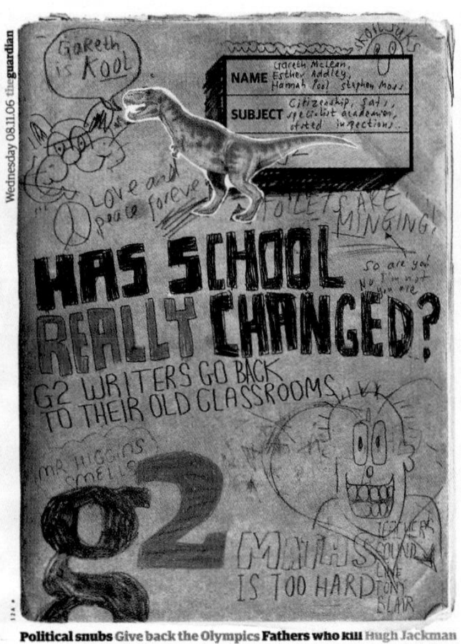

Chapter Three

# MULTIPLE WINNERS

Ganadores múltiples

**ENTRIES WINNING MORE THAN ONE AWARD**
Piezas ganadoras de más de un premio

**ARIZONA DAILY STAR,** Tucson

Jeff Randall, James Gregg, Lindsay Miller, Kelly Presnell, Chiara Bautista, Mike Rice, Rick Wiley, V.W. Vaughan, Staff

**Awards of Excellence**
News, A-Section page, broadsheet, 50,000-174,999
Reprints
Single-subject special coverage
Special news topics, local

Tuitama hurt as Cats play USC tough / Sports

Arizona Daily Star

SERVING TUCSON SINCE 1877 · SUNDAY, SEPTEMBER 24, 2006

STAR INVESTIGATION: SEALING OUR BORDER

# It won't work

Canyons, rivers and shifting sand — plus a multibillion-dollar price tag, more violence and less business — make sealing the border all but impossible

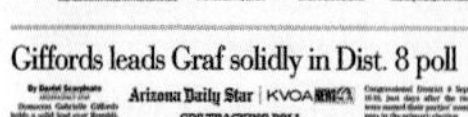

SEALING OUR BORDER

WHY IT WON'T WORK

Giffords leads Graf solidly in Dist. 8 poll

Arizona Daily Star | KVOA

Naming places

The Penobscot Way

How the Penobscots named the lands and waters around us

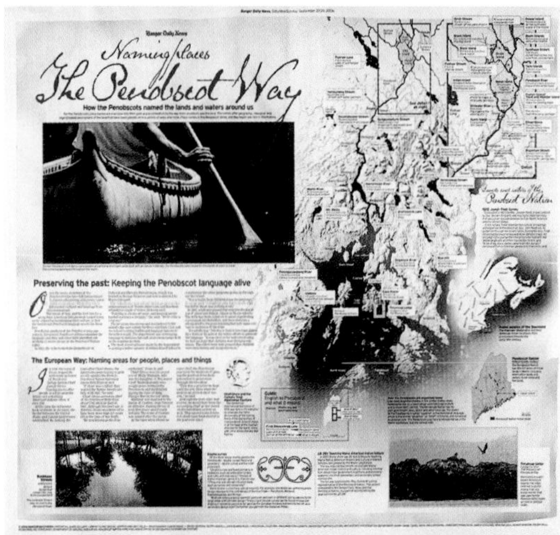

Naming places

The Penobscot Way

How the Penobscots named the lands and waters around us

Preserving the past: Keeping the Penobscot language alive

The European Way: Naming areas for people, places and things

**BANGOR DAILY NEWS** (Maine)

Eric Zelz, Jonathan Ferland, Aimee Dolloff, Scott Haskell, John Clarke Russ, Gabor Degre

**Awards of Excellence**
Mapping, 50,000-174,999
Miscellaneous

Sunday, July 2, 2006 / ARIZONA DAILY STAR · A5

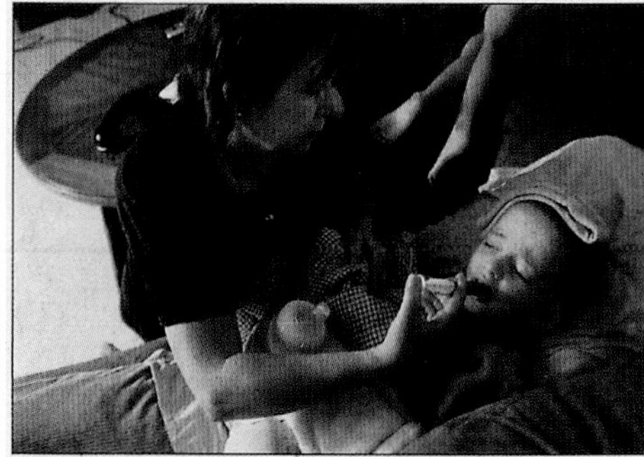

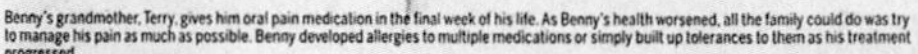

Benny's grandmother, Terry, gives him oral pain medication in the final week of his life. As Benny's health worsened, all the family could do was try to manage his pain as much as possible. Benny developed allergies to multiple medications or simply built up tolerances to them as his treatment progressed.

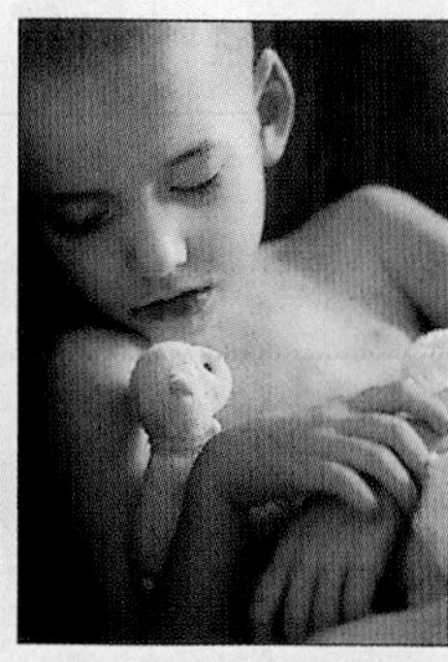

Benny cuddles with his favorite stuffed animal, Lamby, while napping on the living room couch. Often times, when Benny awoke in pain, he would ask for Lamby, who was never far away. Since Benny's death, his mother, Amy, sleeps with Lamby for comfort.

Benny's parents, Derek and Amy, lie in bed with their son's body while waiting for him to be taken to the mortuary. "These pictures are devastating, but beautiful," Amy said later. "They speak nothing but the truth. We think the general public needs to see that this world exists and then maybe they will donate money to find a cure, so no more mothers and fathers have to face the loss of their babies and no more children will suffer like Benny."

*Continued from previous page*

happy, energetic kid once again.

But Benny's good health was brief. The cancer came back in September, growing fast.

More rounds of chemo, most of it useless. Within a few months, the pain moved in, meaning more drugs and radiation to try to control it. In the last stages of pregnancy with her fifth son, Amy remembers how Benny would come over to her if she moaned even once.

"Here he would be in excruciating pain, and he'd come over and ask, 'Mom, are you OK?' " Amy said. "He was always worried about everybody else. Benny was as stubborn as they come. He had a mind of his own, but he was very much the peacekeeper. I always taught my children to treat each other with love and respect, and it was Benny who reminded everybody to do that."

Even as Benny's life force began to wane, he decided to celebrate his fifth birthday not with a party, but by working an "Alex's Lemonade Stand" at Reid Park to raise money for pediatric-cancer research. Setting a goal of about $1,000, the Petz family was astonished when hundreds of Tucsonans, upon hearing of Benny's plight, stopped by to sip juice, give gifts to the little boy in a wheelchair — and donate some $13,000.

Only two weeks later, Benny's breathing turned shallow, late one night, and Amy finally told her child closest to Benny, 6-year-old Jeremia, that his little brother was dying.

Surprising everyone, Benny somehow made it through the night, even rallying the next morning. It was then that Jeremia asked the fateful question Benny overheard.

"Benny let me hold him for the first time in a long time," Amy said. "We talked about heaven, that piggies — oh, he loved pigs — would be there, where clouds were made of Cinnamon Toast Crunch, where he would never be sick again.

"He said he didn't want to go 'because you're not there.' But I told him we would all come as soon as we could."

That talk — that death and heaven and piggies were near — lasted about 20 minutes, until Benny had had enough. He asked one more question: "Will everyone in heaven think I'm cute?" because everyone always had, his whole life.

Of course, Benny, she told him. "They'd be crazy not to."

*Contact reporter Carla McClain at 806-7754 or at cmcclain@azstarnet.com.*

**On StarNet**
View a slideshow of images from the last days of young Benny's life at **azstarnet.com/slideshows**

**In Benny's memory**

The Petz family will continue to support Alex's Lemonade Stand, a nationwide project to raise money for pediatric-cancer research. They plan to set up a stand in Tucson every year on Benny's birthday, May 26.

To donate to Alex's Lemonade Stand For Pediatric Cancer Research in Benny's memory, go to www.alexslemonade.org or to the family's Web site at www.bennylove.com. You may send the family your thoughts via their Web site, too.

"I have to let my baby go," mother Amy says through sobs as she, her husband and her mother comfort each other. With Benny's death came a mix of relief for the end of his suffering and deep sorrow for his shortened life.

**ARIZONA DAILY STAR,** Tucson

Greg Bryan, Jeff Randall, Mike Rice, Rick Wiley, Staff

**Silver:** General news photo
**Award of Excellence:** Photo series

Benny's parents lie in bed with their son's body while waiting for him to be taken to the mortuary. Often you see pictures of the bereaved, and they're very emotional. Here the emotion is subtle, until you read in the caption that the child died of pediatric cancer. We can't imagine the moment when the photographer was there. When we saw it, we hurt.

Los padres de Benny yacen en la cama con el cuerpo de su hijo mientras esperan llevarlo a la funeraria. Muchas veces se ven fotos de los deudos y son muy emotivas. En este caso, la emoción es sutil, hasta que se lee bajo la foto que el niño murió de cáncer infantil. No nos podemos imaginar el momento en que el fotógrafo estuvo presente. Cuando vimos la foto, sentimos dolor.

**THE BUFFALO NEWS** (N.Y.)

Vincent J. Chiaramonte

**Awards of Excellence**

News, inside page, broadsheet, 175,000+

Sports page design, 175,000+

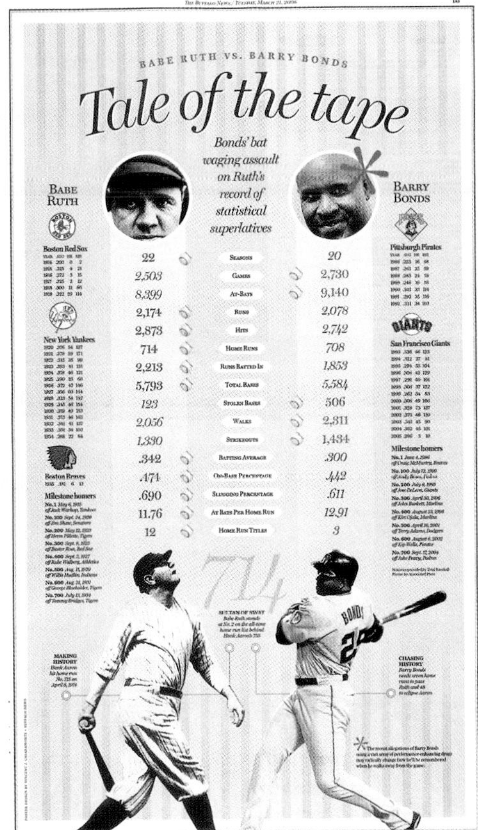

Babe Ruth vs. Barry Bonds

# Tale of the tape

Bonds' bat waging assault on Ruth's record of statistical superlatives

Babe Ruth

Barry Bonds

**THE BULLETIN,** Bend, Ore.

Renee Fullerton, Julie Johnson, Anders Ramberg, Melissa Jansson

**Awards of Excellence**

Home/real estate page, broadsheet, 49,999 & under

Portfolio, feature page design, 49,999 & under, Renee Fullerton

FOOD • HOME • GARDEN

TUESDAY

AT HOME

F

Gardening

# Bonsai

Embrace the ancient art as your own

Getting started:

History:

Cape Cod Times

FORUM

JIM COOGAN

Trust, credibility suffer when public employees cross the line.

INSIDE F

FIVE YEARS LATER

# Lessons of 9/11 burn deep

Don't let terror attacks be hijacked for political gain

Answering a call for help in the night

There were people who hated us. Shouldn't we be talking about why?

I now know that I humbly learned a great lesson that day: When we have an opportunity to extend ourselves to help others, don't be timid, go ahead and reach out.

**CAPE COD TIMES,** Hyannis, Mass.

James Warren

**Awards of Excellence**

Other feature page, broadsheet, 49,999 & under

Single illustration

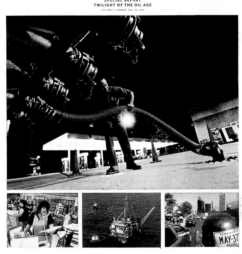

Chicago Tribune

SPECIAL REPORT

TWILIGHT OF THE OIL AGE

# A tank of gas, a world of trouble

What does it take to quench America's mighty thirst for gasoline? Pulitzer Prize-winning Tribune correspondent Paul Salopek found the answer to that question by cracking a closely guarded code of the oil industry: He traced individual tanks of gas pumped at a suburban Marathon station to the fuel's precise sources around the globe, from the fishless waters off the coast of Nigeria to the politically restless fields of Venezuela. In doing so, Salopek reveals how America's oil addiction binds us to some of the most fragile and hostile corners of the planet–and to a petroleum economy edging toward an epic energy crisis.

STORY BY PAUL SALOPEK

TRIBUNE CORRESPONDENT

PHOTOS BY KUNI TAKAHASHI

TRIBUNE STAFF PHOTOGRAPHER

RESEARCH BY BRENDA KILIANSKI

TRIBUNE RESEARCHER

EDITORIALS AND COMMENTARY PAGES APPEAR ON PAGES 14 AND 15; THE PERSPECTIVE SECTION WILL RETURN NEXT WEEK

**CHICAGO TRIBUNE**

Steve Cavendish, Meg Theno, Kuni Takahashi, Adam Zoll, Steve Layton, Paul Salopek, George Papajohn, Flynn McRoberts, Robin Daughtridge, Mike Miner

**Awards of Excellence**

Photo project

Special news topics, international

**THE BOSTON GLOBE**

Chin Wang, Ann Scales, Lane Turner, Dan Zedek

**Awards of Excellence**
Other feature page, broadsheet, 175,000+
Redesign, section

Style & Arts

The Boston Globe Thursday, April 20, 2006

It's all about me!

With personalization on the rise, you can put your stamp on anything. Even stamps.

By Linda Matchan | Globe Staff

Shopping gets chic on Main Street

Stage Review

Roberts gets lost in lackluster 'Three Days'

Redesign, After

Living Arts

The Boston Globe Thursday, October 13, 2005

Alex Beam

A who's who of mistaken identity

Symphony No. 1

A James Levine protege gets a chance to take the podium in Boston

This 'Boy Friend' has style, but needs attitude adjustment

Big names up for National Book Award

Redesign, Before

**THE BOSTON GLOBE**

Brian Gross, Ken Fratus

**Awards of Excellence**
News, inside page, broadsheet, 175,000+
Portfolio, sports page design, 175,000+, Brian Gross
Sports page, broadsheet, 175,000+

The Boston Globe

New Red Sox home run mark

52

David Ortiz, the king of pop, produces a chart-topping record long in the making

The Boston Globe

Style

Cracking the Code

By Carol Beggy | Globe Staff
Illustrations by Pablo

Casual/Dress Casual

Business-Casual/Business

Cocktail

Formal/Black Tie/Creative Black Tie

White Tie

**THE BOSTON GLOBE**

Chin Wang, Pablo, Ann Scales, Dan Zedek

**Awards of Excellence**
Other feature page, broadsheet, 175,000+
Single illustration

Business&Money

Boston Sunday Globe, June 4, 2006

Why are office towers on the rise again in Boston?

Dormant plans to reshape the city's skyline come alive as firms feel squeezed for space

While other sites list airfares, newcomer forecasts where they're headed

Step smart

An eye toward growth

Staying sharp

**THE BOSTON GLOBE**

Grant Staublin, Shirley Leung, Dan Zedek

**Awards of Excellence**
Business page, broadsheet, 175,000+
Portfolio, news page design, 175,000+

**EL CORREO,** Bilbao, Spain

Fernando G. Baptista, José Miguel Benítez, Gonzalo de las Heras, Daniel Garcia, Isabel Toledo, María Almela, Saioa Exteazarra, Bárbara Sarrionainda, Jorge Dragonetti

**Silver:** Portfolio, information graphics, staff, non-breaking news & features, 50,000-174,999
**Award of Excellence:** Information graphics, non-breaking news & features, 50,000-174,999

La Historia avala al Puente de Vizcaya

We read every word of this and thought "wow." These have all been finished well, and they've introduced many elements gently. You notice the details without any stress or difficulty, and that's an art form. The rendering is incredible, the color palettes subtle, and the hierarchy clear. The graphic on boat reconstruction is like an elegant, structured piece of music.

Leímos cada palabra de esta pieza y quedamos atónitos. Todos han sido bien terminados y han presentado muchos elementos de forma delicada. Los detalles se notan sin nada de estrés o dificultad, lo que es todo un formato artístico. El dibujo es increíble, las paletas de color son suaves, y la jerarquía es clara. El grafico de la reconstrucción del barco es como una elegante y estructurada pieza musical.

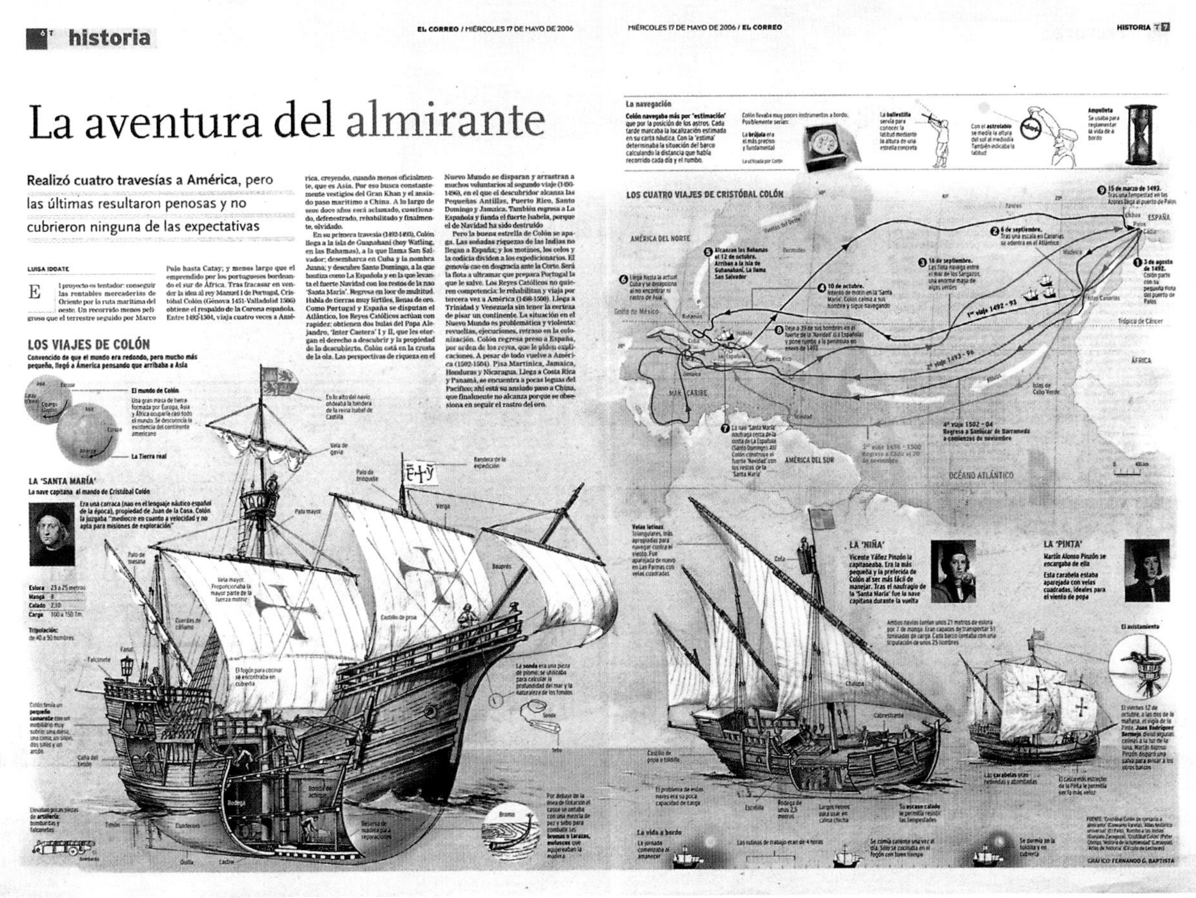
historia

EL CORREO / MIÉRCOLES 17 DE MAYO DE 2006

MIÉRCOLES 17 DE MAYO DE 2006 / EL CORREO

HISTORIA

La aventura del almirante

Realizó cuatro travesías a América, pero las últimas resultaron penosas y no cubrieron ninguna de las expectativas

LOS VIAJES DE COLÓN

LA 'SANTA MARÍA'

LOS CUATRO VIAJES DE CRISTÓBAL COLÓN

LA 'NIÑA'

LA 'PINTA'

POLICIALES

Robo al banco: la historia secreta del golpe más audaz

Cómo se concretó el plan

**CLARÍN,** Buenos Aires, Argentina

Gustavo Lo Valvo, Juan Elissetche, Federico Sosa, Hugo Scapparone, Pablo Ayala, Darío Morel, Martín Marpons, Alejandro Tumas, Pablo Loscri, Jorge Portaz, Staff

**Awards of Excellence**
News, A-Section page, tabloid, 175,000+
Information graphics, breaking news, 175,000+
Portfolio, Information graphics, staff, breaking news, 175,000+

"It's okay to go through this together"

**CONCORD MONITOR** (N.H.)

Dan Habib, Lori Duff, Preston Gannaway, Ken Williams, Tim Lytvinenko, Thomas Whisenand, Brian Lehmann

**Awards of Excellence**
Portfolio, staff photo
Portfolio, individual photo, Preston Gannaway

**THE GUARDIAN,** London

Paul Scruton, Michael Robinson, Simon Rogers, Staff

**Silvers**
Mapping, 175,000+
Portfolio, information graphics, staff, non-breaking news & features, 175,000+

This graphic is beautifully drawn and wonderfully clear, with exceptional contrast between the different types of war deaths. Powerful color leads you through the profound topic. It has such an effect because it brings a far-away topic into common context.

Este gráfico está bellamente dibujado y es maravillosamente claro, con un excepcional contraste entre los diferentes tipos de muerte producto de la guerra. El potente color sirve de guía a través de la profundidad del tema. Produce tal efecto porque pone un tema lejano en un contexto cercano.

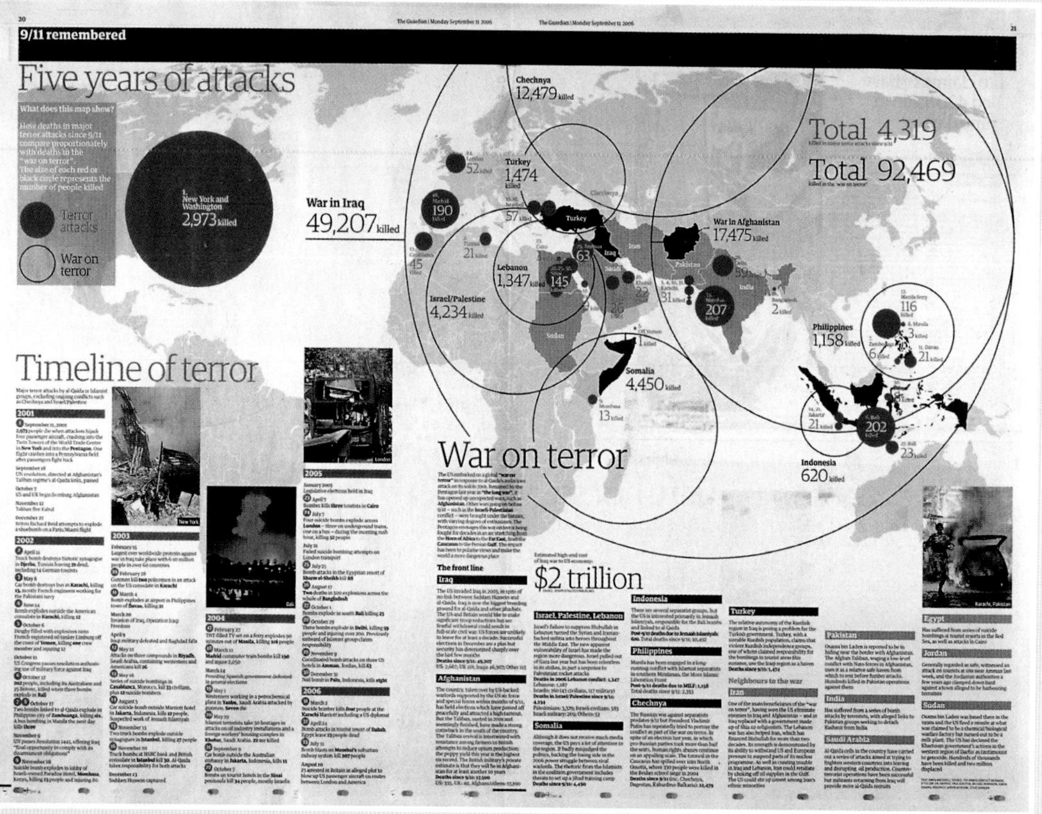
9/11 remembered

Five years of attacks

What does this map show?

Terror attacks

War on terror

New York and Washington 2,973 killed

War in Iraq 49,207 killed

Chechnya 12,479 killed

Turkey 1,474 killed

Lebanon 1,347 killed

Israel/Palestine 4,234 killed

War in Afghanistan 17,475 killed

Somalia 4,450 killed

Philippines 1,158 killed

Indonesia 620 killed

Total 4,319

Total 92,469

Timeline of terror

War on terror

The front line

$2 trillion

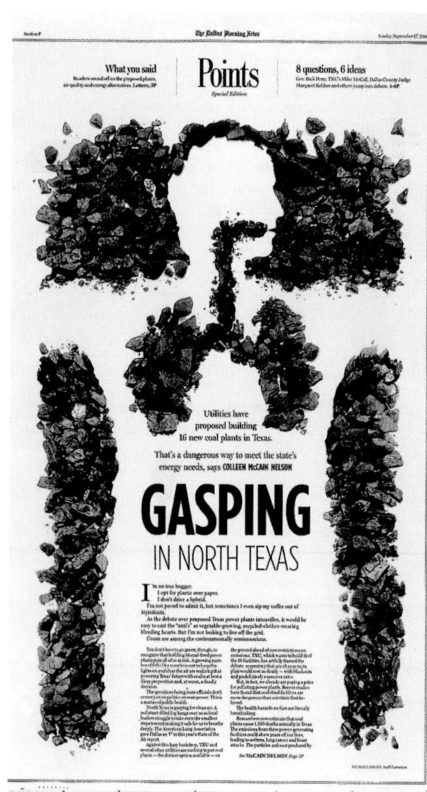
Points

What you said

8 questions, 6 ideas

Utilities have proposed building 16 new coal plants in Texas.

That's a dangerous way to meet the state's energy needs, says COLLEEN McCAIN NELSON

GASPING

IN NORTH TEXAS

**THE DALLAS MORNING NEWS**

G. Noel Gross, Michael Hogue

**Awards of Excellence**
Single illustration
Special coverage, section cover

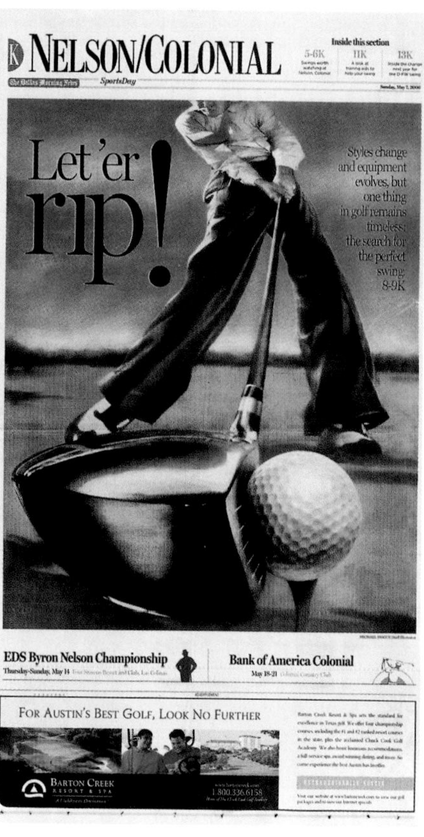
NELSON/COLONIAL

Let'er rip!

Styles change and equipment evolves, but one thing in golf remains timeless: the search for the perfect swing. 8-9K

EDS Byron Nelson Championship

Bank of America Colonial

For Austin's Best Golf, Look No Further

Barton Creek

**THE DALLAS MORNING NEWS**

Rob Schneider, Jason Dugger, Michael Hogue, Noel Nash, Mark Kazlowski, Troy Oxford

**Awards of Excellence**
Special coverage, section cover
Special news topics, sports

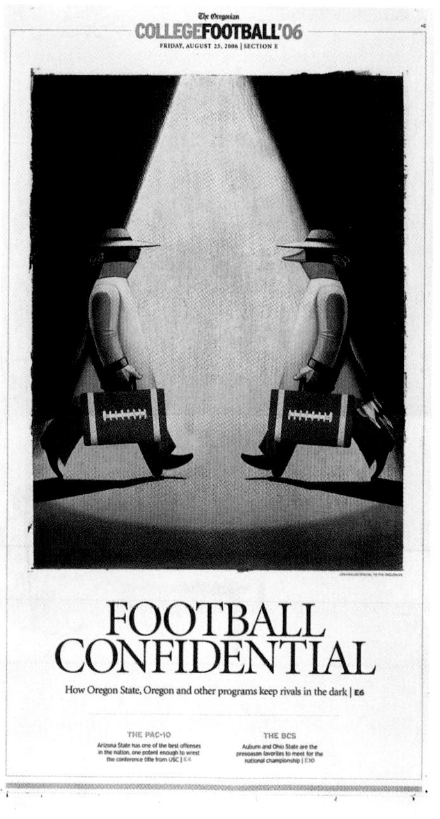
The Oregonian

COLLEGE FOOTBALL '06

FOOTBALL CONFIDENTIAL

How Oregon State, Oregon and other programs keep rivals in the dark | E6

THE PAC-10

THE BCS

**THE OREGONIAN,** Portland

Steve McKinstry, Derrik Quenzer, Steve Cowden, Jon Krause, Eric Baker, Joel Odom, Steve Zimmerman, Dan Uthman

**Awards of Excellence**
Portfolio, illustration, staff
Single illustration
Special coverage, section cover

**SUN JOURNAL,** Lewiston, Maine

Nick Masuda, Pete Gorski, Amber Waterman, Carol Coultas, Rex Rhoades, Judy Meyer, Keith Hagel, Douglas Van Reeth

**Awards of Excellence**
Special coverage, inside page
News, inside page, broadsheet

SEEING GREEN: Fiber, forests, futures

# A glimpse at papermaking a continent away

**A tale of two trees: The tortoise and the hare**

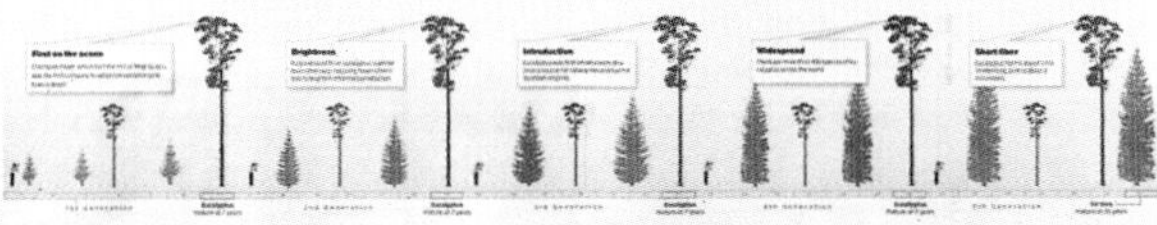

THE NEWS TRIBUNE

**THE NEWS TRIBUNE,** Tacoma, Wash.

Elysia Smith

**Awards of Excellence**
Entertainment page, tabloid, 50,000-174,999
Portfolio, feature page design, 50,000-174,999

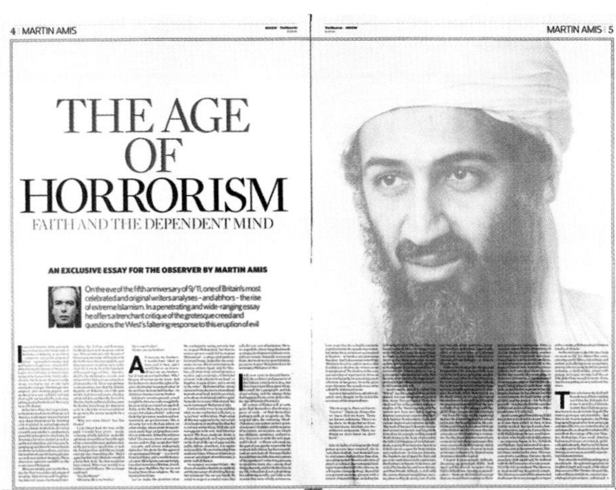

4 MARTIN AMIS

MARTIN AMIS 5

THE AGE OF HORRORISM

FAITH AND THE DEPENDENT MIND

AN EXCLUSIVE ESSAY FOR THE OBSERVER BY MARTIN AMIS

On the eve of the fifth anniversary of 9/11, one of Britain's most celebrated and original writers analyses – and abhors – the rise of extreme Islamism. In a penetrating and wide-ranging essay he offers a trenchant critique of the grotesque creed and questions the West's faltering response to this eruption of evil

**THE OBSERVER,** London

Carolyn Roberts, Lynsey Irvine, Jamie Sage, Anthony Bell

**Awards of Excellence**
Entertainment section, 175,000+
Other feature page, tabloid, 175,000+

LA PRESSE MONTRÉAL SAMEDI 9 SEPTEMBRE 2006

**LA PRESSE,** Montréal

Francis Leveillee, Benoit Giguere, Genevieve Dinel, Alexandre Pratt, Frederic Murphy

**Silver:** Single illustration
**Award of Excellence:** Special coverage, section cover

We like the loose type, the colors and the energy. The typography has a raw and primitive feel. It's very graphic, and there's a youthful energy to it. It's much like a poster with complementary colors.

Nos gusta la tipografía suelta, los colores y la energía. La tipografía tiene una sensación cruda y primitiva. Es muy gráfica y lleva una energía juvenil. Es como un afiche con colores complementarios.

Hartford Courant.

RELL EASILY HOLDS GOVERNOR'S OFFICE

U.S. HOUSE: DEMS RULE
5th: Murphy ousts Johnson
2nd, 4th: Simmons and Shays fighting for survival

U.S. SENATE: SHARP SPLIT
Democrats, riding a wave of voter discontent, cut into Republican majority

INDEPENDENT'S DAY

Lieberman Defeats Lamont

WINNERS AND LOSERS

Democrats Seize Control In House

**HARTFORD COURANT**
(Conn.)

Greg Harmel,
Michael McAndrews,
Richard Messina, Wes Rand,
Melanie Shaffer,
David Grewe, John Scanlan

**Awards of Excellence**
News, A-Section, 175,000+
News, A-Section page, broadsheet, 175,000+
Portfolio, news page design, 175,000+, Greg Harmel

BASEBALL '06

{ PART ONE

Coco Crisp Comes To The Red Sox To Replace Johnny Damon In Center. Given Damon's Popularity, That Could Be A Hairy Situation. But Crisp Has The Name And Many People Think The Game. Meanwhile, The Yankees Bank On Damon.

CRISP, CLEAN LOOK

{ INSIDE: PART TWO
Clubhouses: The Home Away From Home For Major Leaguers. Pages L13-18

**HARTFORD COURANT**
(Conn.)

Timothy Reck,
Suzette Moyer, Mario Zucca

**Awards of Excellence**
Special coverage, section, with ads
Special coverage, section cover

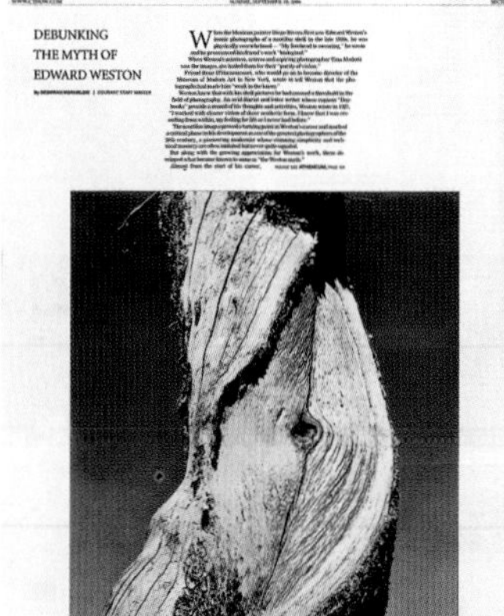

ARTS

DEBUNKING THE MYTH OF EDWARD WESTON

MASKS AND COSTUMES SLOW TIME'S PASSAGE IN ATHENEUM EXHIBIT

**HARTFORD COURANT**
(Conn.)

Nicole Dudka, Beth Bristow

**Awards of Excellence**
Entertainment page, broadsheet, 175,000+
Portfolio, feature page design, 175,000+, Nicole Dudka

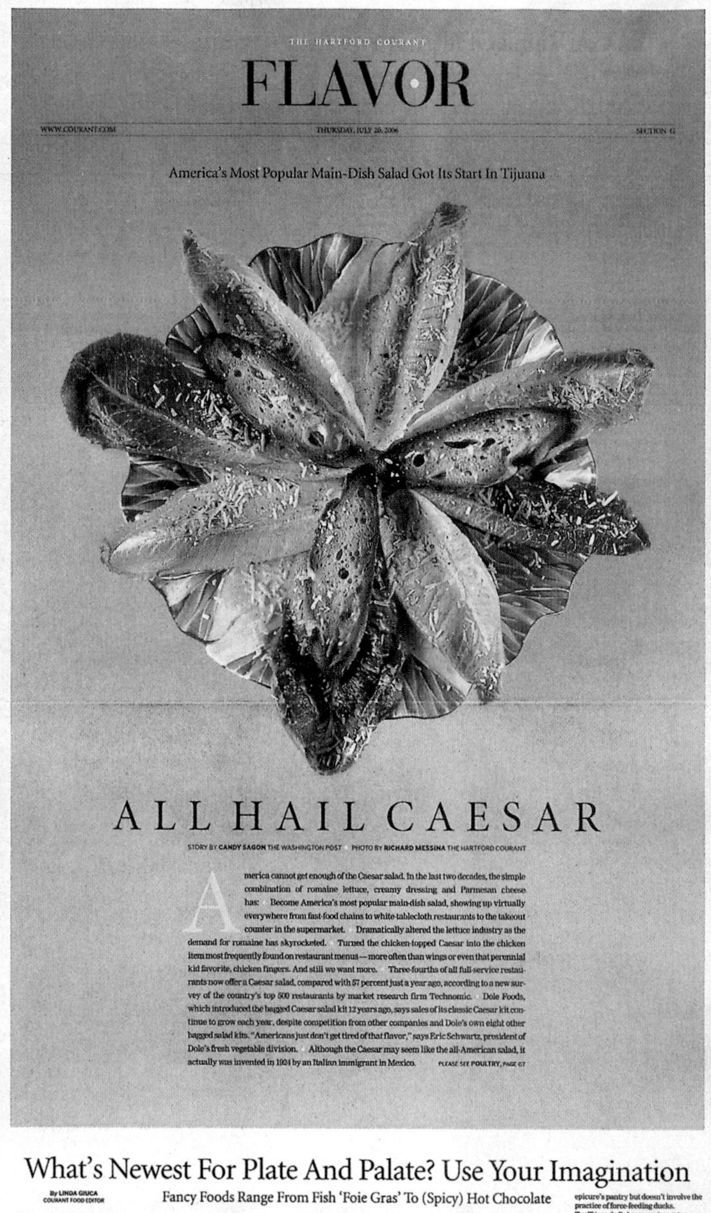

THE HARTFORD COURANT

FLAVOR

WWW.COURANT.COM · THURSDAY, JULY 20, 2006 · SECTION G

America's Most Popular Main-Dish Salad Got Its Start In Tijuana

ALL HAIL CAESAR

STORY BY CANDY SAGON THE WASHINGTON POST · PHOTO BY RICHARD MESSINA THE HARTFORD COURANT

America cannot get enough of the Caesar salad. In the last two decades, the simple combination of romaine lettuce, creamy dressing and Parmesan cheese has: Become America's most popular main-dish salad, showing up virtually everywhere from fast-food chains to white-tablecloth restaurants to the takeout counter in the supermarket. Dramatically altered the lettuce industry as the demand for romaine has skyrocketed. Turned the chicken-topped Caesar into the chicken item most frequently found on restaurant menus — more often than wings or even that perennial kid favorite, chicken fingers. And still we want more. Three-fourths of all full-service restaurants now offer a Caesar salad, compared with 57 percent just a year ago, according to a new survey of the country's top 500 restaurants by market research firm Technomic. Dole Foods, which introduced the bagged Caesar salad kit 12 years ago, says sales of its classic Caesar kit continue to grow each year, despite competition from other companies and Dole's own eight other bagged salad kits. "Americans just don't get tired of that flavor," says Eric Schwartz, president of Dole's fresh vegetable division. Although the Caesar may seem like the all-American salad, it actually was invented in 1924 by an Italian immigrant in Mexico. PLEASE SEE POULTRY, PAGE G7

What's Newest For Plate And Palate? Use Your Imagination

By LINDA GIUCA
COURANT FOOD EDITOR

Fancy Foods Range From Fish 'Foie Gras' To (Spicy) Hot Chocolate

The opening day of the 52nd Summer Fancy Food Show in New York City was all about the Italians, but it had nothing to do with food.

In a show where producers and international trade associations represent more than 160,000 specialty food products, Italy is always a major presence, with aisle after aisle in its pavilion devoted to cheese, olive oil, pasta, condiments and the like.

But even the best aged Parmigiano Reggiano or the darkest-green extra virgin olive oil couldn't compete with the finish of the World Cup soccer match between Italy and France, whose food producers also were well represented at the show.

By 4 p.m. on July 9, the show's opening day, the Italian booths were all but deserted as the faithful's eyes were glued to the flat-screen televisions perched in the common areas. When their countrymen finally captured the title, there was more waving of the red, green and white and shouts of "Italia! Italia!" than sampling or bragging about the quality of Italian gourmet exports.

Even as the soccer contest heated up, the food show went on, as retailers trekked the aisles in search of the new and exciting.

While some may wonder if a truly unique product is possible — haven't we already seen it all? — exhibitors offered some new twists.

One candidate for the "most unusual" label was a foie gras alternative that will probably never become a staple in every epicure's pantry but doesn't involve the practice of force-feeding ducks.

Truffières de Rabasse, an importer based in the Provence region of France, is promoting monkfish liver — la foie de lotte — as an alternative to the rich duck-liver delicacy that has become the subject of laws in California, where force-feeding is prohibited, and in Chicago, where the sale of foie gras is banned.

**HARTFORD COURANT** (Conn.)

Timothy Reck, Suzette Moyer, Richard Messina

**Silver:** Food page, broadsheet, 175,000+
**Award of Excellence:** Portfolio, feature page design, 175,000+, Timothy Reck

This page does just what a food page should. The food looks fresh and crunchy — you want to taste it. The choice of green food on a green background is unusual, but it gives the page a luxurious magazine feel. The food styling is excellent. The plate is beautiful but doesn't overpower the food.

Esta página hace justamente lo que toda página de comida debería lograr. La comida se ve fresca y crujiente; hay que probarla. La elección de comida de color verde contra un fondo del mismo color es poco común, pero le da a la página un toque de revista de lujo. El diseño de la comida es excelente. El plato es bello pero no opaca la comida.

GAMING } **"It kinda fell into my lap** about five years ago. I saw it [the video game Dance Dance Revolution] at a local arcade that I've been going to since I was a little kid. I've been hooked ever since. It's the first game to test your mind and test you physically. You shed the pounds. It's equivalent to miles of running. The game involves club dance music. It really never ends. It's almost impossible to ever beat it. You're constantly upgrading your skills. I'm kind of unofficially retired now; I'm playing keyboard in an industrial band called Intrigue Unique."

Ryan Dest, 18, of Wallingford, was photographed on July 16, 2005, at the ConnectiCon Gaming Convention in the Connecticut Convention Center in Hartford. Dest was DJ'ing the Dance Dance Revolution competition at the convention. This music-based game calls for players get up and move their feet to the music. It features a variety of songs and levels of difficulty.

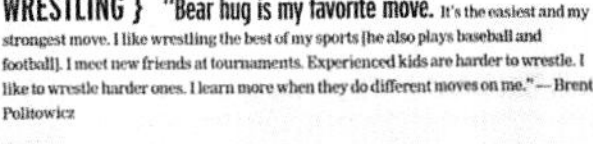

WRESTLING } **"Bear hug is my favorite move.** It's the easiest and my strongest move. I like wrestling the best of my sports [he also plays baseball and football]. I meet new friends at tournaments. Experienced kids are harder to wrestle. I like to wrestle harder ones. I learn more when they do different moves on me." — Brent Politowicz

"Brent is a guy's guy. He's very into camaraderie and his buddies. You don't have to talk about it. You're out on the mat by yourself, and you show your buddies what you can do. Wrestling is very good at teaching the kids respect and empathy. Whether you're a girl or a boy, you're part of the brotherhood. You're always known as a wrestler." — Carolyn Politowicz, Brent's mother

Brent "Tank" Politowicz, 8, of Montville, was photographed on Jan. 9, 2005, during a USA Wrestling Connecticut meet at Southington High School. He has competed with the Montville Youth Wrestling Team for three years. Tank wrestles in the 103 class of the Midget division, and he finished second in the state in his weight class.

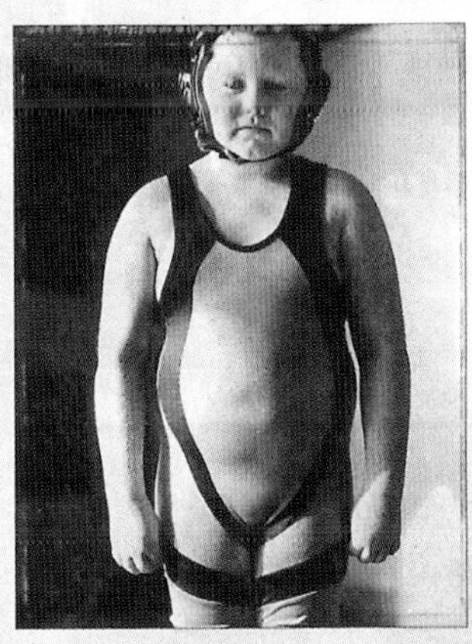

SLED HOCKEY } **"I like all the action.** I've always liked hockey. This was a good opportunity to play. I've been skating on my feet for about five years. I like competing. We play the same teams every month, and it's good to see the same teams getting better and better. I play right wing; I'm stronger with my right hand." — Anthony Kuntz

"Anthony has spina bifida. He played youth soccer until the sixth grade. He needed an outlet. He fell in love with it once he tried it. It's a great outlet for kids who normally wouldn't get a chance to compete." — Richard Kuntz, Anthony's father

Anthony Kuntz, 14, of West Hartford was photographed on Dec. 18, 2004, following a practice of the Connecticut Wolf Pack sled hockey team at the Loomis Chaffee School rink in Windsor. The team plays in the Prudential Northeast Sled Hockey League. Sled hockey, for physically challenged athletes, is played by the same rules as those for players who are not physically challenged.

BODYBUILDING } **"You have to learn your body** when you compete. There's a lot of things you have to know about your body. I do five shows a year. It's just a good experience. You're really competing against yourself. I like meeting a lot of personalities at the meets. Everybody does something different with their workout ethic. It's a very competitive sport. Everybody wants to win. I have Sarcoidosis [an inflammatory disease that can affect major organs and tissues]. I should have been dead 12 years ago. Once I got into lifting weights, it went away. I have no sign of it now, but they say it's always with you. It brings me so much thrill to show people what I've been working hard for."

Rhodes, 34, of Fort Washington, Md., was photographed on Aug. 27, 2005, during a competition at Bristol Eastern High School sponsored by the Organization of Competitive Bodybuilders and the International Fitness Professions Association. He has been weightlifting for 10 years and competing in bodybuilding for three years.

**HARTFORD COURANT** (Conn.)
Bruce Moyer, Suzette Moyer, Thom McGuire

**Silver:** Photo project
**Award of Excellence:** Special coverage, section, no ads

This tells the story of a community through events such as beauty pageants, dog shows, roller derby and fencing. It's a clever way to bring out the diversity of a community, and it all begins with the idea. The image sizes vary, from the full face to the body — it's great portrait photography. It's simply fun and entertaining, and the pages just make you happy.

Se relata la historia de una comunidad a través de eventos tales como concursos de belleza, exhibiciones de perros, y competencias de patinaje y de esgrima. Es una forma inteligente de exhibir la diversidad de una comunidad, y todo comienza con una idea. El tamaño de las imágenes varía, desde el rostro completo hasta el cuerpo entero; los retratos son excelentes. Verdaderamente es divertido y entretenido; las páginas hacen sentirse bien.

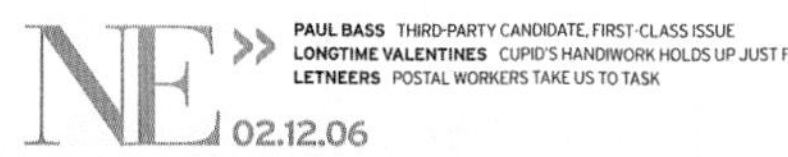

NE
PAUL BASS THIRD-PARTY CANDIDATE, FIRST-CLASS ISSUE
LONGTIME VALENTINES CUPID'S HANDIWORK HOLDS UP JUST FINE
LETNEERS POSTAL WORKERS TAKE US TO TASK
02.12.06


THE FACE OF
COMPETITION

On Teams Or On Their Own, Their Joy Is In The Pursuit, Not The Prize | Photo Essay by Bruce Moyer

RUGBY } **"The physical contact** keeps me sane. It's an aggressive physical activity that allows me to let off steam. It's socially acceptable to hit somebody as hard as you can, and there's no legal recourse. I started playing in 1981, took some time off and then got back into it. Rugby is a community all its own. You'll spot a rugby player by the type of shirts they wear and just start talking. It's very small in the United States but big around the world. I play for a team in Nashville now. I was coming up to Connecticut and timed my visit around a home game so I could play."

Sheryl Turse, 39, now living in Franklin, Kentucky, was photographed on Sept. 18, 2004, after a Hartford Wild Rose Women's Rugby Football Club match at the Glastonbury Elks Club

WHETHER BY CLIMBING OR HIKING, SLOVENES MAKE PILGRIMAGE UP THEIR MOUNTAIN

STORY AND PHOTOS BY DAVID H. WEINH SPECIAL TO THE COURANT

TRAVEL

A TREK IN JULIAN ALPS

BLED, Slovenia — The plan was for Mojca Span of Life-Trek to meet me at Bled's Jezera train station. I was assured that there was no chance of missing one another, and sure enough, I alighted on the gravel rail bed behind a station that was little more than a whistle-stop. Span, whom I had been addressing as "Mr. Span" in my e-mail correspondence (faux pas, there), turned out to be an attractive young woman who grabbed one of my bags, led me to her car and drove me around Lake Bled to the company's offices. • The environs were instantly captivating: a placid, azure lake with a small, chapel-bedecked island in its middle; a 15th-century fortress on one side, perched on a massive outcrop; and mountains on the horizon. Beautiful, photogenic Bled, Austro-Hungarian spa town and favorite getaway of Tito, the late dictator of Yugoslavia. Welcome to Slovenia. • Span and I go over my itinerary, a multiday hut-to-hut backcountry hike and an ascent of Mount Triglav. The tour would be a circuit: up the Vrata Valley from Mojstrana and down the Valley of the Seven Lakes

**HARTFORD COURANT** (Conn.)
Timothy Reck, Suzette Moyer

**Awards of Excellence**
Travel page, broadsheet, 175,000+
Portfolio, feature page design, 175,000+, Timothy Reck

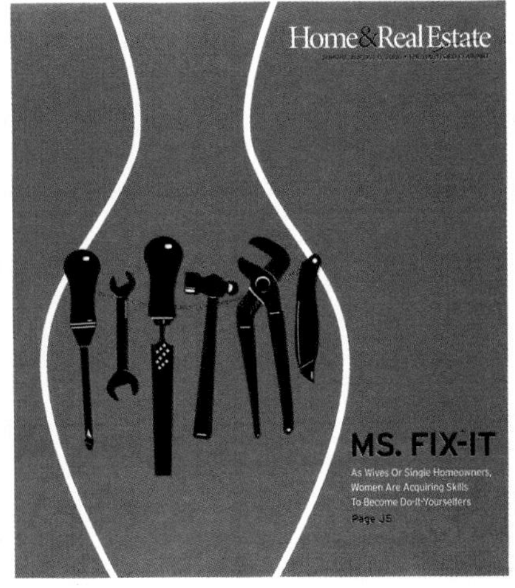

Home&Real Estate
MS. FIX-IT
As Wives Or Single Homeowners, Women Are Acquiring Skills To Become Do-It-Yourselfers
Page J5


**HARTFORD COURANT** (Conn.)
Kristin Lenz, Suzette Moyer

**Awards of Excellence**
Home/real estate page, tabloid, 175,000+
Single illustration

[ The New Foreign Aid : Kenya ]

# Cash and Values From Abroad

LINING UP: Christine Waona's son, Edwin, second from right, and his fellow first graders wait to receive their corrected lessons from their teacher, Judith Odima, at Pinocchio Primary School in Kisumu, Kenya. Edwin lives with two uncles while his mother works abroad to pay for his schooling.

WASHING UP: Edwin gets a bath from his uncle Lucas. The home in Kisumu lacks running water and electricity, so Lucas uses rainwater and candlelight to do the job.

FAMILY VISIT: Susan Waona and niece Faith take a walk near the child's residence, which is protected by a brick wall and razor wire, in Nairobi, the Kenyan capital. Faith lives with her father while her mother, Benta Waona, works in Rome.

While Christine cares for a European child in Rome, family members in Kenya look after her son, Edwin. Like sister Benta, she regularly sends part of her earnings home.

On the web

**LOS ANGELES TIMES**

Don Bartletti, Gail Fisher, Colin Crawford, Michael Whitley, Joseph Hutchinson, Kelli Sullivan

**Silver**
Feature photo

**Awards of Excellence**
News, inside page, broadsheet, 175,000+
Photo series
Photo project

This photo of Kenyan first-graders receiving their corrected lessons just makes you feel good. It's such a beautiful moment, with the children lined up and the great light streaming into the room. Each eager face, including the teacher's, has a story to tell.

Esta foto de estudiantes de primaria de Kenia que reciben sus tareas ciertamente hace sentirse bien. Es un momento tan bello, con los niños en fila y la linda luz que entra a la sala. Cada rostro entusiasta, incluyendo el de quien les enseña, tiene una historia que contar.

[ The New Foreign Aid : Haiti ]

Dozens Living on Emigre's Largess

Haiti by numbers

Lundi has pumped tens of thousands of dollars back into his homeland over the years. 'God blessed me with good fortune,' he says, 'and I have to give it back to Haiti. If I have two dollars, I have to give Haiti one of them.'

**LOS ANGELES TIMES**

Kelli Sullivan, Joseph Hutchinson, Michael Whitley, Gail Fisher, Colin Crawford, Don Barletti

**Awards of Excellence**
News, A-Section page, broadsheet, 175,000+
News, inside page, broadsheet, 175,000+
Photo project
Special news topics, international

**LOS ANGELES TIMES**

Don Bartletti, Gail Fisher, Colin Crawford, Kelli Sullivan, Joseph Hutchinson, Michael Whitley

**Silver:** Feature photo
**Award of Excellence:** Photo page design

We appreciate all the content in this image of a funeral in Haiti — the casket, the cross, the emotion, the grief. It's balanced, with a beginning and an ending, and the cross frames it well. The building on the left adds just the right color palette to offset the casket. After the eyes, the hands next show the feeling and emotion.

Apreciamos todo el contenido de esta imagen de un funeral en Haití; el ataúd, la cruz, la emoción, la pena. Está equilibrada, con un comienzo y un final, y la cruz lo enmarca bien. El edificio de la izquierda añade la paleta de color justa para compensar el ataúd. Tras los ojos, les siguen las manos para mostrar sentimiento y emoción.

## After a family member's death comes mourning, and a search for answers

During the burial of Saintilia Jean in Saint-Louis du Nord, Haiti, above, her oldest daughter, 16-year-old Roselande, collapses in grief as pallbearers, including Dieuseul Lundi, left, carry the casket into the cemetery. Jean, Lundi's half sister, succumbed to an infection stemming from the stillbirth of her 6-month-old fetus. She died in her best friend's arms, in a taxi that lurched along an unpaved road toward the nearest hospital, an hour's drive from her home. Lundi and a brother paid for the burial and other expenses, including new clothes for scores of relatives who attended the funeral. They also hired a 16-piece band that accompanied the funeral procession. Earlier, Lundi, at left, visits the mortician's lab in Port-de-Paix, where Jean's body lies, shortly after her death. Unsatisfied at the lack of a definitive cause of death, he consulted a voodoo priest. The priest concluded that she had been killed by a curse, a death wish cast by a neighbor who was jealous of the secondhand shoes and clothes that Lundi had sent her from Miami over the years. — Don Bartletti

## LOS ANGELES TIMES

Michael Whitley, Joseph Hutchinson, Kelli Sullivan, Mary Cooney, Colin Crawford, Carolyn Cole

**Silver**
News, A-Section page, broadsheet, 175,000+

**Awards of Excellence**
General news photo
News, inside page, broadsheet, 175,000+
Photo project
Portfolio, news page design, 175,000+, Michael Whitley
Special news topics, international

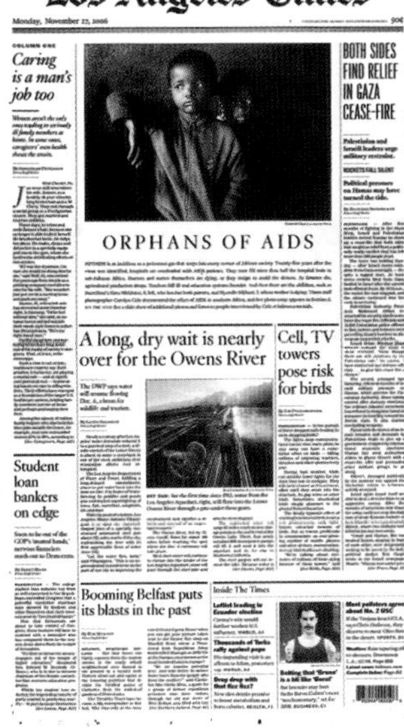

Los Angeles Times

Caring is a man's job too

BOTH SIDES FIND RELIEF IN GAZA CEASE-FIRE

ORPHANS OF AIDS

A long, dry wait is nearly over for the Owens River

Cell, TV towers pose risk for birds

Student loan bankers on edge

Booming Belfast puts its blasts in the past

Inside The Times

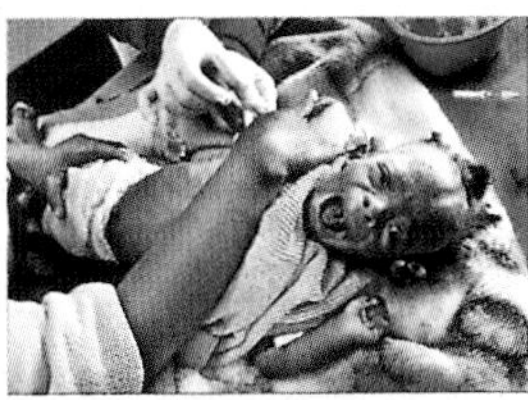

This publication devotes resources to the important issue of AIDS. At 12 columns, you can't ignore the faces of the people who are suffering. You can't help but study their faces. There is a profound sadness that emerges when all the expressions are neutral. The design is seamless and silent, and the front headline and photo are poignant.

Este periódico dedica grandes recursos al importante tema del SIDA. A lo largo de 12 columnas, no es posible ignorar los rostros de las personas en sufrimiento. No queda más que observar sus caras. Una profunda tristeza emerge cuando todas las expresiones son neutrales. El diseño es continuo y silencioso, y el título principal y la fotografía son conmovedores.

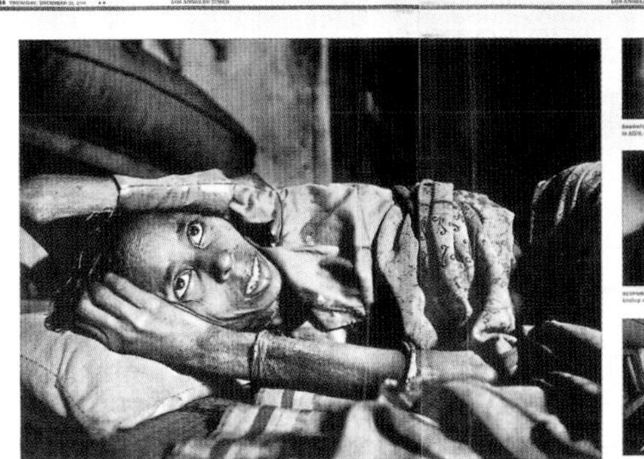

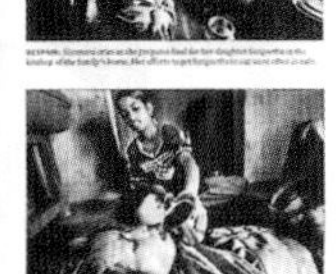

AIDS RAVAGES RURAL INDIA

No country has more people with HIV, and villagers often are unable to access help.

## LOS ANGELES TIMES

Kelli Sullivan, Joseph Hutchinson, Michael Whitley, Gerard Babb, Mary Cooney, Colin Crawford, Francine Orr

**Awards of Excellence**
News, A-Section page, broadsheet, 175,000+
News, inside page, broadsheet, 175,000+
Photo page design

ORPHANS OF AIDS

In southern Africa, children have been cast adrift by disease and victimized by their elders

## LOS ANGELES TIMES

Carolyn Cole, Mary Cooney, Colin Crawford, Michael Whitley, Joseph Hutchinson, Kelli Sullivan

**Awards of Excellence**
Feature photo
News, inside page, broadsheet, 175,000+
Photo page design

**LOS ANGELES TIMES**

Michael Whitley, Joseph Hutchinson, Gail Fisher, Colin Crawford, Rick Loomis

**Awards of Excellence**

News, A-Section page, broadsheet, 175,000+
News, inside page, broadsheet, 175,000+

THE LIFELINE

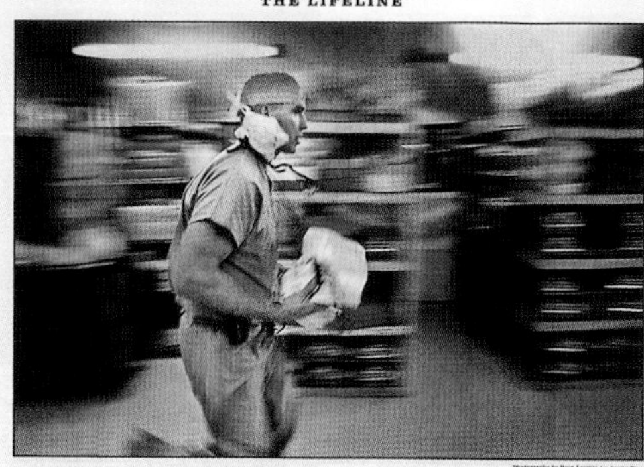

## Medical Victories and Major Losses

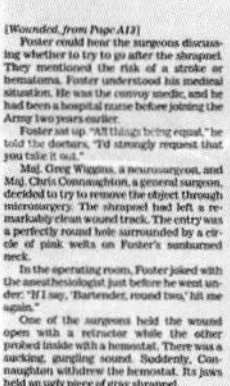

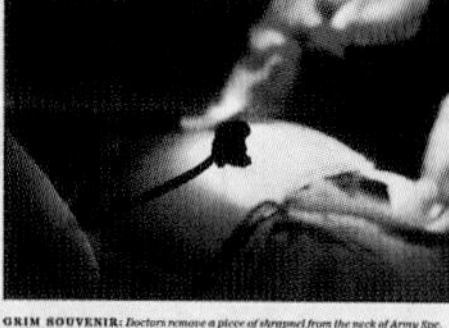

In harm's way

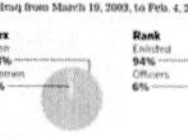

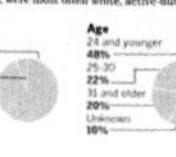

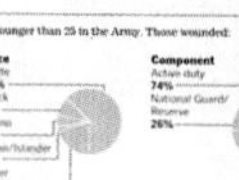

## New Orleans adapts to the 'new normal'

One year after Hurricane Katrina, victims are still repairing damage, searching for belongings

**LOS ANGELES TIMES**

Carolyn Cole, Mary Cooney, Colin Crawford, Michael Whitley, Joseph Hutchinson

**Awards of Excellence**

General news photo
Photo page design
Photo project

A24 SUNDAY, APRIL 2, 2006 ★ LOS ANGELES TIMES

THE LIFELINE

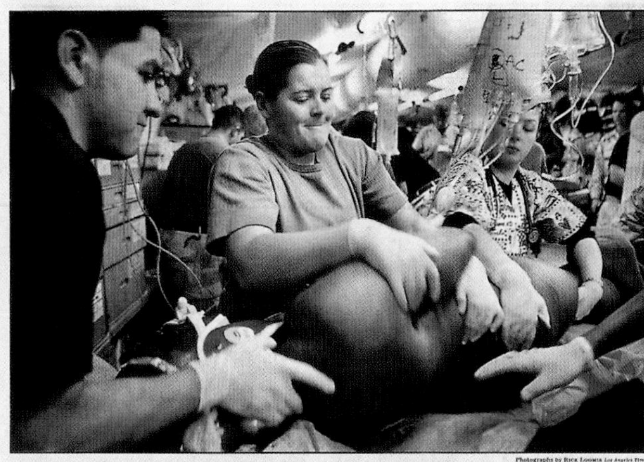

## From Field to Hospital in Minutes

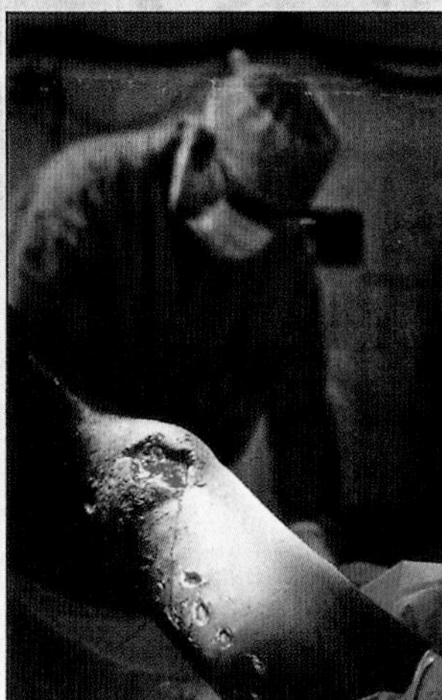

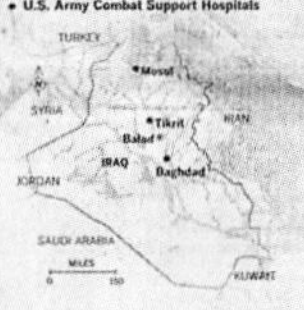

**LOS ANGELES TIMES**

Michael Whitley, Joseph Hutchinson, Gail Fisher, Colin Crawford, Rick Loomis

**Silver**

News, inside page, broadsheet, 175,000+

**Awards of Excellence**

News, A-Section page, broadsheet, 175,000+
Photo project
Photo series

The subject matter and photo content are extraordinary. By devoting resources to covering Iraq and matching that effort with great display, the designers are drawing attention to the subject. The photos are graphic, and they are played appropriately to balance the text on each page.

Los hechos del tema y el contenido fotográfico son extraordinarios. Al dedicar recursos para cubrir Irak y equiparar ese esfuerzo con un gran despliegue, los diseñadores llaman la atención al tema. Las fotos son gráficas y están dispuestas apropiadamente para equilibrar el texto en cada página.

THE LIFELINE

## Patients Quickly Flown to Germany

# SEA LIONS SICKENED BY ALGAE

# DIGGING FOR DATA

RUNOFF NURTURES TOXIC BLOOMS

**LOS ANGELES TIMES**

Kelli Sullivan, Joseph Hutchinson, Michael Whitley, Gail Fisher, Rick Loomis, Colin Crawford

**Silver:** News, inside page, broadsheet, 175,000+
**Award of Excellence:** News, A-Section page, broadsheet, 175,000+

This is the pinnacle of great visual journalism. It's incredible to offer such an amount of space that gives the subject matter its due. The editing and photo play communicate the issue's importance.

Éste es el punto máximo de la excelencia en el periodismo visual. Es increíble dedicar un espacio de tal tamaño para presentar el asunto como corresponde. La edición y el rol de la fotografía comunican la importancia del tema.

Algae, bacteria and jellyfish are thriving

# WORLD'S FISHERIES IN DECLINE

**LOS ANGELES TIMES**

Joseph Hutchinson, Kelli Sullivan, Michael Whitley, Gail Fisher, Rick Loomis, Colin Crawford

**Silver:** News, A-Section page, broadsheet, 175,000+
**Award of Excellence:** Photo project

Beautiful, tightly edited photography makes these pages shine. The spreads flow well together with pacing that mixes photos, graphics, headlines and body type, with overwhelming visuals. On one spread, a series of same-sized photos builds contrast through tight and loose crops.

La bella y bien editada fotografía hace que estas páginas brillen. Los artículos fluyen bien en conjunto con un compás que mezcla fotos, gráficos, tipografía de títulos y texto sin opacar los elementos visuales. En uno de los artículos, una serie de fotos del mismo tamaño crea un contraste por medio de recortes ajustados y sueltos.

# JUNK FOOD DIET DOOMS WILDLIFE

**LOS ANGELES TIMES**

Joseph Hutchinson, Kelli Sullivan, Michael Whitley, Gail Fisher, Rick Loomis, Colin Crawford

**Awards of Excellence**
News, A-Section page, broadsheet, 175,000+
News, inside page, broadsheet, 175,000+
Special news topics, international

**LOS ANGELES TIMES**

Carol Kaufman, Wes Bausmith, Christian Potter Drury, Joseph Hutchinson, Valeria Petrone, Christopher Serra, Franklin Wyandotte, Haydn Cornner, Tomasz Walenta, David Plunket

**Awards of Excellence**
Portfolio, illustration, staff
Single illustration

**LOS ANGELES TIMES**

Lorena Iñiguez, Raoul Rañoa, Thomas Suh Lauder, Cheryl Brownstein-Santiago, Julie Sheer, Les Dunseith

**Awards of Excellence**
Portfolio, information graphics, individual, non-breaking news & features, 175,000+, Lorena Iñiguez
Portfolio, information graphics, staff, extended coverage, 175,000+

B2 TUESDAY, JANUARY 24, 2006 LOS ANGELES TIMES CALIFORNIA

A VISUAL HISTORY OF LOS ANGELES

A landscape of names

After El Camino Real became the Southland's first roadway, the 19th century rancho system and the area's settlers lent their names to many modern-day cities and streets. As part of a periodic series on the birth of L.A., leading up to the 225th anniversary of the city's founding in September, here's a look at some names in our urban landscape, as viewed in a 1930 map published by the L.A.-based Title Insurance and Trust Co.

Old divisions: 1930

Tale of two ranchos

A large tract, almost intact

■ Where Franklin, Coldwater and Benedict canyons' runoff pooled, now near Beverly Drive and Sunset Boulevard, was first called the Gathering of the Waters, or El Rodeo de las Aguas. Maria Rita Valdez de Villa, an Afro Latina soldier's widow, ranched there after her 1838 grant. Burton Green's Rodeo Land and Water Co. developed most of it as Beverly Hills. He and his wife named it after Beverly Farms, Mass.

A large tract that was broken up

■ Juan Jose Dominguez, a retired Spanish soldier, received the Southland's original land grant in 1784. The 75,000-acre Rancho San Pedro eventually passed to his grand-nephew, Manuel Dominguez, an L.A. mayor and L.A. County supervisor. Torrance, Compton, Wilmington, and Carson were settled there. Dominguez heirs' firms still own some of the property.

Pioneers behind some street names today

A Sepulveda Boulevard is probably named for Francisco Sepulveda (1775–1853), an interim L.A. mayor who built Olvera Street's Sepulveda House and got the San Vicente y Santa Monica grant. His son, Jose Andres, got Rancho San Joaquin in what later became the Irvine Ranch.

B Wilshire Boulevard was named by real estate developer H. Gaylord Wilshire (1861–1927). An Ohio native from a wealthy family, Wilshire made and lost fortunes in real estate, farming and gold mining.

C Bandini, a Commerce and Vernon boulevard and a San Pedro street, is named for Peru-born Juan Bandini (1800-1859). He moved here with his father, a Spanish sea captain. A San Diego and Los Angeles civic leader, Bandini owned Rancho Jurupa, where the city of Riverside is now.

D Carson Street was named for John Manuel Carson, a descendant of Juan Jose Dominguez. The younger man was active in the early 20th century in developing the part of Rancho San Pedro that became Carson in 1968.

Sources: San Fernando Valley History Digital Library, Dominguez Rancho Adobe Museum, Riverside County, Los Angeles County Public Library, A Companion to California, L.A. Almanac, the cities of Compton, Simi Valley, Malibu and Irvine, and www.sanleonehistory.com. Graphics reporting by Cheryl Brownstein-Santiago

Recent regional explainer graphics are available at latimes.com/localgraphics

Lorena Iñiguez Los Angeles Times

Sunday, December 10, 2006 Los Angeles Times

BOOK REVIEW

HOLIDAY BOOKS

Jump in, the reading's fine

Looking for that perfect book this season? We've selected 50 of our favorites from the past year. Plus: A return to "Charlotte's Web," and a bookseller reveals how to pick the right gift.

Valeria Petrone For The Times

Los Angeles Times

OTIS CHANDLER | 1927-2006

A Lion of Journalism

**LOS ANGELES TIMES**

Michael Whitley, Kelli Sullivan, Joseph Hutchinson, Robert St. John, Alan Hagman, Mary Cooney, Colin Crawford

**Awards of Excellence**
News, A-Section page, broadsheet, 175,000+
Breaking news, obituaries
News, inside page, broadsheet, 175,000+

E4 SUNDAY, JULY 9, 2006 LOS ANGELES TIMES STYLE & CULTURE

Rasslin' and razzle-dazzle

Far-out flamboyance always prevails at Lucha VaVoom, a spectacle of Mexican freestyle wrestling with an L.A. twist. At its latest stand, Times photographer Francine Orr captures the parade of color and characters.

**LOS ANGELES TIMES**

An Moonen, Paul Gonzales, Christian Potter Drury, Joseph Hutchinson, Francine Orr, Cindy Hively, Kirk McKoy

**Awards of Excellence**
Other feature page, broadsheet, 175,000+
Portrait photo

{ THE OSCARS }

# Fabulous as a formality

{ THE OSCARS }

BEST ACTRESS

Paying homage to a 'real woman'

BEST SUPPORTING ACTRESS

A 'Constant' dig to land the role

BEST ACTOR

A low profile, but a big win

BEST SUPPORTING ACTOR

It's a role worth its weight in gold

Los Angeles Times

HOLLYWOOD

COMMEMORATIVE EDITION

# The Dream Machine

How our town's image factories rose, prospered and conquered the world — and the big challenges they now face. STAR POWER: The glow of lost glamour, Page 14. THE STUDIOS: The system and its discontents, Page 4. CLASSICS: Key films and TV shows that changed the industry, Pages 5 and 16. THE BIZ: A mogul's lament for the old ways, Page 10. PLUS: The new immigrants. Movie worker bees. Tinseltown vs. L.A. Film-tech. A gallery of A-list peccadilloes. A secret history of the town. And test your entertainment IQ.

**LOS ANGELES TIMES**

Christian Potter Drury, Wes Bausmith, Paul Gonzales, Steven R. Hawkins, Kirk Christ, Judy Pryor, Ron Neal, Cindy Hively, Kirk McKoy, Hal Wells, Calvin Hom, Iris Schneider, Alan Hagman, Robert St. John, Richard Derk, Staff

**Silver**
Other news page, broadsheet, 175,000+

**Awards of Excellence**
Breaking news, national
News, inside page, broadsheet, 175,000+
Special coverage, section, with ads

What movie fan wouldn't want to read the Los Angeles Times after the Oscars? There's a "wow" with every turn of the page. These are the moments — not just fashion or who won what award. The editing is so disciplined, with the pacing of long- and short-form storytelling. It's beautifully organized on a tight deadline.

¿Acaso algún fanático del cine no querría leer Los Angeles Times después de los premios Oscar? Hay una exclamación con cada vuelta de página. Éstos son los momentos; no sólo la moda o quién ganó qué premio. La edición es muy disciplinada, con un compás de narración para historias largas y cortas. Está bellamente organizada al filo de la hora de cierre.

**LOS ANGELES TIMES**

Kelli Sullivan, Joseph Hutchinson, Michael Whitley, Judy Pryor, Steven R. Hawkins, Kirk Christ, Steven Sedam, Dave Campbell, Alex Brown, Mary Cooney, Nick Cuccia, Cindy Hively

**Awards of Excellence**
Portfolio, news page design, 175,000+, Kelli Sullivan
Single-subject special coverage
Special coverage, multiple sections, with ads
Special coverage, section, with ads
Special news topics, local

**LOS ANGELES TIMES WEST MAGAZINE**

Heidi Volpe, Joseph Hutchinson, Carol Wakano, Nigel Cox

**Silver:** Magazine inside page
**Award of Excellence:** Portfolio, magazine page design, 175,000+, Heidi Volpe

These pages create art using ordinary objects that appear almost animated in how they are photographed, edited and cropped. It's like a piece from the Museum of Modern Art; every photo is something to frame on a wall. These pages make the pens beautiful and sexy, and you have to have them. The typography is very well done, and color punctuates every page.

Estas páginas crean imágenes por medio del uso de objetos comunes y corrientes que aparecen casi inanimados tal como han sido fotografiados, editados y recortados. Es como una pieza de museo de arte moderno; cada foto merece ser enmarcada en el muro. Estas páginas hace que los bolígrafos sean bellos y sexy, y que se haga imperativo poseerlos. La tipografía está muy bien realizada y el color acentúa cada página.

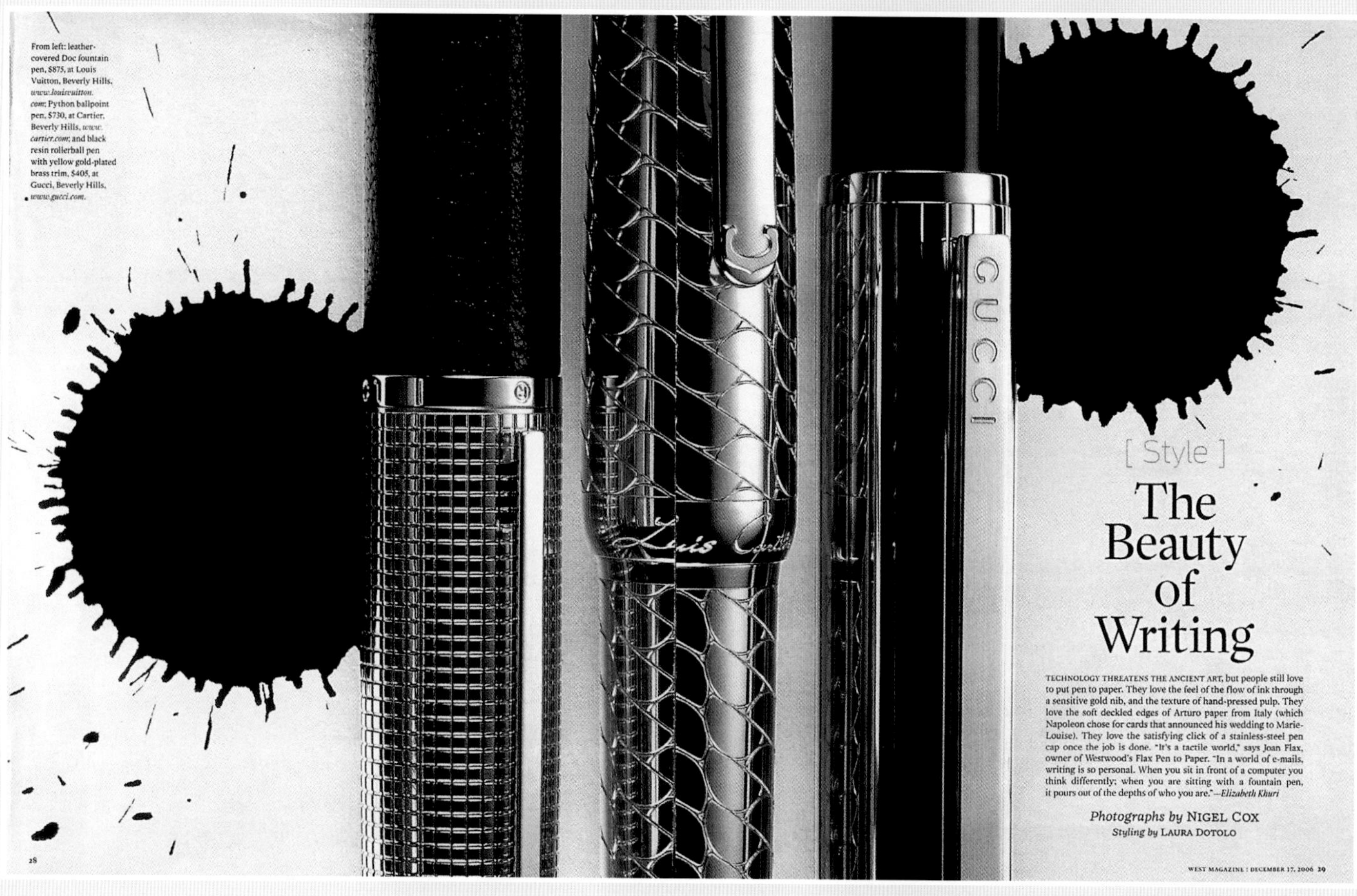

From left: leather-covered Doc fountain pen, $875, at Louis Vuitton, Beverly Hills, *www.louisvuitton.com*; Python ballpoint pen, $730, at Cartier, Beverly Hills, *www.cartier.com*; and black resin rollerball pen with yellow gold-plated brass trim, $405, at Gucci, Beverly Hills, *www.gucci.com*.

[ Style ]

The Beauty of Writing

TECHNOLOGY THREATENS THE ANCIENT ART, but people still love to put pen to paper. They love the feel of the flow of ink through a sensitive gold nib, and the texture of hand-pressed pulp. They love the soft deckled edges of Arturo paper from Italy (which Napoleon chose for cards that announced his wedding to Marie-Louise). They love the satisfying click of a stainless-steel pen cap once the job is done. "It's a tactile world," says Joan Flax, owner of Westwood's Flax Pen to Paper. "In a world of e-mails, writing is so personal. When you sit in front of a computer you think differently; when you are sitting with a fountain pen, it pours out of the depths of who you are."—*Elizabeth Khuri*

*Photographs by* NIGEL COX
*Styling by* LAURA DOTOLO

28 WEST MAGAZINE | DECEMBER 17, 2006 29

**LOS ANGELES TIMES WEST MAGAZINE**

Joseph Hutchinson, Roger Gurbani, Liz Von Hoene

**Awards of Excellence**
Magazine cover design
Magazine cover story

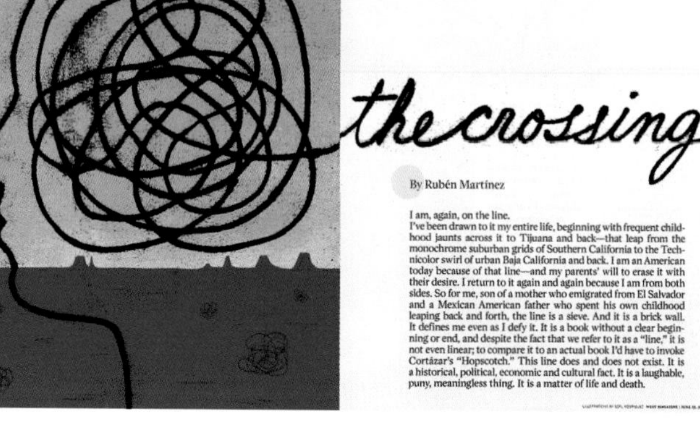

the crossing

By Rubén Martínez

I am, again, on the line.
I've been drawn to it my entire life, beginning with frequent childhood jaunts across it to Tijuana and back—that leap from the monochrome suburban grids of Southern California to the Technicolor swirl of urban Baja California and back. I am an American today because of that line—and my parents' will to erase it with their desire. I return to it again and again because I am from both sides. So for me, son of a mother who emigrated from El Salvador and a Mexican American father who spent his own childhood leaping back and forth, the line is a sieve. And it is a brick wall. It defines me even as I defy it. It is a book without a clear beginning or end, and despite the fact that we refer to it as a "line," it is not even linear; to compare it to an actual book I'd have to invoke Cortázar's "Hopscotch." This line does and does not exist. It is a historical, political, economic and cultural fact. It is a laughable, puny, meaningless thing. It is a matter of life and death.

**LOS ANGELES TIMES**

Heidi Volpe, Liz Hale, Joseph Hutchinson, Edel Rodriguez

**Awards of Excellence**
Magazine inside page
Single illustration

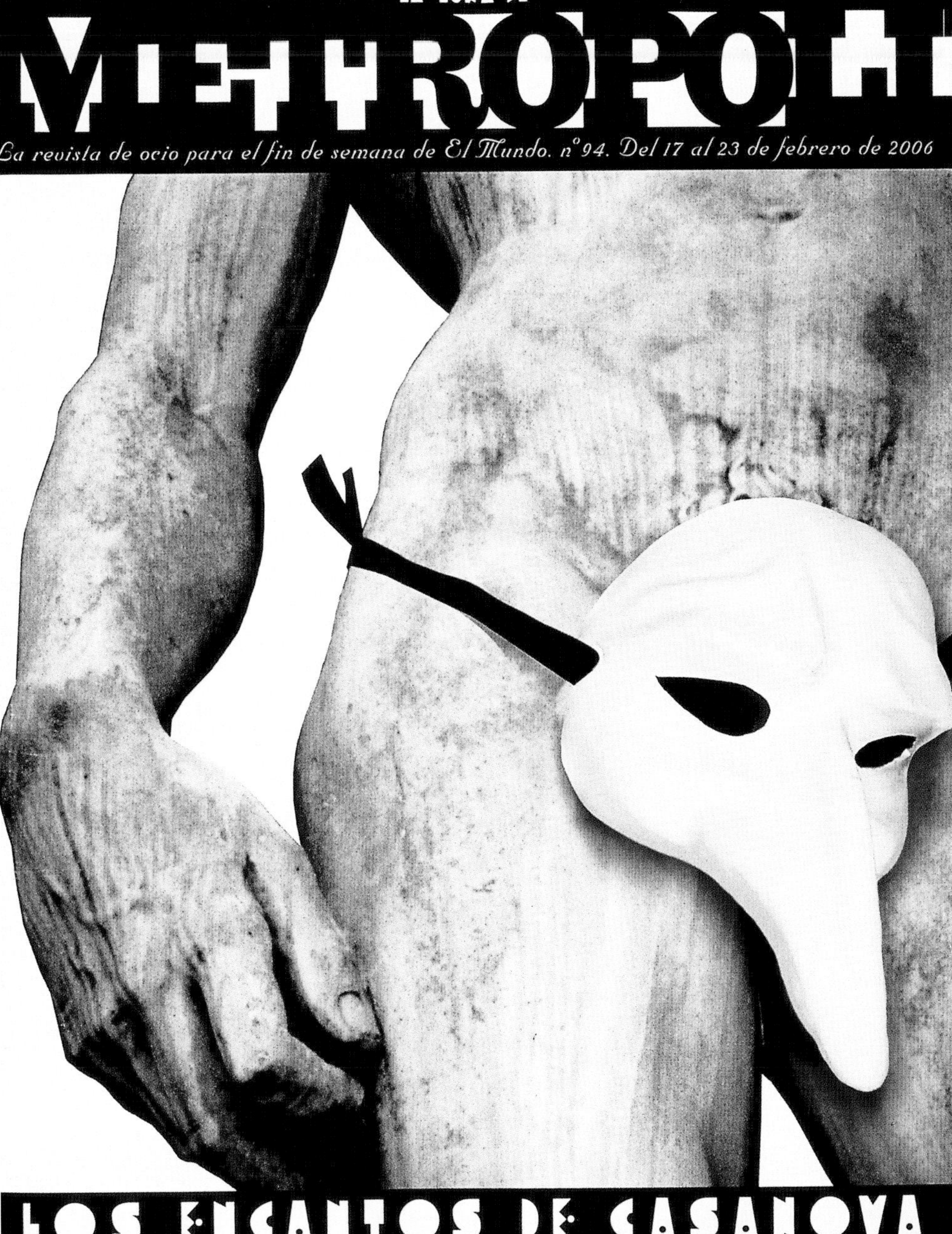


**EL MUNDO MAGAZINE,** Madrid, Spain

Rodrigo Sanchez, Carmelo Caderot, Maria Gonzalez, Javier Sanz, Eva Lopez, Miguel Santamarina

**Awards of Excellence**
Magazine cover design
Magazine special section

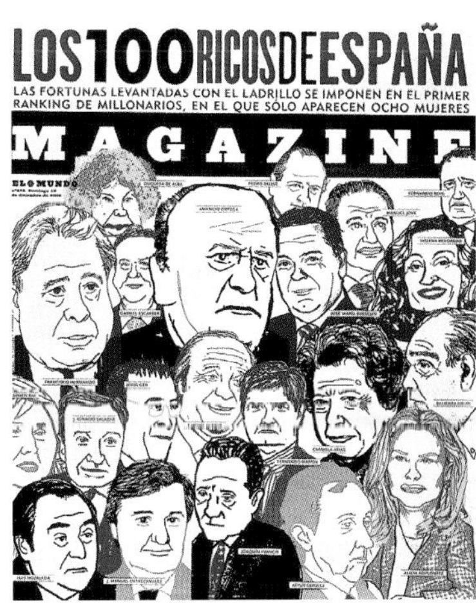


**EL MUNDO METROPOLI,** Madrid, Spain

Rodrigo Sanchez, Carmelo Caderot, Raul Arias

**Awards of Excellence**
Magazine cover design
Portfolio,magazine page design, 175,000+, Rodrigo Sanchez
Single illustration

**EL MUNDO METROPOLI,** Madrid, Spain

Rodrigo Sanchez, Carmelo Caderot, Raul Arias

**Awards of Excellence**
Magazine cover design
Portfolio, magazine page design, 175,000+, Rodrigo Sanchez

**EL MUNDO METROPOLI,** Madrid, Spain

Raul Arias, Rodrigo Sanchez, Carmelo Caderot

**Awards of Excellence**
Single illustration
Magazine cover design
Portfolio, magazine page design, 175,000+, Rodrigo Sanchez

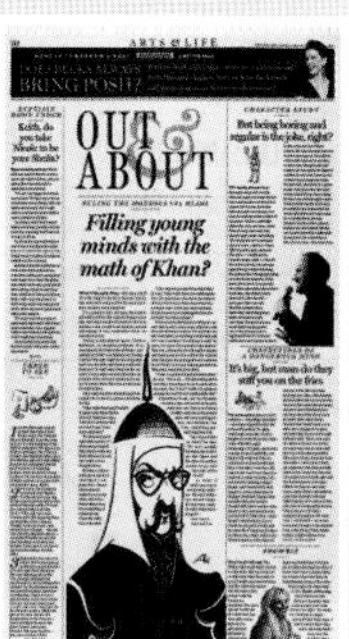
OUT & ABOUT

*Filling young minds with the math of Khan?*

**NATIONAL POST,** Toronto

Doug Kelly, Gayle Grin, Ben Errett, Geneviève Biloski, Antony Hare

**Silver**
Portfolio, illustration, individual, Anthony Hare

**Award of Excellence**
Information graphics, non-breaking news & features, 175,000+

These illustrations are consistent, clean and expressive, with very simple lines. You can identify the caricatures because of the elegant, understated style.

Estas ilustraciones son consistentes, limpias y expresivas, con líneas muy simples. Se puede identificar las caricaturas gracias al estilo elegante y minimizado.

B6

AVENUE

WINNER FAKE ALL!

**Americans may be the ones** heading to the polls today, but more than a quarter-million Canadians will be staying up to see what two of the continent's most respected (albeit fake) news programs have to say about the results as *The Daily Show with Jon Stewart* and *The Colbert Report* join forces for their live Midterm Midtacular (The Comedy Network, 11 p.m. ET). But today marks another milestone for fans of the double dose of satire. It was on Nov. 7 of last year that *The Colbert Report* made its debut on Canadian TV, which means viewers have had exactly one year to choose sides. (Sure, you could just watch both — as many fans do nightly — but isn't fostering non-existent rivalries much more fun?) Here's a look at how the programs stack up. *Basem Boshra, National Post*

HOST

Jon Stewart remains the more polished of the two and is more adept at salvaging a bit that's going nowhere. However, his mugging seems to have ramped up in recent months and his overreliance on a shaky George W. Bush impression (it's really more of an impression of Will Ferrell's Bush impression) can be grating.

Despite his recent Emmy loss (to Barry Manilow, of all people), Colbert is arguably the deftest comedic performer on TV today. The fact that, unlike Stewart, he stays in his blowhard neo-con pundit character for the entire length of the program is an impressive feat (and makes those rare instances when he breaks character all the more gratifying).

CORRESPONDENTS

An exodus of stellar fake reporters over the past couple of years (Steve Carell, Colbert himself, Nate and Rob Corddry, Ed Helms et al.) has hurt, but newcomer John Oliver shows promise and the superlative Samantha Bee remains the team's MVP.

None — unless you count Colbert's long-suffering stage manager Bobby and his recently departed black friend, Alan — which can make the *Report* a bit too much of a one-man show at times. But Colbert puts his *Daily Show* "reporting" skills to good use in a variety of settings that help keep things from getting stale.

INTERVIEWS

Hands down the weakest part of Stewart's show — despite the fact it gets far bigger guests — even ardent fans of the show have a habit of tuning out before the third act. Stewart betrays his stand-up roots during the chat segments, striving for laughs at the expense of eliciting interesting responses from whoever's in the seat of heat.

The quality of the *Report*'s talk segments hinges entirely on whether that night's guest gets and/or plays along with Colbert's shtick. When they don't, the results can be painful to sit through. His intentionally preening sprint to the show's interview set also got real old, real fast.

FEATURES

Lewis Black's painfully predictable rants in Back in Black and the show's increasingly dodgy remote pieces are leavened by the deadpan genius of "resident expert" John Hodgman, Demetri Martin's Trendspotting reports, This Week in God and the newest addition to the roster, Poll Smoking with Dave Gorman.

The show's signature The Word segment varies wildly in quality (and often betrays Colbert's surprisingly sketchy TelePrompTer-reading skills), but rotating bits like the Threatdown, Better Know a District and Tip of the Hat, Wag of the Finger are reliably hilarious.

INFLUENCE

Stewart still gets the bigger ratings and Emmy love, and *TDS*'s Indecision election coverage remains a must-watch not just for fans, but for the politicos it skewers. Anecdotal evidence also suggests "Did you watch Jon Stewart last night?" is still more prevalent around the proverbial water cooler than "Did you watch Colbert?"

From the Colbert-coined "truthiness" becoming part of the popular lexicon to his sly evisceration of the Bush administration at last spring's White House correspondents' dinner, Colbert has stolen plenty of Stewart's thunder in a rather short span, but he still has plenty of ground to make up.

OVERALL

Night in and night out, *The Daily Show* remains the more compelling and entertaining of the two programs, but it's hard not to detect the odd phoned-in installment these days, an indication perhaps that, 10 years in, it's simply harder to keep the satirical skewers sharp.

Definitely still a work in progress, the *Report* remains the more uneven of the two, but, when everything clicks, it's capable of delivering more inspired laughs than Stewart's show. Should Colbert ever decide to cede some of the spotlight to his collaborators, the results could be spectacular.

ILLUSTRATION BY ANTHONY HARE

JON STEWART

STEPHEN COLBERT

**NATIONAL POST,** Toronto

Doug Kelly, Gayle Grin, Laura Koot, Jim Bray, Jeff Wasserman

**Awards of Excellence**
Special coverage, section cover
Sports page, broadsheet, 175,000+

TURIN 2006

S1

Turin will always be the city with thick brown air and the place Canada matured into an Olympic power

FORZA CANADA

**NATIONAL POST,** Toronto

Doug Kelly, Gayle Grin, Stephen Meurice, Jeff Wasserman, John Racovali, Laura Koot, Steven Murray, Kagan McLeod, Andrew Barr, Jonathon Rivait, Kelly McParland, Angela Murphy, Tom Philip

**Awards of Excellence**
News, A-Section, 175,000+
Breaking news, local
Special news topics, local

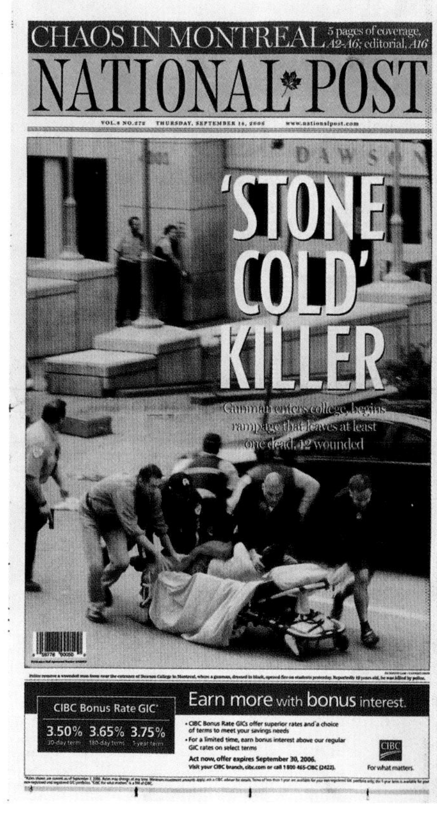
CHAOS IN MONTREAL 5 pages of coverage, A2-A6; editorial, A16

NATIONAL POST

'STONE COLD' KILLER

Gunman enters college, begins rampage that leaves at least one dead, 12 wounded

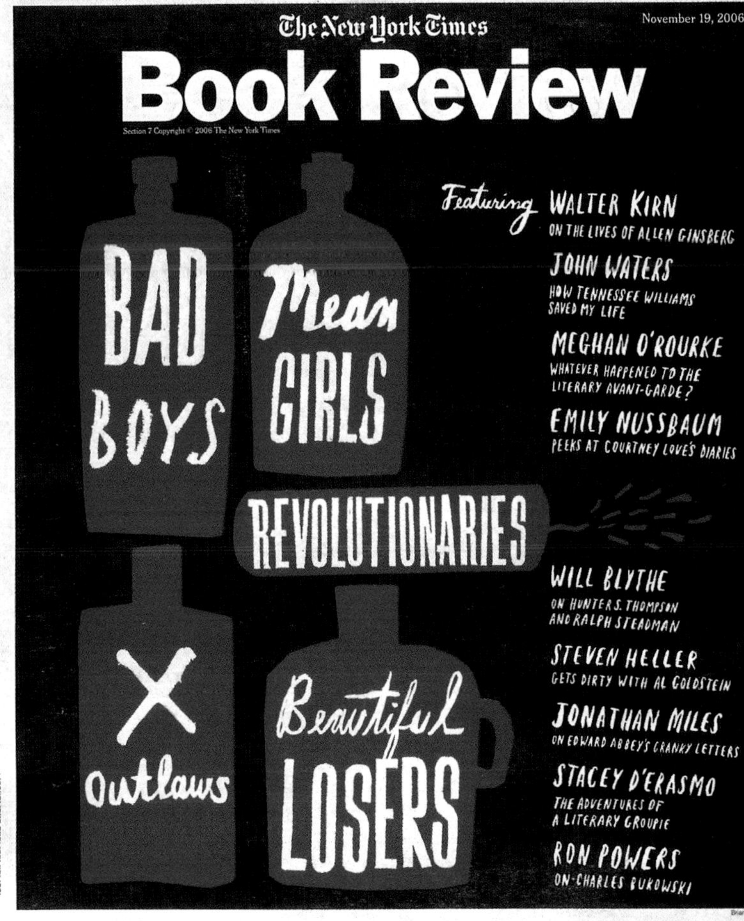

The New York Times

November 19, 2006

Book Review

Section 7 Copyright © 2006 The New York Times

BAD BOYS

Mean GIRLS

REVOLUTIONARIES

X Outlaws

Beautiful LOSERS

Featuring WALTER KIRN ON THE LIVES OF ALLEN GINSBERG

JOHN WATERS HOW TENNESSEE WILLIAMS SAVED MY LIFE

MEGHAN O'ROURKE WHATEVER HAPPENED TO THE LITERARY AVANT-GARDE?

EMILY NUSSBAUM PEEKS AT COURTNEY LOVE'S DIARIES

WILL BLYTHE ON HUNTER S. THOMPSON AND RALPH STEADMAN

STEVEN HELLER GETS DIRTY WITH AL GOLDSTEIN

JONATHAN MILES ON EDWARD ABBEY'S CRANKY LETTERS

STACEY D'ERASMO THE ADVENTURES OF A LITERARY GROUPIE

RON POWERS ON CHARLES BUKOWSKI

Brian Rea

The New York Times

December 17, 2006

Book Review

Section 7 Copyright © 2006 The New York Times

# Wars and a Man

**THE AENEID** *by Virgil. Translated by Robert Fagles. 486 pp. Viking. $40.*

Christoph Niemann

*By Brad Leithauser*

THERE'S a moment in Virgil's "Aeneid" when the Trojan forces are massed like "a cloudburst wiping out the sun, sweeping over the seas toward land." It's an image that evokes another army, likewise intimidating, although this one's composed chiefly of sedentary men, white-haired and bespectacled. Their numbers, too, are unreckonable — those squadrons of scholars who have, over the centuries, translated the "Aeneid."

Has any book been recast into English more times than this tale of Aeneas' wanderings and the eventual establishment of the Roman Empire? Probably not, given both the poem's venerability and the relative accessibility of Latin. When you further consider all the partial or complete versions in private manuscript — often the work of old classics teachers, shared with their students — we indeed confront something that looms over us like a cloudburst.

Robert Fagles, the poem's newest translator, comes to the fray well armed. An emeritus professor of comparative literature at Princeton, he has already translated, with great success, Homer's "Iliad" and "Odyssey." And his publisher for the "Aeneid," Viking, has accoutered

*Continued on Page 10*

IN THIS ISSUE: BOOKS ON WAR

**THE NEW YORK TIMES**

Nicholas Blechman, Tom Bodkin, Brian Rea, Christoph Niemann

**Silvers**

Feature page design, 175,000+
Portfolio, feature page design, 175,000+, Nicholas Blechman

**Awards of Excellence**

Opinion page, broadsheet, 175,000+
Other feature page, tabloid, 175,000+

This portfolio shows range in style, as well as the use of illustration and media. The contents are simple, with great concepts. The illustrations tell the story right away, and they're very smart.

Este portafolio muestra una gran variedad de estilos, como también en el uso de la ilustración y los medios. Los contenidos son simples y tienen grandes conceptos. Las ilustraciones cuentan la historia de inmediato y son muy elegantes.

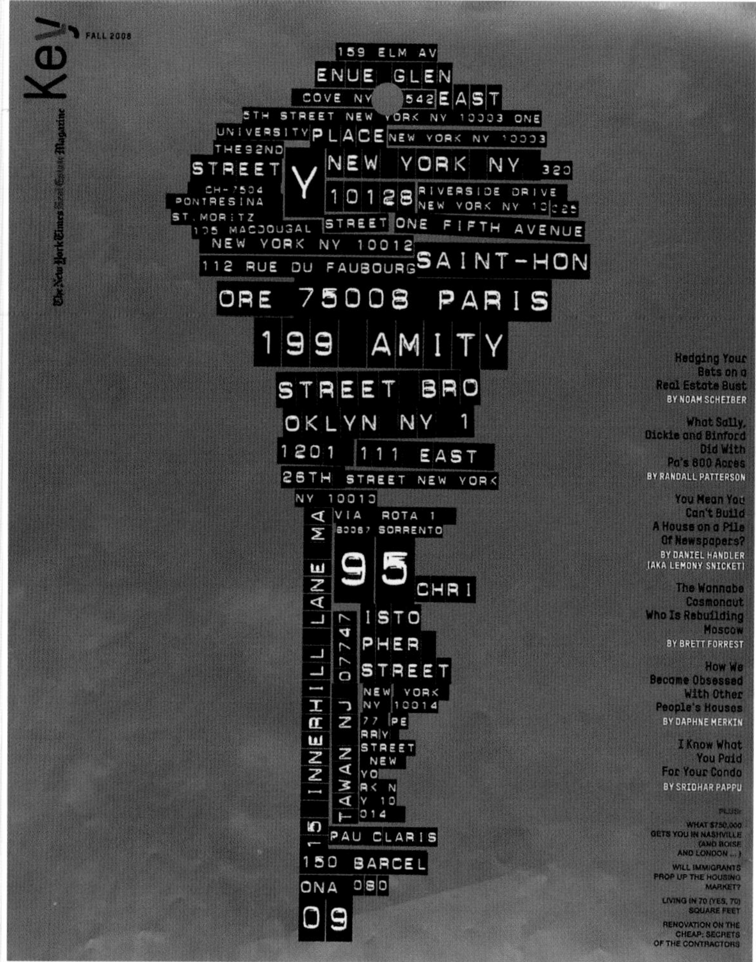


**THE NEW YORK TIMES REAL ESTATE MAGAZINE**

Janet Froelich, Dirk Barnett, Carin Goldberg, Josef Reyes, Dragos Lemnei, Alice Alvez

**Silver:** Magazine cover design
**Award of Excellence:** Magazine special section

This illustration of a key made of street addresses is a puzzle with many levels. You instantly understand its message about real estate, but as you read the addresses, you understand the story is international. And when you look at the image sideways, it's almost a skyline.

Esta ilustración de una llave formada por direcciones de calles es un rompecabezas con varios niveles. El mensaje sobre los bienes raíces se entiende de forma instantánea, pero a medida de que se leen las direcciones, se revela que el relato es internacional. Y cuando se ven las imágenes de lado, es casi como un perfil urbano.

**THE NEW YORK TIMES STYLE MAGAZINE**

Janet Froelich, David Sebbah, Chris Martinez, Elizabeth Spiridakis, Jean-Baptiste Mondino

**Silver:** Overall magazine design
**Award of Excellence:** Magazine cover design

This magazine is classic, but it has spice. Each page includes a spark of quirkiness and creativity that puts it off balance. Great art direction, beautiful photography, tight editing, restrained typography — it's clean, not fussy or gimmicky.

Esta revista es clásica, pero tiene sabor. Cada página contiene una chispa de peculiaridad y creatividad que le rompe el equilibrio. Excelente dirección de arte, bella fotografía, prolija edición, limitada tipografía; es limpia, sin recargos ni artilugios.

The 6th Annual Year in Ideas

The New York Times Magazine
DECEMBER 10, 2006 / SECTION 6




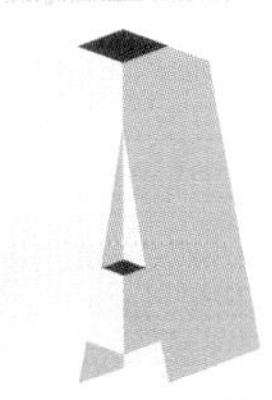

**The 6th Annual Year in Ideas**

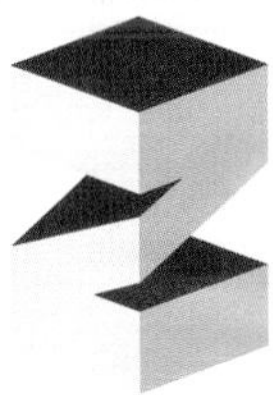

**THE NEW YORK TIMES MAGAZINE**

Janet Froelich, Arem Duplessis, Gail Bichler, Kathy Ryan, Horacio Salinas

**Gold**
Magazine cover story

**Awards of Excellence**
Magazine cover design
Magazine special section

This is an incredibly hard subject to take on, but the newspaper tackled it with fresh excitement. Editors matched the subject matter with a high level of conceptualization for each item, including the cover, which features a light bulb of honey attracting flies. Each visual choice is intelligent and consistent, from the subtle folios to selections for color and typography. The design inspires, just as the content does.

Éste es un tema increíblemente difícil de abordar, pero el diario lo hace con un entusiasmo fresco. Los editores hicieron corresponder el tema con un alto nivel de conceptualización en cada ítem, incluyendo la portada, que muestra una bombilla de miel que atrae moscas. Toda decisión visual es inteligente y consistente, desde los suaves folios hasta la selección del color y la tipografía. El diseño es inspirador, tal como el contenido.

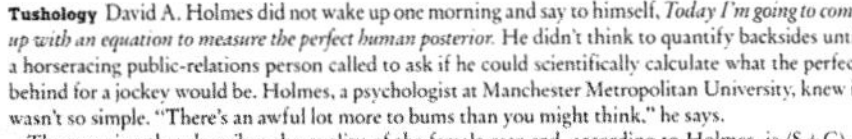


**Tushology** David A. Holmes did not wake up one morning and say to himself, *Today I'm going to come up with an equation to measure the perfect human posterior.* He didn't think to quantify backsides until a horseracing public-relations person called to ask if he could scientifically calculate what the perfect behind for a jockey would be. Holmes, a psychologist at Manchester Metropolitan University, knew it wasn't so simple. "There's an awful lot more to bums than you might think," he says.

The equation that describes the quality of the female rear end, according to Holmes, is (S + C) x (B + F)/T - V, where S = Overall Shape ("including tendency to droop"), C = Circularity, B = Bounce Factor (not to be confused with "wobble"), F = Firmness (with perfect being "like a comfy bed"), T = Skin Texture and V = Vertical Ratio (the goal: "on the top-heavy side of symmetrical"). For the male rear end, the equation replaces bounce, circularity and vertical ratio with M (Muscularity), L (Leanness) and O (Overall Symmetry).

The numbers you plug in to the equation come from a list of descriptions. To calculate B for Bounce: "After one flick it wobbles for 30 secs" gives you a 2, whereas "during aerobics it doesn't even quiver" gives you a 5. And so on. For Holmes, judging posteriors is very serious: "If I can draw attention to people's backsides, they may actually take their overall health more seriously. Because you can dress yourself up in a suit, you can put on your makeup and cover up all of nature's ills and pretend you're in great shape, but if you stand naked and stare backward into the mirror, you have to confront reality."

There's not much debate over the perfect male behind. (Brad Pitt's is pretty much the callipygian ideal.) But the female rear end is a different story. "There is a massive — and I mean massive — disagreement among the public between the larger, motherly, 1950s womanly bum and the impossible small, pert, athletic, rounded one," Holmes says. He calls it "the J. Lo bum verses the Kylie bum," after Jennifer Lopez and the singer Kylie Minogue (who scores close to the ideal). Holmes's personal bottom line: "The J. Lo bum is more feminine and more representative of Woman; the Kylie bum is actually very close to the perfect male bum — it's far more androgynous than people would like to admit."

And jockeys? "They do have wonderful, strong upper thighs," Holmes says, "but their bums tend to be sat on a lot." REBECCA SKLOOT

**Unscratchable Paint** KITT, the talking Trans Am from the 1980s television series "Knight Rider," could crash through a concrete wall without a ding to his sleek, black exterior. Now Nissan has invented a self-healing paint that brings us one step closer to making that archetypal invulnerable car a reality.

These days, a typical auto-body paint job consists of primer, then color, then a shiny acrylic veneer called clear coat. If you back out of a driveway and into a wayward tree branch, the resulting scrape tears the surface in two to reveal the duller undercolor, much to the dismay of any new-car owner. But Nissan's Scratch Guard Coat, made of a dense, highly elastic, urethane-based resin, behaves more like wet glue than dry paint: when nicked, it first absorbs the blow, then slowly flows back together to fill in the gap. The healing process is hurried along by the heat of the sun or, more expediently, warm water. Depending on the severity of the scratch, the surface will return to its original state overnight or by the end of a week.

Scratch Guard is not only self-healing but supposedly more scratch-resistant than traditional clear coats. This is good news for automatic carwashes, which have a reputation for slowly abrading a car's surface, though bad news for auto-body shops, which do a swift business in repairing such damage. Of course, Scratch Guard isn't perfect: it can't protect against gouges that break through the layers beneath, so unfortunate run-ins with mailboxes or with petty vandals prone to "keying" will still require the help of professionals.

Nor is Scratch Guard likely to come to the U.S.A. soon. At present, it is available on the X-Trail S.U.V. — but only in Japan. KATE BOLICK

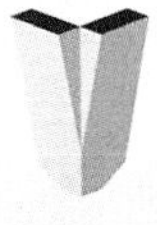

**Visage Problem, The** In August, Mary Ann Sieghart, a columnist for The Times of London, described her battle with the disorder prosopagnosia, also known as face-blindness. She can spend an hour and a half with a new acquaintance at lunch, "furiously trying to imprint his features on my memory," she wrote. "Yet the chances are that the next time I bump into him, I won't know who he is." Like other prosopagnosics, Sieghart finds most human faces to be about as distinguishable as stones in a driveway. The disorder was first fully described in the medical literature in the 1940s and has long been viewed as an exceedingly rare, baffling derangement.

But in a startling development in May, the researchers Ken Nakayama and Richard Russell at Harvard and Bradley Duchaine at University College, London, declared that as many as 2 percent of all humans seem to suffer from face-blindness to some degree. The team recruited some 1,600 volunteers and gave them a battery of tests. In one, the subjects were shown six faces, and then those faces were mixed in with others and the subjects were asked which they had seen before. Fully 1 in 50 of the par-

80

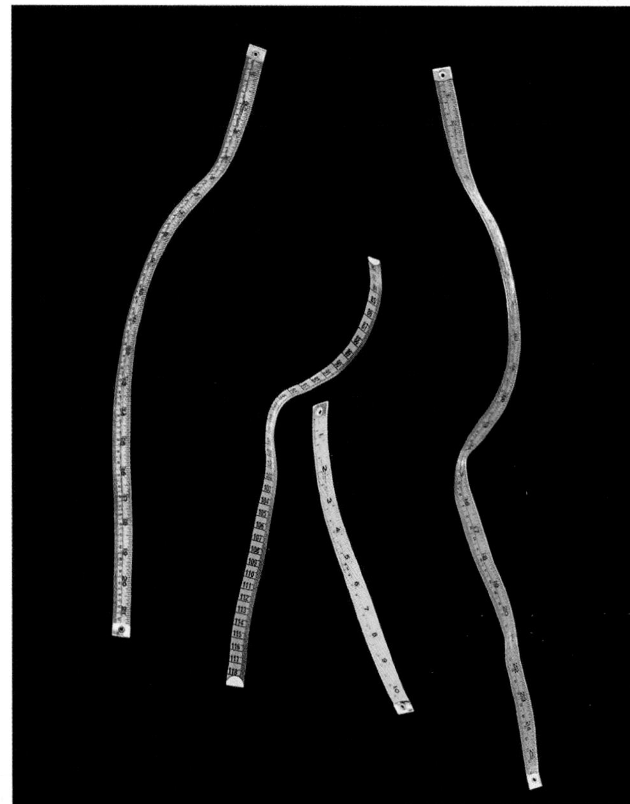

TUSHOLOGY PHOTOGRAPH BY HORACIO SALINAS

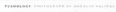

**THE NEW YORK TIMES**

Graham Roberts

**Awards of Excellence**
Information graphics, non-breaking news & features, 175,000+
Portfolio, information graphics, individual, non-breaking news & features, 175,000+

SCIENCE ILLUSTRATED

Refining Vision Surgery for a Sharper Focus

The newest technology in Lasik surgery, commonly called custom Lasik, provides additional accuracy and personalization to the eye correction procedure. Wavescan technology creates a "fingerprint" of the patient's vision, precise enough to capture subtle anomalies in each eye. A guided laser can cut a thinner, more uniform flap, while a corrective laser with variable size beams can reshape the cornea with increased accuracy, keeping on target even as the eye moves. But as with all corrective surgeries, complications can arise. GRAHAM ROBERTS

COMMON VISION PROBLEMS
By reshaping the cornea, Lasik surgery can correct the eye's ability to focus light onto the retina.

NEARSIGHTEDNESS
The eye is too long or the cornea is too curved. Light focuses in front of the retina.

**THE NEW YORK TIMES**

Jonathan Corum

**Awards of Excellence**
Charting, 175,000+
Information graphics, non-breaking news & features, 175,000+

artists inspiration Howard everything four inspired hi Brian Oscar guys father writing Walsh Universal yes nominees woman Paul Richard night please sorry HBO talented person ago Osborne country fellow kids Weta somewhere brought whose start parents story watching Ron Russell mind daughter supported gave Kong helped done husband again bless Ridley together real feel standing hard art Steve DreamWorks said whole dream honored Sony James grateful music Tom script little children special Bill Rob come ever year live son finally brilliant Barrie worked Lisa pictures always give sound part Marshall New Zealand believe day hope Lee Mark vision films members entire man working Fran producer job long name fantastic actors journey wow proud Bob mother heart Scott Jackson director giving share dedicate him home dad producers right think her partner world friend never team David especially Michael friends support time God John mom made cast family beautiful making incredible honor without oh award Peter movie everyone life his say years wonderful wife amazing their work tonight crew everybody thanks know film great love people academy

Each word is scaled proportionally to the number of times it has been used in acceptance speeches at the last six Academy Award ceremonies. Words are included only if they have been used 10 or more times, and some pronouns and other common words have been removed.

thank

Jonathan Corum/The New York Times

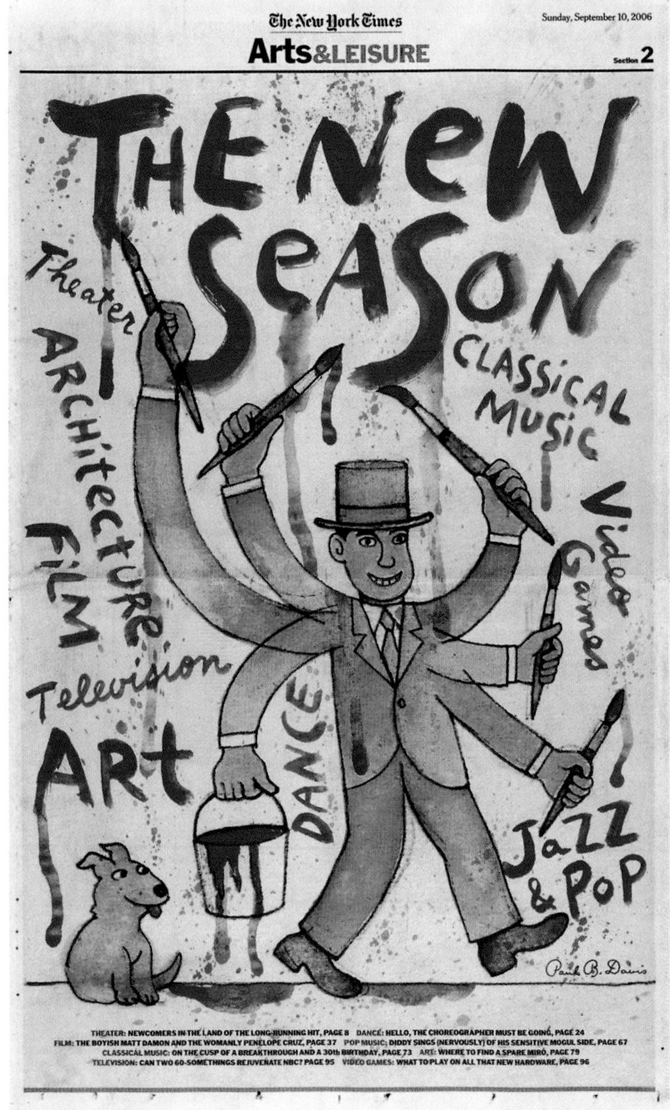


**THE NEW YORK TIMES**

Tom Bodkin, Nicki Kalish, Paul B. Davis

**Awards of Excellence**
Entertainment page, broadsheet, 175,000+
Single illustration

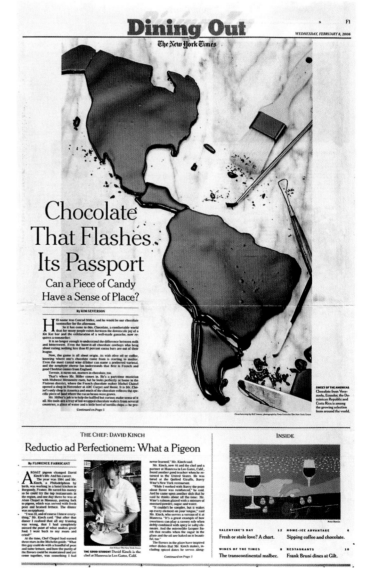

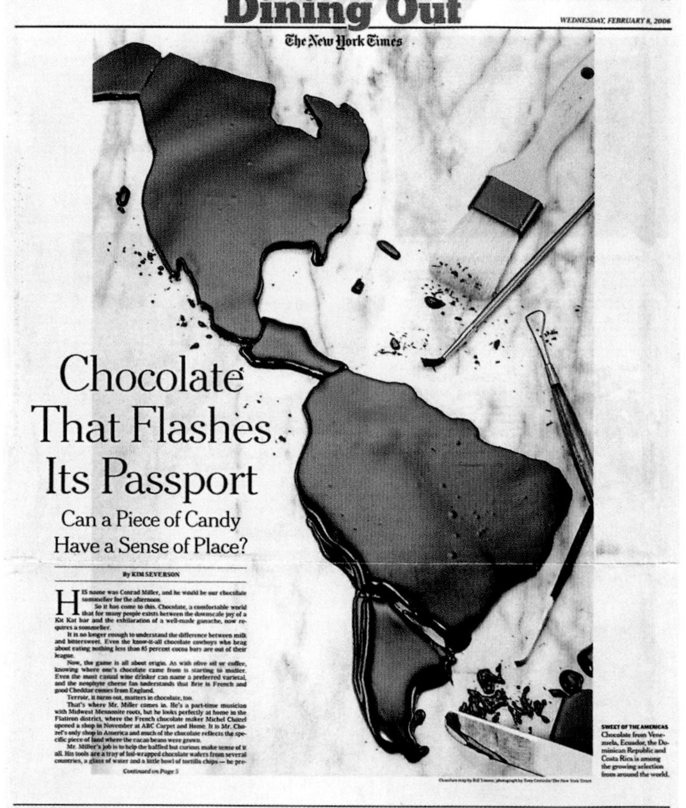


**THE NEW YORK TIMES**

Soo-Jeong Kang, Tony Cenicola, Barbara Richer, Tom Bodkin

**Awards of Excellence**
Food page, broadsheet, 175,000+
Photo illustration

**THE NEW YORK TIMES**

Matthew Ericson

**Awards of Excellence**

Charting, 175,000+

Information graphics, breaking news, 175,000+

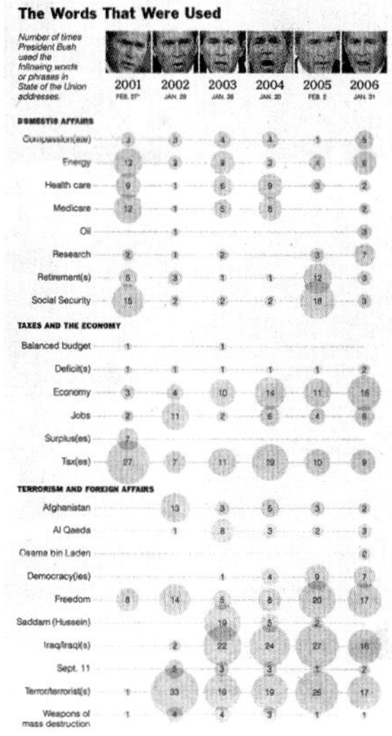


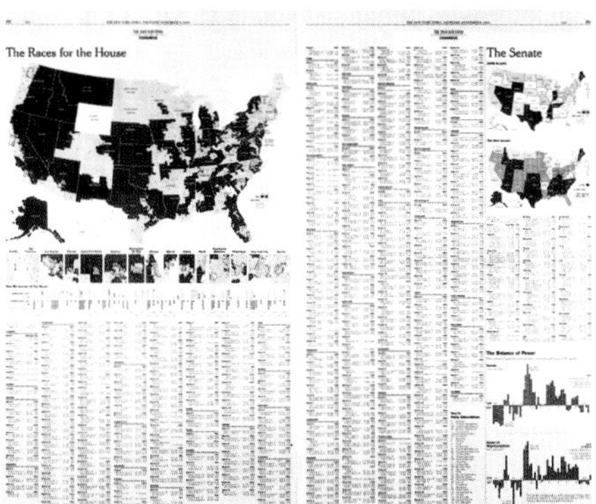


**THE NEW YORK TIMES**

Erin Aigner

**Awards of Excellence**

Information graphics, breaking news, 175,000+

Mapping, 175,000+

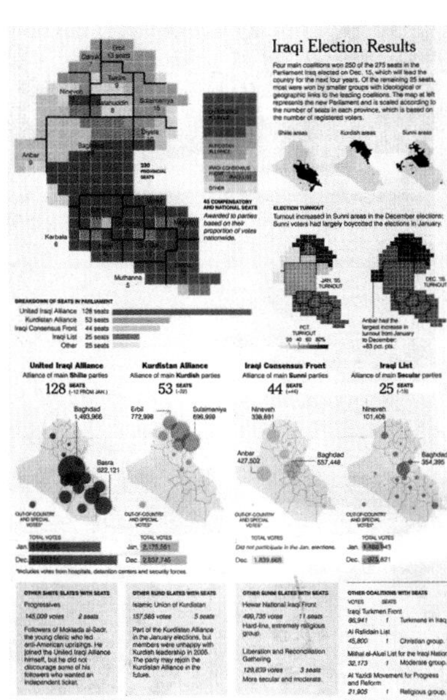


**THE NEW YORK TIMES**

Hannah Fairfield, Archie Tse, Staff

**Awards of Excellence**

Information graphics, breaking news, 175,000+

Portfolio, information graphics, individual, non-breaking news & features, 175,000+, Hannah Fairfield

Portfolio, information graphics, staff, breaking news, 175,000+

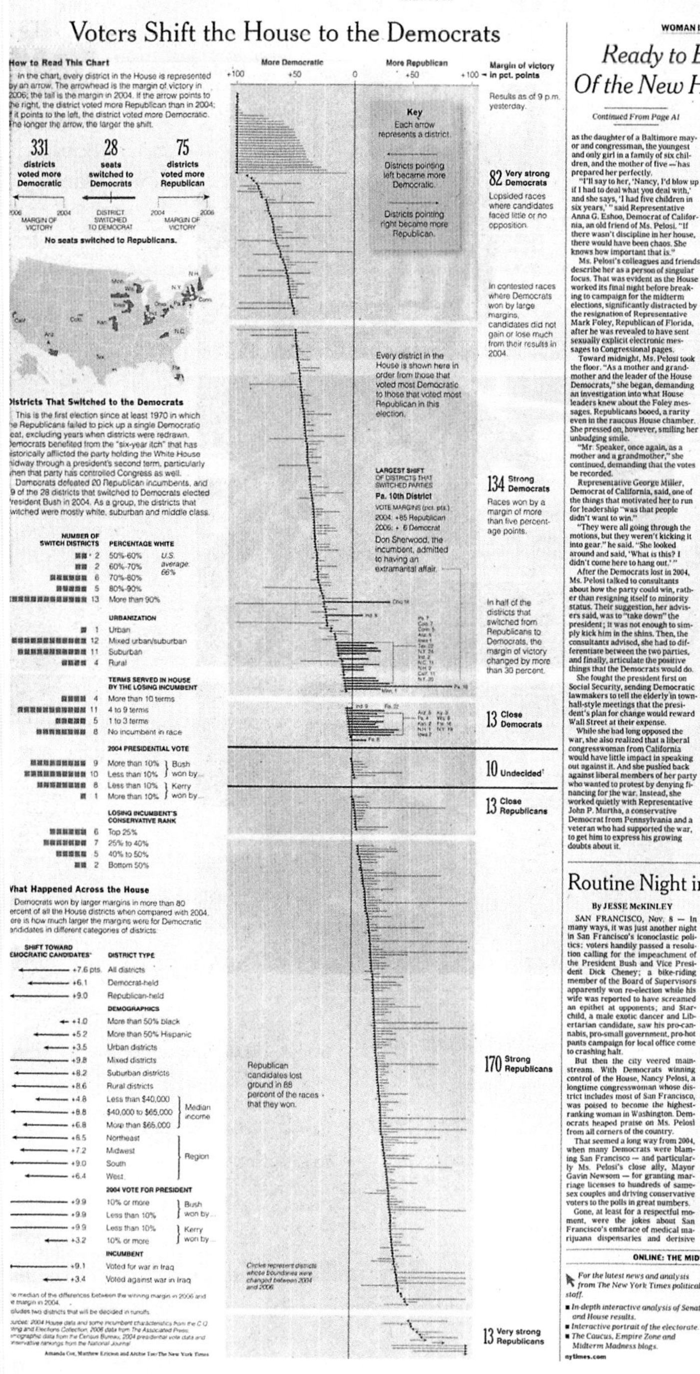

THE 2006 ELECTIONS

THE HOUSE

# Voters Shift the House to the Democrats

WOMAN IN THE NEWS

## Ready to Be the Voice Of the New House Majority

## Routine Night in San Francisco

ONLINE: THE MIDTERM ELECTIONS

**THE NEW YORK TIMES**

Amanda Cox, Archie Tse, Staff

**Silvers**

Charting, 175,000+

Information graphics, breaking news, 175,000+

**Awards of Excellence**

Portfolio, information graphics, individual, non-breaking news & features, 175,000+, Archie Tse

Portfolio, information graphics, staff, breaking news, 175,000+

Portfolio, information graphics, staff, extended coverage, 175,000+

This graphic showing the U.S. House shifting to the Democrats has dense information, but once you look at the key, it's visually understandable. It works on two levels — you can see which party held power in the House over time, or you can really drill into it and get more detail. We've never seen this before. It's enormously clever, deep and quick.

Este gráfico que muestra cómo la Cámara Baja del Congreso norteamericano pasa al control de los demócratas contiene una información densa y profunda, pero una vez que se ve la simbología, es visualmente entendible. Funciona en dos niveles; se puede ver qué partido ha tenido el poder a lo largo del tiempo, o se puede examinar a fondo para informarse con más detalle. No nos habíamos encontrado con algo así hasta ahora. Es tremendamente ingenioso, profundo y agudo.

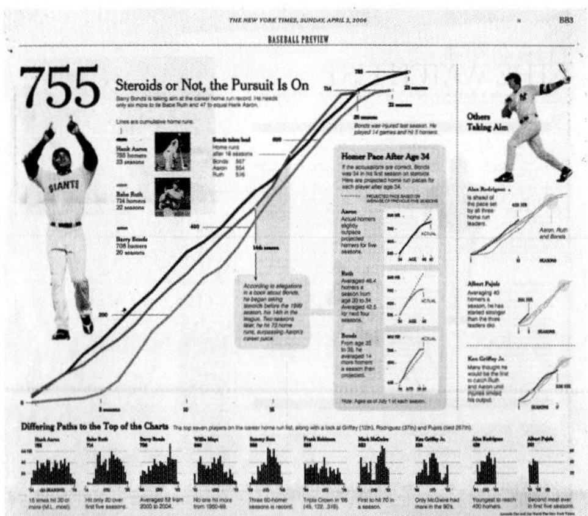

755

Steroids or Not, the Pursuit Is On

Differing Paths to the Top of the Charts

**THE NEW YORK TIMES**

Amanda Cox, Joe Ward

**Awards of Excellence**

Charting, 175,000+

Portfolio, information graphics, individual, non-breaking news & features, 175,000+, Joe Ward

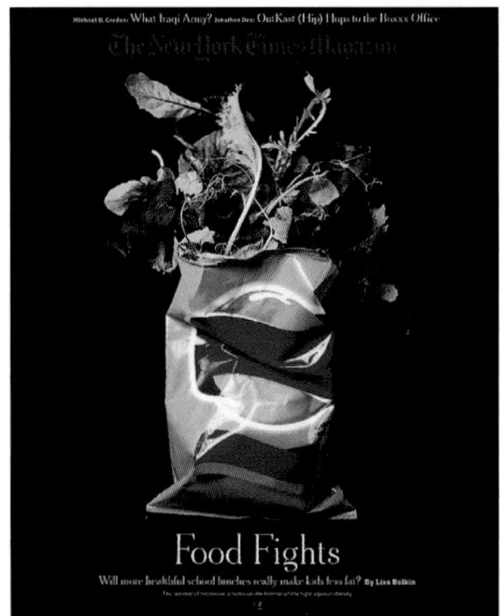



**THE NEW YORK TIMES MAGAZINE**

Janet Froelich, Arem Duplessis, Gail Bichler, Kathy Ryan, Stephen Lewis

**Awards of Excellence**

Magazine cover design

Magazine cover story

The New York Times

Bush Marks 9/11 at Ground Zero as New York Remembers

'WITH A HEAVY HEART'

Broken Ground

Portraits of Grief

In Democrats' Fight for the House, New York Looks Less Promising

Suicide Bomber Kills a Governor In Afghanistan

**THE NEW YORK TIMES**

Tom Bodkin, Aviva Mikhaelov, Staff

**Awards of Excellence**

News, A-Section page, broadsheet, 175,000+

Use of photography

'You have given me your shoulders to stand on to reach for my dreams, dreams I could never have reached without you. Over the last 21 years, I have found you, and I will take you and the memory of you with me for the rest of my life.'

ANDRE AGASSI,
addressing the U.S. Open crowd

SportsMonday D1

MONDAY, SEPTEMBER 4, 2006

The New York Times

# FINAL SCORE IS LOVE

Agassi's All Is Not Good Enough as Career Ends in Four-Set Loss

Andre Agassi could not overcome an aching back and a much younger opponent in the third round of the United States Open yesterday, but he retires with eight Grand Slam titles, including all four majors.

Agassi congratulating Benjamin Becker after his 7-5, 6-7 (4), 6-4, 7-5 victory, and, right, taking his last bows.

**The Art of Tennis**

BY MICHAEL KIMMELMAN

*The Times's senior art critic blogs about the scene at the Open. Also, photographs of Andre Agassi's career, with commentary by Christopher Clarey and remarks from fans.*

nytimes.com/tennis

WILLIAM C. RHODEN/Sports of The Times

*A Champion Leaves Them Cheering With Plenty of Winning Moments*

*"The scoreboard says I lost today. But what the scoreboard doesn't say is what I have found. Over the last 21 years, I have found loyalty."*

THE back pain kicked in almost immediately yesterday afternoon, and Andre Agassi knew this would be a long painful day, and probably the last one of his professional tennis career. He had been able to fight off the bulls twice in this United States Open, defeating Andrei Pavel on Monday and Marcos Baghdatis on Thursday. Saturday's washout provided a reprieve. This was the end.

"The pain came quickly," Agassi said. "It can do that, and it did. I knew I was in trouble at that point."

Members of the news media love a good story, and Agassi certainly has been that. He has taken us on a journey he began as a bratty 16-year-old who was often more style than substance and ended as a 36-year-old senior who taught a generation of younger players how to compete with heart and soul.

U.S. Open

But there always comes a point in sports when the good story must give way to the better player. Benjamin Becker, 25, was bigger, younger and stronger. This would be his victory, but it was clearly Andre Agassi's day. And in the process of losing the match, Agassi supplied wonderful mini-moments. This was a match of emotion and standing ovations.

The match was sprinkled with great Agassi moments. There was the third set, when Agassi

*Continued on Page D2*

From Rebel to Statesman

In 21 years of professional tennis, Andre Agassi rose to No. 1 (1995), sank to No. 141 (1997) and back to No. 1 again (1999). While winning his 60 singles titles, he finished the season ranked in the top 10 16 times and became one of five men to achieve a career Grand Slam (winning the United States, French, Australian Opens and Wimbledon).

KEY: Best ranking, Year-end ranking, Worst ranking; Singles titles; Grand Slam

1988 United States Open · Wimbledon · U.S. Open · Australian Open · French Open · U.S. Open · Australian Open · Australian Open · Agassi and Pete Sampras, 2001 United States Open · Australian Open

1986 1987 1988 1989 1990 1991 1992 1993 1994 1995 1996 1997 1998 1999 2000 2001 2002 2003 2004 2005 2006

Lindsay Davenport comes back to beat Katarina Srebotnik. Page D2.

Andy Roddick advances. Page D4.

BASEBALL — Yankees rout the Twins behind Rasner and Rodriguez. PAGE D7

BASEBALL — Beltrán is feeling better, but Mets, yielding one hit, lose to Astros. PAGE D7

GOLF — Singh shoots a 61 and takes the lead, surging ahead of Woods. PAGE D7

FOOTBALL — Appendectomy puts Roethlisberger out of the Steelers' opener. PAGE D8

**THE NEW YORK TIMES**

Lee Yarosh, Tom Bodkin, Bedel Saget, Jeremiah Bogert

**Silver:** Portfolio, sports page design, 175,000+, Lee Yarosh

**Award of Excellence:** Sports page, broadsheet, 175,000+

This conceptual material is at a higher level than many of the portfolios we saw. It fits the mold of The New York Times, but it is surprising. Each story is well told. You don't need to read the headlines to know what the stories are about.

Este material conceptual es de un nivel superior al de muchos otros portafolios que examinamos. Calza con el estilo de The New York Times, pero es sorprendente. Cada uno de los artículos está bien contado. No es necesario leer los títulos para enterarse de qué se tratan los artículos.

SportsMonday

The New York Times

TURIN PASSES THE TORCH

Lundqvist's Painful Move Saves Sweden

Podium Crashers

Passion a Guest That Wouldn't Stick Around

**THE MIAMI HERALD**

Eddie Alvarez, Paul Cheung, Philip Brooker, Ana Larrauri, Danny Paskin

**Awards of Excellence**
Single-subject special coverage
Special news topics, World Cup

SOCCER

WORLD CUP SPECIAL

FIRST-ROUND MATCHES
• JUNE 10 VS. IVORY COAST
• JUNE 16 VS. SERBIA & MONTENEGRO
• JUNE 21 VS. NETHERLANDS
WORLD CUP ODDS
ARGENTINA IS LISTED AT 7-1

# ARGENTINA

"I don't think you can either have confidence in or underestimate Argentina after what happened in 2002." — Diego Maradona, on Argentina's failure to advance to the Round of 16 four years ago

5 FACTS

**OUTLOOK**

Finished second to Brazil on goal differential in South American qualifying. They have yet to advance past the quarterfinals in the post-Maradona era, and were bounced in the first round four years ago, but with playmaker Juan Román Riquelme and Barcelona's teen phenom Lionel Messi in the middle, and Olympic star Carlos Tévez up front, anything's possible. Argentina won the World Cup in 1978 and 1986, and twice finished runner-up (1930 and 1990).

HERNÁN CRESPO

PROJECTED STARTING LINEUP

WWW.MIAMIHERALD.COM

WORLD CUP 2006

POLITIKEN | KULTUR | NAVNE | SPORT

2

Fremmed

Fremmed var jeg på denne jord
Lige siden jeg kom ud af min mor
Der var så meget jeg ville
Lige fra jeg var lille
Sang jeg med i kæmpernes kor
Om alt det jeg ville
Når jeg engang blev stor

Og nu er mit hår blevet hvidt
Men jeg er ikke kommet et skridt
Nærmere til målet
Min sko er blevet forsålet
Men lommen den er ligeså tom
Og jeg er ligeså hullet
Som den dag da jeg kom

Men jeg er stadig den samme
Hvad der så end sker
Vi er alle sammen fremmede
Men jeg har hjemme her
Vi er alle sammen fremmede
Men jeg har hjemme her

Hjemme er der hvor jeg bor
Mit mellem himmel og jord
Første sal til venstre
Der går der en og venter
Venter på mig
Du skal ikke vente længe
For nu kommer jeg

Og jeg er stadig den samme
Hvad der så end sker
Vi er alle sammen fremmede
Men jeg har hjemme her

*Fra Kim Larsens ny cd, der udkommer på tirsdag.*

'Hjernefri zone' står der på døren til det Medley-studie, hvor Lasse Ellegaard og Roald Als har mødt Kim Larsen. Den alsidige menu byder blandt andet på Flensburger Pilsner, portvin og børnekrydsogtværs, men også Hemingway, Hamsun og Victor Hugo.

Læs side 6-7

Anmeldelse af Kim Larsens ny cd, 'Gammel Hankat', side 9

Tegning: Roald Als

**POLITIKEN,** Copenhagen, Denmark

Søren Nyeland, Roald Als, Peter Sætternissen, Christian Iløse, Uffe Hastrup

**Awards of Excellence**
Entertainment page, broadsheet, 50,000-174,999
Single illustration

Crossroads

Building amid ramps used to serve rails

Surprise or shock?

Hamas victory gives birth to unintended consequences

INSIDE

**MILWAUKEE JOURNAL SENTINEL** (Wis.)

Gary Markstein, Lonnie Turner

**Awards of Excellence**
Opinion page, broadsheet, 175,000+
Single illustration

POLITIKEN

Danmark kom godt fra start med 2-0 over Island i EM-kvalifikationen

# Løkke: Nødhjælp til kommuner

## Vennerne: Rettroende, men ikke fanatiske

Skandia Banken

Giv dig selv en lønforhøjelse

Drømmerejser til Thailand

*Redesign, Before*

POLITIKEN

Lørdag

Druk

Og så findes der et nyt ansigt ved navn Fredrik Reinfeldt. Han er også lidt rund og landsfaderlig. Smukke sørgmodige øjne. Engageret, men ikke udslidt. Det nye arbejderpartis talsmand. Hvorfor ikke? Og så gik det, som det gik.

Et grimt mønster

## Asylboom presser humane Sverige

VINTER DÆK

PHOTOGRAFICA

brdr. friis møbler

*Redesign, After*

**POLITIKEN,** Copenhagen, Denmark

Staff

**Awards of Excellence**
Redesign, overall newspaper
Redesign, section

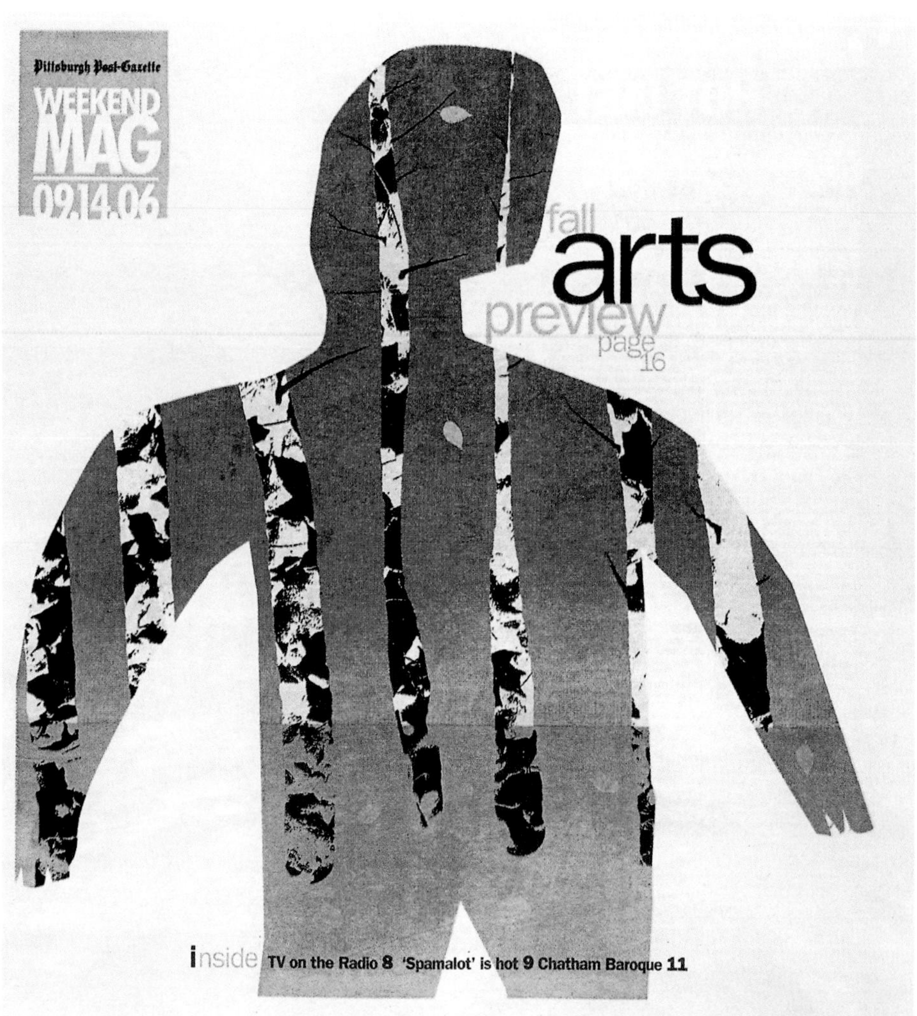
Pittsburgh Post-Gazette

WEEKEND MAG

09.14.06

fall arts preview page 16

inside TV on the Radio 8 'Spamalot' is hot 9 Chatham Baroque 11

**PITTSBURGH POST-GAZETTE**

Daniel Marsula, Stacy Innerst

**Awards of Excellence**

Entertainment page, tabloid, 175,000+

Portfolio, feature page design, 175,000+, Daniel Marsula

FORUM

Section H

COMMENTARY, EDITORIALS, LETTERS • BOOKS • CROSSWORDS • Pittsburgh Post-Gazette • SUNDAY, MARCH 19, 2006

BIG CHICKEN FARMS GAVE BIRDS THE FLU

The industrialization of poultry raising is the culprit, says WENDY ORENT, and migratory birds are usually victims, not carriers

THE TROUBLE WITH THE IRISH

DENNIS RODDY

RESURRECTION

Biographer restores luster to three-time loser William Jennings Bryan.

BOOKS, PAGE H-8

The Rev. Fred Phelps is a vulgar nuisance. But the state Legislature should not trample on bedrock American beliefs, says ROBERT D. RICHARDS, in order to shut him up

Let FREEDOM, however VILE, ring

INSIDE When a libertarian needs a kidney PAGE H-4 | Columns by DAVID SHRIBMAN, SALLY KALSON and JACK KELLY

**PITTSBURGH POST-GAZETTE**

Steve Urbanski, Daniel Marsula, Chris Pett-Ridge

**Awards of Excellence**

Portfolio, news page design, 175,000+, Steve Urbanski

Single illustration

FORUM

Section J

COMMENTARY, EDITORIALS/LETTERS • BOOKS • CROSSWORDS • Pittsburgh Post-Gazette • SUNDAY, JANUARY 29, 2006

LISTEN IN WITH GOOD CAUSE

VICTORIA TOENSING asks: Do Al Gore and other Democrats really want to keep us from finding al-Qaida agents in the United States?

Peduto sells out

DENNIS RODDY

While waving a Terrible Towel, CHARLIE HUMPHREY gazes at the city's psyche

OUR STEELERS, OUR SELVES

In other news:

INSIDE, PAGE H-4

INSIDE 'At Camera's Edge': Taylor Branch concludes his MLK bio. | Columns by DAVID SHRIBMAN, ANN McFEATTERS, JACK KELLY

**PITTSBURGH POST-GAZETTE**

Daniel Marsula, Steve Urbanski

**Awards of Excellence**

Opinion page, broadsheet, 175,000+

Single illustration

the next page

I REMEMBER WHEN THE 9/11 THING HAPPENED. I WAS 5. MY PARENTS WANT US TO GO TO SOME CANDLE-HOLDING EVENT TOMORROW, BUT...

5 YEARS

STORY BY LAWRENCE MERCURIO • ART BY STACY INNERST

WHY DO I HAVE TO THINK ABOUT THAT AGAIN? I REMEMBER HOW CONFUSED I WAS THAT DAY.

ALL THESE PARENTS CAME TO SCHOOL TO PICK UP THEIR KIDS. I WONDERED WHY– IT WASN'T EVEN RECESS YET. WHO WOULD I SIT WITH AT LUNCH?

A LOT OF MY FRIENDS HAD ALREADY LEFT. WHEN MY THIRD-BEST FRIEND MINDY TOLD ME IT WAS BAD! SHE HEARD IT WAS "EL KITTY."

I REMEMBER BEING SO SCARED. USUALLY MONSTERS DIDN'T SCARE ME BUT EL KITTY I HAD NEVER HEARD OF IN MY WHOLE LIFE. DID HE BITE? SCRATCH? WAS HE EVEN A HE? (OR JUST HUNGRY?)

WHEN MY MOM CAME FOR ME, I WAS REALLY HAPPY. I TOLD MINDY HER MOM WOULD COME SOON, EVEN THOUGH I DIDN'T KNOW.

MY MOM TOLD ME THAT EL KITTY WASN'T A CAT, BUT PEOPLE. ANGRY PEOPLE. ANGRY PEOPLE WHO WANT TO HURT US. I THOUGHT OF WHAT I LEARNED ABOUT 'STRANGER DANGER.' I FOUND OUT LATER IT WAS DIFFERENT THAN THAT.

NOW I KNOW THAT SCARY THINGS HAPPEN. SAD THINGS, TOO. MY GYM TEACHER'S HUSBAND WENT TO IRAQ. HE DIDN'T COME BACK. HE DIED.

WELL, I GUESS I'LL GO WITH MY PARENTS TOMORROW. MAYBE MINDY WILL BE THERE. SHE'S NOW MY SECOND-BEST FRIEND. WE'VE BEEN THROUGH A LOT. WE WATCH OUT FOR EACH OTHER.

**PITTSBURGH POST-GAZETTE**

Stacy Innerst

**Awards of Excellence**

Portfolio, illustration, individual

Single illustration

## train jumping:

A DESPERATE JOURNEY

Hundreds of thousands cross the

753-mile border

that separates Mexico from Guatemala and Belize each year.

They are beginning a

1,500-mile odyssey

to the United States.

Last year, Mexican immigration deported

232,157 unauthorized migrants,

mostly from Central America.

Since 2000, the number of unauthorized Central American migrants in the U.S. has increased

56% to 1.1 million.

Records from Grupo Beta show

22,332 migrants rescued

3,919 migrants injured

270 migrants mutilated

between January 2002 and August 2006.

**CREDITS**

Photographer | Gary Coronado
Writer| Christine Evans

Photo Editors | Mark Edelson and Pete Cross
Story Editor | Bill Greer

Research | Melanie Mena
Designer | Nicole Bogdas
Copy Editor | Margaret McKenzie

IN TRAVEL FAMILY TRIP TO JAMAICA Is an all-inclusive resort worth it?

Getting a grip on obesity

WALT DISNEY

The Palm Beach Post

SPECIAL SECTION INSIDE

train jumping A DESPERATE JOURNEY

Riding for their lives

Winners promise populist agenda

GOP sees Crist as bright hope at gloomy time

**THE PALM BEACH POST,** West Palm Beach, Fla.

Gary Coronado, Bruce R. Bennett, Damon Higgins, Bill Ingram, Erik Lunsford, Uma Sanghvi, Lannis Waters, Nicole Bogdas, Mark Edelson

**Gold**
Photo project

**Awards of Excellence**
Special coverage, section, no ads
Portfolio, staff photo
Special coverage, section cover

This work takes the complicated subject of border patrol and tells it through the specific situation of train jumping. The photographer was in danger to get the story, and the emotion in the images puts you there. The photo selection shows command of crops, shapes and sizes, and the right images are played for maximum effect. It's a good job at editing, designing and shooting.

Este trabajo trata del complicado tema del patrullaje fronterizo y lo cuenta a través de la situación específica del salto a los trenes en movimiento. El fotógrafo estuvo en peligro al salir a buscar la historia, y la emoción de las imágenes lo trasporta a uno al lugar. La selección de las fotos demuestra dominio de recorte, forma y tamaño, y las imágenes correctas se usan para lograr el máximo efecto. Es un buen trabajo de edición, diseño y toma fotográfica.

**THE PLAIN DEALER,** Cleveland

David Kordalski, Emmet Smith, Roadell Hickman, Roy Hewitt, David Campbell, Mike Starkey, Bill Gugliotta

**Awards of Excellence**
Portfolio, sports page design, 175,000+, Emmet Smith
Special coverage, section cover
Sports page, broadsheet, 175,000+

NBA PLAYOFFS

Cleveland Cavaliers vs. Washington Wizards

Banner year

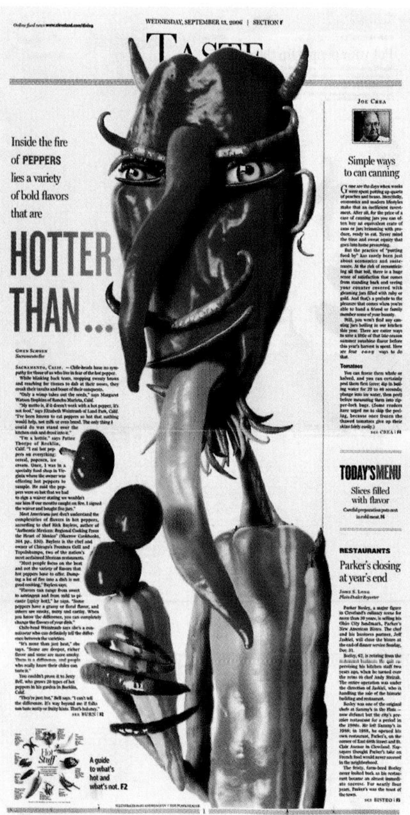

TASTE

Inside the fire of PEPPERS lies a variety of bold flavors that are

HOTTER THAN...

Simple ways to can canning

TODAY'S MENU

Slices filled with flavor

RESTAURANTS

Parker's closing at year's end

A guide to what's hot and what's not. F2

**THE PLAIN DEALER,** Cleveland

Andrea Levy, David Kordalski, Amanda Hamann

**Awards of Excellence**
Food page, broadsheet, 175,000+
Photo illustration
Portfolio, illustration, individual, Andrea Levy

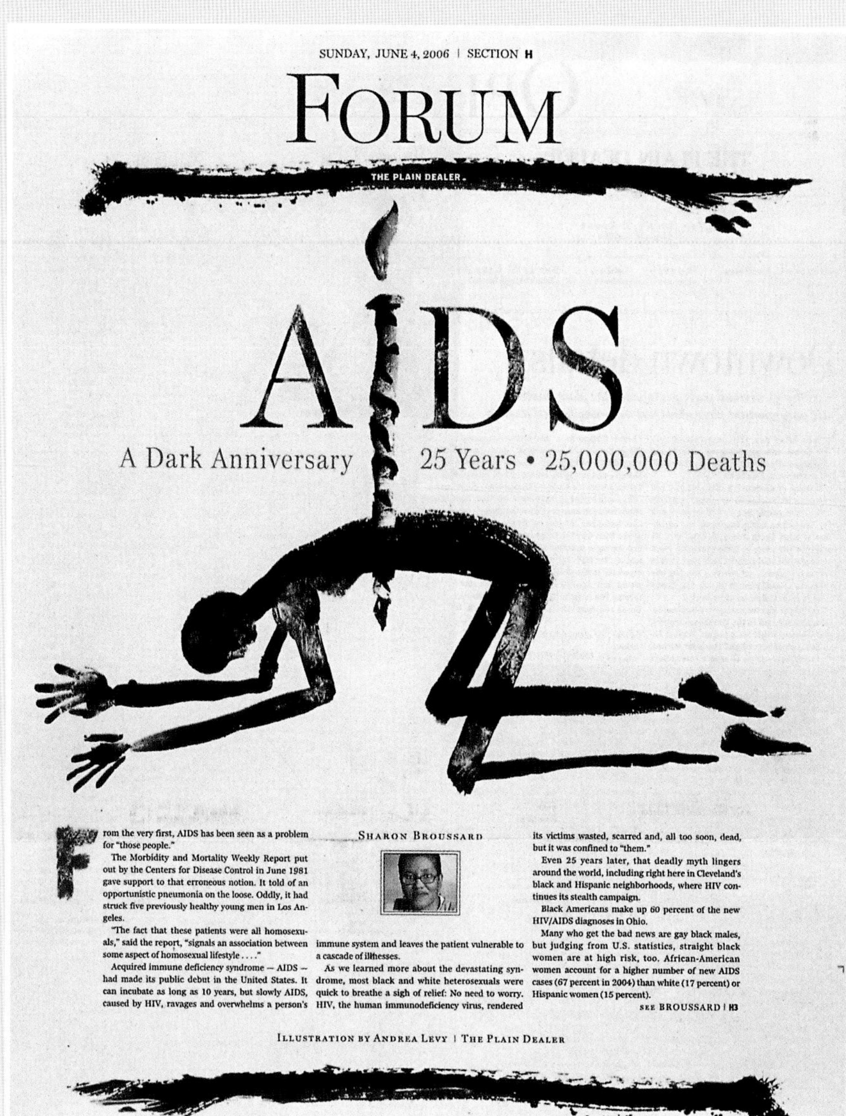

SUNDAY, JUNE 4, 2006 | SECTION H

# FORUM

THE PLAIN DEALER

# AIDS

A Dark Anniversary 25 Years • 25,000,000 Deaths

SHARON BROUSSARD

From the very first, AIDS has been seen as a problem for "those people."

The Morbidity and Mortality Weekly Report put out by the Centers for Disease Control in June 1981 gave support to that erroneous notion. It told of an opportunistic pneumonia on the loose. Oddly, it had struck five previously healthy young men in Los Angeles.

"The fact that these patients were all homosexuals," said the report, "signals an association between some aspect of homosexual lifestyle . . . ."

Acquired immune deficiency syndrome — AIDS — had made its public debut in the United States. It can incubate as long as 10 years, but slowly AIDS, caused by HIV, ravages and overwhelms a person's immune system and leaves the patient vulnerable to a cascade of illnesses.

As we learned more about the devastating syndrome, most black and white heterosexuals were quick to breathe a sigh of relief: No need to worry. HIV, the human immunodeficiency virus, rendered its victims wasted, scarred and, all too soon, dead, but it was confined to "them."

Even 25 years later, that deadly myth lingers around the world, including right here in Cleveland's black and Hispanic neighborhoods, where HIV continues its stealth campaign.

Black Americans make up 60 percent of the new HIV/AIDS diagnoses in Ohio.

Many who get the bad news are gay black males, but judging from U.S. statistics, straight black women are at high risk, too. African-American women account for a higher number of new AIDS cases (67 percent in 2004) than white (17 percent) or Hispanic women (15 percent).

SEE BROUSSARD | H3

ILLUSTRATION BY ANDREA LEVY | THE PLAIN DEALER

## What we don't do for our troops

DICK FEAGLER

My pal Tom Meyrose has a son fighting in Afghanistan. I know the kid slightly. And that's as close as I come to any personal contact with this war on terror. How about you?

The first time Tom's kid went out on a mission, a roadside bomb blew up his Humvee. Tom's kid called home and said he was OK, except for some nerve damage to his arm. He said the bomb was set off by remote control. It seems there is an electronic device that blocks the signal to the bomb, but his Humvee didn't have one.

It is only through Tom that I keep in touch with this war. Mostly, we here at home watch the war on the cable channels, which leaves us confused.

First, we hear somebody saying we're winning over there. Then you hear somebody saying we're not. This is called balanced coverage. Then, after a sliver of news, we have to sit through two male-enhancement commercials and some kind of feminine smell-good ad. And then we're back to what the cable people call the news.

The constant news ought to be that we are a nation at war. They shouldn't give that equal billing with "American Idol."

The trouble is, we are not a whole nation at war. We make, in this war, no sacrifices.

War has changed since I was a child. I remember when the butcher gave you liver instead of beef, and if you groused, he said, "What's the matter, lady, don't you know there's a war on?"

The war I grew up with rationed meat and butter and gasoline. You didn't gripe about the price of gas; you couldn't get any. And if you had a tire that went flat, you took the bus. Rubber had gone to war along with the rest of us.

But in this strange war, most of us make no sacrifice at all. I think that's obscene. I think any time we go off to fight, we all should pay something for a war waged in the name of all of us. Even if we have to pay an extra tax on . . . wood screws, say.

SEE FEAGLER | H3

STRANGE PIECE OF PARADISE

TERRI JENTZ

**BOOKS**

*Book editor Karen Long looks at a woman's search for her would-be murderer and likes what she sees in "Strange Piece of Paradise."* H4



## A little too exciting for the bench

BRENT LARKIN

Christine Russo knows her personal life has become a train wreck, with details of the pileup chronicled in excruciating detail in newspaper stories and television reports.

But the woman with the magic political name that may catapult her from the ranks of a little-known divorce attorney to a seat on the Common Pleas Court bench in Ohio's largest county says voters needn't be alarmed by those messy tales of money laundering, marijuana use, domestic violence and alleged infidelity.

If elected on Nov. 7, Russo resolves to prove us all wrong.

"All these real-life experiences will help," she said the other day. "I will absolutely be a breath of fresh air on the court. I'm a strong, hard-working individual who will only bring positive things to the bench."

Spend a few minutes chatting with Russo and you want desperately to believe her. The 41-year-old Strongsville woman is tough, self-confident and — above all — disarmingly engaging.

Still, it's impossible to ignore all those devilish details.

Prior to the May 2 Democratic primary, Plain Dealer reporters Jim McCarty and Jim Nichols revealed that Russo, a former assistant county prosecutor, was convicted of drug abuse (marijuana) in 1995 and was fined $100. Drug-related allegations resurfaced following what appeared to be a family brawl on Thanksgiving Day 2003. A lawsuit followed, and Christine's brother-in-law eventually produced a tape recording in which she is heard complaining of having to launder the proceeds of her brother-in-law's drug sales.

"I wash a thousand dollars a month," Russo protested to brother-in-law Vince Russo. "I can't take and deposit [your] illegal money" anymore.

The Plain Dealer report on Russo's problems sent many of her supporters diving for cover — including County Prosecutor Bill Mason.

SEE LARKIN | H3

**THE PLAIN DEALER,** Cleveland

Andrea Levy, Mary Lou Sneyd, David Kordalski

**Silver**
Single illustration

**Award of Excellence**
Opinion page, broadsheet, 175,000+

This a great concept for the sensitive topic of AIDS. The primitiveness makes it fragile — you can feel the disease taking over. It's sad, and you experience the pain.

Esté es un gran concepto para un tema sensible como el SIDA. Lo primitivo lo hace frágil; se puede sentir como la enfermedad va ganando terreno. Es triste y se siente el dolor.

ARTS & LIFE

THE PLAIN DEALER

SPRING

The season for eternal hope

SXSW MUSIC FESTIVAL

Past, present and future heat up already-hot town

INSIDE

Doubts cast on Costco's Picassos

Popular ballet

It's extraordinary how the artist sees relationships in individual elements and has a vision to present them. The ideas are original and complex. The work is clean, innovative and fresh.

Es extraordinaria la forma en que el artista ve relaciones entre los elementos individuales y tiene una visión para presentarlas. Las ideas son originales y complejas. El trabajo es limpio, innovador y fresco.

**THE PLAIN DEALER,** Cleveland

Andrea Levy, David Kordalski, Emmet Smith, Roy Hewitt, David Campbell, Mike Starkey, Kristen Davis, Ted Crow, Ellie Rhyner, Amanda Hamann, James M. Lewis, Sharon Yemich, Mary Lou Sneyd, Ken Marshall

**Silver**
Portfolio, individual photo, Andrea Levy

**Awards of Excellence**
Photo illustration
Portfolio, illustration, staff
Sports page, broadsheet, 175,000+

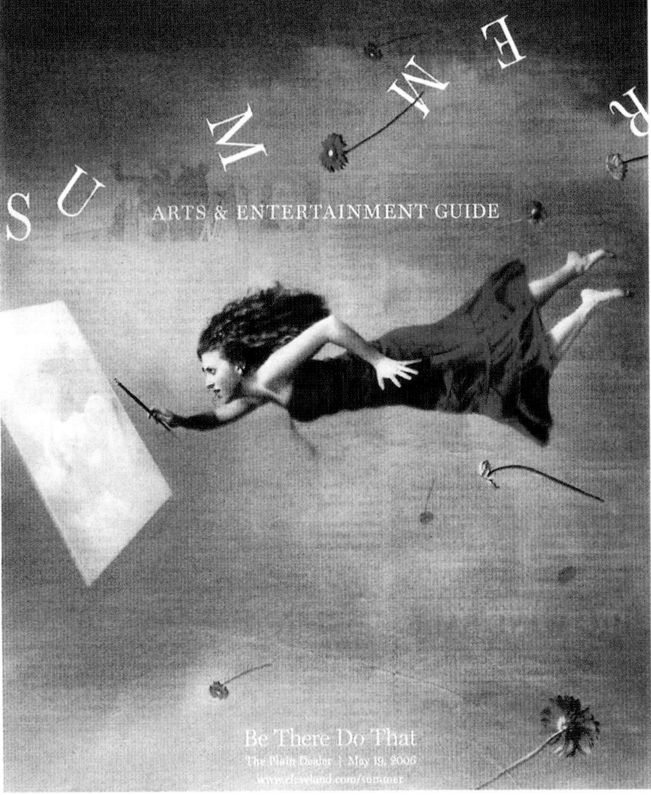


**THE PLAIN DEALER,** Cleveland

David Kordalski, Andrea Levy, Scott Sheldon

**Awards of Excellence**
Entertainment page, tabloid, 175,000+
Photo illustration

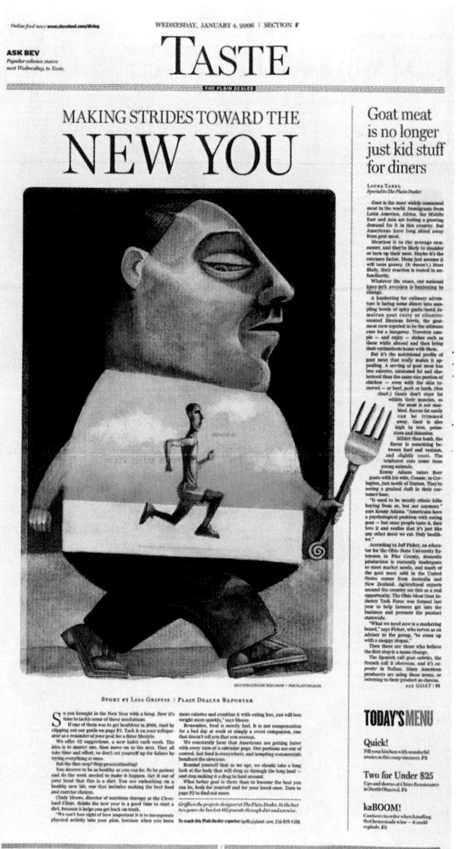
WEDNESDAY, JANUARY 4, 2006 | SECTION F

ASK BEV

# TASTE

THE PLAIN DEALER

MAKING STRIDES TOWARD THE

NEW YOU

Goat meat is no longer just kid stuff for diners

TODAY'S MENU

Quick!

Two for Under $25

kaBOOM!

**THE PLAIN DEALER,** Cleveland

David Kordalski, Lisa Griffis, Ted Crow

**Awards of Excellence**

Food page, broadsheet, 175,000+

Single illustration

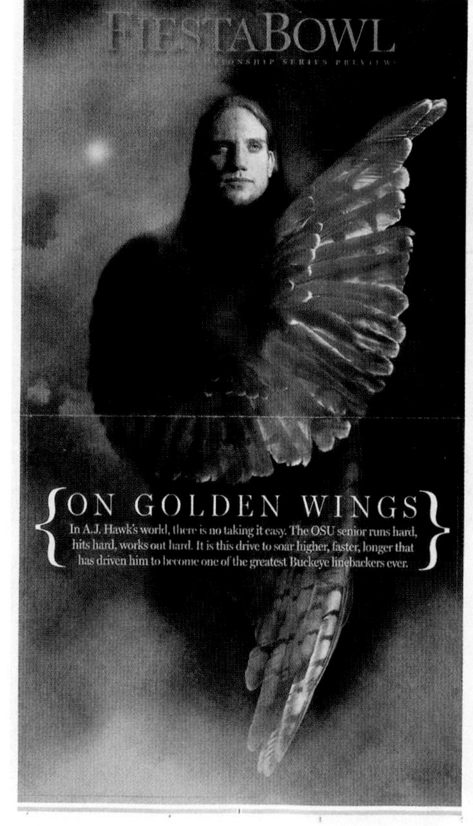
The Plain Dealer | Sunday, January 1, 2006

THE PLAIN DEALER

FIESTA BOWL

ON GOLDEN WINGS

In A.J. Hawk's world, there is no taking it easy. The OSU senior runs hard, hits hard, works out hard. It is this drive to soar higher, faster, longer that has driven him to become one of the greatest Buckeye linebackers ever.

**THE PLAIN DEALER,** Cleveland

Andrea Levy, David Kordalski, Emmet Smith, Roy Hewitt, David Campbell, Mike Starkey

**Awards of Excellence**

Photo illustration

Sports page, broadsheet, 175,000+

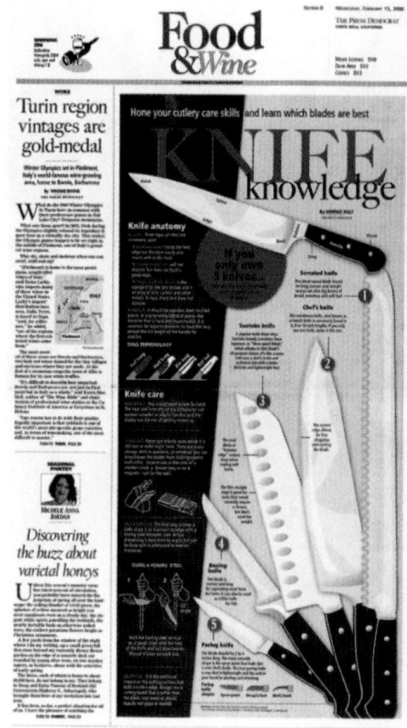
Food & Wine

Turin region vintages are gold-medal

Hone your cutlery care skills and learn which blades are best

KNIFE knowledge

Knife anatomy

Knife care

Discovering the buzz about varietal honeys

**THE PRESS DEMOCRAT,** Santa Rosa, Calif.

Dennis Bolt

**Awards of Excellence**

Food page, broadsheet, 50,000-174,999

Information graphics, non-breaking news & features, 50,000-174,999

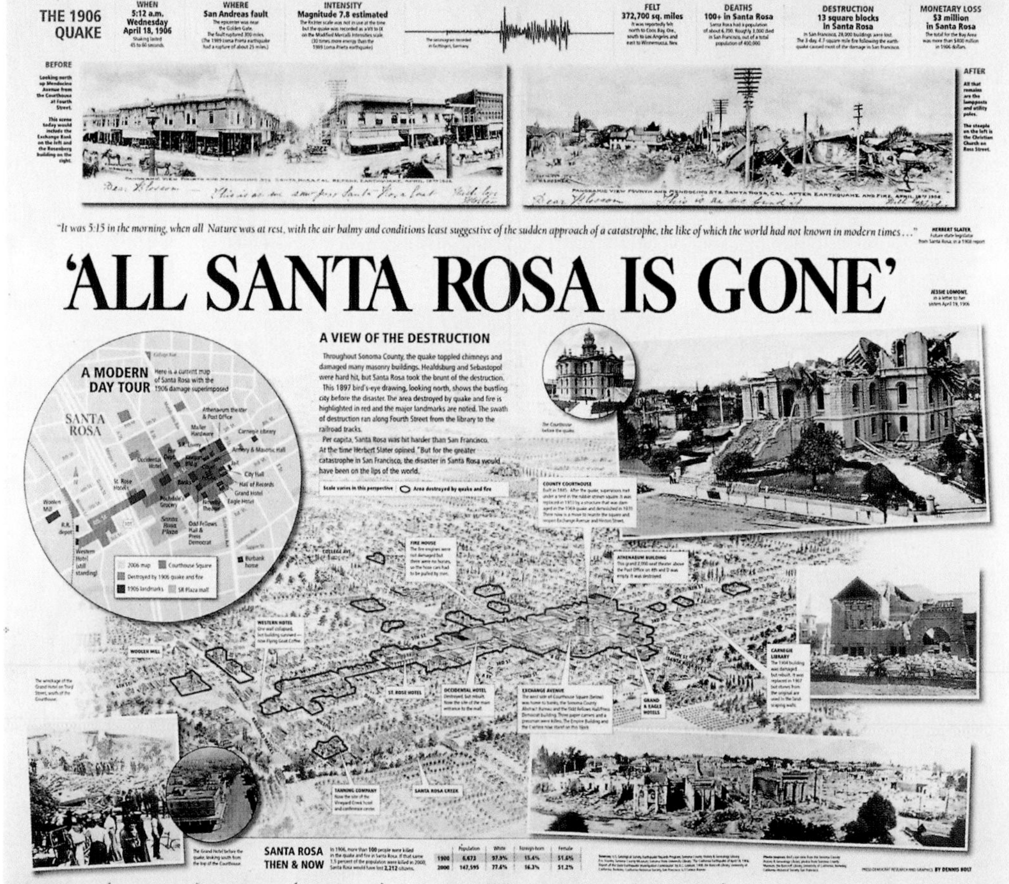
THE 1906 QUAKE

WHEN 5:12 a.m. Wednesday April 18, 1906

WHERE San Andreas fault

INTENSITY Magnitude 7.8 estimated

FELT 372,700 sq. miles

DEATHS 100+ in Santa Rosa

DESTRUCTION 13 square blocks in Santa Rosa

MONETARY LOSS $3 million in Santa Rosa

BEFORE

AFTER

"It was 5:15 in the morning, when all Nature was at rest, with the air balmy and conditions least suggestive of the sudden approach of a catastrophe, the like of which the world had not known in modern times . . ."

# 'ALL SANTA ROSA IS GONE'

A VIEW OF THE DESTRUCTION

Throughout Sonoma County, the quake toppled chimneys and damaged many masonry buildings. Healdsburg and Sebastopol were hard hit, but Santa Rosa took the brunt of the destruction. This 1897 bird's-eye drawing, looking north, shows the bustling city before the disaster. The area destroyed by quake and fire is highlighted in red and the major landmarks are noted. The swath of destruction ran along Fourth Street from the library to the railroad tracks.

Per capita, Santa Rosa was hit harder than San Francisco. At the time Herbert Slater opined, "But for the greater catastrophe in San Francisco, the disaster in Santa Rosa would have been on the lips of the world.

A MODERN DAY TOUR

SANTA ROSA THEN & NOW

**THE PRESS DEMOCRAT,** Santa Rosa, Calif.

Dennis Bolt

**Awards of Excellence**

Information graphics, non-breaking news & features, 50,000-174,999

Mapping, 50,000-174,999

SAN FRANCISCO CHRONICLE | 5.14.06 | DA VINCI CODE | 'POSEIDON' | MARLEY'S GHOST


**SAN FRANCISCO CHRONICLE**

Nanette Bisher, Matt Petty, Shawn Barber, Zach Trenholm, Olaf Hajek, Adam McCauley, Ward Schumaker, Lance Jackson, Sue Adolphson, Joe Brown

**Silvers**
Entertainment page, tabloid, 175,000+
Portfolio, illustration, staff

**Awards of Excellence**
Portfolio, feature page design, 175,000+, Matt Petty
Single illustration

We've seen "Mona Lisa" over and over again with the release of the movie "The Da Vinci Code." This page plays on that familiarity by creating a playful paint-by-the-numbers illustration that invites the reader to participate. Finding the numbers is like cracking the code in the movie. Of all the "Da Vinci" pages, this stands out.

La "Mona Lisa" ha sido vista una y otra vez con el lanzamiento de la película "El Código da Vinci". Esta página toma esta familiaridad al crear una juguetona ilustración para colorear los números, que invita al lector a participar. Encontrar los números es como descifrar el código del filme. Ésta sobresale entre todas las páginas "da Vinci".

SAN FRANCISCO CHRONICLE | 5.21.06 | SUMMER SHAKESPEARE | MATTHEW BARNEY | TAMMY HALL


**SAN FRANCISCO CHRONICLE**

Nanette Bisher, Matt Petty, Shawn Barber, Zach Trenholm, Olaf Hajek, Adam McCauley, Ward Schumaker, Lance Jackson

**Silver:** Illustration, staff
**Award of Excellence:** Portfolio, feature page design, 175,000+, Matt Petty

This entry is quite provocative, exciting and consistent throughout. It shows a broad range of strong illustrations, and it engages readers on many levels.

En toda su extensión, esta pieza es bastante provocadora, estimulante y consistente. Muestra un amplio rango de ilustraciones potentes, y capta la atención de los lectores en varios niveles.

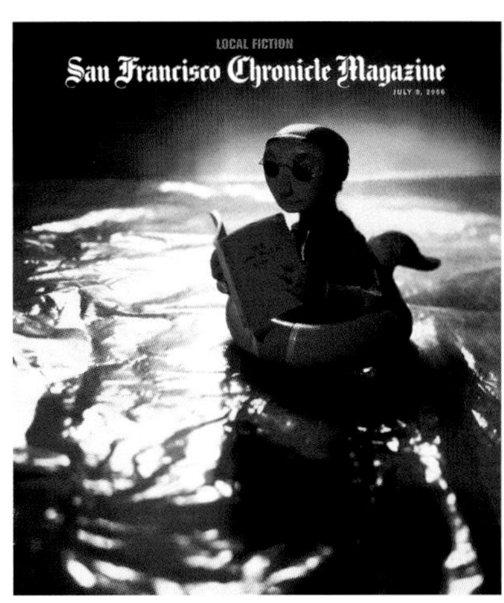


**SAN FRANCISCO CHRONICLE**

Nanette Bisher, Matt Petty, Dorothy Yule, Red Nose Studio, George Russell, Wayne Walters, Jim Merithew, Alison Biggar

**Awards of Excellence**
Magazine cover design
Magazine cover story
Multiple illustrations

**SAN JOSE MERCURY NEWS** (Calif.)

Martin Gee, Stephanie Grace Lim, Jonathon Berlin

**Awards of Excellence**

Entertainment page, broadsheet, 175,000+
Portfolio, illustration, individual, Martin Gee
Single illustration

E
WEDNESDAY

a+e

ARTS + ENTERTAINMENT

INSTRUCTIONS:

MONSTER MASH-UP

NEED A QUICK GET-UP? GRAB SCISSORS. START SNIPPING

NHL PLAYOFFS MEET THE SHARKS

ALL ABOARD THE CHEECHOO TRAIN

# JONATHAN CHEECHOO

First in a series: Each day of a Sharks playoff game, the Mercury News will run another car in the train featuring another Sharks personality. Collect them all.

'CHEECH'
RIGHT WING



**SAN JOSE MERCURY NEWS** (Calif.)

Doug Griswold, Jonathon Berlin, Pai, Matt Mansfield

**Awards of Excellence**

Miscellaneous
Multiple illustrations

F
SATURDAY

OUR GIFT TO YOU

House+Home

Last-Minute Wrapping Paper

HAPPY HOLIDAYS! • HAPPY HOLIDAYS! • HAPPY HOLIDAYS! • HAPPY HOLIDAYS! • HAPPY HOLIDAYS! • HAPPY HOLIDAYS! • HAPPY HOLIDAYS!



**SAN JOSE MERCURY NEWS** (Calif.)

Stephanie Grace Lim, Jonathon Berlin, Matt Mansfield

**Awards of Excellence**

Home/real estate page, broadsheet, 175,000+
Portfolio, feature page design, 175,000+, Stephanie Grace Lim

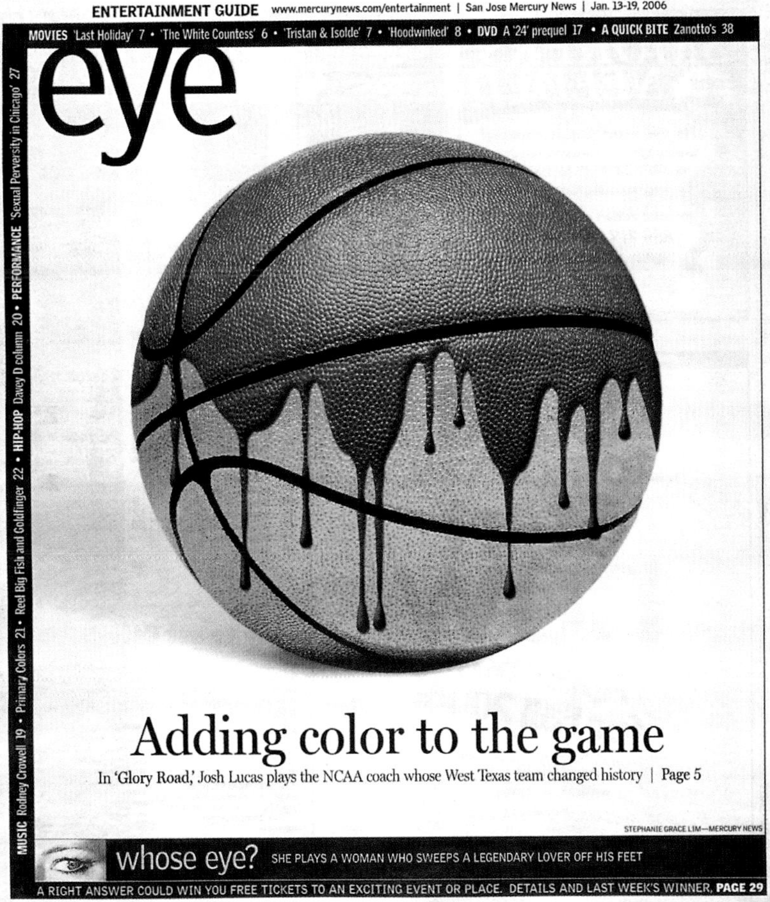
ENTERTAINMENT GUIDE www.mercurynews.com/entertainment | San Jose Mercury News | Jan. 13-19, 2006

MOVIES 'Last Holiday' 7 • 'The White Countess' 6 • 'Tristan & Isolde' 7 • 'Hoodwinked' 8 • DVD A '24' prequel 17 • A QUICK BITE Zanotto's 38

MUSIC Rodney Crowell 19 • Primary Colors 21 • Reel Big Fish and Goldfinger 22 • HIP-HOP Davey D column 20 • PERFORMANCE 'Sexual Perversity in Chicago' 27

eye

Adding color to the game

In 'Glory Road,' Josh Lucas plays the NCAA coach whose West Texas team changed history | Page 5

STEPHANIE GRACE LIM—MERCURY NEWS

whose eye? SHE PLAYS A WOMAN WHO SWEEPS A LEGENDARY LOVER OFF HIS FEET

A RIGHT ANSWER COULD WIN YOU FREE TICKETS TO AN EXCITING EVENT OR PLACE. DETAILS AND LAST WEEK'S WINNER, PAGE 29

**SAN JOSE MERCURY NEWS** (Calif.)

Stephanie Grace Lim, Ray Moses, Jonathon Berlin, Matt Mansfield

**Silvers**
Entertainment page, tabloid, 175,000+
Portfolio, feature page design, 175,000+, Stephanie Grace Lim

This is clever, not cliché, as a metaphor for the issue of race in the basketball movie "Glory Road." The rendering of the basketball is excellent, and the marriage of headline and image completes the concept.

Como metáfora sobre el asunto de la raza en la película sobre baloncesto "Glory Road", es ingeniosa y nada de cliché. El dibujo de la pelota de baloncesto es excelente, y la unión del título y la imagen completa el concepto.

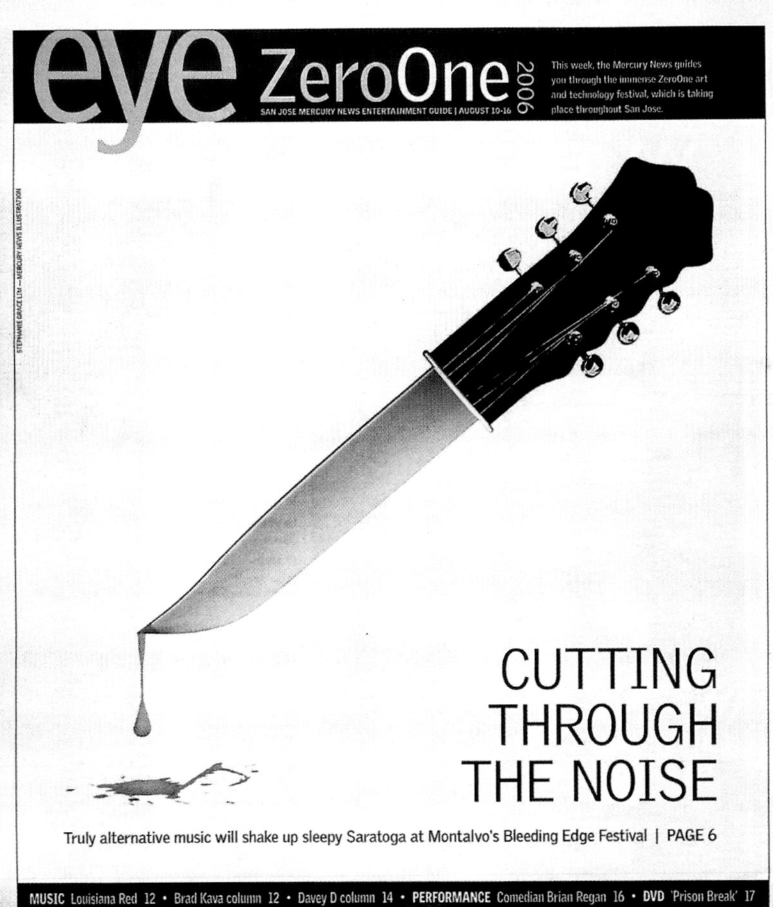
eye ZeroOne 2006

SAN JOSE MERCURY NEWS ENTERTAINMENT GUIDE | AUGUST 10-16

This week, the Mercury News guides you through the immense ZeroOne art and technology festival, which is taking place throughout San Jose.

STEPHANIE GRACE LIM—MERCURY NEWS ILLUSTRATION

CUTTING THROUGH THE NOISE

Truly alternative music will shake up sleepy Saratoga at Montalvo's Bleeding Edge Festival | PAGE 6

MUSIC Louisiana Red 12 • Brad Kava column 12 • Davey D column 14 • PERFORMANCE Comedian Brian Regan 16 • DVD 'Prison Break' 17

**SAN JOSE MERCURY NEWS** (Calif.)

Stephanie Grace Lim, Jonathon Berlin, Matt Mansfield

**Silvers**
Entertainment page, tabloid, 175,000+
Feature page design, 175,000+

The illustration melds a guitar and knife quite naturally to complete the metaphor in the headline. It's a perfect marriage of illustration and words for the Bleeding Edge Festival.

La ilustración funde una guitarra y un cuchillo con gran naturalidad para completar la metáfora del título. Se trata de una perfecta unión entre ilustración y palabras para el Bleeding Edge Festival (Festival del filo sangrante).

**SAN JOSE MERCURY NEWS** (Calif.)

Shan Carter, Doug Griswold, Pai, Karl Kahler, Michael Malone, Geri Migielicz, Jonathon Berlin, Matt Mansfield, A.C. McReynolds

**Awards of Excellence**
Reprints
Single-subject special coverage
Special news topics, local

San Jose Mercury News

FIRST OF FIVE PARTS
A MERCURY NEWS WATCHDOG REPORT

# Tainted trials, stolen justice

By Fredric N. Tulsky

The Santa Clara County criminal justice system failed Miguel Sermeno.

Sermeno was arrested on felony hit-and-run charges after walking the half-block from his house to the scene of an accident. An overzealous deputy district attorney ignored evidence that pointed to a more likely suspect, instead winning a wrongful conviction.

The system failed Bobby Herrera.

Herrera pleaded guilty to assault for a shooting he did not commit, buckling to pressure from an incompetent lawyer who bled his family for thousands of dollars but never investigated the case. Even after the key witness admitted she falsely accused him, indifferent state appellate court justices let his five-year prison sentence stand without explanation.

WWW.MERCURYNEWS.COM: TALES OF FOUR DEFENDANTS BETRAYED BY THE SYSTEM

READ EACH INSTALLMENT AND SHARE YOUR THOUGHTS IN FORUMS, POLLS, CHATS

| TODAY: THE STUDY | MONDAY: PROSECUTION | TUESDAY: DEFENSE | WEDNESDAY: JUDGES | THURSDAY: APPEALS |
| --- | --- | --- | --- | --- |
| Problems plague one-third of trials, but little is done about them | Top officials neglected signs of misconduct, risking wrongful convictions | Some lawyers overlook key evidence or fail to restrain prosecutors | Their rulings have enormous power to tilt trials against defendants | The appellate court goes to surprising lengths to uphold guilty verdicts |

INSIDE: HOW THE SYSTEM WORKS AND WHAT CAN GO WRONG | 4AA HOW THE STUDY WAS CONDUCTED | 8AA

NBC11: SEE ONE DEFENDANT'S SAGA IN A SPECIAL REPORT AT 7 A.M. AND 6 P.M. TODAY

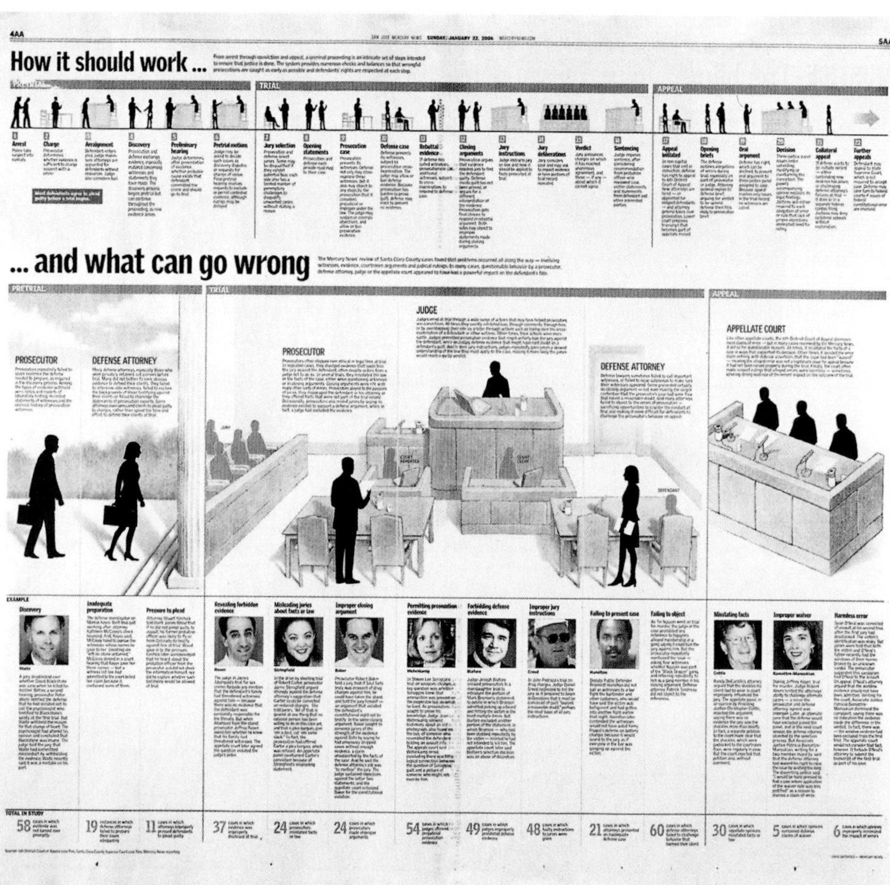

# How it should work ...

PRETRIAL · TRIAL · APPEAL

# ... and what can go wrong

PROSECUTOR · DEFENSE ATTORNEY · JUDGE · APPELLATE COURT



**SAN JOSE MERCURY NEWS** (Calif.)

Shan Carter, Doug Griswold, Pai, Karl Kahler, Jami C. Smith, Geri Migielicz, Jonathon Berlin, Andrea Maschietto, Matt Mansfield, A.C. McReynolds, Michael Malone

**Awards of Excellence**
Special coverage, inside page
Special coverage, section, no ads
Information graphics, staff, extended coverage, 175,000+

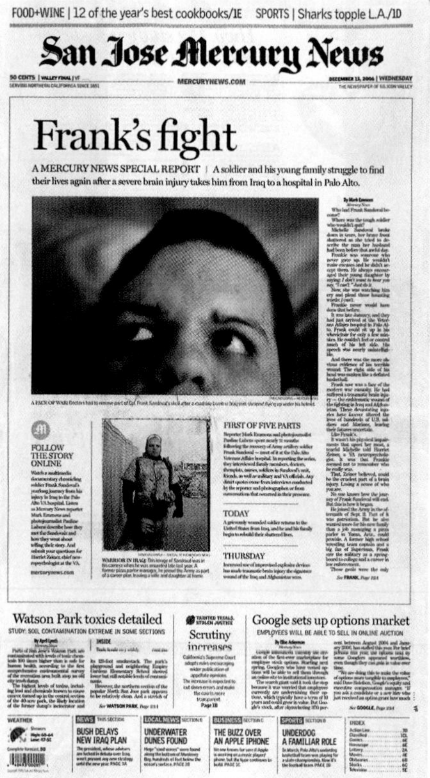

FOOD+WINE | 12 of the year's best cookbooks/1E SPORTS | Sharks topple L.A./1D

San Jose Mercury News

MERCURYNEWS.COM

# Frank's fight

A MERCURY NEWS SPECIAL REPORT | A soldier and his young family struggle to find their lives again after a severe brain injury takes him from Iraq to a hospital in Palo Alto.

FOLLOW THE STORY ONLINE

FIRST OF FIVE PARTS

TODAY

THURSDAY

Watson Park toxics detailed

Scrutiny increases

Google sets up options market

BUSH DELAYS NEW IRAQ PLAN

UNDERWATER DUNES FOUND

THE BUZZ OVER AN APPLE IPHONE

UNDERDOG A FAMILIAR ROLE

**SAN JOSE MERCURY NEWS** (Calif.)

Michael Tribble, Geri Migielicz, Pauline Lubens, Jonathon Berlin, Matt Mansfield

**Awards of Excellence**
News, A-Section page, broadsheet, 175,000+
Special news topics, war on terrorism

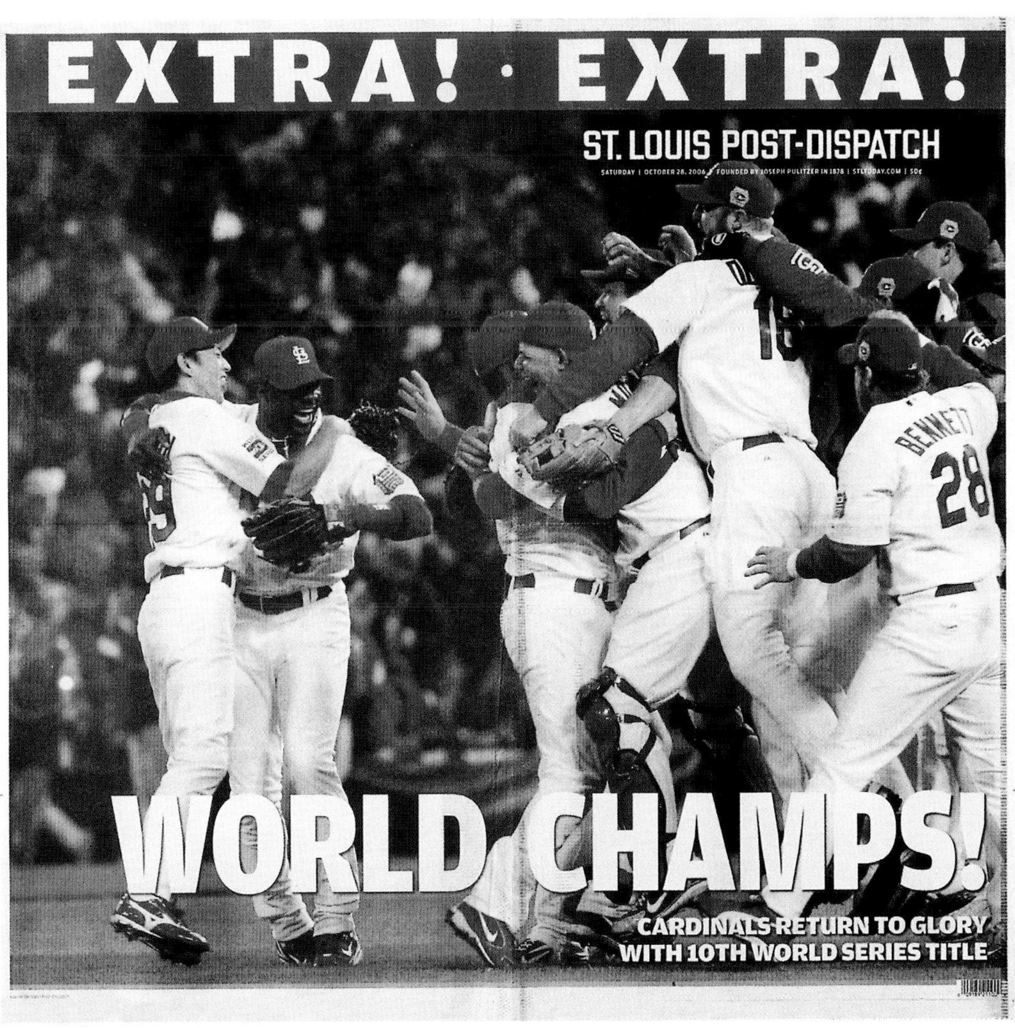

EXTRA! · EXTRA!

ST. LOUIS POST-DISPATCH

SATURDAY | OCTOBER 28, 2006 | FOUNDED BY JOSEPH PULITZER IN 1878 | STLTODAY.COM | 50¢

WORLD CHAMPS!

CARDINALS RETURN TO GLORY WITH 10TH WORLD SERIES TITLE

**ST. LOUIS POST-DISPATCH**

Staff

**Awards of Excellence**

Breaking news, sports

Other news page, broadsheet, 175,000+

Special news topics, sports

The Seattle Times

America's Immigration Dilemma

A SPECIAL REPORT

Understanding Immigration >> A new chapter is being written in America's immigration story. This time, the usual debates about illegal residents, jobs, social services, cultural identity and economics are complicated by national-security fears. The issue, unlike so many in this country, crosses ideological lines, making a solution extremely difficult to find.

A Historical Look

The Border

The Legal Options for Immigrants

More Online

The Numbers

The National Debate

Other Strategies

**THE SEATTLE TIMES**

Denise Clifton, Fred Nelson, Aldo Chan

**Awards of Excellence**

Special coverage, section, no ads

Special coverage, section cover

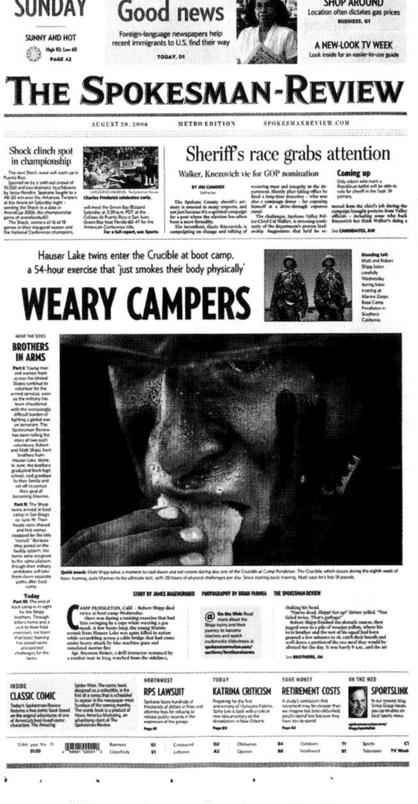

SUNDAY

Good news

Foreign-language newspapers help recent immigrants to U.S. find their way

SHOP AROUND

A NEW-LOOK TV WEEK

THE SPOKESMAN-REVIEW

AUGUST 20, 2006 METRO EDITION SPOKESMANREVIEW.COM

Shock clinch spot in championship

Sheriff's race grabs attention

Walker, Knezovich vie for GOP nomination

Hauser Lake twins enter the Crucible at boot camp, a 54-hour exercise that 'just smokes their body physically'

WEARY CAMPERS

BROTHERS IN ARMS

CLASSIC COMIC

RPS LAWSUIT

KATRINA CRITICISM

RETIREMENT COSTS

SPORTSLINK

**THE SPOKESMAN-REVIEW,** Spokane, Wash.

Geoff Pinnock, Ralph Walter, Brian Plonka, Bart Rayniak

**Awards of Excellence**

Single-subject special coverage

Special news topics, local

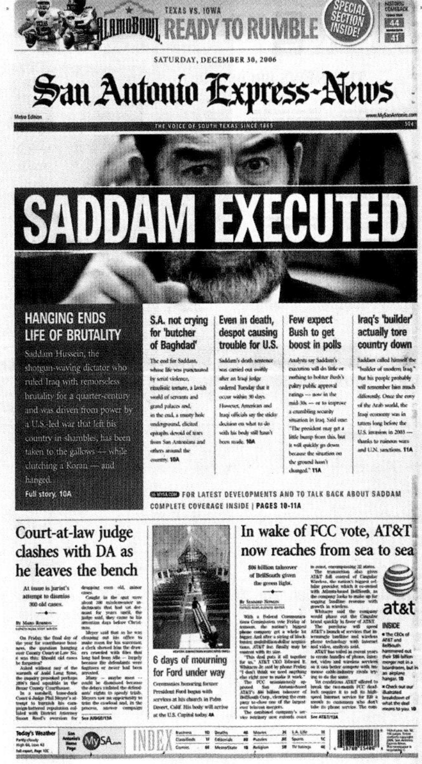

TEXAS VS. IOWA

ALAMOBOWL READY TO RUMBLE

SPECIAL SECTION INSIDE!

SATURDAY, DECEMBER 30, 2006

San Antonio Express-News

THE VOICE OF SOUTH TEXAS SINCE 1865

SADDAM EXECUTED

HANGING ENDS LIFE OF BRUTALITY

Saddam Hussein, the shotgun-waving dictator who ruled Iraq with remorseless brutality for a quarter-century and was driven from power by a U.S.-led war that left his country in shambles, has been taken to the gallows — while clutching a Koran — and hanged.

Full story, 10A

S.A. not crying for 'butcher of Baghdad'

Even in death, despot causing trouble for U.S.

Few expect Bush to get boost in polls

Iraq's 'builder' actually tore country down

FOR LATEST DEVELOPMENTS AND TO TALK BACK ABOUT SADDAM

COMPLETE COVERAGE INSIDE | PAGES 10-11A

Court-at-law judge clashes with DA as he leaves the bench

6 days of mourning for Ford under way

In wake of FCC vote, AT&T now reaches from sea to sea

INDEX

**SAN ANTONIO EXPRESS-NEWS**

Adrian Alvarez, Jason Tyler, Nan Keck, Dean Lockwood

**Awards of Excellence**

Breaking news, international

Breaking news, war on terrorism

OUTLOOK
WHERE YOUR TRASH GOES
HIP-HOP VOICES

**SOUTH FLORIDA SUN-SENTINEL,** Fort Lauderdale
Michael Johnson, John L. White, Chris Mihal, Mary Vignoles, Tim Frank
Other news page, broadsheet, 175,000+

OUTLOOK
YOUR POWER
FISHING FOR FANS

**SOUTH FLORIDA SUN-SENTINEL,** Fort Lauderdale
Omar Vega, Kristian Rodriguez, Mary Vignoles, Tim Frank
**Awards of Excellence**
Other news page, broadsheet, 175,000+
Photo illustration

Outlook
A DAY OF TERROR, AN ERA OF CHANGE

**SOUTH FLORIDA SUN-SENTINEL,** Fort Lauderdale
Kristian Rodriguez, Chris Mihal, Tim Frank
**Awards of Excellence**
Other news page, broadsheet, 175,000+
Single illustration

**SOUTH FLORIDA SUN-SENTINEL,** Fort Lauderdale
Belinda Long, R. Scott Horner, Len De Groot, Tim Frank
**Awards of Excellence**
Information graphics, non-breaking news & features, 175,000+
Portfolio, information graphics, individual, non-breaking news & features, 175,000+, Belinda Long

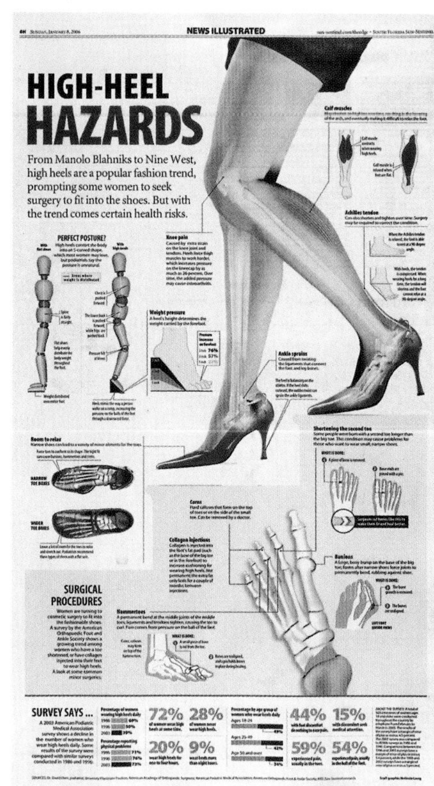
NEWS ILLUSTRATED
HIGH-HEEL HAZARDS
From Manolo Blahniks to Nine West, high heels are a popular fashion trend, prompting some women to seek surgery to fit into the shoes. But with the trend comes certain health risks.
PERFECT POSTURE?
SURGICAL PROCEDURES
SURVEY SAYS ...
72% 28%
20% 9%
44% 15%
59% 54%

Lifestyle
NEW YORK FASHION WEEK
Toning down the hot hues
FAST FRIENDS
Anthony Hopkins and director patch up an old rift to film *Indian*.
THIS CAN'T BE WHAT MUHAMMAD WANTED

*Redesign, Before*

**SOUTH FLORIDA SUN-SENTINEL,** Fort Lauderdale
Christian Font, Robert Duyos, Amy Beth Bennett, Jonathan Boho
**Awards of Excellence**
Sports page, broadsheet, 175,000+
Breaking news, sports

Sun-Sentinel
NBA FINALS | GAME 6 | HEAT 95, MAVERICKS 92
'OUR TIME'
FINALS MVP DWYANE WADE SCORES 36 POINTS, LEADS HEAT TO ITS FIRST NBA TITLE
PAT RILEY FULFILLS PROMISE OF A CHAMPIONSHIP PARADE IN SOUTH FLORIDA
HEAT COMMEMORATIVE SECTION COMING SUNDAY

LIFESTYLE PLAY
YOUR THURSDAY PREVIEW TO THE WEEKEND
You say you want a resolution?
How about a new you for the new year? If you're ready to sweep out unproductive old habits, here's how to get started this weekend.
HOME
HEALTH
RELATIONSHIPS
FINANCES
PARENTING

*Redesign, After*

**SOUTH FLORIDA SUN-SENTINEL,** Fort Lauderdale
Angela Brennan, Gretchen Day-Bryant, Ben Crandell, Susana Sanchez, Tim Frank
**Awards of Excellence**
Other feature page, broadsheet, 175,000+
Redesign, page

**SOUTH FLORIDA SUN-SENTINEL,** Fort Lauderdale

Tim Frank, Mary Vignoles, Tim Rasmussen, Chris Mihal, Robert Mayer

**Awards of Excellence**

Other news page, broadsheet, 175,000+
Photo project
Special news topics, local

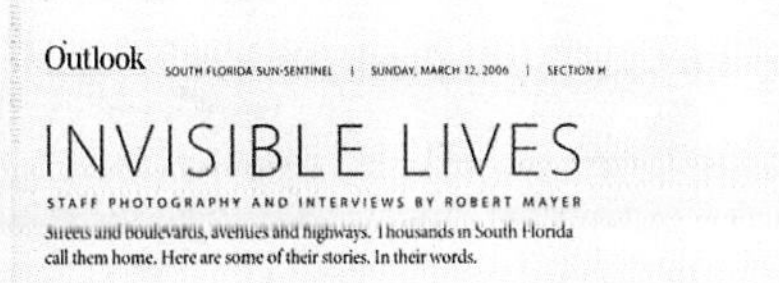

**SOUTH FLORIDA SUN-SENTINEL,** Fort Lauderdale

Tim Frank, Tim Rasmussen, Mary Vignoles, Chris Mihal, Rebekah Monson, Joe Amon, Mike Stocker

**Awards of Excellence**

Photo project
Photo series

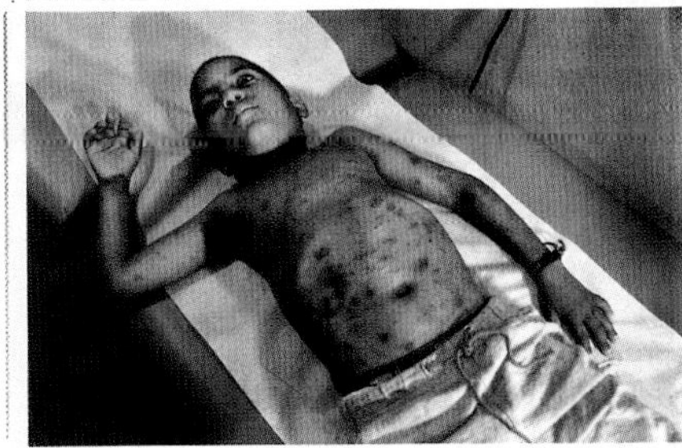

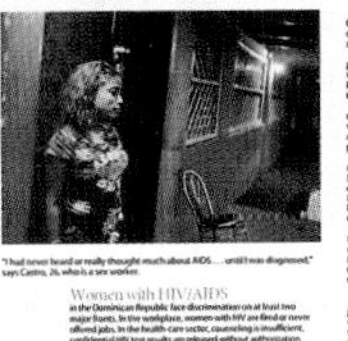

**SOUTH FLORIDA SUN-SENTINEL,** Fort Lauderdale

Chris Mihal, Rebekah Monson, Mike Stocker, Joe Amon, Mary Vignoles, Tim Rasmussen, Tim Frank

**Awards of Excellence**

Special coverage, inside page
Special coverage, multiple sections, no ads

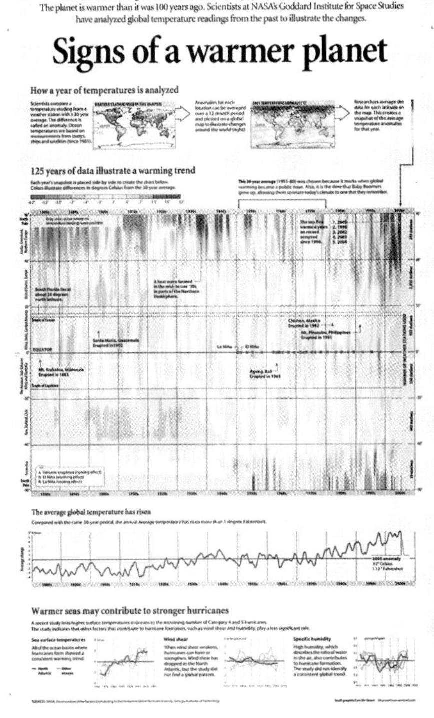

**SOUTH FLORIDA SUN-SENTINEL,** Fort Lauderdale

Len De Groot, R. Scott Horner, Tim Frank

**Awards of Excellence**

Charting, 175,000+
Mapping, 175,000+

**THE VIRGINIAN-PILOT,** Norfolk

Sam Hundley, Chris Curry, Norm Shafer, Charles Apple, Paul Nelson, Deborah Withey, David M. Putney, Martin Smith-Rodden, Judy Le, Paul Nelson

**Awards of Excellence**
News, A-Section page, broadsheet, 175,000+
Special news topics, local

LANDIS IN THE LEAD

The Virginian-Pilot

BLACKWATER

INSIDE AMERICA'S PRIVATE ARMY

ENTER A WORLD where the military has become a business – where citizen soldiers work for a private company whose currency comes from conflict. It's a place sewn subtle and others fear. And it's right in our backyard.

Israel crosses over Lebanese border

FORCES SEIZE VILLAGE; U.N. FEARS GROWING HUMANITARIAN CRISIS

Debate sets tone for main issues in hotly contested Senate race

OUT OF THE SEA!

Capture

The Virginian-Pilot

Welcome to Londonistan, where your mild-mannered neighbor may be an Islamic extremist

Great Britain remains a cauldron of Islamic militants unmatched in Europe

Teenager with cancer ponders life as court date nears

Trail of destruction greets the displaced after 33 days of Israel-Hezbollah warfare

**THE VIRGINIAN-PILOT,** Norfolk

Robert Suhay, Elizabeth Thiel, Paul Nelson, Deborah Withey

**Awards of Excellence**
News, A-Section page, broadsheet, 175,000+
Portfolio, news page design, 175,000+, Robert Suhay

new wave of sound

OUR CD REVIEWS HAVE A BONUS TRACK. **THE DAILY BREAK, E10**

**FRIDAY**
**AUGUST 4, 2006**
141ST YEAR • NO. 257
50 CENTS

# The Virginian-Pilot

Afternoon storms. High in the mid-90s. **Details, D6**

SERVING HAMPTON ROADS AND NORTHEASTERN NORTH CAROLINA

## Silence surrounds Navy's local court system

### Petty officer held in secret for 4 months

BY TIM McGLONE
THE VIRGINIAN-PILOT

NORFOLK — A petty officer has been in the Norfolk Naval Station brig for more than four months facing espionage, desertion and other charges, but the Navy has refused to release details of the case.

The case against Fire Control Technician 3rd Class Ariel J. Weinmann is indicative of the secrecy surrounding the Navy military court here, where public affairs and trial court officials have denied access to basic information including the court docket – a listing of cases to be heard.

**ONLINE**
Should the Navy release details of the case against an imprisoned officer facing espionage and desertion charges? Vote at **pilotonline.com.**

After months of requests, the Navy this week provided The Virginian-Pilot with Weinmann's name, rank and the charges he faces.

In an e-mail, Theodore Brown, a spokesman for Fleet Forces Command, said, "It is sometimes a challenge to balance the desires of the media, the public's right to know, and the rights of an individual accused of a crime."

"In this case," he concluded, the command "is attempting to provide as much unclassified

*Please see* **Court,** *Page* **A7**

INSIDE

Season is downgraded

Hurricane forecaster William Gray now predicts fewer major storms.
**Page A3**

Abduction victims safe

Police seek two men suspected of kidnapping Beach mother and son.
**Hampton Roads**

COMING SUNDAY

**Teachers' pay rivals other professionals'**

An analysis of public teachers' salaries and benefits reveals that a career in the classroom is not what it used to be.

## YOU'VE MADE IT THROUGH TWO OPPRESSIVELY HOT DAYS. JUST ONE TO GO BEFORE A BREAK.

101°

WEDNESDAY
**Record day No. 1**
The temperature hit triple digits for the first time this summer, Aug. 2 became the hottest on record locally, one degree higher than the old mark set in 1942.

102°

THURSDAY
**Record day No. 2**
The last time the area had back-to-back days of record-setting, 100-plus heat was in 1952. It's happened six times since 1871, when continuous observations began.

YOU ARE HERE

94°

TODAY
**Finally, double digits**
The National Weather Service anticipates a high in the mid-90s for Norfolk, a more typical temperature for early August.

84°

SATURDAY
**A return to normal**
High temperatures may drop 10 degrees into the 80s. Next week, forecasters predict highs in the low 90s but say the worst is probably past.

### Electricity usage, calls for help prove heat wave's growing cost

BY STEVE STONE
THE VIRGINIAN-PILOT

Another hot day, another heat record as nature pushed the mercury up one more notch, to 102 in Norfolk.

That follows Wednesday's record of 101. The area hasn't broiled like this in 29 years.

But the bubble is about to burst – or at least vent some hot air – as the region begins a slide back to normalcy.

"It certainly doesn't look as hot as it's been," said Brian Hurley, a meteorologist at the National Weather Service office in Wakefield.

The Weather Service anticipates a high of about 94 this afternoon in Norfolk – not pleasant but lower. Saturday's high is expected to come in about 10 degrees

CHRIS TYREE/THE VIRGINIAN-PILOT
**Jay Cousins, a roofer for Stevens Roofing Corp., cools off Thursday on the job.**

under that.

"The outlook is really for mid- to upper 80s over the weekend," Hurley said. Hampton Roads may see some highs in the lower 90s for a few days early

*Please see* **Heat,** *Page* **A10**

INSIDE
**Eastern U.S. feels the heat**
More than a dozen states from Georgia to Connecticut are under a heat advisory. Since Sunday, at least 25 deaths in 10 states and Washington, D.C., have been connected to the scorching temperatures.

**Mapping the heat**
A look at some of Thursday's high temperatures across the nation.
*Page A10*

## Generals say civil war in Iraq now more likely

### Rumsfeld does not contradict officers

BY THOM SHANKER
THE NEW YORK TIMES

WASHINGTON — The commander of U.S. forces in the Middle East bluntly warned a Senate committee Thursday that sectarian violence in Iraq, especially in Baghdad, had grown so severe that the nation could slide toward civil war.

The commander, Army Gen. John Abizaid, also acknowledged that since the security situation remained so unstable, the significant reductions in U.S. forces were unlikely before the end of this year.

Asked by Sen. Carl Levin of Michigan, the ranking Democrat on the Senate Armed Services Committee, whether Iraq risked falling into civil war, Abizaid replied, "I believe that the sectarian violence is probably as bad as I've seen it, in Baghdad in particular, and that if not stopped, it is possible that Iraq could move towards civil war." But,

*Please see* **War,** *Page* **A12**

**WHAT THEY SAID**
**Gen. Peter Pace,** left, confirmed in a Senate hearing that the situation in Iraq may be evolving into civil war, which he had not anticipated.
**Gen. John Abizaid** said: "I believe that the sectarian violence is probably as bad as I've seen it. ... if not stopped, it is possible that Iraq could move towards civil war."

## Israel readies for push into Lebanon as talks continue

FROM WIRE REPORTS

MAALOT, Israel — The Lebanese militia Hezbollah killed 12 Israelis – eight civilians and four soldiers – on Thursday, making it Israel's deadliest day in more than three weeks of conflict.

As Israeli troops tried to create a narrow buffer zone inside Lebanon and bombed southern Beirut, Hezbollah's leader, Sheik Hassan Nasrallah warned he would send his long-range missiles into Tel Aviv if the Israelis continued airstrikes.

**ATTACKS**
Hezbollah launched more than 100 rockets at northern Israel in less than an hour.

"If you bomb our capital, Beirut, we will bomb the capital of your usurping entity," he said on Lebanese television. "We will bomb Tel Aviv." But he also offered to halt Hezbollah's missile barrage into Israel if it stopped bombing Lebanon.

Israeli Defense Minister Amir Peretz told the army to begin preparing to push to

*Please see* **Israel,** *Page* **A12**

**THE VIRGINIAN-PILOT,** Norfolk

Lori Kelley, Martin Smith-Rodden, Judy Le, Paul Nelson, Deborah Withey

**Awards of Excellence**
News, A-Section page, broadsheet, 175,000+
Portfolio, combination page design, 175,000+, Lori Kelley

THE VIRGINIAN PILOT | A SPECIAL COMMEMORATIVE EDITION

THE WORLD TRADE CENTER | **2,749 KILLED** *

# 911+5

Nothing's changed, you hear people say.

Airport security is a lot tougher, they'll concede, but still, what's so different?

Only everything. Only the meaning behind hundreds of words:

Airplanes.

Box cutters.

Nineteen men.

Let's roll.

The south tower. Structural engineers. Jet fuel.

Jumpers.

If we don't do x, the terrorists will win.

FDNY.

Heroes.

Boeing 757. Pentagon blast.

Jalalabad. Kabul. Kandahar.

Anthrax.

Company ID badges.

Fingernail clippers, scissors, contact lens solution, baby formula, Gatorade.

Madrid trains.

London subways.

A suicide bomber today blew himself up in (world city) at a police checkpoint/busy market/ historic mosque/among mourners at a funeral, killing (number) and wounding (number).

"God Bless America" during the seventh-inning stretch.

Terror level: red, orange, yellow. Elevated.

Flying the flag in defiance.

Burning a candle for the survivors.

You will always remember the person who told you what was happening that morning; you will remember that morning as long as you live.

We are changed.

Place names, tools or toiletries conjure terrorists; a simple sports drink, eye drops or a choppy accent raises suspicions.

When you can write a whole essay about 9/11 and not even mention the subject by name until the second to last paragraph:

We haven't just changed; we've changed deep down inside.

*– Lon Wagner*

* ASSOCIATED PRESS CASUALTY ESTIMATES (NOT INCLUDING THE 19 HIJACKERS) ARE BASED ON INFORMATION COLLECTED FROM THE DEFENSE DEPARTMENT, MEDICAL EXAMINERS, THE COURTS, AP FOREIGN BUREAUS, COMPANIES, FAMILIES, MEMBER NEWSPAPERS, FUNERAL HOMES AND PLACES OF WORSHIP.

**THE VIRGINIAN-PILOT,** Norfolk

Sam Hundley, Paul Nelson, Deborah Withey

**Gold**

News, A-Section page, broadsheet, 175,000+

**Awards of Excellence**

News, A-Section page, broadsheet, 175,000+

Portfolio, combination page design, 175,000+, Sam Hundley

This commemorative front page marking the fifth anniversary of 9/11 lets you feel your own emotions. It simply remembers. The imagery was pared down so much — no red, white and blue, and no stars or planes. The illustration allows you to see what you want to see — the number 5, two towers or a plane flying through two towers. This bold page breaks conventions. It stops you.

Esta primera página que conmemora el quinto aniversario del 11 de septiembre permite sentir las propias emociones. Es simplemente un recuerdo. Se restringió en gran medida el uso de imágenes; no hay rojo, blanco y azul, no hay estrellas ni aviones. La ilustración permite ver lo que se quiere ver; el número cinco, dos torres o un avión que vuela a través de las dos torres. Esta atrevida página rompe con las convenciones. Impone un alto.

**ST. PETERSBURG TIMES** (Fla.)

Jennifer DeCamp, Patty Yablonski, Nikki Life, Patty Cox

**Awards of Excellence**
Food page, broadsheet, 175,000+
Redesign, page

THE DISH

3E

A WORLD OF FLAVORS

Before

St. Petersburg Times

Small bites

EAT YOUR WORDS

*"Full-size candy bars are indeed the Holy Grail of Halloween candy."*

THE DISH

Wednesday, October 25, 2006

CHORIZO JUMPS TO SUSTAINABLE, GOURMET STATUS

Cookbook salute to the South

Snacks to keep you on your diet

A tip about coconut

caramel apple masquerade

Dressing up you gooey apple

After

First Business

Community rules

When planned communities take over enforcement of their covenants, it's often a tough transition

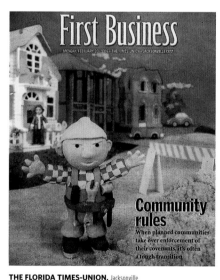

**THE FLORIDA TIMES-UNION,** Jacksonville

M. Jack Luedke, Colleen Flannery, Denise M. Reagan

**Awards of Excellence**
Business page, tabloid, 50,000-174,999
Photo illustration

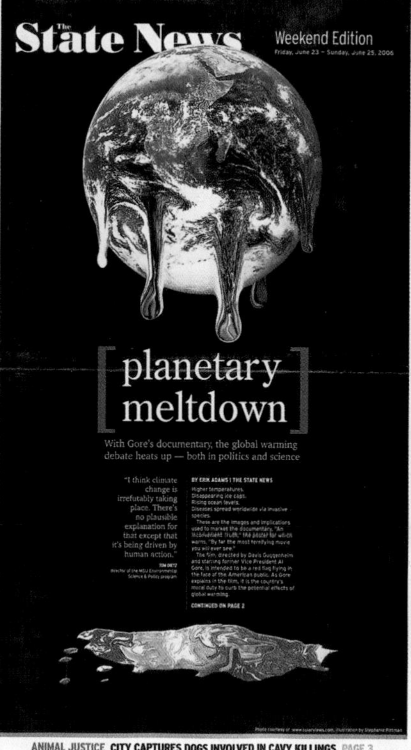

The State News

Weekend Edition

planetary meltdown

With Gore's documentary, the global warming debate heats up — both in politics and science

ANIMAL JUSTICE CITY CAPTURES DOGS INVOLVED IN CAVY KILLINGS. PAGE 3

**THE STATE NEWS,** Michigan State University, East Lansing, Mich.

Stephanie Pittman, Lindy O'Donnell, Nick Mrozowski

**Awards of Excellence**
News, A-Section page, broadsheet, 49,999 & under
Science/technology page, broadsheet, 49,999 & under

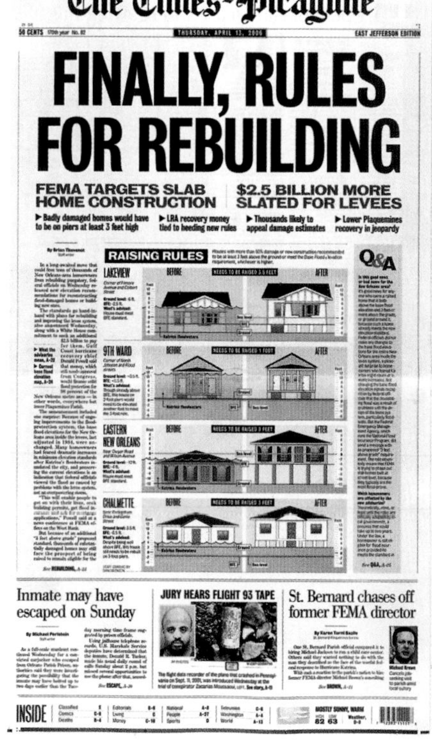

The Times-Picayune

FINALLY, RULES FOR REBUILDING

FEMA TARGETS SLAB HOME CONSTRUCTION

$2.5 BILLION MORE SLATED FOR LEVEES

RAISING RULES

Q&A

Inmate may have escaped on Sunday

JURY HEARS FLIGHT 93 TAPE

St. Bernard chases off former FEMA director

INSIDE

**THE TIMES-PICAYUNE** New Orleans

Anne Webbeking, Terry Baquet

**Awards of Excellence**
News, A-Section page, broadsheet, 175,000+
Breaking news, local

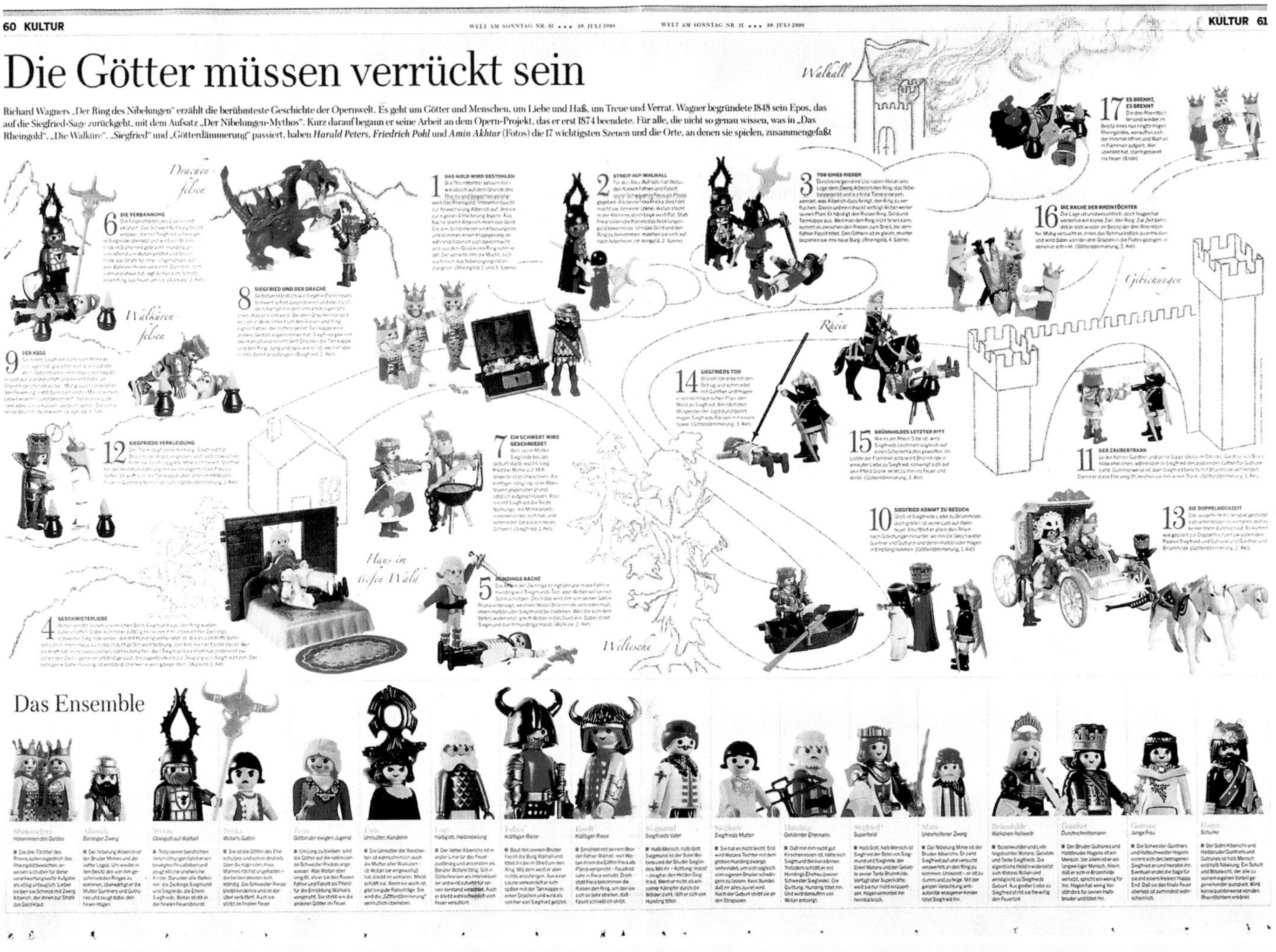

60 KULTUR — WELT AM SONNTAG NR. 31 ••• 30. JULI 2006 — WELT AM SONNTAG NR. 31 ••• 30. JULI 2006 — KULTUR 61

# Die Götter müssen verrückt sein

Richard Wagners „Der Ring des Nibelungen“ erzählt die berühmteste Geschichte der Opernwelt. Es geht um Götter und Menschen, um Liebe und Haß, um Treue und Verrat. Wagner begründete 1848 sein Epos, das auf die Siegfried-Sage zurückgeht, mit dem Aufsatz „Der Nibelungen-Mythos“. Kurz darauf begann er seine Arbeit an dem Opern-Projekt, das er erst 1874 beendete. Für alle, die nicht so genau wissen, was in „Das Rheingold“, „Die Walküre“, „Siegfried“ und „Götterdämmerung“ passiert, haben *Harald Peters, Friedrich Pohl* und *Amin Akhtar* (Fotos) die 17 wichtigsten Szenen und die Orte, an denen sie spielen, zusammengefaßt

Walhall

Drachenfelsen

Walkürenfelsen

Rhein

Gibichungen

Haus im tiefen Wald

Weltesche

1 DAS GOLD WIRD GESTOHLEN

2 STREIT AUF WALHALL

3 TOD EINES RIESEN

5 HUNDINGS RACHE

6 DIE VERBANNUNG

7 EIN SCHWERT WIRD GESCHMIEDET

8 SIEGFRIED UND DER DRACHE

9 DER KUSS

10 SIEGFRIED KOMMT ZU BESUCH

11 DER ZAUBERTRANK

12 SIEGFRIEDS VERKLEIDUNG

13 DIE DOPPELHOCHZEIT

14 SIEGFRIEDS TOD

15 BRÜNNHILDES LETZTER RITT

16 DIE RACHE DER RHEINTÖCHTER

17 ES BRENNT, ES BRENNT

4 GESCHWISTERLIEBE

## Das Ensemble

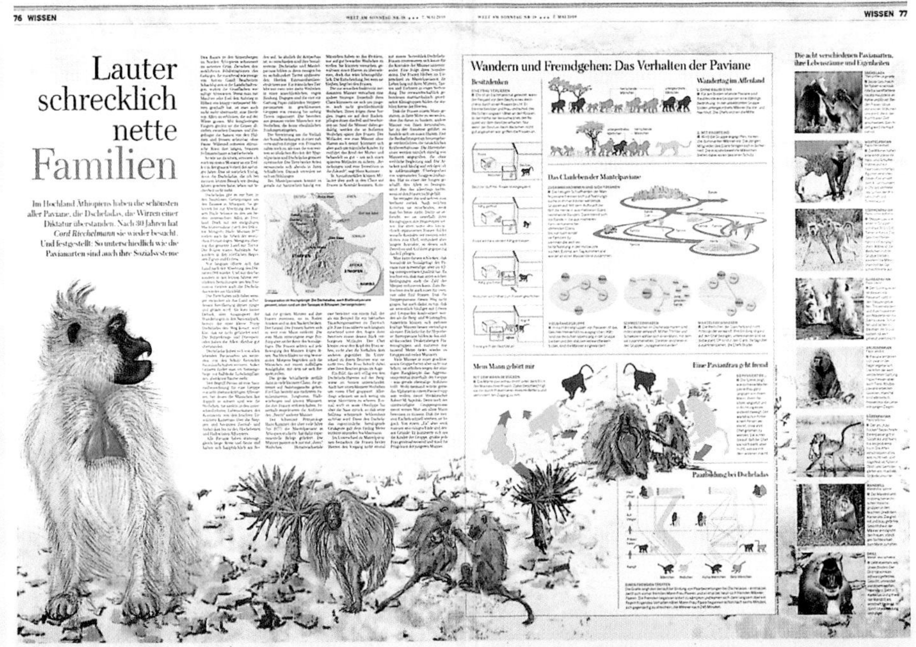


**WELT AM SONNTAG,** Berlin

Jördis Guzmán Bulla, Karin Sturm, Amin Akhtar

**Gold**

Portfolio, combination page design, 175,000+, Jördis Guzmán Bulla

**Silver**

Entertainment page, broadsheet, 175,000+

This work is inspiring. There is a large range of intricate work with every kind of media. The storytelling on these pages is bulletproof. The designer had to work hand-in-hand with graphic artists and photographers to make these pages happen.

Este trabajo es inspirador. Hay una gran variedad de trabajo intrincado con todo tipo de formatos mediales. El relato en estas páginas es a prueba de balas. El diseñador tuvo que trabajar mano a mano con los artistas gráficos y los fotógrafos para lograr estas páginas.

**STAR TRIBUNE,** Minneapolis

Colleen Kelly, Steve Rice

**Awards of Excellence**
Combination page design, 175,000+
Food page, broadsheet, 175,000+

taste

A fresh look at oranges

Take your pick | Recipes | Varieties | Nutrition

Teen makes food presentations really sing

Get ready to write and roll T3

**THE WASHINGTON POST**

News Desk Staff, News Art Staff

**Awards of Excellence**
Special coverage, section, no ads
Special news topics, local

The Washington Post

ELECTION '06

Change of Power

Today's Coverage

DISPATCH FROM THE GOP

Republicans' Angry Factions Point Fingers At Each Other

SPEAKER IN WAITING

Pelosi Steps Into the Spotlight

New House Leader's Agenda, Management Style Take Center Stage

AT THE POLLS

Some Voters Find Lines, And a Certain Satisfaction

VA. SENATE RACE

Changing Pattern Of N.Va. Voting Cited as Pivotal

**THE WALL STREET JOURNAL,** New York

Joe Paschke, David Bamundo, Ketrina Hoskin, Susan McDermott, Manny Velez, Barbara Scott, Ericka Burchett, Michelle Hotchkiss, Mirko Ilic

**Awards of Excellence**
Lifestyle section, 175,000+
Single illustration

STYLE | A Rally in the Mid-Cap Market—for Purses

PURSUITS

THE WALL STREET JOURNAL.

ART

The Secret Sales That Are Rankling Gallery Owners

DINING

Jean-Georges On Where to Get Great Chinese

BOOKS

Francis Fukuyama's About-Face on Iraq

HOME

Creative Outlets: Making Over A Room for $50

DRINKS

Correcting the Record on a Staple Of St. Patrick's Day

PAY FOR PLAYOFFS

*Basketball spending at top colleges is up 12% in a year, driven by rocketing salaries for coaches. Our look at who's getting the most wins for their money*

TRAVEL

The Return Of the Sandinistas

HAFTANIN DUASI

SÖZÜN ÖZÜ

KÜRSÜ

HİS DÜNYASI

ÇOCUK

Haram lokma endişesi insanı titretmelidir

'EVLADIM, ARTIK BAL YEME'

**ZAMAN,** Yenibosna, Turkey

Ekrem Dumanli, Fevzi Yazici, Mustafa Saglam, Osman Turhan, Murat Akkus, Süleyman Sargin

**Awards of Excellence**
Other feature page, broadsheet, 175,000+
Single illustration

AKADEMİ

ZAMAN

İDEAL dava ADAMI

**ZAMAN,** Yenibosna, Turkey

Ekrem Dumanli, Fevzi Yazici, Mustafa Saglam, Osman Turhan, Semsi Açikgöz, Süleyman Sargin

**Awards of Excellence**
Other feature page, broadsheet, 175,000+
Single illustration

Chapter Four

# NEWS

Noticias

**SECTIONS & PAGES**
**A-section / Local News / Sports / Business / Inside / Other**

**BREAKING NEWS & SPECIAL NEWS TOPICS**

SECCIONES Y PÁGINAS
Sección A / Noticias locales / Deportes / Negocios / Crónica / Otros

NOTICIAS DE ÚLTIMA HORA Y TEMAS NOTICIOSOS ESPECIALES

**THE OBSERVER,** London
Carolyn Roberts, Lynsey Irvine, Greg Whitmore
A-Section, 175,000+

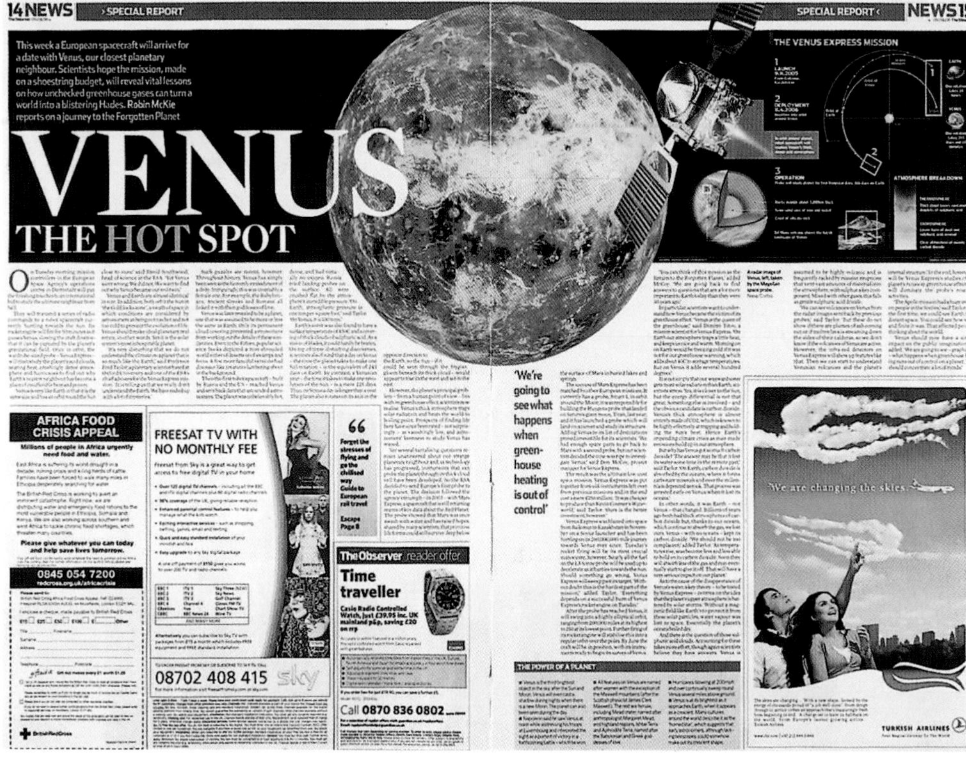
14 NEWS › SPECIAL REPORT
SPECIAL REPORT ‹ NEWS 15

This week a European spacecraft will arrive for a date with Venus, our closest planetary neighbour. Scientists hope the mission, made on a shoestring budget, will reveal vital lessons on how unchecked greenhouse gases can turn a world into a blistering Hades. Robin McKie reports on a journey to the Forgotten Planet

# VENUS
## THE HOT SPOT

THE VENUS EXPRESS MISSION

'We're going to see what happens when green-house heating is out of control'

AFRICA FOOD CRISIS APPEAL

FREESAT TV WITH NO MONTHLY FEE

0845 054 7200

08702 408 415

The Observer reader offer
Time traveller

Call 0870 836 0802

THE POWER OF A PLANET

We are changing the skies.

TURKISH AIRLINES

**SUNDAY HERALD,** Glasgow, Scotland
Stephen Penman, Kathryn Course, Elaine Livingstone
Sports section, 50,000-174,999

FOOTBALL

ONE MAN UNITED

SCOTLAND FROM THE SKIES
FREE AERIAL IMAGE SUPPLEMENT
TAKE YOUR PARTNERS FOR THE sundaybriefing CEILIDH GUIDE
FREE HARDBACK JAMES BOND BOOK WORTH £20

sundayherald

26 November 2006

British spies: we told you Putin could be dangerous

● PRESSURE ON RUSSIA MOUNTS OVER POISONING OF DISSIDENT
● GROWING FEARS OVER KREMLIN'S NETWORK OF SPIES IN BRITAIN
● GOVERNMENT FACING QUESTIONS OVER LETHAL POLONIUM-210

THE NEW COLD WAR SUNDAY HERALD INVESTIGATION: PAGES 8-11

**SUNDAY HERALD,** Glasgow, Scotland
Richard Walker, Roxanne Sorooshian, Elaine Livingstone, John Henderson, Staff
A-Section, 50,000-174,999

KANSAS CITY AND THE AREA
THE KANSAS CITY STAR.
WEDNESDAY, NOVEMBER 8, 2006

Local

MISSOURI BALLOT ISSUES | Voters were rejecting an increase in the state's cigarette tax

# WIDE FAVOR FOR WAGE HIKE

KANSAS GOVERNOR | 'This is a great night'

## Sebelius scores a first by winning second term

Top names lead local races

KANSAS 2ND DISTRICT | Democrat claims an upset

## Boyda ousts U.S. Rep. Jim Ryun

SOCCER VOTE | 'Lies, deception and secrecy were their undoing'

## Proposed Johnson County amateur complex falls hard

FOR MORE NEWS FROM MISSOURI, KANSAS AND SURROUNDING STATES, SEE B3

**THE KANSAS CITY STAR** (Mo.)
Tom Dolphens, Greg Branson, John Kleinow, Staff
Local section, 175,000+

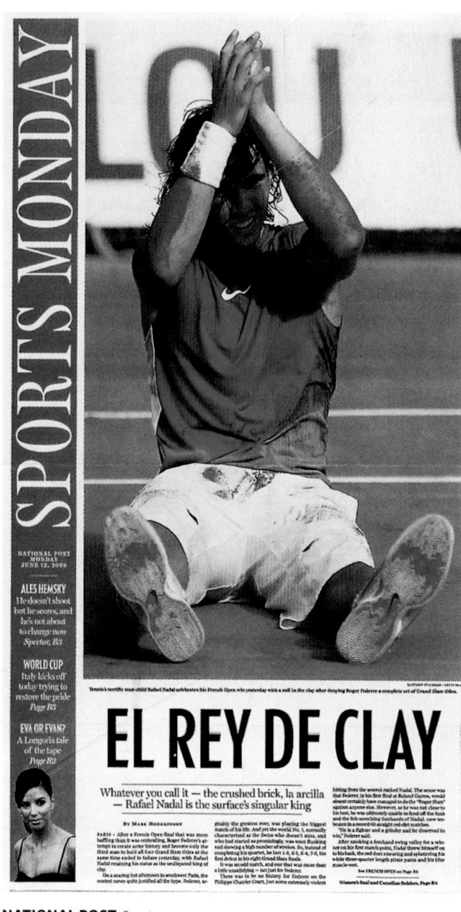
SPORTS MONDAY

NATIONAL POST
MONDAY
JUNE 12, 2006

ALES HEMSKY
He doesn't shoot but he scores, and he's not about to change now
Spector, B3

WORLD CUP
Italy kicks off today trying to restore the pride
Page B2

EVA OR EVAN?
A Longoria tale of the tape
Page B2

# EL REY DE CLAY

Whatever you call it — the crushed brick, la arcilla — Rafael Nadal is the surface's singular king

**NATIONAL POST,** Toronto
Doug Kelly, Gayle Grin, Laura Koot, Jim Bray
Sports section, 175,000+

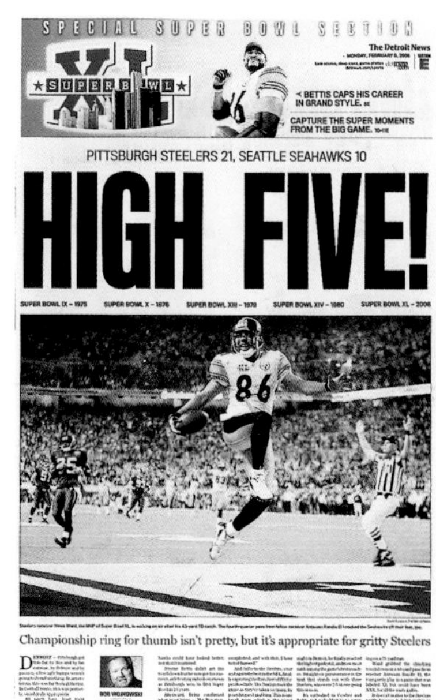
SPECIAL SUPER BOWL SECTION

The Detroit News

BETTIS CAPS HIS CAREER IN GRAND STYLE.
CAPTURE THE SUPER MOMENTS FROM THE BIG GAME.

PITTSBURGH STEELERS 21, SEATTLE SEAHAWKS 10

# HIGH FIVE!

SUPER BOWL IX – 1975 SUPER BOWL X – 1976 SUPER BOWL XIII – 1979 SUPER BOWL XIV – 1980 SUPER BOWL XL – 2006

Championship ring for thumb isn't pretty, but it's appropriate for gritty Steelers

**THE DETROIT NEWS**
Cindy Lacy, Emily Irvine, Erin Spraw, Richard Epps, Eric Millikin, Elizabeth Cusmano, Tyler Rau, Jeff Tarsha, Jason Karas, Ruben Luna
Sports section, 175,000+

The Observer SUNDAY 2 APRIL 2006
SPORT
LONG GAME
TIGER LOOKS AHEAD TO THE MASTERS P12-13
HOORAY HENRY
SURELY ARSENAL WILL KEEP THIERRY NOW P6-7
GINGER SPICE
AINTREE LEGEND'S FAREWELL SALVO P19

GAME ON
Ruud Van Nistelrooy tests Chelsea's nerve by coming off the bench to score the winner for Manchester United at Bolton. On the first weekend of March United were 18 points behind the champions – now the deficit is seven, and the fourth of Chelsea's six remaining games is against United. Reports, pages 2-5

TROUBLED REIGN OF KING MARTIN THE SECOND
On the eve of their autumn international campaign England's captain tells Jon Henderson that recent poor results are not just the fault of the coach
All Blacks right on target but England look wide of the mark
JOHN KIRWAN
Spending will make big savings
FRANCIS BARON
RFU CHIEF EXECUTIVE

## SILVER

**THE OBSERVER,** London

Carolyn Roberts, Lynsey Irvine, Iain Blohm, Jamie Sage

Sports section, 175,000+

This entry captures the essence and energy of sports. It is a large section, but it's cohesive because of typography and color. Even the agate gets attention. The emotion of the design just oozes from it, and it's smart — it doesn't bludgeon you over the head.

Esta pieza capta la esencia y la energía de los deportes. Es una sección grande, pero es cohesiva gracias a la tipografía y el color. Incluso la tipografía agate llama la atención. La emoción del diseño sale a raudales y está hecho con inteligencia; no da un mazazo en la cabeza.

GameDay
Cowboys drop the ball with a series of costly mistakes
Mental block


**FORT WORTH STAR-TELEGRAM** (Texas)

Ellen Alfano, Celeste Williams, Michael Currie, Sports Staff

Sports section, 175,000+

**THE ATLANTA JOURNAL-CONSTITUTION**

Shane Blatt

A-Section page, broadsheet, 175,000+

**THE KANSAS CITY STAR** (Mo.)

Tom Dolphens, Greg Branson, Holly Lawton, Mike Fannin

Sports section, 175,000+

**ZAMAN,** Yenibosna, Turkey
Ekrem Dumanli, Fevzi Yazici, Mustafa Saglam, Semsi Açikgöz
A-Section page, broadsheet, 175,000+

**THE GAZETTE,** Montreal
Nuri Ducassi, Catherine Wallace
Other news section, 50,000-174,999

**THE VIRGINIAN-PILOT,** Norfolk
Robert Suhay, Martin Smith-Rodden, Judy Le, Paul Nelson, Deborah Withey
A-Section page, broadsheet, 175,000+

**THE VIRGINIAN-PILOT,** Norfolk
Robert Suhay, Martin Smith-Rodden, Judy Le, Paul Nelson, Deborah Withey
A-Section page, broadsheet, 175,000+

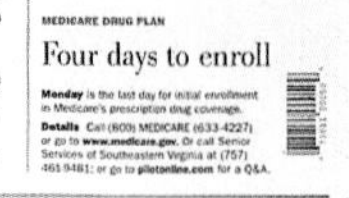

**THE VIRGINIAN-PILOT,** Norfolk
Luis Vilches, Robert Suhay, Vicki Cronis, Norm Shafer, Paul Nelson, Deborah Withey
A-Section page, broadsheet, 175,000+

**THE SEATTLE TIMES**
Staff
Business section, 175,000+

**LA PRESSE,** Montréal
Staff Photographer, Benoit Giguere, Genevieve Dinel, Staff Designer, Alain-Pierre Hovasse, Eric Trottier
A-Section page, broadsheet, 175,000+

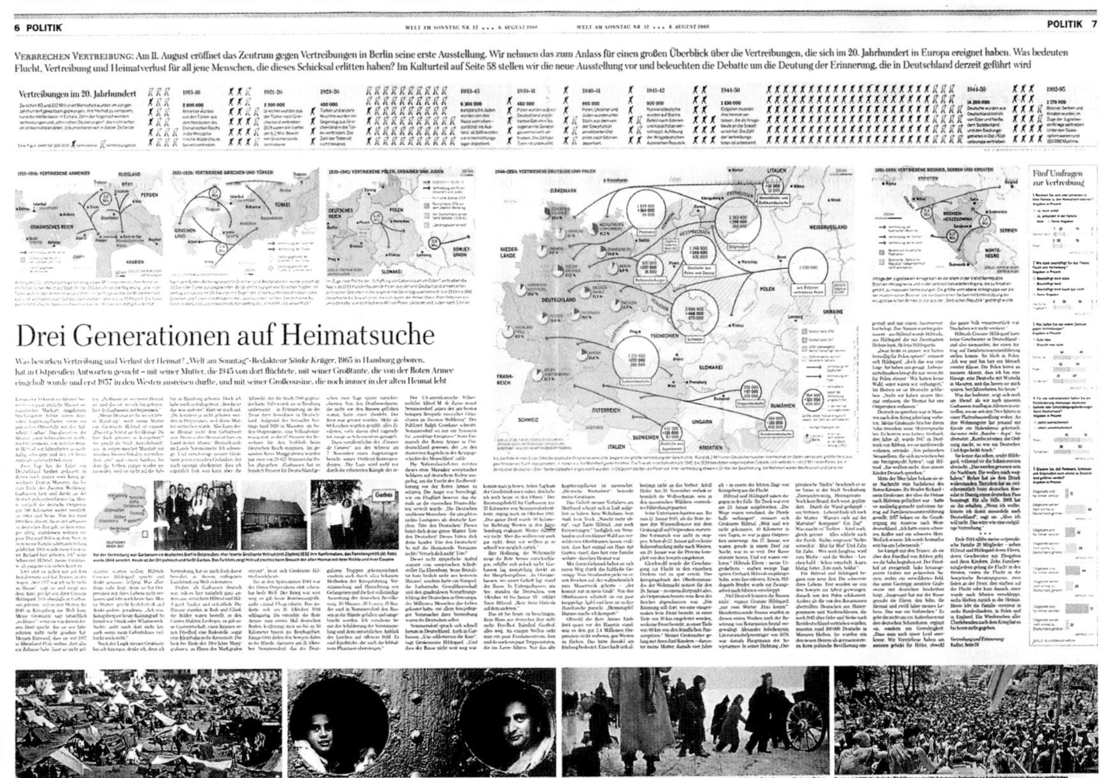

6 POLITIK

WELT AM SONNTAG NR. 32 ... 6. AUGUST 2006

POLITIK 7

VERBRECHEN VERTREIBUNG: Am 11. August eröffnet das Zentrum gegen Vertreibungen in Berlin seine erste Ausstellung. Wir nehmen das zum Anlass für einen großen Überblick über die Vertreibungen, die sich im 20. Jahrhundert in Europa ereignet haben. Was bedeuten Flucht, Vertreibung und Heimatverlust für all jene Menschen, die dieses Schicksal erlitten haben? Im Kulturteil auf Seite 58 stellen wir die neue Ausstellung vor und beleuchten die Debatte um die Deutung der Erinnerung, die in Deutschland derzeit geführt wird

Vertreibungen im 20. Jahrhundert

Fünf Umfragen zur Vertreibung

Drei Generationen auf Heimatsuche

Was bewirken Vertreibung und Verlust der Heimat? „Welt am Sonntag"-Redakteur *Sönke Krüger*, 1965 in Hamburg geboren, hat in Ostpreußen Antworten gesucht – mit seiner Mutter, die 1945 von dort flüchtete, mit seiner Großtante, die von der Roten Armee eingeholt wurde und erst 1957 in den Westen ausreisen durfte, und mit seiner Großcousine, die noch immer in der alten Heimat lebt

## SILVER

**WELT AM SONNTAG,** Berlin

Jördis Guzmán Bulla, Karin Sturm

A-Section page, broadsheet, 175,000+

This story about three generations looking for a name shows the long-term effects of displacement from a home. A well-edited sequence of family and staff photos recreates time. The graphics illustrate migration, and the mapping is tremendous. The typography is simple, and the color palette is reserved.

Esta historia sobre tres generaciones que buscan un nombre muestra los efectos de largo plazo que sufren quienes han sido desplazados de su hogar. Una bien editada secuencia de fotos familiares y del equipo periodístico recrea la época. Los gráficos ilustran la migración y los mapas son impresionantes. La tipografía es simple y la paleta de colores es limitada.

UN SOMMET DE 14 ANS › LE HUARD FILE VERS LES 90 CENTS US *LA PRESSE AFFAIRES* PAGE 1

LA PRESSE

LA COMPLAINTE D'UN BEATLE AU CANADA

La Cour suprême autorise le port du symbole sikh dans les écoles

RENTRÉE EN CLASSE DU KIRPAN

Le couteau cérémonial n'est pas une menace à la sécurité, tranchent les magistrats

Les religieux canadiens critiquent la morale sexuelle catholique

Contraception, avortement et protection contre le sida sont en tête de liste des préoccupations de la Conférence religieuse du Canada

SCANDALE DES COMMANDITES

Mtl-Québec 99$

**LA PRESSE,** Montréal

Staff Photographer, Benoit Giguere, Genevieve Dinel, Staff Designer, Alain-Pierre Hovasse, Eric Trottier

A-Section page, broadsheet, 175,000+

LA PRESSE

AEBISCHER À MONTRÉAL

THÉODORE S'EN VA AU COLORADO

TRANSPORT EN COMMUN LE MAIRE TREMBLAY PROPOSE SON PLAN PAGE A10

POLITIQUE CHRÉTIEN RÉDIGE SES MÉMOIRES PAGE A7

Journée de la femme Pour le respect et un avenir meilleur

ENQUÊTES SUR NORBOURG

La GRC et l'Autorité des marchés financiers jouent du coude

Un lopin de terre pour le sénateur

Pour pouvoir siéger légalement au Sénat, le nouveau ministre conservateur Michael Fortier a dû acheter un petit terrain en Montérégie

70sushi.com (514) 70-SUSHI

**LA PRESSE,** Montréal

Staff Photographer, Benoit Giguere, Genevieve Dinel, Staff Designer, Alain-Pierre Hovasse, Eric Trottier

A-Section page, broadsheet, 175,000+

CARAMBOLAGE MONSTRE SUR LA 40

LA PRESSE

LA NATURE SE DÉCHAÎNE

PAGES A2 À A7

TORINO 2006

MALTAIS PLANCHE VERS LE BRONZE

CINÉMA LA 3D REDONNE VIE AU MANÈGE ENCHANTÉ

TÉLÉVISION LES COÛTS DES TÉLÉSÉRIES

ACTUEL PRINCESSES, PAILLETTES, PATINS

DES BAS TARIFS QUI VOUS MÈNENT PLUS HAUT.

72$ 109$ 134$ 154$

aircanada.com

**LA PRESSE,** Montréal

Staff Photographer, Benoit Giguere, Genevieve Dinel, Staff Designer, Alain-Pierre Hovasse, Eric Trottier

A-Section page, broadsheet, 175,000+

**SAN JOSE MERCURY NEWS** (Calif.)

Michael Tribble, Karen T. Borchers, Geri Migielicz, Jonathon Berlin, Matt Mansfield

A-Section page, broadsheet, 175,000+

Sunday
OLD HAWAII NEW HAWAII
Young QB starting to click
San Jose Mercury News
MERCURYNEWS.COM
CORRUPTION AT THE BORDER
HORRIFIC ATTACK IN BAGHDAD
NEW RUMBLINGS ABOUT BIN LADEN
A WOMAN'S NAZI PAST
TEACHERS OF THE YEAR
BILLOWING FASHIONS
U.S. FAR BEHIND IN RYDER CUP
ADVENTURES OF WOZNIAK
ELECTION 2006
Angelides struggles to save campaign
SIX WEEKS LEFT TO GAIN TRACTION
LAURIE SURVIVED
A vicious crime 21 years ago failed to consume her life
U.S. report ties increase in terrorists to Iraq war

**LOS ANGELES TIMES**

Kelli Sullivan, Alex Brown, Gail Fisher, Colin Crawford, Anne Cusack

A-Section page, broadsheet, 175,000+

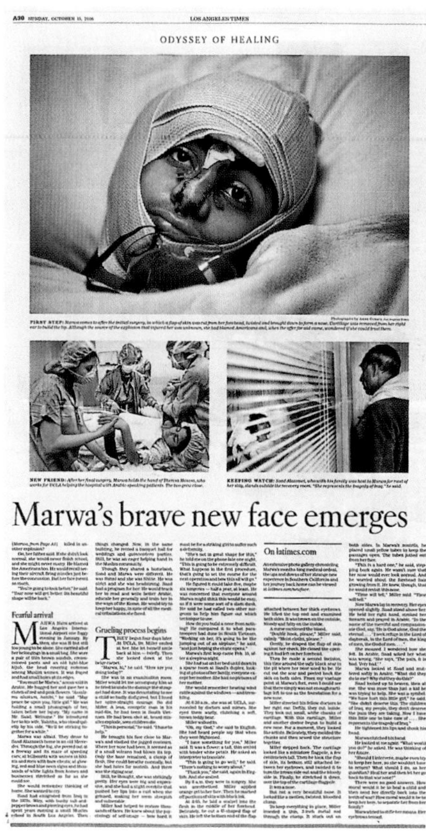
LOS ANGELES TIMES
ODYSSEY OF HEALING
Marwa's brave new face emerges
Fearful arrival
Grueling process begins
On latimes.com

**LA PRESSE**, Montréal

Staff Photographer, Benoit Giguere, Genevieve Dinel, Staff Designer, Alain-Pierre Hovasse, Eric Trottier

A-Section page, broadsheet, 175,000+

POUR UN GOUVERNEMENT CONSERVATEUR L'ÉDITORIAL D'ANDRÉ PRATTE PAGE A16
LA PRESSE
SONDAGE CROP-LA PRESSE-98,5-INFO690-CKAC
POUR TOUT COMPRENDRE
LES TEXTES DE DENIS LESSARD PAGES A2 ET A3
VINCENT MARISSAL Rats le bol du rouge PAGE A3
HUIT CIRCONSCRIPTIONS DÉCORTIQUÉES
TROIS MINISTRE LIBÉRAUX MENACÉS : PIERRE PETTIGREW, LIZA FRULLA ET JEAN LAPIERRE
PERCÉE CONSERVATRICE : JOSÉE VERNER ET MAXIME BERNIER ONT LE VENT DANS LES VOILES
LE BLOC S'IMPOSE DANS BROME-MISSISQUOI ET PAPINEAU
SURPRISE : L'INDÉPENDANT ANDRÉ ARTHUR MÈNE DANS PORTNEUF
SUCCESSION ÉVENTUELLE DE PAUL MARTIN
CAUCHON SORT DE L'OMBRE
Stars 2, Canadien 4 Une équipe transformée
«Karla» ne vaut pas le déplacement
DE BELLES ET BONNES IDÉES POUR RÉCHAUFFER L'HIVER
EN KIOSQUE MAINTENANT

ELECTION 2006
The Times-Picayune
WEDNESDAY, NOVEMBER 8, 2006
195 221 49 46
DEMOS TAKE HOUSE
In Senate, Democrats gain 3 seats; control depends on 3 undecided races
ONE-ASSESSOR AMENDMENT WINS BIG STATEWIDE AND IN NEW ORLEANS
JEFFERSON, KAREN CARTER HEADED FOR RUNOFF
Divided Congress may complicate Bush's last two years
Jindal, Melancon roll to easy second terms
Power shift in House hurts La.
New assessor system will take effect in 2010

**THE TIMES-PICAYUNE,** New Orleans

Adrianna Garcia, Terry Baquet

A-Section page, broadsheet, 175,000+

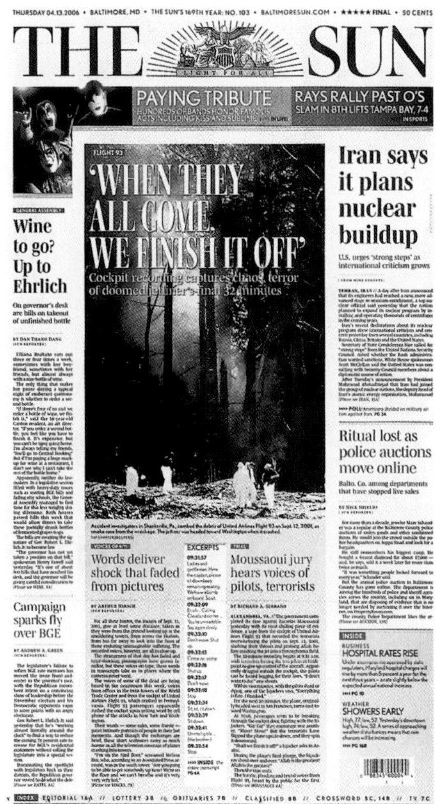
THE SUN
PAYING TRIBUTE
RAYS RALLY PAST O'S
Wine to go? Up to Ehrlich
'WHEN THEY ALL COME, WE FINISH IT OFF'
Cockpit recording captures chaos, terror of doomed jetliner's final 32 minutes
Iran says it plans nuclear buildup
Ritual lost as police auctions move online
Words deliver shock that faded from pictures
Moussaoui jury hears voices of pilots, terrorists
Campaign sparks fly over BGE

**THE BALTIMORE SUN**

Bill Wachsberger, Jay Judge

A-Section page, broadsheet, 175,000+

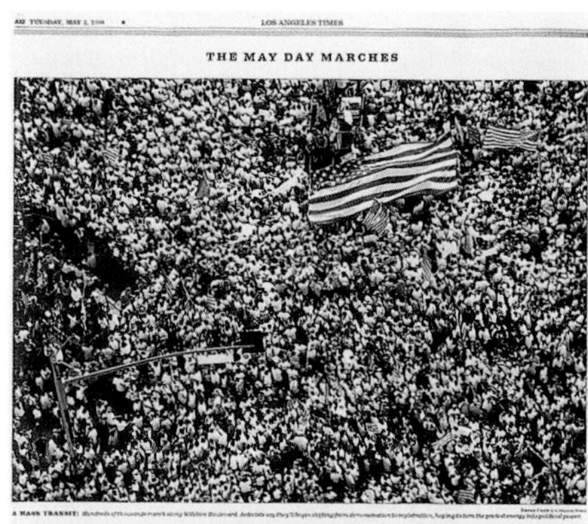
LOS ANGELES TIMES
THE MAY DAY MARCHES

Activists Hope to Build Political Clout
By the numbers
Boycott Turns Panorama City Mall Into Ghost Town

**LOS ANGELES TIMES**

Joseph Hutchinson, Michael Whitley, Kelli Sullivan, Dave Campbell, Bill Sheehan, Lorraine Wang, Alex Brown, Gerard Babb, Robert St. John, Steve Stroud

A-Section page, broadsheet, 175,000+

**HARTFORD COURANT** (Conn.)
Kristin Lenz, Thom McQuire, Melanie Shaffer
A-Section page, broadsheet, 175,000+

Brady Throws 4 TD Passes To Lead Patriots Past Vikings · Sports, C1

Hartford Courant.

## Brass Seek Quit Date

U.S. Officers Warm To Iraq Deadlines

## BLOODY OCTOBER

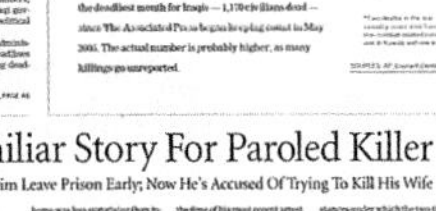

## A Familiar Story For Paroled Killer

## Activist Denies Violating Ban On Ballot Work

**THE TIMES-PICAYUNE,** New Orleans
George Berke, Terry Baquet, Ted Jackson, Bruce Nolan
A-Section page, broadsheet, 175,000+

FORMER BAIL BONDSMAN LOUIS MARCOTTE GETS 38-MONTH SENTENCE

The Times-Picayune

The floodwaters rushed in, putting thousands in a struggle for survival. Six who stayed tell their stories.

## REMEMBERING KATRINA

LANDFALL SURAS • 6:10 A.M. • MONDAY, AUGUST 29, 2005

## At Convention Center, hope for refuge turned to anguish

**ORLANDO SENTINEL** (Fla.)
Todd Stewart, Roberto Gonzalez, Stephen Komives, Bonita Burton
A-Section page, broadsheet, 175,000+

SPORTS FLORIDA'S NFL SPLIT DECISION: RAVENS ROUT BUCS 27-0; JAGS STOP COWBOYS 24-17, D1

Orlando Sentinel

MONDAY, SEPTEMBER 11, 2006

SEPT. 11: FIVE YEARS LATER

## 'ONE DAY I WILL SEE YOU. ONE DAY I WILL LOVE YOU. ONE DAY I WILL KISS AND HUG YOU BECAUSE I LOVE YOU.'

Jevon's story

## Unusual Gulf quake shakes up our world

## $385 million question: What will Magic be willing to pay?

THE TAMPA TRIBUNE

## Feeling Pounded At The Pump?

## Well ... It's Nice, But How About Something Original?

## Front-Runner For CIA Chief Hits Opposition

## More Americans Are Slipping Below The Poverty Line

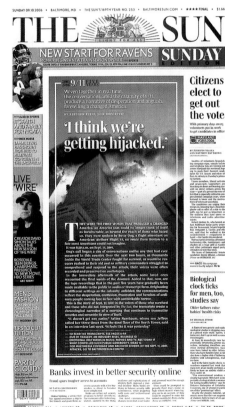

**THE TAMPA TRIBUNE** (Fla.)
Greg Williams
A-Section page, broadsheet, 175,000+

FOOD: A SPECIAL GUIDE TO BROWN-BAGGING – WHAT TO PACK, WHERE TO EAT OUT

San Francisco Chronicle

## DRIVER'S RAMPAGE

Injury and chaos in S.F.

Deadly start of hit-and-run spree

Rampage ends when SUV rammed

**SAN FRANCISCO CHRONICLE**
Tracy Cox, Reid Sams, Gus D'Angelo, Penni Gladstone, Liz Mangelsdorf, Michael Macor, Frank Mina, Nanette Bisher
A-Section page, broadsheet, 175,000+

SUNDAY 09.10.2006 • BALTIMORE, MD • THE SUN'S 169TH YEAR: NO. 253 • BALTIMORESUN.COM • FINAL • $1.66

THE SUN

NEW START FOR RAVENS SUNDAY

9/11

## 'I think we're getting hijacked.'

## Citizens elect to get out the vote

## Biological clock ticks for men, too, studies say

## Banks invest in better security online

**THE BALTIMORE SUN**
Anthony Conroy, Jay Judge, Monty Cook
A-Section page, broadsheet, 175,000+

**HARTFORD COURANT** (Conn.)

Greg Harmel, John Woike, Suzette Moyer, John Scanlan

A-Section page, broadsheet, 175,000+

A-Rod, Jeter Homer To Lead Yankees; Red Sox Rained Out · Sports, Section E

Hartford Courant.

Divided Justices Resume Hearings

Split In Supreme Court Mirrors California Case

SPECIAL REPORT

MENTALLY UNFIT, FORCED TO FIGHT

TODAY: TRAPPED

MONDAY: IGNORED

TUESDAY: DRUGGED

WEDNESDAY: RECYCLED

INSIDE

How Much Do You Know About Mom?

An Ivy Trailblazer

The Big House

'JEFFREY WAS REALLY MESSED UP'

courant.com

**SAN FRANCISCO CHRONICLE**

Frank Mina, Nanette Bisher

A-Section page, broadsheet, 175,000+

San Francisco Chronicle

SUNDAY, FEBRUARY 19, 2006

WALKING THE WALK

SELLING FASTRAK

LOOKING IN HIS SILICON BALL

SPRING HOME DESIGN SPECIAL

STARTING OUT AT THE ENDUP

HOUSING – JUST COOL OR GOING COLD?

As Bay Area sales continue to drop, questions about the market's cycles are taking on a new sense of urgency

Defiant Hamas takes charge

Palestinian Legislative Council says it will not recognize Israel

Westly's history of questionable IPO stock trades

Extra-special education at public expense

**THE WASHINGTON POST**

Beth Broadwater, Dennis Brack, Seth Hamblin, Michael Keegan, Vanessa Barnes Hillian, Phil Bennett

A-Section page, broadsheet, 175,000+

BELLWETHERS | THE BATTLE FOR CONGRESS

Is The GOP Facing A MIDTERM REVERSAL?

Eight Questions That Will Shape The 2006 Elections

1 The Elephant in the Room

HOW BIG A PROBLEM IS PRESIDENT BUSH FOR THE GOP?

2 Money Matters

WILL POCKETBOOK CONCERNS MOVE VOTERS?

3 Rethinking Red States

CAN DEMOCRATS COMPETE IN THE SOUTH?

Real estate giant has 18 names D1 · How does gay marriage affect you? AA1 · China's wild west G1

Pulitzer Prize winner 'Gilead'

The dog issue: Chic, shows, parks and more

StarTribune Sunday

KATRINA REPORT SPREADS BLAME

STUDENTS WALKING AWAY

Senate race puts state in spotlight

TURIN 2006

One down, four to go for Hedrick

ONE LAST SIP, ONE LAST STEP

A walk after a night of drinking has ended in disaster for a dozen young men at college.

Privacy laws jeopardize heart study

Northwest Airlines employees learning to live with a lot less

**STAR TRIBUNE**, Minneapolis

Chris Clonts, Renee Jones Schneider, Peter Koeleman, Cory Powell, Rene Sanchez, Vickie Kettlewell

A-Section page, broadsheet, 175,000+

SUNDAY || COVER STORY

HERE TO STAY?

When Min Chen completes his sentence for the murder of Cecilia Zhang, he may step into a legal no man's land

By Andrew Chung

**TORONTO STAR**

Devin Slater, Alison Uncles, Susan Grimbly, Tony Bock, Andrew Chung

A-Section page, broadsheet, 175,000+

The Miami Herald

MiamiHerald.com

FINAL EDITION

MONDAY, NOVEMBER 13, 2006

DOLPHINS HOLD ON FOR WIN

CHILDREN OF THE AMERICAS

Throwaway children

PROMOTING THE WRITE APPROACH

TEEN COUPLE KILLED IN CRASH

ROCKETS ROUT HEAT

UP FRONT HIGHER EDUCATION

CHINA SEEKS TOURISM GAIN WITH FIU HELP

BROWARD COUNTY

Two deputies shot, 1 killed

CASTRO HEALTH CRISIS

Castro has 18 months to live, U.S. believes

**THE MIAMI HERALD**

Eddie Alvarez, Michael Babin

A-Section page, broadsheet, 175,000+

**NATIONAL POST,** Toronto

Doug Kelly, Gayle Grin, Stephen Meurice, Tom Philip, Kelly McParland, Jeff Wasserman, Angela Murphy

A-Section page, broadsheet, 175,000+

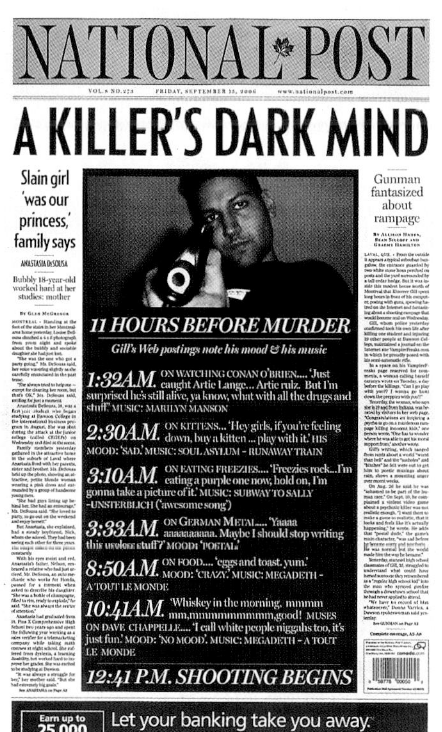

NATIONAL POST

# A KILLER'S DARK MIND

Slain girl 'was our princess,' family says

Gunman fantasized about rampage

11 HOURS BEFORE MURDER

Gill's Web postings note his mood & his music

1:32A.M. ON WATCHING CONAN O'BRIEN.... 'Just caught Artie Lange... Artie rulz. But I'm surprised he's still alive, ya know, what with all the drugs and stuff.' MUSIC: MARILYN MANSON

2:30A.M. ON KITTENS... 'Hey girls, if you're feeling down, buy a kitten... play with it.' HIS MOOD: 'SAD.' MUSIC: SOUL ASYLUM – RUNAWAY TRAIN

3:10A.M. ON EATING FREEZIES.... 'Freezies rock...I'm eating a purple one now, hold on, I'm gonna take a picture of it.' MUSIC: SUBWAY TO SALLY - UNSTERBLICH ('awesome song')

3:33A.M. ON GERMAN METAL.... 'Yaaaa aaaaaaaaa. Maybe I should stop writing this useless stuff?' MOOD: 'POSTAL.'

8:50A.M. ON FOOD.... 'eggs and toast, yum.' MOOD: 'CRAZY.' MUSIC: MEGADETH - A TOUT LE MONDE

10:41A.M. 'Whiskey in the morning, mmmm mm,mmmmmmmmmm,good.' MUSES ON DAVE CHAPPELLE.... 'I call white people niggahs too, it's just fun.' MOOD: 'NO MOOD.' MUSIC: MEGADETH - A TOUT LE MONDE

12:41 P.M. SHOOTING BEGINS



**HARTFORD COURANT** (Conn.)

Kristin Lenz, Melanie Shaffer, Allison Corbet

A-Section page, broadsheet, 175,000+

UCONN MEN BEAT MISSISSIPPI; JIMMIE JOHNSON NEXTEL CUP CHAMPION · SPORTS, C1

Hartford Courant

From 1944 to 1986, 3.9 million tons of uranium ore were mined from the Navajo reservation. Today, its inhabitants are paying an exorbitant price in the form of death and chronic illness.

# A PEOPLE POISONED

Policy Rates: A New Tack

Car, Home Insurance Gets More Complex

Mood Swing On Iraq

Funerals Give Mourners Sticker Shock

Charges Heighten Scrutiny Of Funeral Director Already Under Investigation

Dialogue Follows Pre-Election Enmity

For What Ails You

Gamer Buying Guide

Blue Back Square: An Update

courant.com

**HARTFORD COURANT** (Conn.)

Kristin Lenz, Melanie Shaffer, Allison Corbet

A-Section page, broadsheet, 175,000+

UCONN WOMEN STRUGGLE EARLY, PUT AWAY HOLY CROSS · SPORTS, C1

Hartford Courant

INTERNAL AFFAIRS SYSTEM FOUND RIFE WITH MISCONDUCT

GOVERNOR ORDERS INDEPENDENT PANEL TO OVERSEE REFORM

PROBE COULD RESULT IN CRIMINAL CHARGES AGAINST STATE TROOPERS

# REPORT RIPS STATE POLICE

Dodd Key In Bolton's Departure

U.N. Ambassador Leaving Post Despite President's Efforts

Race-Based School Selection On Trial

U.S. Supreme Court Case Involving Integration Could Affect Sheff Ruling

Pfizer Falls

Saving Land, Forever

Back To The Moon

They're On A Roll

courant.com

SCHOOL THE RETURN

The Virginian-Pilot

MEDICARE PART D can reach a point where recipients shoulder the entire financial burden for drug prescriptions. If you're one of those estimated 3.4 million Americans, YOU ARE HERE.

# The doughnut hole

Randolph-Macon Woman's alums, students: We're ready for a fight

Trustees' move to go coed draws ire and protests

"Our whole passion is to be on this planet is to educate people about wildlife. I will die doing that." STEVE IRWIN

'Crocodile Hunter' made a career out of close calls

REVILED

He's used to it. He's an atheist. But that doesn't make it easy.

Study: Father's age affects autism rate

**THE VIRGINIAN-PILOT,** Norfolk

Robert Suhay, Elizabeth Thiel, Paul Nelson, Deborah Withey

A-Section page, broadsheet, 175,000+

The Washington Post

BEING A BLACK MAN

A Unique Bond, From the Streets to The Halls of Power

In popular culture, an image that inspires both fascination and fear

For an enduring brotherhood, new opportunities and new dangers

1619–1776 · 1780–1860 · 1860–1900 · 1900–1950 · 1950–1970 · 1970–2006

**THE WASHINGTON POST**

Beth Broadwater, Kevin Merida, Dennis Brack, Michel du Cille, Marvin Joseph, Marcia Davis, Phil Bennett

A-Section page, broadsheet, 175,000+

**TORONTO STAR**
Charlie Kopun, Diana Zlomislic, Aaron Lynett, Rita Daly
A-Section page, broadsheet, 175,000+

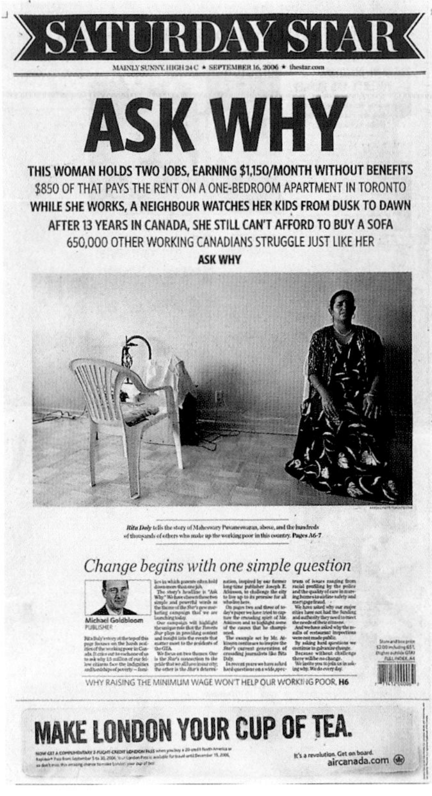

SATURDAY STAR

MAINLY SUNNY, HIGH 24 C ★ SEPTEMBER 16, 2006 ★ thestar.com

ASK WHY

THIS WOMAN HOLDS TWO JOBS, EARNING $1,150/MONTH WITHOUT BENEFITS
$850 OF THAT PAYS THE RENT ON A ONE-BEDROOM APARTMENT IN TORONTO
WHILE SHE WORKS, A NEIGHBOUR WATCHES HER KIDS FROM DUSK TO DAWN
AFTER 13 YEARS IN CANADA, SHE STILL CAN'T AFFORD TO BUY A SOFA
650,000 OTHER WORKING CANADIANS STRUGGLE JUST LIKE HER
ASK WHY

Change begins with one simple question

Michael Goldbloom
PUBLISHER

WHY RAISING THE MINIMUM WAGE WON'T HELP OUR WORKING POOR, H6

MAKE LONDON YOUR CUP OF TEA.

It's a revolution. Get on board.
aircanada.com

**SAN FRANCISCO CHRONICLE**
Frank Mina, Nanette Bisher
A-Section page, broadsheet, 175,000+

San Francisco Chronicle

SERVING UP THE WORLD CUP

GENIE IN CYBERSPACE

ACCORDION AMBASSADOR

BAY AREA MOVIE LISTING CORRECTION

AIDS AT 25

17 arrested in Canada terror plot

CAMPAIGN 2006
Democrats turn to big guns and foot soldiers

Money man's big task: Make Stanford richer

IN COMPTON, OAKLAND SEES HOPE TO STOP THE KILLINGS

**HARTFORD COURANT** (Conn.)
Kristin Lenz, Melanie Shaffer, David Grewe, Thom McGuire
A-Section page, broadsheet, 175,000+

2006 Campaign

GREEN PARTY TRIES A NEW APPROACH

ATTORNEY GENERAL NANCY BURTON

LIEUTENANT GOVERNOR JEAN M. DE SMET

U.S. SENATE RALPH FERRUCCI

GOVERNOR CLIFFORD W. THORNTON JR.

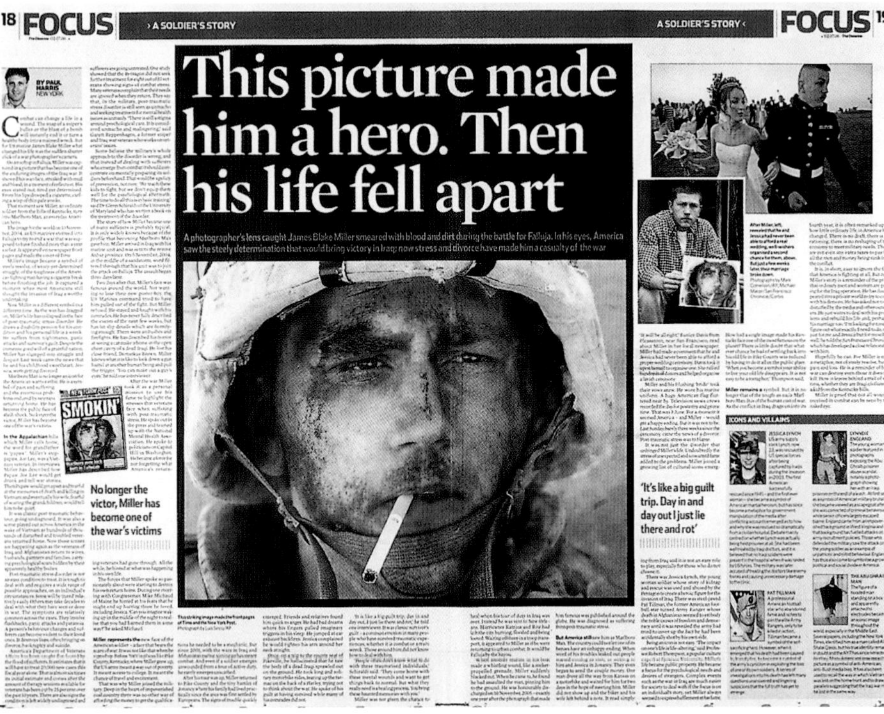

18 FOCUS | A SOLDIER'S STORY

A SOLDIER'S STORY | FOCUS 19

This picture made him a hero. Then his life fell apart

A photographer's lens caught James Blake Miller smeared with blood and dirt during the battle for Falluja. In his eyes, America saw the steely determination that would bring victory in Iraq; now stress and divorce have made him a casualty of the war

No longer the victor, Miller has become one of the war's victims

'It's like a big guilt trip. Day in and day out I just lie there and rot'

ICONS AND VILLAINS

**THE OBSERVER,** London
Lynsey Irvine, Carolyn Roberts, Greg Whitmore
A-Section page, broadsheet, 175,000+

SOX'S SCHILLING GETS 200TH CAREER WIN; YANKEES DEFEAT ROYALS • SPORTS, E1

Hartford Courant.

FOR CONNECTICUT MARINES, THE ENEMY IS EVERYWHERE

Special Report: On The Ground With Charlie Company

"Treat them as our counterparts, but be ready to kill them, if necessary." – 1st Sgt. Ben Grainger, referring to Iraqi security forces

IN CONNECTICUT
Five Die In Crash

COMMENTARY
Iran, U.S. And Rights

IN LIFE
Urban Obstacles

IN BUSINESS
Pilot's Mystery

THE WORLD
Deadly Earthquake

**HARTFORD COURANT** (Conn.)
Greg Harmel, Suzette Moyer, Tom Brown, Bruce Moyer, John Scanlan
A-Section page, broadsheet, 175,000+

**CHICAGO TRIBUNE**

Bill McDonald, Danielle Mollette-Parks, Ryan Smith, Stephan Benzkofer

A-Section page, broadsheet, 175,000+

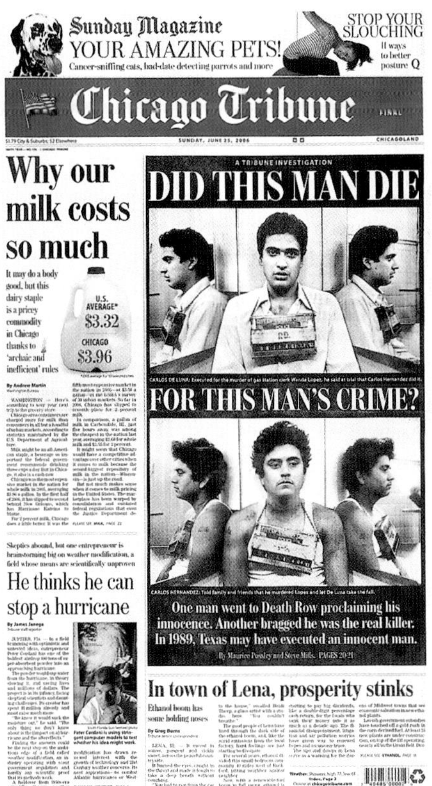

Sunday Magazine
YOUR AMAZING PETS!
STOP YOUR SLOUCHING
Chicago Tribune
Why our milk costs so much
U.S. AVERAGE* $3.32
CHICAGO $3.96
A TRIBUNE INVESTIGATION
DID THIS MAN DIE
FOR THIS MAN'S CRIME?
One man went to Death Row proclaiming his innocence. Another bragged he was the real killer. In 1989, Texas may have executed an innocent man.
He thinks he can stop a hurricane
In town of Lena, prosperity stinks

**HARTFORD COURANT** (Conn.)

Kristin Lenz, Melanie Shaffer, David Grewe

A-Section page, broadsheet, 175,000+

Hartford Courant.

GERALD R. FORD JR 1913 - 2006
A GENTLE, GRACIOUS LIFE
Next On The Shopping List: Me
Gift-Givers Look For A Little Something For Themselves
Larson Powers Up His Career
Networking Savvy Works To Congressman's Advantage
A Lifetime Of Humor
Who Makes These %!@#! Rules?
courant.com

**RICHMOND TIMES-DISPATCH** (Va.)

Jeremy Glover, Brice Anderson, James Wallace, John Witt, Rick Thornton, Danny Finnegan

A-Section page, broadsheet, 175,000+

REMEMBERING A PRESIDENT
Richmond Times-Dispatch
GERALD R. FORD: 1913 – 2006

AMERICA'S HEALING HAND

Yule wait for iTunes songs
Career, technical-education proposal worries educators

UTAH'S INDEPENDENT VOICE SINCE 1871
The Salt Lake Tribune
FISHER POWER
CATERING TO YOUR TASTES
★★ Election '06 ★★
Dems seize the House
Americans speak out on failures of GOP
Utah lawmakers
D.C. incumbents back; Curtis survives
Judicial retention
Voters have enough of Judge Lewis
Hot races
Winder triumphs in sheriff campaign
MORE ONLINE: UPDATED OVERNIGHT RESULTS AND COVERAGE AT SLTRIB.COM

Ex-ruler back in court
Bennett: Rumsfeld out

**THE SALT LAKE TRIBUNE,** Salt Lake City

Josh Awtry, Colin Smith, Scott Sommerdorf, Todd Adams

A-Section page, broadsheet, 50,000-174,999

It should crest today
The Virginian-Pilot
N. Korea says it has the bomb. Now what?
YOUR DAILY NEWS DIGEST RETURNS
Attacks punctuate last debate
Groups use faith to back both sides of the issue

**THE VIRGINIAN-PILOT,** Norfolk

Robert Suhay, Martin Smith-Rodden, Judy Le, Paul Nelson, Deborah Withey

A-Section page, broadsheet, 175,000+

Join in a student's mission of mercy
The Virginian-Pilot
Mark Warner for president?
Nope
Guard found dead near Wesleyan dining hall
Another thing you can't sell on eBay: mummified remains
Ex-governor says 2008 race would strain family
Europe's first new land critter in decades: the Cypriot mouse
MEET THE ADMIRALS
Jones Institute focus of show
READ ON THE RUN

**THE VIRGINIAN-PILOT,** Norfolk

Robert Suhay, Martin Smith-Rodden, Judy Le, Paul Nelson, Deborah Withey

A-Section page, broadsheet, 175,000+

**THE VIRGINIAN-PILOT,** Norfolk
Lori Kelley, Martin Smith-Rodden, Judy Le, Paul Nelson, Deborah Withey, Brian Root
A-Section page, broadsheet, 175,000+

Meet the smart kids

The Virginian-Pilot

IT'S JUST YOU AGAINST THE STORM

HOW TO GET PREPARED

Are you ready? Brace for a week or more, authorities say

Initial report says Marine officers lied about deaths

"Wonky" executive thinks it's his time

One woman dead. One hurt. One unthinkable error.

Pigskin fans on the sand

Katie Couric bids farewell

**ARIZONA DAILY STAR,** Tucson
Jeff Randall, Mike Rice, Rick Wiley, Staff
A-Section page, broadsheet, 50,000-174,999

DIAMONDBACKS UNVEIL NEW LOOK

WII, PS3 VIE FOR GAMERS' DOLLARS

Arizona Daily Star

SERVING TUCSON SINCE 1877 • THURSDAY, NOVEMBER 9, 2006

RUMSFELD RESIGNS

The announcement

The nominee

The response

MORE COVERAGE ON PAGE A11

U.S. SENATE CONTROL TILTS TOWARD DEMOCRATS

AP declares GOP loss in Va.; Montana Demo claims victory

SAME-SEX MARRIAGE

Prop. 107 trails with plenty of votes to go

THE LATEST COUNT

49 49 2

MORE COVERAGE ON PAGES A12-A13

PRESIDENT BUSH'S PRESS CONFERENCE

A LOOK AHEAD AT BUSH'S FINAL TWO YEARS IN OFFICE, PAGE A11

MORE INSIDE

COMING UP, DON'T MISS...

Arts & Crafts Festival

**THE NEWS TRIBUNE,** Tacoma, Wash.
David Montesino, Fred Matamoros
A-Section page, broadsheet, 50,000-174,999

THE NEWS TRIBUNE

MEMORIAL DAY 2006

REMEMBER THE SACRIFICE

We've got no time for this old virtue

Baarsma waves green flag for NASCAR speedway

BONDS PASSES BABE RUTH

THE SUN

Enough.

Traveil Williams
16 years old

Anthony Michael Ramirez
11 years old

Anthony Johnson
17 years old

Jarred Mitchell
14 years old

Glyn Fergerson Jr.
17 years old

Christopher Paul Ransom
15 years old

Dustin Michael-Roy Namanny
14 years old

Melanie Miers
16 years old

Mynisha Crenshaw
11 years old

This community has had enough — of people dying, of children dying, of gangs and shootings and inhumanity beyond what words can describe.
Today, The Sun is burning over much of our newspaper to what we can do as a community to end the violence.
In the end, that's our most powerful weapon — community.
We want to hear from you.
If you have ideas, thoughts or suggestions on what all of us can do to make this a safer community, e-mail us at voice@sbsun.com.

**THE SUN,** San Bernardino, Calif.
Gina Dvorak
A-Section page, broadsheet, 50,000-174,999

WHO'S TO BLAME IN FIRE RECRUIT'S DEATH? STORY BELOW

The Florida Times-Union

Friday, August 11, 2006 JACKSONVILLE www.jacksonville.com

THE PLOT
Suspects wanted to use liquid explosives to bring down airliners

THE TARGETS
Commercial flights coming into the U.S. from Britain

THE BOMBS
Flammable peroxide-based mix sparked by small electronic devices

THE REACTION
Frenzied airports, expanded searches, bans on most carry-on liquids

New threat in air

10 jets were to be hit with liquid explosives

WHAT IT MEANS TO YOU

No longer permitted

Crazed day at airports

State finds Jacksonville fire recruit died after pushed past his limits

**THE FLORIDA TIMES-UNION,** Jacksonville
Derek Hembd, Will Dickey, Kelly Jordan, Denise M. Reagan, Mike Marino, Staff
A-Section page, broadsheet, 50,000-174,999

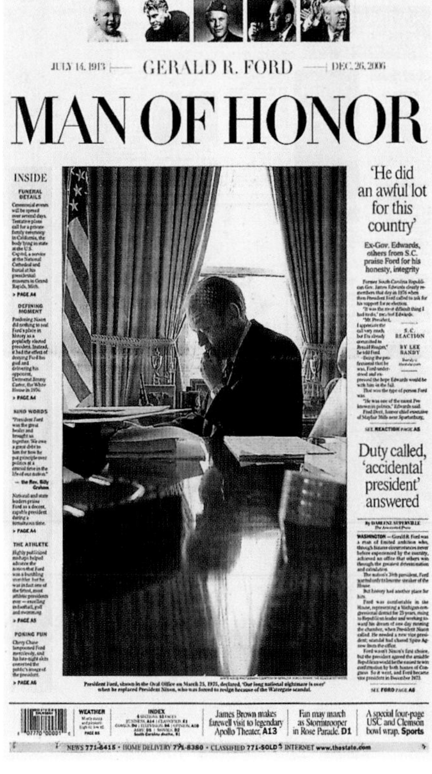

The State

Thursday, December 28, 2006

JULY 14, 1913 — GERALD R. FORD — DEC. 26, 2006

MAN OF HONOR

INSIDE

'He did an awful lot for this country'

Duty called, 'accidental president' answered

James Brown makes farewell visit to legendary Apollo Theater A13

Fan may march as Stormtrooper in Rose Parade D1

A special four-page USC and Clemson bowl wrap Sports

**THE STATE,** Columbia, S.C.
Tim Chamberlin
A-Section page, broadsheet, 50,000-174,999

**POLITIKEN,** Copenhagen, Denmark

Søren Nyeland, Frederik Storm, Jens Mørch, Torben Benner, Flemming Christiansen

A-Section page, broadsheet, 50,000-174,999

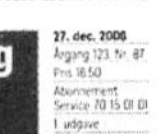

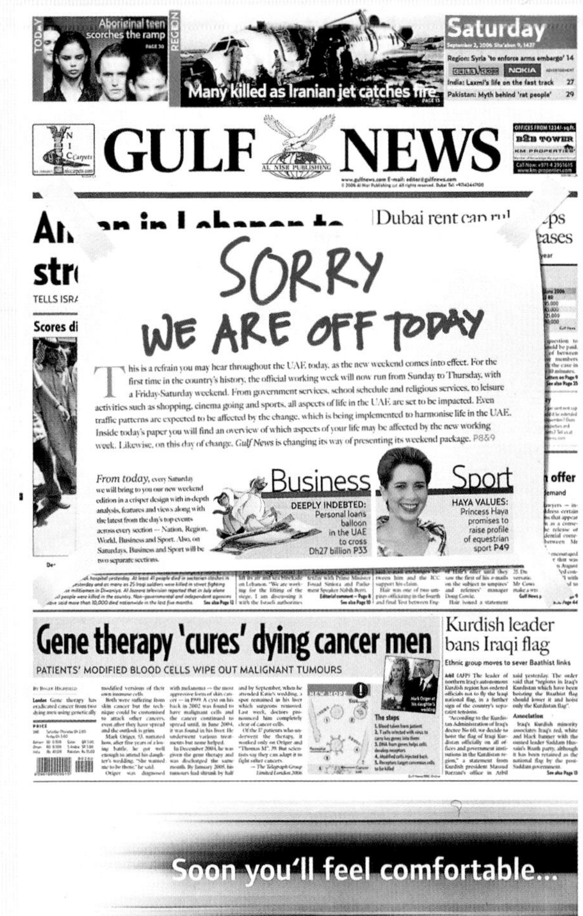


SILVER

**GULF NEWS,** Dubai, United Arab Emirates

Talib Jariwala, Ramachandra Babu, Dwynn Ronald Trazo, Chiranjib Sengupta, Aelred Luis, Shyam Krishna, Miguel Angel Gomez, Abdul Hamid Ahmad

A-Section page, broadsheet, 50,000-174,999

This story on the shift in the work week is illustrated to show procrastination. The execution of this page is technically perfect. It looks as if the tape were really there. The designers took a chance, and it paid off. You want to read the story.

Este relato sobre los turnos semanales de trabajo está ilustrada para mostrar la pérdida de tiempo. La realización de esta página es técnicamente perfecta. Parece como si la cinta realmente estuviera ahí. Los diseñadores tomaron un riesgo y el resultado fue positivo. El artículo llama a la lectura.

**THE SPOKESMAN-REVIEW,** Spokane, Wash.

Geoff Pinnock, Larry Reisnouer, Brian Plonka, Ralph Walter

A-Section page, broadsheet, 50,000-174,999

**ARIZONA DAILY STAR,** Tucson

Mark Brunton, Jeff Randall, Mike Rice, Dean Knuth, Rick Wiley, Staff

A-Section page, broadsheet, 50,000-174,999

**THE GAZETTE,** Montreal
Nuri Ducassi, Catherine Wallace
A-Section page, broadsheet, 50,000-174,999

GARDENS
A 5-PAGE SPECIAL SECTION, WEEKEND LIFE
The Gazette
the big butt-out
25 quitting days until smoking is banned in Montreal bars and restaurants! Aaron Derfel looks at the science, the psychology and the support needed to give up the evil weed, and smokin' comedian Joey Elias vows to jump on the wagon – any day now…
SATURDAY EXTRA
Brault jailed for Adscam
SENTENCED TO 30 MONTHS
Judge says executive was major player in federal scandal
BLACK WATCH PARADE
Post-9/11 rule scotches route
IN FOCUS
QUOTE OF THE DAY
INDEX
WEATHER
SPORTS
NATION
WORLD
WE CAN HELP
YOU PAY YOUR MORTGAGE FASTER.

**THE GAZETTE,** Montreal
Nuri Ducassi, Catherine Wallace
A-Section page, broadsheet, 50,000-174,999

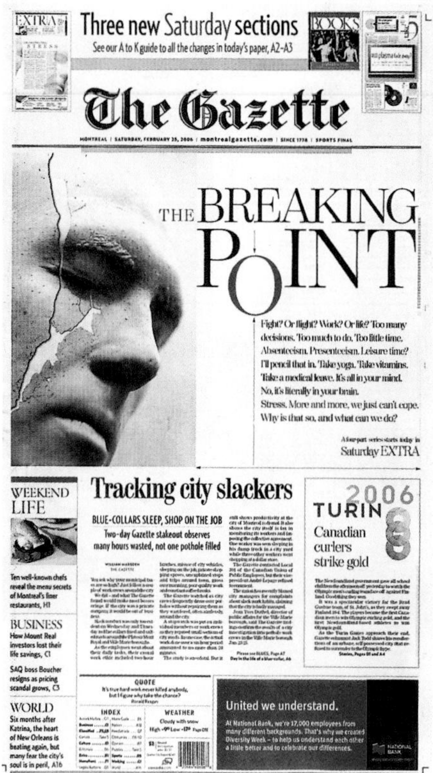
Three new Saturday sections
See our A to K guide to all the changes in today's paper, A2-A3
The Gazette
THE BREAKING POINT
Fight? Or flight? Work? Or life? Too many decisions. Too much to do. Too little time. Absenteeism. Presenteeism. Leisure time? I'll pencil that in. Take yoga. Take vitamins. Take a medical leave. It's all in your mind. No, it's literally in your brain. Stress. More and more, we just can't cope. Why is that so, and what can we do?
Saturday EXTRA
WEEKEND LIFE
Tracking city slackers
BLUE-COLLARS SLEEP, SHOP ON THE JOB
Two-day Gazette stakeout observes many hours wasted, not one pothole filled
2006 TURIN
Canadian curlers strike gold
BUSINESS
WORLD
INDEX
WEATHER
United we understand.

**ESTADO DE MINAS,** Belo Horizonte, Brazil
Júlio Moreira
A-Section page, broadsheet, 50,000-174,999

POLÍTICA
Demissão do titular da Fazenda é ponto alto da crise detonada pela violação da conta do caseiro e encerra gestão de 39 meses, marcada por polêmica na política econômica
Sigilo derruba PALOCCI
"Estou convencido de que minha permanência não mais contribui para o avanço da obra do governo"

EXCELSIOR
EL PERIÓDICO DE LA VIDA NACIONAL
ZAFARRANCHO Y TOMA DE TRIBUNA EN SAN LÁZARO
Revienta la Cámara
PARA QUE FUNCIONE DE VERDAD
Ponen vigía al gabinete
DIÁLOGO PARLAMENTARIO
PAN y PRD se diputaron ayer, a golpes, el sitio en el que está programada la toma de posesión de Felipe Calderón; al menos cinco diputados fueron a dar a la enfermería
Labor de expertos
Detienen a hermano del líder de la APPO
3 MINUTOS
COLUMNAS
OPINIÓN

**EXCELSIOR,** México City
Abraham Solís, Erik Meza, Marco Gonsen, Gunther Sahagún, Luzma Díaz de León Reyes, Marco A. Román, Alexandro Medrano, Gerardo Galarza, Pascal Beltrán del Río, Ernesto Rivera
A-Section page, broadsheet, 50,000-174,999

EXCELSIOR
EL PERIÓDICO DE LA VIDA NACIONAL
GOBERNADORES
Relegan plan de combate al narco
Diálogo, hasta de la reforma energética
OFRENDA POR NUEVA YORK
Estrenan el mercado de cohetes… y estalla
3 MINUTOS

**EXCELSIOR,** México City
Abraham Solís, Marco Gonsen, Gunther Sahagún, Luzma Díaz de León Reyes, Marco A. Román, Alexandro Medrano, Gerardo Galarza, Pascal Beltrán del Río, Ernesto Rivera
A-Section page, broadsheet, 50,000-174,999

EXCELSIOR
EL PERIÓDICO DE LA VIDA NACIONAL
NI SIQUIERA UN EXHORTO HARÁ EL SENADO
Oaxaca: matan a otro y van 10
Paisanos dan sólo 10% a familias
SERÉ CAMPEÓN DEL MUNDO
Clases con guaruras
Si rechazas el ADN… el niño es tuyo
3 MINUTOS

**EXCELSIOR,** México City
Abraham Solís, Javier Otaola, Marco Gonsen, Gunther Sahagún, Luzma Díaz de León Reyes, Marco A. Román, Alexandro Medrano, Gerardo Galarza, Pascal Beltrán del Río, Ernesto Rivera
A-Section page, broadsheet, 50,000-174,999

**THE GAZETTE,** Montreal
Nuri Ducassi, Catherine Wallace
A-Section page, broadsheet, 50,000-174,999

CULTURE

If Serge Losique's life was an old, black-and-white western, it would be called Return of the Maverick. On the eve of the 30th annual Montreal World Film Festival, his feisty founder proves he's not ready to ride off into the sunset.

# The Gazette

MONTREAL | SATURDAY, AUGUST 19, 2006 | montrealgazette.com | SINCE 1778 | SPORTS FINAL

## Lured by salmon, hooked on history

A 55½-pound fish, a princess and a pauper, a murdered millionaire: tales of the Grand Cascapédia River. SATURDAY EXTRA

## PROVINCE TO REFUND ABORTIONS

$13 MILLION TO 45,000 WOMEN
Private clinics covered, court rules

## Distraught mother pleads not guilty

WAKE-UP CALL ON AIDS

IN FOCUS

QUOTE OF THE DAY

"From my experience of life, I believe my personal motto should be: 'Beware of men bearing flowers.'"

WEATHER

INDEX

WEEKEND LIFE · BUSINESS · NATION · SPORTS

WE CAN HELP DEVELOP YOUNG TENNIS TALENT.

NATIONAL BANK

**THE GAZETTE,** Montreal
Nuri Ducassi, Catherine Wallace
A-Section page, broadsheet, 50,000-174,999

THE POP TARTS THAT COULD
How bubblegum stars like Hilary Duff, Jessica Simpson and Lindsay Lohan keep a lock on the charts, D1

SPECIAL HOCKEY PIN OFFER
Unique Maple Leaf commemorative pin is No. 8 in our Hockey Canada 2006 collection. Coupon on C6

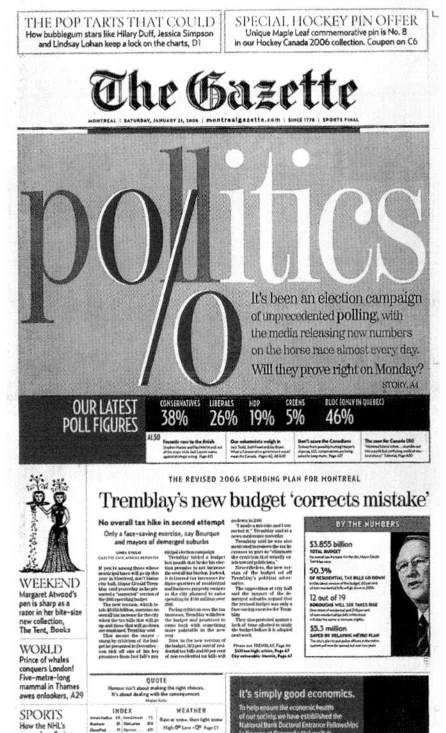

# The Gazette

MONTREAL | SATURDAY, JANUARY 21, 2006 | montrealgazette.com | SINCE 1778 | SPORTS FINAL

## pol%itics

It's been an election campaign of unprecedented polling, with the media releasing new numbers on the horse race almost every day. Will they prove right on Monday? STORY, A4

| OUR LATEST POLL FIGURES | CONSERVATIVES | LIBERALS | NDP | GREENS | BLOC (ONLY IN QUEBEC) |
|---|---|---|---|---|---|
| | 38% | 26% | 19% | 5% | 46% |

THE REVISED 2006 SPENDING PLAN FOR MONTREAL

## Tremblay's new budget 'corrects mistake'

No overall tax hike in second attempt

BY THE NUMBERS

WEEKEND
Margaret Atwood's pen is sharp as a razor in her bite-size new collection, The Tent, Books

WORLD
Prince of whales conquers London! Five-metre-long mammal in Thames awes onlookers, A29

SPORTS
How the NHL's new rule collaring free-range goalies has changed the game, C1

INDEX · WEATHER

It's simply good economics.

NATIONAL BANK

# EXCELSIOR

EL PERIÓDICO DE LA VIDA NACIONAL

FELIPE CALDERÓN

## Día 1

El candidato que enarboló el empleo como bandera de campaña tiene a partir de hoy el reto de cumplir. Su primer escollo a superar se llama crispación social.

ENTREGA EL PODER

CONTRATADO

LAS TUERCAS POR APRETAR

BODA LOUNGE

Cae el Águila

COLUMNAS · OPINIÓN

**EXCELSIOR,** México City
Abraham Solís, Marco Gonsen, Gunther Sahagún, Luzma Díaz de León Reyes, Marco A. Román, Alexandro Medrano, Gerardo Galarza, Pascal Beltrán del Río, Ernesto Rivera
A-Section page, broadsheet, 50,000-174,999

# EXCELSIOR

EL PERIÓDICO DE LA VIDA NACIONAL

NIÑA BIEN · EL AUTO INCREÍBLE · LAS PENAS, CON PAN

TARJETA DE IDENTIDAD

## Buscan frenar el *chip* de SHCP

El IFAI verificará que no se viole la privacidad de los ciudadanos; diputados exigen congelar el plan

Y DESPUÉS DEL DERRUMBE...

Elecciones EU 2006

## Auditoría a Oaxaca, entre amigos

ESE APOYO NO SE VE

Congreso de Quintana Roo

## Declaran *non grato* a ex gobernador

3 MINUTOS

UN VICIO PERMITIDO

**EXCELSIOR,** México City
Abraham Solís, Marco Gonsen, Luzma Díaz de León Reyes, Marco A. Román, Alexandro Medrano, Gerardo Galarza, Pascal Beltrán del Río, Ernesto Rivera
A-Section page, broadsheet, 50,000-174,999

# EXCELSIOR

EL PERIÓDICO DE LA VIDA NACIONAL

EN SÓLO CINCO MINUTOS

CALDERÓN SUPERÓ EL CERCO EN SAN LÁZARO

## ...y protestó

En un entorno caótico, Felipe Calderón cumplió la obligación constitucional en el Congreso y asumió la Presidencia. En su primer mensaje a la nación, en el Auditorio Nacional, llamó de nuevo a la concordia, aunque advirtió: "No esperaré el diálogo para ponerme a trabajar"

SU FAMILIA

LA OPOSICIÓN

De antología

El interlocutor

COLUMNAS · OPINIÓN

**EXCELSIOR,** México City
Abraham Solís, Erik Meza, Marco Gonsen, Gunther Sahagún, Luzma Díaz de León Reyes, Marco A. Román, Alexandro Medrano, Gerardo Galarza, Pascal Beltrán del Río, Ernesto Rivera
A-Section page, broadsheet, 50,000-174,999

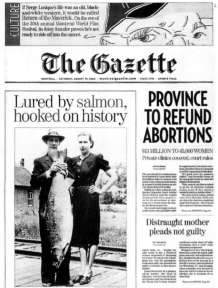

**THE GAZETTE,** Montreal
Nuri Ducassi, Catherine Wallace
A-Section page, broadsheet, 50,000-174,999

THE VANISHING SUMMER COTTAGE, IN SATURDAY EXTRA

The Gazette

MONTREAL | SATURDAY, JULY 22, 2006 | montrealgazette.com | SINCE 1778 | SPORTS FINAL

ISRAEL-HEZBOLLAH CONFLICT ENTERS DAY 11

TENSIONS MOUNT

SAFE AT HOME

TEARS AND KISSES fill the arrivals lounge at Trudeau airport as the first wave of Montrealers end a long journey from war-torn Lebanon. Page A6

ON THE GROUND

SOLDIERS AND TANKS line the Israeli-Lebanese border, raising fears of an extensive ground invasion as the U.S. rejects calls for a ceasefire. Page A3

LIFE & DEATH

FOOD AND MEDICINE are in short supply and in the face of a mounting humanitarian crisis, Israel has vowed to clear the way for crucial aid. Page A4

IN FOCUS

QUOTE OF THE DAY

WEATHER

INDEX

TRAVEL

MONTREAL

SPORTS

ARTS & LIFE

WE CAN HELP

MAKE YOUR DREAM PATIO A REALITY.

**THE FLORIDA TIMES-UNION,** Jacksonville
Denise M. Reagan, Jon M. Fletcher, Kelly Jordan, Kyle Alcott, Staff
A-Section page, broadsheet, 50,000-174,999

Man charged in shooting death of book-reading teen

READY FOR ERNESTO

Why Karr won't be charged in JonBenet killing

The Florida Times-Union

Tuesday, August 29, 2006

JACKSONVILLE

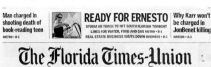

The bond that Katrina couldn't break

The bayou rose, as before. Water swallowed homes, as before. But one year ago, it threatened to stop the cycle of rebuilding.

Turn to the back page to compare

Today

Weather

93 25%

**THE FLORIDA TIMES-UNION,** Jacksonville
Phillippe Diokno, Kelly Jordan, Denise M. Reagan, Bob Self
A-Section page, broadsheet, 50,000-174,999

NEW TV BOOK DEBUTS MORE FEATURES, BETTER LISTINGS

EMMYS ROUNDUP

STARTER PAINS

Offense struggles again in first half

COLLEGE FOOTBALL PREVIEW

The Florida Times-Union

Sunday, August 27, 2006

JACKSONVILLE

NEW ORLEANS, ONE YEAR AFTER HURRICANE KATRINA

SOUNDS of REVIVAL

Weather

89 35%

EXCELSIOR

EL PERIÓDICO DE LA VIDA NACIONAL

EL GOBIERNO DEL CAMBIO

SE ACABÓ

Pensar en el día siguiente

Polémico desde que inició su gestión, Vicente Fox cumple hoy su último día como Presidente de la República, el primero no emanado del partido que energizó hegemónico al término de la Revolución Mexicana. Ejerció el poder con su muy particular estilo, el cual concitó críticas y simpatías. Sometido a permanente escrutinio, llegó el turno del que hará la Historia.

Lo que queda

CUENTA REGRESIVA

1 DÍA

Retiran la última barricada

3 MINUTOS

**EXCELSIOR,** México City
Abraham Solís, Marco Gonsen, Gunther Sahagún, Luzma Díaz de León Reyes, Marco A. Román, Alexandro Medrano, Gerardo Galarza, Pascal Beltrán del Río, Ernesto Rivera
A-Section page, broadsheet, 50,000-174,999

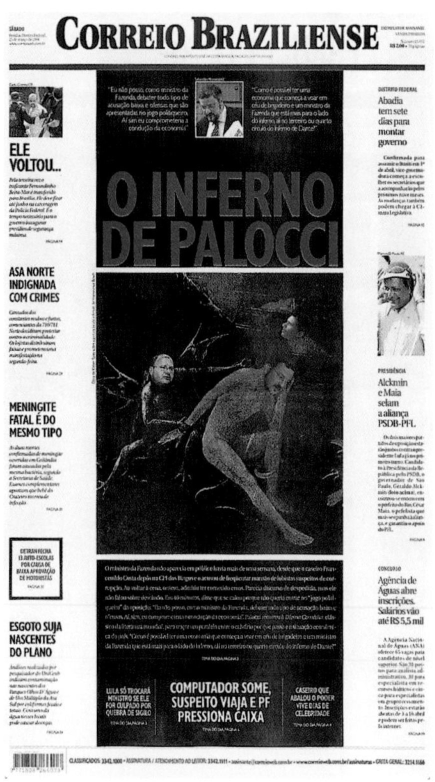
CORREIO BRAZILIENSE

ELE VOLTOU...

O INFERNO DE PALOCCI

ASA NORTE INDIGNADA COM CRIMES

MENINGITE FATAL É DO MESMO TIPO

ESGOTO SUJA NASCENTES DO PLANO

COMPUTADOR SOME, SUSPEITO VIAJA E PF PRESSIONA CAIXA

Abadia tem sete dias para montar governo

Alckmin e Maia selam aliança PSDB-PFL

Agência de Águas abre inscrições. Salários vão até R$ 5,5 mil

**CORREIO BRAZILIENSE,** Brasília, Brazil
Josemar Gimenez, Ana Dubeux, Carlos Marcelo, João Bosco Adelino de Almeida, Luís Tajes, Kleber Salles
A-Section page, broadsheet, 50,000-174,999

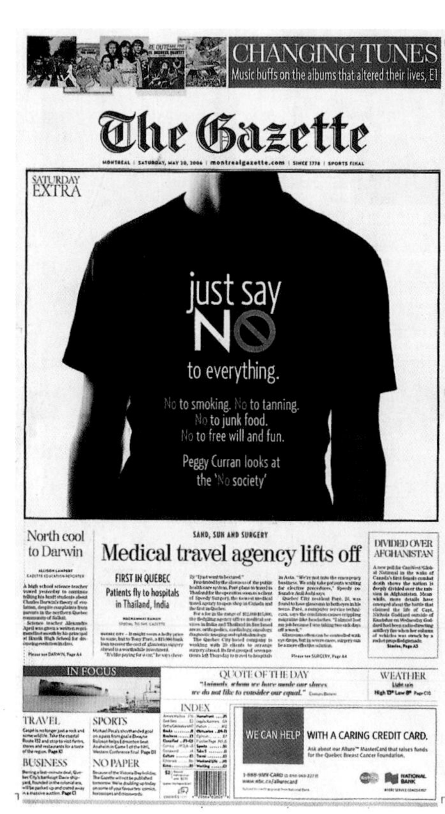
CHANGING TUNES

Music buffs on the albums that altered their lives, E1

The Gazette

MONTREAL | SATURDAY, MAY 20, 2006 | montrealgazette.com | SINCE 1778 | SPORTS FINAL

SATURDAY EXTRA

just say NO to everything.

No to smoking. No to tanning. No to junk food. No to free will and fun.

Peggy Curran looks at the 'No society'

North cool to Darwin

SAND, SUN AND SURGERY

Medical travel agency lifts off

FIRST IN QUEBEC

Patients fly to hospitals in Thailand, India

DIVIDED OVER AFGHANISTAN

IN FOCUS

QUOTE OF THE DAY

WEATHER

INDEX

TRAVEL

SPORTS

BUSINESS

NO PAPER

WE CAN HELP

WITH A CARING CREDIT CARD.

**THE GAZETTE,** Montreal
Nuri Ducassi, Catherine Wallace
A-Section page, broadsheet, 50,000-174,999

**ROCKY MOUNTAIN NEWS,** Denver

Dean Lindoerfer

A-Section page, tabloid, 175,000+

Rocky Mountain News

FIVE YEARS AFTER 9/11

**Words of comfort, resolve**

Nation remembers the pain as Bush vows to defeat terror

Special coverage begins on 26A

Cops Shoot Suspect at Brooklyn Party A6

Newsday

NEW YORK CITY

MOST POWER'S BACK, BUT . . .

**Watt a Mess!**

As politicians rage, residents clean up, fill out forms and worry A4-5

**NEWSDAY,** Melville, N.Y.

Jeff Massaro, Richard Loretoni, Wayne McClean

A-Section page, tabloid, 175,000+

Rocky Mountain News

**Unspeakable**

■ Gunman kills girl, himself after storming Bailey high school, sexually assaulting hostages. 4A

**ROCKY MOUNTAIN NEWS,** Denver

Dean Lindoerfer

A-Section page, tabloid, 175,000+

**EL CORREO,** Bilbao, Spain

Diego Zúñiga, María del Carmen Navarro, Mikel García Macías, Aurelio Garrote, Ana Espligares, Noelia Martínez, Juan Antonio Salazar, Laura Piedra, Pacho Igartua

A-Section page, tabloid, 50,000-174,999

EL CORREO

Hallado muerto en Guipúzcoa un ex preso de ETA que desapareció hace cuatro meses

Ferrovial lanza una OPA de 12.400 millones por el mayor gestor mundial de aeropuertos

Cultura descarta trasladar el 'Guernica' para su exhibición temporal en Euskadi

**Zapatero remodela el Gobierno para afrontar el proceso de paz**

Sitúa a Rubalcaba en Interior y traslada a Alonso a Defensa para gestionar el alto el fuego de ETA

La insistencia de Bono en dejar la política activa precipita la crisis

Otegi, Olano y Petrikorena dejan la cárcel tras pagar la fianza

EL ENCAJE DE SAN MAMÉS

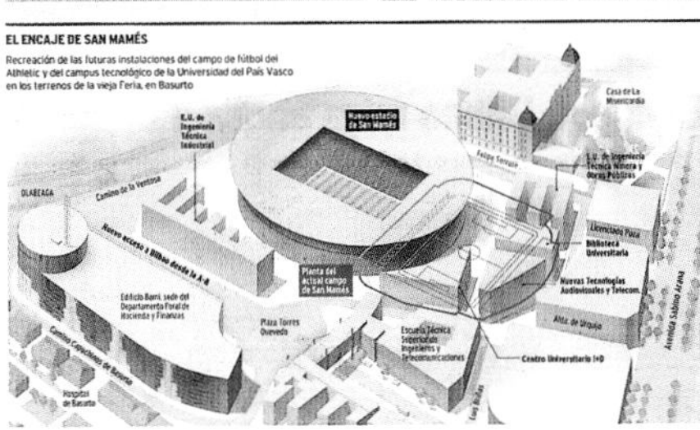

**Azkuna da al Athletic tres años para empezar el nuevo campo**

El derribo de la Feria tras el verano permite a la UPV iniciar el próximo año el campus tecnológico para 8.000 estudiantes

enlace

Defiende la camiseta de enlaCe en el mundial de fútbol Jogá de Ronaldo

**BERGENS TIDENDE,** Bergen, Norway

Arne Edvardsen, Walter Jensen, Geir Goosen

A-Section page, tabloid, 50,000-174,999

LØRDAG

STERKE MENINGER: Piggdekk-gebyret utløste leserstorm på bt.no.

Bergens Tidende

101 GRUNNER TIL Å ♥ BERGEN

DENNE UKEN HAR DET IKKE VÆRT LETT Å VÆRE BERGENSER. BRANN TAPTE GULLET, OG HØSTSTORMENE HERJER. MEN FORTVIL IKKE! DAGENS BTMAGASIN ER EN PÅMINNELSE OM AT BERGEN FORTSATT E BEST ... FORDI **BERGEN ER VAKKER** OGSÅ I ORD ... FORDI VI GÅR OG GÅR ... FORDI LOTTE VISER OSS FAVORITTLISTEN ... FORDI **VI LEVER** MODERNE I GAMLE HUS ... FORDI ELSE HAR VÆRT **LYKKELIG HER** ... FORDI OLE BULL VAR NORGES FØRSTE SUPERSTJERNE ... FORDI NARKOMANE HAR SIN EGEN PARK VERDT 250 MILLIONER ... VEL, SE DEG **RUNDT** ... FORDI VI FORTSATT ER FORVIRRET OM **SYV FJELL** ... FORDI VI ER STØRST PÅ SKARRING ... FORDI **VI ELSKER OSS SELV** HØYERE, JO MER RESTEN AV LANDET HATER OSS ... FORDI ORDFØREREN HENGER **PÅ TORGALLMENNINGEN** ... FORDI VI HAR ET SLOTT SOM SER UT SOM ET SLOTT ... FORDI NOEN AV OSS KAN LØPE **FRA SJØ TIL FJELL** PÅ TI MINUTTER ... FORDI AGNAR MYKLE SKREV EROTISK HER LENGE FØR ANNE B. RAGDE VAR FØDT ... FORDI BØRS KAFE ER ET STED DER MAN ALDRI GIR OPP ... FORDI VI HAR HATT 21 DAGER **I KLARVÆR** ... FORDI VI PLASSERTE EN RUNDKJØRING I HAGEN ... OG FORDI VI IKKE SLUTTER Å TRO PÅ MIRAKLER **ELLER** BRANN ... VI GÅR OG GÅR I LANDETS FINESTE **SJØSTØVLER** ... FORDI VI HAR FÅTT EN SLAGS MOSKÉ ... FORDI BIRGITTE (5) HAR LIVET FORAN SEG ... FORDI VI **KAN** GÅ OVER FJELLET HJEM FRA JOBB ... FORDI VI HAR **LANDETS PENESTE** VAREHUS MIDT I BYEN ... FORDI **JENTER FRA BERGEN** E NÅKKE FOR SEG ... FORDI VI HAR LANDETS BESTE MUSIKKMILJØ ... FORDI VI KAN **PRATE HÅLL I HOVVE PÅ FOLK** ... FORDI VI ALLTID VENDER HJEM ... FORDI BERGENSERE ALLTID HAR BODD **I NORGES EGENTLIGE HOVEDSTAD**

UTAH'S INDEPENDENT VOICE SINCE 1871

The Salt Lake Tribune

SUNDAY ✦ AUGUST 6, 2006

OLIVER STONE DEPICTS 9/11 HEROISM D1

DAWN OF A DREAM

REAL MADRID HAS BECOME A GLOBAL PHENOMENON

HOME STAGING: HITS THE MARK

FLDS verdict not seen as gauge

GLOBAL WARMING

**A CLIMATE OF UNCERTAINTY**

The Earth is heating up, a trend that has ramifications all over the globe as well as in Utah and the West

France, U.S. push Mideast truce pact

Handling of conflict splits Utahns with Mideast ties

» We begin a week of global climate change coverage on Pages B8-B9

**THE SALT LAKE TRIBUNE,** Salt Lake City

Josh Awtry, Colin Smith

A-Section page, broadsheet, 50,000-174,999

EXCELSIOR

EL PERIÓDICO DE LA VIDA NACIONAL

LA APPO ABANDONA EL ZÓCALO DE LA CAPITAL

Licitan tarjeta de ID

**PFP toma Oaxaca**

Las fuerzas federales asumieron el control del centro histórico tras el retiro de los inconformes, quienes denunciaron la muerte de dos personas

Dictan formal prisión a secuaz de Napoleón

3 MINUTOS

**EXCELSIOR,** México City

Damián Martínez, Javier Otaola, Marco Gonsen, Gunther Sahagún, Luzma Díaz de León Reyes, Marco A. Román, Alexandro Medrano, Gerardo Galarza, Pascal Beltrán del Río, Ernesto Rivera

A-Section page, broadsheet, 50,000-174,999

ZONA tema del domingo

DE 0 A 10 PUNTOS, EL PROMEDIO DE EXPECTATIVAS QUEDO EN 7,38

# Disfrutar más, la meta de los argentinos para 2007

8,1 Pareja y sexo

8,4 Trabajo

6,2 Bienes materiales

7,2

6,8

6,6

7,5 Cultura y tiempo libre

**CLARÍN,** Buenos Aires, Argentina
Gustavo Lo Valvo, Juan Elissetche, Federico Sosa, Hugo Scapparone, Pablo Ayala, Darío Morel, Martín Marpons
A-Section page, tabloid, 175,000+

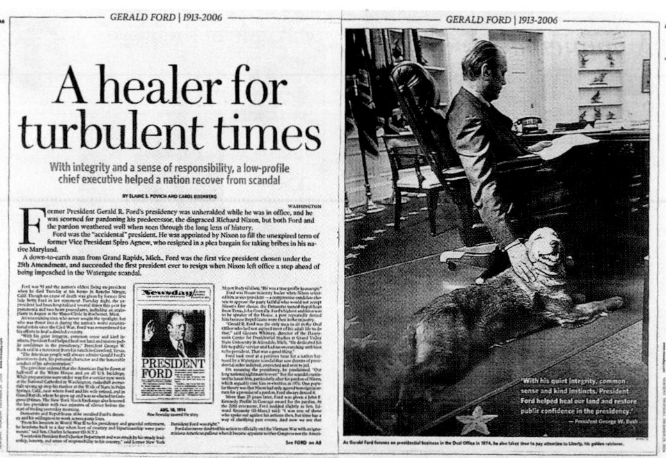
GERALD FORD | 1913-2006

# A healer for turbulent times

With integrity and a sense of responsibility, a low-profile chief executive helped a nation recover from scandal

PRESIDENT FORD

**NEWSDAY,** Melville, N.Y.
Seth Mates, Richard Loretoni, Karen Bailis, Douglas Wolfson, John Keating
A-Section page, tabloid, 175,000+

CULTURA

# Logias, secretos, misterios: el auge de los relatos conspirativos

Cinco clásicos de la intriga organizada

Docentes de colegios secundarios de todo el país.

Los invitamos a concurrir con los alumnos

**CLARÍN,** Buenos Aires, Argentina
Gustavo Lo Valvo, Juan Elissetche, Federico Sosa, Hugo Scapparone, Pablo Ayala, Darío Morel, Martín Marpons
A-Section page, tabloid, 175,000+

SOCIEDAD

# Crece el uso de videopíldoras para diagnósticos

"Me grabaron la panza"

"Permiten ahorrar tiempo y dinero"

Cuba: nueva droga contra el sida

**CLARÍN,** Buenos Aires, Argentina
Gustavo Lo Valvo, Juan Elissetche, Federico Sosa, Hugo Scapparone, Pablo Ayala, Darío Morel, Martín Marpons
A-Section page, tabloid, 175,000+

DROGA KRZYŻOWA

# Jezus umrze dziś za Ciebie

**FAKT,** Warsaw, Poland
Piotr Grzybowski, Grzegorz Jankowski, Przemyslaw "Trust" Truscinski
A-Section page, tabloid, 175,000+

# Hoy se define si el sistema solar tiene ocho o nueve planetas

China y Rusia podrían llegar juntos a Marte en 2009

Una larga discusión histórica

# La mayoría de la gente, a favor de los espacios libres de humo

Ordenan operar a una nena de 4 años

**CLARÍN,** Buenos Aires, Argentina
Gustavo Lo Valvo, Juan Elissetche, Federico Sosa, Hugo Scapparone, Pablo Ayala, Darío Morel, Martín Marpons
A-Section page, tabloid, 175,000+

**REDEYE,** Chicago
Chris Courtney
A-Section page, tabloid, 50,000-174,999

**CLARÍN,** Buenos Aires, Argentina
Gustavo Lo Valvo, Juan Elissetche, Federico Sosa, Hugo Scapparone, Pablo Ayala, Darío Morel, Martín Marpons
A-Section page, tabloid, 175,000+

EL MUNDO

Guerra en Oriente Medio

CONFUNDIERON DOS MAQUINAS PARA EXTRAER AGUA CON PLATAFORMAS DE MISILES

# El centro de Beirut, por primera vez bajo las bombas israelíes

▸ En uno de los días más sangrientos desde el inicio de la ofensiva, aviones israelíes dispararon sobre dos camiones estacionados entre hoteles y cafeterías. La enviada de Clarín estaba allí y cuenta lo que vio.

Guerra en Oriente Medio

Estietes

OCHO DIAS DE ATAQUES

Evacuados

EL CONFLICTO EN GAZA

**REDEYE,** Chicago
Chris Courtney
A-Section page, tabloid, 50,000-174,999

UPPSALA

# 3 867 cyklar

Synen vid Centralstationen i Uppsala är bekant för de flesta. Cyklar, cyklar, cyklar. Överallt. 3 867 stycken närmare bestämt, en vanlig vardagsmorgon vid 9-tiden. UNT synar cykelkaoset i stan.

"Cyklisterna tycks anse att vissa parkeringar är för långt bort."

Så här många cyklar stod det vid Centralstationen när UNT gick runt och räknade

Flera nya bilbränder i helgen

Knutbygrav blir kammarrättsärende

Hot mot UNT-reporter polisanmäldes

Barn hittades

Fel smärtmedicin sändes från apotek

HD avslår Mostens överklagan

Tjuv kröp under galler

**UPSALA NYA TIDNING,** Uppsala, Sweden
Staff Designer, Rolf Hamilton
A-Section page, tabloid, 50,000-174,999

**REDEYE,** Chicago
Chris Courtney
A-Section page, tabloid, 50,000-174,999

**NEWSDAY,** Melville, N.Y.
Richard Loretoni, Doug Dutton, John Keating
A-Section page, tabloid, 175,000+

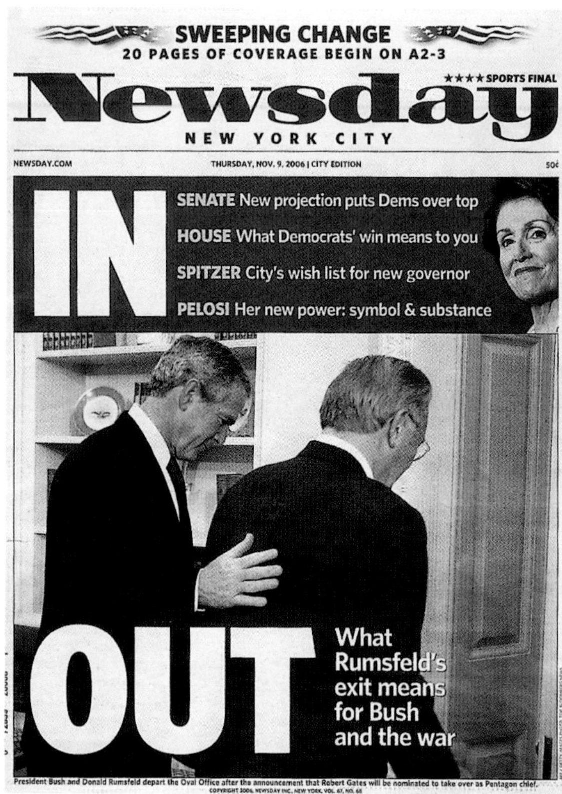
SWEEPING CHANGE
20 PAGES OF COVERAGE BEGIN ON A2-3

Newsday
NEW YORK CITY
★★★★ SPORTS FINAL
NEWSDAY.COM THURSDAY, NOV. 9, 2006 | CITY EDITION

IN

SENATE New projection puts Dems over top
HOUSE What Democrats' win means to you
SPITZER City's wish list for new governor
PELOSI Her new power: symbol & substance

OUT

What Rumsfeld's exit means for Bush and the war

President Bush and Donald Rumsfeld depart the Oval Office after the announcement that Robert Gates will be nominated to take over as Pentagon chief.

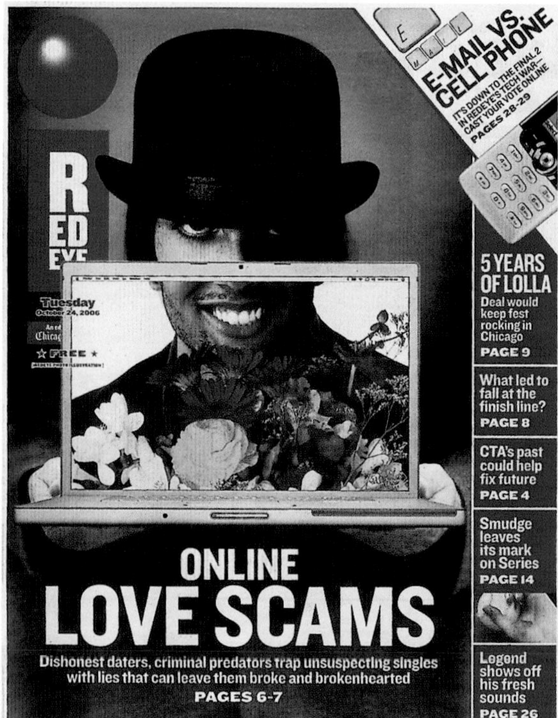
RED EYE
Tuesday
October 24, 2006
Chicago
★ FREE ★

E-MAIL VS. CELL PHONE
IT'S DOWN TO THE FINAL 2 IN REDEYE'S TECH WAR. CAST YOUR VOTE ONLINE
PAGES 28-29

5 YEARS OF LOLLA
Deal would keep fest rocking in Chicago
PAGE 9

What led to fall at the finish line?
PAGE 8

CTA's past could help fix future
PAGE 4

Smudge leaves its mark on Series
PAGE 14

Legend shows off his fresh sounds
PAGE 26

ONLINE
LOVE SCAMS
Dishonest daters, criminal predators trap unsuspecting singles with lies that can leave them broke and brokenhearted
PAGES 6-7

**REDEYE,** Chicago
Chris Courtney
A-Section page, tabloid, 50,000-174,999

**NEWSDAY,** Melville, N.Y.
Richard Loretoni, Tim Drachlis, Jeff Schamberry
A-Section page, tabloid, 175,000+

TWAflight800 10 YEARS LATER

RELIVING THE HORROR

When tragedy filled the sky
BY STEVE WICK | STAFF WRITER

230 people died on Flight 800
12 Long Islanders were on the plane
49 months of investigation
$67M NTSB inquiry's price tag

THE PLANE'S ILL-FATED JOURNEY | A4-5

EL MUNDO

Guerra en Oriente Medio

Israel aceptó un cese del fuego pero aún no frenó los ataques

El primer ministro Ehud Olmert aprobó la resolución de la ONU que prevé el retiro gradual de sus tropas del sur libanés. Mañana la tratará el gabinete. Entretanto, seguirán las acciones bélicas.

Guerra en Oriente Medio

Treinta días de conflicto

**CLARÍN,** Buenos Aires, Argentina
Gustavo Lo Valvo, Juan Elissetche, Federico Sosa, Hugo Scapparone, Pablo Ayala, Darío Morel, Martín Marpons
A-Section page, tabloid, 175,000+

Newsday
BEHIND THE HEADLINES THE FOLD WEST BANK OUTPOST

The battle at Amona

**NEWSDAY,** Melville, N.Y.
Tim Healy, Jeff Schamberry
A-Section page, tabloid, 175,000+

**THE BOSTON GLOBE**

David Schutz, David Filipov, Thea Breite

Local page, broadsheet, 175,000+

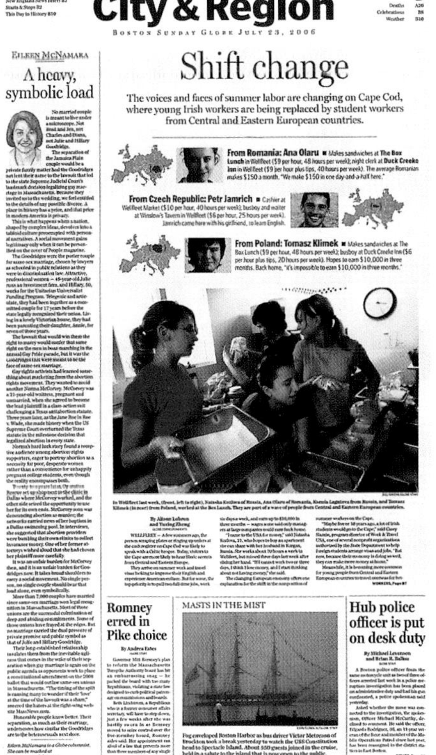

City & Region

Boston Sunday Globe July 23, 2006

Eileen McNamara

A heavy, symbolic load

Shift change

The voices and faces of summer labor are changing on Cape Cod, where young Irish workers are being replaced by student workers from Central and Eastern European countries.

From Romania: Ana Olaru

From Czech Republic: Petr Jamrich

From Poland: Tomasz Klimek

Romney erred in Pike choice

Masts in the mist

Hub police officer is put on desk duty

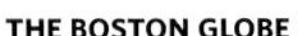

**THE BOSTON GLOBE**

George Patisteas, Dan Zedek

Local page, broadsheet, 175,000+

Globe North

The Boston Globe Thursday, October 12, 2006

Reign of the Monarchs

Nourishing hand expanded campus

Inside

Seeking comfort in memorials to fallen

**THE BOSTON GLOBE**

David Schutz, David Filipov, Thea Breite

Local page, broadsheet, 175,000+

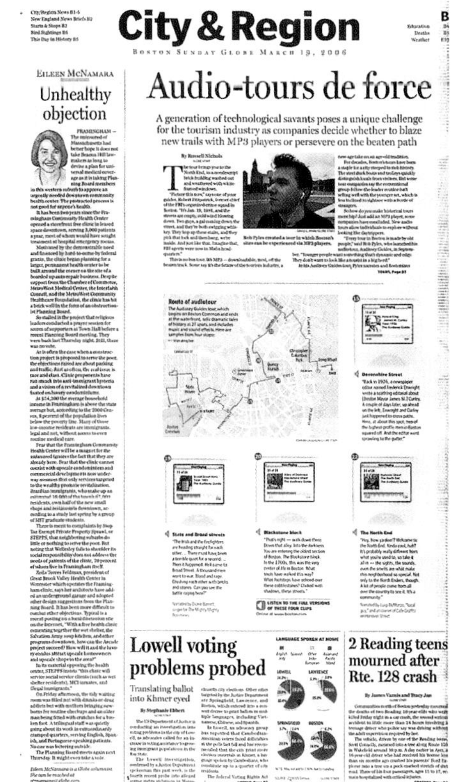

City & Region

Boston Sunday Globe March 19, 2006

Eileen McNamara

Unhealthy objection

Audio-tours de force

A generation of technological savants poses a unique challenge for the tourism industry as companies decide whether to blaze new trails with MP3 players or persevere on the beaten path

Lowell voting problems probed

2 Reading teens mourned after Rte. 128 crash

brasil

Folha de S.Paulo

Eleições 2006 / Presidência

Vacilante, Alckmin vê 'hora da arrancada'

Aliados de tucano evitam hostilizar Lula

**FOLHA DE SÃO PAULO** (Brazil)

Massimo Gentile, Fabio Marra, Marcelo Pliger, Mario Kanno

Local page, broadsheet, 175,000+

Emotion at Vass inquest B2 Jim Coyle B3

GTA

16 days to go for the GTA Municipal Election.

The James Report: Our columnist takes a hard look at who's wanted and who leaves us wanting at City Hall . . .

. . . and picks 10 (mostly) fresh faces who deserve a chance

Royson James

Sonali Verma · Mohamed Dhanani · Rowena Santos · John Sewell · Alejandra Bravo

Adam Vaughan · Chin Lee · Diana Hall · Keith Sweeney · Cadigia Ali

ontario place: over $3,000 in prizes available to be won!

Enter for your chance to WIN!

Simply visit www.ontarioplace.com and complete the 5 minute survey for your chance to win.

**TORONTO STAR**

Miguel Vadillo, Greg Smith, Royson James, Rene Johnston, Catherine Pike, Martin Regg Cohn, Steve Tustin

Local page, broadsheet, 175,000+

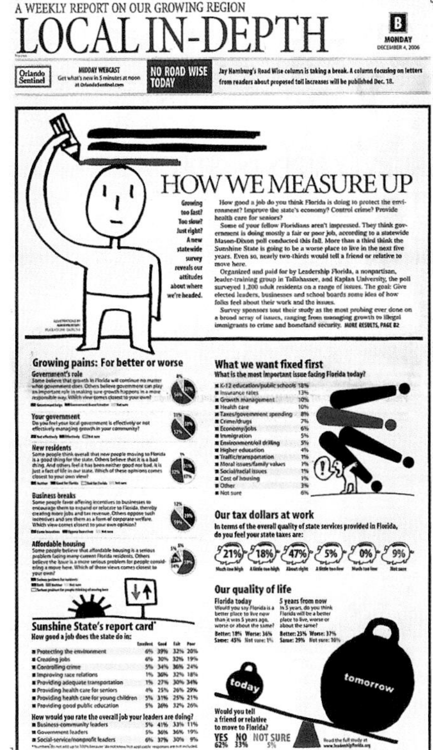

A weekly report on our growing region

LOCAL IN-DEPTH

B Monday December 4, 2006

How we measure up

Growing pains: For better or worse

What we want fixed first

Our tax dollars at work

Our quality of life

Sunshine State's report card

**ORLANDO SENTINEL** (Fla.)

Melissa Angle, Stephen Komives, Bonita Burton

Local page, broadsheet, 175,000+

**THE GLOBE AND MAIL,** Toronto

David Woodside, David Pratt, Cathrin Bradbury, Carol Toller

Local page, broadsheet, 175,000+

Globe Toronto

ALL THE PRETTY HORSES — BUT DO WE NEED THEM ON THE FORCE? SEE STORY, M4

Small classes, big woes

PETER CHENEY REPORTS

He's taken on CSIS, the Toronto police, the Canadian government and the Queen. Is Keyvan Nourhaghighi the most relentless plaintiff in the city? Ask his neighbours, M3

Today's special: roo stew

Today, York. Tomorrow, Yorkdale!

**THE GLOBE AND MAIL,** Toronto

David Woodside, David Pratt, Cathrin Bradbury, Carol Toller, Arantxa Cedillo

Local page, broadsheet, 175,000+

POSTCARDS FROM THE EDGE

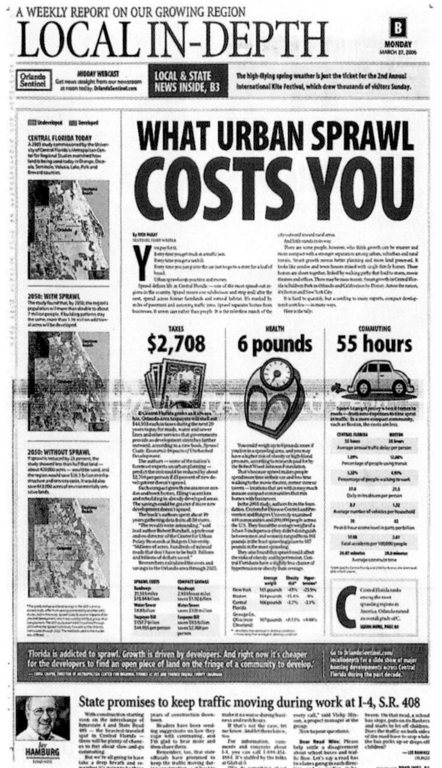

A WEEKLY REPORT ON OUR GROWING REGION

LOCAL IN-DEPTH

WHAT URBAN SPRAWL COSTS YOU

$2,708

6 pounds

55 hours

State promises to keep traffic moving during work at I-4, S.R. 408

**ORLANDO SENTINEL** (Fla.)

Sara Reeves, Lisa Frasier, Stephen Komives, Bonita Burton

Local page, broadsheet, 175,000+

A WEEKLY REPORT ON OUR GROWING REGION

LOCAL IN-DEPTH

Hang up and drive or face fine

A CRANE'S EYE VIEW

Towers do heavy lifting for growth

**ORLANDO SENTINEL** (Fla.)

Melissa Angle, Dana Fasano, Roberto Gonzalez, Reggie Myers, Stephen Komives, Bonita Burton

Local page, broadsheet, 175,000+

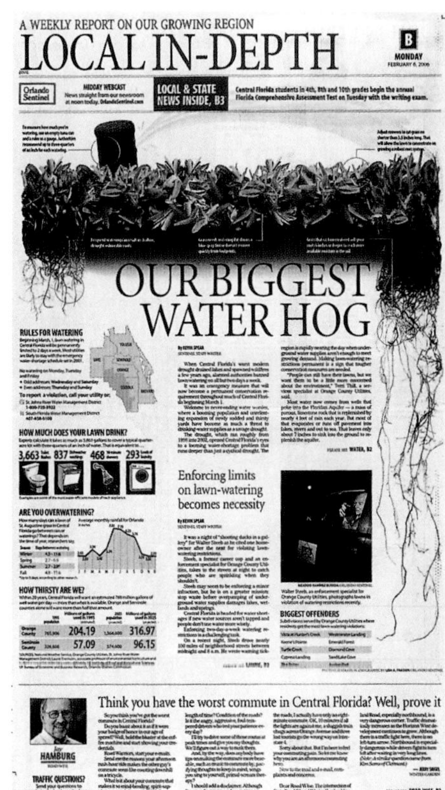

A WEEKLY REPORT ON OUR GROWING REGION

LOCAL IN-DEPTH

OUR BIGGEST WATER HOG

Enforcing limits on lawn-watering becomes necessity

Think you have the worst commute in Central Florida? Well, prove it

**ORLANDO SENTINEL** (Fla.)

Melissa Angle, Lisa Frasier, Stephen Komives, Bonita Burton

Local page, broadsheet, 175,000+

**ST. LOUIS POST-DISPATCH**

Norma Klingsick

Local page, broadsheet, 175,000+

ST. LOUIS POST-DISPATCH **Metro** | THURSDAY | OCTOBER 26, 2006 | SECTION B |

# Panel seeks more oversight

State-run homes | In wake of abuse of disabled people, task force drafts rules

# FORGET THE BIRDS, BEES ARE THE BUZZ

Genome is decoded

# 'Go Cardnals'

MLB fights knockoffs, bogus collectibles

Trademarketing

It's big money

SYLVESTER BROWN JR.

Faced with great loss, she preaches forgiveness

TOP NEWS

INSIDE

ONLINE

COME BACK TOMORROW

Who do you think you are?

**THE BOSTON GLOBE**

Lesley Becker, Dan Zedek

Local page, broadsheet, 175,000+

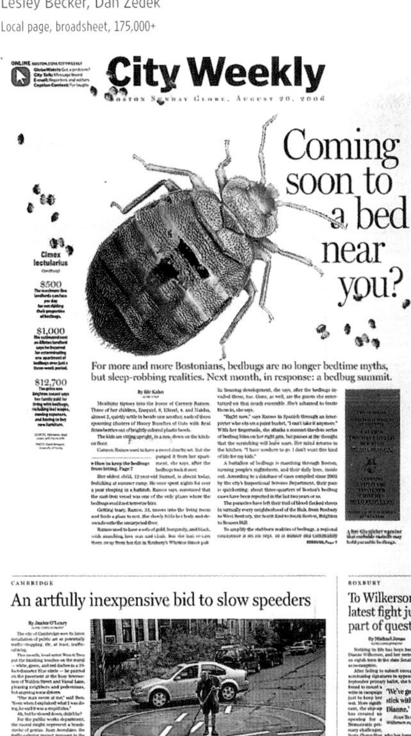

# City Weekly

BOSTON SUNDAY GLOBE, AUGUST 20, 2006

# Coming soon to a bed near you?

Cimex lectularius

$500

$1,000

$12,700

For more and more Bostonians, bedbugs are no longer bedtime myths, but sleep-robbing realities. Next month, in response: a bedbug summit.

CAMBRIDGE

## An artfully inexpensive bid to slow speeders

ROXBURY

## To Wilkerson, latest fight just part of quest

**Inside**

**THE NEW YORK TIMES**

Tom Bodkin, John Cayea

Local page, broadsheet, 175,000+

# The Quarrel

'I hate to go back all these years,' Pilar Montero says firmly. 'It turns my stomach.'

A Sore Point

**THE BOSTON GLOBE**

David Schutz, David Filipov, Thea Breite

Local page, broadsheet, 175,000+

# City & Region

BOSTON SUNDAY GLOBE JANUARY 8, 2006

EILEEN McNAMARA

## Reilly's lapse in judgment

# Big Dig. Done.

(Well, almost)

Day 1 May 13, 1991

Day 5,352 Jan. 5, 2006

So, what's left to be done?

Maynard teacher is accused of rape

Community center in line for $80m

## 'Watch out!' — and the stones rained down

N.H. survivors describe fatal avalanche on Mt. Kilimanjaro

**ST. PAUL PIONEER PRESS** (Minn.)

Steve Thomas, Ben Ramsden

Local page, broadsheet, 175,000+

ST. PAUL PIONEER PRESS | SUNDAY, DECEMBER 10, 2006 | WWW.TWINCITIES.COM

# LOCAL NEWS

INSIDE CALLS TO LOCAL POLICE AND THINGS TO DO IN YOUR NEIGHBORHOOD 2B

## Crash prompts bus checks

School board asks that similar models be grounded until brake inspections can be completed

## Law targets brutal form of abuse

# iGod

You don't have to sit in a pew to hear messages about your faith. Just download a 'godcast.'

## In our healthy state, Ialutefisk isn't funny

## Rush River vineyard divides neighbors

IN THE TWIN CITIES HOW DO LOCAL RESTAURANTS FARE IN INSPECTIONS? 1A 7-YEAR-OLD'S QUICK THINKING SAVED MOTHER 1A

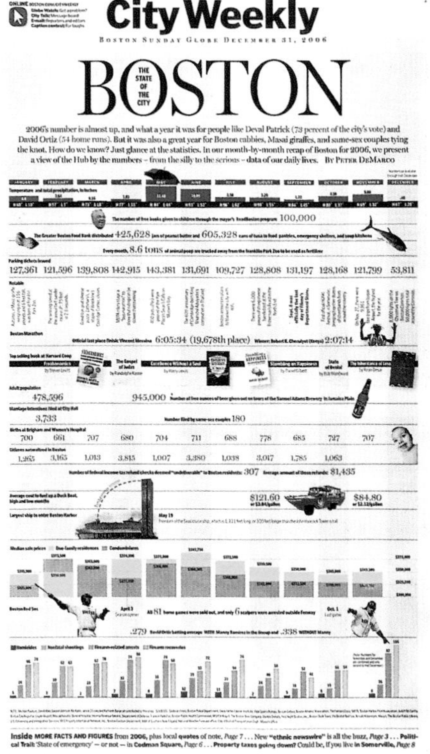

# City Weekly

BOSTON SUNDAY GLOBE DECEMBER 31, 2006

# BOSTON

THE STATE OF THE CITY

2006's number is almost up, and what a year it was for people like Deval Patrick (73 percent of the city's vote) and David Ortiz (54 home runs). But it was also a great year for Boston cabbies, Masai giraffes, and same-sex couples tying the knot. How do we know? Just glance at the statistics. In our month-by-month recap of Boston for 2006, we present a view of the Hub by the numbers — from the silly to the serious — data of our daily lives. By PETER DeMARCO

**THE BOSTON GLOBE**

Lesley Becker, Dan Zedek

Local page, broadsheet, 175,000+

**CORREIO BRAZILIENSE,** Brasília, Brazil

Josemar Gimenez, Ana Dubeux, Carlos Marcelo, João Bosco Adelino de Almeida, Luís Tajes, Marcelo Ramos, Conceição Freitas

Local page, broadsheet, 50,000-174,999

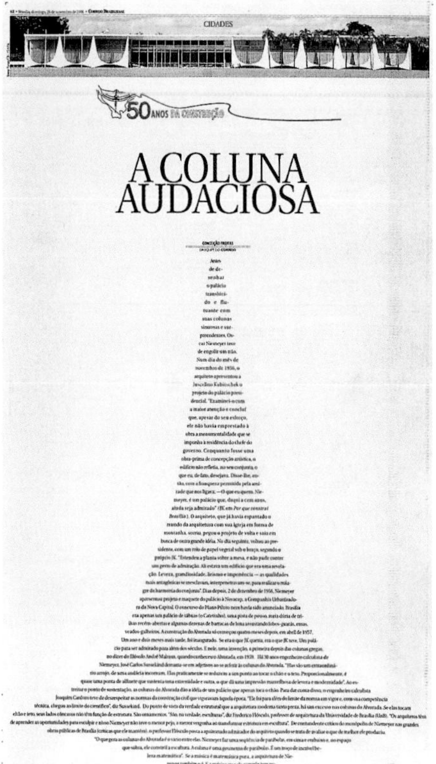

**THE BOSTON GLOBE**

Lesley Becker, Dan Zedek

Local page, broadsheet, 175,000+

**KESKISUOMALAINEN,** Jyvaskyla, Finland

Pentti Rytkönen, Pieta Forssell, Down Leikkonen

Local page, broadsheet, 50,000-174,999

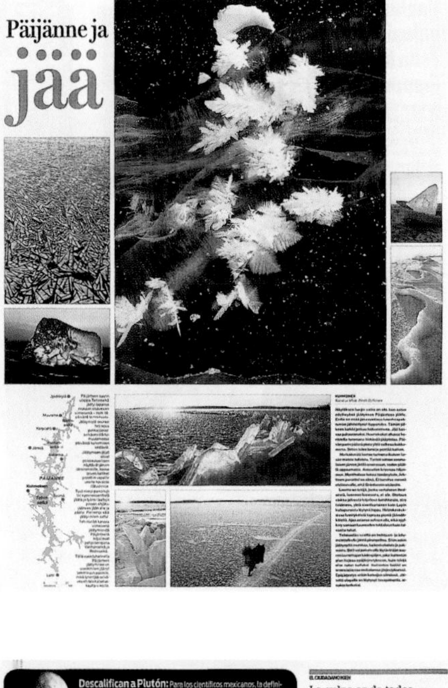

**EXCELSIOR,** México City

Juan Carlos Gutiérrez Alvarez, Alejandro Rodríguez, Paris Martínez, María Luisa López, Luzma Díaz de León Reyes, Marco A. Román, Alexandro Medrano, Ma. Luisa Díaz de León, Pascal Beltrán del Río, Ernesto Rivera

Local page, broadsheet, 50,000-174,999

**EXCELSIOR,** México City

Javier Uribe, Julio Aguilar, María Luisa López, Luzma Díaz de Léon Reyes, Marco A. Román, Alexandro Medrano, Ma. Luisa Díaz de León, Pascal Beltrán del Río, Ernesto Rivera

Local page, broadsheet, 50,000-174,999

**EXCELSIOR,** México City

Deneb Jacome, Ramíro Cháves, Paris Martínez, María Luisa López, Luzma Díaz de León Reyes, Marco A. Román, Alexandro Medrano, Ma. Luisa Díaz de León, Pascal Beltrán del Río, Ernesto Rivera

Local page, broadsheet, 50,000-174,999

**TORONTO STAR**

Staff, Tonia Conan, Catherine Farley, Dale Brazao, John Duncanson, Tracy Huffman, Nick Pron, Kevin Scanlon, Greg Smith, Alex Tavsunsky

Local page, broadsheet, 175,000+

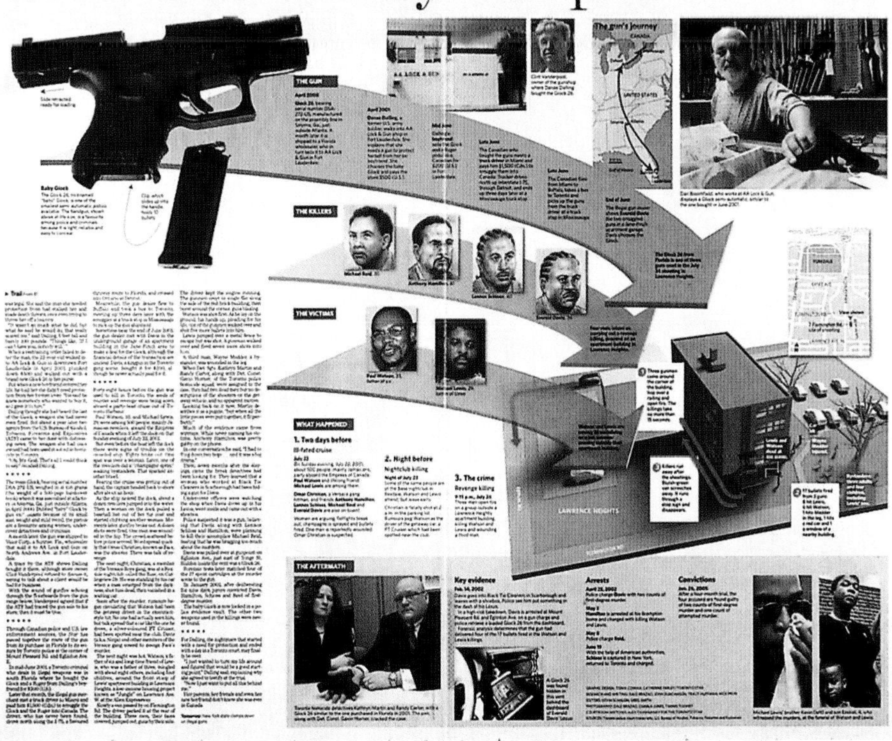

Trail of a deadly weapon

THE GUN

THE KILLERS

THE VICTIMS

WHAT HAPPENED

THE AFTERMATH

**ST. PAUL PIONEER PRESS** (Minn.)

Amanda Willis, Photo Staff

Local page, broadsheet, 175,000+

ST. PAUL PIONEER PRESS | SUNDAY, DECEMBER 31, 2006 | WWW.TWINCITIES.COM

LOCAL NEWS

INSIDE CALLS TO LOCAL POLICE AND THINGS TO DO IN YOUR NEIGHBORHOOD 2B

Schools dig into pasts of volunteers

New club in old trouble spot worries neighbors

Fruitcakes found in 'food desert'

2006 YEAR IN REVIEW

WHAT WE'LL REMEMBER

MORE YEAR IN REVIEW ON PAGES 6-7B

More than 1,000 protest conflict in Somalia

City Weekly

GOTCHA!

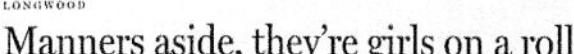

Speed traps that snag hot dogs going 70-80 miles per hour on the highway are one thing, but snares set on city streets, where most of us are happy just to break out of a crawl once in a while? The traps are out there; here's where.

Manners aside, they're girls on a roll

Can a Southie guy's Asian magazine fly?

**THE BOSTON GLOBE**

Lesley Becker, Dan Zedek

Local page, broadsheet, 175,000+

METRO

Tax Relief Solutions Suggested

Who Has Charlie's Ear?

For 3 Generations, Cutting Hair 'Runs In The Blood'

Grinch Who Stole Christmas Tree In Port Tampa To Plant Another

**THE TAMPA TRIBUNE** (Fla.)

Fred Stone

Local page, broadsheet, 175,000+

GlobeSouth

Terns, terns, terns

A haven for endangered species, Bird Island shrinks while a $3.8m fix is snared in red tape

Pilgrim mandate is up for debate

Court clerk, 82, wants another term

**THE BOSTON GLOBE**

George Patisteas, Dan Zedek

Local page, broadsheet, 175,000+

**THE BUFFALO NEWS** (N.Y.)
Vincent J. Chiaramonte, Dennis Danheiser, Howard Smith
Sports page, broadsheet, 175,000+

GRAND DRURY

*Suddenly, speed demons are exorcised*

Wild OT victory gets Sabres off and running

COMUNIDAD

SOCIEDADES DE CONVIVENCIA

SÍ

...PERO

Nutren el cómic con leyendas indígenas

Marcelo y Mariagna inician gira por Europa

**EXCELSIOR,** México City
Juan Carlos Gutierrez Alvarez, Paris Martínez, Óscar Cedillo, Luzma Díaz de Léon Reyes, Marco A. Román, Alexandro Medrano, Ma. Luisa Díaz de León, Pascal Beltrán del Río, Ernesto Rivera
Local page, broadsheet, 50,000-174,999

The Boston Globe

110TH BOSTON MARATHON

COUNTRY CLUB

**THE BOSTON GLOBE**
Brian Gross
Sports page, broadsheet, 175,000+

**NATIONAL POST,** Toronto
Doug Kelly, Gayle Grin, Laura Koot, Jim Bray, Jeff Wasserman
Sports page, broadsheet, 175,000+

OLYMPIC AVENUE

EXHAUSTED

SPORTS

NATIONAL POST, FRIDAY, JUNE 16, 2006

CFL PREVIEW

THE YEAR AHEAD | THE WRIGHT STUFF | MORE SPORTS

**NATIONAL POST,** Toronto
Doug Kelly, Gayle Grin, Laura Koot, Jim Bray, Peter J. Thompson
Sports page, broadsheet, 175,000+

**THE BALTIMORE SUN**
Lloyd Fox, Monty Cook
Sports page, broadsheet, 175,000+

PREAKNESS

SATURDAY 05.20.2006
THE SUN · BALTIMORESUN.COM

The Undefeated

Barbaro has won all six of his races, including a Kentucky Derby runaway. A victory today at Pimlico could mean he's the perfect horse to pull off the first Triple Crown sweep since 1978.

PIMLICO RACE COURSE «» TODAY «» 6:15 P.M. POST TIME

>>> GUIDE TO GETTING THERE, BETTING, MORE PAGE 7M
>>> BARBARO'S HOME HAS RICH HISTORY PAGE 8M
>>> WHEN NEW YORK HAD THE PREAKNESS PAGE 9M
>>> COMPLETE LOOK AT TODAY'S FIELD PAGE 12M

EASTERN CONFERENCE FINALS

Heat vs. Pistons

GAME 6

REDEMPTION

AFTER 18 YEARS, HEAT REACHES THE NBA FINALS

FINALLY IT'S THE HEAT'S TIME

Wade ailing, but Williams, O'Neal step up

**SOUTH FLORIDA SUN-SENTINEL,** Fort Lauderdale
Craig Davis, Robert Duyos, Amy Beth Bennett, Jonathan Boho
Sports page, broadsheet, 175,000+

**EXCELSIOR,** México City

Juan Carlos Gutiérrez Alvarez, Alejandro Rodríguez, Trinidad Ferreiro, Óscar Cedillo, Luzma Díaz de León Reyes, Marco A. Román, Alexandro Medrano, Ma. Luisa Díaz de León, Pascal Beltrán del Río, Ernesto Rivera

Local page, broadsheet, 50,000-174,999

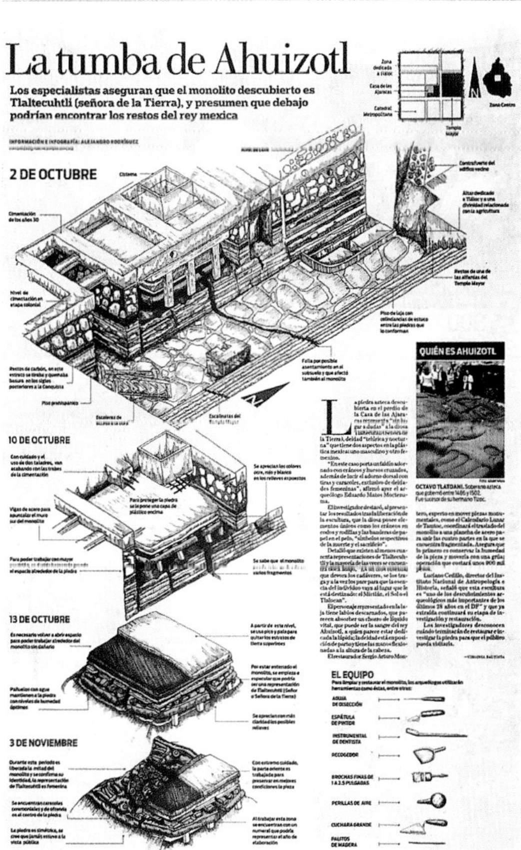

# La tumba de Ahuizotl

**Los especialistas aseguran que el monolito descubierto es Tlaltecuhtli (señora de la Tierra), y presumen que debajo podrían encontrar los restos del rey mexica**

2 DE OCTUBRE

10 DE OCTUBRE

13 DE OCTUBRE

3 DE NOVIEMBRE

QUIÉN ES AHUIZOTL

EL EQUIPO

**CLAVE,** Santo Domingo, Dominican Republic

Karen Cortez, Juan Manuel Sánchez, Victor Bautista, Fausto Rosario Adames

Local page, tabloid, 50,000-174,999

actualidad

79.8% 42.7% 2,500

# ¿Qué pasa con la imagen del país?

**Diplomáticos critican a la Justicia y la falta de institucionalidad**

Empresa de origen español denuncia obstáculos

Visión del país desde el extranjero

Inversiones crecen y el comercio baja

Oferta del país en Europa

# Cuatro muertos al arrasar el fuego una pensión en Bilbao

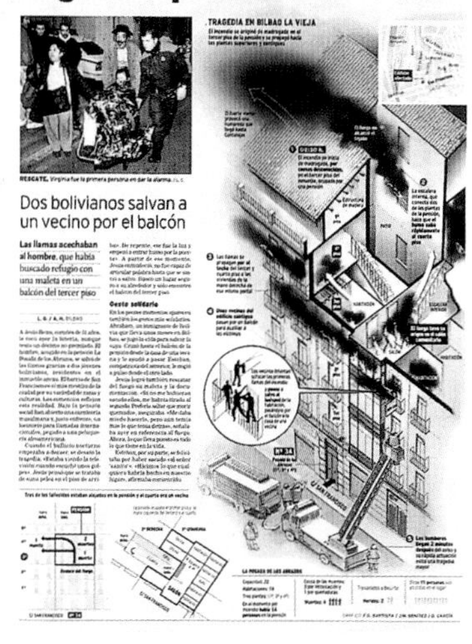

Dos bolivianos salvan a un vecino por el balcón

**EL CORREO,** Bilbao, Spain

Diego Zúñiga, María del Carmen Navarro, Mikel García Macías, Aurelio Garrote, Ana Espligares, Noelia Martínez, Juan Antonio Salazar, Laura Piedra, Pacho Igartua

Local page, tabloid, 50,000-174,999

LEGADO POLÍTICO:

# COMUNIDAD

Apoyo a la poesía indígena

PREMIO NOBEL DE LITERATURA 2006 Orhan Pamuk, el turco disidente

FESTIVAL CERVANTINO 2006 FAUSTO AL CUBO

Piden usar tarjeta de viejitos en mercados

# BELLOS HORRORES

Llega al DF la exposición World Press Photo 2006, con las mejores imágenes captadas por reporteros gráficos en los conflictos vividos en el mundo en 2005

AUSTERIDAD FÚNEBRE

VISOR

**EXCELSIOR,** México City

Juan Carlos Gutierrez Alvarez, Paris Martínez, María Luisa López, Luzma Díaz de León Reyes, Marco A. Román, Alexandro Medrano, Ma. Luisa Díaz de León, Pascal Beltrán del Río, Ernesto Rivera

Local page, broadsheet, 50,000-174,999

# Colección Cisneros

*"Ecos y contrastes"*

Arte contemporáneo en El Salvador

LA COLECCIÓN CISNEROS, DE VENEZUELA, UNA DE LAS MUESTRAS DE ARTE CONTEMPORÁNEO MÁS IMPORTANTES DE AMÉRICA LATINA, ESTÁ EN EL PAÍS. ARTE QUE ROMPIÓ LOS ESQUEMAS CLÁSICOS DE LA CREACIÓN ARTÍSTICA. SON 48 OBRAS QUE REFLEJAN PROBLEMAS DE IDENTIDADES, PAISAJES PECULIARES Y ABSTRACCIONES. EL MUSEO DE ARTE DE EL SALVADOR (MARTE) ABRE ESTE DÍA TRES DE SUS SALAS PARA SU EXHIBICIÓN.

Santos y profetas 1995

Romper esquemas

CUATRO SEMANAS TIENEN LAS OBRAS DE LA Colección Cisneros DE ESTAR EN EL PAÍS, ACOMPAÑADAS DE CURADORES Y MUSEÓGRAFOS.

LA MUESTRA

**LA PRENSA GRÁFICA,** Antiguo Cuscatlán, El Salvador

Enrique Contreras, Héctor Ramírez, Gabriel Trillos

Local page, tabloid, 50,000-174,999

**THE BUFFALO NEWS** (N.Y.)
Vincent J. Chiaramonte, Steve Jones, Howard Smith
Sports page, broadsheet, 175,000+

**THE OBSERVER,** London
Carolyn Roberts, Iain Blohm
Sports page, broadsheet, 175,000+

12 SPORT RUGBY UNION | RUGBY UNION SPORT 13

# ONWARD WITH ROB

Rob Andrew used to be a well-organised fly-half who served his country with distinction before going into management at Newcastle. Now, installed in one of the toughest jobs in English rugby, he tells Eddie Butler the past is a banned subject – and anyone who looks back is out. He also refuses to be drawn into a tit-for-tat spat with Sir Clive Woodward. Portrait by Chris Barry

ROB ANDREW INTERVIEW

'I thought the line in the sand would have been drawn last April. It wasn't'

Sweet - and tough

SECTION D

SPORTS

THE BUFFALO NEWS

Bob DiCesare

Bills buying family plan from Jauron

.339 | .417 | 199 | 110

DEREK JETER HAS THE NUMBERS TO BACK HIS CANDIDACY FOR MOST VALUABLE PLAYER IN THE AMERICAN LEAGUE. IT'S HARD TO BELIEVE HE'S NEVER WON ONE, AS THE YANKEES HAVE NEVER MISSED THE POSTSEASON IN HIS CAREER.

MVP

Woods, Furyk: a fine mesh

Odd coupling may hold key to U.S. Ryder Cup hopes

Peters' goal: drop pounds, add minutes

INSIDE: Bills' Parrish is a touchdown waiting to happen / Page D3 • NFL leaders / Page D3

Yankees magic number down to one / Page D4 • Twins close in on Tigers / Page D5

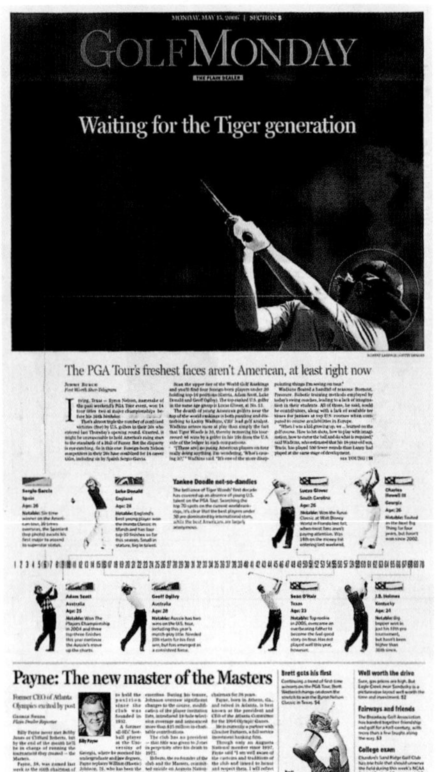

GOLF MONDAY

Waiting for the Tiger generation

The PGA Tour's freshest faces aren't American, at least right now

Payne: The new master of the Masters

**THE PLAIN DEALER,** Cleveland
David Kordalski, Roy Hewitt, Ryan Powell
Sports page, broadsheet, 175,000+

NBA FINALS

Heat vs. Mavericks

GAME 4

# TURNAROUND

TENACIOUS DEFENSE HELPS HEAT EVEN SERIES AT 2

DAVE HYDE | SUMMARY | SLUGFEST | STORY OF DAVID | MEN AT WORK

COMPLETE SPORTS SECTION INSIDE: COLIN MONTGOMERIE LEADS U.S. OPEN; TIGER WOODS STRUGGLES | 8C

**SOUTH FLORIDA SUN-SENTINEL,** Fort Lauderdale
Christian Font, Robert Mayer, Amy Beth Bennett, Jonathan Boho
Sports page, broadsheet, 175,000+

TURIN '06

San Jose Mercury News

SPORTS INSIDE

# Sparkle, and fade

Coming home with her Kleenex

Gold for Swedes and an Italian skier

One final salute to our medalists

U.S. MEDAL COUNT | MEDALISTS, BACK PAGE

**SAN JOSE MERCURY NEWS** (Calif.)
Tim Ball
Sports page, broadsheet, 175,000+

**LA PRESSE,** Montréal

Francis Leveillee, Benoit Giguere, Genevieve Dinel, Jean-Pascal Beaupre, Jean-Sebastien Gagnon, Paul Journet

Sports page, broadsheet, 175,000+

SPORTS PLUS JUNIOR

LE SKI CROSS AUX OLYMPIQUES

DES QUÉBÉCOIS SUR LE PODIUM?

ANIK DEMERS première et dernière chance

**SAN JOSE MERCURY NEWS** (Calif.)

Tim Ball

Sports page, broadsheet, 175,000+

TURIN '06

San Jose Mercury News

SPORTS INSIDE

ALPINE SKIING

Austrians, Americans cap their blowouts

SHORT TRACK

'Perfect'

OHNO WINS TWO MEDALS AND LIFTS FORTUNES OF U.S. OLYMPIC TEAM

U.S. MEDAL COUNT

SOAK IT UP; 'CAUSE THIS IS IT, FOLKS

JAMAICA TO CANADA? WORTH IT?

FOR THOSE WHO INSIST ON 'TORINO'

MAKE YOUR VOICE HEARD, HEAR OURS

**THE BOSTON GLOBE**

Brian Gross

Sports page, broadsheet, 175,000+

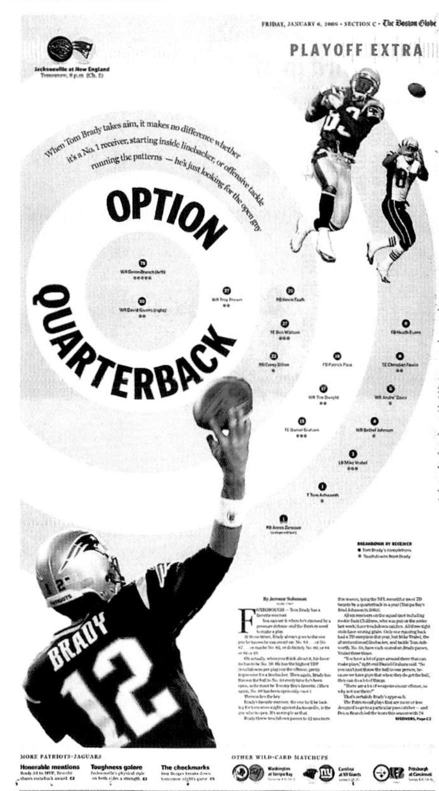

The Boston Globe

PLAYOFF EXTRA

When Tom Brady takes aim, it makes no difference whether it's a No. 1 receiver, starting inside linebacker, or offensive tackle running the patterns — he's just looking for the open guy

OPTION QUARTERBACK

BRADY 12

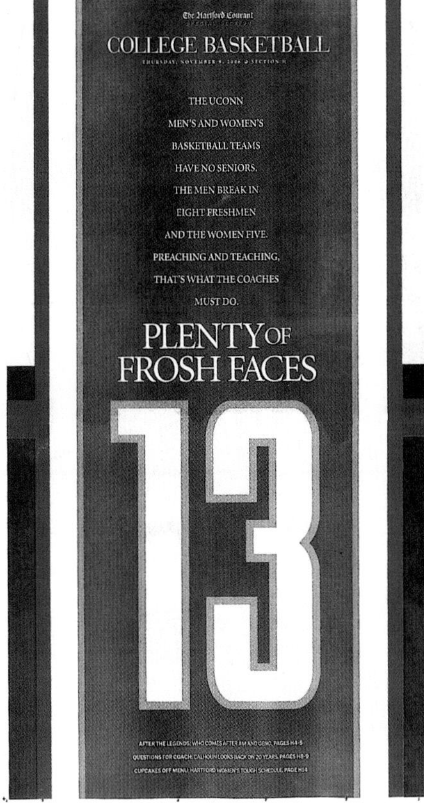

The Hartford Courant

COLLEGE BASKETBALL

THE UCONN MEN'S AND WOMEN'S BASKETBALL TEAMS HAVE NO SENIORS. THE MEN BREAK IN EIGHT FRESHMEN AND THE WOMEN FIVE. PREACHING AND TEACHING, THAT'S WHAT THE COACHES MUST DO.

PLENTY OF FROSH FACES

13

**HARTFORD COURANT** (Conn.)

Chris Moore, Vada Crosby, Sean Kelly

Sports page, broadsheet, 175,000+

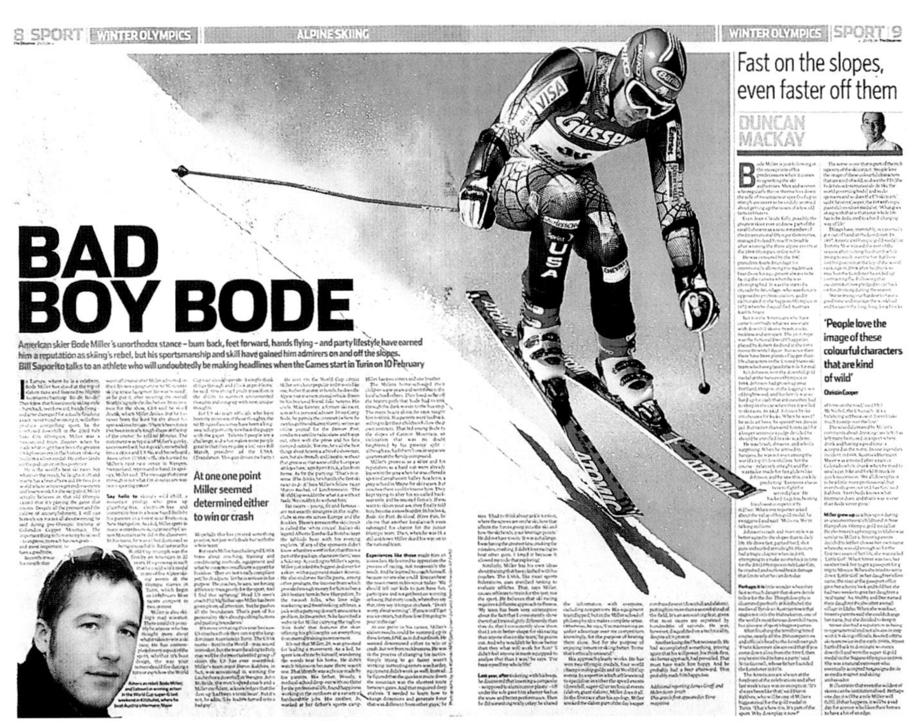

8 SPORT WINTER OLYMPICS ALPINE SKIING WINTER OLYMPICS SPORT 9

BAD BOY BODE

American skier Bode Miller's unorthodox stance – bum back, feet forward, hands flying – and party lifestyle have earned him a reputation as skiing's rebel, but his sportsmanship and skill have gained him admirers on and off the slopes. Bill Saporito talks to an athlete who will undoubtedly be making headlines when the Games start in Turin on 10 February

At one one point Miller seemed determined either to win or crash

Fast on the slopes, even faster off them

DUNCAN MACKAY

'People love the image of these colourful characters that are kind of wild'

**THE OBSERVER,** London

Carolyn Roberts, Dominic Thompson

Sports page, broadsheet, 175,000+

**THE GLOBE AND MAIL,** Toronto
David Woodside, David Pratt, Steve McAllister, Randall Moore
Sports page, broadsheet, 50,000-174,999

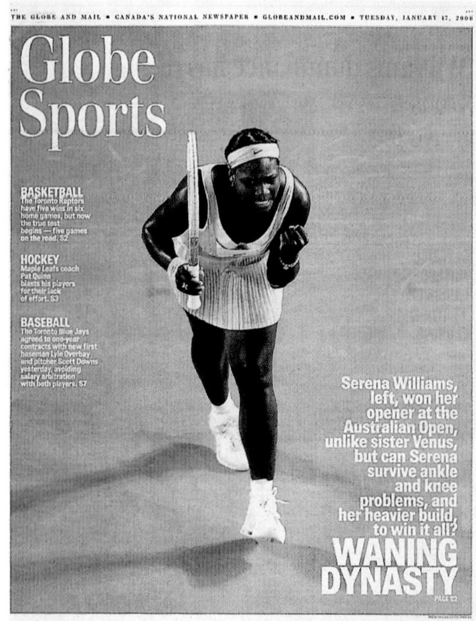
THE GLOBE AND MAIL • CANADA'S NATIONAL NEWSPAPER • GLOBEANDMAIL.COM • TUESDAY, JANUARY 17, 2006

Globe Sports

BASKETBALL
The Toronto Raptors have five wins in six home games, but now the true test begins — five games on the road. S2

HOCKEY
Maple Leafs coach Pat Quinn blasts his players for their lack of effort. S3

BASEBALL
The Toronto Blue Jays agreed to one-year contracts with new first baseman Lyle Overbay and pitcher Scott Downs yesterday, avoiding salary arbitration with both players. S7

Serena Williams, left, won her opener at the Australian Open, unlike sister Venus, but can Serena survive ankle and knee problems, and her heavier build, to win it all?

WANING DYNASTY

CFL's pot already on the boil

It's only a winter meeting, but the league's governors may be sharpening their knives for commissioner Wright

Disparate clubs will be asked to find consensus on meaningful salary cap

STEPHEN BRUNT
THE GAME

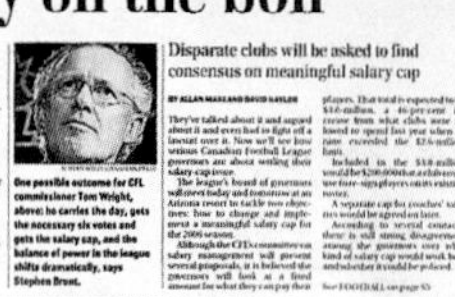
One possible outcome for CFL commissioner Tom Wright, above: he carries the day, gets the necessary six votes and gets the salary cap, and the balance of power in the league shifts dramatically, says Stephen Brunt.

**STAR TRIBUNE,** Minneapolis
Chris Carr, Glen Crevier
Sports page, broadsheet, 175,000+

.318 | 2,304 | .344 | 5 | 7

« HE'S GIVEN MINNESOTA SO MANY MAGICAL MOMENTS. BUT I THINK IT'S HIS SMILE MORE THAN ANYTHING ELSE THAT WILL ALWAYS BE IN EVERYBODY'S MEMORY. »
Former governor Arne Carlson

Unforgettable

.339 | 10 | 2 | 6 | 82.14

**THE STATE,** Columbia, S.C.
Merry Eccles, Rick Millians
Sports page, tabloid, 50,000-174,999

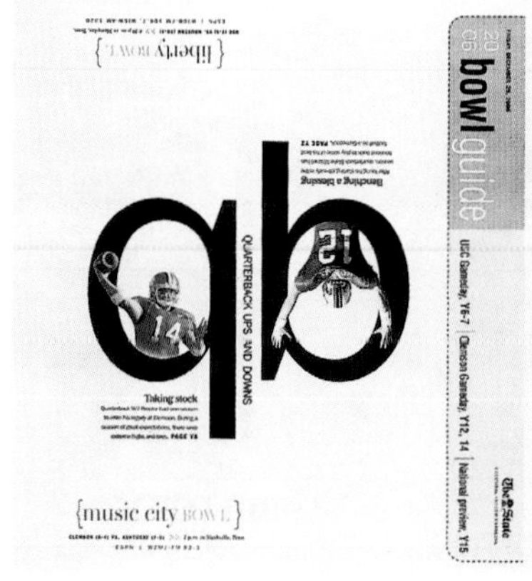
bowl guide

qb

QUARTERBACK UPS AND DOWNS

Taking stock

{music city BOWL}

Fußball WM 2006

Ab in die Wagenburg | Alles war Fußball | Alles über die Teams | Einer für alle

Nun spielt mal schön!

**FRANKFURTER ALLGEMEINE SONNTAGSZEITUNG**
Frankfurt am Main, Germany
Peter Breul, Volker Stumpe, Andreas Kuther
Sports page, broadsheet, 175,000+

The State

{20 06} college WORLD SERIES

series schedule

DOUBLE ELIMINATION

Armed forces

Clemson's starting rotation might not be as intimidating as 1996's big-league-bound staff, but it is the reason the Tigers are back in Omaha

COMPARING THE STARTERS

2006

1996

CHAMPIONSHIP SERIES BEST-OF-THREE

Burning love

Jack Leggett has mellowed after 13 years at Clemson — but not much

Bob Spear

INSIDE | Tiger Woods struggles mightily at the U.S. Open. Page C3

SPORTS

**THE STATE,** Columbia, S.C.
Merry Eccles, Rick Millians
Sports page, broadsheet, 50,000-174,999

FASTLANE

LAST STAND | Sunday's race at Texas Motor Speedway should be the 84th and final Cup series start for Terry Labonte. Page C5

The State

SPORTS

FRIDAY, NOVEMBER 3, 2006 • SECTION C

CLEMSON FOOTBALL | Chris McDuffie draws praise for his starting debut on the offensive line. Page C4

With his long field goals and movie-star good looks, USC's sophomore kicker is turning a lot of heads on campus

STYLE, SUBSTANCE & SUCCOP

USC'S LONGEST FIELD GOALS

| MARK FLEETWOOD | RYAN SUCCOP | SCOTT HAGLER | SCOTT HAGLER | COLLIN MACKIE | MARK FLEETWOOD | RYAN SUCCOP | SCOTT HAGLER | COLLIN MACKIE | MARTY SIMPSON |
|---|---|---|---|---|---|---|---|---|---|
| 58 | 55 | 54 | 52 | 52 | 51 | 50 | 50 | 50 | 50 |

Fans' misdeeds give USC little to crow over

Ron Morris

INSIDE

Retired coaches learn new ways to satisfy weekend itch in the fall

TV marathons and road trips as a fan provide them access and an outlet for their passion

Carolina Fall Saturdays

WWW.GOGAMECOCKS.COM • WWW.THESTATE.COM

**THE STATE,** Columbia, S.C.
Merry Eccles, Rick Millians
Sports page, broadsheet, 50,000-174,999

SPORTS

INSIDE: MOTORSPORTS

Padres suit Maddux fine this time

Future Hall of Fame pitcher formally introduced to San Diego community

THE GOLDEN STANDARD

"Last year, I felt very good. Last year, I felt as good as I have ever felt."

Tim Sullivan

No gas guzzler, Maddux may be Prius of pitchers

1933 Lamar Hunt 2006

Kansas City Chiefs owner was pioneer of modern NFL

Football's "Golden Boy,"

**THE SAN DIEGO UNION-TRIBUNE**
Paul Wallen, Liz Grauman
Sports page, broadsheet, 175,000+

**THE STATE,** Columbia, S.C.

Merry Eccles, Rick Millians

Sports page, broadsheet, 50,000-174,999

The State

SPORTS

SATURDAY, MAY 27, 2006 • SECTION C

NASCAR

Mister, can you spare a Bodine?

With a few owners hoarding talent, new teams are desperate to sign good drivers

What you gonna do with all that junk? All that junk inside your trunk?

Can your rear fit here?

Ron Morris

USC BASEBALL

Hits just keep on coming for foes

Georgia scores 14 unanswered runs to obliterate USC's early nine-run lead

CLEMSON BASEBALL

Coming through in a pinch

Ben Hall has a history of bailing out the Tigers with timely pinch hits

TIGERS VS. YELLOW JACKETS

SOME BIG NUMBERS

COCA-COLA 600

INSIDE

BASEBALL C4 • GOLF C5 • NBA C8 • NHL C8 • WWW.THESTATE.COM

**GULF NEWS,** Dubai, United Arab Emirates

Douglas Okasaki, Paul Velasco, Robin Chatterjee, Gautam Bhattacharyya, Sanjib Das, AK. Satish, Miguel Angel Gomez, Abdul Hamid Ahmad, Leslie Wilson

Sports page, broadsheet, 50,000-174,999

38 Sport Special

Sport Special 39

6 NATIONS RUGBY

GILBERT

1 WALES

2 IRELAND

3 FRANCE

4 ENGLAND

5 SCOTLAND

6 ITALY

There's no doubting Thomas

Ruck and roll!

Ireland boosted by O'Driscoll's return

adrenalina

Cerca de Alemania > La recuperación de Wayne Rooney va viento en popa. Hoy se realizará más estudios > 07

"Ellos no van a salir a atacar. Es un equipo difícil de analizar. Te cambian constantemente el esquema".

CONTRA IRÁN...

¡AL ATAQUE!

El técnico de la Selección Nacional dijo, que México será quien proponga el partido del domingo 11 de junio > 04-05

a06 Nuestro Mundial comienza antes

Cardozo se perderá la Copa del Mundo

Federer continúa por buen camino

Dallas y Miami, del sótano a la cima

COLUMNAS

**EXCELSIOR,** México City

Horacio Trejo Rivera, Mauricio Belman, Carlos Uriegas, Luzma Díaz de León Reyes, Marco A. Román, Alexandro Medrano, Ma. Luisa Díaz de León, Pascal Beltrán del Río, Ernesto Rivera

Sports page, broadsheet, 50,000-174,999

Emotivo festejo > Jorge Vergara lloró de alegría junto a sus jugadores > 4 y 5

adrenalina

MÁS SAGRADO QUE NUNCA

El Rebaño consiguió ayer su undécimo título y se convirtió en el equipo más ganador del futbol mexicano

COLUMNAS

**EXCELSIOR,** México City

Eduardo César Mendoza, Ricardo Puig, Luzma Díaz de León Reyes, Marco A. Román, Alexandro Medrano, Ma. Luisa Díaz de León, Pascal Beltrán del Río, Ernesto Rivera

Sports page, broadsheet, 50,000-174,999

adrenalina

Aupa Osasuna > Los rojillos ganaron y están en el segundo lugar de la Liga de España > 04

Cuauhtémoc Blanco está resignado a su suerte. Tras conocer que La Volpe no piensa en él, afirmó que, si México fracasa, "será su culpa, no la mía"

SE ACABÓ

Óliver y Rodrigo abrirán.

Ultra decepción universitaria

Toluca dio un gran paso hacia Japón

Imágenes que revolucionan la televisión

**EXCELSIOR,** México City

Horacio Trejo Rivera, Martín Del Palacio, Luzma Díaz de León Reyes, Marco A. Román, Alexandro Medrano, Ma. Luisa Díaz de León, Pascal Beltrán del Río, Ernesto Rivera

Sports page, broadsheet, 50,000-174,999

**EXCELSIOR,** México City

Horacio Trejo Rivera, Ricardo Puig, Luzma Díaz de León Reyes, Marco A. Román, Alexandro Medrano, Ma. Luisa Díaz de León, Pascal Beltrán del Río, Ernesto Rivera

Sports page, broadsheet, 50,000-174,999

adrenalina

Reconocen a Wade > El jugador de Miami será nombrado mejor deportista del año > 8

CHIVAS LAMENTA EL RESULTADO

¡DIABLOS!

LE MONDE ACUSA AL BARÇA Y AL MADRID DE DOPAJE

GUADALAJARA NO PUDO SACAR VENTAJA EN CASA Y AHORA DEBERÁ GANAR EL DOMINGO EN LA BOMBONERA, ESTADIO EN EL QUE CHIVAS NO CONSIGUE UN TRIUNFO DESDE EL VERANO 97, CUANDO FUE CAMPEÓN > 2 y 3

ARGONADO VAMPIRO

PITTSBURGH VENCIÓ 27-7 A CLEVELAND

Parker fundió récord de Acereros

COLUMNAS

**EXCELSIOR,** México City

Horacio Trejo Rivera, Fernando Ruíz, Luzma Díaz de León Reyes, Marco A. Román, Alexandro Medrano, Ma. Luisa Díaz de León, Pascal Beltrán del Río, Ernesto Rivera

Sports page, broadsheet, 50,000-174,999

PEKÍN AÚN VIVE SU COMUNISMO PATRIÓTICO

Entre la vergüenza y el honor

La capital china avanza rápidamente en los preparativos para los Juegos Olímpicos de 2008. Conforme se acerca la fecha, comienza el debate sobre si el país asiático puede manifestar abiertamente su ideología política en medio de un evento internacional de tal envergadura, el primero en suelo comunista desde los juegos de Moscú en 1980

Krámnik, sospechoso de trampas contra Topálov

Ponen en duda a Vinokourov

Moscú 80, los primeros juegos del comunismo

7: adrenalina

PABLO CARRILLO

Qué chula es Puebla

Federaciones piden cambio al calendario

Brent Cass · Alison Cheney · Dez Curet · Sara Hemmings · Aric Goodman

Danielle Kachulis · Geoff Heller · Kristen Kugler · Jacob Houghton · Lauren Miller

John Kyed · Lindsey Meller · Robby Pride · Justine Sanderfield · Lane Waslegen

Honoring the state's best on and off the field

The Steinmark Award

Steinmark finalists capsules, 4P

**ROCKY MOUNTAIN NEWS,** Denver

Amy Speer

Sports page, tabloid, 175,000+

adrenalina

Arranca el beis > Hoy lanzan mexicanos en Grandes Ligas > 08

¡PUMAS POR FIN GANÓ!

TODOS AL ÁNGEL

Los universitarios sorprendieron al superlíder con un buen planteamiento de su nuevo técnico, Memo Vázquez. Increíblemente, aún aspiran a calificar > 3

2-1

¿Qué pasó celestes? > Cruz Azul cayó en San Luis 2-1 pese a tener un hombre más durante cuarenta minutos > 04

Con el grito en la garganta

La Volpe dio la lista

Llegan los resultados

Osasuna se derrumba

**EXCELSIOR,** México City

Horacio Trejo Rivera, Martín Del Palacio, Luzma Díaz de León Reyes, Marco A. Román, Alexandro Medrano, Ma. Luisa Díaz de León, Pascal Beltrán del Río, Ernesto Rivera

Sports page, broadsheet, 50,000-174,999

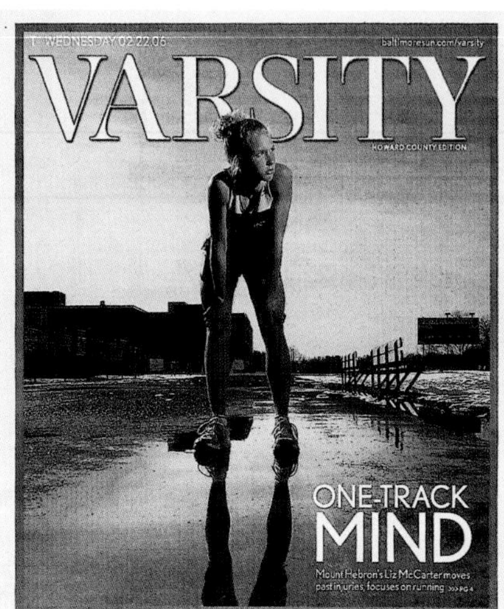

WEDNESDAY 02.22.06

baltimoresun.com/varsity

VARSITY

HOWARD COUNTY EDITION

ONE-TRACK MIND

Mount Hebron's Liz McCarter moves past injuries, focuses on running

**THE BALTIMORE SUN**

Heather Sigle, Doug Kapustin

Sports page, tabloid, 175,000+

**THE GAZETTE,** Montreal

Nuri Ducassi, Stu Cowan

Sports page, tabloid, 50,000-174,999

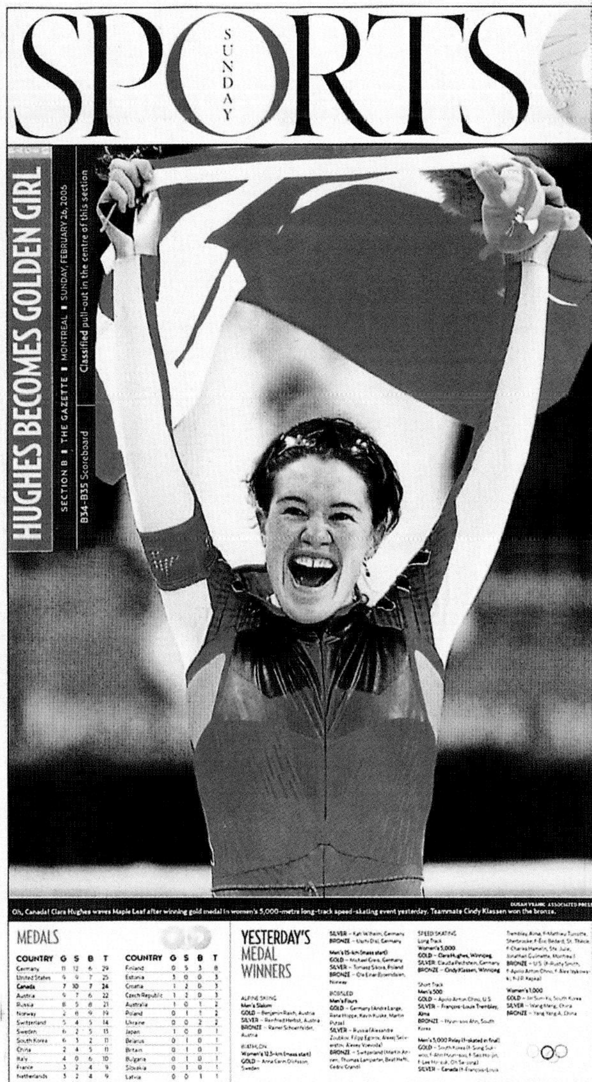

SPORTS SUNDAY

HUGHES BECOMES GOLDEN GIRL

SECTION B ■ THE GAZETTE ■ MONTREAL ■ SUNDAY, FEBRUARY 26, 2006

B34-B35 Scoreboard

Classified pull-out in the centre of this section

Oh, Canada! Clara Hughes waves Maple Leaf after winning gold medal in women's 5,000-metre long-track speed-skating event yesterday. Teammate Cindy Klassen won the bronze.

MEDALS

YESTERDAY'S MEDAL WINNERS

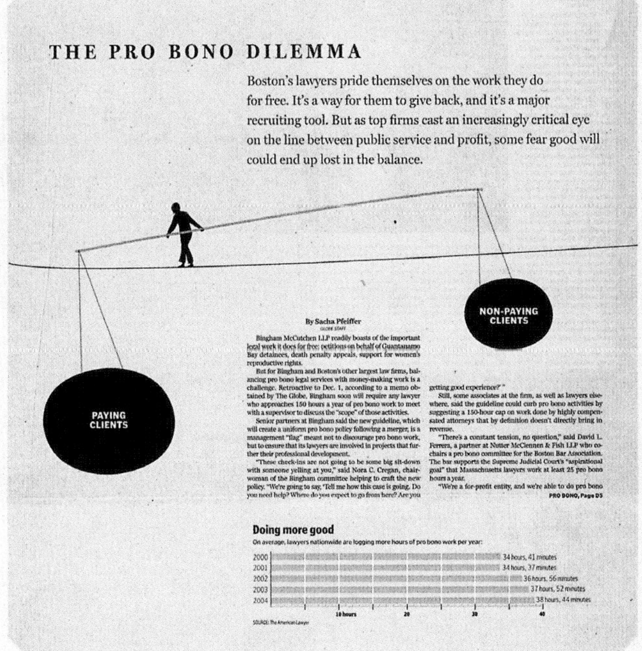

# Business&Money

BOSTON SUNDAY GLOBE MARCH 5, 2006

## THE PRO BONO DILEMMA

Boston's lawyers pride themselves on the work they do for free. It's a way for them to give back, and it's a major recruiting tool. But as top firms cast an increasingly critical eye on the line between public service and profit, some fear good will could end up lost in the balance.



By Sacha Pfeiffer
GLOBE STAFF

Bingham McCutchen LLP readily boasts of the important legal work it does for free: petitions on behalf of Guantanamo Bay detainees, death penalty appeals, support for women's reproductive rights.

But for Bingham and Boston's other largest law firms, balancing pro bono legal services with money-making work is a challenge. Retroactive to Dec. 1, according to a memo obtained by The Globe, Bingham soon will require any lawyer who approaches 150 hours a year of pro bono work to meet with a supervisor to discuss the "scope" of those activities.

Senior partners at Bingham said the new guideline, which will create a uniform pro bono policy following a merger, is a management "flag" meant not to discourage pro bono work, but to ensure that its lawyers are involved in projects that further their professional development.

"These check-ins are not going to be some big sit-down with someone yelling at you," said Nora C. Cregan, chairwoman of the Bingham committee helping to craft the new policy. "We're going to say, 'Tell me how this case is going. Do you need help? Where do you expect to go from here? Are you getting good experience?' "

Still, some associates at the firm, as well as lawyers elsewhere, said the guideline could curb pro bono activities by suggesting a 150-hour cap on work done by highly compensated attorneys that by definition doesn't directly bring in revenue.

"There's a constant tension, no question," said David L. Ferrera, a partner at Nutter McClennen & Fish LLP who co-chairs a pro bono committee for the Boston Bar Association. The bar supports the Supreme Judicial Court's "aspirational goal" that Massachusetts lawyers work at least 25 pro bono hours a year.

"We're a for-profit entity, and we're able to do pro bono

PRO BONO, Page D5

**Doing more good**

On average, lawyers nationwide are logging more hours of pro bono work per year:

| | |
|---|---|
| 2000 | 34 hours, 41 minutes |
| 2001 | 34 hours, 37 minutes |
| 2002 | 36 hours, 56 minutes |
| 2003 | 37 hours, 52 minutes |
| 2004 | 38 hours, 44 minutes |

SOURCE: The American Lawyer

STEPHEN J. DUBNER AND STEVEN D. LEVITT

**Freakonomics**

### If real estate is prospering, chances are your agent isn't

It is hard to think of many occupations that garner less good will these days than the real estate agent.

A great many of these agents and brokers, more than 1.2 million, belong to the National Association of Realtors, which the Department of Justice accused in a recent lawsuit of behaving like a cross between a cartel and a mafia, hoarding access to home-sale databases and harassing competitors who dared to offer discounted commissions.

Even if you believe all these terrible things about real estate agents, however, you should try to find in your heart a bit of sympathy for them. There are two reasons for this.

To examine the first reason, ask this question: Who has prospered during the recent real-estate boom? Home sellers, to be sure, along with developers, mortgage brokers — and also, you would assume, your average real estate agent.

These agents have rung up millions of sales while home prices have been doubling and even tripling. Since an agent's commission is usually based on a fixed percentage of the sale price — typically 5 percent or 6 percent, of which about half goes to the listing agent and half to the buyer's agent — agents' fees have climbed along with home prices, even though they probably don't have to work any harder to sell an $800,000 house than

Most realtors don't make much money in a boom.

REALTORS, Page D5

**Consumer Beat**

### As oil prices fall, price caps become a hot-button issue

By Bruce Mohl
GLOBE STAFF

Heating oil prices are down from their fall peak, but some consumers with price caps are complaining that their dealers aren't passing along the savings to them.

Kathryn Wilson of Andover thought her price cap protection was finally going to come into play recently when her dealer, Alliance Express, pulled up for a delivery. She had signed a cap last fall guaranteeing her that she wouldn't pay more than $2.69 all winter and that she would pay less if the retail price fell below that level.

Just before her dealer arrived, Wilson had read in the newspaper that a survey by the state's Division of Energy Resources indicated the average price of heating oil in Massachusetts was $2.31 a gallon. The survey price was adjusted upward a week later to $2.35, but either way the price was well below her cap.

Yet when Wilson received her bill from Alliance she was charged her cap price of $2.69 a gallon. Alliance said its retail price — what it's currently charging customers — was $2.84 a gallon, nowhere near the statewide average. Wilson complained, but was told that Alliance was not included in the statewide survey and that its results had no bearing on the firm's costs.

"It's really hard for consumers to know what's going on," Wilson said. "If you have a price cap, how do you know what the real price is for that company?"

Caps sounded great last fall, when energy

Some say dealers aren't passing along savings.

CONSUMER BEAT, Page D4

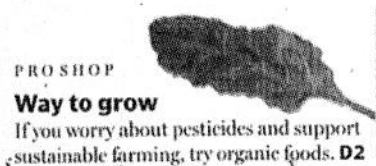

PRO SHOP

**Way to grow**

If you worry about pesticides and support sustainable farming, try organic foods. D2

ON THE HOT SEAT

**King of the malls**

Simon Property Group's Richard S. Sokolov talks about the future of department stores. D3

ETIQUETTE AT WORK

**Do not disturb**

Get your cubicle neighbors to keep the noise down without antagonizing them. D2

ALSO

**BostonWorks** Try a few careers until you're sure. G1

**Real Estate** Lowell's latest renewal is luring homeowners. H1

SILVER

**THE BOSTON GLOBE**

Grant Staublin, Shirley Leung, Dan Zedek

Business page, broadsheet, 175,000+

Hitting all areas is this story on the tension between pro bono work and billing your firm — the stripped-down illustration style, the simple charting and the lovely typography. The secondary stories don't compete despite a very reserved centerpiece.

Este artículo toca todos los ángulos sobre la tensión entre el trabajo pro bono -sin fines de lucro que hacen los abogados-, y el cobro a la firma, con el estilo puro de la ilustración, las sencillas tablas y la linda tipografía. Los artículos secundarios no compiten con el principal, pese a ser restringido.

Goodbye, Kirby

**STAR TRIBUNE,** Minneapolis

Chris Carr, Derek Simmons, Cory Powell, Glen Crevier

Sports page, broadsheet, 175,000+

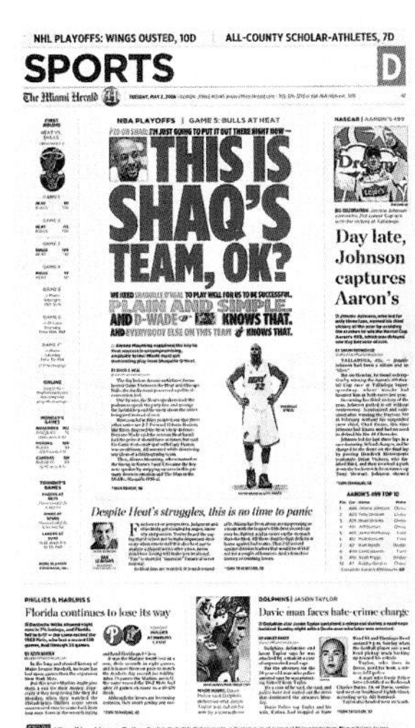

NHL PLAYOFFS: WINGS OUSTED, 10D | ALL-COUNTY SCHOLAR-ATHLETES, 7D

SPORTS D

The Miami Herald

NBA PLAYOFFS | GAME 5: BULLS AT HEAT

THIS IS SHAQ'S TEAM, OK?

Day late, Johnson captures Aaron's

*Despite Heat's struggles, this is no time to panic*

Florida continues to lose its way

Davie man faces hate-crime charge

**THE MIAMI HERALD**

Eddie Alvarez, Robert Cohn

Sports page, broadsheet, 175,000+

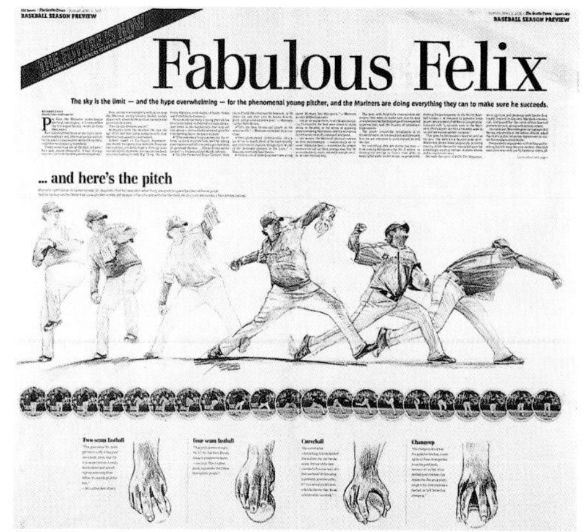

BASEBALL SEASON PREVIEW

# Fabulous Felix

The sky is the limit — and the hype overwhelming — for the phenomenal young pitcher, and the Mariners are doing everything they can to make sure he succeeds.

... and here's the pitch

Two-seam fastball

Four-seam fastball

Curveball

Changeup

**THE SEATTLE TIMES**
Mark McTyre, Susan Jouflas, Rod Mar
Sports page, broadsheet, 175,000+

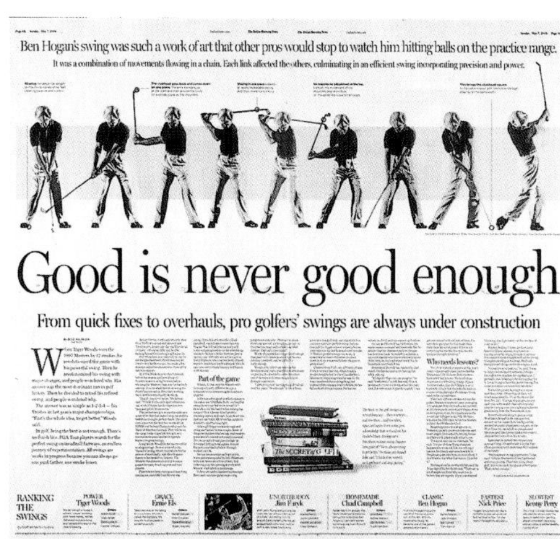

Ben Hogan's swing was such a work of art that other pros would stop to watch him hitting balls on the practice range.

It was a combination of movements flowing in a chain. Each link affected the others, culminating in an efficient swing incorporating precision and power.

# Good is never good enough

From quick fixes to overhauls, pro golfers' swings are always under construction

Part of the game

Who needs lessons?

RANKING THE SWINGS

Tiger Woods · Ernie Els · Jim Furyk · Chad Campbell · Ben Hogan · Nick Price · Kenny Perry

**THE DALLAS MORNING NEWS**
Rob Schneider, Troy Oxford, Noel Nash, Bill Nicholls
Sports page, broadsheet, 175,000+

**HARTFORD COURANT** (Conn.)
Kristin Lenz, Suzette Moyer
Business page, broadsheet, 175,000+

# BUSINESS

## 'Our Rules Are Out Of Date'

SEC Moves To Require Companies To Provide More Details On Executives' Pay, Perks

## UTC Exec Steps Aside

Fire & Security Chief To Answer Allegations Of Misconduct In France

## Technology Bellwethers Take A Hit

3 Firms' Results Signal Sector May Go Lower

## TASTING CELEBRITY

Trump, Others Popping Up In Branding Deals With Wilton Beverage Distributor

IN THE NEWS

Winchester Plant Closing

Walgreen In Windsor

courant.com

# Business

mercurynews.com/business

## libertarian Republican Friedman

THE MERCURY NEWS INTERVIEW

THE PIED PIPER OF FREE MARKETS HELPED LEAD 'REAGAN REVOLUTION'

NOBEL PRIZE WINNER EXPOUNDS ON EDUCATION, HEALTH CARE, IRAQ

## Seeking health care abroad

**SAN JOSE MERCURY NEWS** (Calif.)
Emmet Smith, Jonathon Berlin, Matt Mansfield
Business page, broadsheet, 175,000+

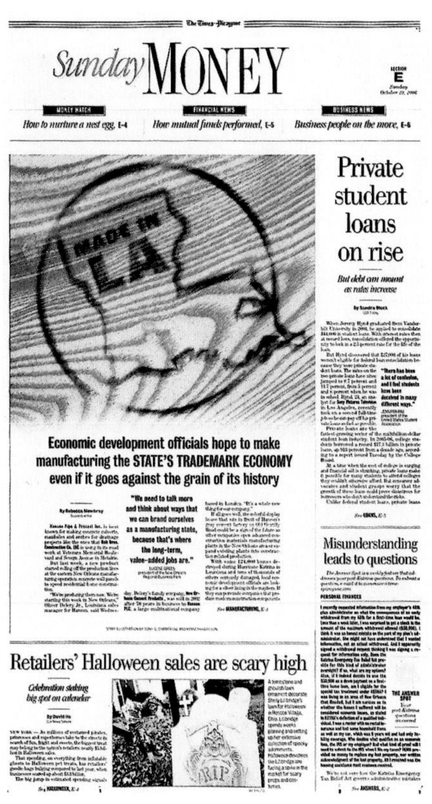

The Times-Picayune

# Sunday MONEY

SECTION E

MONEY WATCH — How to nurture a nest egg, E-4

FINANCIAL NEWS — How mutual funds performed, E-5

BUSINESS NEWS — Business people on the move, E-6

## Private student loans on rise

But debt can mount as rates increase

## Economic development officials hope to make manufacturing the STATE'S TRADEMARK ECONOMY even if it goes against the grain of its history

"We need to talk more and think about ways that we can brand ourselves as a manufacturing state, because that's where the long-term, value-added jobs are."

## Misunderstanding leads to questions

## Retailers' Halloween sales are scary high

Celebration sloshing big spot on calendar

**THE TIMES-PICAYUNE,** New Orleans
Tiffany Bennett Leashore, Tony O. Champagne, Kenny Harrison, Kim Quillen
Business page, broadsheet, 175,000+

# Business & Innovation

The Boston Globe Monday, November 27, 2006

## Sold: 1 open-air parking space in the Back Bay

A home for a car may cost a small fortune in Boston

$250,000

$561.07 | $1,736.11

## Software streams music from PCs to cellphones

Product can tap into multiple computers

## Cambridge nonprofit cuts nursing turnover

PAGE 2

Have germs, will travel

Worth the gamble

Skype wirelessly

**THE BOSTON GLOBE**
Vic DeRobertis, David Ryan, Dan Zedek
Business page, broadsheet, 175,000+

SILVER

**LA PRESSE,** Montréal

Philippe Tardif, Stephanie Grammond, Benoit Giguere, Genevieve Dinel, Stephane Lavallee

Business page, broadsheet, 175,000+

The tone of these pages, with their playful illustrations, is very different from other business pages. The alternative storytelling propels this entry to the award. A snakes-and-ladders theme, plus almost invisible chunks of type, help you understand the 35 worst financial actions you can take.

El tono de estas páginas, con sus juguetonas ilustraciones, es muy diferente al de otras páginas de negocios. La narración alternativa hace que esta pieza resulte premiada. Un tema como de juego de escaleras y resbalones, junto a tipografías casi invisibles, ayuda a entender los 35 peores actos financieras que se puede cometer.

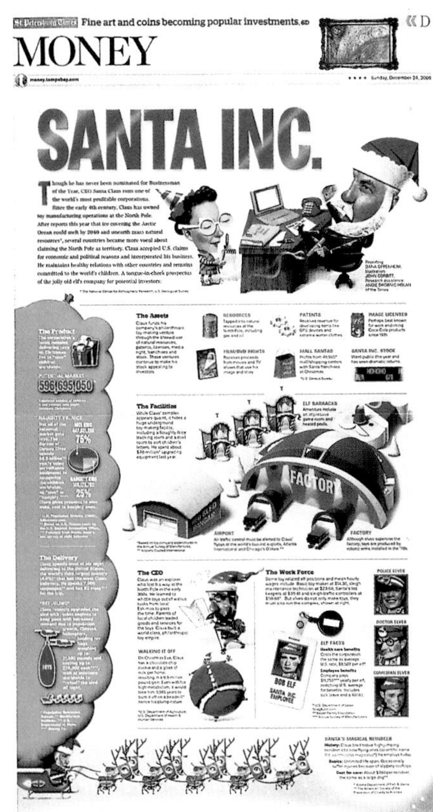

**ST. PETERSBURG TIMES** (Fla.)

John Corbitt, Dana Oppenheim, Jeff Harrington, Angie Drobnic Holan, Terry Chapman

Business page, broadsheet, 175,000+

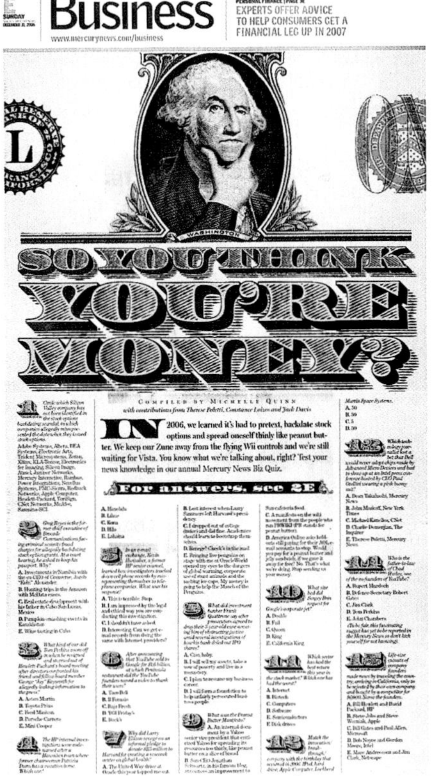

**SAN JOSE MERCURY NEWS** (Calif.)

Emmet Smith, Michael Swartz, Jonathon Berlin, Matt Mansfield

Business page, broadsheet, 175,000+

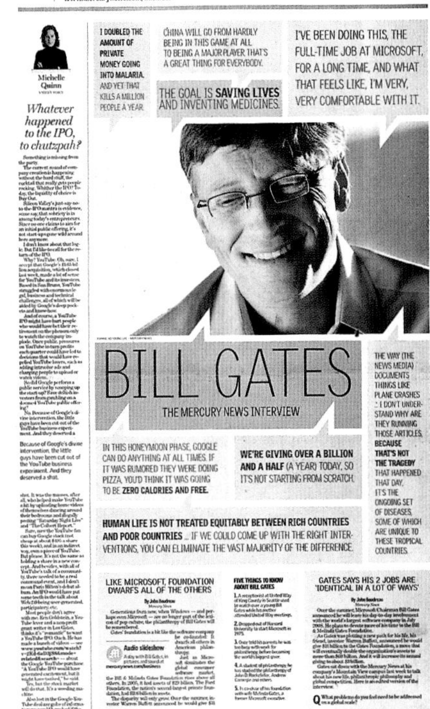

**SAN JOSE MERCURY NEWS** (Calif.)

Emmet Smith, Joanne Ho-Young Lee, Jonathon Berlin, Matt Mansfield

Business page, broadsheet, 175,000+

**THE PLAIN DEALER,** Cleveland
David Kordalski, Andrea Levy, Sharon Yemich, Roger Metzger
Business page, broadsheet, 175,000+

BUSINESS MONDAY

MONEY MATTERS

Bank messed up, but now prove it

Femininitee

Golf can help businesswomen compete in the gender game

MY BIGGEST MISTAKE ...

... AND HOW I FIXED IT

Work with experienced lawyer before opening firm

Local rates for 5-year CDs

INSIDE

**LA PRESSE,** Montréal
Julien Chung, Vincent-Brousseau Pouliot, Benoit Giguere, Genevieve Dinel, Stephane Lavallee
Business page, broadsheet, 175,000+

À VOS AFFAIRES

CONSOMMATION QUAND LES FRAIS BANCAIRES FONT SURSAUTER! PAGE 6

LE GUIDE DU NOUVEAU TRAVAILLEUR

VINCENT BROUSSEAU-POULIOT

LES DÉCISIONS À PRENDRE ET LES GESTES À FAIRE LORSQUE LES PREMIERS CHÈQUES DE PAIE ARRIVENT

LES BONS COMPTES

SOUS LA LOUPE

MICHEL GIRARD

FINANCES PERSONNELLES

LIVRES

**FRANKFURTER ALLGEMEINE SONNTAGSZEITUNG,** Frankfurt am Main, Germany
Peter Breul, Rainer Hank, Andreas Kuther
Business page, broadsheet, 175,000+

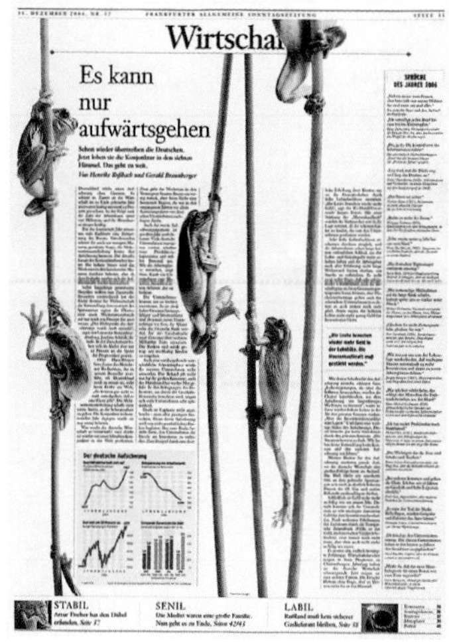
Wirtschaft

Es kann nur aufwärtsgehen

STABIL

SENIL

LABIL

MONEY & BUSINESS

No Kidding: It's Time We *Raised* Gasoline Taxes

PIECES OF THE PAST

**HARTFORD COURANT** (Conn.)
Kristin Lenz, Suzette Moyer, Bruce Moyer
Business page, broadsheet, 175,000+

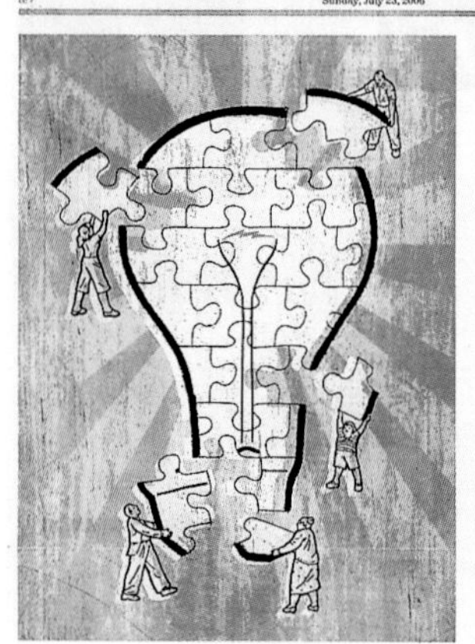
Los Angeles Times

BUSINESS

Latino-Owned Banks Seek to Fill Void in L.A.

Niche markets

Divine Inspiration From the Masses

Open-source programming's organizing principle has been embraced in medical research, engineering — even religion

Unsettling Days for King of Class Actions

INSIDE

**LOS ANGELES TIMES**
Mark Sims, Kelli Sullivan, Michael Whitley, Steven Sedam
Business page, broadsheet, 175,000+

BUSINESS & TECHNOLOGY

Too many strings?

ONLINE FREEBIES

Lightly regulated operators often rely on an array of anything-but-free marketing ploys

FIRST-PERSON ACCOUNT

Sure, it's a big sales pitch. But do you at least get the freebie? Our reporter aims to find out

TECH TRENDS

Dual-lens camera creates big results in small space

THINK YOU'RE THE NEXT QUENTIN TARANTINO?

HELP DESK

Desktop search tool has lame but effective fix

**THE VIRGINIAN-PILOT,** Norfolk
Josh Bohling, Chris Dinsmore, Paul Nelson, Deborah Withey
Business page, broadsheet, 175,000+

Business & Innovation

Spy vs. Spy

Internet adware companies are trying to reform themselves before politicians and angry consumers do it for them

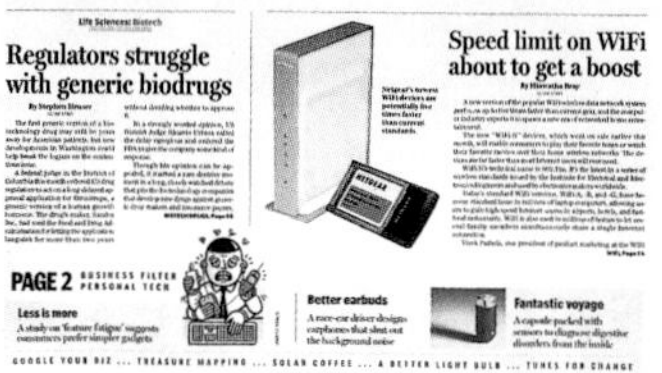
Regulators struggle with generic biodrugs

Speed limit on WiFi about to get a boost

**THE BOSTON GLOBE**
Vic DeRobertis, Dan Zedek
Business page, broadsheet, 175,000+

**THE BOSTON GLOBE**

Vic DeRobertis, Dan Zedek

Business page, broadsheet, 175,000+

C5

# Business
## & Innovation

The Boston Globe Monday, May 29, 2006

## Why Google makes everyone else nervous

Firm's ad-based software is changing the media landscape

By Robert Weisman

*Google is causing disruption. . . . Things that have long been fee-based now have the potential to be free to consumers and supported by ads.*

Life Sciences: Biotech

## Start-ups turning to hedge funds

Shift is challenge to venture capital

By Stephen Heuser

## Cambridge company offers cellphone fix

By Keith Reed

**PAGE 2** BUSINESS FILTER PERSONAL TECH

**Takes two to Roomba**

iRobot envisions its robots as caregiving companions for the elderly

**No sweat shirt**

New 'performance shirt' has clever hideaways for your gadgets

**Teasing the brain**

A Nintendo DS game challenges your mind while you play

BLOG ON, GIRL . . . THE SKINNY ON SMART PHONES . . . RUNNING ITUNES . . . FANTASTIC PLASTIC . . . FOOT POWER

Dodge Challenger should please fans

BUSINESS & MONEY

How one man could change GM's destiny

Health group assists needy

A Renault-Nissan union would give financier authority

**DETROIT FREE PRESS**

Courtney Ruiz, John W. Fleming, Steve Dorsey

Business page, broadsheet, 175,000+

business

Enron CEOs committed no crime, lawyers say

Here comes HELICOPTER BEN

**STAR TRIBUNE,** Minneapolis

Kim Vu, Paul Carbo, Duchesne Drew

Business page, broadsheet, 175,000+

The Seattle Times

# BUSINESS
## »PERSONAL FINANCE«

seattletimes.com/businesstechnology | APRIL 16, 2006 | SUNDAY

WEEK'S CLOSES | Dow 11,137.65 up 17.61, +0.16% | Nasdaq 2,326.11 down 12.91, -0.55% | Seattle Times NW 1,546.66 down 4.28, -0.28% | 10-year Treasury 5.05% yield, +0.07 | Currencies 118.60 yen = $1 1 euro = $1.2113

THE SEATTLE TIMES AND SEATTLE POST-INTELLIGENCER

Researching a Northwest company? Find out more from our annual ranking seattletimes.com/nw100

**In this section >**

**TIMES WATCH:** Trading up with China

**TRACKING YOUR REFUND:** Tax tips

**CHARITY AS BUSINESS:** Philanthropy's role

*NEW TECH COLUMN Brier Dudley's debut ... and what he has to say about Bill Gates > Monday in Business*

## Sirius CEO's goal? Make a profit

PROFILE | Mel Karmazin

*Mel Karmazin is CEO of Sirius Satellite Radio*

SILVER

**THE SEATTLE TIMES**

Boo Davis, Drew DeSilver, Whitney Stensrud

Business page, broadsheet, 175,000+

This unusual style of storytelling is very informative, and it attracts a different audience than the standard business-page reader. Just think of the integration and editing that must have gone into this stylized cartoon.

Esta inusual manera de contar una historia es muy informativa y atrae una lectoría diferente a la de las corrientes páginas de negocios. Basta con imaginar la integración y la edición que se debe haber dedicado a esta estilizada historieta.

**HARTFORD COURANT** (Conn.)
Kristin Lenz, Suzette Moyer, Melanie Shaffer
Business page, broadsheet, 175,000+

BUSINESS

Koreans Snap Up Property In U.S.

Investors Bet Dollar Will Rise, Increasing Value Of Purchases

How A Blogger Used Web Celebrity And Dumb Luck To Fulfill A Quest. It all began by trading ONE RED PAPER CLIP for ...

ONE HOUSE

Casino Making Moves At Top

Responding To Growth, Foxwoods Hires One President, Seeks Another

Cancer Study Enrollment Lagging

Review Of Cases At Pratt Still Lacks Sufficient Participation

INSIDE

House Approves Online Gambling Bill

Microsoft Faces European Penalty

Aetna To Offer New Health Plan

courant.com

**HARTFORD COURANT** (Conn.)
Kristin Lenz, Suzette Moyer, Melanie Shaffer, Dan Haar, Ritu Kalra
Business page, broadsheet, 175,000+

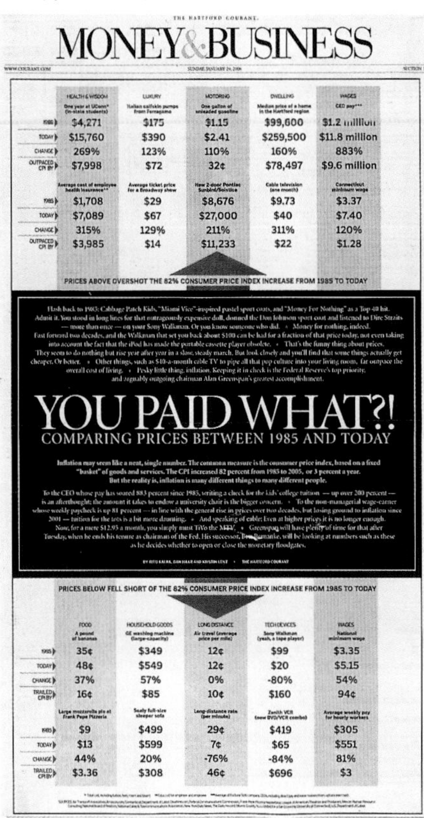

THE HARTFORD COURANT

MONEY & BUSINESS

| | HEALTH & WISDOM | LUXURY | MOTORING | DWELLING | WAGES |
|---|---|---|---|---|---|
| 1985 | $4,271 | $175 | $1.15 | $99,600 | $1.2 million |
| TODAY | $15,760 | $390 | $2.41 | $259,500 | $11.8 million |
| CHANGE | 269% | 123% | 110% | 160% | 883% |
| OUTPACED CPI BY | $7,998 | $72 | 32¢ | $78,497 | $9.6 million |
| 1985 | $1,708 | $29 | $8,676 | $9.73 | $3.37 |
| TODAY | $7,089 | $67 | $27,000 | $40 | $7.40 |
| CHANGE | 315% | 129% | 211% | 311% | 120% |
| OUTPACED CPI BY | $3,985 | $14 | $11,233 | $22 | $1.28 |

PRICES ABOVE OVERSHOT THE 62% CONSUMER PRICE INDEX INCREASE FROM 1985 TO TODAY

YOU PAID WHAT?!

COMPARING PRICES BETWEEN 1985 AND TODAY

PRICES BELOW FELL SHORT OF THE 62% CONSUMER PRICE INDEX INCREASE FROM 1985 TO TODAY

| | FOOD | HOUSEHOLD GOODS | LONG DISTANCE | TECHNOLOGY | WAGES |
|---|---|---|---|---|---|
| 1985 | 35¢ | $349 | 12¢ | $99 | $3.35 |
| TODAY | 48¢ | $549 | 12¢ | $20 | $5.15 |
| CHANGE | 37% | 57% | 0% | -80% | 54% |
| TRAILED CPI BY | 16¢ | $85 | 10¢ | $160 | 94¢ |
| 1985 | $9 | $499 | 29¢ | $419 | $305 |
| TODAY | $13 | $599 | 7¢ | $65 | $551 |
| CHANGE | 44% | 20% | -76% | -84% | 81% |
| TRAILED CPI BY | $3.36 | $308 | 46¢ | $696 | $3 |

**THE SEATTLE TIMES**
Michele Lee McMullen, Denise Clifton, Whitney Stensrud
Business page, broadsheet, 175,000+

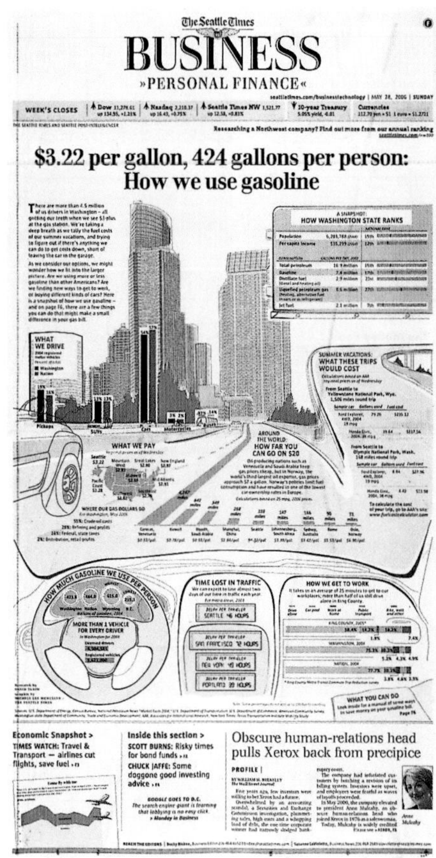

The Seattle Times

BUSINESS

»PERSONAL FINANCE«

$3.22 per gallon, 424 gallons per person: How we use gasoline

HOW WASHINGTON STATE RANKS

WHAT WE DRIVE

WHAT WE PAY

SUMMER VACATIONS: WHAT THESE TRIPS WOULD COST

HOW MUCH GASOLINE WE USE PER PERSON

TIME LOST IN TRAFFIC

HOW WE GET TO WORK

Economic Snapshot

Inside this section

Obscure human-relations head pulls Xerox back from precipice

**SAN JOSE MERCURY NEWS** (Calif.)
Daymond Gascon, Jonathon Berlin, Matt Mansfield
Business page, broadsheet, 175,000+

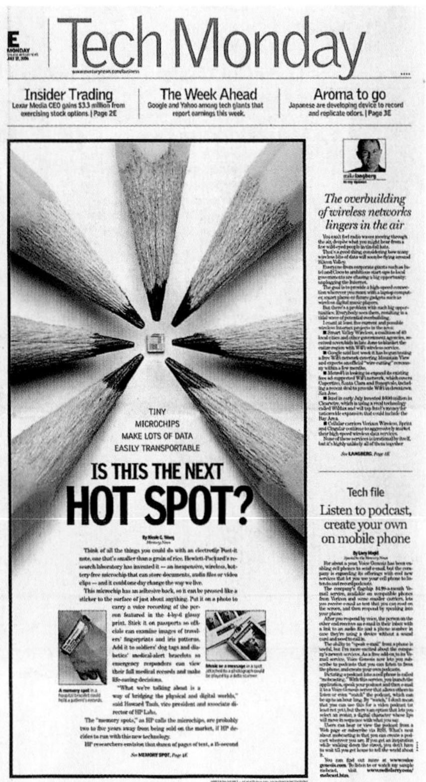

E | Tech Monday

Insider Trading

The Week Ahead

Aroma to go

The overbuilding of wireless networks lingers in the air

TINY MICROCHIPS MAKE LOTS OF DATA EASILY TRANSPORTABLE

IS THIS THE NEXT HOT SPOT?

Tech file

Listen to podcast, create your own on mobile phone

**ORLANDO SENTINEL** (Fla.)
Janel Jacobs, Lisa Frasier, Bonita Burton
Business page, broadsheet, 175,000+

YOUR MONEY

SUNDAY FEBRUARY 26, 2006

YOUR COST OF LIVING: PAYING THE PRICE FOR PETS

$519

That's what the average household that includes pets spent last year on food, health care, and other things for those animal occupants. Since 1994, Americans' spending on pets has more than doubled. The biggest category? Veterinary care, followed by food.

THIS WEEK

TYING THE FINANCIAL KNOT

How you mingle your money after marriage can lead to a lifetime of wedded bliss or a day in divorce court. You decide.

CLIPPER FUND DIRECTORS TAKE A STAND

**THE PLAIN DEALER,** Cleveland
David Kordalski, Andrea Levy, Sharon Yemich, John Kroll
Business page, broadsheet, 175,000+

BUSINESS

Watch your step

You may not see it, but you're leaving a carbon footprint on the planet

New York blocks Ohio driver's license

Custom cards

**THE PLAIN DEALER,** Cleveland

David Kordalski, Andrea Levy, Sharon Yemich

Business page, broadsheet, 175,000+

BUSINESS

SUNDAY, DECEMBER 24, 2006 | SECTION G

THE PLAIN DEALER

Perfect pitch

Success with selling means being bright, aggressive, lucky ... and just a bit more

About the series

PLAIN DEALING

My holiday gift to you: A list of Ohio politicians who sold you out

**SAN JOSE MERCURY NEWS** (Calif.)

Michael Tribble, Rob Hernandez, Jonathon Berlin, Matt Mansfield

Business page, broadsheet, 175,000+

Business

www.mercurynews.com/business

KNOWING WHAT TO BUY WHEN CAN SAVE YOU A TIDY SUM

MOVING TOWARD AN IDEA ECONOMY

Google going after Microsoft and Apple

CATCHING UP WITH MICHAEL ARRINGTON

Web 2.0: 'a read and write mechanism'

Silicon Valley stops the loss of jobs

SILICON VALLEY JOBS

HIGH SCHOOL GRADUATION

VENTURE CAPITAL DOLLARS

PATENTS

**THE VIRGINIAN-PILOT,** Norfolk

Lori Kelley, Bill Choyke, Paul Nelson, Deborah Withey

Business page, broadsheet, 175,000+

BUSINESS & FINANCE

UP 56.1%

THE SLIDE OF THE F-SERIES

For a line of trucks that just 4½ months ago was touted for its unassailable strength, Ford's big-truck series has had a bumpy ride. The trucks include the F-150, still rolling off the assembly line in Norfolk – for now.

WHERE DID THE CUSTOMERS GO?

WHY DID FORD PULL BACK ON THE F-SERIES?

DOWN 45.6%

PERSONAL FINANCE

After its tacky tips for job loss, Northwest needs guide on tact

You've got data. Now, researchers wonder whether they should open it.

Clean-air police state

The new Tory bill goes too far. Terence Corcoran, FP15

FINANCIAL POST

NATIONAL POST, SATURDAY, OCTOBER 21, 2006

Ports around the world anxiously await results of Panama vote. FP4

SHIPPING NEWS

Tim's world

Ron Joyce on his inside story of the Canadian coffee empire. FP3

MEDIA

MOTION PICTURE SUITOR STILL KEEN

The mortgage bite

Want the detached house and the picket fence but can't make the payments? There are new mortgages that can help ... if you ignore the downside for 40 years

Move to RBC Direct Investing and we'll invest in you.

**NATIONAL POST,** Toronto

Doug Kelly, Gayle Grin, Charles Lewis, Ian Karleff, Ron Wadden

Business page, broadsheet, 175,000+

Toronto Expo madness

Will Ottawa back boondoggle? Terence Corcoran, FP15

FINANCIAL POST

NATIONAL POST, SATURDAY, OCTOBER 28, 2006

Glittering Tribune media empire prize in high-profile corporate battle in U.S. FP5

'TRIB' TROPHY

Golden deal

Ivanhoe's Friedland on Rio Tinto backing. Diane Francis, FP2

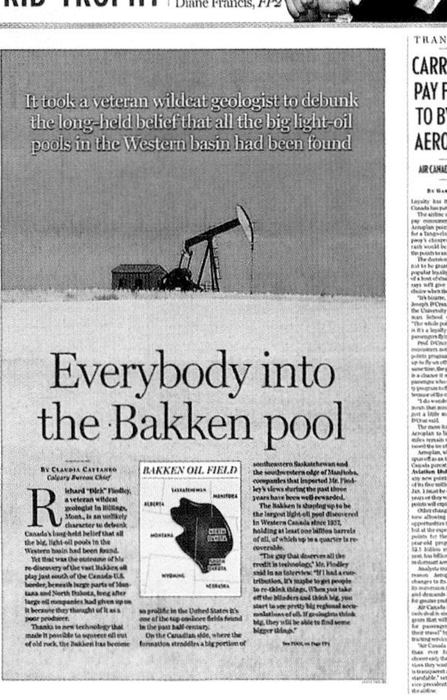

It took a veteran wildcat geologist to debunk the long-held belief that all the big light-oil pools in the Western basin had been found

Everybody into the Bakken pool

BAKKEN OIL FIELD

TRANSPORT

CARRIER TO PAY FLYERS TO BYPASS AEROPLAN

**NATIONAL POST,** Toronto

Doug Kelly, Gayle Grin, Charles Lewis, Ian Karleff, Ron Wadden

Business page, broadsheet, 175,000+

Rona Brockovich?

Ambrose buys into claims of 'toxic nation' report. FP19

FINANCIAL POST

NATIONAL POST, SATURDAY, JUNE 3, 2006

Is Beaudoin justified in blaming rising loonie for Bombardier's woes? FP2

DOSSIER

On a roll

WestJet apology latest in string of wins for ACE's Milton. FP3

WORLD CUP '06: THE BEAUTIFUL BUSINESS

The Cup runneth over

The most popular sporting event on the planet, soccer's crown jewel is a 'really impressive example of successful globalization of the First and Third World'

**NATIONAL POST,** Toronto

Doug Kelly, Gayle Grin, Charles Lewis, Ian Karleff, Ron Wadden

Business page, broadsheet, 175,000+

**LA GACETA,** San Miguel de Tucuman, Argentina
Ruben Falci, Sergio Fernandez
Business page, broadsheet, 50,000-174,999

LA GACETA

ECONOMIA

1,5
MILLON de habitantes de los 35 aglomerados urbanos del país están sin empleo. La tasa es del 10,4% y sigue en descenso.

En Tucumán, el Estado y la actividad comercial concentran el 55% de la fuerza laboral, compuesta por algo más de 275.000 trabajadores. Es en estos sectores donde se genera la mayoría de los nuevos puestos de trabajo, aunque no todos son de calidad. Rigidez en la normativa laboral argentina, la presión fiscal y lo oneroso y burocrático que significa crear un nuevo puesto de trabajo, son algunos de los factores que economistas, empresarios y sindicalistas consultados por LA GACETA consideran que atentan contra la generación de empleos registrados. Se pierde una oportunidad

275.453
trabajadores conforman la fuerza laboral de Tucumán. De ese total, un 50,9% se desempeña en la informalidad.

37.000
personas que viven en el Gran San Miguel de Tucumán están desocupadas. Es el 11,7% de la población económicamente activa.

EL SISTEMA
DESALIENTA
LA GENERACION DE EMPLEO DE CALIDAD

PAGINAS 2 y 3

**SAN JOSE MERCURY NEWS** (Calif.)
Michael Swartz
Business page, broadsheet, 175,000+

E
MONDAY
Tech Monday

Insider trading
The week ahead
'Tetris' grows up

HOW MANY WAYS DO MY PORES BETRAY ME?
LET THIS MACHINE COUNT THE DIPS AND BUMPS

POWER SCANNER
SHINES LIGHT ON
IMPERFECTIONS

Same-day gratification for online shoppers

*Buying a PC is hard, even more complicated for Vista*

**SAN JOSE MERCURY NEWS** (Calif.)
Jonathon Berlin, Matt Mansfield
Business page, broadsheet, 175,000+

GUIDE TO BUYING A HOME

WHAT CAN
YOU AFFORD?

$660,000
2,930
37

HERE'S HOW TO FIND OUT
Meet lender face to face and get 'pre-approved'

AND WHAT TO THINK ABOUT
Strategy helps buyers' navigate market

MORE INSIDE
BUYING, SELLING WITH LOW STRESS
MANAGING MONEY WHILE BUYING
LOAN APPLICATION DOS AND DON'TS
AUDIO: SUE MCCALLISTER ON THE CHANGING MARKET

Business
& Innovation
The Boston Globe Monday, May 22, 2006

Kits let kids add science, engineering, math to art explorations

YOUR AD HERE
YOUR AD HERE
YOUR AD HERE
ADVERTISERS ARE FINDING CREATIVE NEW WAYS TO REACH CONSUMERS ONLINE
YOUR AD HERE [BLOGS]
YOUR AD HERE [THE WEB]

Long-term care nurses enlisting BlackBerrys in fight for referrals

PAGE 2
In translation
Espresso & Poo
Solar power

**THE BOSTON GLOBE**
Dan Zedek
Business page, broadsheet, 175,000+

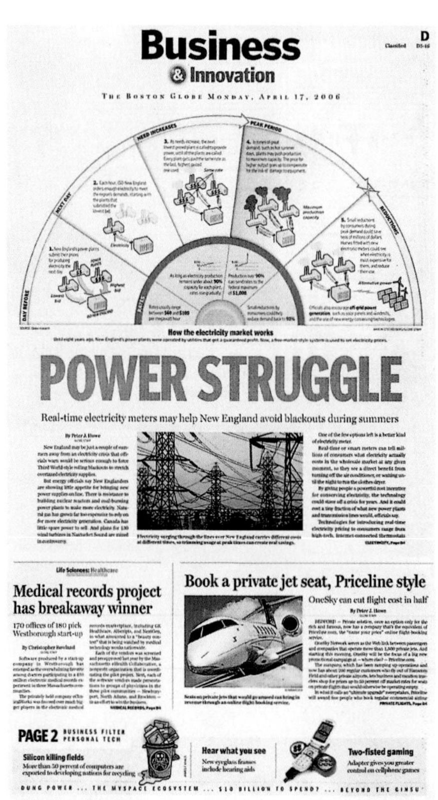
Business
& Innovation
The Boston Globe Monday, April 17, 2006

How the electricity market works

POWER STRUGGLE
Real-time electricity meters may help New England avoid blackouts during summers

Medical records project has breakaway winner

Book a private jet seat, Priceline style

PAGE 2
Silicon killing fields
Hear what you see
Two-fisted gaming

**THE BOSTON GLOBE**
Vic DeRobertis, Dan Zedek
Business page, broadsheet, 175,000+

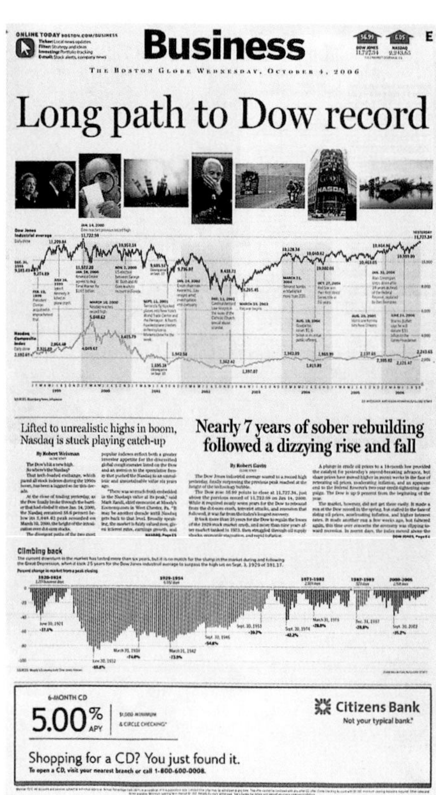
Business
The Boston Globe Wednesday, October 4, 2006

Long path to Dow record

Lifted to unrealistic highs in boom, Nasdaq is stuck playing catch-up

Nearly 7 years of sober rebuilding followed a dizzying rise and fall

Climbing back

5.00% APY
Citizens Bank
Not your typical bank.
Shopping for a CD? You just found it.

**THE BOSTON GLOBE**
Anthony Schultz
Business page, broadsheet, 175,000+

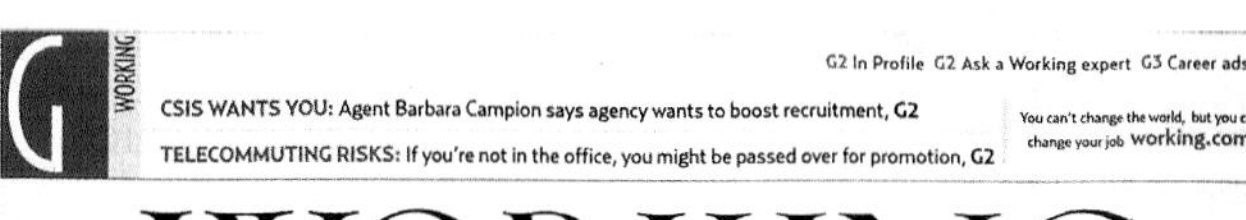


# WORKING

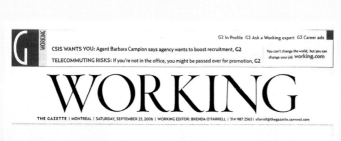

THE GAZETTE | MONTREAL | SATURDAY, SEPTEMBER 23, 2006 | WORKING EDITOR: BRENDA O'FARRELL | 514 987 2563 | ofarrell@thegazette.canwest.com

A co-worker gets a cushy assignment. Or, lands a lucrative promotion. You feel jealous.
Perhaps, you're envious. It's not uncommon in the workplace. In fact,
research shows the hardest-working people are more
prone to these nasty feelings

# WHEN GREEN EYES ARE CONNIVING

DONNA NEBENZAHL THE GAZETTE

It's the green-eyed monster, no less insidious and disheartening in our work life than it is in our social life. Let's face it, we spend half our waking days at work. So when jealousy and envy strike, the workplace is a terrible place to come under its spell.

And do we ever.

According to research cited by University of Notre Dame management professor Robert P. Vecchio, who specializes in studying envy in the workplace, 77 per cent of employees surveyed have witnessed jealousy around the office within the past month. To make matters worse, more than half admitted to being directly involved.

"It's pretty commonly reported," Vecchio said. "Often times, it's about who gets the cushiest or most desirable assignments, who gets promotions.

"The problem is that people feel it's inappropriate or childish to carry these feelings around."

So instead of talking about it or looking for ways to cope with it, Vecchio said, they withhold efforts. Recent research on loafing in groups, he says, shows those who felt more envy were doing more loafing.

"They're evening up the score by withholding their contribution," he said.

At the very least, those who feel envy or jealousy will monitor others' behaviour to conform to what they're feeling.

And because there is such a lack of sensitivity about how people feel – a taboo subject in the workplace – there is also a lack of awareness about the impact of jealousy and envy.

It can't be ignored, said Vecchio, whose research shows that people who feel envious and resentful express stronger interest in looking for alternative employment.

So where do these feelings come from?

In his survey of more than 100 first-level supervisors, Vecchio found that lack of consideration from a supervisor fuelled more jealousy and envy among subordinates than did bosses who were perceived as nurturing.

And while a strong work ethic is a great asset in the workplace, there is a downside as far as the green-eyed monster is concerned. Turns out that people with this attitude about work are also prone to be more envious and jealous in the workplace. In fact, they generally react more emotionally to a variety of office situations.

"These are people who worry more about work. They're more sensitive to it," he said. "The other group is the low self-esteemers and the people who think work is very competitive, where people are pitted against each other."

Women, it seems are more jealous than men, while males express more workplace envy. Vecchio suspects this is because men are more attuned to threats to competitive standing, while women seem to care more about threats to social relationships.

"Jealousy is actually like a three-way system, in which you have the focal person, then you have the rival. In this case, the rival is working toward gaining advantage in a relationship with a third party. For instance, a new person who is getting a lot of attention from the boss.

"Envy is only two-party," he said, and it's based on competitiveness, as in "how do I stand against this person?"

These nasty feelings arise less frequently in large offices than in small, he said, possibly because people are not as possessive in larger groups and because those who work in a big organization are more likely to shrug off inequities as an element of inefficient bureaucracy.

In most cases, envy and jealousy are about the fear of losing social standing.

"Your sense of value is being threatened by the data you're getting," Vecchio said. "I've found that people with high self-esteem report fewer problems."

So can it be fixed?

One obvious way is to bolster your self-esteem, by modifying your thoughts to focus on the good things in your life, Vecchio said.

And managers, who hold so much power in this area, can work to create more of a team culture, one in which people work co-operatively.

"You could argue that the management of envy underlies a lot of work in management today," he said. "But no one wants to talk about the management of emotion.

"In reality, there are a lot of emotions and feelings out there."

So in an workplace setting, managers can create shared purpose through teams and engage in a lot more sharing and decision-making.

"Explain decisions, get input," he said. "Don't let people speculate resentfully. If something comes up, say you need to make a tough decision, and put possible feelings on the table."

"Let's all unite around that decision we need to make."

dnebenzahl@thegazette.canwest.com

## We all experience envy. But how envious are you?

**Are you an envious person?**

It's clear that we all envy to a varying degree. Question is, how do you know if you're feeling envy?

The following questions, designed by organizational analyst J. Gerald Suarez, will help you to conduct a self-assessment and reflect about the possible presence and intensity of your envy.

1. Do you feel discomfort because of another person's promotion?
2. Do you find yourself constantly thinking about what you lack?
3. Do you resent people who do not come to you for help and advice?
4. Do you find that you want to put down people who are more succesful than you are?
5. Do you hide or try to ignore your envious feelings from yourself?

**Do you encourage envy?**

Suarez points out that many managers are often unaware of the effects of their actions in creating an atmosphere that fosters envy. As a manager, he asks:

1. Do you favour some employees over others?
2. Do you stereotype employees?
3. Do you pretend all employees are the same?
4. Do you make verbal comparisons?
5. Do you not pay attention to current employees when a new employee is hired?

If the answers to these questions are yes, it's time to take stock and rethink your behaviour.

SILVER

**THE GAZETTE,** Montreal

Susan Ferguson, Nuri Ducassi, Brenda O'Farrell

Business page, broadsheet, 50,000-174,999

This story about envy in the workplace helps transform typical business content. This could have been a really boring picture. Instead it is a striking image that appeals to all kinds of readers.

Este artículo sobre la envidia en la oficina ayuda a transformar el típico contenido sobre negocios. Podría haber sido una foto muy aburrida, pero en cambio es una imagen impactante que llama la atención de todo tipo de lectores.

WORKING

Raising the raise issue

JEAN TREMBLAY
SENIOR ACCOUNTS MANAGER

BUSINESS CARDS

KEEPING THEM SIMPLE CAN SAY A LOT ABOUT THE PERSON OR COMPANY

**THE GAZETTE,** Montreal

Susan Ferguson, Nuri Ducassi, Brenda O'Farrell

Business page, broadsheet, 50,000-174,999

DINERO

EL MERCADO ARCOIRIS

Por su poder de compra la comunidad homosexual es una de las más deseadas por las empresas. >06

Ponen *la lana* para carreteras

El DF, entre los peores en calidad de vida

HOY EN LAS COLUMNAS

**EXCELSIOR,** México City

Ricardo Peña, Alejandro Rodríguez, Mildred Ramo, Héctor Rendón, Luzma Díaz de León Reyes, Marco A. Román, Alexandro Medrano, Gerardo Galarza, Pascal Beltrán del Río, Ernesto Rivera

Business page, broadsheet, 50,000-174,999

[FINANZAS PERSONALES]

EL CO$TO DE LA SEPARACIÓN

En el DIF los trámites son gratuitos

100 MIL 25 MIL 10 MIL

**EL UNIVERSAL,** México City

Roberto Rock L., Francisco Santiago, Oscar Santiago Méndez, Rubén Álvarez, Roberto Aguilar, Romina Román, Francisco Vega, Beatriz García, Luis Miguel Cruz Ceballos, Rodolfo Hernández

Business page, broadsheet, 50,000-174,999

**EXCELSIOR,** México City

Ricardo Peña, Cristina Medrano, Mildred Ramo, Héctor Rendón, Luzma Díaz de León Reyes, Marco A. Román, Alexandro Medrano, Gerardo Galarza, Pascal Beltrán del Río, Ernesto Rivera

Business page, broadsheet, 50,000-174,999

EXCELSIOR

DINERO

Los lucrativos 80

EN MÉXICO, COMO EN EL RESTO DEL MUNDO, LOS ADULTOS DE MAYOR PODER ADQUISITIVO QUIEREN RECORDAR SU ADOLESCENCIA: SON UN SEGMENTO RENTABLE >06

RESULTAN ELEVADAS

Se aprovechan bancos del mercado: Ortiz

MIRILLA

AEROPUERTOS

ENERGÍA

MAIZ

BRONCAS EN EL AIRE

EL RUBRO DE COSTOS Y PAGOS SUELE SER UN TEMA DE TENSIÓN ENTRE LAS AEROLÍNEAS Y TERMINALES AÉREAS. SEGUNDA Y ÚLTIMA PARTE DE LA MESA DE ANÁLISIS >08

Evalúa el mercado de las Afores

INDUSTRIALES

Vienen seis años maravillosos: Fox

OPINIÓN

**EXCELSIOR,** México City

Ricardo Peña, Cristina Medrano, Mildred Ramo, Héctor Rendón, Luzma Díaz de León Reyes, Marco A. Román, Alexandro Medrano, Gerardo Galarza, Pascal Beltrán del Río, Ernesto Rivera

Business page, broadsheet, 50,000-174,999

EXCELSIOR

DINERO

¿Y CUÁNTO SE EVADE?

EN LAS VÍSCERAS DEL DRAGÓN

Aunque su economía ha crecido a una tasa promedio de 9%, no ha sido suficiente para eliminar su alto índice de pobreza e ilegalidad >6 y 7

CONTROVERSIA PRESUPUESTAL

Economía nacional, blindada: Carstens

PRESUPUESTO EN LINTANTÁNEAS

MIRILLA

PYMES

CEPAL

SALAROS

DE MILLONARIO A PRESIDIARIO

MIKHAIL KHODORKOVSKY, EX DIRECTOR GENERAL DE YUKOS

HOY EN LAS COLUMNAS

**ARIZONA DAILY STAR,** Tucson

Mark Brunton, Mike Rice, Staff

Business page, broadsheet, 50,000-174,999

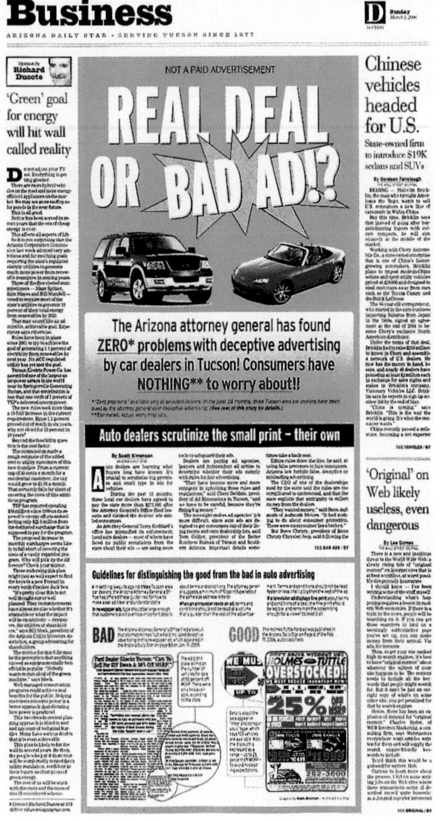

Business

ARIZONA DAILY STAR

'Green' goal for energy will hit wall called reality

NOT A PAID ADVERTISEMENT

REAL DEAL OR BAD AD!?

The Arizona attorney general has found ZERO* problems with deceptive advertising by car dealers in Tucson! Consumers have NOTHING** to worry about!!

Auto dealers scrutinize the small print – their own

Chinese vehicles headed for U.S.

'Original' on Web likely useless, even dangerous

Guidelines for distinguishing the good from the bad in auto advertising

BAD

GOOD

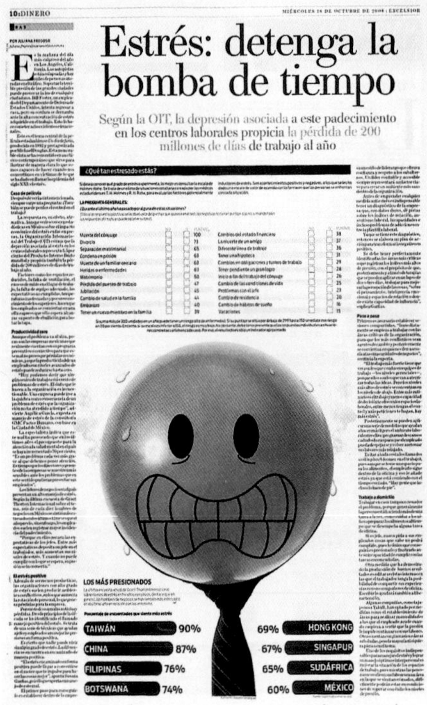

10 DINERO

Estrés: detenga la bomba de tiempo

Según la OIT, la depresión asociada a este padecimiento en los centros laborales propicia la pérdida de 200 millones de días de trabajo al año

¿Qué tan estresado estás?

LOS MÁS PRESIONADOS

| | |
|---|---|
| TAIWÁN | 90% |
| CHINA | 87% |
| FILIPINAS | 76% |
| BOTSWANA | 74% |
| HONG KONG | 69% |
| SINGAPUR | 67% |
| SUDÁFRICA | 65% |
| MÉXICO | 60% |

**EXCELSIOR,** México City

Adriana Carrillo, Alejandro Rodríguez, Ricardo Peña, Victor Torres, Luzma Díaz de León Reyes, Marco A. Román, Alexandro Medrano, Gerardo Galarza, Pascal Beltrán del Río, Ernesto Rivera

Business page, broadsheet, 50,000-174,999

10 DINERO

El blindaje como prestación laboral

EL CASO JOSÉ CUERVO

Meseros con formación universitaria

Antes, la membresía a clubes deportivos era un buen estímulo para los altos ejecutivos de empresa. Hoy prefieren la seguridad personal

UN PAÍS BLINDADO

25 A 75%

ENTRE 24MIL Y 100MIL

**EXCELSIOR,** México City

Adriana Carrillo, Alejandro Rodríguez, Ricardo Peña, Victor Torres, Luzma Díaz de León Reyes, Marco A. Román, Alexandro Medrano, Gerardo Galarza, Pascal Beltrán del Río, Ernesto Rivera

Business page, broadsheet, 50,000-174,999

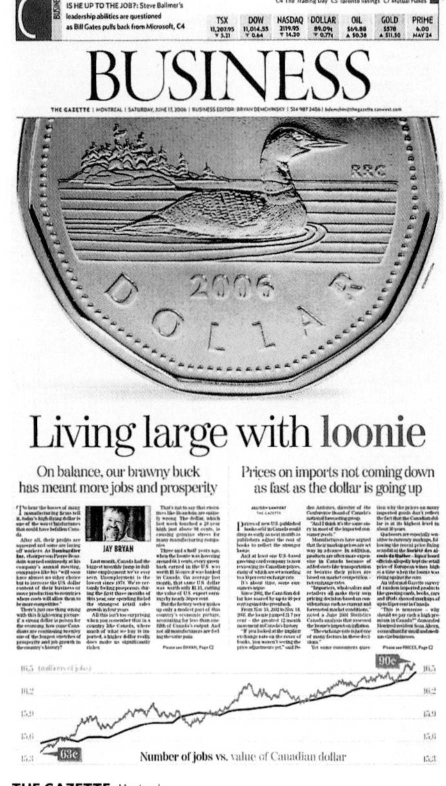

IS HE UP TO THE JOB?: Steve Ballmer's leadership abilities are questioned as Bill Gates pulls back from Microsoft, C4

BUSINESS

THE GAZETTE | MONTREAL

Living large with loonie

On balance, our brawny buck has meant more jobs and prosperity

Prices on imports not coming down as fast as the dollar is going up

JAY BRYAN

Number of jobs vs. value of Canadian dollar

**THE GAZETTE,** Montreal

Susan Ferguson, Nuri Ducassi, Bryan Demchinsky

Business page, broadsheet, 50,000-174,999

**THE ORANGE COUNTY REGISTER,** Santa Ana, Calif.
Kyle Sackowski, Karen Kelso, Neil C. Pinchin, Brenda Shoun
Business page, tabloid, 175,000+

THE ORANGE COUNTY REGISTER
BUSINESS MONDAY
BUSINESSWOMEN WORK TO DISTINGUISH THEIR FIRMS FROM THE CROWD. **PAGE 10**

in good company

IT'S YOUR BUSINESS / 3 · WORK & LIFE / 8 · CAREER CHAT / 13

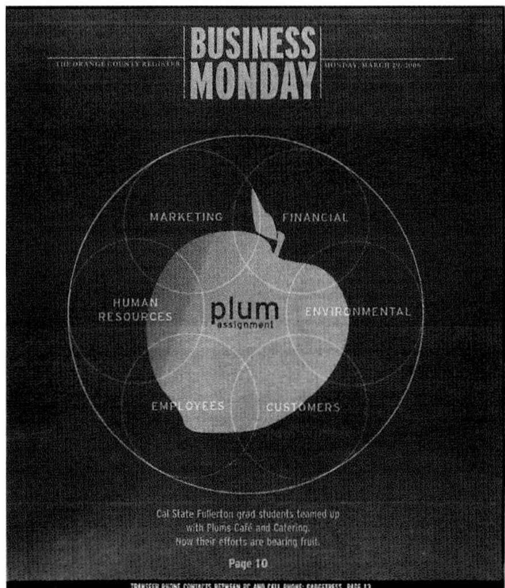
THE ORANGE COUNTY REGISTER
BUSINESS MONDAY
MONDAY, MARCH 20, 2006



Cal State Fullerton grad students teamed up with Plums Café and Catering. Now their efforts are bearing fruit.
Page 10

**THE ORANGE COUNTY REGISTER,** Santa Ana, Calif.
Kyle Sackowski, Karen Kelso, Neil C. Pinchin, Brenda Shoun
Business page, tabloid, 175,000+

THE ORANGE COUNTY REGISTER
BUSINESS MONDAY
MONDAY, MARCH 27, 2006

Doctor moms
Pediatric office lets its staff of mostly mothers work family-friendly hours.
Page 8

IT'S YOUR BUSINESS | 3 — TIPS FOR THOSE WHO OPERATE MORE THAN ONE COMPANY.
WORK & LIFE | 6 — MEET OUR NEW COLUMNIST, MICHELE HIMMELBERG.
CAREER CHAT | 11 — MY SON'S TRYING TO CHOOSE A MAJOR. CAN YOU HELP?

**THE ORANGE COUNTY REGISTER,** Santa Ana, Calif.
Kyle Sackowski, Karen Kelso, Neil C. Pinchin, Brenda Shoun
Business page, tabloid, 175,000+

**EXCELSIOR,** México City
Oscar Hernández, Ricardo Peña, Ángeles Barajas, Mildred Ramo, Luzma Díaz de León Reyes, Marco A. Román, Alexandro Medrano, Gerardo Galarza, Pascal Beltrán del Río, Ernesto Rivera
Business page, broadsheet, 50,000-174,999

DINERO

APUESTAN POR EL RIESGO
LOS ACAUDALADOS DEL MUNDO ESTÁN DISPUESTOS A INVERTIR EN PROYECTOS NOVEDOSOS Y CON ALTAS PROBABILIDADES DE ÉXITO

HACKER

LUCENT CONVERGE
LA EMPRESA BUSCA EN MÉXICO A LAS CABLERAS PARA OFRECER SUS SERVICIOS, EN UN CONTEXTO DE ALIANZAS QUE LA INDUSTRIA HA EMPRENDIDO PARA JUGAR EL PARTIDO DE LAS TRES BANDAS DE NEGOCIO >11

COMPETENCIA ECONÓMICA
Monopolios afectan el desarrollo: Ortiz

MIRILLA
OPINIÓN

**EXCELSIOR,** México City
Adriana Carrillo, Alejandro Rodríguez, Ricardo Peña, Victor Torres, Luzma Díaz de León Reyes, Marco A. Román, Alexandro Medrano, Gerardo Galarza, Pascal Beltrán del Río, Ernesto Rivera
Business page, broadsheet, 50,000-174,999

2007, el año del alto potencial
Conozca las nuevas tendencias de desarrollo y capacitación para empleados

Con la juventud en contra

LOS MODELOS DE LA PRÓXIMA TEMPORADA
Rutas · Coaching · E-learning · Internet

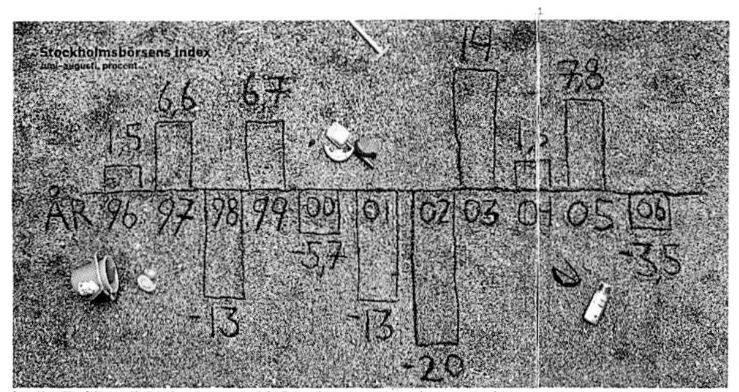


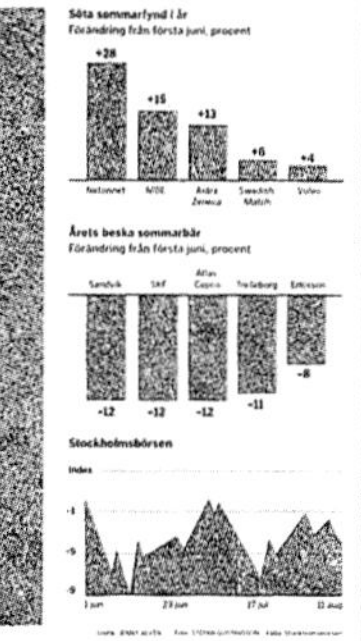
Sålda sommarfynd i år
Årets bästa sommarbör
Stockholmsbörsen

INTERVJUN
Affischerna har bara text, varför?

Kylig börs trots het sommar

631 · Explosion i vapenexporten · Terrorhotet gör saken bara ännu mer orovackande. · 39 · Vi ska snickra på torpet · Attraktion vid kusten

4 N | SÖNDAG · SÖNDAG | N 5

**SVENSKA DAGBLADET,** Stockholm, Sweden
Jenney Alvén, Jan Almgren
Business page, tabloid, 175,000+

REPORTAGEM

# O dinheiro está no ar

Os novos parques eólicos da EDP vão produzir electricidade para 1/4 dos portugueses

"40% dos investimentos são nas renováveis"

Moura líder mundial na fotovoltaica

P&R

**EXPRESSO,** Lisbon, Portugal
Marco Grieco, Pedro Figueiral, Luís Miguel Ribeiro, Jaime Figueiredo
Business page, tabloid, 50,000-174,999

**THE ORANGE COUNTY REGISTER,** Santa Ana, Calif.
Kyle Sackowski, Karen Kelso, Neil C. Pinchin, Brenda Shoun
Business page, tabloid, 175,000+

THE ORANGE COUNTY REGISTER
BUSINESS MONDAY
SPHERE OF INFLUENCE
Entrepreneur's vision drives her success with her company and with her family. Page 8

IT'S YOUR BUSINESS | 3 BIG IDEA, BIG BOWS, BIG BUSINESS.
WORK & LIFE | 6 THE BENEFITS AND DRAWBACKS OF UNCONVENTIONAL SCHEDULES.
ASK MICHELE | 11 WHY SAFETY ON THE JOB IS IMPORTANT.

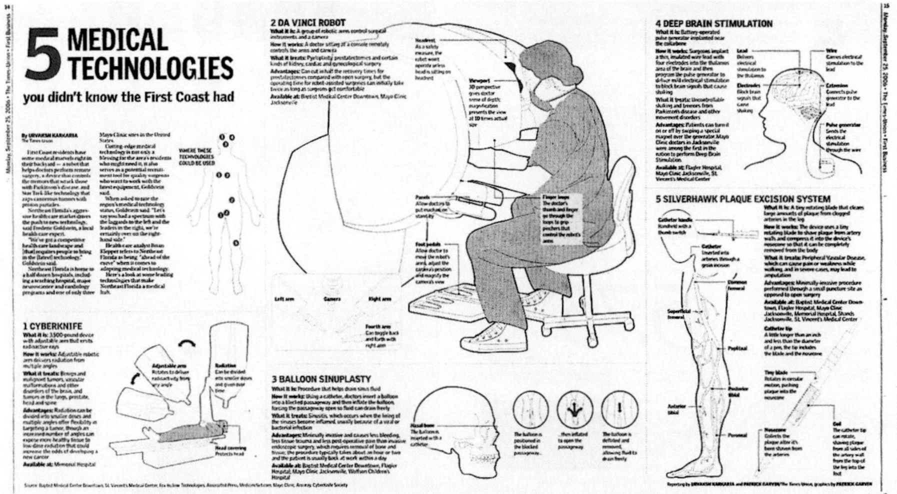
5 MEDICAL TECHNOLOGIES
you didn't know the First Coast had
1 CYBERKNIFE
2 DA VINCI ROBOT
3 BALLOON SINUPLASTY
4 DEEP BRAIN STIMULATION
5 SILVERHAWK PLAQUE EXCISION SYSTEM

**THE FLORIDA TIMES-UNION,** Jacksonville
Patrick Garvin, Denise M. Reagan, Steve Nelson, Jennifer Merritt, Paul Mattson, Urvaksh Karkaria, Robert Davis
Business page, tabloid, 50,000-174,999

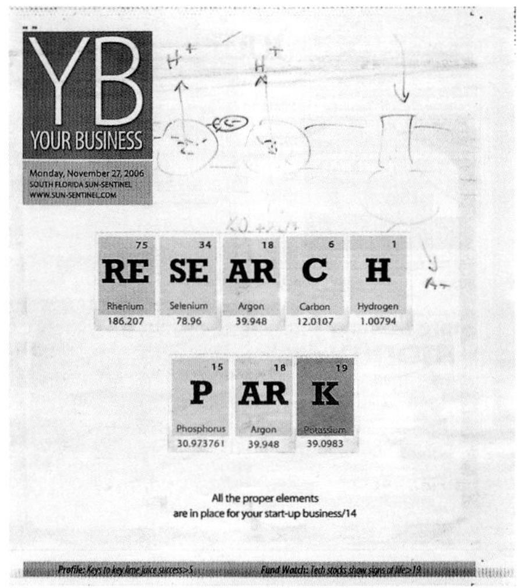
YB
YOUR BUSINESS
Monday, November 27, 2006
SOUTH FLORIDA SUN-SENTINEL
WWW.SUN-SENTINEL.COM

All the proper elements are in place for your start-up business/14

**SOUTH FLORIDA SUN-SENTINEL,** Fort Lauderdale
Kristian Rodriguez, Chris Mihal, Tim Frank
Business page, tabloid, 175,000+

EMPRESAS OPA SONAE / PT
# E agora?
O Governo é o próximo interveniente a convencer
Paulo Azevedo presidente da Sonaecom
"Estes não são os meus remédios"
ACCIONISTAS DA PT DIZEM QUE OPA DIMINUI CONCORRÊNCIA
O DESEJO DE CONQUISTAR A PT MUDOU O DISCURSO DA SONAE

**EXPRESSO,** Lisbon, Portugal
Marco Grieco, Pedro Figueiral, João Paulo Galacho, Alberto Frias
Business page, tabloid, 50,000-174,999

Real Estate
www.mercurynews.com/realestate
SQUARE FEET BLOG
# Gay Golden Years
Retirement homes cater to gays who want to stay out of the closet | Page 8
BIGGEST SALES | FANTASY HOME | REAL ESTATE CLASSIFIEDS
SAN JOSE MERCURY NEWS SATURDAY, JULY 8, 2006

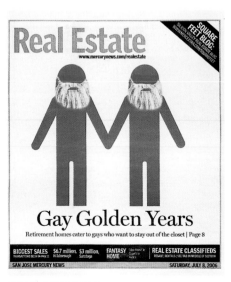

**SAN JOSE MERCURY NEWS** (Calif.)
Jeff Hindenach, Jonathon Berlin, Matt Mansfield
Business page, tabloid, 175,000+

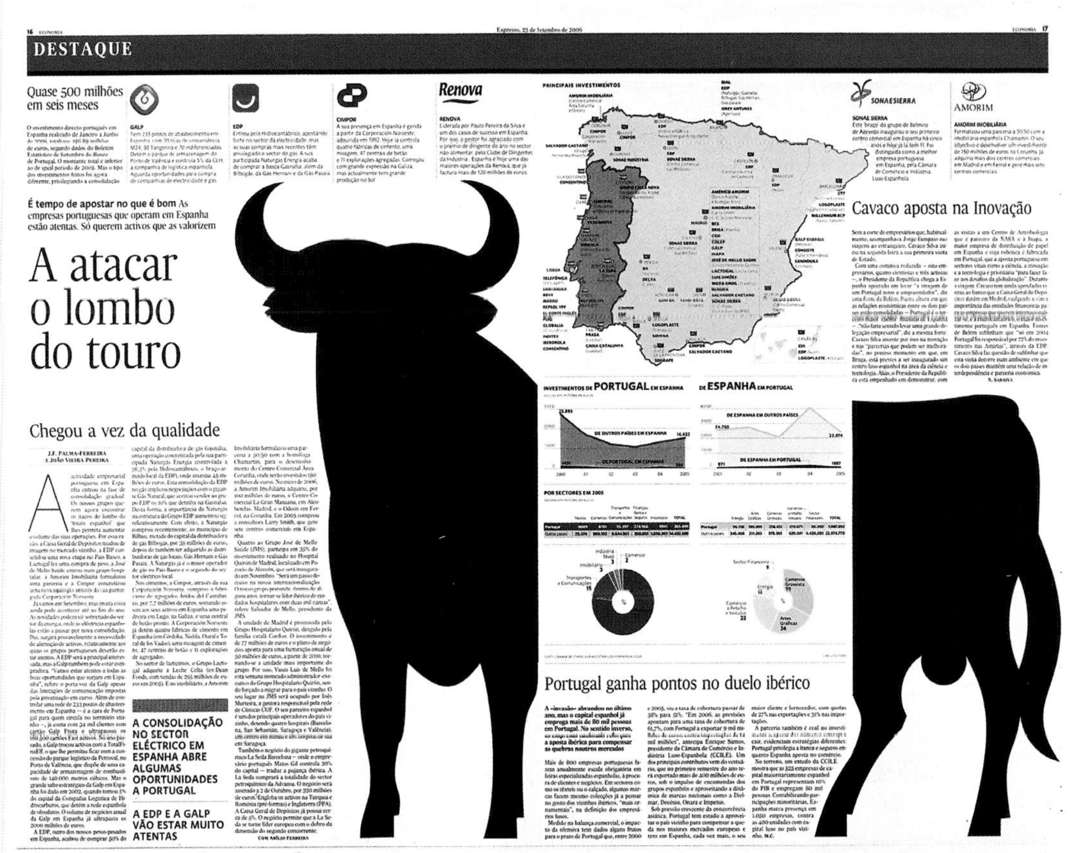

DESTAQUE

Quase 500 milhões em seis meses

É tempo de apostar no que é bom. As empresas portuguesas que operam em Espanha estão atentas. Só querem activos que as valorizem

# A atacar o lombo do touro

Chegou a vez da qualidade

A CONSOLIDAÇÃO NO SECTOR ELÉCTRICO EM ESPANHA ABRE ALGUMAS OPORTUNIDADES A PORTUGAL

A EDP E A GALP VÃO ESTAR MUITO ATENTAS

Cavaco aposta na Inovação

Portugal ganha pontos no duelo ibérico

SILVER

**EXPRESSO,** Lisbon, Portugal

Marco Grieco, Pedro Figueiral, João Paulo Galacho, Carlos Esteves

Business page, tabloid, 50,000-174,999

The illustration, which helps package the graphic information, complements the headline "Attacking the bull." A page such as this shows how all crafts must work together closely.

La ilustración, que ayuda a empaquetar la información gráfica, complementa el título "Atacando el toro". Una página como ésta muestra la forma en que todas las partes deben funcionar como un todo.

# RUSSIA'S BEER REVOLUTION

**SUNDAY HERALD,** Glasgow, Scotland

Jill Myormalk, Elaine Livingstone, Roxanne Sorooshian

Business page, tabloid, 50,000-174,999

REPORTAGE ENRON-EFFEKTEN

I MORGON ÅRETS MERCURIUS

# Cheferna till skranket i Enron-skandalen

**DAGENS INDUSTRI,** Stockholm, Sweden

Staff, Kicki Siösteen

Business page, tabloid, 50,000-174,999

INVESTIMENTO

# Bolsas estão de novo muito quentes

Tertir, Altri e Soares da Costa são as campeãs este ano

Acções não estão propriamente baratas mas subidas vão continuar

**EXPRESSO,** Lisbon, Portugal

Marco Grieco, Pedro Figueiral, Luís Miguel Ribeiro

Business page, tabloid, 50,000-174,999

REPORTAGEM

# Abandono do olival dispara importações

Portugal já tem cinco azeites DOP

Só produzimos metade do que precisamos

Breve história do precioso líquido

**EXPRESSO,** Lisbon, Portugal

Marco Grieco, Pedro Figueiral, Paula Bouças, Tiago Miranda

Business page, tabloid, 50,000-174,999

HOCKEY | SPORTS • S5

DUHATSCHEK ON HOCKEY SHOOTING SEASON

POWER RANKINGS

**THE GLOBE AND MAIL,** Toronto

David Woodside, David Pratt, Steve McAllister, Randall Moore

Inside page, broadsheet, 175,000+

**EXPRESSO,** Lisbon, Portugal

Marco Grieco, Pedro Figueiral, João Paulo Galacho, Jaime Figueiredo

Business page, tabloid, 50,000-174,999

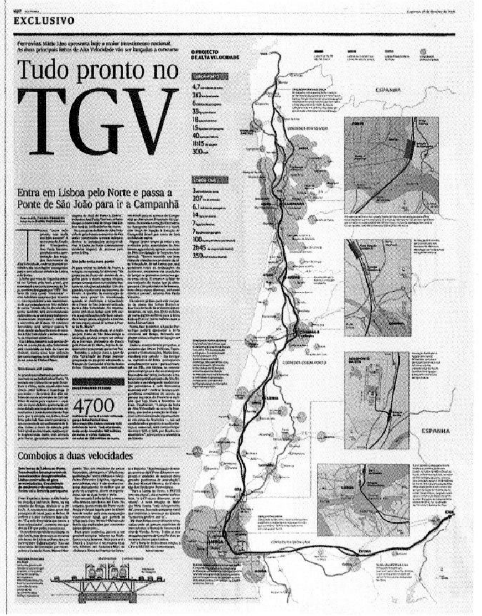

EXCLUSIVO

Tudo pronto no TGV

Entra em Lisboa pelo Norte e passa a Ponte de São João para ir a Campanhã

4700

Comboios a duas velocidades

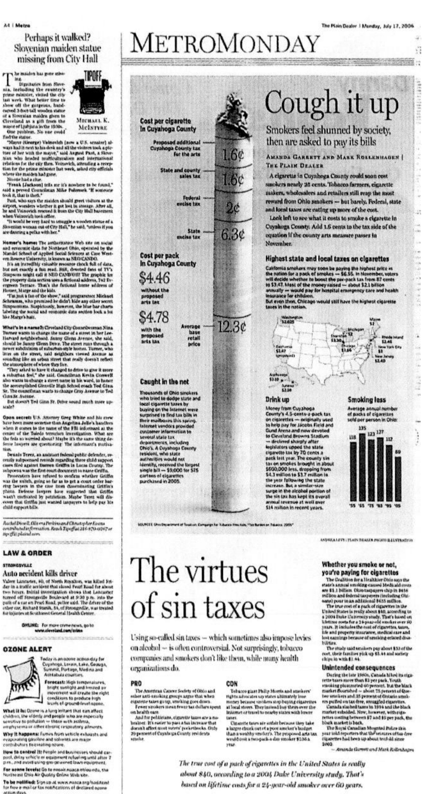

METROMONDAY

Perhaps it walked? Slovenian maiden statue missing from City Hall

Cough it up

Smokers feel shunned by society, then are asked to pay its bills

The virtues of sin taxes

LAW & ORDER

OZONE ALERT

**THE PLAIN DEALER,** Cleveland

David Kordalski, Bill Lammers, Andrea Levy, Ken Marshall, Debbie Van Tassel, Kathryn Kroll, Daryl Kannberg

Inside page, broadsheet, 175,000+

**SVENSKA DAGBLADET,** Stockholm, Sweden

Joakim Larsson

Business page, tabloid, 175,000+

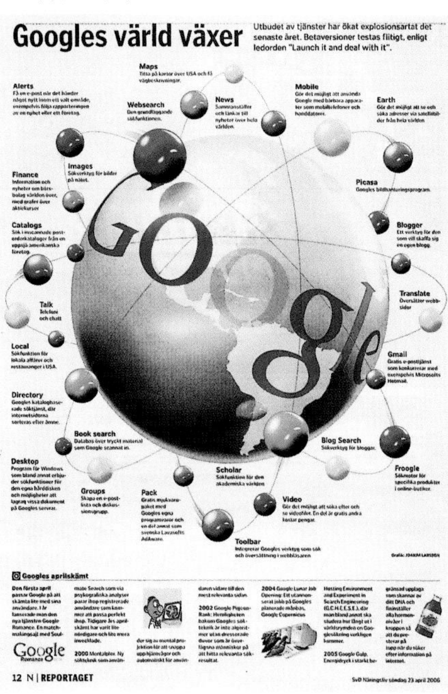

Googles värld växer

Utbudet av tjänster har ökat explosionsartat det senaste året. Betaversioner testas flitigt, enligt ledorden "Launch it and deal with it".

Googles aprilskämt

12 N | REPORTAGET

NBA FINALS GAME 6: HEAT 95, MAVERICKS 92

QUARTER-BY-QUARTER

INSIDE THE BOXSCORE

SHOT CHART

MVP WATCH

THE SERIES | HEAT WINS 4-2

**THE MIAMI HERALD**

Eddie Alvarez, Michael Babin

Inside page, broadsheet, 175,000+

**THE MIAMI HERALD**
Eddie Alvarez, Paul Cheung, Philip Brooker, Ana Larrauri, Danny Paskin
Inside page, broadsheet, 175,000+

**THE MIAMI HERALD**
Eddie Alvarez, Paul Cheung, Samantha Riepe
Inside page, broadsheet, 175,000+

**STAR TRIBUNE,** Minneapolis
Colleen Kelly
Inside page, broadsheet, 175,000+

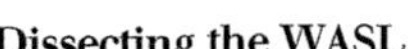

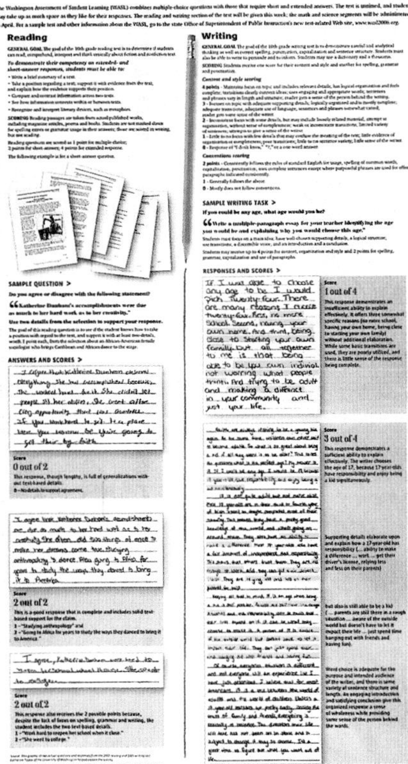

**THE SEATTLE TIMES**
Aldo Chan, Whitney Stensrud
Inside page, broadsheet, 175,000+

**RICHMOND TIMES-DISPATCH** (Va.)
Jeremy Glover, Tom Roberts, Andrew I. Cain
Inside page, broadsheet, 175,000+

**ORLANDO SENTINEL** (Fla.)
Stephen Komives, Bonita Burton
Inside page, broadsheet, 175,000+

**THE NEW YORK TIMES**
Tom Bodkin, Margaret O'Connor, Steve Wolgast
Inside page, broadsheet, 175,000+

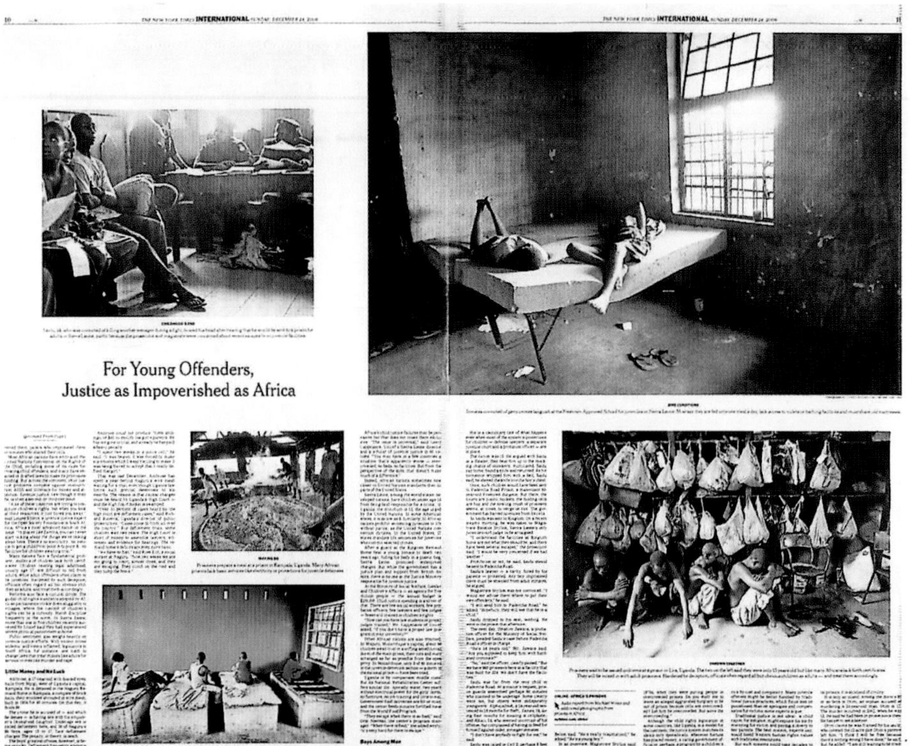

**THE VIRGINIAN-PILOT,** Norfolk
Xinning Huang, Charles Apple, Paul Nelson, Deborah Withey
Inside page, broadsheet, 175,000+

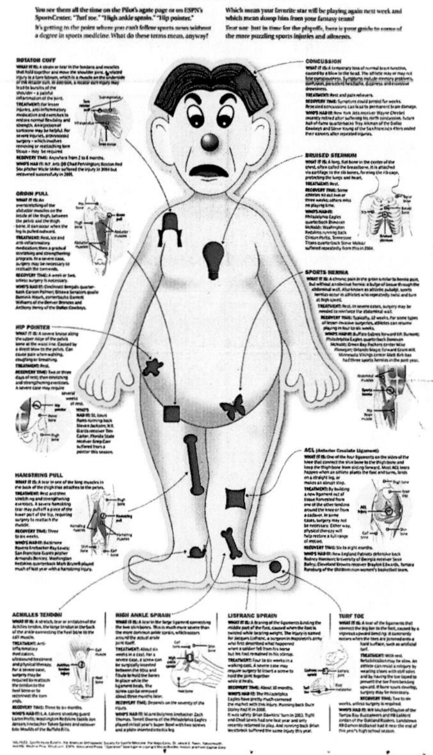

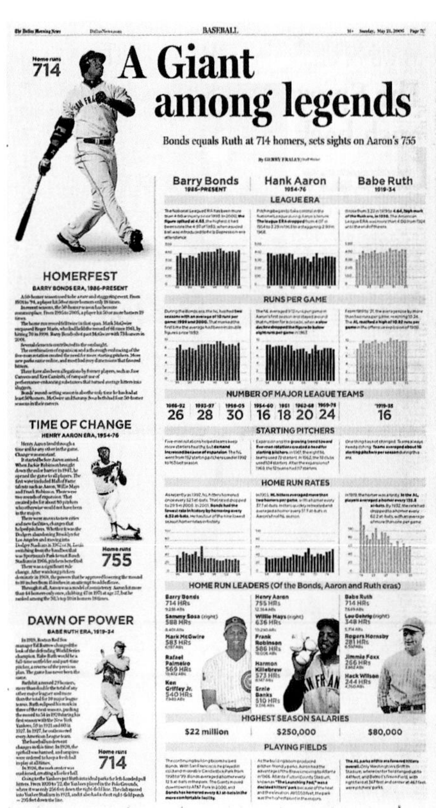

**THE DALLAS MORNING NEWS**
Christopher Velez, Rob Schneider, Gerry Fraley
Inside page, broadsheet, 175,000+

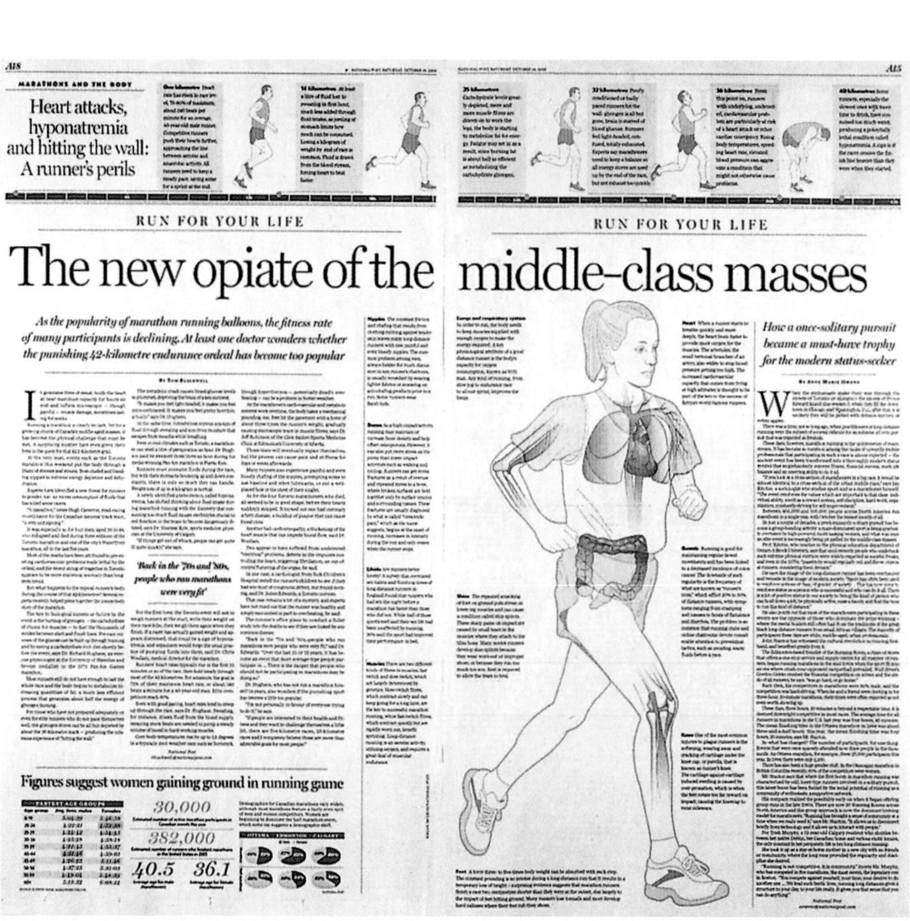

**NATIONAL POST,** Toronto
Doug Kelly, Gayle Grin, Kagan McLeod, Stephen Meurice
Inside page, broadsheet, 175,000+

**SAN JOSE MERCURY NEWS** (Calif.)

Michael Tribble, Susanna Frohman

Inside page, broadsheet, 175,000+

# Indian widows focus on devotion, fatalism

**THE BUFFALO NEWS** (N.Y.)

Vincent J. Chiaramonte

Inside page, broadsheet, 175,000+

MONDAY EXTRA

*The Buffalo News / Monday, January 9, 2006 • Page D6*

# MARVISMS

## *The wit and wisdom of Marv Levy*

Marv Levy returned to Buffalo last week to run the Bills' football operations and offer his unique perspective on life and football. Levy snapped off more one-liners in his introductory, 30-minute news conference than the past three Bills head coaches – Mike Mularkey, Gregg Williams and Wade Phillips – did over the past eight years. Here are the highlights of Levy's words of wisdom:

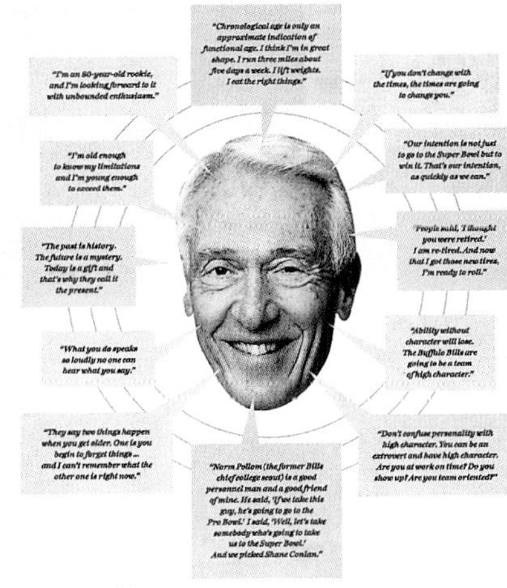

***What makes you think you have the physical stamina and the mental acuity to do the job?*** "Uuuuhhhh (pretending to be confused) ... will you repeat that question, please?"

***At one time you hid your age, now you seem to celebrate it. What happened?*** "I came out of the closet on it, I guess. Way back when I was hired in 1986, I was 61 years of age, and it sounded too old so I lied and said I was 58. Finally I cleared that up. Maybe as I matured I came to realize it wasn't a factor. It's what you can do that counts."

POSTER DESIGN BY VINCENT J. CHIARAMONTE / BUFFALO NEWS

# LBJ5K

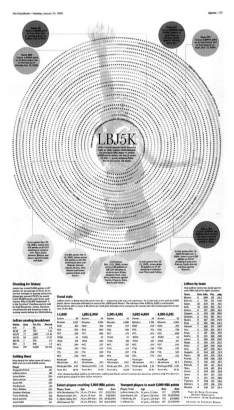

**THE PLAIN DEALER**, Cleveland

David Kordalski, Emmet Smith, Stephen J. Beard, Dennis Manoloff, Rich Fletcher, Tim Bennet, Jesse Haberman, Mike Starkey, Ken Marshall, Ryan Powell

Inside page, broadsheet, 175,000+

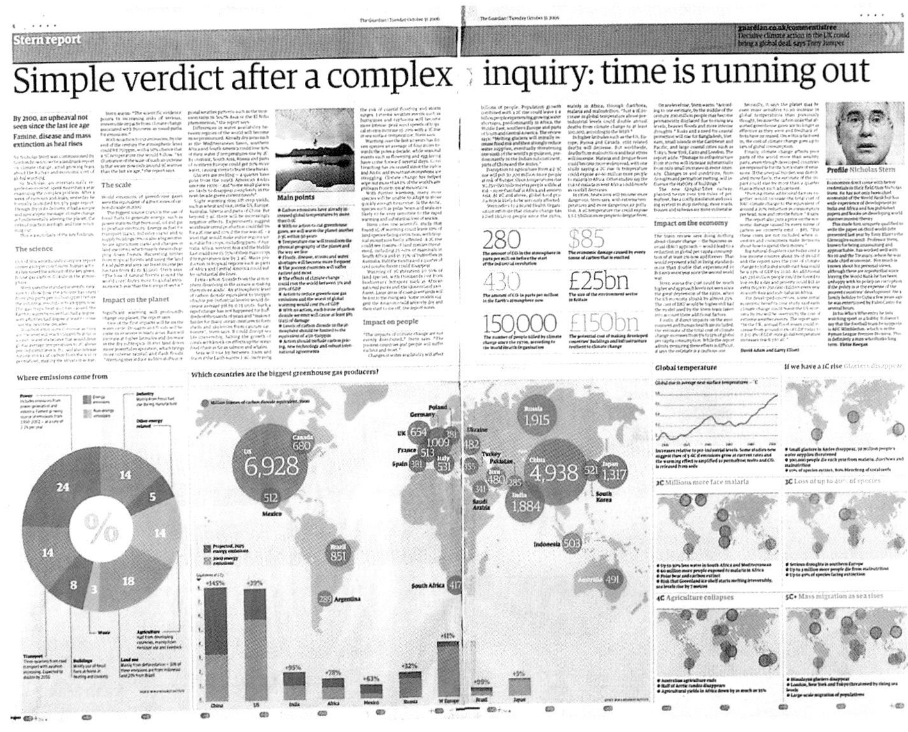

Stern report

# Simple verdict after a complex inquiry: time is running out

**THE GUARDIAN**, London

Staff

Inside page, broadsheet, 175,000+

**THE GUARDIAN,** London

Kevin Wilson

Inside page, broadsheet, 175,000+

Special report Europe's migrant workers

Migrants' stories

'We can't go back; there's nothing to go back to. We were hungry'

**THE WASHINGTON POST**

Jon Wile, Beth Broadwater, Dennis Brack, Larry Nista, Laura Stanton

Inside page, broadsheet, 175,000+

William Jewell

Michael Johnson

BEING A BLACK MAN

Poll uncovers great contradictions

KREATIV ERHVERV

Kan Danmark sælges?

**POLITIKEN,** Copenhagen, Denmark

Søren Nyeland, Tomas Østergren, Michael Jarlner, Michael Olsen, Bjarke Møller

Inside page, broadsheet, 50,000-174,999

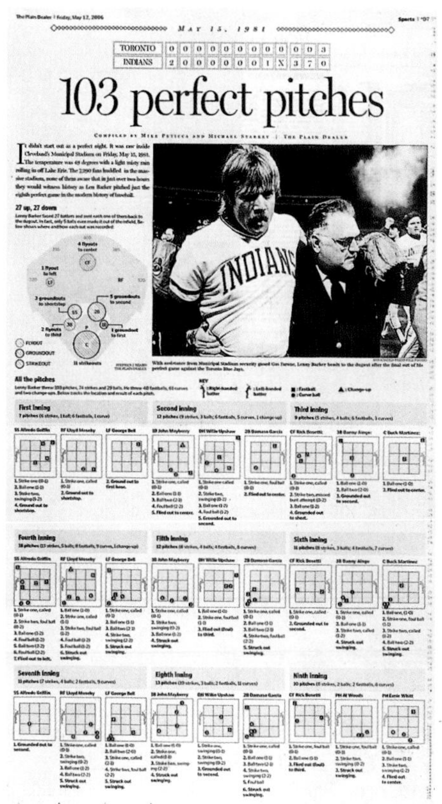
May 15, 1981

103 perfect pitches

**THE PLAIN DEALER,** Cleveland

David Kordalski, Roy Hewitt, Mike Starkey, Mike Peticca, Emmet Smith, Stephen J. Beard, Ken Marshall

Inside page, broadsheet, 175,000+

SUNDAY

Los Angeles Times

SUNDAY, APRIL 16, 2006

Backers of Ads Skirt Rules on Disclosure

The New Foreign Aid: Mexico

States Acting to Protect Private Property

The Seeds of Promise

Wristwatches Get the Back of the Hand

Inland Empire: Where the L.A. Dream Landed

INSIDE

**LOS ANGELES TIMES**

Joseph Hutchinson, Kelli Sullivan, Michael Whitley, Gail Fisher, Colin Crawford, Don Bartletti

Inside page, broadsheet, 175,000+

**EL UNIVERSAL,** México City

Roberto Rock L., Francisco Santiago, Oscar Santiago Méndez, Rubén Álvarez, María Elena Matadamas, Nilton Torres Pérez, Omar Canek Páramo Kañetas, Rafael Sotomayor, Ángel Boligán

Inside page, broadsheet, 50,000-174,999

CULTURA

SECCIÓN F

Alí CHUMACERO A PRUEBA DEL TIEMPO

Amigos del poeta nayarita trazan un perfil del también editor, quien recibirá un doble homenaje: en su tierra natal y en Bellas Artes, este jueves

EL HORROR ATRAPADO EN IMÁGENES

**EXCELSIOR,** México City

Juan Carlos Gutiérrez Alvarez, Ernesto Alcántara, Dulce Liz Moreno, Luzma Díaz de León Reyes, Marco A. Román, Alexandro Medrano, Gerardo Galarza, Pascal Beltrán del Río, Ernesto Rivera

Inside page, broadsheet, 50,000-174,999

2 TEMA DEL DÍA

LES CIERRAN PUERTAS Y SE CIERRAN LA VIDA

La Procuraduría capitalina supone que una ola de suicidios recientes se debe a frustración extrema por fracaso escolar

Sobrepuesta a las caídas

Cuatro veces rechazado

58%

7%

11%

PRIMERA SECCIÓN | EXCELSIOR

PUBLICIDAD 5705 4444 5128 3000

Clasificados: 4234 y 4248

Atención a Clientes: 4236 y 4232

www.nuevoexcelsior.com.mx

**EXCELSIOR,** México City

Daniel González Hernández, Ángeles Barajas, Iván Ventura, Juan Carlos Gutiérrez, Luzma Díaz de León Reyes, Marco A. Román, Alexandro Medrano, Gerardo Galarza, Pascal Beltrán del Río, Ernesto Rivera

Inside page, broadsheet, 50,000-174,999

CHINA, OBSESIONADA CON LA NUMEROLOGÍA

Una matrícula de circulación que lleve el número ocho se ha convertido en un símbolo de estatus, casi en la misma medida que un auto deportivo del año, de las mejores marcas. Aquellos que lo acumulen varias veces en su placa es sinónimo de una persona acaudalada.

POR JIM YARDLEY

CÓDIGO

María Luisa Mendoza, colaboradora de Excélsior, evoca las andanzas del Ingenioso Hidalgo y alude a la vigencia de la obra universal de Cervantes, al comparar las batallas cotidianas del siglo XXI con las que libraba el caballero de la triste figura con sus molinos de viento

LA FERMOSURA DE DON QUIJOTE EN TIERRAS GUANAJUATENSES

POR MARÍA LUISA MENDOZA

CÓDIGO | EXCELSIOR

**EXCELSIOR,** México City

Daniel González Hernández, Cristina Medrano, Mario Carboneli, Juan Carlos Gutiérrez Alvarez, Luzma Díaz de León Reyes, Marco A. Román, Alexandro Medrano, Gerardo Galarza, Pascal Beltrán del Río, Ernesto Rivera

Inside page, broadsheet, 50,000-174,999

In Depth 7

Finding jobs for UAE nationals

LABOUR MINISTRY'S STRATEGY OF EMIRATISING SELECTIVE PROFESSIONS IN THE COUNTRY IS BEARING FRUIT

Emiratisation policies

Cost of hiring

Statistics

800,000

600,000

450,000

150,000

27,300

36,000

Two-thirds of national women are unemployed

Some private firms 'lack commitment'

**GULF NEWS,** Dubai, United Arab Emirates

Syed Mohd. Arshad, Abbas Al Lawati, Wafa Issa, Meher Murshed, Miguel Angel Gomez, Abdul Hamid Ahmad

Inside page, broadsheet, 50,000-174,999

**EXCELSIOR,** México City

Juan Carlos Gutiérrez Alvarez, Ernesto Alcántara, Óscar Cedillo, Luzma Díaz de León Reyes, Marco A. Román, Alexandro Medrano, Gerardo Galarza, Pascal Beltrán del Río, Ernesto Rivera

Inside page, broadsheet, 50,000-174,999

BOTELLA LLENA, CORAZÓN CONTENTO

La frecuencia, y no la cantidad, hace que la mujer prevenga problemas cardiacos: una copa de alcohol a la semana le puede salvar la vida

PRIMERA SECCIÓN

EXCELSIOR

PUBLICIDAD

5705 4444 5128 3000

Clasificados: 4234 y 4248

Atención a Clientes: 4236 y 4232

**CORREIO BRAZILIENSE,** Brasília, Brazil

Josemar Gimenez, Ana Dubeux, Carlos Marcelo, João Bosco Adelino de Almeida, Luís Tajes, Maurenilson Freire

Inside page, broadsheet, 50,000-174,999

POLÍTICA

PSOL

No comando do partido e da campanha de Heloísa Helena à Presidência, ex-petistas dividem-se entre a empolgação e a descrença com a política

A INCRÍVEL ARMADA DE HELOÍSA HELENA

ELEIÇÕES 2006

GOVERNO NO ALVO

**ESTADO DE MINAS,** Belo Horizonte, Brazil

Janey Costa, Júlio Moreira

Inside page, broadsheet, 50,000-174,999

POLÍTICA

ELEIÇÕES 2006

Não posso passar um mês de campanha apanhando por causa deste dossiê. Vocês precisam resolver isso

BERZOINI

CABEÇA DA VÉZ

Executiva do partido discute expulsão de todos os envolvidos com a compra do dossiê antitucano, os que foram chamados de 'aloprados'

Muitos setores do partido entendem que Berzoini tem responsabilidade política pelo que aconteceu

Vicios privados | Virtudes públicas

HÉCTOR FALCÓN

ENVICIADO por el ARTE

Como estudiante de diseño, el creador visual comprendió que plegarse a los criterios comerciales no era lo suyo, y el trabajar como modelo de pasarela lo llevó a reflexionar sobre la simbología del cuerpo: es a partir de ambas experiencias que desarrolló su propuesta estética de transgresión

1-800 SOFT SEX

¿QUIÉN ES?

**EL UNIVERSAL,** México City

Roberto Rock L., Francisco Santiago, Oscar Santiago Méndez, Rubén Álvarez, María Elena Matadamas, Nilton Torres Pérez, Patricia Velázquez Yebra, Rafael Sotomayor, Jorge Manjarrez, Roberto Hernández Gutierrez

Inside page, broadsheet, 50,000-174,999

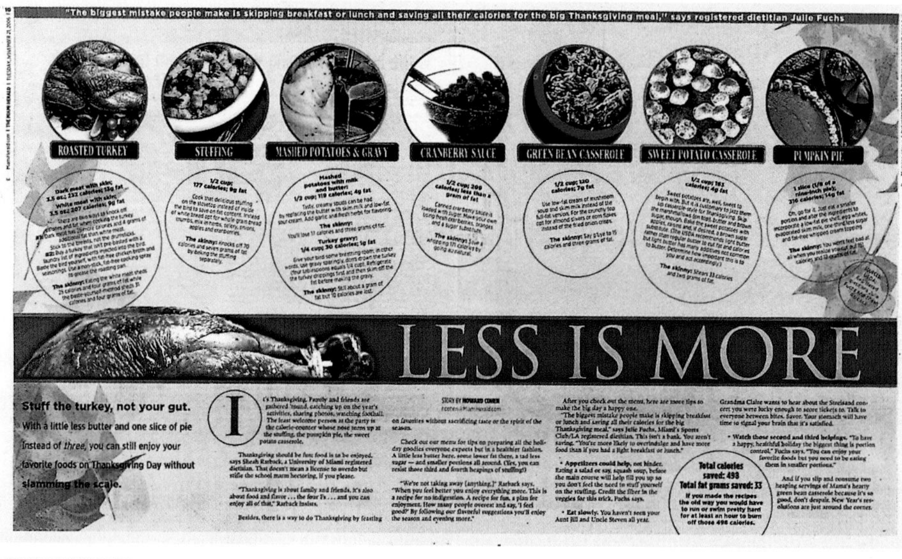

"The biggest mistake people make is skipping breakfast or lunch and saving all their calories for the big Thanksgiving meal," says registered dietitian Julie Fuchs

ROASTED TURKEY | STUFFING | MASHED POTATOES & GRAVY | CRANBERRY SAUCE | GREEN BEAN CASSEROLE | SWEET POTATO CASSEROLE | PUMPKIN PIE

LESS IS MORE

Stuff the turkey, not your gut. With a little less butter and one slice of pie instead of three, you can still enjoy your favorite foods on Thanksgiving Day without slamming the scale.

Total calories saved: 498

Total fat grams saved: 33

**THE MIAMI HERALD**

Eddie Alvarez, Paul Cheung, Ana Larrauri

Inside page, tabloid, 175,000+

THE TIME COMES IN A MAN'S LIFE WHEN HE MUST PUT AWAY CHILDISH THINGS — THE LOW-SLUNG JEANS, THE FUNKY HAIR, THE ROUGH MANNERS — AND ACT LIKE, WELL, A GENTLEMAN. IT'S ALL ABOUT ROMANCE (FROM COURTSHIP THROUGH MARRIAGE) AND CAREER (DRESS CODE FOR JOB INTERVIEW). SO HERE ARE SOME SUGGESTIONS ON HOW TO CLEAN UP NICELY.

a gentleman's guide

How to impress in 10 easy steps

THE SUIT | THE PEN IS MIGHTIER THAN THE LAPTOP | THE HAIRCUT | THE TUX | THE ACCESSORIES | THE CRIB | THE SHOE REPAIR | THE SHOES | THE FLOWERS | THE WHEELS

**THE MIAMI HERALD**

Eddie Alvarez, Paul Cheung, Ana Larrauri

Inside page, tabloid, 175,000+

**HERALDO DE ARAGÓN,** Zaragoza, Spain
Kristina Urresti, Irán Santos, Pilar Ostalé, Jorge Luis Mora, Pedro Zapater
Inside page, tabloid, 50,000-174,999

42 | Martes 3 de octubre de 2006 | Heraldo de Aragón

# GALERIA

*"Quien posee mujer e hijos ha entregado rehenes a la fortuna". Francis Bacon, filósofo británico (1561-1626).*

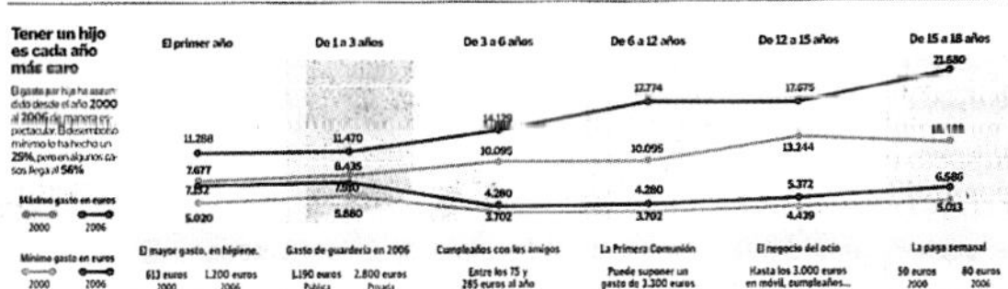

## Mantener a un hijo y otras ruinas

Un informe de la Ceaccu desvela que cada vástago cuesta entre 98.000 y 310.000 euros desde que nace hasta los 18 años

**EXPRESSO,** Lisbon, Portugal
Marco Grieco, Pedro Figueiral, Jorge Simão
Inside page, tabloid, 50,000-174,999

CARA-A-CARA

O que foi mais difícil em Portugal?
Scolari "A minha renovação de contrato"
F. Pinto "Aí nós temos exactamente a mesma opinião! Igualzinho!"

52 | Domingo 22 de octubre de 2006 | Heraldo de Aragón

# GALERIA

*"Todo error contiene un núcleo de verdad, y toda verdad puede ser semilla de error". Friedrich Rückert, escritor alemán (1788-1866).*

## La suelta del visón americano amenaza al autóctono, en peligro de extinción

Desde ecologistas hasta peleteros denuncian que se libere una especie invasora tan dañina para el ecosistema

**Un pariente problemático**

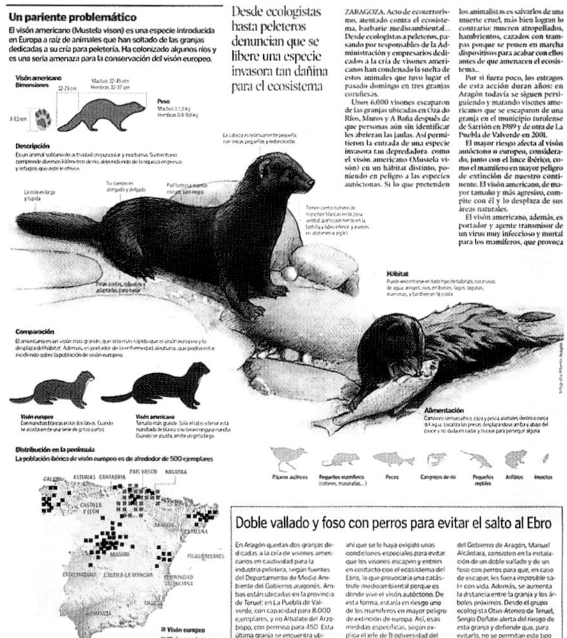

**Doble vallado y foso con perros para evitar el salto al Ebro**

DESTAQUE EXPRESSO

## A vida difícil dos tribunais

Juízes carregam processos em malas de viagem

Tribunal ideal

**EXPRESSO,** Lisbon, Portugal
Marco Grieco, Pedro Figueiral, Paula Bouças, Ana Serra
Inside page, tabloid, 50,000-174,999

**HERALDO DE ARAGÓN,** Zaragoza, Spain
Kristina Urresti, Irán Santos, Pilar Ostalé, Jorge Luis Mora, Pedro Zapater, Alberto Aragón
Inside page, tabloid, 50,000-174,999

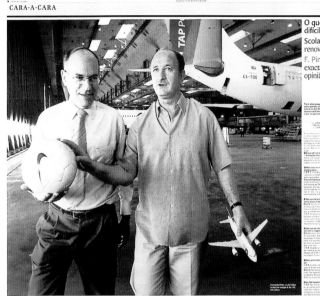

VENEZUELA

CHÁVEZ VICTORIA DE VENEZUELA

# «Muy» doidos por Chávez

Combate à exclusão social e aposta na saúde e educação resultaram

ATÉ POLÍCIAS SÃO OBRIGADOS A IR AOS COMÍCIOS DO CHEFE DE ESTADO

O RIVAL MANUEL ROSALES QUER O REGRESSO DO INVESTIMENTO ESTRANGEIRO

## O músculo guerrilheiro da revolução

## Pecados da 'monarquia' chavista

Internet e Propriedade Intelectual

**EXPRESSO,** Lisbon, Portugal
Marco Grieco, Pedro Figueiral, Paula Bouças, João Paulo Galacho
Inside page, tabloid, 50,000-174,999

**EXPRESSO,** Lisbon, Portugal
Marco Grieco, Pedro Figueiral, Paula Bouças
Inside page, tabloid, 50,000-174,999

INVESTIGAÇÃO EXPRESSO

Correspondência dos EUA sobre o 28 de Setembro de 1974 comprova pedidos de auxílio

# Spínola pediu invasão militar da NATO

Documentos secretos desclassificados revelam segredos

O fantasma do Vietname

## As três sugestões de Spínola

## Kissinger inquieto



**EXPRESSO,** Lisbon, Portugal
Marco Grieco, Pedro Figueiral, Luis Grañena
Inside page, tabloid, 50,000-174,999

DESTAQUE EXPRESSO

Ruptura da coligação com o CDS deixa PSD sem maioria na maior Câmara do país. Partidos dizem querer cumprir o mandato, mas o risco de eleições antecipadas não está afastado

# Carmona aceita ir a votos

Presidente da Câmara está refém das oposições

CARMONA DECIDIU CHAMAR A SI O PLANO DA BAIXA-CHIADO, QUE ERA A 'MENINA DOS OLHOS' DE NOGUEIRA PINTO

COM A RUPTURA NA COLIGAÇÃO, O PROJECTO PASSA PARA AS MÃOS DO PRESIDENTE. A VEREADORA DO CDS É ACUSADA DE ÂNSIA DE PROTAGONISMO

Oposição a Mendes cavalga a crise

"Quero fazer o melhor para cumprir o mandato"

"Tiraram-me a Basílica da Estrela de cima"

www.ina.pt

Conhecimento e Cooperação Internacional

**SOUTH FLORIDA SUN-SENTINEL,** Fort Lauderdale
Rebekah Monson, Tom Peyton, Tim Frank
Other news page, broadsheet, 175,000+

Outlook
JANUARY 29, 2006

REPAIR.
REPLANT.
**REBUILD.**

A guide to **fixing without fear** after hurricane season.

NEWS ILLUSTRATED, 20H

**SOUTH FLORIDA SUN-SENTINEL,** Fort Lauderdale
Victoria Ballard, Tom Peyton, Chris Mihal, Tim Frank
Other news page, broadsheet, 175,000+

Outlook
SOUTH FLORIDA SUN-SENTINEL | SUNDAY | JULY 2, 2006 | SECTION H

*O say, did you know, that our national song*

*Once had a life, as an English drinking tune? But then Francis Scott Key, saw a banner so strong*
*That it held up through bombs, in our country's time of gloom? He decided to write, 'bout a young nation's fight*
*And a flag that survived to the Brit's cannon might. O say that's how our song was born, from verses Key gave,*
*And after 1931, it became all the rave.*

NO, THOSE AREN'T THE WORDS to our national anthem. But a poll conducted by Harris Interactive suggests two out of three Americans wouldn't know the difference. Staff Writer Jean-Paul Renaud explores the anthem's history. 3H

VIEW EXCLUSIVE VIDEO of South Floridians singing *The Star-Spangled Banner*. www.sun-sentinel.com/anthem

**SAN FRANCISCO CHRONICLE**
Rick Nobles, Frank Mina, Randy Greenwell, Nanette Bisher, Kathleen Hennessy, Lacy Atkins, Jim Finefrock
Other news page, broadsheet, 175,000+

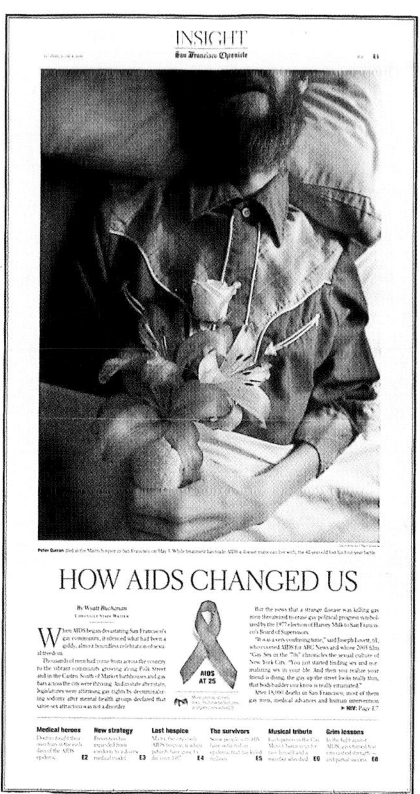
INSIGHT
San Francisco Chronicle

HOW AIDS CHANGED US

AIDS AT 25

Medical heroes | New strategy | Last hospice | The survivors | Musical tribute | Grim lessons

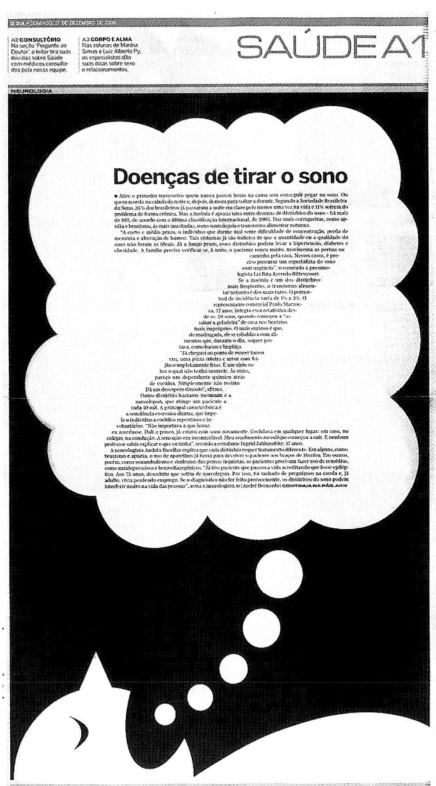
SAÚDE A1

NEUROLOGIA

Doenças de tirar o sono

**O DIA,** Rio de Janeiro, Brazil
André Hippertt, Luisa Bousada
Other news page, broadsheet, 175,000+

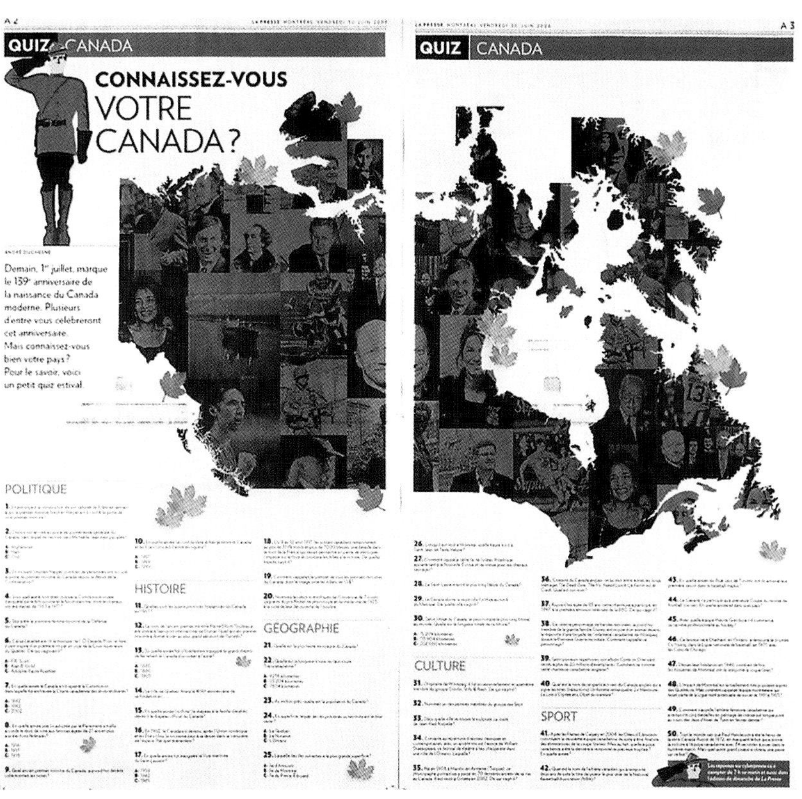
QUIZ CANADA

CONNAISSEZ-VOUS VOTRE CANADA?

Demain, 1er juillet, marque le 139e anniversaire de la naissance du Canada moderne. Plusieurs d'entre vous célébreront cet anniversaire. Mais connaissez-vous bien votre pays? Pour le savoir, voici un petit quiz estival.

POLITIQUE

HISTOIRE

GÉOGRAPHIE

CULTURE

SPORT

**LA PRESSE,** Montréal
Yanick Nolet, Benoit Giguere, Genevieve Dinel, Andre Duchesne
Other news page, broadsheet, 175,000+

**EXCELSIOR,** México City

Elizabeth Medina Martínez, Cecilia Estrada Medina, Luzma Díaz de León Reyes, Marco A. Román, Alexandro Medrano, Gerardo Galarza, Pascal Beltrán del Río, Ernesto Rttivera

Other news page, broadsheet, 50,000-174,999

Hoy en agenda: La Corte Suprema de EU estudia la legalidad de la discriminación positiva que realizan algunas escuelas primarias públicas para respetar la diversidad racial entre sus alumnos.

EXCELSIOR

GLOBAL

SEGUIRÁ EN EL PODER

El mandatario de Venezuela aventajaba en la elección presidencial con 61.35 por ciento a su opositor, el socialdemócrata Manuel Rosales. >04

Alta cocina en el espacio

Pinochet responde favorablemente

Buscan deportar a esposa de senador

2005

BONDADES DEL VINO TINTO

OPINIÓN

**EXCELSIOR,** México City

Daniel González Hernández, Cecilia Estrada Medina, Luzma Díaz de León Reyes, Marco A. Román, Alexandro Medrano, Gerardo Galarza, Pascal Beltrán del Río, Ernesto Rivera

Other news page, broadsheet, 50,000-174,999

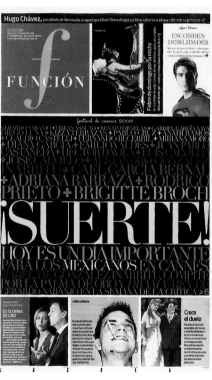

Hoy en agenda: El presidente de Estados Unidos, George W. Bush, recibe en la Casa Blanca al presidente electo de México, Felipe Calderón Hinojosa.

EXCELSIOR

GLOBAL

Elecciones EU 2006

BUSH SACRIFICA A RUMSFELD

PRIMERA BAJA

El secretario de Defensa se convirtió en víctima de las elecciones legislativas, mientras que el Presidente admitió su responsabilidad por la derrota en las urnas. >6-7

Desfile *gay* causa revuelo en Jerusalén

El Vaticano pide cancelar marcha

MATANZA ISRAELÍ EN BEIT HANUN

OPINIÓN

**LEXINGTON HERALD-LEADER** (Ky.)

Dennis Varney, Chris Ware, Scott Shive

Other news page, broadsheet, 50,000-174,999

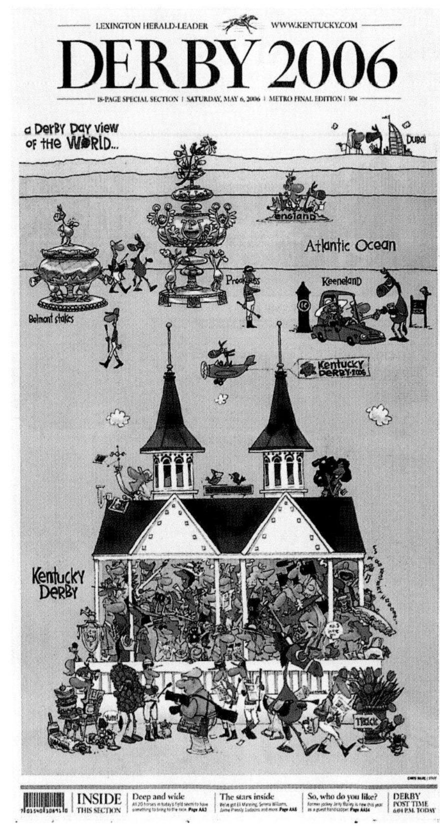

LEXINGTON HERALD-LEADER WWW.KENTUCKY.COM

DERBY 2006



INSIDE THIS SECTION

Deep and wide

The stars inside

So, who do you like?

DERBY POST TIME

**EXCELSIOR,** México City

Nancy Araiza, Mario Palomera, Carlos Meraz, Luzma Díaz de León Reyes, Marco A. Román, Alexandro Medrano, Ma. Luisa Díaz de León, Pascal Beltrán del Río, Ernesto Rivera

Other news page, broadsheet, 50,000-174,999

¡Magazo! El mexicano Jorge Ramírez dirigirá al irlandés Michael Gambon, quien caracterizó a Albus Dumbledore en *Harry Potter* >7

EXCELSIOR

FUNCIÓN

DUERME CALIENTITO

robbie williams

SHOWMAN CON ÁNGEL

Pequeños manjares

Dirigida al metrosexual

Lo encontrarás en un musical

**EXCELSIOR,** México City

Nancy Araiza, Ana Maria Prado, Carlos Meraz, Luzma Díaz de León Reyes, Marco A. Román, Alexandro Medrano, Ma. Luisa Díaz de León, Pascal Beltrán del Río, Ernesto Rivera

Other news page, broadsheet, 50,000-174,999

**THE GAZETTE,** Montreal

Nuri Ducassi, John Mahoney, Catherine Wallace

Other news page, broadsheet, 50,000-174,999

EXTRA SATURDAY

COMMENTARY

LIFE INSIDE AN AMERICAN PRISON CAMP

MONTREAL DIARY

PLEASE justify your existence

REPORT ON ...

FROM SEA TO SEA is one ocean short

EXTREME MEASURES

TONIGHT in Las Vegas, fans are paying up to $450 U.S. to see a Quebec athlete few Quebecers have heard of.

The Pharmaceutical Industry in Canada

The Legal Aspects of e-Governance

McGill

**THE GAZETTE,** Montreal

Nuri Ducassi, Dawn Lemieux, Marilyn Mill, Phil Carpenter, Catherine Wallace

Other news page, broadsheet, 50,000-174,999

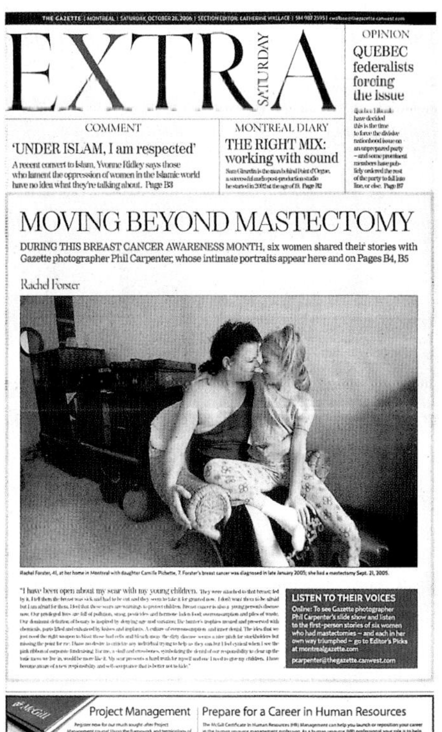
EXTRA SATURDAY

OPINION
QUEBEC federalists forcing the issue

COMMENT
'UNDER ISLAM, I am respected'

MONTREAL DIARY
THE RIGHT MIX: working with sound

MOVING BEYOND MASTECTOMY

DURING THIS BREAST CANCER AWARENESS MONTH, six women shared their stories with Gazette photographer Phil Carpenter, whose intimate portraits appear here and on Pages B4, B5

Rachel Forster

LISTEN TO THEIR VOICES

Project Management

Prepare for a Career in Human Resources

McGill

**EXCELSIOR,** México City

Daniel González Hernández, Ivan Ventura Cancio, Luzma Díaz de León Reyes, Marco A. Román, Alexandro Medrano, Gerardo Galarza, Pascal Beltrán del Río, Ernesto Rivera

Other news page, broadsheet, 50,000-174,999

GLOBAL

Borracho abraza y muerde a Gu Gu

EU hace operativos contra inmigrantes

115

DESOBEDECEN LA LEY

FRONTERA MÉXICO-ESTADOS UNIDOS

PREPARAN DOBLE MURO

En el Senado estadunidense se discute la construcción de una barda, que mediría mil 120 kilómetros. >04

Pobreza obliga a los beliceños a delinquir

TIENEN NUEVOS RECLUTAS

Agresor de JP II alerta a Benedicto

OPINIÓN

**EXCELSIOR,** México City

Rodolfo Preciado, Abraham Solís, Óscar Cedillo, Luzma Díaz de León Reyes, Marco A. Román, Alexandro Medrano, Gerardo Galarza, Pascal Beltrán del Río, Ernesto Rivera

Other news page, broadsheet, 50,000-174,999

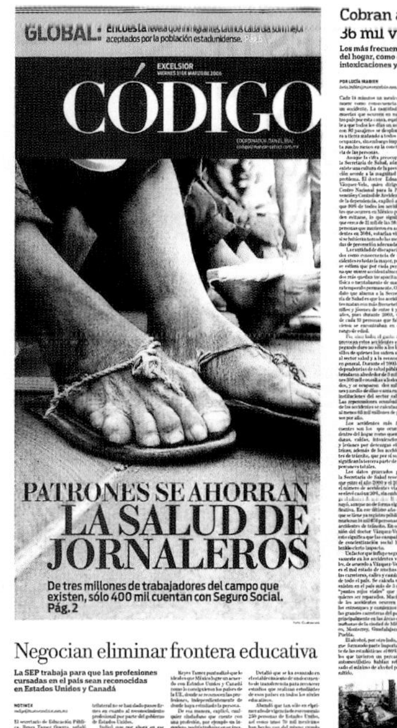
GLOBAL:

CÓDIGO

Cobran accidentes 36 mil vidas al año

PATRONES SE AHORRAN LA SALUD DE JORNALEROS

De tres millones de trabajadores del campo que existen, sólo 400 mil cuentan con Seguro Social. Pág. 2

3 mil

1

70 mil

60%

14 mil

Negocian eliminar frontera educativa

Moda de verdad.

FUNCIÓN

Juegos sexuales

putumayo

sonidos sin fronteras

EL SELLO DISCOGRÁFICO, CREADO POR DAN STORPER, HA PUESTO EN BOGA LA MÚSICA ÉTNICA CON MÁS DE CENTENAR DE ÁLBUMES, A LOS QUE SE SUMAN CUATRO NUEVOS LANZAMIENTOS >4

Rechazó ser el 007

Tiene un cita con Oprah

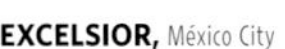

**EXCELSIOR,** México City

Carolina Kopeloff, Mario Palomera, Carlos Meraz, Luzma Díaz de León Reyes, Marco A. Román, Alexandro Medrano, Ma. Luisa Díaz de León, Pascal Beltrán del Río, Ernesto Rivera

Other news page, broadsheet, 50,000-174,999

8: CINE

LUCERO SOLORZANO

Cine: Elsa y Fred

viernes 13

La fórmula del horror

La industria del cine se enfrenta cada vez a más retos a la hora de hacer filmes de terror debido a que hoy al ser humano es más difícil convencerlo y asustarlo; sin embargo, ya existe una ecuación que te hará temblar frente a la pantalla

Tributo fílmico

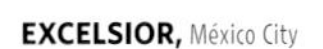

9: cine

VA DE COMPRAS

LE DAN SU ESTRELLA

Con temple latino

**EXCELSIOR,** México City

Carolina Kopeloff, Mario Palomera, Arturo Aguilar, Luzma Díaz de León Reyes, Marco A. Román, Alexandro Medrano, Ma. Luisa Díaz de León, Pascal Beltrán del Río, Ernesto Rivera

Other news page, broadsheet, 50,000-174,999

**EXCELSIOR,** México City

Daniel González Hernández, Israel López Gutiérrez, Luzma Díaz de León Reyes, Marco A. Román, Alexandro Medrano, Gerardo Galarza, Pascal Beltrán del Río, Ernesto Rivera

Other news page, broadsheet, 50,000-174,999

GLOBAL

202 MUERTOS

DUELO EN BAGDAD

Hacen pasteles para perros

Bachelet fortalece su política social

Pinochet cumple 91 años de edad

Toma caricaturista oficinas del *Herald*

MARAVILLAS DE LA NATURALEZA

28 MMD

OPINIÓN

**EXCELSIOR,** México City

Daniel González Hernández, Ivan Ventura Cancio, Luzma Díaz de León Reyes, Marco A. Román, Alexandro Medrano, Gerardo Galarza, Pascal Beltrán del Río, Ernesto Rivera

Other news page, broadsheet, 50,000-174,999

GLOBAL

EL INGLÉS, IDIOMA OFICIAL EN EU

WHAT?

El strip-tease es un arte

"No se manipuló la salud de Pinochet"

Ex director de la DINA

Advierten de una guerra regional

LA LUNA SERÁ COLONIZADA

Condiciona Chávez diálogo con Bush

OPINIÓN

**EXCELSIOR,** México City

Daniel González Hernández, Israel López Gutiérrez, Luzma Díaz de León Reyes, Marco A. Román, Alexandro Medrano, Gerardo Galarza, Pascal Beltrán del Río, Ernesto Rivera

Other news page, broadsheet, 50,000-174,999

GLOBAL

Prefieren cervezas que mujeres

DISCRIMINACIÓN EN GRAN BRETAÑA

BLAIR VA CONTRA EL VELO

Chile busca candidato de consenso en AL

112

78

EU tiene más de 300 millones de habitantes

DISTURBIOS EN EL MAUSOLEO

OPINIÓN

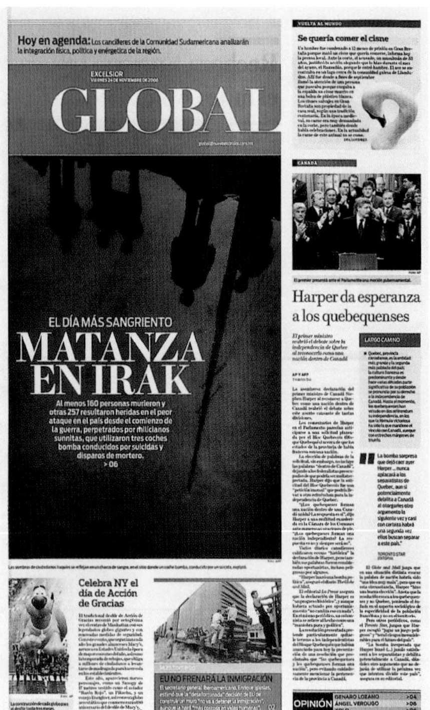

GLOBAL

EL DÍA MÁS SANGRIENTO

MATANZA EN IRAK

Se quería comer el cisne

Harper da esperanza a los quebequenses

Celebra NY el día de Acción de Gracias

EU NO FRENARÁ LA INMIGRACIÓN

OPINIÓN

**EXCELSIOR,** México City

Daniel González Hernández, Cecilia Estrada Medina, Luzma Díaz de León Reyes, Marco A. Román, Alexandro Medrano, Gerardo Galarza, Pascal Beltrán del Río, Ernesto Rivera

Other news page, broadsheet, 50,000-174,999

CÓDIGO

LOS HOMBRES DEL PRESIDENTE

El diario de un "loco"

Rabinos diferentes

SEP se pone de tarea retener a los alumnos

**EXCELSIOR,** México City

Alan Meraz, Alejandro Rodríguez, Óscar Cedillo, Juan Carlos Gutiérrez Alvarez, Luzma Díaz de León Reyes, Marco A. Román, Alexandro Medrano, Gerardo Galarza, Pascal Beltrán del Río, Ernesto Rivera

Other news page, broadsheet, 50,000-174,999

GLOBAL

ELECCIONES EN ESTADOS UNIDOS

KERRY SE RETIRA

Falla el hechizo de una bruja

Chávez adelanta a los burócratas aguinaldo

3 mdd

CEDEN SU LUGAR A PANAMÁ

OPINIÓN

**EXCELSIOR,** México City

Daniel González Hernández, Ivan Ventura Cancio, Luzma Díaz de León Reyes, Marco A. Román, Alexandro Medrano, Gerardo Galarza, Pascal Beltrán del Río, Ernesto Rivera

Other news page, broadsheet, 50,000-174,999

**EXCELSIOR,** México City

Elizabeth Medina Martínez, Daniel González Hernández, Cecilia Estrada Medina, Luzma Díaz de León Reyes, Marco A. Román, Alexandro Medrano, Gerardo Galarza, Pascal Beltrán del Río, Ernesto Rivera

Other news page, broadsheet, 50,000-174,999

GLOBAL

VISIÓN SOMBRÍA

"LA VICTORIA EN IRAK NO ES POSIBLE"

Remedio contra la impotencia

Viciado de origen, el juicio a Hussein

Restablecerían el servicio militar obligatorio

Chirac pierde apoyo de los franceses

TERMINA LA CUMBRE DE APEC

Evo Morales enfrenta otra crisis

OPINIÓN

**EXCELSIOR,** México City

Mario Palomera, Ángeles Barajas, Carlos Meraz, Luzma Díaz de León Reyes, Marco A. Román, Alexandro Medrano, Ma. Luisa Díaz de León, Pascal Beltrán del Río, Ernesto Rivera

Other news page, broadsheet, 50,000-174,999

Jaime Camil y Reyli

FUNCIÓN

El lado oscuro del 007

octubre musical

Un corsario le roba el corazón

DOCADO DE NIÑOS

¡LARARÁ!

La hazaña de un regreso

**EXCELSIOR,** México City

Nancy Araiza, Carlos Meraz, Ernesto Alcántara, Luzma Díaz de León Reyes, Marco A. Román, Alexandro Medrano, Ma. Luisa Díaz de León, Pascal Beltrán del Río, Ernesto Rivera

Other news page, broadsheet, 50,000-174,999

Desembarcan con gracia.

FUNCIÓN

Loco por Madonna

simplemente sexo

EL juego QUE TODOS JUEGAN

SE SALE DEL CINE

Para no mojarte

Teléfono ocupado.

Le prohíben las fiestas

EL DIABLO LOS HACE... Y ELLOS SE JUNTAN

7: cine

SIMPATÍA POR EL DIABLO

la profecía

El mal se vende bien

Hoy se estrena el remake del clásico de 1976 con la historia de la infancia del anticristo

Organiza su Halloween

UN ESTRENO A MALA HORA

**EXCELSIOR,** México City

Mario Palomera, Carlos Meraz, Luzma Díaz de León Reyes, Marco A. Román, Alexandro Medrano, Ma. Luisa Díaz de León, Pascal Beltrán del Río, Ernesto Rivera

Other news page, broadsheet, 50,000-174,999

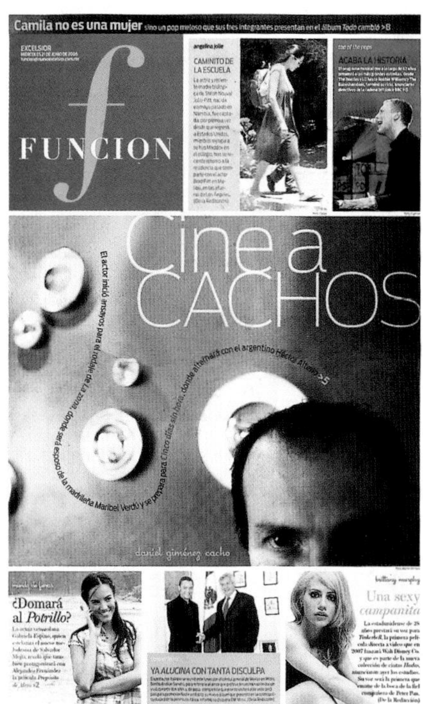

Camila no es una mujer

FUNCIÓN

CAMINITO DE LA ESCUELA

ACABA LA HISTORIA

Cine a CACHOS

¿Domará al Potrillo?

YA ALUCINA CON TANTA DISCULPA

Una sexy campanita

**EXCELSIOR,** México City

Mario Palomera, Walter Shintani, Carlos Meraz, Luzma Díaz de León Reyes, Marco A. Román, Alexandro Medrano, Ma. Luisa Díaz de León, Pascal Beltrán del Río, Ernesto Rivera

Other news page, broadsheet, 50,000-174,999

**CLAVE,** Santo Domingo, Dominican Republic
Juan Manuel Sánchez, Victor Bautista, Fausto Rosario Adames
Other news page, tabloid, 50,000-174,999

C2
La revista de Clave.
10 AGO 2006.

Riesgos de negocios familiares

Mil fotos vistas en septiembre

Relajación: del SPA a la casa

RD será la capital de científicos del Caribe

"A NADIE LE VENDÍ UTOPÍAS"

Clínica Oftalmológica de Santo Domingo

**CLAVE,** Santo Domingo, Dominican Republic
Marcos Nova, Juan Manuel Sánchez, Victor Bautista, Fausto Rosario Adames
Other news page, tabloid, 50,000-174,999

C2
La revista de Clave.
14 DIC 2006.

POR LAS SENDAS DEL ARTE

**Museo:** Al MAM le falta espacio para resguardar obras de arte. **Fotografía:** Polibio Díaz sumergido en el interior de las casas. Ricardo Briones, Víctor Siladi, Ricardo Piantini, José Alejandro Álvarez y Nemanja Brancovic ofrecen fotos a los viajeros. **Pintura:** Tras el origen de los paisajes de Miguel Angel Sierra. Seis pintores cubanos en una galería. Miguel Núñez, amor de cordillera. Fabré del mar. El otoño de Bidó. Patutus invita a su baby shower. **Cerámica:** Más días para la la III Trienal Internacional de Tile Cerámico.

Reserva mundial bajo gran amenaza

Diálogo sobre la energía y el futuro

Perlas, muy "in" en esta época

Clínica Oftalmológica de Santo Domingo

**SAN FRANCISCO CHRONICLE**
Nanette Bisher, Frank Mina, Tracy Cox, John Curley, Jay Johnson, Reid Sams, Steve Hornbostel, Chris Crescibene, Dan Jung
Breaking news, war on terrorism

San Francisco Chronicle

GUIDE FOR AIR TRAVELERS: TIPS FOR A SMOOTH JOURNEY IN TURBULENT TIMES A21

ON ALERT

WAR ON TERROR: A plot to blow up planes headed for the U.S. is foiled in England, authorities say, leading to tough new security measures for airline passengers that disrupt travel in both nations

THE PLOT

PLANS UNCOVERED: How investigators, tracking dozens of suspects for months, discovered a scheme to rival Sept. 11

SECURITY

CALIFORNIA: Governor sends Guard to four major airports — CHP to keep an eye on bridges, other possible targets

TRAVEL

NEW RULE: Ban on carrying liquids onto planes creates chaos at U.S. airports — experts predict more sophisticated screening of passengers A22, A23

ONLINE: FOR LATEST DETAILS ON THE PLOT AND UPDATES ON THE TRAVEL SITUATION, GO TO SFGate.com

Greenland's ice cap is melting at a frighteningly fast rate

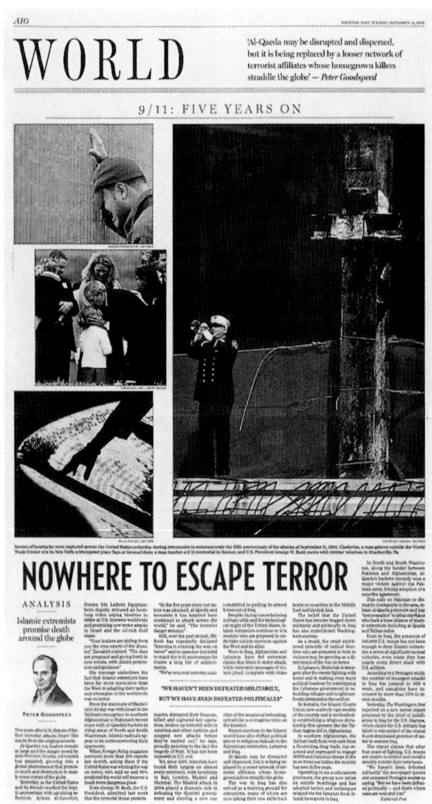
WORLD

'Al-Qaeda may be disrupted and dispersed, but it is being replaced by a looser network of terrorist affiliates whose homegrown killers straddle the globe' — Peter Goodspeed

9/11: FIVE YEARS ON

NOWHERE TO ESCAPE TERROR

ANALYSIS

Islamic extremists promise death around the globe

'WE HAVEN'T BEEN DEFEATED MILITARILY, BUT WE HAVE BEEN DEFEATED POLITICALLY'

**NATIONAL POST,** Toronto
Doug Kelly, Gayle Grin, Stephen Meurice, Tom Philip, Kelly McParland, Jeff Wasserman, Laura Koot, Angela Murphy
Breaking news, war on terrorism

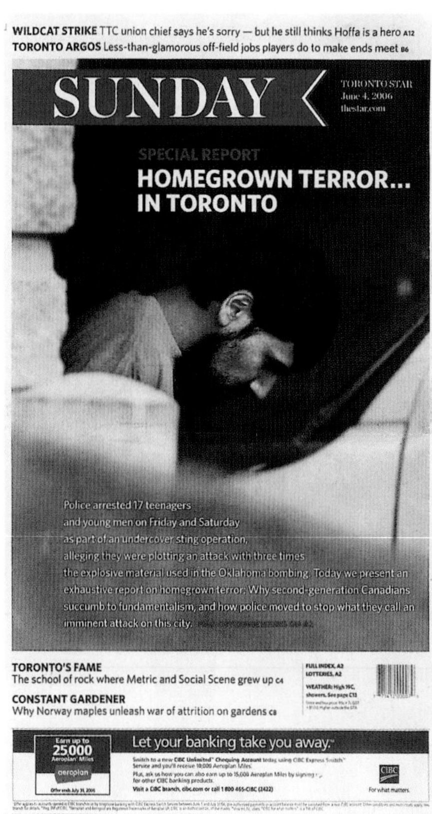
WILDCAT STRIKE TTC union chief says he's sorry — but he still thinks Hoffa is a hero A12
TORONTO ARGOS Less-than-glamorous off-field jobs players do to make ends meet B6

SUNDAY
TORONTO STAR
June 4, 2006

SPECIAL REPORT
HOMEGROWN TERROR... IN TORONTO

Police arrested 17 teenagers and young men on Friday and Saturday as part of an undercover sting operation, alleging they were plotting an attack with three times the explosive material used in the Oklahoma bombing. Today we present an exhaustive report on homegrown terror. Why second-generation Canadians succumb to fundamentalism, and how police moved to stop what they call an imminent attack on this city.

TORONTO'S FAME
The school of rock where Metric and Social Scene grew up C4

CONSTANT GARDENER
Why Norway maples unleash war of attrition on gardens C8

Earn up to 25000 Aeroplan Miles
Let your banking take you away.

**TORONTO STAR**
Devin Slater
Breaking news, war on terrorism

The Virginian-Pilot

THE REPORT'S OPENING LINE "The situation in Iraq is grave and deteriorating."

IRAQ STUDY GROUP REPORT

Is this the fix?

Bipartisan panel makes 79 recommendations

Beach Marine one of four killed in Iraq copter crash

Leaving the peak, but not the Hill

Submariner in spy case sentenced to 12 years

Peace after Pearl Harbor

Chance that water flows on Mars

**THE VIRGINIAN-PILOT,** Norfolk
Lori Kelley, Lauren Antonelli, Martin Smith-Rodden, Brian Cleveland, Paul Nelson, Deborah Withey
Breaking news, war on terrorism

CONMOCIÓN EN LAREDO

# Una explosión de gas lleva el

TRAGEDIA EN LA COSTA CÁNTABRA

Tres miembros de una familia de Bilbao y dos vecinas de Getxo mueren intoxicados por el humo

Unos cuarenta inquilinos fueron desalojados tras permanecer una hora atrapados por las llamas

La urbanización 'Jai-Alai'

1 EL INICIO: LA EXPLOSIÓN

2 EL INCENDIO Y EL RESCATE

Situación límite

CONMOCIÓN EN LAREDO

# horror al verano de Laredo

HURACÁN DE FUEGO.

Llegada de los bomberos

3 LOS FALLECIDOS

Planta del tercer piso

Unos 40.000 vascos, sobre todo vizcaínos, veranean en el municipio

Un niño de 4 años, con graves quemaduras

SILVER

**EL CORREO,** Bilbao, Spain

Diego Zúñiga, María del Carmen Navarro, Mikel García Macías, Aurelio Garrote, Ana Espligares, Noelia Martínez, Juan Antonio Salazar, Laura Piedra, Pacho Igartua

Breaking news, local

Designers clearly went into this with a game plan. In a turnaround of this complexity, it's impressive to get this level of presentation and integrate it into the coverage on deadline. Standing out are the photo editing and range of image sizes. The work is well layered, starting with three big stories and alternate forms — there's some real consumer-oriented content. The stories aren't long, with digestible pieces on each spread. It just doesn't feel like breaking news. It is very digestible and edited.

Claramente, los diseñadores abordaron este artículo con un plan de acción. Como resultado de esta complejidad, es impresionante lograr tal nivel de presentación visual e integrarla en la cobertura noticiosa contra la hora de cierre. Se destacan la edición fotográfica y la variedad de tamaños de las imágenes. El trabajo está bien estructurado al comenzar con tres grandes artículos y fuentes tipográficas alternadas. El contenido ciertamente está orientado al público objetivo. Los artículos no son largos y tienen piezas digeribles en cada par de páginas enfrentadas. No se siente como una noticia de última hora. El artículo está bien procesado y editado.

LIBAN ÉCHEC DES DISCUSSIONS À L'ONU PAGE A13

LA PRESSE

ALERTE ROUGE

LA GRANDE-BRETAGNE DÉJOUE UN COMPLOT VISANT À FAIRE EXPLOSER DES AVIONS EN VOL VERS LES ÉTATS-UNIS

10 PAGES À LIRE

UNE BOMBE LIQUIDE

CHAOS À HEATHROW

LA SIGNATURE DAL-QAEDA

VOUS NE GAGNEREZ PAS!

PANIQUE POUR DU VENT

De toute beauté.

**LA PRESSE,** Montréal

Genevieve Dinel, Genevieve Lapointe, Yanick Nolet, Benoit Giguere, Eric Trottier

Breaking news, war on terrorism

SPORTSDAY

BYRON NELSON: 1912-2006

Lord & masterful

Golf legend leaves lasting impression

No argument: Nelson one of sports's kings

NELSON BY THE NUMBERS

52 | 11 | 113 | 18 | $94 million

Dirk will begin camp with $60 million bang

**THE DALLAS MORNING NEWS**

Rob Schneider, Jason Dugger, Chuck Stewart, Kevin Lueb, Joel Moore, Michael Hogue

Breaking news, obituaries

Sports

BOSTON SUNDAY GLOBE OCTOBER 29, 2006

Arnold 'Red' Auerbach

1917-2006

Tough man had a tender side

For decades, he lit up our lives

Pound of prevention

Revolution put out Fire

**THE BOSTON GLOBE**

Brian Gross, Greg Lang

Breaking news, obituaries

**THE PLAIN DEALER,** Cleveland

David Kordalski, Daryl Kannberg, Chuck Caton, Bill Gugliotta, Jeff Greene, Photography Staff, Ken Marshall, James Owen, Stephen J. Beard, Haki Crisden

Breaking news, local

CLEVELAND GRAND PRIX WEEKEND TAKES OFF. D1

TRIBE BATS QUIET IN 3-0 LOSS TO REDS

THE PLAIN DEALER

SATURDAY, JUNE 24, 2006

# Storms left a mess

'I lost everything': Memories, hopes buried under mud

Cuyahoga River reaches a record height

Region swamped, staggered by worst flooding in decades

INSIDE

TV producer Aaron Spelling dies

Cabinet member to step down

Terror plot stopped early on, officials say

**THE VIRGINIAN-PILOT,** Norfolk

Robert Suhay, Laura Michalski, Martin Smith-Rodden, Judy Le, Paul Nelson, Deborah Withey

Breaking news, local

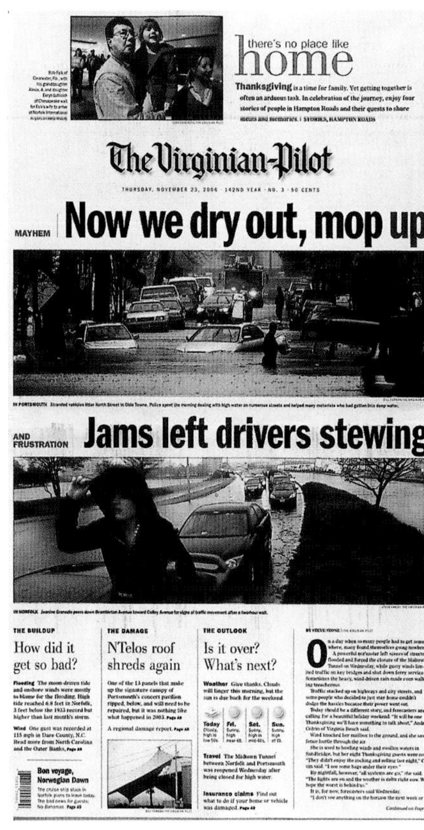

there's no place like home

The Virginian-Pilot

MAYHEM

# Now we dry out, mop up

AND FRUSTRATION

Jams left drivers stewing

THE BUILDUP — How did it get so bad?

THE DAMAGE — NTelos roof shreds again

THE OUTLOOK — Is it over? What's next?

**THE NEWS-PRESS,** Fort Myers, Fla.

Theresa Trenkamp, Kinfe Moroti, Valerie Roche, John David Emmett, Todd Stubing, Amanda Inscore, Terry Williams, Javier Torres, Staff

Breaking news, local

NFL TEAMS BUILD FOR THE FUTURE

WHO'S WATCHING?

THE NEWS-PRESS

SPECIAL COVERAGE | BRUSH FIRES ENGULF AREA

# LEHIGH BURNING

2,000 acres charred, 10 homes destroyed, scores forced to evacuate

Other blaze contained in North Fort Myers

MORE INSIDE

news-press.com

Condos king

Wine country

your Kitchen

239-332-3020

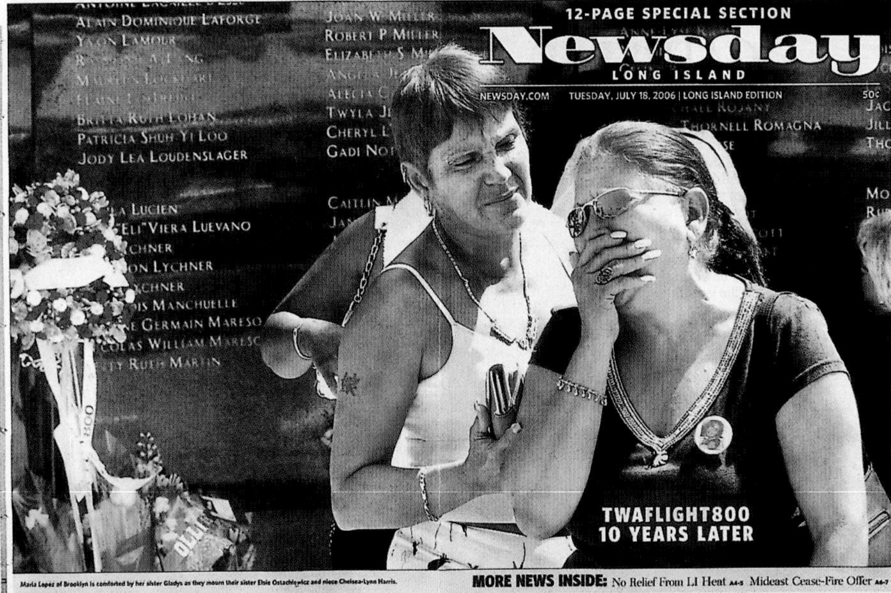

12-PAGE SPECIAL SECTION

Newsday

LONG ISLAND

NEWSDAY.COM TUESDAY, JULY 18, 2006 | LONG ISLAND EDITION

TWA FLIGHT 800 10 YEARS LATER

MORE NEWS INSIDE: No Relief From LI Heat A4-5 Mideast Cease-Fire Offer A6-7

**NEWSDAY,** Melville, N.Y.

Jeff Massaro, Doug Dutton, Karen Bailis, Martha Guevara, John Keating, David L. Pokress

Breaking news, local

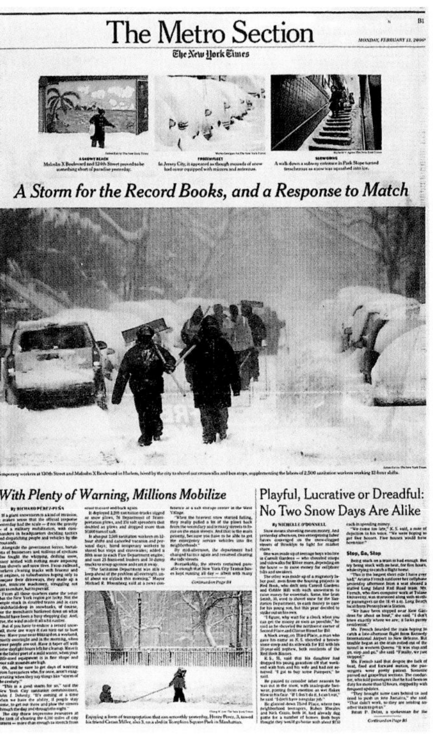

The Metro Section

The New York Times

*A Storm for the Record Books, and a Response to Match*

*With Plenty of Warning, Millions Mobilize*

Playful, Lucrative or Dreadful: No Two Snow Days Are Alike

**THE NEW YORK TIMES**

Tom Bodkin, Michael Kolomatsky, John Payne

Breaking news, local

**LOS ANGELES TIMES**

Joseph Hutchinson, Michael Whitley, Kelli Sullivan, Dave Campbell, Bill Sheehan, Lorraine Wang, Alex Brown, Gerard Babb, Robert St. John, Steve Stroud

Breaking news, local

Los Angeles Times

TUESDAY, MAY 2, 2006

# Marchers Fill L.A.'s Streets

At One With Dual Devotion

Next: Converting the Energy of Protest to Political Clout

Immigrants Demonstrate Peaceful Power

Throngs Show Their Potent Role in Economy

'When I See This, I See Strength'

INSIDE

**THE MIAMI HERALD**

Eddie Alvarez, Nathan Estep

Breaking news, local

The Miami Herald

MiamiHerald.com FINAL EDITION

TUESDAY, AUGUST 1, 2006

GADGETS FOR COLLEGE

LABOR OF LOVE

# CASTRO CEDES POWER

- AILING LEADER TRANSFERS AUTHORITY TO BROTHER RAUL
- FIDEL CASTRO HAS SURGERY FOR AN 'INTESTINAL CRISIS'
- CUBAN EXILES CELEBRATE POSSIBLE END OF AN ERA

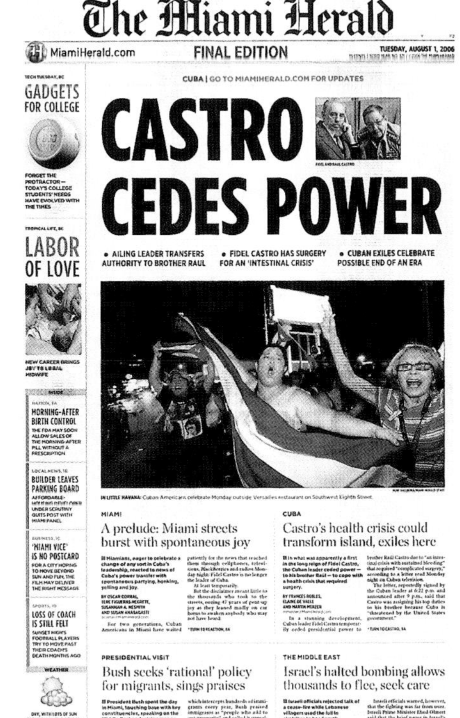

A prelude: Miami streets burst with spontaneous joy

Castro's health crisis could transform island, exiles here

Bush seeks 'rational' policy for migrants, sings praises

Israel's halted bombing allows thousands to flee, seek care

**THE DES MOINES REGISTER** (Iowa)

Jon Benedict, Nathan Groepper, Suzanne Behnke

Breaking news, local

The Des Moines Register

DEMOCRATS WIN U.S. HOUSE

# CULVER COASTS TO TERRACE HILL

DEMOCRATS SWEEP STATEHOUSE, GOVERNORSHIP

LOEBSACK ENDS LEACH'S 30-YEAR RUN IN CONGRESS

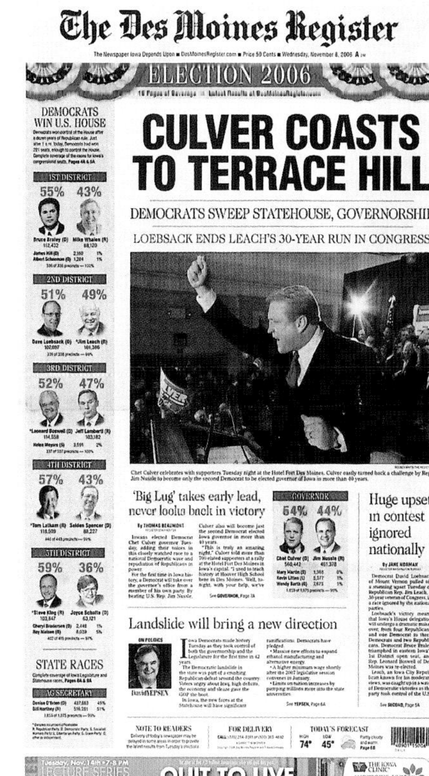

'Big Lug' takes early lead, never looks back in victory

Huge upset in contest ignored nationally

Landslide will bring a new direction

STATE RACES

QUIT TO LIVE

FORD PLANT TO CLOSE

"The way this country is going, nobody's safe," one worker says

FORD'S HISTORY IN NORFOLK

**THE VIRGINIAN-PILOT,** Norfolk

Ryan Healy, Robert Suhay, Lori Kelley, Robert D. Voros, Martin Smith-Rodden, Judy Le, Paul Nelson, Charles Apple, Deborah Withey

Breaking news, local

FEATURES | E1 Emmys: '24' named best drama, 'The Office' best comedy

The Courier-Journal

MONDAY

courier-journal.com

# Runways mixed up in Lexington crash

The lives behind the seat numbers

Lexington/Blue Grass Airport

Comair jet hits field; 49 killed

**THE COURIER-JOURNAL,** Louisville, Ky.

Mike Stollhaus, Steve Reed, Patty Pitts

Breaking news, local

FOLHA COTIDIANO

GUERRA URBANA

# PCC ataca ônibus e bancos,

promove megarrebelião

e amplia medo no Estado

74 mortes

156 ataques

80 rebeliões

**FOLHA DE SÃO PAULO** (Brazil)

Massimo Gentile, Fabio Marra, Clayton Bueno, Clauton Danelli de Souza, Viviane Jorge

Breaking news, local

**LOS ANGELES TIMES**
Joseph Hutchinson, Michael Whitley, Kelli Sullivan, Lorraine Wang, Mark Yemma, Dave Campbell, Mike McKay, David Rose, Editing Staff
Breaking news, local

DEADLY WILDFIRE: TRAGEDY IN THE SAN JACINTO MOUNTAINS

# Fast-moving fire routs hundreds

"The fire all of a sudden turned direction and headed straight toward our home."

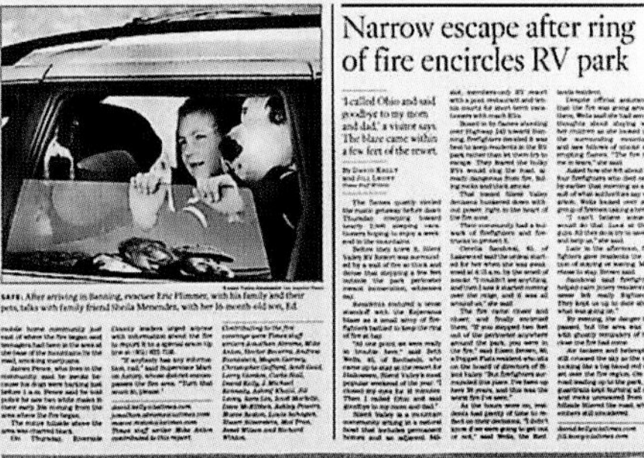

# Narrow escape after ring of fire encircles RV park

**HERALDO DE ARAGÓN,** Zaragoza, Spain
Kristina Urresti, Irán Santos, Pilar Ostalé, Jorge Luis Mora, Pedro Zapater
Breaking news, national

DIARIO INDEPENDIENTE • FUNDADO EN 1895

# HERALDO
DE ARAGON

# El vuelco de un convoy del metro de Valencia causa 41 muertos

HERIDOS Otras 47 personas resultaron con daños de diversa gravedad y 150 fueron evacuadas | INVESTIGACIÓN El exceso de velocidad y la rotura de una de las ruedas, posibles causas del siniestro | CONDOLENCIAS El Papa reza por las víctimas en vísperas de su visita y Zapatero regresa de la India

"Iba muy fuerte y ha golpeado con el andén en la curva de la estación"

El PSE y Batasuna aplazan su cita de hoy que el PP considera ilegal

"Tener a Víctor como míster es sinónimo de buen fútbol"

GTA WINNERS: FLAHERTY, STRONACH, IGNATIEFF, B1-B16
NDP SUCCESS: LAYTON LEADS PARTY TO GAINS, INCLUDING CHOW A6
QUEBEC: CONSERVATIVES FINALLY SCORE MAJOR BREAKTHROUGH A7
POLL 37: TURNOUT MORE THAN DOUBLES IN NORTH ETOBICOKE A15

# TORONTO STAR

# FRAGILE MINORITY

CON 124
LIB 103
BLOC 51
NDP 29

Martin stepping down as Liberal leader

Stephen Harper: The outsider comes in

GTA stays true to form

Cautious voters keep new PM on tight leash

**TORONTO STAR**
John Ferri, Charlie Kopun
Breaking news, national

# VÔO 1907

# DESASTRE NO AR

Mortos devem chegar a 155 no maior acidente aéreo da história do país

3 PERGUNTAS SEM RESPOSTA

**FOLHA DE SÃO PAULO** (Brazil)
Massimo Gentile, Fabio Marra, Marcio Freitas, Mario Kanno, Alex Argozino, Clayton Bueno
Breaking news, national

# Los Angeles Times

Wednesday, November 8, 2006

# DEMOCRATS CAPTURE HOUSE
## SCHWARZENEGGER WINS AND LOOKS AHEAD

TIMES EDITOR IS OUT AFTER FIGHTING CUTS

MADAM SPEAKER

A landslide for Feinstein and governor

Schwarzenegger can focus on legacy

GOP ceded the center and paid the price

**LOS ANGELES TIMES**
Joseph Hutchinson, Michael Whitley, Kelli Sullivan, Dan Santos, Mark Yemma, Dave Campbell, Alex Brown, Mike McKay, Bill Sheehan, Photo Editing Staff
Breaking news, national

Middle East crisis

# 'Is Hizbullah here? Only children here.' City mourns air strike dead

Israeli attacks on Lebanon port hit canal near Palestinian refugee camp

Streets empty as civilians in missile range hunker down

Diplomacy

## West flounders as old divisions resurface

Explainer UN force

Proposal met with hostility

Iran

Tehran benefits but role still unproven

The graphic's level of detail is impressive, and so are the images — every time you turn the page. There's great packaging and incredible imagery on deadline.

El nivel de detalle del gráfico es impresionante, tal como el de las imágenes, a cada vuelta de página. El excelente empaquetamiento informativo y las increíbles imágenes han sido realizadas contra la hora de cierre.

SILVER

**THE GUARDIAN,** London

Staff

Breaking news, international

BUDGET 2006

Blue Jays vow to 'examine options' for fans who paid GST on future tickets

Tax cuts will increase consumer confidence in buying a home: Real Estate Association

# THE BUDGET AT A GLANCE

PROVINCES

Quebec favoured, Ontario alleges

SIN TAX

Smokers, drinkers to foot GST bill

MILITARY

Forces will have to wait until 2008 for full fiscal boost

LAW & ORDER

Policing, border security get $1B shot in the arm

**NATIONAL POST,** Toronto

Doug Kelly, Gayle Grin, Steven Murray, Kagan McLeod, Andrew Barr, Jonathon Rivait, Stephen Meurice, Laura Koot, Jeff Wasserman, Kelly McParland

Breaking news, national

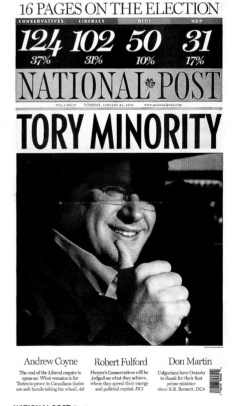

16 PAGES ON THE ELECTION

| CONSERVATIVES | LIBERALS | BLOC | NDP |
|---|---|---|---|
| 124 | 102 | 50 | 31 |
| 37% | 31% | 10% | 17% |

NATIONAL POST

# TORY MINORITY

Andrew Coyne — The end of the Liberal empire is upon us: What remains is for Tories to prove to Canadians theirs are safe hands taking the wheel. A3

Robert Fulford — Harper's Conservatives will be judged on what they achieve, where they spend their energy and political capital. DC1

Don Martin — Calgarians have Ontario to thank for their first prime minister since R.B. Bennett. DC4

**NATIONAL POST,** Toronto

Doug Kelly, Gayle Grin, Stephen Meurice, Kelly McParland, Jeff Wasserman, Laura Koot, Gary Clement

Breaking news, national

**THE GUARDIAN,** London
Staff
Breaking news, international

Has Kate lost her sense of style?
The England coach must have passion
John Terry interview
the guardian
Newspaper of the year
'They found them huddled together'
Israel calls off air strikes after raid on Lebanese town kills more than 60 people, including 34 children
Deadly day
National
PM: 'cross-dressing' on policy the norm
International
Spain and UK to sign Gibraltar treaty
Financial
Calls grow for £15bn pension payout
Sport
Drugs breach may end Gatlin's career
Young cartoonists

**FOLHA DE SÃO PAULO** (Brazil)
Massimo Gentile, Fabio Marra, Alex Argozino, Kleber Bonjoan
Breaking news, international

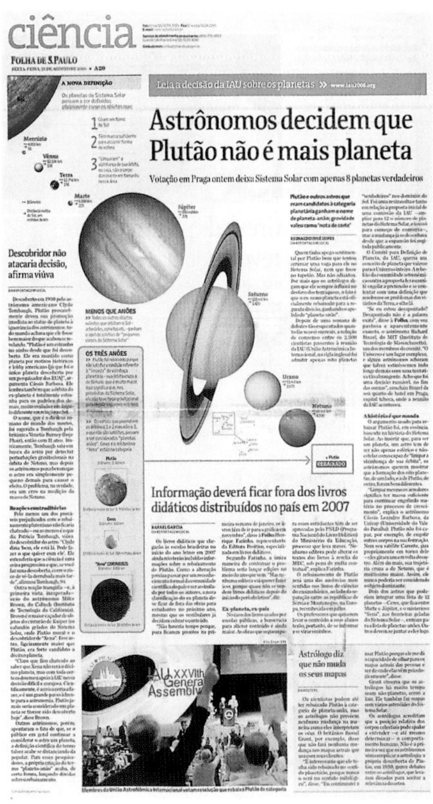
ciência
FOLHA DE S.PAULO
Leia a decisão da IAU sobre os planetas
Astrônomos decidem que Plutão não é mais planeta
Votação em Praga ontem deixa Sistema Solar com apenas 8 planetas verdadeiros
Descobridor não atacaria decisão, afirma viúva
Informação deverá ficar fora dos livros didáticos distribuídos no país em 2007
Astrólogo diz que não muda os seus mapas

**ORLANDO SENTINEL** (Fla.)
Chris Olds
Breaking news, sports

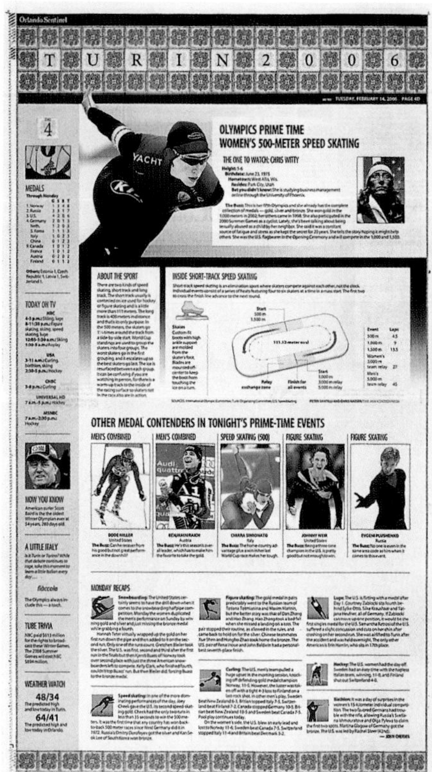
Orlando Sentinel
TURIN 2006
OLYMPICS PRIME TIME
WOMEN'S 500-METER SPEED SKATING
MEDALS
ABOUT THE SPORT
INSIDE SHORT-TRACK SPEED SKATING
TODAY ON TV
OTHER MEDAL CONTENDERS IN TONIGHT'S PRIME-TIME EVENTS
MEN'S COMBINED
MEN'S COMBINED
SPEED SKATING (500)
FIGURE SKATING
FIGURE SKATING
DID YOU KNOW
A LITTLE ITALY
TURIE TRIVIA
MONDAY RECAPS
WEATHER WATCH
48/34
64/41

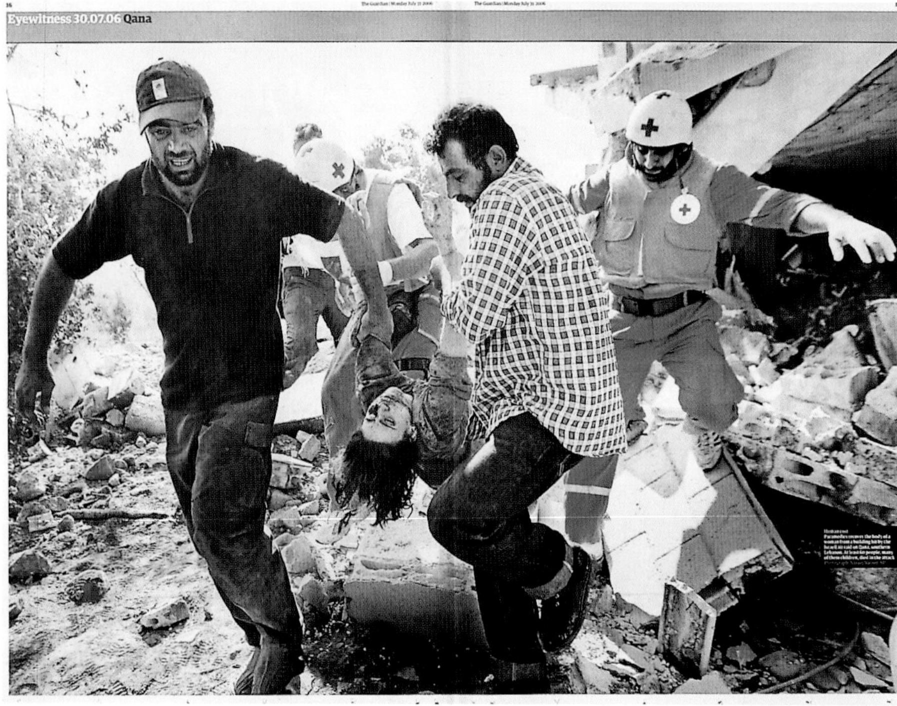
Eyewitness 30.07.06 Qana

**THE GUARDIAN,** London
Staff
Breaking news, international

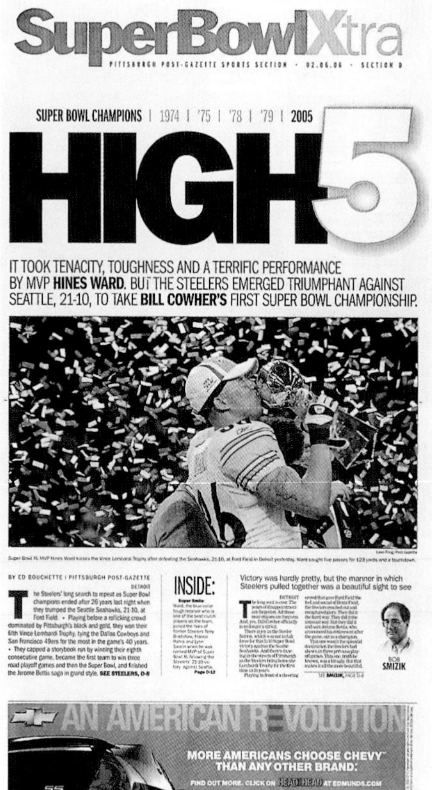
SuperBowlXtra
PITTSBURGH POST-GAZETTE SPORTS SECTION • 02.06.06 • SECTION D
SUPER BOWL CHAMPIONS | 1974 | '75 | '78 | '79 | 2005
HIGH 5
IT TOOK TENACITY, TOUGHNESS AND A TERRIFIC PERFORMANCE BY MVP HINES WARD. BUT THE STEELERS EMERGED TRIUMPHANT AGAINST SEATTLE, 21-10, TO TAKE BILL COWHER'S FIRST SUPER BOWL CHAMPIONSHIP.
INSIDE:
Victory was hardly pretty, but the manner in which Steelers pulled together was a beautiful sight to see


**PITTSBURGH POST-GAZETTE**
Ben Howard
Breaking news, sports

THE EXECUTION OF SADDAM HUSSEIN

# 'THIS IS MY END, DEATH DOESN'T FRIGHTEN ME'

PART ONE **THE HANGING** BY NEIL MACKAY

ON OTHER PAGES
4&5 PART TWO: THE FALLOUT BY DAVID PRATT
6&7 PART THREE: THE LEGACY OF SADDAM BY TREVOR ROYLE
8&9 PART FOUR: WAS IT LEGAL? BY JOHN SCOTT
34 MILESTONE OR MILLSTONE? EDITORIAL

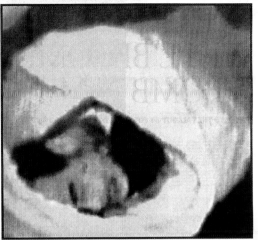

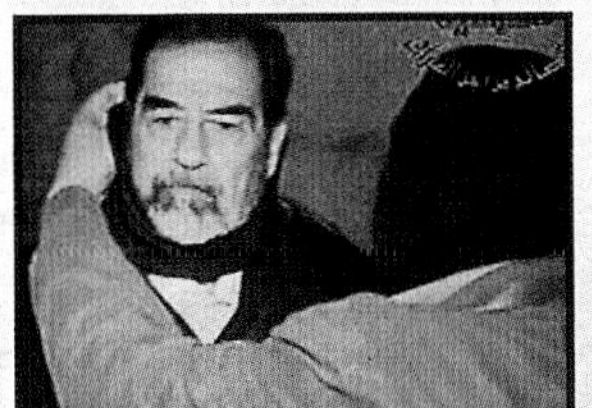

Some witnesses report Saddam seeming stoical at death, others a broken man. Photographs: AP

REACTION

"Bringing Saddam Hussein to justice will not end the violence in Iraq, but it is an important milestone on Iraq's course to becoming a democracy that can govern, sustain, and defend itself. Many difficult choices and further sacrifices lie ahead"
US PRESIDENT
GEORGE BUSH

"You don't fight barbarism with acts that I deem as barbaric. The death penalty is not compatible with democracy"
LOUIS MICHEL,
THE EUROPEAN UNION'S AID AND DEVELOPMENT COMMISSIONER

SILVER

**SUNDAY HERALD,** Glasgow, Scotland
Richard Walker, Elaine Livingstone, Staff
Breaking news, international

This coverage of the execution of Saddam Hussein is presented in three digestible parts, with a commitment to word pages and visual pages. The typography is clean and beautiful, and it unifies the package. The headings are like chapters in a book, and the high-effect photographs work hand in hand with the type. It's very simple, very straightforward, very direct.

Esta cobertura de la ejecución de Saddam Hussein está presentada en tres partes digeribles, con una dedicación tanto a las páginas con texto como con imágenes. La tipografía es limpia y bella, y unifica el paquete informativo. Los encabezados son como capítulos de un libro, y las fotos de alto impacto funcionan a la par con la tipografía. Es muy simple, al grano y directa.

TORINO GAMES
THE 20TH WINTER OLYMPICS | TURIN, ITALY

Yes, it's ladies night

Tough Finnish

Stars' Modano expresses discontent after U.S. loss

"We said, 'Let's enjoy it and may the better one win.' Today it was me. Sorry, Simon."

Don't miss ...

**FORT WORTH STAR-TELEGRAM** (Texas)
Michael Currie, Celeste Williams, Terry Bigham, Seth Schrock
Breaking news, sports

TORINO GAMES
THE 20TH WINTER OLYMPICS | TURIN, ITALY

Kwan is skating on thin ice

First strike

'Texas' Hedrick skates to a gold medal in his Olympic debut

3rd

Don't miss ...

Drive for five

**FORT WORTH STAR-TELEGRAM** (Texas)
Michael Currie, Celeste Williams, Terry Bigham
Breaking news, sports

TORINO GAMES
THE 20TH WINTER OLYMPICS | TURIN, ITALY

Bode made us all look like fools

Take 2

Ohno grabs a stunning victory in the 500, then leads U.S. relay team to a bronze

Hays wraps up sled career

**FORT WORTH STAR-TELEGRAM** (Texas)
Michael Currie, Celeste Williams, Terry Bigham
Breaking news, sports

**LA PRESSE,** Montréal

Andre Rivest, Benoit Giguere, Genevieve Dinel, Jean-Pascal Beaupre, Jean-Sebastien Gagnon, Yanick Nolet, Michel Marois

Breaking news, sports

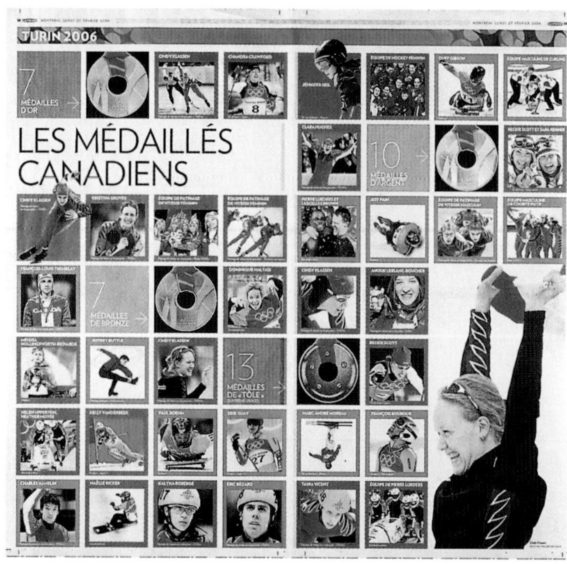


**LA PRESSE,** Montréal

Francis Leveillee, Benoit Giguere, Genevieve Dinel, Jean-Pascal Beaupre, Jean-Sebastien Gagnon, David Lambert

Breaking news, sports

**LA PRESSE,** Montréal

Andre Rivest, Benoit Giguere, Genevieve Dinel, Jean-Pascal Beaupre, Jean-Sebastien Gagnon

Breaking news, sports

**SUR,** Malaga, Spain

Baldomero Villanueva, Rafael Ruiz, Mª Dolores de la Vega, Javier Romero, Antonio Salas, Carlos Moret, Fernando González, Francisco Sánchez Ruano, Alberto Torregrosa

Breaking news, sports

**LA PRENSA GRÁFICA,** Antiguo Cuscatlán, El Salvador

Enrique Contreras, Héctor Ramírez, Erick Cortez, Denis García Márquez, Ricardo Orellana

Breaking news, sports

**THE GLOBE AND MAIL,** Toronto

David Woodside, David Pratt, Steve McAllister, Randall Moore

Breaking news, sports

**ST. LOUIS POST-DISPATCH**
Staff
Breaking news, sports

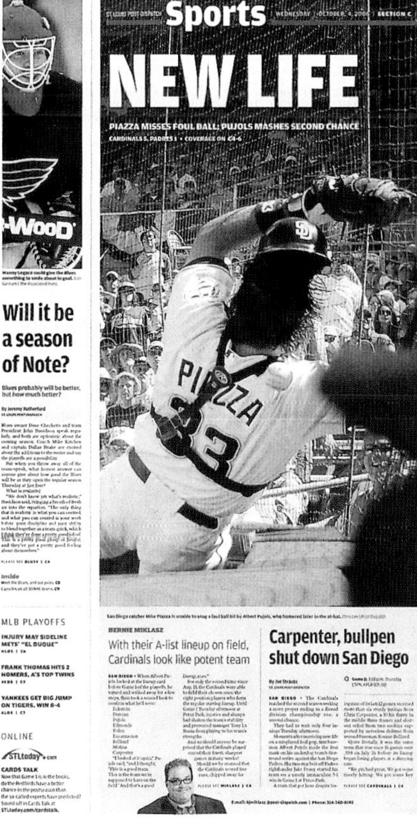

ST. LOUIS POST-DISPATCH **Sports** WEDNESDAY, OCTOBER 4, 2006 | SECTION C

# NEW LIFE

PIAZZA MISSES FOUL BALL; PUJOLS MASHES SECOND CHANCE

CARDINALS 5, PADRES 1 • COVERAGE ON C4-6

**Will it be a season of Note?**

Blues probably will be better, but how much better?

MLB PLAYOFFS

BERNIE MIKLASZ

With their A-list lineup on field, Cardinals look like potent team

**Carpenter, bullpen shut down San Diego**

ONLINE

STLtoday.com

**ST. LOUIS POST-DISPATCH**
Staff
Breaking news, sports

ST. LOUIS POST-DISPATCH **Sports** | SUNDAY | OCTOBER 15, 2006 | SECTION C

# SUP-ERB!

SUPPAN TAMES THE METS WITH HIS BAT AND HIS ARM

CARDINALS 3, METS 0 • COVERAGE ON C4-8

BERNIE MIKLASZ

It's a red letter night for Redbirds

**Cards take 2-1 series lead**

BRYAN BURWELL

Maybe it's in cards for Cards

MIZZOU

UNDEFEATED NO MORE

ALCS

TIGERS REACH WORLD SERIES

ONLINE

**THE GLOBE AND MAIL**, Toronto
David Woodside, David Pratt, Steve McAllister, Randall Moore
Breaking news, sports

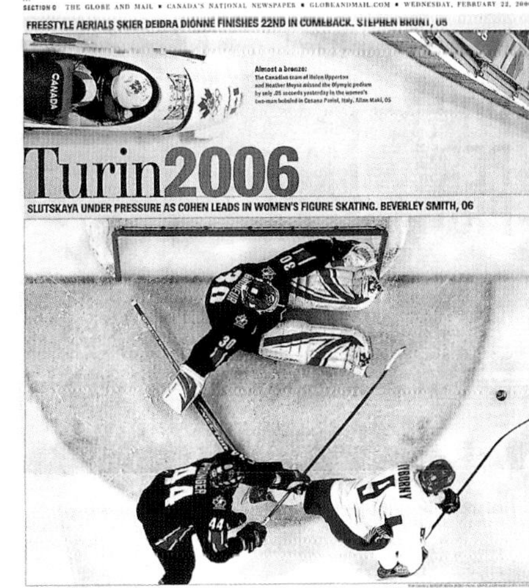

SECTION S THE GLOBE AND MAIL • CANADA'S NATIONAL NEWSPAPER • GLOBEANDMAIL.COM • WEDNESDAY, FEBRUARY 22, 2006

FREESTYLE AERIALS SKIER DEIDRA DIONNE FINISHES 22ND IN COMEBACK. STEPHEN BRUNT, S5

Turin**2006**

SLUTSKAYA UNDER PRESSURE AS COHEN LEADS IN WOMEN'S FIGURE SKATING. BEVERLEY SMITH, S6

# 'Win or go home'

Canada ends round robin with a 5-2 victory and will face high-flying Russians in the quarter-finals, ROY MacGREGOR reports

QUARTER-FINALS TODAY

LOS ANGELES TIMES

20TH WINTER OLYMPIC GAMES

torino 2006

# Cohen Was Undeserving of a Medal

**LOS ANGELES TIMES**
Vic Seper, Athan Atsales, Michael Whitley, George Wilhelm, Alex Gallardo, Calvin Hom, Dave Bennett, Raoul Rañoa
Breaking news, sports

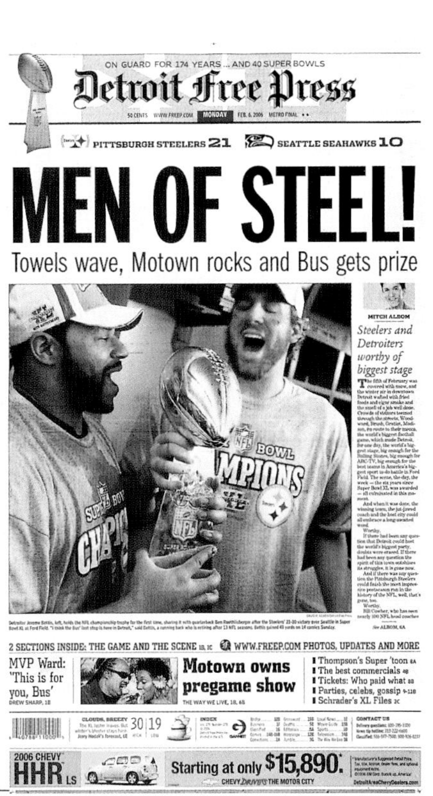

ON GUARD FOR 174 YEARS ... AND 40 SUPER BOWLS

Detroit Free Press

MONDAY FEB. 6, 2006

PITTSBURGH STEELERS 21 SEATTLE SEAHAWKS 10

# MEN OF STEEL!

Towels wave, Motown rocks and Bus gets prize

MITCH ALBOM

*Steelers and Detroiters worthy of biggest stage*

2 SECTIONS INSIDE: THE GAME AND THE SCENE | WWW.FREEP.COM PHOTOS, UPDATES AND MORE

MVP Ward: 'This is for you, Bus'

**Motown owns pregame show**

Thompson's Super 'toon
The best commercials
Tickets: Who paid what
Parties, celebs, gossip
Schrader's XL Files

2006 CHEVY HHR LS Starting at only $15,890.

**DETROIT FREE PRESS**
Staff, Robert Huschka, Mauricio Gutierrez, Ryan Ford, Steve Anderson, Steve Dorsey
Breaking news, sports

SECTION S

THE GLOBE AND MAIL

Turin**2006**

There's a new confidence, a new attitude among Canadians, STEPHEN BRUNT writes. Call it an unwillingness to settle for a respectable top-10 finish

**54 years 282 days**

**100+**

**252**

To our athletes in Torino, Canada is cheering for you!

Putting athletes first since 1947

**THE GLOBE AND MAIL**, Toronto
David Woodside, David Pratt, Steve McAllister, Randall Moore
Breaking news, sports

**EL GRÁFICO,** Antiquo Cuscatlan, El Salvador
Agustín A. Palacios, Oscar Guerra
Breaking news, sports

GOL INTERNACIONAL

"No culpo a los jugadores, yo soy el único responsable. Algunos jugadores están confundidos y yo he participado en su confusión. No me han gustado muchas de las actuaciones de los últimos días y debo echarme la culpa a mí mismo."

# Destrucción galáctica

Florentino Pérez renunció como presidente del Real Madrid, echándose para sí la culpa de todo lo malo que le ha pasado al equipo.

# El nuevo presidente

Fernando Martín toma las riendas del Real Madrid.

"Fernando Martín continuará con mi labor y le deseo suerte y que creo que está capacitado para este desafío"

"Hemos hecho una plantilla de grandes jugadores de la que soy el responsable. Los he maleducado y se han confundido. He actuado como los padres por darle lo mejor a los niños y se confunden."

**AUSTIN AMERICAN-STATESMAN** (Texas)
Chris Hanna, Tom Widlowski, Jason Whaley, Scott Ladd, Jay Godwin, Zach Ryall, Deborah Cannon, Ralph Barrera, Jay Janner, Rodolfo Gonzalez
Breaking news, sports

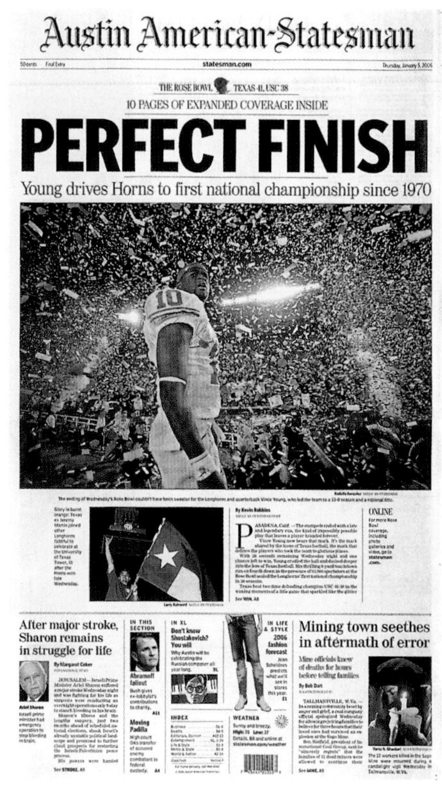
Austin American-Statesman

statesman.com

THE ROSE BOWL TEXAS 41, USC 38

10 PAGES OF EXPANDED COVERAGE INSIDE

# PERFECT FINISH

Young drives Horns to first national championship since 1970

After major stroke, Sharon remains in struggle for life

Mining town seethes in aftermath of error

World Cup 2006 47

ITALY

GHANA

US

CZECH

BEST XI

THE SQUAD

TOP MAN

**GULF NEWS,** Dubai, United Arab Emirates
Douglas Okasaki, Gautam Bhattacharyya, Sanjib Das, A.K. Satish, Paul Velasco, Syed Mohd. Arshad, Robin Chatterjee, Miguel Angel Gomez, Abdul Hamid Ahmad
Special news topics, World Cup

El Diario de Hoy

2006

Cristiano RONALDO

CON EL PENAL EJECUTADO LE DIO AYER EL PASE A PORTUGAL A LAS SEMIFINALES. SU HABILIDAD EN VELOCIDAD LO HACE IMPREVISIBLE PARA CUALQUIER DEFENSA. HA REALIZADO UN GOL EN EL MUNDIAL Y ES CANDIDATO AL PREMIO FIFA DEL MEJOR JUGADOR JOVEN DEL TORNEO.

**EL DIARIO DE HOY,** San Salvador, El Salvador
Juan Durán, Teodoro Wilson Torres, Jorge Castillo, Alicia Dubón, Hugo Rodríguez, Staff de Deportes
Special news topics, World Cup

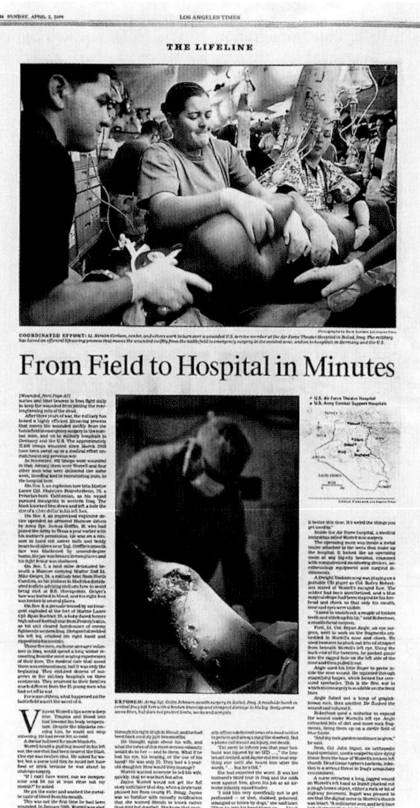
LOS ANGELES TIMES

THE LIFELINE

# From Field to Hospital in Minutes

**LOS ANGELES TIMES**
Michael Whitley, Joseph Hutchinson, Gail Fisher, Colin Crawford, Rick Loomis
Special news topics, war on terrorism

El día que cambió nuestras vidas La 'Nueva Economía del Terror'

# ¿CÓMO SE FINANCIA LA RED DE AL QAEDA?

El terrorismo islámico se nutre del crimen y de donaciones de estados, empresas y particulares

Serie especial Última entrega 11.09.2001

## El complejo entramado económico del terrorismo islamista

## La *hawala*: el circuito financiero oculto del terrorismo islamista

Un sistema milenario sirve a Al Qaeda para transferir dinero sin dejar rastro

150.000 MILLONES DE EUROS.

SILVER

**EL ECONOMISTA,** Madrid, Spain

Miguel Buckenmeyer, Gorka Sampedro, Susana Millan, Maria Verde, Victor Arias, Amaya Verde, Raquel Nieto, Javier Checa, Barbara Martinez, Juanjo Santacana

Special news topics, war on terrorism

11.09.2001
EL DÍA QUE CAMBIÓ NUESTRAS VIDAS


We like the multiple story-telling devices in this entry on the five-year anniversary of the Sept. 11 attacks. It's very easy to navigate. It offers great photo play, good type contrast and strong consistency. What we also liked was the pictures — the editors didn't just go with bold images to carry the spread, but they used photos that really told the story. They didn't take the easy way on a topic of importance.

Nos gustan los dispositivos de relato múltiple en esta pieza sobre el quinto aniversario de los ataques del 11 de septiembre. Es muy fácil de navegar. Tiene un muy buen uso de la fotografía, un buen contraste tipográfico y una sólida consistencia. También nos gustaron las fotos: los editores no seleccionaron simplemente imágenes audaces para sostener las páginas enfrentadas, sino que usaron fotos que realmente relataban lo ocurrido. No se fueron por el camino fácil para contar un tema de importancia.

En Afganistán se cumplirán pronto cinco años del inicio de la intervención militar estadounidense, que provocó la caída del régimen Talibán. En la actualidad, esos grupos extremistas aún tienen presencia en la parte sur de ese país, aún sumergido en la pobreza. Los afganos reclaman más ayuda a la comunidad internacional

**EL DIARIO DE HOY,** San Salvador, El Salvador

Juan Durán, Teodoro Wilson Torres, Jorge Castillo, Remberto Rodríquez, Marjorie Melqar

Special news topics, war on terrorism

**EL DIARIO DE HOY,** San Salvador, El Salvador

Juan Durán, Teodoro Wilson Torres, Jorge Castillo, Alicia Dubón, Hugo Rodríguez, Staff de Deportes

Special news topics, World Cup

**THE OREGONIAN,** Portland

Steve McKinstry, Derrik Quenzer, Steve Cowden, Michael Mode

Special news topics, Olympics

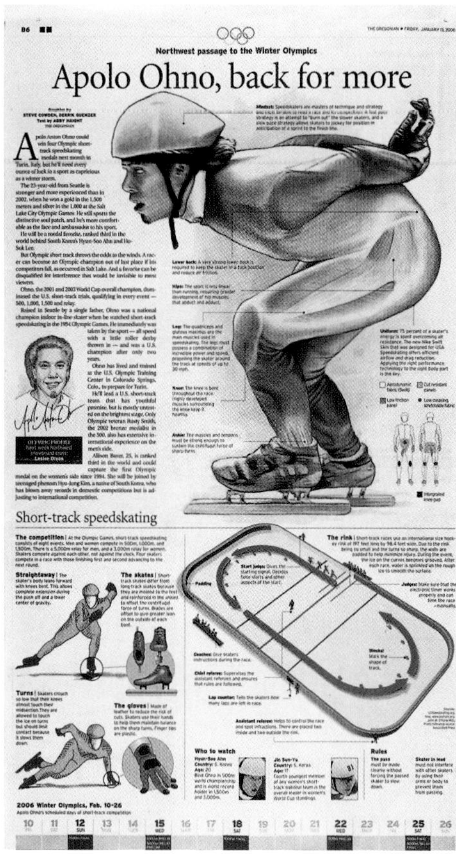

Northwest passage to the Winter Olympics

Apolo Ohno, back for more

Short-track speedskating

2006 Winter Olympics, Feb. 10-26

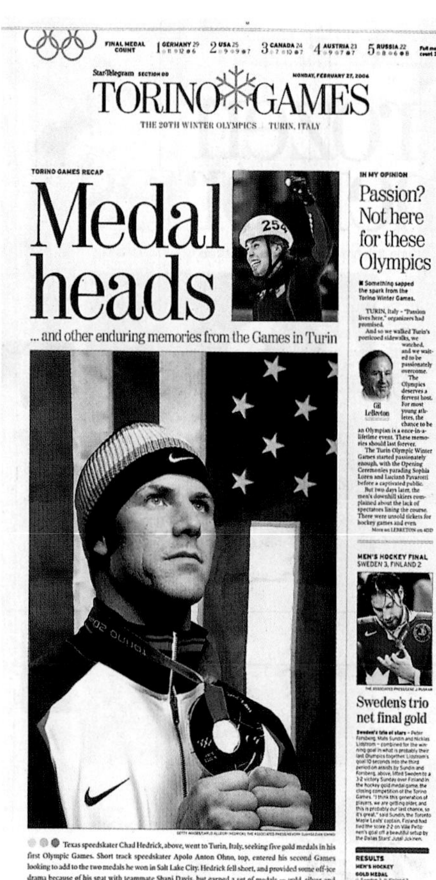

TORINO GAMES

THE 20TH WINTER OLYMPICS | TURIN, ITALY

Medal heads

... and other enduring memories from the Games in Turin

IN MY OPINION

Passion? Not here for these Olympics

MEN'S HOCKEY FINAL SWEDEN 3, FINLAND 2

Sweden's trio net final gold

**FORT WORTH STAR-TELEGRAM** (Texas)

Michael Currie, Celeste Williams, Terry Bigham, Seth Schrock

Special news topics, Olympics

**EL GRÁFICO,** Antiguo Cuscatlan, El Salvador

Agustín A. Palacios, Alexander Rivera, Humberto Rodríguez, Gabriel Orellana, Ernesto Quan, Rosemberg Girón, Yanira Segovia, Juan José

Special news topics, World Cup

Resumen GRUPO D Primera fase

LA FIGURA

Momento de lusos y mariachis

Ante los titubeos de Irán y sobre todo de Angola, que no se afirmó nunca para pelear un puesto, este grupo D terminó siendo fácil para Portugal y México.

Luis Figo

México sufrido

ALEMANIA 2006

MOMENTO ANÍMICO

CAMBIO GENERACIONAL

GRUPO C

SE GUARDAN A LOS AMONESTADOS

EN CONDICIONES IGUALES

[DELANTERA NUEVA] POR LO EXPUESTO POR JOSÉ PEKERMAN Y DADAS LAS AMARILLAS QUE PESAN SOBRE HERNÁN CRESPO Y JAVIER SAVIOLA, LA DELANTERA ARGENTINA SERÁ PRIMERIZA EN ALEMANIA 2006.

[DEFENSA NUEVA] DADA LA LESIÓN DE JOHNNY HEITINGA Y LAS AMARILLAS DE GIOVANNI VAN BRONCKHORST Y JORIS MATHIJSEN, LA DEFENSA DE HOLANDA HOY TENDRÁ UNA NUEVA CARA.

VAN DER SAR AL 112

**LA PRENSA GRÁFICA,** Antiguo Cuscatlán, El Salvador

Enrique Contreras, Héctor Ramírez, Erick Cortez

Special news topics, World Cup

GRUPO A [ECUADOR • COSTA RICA]

Cruzó el Ecuador

El equipo sudamericano eliminó a los ticos y logró una histórica clasificación

La figura...

"Tin" Delgado

3-0

**EL DIARIO DE HOY,** San Salvador, El Salvador

Juan Durán, Teodoro Wilson Torres, Jorge Castillo, Alicia Dubón, Hugo Rodríguez, Staff de Deportes

Special news topics, World Cup

**STAR TRIBUNE,** Minneapolis
Staff
Special news topics, Olympics

THE XX WINTER OLYMPIAD
FEBRUARY 10-26 • TURIN, ITALY
WHO WILL SHINE?
Janica Kostelic
Apolo Anton Ohno
Sasha Cohen
Bode Miller
Past stars
An Olympic retrospective

**SVENSKA DAGBLADET,** Stockholm, Sweden
Bengt Sazomonson, Kristofer Gustafsson
Special news topics, Olympics

1435 meter på 56 sekunder
OS i dag
Det jäser i områden runt Turin! Lugn, så är det alltid.
Alkohol kan skada din hälsa.

[LOS GRITOS DEL MUNDIAL]
En el Mundial se llevan convertidos 65 goles. El grito sagrado del fútbol en toda su dimensión, con festejos para todos los gustos y de los más variados. Una recorrida gráfica por el momento más deseado de jugadores y aficionados.
GOLES SON AMORES

**EL DIARIO DE HOY,** San Salvador, El Salvador
Juan Durán, Teodoro Wilson Torres, Jorge Castillo, Alicia Dubón, Hugo Rodríguez, Sports Staff
Special news topics, World Cup

NATIONAL POST
MONDAY, FEBRUARY 27, 2006
7 10 7
CANADA, KLASSEN CELEBRATE GAMES RECORDS
STAGE SET FOR 2010
INSIDE
SWEDES WIN GOLD

**NATIONAL POST,** Toronto
Doug Kelly, Gayle Grin, Stephen Meurice, Tom Philip, Kelly McParland, Jeff Wasserman, Laura Koot, Angela Murphy, Jim Bray
Special news topics, Olympics

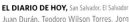

El 25 de septiembre, 3 mil hombres, entre policías, soldados y carceleros recuperaron Pavón, la cárcel "modelo" guatemalteca que desde hacía diez años estaba en manos de un comité de presos. El lugar era más bien un feudo donde se vivía con lujos y se controlaba un abanico de crímenes.
El escándalo de Pavón
Palacio arrebatado a la mafia
Jefe con derecho de pernada

**EL DIARIO DE HOY,** San Salvador, El Salvador
Juan Durán, Teodoro Wilson Torres, Jorge Castillo, José Santos, Remberto Rodríguez, Ricardo Antonio Saravia
Special news topics, local

**SAN FRANCISCO CHRONICLE**

Nanette Bisher, Frank Mina, Matt Petty, Rick Nobles, Elizabeth Burr, Kathleen Hennessy, Gus D'Angelo, Joe Shoulak, John Blanchard, Kat Wade

Special news topics, local

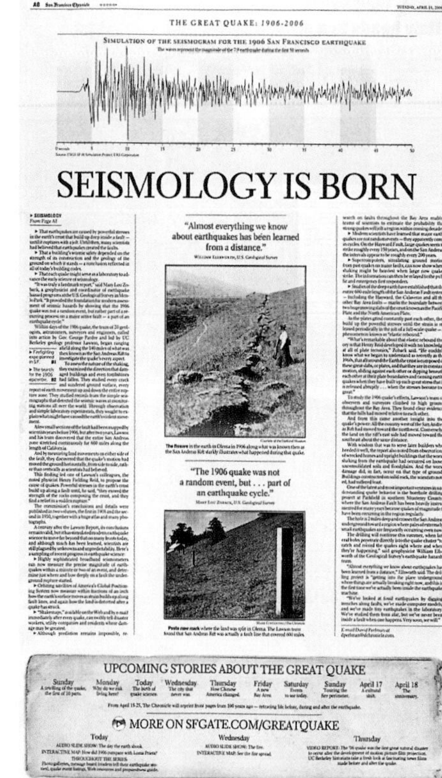

THE GREAT QUAKE: 1906-2006

SIMULATION OF THE SEISMOGRAM FOR THE 1906 SAN FRANCISCO EARTHQUAKE

# SEISMOLOGY IS BORN

"Almost everything we know about earthquakes has been learned from a distance."

"The 1906 quake was not a random event, but . . . part of an earthquake cycle."

UPCOMING STORIES ABOUT THE GREAT QUAKE

MORE ON SFGATE.COM/GREATQUAKE

**LA PRESSE,** Montréal

Benoit Giguere, Genevieve Dinel, Alain-Pierre Hovasse, Eric Trottier, Staff

Special news topics, local

LA PRESSE

15 PAGES /// LA TRAGÉDIE EN MOTS ET EN PHOTOS

# FUSILLADE AU COLLÈGE DAWSON

UN FORCENÉ PREND D'ASSAUT LE CÉGEP DU CENTRE-VILLE

/// Une élève tuée
/// Une vingtaine de blessés
/// Le tireur perd la vie

Portrait du tireur, compte rendu et analyses d'une journée d'horreur

'06

San Jose Mercury News

SPECIAL ELECTION SECTION

# DEMOCRATS HALT GOP DOMINANCE

Pelosi and party celebrate House triumph, Senate gains

SAN JOSE MAYOR'S RACE

CALIFORNIA GOVERNOR'S RACE

Chuck Reed sails to easy win

Schwarzenegger starts 'sequel'

National — How Congress has changed

California — Several close races for state offices

For results, go to mercurynews.com

Bay Area — Carr wins county DA race

San Jose — Licardo defeats Diaz in District 3

**SAN JOSE MERCURY NEWS** (Calif.)

Staff

Special news topics, local

PORTRAIT OF DIGNITY

CORETTA SCOTT KING / 1927-2006

# 'She lived a graceful and beautiful life.'

ANDREW YOUNG, former U.N. ambassador and Atlanta mayor



"Seeing her stoic demeanor and gentleness throughout my life makes me so very proud to be an African-American woman raising an African-American young lady. My 7-year-old said this morning, 'Mommy, I want to go to Mrs. King's funeral to say goodbye.'"

ETHEL SANDERS, Roswell

"She was nonviolent to the end. No struggle. Peace."

EDYTHE SCOTT BAGLEY, sister

**THE ATLANTA JOURNAL-CONSTITUTION**

Staff

Special news topics, local

LIVING VISIONS

"Don't you know that your body is the temple of the Holy Spirit, who lives in you and was given to you by God? You do not belong to yourself, for God bought you with a high price. So you must honor God with your body."

1 Corinthians 6:19-20

I exhort therefore, that, first of all, supplications, prayers, intercessions, and giving of thanks, be made for all men; For kings, and for all that are in authority; that we may lead a quiet and peaceable life in all godliness and honesty. For this is good and acceptable in the sight of God our Saviour;

I Timothy 2:1-3

Photography Alan Spearman

**THE COMMERCIAL APPEAL,** Memphis, Tenn.

Richard Robbins, Alan Spearman, John Sale

Special news topics, local

**THE SAN DIEGO UNION-TRIBUNE**

Michael Canepa, Cristina Martinez Byvik, Michael Price, Crissy Pascual, Michael Franklin, Michael James Rocha

Special news topics, local

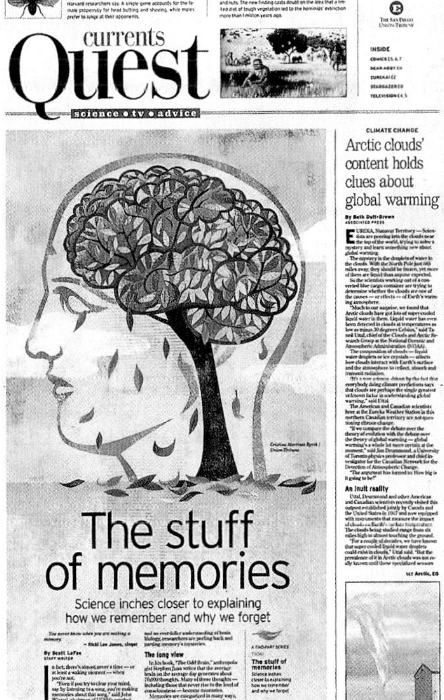

GIRLS HEAD-BUTT: BOYS LUNGE

VARIED DIET: TEETH TELL THE STORY

THURSDAY November 16, 2006

currents Quest

science • tv • advice

CLIMATE CHANGE

Arctic clouds' content holds clues about global warming

The stuff of memories

Science inches closer to explaining how we remember and why we forget

PIERCE LEADS CELTICS TO FIFTH STRAIGHT WIN

Stepping up

SUNDAY CAPE COD TIMES

POISON BULLETS

How TUNGSTEN missed the MARK

Army failed to share information that bullets can pollute soil and water supply

Shuttle crew repairs station

Fund helps young couple pay the bills

**CAPE COD TIMES,** Hyannis, Mass.

Eric Gongola, James Warren

Special news topics, local

Fredag 5. maj 2006 ■ Årgang 122 Nr. 214 ■ Pris 19,50 ■ AbonnementService 70 15 01 01 ■ www.politiken.dk

# POLITIKENFREDAG

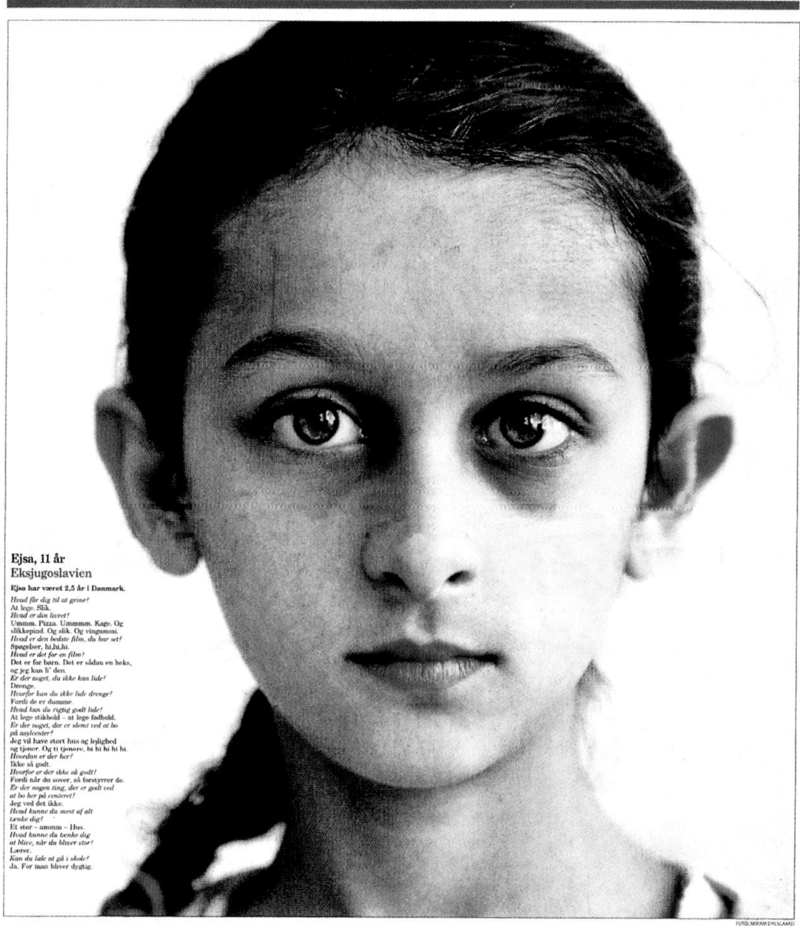

**Ejsa, 11 år**
Eksjugoslavien

**Ejsa har været 2,5 år i Danmark.**

*Hvad får dig til at grine?*
At lege. Slik.
*Hvad er din livret?*
Ummm. Pizza. Ummmm. Kage. Og slikkepind. Og slik. Og vingummi.
*Hvad er den bedste film, du har set?*
Spøgelser, hi,hi,hi.
*Hvad er det for en film?*
Det er for børn. Det er sådan en heks, og jeg kan li' den.
*Er der noget, du ikke kan lide?*
Drenge.
*Hvorfor kan du ikke lide drenge?*
Fordi de er dumme.
*Hvad kan du rigtig godt lide?*
At lege stikbold - at lege fodbold.
*Er der noget, der er slemt ved at bo på asylcenter?*
Jeg vil have stort hus og lejlighed og tjener. Og ti tjenere, hi hi hi hi hi.
*Hvordan er der her?*
Ikke så godt.
*Hvorfor er der ikke så godt?*
Fordi når du sover, så forstyrrer de.
*Er der nogen ting, der er godt ved at bo her på centeret?*
Jeg ved det ikke.
*Hvad kunne du mest af alt tænke dig?*
Et stor - ammm - Hus.
*Hvad kunne du tænke dig at blive, når du bliver stor?*
Lærer.
*Kan du lide at gå i skole?*
Ja. For man bliver dygtig.

FOTO: MIRIAM DALSGAARD

## Mød Ejsa og 31 andre asylbørn

**Debatten om børns forhold på asylcentrene har splittet Danmark på tværs af politiske fløje. Men hvem er børnene? Læs om dem i dag.**

Historien om de danske asylcentre er historien om alt for mange mennesker på alt for lidt plads i alt for lang tid. Og selv om alle er enige om, at børn og voksne bliver fysisk og psykisk syge af at bo der, tyder intet på, at der vil ske nævneværdige forandringer i den kommende tid.

Statsminister Anders Fogh Rasmussen (V) har siden påske to gange slået fast, at ansvaret for børnenes trivsel er forældrenes. Som han sagde i går i Folketinget: »Vi taler om sager, hvor der er givet afslag. Det betyder, at så har forældrene ansvaret for at vende tilbage, så børnene kan vokse op under andre forhold«.

Ifølge Fogh skal det ikke være sådan, »at jo længere tid man opholder sig i centrene, desto bedre vilkår kan man tilkæmpe sig, fordi så bryder hele systemet sammen«.

Det var Foghs partifælle Ejvind Vesselbo og Henriette Kjær fra de konservative, der satte ny ild til en gammel debat. De to havde som medlemmer af Folketingets Integrationsudvalg besøgt asylcentrene og var rystede over forholdene.

»Lige meget hvilken status du har i Danmark - om du er afvist eller søger asyl - har vi altså ansvar for, at dem der bor her, lever under nogle forhold, som vi kan forsvare, og det mener jeg sådan set ikke er tilfældet på nuværende tidspunkt«, sagde Ejvind Vesselbo 15. april til Politiken, og Henriette Kjær sagde til Ritzau:

»Forholdene på de danske asylcentre er rystende ringe og uværdige. Det kan vi ikke være bekendt at byde andre mennesker og jeg vil derfor arbejde på at få forbedret forholdene hurtigst muligt«.

Anders Fogh Rasmussen har ikke besøgt centrene, og har heller ikke »nogen faste planer vedrørende besigtigelse af asylcentre«.

Men Henriette Kjær står fast. Hun sagde til Information i går: »Jeg holder fast i, at de folk, der bor på asylcentre i Danmark, dem skal vi behandle ordentlig, uanset hvorfor de er i landet. Jeg er enig i, at de voksne har et ansvar i forhold til deres egen situation. De vil ikke rejse hjem, og det kan der være så mange forklaringer på. Men én ting er forældrene, noget andet er børnene«.

**Lea Korsgaard og Olav Hergel har mødt Kongelundens børn. Fire sider inde i 1. SEKTION**

**Ledende artikel 2. SEKTION side 10**

### Fogh vil ikke besøge asylbørn

Af Tanja Parker Astrup

**VEJRET.** Tørt og solrigt med kun få skyer. 18-23 grader.

**LÆS OGSÅ**



SILVER

**POLITIKEN,** Copenhagen, Denmark

Søren Nyeland, Per Folkver, Claus Skovhus, Miriam Dalsgaard, Per Bülow, Liv Olsen, Heidi Højgaard, Olav Hergel

Special news topics, local

This package tells the stories of children in asylums, places a politician won't visit. How can you turn your back? The poses and variations in the portraits show much about their personalities. It's very touching, very documentary. We don't know how you could approach this topic with more poignancy. You can't ignore these children.

Esta unidad noticiosa cuenta la historia de los niños en los asilos, lugares que un político no visitaría. ¿Cómo se les podría dar la espalda? Las posturas y las variaciones en los retratos enseñan mucho sobre sus personalidades. Es muy conmovedor, muy documental. No sabemos cómo se podría tocar este tema de forma más conmovedora. Estos niños no pueden ser simplemente ignorados.

ASYLBØRN

**LA PRESSE,** Montréal

Philippe Tardif, Martin Tremblay, Pascale Breton, Silvia Galipeau, Benoit Giguere, Genevieve Dinel, Marie-Claude Malboeuf, Alain-Pierre Hovasse, Marie-Claude Lortie

Special news topics, local

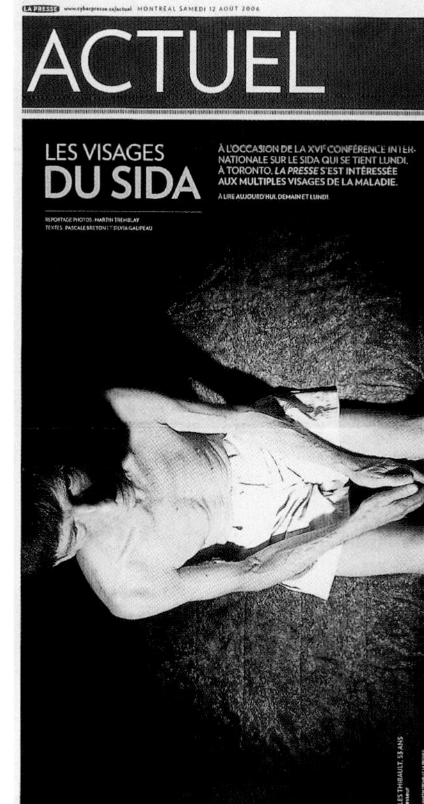

MONTRÉAL SAMEDI 12 AOÛT 2006

ACTUEL

LES VISAGES DU SIDA

À L'OCCASION DE LA XVI[e] CONFÉRENCE INTERNATIONALE SUR LE SIDA QUI SE TIENT LUNDI À TORONTO, *LA PRESSE* S'EST INTÉRESSÉE AUX MULTIPLES VISAGES DE LA MALADIE.

À LIRE AUJOURD'HUI, DEMAIN ET LUNDI

**THE VIRGINIAN-PILOT,** Norfolk

Ryan Healy, Sam Hundley, Lori Kelley, Robert Suhay, Robert D. Voros, Martin Smith-Rodden, Judy Le, Charles Apple, Paul Nelson, Deborah Withey

Special news topics, local

FORD PLANT TO CLOSE

The Virginian-Pilot

Workers, Norfolk stunned; 2,400 to lose jobs by 2008

THE REASONS East Coast location, inability to build bigger pickups seen as liabilities

WHAT'S NEXT Provisions for workers unclear; 400,000 vehicles to be produced before close

"We got families going to lose their houses ... everything they worked for."

TAKING A HIT Loss of big taxpayer will upset city budget

SADNESS, DISBELIEF Workers try to figure out their futures

MORE INSIDE FIVE PAGES OF COVERAGE

AN ERA TO END Popular trucks can't save plant

**EL ECONOMISTA,** Madrid, Spain

Miguel Buckenmeyer, Gorka Sampedro, Juanjo Santacana, Elisabeth Nogales, Rosa Rey, Graphics Staff

Special news topics, local

Un año récord BOLSA & INVERSIÓN

La bolsa hace historia

E F M A M J

Enero Comienza el baile de opas

Febrero Aterrizan los 'alemanes'

Marzo Telefónica mueve ficha

Abril Abertis flirtea con Autostrade

Mayo El peor mes del año

Junio Nace el índice Eco10

El Ibex en 2006

SEGRE

Catalunya elige nuevo President

Los cinco candidatos se reúnen para posar en el día de reflexión

El Barça se complica su futuro europeo

Eurocasion

**SEGRE,** Lerida, Spain

Santiago Costa Miranda, Anna Barcala Sirvent, Glòria Farré Lorente, Anna Gómez Marsol, Joan Miras Montadas

Special news topics, local

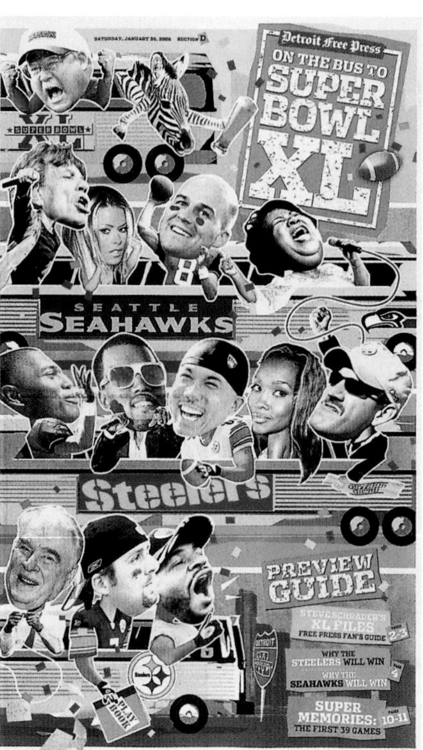



**DETROIT FREE PRESS**

Rick Nease, Mark Francescutti, Gene Myers, Diane Weiss, Steve Dorsey

Special news topics, sports

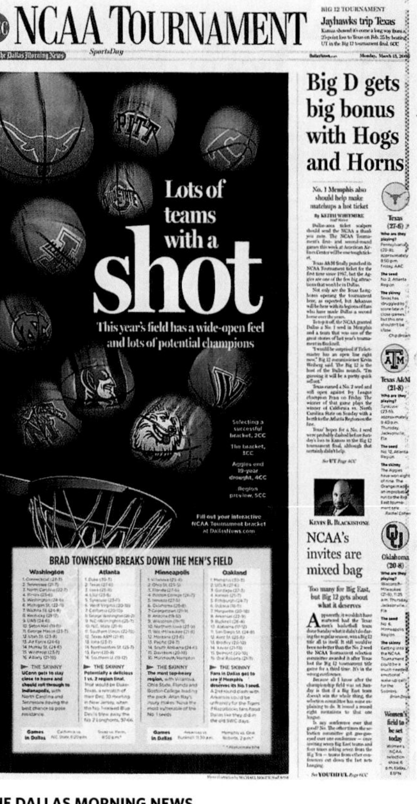

NCAA TOURNAMENT

Big D gets big bonus with Hogs and Horns

Lots of teams with a shot

This year's field has a wide-open feel and lots of potential champions

BRAD TOWNSEND BREAKS DOWN THE MEN'S FIELD

NCAA's invites are mixed bag

**THE DALLAS MORNING NEWS**

Rob Schneider, Jason Dugger, Christopher Velez, Michael Hogue, Mark Konradi, Brad Townsend, Carl Ellis, Joel Moore

Special news topics, sports

**EL DIARIO DE HOY,** San Salvador, El Salvador

Juan Durán, Teodoro Wilson Torres, Jorge Castillo, Edgardo Mendoza, Carlos Alvizures, José Elias Rivera, José Roberto Santo

Special news topics, international

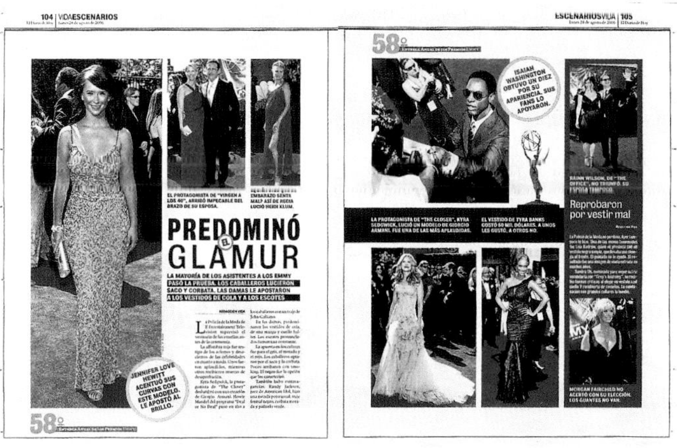

PREDOMINÓ EL GLAMUR

Reprobaron por vestir mal

**EL DIARIO DE HOY,** San Salvador, El Salvador

Juan Durán, Teodoro Wilson Torres, Jorge Castillo, Edgardo Mendoza, José Alejandro Ibarra, José Elias Rivera, Rosemarie Mixco

Special news topics, international

VIDA

Un final INESPERADO

CONTRA TODOS LOS PRONÓSTICOS, *CRASH* GANÓ EL PREMIO A LA MEJOR PELÍCULA Y SILENCIÓ A *SECRETO EN LA MONTAÑA*, EL FILME DE LOS VAQUEROS GAY

ORGULLOSOS CON SUS PREMIOS

LOS GANADORES

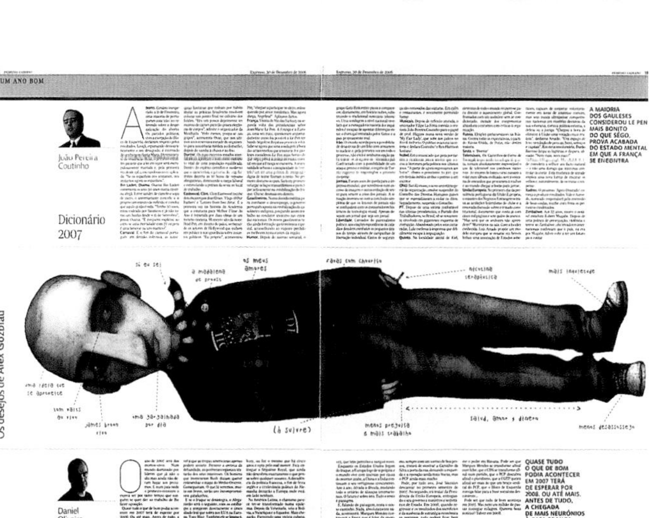

UM ANO BOM

Dicionário 2007

Os desejos de Alex Gozblau

Talvez em 2008

**EXPRESSO,** Lisbon, Portugal

Marco Grieco, Pedro Figueiral, João Paulo Galacho, Alex Gozblau, Goncalo Viana, Cristina Sampaio, Alexandre Farto

Special news topics, international

CRISIS IN THE MIDDLE EAST

'We left everything behind. I tried to keep my children calm but it was very hard'

PART THREE: THE EVACUEES BY CHARLES CHARALAMBOUS

Don't blame us ... this is not our fight

**SUNDAY HERALD,** Glasgow, Scotland

Richard Walker, Elaine Livingstone, Staff

Special news topics, international

INTERNACIONAL

FIDEL

Tres corrientes VAN POR EL PODER

Fidel Castro abandona la UCI

**EL DIARIO DE HOY,** San Salvador, El Salvador

Juan Durán, Teodoro Wilson Torres, Jorge Castillo, José Santos, Remberto Rodríguez, Enrique Peña, Mauricio Vaquez

Special news topics, international

THE START

Shouldering the load

LEBRON JAMES' BODY OF WORK

**THE PLAIN DEALER,** Cleveland

David Kordalski, Roy Hewitt, Mike Starkey, Emmet Smith, Roadell Hickman, Marvin Fong, John Kuntz, Bill Gugliotta, Stephen J. Beard, Rich Fletcher

Special news topics, sports

**FOLHA DE SÃO PAULO** (Brazil)
Massimo Gentile, Fabio Marra, Mario Kanno, Rubens Paiva
Special news topics, international

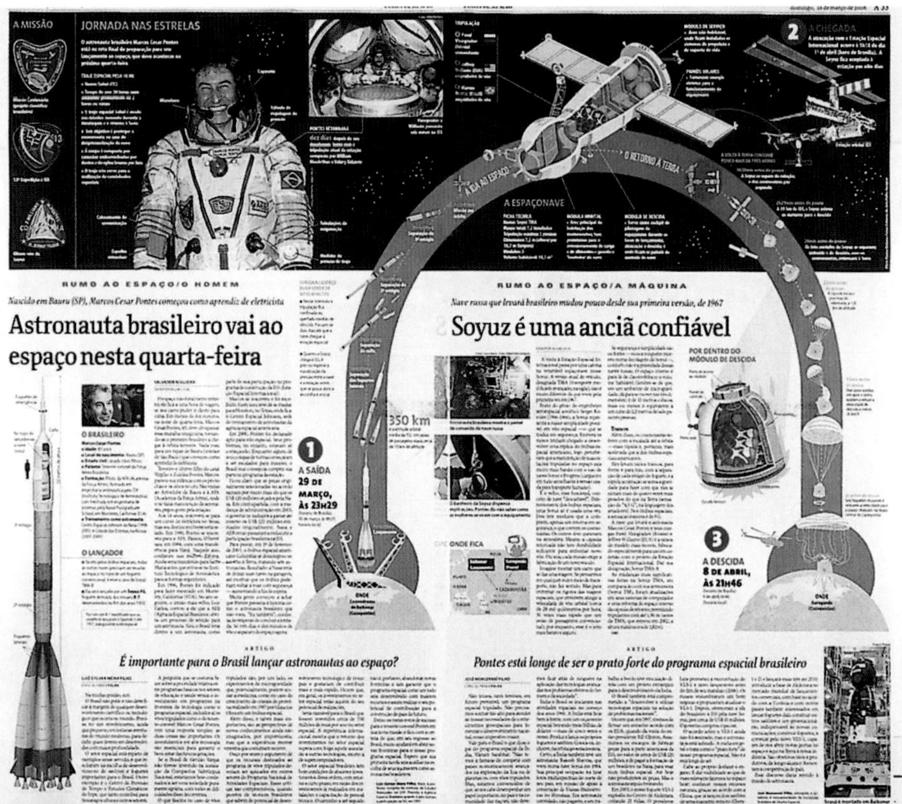
JORNADA NAS ESTRELAS

A ESPAÇONAVE

RUMO AO ESPAÇO/O HOMEM

Astronauta brasileiro vai ao espaço nesta quarta-feira

RUMO AO ESPAÇO/A MÁQUINA

Soyuz é uma anciã confiável

É importante para o Brasil lançar astronautas ao espaço?

Pontes está longe de ser o prato forte do programa espacial brasileiro

**SEATTLE POST-INTELLIGENCER**
Staff
Special news topics, sports

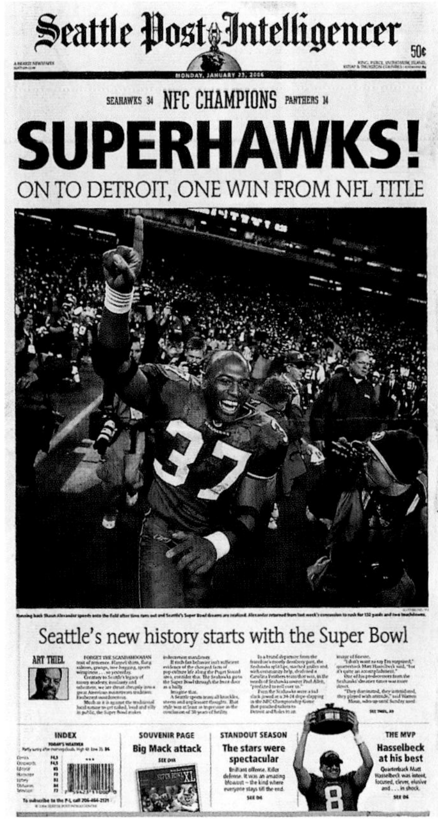
Seattle Post-Intelligencer

SEAHAWKS 34 NFC CHAMPIONS PANTHERS 14

SUPERHAWKS!

ON TO DETROIT, ONE WIN FROM NFL TITLE

Seattle's new history starts with the Super Bowl

LA PRENSA GRÁFICA

LUNES DEPORTIVO

MUNDIAL DE CORTE INGLÉS

ASESUISA
Asegura su tranquilidad

**LA PRENSA GRÁFICA,** Antiguo Cuscatlán, El Salvador
Enrique Contreras, Héctor Ramírez, Erick Cortez, Ricardo Orellana, Manuel Orantes
Special news topics, sports

Suplemento de Deportes de HERALDO DE ARAGÓN

HD.

Alicante ELIMINADO

Xerez ELIMINADO

Atlético de Madrid ELIMINADO

Barcelona ELIMINADO

Real Madrid ELIMINADO

Santiago Bernabéu, 21.30 (Tele 5)

Espanyol - Real Zaragoza

Remate final

Tras un brillantísimo torneo, en el que ha dejado en la cuneta a los más grandes equipos españoles, el Real Zaragoza afronta esta noche, en el Bernabéu (21.30), el último peldaño de la competición: la gran final, ante el Espanyol

El cuadro de Víctor Muñoz afronta el duelo con etiqueta de favorito, pero nadie se fía. Más de 35.000 aficionados zaragocistas acuden a la capital de España para arropar al equipo en su nuevo reto: la conquista de la Séptima

**HERALDO DE ARAGÓN,** Zaragoza, Spain
Kristina Urresti, Irán Santos, Pilar Ostalé, Jorge Luis Mora, Pedro Zapater
Special news topics, sports

One New Orleans Home Reborn, With Grit and Persistence

Then and Now

**THE NEW YORK TIMES**
Tom Bodkin, Margaret O'Connor, Brian Fidelman
Special news topics, national

**THE GUARDIAN,** London
Kevin Wilson, John Reardon/IPG
Special news topics, national

Special report

# Racism, recruitment and how the BNP believes it is just 'one crisis away from power'

Yesterday we reported how Ian Cobain went undercover to explore the secretive world of the British National party. Using a false identity, he joined the party last June, and within three months had been appointed central London organiser. Today, he describes the members he met, reveals the long-term strategy behind the repackaging of the BNP ... and goes to the Christmas party

'It will be ... an age of scarcity, an age in which a well-organised nationalist party could really make an impact'

'We do not have centuries in which to gradually achieve our aims ... we have a limited amount of time available to us'

Indblik

# Menneskehedens 10 største erkendelser

**MORGENAVISEN JYLLANDS-POSTEN,**
Viby, Denmark
Rina Kjeldgaard, Pierre Collignon, Arne E. Mathiesen
Special news topics, national

REPORTAGE ALL TIME HIGH FÖR H&M

# 350 000 procent upp för H&M-aktien

"Finansiellt har vi inga begränsningar, inte heller geografiskt."

80 Mkr

280 000 Mkr

Över 1 300 butiker i tre världsdelar

**DAGENS INDUSTRI,** Stockholm, Sweden
Lotta Andersson, Anna Byström, Fredrik Björnsson, Kicki Siösteen
Special news topics, national

# ASESINATOS
ANTIMOTINES SON ACRIBILLADOS

Saca acusa al FMLN

**EL DIARIO DE HOY,** San Salvador, El Salvador
Juan Durán, Teodoro Wilson Torres, Jorge Castillo, José Santos, Remberto Rodríguez, Hugo Rodríguez
Special news topics, national

CARLOS PERLA:

# "Orellana nos engañó"

El extraditado no pidió privilegios ni ser trasladado a un sitio específico

Carlos Perla, el hombre más famoso del momento en El Salvador, se sentó tranquilamente frente a los micrófonos. Eran las seis y media de la tarde cuando las preguntas de los periodistas cayeron como lluvia. Como si las esperara con mucha antelación, el ex funcionario extraditado comenzó a responderlas una a una. Estas son, en síntesis, sus palabras, que a continuación resume El Diario de Hoy

**EL DIARIO DE HOY,** San Salvador, El Salvador
Juan Durán, Teodoro Wilson Torres, Jorge Castillo, José Santos, Remberto Rodríguez, Enrique Peña
Special news topics, national

EL TERRORISMO DE ETA CLAVES DE ANÁLISIS

Miguel Sanz · Josu Jon Imaz · Gabriel Elorriaga · Nicolás Redondo · Joseba Arregi · Francisco José Alcaraz · Patxi López

JULEN DE MADARIAGA
FUNDADOR DE ETA Y MILITANTE DE ARALAR

# "ETA se debilita porque el pueblo vasco le da la espalda, no por la represión"

**HERALDO DE ARAGÓN,** Zaragoza, Spain
Kristina Urresti, Irán Santos, Pilar Ostalé, Jorge Luis Mora, Pedro Zapater
Special news topics, national

**SAN JOSE MERCURY NEWS** (Calif.)
Michael Tribble, Pai, Geri Migielicz, Jonathon Berlin, Matt Mansfield
Special news topics, national

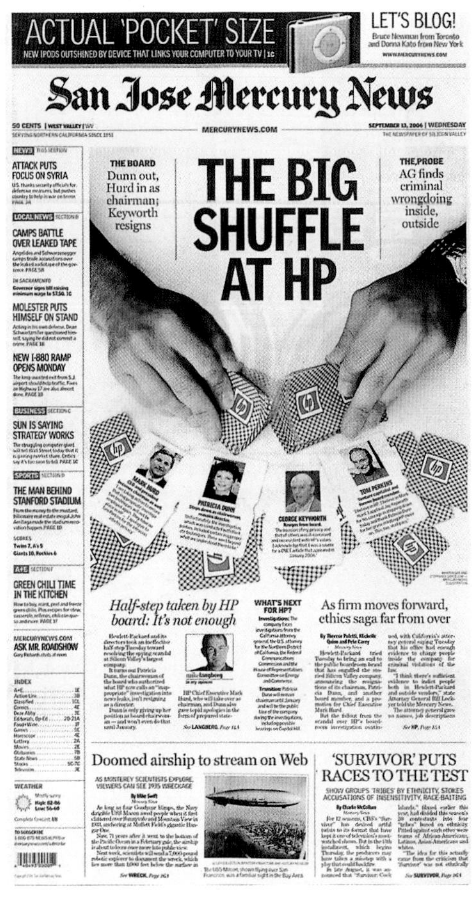
ACTUAL 'POCKET' SIZE

LET'S BLOG!

San Jose Mercury News

THE BIG SHUFFLE AT HP

Half-step taken by HP board: It's not enough

As firm moves forward, ethics saga far from over

Doomed airship to stream on Web

'SURVIVOR' PUTS RACES TO THE TEST

**FOLHA DE SÃO PAULO** (Brazil)
Massimo Gentile, Fabio Marra, Clayton Jr.
Special news topics, national

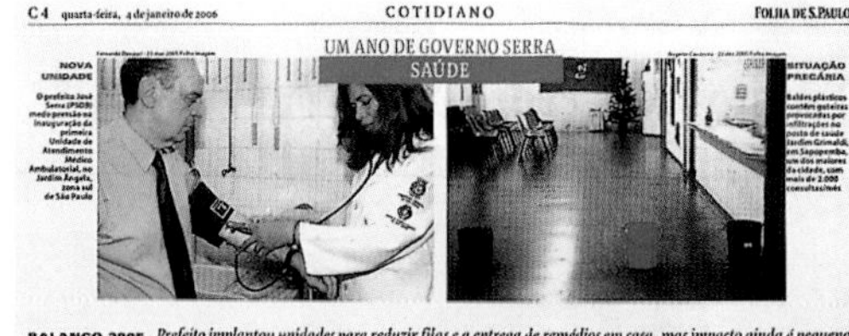
COTIDIANO

UM ANO DE GOVERNO SERRA

SAÚDE

Programas de Serra estão em ritmo lento

Situação não muda em posto e hospital

Parceria é a saída para setor, defende prefeito

**SAN JOSE MERCURY NEWS** (Calif.)
Karl Kahler, Pai, Geri Migielicz, Jonathon Berlin, Matt Mansfield, Michael Tribble
Special news topics, national

SEPT. 11: FIVE YEARS LATER

DAY TO MOURN

Tears, solemn moments mark the sites where terrorists struck

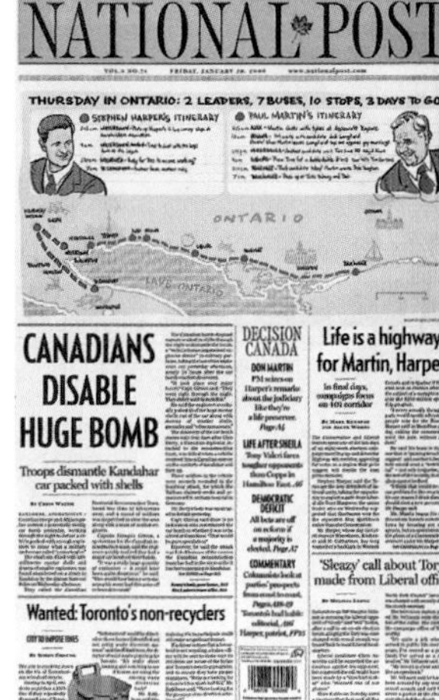
LOVE MATCH

NATIONAL POST

CANADIANS DISABLE HUGE BOMB

Life is a highway for Martin, Harper

**NATIONAL POST,** Toronto
Doug Kelly, Gayle Grin, Stephen Meurice, Tom Philip, Kelly McParland, Jeff Wasserman, Laura Koot, Angela Murphy, Kagan McLeod, Gary Clement
Special news topics, national

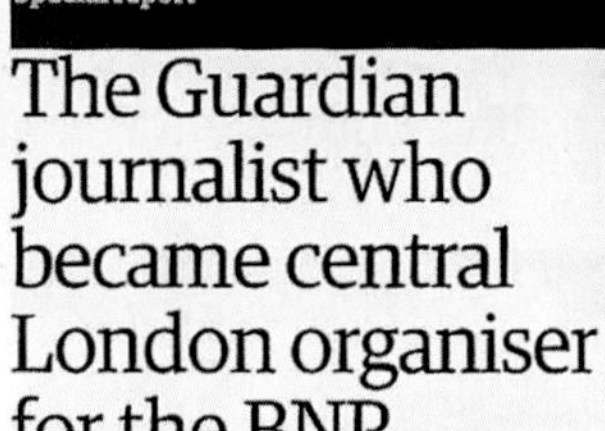
Special report

The Guardian journalist who became central London organiser for the BNP

Reporter Ian Cobain went undercover for seven months to explore the clandestine world of the British National party: how it operates, recruits and holds meetings. Who its members are – from businessmen to ballerinas – and what they say in private. He found a party desperate to persuade the public that the image of the shaven-headed football hooligan is a thing of the past. But in private it is a party that operates unlike any other: using false names, encryption software, secret lists and counter-surveillance techniques

The first meeting

I would say, quite truthfully: 'Trust me, if you knew what I did for a living you would understand why I can't tell you'

The activists

The members

The Orange Tree pub

Who is watching?

Central London organiser

The South Africans will never stage a proper World Cup, how could they? They're a black country'

SATURDAY STAR

WHO WE ARE

WHO WE'LL BE

A groundbreaking poll of Canadian immigrants shows a country pointed in a fresh direction. Our nation's newest builders are younger, smarter, healthier and committed to Canada.

Want to save $20? The choice is yours.

**THE GUARDIAN,** London
Kevin Wilson, John Reardon
Special news topics, national

**TORONTO STAR**
Charlie Kopun, Spencer Wynn, Francine Kopun, Lucas Oleniuk, Lynn McAuley, Giles Gherson
Special news topics, national

Chapter Five

# FEATURES & MAGAZINES

Reportajes y revistas

**FEATURES**
**Opinion / Lifestyle / Entertainment / Food / Fashion**
**Home/Real Estate / Travel / Science/Technology**

**MAGAZINES**
**Covers / Pages / Special Sections / Overall**

REPORTAJES
Opinión / Estilo de vida / Entretención / Comida / Moda
Hogar/Inmobiliaria / Viajes / Ciencia/Tecnología

REVISTAS
Portadas / Páginas / Secciones especiales / Total

**THE DALLAS MORNING NEWS**

Douglas Jones, Laura Schwed, John Lose, Michael Mulvey, Michael Hamtil, Marilyn Bishkin

Other feature section, 175,000+

The Dallas Morning News

Solutions

SUDOKU

CLEAN SWEEP

The new generation of vacuum cleaners 4

SIMPLIFY: DESPERATION DINNERS Banish dinner doldrums with morning favorites 8
INSPIRE ME: TASTING MEMORIES Savoring apples and the thoughts that come with them 9
ONLINE: HELP FOR PARENTS Visit DallasNews.com/familyblog

**THE OBSERVER,** London

Carolyn Roberts, Caroline Costello

Travel section, 175,000+

The Observer SUNDAY 8 JANUARY 2006

ESCAPE

TIME TO GET HIGH | THE £200 CHALLENGE | THE GUIDE: DUBAI ON THE CHEAP

My favourite place in the world

They've travelled all over the globe but if they could return to just one special place which would it be? Carl Wilkinson asked 15 of the world's top travel writers to choose their all-time favourite destination

COLIN THUBRON KHOTAN, CHINA

world domination

international calls for local prices

it's a different world

Telewest

**THE KANSAS CITY STAR** (Mo.)

Tom Dolphens, Greg Branson, Barbara Hill-Meyer, Randy Wyrick, Staff

Food section, 175,000+

THE KANSAS CITY STAR

Start your ovens

Eating for Life

Food

OLD FAVORITES | A tender topper for chicken

DELIGHTFUL DUMPLINGS

BE LIKE PETER, THE PUMPKIN EATER

THURSDAY IN PREVIEW

K

"My reward comes when the girls have a great performance." K9

Better health

TAKE CARE OF YOURSELF & YOUR FAMILY

ajc On ajc.com/health: Check for daily updates at our redesigned health channel, and sign up to receive our e-newsletter.

Which teas can save your life?

PAGE K6

PLUS Yerba maté may be good for you, but it's an acquired taste. PAGE K5

FOOD & NUTRITION
Don't blow your diet at happy hour. Know which cocktails are a calorie-counter's nightmare. / K4

GOOD FORM
Fitness trainer Cynthia Phillips shows you how to stay fit without leaving your hotel room. / K4

TRUE OR FALSE
Does working the night shift increase your chance of breast cancer? / K8

7.2

**THE ATLANTA JOURNAL-CONSTITUTION**

Will Alford, Cindy Deifenderfer, Evelyn Ortego, Karen Park

Other feature section, 175,000+

Style & Arts

The Boston Globe Thursday, March 9

H

SPRING FASHION REPORT

BOLD ENOUGH FOR YOU?

THINK FLORAL

THINK MOD

THINK STRIPES

INSIDE

PICTURED

ART REVIEW

Pictures that are worth a thousand gonzo words

**THE BOSTON GLOBE**

Chin Wang, Lane Turner, Ann Scales, Dan Zedek

Other feature section, 175,000+

**THE OTTAWA CITIZEN**

Paula McLaughlin, Carl Neustaedter, Susan Allan, Susan McDonough, Scott Anderson

Other feature section, 50,000-174,999

THE CITIZEN'S

# WEEKLY

SUNDAY, JANUARY 22, 2006 • SECTION B

## The winter of our disconnect

While this campaign turned surprisingly substantive, it avoided the deeper issues that face our fragile country and a burning world. Canadians, as always, want change while staying the same. This time, ANDREW COHEN observes, we want liberalism without Liberals, or more likely, Conservatives without conservatism.

And so it ends, this long, cold campaign stretching from the dead of autumn to the hollow of winter, its armies of partisans sustained through darkness and snow by the promise of a bright political spring. For one of them, it arrives tomorrow.

Like the visit of the pushy cousin who comes for Advent and stays through Christmas, New Year's and Epiphany, this was a campaign that seemed to go on forever. The experts sniffed that it would be shallow, predictable, nasty and inconsequential. Actually, it has turned out to be substantive, surprising and relatively civil, if uninspiring. Most important for the electors of Canada, it looks to be decisive.

Today, we welcome the election like an ailing soul welcomes the morning. Collectively, we sense who will win but don't know exactly how or where. For all the feverish advertising and the high-blown rhetoric, the election of 2006 doesn't feel like a watershed. If it does turn out to be a historic realignment of priorities and politics — and an ambitious government with "a hidden agenda" might well make it so — it isn't because either major party promised a sea change or the people demanded it.

Story continues on PAGE B10

## Election GUIDE

'Hey, didn't Harper have a rocky start? How did he end up in front?'

Eight weeks is a long time on the hustings. Relive the highs, lows and the dubious achievements. See the quotes, cartoons and turning points on the campaign trail.

The Campaign: B2-3

'Never mind the leaders, battles are won in ridings like mine in Ottawa.'

Patrick Dare goes to the frontline of the local races and finds Liberals fighting a surging Tory tide.
Plus: Key races to watch in town and across the country.

The Races: B4-5

'But I want to vote based on the issues. Where does each party stand?'

Still haven't read the platforms? That's OK, we did the hard work, then created a cheat sheet: Catch up on five parties and 11 issues in the time it takes to have coffee and toast.

The Issues: B6-7

'I've got it all figured out. Just tell me where to vote.'

Can't find your Elections Canada card? Don't know where to go? Never voted before? Rather eat your ballot? We can help. Plus: Where to go for results and analysis tomorrow night. BONUS! TV-watcher's bingo card!

Voter Guide: B8-9

# SONNTAG



Was 2006 die Menschen dieser Welt bewegte: Demonstrationen und Parolen im **Jahresrückblick**

WWW.TAGESSPIEGEL.DE/SONNTAG

Oliver Kahn, 37, ist Torwart beim FC Bayern, sieben Meistertitel und fünf Pokalsiege feierte er dort. Dreimal wurde er zum besten Torhüter der Welt gewählt. 86-mal spielte er in der deutschen Nationalmannschaft. Bei dieser Fußball-WM hatte er nur einen Einsatz: Beim siegreichen Spiel um den dritten Platz gegen Portugal.

INTERVIEW: NORBERT THOMMA

## „Ich bin Herrn Klinsmann gar nicht dankbar"

Oliver Kahn wurde zur Nummer 2 degradiert, im Juli nahm er seinen Abschied. Wie war sein Jahr? Menschlich toll, sagt er, und: „Ich hätte diese WM gewonnen."

**DER TAGESSPIEGEL,** Berlin

Bettina Seuffert, Norbert Thomma

Other feature section, 50,000-174,999

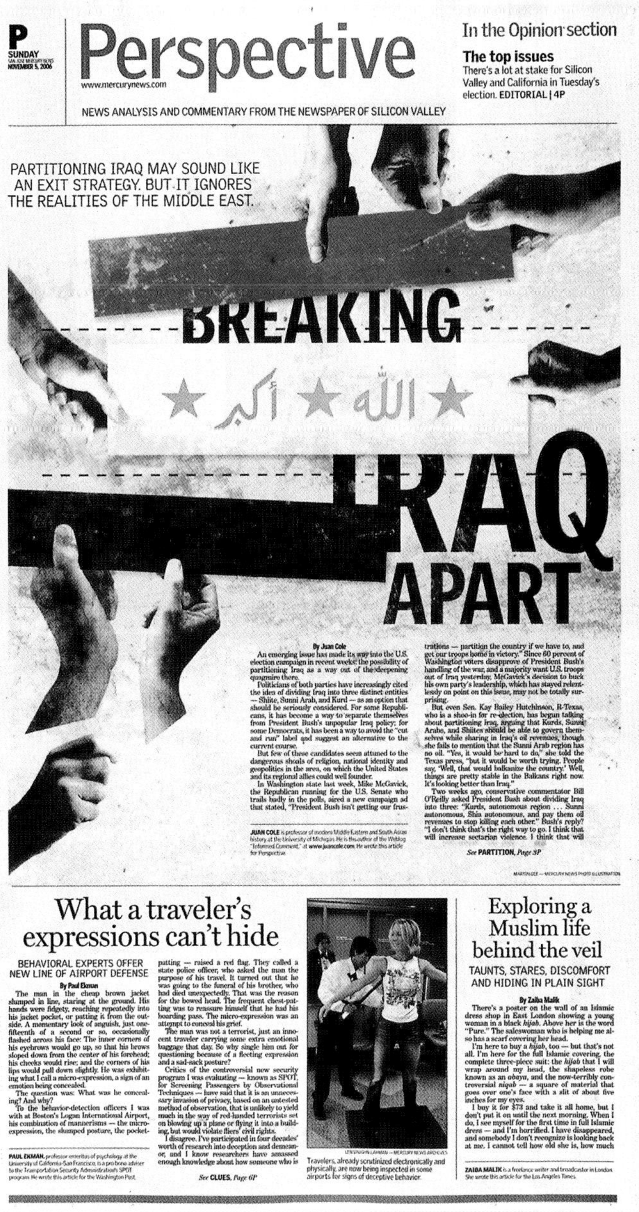

P
SUNDAY
NOVEMBER 5, 2006

# Perspective

www.mercurynews.com

NEWS ANALYSIS AND COMMENTARY FROM THE NEWSPAPER OF SILICON VALLEY

In the Opinion section

**The top issues**
There's a lot at stake for Silicon Valley and California in Tuesday's election. **EDITORIAL | 4P**

PARTITIONING IRAQ MAY SOUND LIKE AN EXIT STRATEGY. BUT IT IGNORES THE REALITIES OF THE MIDDLE EAST.

## BREAKING IRAQ APART



By Juan Cole

An emerging issue has made its way into the U.S. election campaign in recent weeks: the possibility of partitioning Iraq as a way out of the deepening quagmire there.

Politicians of both parties have increasingly cited the idea of dividing Iraq into three distinct entities — Shiite, Sunni Arab, and Kurd — as an option that should be seriously considered. For some Republicans, it has become a way to separate themselves from President Bush's unpopular Iraq policy; for some Democrats, it has been a way to avoid the "cut and run" label and suggest an alternative to the current course.

But few of these candidates seem attuned to the dangerous shoals of religion, national identity and geopolitics in the area, on which the United States and its regional allies could well founder.

In Washington state last week, Mike McGavick, the Republican running for the U.S. Senate who trails badly in the polls, aired a new campaign ad that stated, "President Bush isn't getting our frustrations — partition the country if we have to, and get our troops home in victory." Since 60 percent of Washington voters disapprove of President Bush's handling of the war, and a majority want U.S. troops out of Iraq yesterday, McGavick's decision to buck his own party's leadership, which has stayed relentlessly on point on this issue, may not be totally surprising.

But even Sen. Kay Bailey Hutchinson, R-Texas, who is a shoo-in for re-election, has begun talking about partitioning Iraq, arguing that Kurds, Sunni Arabs, and Shiites should be able to govern themselves while sharing in Iraq's oil revenues, though she fails to mention that the Sunni Arab region has no oil. "Yes, it would be hard to do," she told the Texas press, "but it would be worth trying. People say, 'Well, that would balkanize the country.' Well, things are pretty stable in the Balkans right now. It's looking better than Iraq."

Two weeks ago, conservative commentator Bill O'Reilly asked President Bush about dividing Iraq into three: "Kurds, autonomous region ... Sunni autonomous, Shia autonomous, and pay them oil revenues to stop killing each other." Bush's reply? "I don't think that's the right way to go. I think that will increase sectarian violence. I think that will

See PARTITION, Page 3P

JUAN COLE is professor of modern Middle Eastern and South Asian history at the University of Michigan. He is the author of the Weblog "Informed Comment," at www.juancole.com. He wrote this article for Perspective.

MARTIN GEE — MERCURY NEWS PHOTO ILLUSTRATION

## What a traveler's expressions can't hide

BEHAVIORAL EXPERTS OFFER NEW LINE OF AIRPORT DEFENSE

By Paul Ekman

The man in the cheap brown jacket slumped in line, staring at the ground. His hands were fidgety, reaching repeatedly into his jacket pocket, or patting it from the outside. A momentary look of anguish, just one-fifteenth of a second or so, occasionally flashed across his face: The inner corners of his eyebrows would go up, so that his brows sloped down from the center of his forehead; his cheeks would rise; and the corners of his lips would pull down slightly. He was exhibiting what I call a micro-expression, a sign of an emotion being concealed.

The question was: What was he concealing? And why?

To the behavior-detection officers I was with at Boston's Logan International Airport, his combination of mannerisms — the micro-expression, the slumped posture, the pocket-patting — raised a red flag. They called a state police officer, who asked the man the purpose of his travel. It turned out that he was going to the funeral of his brother, who had died unexpectedly. That was the reason for the bowed head. The frequent chest-patting was to reassure himself that he had his boarding pass. The micro-expression was an attempt to conceal his grief.

The man was not a terrorist, just an innocent traveler carrying some extra emotional baggage that day. So why single him out for questioning because of a fleeting expression and a sad-sack posture?

Critics of the controversial new security program I was evaluating — known as SPOT, for Screening Passengers by Observational Techniques — have said that it is an unnecessary invasion of privacy, based on an untested method of observation, that is unlikely to yield much in the way of red-handed terrorists set on blowing up a plane or flying it into a building, but would violate fliers' civil rights.

I disagree. I've participated in four decades' worth of research into deception and demeanor, and I know researchers have amassed enough knowledge about how someone who is

See CLUES, Page 6P

PAUL EKMAN, professor emeritus of psychology at the University of California-San Francisco, is a pro bono adviser to the Transportation Security Administration's SPOT program. He wrote this article for the Washington Post.

Travelers, already scrutinized electronically and physically, are now being inspected in some airports for signs of deceptive behavior.

## Exploring a Muslim life behind the veil

TAUNTS, STARES, DISCOMFORT AND HIDING IN PLAIN SIGHT

By Zaiba Malik

There's a poster on the wall of an Islamic dress shop in East London showing a young woman in a black *hijab*. Above her is the word "Pure." The saleswoman who is helping me also has a scarf covering her head.

I'm here to buy a *hijab*, too — but that's not all. I'm here for the full Islamic covering, the complete three-piece suit: the *hijab* that I will wrap around my head, the shapeless robe known as an *abaya*, and the now-terribly controversial *niqab* — a square of material that goes over one's face with a slit of about five inches for my eyes.

I buy it for $73 and take it all home, but I don't put it on until the next morning. When I do, I see myself for the first time in full Islamic dress — and I'm horrified. I have disappeared, and somebody I don't recognize is looking back at me. I cannot tell how old she is, how much

ZAIBA MALIK is a freelance writer and broadcaster in London. She wrote this article for the Los Angeles Times.

SILVER

**SAN JOSE MERCURY NEWS** (Calif.)

Martin Gee

Opinion page, broadsheet, 175,000+

This presentation shows Iraq literally breaking apart. The headline is integrated into the illustration. The whole concept is very well communicated, and it doesn't take the whole page to do it.

Esta presentación muestra como Irak literalmente se rompe en pedazos. El título forma parte de la ilustración. Todo el concepto está muy bien comunicado, y no toma toda la página para lograrlo.

**ZAMAN,** Yenibosna, Turkey

Ekrem Dumanli, Fevzi Yazici, Mustafa Saglam, Babür Boysal, Cem Kiziltug

Opinion page, broadsheet, 175,000+

ZAMAN 18 — YORUM — 26 MART 2006 PAZAR

Türk muhafazakârlığı: Yenilikçi ve değişimci (2)

**LA REPUBBLICA,** Rome

Angelo Rinaldi, Silvia Rossi, Stefano Cipolla, Isabella Maoloni

Other feature section, 175,000+

SPETTACOLI

"La mia vita in settanta souvenir"

Il vestito strappato della "Ciociara"

Sophia Loren

Perspective

Border politics

Will a new Congress finally confront real immigration reform?

Facing the war on terrorism

Israel's deep identity crisis

**SAN JOSE MERCURY NEWS** (Calif.)

Martin Gee, Jonathon Berlin

Opinion page, broadsheet, 175,000+

WATCHING THE SEAS F3 CATS AND DOGS F4

National Report

Tempting the cities

Watch the little birdie while you can

**TORONTO STAR**

Sharis Shahmiryan, Raffi Anderian, Catherine Pike, Rick Haliechuk

Opinion page, broadsheet, 175,000+

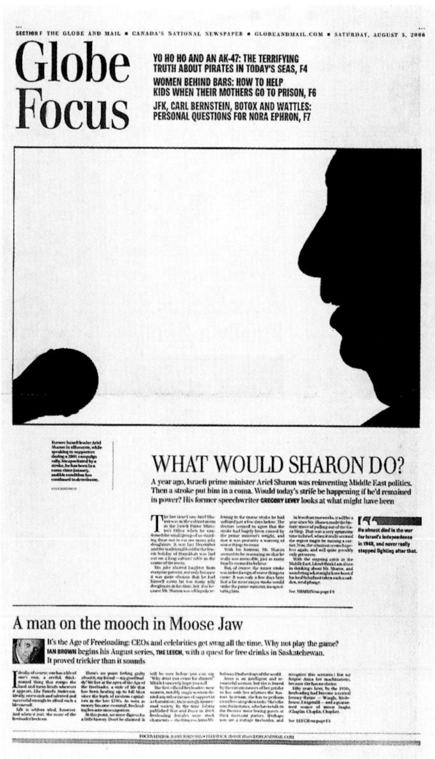

Globe Focus

WHAT WOULD SHARON DO?

A man on the mooch in Moose Jaw

**THE GLOBE AND MAIL,** Toronto

Cinders McLeod, David Pratt, Cathrin Bradbury, Jerry Johnson, Brian Kerrigan

Opinion page, broadsheet, 175,000+

**SAN FRANCISCO CHRONICLE**
Rick Nobles, Jim Finefrock, Nanette Bisher
Opinion page, broadsheet, 175,000+

**SAN JOSE MERCURY NEWS** (Calif.)
Daymond Gascon
Opinion page, broadsheet, 175,000+

**CHICAGO SUN-TIMES**
Guillermo Munro
Opinion page, broadsheet, 175,000+

**THE NEWS & OBSERVER,** Raleigh, N.C.
Steve Allen, Tim Lee
Opinion page, broadsheet, 175,000+

**SAN FRANCISCO CHRONICLE**
Rick Nobles, Lance Jackson, Jim Finefrock, Nanette Bisher
Opinion page, broadsheet, 175,000+

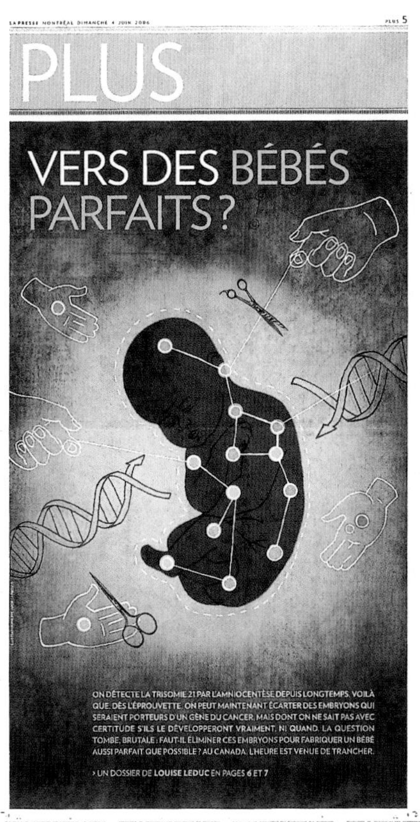

**LA PRESSE,** Montréal
Philippe Tardif, Louise Leduc, Benoit Giguere, Genevieve Dinel, Marie-Claude Malboeuf
Opinion page, broadsheet, 175,000+

**ZAMAN,** Yenibosna, Turkey
Ekrem Dumanli, Fevzi Yazici, Mustafa Saglam, Babür Boysal, Cem Kiziltuga
Opinion page, broadsheet, 175,000+

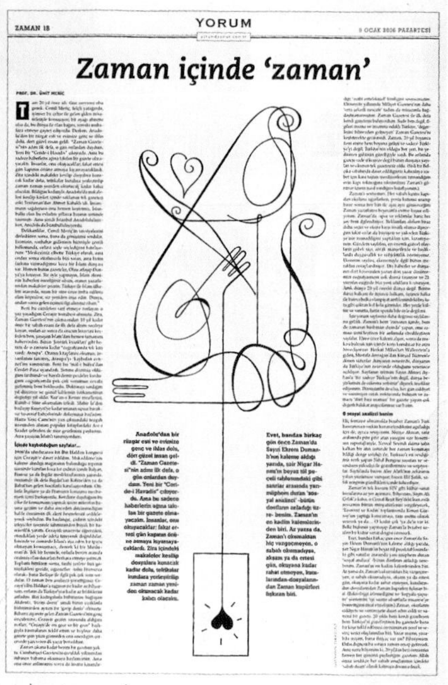
ZAMAN 18 YORUM 9 OCAK 2006 PAZARTESİ

Zaman içinde 'zaman'

**LA NACIÓN,** Buenos Aires, Argentina
Carlos Guyot, Silvana Segú, Mariana Trigo Viera
Opinion page, broadsheet, 175,000+

LA NACION

7 Enfoques

DEL PAÍS & DEL MUNDO

A 70 años del día en que estalló España

Kim Jong-Il, el insondable hombre fuerte de Pyongyang

El Código Penal y el debate por la reforma

[ POLITICA ]

ASEDIO A LA PRENSA

Qué hay detrás de la estrategia K

Desde el Gobierno se asegura que no hay un plan montado detrás de la andanada de ataques a diarios y periodistas, pero la virulencia y coordinación de la embestida sugieren otras lecturas. Cuánto tuvieron que ver el debate por los superpoderes, la reglamentación de los decretos y la irrupción mediática de Lavagna Por Laura Di Marco

**THE PLAIN DEALER,** Cleveland
Mary Lou Sneyd, Andrea Levy, David Kordalski
Opinion page, broadsheet, 175,000+

FORUM

AMERICAN No. 300,000,000

Let's invite him here

SEX

AGE

RACE

LATINO

FAMILY

Why a hush falls over judge elections

INSIDE

Elizabeth Auster

Eye on the World

We call it fall, but it's uplifting

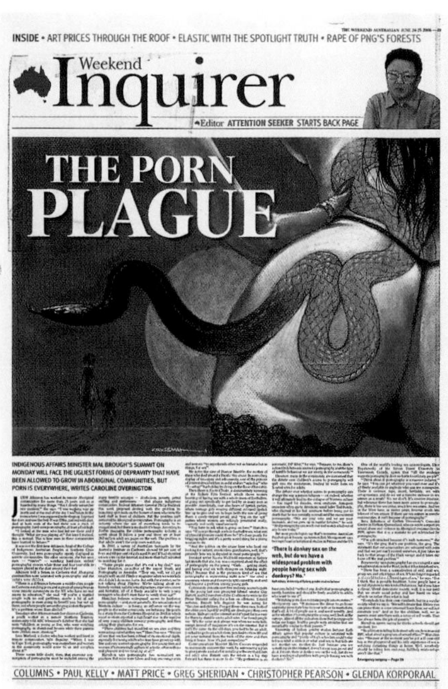
INSIDE • ART PRICES THROUGH THE ROOF • ELASTIC WITH THE SPOTLIGHT TRUTH • RAPE OF PNG'S FORESTS

Weekend Inquirer

Editor: ATTENTION SEEKER STARTS BACK PAGE

THE PORN PLAGUE

COLUMNS • PAUL KELLY • MATT PRICE • GREG SHERIDAN • CHRISTOPHER PEARSON • GLENDA KORPORAAL

**THE AUSTRALIAN,** Sydney
Jason Bitneris, Sturt Krygsman
Opinion page, broadsheet, 175,000+

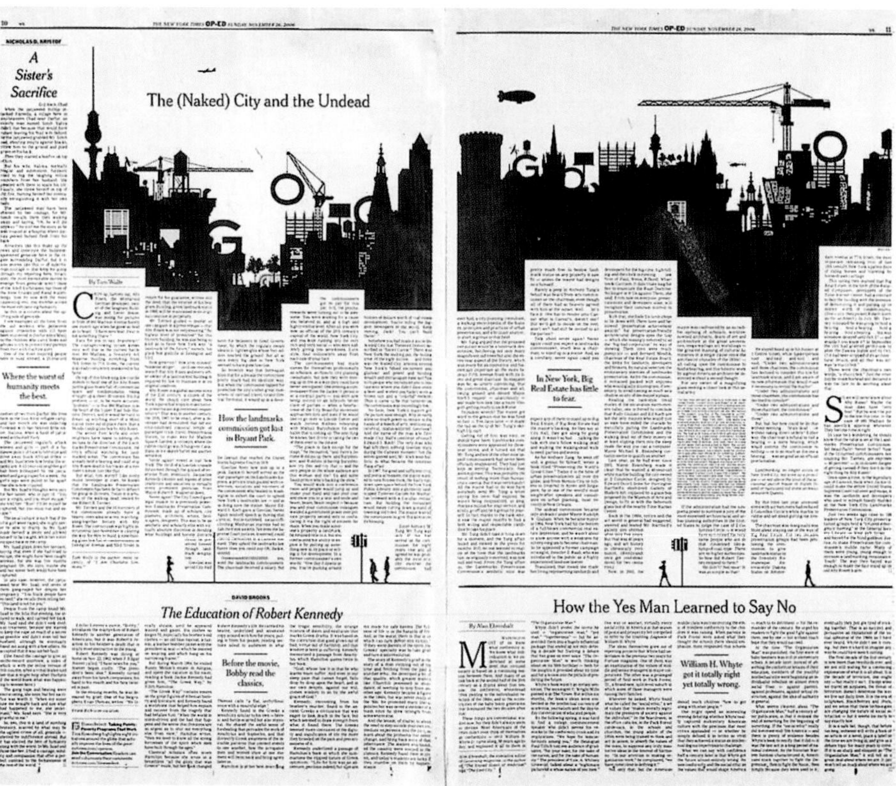
THE NEW YORK TIMES OP-ED

A Sister's Sacrifice

The (Naked) City and the Undead

Where the worst of humanity meets the best.

How the landmarks commission got lost in Bryant Park.

In New York, Big Real Estate has little to fear.

The Education of Robert Kennedy

Before the movie, Bobby read the classics.

How the Yes Man Learned to Say No

William H. Whyte got it totally right yet totally wrong.

**THE NEW YORK TIMES**
Tom Bodkin, Brian Rea, Marc Alary, Sam Weber
Opinion page, broadsheet, 175,000+

**THE GLOBE AND MAIL,** Toronto
Cinders McLeod, David Pratt, Cathrin Bradbury, Jerry Johnson, Brian Kerrigan
Opinion page, broadsheet, 175,000+

Globe Focus

CHINA WRITHING: ARE SUICIDES THE PRICE OF THE BOOM? F3
FOOD OF THE FUTURE: BENEFICIAL BUT BORING, F6
WORKERS' PLAYTIME: THE NEW ON-THE-JOB LEISURE, F8

THE POPE NOBODY KNOWS

**THE VIRGINIAN-PILOT,** Norfolk
Ryan Healy, Paul Nelson, Deborah Withey
Opinion page, broadsheet, 175,000+

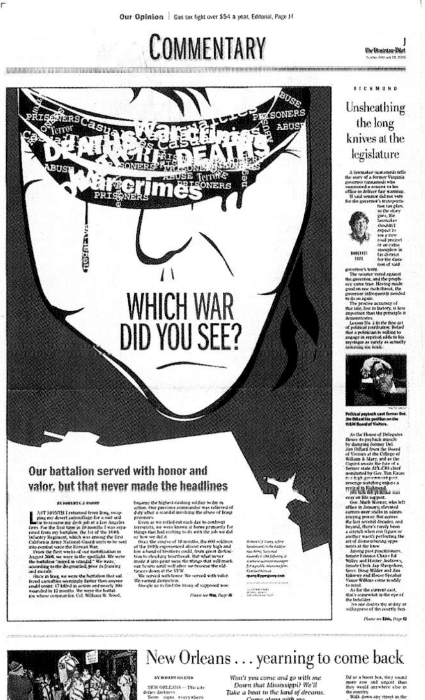
COMMENTARY

WHICH WAR DID YOU SEE?

Our battalion served with honor and valor, but that never made the headlines

Unsheathing the long knives at the legislature

New Orleans . . . yearning to come back

**CHICAGO SUN-TIMES**
Guillermo Munro
Opinion page, broadsheet, 175,000+

How love, con and baggage affect the artistic muse during a May-December romance between writers abroad

A FOREIGN AFFAIR

At 32, Delhi-bred Dawesar can be applauded for injecting raging libidos in her elderly protagonist and his peers. Still, it's a little difficult to believe (they) are the type of geriatric studmuffins akin to Mick Jagger.

For children

INSIGHT
OPINION & COMMENTARY

IDENTITY CRISIS
The FBI struggles to succeed with its post-9/11 transition to counterterrorism

BUSH ARGUES HIS CASE ON IMMIGRATON

**THE SAN DIEGO UNION-TRIBUNE**
Gloria Orbegozo, Chris Ross
Opinion page, broadsheet, 175,000+

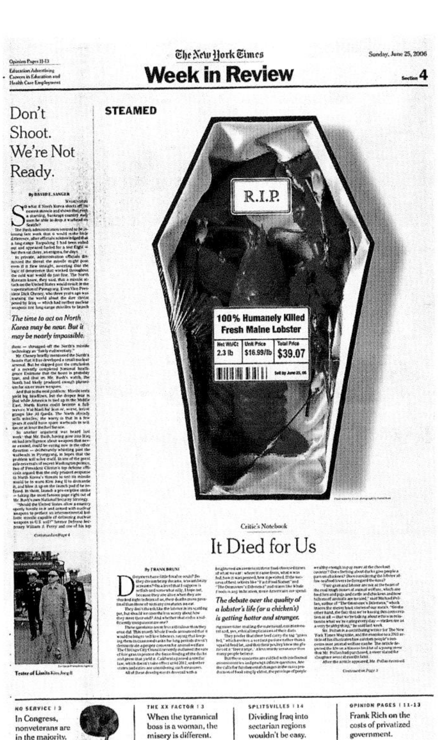
The New York Times
Week in Review

Don't Shoot. We're Not Ready.

STEAMED

R.I.P.

100% Humanely Killed Fresh Maine Lobster

It Died for Us

**THE NEW YORK TIMES**
Tom Bodkin, Nicholas Blechman, Ji Lee, Daniel Root, Shelly Camhi
Opinion page, broadsheet, 175,000+

Shopping

0 10000 00102 5

Think outside the Boxing sales

**TORONTO STAR**
Jo-Ann Dodds, David Graham, Rita Zekas, Lesley Taylor
Lifestyle page, broadsheet, 175,000+

**LA PRESSE,** Montréal
Francis Leveillee, Katia Gagnon, Benoit Giguere, Genevieve Dinel, Marie-Claude Malboeuf
Opinion page, broadsheet, 175,000+

**THE NEW YORK TIMES**
Tom Bodkin, Nicholas Blechman, Christoph Niemann, Shelly Camhi
Opinion page, broadsheet, 175,000+

**ZAMAN,** Yenibosna, Turkey
Ekrem Dumanli, Fevzi Yazici, Mustafa Saglam, Betül Tanrikulu
Opinion page, broadsheet, 175,000+

YORUM

27 EKİM 2006 CUMA ZAMAN

Fransız Meclisi'ndeki oylama ışığında tarih, siyaset ve 1915 trajedisi (II)

The New York Times

Week in Review

Sunday, April 23, 2006

MELTDOWN

Yelling 'Fire' On A Hot Planet

Why not bring the debate on global warming down to earth?

What We Know

Spell 'No Comment' for Us, Please

LITTLE OIL | 3
Chad's problems are everyone's problems.

HERE AND THERE | 4
Mr. Hu goes to Washingtons.

SEPARATE WAYS | 4
The states agree to disagree.

OPINION PAGES | 11-13
Nicholas D. Kristof on China's responsibility.

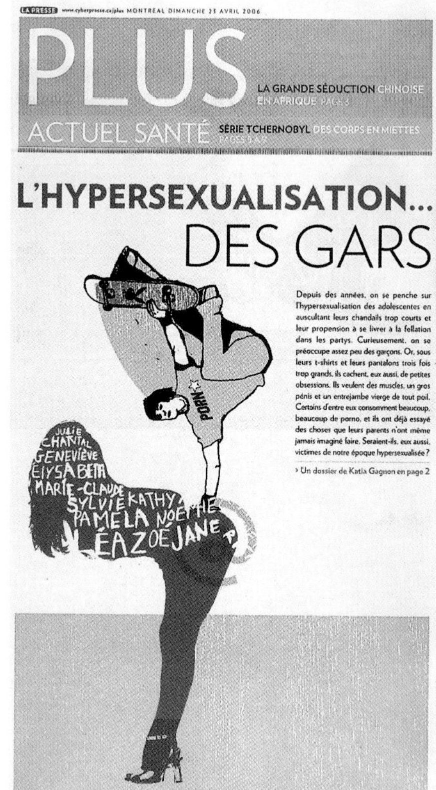
LA PRESSE

MONTRÉAL DIMANCHE 23 AVRIL 2006

PLUS

ACTUEL SANTÉ

LA GRANDE SÉDUCTION CHINOISE EN AFRIQUE PAGE 3

SÉRIE TCHERNOBYL DES CORPS EN MIETTES PAGES 8 À 9

L'HYPERSEXUALISATION... DES GARS

Depuis des années, on se penche sur l'hypersexualisation des adolescentes en auscultant leurs chandails trop courts et leur propension à se livrer à la fellation dans les partys. Curieusement, on se préoccupe assez peu des garçons. Or, sous leurs t-shirts et leurs pantalons trois fois trop grands, ils cachent, eux aussi, de petites obsessions. Ils veulent des muscles, un gros pénis et un entrejambe vierge de tout poil. Contains d'entre eux consomment beaucoup, beaucoup de porno, et ils ont déjà essayé des choses que leurs parents n'ont même jamais imaginé faire. Seraient-ils, eux aussi, victimes de notre époque hypersexualisée?

> Un dossier de Katia Gagnon en page 2

Boston Sunday Globe

Ideas

MAY 7, 2006

&Books

Editorials, Letters, & Op-eds

OUR ALLERGIES, OURSELVES

Bonds, the Babe, and how the homer changed the game

Oy vey, can you see...

Martin Amis's 9/11

The Word Survey: Results are in!

Are we allergic because of pollution? Because we wash our hands too much? There's a surprising lack of consensus as to why allergies are on the rise, but some scientists suggest we have only ourselves to blame.
By Drake Bennett

Unconventional

The real John Kenneth Galbraith | By Richard Parker

**THE BOSTON GLOBE**
Gregory Klee, Dan Zedek
Opinion page, broadsheet, 175,000+

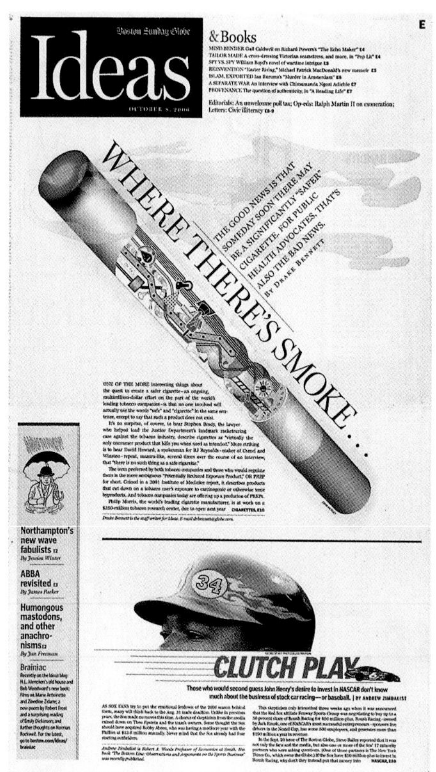
Boston Sunday Globe

Ideas

OCTOBER 8, 2006

&Books

WHERE THERE'S SMOKE...

The good news is that someday soon there may be a significantly "safer" cigarette. For public health advocates, that's also the bad news.
By Drake Bennett

Northampton's new wave fabulists

ABBA revisited

Humongous mastodons, and other anachronisms

CLUTCH PLAY

These who would second guess John Henry's desire to invest in NASCAR don't know much about the business of stock car racing — or baseball.

**THE BOSTON GLOBE**
Gregory Klee, Dan Zedek
Opinion page, broadsheet, 175,000+

LA NACION

7

Enfoques

DEL PAÍS & DEL MUNDO

[ ISLAM Y OCCIDENTE ]

CONVIVENCIA AMENAZADA

Las violentas reacciones en el mundo islámico por la publicación de las caricaturas de Mahoma despertó un profundo debate entre quienes llaman a la moderación y la responsabilidad y quienes creen que ya es hora de que Europa le ponga límites al avance musulmán sobre los valores occidentales
Por Juana Libedinsky

El derecho a la irreverencia

Por Mario Vargas Llosa

**LA NACIÓN,** Buenos Aires, Argentina
Carlos Guyot, Silvana Segú
Opinion page, broadsheet, 175,000+

**THE STAR-LEDGER,** Newark, N.J.
Bob Bogert, Bumper DeJesus, Pablo Colon, John Hassell
Opinion page, broadsheet, 175,000+

# Perspective

Sorting the mess at UMDNJ

SURVEILLANCE NATION

Addiction, withdrawal and the BlackBerry

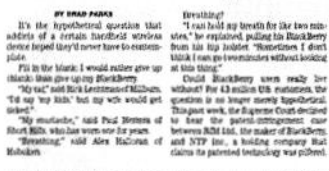

**CHICAGO SUN-TIMES**
Guillermo Munro
Opinion page, broadsheet, 175,000+

CONTROVERSY

ON THE BACK: BOOKS

STEAL TRAPS

Sleuthing software makes it easier than ever to catch a plagiarist, so why do writers keeping ripping off the words of others?

**MILWAUKEE JOURNAL SENTINEL** (Wis.)
Gary Markstein, Lonnie Turner
Opinion page, broadsheet, 175,000+

For many, MPS remains their No. 1 choice

Crossroads

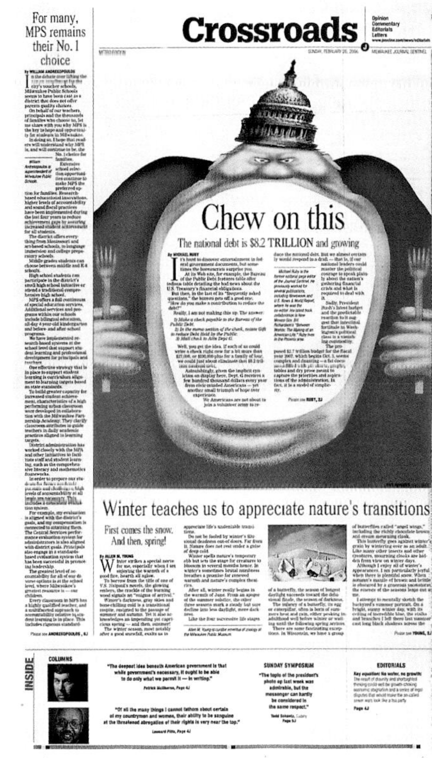

Chew on this

The national debt is $8.2 TRILLION and growing

Winter teaches us to appreciate nature's transitions

THOMAS WALKOM F5 STILL WAITING FOR CONTACT F4

# National Report

THE INVESTIGATION: Nearly two years of undercover work culminate in mass arrests

The Spy Game

James Travers F2 Fighting radical Islam F2 Terror was the story F3

**TORONTO STAR**
Catherine Pike, Catherine Farley, Sean Stanleigh, David Walmsley, Rick Haliechuk, Steve Russell, Michelle Shephard
Opinion page, broadsheet, 175,000+

CURRENT

Los Angeles Times

**LOS ANGELES TIMES**
Tom Trapnell, Mark Alan, Michael Whitley, Joseph Hutchinson
Opinion page, broadsheet, 175,000+

Q:

Topic Two

Ugly past echoes in Duke case

TOLLS AHEAD?

User fees could pave the way for two long-delayed highway projects in the Triangle

**THE NEWS & OBSERVER,** Raleigh, N.C.
Shannon Niedling
Opinion page, broadsheet, 175,000+

**THE OTTAWA CITIZEN**

Jacqueline Beingessner, Scott Anderson, Derek Shelly, Ryan MacDonald, Susan McDonough

Opinion page, broadsheet, 50,000-174,999

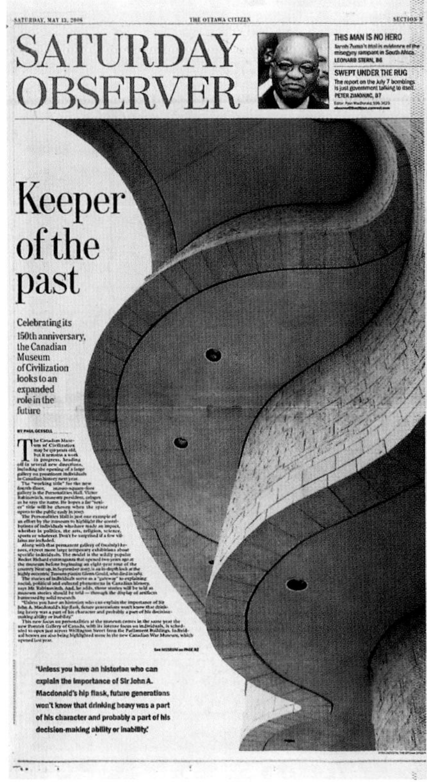

SATURDAY OBSERVER

THIS MAN IS NO HERO

SWEPT UNDER THE RUG

Keeper of the past

Celebrating its 150th anniversary, the Canadian Museum of Civilization looks to an expanded role in the future

"Unless you have an historian who can explain the importance of Sir John A. Macdonald's hip flask, future generations won't know that drinking heavy was a part of his character and probably a part of his decision-making ability or inability."

**GULF NEWS,** Dubai, United Arab Emirates

Talib Jariwala, Dwynn Ronald Trazo, Miguel Angel Gomez, Abdul Hamid Ahmad, Najla Al Rostamani, Vinta Baharadwaj

Opinion page, broadsheet, 50,000-174,999

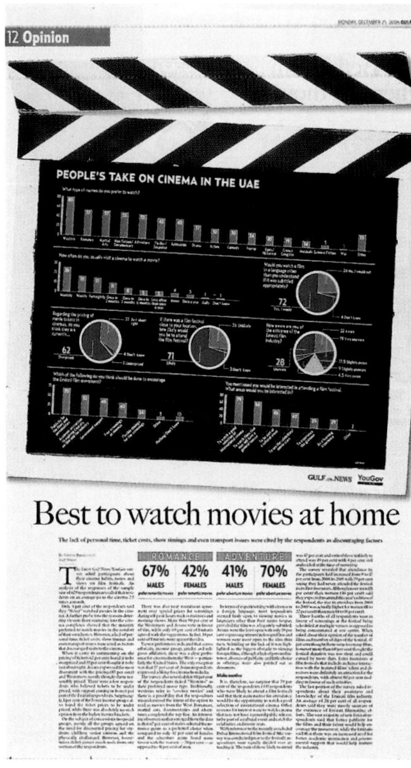

12 Opinion

PEOPLE'S TAKE ON CINEMA IN THE UAE

Best to watch movies at home

| ROMANCE | | ADVENTURE | |
|---|---|---|---|
| 67% | 42% | 41% | 70% |
| MALES | FEMALES | MALES | FEMALES |

**WINNIPEG FREE PRESS** (Canada)

Gordon Preece

Opinion page, broadsheet, 50,000-174,999

Winnipeg Free Press

PERSPECTIVE

Legions of solvent abusers in Winnipeg's core exist only to find their next poisonous fix; the Downtown BIZ is taking steps to do something about the problem

HIGH AND HOPELESS

THE MISSING AND THE DEAD OF MAIN STREET

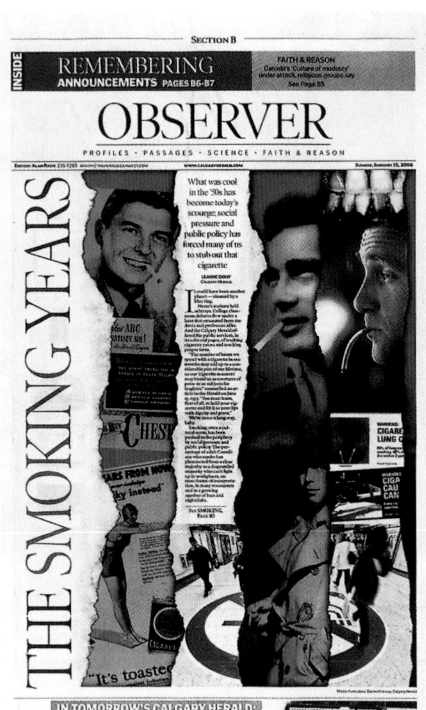

SECTION B

INSIDE

REMEMBERING

ANNOUNCEMENTS PAGES B6-B7

FAITH & REASON

OBSERVER

PROFILES • PASSAGES • SCIENCE • FAITH & REASON

THE SMOKING YEARS

What was cool in the '50s has become today's scourge; social pressure and public policy has forced many of us to stub out that cigarette

IN TOMORROW'S CALGARY HERALD:

Check out all the winners from Calgary Minor Hockey Week

**CALGARY HERALD** (Alberta, Canada)

Darren Francey, Alan Rach, Janet Matiisen, Lorne Motley, Monica Zurowski

Opinion page, broadsheet, 50,000-174,999

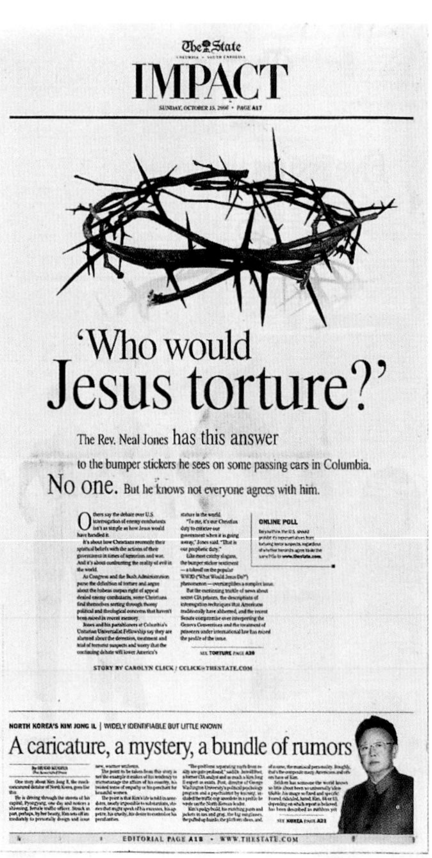

The State

IMPACT

'Who would Jesus torture?'

The Rev. Neal Jones has this answer to the bumper stickers he sees on some passing cars in Columbia. No one. But he knows not everyone agrees with him.

ONLINE POLL

NORTH KOREA'S KIM JONG IL | WIDELY IDENTIFIABLE BUT LITTLE KNOWN

A caricature, a mystery, a bundle of rumors

EDITORIAL PAGE A18 • WWW.THESTATE.COM

**THE STATE,** Columbia, S.C.

William Campling

Opinion page, broadsheet, 50,000-174,999

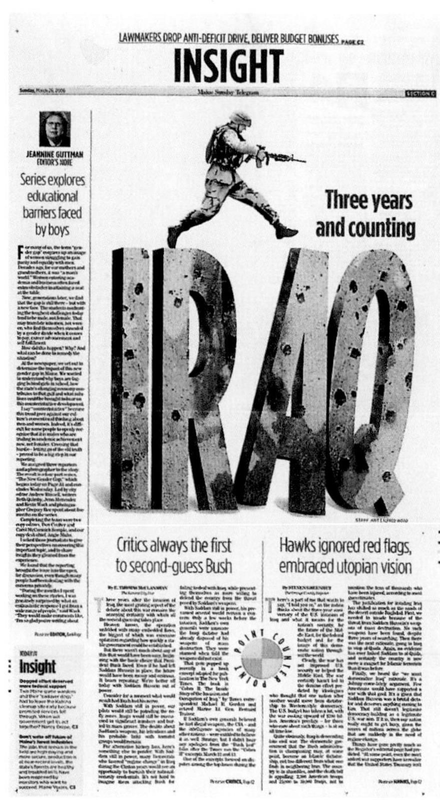

LAWMAKERS DROP ANTI-DEFICIT DRIVE, DELIVER BUDGET BONUSES PAGE C2

INSIGHT

Maine Sunday Telegram

JEANNINE GUTTMAN EDITOR'S NOTE

Series explores educational barriers faced by boys

Three years and counting

IRAQ

Critics always the first to second-guess Bush

Hawks ignored red flags, embraced utopian vision

Insight

**PORTLAND PRESS HERALD** (Maine)

Alfred Wood

Opinion page, broadsheet, 50,000-174,999

06 RAPORTTI

HUKASSA

EU etsii johtajaa

EUROOPPA | Unioni on syöksynyt tylsien päätösten aikaan, jota leimaa suurten johtajien puuttuminen. Suomen alkavasta puheenjohtajuudesta on tulossa väritön viimenokausi. Euroopan pelastajaksi on tarjolla vain Angela Merkel

**AAMULEHTI,** Tampere, Finland
Elina Saarikoski, Ari Kinnari, Kaija Toivonen
Opinion page, tabloid, 50,000-174,999

ACTUEL

LA FEMME NOUVELLE EST ARRIVÉE

LA MAMAN ET LA PUTAIN



**LA PRESSE,** Montréal
Catherine Bernard, Benoit Giguere, Genevieve Dinel, Michele Ouimet, Marie Claude Lortie
Lifestyle page, broadsheet, 175,000+

INTERNACIONAL ESTADOS UNIDOS

LAS ELECCIONES PRESIDENCIALES DE 2008

¿QUIÉN SUCEDERÁ A BUSH?

Los lastres de McCain y Giuliani

**LA PRENSA GRÁFICA,** Antiguo Cuscatlán, El Salvador
Enrique Contreras, Héctor Ramírez, Giovanni Paniagua, Mauricio Duarte
Opinion page, tabloid, 50,000-174,999

ACTUEL

LES MOQUETTES COQUETTES LE JARDIN PAGE 4

LES ACCROS DU SEXE

QUAND LE SEXE DEVIENT UNE OBSESSION

**LA PRESSE,** Montréal
Philippe Tardif, Annabelle Nicoud, Benoit Giguere, Genevieve Dinel, Michele Ouimet, Marie-Claude Lortie
Lifestyle page, broadsheet, 175,000+

tribuna

Claroscuros en el umbral del nuevo año

Seres de encuentro

El deleite del pensamiento

El pensamiento es un deleite, y un arma que hace apto al sujeto en cualquier situación de indefensión

¿SERÁ APROBADO ESTE AÑO EL PRESUPUESTO DE 2007?

**CLAVE,** Santo Domingo, Dominican Republic
Staff, Rafael Nuñez Grassals, Juan Manuel Sánchez, Victor Bautista, Fausto Rosario Adames
Opinion page, tabloid, 50,000-174,999

**THE KANSAS CITY STAR** (Mo.)
Charles Bloom, Tom Dolphens, Barbara Hill-Meyer
Lifestyle page, broadsheet, 175,000+

WWW.KANSASCITY.COM THE KANSAS CITY STAR. TUESDAY, OCTOBER 10, 2006 E

It's a dirty job

The Scream Awards

Halloween events

FYI

CONTEST | Haunting Kansas City

# GET IN THE SPIRIT

Have you seen a ghost? Tell us about it, and you could win a Halloween prize.

HOW TO ENTER

STARGAZING | WEIRD NEWS | COMMENTARY | BY THE NUMBERS

DON'T GET BEHIND THE 8-BALL

JENEÉ OSTERHELDT

WEDNESDAY IN FYI: JAZZ PROGRAM TEACHES YOUTHS TO MAKE MUSIC OF THEIR LIVES

**FORT WORTH STAR-TELEGRAM** (Texas)
Deborah Overton, Mark Hoffer, Andrew Marton
Lifestyle page, broadsheet, 175,000+

Life&Arts

SNEAK PEEK This weekend's Texas Ballet Theater program of shorts is oh, so on pointe

SPORTS FASHION

Olympics showcase Italian style

ROPIN' THE OSCARS

Batman Begins

GROOMING

# 2006: A FACE ODYSSEY

The five-bladed 'Fusion' is billed as the Ferrari of razors, the latest in shaving technology – but is it really a cut above? Our reporter risks taking it on the chin in his quest for the bare truth.

By ANDREW MARTON

Putting razors to the test

WHAT DO YOU THINK?

YOUR FAVORITE SECTIONS | WHAT'S UP IN THE WEEK AHEAD

**THE PHILADELPHIA INQUIRER**
Beto Alvarez, Lisa Zollinger, Kevin Burkett
Lifestyle page, broadsheet, 175,000+

Magazine

What does "the pursuit of happiness" mean? Readers and others tell us.

"To fill the hour – that is happiness."

"The ability to choose how I live."

"Happiness, for me, is a metaphorical blank page. It's the ability to turn the unknown into pleasure that gets me every time."

"If what I like doesn't harm anyone else, I should be able to pursue it."

"Independence is happiness."

"It's the right to do nothing or do something."

"The struggle to live for something outside yourself."

FINAL WEEKS! Andrew Wyeth MEMORY AND MAGIC

TICKETS STILL AVAILABLE! Philadelphia Museum of Art

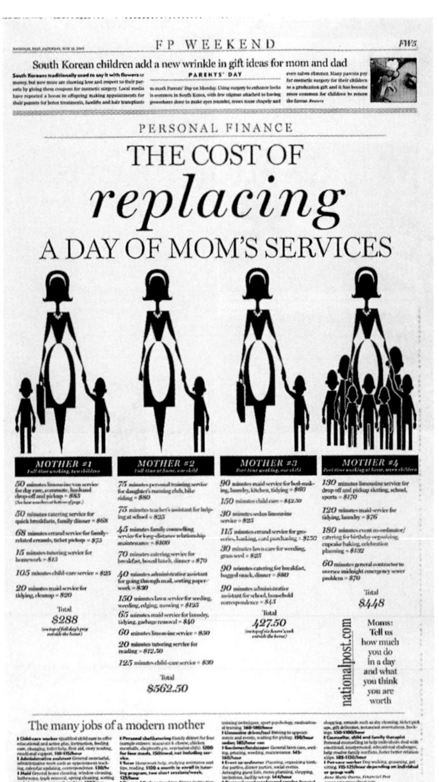
FP WEEKEND

South Korean children add a new wrinkle in gift ideas for mom and dad

PERSONAL FINANCE

# THE COST OF *replacing* A DAY OF MOM'S SERVICES

MOTHER #1 | MOTHER #2 | MOTHER #3 | MOTHER #4

Total $288

Total $562.50

Total $427.50

Total $448

Moms: Tell us how much you do in a day and what you think you are worth

nationalpost.com

The many jobs of a modern mother

**NATIONAL POST,** Toronto
Doug Kelly, Gayle Grin, Deborah Stokes, Gigi Suhanic
Lifestyle page, broadsheet, 175,000+

7pm LIFE 2·9 7:30pm

blas·phe·my

[ˈblasfəmē]

Passing Along His Knowledge Of Opera

fashion

Lauren's Menswear On Target

'TV EYE': CHECK OUT THE SUPER-SIZE SKULL ON 'SURVIVOR,' D2 | TECH: CYBERSPACE IS BUSY WITH THE WINTER OLYMPICS, D3

**HARTFORD COURANT** (Conn.)
Melanie Shaffer
Lifestyle page, broadsheet, 175,000+

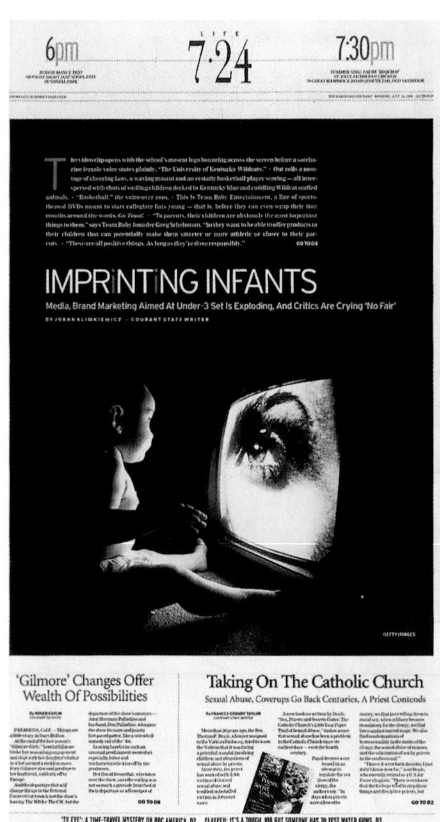
6pm LIFE 7·24 7:30pm

IMPRINTING INFANTS

Media, Brand Marketing Aimed At Under-3 Set Is Exploding, And Critics Are Crying 'No Fair'

'Gilmore' Changes Offer Wealth Of Possibilities

Taking On The Catholic Church

Sexual Abuse, Coverups Go Back Centuries, A Priest Contends

'TV EYE': A TIME-TRAVEL MYSTERY ON BBC AMERICA, D2 | PLAYER: IT'S A TOUGH JOB BUT SOMEONE HAS TO TEST WATER GUNS, D3

**HARTFORD COURANT** (Conn.)
Timothy Reck, Suzette Moyer, Beth Bristow
Lifestyle page, broadsheet, 175,000+

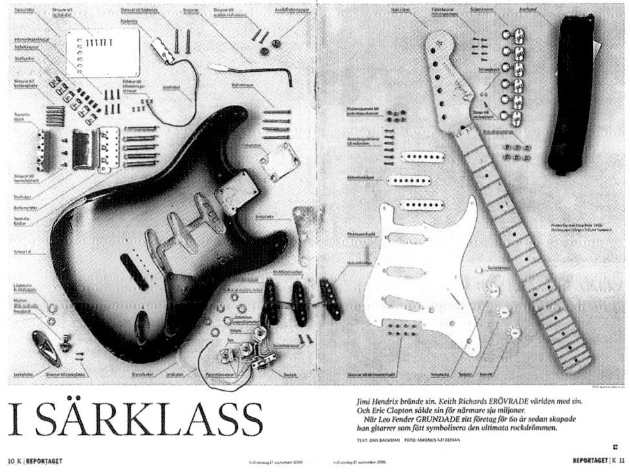
I SÄRKLASS

*Jimi Hendrix brände sin. Keith Richards ERÖVRADE världen med sin. Och Eric Clapton sålde sin för närmare sju miljoner. När Leo Fender GRUNDADE sitt företag för 60 år sedan skapade han gitarrer som fått symbolisera den ultimata rockdrömmen.*

10 K | REPORTAGET REPORTAGET | K 11

**SVENSKA DAGBLADET,** Stockholm, Sweden
Lena K. Samuelsson, Mats-Eric Nilsson, Anna W. Thurfjell, Anders Lindgren, Ann Axelsson, Staffan Löwstedt, Mathias Karlsson
Lifestyle page, tabloid, 175,000+

K
SvD KULTUR
Söndag den 21 maj 2006

Slutpunkt

Avgångselever på konstnärliga skolor visar sina verk

SAMUEL BECKETT i ny närbild

Dykning ett LYFT för hela familjen

Möt enmans-armén THORSTEN FLINCK

**SVENSKA DAGBLADET,** Stockholm, Sweden
Lena K. Samuelsson, Mats-Eric Nilsson, Anna W. Thurfjell, Anders Lindgren, Ann Axelsson, Staffan Löwstedt, Dan Hansson
Lifestyle page, tabloid, 175,000+

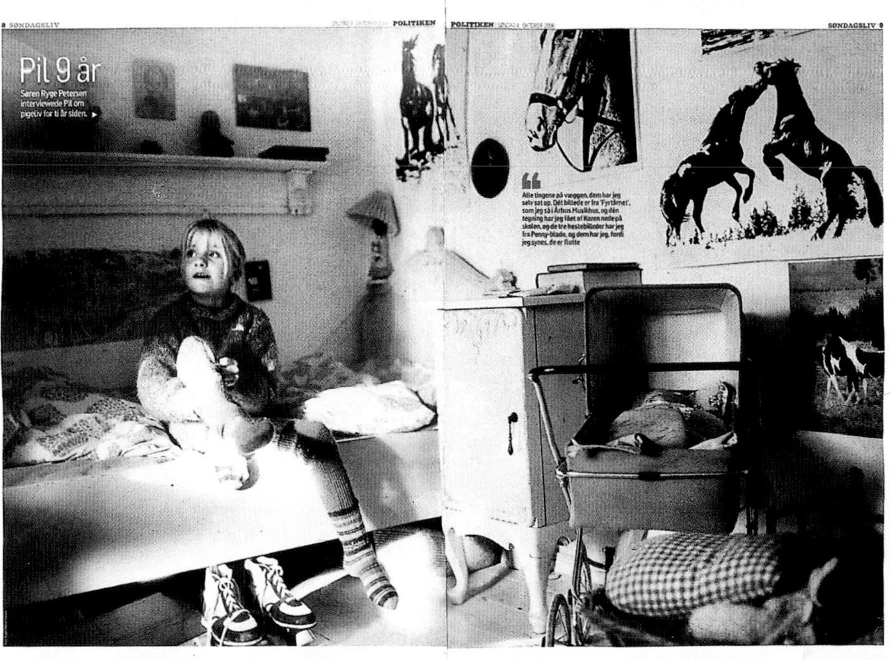
SØNDAGSLIV POLITIKEN

Pil 9 år

Søren Ryge Petersen interviewede Pil om pigeliv for 9 år siden.

**POLITIKEN,** Copenhagen, Denmark
Søren Nyeland, Mai-Britt Bernt Jensen, Ole Gravesen, Liv Olsen, Annette Nyvang, Per Munch
Lifestyle page, tabloid, 50,000-174,999

K
SvD KULTUR
Söndag den 29 oktober 2006

Hetsig jakt på den rätta tar död på romantiken

NÄTSHOPPING kittlar modelejonets nerver

Dyk bland favoriter vid THAILANDS öar

USA dominerar bok om FILMFAVORITER

**SVENSKA DAGBLADET,** Stockholm, Sweden
Lena K. Samuelsson, Mats-Eric Nilsson, Anna W. Thurfjell, Anders Lindgren, Ann Axelsson, Staffan Löwstedt
Lifestyle page, tabloid, 175,000+

C2 Batidora

MIS COSAS Y YO

Sixto Minier

Tristeza y desengaño

Futuro y ayuda

Juguetes sonoros

Retomba el espíritu

**CLAVE,** Santo Domingo, Dominican Republic
Ruth Ester Jiménez, Juan Manuel Sánchez, Victor Bautista, Fausto Rosario Adames
Lifestyle page, tabloid, 50,000-174,999

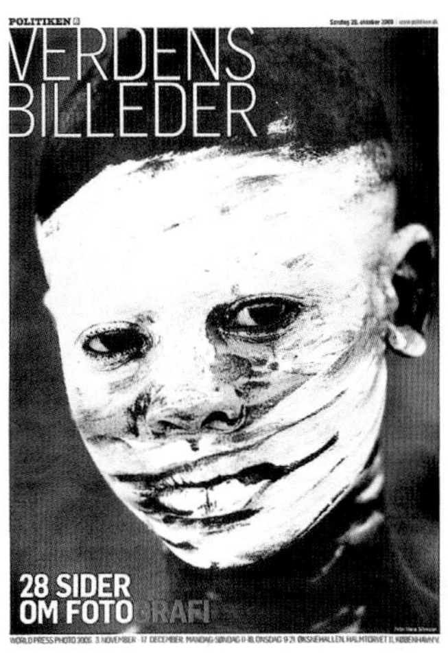
POLITIKEN

VERDENS BILLEDER

28 SIDER OM FOTOGRAFI

**POLITIKEN,** Copenhagen, Denmark
Søren Nyeland, Liv Olsen, Christian Ilsøe, Søren Hansen, Per Folkver
Lifestyle page, tabloid, 50,000-174,999

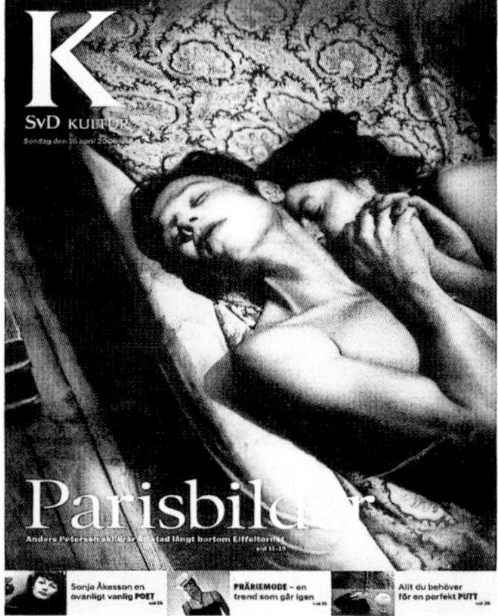
K
SvD KULTUR

Parisbilder

Sonja Åkesson en ovanligt vanlig POET

PRÄRIEMODE – en trend som går igen

Allt du behöver för en perfekt PUTT

**SVENSKA DAGBLADET,** Stockholm, Sweden
Lena K. Samuelsson, Mats-Eric Nilsson, Anna W. Thurfjell, Henrik Matern-Lindewald, Ann Axelsson, Staffan Löwstedt, Anders Petersen/Silver
Lifestyle page, tabloid, 175,000+

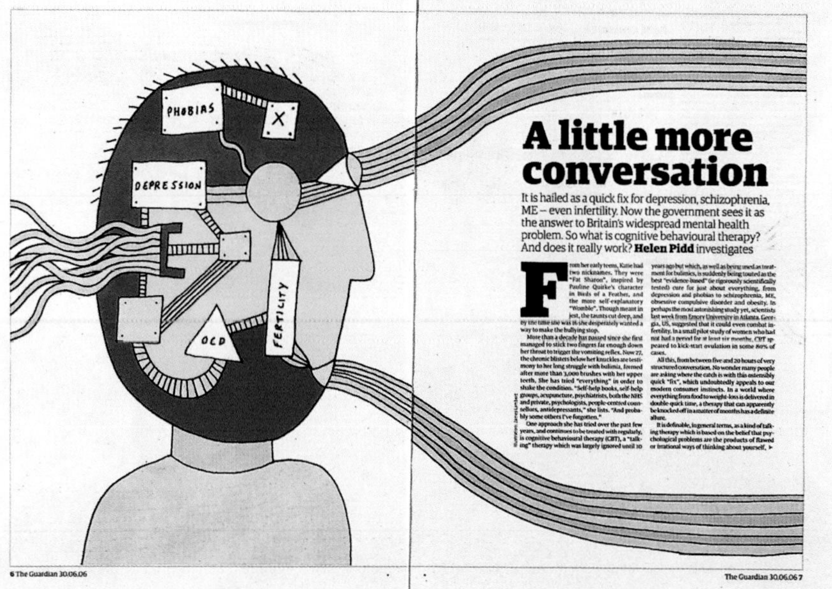

# A little more conversation

It is hailed as a quick fix for depression, schizophrenia, ME – even infertility. Now the government sees it as the answer to Britain's widespread mental health problem. So what is cognitive behavioural therapy? And does it really work? **Helen Pidd** investigates

From her early teens, Katie had two nicknames. They were "Fat Sharon", inspired by Pauline Quirke's character in Birds of a Feather, and the more self-explanatory "Womble". Though meant in jest, the taunts cut deep, and by the time she was 16 she desperately wanted a way to make the bullying stop.

More than a decade has passed since she first managed to stick two fingers far enough down her throat to trigger the vomiting reflex. Now 27, the chronic blisters below her knuckles are testimony to her long struggle with bulimia, formed after more than 3,000 brushes with her upper teeth. She has tried "everything" in order to shake the condition. "Self-help books, self-help groups, acupuncture, psychiatrists, both the NHS and private, psychologists, people-centred counsellors, antidepressants," she lists. "And probably some others I've forgotten."

One approach she has tried over the past few years, and continues to be treated with regularly, is cognitive behavioural therapy (CBT), a "talking" therapy which was largely ignored until 10 years ago but which, as well as being used as treatment for bulimics, is suddenly being touted as the best "evidence-based" (ie rigorously scientifically tested) cure for just about everything, from depression and phobias to schizophrenia, ME, obsessive compulsive disorder and obesity. In perhaps the most astonishing study yet, scientists last week from Emory University in Atlanta, Georgia, US, suggested that it could even combat infertility. In a small pilot study of women who had not had a period for at least six months, CBT appeared to kick-start ovulation in some 80% of cases.

All this, from between five and 20 hours of very structured conversation. No wonder many people are asking where the catch is with this ostensibly quick "fix", which undoubtedly appeals to our modern consumer instincts. In a world where everything from food to weight-loss is delivered in double-quick time, a therapy that can apparently be knocked off in a matter of months has a definite allure.

It is definable, in general terms, as a kind of talking therapy which is based on the belief that psychological problems are the products of flawed or irrational ways of thinking about yourself. ➤

6 The Guardian 30.06.06 | The Guardian 30.06.06 7



**THE GUARDIAN,** London
Richard Turley
Opinion page, tabloid, 175,000+

**STAR TRIBUNE,** Minneapolis
Tippi Thole, Lisa Clausen
Lifestyle page, broadsheet, 175,000+

# source how·to

# Stalking bamboo

• Retailers looking to satisfy our with to be "green" have embraced these trendy new products. But are we being bamboozled?

DOLLARS & SENSE
JOHN EWOLDT

Bamboo is used to make a variety of products ranging from T-shirts to jewelry. Test your skill by identifying the items shown here. Answers are below.

## Etiquette lessons give kids the social graces

• A short course on manners helps kids prepare for life.

No magic 'Idol' moment yet E8

Web search: The Big One in '06 E2

# Ipanema se divide para reinar no verão

*Grupos de gays, estrangeiros, pit boys e endinheirados se espalham pelo bairro e têm até locais delimitados na areia da praia*

COTIDIANO

PRAIA DE IPANEMA

LAGOA RODRIGO DE FREITAS

ENDEREÇOS DE IPANEMA

Gays chegam do Brasil e de fora

Na rua mais cara, tapete vermelho

**FOLHA DE SÃO PAULO** (Brazil)
Massimo Gentile, Fabio Marra, Felipe Jardim, Eduardo Asta
Lifestyle page, broadsheet, 175,000+

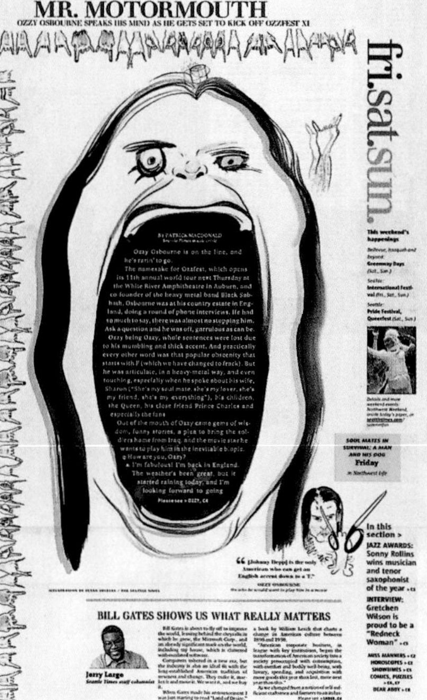

The Seattle Times

# Northwest LIFE

seattletimes.com/living | JUNE 22, 2006 | THURSDAY

# MR. MOTORMOUTH

OZZY OSBOURNE SPEAKS HIS MIND AS HE GETS SET TO KICK OFF OZZFEST XI

fri.sat.sun.

BILL GATES SHOWS US WHAT REALLY MATTERS

**THE SEATTLE TIMES**
Jeff Paslay
Lifestyle page, broadsheet, 175,000+

LES QUATRE VICTIMES OUBLIÉES

# La vie brisée de Mme Gill

La tragédie du collège Dawson

**LA PRESSE,** Montréal
Francis Leveillee, Benoit Giguere, Genevieve Dinel, Michele Ouimet, Josee Lapointe
Lifestyle page, broadsheet, 175,000+

**NATIONAL POST,** Toronto
Doug Kelly, Gayle Grin, Ben Errett, Steven Murray, Laura Koot
Lifestyle page, broadsheet, 175,000+

B9

# AVENUE

By Steven Murray

*Push the envelope, then lick it, seal it and send it outside the box. Then give yourself a raise, chump.* • Participate in nature's greatest miracle, childbirth, either as a mother, father or child. • Love like there's no tomorrow when she's out of the room. • Do the Dew all over again. • *Let your mouth write cheques your body CAN cash.* • Serenade more often and with saucier numbers. • **Vote more, whether it be for Prime Minister or determining America's Best Cat.** • *Play more sports on your wicked awesome XBOX 360.* • Make the leap from Timmy's to Starbucks. Learn how to order a Ventini Cafelona, w/ extra Espranzzo. • How much is that puppy in the window? Who cares? Buy that awesome dude. Now pet. Repeat. • *Throw out any 2005-model dogs that may be left over in the new year.* • **Laugh more. Stop watching Two and a Half Men.** • *Support the ailing Hollywood studios and spring for the $9 bag of popcorn.* • Start thinking about your 2007 resolutions. • Start an office "fight club." Don't tell anyone in the office until the first punch is thrown, by you. • Get a lower back tattoo. Something that sums up your feelings about your lower back. • *Listen to your heart more. Can't hear it? Then stop drinking Baconshakes™.* • **Tell your wife that you love her more often.** • Tell your husband that you love him more often. • *Introduce your wife to your husband. Turn the lights down real low and wait for the magic.* • **Bowl For The Cure. The disease? Not bowling enough! Strike!** • *Stop yelling "strike" when there's clearly many pins still standing.* • Upgrade your cellphone plan from "Friendless Savings."

# RESOLUTIONS

*Give me a call sometime.* • Get your tickets now for Superman Returns, opening this summer. There may not be enough to go around. • **Write more letters to the National Post complaining about their lack of coverage of Superman Returns. Does his skin-tight costume bring out certain feelings in the paper that they refuse to acknowledge? Hmm?** • *Bake more, don't just heat your Chips Ahoy bag in the microwave.* • Remember that breakfast is the most important meal of the day. Refuse to acknowledge lesser meals like lunch and supper. • Would you PLEASE start doing your part to fight terror? • Petition to bring back Arrested Development, watch it get cancelled again, repeat. • *Stop COVETING your neighbour's wife and just do it already! The sexual tension is killing me.* • **Expand your reading material. Have you seen our sizzlin' Sports section? Sizzzzzzzle.** • Take more road trips, even if it's just to the corner store for some Doritos and adult magazines (Harper's, The Economist, etc.) • *Start your own newspaper! Canada can never have enough.* • Start protesting the next war in Iraq. • Grow more beards, all over your body if necessary. • *Treat your body like a temple. Fill it with incense and congregations of worshippers.* • Finally recognize yourself as being a beautiful and unique snowflake. The kind of snowflake that has a lot of extra skin flaps and chronic dandruff. Hey, dandruff is kind of like snowflakes! Snowflakes within a snowflake! Beautiful. • **Constantly compliment the other guys in the gym on their stellar physiques. They'll appreciate the encouragement.** • *Eat. More. Tacos. Seriously, Taco Bell practically gives them away. What's your excuse for living this non-taco lifestyle?* • Stop smoking. It's like I'm kissing an ashtray. A sexy, soft ashtray that anticipates all my needs and takes me to places I've never been to before. God, I need a cigarette. • *Start a book club where "books" can be replaced with movies or video games. And "club" can just be you.* • Nobody likes a crybaby, so silicone-seal your tear ducts. • Become a male model, overcoming the fact that you're an unattractive woman. • Finally complete the long-awaited addition to your house, a "bath-room." Clean the rest of the house thoroughly. • *Pick a number, any number. Was that number 26? If so, spend the year developing your supernatural talents. If not, then make yourself useful and get me a beer, you unremarkable failure. Hey, if you were psychic I'd already have that beer in my hand, wouldn't I? Move it.* • Spend $200-million dollars and re-make an old B-movie with a running time of three hours. • Check yourself before you wreck yourself.

**STAR TRIBUNE,** Minneapolis
Tippi Thole, Lisa Clausen
Lifestyle page, broadsheet, 175,000+

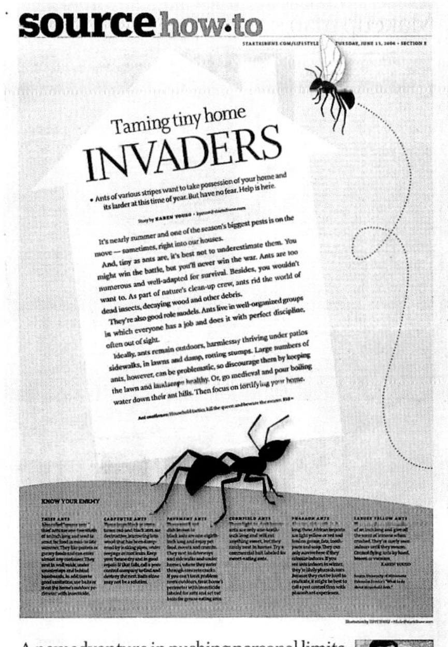


**THE ORANGE COUNTY REGISTER,** Santa Ana, Calif.
Rick Ngoc Ho, Peter Nguyen, Neil C. Pinchin, Brenda Shoun
Lifestyle page, broadsheet, 175,000+

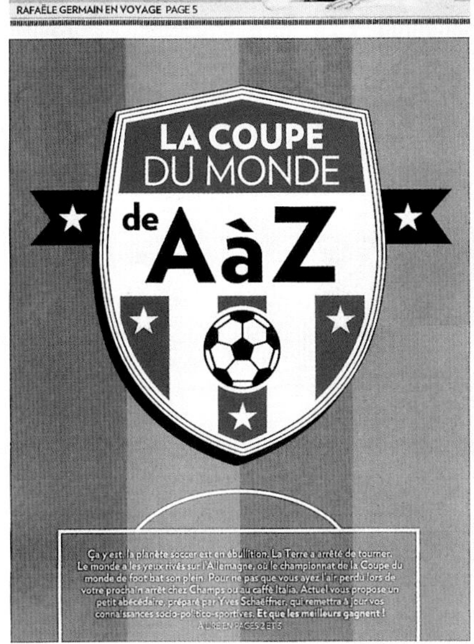

**LA PRESSE,** Montréal
Yanick Nolet, Yves Schaeffner, Benoit Giguere, Genevieve Dinel, Michele Ouimet, Marie-Claude Lortie
Lifestyle page, broadsheet, 175,000+

**LA PRESSE,** Montréal
Genevieve Lapointe, Sylvie St-Jacques, Benoit Giguere, Genevieve Dinel, Michele Ouimet, Marie-Claude Lortie
Lifestyle page, broadsheet, 175,000+

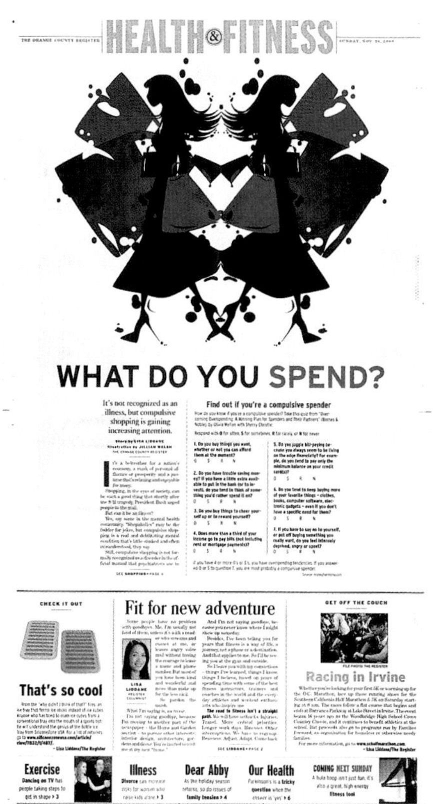


**THE ORANGE COUNTY REGISTER,** Santa Ana, Calif.
Jillian Welsh, Rick Ngoc Ho, Karen Kelso, Neil C. Pinchin, Brenda Shoun
Lifestyle page, broadsheet, 175,000+

**STAR TRIBUNE,** Minneapolis
Tippi Thole
Lifestyle page, broadsheet, 175,000+

source relationships

Poem for the holidays

Real letters and tips to improve your own

Daddy's girl

One woman's encounter with carbon monoxide poisoning

Video games: 'Viva Piñata' is 'The Sims' for little kids. Faith & Values: Converting as adults.

**THE NEW YORK TIMES**
Tom Bodkin, Bernadette Dashiell, Tony Cenicola
Lifestyle page, broadsheet, 175,000+

Big Bag
Bigger, Biggest

TIFFANY & CO.

**THE SEATTLE TIMES**
Jeff Paslay
Lifestyle page, broadsheet, 175,000+

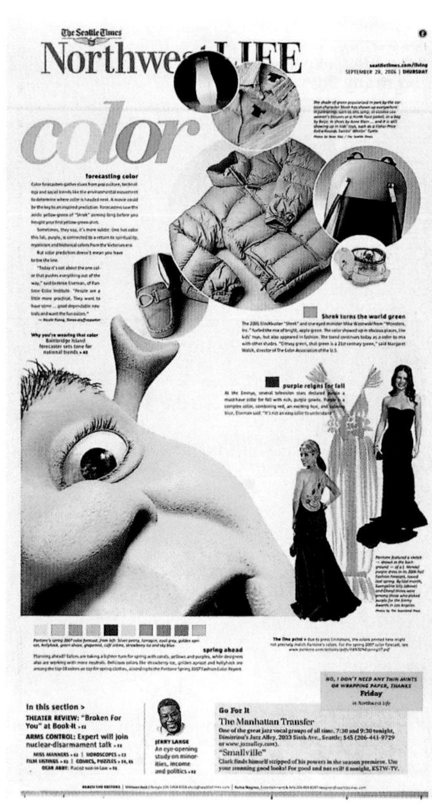

Northwest LIFE

color

In this section

Go For It
The Manhattan Transfer
"Smallville"

1pm 1:28 8pm

COLD HEARTS

As Winter Settles In, Romance Often Goes South;
With Valentine's Day Looming, It's Time For Tough Decisions

A Flamethrower For All Seasons

Helping Patients
Help Themselves

**THE HARTFORD COURANT** (Conn.)
Suzette Moyer, Nicole Dudka
Lifestyle page, broadsheet, 175,000+

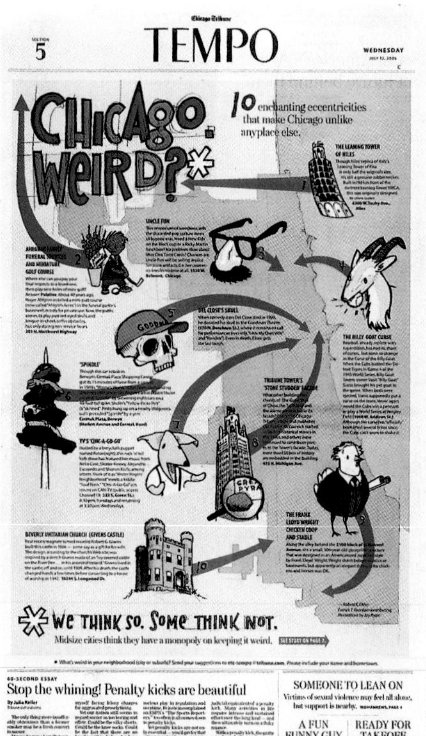

5 TEMPO

CHICAGO WEIRD?

10 enchanting eccentricities that make Chicago unlike anyplace else.

WE THINK SO. SOME THINK NOT.

Stop the whining! Penalty kicks are beautiful

SOMEONE TO LEAN ON

A FUN FUNNY GUY

READY FOR TAKEOFF

**CHICAGO TRIBUNE**
Tom Heinz, Jay Ryan, Robert K. Elder, Patrick T. Reardon, Cassandra West
Lifestyle page, broadsheet, 175,000+

LifeStyle

ARTS+ENTERTAINMENT | STYLE | BOOKS

PERFORMANCE ARTIST USES A LOT TO SAY RATHER LITTLE
DESPITE ITS TITLE, 'DRAWING RESTRAINT' GIVES MATTHEW BARNEY FREE REIN WITH VASELINE

'CLERKS' GROW UP IN MOVIE SEQUEL
LIKE HIS PROTAGONISTS, DIRECTOR KEVIN SMITH DISPLAYS A MATURING PERSPECTIVE

Curling up with a good bookstore

A Bay Area book lover takes us on a magical history tour in his memoir 11D

Style
SHOW THEM THE MONEY
MANY OF TODAY'S COUPLES REQUEST CASH IN LIEU OF TRADITIONAL WEDDING GIFTS

Fashion
BEST-DRESSED GUEST
WHAT TO WEAR WHEN SUMMER BRINGS A SLEW OF WEDDING INVITATIONS

**SAN JOSE MERCURY NEWS** (Calif.)
Stephanie Grace Lim, Jonathon Berlin, Matt Mansfield
Lifestyle page, broadsheet, 175,000+

**SAN JOSE MERCURY NEWS** (Calif.)
Stephanie Grace Lim, Pam Moreland, Jonathon Berlin, Matt Mansfield
Lifestyle page, broadsheet, 175,000+

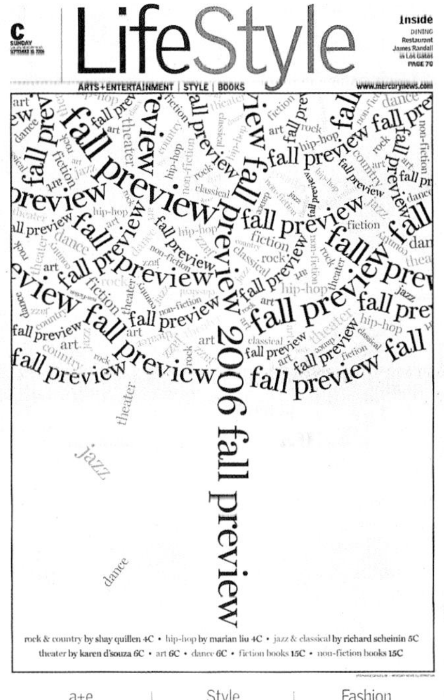
C SUNDAY

LifeStyle

ARTS + ENTERTAINMENT | STYLE | BOOKS

www.mercurynews.com

2006 fall preview

rock & country by shay quillen 4C • hip-hop by marian liu 4C • jazz & classical by richard scheinin 5C
theater by karen d'souza 6C • art 6C • dance 6C • fiction books 15C • non-fiction books 15C

a+e
RECESS IS OVER FOR 'THE WIRE'

Style
P.A. TEEN GETS MODELING JOB

Fashion
OLD MATERIAL, NEW APPEAL

**THE NEWS & OBSERVER,** Raleigh, N.C.
Andrea Jones
Lifestyle page, broadsheet, 175,000+

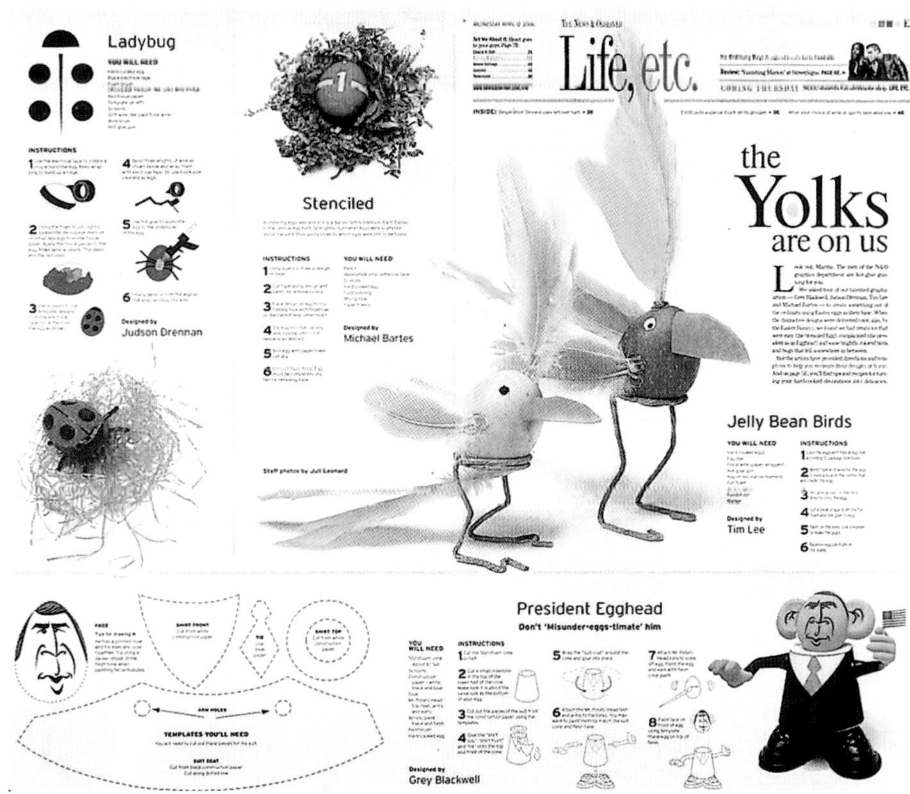
Ladybug

Designed by Judson Drennan

Stenciled

Designed by Michael Bartes

Staff photos by Juli Leonard

Life, etc.

the Yolks are on us

Jelly Bean Birds

Designed by Tim Lee

TEMPLATES YOU'LL NEED

President Egghead
Don't 'Misunder-eggs-timate' him

Designed by Grey Blackwell

codependencia emocional

¿Amar duele?

15: núcleo

ETHEL SORIANO
DE MITOS Y REALIDADES

Nadie me entiende

CAUSAS

¿CÓMO IDENTIFICARLOS?

RELACIONES SANAS

PASOS PARA LA RECUPERACIÓN

DISCIPLINA ESTRELLA

**EXCELSIOR,** México City
Griselda Main, Mario Palomera, Lucía Castañeda, Luzma Díaz de León Reyes, Marco A. Román, Alexandro Medrano, Ma. Luisa Díaz de León, Pascal Beltrán del Río, Ernesto Rivera
Lifestyle page, broadsheet, 50,000-174,999

source how-to

KEEP THE WAVE IN OLD GLORY

A snapping display of the Stars and Stripes is especially inspiring on our nation's birthday. The U.S. Flag Code directs us in proper and respectful display of the flag, and experience guides us in its care and use. Here's what you need to know for flag-flying today.

HOW TO DISPLAY THE FLAG

HOW TO MAINTAIN AND STORE THE FLAG

HOW TO DISPOSE OF THE FLAG PROPERLY

For step-by-step instructions on how to fold the U.S. flag, turn to E10

Cool activities make summer fun

With a little ingenuity and these fun ideas, you can keep things simple and still show your kids a good time.

**STAR TRIBUNE,** Minneapolis
Tippi Thole, Lisa Clausen
Lifestyle page, broadsheet, 175,000+

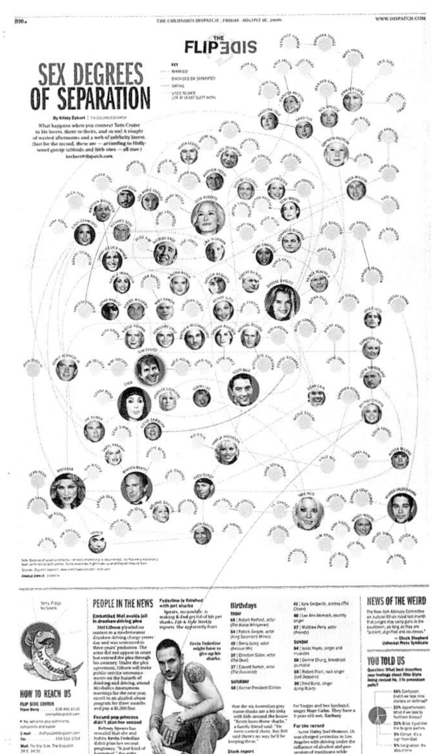
FLIPSIDE

SEX DEGREES OF SEPARATION

PEOPLE IN THE NEWS

Birthdays

NEWS OF THE WEIRD

YOU TOLD US

HOW TO REACH US

**THE COLUMBUS DISPATCH** (Ohio)
Charlie Zimkus, Kristy Eckert, Steve Berry, Scott Minister
Lifestyle page, broadsheet, 175,000+

**LA PRESSE,** Montréal
Francis Leveillee, Sylvie St-Jacques, Benoit Giguere, Michele Ouimet, Marie-Claude Lortie
Lifestyle page, broadsheet, 175,000+

ACTUEL

ACTUELITÉS PAGE 5

LES MOQUETTES COQUETTES : AUX URNES, CANADIENS ! PAGE 4

40 idées pour gens fauchés

Les guirlandes sont retournées dans leurs boîtes. On a achevé tous les restes de dinde. Le sapin séché a échoué sur le trottoir, et le taux de sucre des enfants s'est finalement rétabli. Mais voilà que se pointe un défilé de factures salées qui annonce des mois de frugalité forcée. Actuel lance pour vous 40 idées, pêle-mêle, dont le but avoué est de vous aider à vous remettre de vos excès pécuniaires, sans sombrer dans l'austérité ni racler les fonds de tiroirs.

TEXTES : SYLVIE ST-JACQUES

Le magazine de la déco créative

EN KIOSQUE DÈS MAINTENANT !

inspirations

**ST. PETERSBURG TIMES** (Fla.)
Jessica Parker Gilbert
Lifestyle page, broadsheet, 175,000+

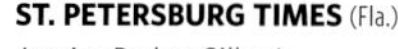

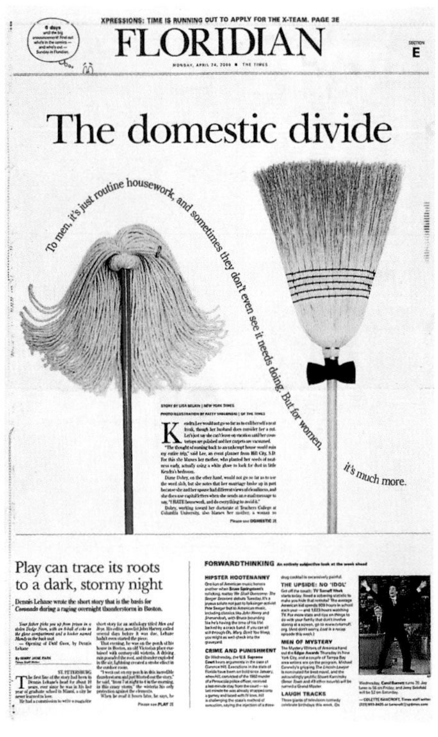
FLORIDIAN

E

The domestic divide

To men, it's just routine housework, and sometimes they don't even see it needs doing. But for women, it's much more.

Play can trace its roots to a dark, stormy night

FORWARD THINKING

**STAR TRIBUNE,** Minneapolis
Laurie Harker, Lisa Clausen
Lifestyle page, broadsheet, 175,000+

signature

What's in the cards?

fashion E8

style E2

drinking trends E3

fitness E6

dates to celebrate E4

2006

7:30pm

7·21

8pm

INTO THE DEEP END

When A Critic Walks Out Of A Movie

Siegel Blasted For Noisy "Clerks II" Departure

**HARTFORD COURANT** (Conn.)
Timothy Reck, Suzette Moyer
Lifestyle page, broadsheet, 175,000+

ARTS&LIFE

Bank error transformed slacker's life

BILL BROWNSTEIN

STILL A STIGMA about a little word that's synonymous with a double standard

Is she a slut?

**THE GAZETTE,** Montreal
Nuri Ducassi
Lifestyle page, broadsheet, 50,000-174,999

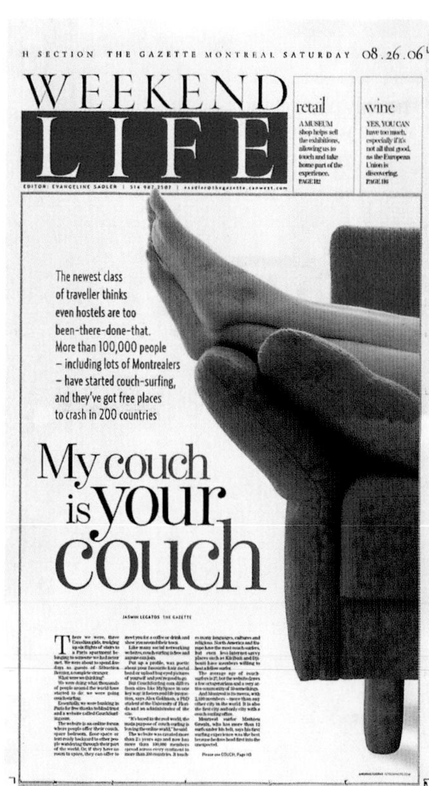
THE GAZETTE MONTREAL SATURDAY 08.26.06

WEEKEND LIFE

retail

wine

The newest class of traveller thinks even hostels are too been-there-done-that. More than 100,000 people – including lots of Montrealers – have started couch-surfing, and they've got free places to crash in 200 countries

My couch is your couch

**THE GAZETTE,** Montreal
Susan Ferguson, Nuri Ducassi, Evangeline Sadler
Lifestyle page, broadsheet, 50,000-174,999

Nick Cave har skrevet en komedie der ikke er spor sjov.

KULTUR 2

Er denne lampe farlig?

**POLITIKEN,** Copenhagen, Denmark
Søren Nyeland, Krisfoffer Løve Østerbye, Christian Ilsøe, Henrlette Llnd
Lifestyle page, broadsheet, 50,000-174,999

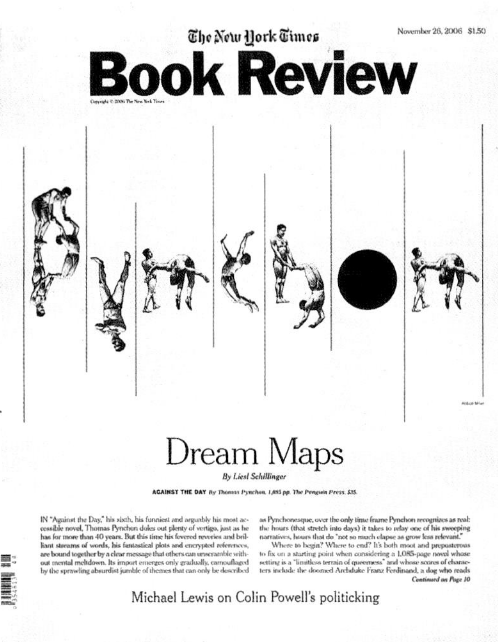

The New York Times — November 26, 2006 $1.50

Book Review

Dream Maps

Michael Lewis on Colin Powell's politicking

**THE NEW YORK TIMES**
Tom Bodkin, Nicholas Blechman, Abbott Miller
Opinion page, broadsheet, 175,000+

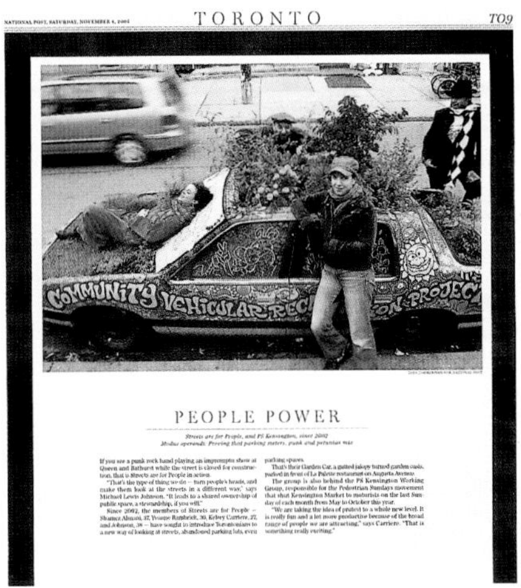

TORONTO — TO9

PEOPLE POWER

**NATIONAL POST,** Toronto
Doug Kelly, Gayle Grin, Jeff Wasserman, Geneviève Biloski, Sarah Murdoch, Rob Roberts, Peter J. Thompson, Tyler Anderson, Tory Zimmerman, Brent Foster
Lifestyle page, tabloid, 175,000+

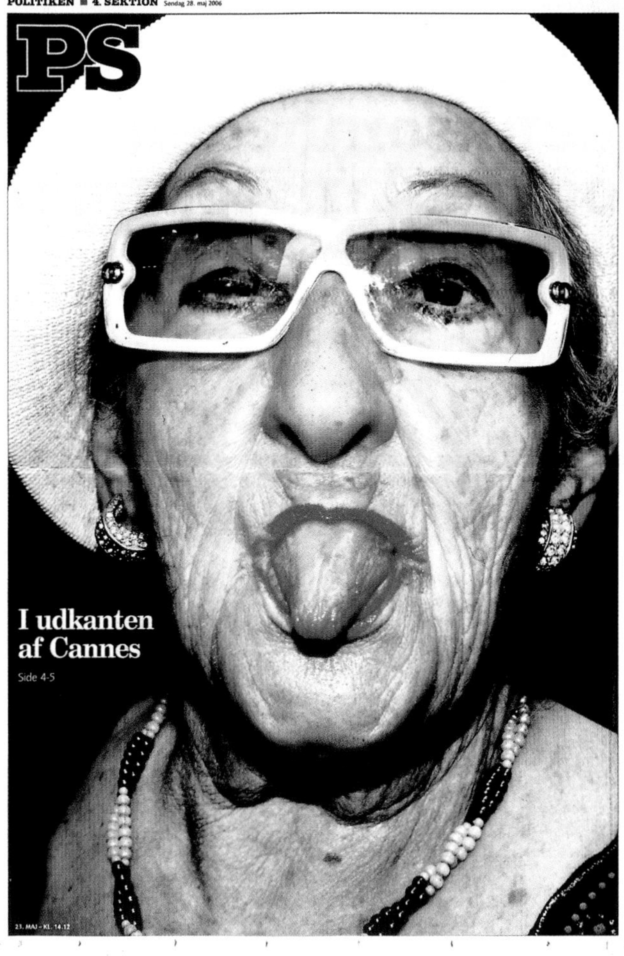

POLITIKEN ■ 4. SEKTION Søndag 28. maj 2006

PS

I udkanten af Cannes

Side 4-5

## SILVER

**POLITIKEN,** Copenhagen, Denmark
Søren Nyeland, Martin Bubandt Jensen, Kjeld Hybel, Bo Søndergaard, Kristoffer Løve Østerbye
Lifestyle page, broadsheet, 50,000-174,999

The bold, irreverent photo illustrating the senior community in Cannes, France, is played at a grand scale, both irreverent and unapologetic. It has a lot of attitude, quite shocking for a cover. You'd find this in the paper and put it on your wall as a poster.

La atrevida e irreverente foto que ilustra la comunidad de tercera edad en Cannes, Francia, está presentada a gran escala, en forma irreverente y sin pedir disculpas. Tiene mucho arrojo, lo que es bastante chocante para una portada. Si se encontrara en un diario, se colgaría en el muro como un afiche.

**SEATTLE POST-INTELLIGENCER**
Bridget Sawicki
Lifestyle page, broadsheet, 50,000-174,999

LIFE AND ARTS
TECHNOLOGY
GROOMING
COMING UP
CALLING FOR HELP
More people are turning to coaches to help define and achieve their goals
Effort builds to get DBP banned from nail polish
IN THE GALLERIES
AUGUST

**THE NEWS-PRESS,** Fort Myers, Fla.
Heather Shlje, Javier Torres
Lifestyle page, broadsheet, 50,000-174,999

LIFESTYLES
FILM GREATS
DREW STERWALD
This year, standard fir isn't option
There are other different ways to decorate for holiday season
All you need is RED
Fight against AIDS supported by various red products
THE "IT" LIST
SUNNY-SIDE UP
SHOW. SHOW. SHOW.

**ARGUS LEADER,** Sioux Falls, S.D.
Sarah Beatty Carlson
Lifestyle page, broadsheet, 50,000-174,999

LIFE SUNDAY
TERRY WOSTER
culture
getaway
books
HAUNTED PLACES
Orpheum, one of state's spooky spots, frightens with noises
Inside
SPOOK ROAD
@argusleader.com

POLITIKEN 2. SEKTION
Hul til Evighedens Hus
KULTUR
2
Den danske mand

**POLITIKEN,** Copenhagen, Denmark
Søren Nyeland, Tomas Østergren, Christian Ilsøe, Peter Lembo
Lifestyle page, broadsheet, 50,000-174,999

POLITIKEN KULTUR OPINION NAVNE SPORT
2
En mageløs rejse i tankens mangfoldighed
SÆLGER TIL DESIGNMØBLER
OLSSØN

**POLITIKEN,** Copenhagen, Denmark
Søren Nyeland, Peter Sætternissen, Christian Ilsøe, Mette Olsen
Lifestyle page, broadsheet, 50,000-174,999

LIFE AND ARTS
BOOKS
RIDES
COMING UP
SEATTLE IMPRESSIONS
P-I PHOTOS BY MIKE KANE

**SEATTLE POST-INTELLIGENCER**
Jim Woolace, Mike Kane, Eustacio Humphrey
Lifestyle page, broadsheet, 50,000-174,999

**ESTADO DE MINAS,** Belo Horizonte, Brazil
Jefferson Coutinho, Valf
Lifestyle page, broadsheet, 50,000-174,999

BEM VIVER

Você tem medo de quê?

ESPECIALISTAS AFIRMAM QUE JÁ EXISTEM MAIS DE 2 MIL OBJETOS DESCRITOS QUE PROVOCAM FOBIAS, DISTÚRBIOS GERALMENTE RELACIONADOS ÀS PERDAS E FRUSTRAÇÕES HUMANAS

**THE FLORIDA TIMES-UNION,** Jacksonville
Gary T. Mills, Denise M. Reagan, Jeff Reece, Patrick Garvin
Lifestyle page, broadsheet, 50,000-174,999

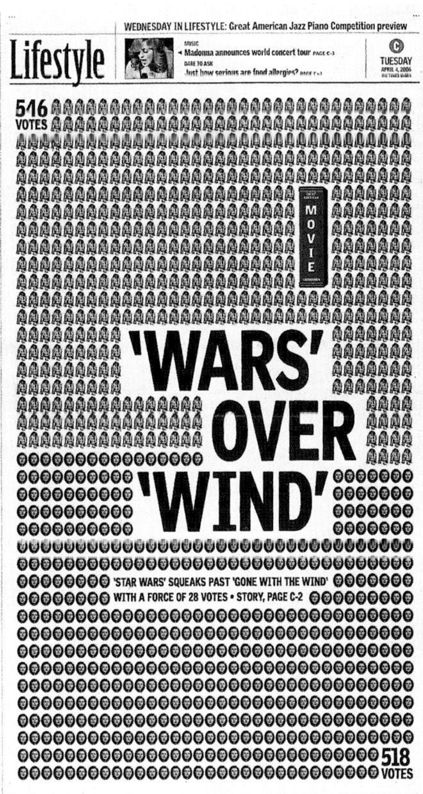
WEDNESDAY IN LIFESTYLE: Great American Jazz Piano Competition preview

Lifestyle

Madonna announces world concert tour

TUESDAY APRIL 4, 2006

516 VOTES

MOVIE

'WARS' OVER 'WIND'

'STAR WARS' SQUEAKS PAST 'GONE WITH THE WIND' WITH A FORCE OF 28 VOTES • STORY, PAGE C-2

518 VOTES

**ESTADO DE MINAS,** Belo Horizonte, Brazil
Júlio Moreira
Lifestyle page, broadsheet, 50,000-174,999

BEM VIVER

Preocupação com qualidade de vida e bem-estar amplia a demanda por alimentos funcionais, fortificados ou biologicamente modificados, capazes de prevenir doenças e evitar carências nutricionais

MAIS SAUDÁVEIS

H SECTION THE GAZETTE MONTREAL SATURDAY 11.04.06

WEEKEND LIFE

food

wine

Is extra large the new medium?

Finding the right size in women's clothing can be a headache – especially if you don't fit impossible fashion ideals – with the numbers changing from one store to another as your waist stays the same



**THE GAZETTE,** Montreal
Susan Ferguson, Nuri Ducassi, Evangeline Sadler
Lifestyle page, broadsheet, 50,000-174,999

LA GACETA

ACTUALIDAD

El consumo cultural de los jóvenes

Páginas 2, 3, 4 y 5



**LA GACETA,** San Miguel de Tucuman, Argentina
Daniel Fontanarrosa, Sergio Fernandez
Lifestyle page, broadsheet, 50,000-174,999

HAPPY THOUGHTS

worry less or not at all!

The Desert Sun

DESERT LIVING

GHASTLY PRICES PER GALLON

BEAUTY

FOOD & DRINK

HEALTH

HOME



**THE DESERT SUN,** Palm Springs, Calif.
Kris Dale
Lifestyle page, broadsheet, 50,000-174,999

**THE COLUMBUS DISPATCH** (Ohio)
Patrick Kastner, Scott Minister
Lifestyle page, broadsheet, 175,000+

Life

PLAYING THE DON

Spinoff of mob film arrives late, packed with extra violence

Would-be henchmen should apply here

Only bartender can beat ex-Buckeye in NCAA contest

**ESTADO DE MINAS,** Belo Horizonte, Brazil
Júlio Moreira, Emmanuel Pinheiro
Lifestyle page, broadsheet, 50,000-174,999

BEM VIVER

DEPRESSÃO
INSÔNIA
DOR DE CABEÇA
ALERGIAS
CANSAÇO
RAIVA
ARREPENDIMENTO
CULPA
ISOLAMENTO SOCIAL
HOSTILIDADE
SENSAÇÃO DE FRACASSO
FRUSTRAÇÃO
DECEPÇÃO
ANSIEDADE
FALTA DE PACIÊNCIA

a profissão é um exercício de paciência, amor, compreensão e esforço pessoal

NO LIMITE

**ARIZONA DAILY STAR,** Tucson
Hugo Torres, Mike Rice, Staff
Lifestyle page, broadsheet, 50,000-174,999

Accent

I INTENDED TO WRITE A STORY ABOUT PROCRASTINATION LAST WEEK . . . I DIDN'T. SO THIS IS VERY LAST-MINUTE. FAILED TO ASK FOR COOL PHOTOS, GRAPHICS, TOO. SORRY.

NATIONAL PROCRASTINATION WEEK
MARCH 6-12, 2006

You can pinch pennies and still be stylish

Ripped off on eBay? Web site has answer

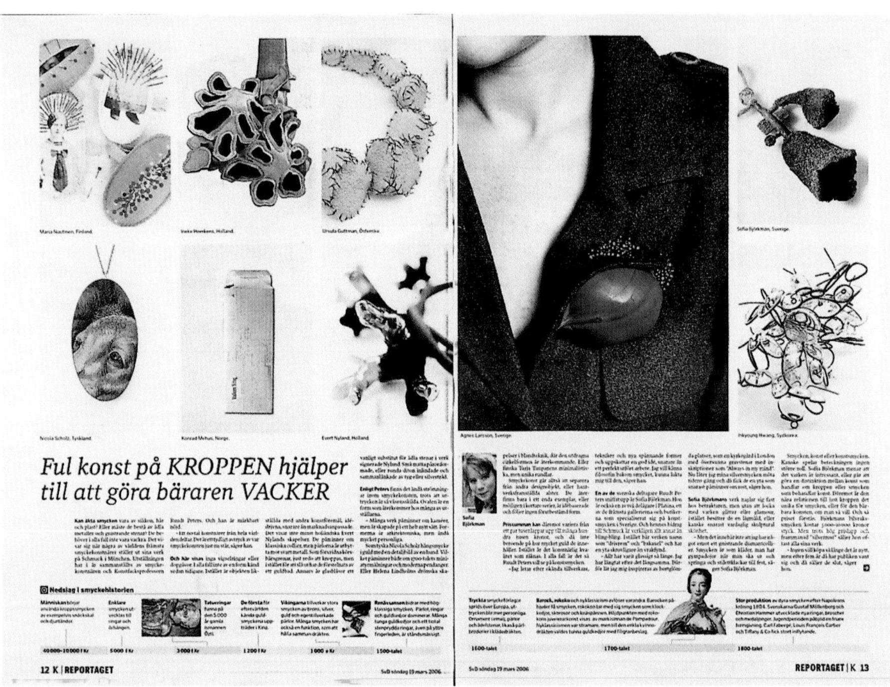
Ful konst på KROPPEN hjälper till att göra bäraren VACKER

12 K | REPORTAGET

REPORTAGET | K 13

**SVENSKA DAGBLADET,** Stockholm, Sweden
Lena K. Samuelsson, Mats-Eric Nilsson, Anna W. Thurfjell, Anders Lindgren, Ann Axelsson, Staffan Löwstedt, Schmuck
Lifestyle page, tabloid, 175,000+

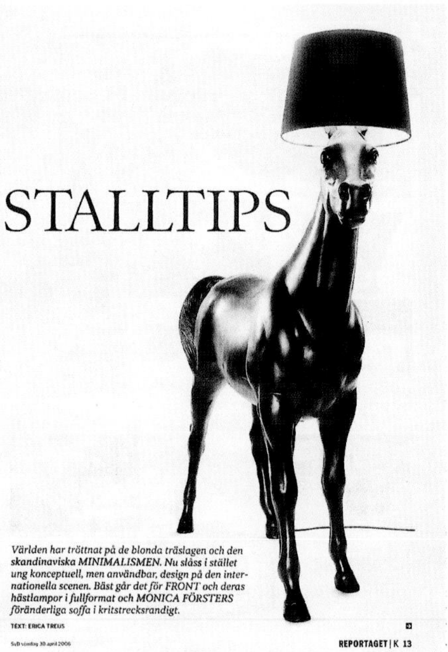
STALLTIPS

*Världen har tröttnat på de blonda träslagen och den skandinaviska MINIMALISMEN. Nu slåss i stället ung konceptuell, men användbar, design på den internationella scenen. Båst går det för FRONT och deras hästlampor i fullformat och MONICA FÖRSTERS föränderliga soffa i kritstrecksrandigt.*

REPORTAGET | K 13

**SVENSKA DAGBLADET,** Stockholm, Sweden
Lena K. Samuelsson, Mats-Eric Nilsson, Anna W. Thurfjell, Malin S. Anell, Ann Axelsson, Staffan Löwstedt, Tommy Bäcklin
Lifestyle page, tabloid, 175,000+

**SVENSKA DAGBLADET,** Stockholm, Sweden
Lena K. Samuelsson, Mats-Eric Nilsson, Anna W. Thurfjell, Malin S. Anell, Ann Axelsson, Staffan Löwstedt
Lifestyle page, tabloid, 175,000+

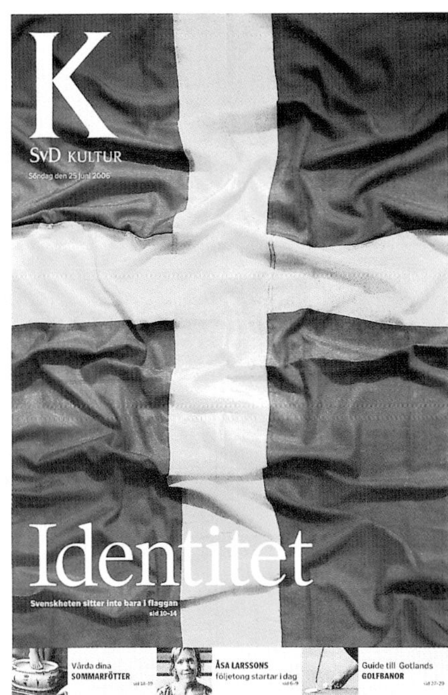
K
SvD KULTUR
Söndag den 25 juni 2006
Identitet
Svenskheten sitter inte bara i flaggan
Vårda dina SOMMARFÖTTER
ÅSA LARSSONS följetong startar i dag
Guide till Gotlands GOLFBANOR

K
SvD KULTUR
Söndag den 5 november 2006
Smärta
Fotografen Lauren Greenfield har följt unga kvinnors kamp mot ätstörningar
LENA ADELSOHN LILJEROTH har ett kall
Turister hittar till kinesiska YUNNAN
Affärer och designer trivs TILLSAMMANS

**SVENSKA DAGBLADET,** Stockholm, Sweden
Lena K. Samuelsson, Mats-Eric Nilsson, Anna W. Thurfjell, Malin S. Anell, Ann Axelsson, Staffan Löwstedt, Lauren Greenfield
Lifestyle page, tabloid, 175,000+

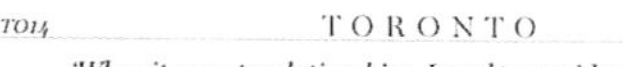
TO14 TORONTO
*'When it came to relationships, I used to consider myself jealous. That's why I couldn't fathom myself doing these things. In the end it made our own love life stronger' — the husband*

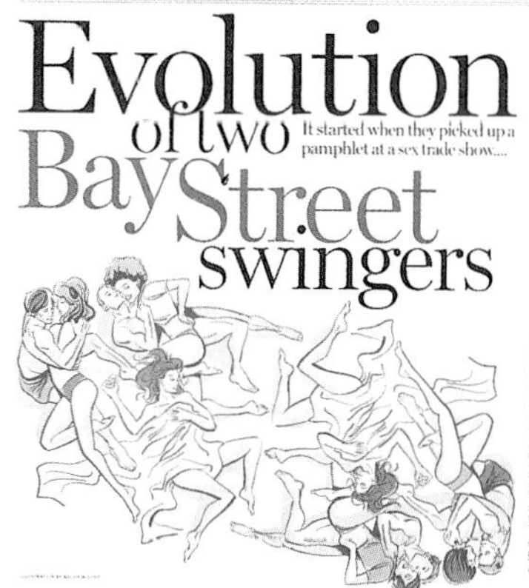
Evolution of two Bay Street swingers
It started when they picked up a pamphlet at a sex trade show...

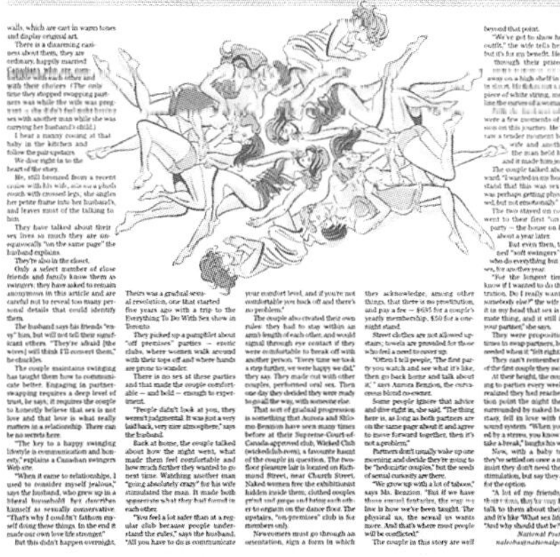
TORONTO TO15
*'For the longest time I didn't know if I wanted to do the full penetration. Do I really want to be with somebody else? I had it in my head that sex is a very intimate thing, and it still is, but with your partner' — the wife*

**NATIONAL POST,** Toronto
Doug Kelly, Gayle Grin, Geneviève Biloski, Rob Roberts, Kagan McLeod, Sarah Murdoch
Lifestyle page, tabloid, 175,000+

TO8 TORONTO
TORONTO TO9
Number of fares collected on an average day: 1,397,000
MY LONG COMMUTE
FOR THREE MONTHS THIS SPRING AND SUMMER DAVID TOPPING FOUGHT BOREDOM AND OFFICIALDOM IN HIS QUEST TO PHOTOGRAPH ALL 69 TTC STATIONS

**NATIONAL POST,** Toronto
Doug Kelly, Gayle Grin, Geneviève Biloski, Rob Roberts
Lifestyle page, tabloid, 175,000+

C2 lecturas
Centinelas de óperas, sinfonías y nostalgias
Max Pou
"Escucho el piano desde antes de nacer"
Mario Emilio Pérez
"Llegué a tener 400 discos de larga duración, mi destino es coleccionar"
Julio Serrallés
"Tengo más de medio siglo sin escuchar música popular, vivo entre melodías"
Angelo Porcella
"Al actuar en dos óperas siento que mis sueños ya se han realizado"
Alberto Perdomo
"La ópera es un espectáculo y como tal se tiene que coleccionar"

**CLAVE,** Santo Domingo, Dominican Republic
Glenny Veloz, Juan Manuel Sánchez, Victor Bautista, Fausto Rosario Adames
Lifestyle page, tabloid, 50,000-174,999

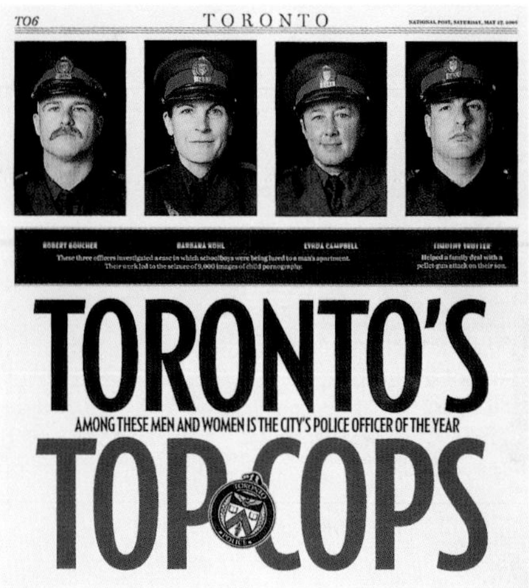
TORONTO

TORONTO'S

AMONG THESE MEN AND WOMEN IS THE CITY'S POLICE OFFICER OF THE YEAR

TOP COPS

**NATIONAL POST,** Toronto
Doug Kelly, Gayle Grin, Geneviève Biloski, Rob Roberts
Lifestyle page, tabloid, 175,000+

Sunday Life

COMICS

BECOMING FU YANG'S DAD

Oct. 2003 at Medical City, Dallas; We were strangers, but our bond was immediate

8

**THE DALLAS MORNING NEWS**
Mary Jennings, Louis DeLuca, Michael Hamtil, Michael Merschel, Marilyn Bishkin
Lifestyle page, tabloid, 175,000+

ACCENT

SAVANNAH SPOKEN WORD FESTIVAL

DREAM IT. PLAN IT. THINK IT. BE IT.

SPEAK IT. SAY IT. RAP IT. SCREAM IT!

CALENDAR

TRENDS

MONEY

CONTACT US

'School's Out Graduation Jam'

What message is your license plate sending?

Are you a penny hoarder?

**SAVANNAH MORNING NEWS** (Ga.)
Sam Morgan
Lifestyle page, tabloid, 50,000-174,999

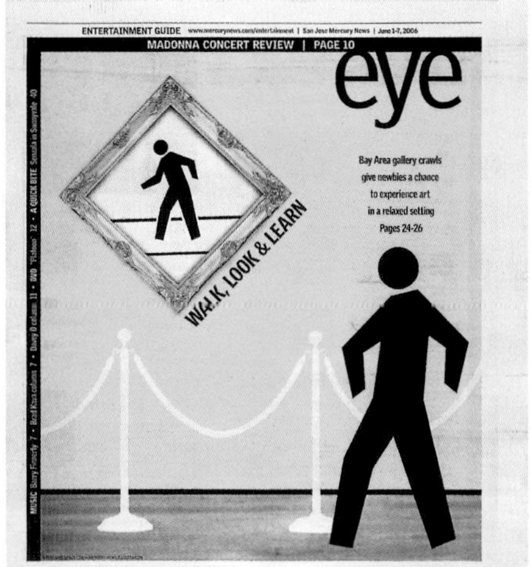
ENTERTAINMENT GUIDE

MADONNA CONCERT REVIEW | PAGE 10

eye

WALK, LOOK & LEARN

Bay Area gallery crawls give newbies a chance to experience art in a relaxed setting Pages 24-26

**SAN JOSE MERCURY NEWS** (Calif.)
Stephanie Grace Lim, Jonathon Berlin, Matt Mansfield
Entertainment page, tabloid, 175,000+

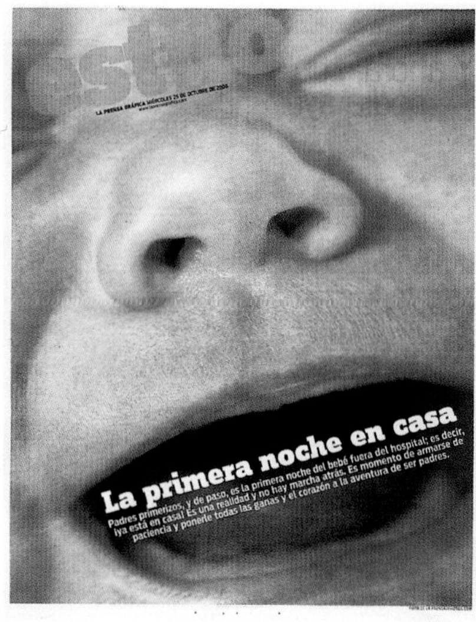
La primera noche en casa

**LA PRENSA GRÁFICA,** Antiguo Cuscatlán, El Salvador
Enrique Contreras, Florence Romero
Lifestyle page, tabloid, 50,000-174,999

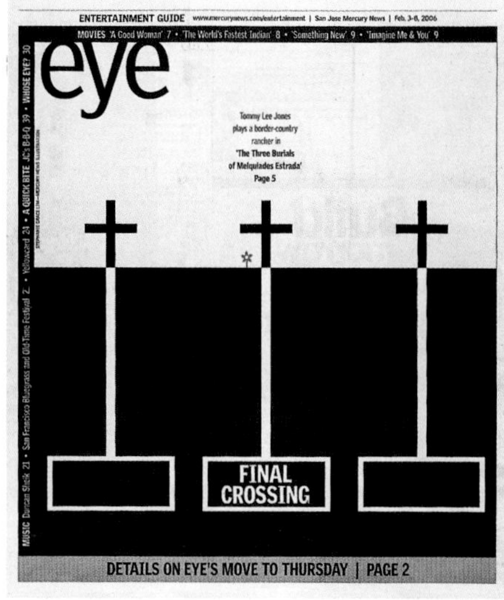
ENTERTAINMENT GUIDE

eye

Tommy Lee Jones plays a border-country rancher in 'The Three Burials of Melquiades Estrada' Page 5

FINAL CROSSING

DETAILS ON EYE'S MOVE TO THURSDAY | PAGE 2

**SAN JOSE MERCURY NEWS** (Calif.)
Stephanie Grace Lim, Jonathon Berlin, Matt Mansfield
Entertainment page, tabloid, 175,000+

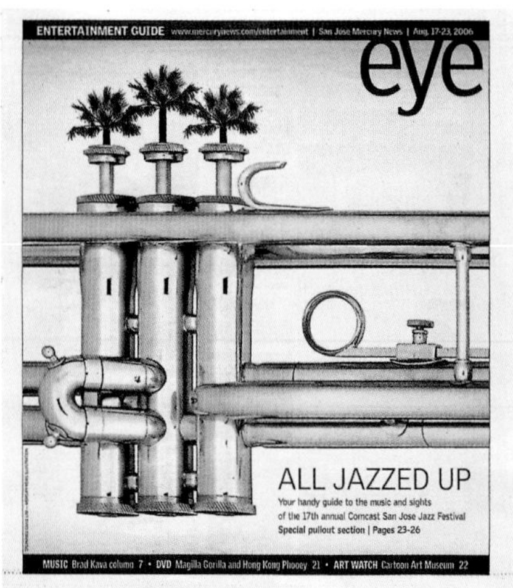
ENTERTAINMENT GUIDE

eye

ALL JAZZED UP

Your handy guide to the music and sights of the 17th annual Comcast San Jose Jazz Festival

Special pullout section | Pages 23-26

**SAN JOSE MERCURY NEWS** (Calif.)
Stephanie Grace Lim, Jonathon Berlin, Matt Mansfield
Entertainment page, tabloid, 175,000+

cal

james blunt dives into heartache page 8

**HARTFORD COURANT** (Conn.)
Nicole Dudka
Entertainment page, tabloid, 175,000+

YOUR GUIDE TO CINEQUEST

eye

COMICS AND TV LISTINGS: PULLOUT SECTION INSIDE

**SAN JOSE MERCURY NEWS** (Calif.)
Stephanie Grace Lim, Jonathon Berlin, Matt Mansfield
Entertainment page, tabloid, 175,000+

**AKZIA,** Moscow
Konstantin Lukjanov, Alla Gorobets, Igor Sadreev, Svetlana Maximchenko
Entertainment page, tabloid, 175,000+

enterкино
6
ДВА 07
Фильмы про Джеймса Бонда появляются не каждый год — и уж тем более не каждый год создатели проводят ему такой колоссальный ребрендинг. Новогоднюю вечеринку в стиле «бондианы» придумал Сергей Долгов, креативный директор агентства eventBRAND.

**THE DALLAS MORNING NEWS**
Jamie Huckaby, Troy Oxford
Entertainment page, broadsheet, 175,000+

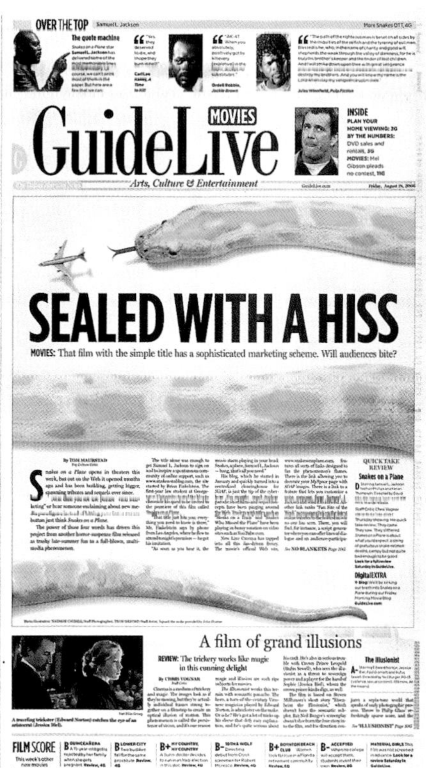
OVER THE TOP
GuideLive
MOVIES
Arts, Culture & Entertainment
SEALED WITH A HISS
MOVIES: That film with the simple title has a sophisticated marketing scheme. Will audiences bite?
A film of grand illusions
FILM SCORE

**THE VIRGINIAN-PILOT,** Norfolk
Sam Hundley, Paul Nelson, Deborah Withey
Entertainment page, broadsheet, 175,000+

THE DAILY BREAK
frisatsun
David Copperfield
A little bit on Mozart
Virginia Flower & Garden Show
GO!

ARTS
winter movies
Big-Screen Blizzard
Hollywood Studios Turn Serious – In Serious Pursuit Of An Oscar

**HARTFORD COURANT** (Conn.)
Melanie Shaffer, Nicole Dudka
Entertainment page, broadsheet, 175,000+

The New York Times
Arts&LEISURE
Section 2
A LOOK BACK AT THE YEAR IN
POP MUSIC
ARCHITECTURE
VIDEO GAMES
DANCE
CLASSICAL
FILM
TELEVISION
The Year in Culture
4 THEATER 7 FILM 28 CLASSICAL MUSIC 30 POP/JAZZ 32 DANCE 34 ART/ARCHITECTURE 37 TELEVISION 38 VIDEO GAMES

**THE NEW YORK TIMES**
Tom Bodkin, Paul Jean, Post Typography
Entertainment page, broadsheet, 175,000+

ARTS
LEAVES OF GLOSS OR DROSS?
Fall Movies May Be More Serious Stuff, But That's No Guarantee Of Success
CRANK
SAW III
BANDIDAS
Texas Chainsaw Massacre: The Beginning
The Prestige
the last kiss

**HARTFORD COURANT** (Conn.)
Chris Moore, Nicole Dudka
Entertainment page, broadsheet, 175,000+

**TORONTO STAR**
Spencer Wynn, Malene Arpe
Entert ainment page, broadsheet, 175,000+

A&E

At age 40, still thinking like a kid

Started as YPT, theatre marks 4 decades with gala

Survived spitballs and a name change to create legacy

Do what?

Go ahead.
We dare you.
Turn off your TV for a week.
To help fill the void, we offer 97 nuggets of tube-style wisdom.
H18-H19

BLUE MAN GROUP "A SENSATION!"

**ROCKY MOUNTAIN NEWS,** Denver
Julie Lovell
Entertainment page, broadsheet, 175,000+

spotlight

Spot check

Bada-Bang!

The Sopranos returns to HBO after nearly two years, and something's not quite right in mob land

With 'Dust,' Towne adapts the 'best' L.A. story

Angry novel's journey to screen took decades

Home Front: 4-page liftout section inside

In Store Warehouse CLEARANCE

**SAN FRANCISCO CHRONICLE**
Nanette Bisher, Matt Petty, David Wiegand, Joel Selvin
Entertainment page, broadsheet, 175,000+

San Francisco Chronicle

DATEBOOK

REUNION TOUR! KIND OF

THE WHO NO, REALLY WHO?

DEAD KENNEDYS SOMEBODY'S

QUEEN SOME OTHER ROYAL FIGURE

It happens: Great rockers split and bands adapt. But the Dead Kennedys minus Jello Biafra? That's not right.

MUSIC REVIEW

MOVIE REVIEW

MOVIE REVIEW

MARK MORFORD

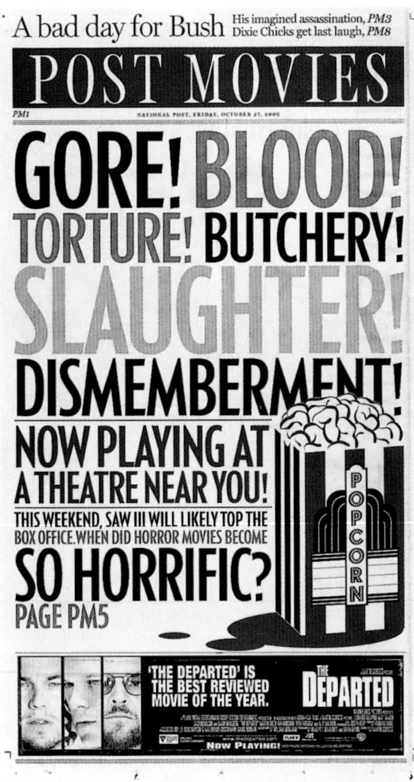
A bad day for Bush His imagined assassination, PM3 Dixie Chicks get last laugh, PM8

POST MOVIES

GORE! BLOOD! TORTURE! BUTCHERY! SLAUGHTER! DISMEMBERMENT! NOW PLAYING AT A THEATRE NEAR YOU!

THIS WEEKEND, SAW III WILL LIKELY TOP THE BOX OFFICE. WHEN DID HORROR MOVIES BECOME SO HORRIFIC?

PAGE PM5

POPCORN

"THE DEPARTED" IS THE BEST REVIEWED MOVIE OF THE YEAR.

THE DEPARTED

NOW PLAYING!

**NATIONAL POST,** Toronto
Doug Kelly, Gayle Grin, Charles Lewis, Ian Karleff, Ron Wadden
Business page, broadsheet, 175,000+

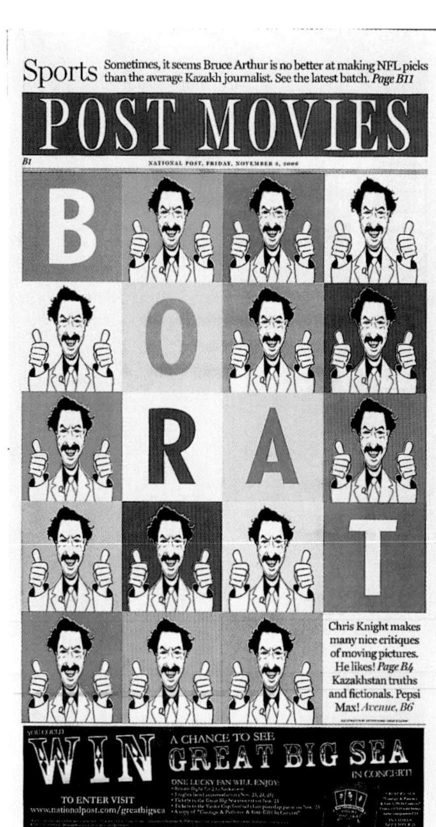
Sports Sometimes, it seems Bruce Arthur is no better at making NFL picks than the average Kazakh journalist. See the latest batch. Page B11

POST MOVIES

B O R A T

Chris Knight makes many nice critiques of moving pictures. He likes! Page B4 Kazakhstan truths and fictionals. Pepsi Max! Avenue, B6

WIN A CHANCE TO SEE GREAT BIG SEA IN CONCERT!

TO ENTER VISIT www.nationalpost.com/greatbigsea

**NATIONAL POST,** Toronto
Doug Kelly, Gayle Grin, Ben Errett, Geneviève Biloski, Antony Hare
Entertainment page, broadsheet, 175,000+

Movies

Boston Sunday Globe July 30, 2006

TWO FOR THE ROAD

FOR THESE MUSIC VIDEO DIRECTORS, 'LITTLE MISS SUNSHINE' REPRESENTS A REAL DEPARTURE

Will Ferrell spoofs NASCAR in new film but plays it straight in real life

Stock card

Now this week

**THE BOSTON GLOBE**
Tito Bottitta
Entertainment page, broadsheet, 175,000+

**NATIONAL POST,** Toronto
Doug Kelly, Gayle Grin, Ben Errett, Geneviève Biloski
Entertainment page, broadsheet, 175,000+

Those mighty Ducks
How Brian Burke changed the losing culture in Anaheim. B8
POST MOVIES
B1
NATIONAL POST, FRIDAY, MARCH 24, 2006
COME TO WHERE THE FUNNY IS
CHRIS KNIGHT'S WARNING:
Thank You For Smoking is addictive, morally vacant and three-and a-half ashtrays full of giddy laughs. Page B3
Because executive material is cut from a different cloth
To advertise call 1 866 588-3678

**CONTRA COSTA TIMES,** Walnut Creek, Calif.
Dave Johnson, Jennifer Schaefer, Chuck Todd
Entertainment page, broadsheet, 175,000+

DECEMBER 24, 2006
THE SUNDAY TIMES
SECTION C
A&E
THE BEST
AND WORST
2006
ARTS & ENTERTAINMENT FOR THE BAY AREA

**THE HARTFORD COURANT** (Conn.)
Nicole Dudka, Suzette Moyer, John Woike, Beth Bristow
Entertainment page, broadsheet, 175,000+

ARTS
Bloody Sunday
The Dark World Of Tony Soprano & Co. Dawns For Final Time
A Lot Of Love In New HBO Series About Family

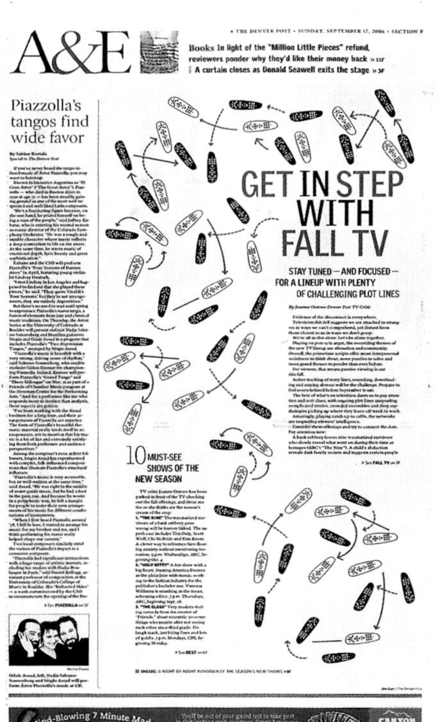
A&E
Books In light of the "Million Little Pieces" refund, reviewers ponder why they'd like their money back
A curtain closes as Donald Seawell exits the stage
Piazzolla's tangos find wide favor
GET IN STEP WITH FALL TV
STAY TUNED — AND FOCUSED — FOR A LINEUP WITH PLENTY OF CHALLENGING PLOT LINES
10 MUST-SEE SHOWS OF THE NEW SEASON
Mind-Blowing 7 Minute Madness
CANTON CASINO

**THE DENVER POST**
Jim Carr
Entertainment page, broadsheet, 175,000+

ARTS
The Stories Are Light, And The Literary Luggage Rides Loaded So Lie Back, Relax And Get Reading
SUMMER READS

**HARTFORD COURANT** (Conn.)
Nicole Dudka
Entertainment page, broadsheet, 175,000+

arts+entertainment
MAXIMUM EXPOSURE

Crosby, Stills, Nash & Young gets political F7
Musical has a 'Wicked' case of success

**STAR TRIBUNE,** Minneapolis
Tippi Thole, Claude Peck, Lisa Clausen
Entertainment page, broadsheet, 175,000+

**THE BOSTON GLOBE**
Jane Simon, Dina Rudick, James Reed, Lane Turner
Entertainment page, tabloid, 175,000+

**THE OREGONIAN,** Portland
Molly Swisher, Pablo Lobaton, Nancy Casey
Entertainment page, tabloid, 175,000+

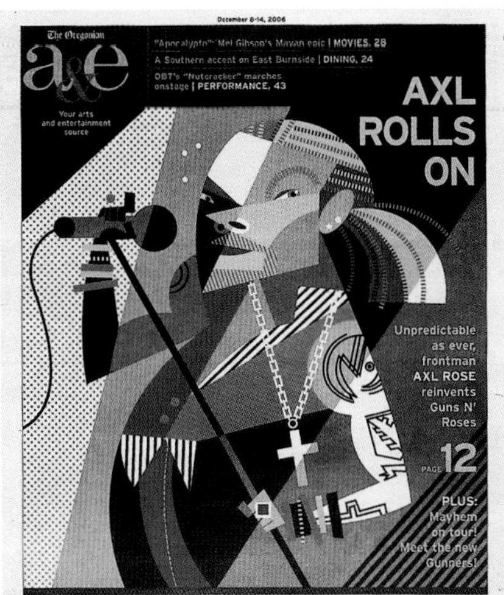


**PITTSBURGH POST-GAZETTE**
Daniel Marsula
Entertainment page, tabloid, 175,000+

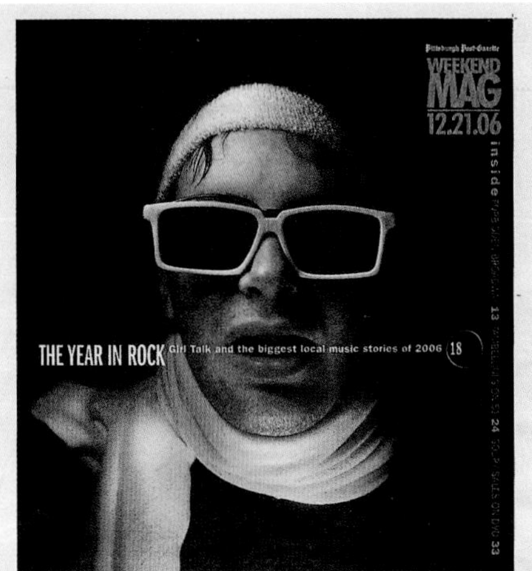

**THE CHARLOTTE OBSERVER** (N.C.)
Luke Trautwein, Denise Renfro, Theoden Janes, Eric Edwards
Entertainment page, tabloid, 175,000+

**SAN FRANCISCO CHRONICLE**
Nanette Bisher, Matt Petty, Sue Adolphson, Meredith White, Ward Schumaker
Entertainment page, tabloid, 175,000+

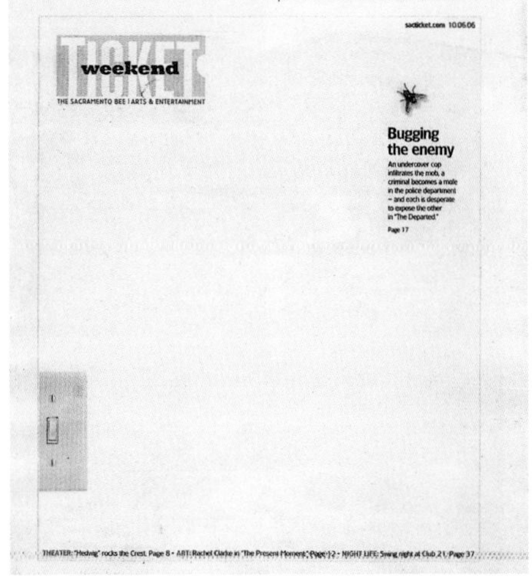


**THE SACRAMENTO BEE** (Calif.)
Margaret Spengler, Val Mina, Barbara Stubbs, Pam Dinsmore
Entertainment page, tabloid, 175,000+

**HARTFORD COURANT** (Conn.)
Nicole Dudka
Entertainment page, tabloid, 175,000+

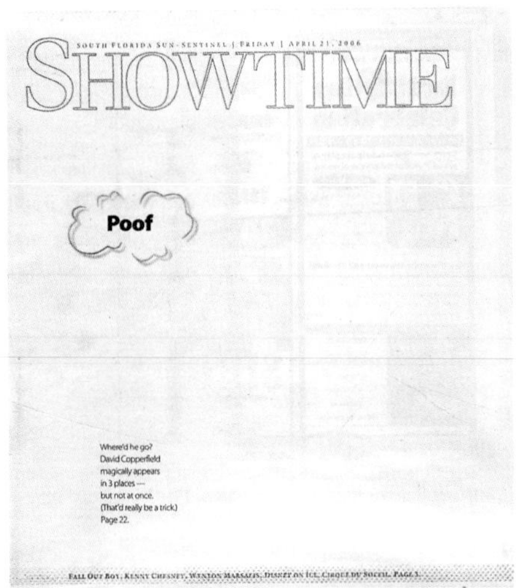


**SOUTH FLORIDA SUN-SENTINEL,** Fort Lauderdale
Vanessa Cordo, Ben Crandell, Tim Frank, Oline Cogdill
Entertainment page, tabloid, 175,000+

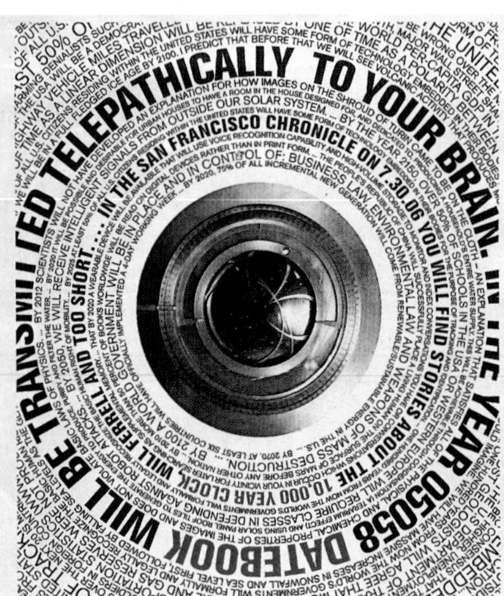


**SAN FRANCISCO CHRONICLE**
Nanette Bisher, Matt Petty, Sue Adolphson
Entertainment page, tabloid, 175,000+

**HARTFORD COURANT** (Conn.)
Nicole Dudka
Entertainment page, broadsheet, 175,000+

**CORREIO BRAZILIENSE,** Brasilia, Brazil
Josemar Gimenez, Ana Dubeux, Carlos Marcelo, João Bosco Adelino de Almeida, Maurenilson Freire, Severino José da Paz
Entertainment page, broadsheet, 50,000-174,999

**LA GACETA,** San Miguel de Tucuman, Argentina
Daniel Fontanarrosa, Sergio Fernandez
Entertainment page, broadsheet, 50,000-174,999

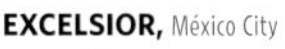

**EXCELSIOR,** México City
Nancy Araiza, Mario Palomera, Carlos Meraz, Luzma Díaz de León Reyes, Marco A. Román, Alexandro Medrano, Ma. Luisa Díaz de León, Pascal Beltrán del Río, Ernesto Rivera
Entertainment page, broadsheet, 50,000-174,999

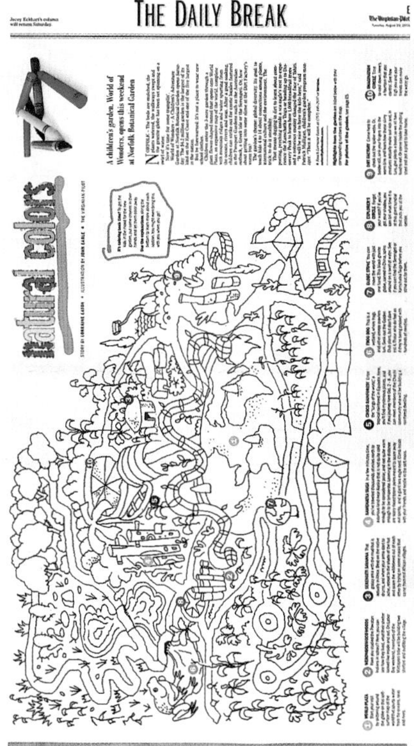

**THE VIRGINIAN-PILOT,** Norfolk
Josh Bohling, John Earle, Paul Nelson, Deborah Withey
Lifestyle page, broadsheet, 175,000+

**SAN JOSE MERCURY NEWS** (Calif.)
Stephanie Grace Lim, Jonathon Berlin, Matt Mansfield
Entertainment page, tabloid, 175,000+

ENTERTAINMENT GUIDE

eye

flea market savvy

From San Jose to De Anza, here's everything you need to know about the area's biggest swap meets
Pages 24-25

**SAN JOSE MERCURY NEWS** (Calif.)
Stephanie Grace Lim, Jonathon Berlin, Matt Mansfield
Entertainment page, tabloid, 175,000+

ENTERTAINMENT GUIDE

eye

SUMMER MOVIE PREVIEW

Hollywood aims at our hearts and wallets with a power-packed lineup of big stars, big effects and big budgets | Pages 22-23

**SAN JOSE MERCURY NEWS** (Calif.)
Stephanie Grace Lim, Martin Gee, Jonathon Berlin, Matt Mansfield
Entertainment page, tabloid, 175,000+

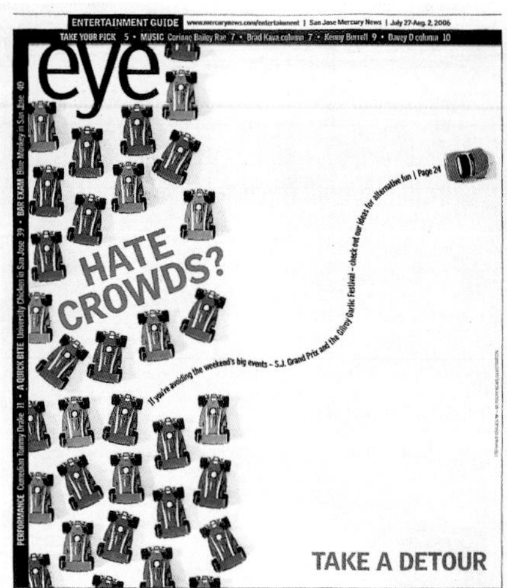

ENTERTAINMENT GUIDE

eye

HATE CROWDS?

TAKE A DETOUR

fiona apple

The eccentric songwriter steps out of her head and back into music. Page 8

caL

**HARTFORD COURANT** (Conn.)
Nicole Dudka
Entertainment page, tabloid, 175,000+

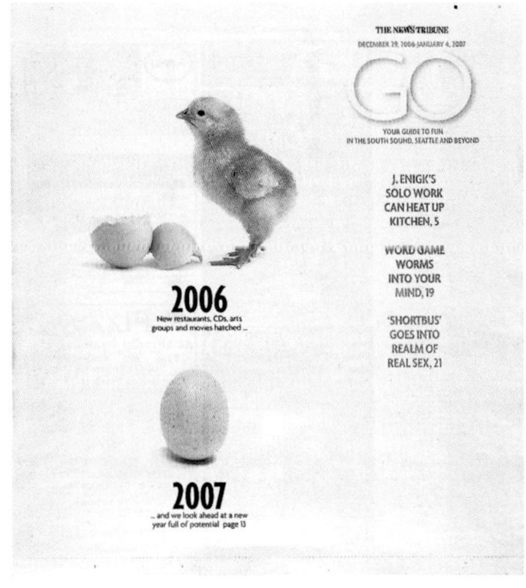

THE NEWS TRIBUNE

GO

J. ENIGK'S SOLO WORK CAN HEAT UP KITCHEN, 5

WORD GAME WORMS INTO YOUR MIND, 19

'SHORTBUS' GOES INTO REALM OF REAL SEX, 21

2006

New restaurants, CDs, arts groups and movies hatched ...

2007

... and we look ahead at a new year full of potential page 13

**THE NEWS TRIBUNE,** Tacoma, Wash.
Elysia Smith
Entertainment page, tabloid, 50,000-174,999

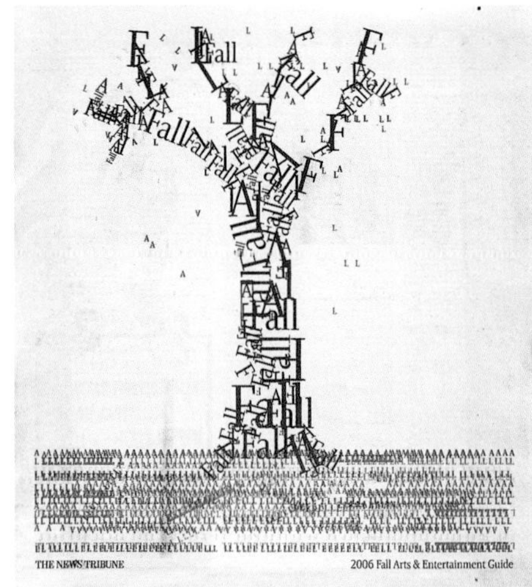

Fall

THE NEWS TRIBUNE

2006 Fall Arts & Entertainment Guide

**THE NEWS TRIBUNE,** Tacoma, Wash.
Elysia Smith
Entertainment page, tabloid, 50,000-174,999

liza minnelli

The indomitable diva performs at Mohegan Sun Arena

Page 8

caL

**THE HARTFORD COURANT** (Conn.)
Nicole Dudka
Entertainment page, tabloid, 175,000+

LA PRENSA GRÁFICA

CULTURA

Ganadores de libros de "El delfín"

Monólogos de la vagina en el Poma

La séptima temporada Poma se reanuda a partir de la próxima semana con "Los monólogos de la vagina".

Oferta variopinta

Encontrando espacios

Obras, fechas y autores

**LA PRENSA GRÁFICA,** Antiguo Cuscatlán, El Salvador
Enrique Contreras, Florence Natsumi, Francesca Zometa
Entertainment page, tabloid, 50,000-174,999

MUÉVETE 162

HERALDO DE ARAGON

Volvemos en septiembre

MODA: LOS HOMBRES ENSEÑAN LAS PIERNAS

CINE: SI HACE CALOR, REFRESCA EL CEREBRO

FESTIVALES: SUMMERCASE, MONEGROS, APTC

**HERALDO DE ARAGÓN,** Zaragoza, Spain
Kristina Urresti, Irán Santos, Pilar Ostalé, Jorge Luis Mora, Pedro Zapater
Entertainment page, tabloid, 50,000-174,999

Jewish Book Festival
Stories from the Jewish experience that speak to us all
Page 8
THE HARTFORD COURANT • OCTOBER 26 - NOVEMBER 1, 2006
caL


SILVER

**HARTFORD COURANT** (Conn.)

Nicole Dudka, Chris Moore

Entertainment page, tabloid, 175,000+

It's clever and inventive to arrange books as a Star of David to illustrate a Jewish book festival. It doesn't feel gimmicky. Even the typography is close to a Jewish script. The page communicates quickly.

Es ingenioso y creativo organizar los libros como una Estrella de David para ilustrar un festival de libros judíos. Y no se ve artificioso. Incluso la tipografía se parece al alfabeto hebreo. Esta página comunica de forma rápida.

¡EXTRA!

MÁS NOTICIAS ESPECTACULARES > 2, 4, 8 y 9

FUNCIÓN

Daily Planet

JUEVES 6 DE JULIO DE 2006

SUPERMAN LLEGA HOY A SALVARNOS

CON LA PRIMERA PELÍCULA EN EL SIGLO XXI DEL *HOMBRE DE ACERO*, LA SAGA DE AVENTURAS ATERRIZA EN ESTA METRÓPOLI CON SU PROTAGONISTA BRANDON ROUTH

Sale avante

Super música

Siéntete héroe

Su grandeza

Siete malditos

Sabías qué...

Héroe de papel

Conoce a los cuatro fantásticos

EN PALABRAS DE LUISA LANE

**EXCELSIOR,** México City

Nancy Araiza, Mario Palomera, Carlos Meraz, Luzma Díaz de León Reyes, Marco A. Román, Alexandro Medrano, Ma. Luisa Díaz de León, Pascal Beltrán del Río, Ernesto Rivera

Entertainment page, broadsheet, 50,000-174,999

CINERAMA

PROMOCIÓN

LA FRASE

"Un buen vino es como una buena película: dura un instante y te deja en la boca un sabor a gloria"

1. Francamente querida, me importa un bledo. Rhett Butler (Clarck Gable) en Lo que el viento se llevó (1939)
2. Voy a hacerle una oferta que no podrá rechazar. Vito Corleone (Marlon Brando) en El Padrino (1972)
3. ¡Tú no entiendes! Podría haber tenido clase. Podría haber sido un contendiente. Pude haber sido alguien en lugar del vago que soy. Terry Malloy (Marlon Brandon) en Nido de ratas. 1954
4. TOTO, TENGO EL PRESENTIMIENTO DE QUE YA NO ESTAMOS EN KANSAS. DOROTHY (JUDY GARLAND) EN EL MAGO DE OZ (1939)
5. Here's looking at you, kid. (Aquí me tienes. Mirándote, niña) Rick Blaine (Humphrey Bogart) en Casablanca (1942)
6. GO AHEAD, MAKE MY DAY (ADELANTE, HAZME EL DÍA). HARRY "DIRTY" CALLAHAN (CLINT EASTWOOD) EN IMPACTO FULMINANTE (1983)
7. Muy bien Mr. DeMille, estoy lista para mi close up. Norma Desmond (Gloria Swanson) en Sunset Boulevard (1950)
8. MAY THE FORCE BE WITH YOU (QUE LA FUERZA TE ACOMPAÑE). PRINCESA LEIA (CARRIE FISHER) EN LA GUERRA DE LAS GALAXIAS (1977)
9. *Abrochen sus cinturones. Va a ser una noche movida. Margo Channing (Bette Davies) en Eva al desnudo (1950)*
10. Are you talking to me? (¿Me estás hablando a mí?) Robert de Niro en Taxi Driver (1976)
11. Lo que tenemos aquí es un problema de comunicación. Capitán Road Prison 36 (Strother Martin) en La leyenda del indomable (1967)
12. Amo el olor del napalm en la mañana. Coronel Bill Kilgore (Robert Duvall) en Apocalipsis ahora (1979)
13. *Amor es nunca tener que decir: "lo siento". Oliver Barrett (Ryan O'Neal) en Historia de amor (1970)*
14. Esa cosa de la que están hechos los sueños. Sam Spade (Humphrey Bogart) en El halcón maltés (1941)
15. E.T. Phone Home (Extraterrestre, teléfono, casa) en la película El Extraterrestre (1982)
16. ¡Me llaman el sr. Tibbs! Detective Virgil Tibbs (Sidney Poitier) en El calor de la noche (1967)
17. *Rosebud. Charles Foster Kane (Orson Welles) en El ciudadano Kane (1941)*
18. ¡Lo hice, Ma! En la cima del mundo. Raoul Walsh (James Cagney) en Al rojo vivo (1949)

LAS 40 FRASES MÁS MEMORABLES DEL CINE

Por su ingenio, gracia, sabiduría o emotividad una frase insertada en el diálogo de una película sobresale de las demás. Se queda grabada en la memoria cinéfila para la posteridad porque encierra un momento imperecedero digno de recordar. Cuando el cine cumplió su primer centenario de vida, el American Film Institute (AFI) recopiló esas palabras inmortales de entre los recuerdos de mil 500 críticos, directores y actores. El resultado arrojó 4 mil frases candidatas y éstas son las primeras 40 más recordadas de todos los tiempos.

20. *Luis, creo que éste es el comienzo de una hermosa amistad. Rick Blaine (Humphrey Bogart) en Casablanca (1942)*
22. Bond. James Bond. El Agente 007 (Sean Connery) en El satánico Dr. No (1962)
23. No hay lugar como el hogar. Dorothy (Judy Garland) en El Mago de Oz (1939)
25. Show me the money! (¡Muéstrame el dinero!) Rod Tidwell (Cuba Gooding, Jr.) en Jerry Maguire: amor y desafío (1996)
26. ¿Por qué no vienes un día a verme? Lady Lou (Mae West) en Nacida para pecar (1933)
28. Play it, Sam. Play "As Time Goes By" (Tócala Sam. Toca "Mientras pasa el tiempo") Rick Blaine (Humphrey Bogart) en Casablanca (1942)
29. You can't handle the truth! (¡No puedes soportar la verdad!) Nathan R. Jessep (Jack Nicholson) en Cuestión de honor (1992)
30. I want to be alone (Quiero estar sola) Grusinskaya (Greta Garbo) en Gran Hotel (1932)
31. ¡Después de todo, mañana será otro día! Scarlett O'Hara (Vivien Leigh) en Lo que le viento se llevó (1939)
32. *Detenga a los sospechosos de siempre. Capitán Renault (Claude Rains) en Casablanca (1942)*
33. Quiero lo mismo que ella. La anciana (Stelle Reiner) al mesero en la escena orgásmica de Cuando Harry conoce a Sally (1989)
35. Vas a necesitar un bote más grande. Lorraine Gary (Ellen Brody) en Tiburón (1975)
37. I'll be back (Volveré) The Terminator (Arnold Schwarzenegger) en The Terminator (1984)
39. If you build it, he will come. (Si lo construyes, él vendrá.) La voz (Lee Garlington) en Campo de sueños (1989)
40. *Mamá dice que la vida es como una caja de chocolates. Nunca sabes lo que te vas a encontrar. Forrest Gump (Tom Hanks) (1967)*

**EL UNIVERSAL,** México City

Roberto Rock L., Francisco Santiago, Oscar Santiago Méndez, Rubén Álvarez, Felipe Morales, Rosalinda Palmeque, Nilton Torres Pérez, Omar Pulído

Entertainment page, broadsheet, 50,000-174,999

enter.akzia.ru

ENTERTAINMENT

27 марта – 9 апреля 2006

«Прощай, детка!»

enterкино /5

enterмузыка /6

enterкниги /6

enterтеатр /7

enterарт /8

**AKZIA,** Moscow

Tatyana Sokolova, Igor Sadreev, Svetlana Maximchenko, Alla Gorobets

Entertainment page, tabloid, 175,000+

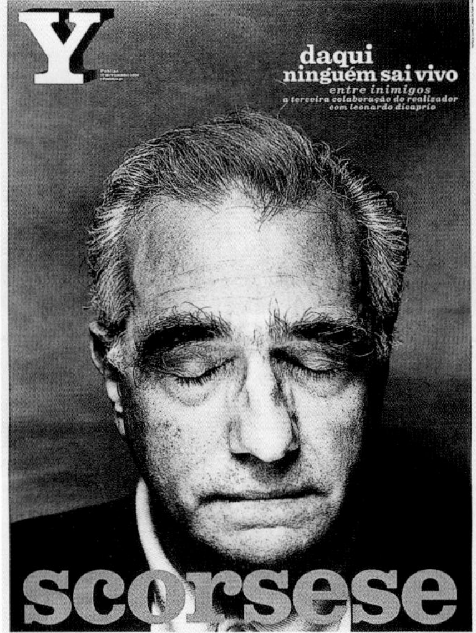


**PÚBLICO,** Quinta do Lambert, Portugal
Hugo Pinto, Ana Carvalho, Marco Ferreira
Entertainment page, tabloid, 50,000-174,999

**PÚBLICO,** Quinta do Lambert, Portugal
Sónia Matos, Hugo Pinto, Ana Carvalho, Marco Ferreira
Entertainment page, tabloid, 50,000-174,999

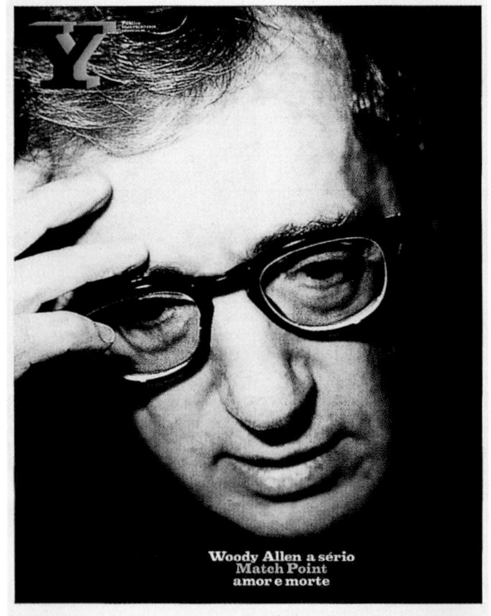


**PÚBLICO,** Quinta do Lambert, Portugal
Sónia Matos, Hugo Pinto, Ana Carvalho, Marco Ferreira
Entertainment page, tabloid, 50,000-174,999

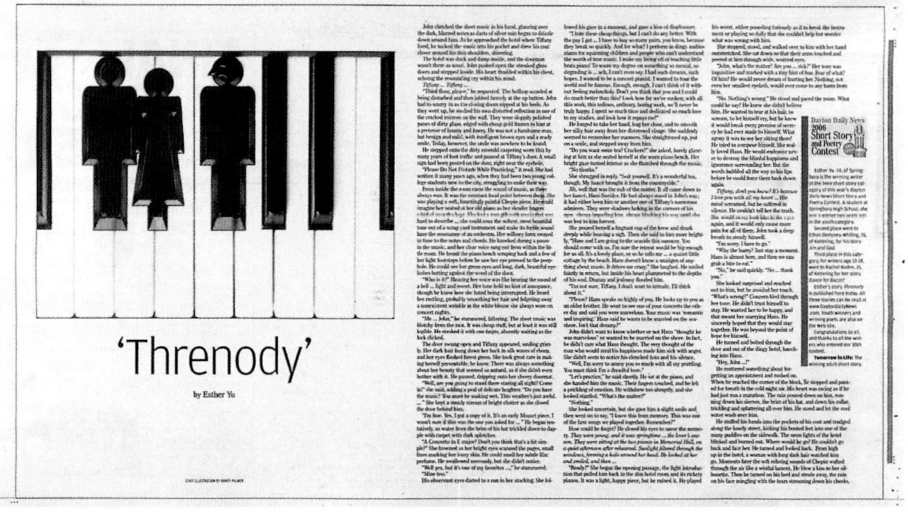


**DAYTON DAILY NEWS** (Ohio)
Randy Palmer, Michelle Fong, Brian Glass
Entertainment page, tabloid, 50,000-174,999

**PÚBLICO,** Quinta do Lambert, Portugal
Hugo Pinto, Ana Carvalho, Marco Ferreira
Entertainment page, tabloid, 50,000-174,999

**PÚBLICO,** Quinta do Lambert, Portugal
Hugo Pinto, Ana Carvalho, Marco Ferreira
Entertainment page, tabloid, 50,000-174,999

**PÚBLICO,** Quinta do Lambert, Portugal
Hugo Pinto, Ana Carvalho, Marco Ferreira
Entertainment page, tabloid, 50,000-174,999

**PÚBLICO,** Quinta do Lambert, Portugal
Hugo Pinto, Ana Carvalho, Marco Ferreira
Entertainment page, tabloid, 50,000-174,999

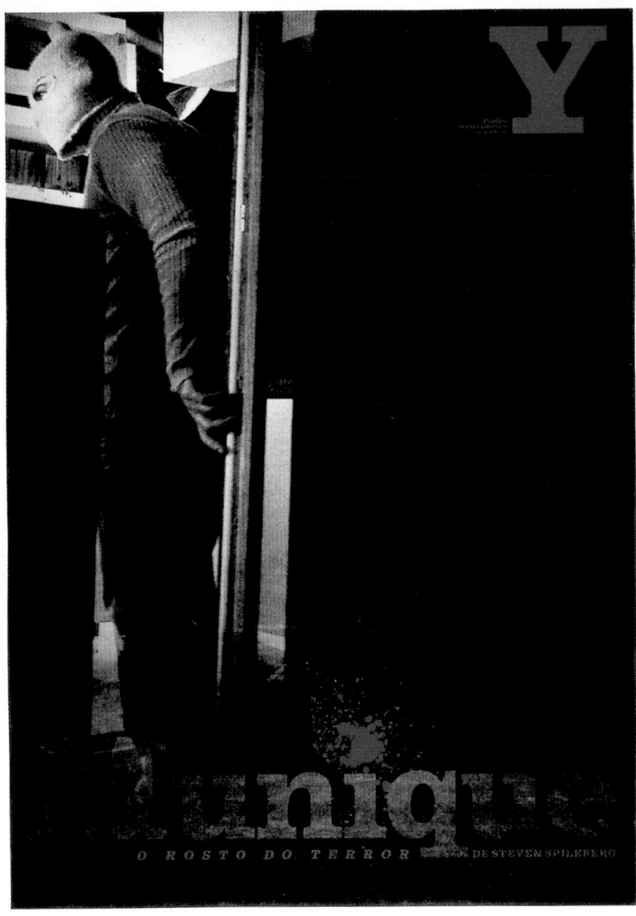


SILVER

**PÚBLICO,** Quinta do Lambert, Portugal
Sónia Matos, Hugo Pinto, Ana Carvalho, Marco Ferreira
Entertainment page, tabloid, 50,000-174,999

This cover illustrating the movie "Munich" uses placement and direction to create tension and to communicate the movie's subject matter of terrorism and revenge. The very subtle color of the headline is a triumph in printing.

Esta portada que ilustra la película "Munich" usa la locación y la dirección para crear tensión y comunicar el tema del filme; el terrorismo y la venganza. El color muy suave del título es todo un logro en impresión.

**PÚBLICO,** Quinta do Lambert, Portugal
Sónia Matos, Hugo Pinto, Ana Carvalho, Marco Ferreira
Entertainment page, tabloid, 50,000-174,999

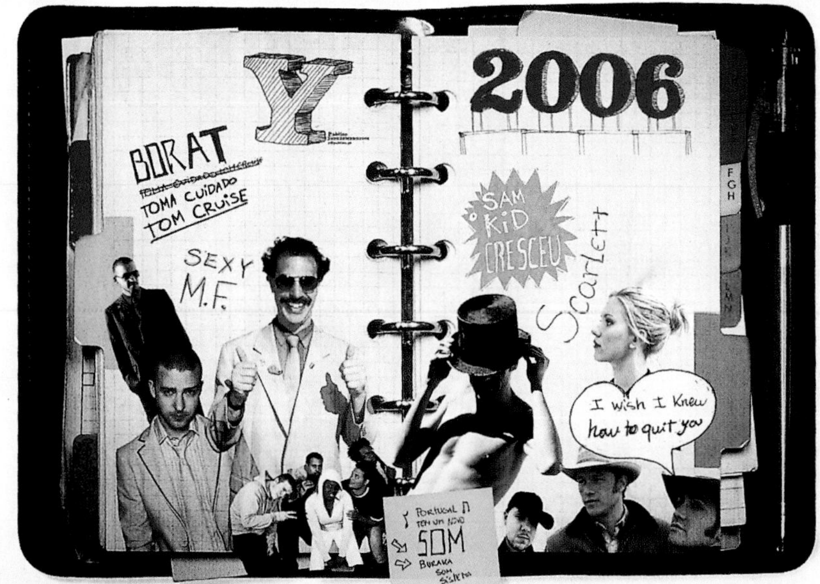


**PÚBLICO,** Quinta do Lambert, Portugal
Hugo Pinto, Ana Carvalho, Marco Ferreira
Entertainment page, tabloid, 50,000-174,999

**PÚBLICO,** Quinta do Lambert, Portugal
Hugo Pinto, Ana Carvalho, Marco Ferreira
Entertainment page, tabloid, 50,000-174,999

**PÚBLICO,** Quinta do Lambert, Portugal
Hugo Pinto, Ana Carvalho, Marco Ferreira
Entertainment page, tabloid, 50,000-174,999

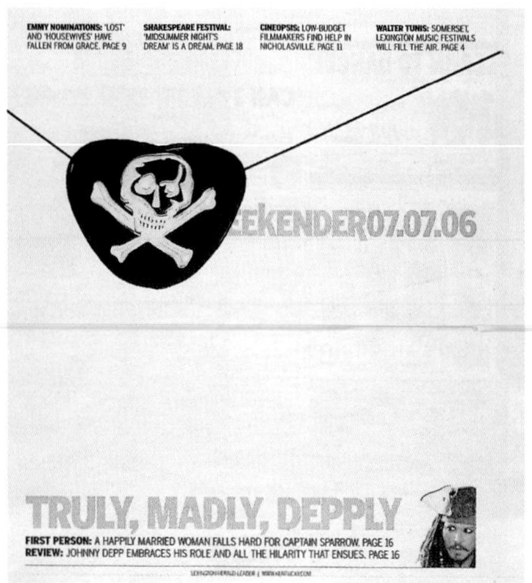


**LEXINGTON HERALD-LEADER** (Ky.)
Randy Medema
Entertainment page, tabloid, 50,000-174,999

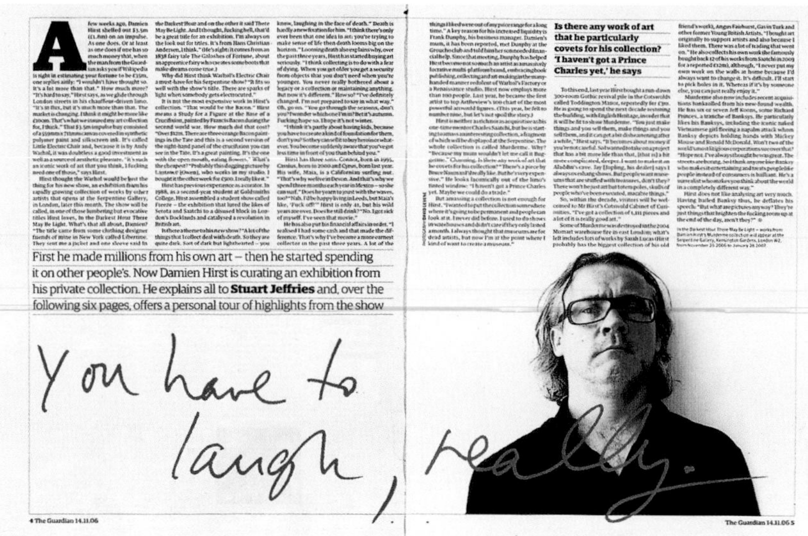


**THE GUARDIAN,** London
Richard Turley
Entertainment page, tabloid, 175,000+

cinema/o tempo que resta

o tempo que resta/cinema

Melvil Poupaud

nascido no cinema

**PÚBLICO,** Quinta do Lambert, Portugal
Sónia Matos, Hugo Pinto, Ana Carvalho, Marco Ferreira
Entertainment page, tabloid, 50,000-174,999

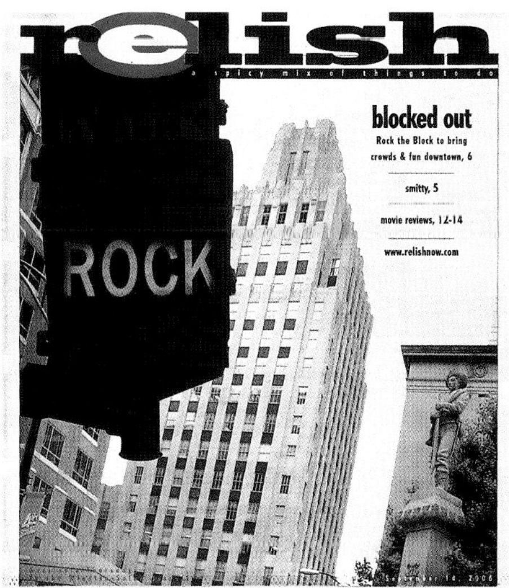

relish

a spicy mix of things to do

blocked out

Rock the Block to bring crowds & fun downtown, 6

smitty, 5

movie reviews, 12-14

www.relishnow.com



**WINSTON-SALEM JOURNAL** (N.C.)
Nicholas Weir, Richard Boyd
Entertainment page, tabloid, 50,000-174,999

cinema/capa

capa/cinema

quando jack nicholson e michelangelo antonioni tomaram um chá no deserto

**PÚBLICO,** Quinta do Lambert, Portugal
Sónia Matos, Hugo Pinto, Ana Carvalho, Marco Ferreira
Entertainment page, tabloid, 50,000-174,999

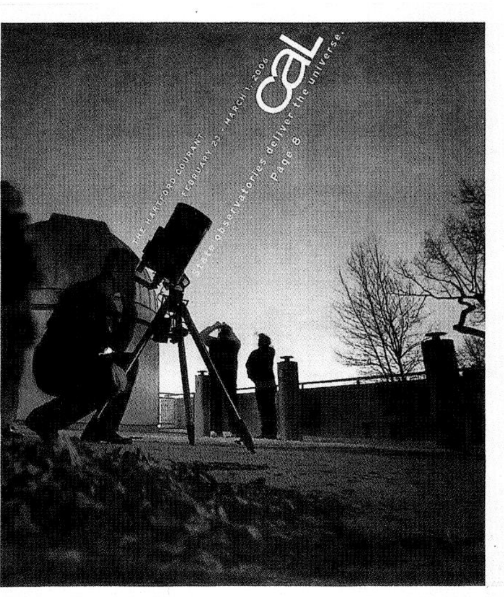

cal

Page 8

**HARTFORD COURANT** (Conn.)
Nicole Dudka
Entertainment page, tabloid, 175,000+

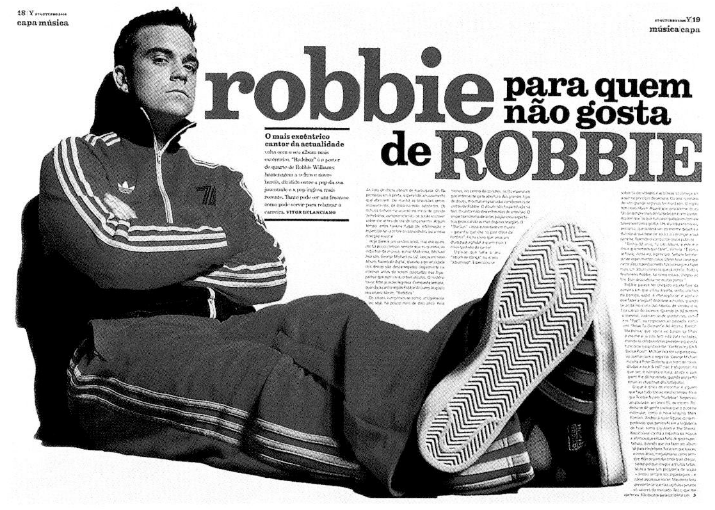

capa/música

música/capa

robbie para quem não gosta de ROBBIE

**PÚBLICO,** Quinta do Lambert, Portugal
Sónia Matos, Hugo Pinto, Ana Carvalho, Marco Ferreira
Entertainment page, tabloid, 50,000-174,999

WEEKEND

The Desert Sun

OCT. 6-12, 2006 >> A CALENDAR OF THINGS TO DO AND PLACES TO GO IN SOUTHERN CALIFORNIA

THEBLACKCROWES

'90s rockers bring '70s vibe to the desert HAPPENINGS page 24

**THE DESERT SUN,** Palm Springs, Calif.
Karla Brown-Garcia
Entertainment page, tabloid, 50,000-174,999

**ÖSTGÖTA CORRESPONDENTEN,** Linkoping, Sweden
Ann-Charlotte Irhede
Entertainment page, tabloid, 50,000-174,999

Corren ■ Linköpingsband rockar på SRF C12 — Fredag 9 juni 2006

FREDAG C



Emelie Wedhäll fångar vardagens förtretligheter C2

**PÚBLICO,** Quinta do Lambert, Portugal
Sónia Matos, Hugo Pinto, Ana Carvalho, Marco Ferreira
Entertainment page, tabloid, 50,000-174,999

músicacapa

As estrelas que vêm pela net

De e-mail para e-mail, como um vírus, grupos como os Clap Your Hands Say Yeah, Arctic Monkeys ou os portugueses Linda Martini dão-se a conhecer na rede, através de comunidades virtuais como o MySpace. Os canais clássicos de promoção e as editoras sofrem mas os internautas bandam. VITOR BELANCIANO

capa música

CIBELLE

Ao segundo album, a brasileira Cibelle reinventa-se

a vida numa caixa de música

**PÚBLICO,** Quinta do Lambert, Portugal
Hugo Pinto, Ana Carvalho, Marco Ferreira
Entertainment page, tabloid, 50,000-174,999

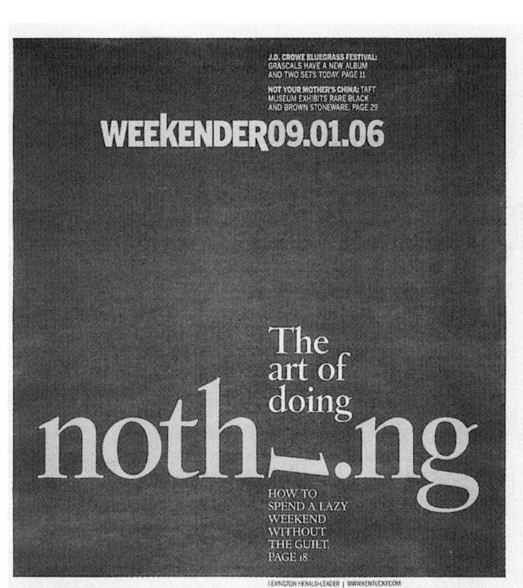

J.D. CROWE BLUEGRASS FESTIVAL: GRASCALS HAVE A NEW ALBUM AND TWO SETS TODAY. PAGE 11

NOT YOUR MOTHER'S CHINA: TAFT MUSEUM EXHIBITS RARE BLACK AND BROWN STONEWARE. PAGE 29

WEEKENDER09.01.06

The art of doing noth_ng

HOW TO SPEND A LAZY WEEKEND WITHOUT THE GUILT. PAGE 18

**LEXINGTON HERALD-LEADER** (Ky.)
Randy Medema
Entertainment page, tabloid, 50,000-174,999

**PITTSBURGH POST-GAZETTE**
Diane Juravich, Steve Mellon
Food page, broadsheet, 175,000+

Food&Flavor

THE ROGUE'S GALLERY

Heirloom tomatoes can look gnarly, but don't be fooled: The taste is out of this world

West End and its cornucopia of businesses should not be bypassed

Easy Gourmet!

MARKET DISTRICT

**THE CHARLOTTE OBSERVER** (N.C.)
Christine Long, Kathleen Purvis, T. Ortega Gaines
Food page, broadsheet, 175,000+

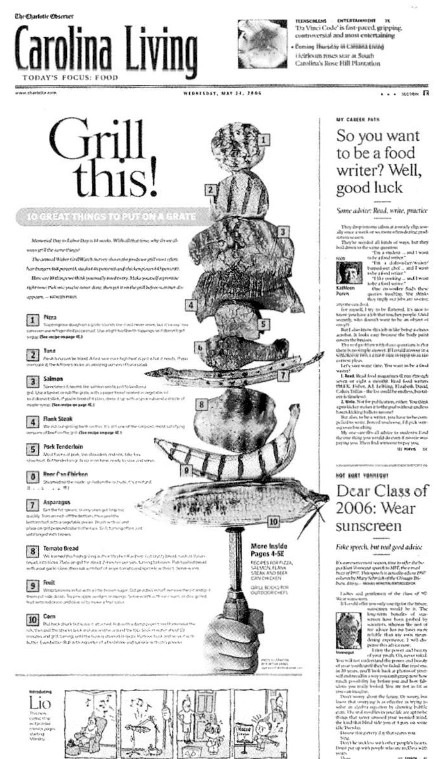
Carolina Living

TODAY'S FOCUS: FOOD

Grill this!

10 GREAT THINGS TO PUT ON A GRATE

So you want to be a food writer? Well, good luck

Dear Class of 2006: Wear sunscreen

**LAS VEGAS REVIEW-JOURNAL**
Melissa Nunnery, Jeff Scheid
Food page, broadsheet, 175,000+

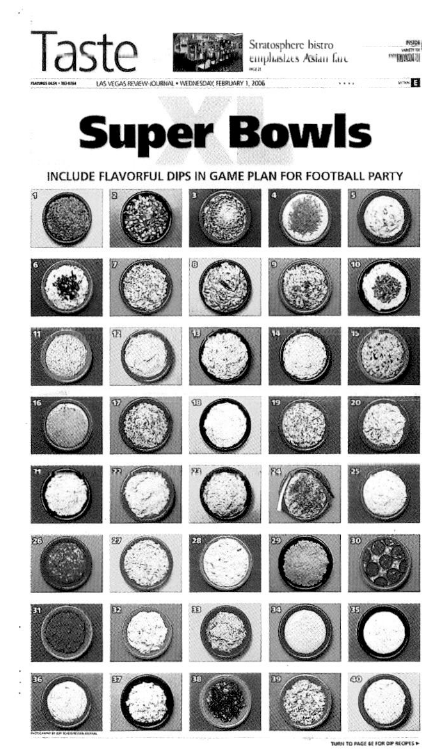
Taste

Stratosphere bistro emphasizes Asian fare

Super Bowls

INCLUDE FLAVORFUL DIPS IN GAME PLAN FOR FOOTBALL PARTY

F WEDNESDAY 02.08.2006

TASTE

Oranges piled high? It's 'twofer' cake to the rescue

A romantic midday repast may be just the ticket this Valentine's Day

A Lovers' Lunch

Single-minded chocolate connoisseurs

**THE BALTIMORE SUN**
Tracey Dieter, Emily Morrow, Joannah Hill
Food page, broadsheet, 175,000+

Los Angeles Times

FOOD

A big sip of Vegas reality

Hummus? It *can* be sublime

SEDUCTION BY FIG

Now that so many Americans are discovering its pleasures, farmers are sending more fresh fruit to market and developing delicious — and gorgeous — new varieties.

**LOS ANGELES TIMES**
Jan Molen, Wes Bausmith, Christian Potter Drury, Ken Hively
Food page, broadsheet, 175,000+

FLAVOR

COOKS & CORKS

Fill That Wait

Till The Midnight Hour

While Easing Your Duties As Host:

Make The Food Preparation Part Of The Party

**HARTFORD COURANT** (Conn.)
Timothy Reck, Suzette Moyer, Mark Mirko, Beth Bristow
Food page, broadsheet, 175,000+

**CHICAGO TRIBUNE**
Catherine Nichols, Bob Fila, Corrine Kozlak, Carol Haddix
Food page, broadsheet, 175,000+

7 GOOD EATING

EAT LIKE AN EGYPTIAN
DOWN, CHOLESTEROL, DOWN!
CHILLING OUT

The original non-stick pan

Time-tested, versatile, durable, fun to use—and cheap too. Why the wok is the only pan you really need.

**THE COLUMBUS DISPATCH** (Ohio)
Scott Minister, Shari Lewis, Robin Davis
Food page, broadsheet, 175,000+

Food

G

CUTTING EDGE

PIZZAS ON THE EDGE

Pie makers are getting more daring, creative with toppings

Perfect crust

**THE BOSTON GLOBE**
Jane Martin, Lane Turner, Jonathan Wiggs, Sheryl Julian
Food page, broadsheet, 175,000+

Food

The Boston Globe Wednesday, August 9, 2006

SUMMER

AT ITS MOST

SUMPTUOUS

A variety of crisp, sweet, and luscious melons are ready for prime time right now at local farmstands and grocers

INSIDE

SPECIAL SAUCE

EVERY WHICH WAY

GARLIC BREATH

LIVING

MONEY

TODAY: FOOD

C

Life on the Isle of Denial

They're hardy, delicious and versatile enough to star in a wide range of dishes

big on summer squash

MIRLITON

ZUCCHINI

PATTYPAN

YELLOW SQUASH

THROWING IN THE TOWEL

**THE TIMES-PICAYUNE,** New Orleans
Jean McIntosh, George Berke, James O'Byrne, Mark Larando, Mary Lou Atkinson, Ted Jackson, Kenny Harrison, Judy Walker
Food page, broadsheet, 175,000+

WINE REVIEWS F2 BOGOTA'S FAMOUS SOUP F6

Food

STRANGE BREWS

Thought this spice of life was plain and purely practical? Look again and join the gourmet salt revival

Salts of the earth and sea

**TORONTO STAR**
Lesley Taylor, Jennifer Bain, Susan Sampson, Jo-Ann Dodds, Keith Beaty
Food page, broadsheet, 175,000+

DARING PAIRING
THE ASIAN GRILL
JUST FOR HER

7 GOOD EATING

WEDNESDAY

Is this polenta ...or just mush?

It's both! Corn in its many ground forms is ubiquitous, and, oh, so trendy ...

**CHICAGO TRIBUNE**
Elaine Melko, Carol Haddix, Bob Fila
Food page, broadsheet, 175,000+

**SAN FRANCISCO CHRONICLE**
Ellie Winter, Hulda Nelson, Nanette Bisher, Jim Merithew, Craig Lee
Food page, broadsheet, 175,000+

WINE
Elegance in a glass
Aged for decades, Cognac ends a meal with style
INSIDE
Get more blanc for your buck

**TORONTO STAR**
Lesley Taylor, Jennifer Bain, Susan Sampson, Jo-Ann Dodds, Louise Ferguson
Food page, broadsheet, 175,000+

Food
The waiting game
A longtime restaurant worker plays eye-spy and serves up some vignettes of life on both sides of the business

**CHICAGO TRIBUNE**
Elaine Melko, Carol Haddix, Bob Fila
Food page, broadsheet, 175,000+

GOOD EATING
The search for the PERFECT LOAF

Food
THE ESSENTIAL THANKSGIVING
At the Broadmoor, a lofty new pinnacle
$1 OFF THANKSGIVING PIES

**THE DENVER POST**
Maureen Scance, Glenn Asakawa
Food page, broadsheet, 175,000+

L'ASSIETTE DES CANADIENS
SONDAGE CANADIEN SUR L'ALIMENTATION
UN CANADIEN SUR QUATRE
100 GRAMMES DE VIANDE PAR JOUR
LES VILLES CANADIENNES ONT DE PLUS FAIBLES TAUX D'OBÉSITÉ
COMBIEN DE CALORIES?
LES PRODUITS CÉRÉALIERS
LE CANADA PASSE À TABLE
ATTENTION AUX LIPIDES

**LA PRESSE,** Montréal
Andre Rivest, David Lambert, Benoit Giguere, Genevieve Dinel, Stephanie Berube
Food page, broadsheet, 175,000+

**THE ATLANTA JOURNAL-CONSTITUTION**
Joanne Sosangelis
Food page, tabloid

ajc Home&Garden
The Atlanta Journal-Constitution
Friday, April 14, 2006
pots of gold
Big or small, containers cradle a wealth of options
PAGE 6
ALSO INSIDE: Bring spring to your table: Ideas for seasonal decorations PAGE 12

**HARTFORD COURANT** (Conn.)
Timothy Reck, Suzette Moyer, Bob MacDonnell
Food page, broadsheet, 175,000+

FLAVOR
When Is Divorce Good For Fresh Greens?
{ Hydroponics }
Noun: Cultivation Of Plants In Nutrient Solution Rather Than In Soil
Two Guys From Connecticut Can Answer That

**THE COLUMBUS DISPATCH** (Ohio)
Scott Minister, Robin Davis
Food page, broadsheet, 175,000+

Food
Alternatives to spinach available in bunches
'FARM-TO-FORK' movement seeks to improve menus with fresh local ingredients
THE CLOSER, THE BETTER

FOODDAY
THE BEST AT THE MARKET, IN YOUR KITCHEN, AND ON YOUR TABLE
In the spa spirit
You don't need to leave home to restore your spirit and renew your commitment to healthy eating
DON'T TIP SCALES: TRY EXPERT'S EATING TIPS
Trans fat joins nutrition label lineup
2 Pairings
3 Mellow yellow
4 In Season

**THE OREGONIAN,** Portland
Molly Swisher, Nancy Casey, Stephanie Yao
Food page, broadsheet, 175,000+

Chicago Tribune
7 GOOD EATING
TWO-BUCK CHUCKWAGON
THAI DUO
FISH, DECONSTRUCTED
HEALTH WATCH
Shaking our salt addiction
Sodium looms as a dietary danger, but oh, how we love what it does to food

**CHICAGO TRIBUNE**
Catherine Nichols, Bob Fila, Corrine Kozlak, Carol Haddix
Food page, broadsheet, 175,000+

Dining In
The New York Times
Just Registered
Marriage can be many things, including a chance for friends to outfit your dream kitchen.

**THE NEW YORK TIMES**
Tom Bodkin, Barbara Richer, Tony Cenicola, Soo-Jeong Kang, Phaedra Brown
Food page, broadsheet, 175,000+

**THE TIMES OF NORTHWEST INDIANA,** Munster
David Windisch
Food page, broadsheet, 50,000-174,999

foodFare

from the farm

Chili cook-off just around the corner

tea-licious

tea market growing, flowing with new flavors and blends

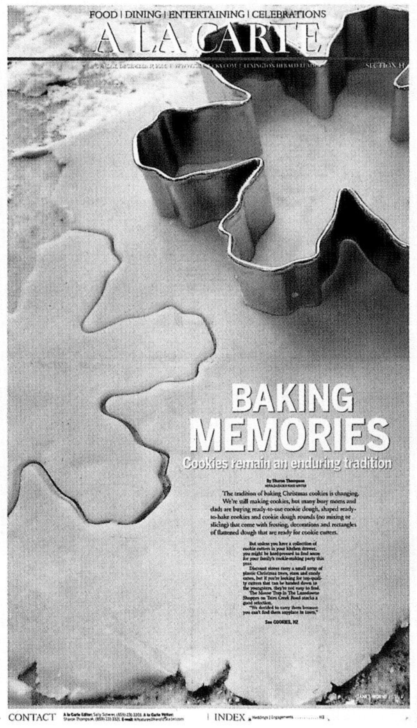
FOOD | DINING | ENTERTAINING | CELEBRATIONS

A LA CARTE

BAKING MEMORIES

Cookies remain an enduring tradition

**LEXINGTON HERALD-LEADER** (Ky.)
May May Barton
Food page, broadsheet, 50,000-174,999

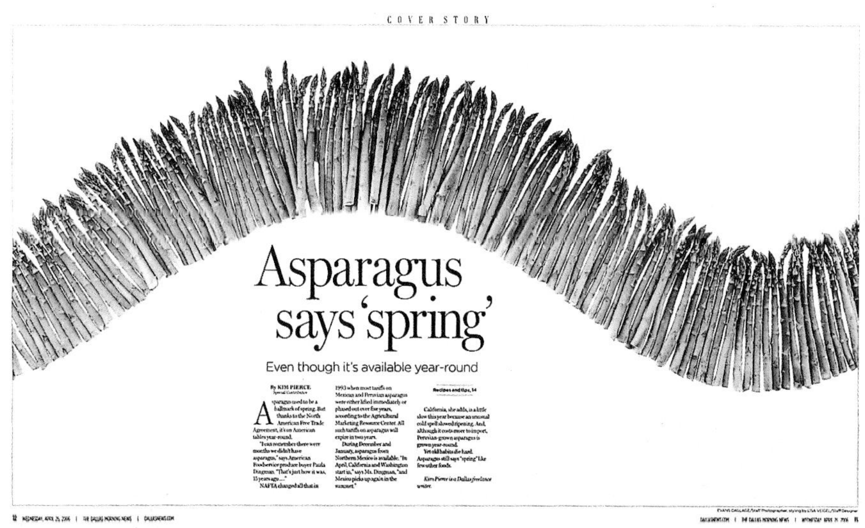
COVER STORY

Asparagus says 'spring'

Even though it's available year-round

**THE DALLAS MORNING NEWS**
Lisa Veigel, Evans Caglage
Food page, tabloid, 175,000+

Sovs

**POLITIKEN, COPENHAGEN,** Denmark
Søren Nyeland, Ole Gravesen, Annette Nyvang, Per Munch, Lars Skaaning
Food page, tabloid, 50,000-174,999

¿Para hoy o para mañana?

En el súper con el chef

11: de antojo

AL GUSTO MARISCOS

El changarro argentino

ZABALETA TE RECOMIENDA

**EXCELSIOR,** México City
Nancy Araiza, Jimena Guarque, Luzma Díaz de León Reyes, Marco A. Román, Alexandro Medrano, Ma. Luisa Díaz de Léon, Pascal Beltrán del Río, Ernesto Rivera
Food page, broadsheet, 50,000-174,999

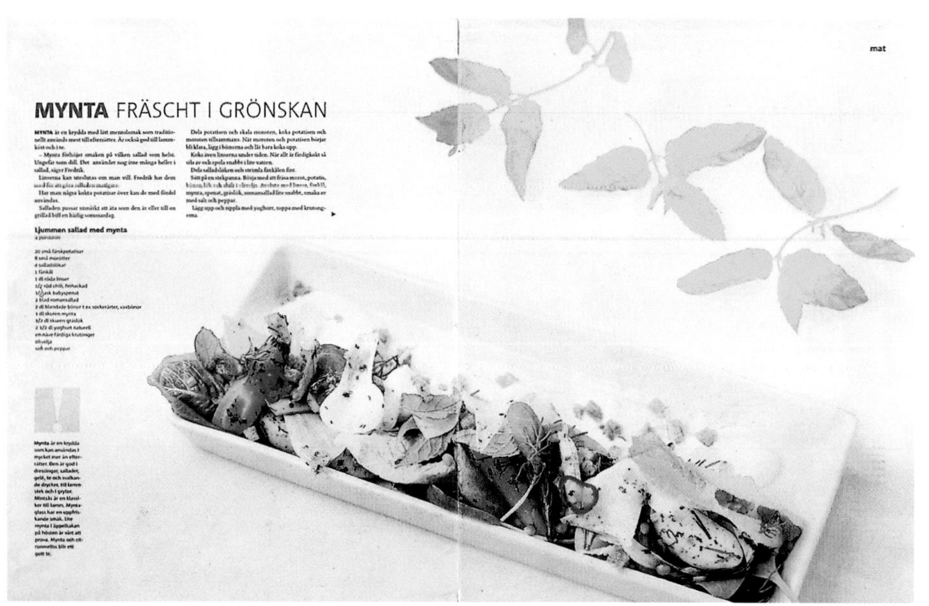


**GÖTEBORGS-POSTEN,** Goteborg, Sweden
Karin Teghammanr Arell, Tomas Yeh
Food page, tabloid, 175,000+

**SEATTLE POST-INTELLIGENCER**
Staff
Food page, broadsheet, 50,000-174,999

We claim to be a nation of foodies, yet vegetables still mystify many cooks – especially those weird specimens that turn up in the weekly organic box. What exactly do you do with chard or salsify? Do turnips have to be a turnoff? Zoe Williams gets out the pots and pans
First catch your radish...
Squash
Salsify
RADISHES
Celeriac
The Guardian 20.11.06


**THE GUARDIAN,** London
Richard Turley
Food page, tabloid, 175,000+

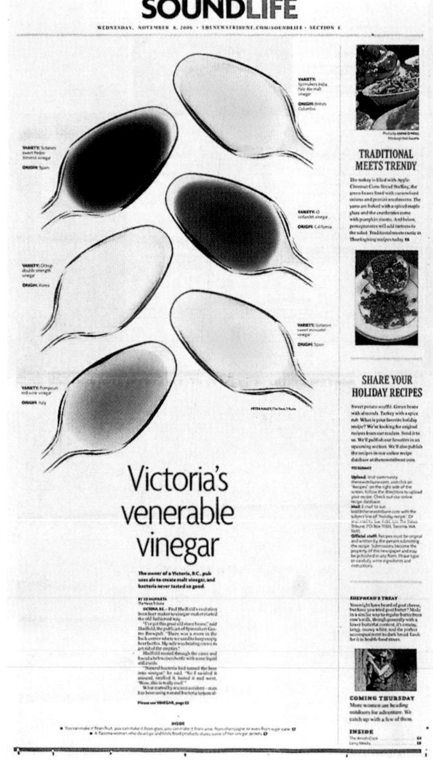


**THE NEWS TRIBUNE,** Tacoma, Wash.
John Ellingson, Peter Haley
Food page, broadsheet, 50,000-174,999

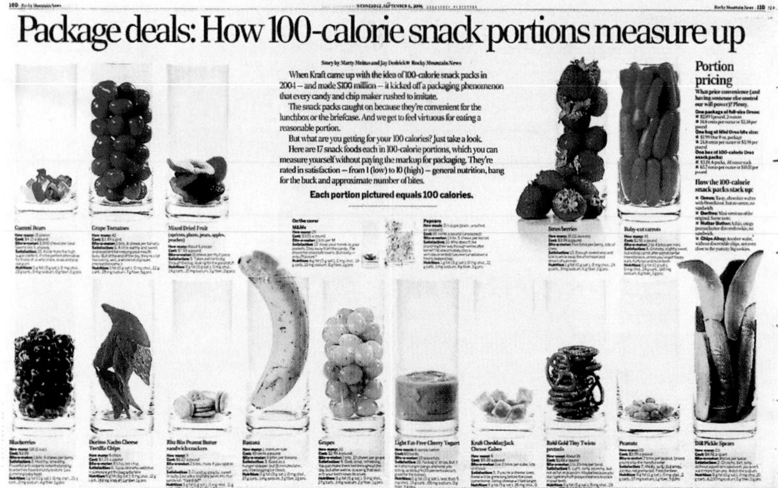


**ROCKY MOUNTAIN NEWS,** Denver
Christine Birch Ferrelli
Food page, tabloid, 175,000+

SILVER

**GÖTEBORGS-POSTEN,** Goteborg, Sweden
Albert Rosander, Tomas Yeh
Food page, tabloid, 175,000+

It's so unusual for a newspaper to use this sort of treatment for food. The typography, the colors, the food styling, the photo editing, the design — you can see the level of planning behind these light, airy pages.

No es usual que un periódico recurra a este estilo para tratar temas de comida. La tipografía, los colores, el diseño de la comida, la edición fotográfica, el diseño; es evidente el nivel de planificación que hay detrás de estas páginas livianas y espaciosas.

mat

Sill

mat

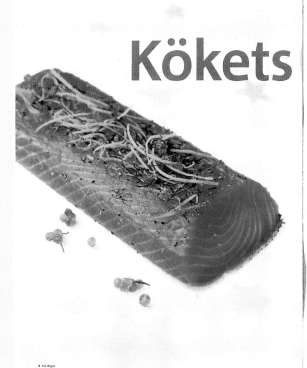

# Kökets julstjärnor

Sex av Göteborgs skarpaste kockar fick uppdraget att presentera varsin favorit till julbordet. Två Dagars matskribent Helena Werner och matfotografen Tomas Yeh lotsar oss genom resultatet, som självklart är: Göteborgs godaste julbord.

## Lax

**HANS BORÉN PÅ STJÄRNKROGEN 28+** firar jul tillsammans med sambons släkt. Det innebär att de reser bort, för släkten finns på ostkusten. Restaurangen har stängt i fyra dar över själva julhelgen och Hans brukar plussa på med några dagar så att ledigheten blir längre. Han brukar vara ganska trött för december är en tuff månad på jobbet.

Ansvaret för julmaten delar de upp. Laxen och ålen är Hans område. Han har bett att få ta hand om dem.

– Har man en uppgift går man ju in för den.

De har alltid gravad lax plus rökt och helst inkokt också. Apelsingravad blev laxen när Hans tröttnade på det vanliga, dill och vitpeppar.

Sill, lax och ål äter han helst på julbordet. Sherrysillen är ett måste. Liksom snapsen, helst Läckö, "så lokalt som möjligt", annars OP. Efter det brukar han känna sig ganska mätt.

Drömmen är att det blir kallt och is på jul. Då åker långfärdsskridskorna på.

– Har du åkt på Göta kanal någon gång? undrar han. Det är häftigt. De plogar en bana om det har snöat. Ungefär fyra mil lång.

Blir det snöfritt hoppas han på golfväder, en relativt ny vurm på fritiden.

**Namn:** Hans Borén.
**Ålder:** 37 år.
**Vem är han?** Doldis som i tio år stått för ett av Sveriges mest renommerade gourmetkök, 28+. Fick i år Västra Gastronomiska Akademins stora pris med motiveringen "För osviklig kreativitet, raffinerade och harmoniska rätter och högklassiska produkter valda med största omsorg, kunnande och medvetenhet."

### Sockersaltad lax med apelsin
10–12 personer

1 kilo laxfilé
2 msk svartpepparkorn
1 dl socker
3/4 dl salt
skal och saft av 1 apelsin
persiljestjälkar
laxrom
persiljeblad

Rensa laxen fri från ben men låt skinnet vara kvar. Skölj fisken och torka med hushållspapper. Gör några snitt med kniv på skinnsidan.

Rosta svartpepparn försiktigt i torr teflonpanna. Stöt i mortel. Blanda socker och salt, svartpeppar, apelsinskal och -saft. Låt blandningen ligga i rumstemperatur tills den löser sig.

Lägg fiskfilén i en bunke eller plastpåse tillsammans med salt-sockerlagen och persiljestjälkar. Täck bunken eller slut till påsen. Ställ i kylen. Vänd några gånger. Tiden för gravningen beror på laxfiléns tjocklek. En laxsida av den här storleken tar cirka tre dagar. Häll av vätskan, annars fortsätter gravningen och laxen blir hård. Skrapa av svartpepparkornen. Dekorera med laxrom och finstrimlade persiljeblad.

**tips!** Glöm inte att få laxen fjällad när du köper den.

Livsmedelsverket rekommenderar att laxen fryses i minst ett dygn före eller efter gravningen.

Laxen räcker gott och väl till en liten god förrätt på juldagen. Hos Hans Borén före kalkonen.

Köp inte färdig gravlaxsås – gör din egen. ▶

4 två dagar

två dagar 5

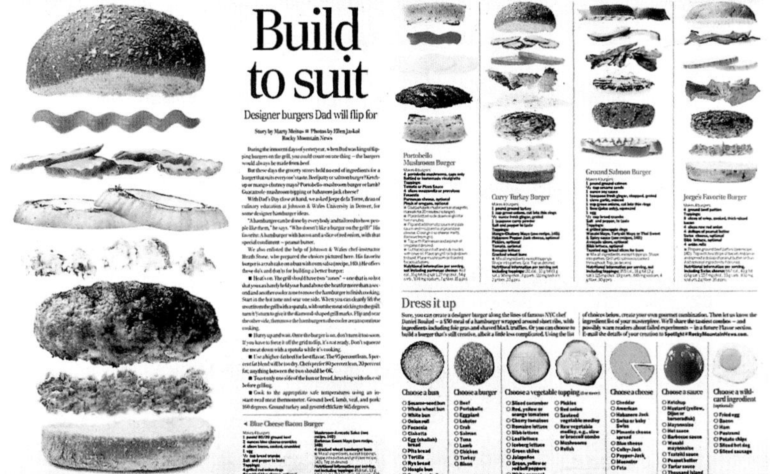

Build to suit
Designer burgers Dad will flip for
Dress it up


**ROCKY MOUNTAIN NEWS,** Denver
Christine Birch Ferrelli
Food page, tabloid, 175,000+

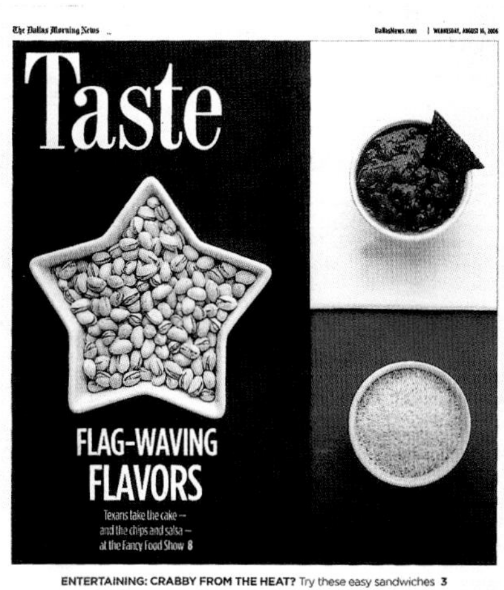

The Dallas Morning News
Taste
FLAG-WAVING FLAVORS
Texans take the cake – and the chips and salsa – at the Fancy Food Show 8
ENTERTAINING: CRABBY FROM THE HEAT? Try these easy sandwiches 3
NUTRITION: SOUL-FOOD SALVATION A free book lightens the load 6
ONLINE: HEATH BAR CAKE Perfect for potluck, at DallasNews.com/taste


**THE DALLAS MORNING NEWS**
Lisa Veigel, Smiley N. Pool
Food page, tabloid, 175,000+

**HOUSTON CHRONICLE**
Kellye Sanford, Kyrie O'Connor, Melissa Ward Aguilar, Molly Glentzer, Nick de la Torre
Fashion page, broadsheet, 175,000+

**THE DALLAS MORNING NEWS**
Kerri Abrams, Richard Krall, Tammy Theis
Fashion page, broadsheet, 175,000+

**THE DALLAS MORNING NEWS**
Kerri Abrams, Richard Krall, Tammy Theis
Fashion page, broadsheet, 175,000+

**THE GLOBE AND MAIL,** Toronto
Cinders McLeod, David Pratt, Cathrin Bradbury, Sheree-Lee Olson, Roger Hallett, Rachel Ann Lindsay
Fashion page, broadsheet, 175,000+

**THE DALLAS MORNING NEWS**

Kerri Abrams, Richard Krall, Tammy Theis

Fashion page, broadsheet, 175,000+

THE LUXE SURVEY: INTERIOR DESIGNERS FIND ROMANCE | ICED, ICED, BABY | SWEET TREATS FROM DALLAS' TOP BAKERS
KISS AND MAKEUP | COSMO ROUGE RAISES THE BAR | AT HOME: A MODERN CLASSIC IN NORTH DALLAS | GEM DANDIES

F!D luxe

The Dallas Morning News FEBRUARY 2006

Share the love

**THE BOSTON GLOBE**

Chin Wang, Lane Turner, Essdras M. Suarez, Ann Scales, Dan Zedek

Fashion page, broadsheet, 175,000+

THURSDAY, FEBRUARY 16, 2006 THE BOSTON GLOBE Style H3

COMING ROUND AGAIN

WELL-HEELED

High heel

Low or kitten heel

Wedge

Ballerina flat

Chunky heel

WHERE TO BUY

SECTION L THE GLOBE AND MAIL • CANADA'S NATIONAL NEWSPAPER • GLOBEANDMAIL.COM • SATURDAY, NOVEMBER 25, 2006

Globe Style

they're making a list...

JEANNE BEKER wants feathered shoes
RUSSELL SMITH wants a fancy pen
REBECCA ECKLER wants a red iPod
LEANNE DELAP wants a plaid hat
KAREN von HAHN wants a big chandelier
JANICE LINDSAY wants a ruffled cushion
LEAH McLAREN wants a kick-ass vacuum
LUCY WAVERMAN wants a sushi knife
JOANNE KATES wants a truckful of gelato
BEPPI CROSARIOL wants ceramic cheese flags
MARJORIE HARRIS wants a nifty spade
For what our columnists are craving this holiday season, see pages L6-L9



**THE GLOBE AND MAIL,** Toronto

Cinders McLeod, David Pratt, Cathrin Bradbury, Sheree-Lee Olson, Roger Hallett, Fernando Morales

Fashion page, broadsheet, 175,000+

POLITIKEN

Søndag 10. december 2006 | www.politiken.dk

søndagsliv

Fightercontrol 8
Swingerfrokost 14
Slip stressen 18
Lakridsboller 22

En hund efter frakker
Max Maras direktør om klassisk mode

**POLITIKEN,** Copenhagen, Denmark

Søren Nyeland, Nanna Skytte, Annette Nyvang, Per Munch

Fashion page, tabloid, 50,000-174,999

**TORONTO STAR**
Bernadette Morra, Kate Robertson, Sharis Shahmiryan, Keith Beaty, Lesley Taylor, Catherine Pike
Fashion page, broadsheet, 175,000+

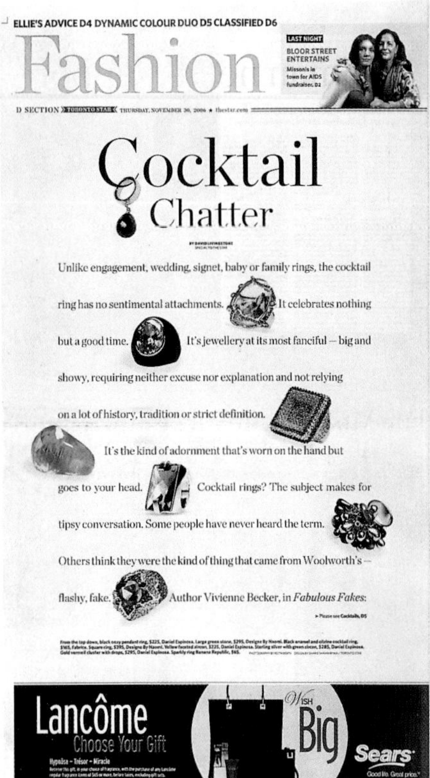

ELLIE'S ADVICE D4 DYNAMIC COLOUR DUO D5 CLASSIFIED D6

Fashion

LAST NIGHT
BLOOR STREET ENTERTAINS
Missonis in town for AIDS fundraiser. D2

D SECTION TORONTO STAR THURSDAY, NOVEMBER 30, 2006 ★ thestar.com

Cocktail Chatter

Unlike engagement, wedding, signet, baby or family rings, the cocktail ring has no sentimental attachments. It celebrates nothing but a good time. It's jewellery at its most fanciful – big and showy, requiring neither excuse nor explanation and not relying on a lot of history, tradition or strict definition. It's the kind of adornment that's worn on the hand but goes to your head. Cocktail rings? The subject makes for tipsy conversation. Some people have never heard the term. Others think they were the kind of thing that came from Woolworth's – flashy, fake. Author Vivienne Becker, in *Fabulous Fakes*.

► Please see Cocktails, D5



**THE BOSTON GLOBE**
Chin Wang, Lane Turner, Dina Rudick, Ann Scales, Dan Zedek
Fashion page, broadsheet, 175,000+

THURSDAY, MAY 18, 2006 THE BOSTON GLOBE Style D5

hefty bags

Let's call it a big trend. Status handbags, like homes and cars that signify wealth, have become enormous lately.

A Prada shoulder bag is the size of carry-on luggage. A Marc Jacobs purse, built like a tank, could house at least three Chihuahuas. And Chloe's "Paddington" satchel, this year's "it" bag, might double as a gym tote. But all that bulk comes with a weighty problem: These bags are heavy, even before women stuff wallets, Palms, cellphones, keys, lipsticks, mirrors, glasses, or even lunch into them. We brought a scale to Neiman Marcus to measure nearly a dozen designer bags from which we removed their paper stuffing and felt storage containers to gauge the most accurate reading.

BY TINA CASSIDY | GLOBE CORRESPONDENT

**TORONTO STAR**
Bernadette Morra, Kate Robertson, Sharis Shahmiryan, Raffi Anderian, Lesley Taylor, Catherine Pike
Fashion page, broadsheet, 175,000+

CLASSIFIED D7 ELLIE D2 BEAUTY COUNTER MAKEOVERS D2

Fashion

NOTEBOOK
BRAVE BROWN BAG

D SECTION TORONTO STAR THURSDAY, DECEMBER 14, 2006 ★ thestar.com

Lash Out

All eyes are on lashes this holiday season with a range of options, from old-fashioned glue-on strips to new-fangled root perms to the lash extensions that are sprouting in beauty salons across the GTA. *Rita Zekas* eyeballs the latest in lashes on D4

Life writer Trish Crawford, who wore the same suit for a month, discusses last Saturday's Life story with Bernadette Morra today at thestar.com/nakedlunch

**UPSALA NYA TIDNING,** Uppsala, Sweden
Jonas Kihlander, Mikael Bigun
Fashion page, tabloid, 50,000-174,999

SUNDAY
LIFE ✲ ARTS ✲ TRAVEL ✲ SECTION G
SUNDAY, SEPTEMBER 17, 2006 • THE PATRIOT-N… HARRISBURG, PA • PENNLIVE.COM

Life
GET A LEG UP ON COLOR
BLACK MAKES A COMEBACK. YOU'LL ALSO FIND CHARCOAL GRAYS, TEALS, BURGUNDYS, PURPLES AND REDS AS GIRLIE SHADES FALL TO SOPHISTICATED STYLE. PAGE G3

Arts
'IDOL' THOUGHTS
SEASON FIVE OF 'AMERICAN IDOL' WAS A TV PHENOM. THE CLASS OF 2006'S LIVE TOUR HAS SOLD OUT ACROSS THE COUNTRY. NOW, EVEN THE 'LOSERS' HAVE A CHANCE OF WINNING. PAGE G16

Travel
SETTING SAIL
WINDJAMMER BAREFOOT CRUISES — THESE AIN'T NO 'FOO FOO' SHIPS. PAGE G23

CAPTAIN, MY CAPTAIN
SANDY FENTON CRUISES WITH CAPT. STUBING AND ASKS THE QUESTIONS YOU NEED TO ANSWER BEFORE TAKING A CRUISE. PAGE G23

FALL FASHION
BACK TO the '80s

**THE PATRIOT-NEWS,** Harrisburg, Pa.
Sue Stine
Fashion page, broadsheet, 50,000-174,999

DE ÚLTIMA

UN VISTAZO AL VERANO
PÁGS. 12 -14

**EL UNIVERSAL,** México City

Roberto Rock L., Francisco Santiago, Oscar Santiago Méndez, Rubén Álvarez, Celia Marín, Rubén Hernández, Héctor Fule, Nilton Torres Pérez, Adriana Peña

Fashion page, tabloid, 50,000-174,999

18 Presso

I'm a roadrunner, honey!

"Hei kamoon, pientä rajaa sen fotaamisen kanssa!"

**KAUPPALEHTI PRESSO,** Helsinki, Finland

Markus Frey, Juha Törmälä, Tommi Aitio

Fashion page, tabloid, 50,000-174,999

POLITIKEN | SØNDAG 19. NOVEMBER 2006 SØNDAGSLIV 17

90 kroner senere

Der er penge at spare på frisørregningen, javel, men hvor meget mere får man for pengene, når man vælger den dyre frisør frem for den billige? Søndagsliv sendte to mænd i byen for et svar. ▶

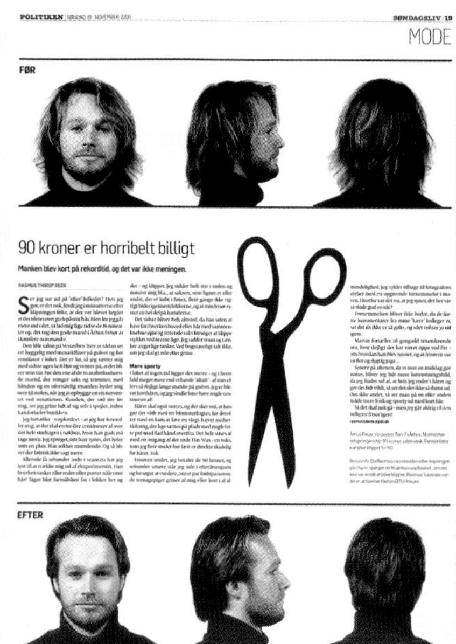

MODE

FØR

90 kroner er horribelt billigt

Manken blev kort på rekordtid, og det var ikke meningen.

EFTER

SILVER

**POLITIKEN,** Copenhagen, Denmark

Søren Nyeland, Mai-Britt Bernt Jenson, Annette Nyvang, Per Munch, Rasmus Baaner

Fashion page, tabloid, 50,000-174,999

This story, "$14 later," shows the evolution of a haircut. The photos create a timeline that lets you see the changes. The repeated pairs of scissors in the background are a fun touch. It is nice to see a man as the subject since these kinds of fashion stories are usually told using women.

Este artículo, "$14 después" muestra la evolución del corte de cabello. Las fotos crean una línea de tiempo que permite ver los cambios. El par de tijeras que se repite en el fondo es un toque con gracia. Nos alegra ver un hombre como sujeto del tema, porque este tipo de relatos sobre moda corrientemente se vale de mujeres.

Home&Real Estate

SUNDAY, MAY 14, 2006 • THE HARTFORD COURANT

10 HOME REPAIRS TO NAIL DOWN

REIGNITE A PILOT LIGHT

REPLACE FURNACE FILTERS

PATCH A HOLE

REPAIR EXTERIOR SIDING

FIND SEPTIC TANK COVER

STOP A DRIPPING FAUCET

REPLACE AN ELECTRICAL OUTLET

FIX BOARDS ON THE DECK

LOCATE UTILITY SHUT-OFFS

REPAIR GUTTERS

PAGE J5

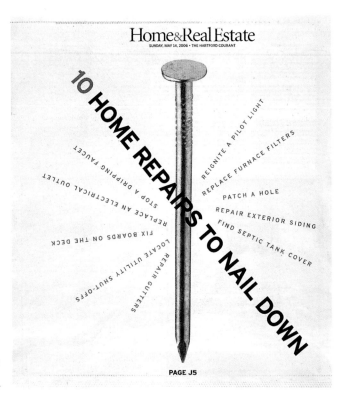

**HARTFORD COURANT** (Conn.)

Kristin Lenz, Suzette Moyer

Home/real estate page, tabloid, 175,000+

**TORONTO STAR**

Gale Beeby, Keith Beaty

Home/real estate page, broadsheet, 175,000+

Your Home

The scoop on poop

You can get help when it comes time to clean up that ugly mess in the backyard, reports *Barbara Turnbull*

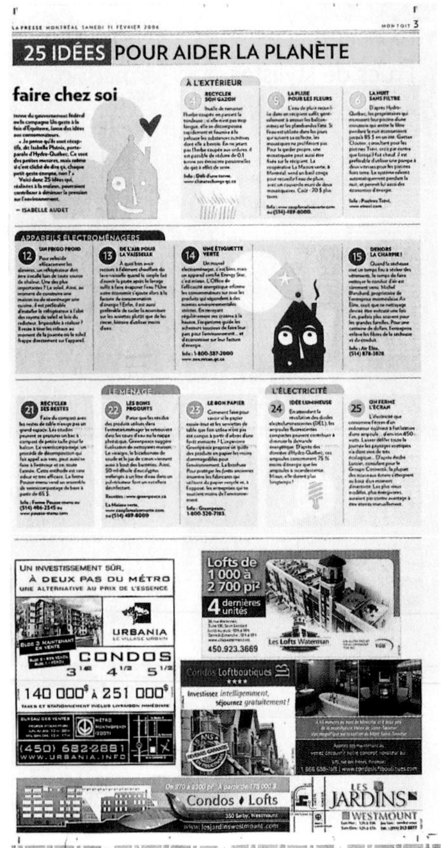

25 IDÉES POUR AIDER LA PLANÈTE

faire chez soi

**LA PRESSE,** Montréal

Julien Chung, Isabelle Audet, Benoit Giguere, Genevieve Dinel, Marc Dore, Eric-Pierre Gibeault

Home/real estate page, broadsheet, 175,000+

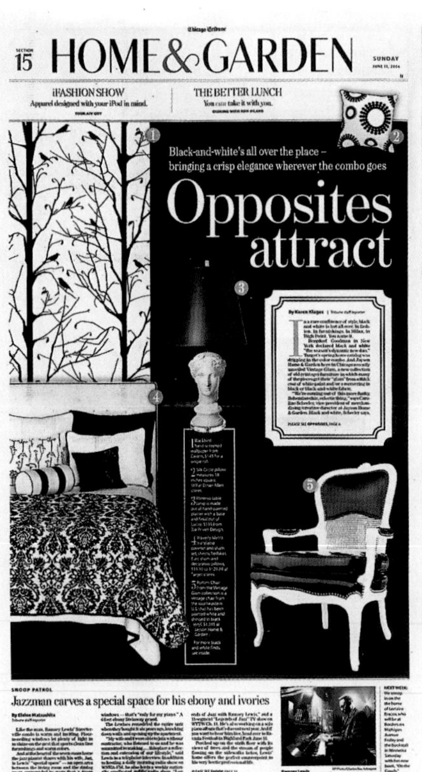

HOME&GARDEN

Black-and-white's all over the place – bringing a crisp elegance wherever the combo goes

Opposites attract

Jazzman carves a special space for his ebony and ivories

**CHICAGO TRIBUNE**

Lana Gwinn, Elaine Matsushita

Home/real estate page, broadsheet, 175,000+

SektöReel

rekabetten estetik çıkıyor

**ZAMAN,** Yenibosna, Turkey

Ekrem Dumanli, Fevzi Yazici, Mustafa Saglam, Seyfulah Öztürk

Home/real estate page, broadsheet, 175,000+

**STAR TRIBUNE,** Minneapolis
Nancy Entwistle, Kim Palmer, Derek Simmons
Home/real estate page, broadsheet, 175,000+

home+garden

Outsourcing at home

trendspotter

Better gnomes and gardens

**THE KANSAS CITY STAR** (Mo.)
Randy Wyrick, Tom Dolphens, Barbara Hill-Meyer, Cindy Hoedel, John Mutrux
Home/real estate page, broadsheet, 175,000+

electronics

h+h house and home

A VINTAGE BREAKOUT

cindy's house

trick the eye

nursery decor

local color

beyond the simple pumpkin

**STAR TRIBUNE,** Minneapolis
Nancy Entwistle, Lynn Underwood, Derek Simmons
Home/real estate page, broadsheet, 175,000+

home+garden

Cheery blossoms

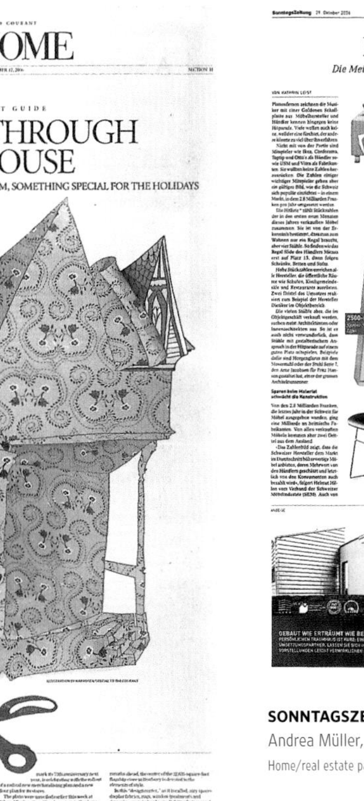
AT HOME

HOLIDAY GIFT GUIDE

ALL THROUGH THE HOUSE

FOR EVERY ROOM, SOMETHING SPECIAL FOR THE HOLIDAYS

Mix & Match New Mantra At Ethan Allen

**HARTFORD COURANT** (Conn.)
Chris Moore, Kim Rosen
Home/real estate page, broadsheet, 175,000+

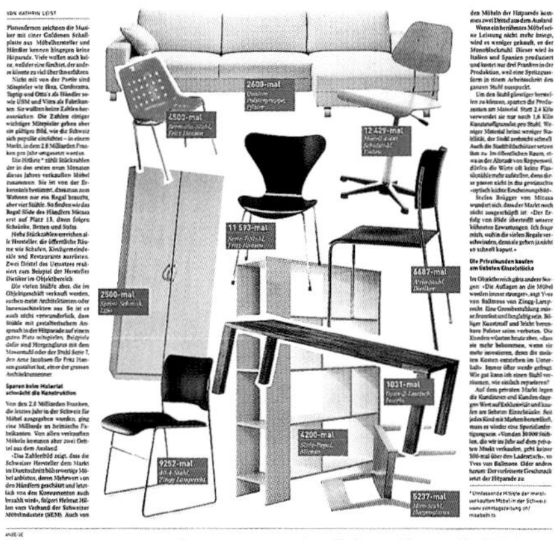
IMMOBILIEN-EXTRA 135

Die vermöbelte Schweiz

*Die Meistgekauften: Eine Hitparade der Stühle, Regale, Tische und Bänke*

**SONNTAGSZEITUNG,** Zürich, Switzerland
Andrea Müller, Benjamin Ogg
Home/real estate page, broadsheet, 175,000+

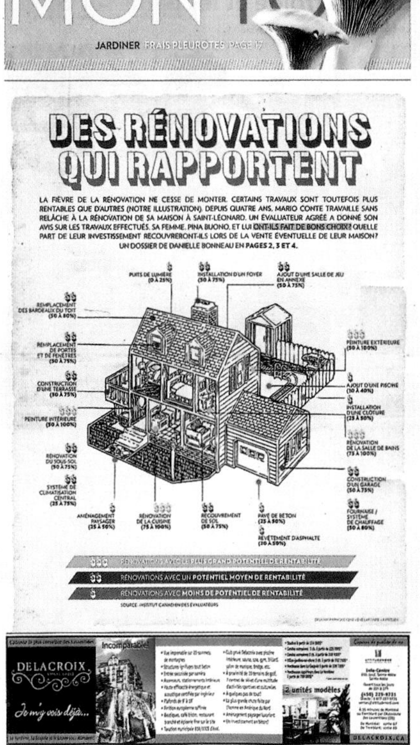
MONTRÉAL SAMEDI 4 NOVEMBRE 2006

MON TOIT

JARDINER FRAIS PLEUROTES

DES RÉNOVATIONS QUI RAPPORTENT

LA FIÈVRE DE LA RÉNOVATION NE CESSE DE MONTER. CERTAINS TRAVAUX SONT TOUTEFOIS PLUS RENTABLES QUE D'AUTRES (NOTRE ILLUSTRATION). DEPUIS QUATRE ANS, MARIO CONTE TRAVAILLE SANS RELÂCHE À LA RÉNOVATION DE SA MAISON À SAINT-LÉONARD. UN ÉVALUATEUR AGRÉÉ A DONNÉ SON AVIS SUR LES TRAVAUX EFFECTUÉS. SA FEMME, PINA BUONO, ET LUI ONT-ILS FAIT DE BONS CHOIX? QUELLE PART DE LEUR INVESTISSEMENT RÉCOUVRERONT-ILS LORS DE LA VENTE ÉVENTUELLE DE LEUR MAISON? UN DOSSIER DE DANIELLE BONNEAU EN PAGES 2, 3 ET 4.

RÉNOVATIONS AVEC UN POTENTIEL MOYEN DE RENTABILITÉ

RÉNOVATIONS AVEC MOINS DE POTENTIEL DE RENTABILITÉ

DELACROIX

**LA PRESSE,** Montréal
Genevieve Lapointe, Danielle Bonneau, Benoit Giguere, Genevieve Dinel, Marc Dore, Eric-Pierre Gibeault
Home/real estate page, broadsheet, 175,000+

**THE PLAIN DEALER,** Cleveland
David Kordalski, Amanda Hamann, Ellie Rhyner, Jon Fobes
Home/real estate page, broadsheet, 175,000+

THURSDAY, FEBRUARY 2, 2006 | SECTION E

INSIDE&OUT

FULL HOUSE

THE 63RD ANNUAL NATIONAL CITY CLEVELAND HOME & GARDEN SHOW

A Dutch treat

INSIDE

Spring is in the air, even if it's just a temporary reprieve from winter's gloom, at the annual International Exposition Center extravaganza.

**TORONTO STAR**
Gale Beeby, Keith Beaty
Home/real estate page, broadsheet, 175,000+

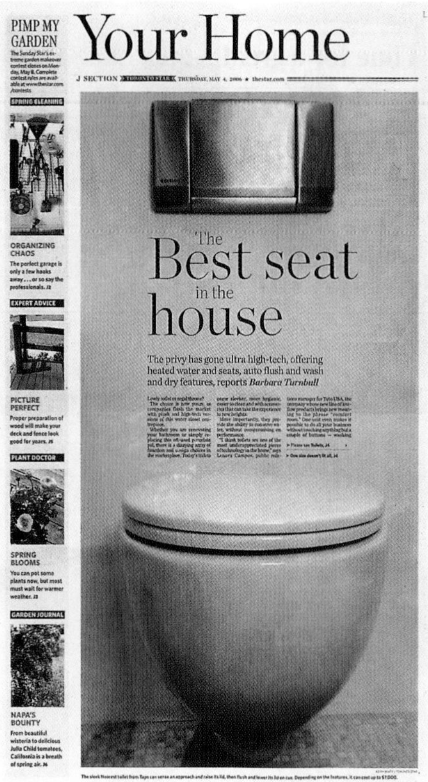

PIMP MY GARDEN

Your Home

SPRING CLEANING

ORGANIZING CHAOS

EXPERT ADVICE

PICTURE PERFECT

PLANT DOCTOR

SPRING BLOOMS

GARDEN JOURNAL

NAPA'S BOUNTY

The Best seat in the house

The privy has gone ultra high-tech, offering heated water and seats, auto flush and wash and dry features, reports Barbara Turnbull

**CHICAGO TRIBUNE**
Hugo Espinoza, Carmel Carrillo, Mary Umberger
Home/real estate page, broadsheet, 175,000+

Chicago Tribune

SECTION 16

REAL ESTATE

SUNDAY

CHICAGOTRIBUNE.COM/HOMES

OPEN SEASON

In shift toward buyer's market, shoppers are more choosy

Mary Umberger

WHAT THE AGENTS SAY

INSIDE AND ONLINE

NEXT WEEK

THE 2007 FORECAST

CHRISTMAS CHEER

NOSTALGIA IS IN STYLE

MISTLETOE

THE KISSING BOUGH

Your Home

Five easy pieces

No longer just an L-shaped sofa, the new sectionals command our attention, reports Barbara Turnbull

**TORONTO STAR**
Gale Beeby
Home/real estate page, broadsheet, 175,000+

Los Angeles Times

HOME

Thursday, June 1, 2006

THE CALIFORNIA GARDEN

Such harsh beauty

Towering aloes, graceful agaves and prickly golden barrels are living sculptures — increasingly popular choices for those looking to blend the practical and the exotic.

INTERIOR MONOLOGUE

A rockin' pad off the Sunset Strip

**LOS ANGELES TIMES**
Judy Pryor, Steven R. Hawkins, Christian Potter Drury, Joseph Hutchinson, Iris Schneider
Home/real estate page, broadsheet, 175,000+

LA PRESSE MONTRÉAL SAMEDI 29 JUILLET 2006

MON TOIT

JARDINER

PLACE AU GYM COCOONING

PAR MANQUE DE TEMPS OU PAR SIMPLE ENVIE DE S'ENTRAÎNER EN TOUTE INTIMITÉ, ILS SONT DE PLUS EN PLUS NOMBREUX À CHOISIR D'AMENER LE GYM CHEZ EUX PLUTÔT QUE D'Y ALLER. TROUVEZ TOUT CE QU'IL VOUS FAUT POUR VOUS ENTRAÎNER DANS LE CONFORT DE VOTRE MAISON.

PAGES 2 ET 3

SHERBROOKE

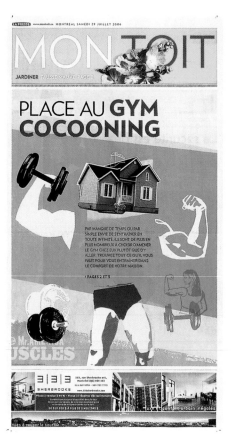

**LA PRESSE,** Montréal
Philippe Tardif, Sebastien Templier, Benoit Giguere, Genevieve Dinel, Marc Dore, Eric-Pierre Gibeault
Home/real estate page, broadsheet, 175,000+

**LOS ANGELES TIMES**
Kelli Sullivan, Joseph Hutchinson, Michael Whitley, Mary Cooney
Home/real estate page, broadsheet, 175,000+

Los Angeles Times

HOME

COMMEMORATIVE EDITION

Magnificent obsession

It's the California dream: a plot of land, a home, some space. It's drawn millions of us here for more than a century. It's fueled dreams and ruined fortunes. And it defines us like nothing else. **LAND RUSH!** The first time Angelenos went real-estate crazy? Try 1886, Page 4. **HISTORY OF PARADISE:** From Mulholland to Jarvis, Page 16. **THE GLASS WALL:** L.A.'s architectural signature, Page 8. **STATE OF DENIAL:** Flood, fire, earthquake — just deal with it, Page 40. **PLUS:** 125 years of Hot Property, lost history, Hollywood mansions and more.

**THE PLAIN DEALER,** Cleveland
David Kordalski, Andrea Levy, Ellie Rhyner, Amanda Hamann
Home/real estate page, broadsheet, 175,000+

HOMES

MORTGAGE RATES

Nasty habitat

A smoker's house can be a real-estate nightmare

Unsmoking the house

OPEN HOUSE

Westlake Tudor enhanced with updates

**THE SACRAMENTO BEE** (Calif.)
Margaret Spengler, Val Mina, Barbara Stubbs, Pam Dinsmore
Home/real estate page, tabloid, 175,000+

California Life

HOME & GARDEN

It's not easy being clean

How to keep a messy house from weighing on your mind

Page 12

Play it safe: 10 tips for displaying holiday lights Page 4 • How to create magical and soothing floral displays. Page 5

Los Angeles Times

REAL ESTATE

Hot Property

She's not wedded to the beach

A building fee-for-all

Behind every successful remodel: A homeowner and a contractor who share a vision and know how to communicate with each other.

A job built on respect

**LOS ANGELES TIMES**
Jim Brooks, Wes Bausmith, Christian Potter Drury, Peter Bennett
Home/real estate page, broadsheet, 175,000+

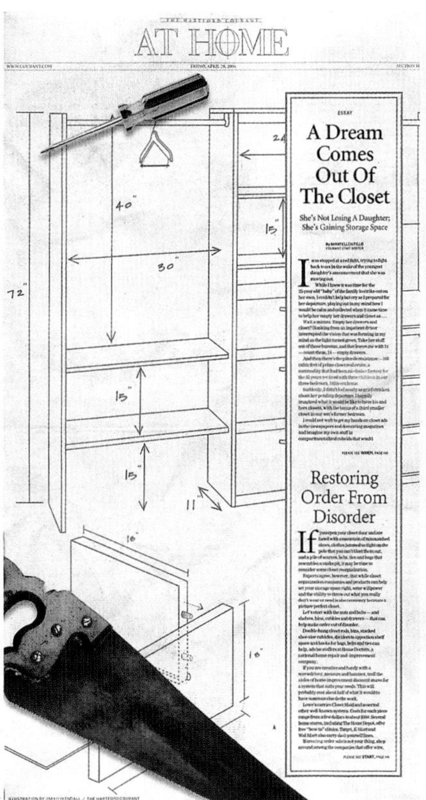

THE HARTFORD COURANT

AT HOME

ESSAY

A Dream Comes Out Of The Closet

She's Not Losing A Daughter; She's Gaining Storage Space

Restoring Order From Disorder

**HARTFORD COURANT** (Conn.)
Vada Crosby, Suzette Moyer, Jim Kuykendall
Home/real estate page, broadsheet, 175,000+

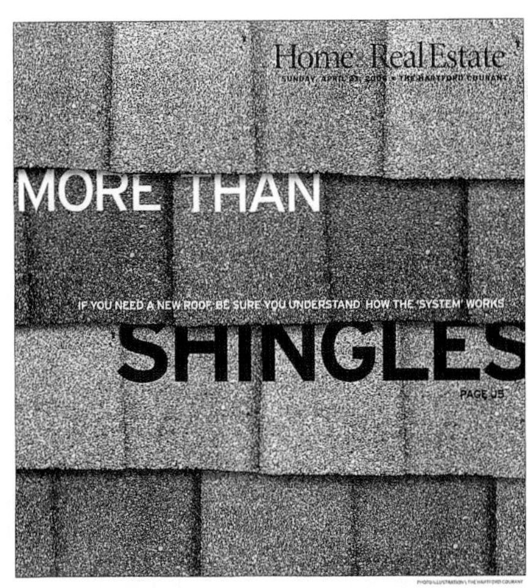

Home Real Estate

MORE THAN SHINGLES

IF YOU NEED A NEW ROOF, BE SURE YOU UNDERSTAND HOW THE 'SYSTEM' WORKS

**HARTFORD COURANT** (Conn.)
Kristin Lenz, Suzette Moyer
Home/real estate page, tabloid, 175,000+

**HARTFORD COURANT** (Conn.)
Vada Crosby, Suzette Moyer
Home/real estate page, broadsheet, 175,000+

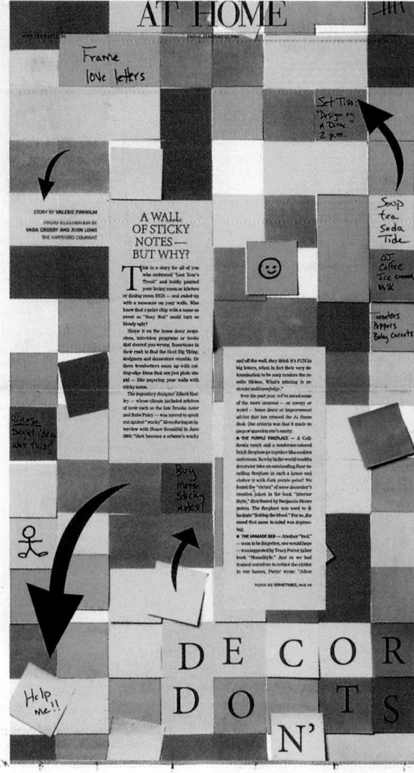
AT HOME

A WALL OF STICKY NOTES — BUT WHY?

DECOR DON'TS

**THE STRAITS TIMES,** Singapore
Andrew Tan, Peter Thomas Williams
Home/real estate page, broadsheet, 175,000+

Some assembly required

An eight-step DIY guide to the charms of Scandinavian style. ANDREW TAN puts together the nuts and bolts

1 Stack & pack

2 Clean lines

3 Curvy forms

4 Seasonal colours

5 Casual looks

6 Organic patterns

7 Natural materials

8 Traditional crafts

**THE SAN DIEGO UNION-TRIBUNE**
Tara Stone, Michael Price, Michael James Rocha
Travel page, broadsheet, 175,000+

travel

adventure • escape

HOSTEL MAKEOVER

Operators counter Spartan image with stricter standards, privacy improvements and even pancakes

"There's been a recognition that hostelling has reached critical mass and gone beyond just cheap places to stay."

130 IMMOBILIEN-EXTRA

Starker Charakter

*Nächstes Wochenende werden am Designer's Saturday in Langenthal Leuchten, Sessel und Stauraum junger Labels und bekannter Firmen zu sehen sein. ARIANA PRADAL stellt die besten Modelle vorab vor*

HELLE SPERMIEN

ECHTER STREBER

STARKER AUFTRITT

ELEGANTE RUNDUNGEN

BEWEGTE FORM

POETISCHES LICHT

PRÄZISE FÜGUNG

FLEXIBLES STAUMÖBEL

UNVERWÜSTLICHE SCHÖNHEIT

HANDGEMACHTES FALTENSPIEL

PERFEKTE TÄUSCHUNG

**SONNTAGSZEITUNG,** Zürich, Switzerland
Andrea Müller, Benjamin Ogg
Home/real estate page, broadsheet, 175,000+

TRAVEL

2006 FREE PRESS DETROIT METRO airport GUIDE

STORIES BY ELLEN CREAGER | FREE PRESS TRAVEL WRITER

EVERYTHING YOU NEED TO KNOW BEFORE YOU BOARD A HOLIDAY FLIGHT

WHAT YOU'LL FIND INSIDE

FREE PRESS PHOTOS BY AMY LEANG

**DETROIT FREE PRESS**
Patrick Sedlar, Amy Leang
Travel page, broadsheet, 175,000+

**HARTFORD COURANT** (Conn.)
Timothy Reck, Suzette Moyer, Leo Espinosa
Travel page, broadsheet, 175,000+

THE HARTFORD COURANT
TRAVEL

a spring cruise

Booking A Cabin Without An Ocean View Yields Significant Savings Without Much Sacrifice

INSIDE PASSAGE

The Art Of Relaxed Sailing Along Caribbean Ports Of Call

More Travelers Are Choosing A Trip That Lasts A While

**STAR TRIBUNE,** Minneapolis
Colleen Kelly, Chris Welsch
Travel page, broadsheet, 175,000+

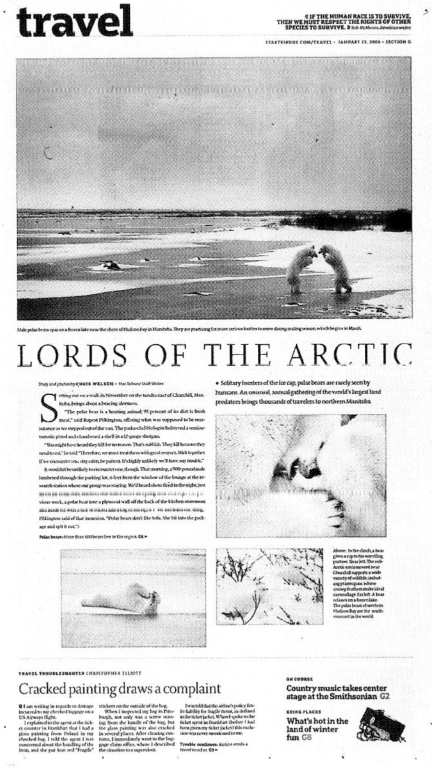
travel

LORDS OF THE ARCTIC

Cracked painting draws a complaint

Country music takes center stage at the Smithsonian G2

What's hot in the land of winter fun G8

**SOUTH FLORIDA SUN-SENTINEL,** Fort Lauderdale
Ben Crandell, Tim Frank
Travel page, broadsheet, 175,000+

SOUTH FLORIDA SUN-SENTINEL | SUNDAY | MARCH 5, 2006 | SECTION G

Travel

Big Sail

Chasing the wind between Italian ports aboard the *Royal Clipper.* Page 10

SUMMER AT SEA

THE PERFECT SHIP FOR YOU Page 3

GORGING ON CHINA Page 6

GORGING ONBOARD Page 4

TRAVEL

From Blue Lagoon to endless other sights, more foreigners are discovering the country.

WARM UP TO ICELAND

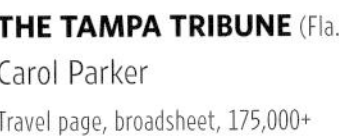

**THE TAMPA TRIBUNE** (Fla.)
Carol Parker
Travel page, broadsheet, 175,000+

travel

ALASKA

Road trip: In America's biggest national park, a ghost town discovery G8

Denali: Walking the fine line between adventure and foolish risk G5

Going Places: Staying safe in Arctic wildernesses and urban jungles G6

**STAR TRIBUNE,** Minneapolis
Colleen Kelly, Chris Welsch
Travel page, broadsheet, 175,000+

THE HARTFORD COURANT
TRAVEL

Give Bugs The Boot

No Weighting

No-Grab Bags

Carry A Charge

GEAR UP AND GET GOING

Super Suds

Up And Aweigh

Dinner Combo

Pocket Socket

Easy Lifting

Your Bag Or Mine?

**HARTFORD COURANT** (Conn.)
Timothy Reck, Suzette Moyer
Travel page, broadsheet, 175,000+

**THE BOSTON GLOBE**

Josue Evilla, Doug Warren, Dan Zedek, Leanne Burden

Travel page, broadsheet, 175,000+

Chill

AIR TIME

EASY DOES IT

BOARD BUZZ

GET THE LOOK

PERFECT FIT

A NEW EDGE

**THE BOSTON GLOBE**

Josue Evilla, Doug Warren, Dan Zedek, Leanne Burden, Jonathan Wiggs

Travel page, broadsheet, 175,000+

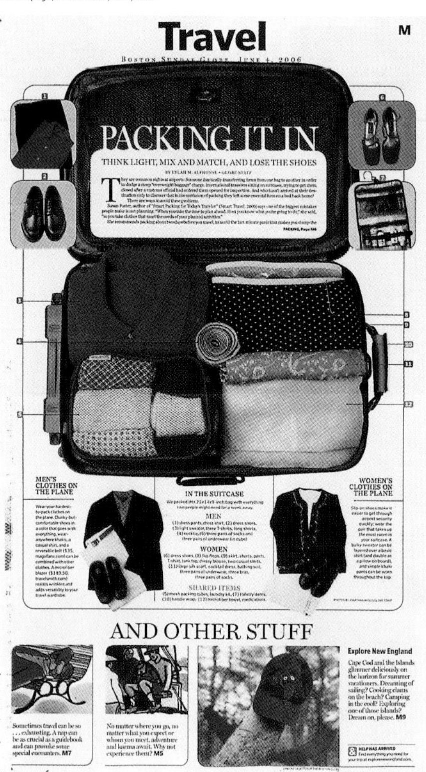

Travel

PACKING IT IN

THINK LIGHT, MIX AND MATCH, AND LOSE THE SHOES

MEN'S CLOTHES ON THE PLANE

IN THE SUITCASE

WOMEN'S CLOTHES ON THE PLANE

AND OTHER STUFF

Explore New England

**SAN JOSE MERCURY NEWS** (Calif.)

Daymond Gascon, Stephanie Grace Lim, Martin Gee, Jonathon Berlin, Matt Mansfield

Travel page, broadsheet, 175,000+

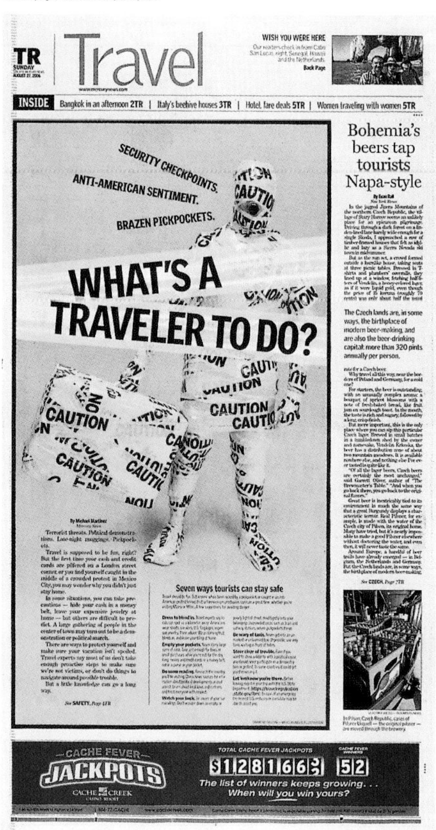

TR

Travel

INSIDE Bangkok in an afternoon 2TR | Italy's beehive houses 3TR | Hotel, fare deals 5TR | Women traveling with women 5TR

SECURITY CHECKPOINTS.

ANTI-AMERICAN SENTIMENT.

BRAZEN PICKPOCKETS.

WHAT'S A TRAVELER TO DO?

Bohemia's beers tap tourists Napa-style

Seven ways tourists can stay safe

JACKPOTS

$1281166 52

The list of winners keeps growing. . . When will you win yours?

TRAVEL

GRAND VIEWS OF GOTHAM

BLACK FAMILY REUNIONS ARE FLOURISHING

Get-Togethers Are Often Three-Day Events, With Parties, Gospel Singing, Prayer And Worship

**HARTFORD COURANT** (Conn.)

Timothy Reck, Suzette Moyer, Richard Messina

Travel page, broadsheet, 175,000+

THE CARIBBEAN

Travel

ahhhhhhh

Luxurious Jammin' on Strawberry Hill

A Margarita in Venezuela PAGE 6G

San Juan: The capital of Reggaeton PAGE 7G

Bargain beauty on Anguilla PAGE 10G

**SOUTH FLORIDA SUN-SENTINEL,** Fort Lauderdale

Susana Sanchez, Ben Crandell, Tim Frank

Travel page, broadsheet, 175,000+

TRAVEL

miniature GOLFER'S PARADISE

Fiery dragons and Tidy Bowl waterfalls are serious business in Myrtle Beach, S.C.

**SAN FRANCISCO CHRONICLE**

Nanette Bisher, Matt Petaty, Hulda Nelson, John Flinn, Jeanne Cooper, Martha Rich

Travel page, broadsheet, 175,000+

**THE NEW YORK TIMES**
Tom Bodkin, Rodrigo Honeywell, Robert Neubecker, Lonnie Schlein
Travel page, broadsheet, 175,000+

**CHICAGO TRIBUNE**
Hugo Espinoza, Randall Curwen, Margaret Backenheimer
Travel page, broadsheet, 175,000+

**POLITIKEN,** Copenhagen, Denmark
Søren Nyeland, Per Bergsbo, Allan Gravbæk
Travel page, tabloid, 50,000-174,999

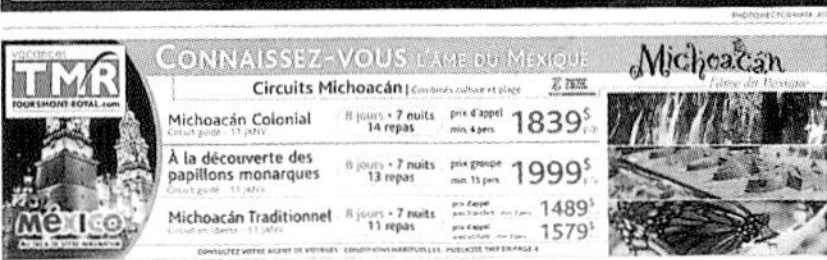


**LA PRESSE,** Montréal
Julien Chung, Rejean Bourdeau, Benoit Giguere, Genevieve Dinel, Marc Dore, Andree Lebel
Travel page, broadsheet, 175,000+

**SAN JOSE MERCURY NEWS** (Calif.)
Martin Gee, Stephanie Grace Lim
Travel page, broadsheet, 175,000+

**THE SAN DIEGO UNION-TRIBUNE**
Gregory Schmidt, Cristina Martinez Byvik, Michael Price, Michael James Rocha
Travel page, broadsheet, 175,000+

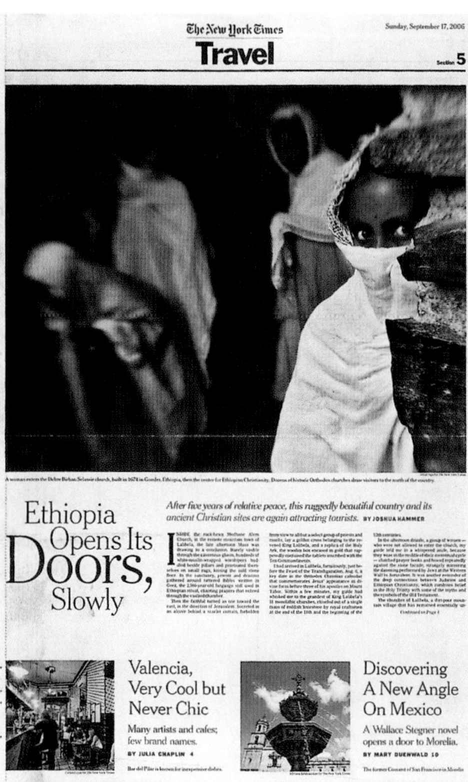
The New York Times
Sunday, September 17, 2006
Travel
Section 5

Ethiopia Opens Its Doors, Slowly

After five years of relative peace, this raggedly beautiful country and its ancient Christian sites are again attracting tourists. BY JOSHUA HAMMER

Valencia, Very Cool but Never Chic
Many artists and cafes; few brand names.
BY JULIA CHAPLIN 4

Discovering A New Angle On Mexico
A Wallace Stegner novel opens a door to Morelia.
BY MARY DUENWALD 10

**THE NEW YORK TIMES**
Tom Bodkin, John Cohoe
Travel page, broadsheet, 175,000+

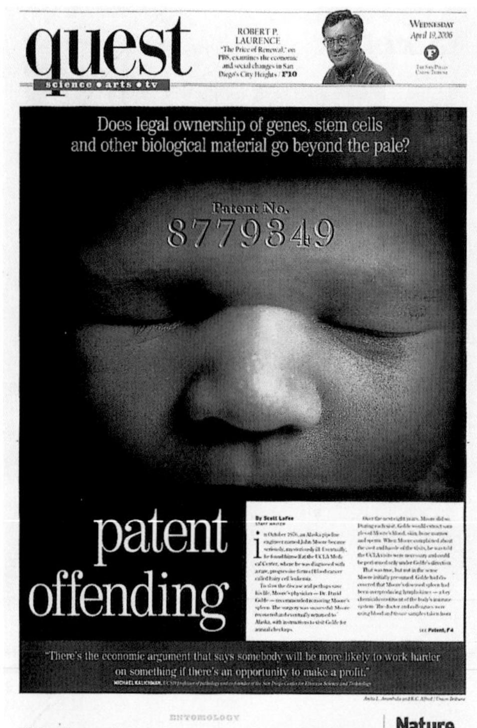
quest
science • arts • tv
ROBERT P. LAURENCE
"The Price of Renewal" on PBS, examines the economic and social changes in San Diego's City Heights · F10
Wednesday April 19, 2006

Does legal ownership of genes, stem cells and other biological material go beyond the pale?

Patent No. 8779349

patent offending

By Scott LaFee

"There's the economic argument that says somebody will be more likely to work harder on something if there's an opportunity to make a profit."

Wingless gliders hint of early insect flight

Nature & Eye
IT'S BIGGER THAN EVER

**THE SAN DIEGO UNION-TRIBUNE**
Martina Schimitschek, Anita L. Arambula, K.C. Alfred, Michael James Rocha
Science/technology page, broadsheet, 175,000+

**SYDSVENSKAN,** Malmö, Sweden
Roger Brinck, Christoffer Rehn
Travel page, tabloid, 50,000-174,999

Resor

Döden i Himalaya

För drygt tre veckor sedan omkom den svenske bergsklättraren Tomas Olsson på Mount Everest. Han är inte den ende. Varje år söker mängder av klättrare allt extremare upplevelser på Himalayas högsta toppar. Och varje år skördas nya offer.

Fortsättning på nästa uppslag

WEST SIDE STORY

1975 kom Två Dagars Peder Grell till New York första gången. Nu har han varit där 45 gånger och vi bad honom skriva om sitt New York. Det blev en West Side Story.

**GÖTEBORGS-POSTEN,** Goteborg, Sweden
Gunilla Wernhamn, Jonny Mattsson
Travel page, tabloid, 175,000+

TRAVEL

MOUNTAINS OF SAND

NATIONAL PARK IN SOUTHERN COLORADO HAS NORTH AMERICA'S HIGHEST DUNES

**HARTFORD COURANT** (Conn.)
Timothy Reck, Suzette Moyer
Travel page, broadsheet, 175,000+

92 WISSEN

# Ganz natürliche Inspiration

*Pflanzen und Tiere dienen als Vorbild für neue Produkte. Mit Hilfe der Bionik werden Flugzeuge oder Klebstoffe entwickelt*

EINSATZGEBIETE DER BIONIK

WAS IST BIONIK?

KÜNSTLICHE GECKOHAARE KOPIEREN DAS REALE VORBILD

**SONNTAGSZEITUNG,** Zürich, Switzerland
Stefan Semrau
Science/technology page, broadsheet, 175,000+

**AKZIA,** Moscow
Konstantin Lukjanov, Svetlana Maximchenko
Science/technology page, tabloid, 175,000+

ГАЗЕТА

# АКЦИЯ

БУДУЩЕЕ В НАСТОЯЩЕМ

Чулпан Хаматова
Елочные игрушки
Линда
ENTERTAINMENT

издается с 12 апреля 2001 года | №50 (60) 16 октября | www.akzia.ru

НАУЧПОП

Чего не хватает современной российской науке?

K8 EL UNIVERSAL · AUTOPISTAS · EL UNIVERSAL K9

HUMMER

220

20

39,329

90%

LO QUE OFRECE

Kalina

Se complica la llegada de marca rusa por impuestos

# Misma actitud en MENOR TAMAÑO

LAS ENTRAÑAS

CALIFICACIÓN

**EL UNIVERSAL,** México City
Roberto Rock L., Francisco Santiago, Oscar Santiago Méndez, Rubén Álvarez, Nilton Torres Pérez, Marco A. Trejo C., Ricardo Gutiérrez Loyola, Tomás Benítez Contreras
Science/technology page, broadsheet, 50,000-174,999

LA GACETA

4 ACTUALIDAD

# El esfuerzo vale la pena

**LA GACETA,** San Miguel de Tucuman, Argentina
Daniel Fontanarrosa, Sergio Fernandez
Science/technology page, broadsheet, 50,000-174,999

86 WISSEN

# Gottes Werk und Doktors Beitrag

*Künstliche Hände aus der Robotertechnik, Augenprothesen, die sehen können – das menschliche Ersatzteillager wird immer ausgefeilter*

Wie die Prothesen laufen lernten

**SONNTAGSZEITUNG,** Zürich, Switzerland
Stefan Semrau
Science/technology page, broadsheet, 175,000+

WISSEN

85

WELTALL
SATELLITEN WARNEN VOR BERGSTÜRZEN

ANDALUSIEN
GEWINNEN SIE EINE REISE IM MONATSQUIZ

WIE SICH KREBS AUSBREITET

# Den Wanderzellen auf der Spur

*Mit neuen Ansätzen soll die Verbreitung von Krebs im Körper enträtselt werden*

RECHTZEITIG FENSTER SANIEREN UND HEIZKOSTEN SPAREN!

Internorm

**SONNTAGSZEITUNG,** Zürich, Switzerland
Andrea Müller, Edith Huwiler
Science/technology page, broadsheet, 175,000+

**THE CHRONICLE OF HIGHER EDUCATION,** Washington

Robert Bryson

Science/technology page, tabloid, 50,000-174,999

VERBATIM

RESEARCH

## Researchers Explore New Visions for Hallucinogens

After a long hiatus, medical investigators return to studying the benefits of once-banned compounds

**EL UNIVERSAL,** México City

Roberto Rock L., Francisco Santiago, Oscar Santiago Méndez, Rubén Álvarez, Nilton Torres Pérez, Ricardo Gutiérrez Loyola, Mauricio González García, Bernardo Mendoza Ruiz

Science/technology page, broadsheet, 50,000-174,999

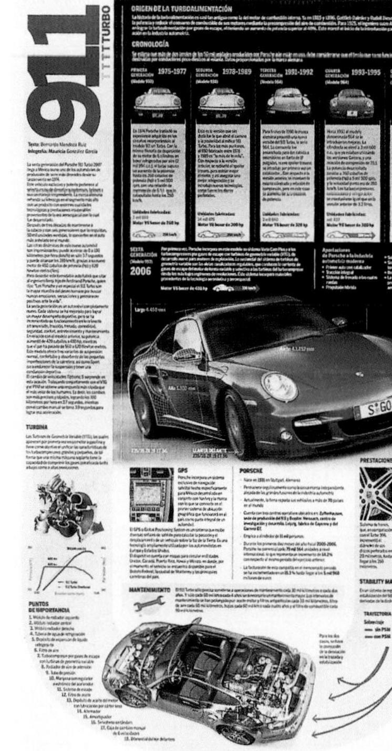

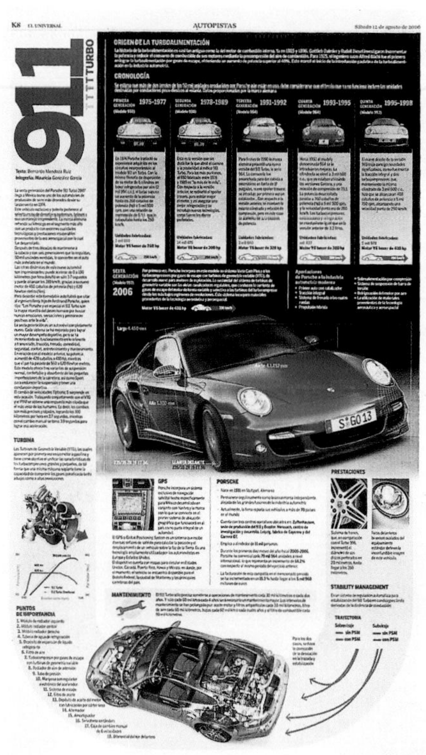


**THE SAN DIEGO UNION-TRIBUNE**

Michael Canepa, Cristina Martinez Byvik, Michael Price, Michael James Rocha

Science/technology page, broadsheet, 175,000+

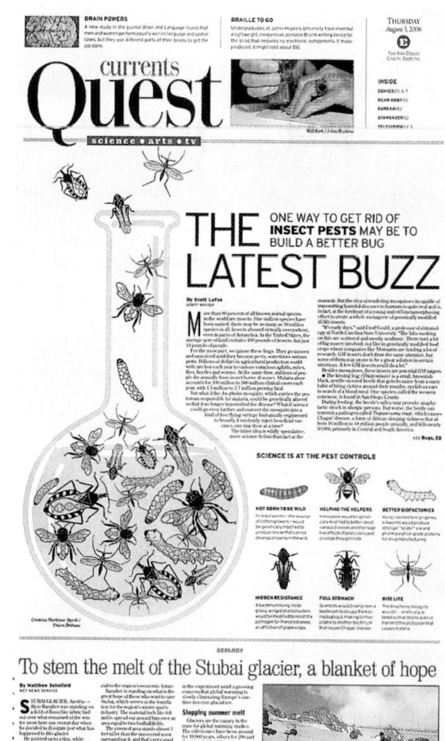

## To stem the melt of the Stubai glacier, a blanket of hope

WISSEN

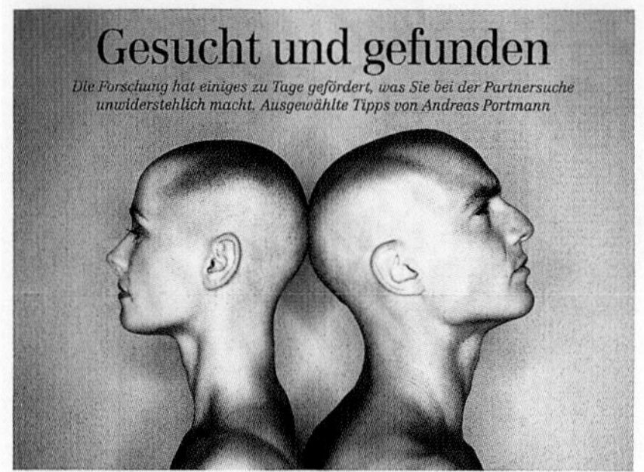

**SONNTAGSZEITUNG,** Zürich, Switzerland

Tobias Peier, Stefan Semrau

Science/technology page, broadsheet, 175,000+

**EL UNIVERSAL,** México City

Roberto Rock L., Francisco Santiago, Oscar Santiago Méndez, Rubén Álvarez, María Elena Matadamas, Nilton Torres Pérez, Patricia Velázquez Yebra, Rafael Sotomayor, Jorge Manjarrez, Roberto Hernández Gutierrez

Science/technology page, broadsheet, 50,000-174,999

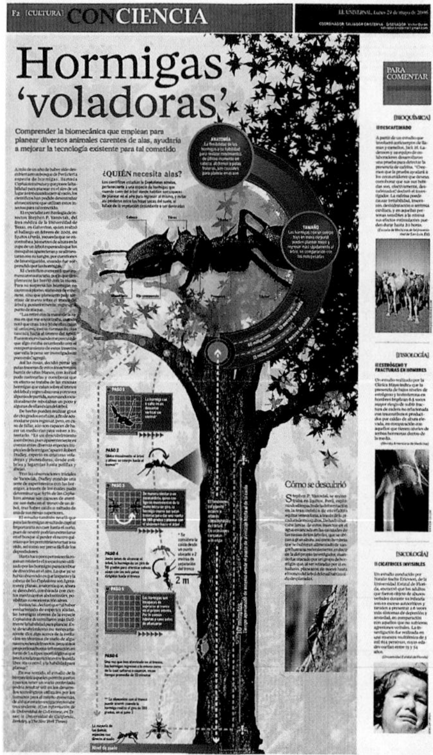

**EL UNIVERSAL,** México City

Roberto Rock L., Francisco Santiago, Oscar Santiago Méndez, Rubén Álvarez, María Elena Matadamas, Nilton Torres Pérez, Omar Canek Páramo Kañetas, Víctor M. Durán Méjia, Luis Miguel Cruz Ceballos, Salvador Cristerna Romo

Science/technology page, broadsheet, 50,000-174,999

**THE BALTIMORE SUN**

Anthony Conroy

Science/technology page, broadsheet, 175,000+

D FRIDAY 09.29.2006 baltimoresun.com/healthscience

HEALTH & SCIENCE

FOREMAN >>> RESEARCH SUPPORTS REMEDY FOR URINARY TRACT INFECTIONS

EXTINCT NO MORE? IVORY-BILLED WOODPECKER SIGHTED IN FLORIDA

New issue shuts down camera on Hubble

NASA hopes instrument will be working next week

TARGETING TASTE

Researchers are beginning to understand how the tongue's sensors discern sour, bitter, sweet and other flavors — and it has nothing to do with the famous 'mouth map'

TWO TESTS PREDICT INHERITED CANCER RISK

Free written screening determines likelihood of developing colon disease

Synthesized corneas may restore sight to cloudy eyes

Bioengineers say substitutes may be available in a few years

San Francisco Chronicle

TECHNOLOGY AND BUSINESS

Section F

David Einstein

Clear your cell before donating it

Seeking readers via 'book trailer'

Publisher tries out movie-style preview to market new title

Coming soon to your screen

Getting started

San Francisco Chronicle | CNET.com

Apple's new toys are here

**SAN FRANCISCO CHRONICLE**

Ed Rachles, Tracy Cox, Frank Mina, Nanette Bisher

Science/technology page, broadsheet, 175,000+

E2 [CULTURA] PROYECTO UNAM

EL UNIVERSAL, jueves 18 de mayo de 2006

EDITOR RESPONSABLE: ROBERTO GUTIÉRREZ ALCALÁ

DISEÑO: VÍCTOR M. DURÁN MEJÍA

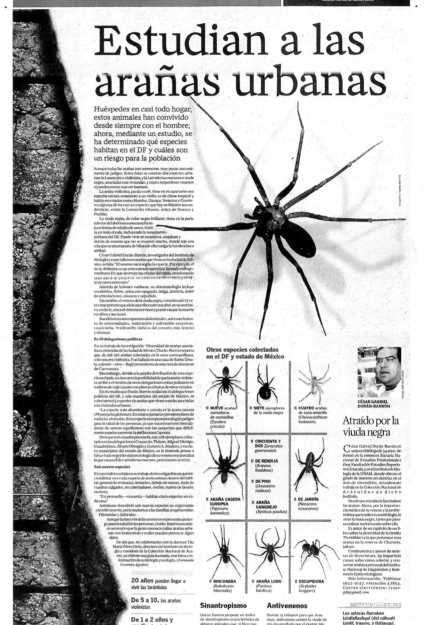

# Estudian a las arañas urbanas

Huéspedes en casi todo hogar, estos animales han convivido desde siempre con el hombre; ahora, mediante un estudio, se ha determinado qué especies habitan en el DF y cuáles son un riesgo para la población

Otras especies colectadas en el DF y estado de México

NUEVE arañas comedoras de cochinillas (Dysdera crocata)

SIETE ejemplares de la viuda negra

CUATRO arañas de saco amarillo (Cheiracanthium inclusum).

CINCUENTA Y DOS Zorocrates guerrerensis

DE RENDIJA (Araneus thaddeus)

DE PISO (Urozelotes rusticus)

ARAÑA CASERA EUROPEA (Tegenaria domestica)

ARAÑA CANGREJO (Xysticus paiutus)

DE JARDÍN (Neoscona oaxacensis)

RINCONERA (Kukulcania hibernalis)

ARAÑA LOBO (Pardosa falcifera)

ESCUPIDORA (Scytodes longipes)

CÉSAR GABRIEL DURÁN-BARRÓN

Atraído por la viuda negra

20 años pueden llegar a vivir las tarántulas

De 5 a 10, las arañas violinistas

De 1 a 2 años y medio, las viudas negras

3 mil personas sufren cada año la mordedura de una viuda negra en México

De 10 a 20 personas, en su mayoría niños, mueren

Sinantropismo

Antivenenos

Los aztecas llamaban tzintlatlauhqui (del náhuatl tzintli, trasero, y tlatlauqui, rojo) a la viuda negra.

El macho, después de copular, se deja comer por la hembra que fecundó, para que ella produzca huevecillos con mayor vitelo (nutriente) y sus hijos nazcan y crezcan más sanos.

SILVER

**EL UNIVERSAL**, México City

Roberto Rock L., Francisco Santiago, Oscar Santiago Méndez, Rubén Álvarez, María Elena Matadamas, Nilton Torres Pérez, Omar Canek Páramo Kañetas, Víctor M. Durán Mejía, Tomás Benítez Contreras, Roberto Hernández Gutierrez

Science/technology page, broadsheet, 50,000-174,999

Many layers of information are packaged onto one page, but they don't overpower. A natural background doesn't overpower. The small spider grid is nicely done and doesn't feel blocky. This is how these pages should be handled.

Muchos niveles de información han sido empaquetados en una sola página, pero no la abruman. Un fondo natural no abruma. La pequeña telaraña está hecha con gracia y no se siente pesada. Así deberían manejarse estas páginas.

90 WISSEN

# Erst der Himmel ist die Grenze

*Die Ära der Super-Wolkenkratzer steht bevor. Die Rekordhöhe wird weniger von der Statik als von den Kosten limitiert*

**SONNTAGSZEITUNG,** Zürich, Switzerland
Stefan Semrau, Bruno Muff
Science/technology page, broadsheet, 175,000+

WISSEN OLYMPIA-EXTRA

SPORTMEDIZIN
SWISS-OLYMPIC-TEAMARZT BEAT VILLIGER IM GESPRÄCH
SEITE 75

SPORTPHYSIK
AUS DEM ETH-LABOR KOMMEN BESSERE EISHOCKEY-STÖCKE
SEITE 72

# Simulieren geht über Probieren

*Mit Hilfe von Computeranimationen wollen Schweizer Ski-Akrobaten Olympiamedaillen gewinnen*

**SONNTAGSZEITUNG,** Zürich, Switzerland
Stefan Semrau
Science/technology page, broadsheet, 175,000+

66 KULTUR | KULTUR 67

# Wohltätig ist des Feuers Macht, wenn sie der Mensch bezähmt, bewacht

**WELT AM SONNTAG,** Berlin
Jördis Guzmán Bulla, Beate Nowak, Jutta Setzer, Jörn Baumgarten
Science/technology page, broadsheet, 175,000+

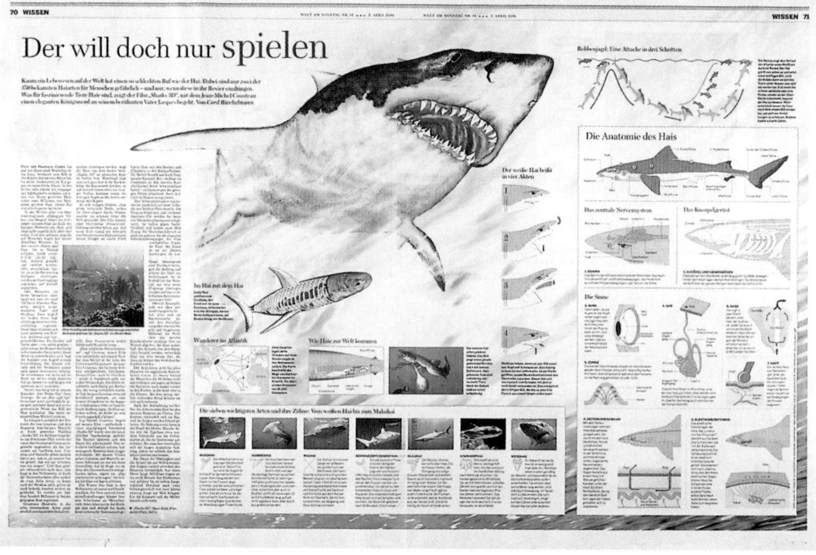
70 WISSEN | WISSEN 71

# Der will doch nur spielen

Die Anatomie des Hais

**WELT AM SONNTAG,** Berlin
Jördis Guzmán Bulla, Karin Sturm
Science/technology page, broadsheet, 175,000+

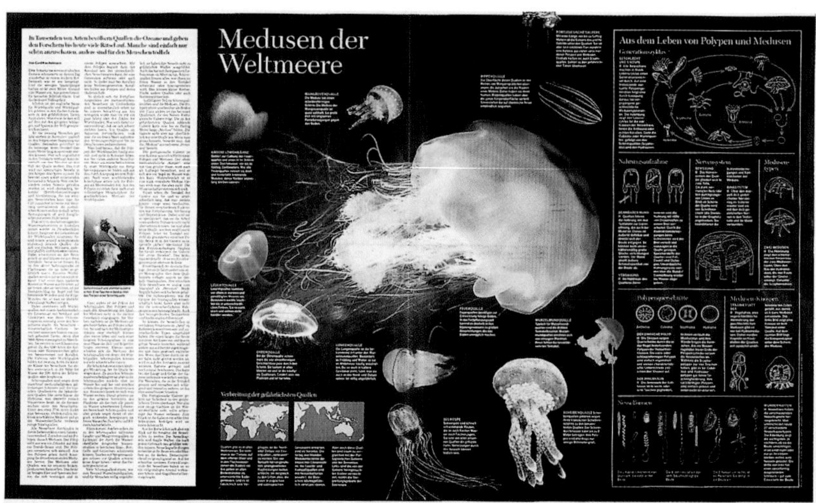
# Medusen der Weltmeere

Aus dem Leben von Polypen und Medusen

**WELT AM SONNTAG,** Berlin
Jördis Guzmán Bulla, Tilman Jersch
Science/technology page, broadsheet, 175,000+

**THE SAN DIEGO UNION-TRIBUNE**

Chris Barber, Jacie Landeros, Michael Price, Michael James Rocha

Other feature page, broadsheet, 175,000+

currents

health

fitness • wellness

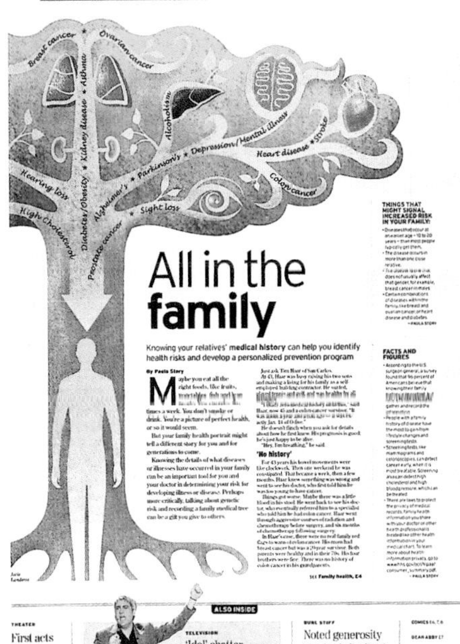

All in the family

Knowing your relatives' medical history can help you identify health risks and develop a personalized prevention program

First acts

'Idol' chatter

Noted generosity

**O GLOBO,** Rio de Janeiro, Brazil

Luciane Costa, Claudio Duarte, Léa Cristina

Other feature page, broadsheet, 175,000+

O GLOBO

BOA CHANCE

Executivos descobrem Jesus

Quatro livros lançados no país dizem que exemplo de liderança do filho de Deus deve ser seguido nas empresas. Vendas superam expectativas

'Jesus convenceu um terço da humanidade'

FGV CADEMP

FUNDAÇÃO GETULIO VARGAS

**THE NEW YORK TIMES**

Tom Bodkin, Kelly Doe, Catherine Chalmers

Science/technology page, broadsheet, 175,000+

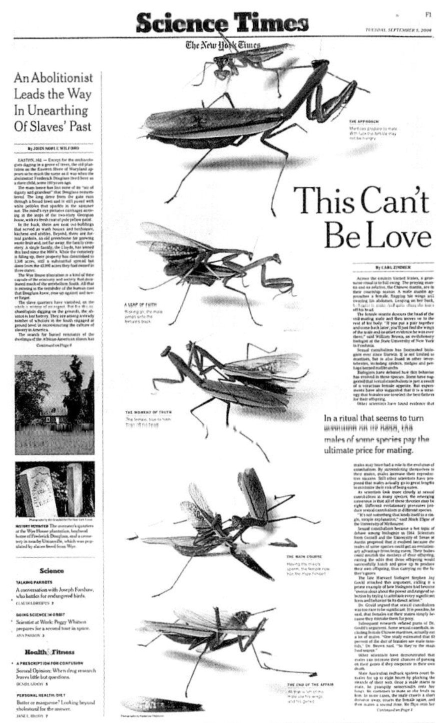

Science Times

The New York Times

An Abolitionist Leads the Way In Unearthing Of Slaves' Past

This Can't Be Love

In a ritual that seems to turn courtship on its head, the males of some species pay the ultimate price for mating.

The Boston Globe

IN GOOD SHAPE

**THE BOSTON GLOBE**

Chin Wang, Lane Turner, Essdras M. Suarez, Ann Scales, Dan Zedek

Other feature page, broadsheet, 175,000+

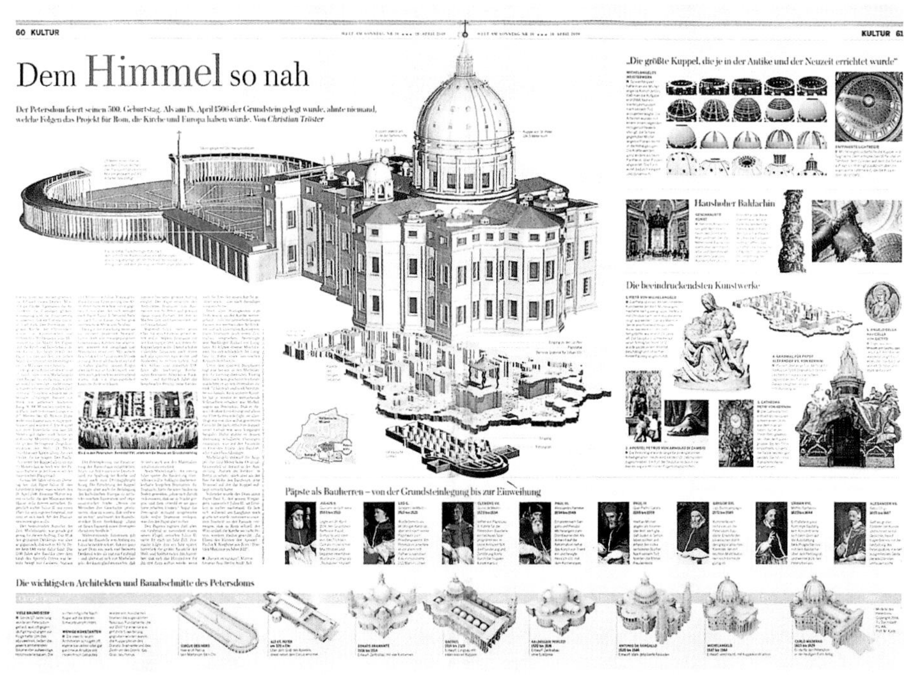

60 KULTUR

KULTUR 61

Dem Himmel so nah

„Die größte Kuppel, die je in der Antike und der Neuzeit errichtet wurde"

Hauslscher Baldachin

Die beeindruckendsten Kunstwerke

Päpste als Bauherren – von der Grundsteinlegung bis zur Einweihung

Die wichtigsten Architekten und Bauabschnitte des Petersdoms

**WELT AM SONNTAG,** Berlin

Jördis Guzmán Bulla, Ralf Powierski, T.U. Darmstadt

Science/technology page, broadsheet, 175,000+

**TORONTO STAR**

Spencer Wynn, Susan Grimbly, Peter Scowen, Leslie Scrivener

Other feature page, broadsheet, 175,000+

TORONTO STAR DECEMBER 24, 2006 SECTION D

IDEAS

GIFT-WRAPPED AND BOW-TIED

2 THE FIRST RULE OF THEATRE Don't drop the Mouse King: On-stage mishaps with the Mayor

BOOKS PRIME EGGERS 7 The storyteller's latest heartbreaking work of staggering genius

MICROSCOPE Sexy skunks, Edison's light bulbs, and a mole that's nothing to sniff at. D3

10 THINGS WE LEARNED THIS WEEK

Though we may pine for the humble Christmas of long ago, the season has been an extravagant, luxury-driven, excessive celebration for a very long time. By Leslie Scrivener

The commercialization of Christmas: A history

Liberating an era's forbidden portraits

A historic record of an era's shame comes to light

**THE BOSTON GLOBE**

Chin Wang, Lane Turner, Dina Rudick, Ann Scales, Dan Zedek

Other feature page, broadsheet, 175,000+

E4 Style THE BOSTON GLOBE

singing the blues

**ST. PETERSBURG TIMES** (Fla.)

Jessica Parker Gilbert

Other feature page, broadsheet, 175,000+

SUNDAY ARTS

underCURRENT

overVIEW

A new height of sophistication

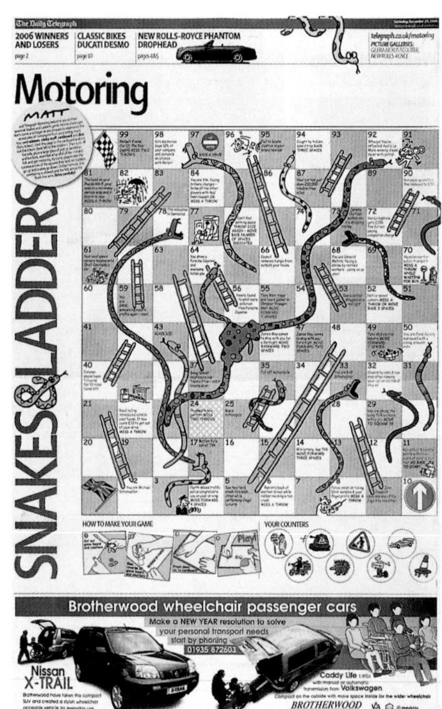

The Daily Telegraph

2006 WINNERS AND LOSERS | CLASSIC BIKES DUCATI DESMO | NEW ROLLS-ROYCE PHANTOM DROPHEAD

Motoring

SNAKES & LADDERS

HOW TO MAKE YOUR GAME

YOUR COUNTERS

Brotherwood wheelchair passenger cars

Make a NEW YEAR resolution to solve your personal transport needs

Nissan X-TRAIL

Caddy Life

BROTHERWOOD

**THE DAILY TELEGRAPH,** London

Staff

Other feature page, broadsheet, 175,000+

自由時報

足球熱

**LIBERTY TIMES,** Taipei, Taiwan

Sung Hsin-Hong

Other feature page, broadsheet, 175,000+

KÜRSÜ

KÜÇÜK VESİLELER AFFA KAPI AÇABİLİR

HEY GİDİ GÜNLER HOCAEFENDİ İLE TANIŞMAMI SAĞLAYAN HACI KEMAL ABİYDİ

Şuuraltıyla ölür şuuraltıyla diriliriz

**ZAMAN,** Yenibosna, Turkey

Ekrem Dumanli, Fevzi Yazici, Mustafa Saglam, Osman Turhan, Murat Akkus, Süleyman Sargin

Other feature page, broadsheet, 175,000+

**LA PRESSE,** Montréal
Yanick Nolet, Benoit Giguere, Genevieve Dinel, Michel Marois, Mathilde Monterosso
Other feature page, broadsheet, 175,000+

**THE SAN DIEGO UNION-TRIBUNE**
Chris Barber, Cristina Martinez Byvik, Michael Price, Michael James Rocha
Other feature page, broadsheet, 175,000+

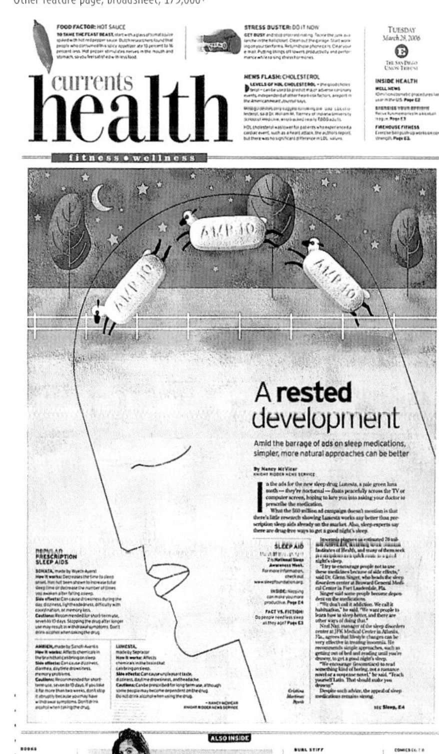

**THE BOSTON GLOBE**
Chin Wang, Lane Turner, Essdras M. Suarez, Ann Scales, Dan Zedek
Other feature page, broadsheet, 175,000+

**THE BOSTON GLOBE**
Chin Wang, LULU☆, Lane Turner, Ann Scales, Dan Zedek
Other feature page, broadsheet, 175,000+

**THE BOSTON GLOBE**
Chin Wang, Scott Menchin, Ann Scales, Dan Zedek
Other feature page, broadsheet, 175,000+

**SONNTAGSZEITUNG**, Zürich, Switzerland
Stefan Semrau
Other feature page, broadsheet, 175,000+

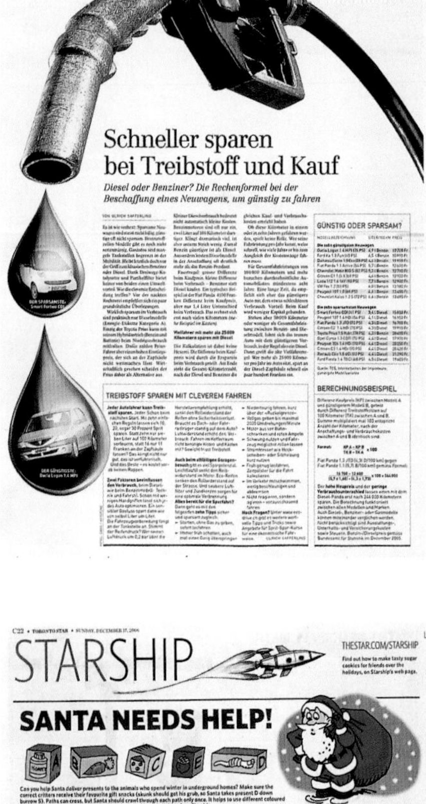
90 AUTO

# Schneller sparen bei Treibstoff und Kauf

*Diesel oder Benziner? Die Rechenformel bei der Beschaffung eines Neuwagens, um günstig zu fahren*

GÜNSTIG ODER SPARSAM?

TREIBSTOFF SPAREN MIT CLEVEREM FAHREN

BERECHNUNGSBEISPIEL

**NATIONAL POST**, Toronto
Doug Kelly, Gayle Grin, Ben Errett, Geneviève Biloski
Other feature page, broadsheet, 175,000+

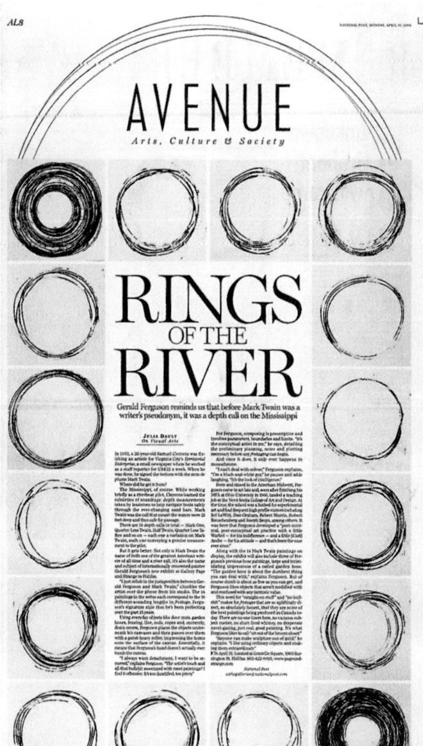
AL8

# AVENUE

*Arts, Culture & Society*

# RINGS OF THE RIVER

Gerald Ferguson reminds us that before Mark Twain was a writer's pseudonym, it was a depth call on the Mississippi

**NATIONAL POST**, Toronto
Doug Kelly, Gayle Grin, Ben Errett
Other feature page, broadsheet, 175,000+

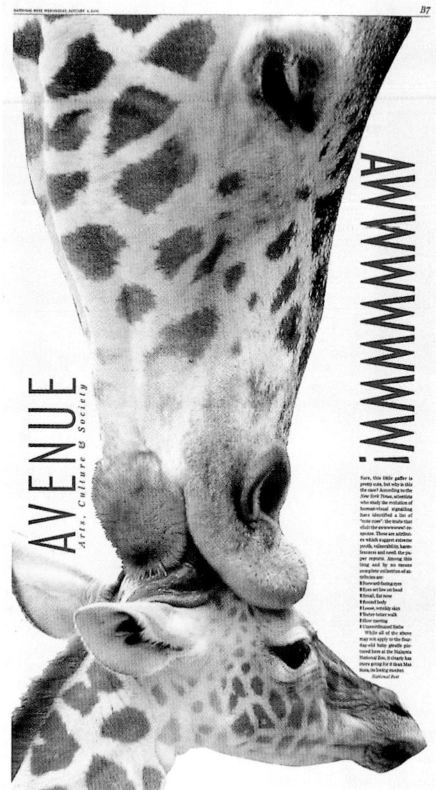
B7

AVENUE

*Arts, Culture & Society*

# AWWWWWWWW!

C22

# STARSHIP

THESTAR.COM/STARSHIP

## SANTA NEEDS HELP!

CLICK PICKS

Hanukkah, Kwanzaa and Christmas are festivals for lighting up the holidays

**TORONTO STAR**
John Robinson, Susan Grimbly, Tak
Other feature page, broadsheet, 175,000+

B7

# AVENUE

*Arts, Culture & Swine*

# ...AND THIS LITTLE PIGGY GLOWS GREEN

**NATIONAL POST**, Toronto
Doug Kelly, Gayle Grin, Ben Errett
Other feature page, broadsheet, 175,000+

B14

# AVENUE

Did His Holiness really write a sassy guide to modern fashion?

Or is that Lemony Snicket hiding under those papal vestments?

**NATIONAL POST**, Toronto
Doug Kelly, Gayle Grin, Ben Errett, Geneviève Biloski
Other feature page, broadsheet, 175,000+

**LA REPUBBLICA,** Rome

Angelo Rinaldi, Silvia Rossi, Stefano Cipolla, Isabella Maoloni

Other feature page, tabloid, 175,000+

**ZAMAN,** Yenibosna, Turkey

Ekrem Dumanli, Fevzi Yazici, Mustafa Saglam, Osman Turhan, Murat Akkus, Süleyman Sargin

Other feature page, broadsheet, 175,000+

**LA PRESSE,** Montréal

Kevin Masse, Benoit Giguere, Genevieve Dinel, Michel Marios, Jade Berube

Other feature page, broadsheet, 175,000+

**ST. PETERSBURG TIMES** (Fla.)

Joshua Engleman, Mike Wilson, Nikki Life

Other feature page, broadsheet, 175,000+

**LA PRESSE,** Montréal

Yanick Nolet, Benoit Giguere, Genevieve Dinel, Michel Marois, Jade Berube

Other feature page, broadsheet, 175,000+

LA PRESSE MONTRÉAL DIMANCHE 28 MAI 2006 7

OUPS DOSSIER

COMMENT TROUVER VOTRE PREMIER EMPLOI D'ÉTÉ

VOTRE PHOTO ICI

Frédéric Fortin, conseiller à l'emploi dans un Carrefour jeunesse-emploi (CJE), répond à nos questions.

**THE VIRGINIAN-PILOT,** Norfolk

Lori Kelley, Toni Guagenti, Paul Nelson, Deborah Withey

Other feature page, broadsheet, 175,000+

WHAT DO YOU HAVE TO SAY?

TEENS COVER THE CODE 757

AFTER THE ATTACKS I WAS ALWAYS AFRAID I WAS TERRIFIED I WAS IN SHOCK I FELT SCARED

I WAS AFRAID THAT I WOULD DIE YOUNG BEFORE THAT DAY I KNEW NOTHING ABOUT TERRORISM I'LL NEVER FORGET THIS WA CATASTROPH IT WAS SCA

GROWING UP WITH SEPT. 11

**CORPUS CHRISTI CALLER-TIMES** (Texas)

Patrick Birmingham, Libby Averyt, Shane Fitzgerald, Jorge Vidrio, Joel Gonzalez

Other feature page, broadsheet, 50,000-174,999

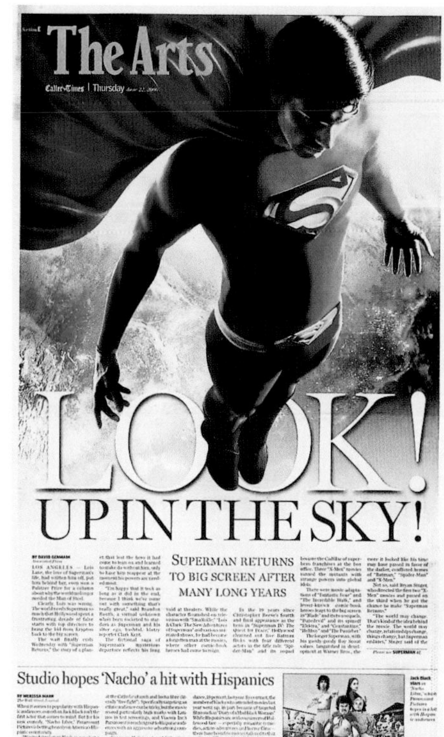

The Arts

Caller-Times | Thursday

LOOK! UP IN THE SKY!

SUPERMAN RETURNS TO BIG SCREEN AFTER MANY LONG YEARS

Studio hopes 'Nacho' a hit with Hispanics

POLITIKEN

PS

Per tabte kampen mod overlægerne

**POLITIKEN,** Copenhagen, Denmark

Søren Nyeland, Mai-Britt Bernt Jensen, Bo Søndergaard

Other feature page, broadsheet, 50,000-174,999

LA GACETA

ACTUALIDAD

Fumar es un placer. Genial, sensual. Adormecida, tendida. Para la amante que el tango recitó, fumar es un edén. Ignora los efectos devastadores del tabaco sobre la salud. Los personajes del arte, la literatura y la publicidad son los únicos que no languidecen tras humo del cigarro. Pero, el tiempo para el consumo de tabaco en lugares públicos se acaba. A partir del 1 de julio entrará en rigor la ley contra el tabaquismo. ¿Cómo dejar de fumar aprovechando la norma? Los especialistas dicen que el proceso comienza fijando una fecha concreta. Intentar dejarlo de manera progresiva, fumando cada día un poco menos, no suele funcionar. En este Suplemento, se brindan consejos para abandonar el vicio

Fumando espero, al hombre que yo quiero...

Fumando espero

Páginas 2, 3 y 5

¿Te has preguntado últimamente a quién le confías tu salud y la de tu familia?

InterSalud

**LA GACETA,** San Miguel de Tucuman, Argentina

Daniel Fontanarrosa, Sergio Fernandez

Other feature page, broadsheet, 50,000-174,999

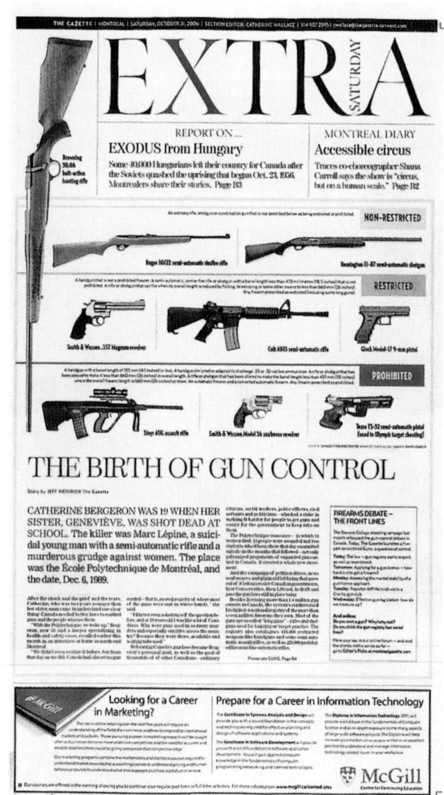

EXTRA SATURDAY

REPORT ON... EXODUS from Hungary

MONTREAL DIARY Accessible circus

NON-RESTRICTED

RESTRICTED

PROHIBITED

THE BIRTH OF GUN CONTROL

CATHERINE BERGERON WAS 19 WHEN HER SISTER, GENEVIÈVE, WAS SHOT DEAD AT SCHOOL. The killer was Marc Lépine, a suicidal young man with a semi-automatic rifle and a murderous grudge against women. The place was the École Polytechnique de Montréal, and the date, Dec. 6, 1989.

FIREARMS DEBATE – THE FRONT LINES

Looking for a Career in Marketing?

Prepare for a Career in Information Technology

McGill

**THE GAZETTE,** Montreal

Dawn Lemieux, Nuri Ducassi, Marilyn Mill

Other feature page, broadsheet, 50,000-174,999

**THE ATLANTA JOURNAL-CONSTITUTION**
Will Alford
Other feature page, broadsheet, 175,000+

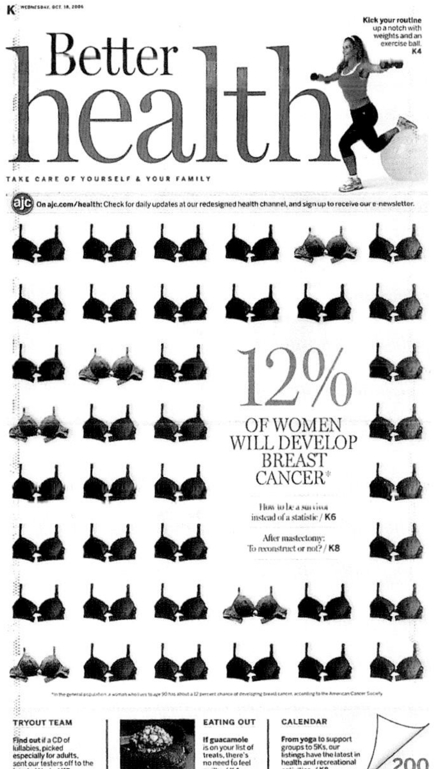
K

Kick your routine up a notch with weights and an exercise ball. K4

# Better health

TAKE CARE OF YOURSELF & YOUR FAMILY

ajc On ajc.com/health: Check for daily updates at our redesigned health channel, and sign up to receive our e-newsletter.

12% OF WOMEN WILL DEVELOP BREAST CANCER*

How to be a survivor instead of a statistic / K6

After mastectomy: To reconstruct or not? / K8

TRYOUT TEAM
Find out if a CD of lullabies, picked especially for adults, sent our testers off to the Land of Nod. / K3

EATING OUT
If guacamole is on your list of treats, there's no need to feel guilty. / K4

CALENDAR
From yoga to support groups to 5Ks, our listings have the latest in health and recreational activities. / K8

200

**LIBERTY TIMES,** Taipei, Taiwan
Sung Hsin-Hong
Other feature page, broadsheet, 175,000+

自由時報

兒子絕不是筆下的人物

手機遺忘錄

可愛的衣服

駭人怪物死了以後？

男身女相

**LIBERTY TIMES,** Taipei, Taiwan
Sung Hsin-Hong
Other feature page, broadsheet, 175,000+

自由時報

蛇

名牌仿冒店

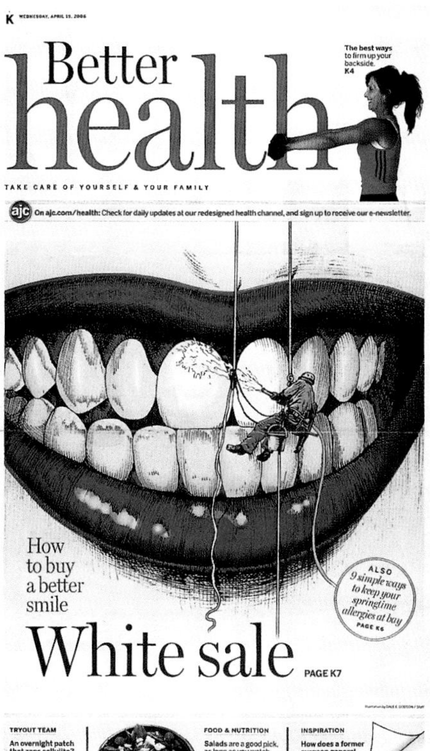
K

The best ways to firm up your backside. K4

# Better health

TAKE CARE OF YOURSELF & YOUR FAMILY

ajc On ajc.com/health: Check for daily updates at our redesigned health channel, and sign up to receive our e-newsletter.

How to buy a better smile

ALSO 9 simple ways to keep your springtime allergies at bay PAGE K4

White sale PAGE K7

TRYOUT TEAM
An overnight patch that zaps cellulite? Our intrepid testers are firm in their assessments. / K3

FOOD & NUTRITION
Salads are a good pick, as long as you watch the toppings and dressing, says dietitian Carolyn O'Neil. / K4-5

INSPIRATION
How does a former surgeon general relax, beat stress and stay fit, body and soul? / K9

115

**THE ATLANTA JOURNAL-CONSTITUTION**
Will Alford, Dale E. Dodson
Other feature page, broadsheet, 175,000+

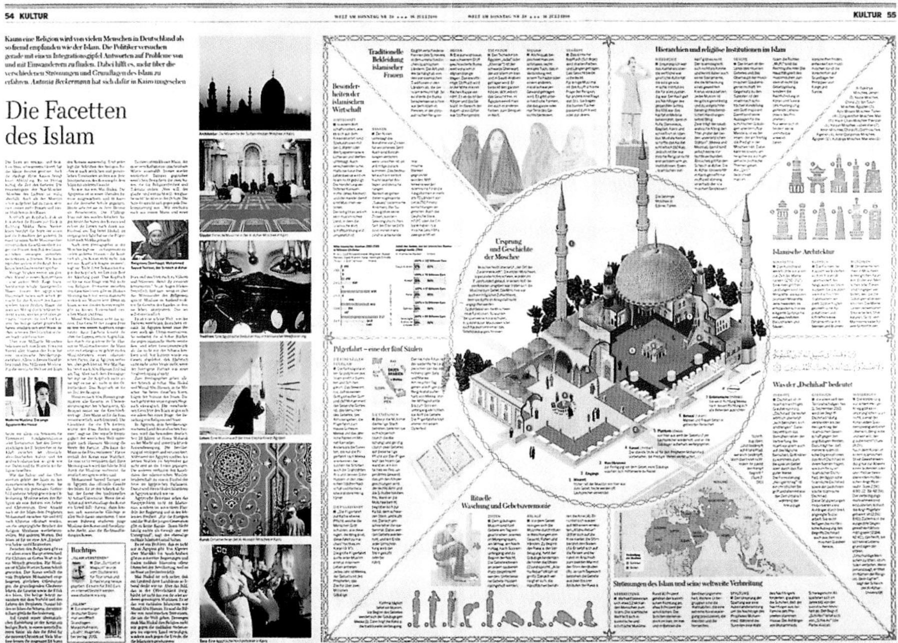
54 KULTUR

KULTUR 55

Die Facetten des Islam

Traditionelle Bekleidung islamischer Frauen

Hierarchien und religiöse Institutionen im Islam

Ursprung und Geschichte der Moschee

Islamische Architektur

Pilgerfahrt – eine der fünf Säulen

Rituelle Waschung und Gebetszeremonie

Was der „Dschihad" bedeutet

Strömungen des Islam und seine weltweite Verbreitung

**WELT AM SONNTAG,** Berlin
Jördis Guzmán Bulla, Silke Meyer
Other feature page, broadsheet, 175,000+

**EXCELSIOR,** México City

Paola Rodríguez Hernández, Iván Ventura Cancio, Ernesto Alcántara, Luzma Díaz de León Reyes, Marco A. Román, Alexandro Medrano, Gerardo Galarza, Pascal Beltrán del Río, Ernesto Rivera

Other feature page, broadsheet, 50,000-174,999

# El doctor que nunca perdió a un paciente

Irving Chais ha dedicado toda su vida a restaurar muñecos antiguos en su Hospital de Manhattan

**CORPUS CHRISTI CALLER-TIMES** (Texas)

Patrick Birmingham, Libby Averyt, Shane Fitzgerald, Jorge Vidrio, Lauren Ruffner

Other feature page, broadsheet, 50,000-174,999

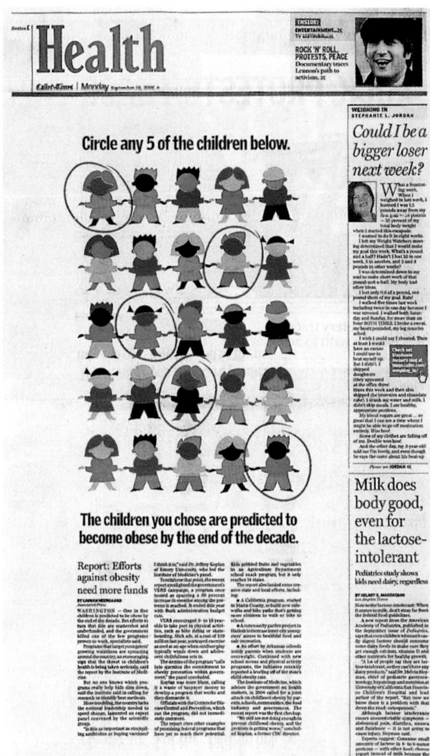

# Health

Circle any 5 of the children below.

The children you chose are predicted to become obese by the end of the decade.

Report: Efforts against obesity need more funds

Could I be a bigger loser next week?

Milk does body good, even for the lactose-intolerant

**LA GACETA,** San Miguel de Tucuman, Argentina

Daniel Fontanarrosa, Sergio Fernandez

Other feature page, broadsheet, 50,000-174,999

LA GACETA

ACTUALIDAD 5

# El lado oscuro de la noche

Páginas 2, 3, 4, 5 y 6

LA GACETA

ACTUALIDAD

# Fábrica de angustias

Páginas 2, 3 y 5

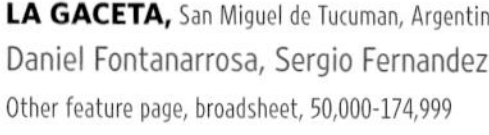

Te damos más ... que una mano

InterSalud

Cobertura real con acceso a red de prestadores a tu elección

**LA GACETA,** San Miguel de Tucuman, Argentina

Daniel Fontanarrosa, Sergio Fernandez

Other feature page, broadsheet, 50,000-174,999

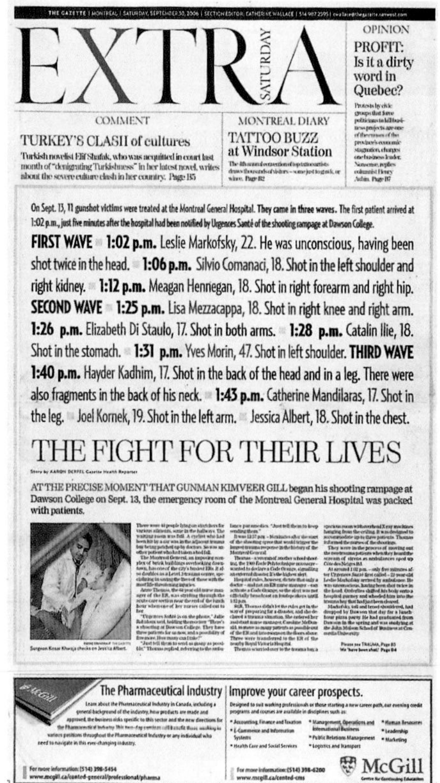

# EXTRA

SATURDAY

OPINION

PROFIT: Is it a dirty word in Quebec?

COMMENT

TURKEY'S CLASH of cultures

MONTREAL DIARY

TATTOO BUZZ at Windsor Station

On Sept. 13, 11 gunshot victims were treated at the Montreal General Hospital. They came in three waves. The first patient arrived at 1:02 p.m., just five minutes after the hospital had been notified by Urgences Santé of the shooting rampage at Dawson College.

**FIRST WAVE** 1:02 p.m. Leslie Markofsky, 22. He was unconscious, having been shot twice in the head. 1:06 p.m. Silvio Comanaci, 18. Shot in the left shoulder and right kidney. 1:12 p.m. Meagan Hennegan, 18. Shot in right forearm and right hip. **SECOND WAVE** 1:25 p.m. Lisa Mezzacappa, 18. Shot in right knee and right arm. 1:26 p.m. Elizabeth Di Staulo, 17. Shot in both arms. 1:28 p.m. Catalin Ilie, 18. Shot in the stomach. 1:31 p.m. Yves Morin, 47. Shot in left shoulder. **THIRD WAVE** 1:40 p.m. Hayder Kadhim, 17. Shot in the back of the head and in a leg. There were also fragments in the back of his neck. 1:43 p.m. Catherine Mandilaras, 17. Shot in the leg. Joel Kornek, 19. Shot in the left arm. Jessica Albert, 18. Shot in the chest.

## THE FIGHT FOR THEIR LIVES

AT THE PRECISE MOMENT THAT GUNMAN KIMVEER GILL began his shooting rampage at Dawson College on Sept. 13, the emergency room of the Montreal General Hospital was packed with patients.

The Pharmaceutical Industry | Improve your career prospects.

McGill

**THE GAZETTE,** Montreal

Dawn Lemieux, Nuri Ducassi, Marilyn Mill

Other feature page, broadsheet, 50,000-174,999

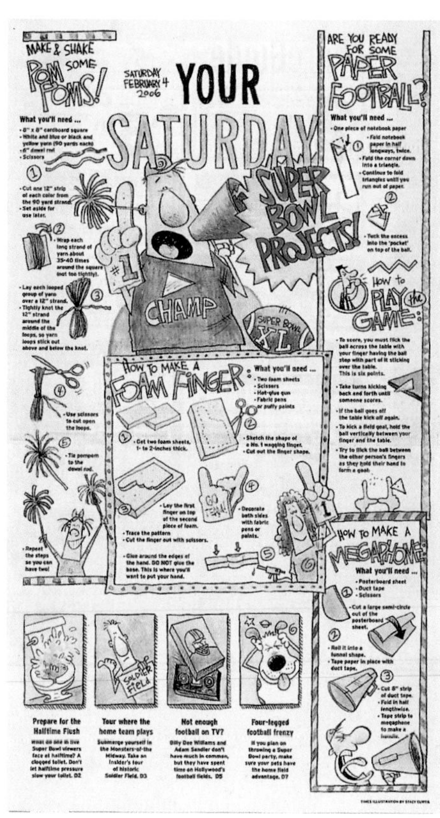



**THE TIMES OF NORTHWEST INDIANA,** Munster

Stacy Curtis, Bill Thornbro, Karin Saltanovitz, David Windisch

Other feature page, broadsheet, 50,000-174,999

**THE GAZETTE,** Montreal
Dawn Lemieux, Nuri Ducassi, Marilyn Mill
Other feature page, broadsheet, 50,000-174,999

EXTRA SATURDAY

COMMENT
EUTHANASIA. Mercy vs. murder

MONTREAL DIARY
ROUGH SKATING: roller derby revival

REPORT ON ...
HOW COOL – a cigarette!

NO

NO SMOKING. NO JAYWALKING. NO FUN?

THE BIG BUTT-OUT
COUNTDOWN TO MAY 31

Does a career in translation interest you?

Improve your career prospects.

McGill

**ESTADO DE MINAS,** Belo Horizonte, Brazil
Ed Rodrigues, Alexandre Péres
Other feature page, broadsheet, 50,000-174,999

CLASSIFICADOS

EMPREGO
ESTADO DE MINAS

Convivência pode ser harmoniosa se a empresa souber mesclar profissionais jovens e experientes

Diversidade nas organizações

**LA GACETA,** San Miguel de Tucuman, Argentina
Daniel Fontanarrosa, Sergio Fernandez
Other feature page, broadsheet, 50,000-174,999

LA GACETA
ACTUALIDAD

ruido

PÁGINAS 2, 3 Y 5

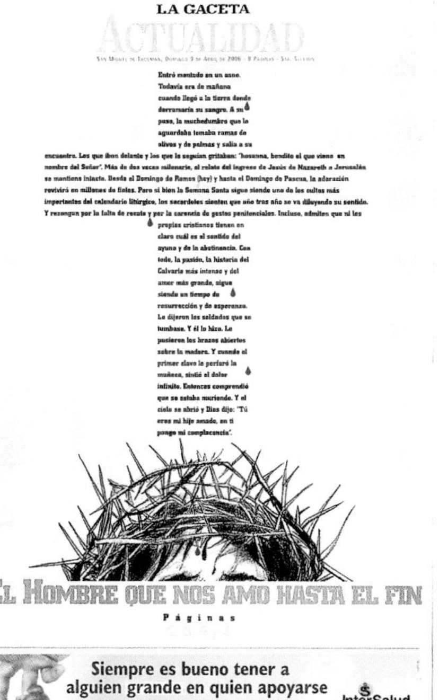

LA GACETA
ACTUALIDAD

EL HOMBRE QUE NOS AMÓ HASTA EL FIN

Páginas

Siempre es bueno tener a alguien grande en quien apoyarse

InterSalud

**LA GACETA,** San Miguel de Tucuman, Argentina
Daniel Fontanarrosa, Sergio Fernandez
Other feature page, broadsheet, 50,000-174,999

12: ponte cómodo

LA VIDA EN UN SILLÓN

¿TELEVISIÓN POR CABLE?

A menos de una semana de que arranque el Mundial, tu sensei te dice por qué contratar cable

GLOSARIO DE TÉRMINOS

La próxima semana, El Rollas te dará los secretos para disfrutar tu primer Mundial desde el sillón

**EXCELSIOR,** México City
Horacio Trejo Rivera, Ernesto Alcántara, Salomón Ramírez, Luis López, Luzma Díaz de León Reyes, Marco A. Román, Alexandro Medrano, Ma. Luisa Díaz de León, Pascal Beltrán del Río, Ernesto Rivera
Other feature page, broadsheet, 50,000-174,999

AGENDA

Rostendes Gold

Russisches Geld

Macht nix

**FINANCIAL TIMES DEUTSCHLAND,** Hamburg, Germany
Staff
Other feature page, broadsheet, 50,000-174,999

**THE GAZETTE,** Montreal
Dawn Lemieux, Nuri Ducassi, Peter Cooney
Other feature page, broadsheet, 50,000-174,999

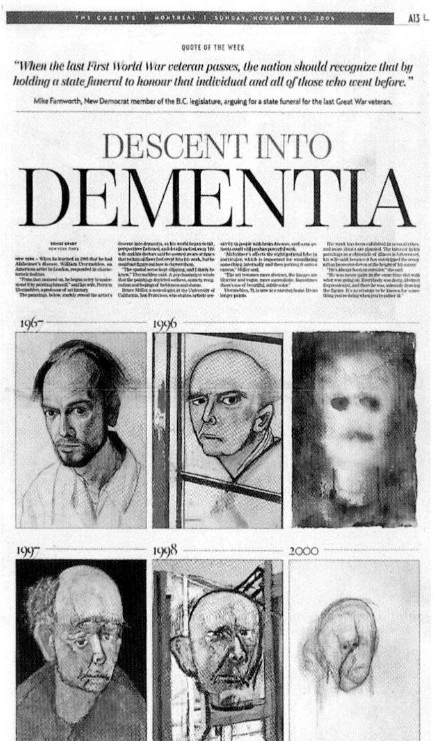

THE GAZETTE | MONTREAL | SUNDAY, NOVEMBER 12, 2006 A13

QUOTE OF THE WEEK

*"When the last First World War veteran passes, the nation should recognize that by holding a state funeral to honour that individual and all of those who went before."*

Mike Farnworth, New Democrat member of the B.C. legislature, arguing for a state funeral for the last Great War veteran.

DESCENT INTO
DEMENTIA

1967 — 1996

1997 — 1998 — 2000

**THE OTTAWA CITIZEN**
Paula McLaughlin, Carl Neustaedter, Susan Allan, Susan McDonough, Scott Anderson
Other feature page, broadsheet, 50,000-174,999

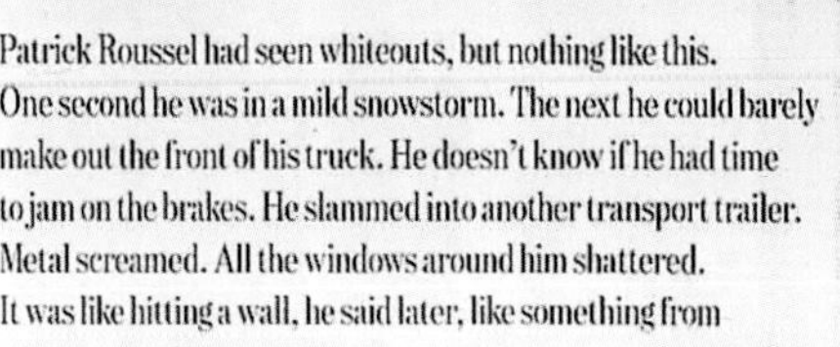

Patrick Roussel had seen whiteouts, but nothing like this. One second he was in a mild snowstorm. The next he could barely make out the front of his truck. He doesn't know if he had time to jam on the brakes. He slammed into another transport trailer. Metal screamed. All the windows around him shattered. It was like hitting a wall, he said later, like something from

Mad Max – only in winter

ALAIN LAPENSÉE

PHIL ROY

PATRICK ROUSSEL

STEVE HALL

MATHIEU CHARLEBOIS

PATRICK DUSSAULT

Health

Caller-Times | Monday July 10, 2006

COMFORTABLE WITH LESS SKIN

DON'T SWEAT THE SMALL STUFF
RICHARD CARLSON

*Bad mood? Recognize it, then let it be; time cures it*

Living in
solitude

AS SOCIAL CIRCLES SHRINK, MANY SAY THEY HAVE NO ONE TO TURN TO IN TIME OF NEED

New lens implant can replace glasses

Multifocals correct close and distant vision problems

**CORPUS CHRISTI CALLER-TIMES** (Texas)
Patrick Birmingham, Libby Averyt, Shane Fitzgerald, Jorge Vidrio, Lauren Ruffner
Other feature page, broadsheet, 50,000-174,999

S!

Clarín

IGGY

LA GRAN BESTIA

EXCLUSIVO, DESPUÉS DE DIEZ AÑOS Y AL FRENTE DE LOS LEGENDARIOS THE STOOGES, VUELVE A BUENOS AIRES COMO ESTRELLA INVITADA DEL PEPSI MUSIC. VIDA Y OBRAS DE UN SOBREVIVIENTE.

POP

POSTER DESPLEGABLE + ENTREVISTA TOTAL AL PADRINO DEL PUNK

**CLARÍN,** Buenos Aires, Argentina
Gustavo Lo Valvo, Carlos Vázquez, Mariana Zerman
Other feature page, tabloid, 175,000+

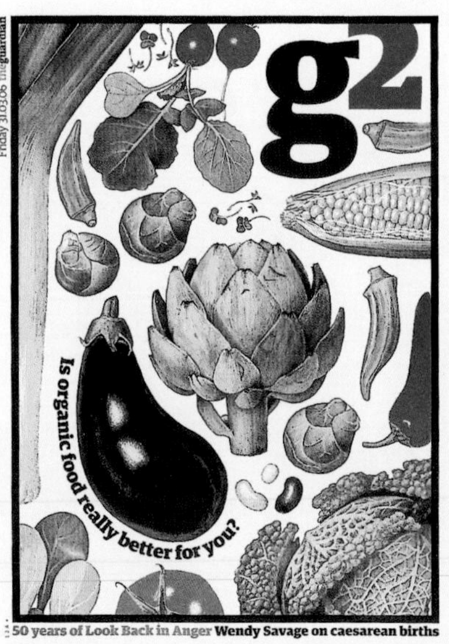

g2

Friday 31.03.06 theguardian

Is organic food really better for you?

50 years of Look Back in Anger Wendy Savage on caesarean births

**THE GUARDIAN,** London
Richard Turley
Other feature page, tabloid, 175,000+

reportage

Döden undgår ingen. Det kan vi vara helt säkra på. Men det är egentligen också det enda. Det mesta som rör livets slut har vi bara en vag, dimmig uppfattning om. Ändå talar många av oss inte gärna om döden.

# SLUTET

DET ÄR MITT I VECKAN och ugnarna på krematoriet har kommit upp i ordentlig arbetstemperatur. Allra bäst går de i slutet av veckan; genomvarm utrustning innebär kortare kremeringstid och lägre bränsleåtgång. Måndag morgon är det tvärtom efter att ugnarna hunnit svalna helt under helgen.

Lyckligtvis sammanfaller denna praktiska detalj med att antalet kremeringar är som störst i slutet av veckan, eftersom många anhöriga vill arrangera med begravning i anslutning till helgen.

Richard Watson kör fram kistan till ugnen. Luckan öppnas automatiskt och han ställer försiktigt ned kistan på hällen därinne. Sedan går han runt på baksidan för att övervaka kremeringen.

På bänken står dagens urnor uppställda i väntan på att respektive kremering ska bli klar. Några är enkla plastbehållare, andra är snidade träurnor med graverade metallplattor. Innehållet är det däremot ingen skillnad på. I döden är det inte mycket som skiljer oss åt.

– Nej, den ena askan är den andra lik. Men vi använder id-plattor i keramik som följer med kroppen från det att den anländer hit till dess att vi lämnar ut urnan. Vi förväxlar ingen här, det kan jag garantera, säger han.

Invändigt är krematoriet på Kvibergs kyrkogård ljust och luftigt. Det ombyggda gamla kapellet har högt i tak och stenväggar och stengolv skapar ett lätt eko när man pratar. Men rummets centralgestalter, de stora, stålgrå ugnarna, hörs inte. De är väl isolerade och arbetar på i tysthet.

Några obehagliga lukter går inte att urskilja. Ingen liklukt i vare sig kremeringsrummet eller lagerutrymmet. Någon enskild gång kan man ana det, berättar Richard, men då är det för att

4 två dagar

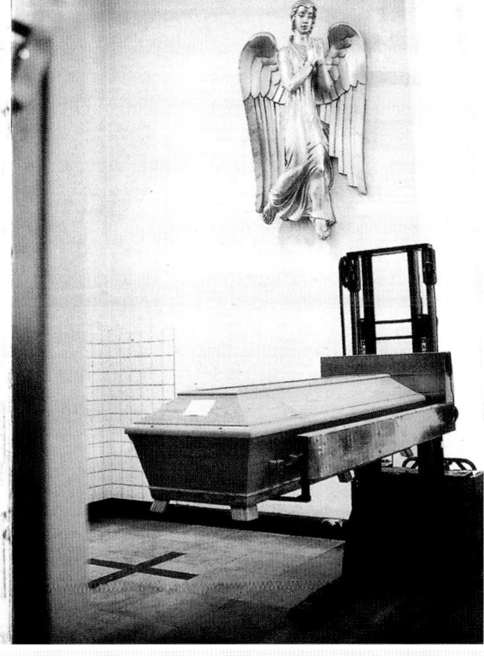

SILVER

**GÖTEBORGS-POSTEN,** Goteborg, Sweden

Albert Rosander, Adam Haglund

Other feature page, tabloid, 175,000+

Both sad and beautiful, these pages offer a sense of rhythm, and there are many lovely details, such as the text building a cross.

Tristes y bellas a la vez, estas páginas entregan un sentido de ritmo. Hay muchos detalles atractivos, como el texto que forma una cruz.

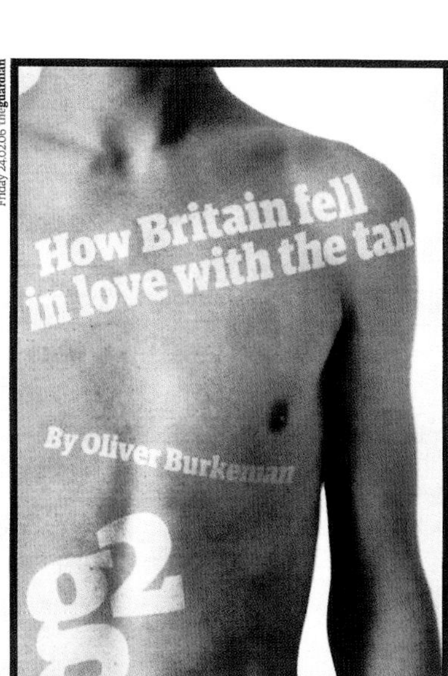


**THE GUARDIAN,** London

Richard Turley

Other feature page, tabloid, 175,000+

**CLARÍN,** Buenos Aires, Argentina

Gustavo Lo Valvo, Carlos Vázquez, Mariana Zerman

Other feature page, tabloid, 175,000+

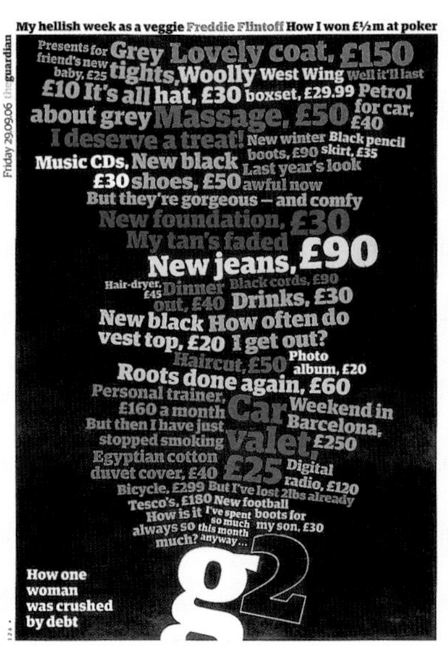


**THE GUARDIAN,** London

Richard Turley

Other feature page, tabloid, 175,000+

**SVENSKA DAGBLADET,** Stockholm, Sweden
Lena K. Samuelsson, Mats-Eric Nilsson, Anna W. Thurfjell, Knut Brunnberg, Martin Jönsson, Gunvor Frykholm, Kalle Kallström
Other feature page, tabloid, 175,000+

5,6 %

21 %

Vem räknar rätt?

**CLARÍN,** Buenos Aires, Argentina
Gustavo Lo Valvo, Carlos Vázquez, Mariana Zerman
Other feature page, tabloid, 175,000+

SI

POSTER DESPLEGABLE + ENTREVISTA TOTAL

ARBOL

QUE SE VENGAN LOS CHICOS

EL CREDITO DE HAEDO ES EL FUROR DE UN ROCK QUE YA NO RECONOCE LIMITES DE EDAD. A SOLAS CON EL SR, CUENTAN SU SECRETO: "HOMENAJE Y SACRILEGIO".

"Es muy difícil ser distinta al 95% de la gente"

**CLARÍN,** Buenos Aires, Argentina
Gustavo Lo Valvo, Carlos Vázquez, Mariana Zerman
Other feature page, tabloid, 175,000+

Rättvisa på väg?

**SVENSKA DAGBLADET,** Stockholm, Sweden
Lena K. Samuelsson, Mats-Eric Nilsson, Anna W. Thurfjell, Knut Brunnberg, Martin Jönsson, Gunvor Frykholm, Stefan Gustavson, Frida Hedberg
Other feature page, tabloid, 175,000+

tvådagar

10 JUNI 2006

GODASTE GRILLEN

Dags att lägga på ett kol, eller snarare briketter. Grillsäsongen är här. För att hjälpa er har vi laddat med recept och goda råd. Dessutom har vi gått på grillkurs hos en riktig expert.

Göteborgs-Posten

**GÖTEBORGS-POSTEN,** Goteborg, Sweden
Roger Olsson
Other feature page, tabloid, 175,000+

Ett lyft miljonprojekt

**SVENSKA DAGBLADET,** Stockholm, Sweden
Lena K. Samuelsson, Mats-Eric Nilsson, Anna W. Thurfjell, Asa Lempert, Anna Julius, Joakim Stahl, Karin Malvhav
Other feature page, tabloid, 175,000+

**LA REPUBBLICA,** Rome
Angelo Rinaldi, Silvia Rossi, Stefano Cipolla, Isabella Maoloni
Other feature page, tabloid, 175,000+

SPETTACOLI

Lucio Battisti

L'avventura del dopo-Mogol

**GÖTEBORGS-POSTEN,** Goteborg, Sweden
Staff
Other feature page, tabloid, 175,000+

Göteborgs-Posten

MÅNDAG 4 DECEMBER 2006

3

Kultur · Gränslöst
Nöje · TV · Guiden
Världens gång

kultur
DE SOM BORDE FÅ AUGUST-PRISET ...

gränslöst
... OCH MÄNNEN SOM FÅR DET

nöje
STURE ALLÉN VILL INTE VARA ETT DANSBAND

världens gång
950 KRONOR FÖR EN ETTA

nöje
FREJA
Kjellberg Borchies om livet efter Top Model

Utropstecknet är osnyggt. Billigt. Dålig reklam. På 50-talet tog punkten över. En VW-annons bröt marken. Hur gick det sen?

reportage

# HJUL-STRUL
## I STORSTADEN

■■ Kullerstenar, höga trottoarkanter, rullstolsförbud på viss kollektivtrafik, trappor och höga trösklar till förbanneise. Göteborg är en handikappad stad.
■■ Två Dagar satte reportern Fredric Askerup i en rullstol under en helt vanlig dag för att göra helt vanliga saker och åtminstone försöka se lite positivt på det hela. Läs hans rapport från gatan. ▸

**GÖTEBORGS-POSTEN,** Goteborg, Sweden
Stefan Renstrom, Camilla Iliefski, Jon Olmeskog
Other feature page, tabloid, 175,000+

**THE OBSERVER,** London
Carolyn Roberts
Other feature page, tabloid, 175,000+

22 FOTOPREIS

FOTOPREIS 23

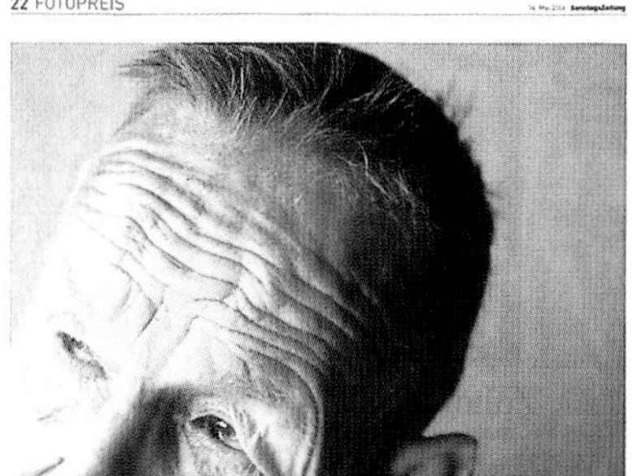

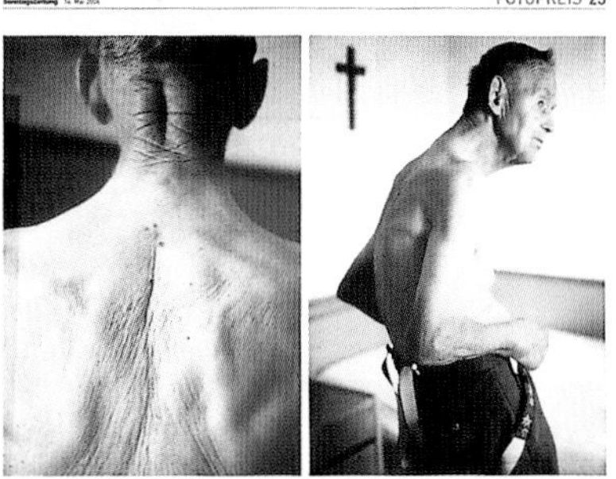

# Ein Knecht in Pension

*Unspektakuläre Annäherung an einen Betagten: Die Bilder von Carmela Odoni sind mit dem Fotopreis der SonntagsZeitung ausgezeichnet worden*

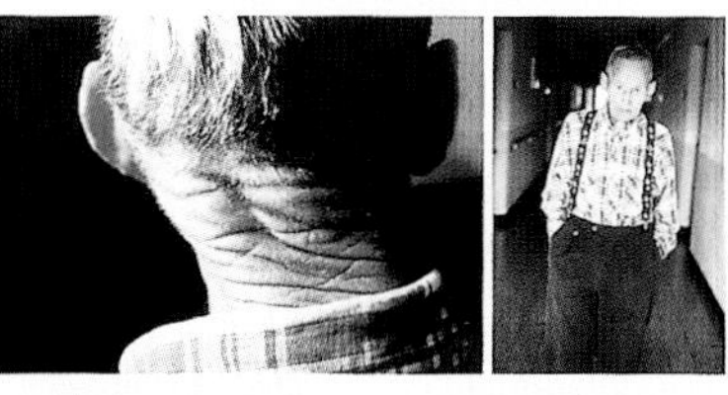

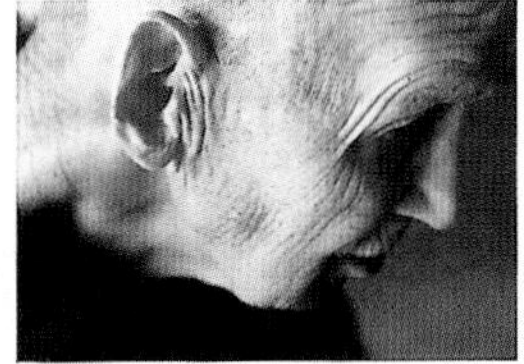

**SONNTAGSZEITUNG,** Zürich, Switzerland
Andrea Müller
Other feature page, tabloid, 175,000+

**CLARÍN,** Buenos Aires, Argentina
Gustavo Lo Valvo, Carlos Vázquez, Mariana Zerman
Other feature page, tabloid, 175,000+

**THE GUARDIAN,** London
Richard Turley, Izabella Bielawska
Other feature page, tabloid, 175,000+

**LA PRENSA GRÁFICA,** Antiguo Cuscatlán, El Salvador
Enrique Contreras, Florence Romero, Giovanni Paniagua, Mauro Arias
Other feature page, tabloid, 50,000-174,999

**THE CHRONICLE OF HIGHER EDUCATION,** Washington
Daphne Sterling
Other feature page, tabloid, 50,000-174,999

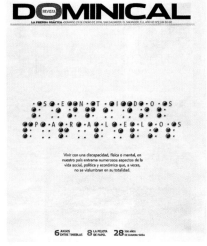

DOMINICAL
REVISTA

Vivir con una discapacidad, física o mental, en nuestro país entrama numerosos aspectos de la vida social, política y económica que, a veces, no se vislumbran en su totalidad.

6 JUEGOS ENTRE TINIEBLAS 8 LA PELOTA DE PAPEL 28

**LA PRENSA GRÁFICA,** Antiguo Cuscatlán, El Salvador
Enrique Contreras, Florence Romero, Francesca Zometa
Other feature page, tabloid, 50,000-174,999

**AAMULEHTI,** Tampere, Finland
Rami Hanafi, Riina Hautala, Ari Kinnari
Other feature page, tabloid, 50,000-174,999

**LA REPUBBLICA,** Rome
Angelo Rinaldi, Silvia Rossi, Stefano Cipolla, Isabella Maoloni
Other feature page, tabloid, 175,000+

**HARTFORD COURANT** (Conn.)
Vada Crosby, Suzette Moyer
Other feature page, tabloid, 175,000+

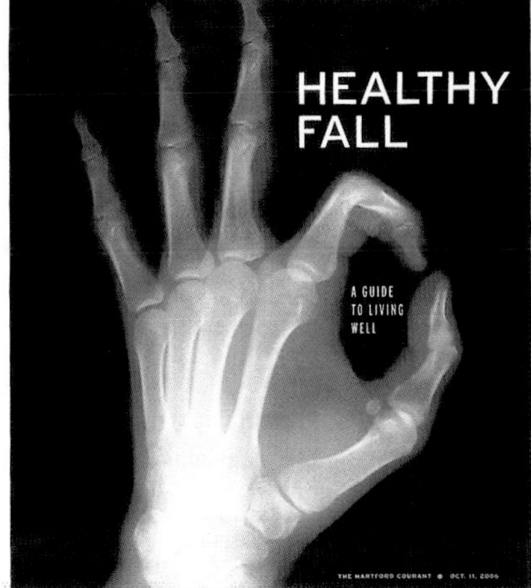


**ALBUQUERQUE JOURNAL** (N.M.)
Jennifer Swanson, Judy Giannettino, Joe Kirby, Leah Derrington, Jim Frost
Other feature page, tabloid, 50,000-174,999

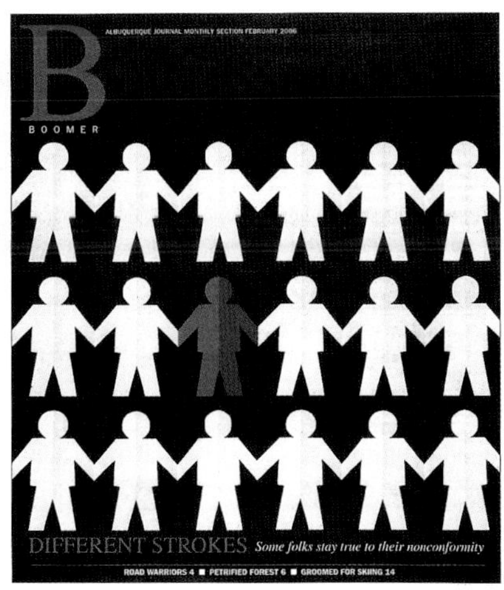


**THE GUARDIAN,** London
Richard Turley
Other feature page, tabloid, 175,000+

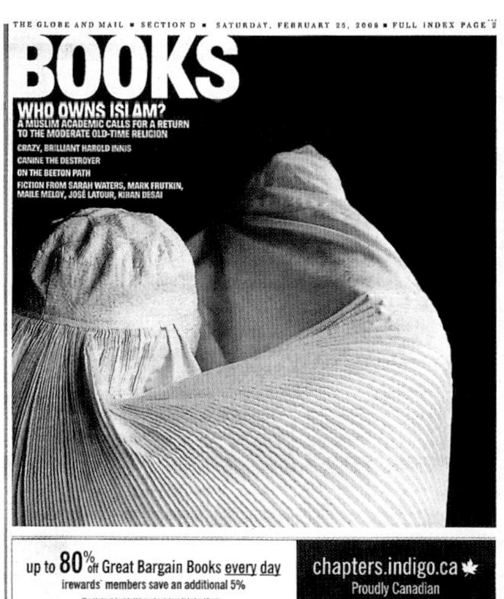


**THE GLOBE AND MAIL,** Toronto
David Woodside, David Pratt, Martin Levin, Patrick Martin, Roger Hallett
Other feature page, tabloid, 175,000+

**DETROIT FREE PRESS**
Rosa E. Castellanos, Mauricio Gutierrez, Steve Dorsey, Sally Tato, Greg Crawford
Other feature page, tabloid, 175,000+

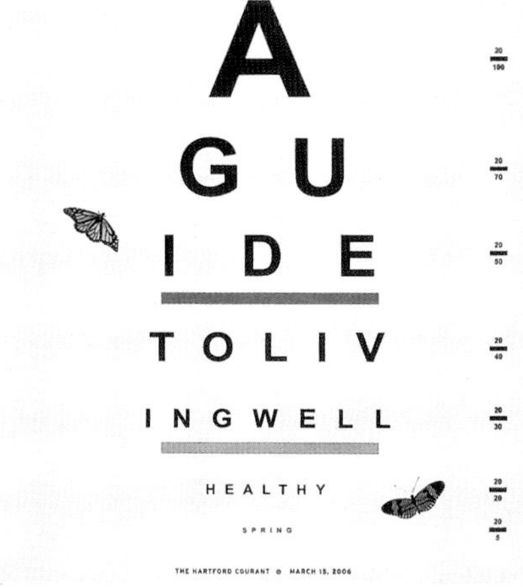


**HARTFORD COURANT** (Conn.)
Vada Crosby, Suzette Moyer
Other feature page, tabloid, 175,000+

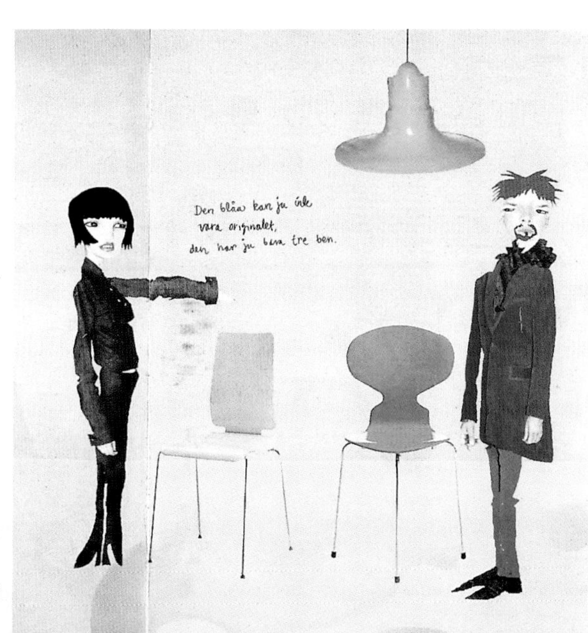

reportage

Den amerikanska gitarrtillverkaren Fender har tagit hand om piratkopiorna genom att själva tillverka dem. Störst vinst lär de göra på de Squire-gitarrer som tillverkas i Kina.

**GÖTEBORGS-POSTEN,** Goteborg, Sweden
Gunilla Wernhamn, Cissi Welin
Other feature page, tabloid, 175,000+

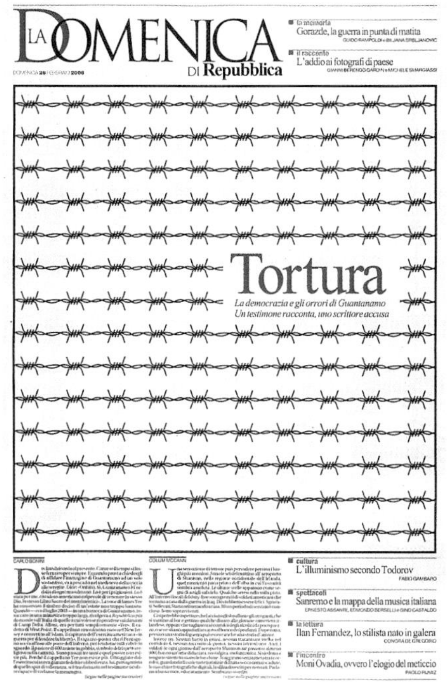


**LA REPUBBLICA,** Rome
Angelo Rinaldi, Silvia Rossi, Stefano Cipolla, Isabella Maoloni
Other feature page, tabloid, 175,000+

**SVENSKA DAGBLADET,** Stockholm, Sweden
Lena K. Samuelsson, Mats-Eric Nilsson, Anna W. Thurfjell, Carl-Johan Bilkenroth, Martin Jönsson, Jan Almgren, Stefan Gustavsson, Björn Larsson Ask
Other feature page, tabloid, 175,000+

**STUTTGARTER ZEITUNG** (Germany)
Stefanie Schönfeld, Heinz Heiss, Achim Wörner, Dirk Steininger
Other feature page, tabloid, 50,000-174,999

**STUTTGARTER ZEITUNG** (Germany)
Stefanie Schönfeld, Heinz Heiss, Achim Wörner, Dirk Steininger
Other feature page, tabloid, 50,000-174,999

**THE CHRONICLE OF HIGHER EDUCATION,** Washington
Daphne Sterling, Steve Brodner
Other feature page, tabloid, 50,000-174,999

**BERGENS TIDENDE,** Bergen, Norway
Arne Edvardsen, Walter Jensen, Roar Christiansen, Arne Størksen, Anneli Solberg, Hilde Sandvik
Other feature page, tabloid, 50,000-174,999

**SVENSKA DAGBLADET,** Stockholm, Sweden
Lena K. Samuelsson, Mats-Eric Nilsson, Anna W. Thurfjell, Elisabeth Mård, Jan Almgren, Staffan Löwstedt, Tomas Oneborg
Other feature page, tabloid, 175,000+

**THE WICHITA EAGLE** (Kan.)
Coryanne Graham
Other feature page, tabloid, 50,000-174,999

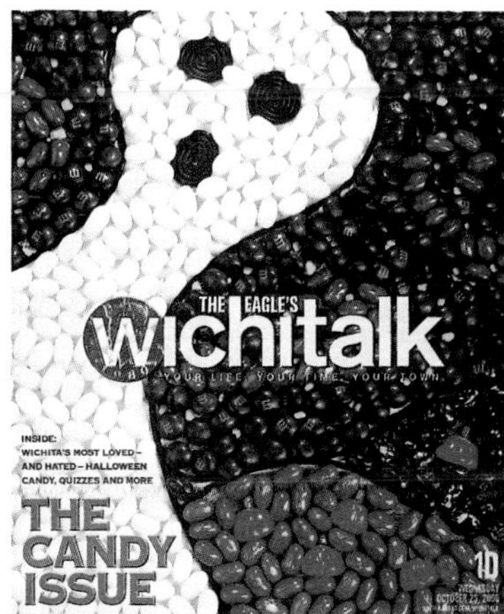


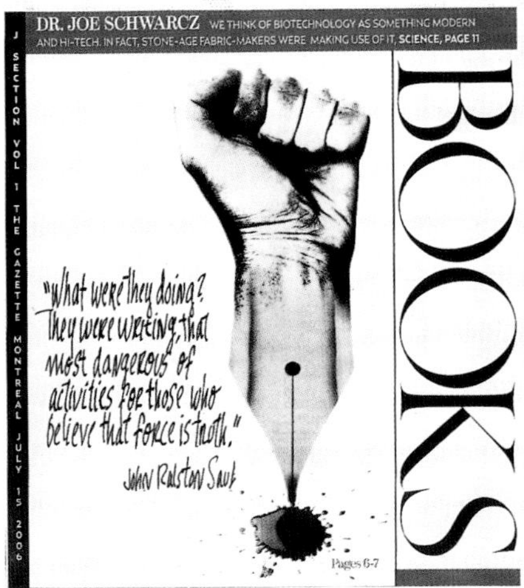


**THE GAZETTE,** Montreal
Nuri Ducassi, Edie Austen
Other feature page, tabloid, 50,000-174,999

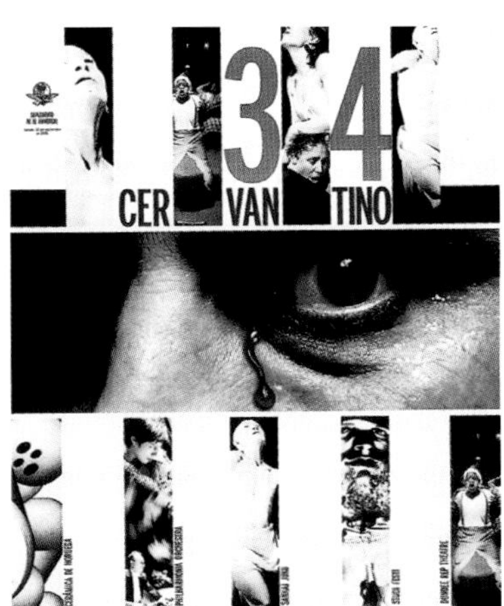


**EL UNIVERSAL,** México City
Roberto Rock L., Francisco Santiago, Oscar Santiago Méndez, Rubén Álvarez, María Elena Matadamas, Nilton Torres Pérez, Amelia González, Victor M. Durán Mejía
Other feature page, tabloid, 50,000-174,999

SILVER

**POLITIKEN,** Copenhagen, Denmark
Søren Nyeland, Nicolai Fontain, Claus Bech-Petersen
Other feature page, tabloid, 50,000-174,999

The publication introduces readers to its new typography by transforming the letter "g" into a friendly face. It gives them something to relate to while giving personality to the type. The character looks like an intellectual. It seems so simple, and it looks effortless.

El periódico presenta su nueva tipografía a los lectores al transformar la letra "g" por una cara amistosa. Les da algo para identificarse con la tipografía a la vez que se le da personalidad. El carácter se ve como un intelectual. Se ve sencillo y no forzado.

FEATURES

MUSIC WHEN JOOLS HOLLAND'S NOT SUPPRESSING REBELLIONS IN KENT, HE'S LISTING THE SERVICE STATIONS HE'S VISITED OR PLAYING BOOGIE-WOOGIE. WHATEVER HAPPENED TO ROCK'N'ROLL? ASKS NIGEL FARNDALE

PORTRAIT BY DAVID SPERO

# A MAN IN TOUCH WITH HIS INNER ANORAK

14 Seven 19 NOVEMBER 2006

**THE SUNDAY TELEGRAPH SEVEN MAGAZINE,** London
David Riley, Alex McFadyen, Nicky Catley
Overall magazine design

medbiz 06
Schwerpunkt
Magazin für Gesundheitswirtschaft
Suche Anschluss
Warum die Vernetzung der deutschen Gesundheitsbranche so langsam vorankommt
Datenbank
Welche Informationen sich aus Krebszellen ablesen lassen
Pharma
Warum Pfizer ein Demenzprojekt mit Krankenkassen startet
Manager
Wer mit Check-ups für Führungskräfte Geld verdient
Karriere
Wie Wolfgang Reim mit Dräger Medical weiter expandiert
FINANCIAL TIMES DEUTSCHLAND



**FINANCIAL TIMES DEUTSCHLAND,** Hamburg, Germany
Staff
Overall magazine design

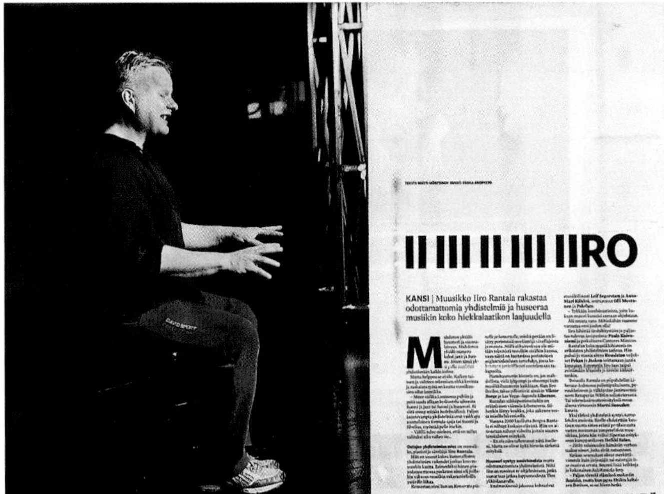

# IIIII II III IIRO

KANSI | Muusikko Iiro Rantala rakastaa odottamattomia yhdistelmiä ja huseeraa musiikin koko hiekkalaatikon laajuudella

**AAMULEHTI,** Tampere, Finland
Eriika Ahopelto, Riina Hautala, Ari Kinnari
Other feature page, tabloid, 50,000-174,999

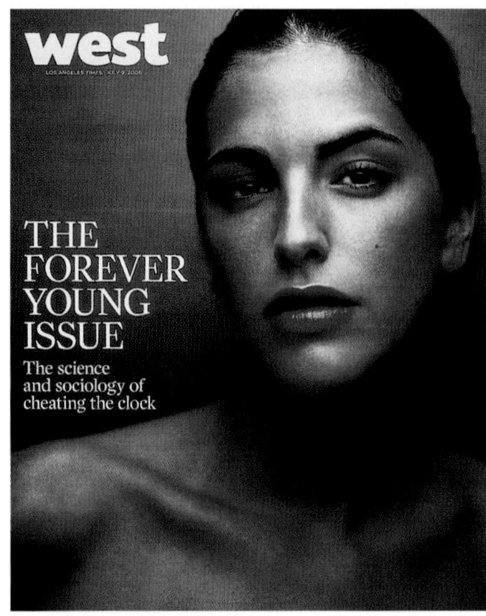

west
THE FOREVER YOUNG ISSUE
The science and sociology of cheating the clock



**LOS ANGELES TIMES WEST MAGAZINE**
Heidi Volpe, Joseph Hutchinson, Liz Hale, Carol Wakano, Russell Devita, Roger Gurbani
Overall magazine design

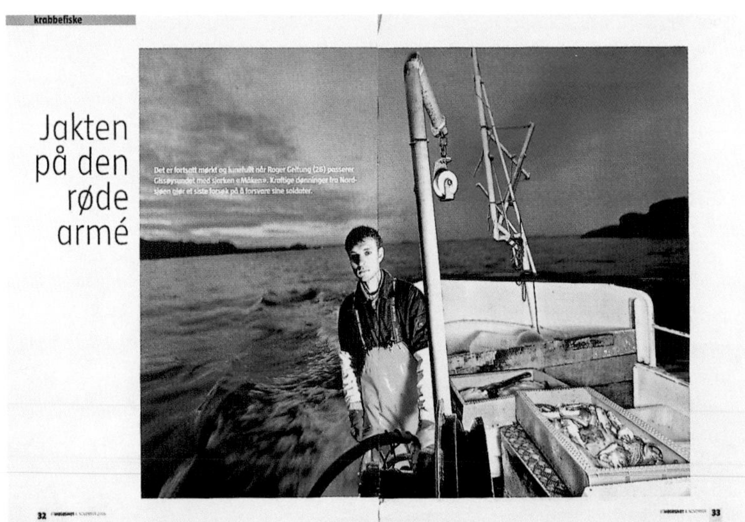

krabbefiske

# Jakten på den røde armé

32 ... 33

**BERGENS TIDENDE,** Bergen, Norway
Arne Edvardsen, Walter Jensen, Christina Pletten, Anneli Solberg, Arne Størksen, Aina Wasmuth, Anne Brun
Overall magazine design

**EL MUNDO MAGAZINE,** Madrid, Spain

Rodrigo Sanchez, Carmelo Caderot, Maria Gonzalez, Javier Sanz, Eva Lopez

Magazine special section

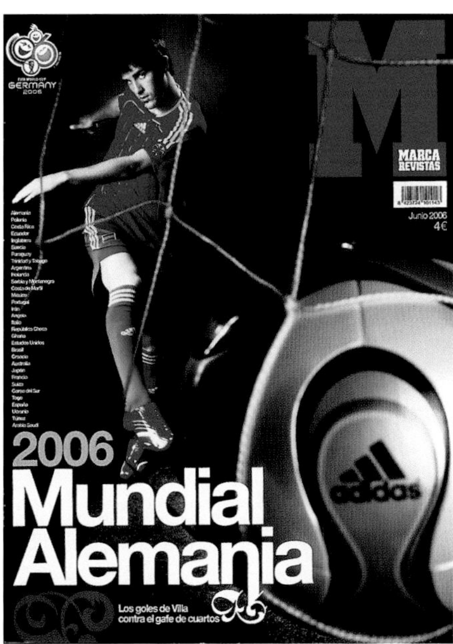


**MARCA,** Madrid, Spain

José Juan Gámez, Antonio Martín Hervás, Pedro Pablos Lorenzana, Blanca Serrano, Mercedes Suils, Elsa Martín, Izaskun G. Alegre, Carolina Díaz, Carlos F. Estébanez, Juanma Castillo

Magazine special section

**EL MUNDO MAGAZINE,** Madrid, Spain

Rodrigo Sanchez, Carmelo Caderot, Maria Gonzalez, Javier Sanz, Eva Lopez

Magazine special section

**MING PAO,** Hong Kong

Ming Chit Yeung, Ping Hsian Wang

Magazine special section

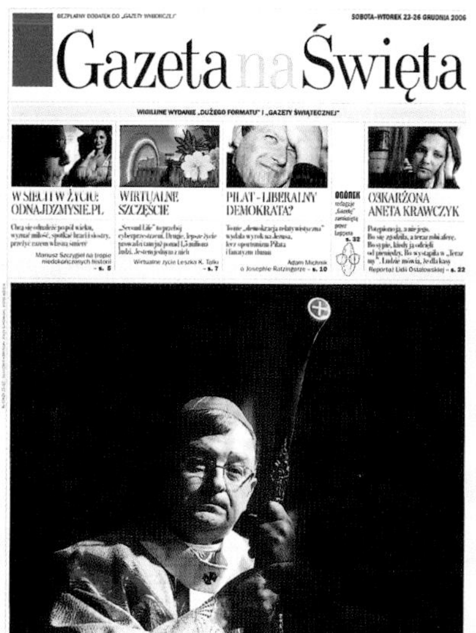


**GAZETA WYBORCZA,** Warsaw, Poland

Maciej Kalkus

Magazine special section

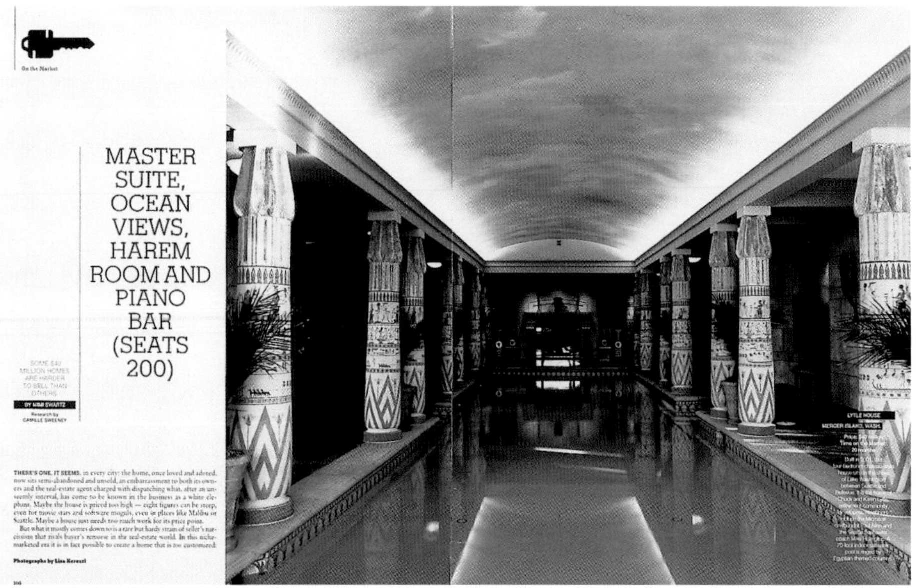

MASTER SUITE, OCEAN VIEWS, HAREM ROOM AND PIANO BAR (SEATS 200)

**THE NEW YORK TIMES MAGAZINE**
Janet Froelich, Arem Duplessis, Jeff Glendenning, Kathy Ryan
Magazine special section

The young, beautiful Elvis as you've never seen him | Weingarten tries to pick up an Artificial Intelligence

The Washington Post Magazine

OCTOBER 22, 2006



Getting to Know Garry Trudeau. Finally.

BY GENE WEINGARTEN

**THE WASHINGTON POST MAGAZINE**
J. Porter, Evan Jane Kriss, Jennifer Beeson, Leslie Garcia, Michael Williamson, Garry Trudeau
Magazine cover design

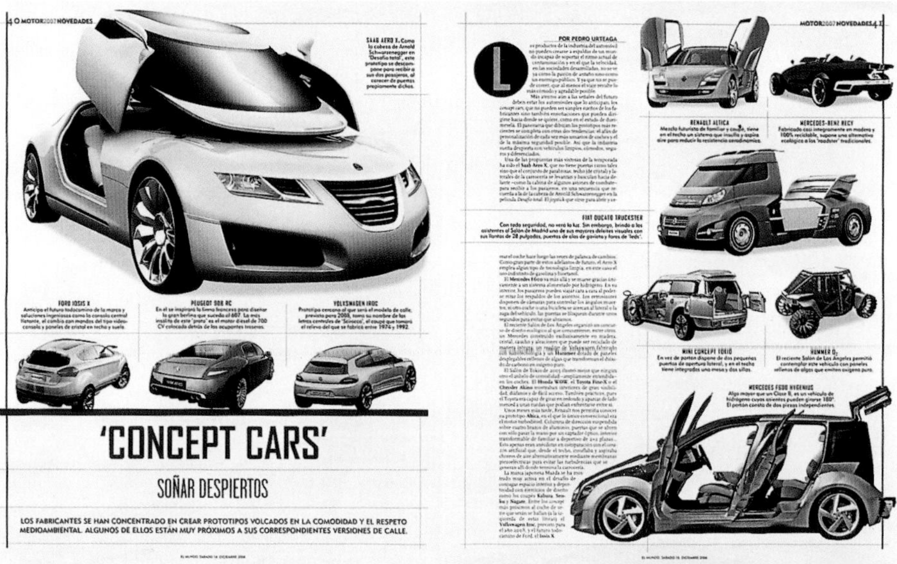

POR PEDRO URTEAGA

'CONCEPT CARS'

SOÑAR DESPIERTOS

LOS FABRICANTES SE HAN CONCENTRADO EN CREAR PROTOTIPOS VOLCADOS EN LA COMODIDAD Y EL RESPETO MEDIOAMBIENTAL. ALGUNOS DE ELLOS ESTÁN MUY PRÓXIMOS A SUS CORRESPONDIENTES VERSIONES DE CALLE.

**EL MUNDO MOTOR,** Madrid, Spain
Carmelo Caderot, Manuel De Miguel, Jose Carlos Saiz
Magazine special section

tendencias RAMBLAS

El latido de Barcelona se mide en Las Ramblas. La calle más emblemática y conocida de la Ciudad Condal acoge multitud de historias que muestran un punto de encuentro entre diferentes formas de vida

un escenario en plena calle

en el corazón de la ciudad...

**GACETA UNIVERSITARIA,** Madrid, Spain
Staff
Overall magazine design

SILVER

**EL MUNDO MAGAZINE,** Madrid, Spain

Rodrigo Sanchez, Maria Gonzalez, Javier Sanz, Eva Lopez, Carmelo Caderot

Overall magazine design

This is one of the best magazines we've seen. It has so much graphic appeal. The use of typography is very risky and very appropriate for subject matter. The photo editing is very good — not just pretty pictures, but packed with information. It feels complete. The pages are fun, new and energizing.

Ésta es una de las mejores revistas que hemos visto. Tiene mucho atractivo visual. El uso de la tipografía es muy arriesgado y muy apropiado para el tema. La edición de la fotografía es muy buena; no son sólo fotos bellas, sino llenas de información. Se siente completa. Las páginas son entretenidas, novedosas y energizantes.

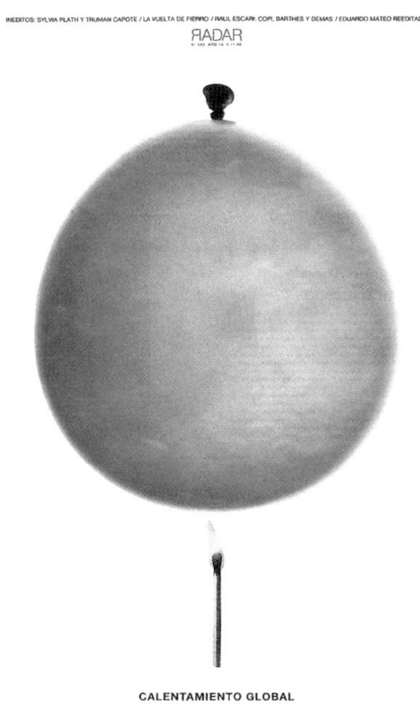


**RADAR. PÁGINA/12 LEISURE MAGAZINE,** Buenos Aires, Argentina

Alejandro Ros

Magazine cover design

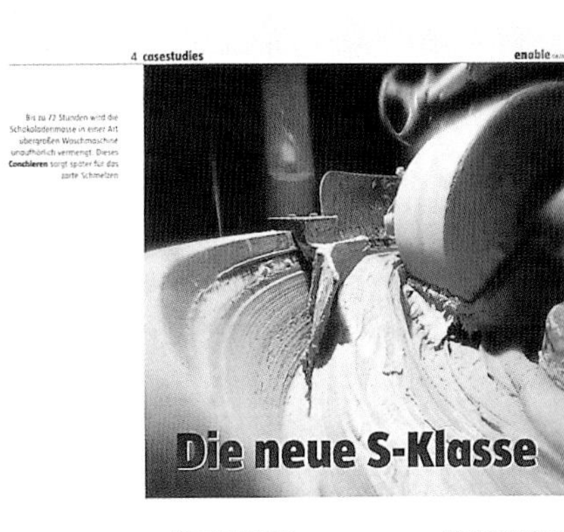


Der Markt für Luxusschokolade wächst. Hosso Nauck tut alles, damit das so bleibt. Der Bremer Schokoladenhersteller erfindet für die Traditionsmarken Hachez und Feodora daher ständig neue Produkte

Von Gunthild Kupitz

enable casestudies 5

"Wir wollen keine braune Masse in hübsch bedrucktes Papier packen. Wir wollen Luxusgüter verkaufen"

Der Enkel übernimmt

**FINANCIAL TIMES DEUTSCHLAND,** Hamburg, Germany

Staff

Overall magazine design

**EXPRESSO,** Lisbon, Portugal
Marco Grieco, Pedro Figueiral, Teresa Hasse e Silva
Magazine cover design

**THE NEW YORK TIMES STYLE MAGAZINE**
Janet Froelich, David Sebbah, Chris Martinez, Raymond Meier
Magazine cover design

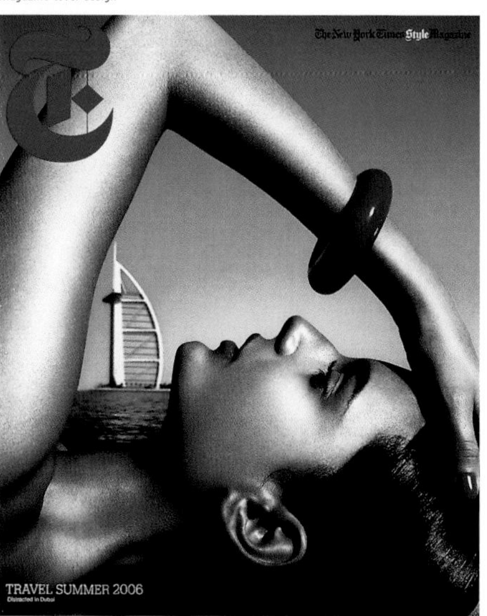


METROPOLI

¿Qué tienen que ver Jesucristo, María Magdalena, sus posibles descendientes, los Templarios y el Opus Dei con Ron Howard, Tom Hanks y Audrey Tautou? La clave, como 10 millones de lectores saben, se halla oculta en el Museo del Louvre y en la obra "La Última Cena". Ni siquiera Da Vinci lo hubiera imaginado...

El Código Da Vinci

el mayor bestseller de la Historia convertido en una película supertaquillera y polémica

**EL MUNDO METROPOLI,** Madrid, Spain
Rodrigo Sanchez, Carmelo Caderot
Magazine cover design

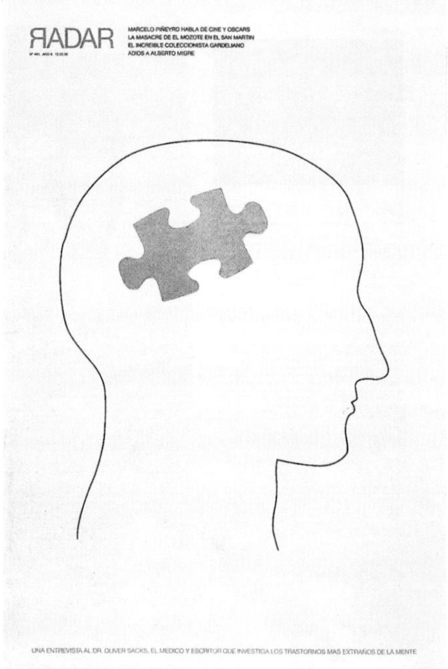


**RADAR. PÁGINA/12 LEISURE MAGAZINE,** Buenos Aires, Argentina
Alejandro Ros
Magazine cover design

**LAS/12. PÁGINA/12 WOMEN MAGAZINE,** Buenos Aires, Argentina
Alejandro Ros
Magazine cover design

**THE NEW YORK TIMES MAGAZINE**
Janet Froelich, Arem Duplessis, Jeff Glendenning, Kathy Ryan
Magazine special section

**EL MUNDO MAGAZINE,** Madrid, Spain
Rodrigo Sanchez, Carmelo Caderot, Maria Gonzalez, Javier Sanz, Eva Lopez
Magazine special section

**LA PRENSA GRÁFICA,** Antiguo Cuscatlán, El Salvador
Enrique Contreras, Héctor Ramírez, Giovanni Paniagua
Other feature page, tabloid, 50,000-174,999

NAVIDADES PARA COMPARTIR
MAGAZINE
EL MUNDO
NO TE EQUIVOQUES: EL REGALO PERFECTO SEGÚN SU HORÓSCOPO
VIVA LA TRADICIÓN: JAMÓN, PAVO, BESUGO Y TURRÓN
PON BUENA CARA: LOS COSMÉTICOS QUE NO FALLAN
ÚNETE A LA MODA: ROPA ÍNTIMA, LO QUE MÁS VENDE
+ 1.000 IDEAS PARA TODOS LOS PÚBLICOS
YO TE REGALO, TÚ ME REGALAS...
...FONSI NIETO A SU MUJER: UN VUELO EN UNA AVIONETA PILOTADA POR ÉL ...EL FUTBOLISTA SEEDORF, UNA CASA DE CAPRICHO PARA SU PAREJA

SILVER
**EL MUNDO MAGAZINE,** Madrid, Spain
Rodrigo Sanchez, Carmelo Caderot, Maria Gonzalez, Javier Sanz, Eva Lopez
Magazine special section

This is exciting — the color, the design, everything. Every department is beautifully art directed. The design is quite ornamental but not overpowering. Even the ads are well chosen.

Es excitante; el color, el diseño, todo. La dirección de arte de cada departamento está bellamente ejecutada. El diseño es bastante ornamental pero no sobrecargado. Incluso los avisos están bien elegidos.

**O GLOBO,** Rio de Janeiro, Brazil
Cristina Flegner
Magazine cover design

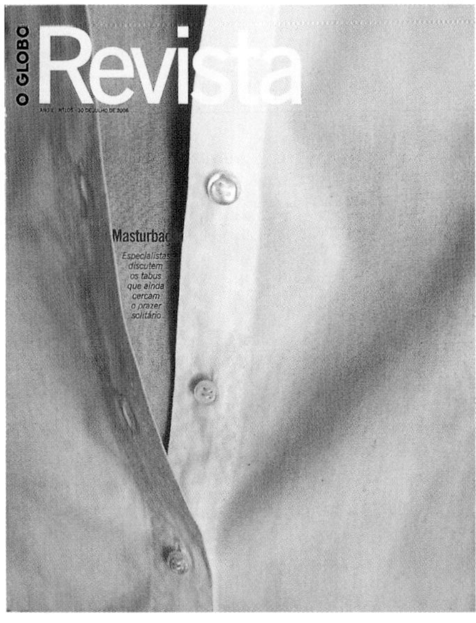


**GACETA UNIVERSITARIA,** Madrid, Spain
Ricardo Mendi
Magazine cover design

**GACETA UNIVERSITARIA,** Madrid, Spain
Antonio Martín Hervás, Leticia Chiarri
Magazine cover design

**GACETA UNIVERSITARIA,** Madrid, Spain
Antonio Martín Hervás, Ramón Franco Sierra
Magazine cover design

**LAS/12. PÁGINA/12 WOMEN MAGAZINE,** Buenos Aires, Argentina
Alejandro Ros
Magazine cover design

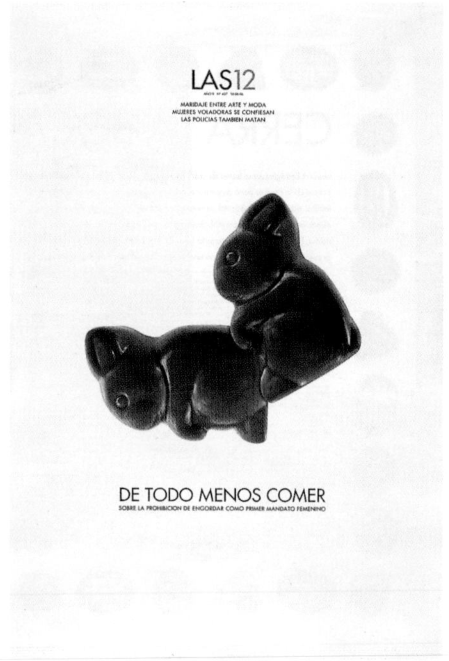


**LAS/12. PÁGINA/12 WOMEN MAGAZINE,** Buenos Aires, Argentina
Alejandro Ros
Magazine cover design

**EL MUNDO METROPOLI**, Madrid, Spain
Rodrigo Sanchez, Carmelo Caderot, Raul Arias
Magazine cover design

**THE SUNDAY TELEGRAPH**, London
David Riley, Alex McFadyen, Nicky Catley
Magazine cover design

**HERALD ON SUNDAY, AUCKLAND**, New Zealand
Rob Cox, Matthew Straker
Magazine cover design

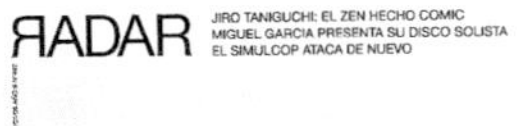

**BERGENS TIDENDE**, Bergen, Norway
Arne Edvardsen, Walter Jensen, Christina Pletten, Aina Wasmuth, Ketil Johnsen
Magazine cover design

**RADAR. PÁGINA/12 LEISURE MAGAZINE**, Buenos Aires, Argentina
Alejandro Ros
Magazine cover design

**THE CHICAGO TRIBUNE MAGAZINE**
Joseph Darrow, David Syrek, John McArthur
Magazine cover design

**EL MUNDO MAGAZINE,** Madrid, Spain
Rodrigo Sanchez, Carmelo Caderot, Alvaro Villarrubia
Magazine cover design

**EXPRESSO,** Lisbon, Portugal
Marco Grieco, Pedro Figueiral, Ana Baião
Magazine cover design

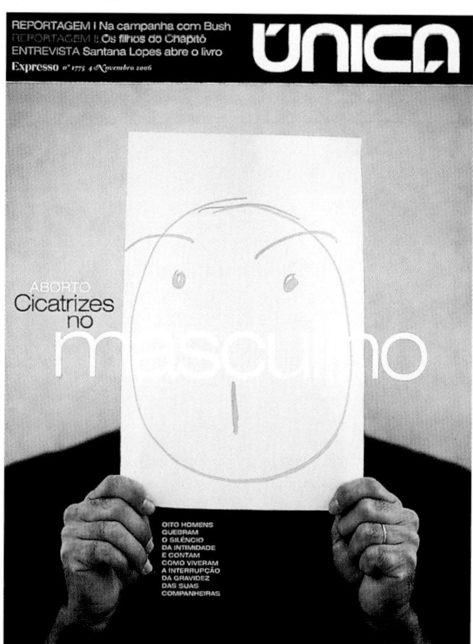

**EL MUNDO METROPOLI,** Madrid, Spain
Rodrigo Sanchez, Carmelo Caderot, Raul Arias
Magazine cover design

**EL MUNDO METROPOLI,** Madrid, Spain
Rodrigo Sanchez, Carmelo Caderot, Raul Arias
Magazine cover design

**EL MUNDO METROPOLI,** Madrid, Spain
Rodrigo Sanchez, Carmelo Caderot
Magazine cover design

**EXPRESSO,** Lisbon, Portugal
Marco Grieco, Pedro Figueiral, Teresa Hasse e Silva, Pedro Pimentel
Magazine cover design

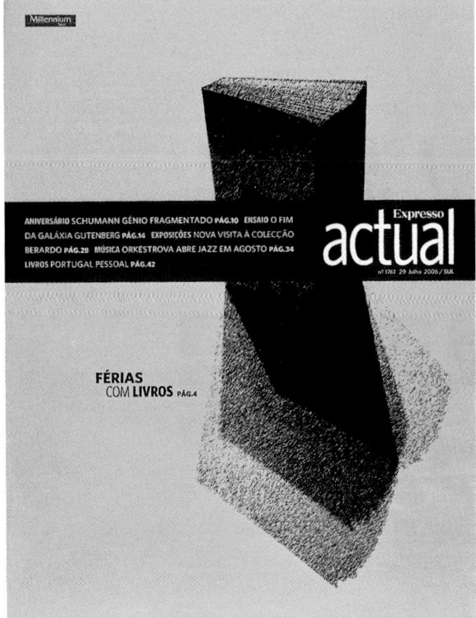


**HERALD ON SUNDAY,** Auckland, New Zealand
Matthew Straker, Naomi Rowley, Chris Skelton, Joel Hammonds
Magazine cover design

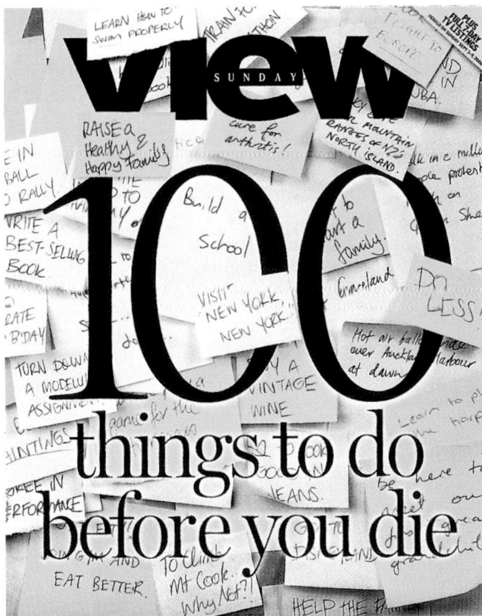


**ZAMAN,** Yenibosna, Turkey
Ekrem Dumanli, Fevzi Yazici, Mustafa Saglam, Nurettin Aslantas, Serhat Seftali
Magazine cover design

**EL MUNDO METROPOLI,** Madrid, Spain
Rodrigo Sanchez, Carmelo Caderot
Magazine cover design

**PÚBLICO,** Quinta do Lambert, Portugal
Hugo Pinto, Ana Carvalho, Marco Ferreira
Magazine cover design

**EXPANSIÓN,** Madrid, Spain
Emilia Peñalba
Magazine cover design

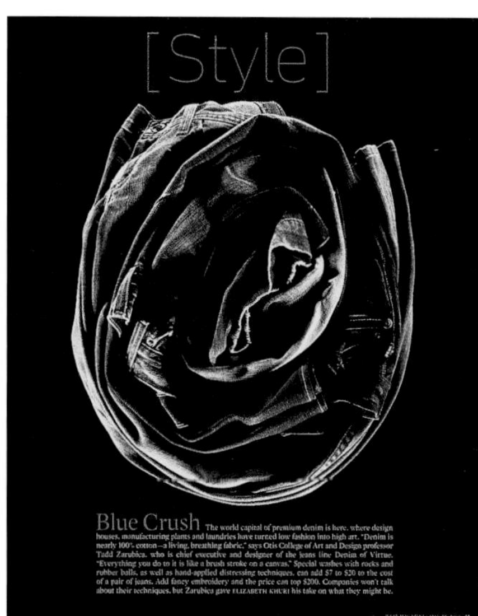


**LOS ANGELES TIMES WEST MAGAZINE**
Heidi Volpe, Joseph Hutchinson, Russell Devita, Nigel Cox
Magazine inside page

**LA NACIÓN,** Buenos Aires, Argentina
Carlos Guyot, Jesica Rizzo, Daniel Merle, Sebastián Menéndez
Magazine inside page

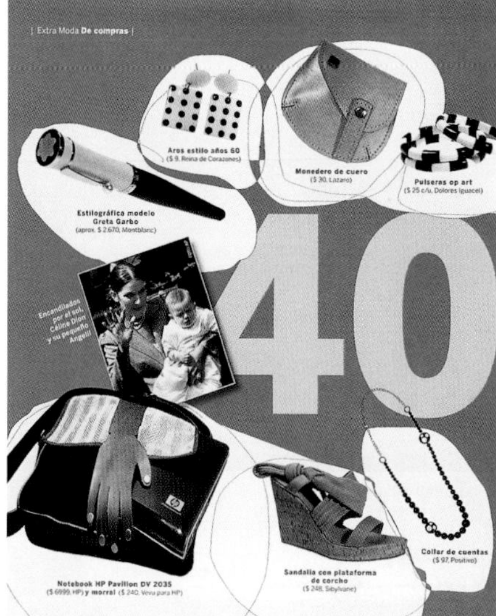


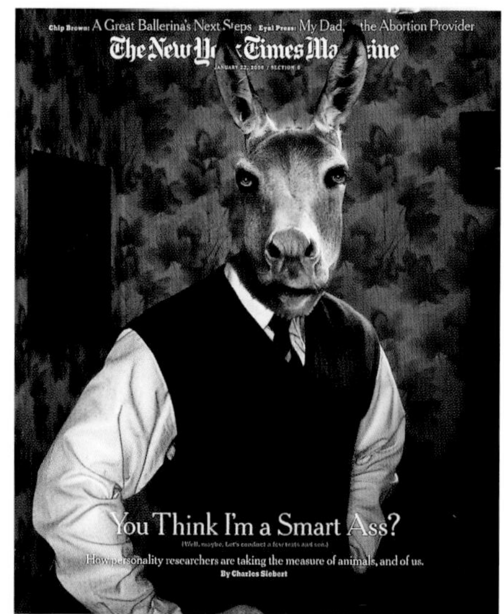


**THE NEW YORK TIMES MAGAZINE**
Janet Froelich, Arem Duplessis, Jeff Glendenning, Kathy Ryan, Erwin Olaf
Magazine cover story

**ASBURY PARK PRESS,** Neptune, N.J.
Harris Siegel, John Workman, Mark Voger, James J. Connolly
Magazine cover story

**GACETA UNIVERSITARIA,** Madrid, Spain
Antonio Martín Hervás, Leticia Chiarri
Magazine cover story

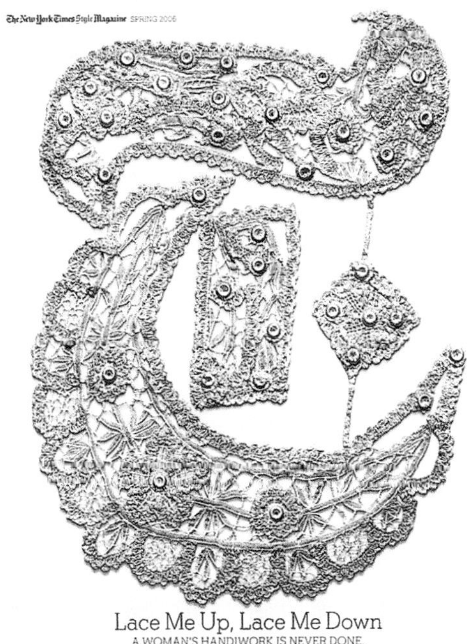

Lace Me Up, Lace Me Down
A WOMAN'S HANDIWORK IS NEVER DONE.

SPRING 2006
Easy as Cherry Pie
RECIPES FOR LIVING THE GOOD LIFE.
PHOTOGRAPH BY JAMES WOJCIK


**THE NEW YORK TIMES STYLE MAGAZINE**
Janet Froelich, David Sebbah, Chris Martinez, James Wojcik, Michael Dal Vecchio, Fernando Campana, Humberto Campana, Andrew Bettles
Magazine inside page

**EL MUNDO METROPOLI,** Madrid, Spain
Rodrigo Sanchez, Carmelo Caderot
Magazine cover design

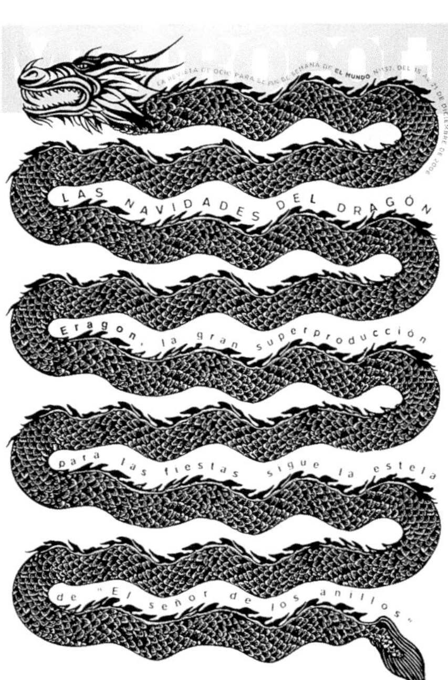


**EL MUNDO METROPOLI,** Madrid, Spain
Rodrigo Sanchez, Carmelo Caderot, Raul Arias
Magazine cover design

**EL MUNDO METROPOLI,** Madrid, Spain
Rodrigo Sanchez, Carmelo Caderot, Angel Becerril
Magazine cover design

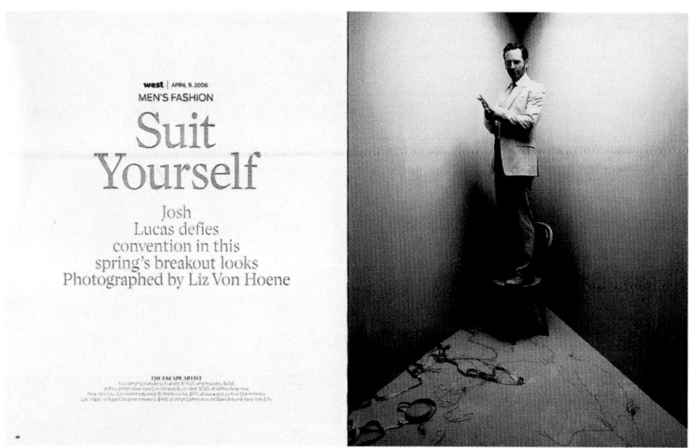

west | APRIL 9, 2006
MEN'S FASHION

Suit Yourself

Josh Lucas defies convention in this spring's breakout looks
Photographed by Liz Von Hoene

**LOS ANGELES TIMES WEST MAGAZINE**
Joseph Hutchinson, Roger Gurbani, Liz Von Hoene
Magazine inside page

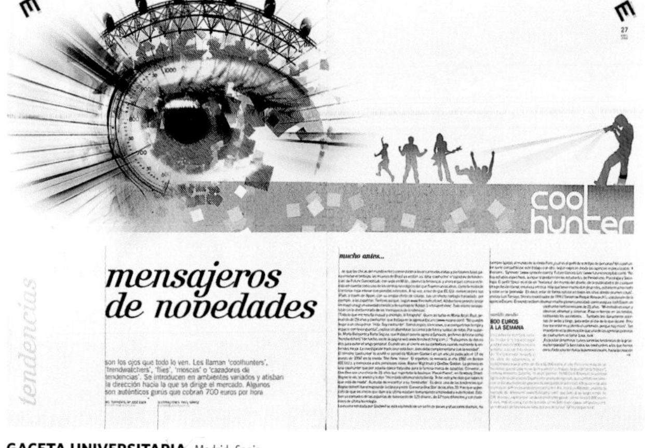

coolhunter

tendencias

mensajeros de novedades

son los ojos que todo lo ven. Los llaman 'coolhunters', 'trendwatchers', 'fíes', 'mescas' o 'cazadores de tendencias'. Se introducen en ambientes variados y atisban la dirección hacia la que se dirige el mercado. Algunos son auténticos gurús que cobran 700 euros por hora

**GACETA UNIVERSITARIA,** Madrid, Spain
Raúl Gámez, Antonio Martín Hervás
Magazine inside page

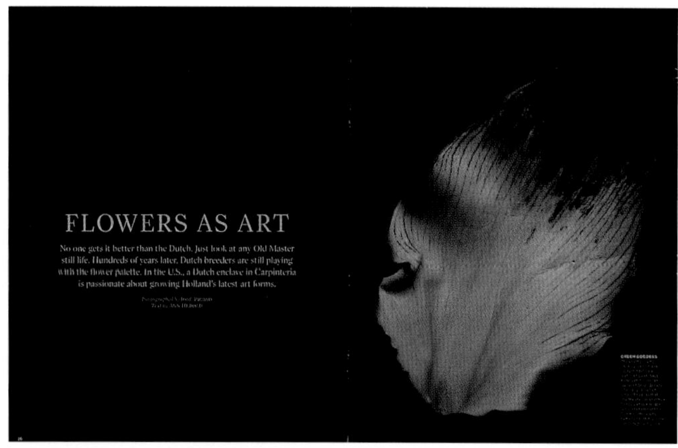

FLOWERS AS ART

No one gets it better than the Dutch. Just look at any Old Master still life. Hundreds of years later, Dutch breeders are still playing with the flower palette. In the U.S., a Dutch enclave in Carpinteria is passionate about growing Holland's latest art forms.

**LOS ANGELES TIMES WEST MAGAZINE**
Joseph Hutchinson, Carol Wakano, José Picayo
Magazine inside page

BOSTON'S EARTHQUAKE PROBLEM

IT'S NOT THE LIKELIHOOD OF A MAJOR EARTHQUAKE THAT MAKES EXPERTS TREMBLE – THOUGH IT'S WORSE THAN YOU THINK. IT'S THE DAMAGE ONE WOULD DO – BECAUSE IT'S MUCH WORSE THAN YOU THINK.

BY JEREMY MILLER

**THE BOSTON GLOBE MAGAZINE**
Emily Reid Kehe, Doug Most, Brendan Stephens
Magazine inside pagea

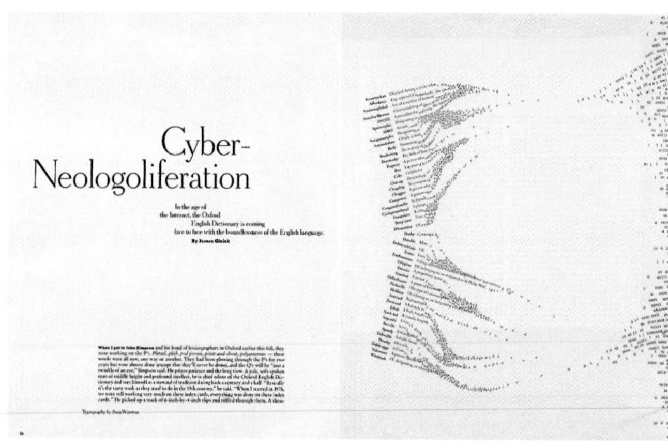

Cyber-Neologoliferation

In the age of the Internet, the Oxford English Dictionary is coming face to face with the boundlessness of the English language.
By James Gleick

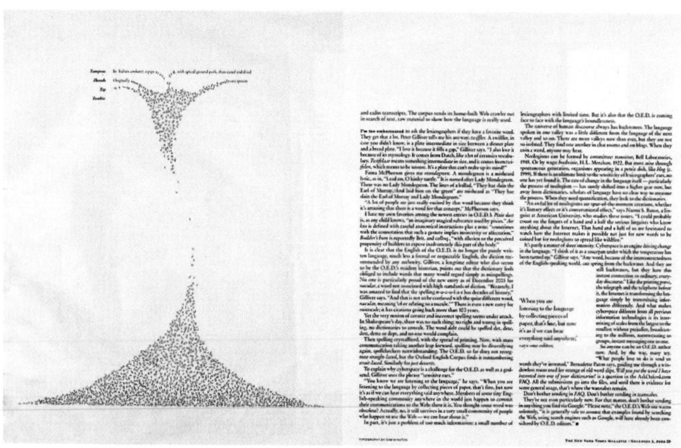

**THE NEW YORK TIMES MAGAZINE**
Janet Froelich, Arem Duplessis, Gail Bichler, Kathy Ryan, Sam Winston
Magazine inside page

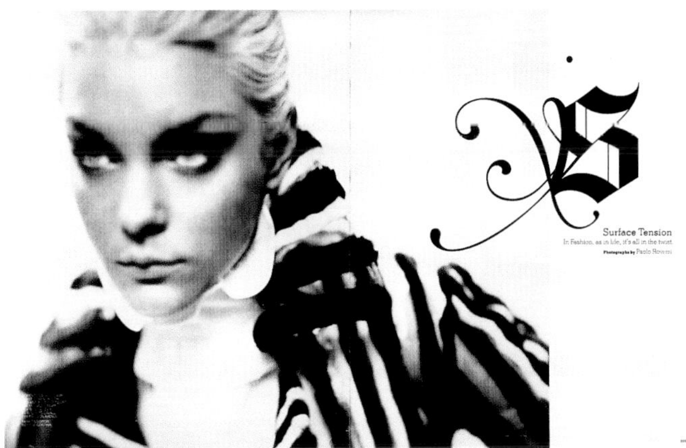


**THE NEW YORK TIMES STYLE MAGAZINE**
Janet Froelich, David Sebbah, Chris Martinez, Paolo Roversi
Magazine inside page

**THE NEW YORK TIMES STYLE MAGAZINE**
Janet Froelich, David Sebbah, Chris Martinez, Elizabeth Spiridakis, Nadav Kander
Magazine inside page

**PÚBLICO,** Quinta do Lambert, Portugal
Sónia Matos, Hugo Pinto, Ana Carvalho, Marco Ferreira
Magazine inside page

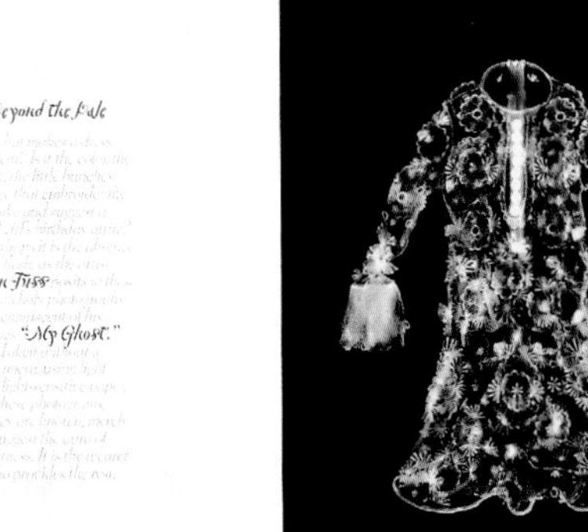


**THE NEW YORK TIMES STYLE MAGAZINE**
Janet Froelich, David Sebbah, Chris Martinez, Adam Fuss
Magazine inside page

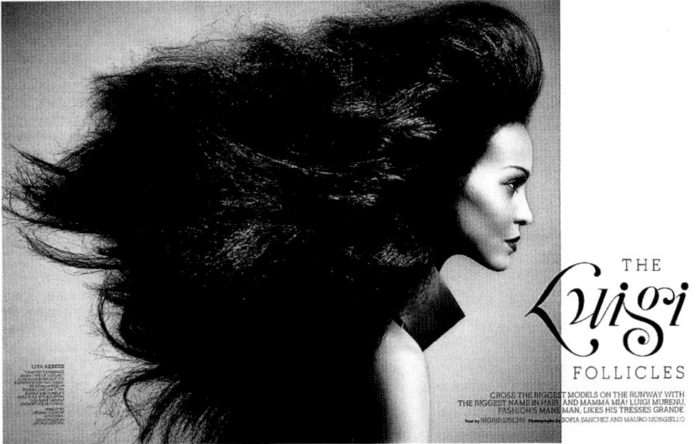


**THE NEW YORK TIMES STYLE MAGAZINE**
Janet Froelich, David Sebbah, Chris Martinez, Sofia Sanchez, Mauro Mongiello
Magazine inside page

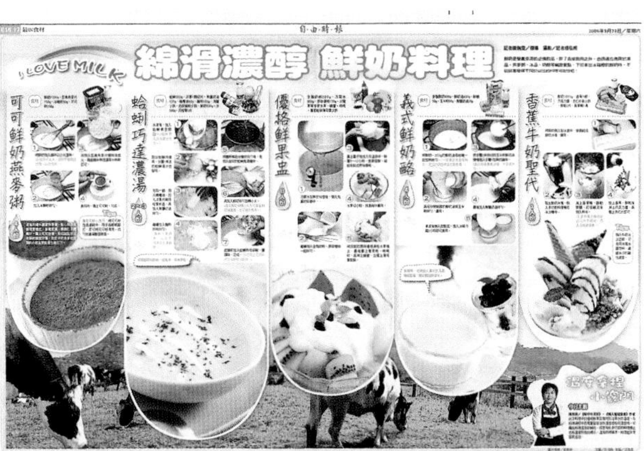


**LIBERTY TIMES,** Taipei, Taiwan
Chin Chang-Ling, Chiu Ching-Shun
Magazine inside page

**LOS ANGELES TIMES WEST MAGAZINE**
Heidi Volpe, Joseph Hutchinson, Russell Devita, Matt Black
Magazine inside page

**LOS ANGELES TIMES WEST MAGAZINE**
Heidi Volpe, Joseph Hutchinson, Carol Wakano, Russell Devita, Liz Hele, Palo Marchesi, Craig Cameron Olson, Jeff Lipsky
Magazine inside page

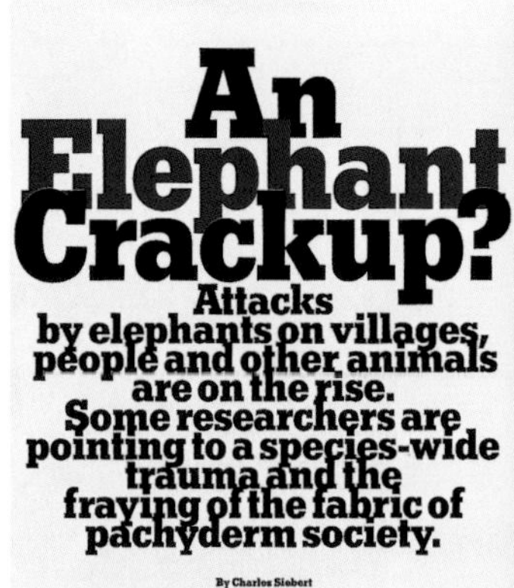

**THE NEW YORK TIMES MAGAZINE**
Janet Froelich, Arem Duplessis, Cathy Gilmore-Barnes, Kathy Ryan, Andres Serrano
Magazine inside page

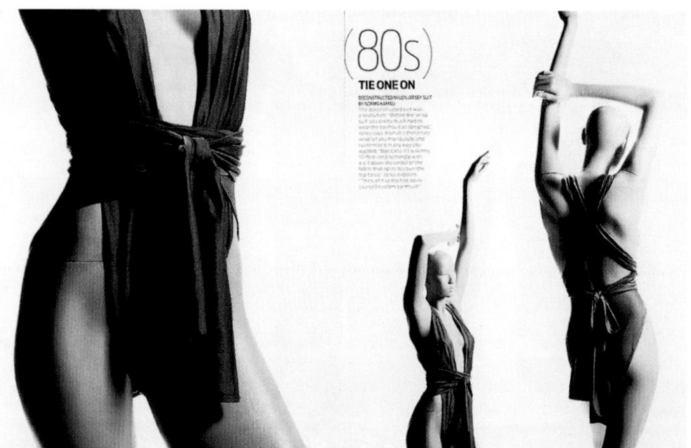


**LOS ANGELES TIMES WEST MAGAZINE**
Heidi Volpe, Joseph Hutchinson, Carol Wakano, Russell Devita, Liz Hele, Shay Peretz
Magazine inside page

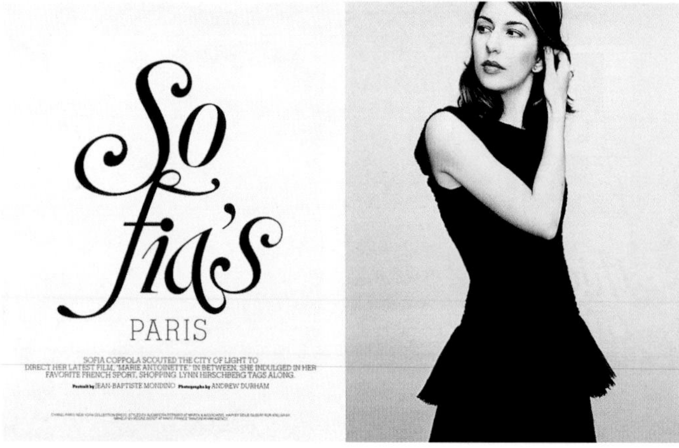


**THE NEW YORK TIMES STYLE MAGAZINE**
Janet Froelich, David Sebbah, Chris Martinez, Andrew Durham
Magazine inside page

**THE NEW YORK TIMES MAGAZINE**
Janet Froelich, Arem Duplessis, Cathy Gilmore-Barnes, Kathy Ryan, Ruven Afanador
Magazine inside page

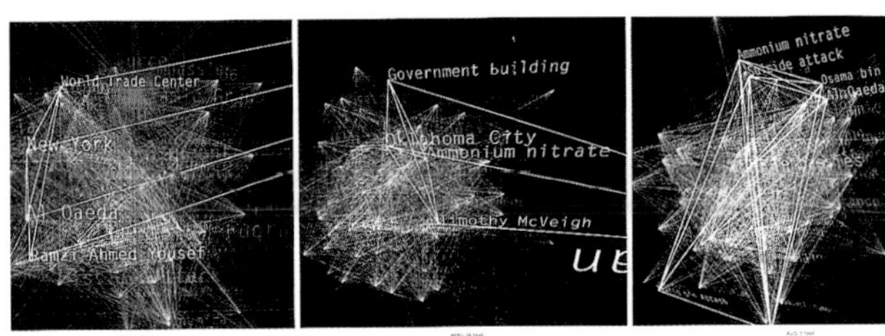

Open-Source Spying

**THE NEW YORK TIMES MAGAZINE**

Janet Froelich, Arem Duplessis, Jeff Glendenning, Kathy Ryan, Lisa Strausfeld, James Nick Sears

Magazine cover story

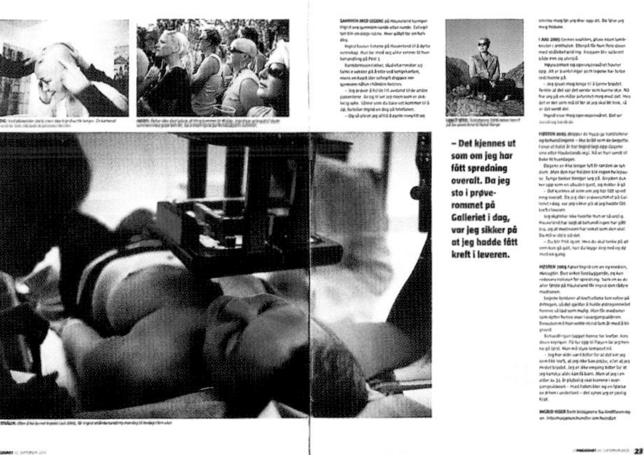

– Det kjennes ut som om jeg har fått spredning overalt. Da jeg sto i prøverommet på Galleriet i dag, var jeg sikker på at jeg hadde fått kreft i leveren.

**BERGENS TIDENDE,** Bergen, Norway

Arne Edvardsen, Walter Jensen, Anneli Solberg, Irina Lee, Christina Pletten, Anne Gjerde, Fred Ivar Klemmetsen

Magazine inside page

INOCENTES PALOMITAS

SÍ QUE SE DEJARON ENGAÑAR, Y RECIBIERON COMO RECOMPENSA RISA EN EL MEJOR DE LOS CASOS, DEUDAS, DESILUSIÓN E INDIGNACIÓN EN EL PEOR. ASÍ SE LAS APLICARON...

BANDA SANGRE

CAEN MEDIOS EN LA TRAMPA

PUBLI XIII

LES BAILAN LA LANA

**EXCELSIOR,** México City

Mauricio Belmán, Rosario Cruz, René Piña, Luzma Díaz de León Reyes, Marco A. Román, Alexandro Medrano, Ma. Luisa Díaz de León, Pascal Beltrán del Río, Ernesto Rivera

Magazine cover story

I DREAMT I WAS BEING PECKED BY BIRDS

THEATRE FIRST CAME A PANICKY TRIP TO MISSISSIPPI. THEN THE NIGHTMARES. ROSAMUND PIKE TELLS NIGEL FARNDALE ABOUT THE PAIN AND PLEASURE OF TAKING ON TENNESSEE WILLIAMS

PORTRAIT BY HARRY BORDEN

**THE SUNDAY TELEGRAPH SEVEN MAGAZINE,** London

David Riley, Stephen Jenkins, Alex McFadyen, Harry Borden, Sasha Lehrfreund

Magazine cover story

THE IDIOM OF TODAY'S ALIENATED (OR ANYWAY, HIPSTER) YOUTH ISN'T ART OR MUSIC OR LITERATURE. IT'S TURNING AN IDEA YOU HAVE – OR MAYBE YOUR SELF – INTO A PRODUCT.

THE BRAND UNDERGROUND

BY ROB WALKER

**THE NEW YORK TIMES MAGAZINE**

Janet Froelich, Arem Duplessis, Jeff Glendenning, Kathy Ryan, Tom Schierlitz

Magazine cover story

Jerry Bruckheimer

8

**LOS ANGELES TIMES WEST MAGAZINE**

Heidi Volpe, Joseph Hutchinson, Russell Devita, Carol Wakano, Liz Hele

Magazine cover story

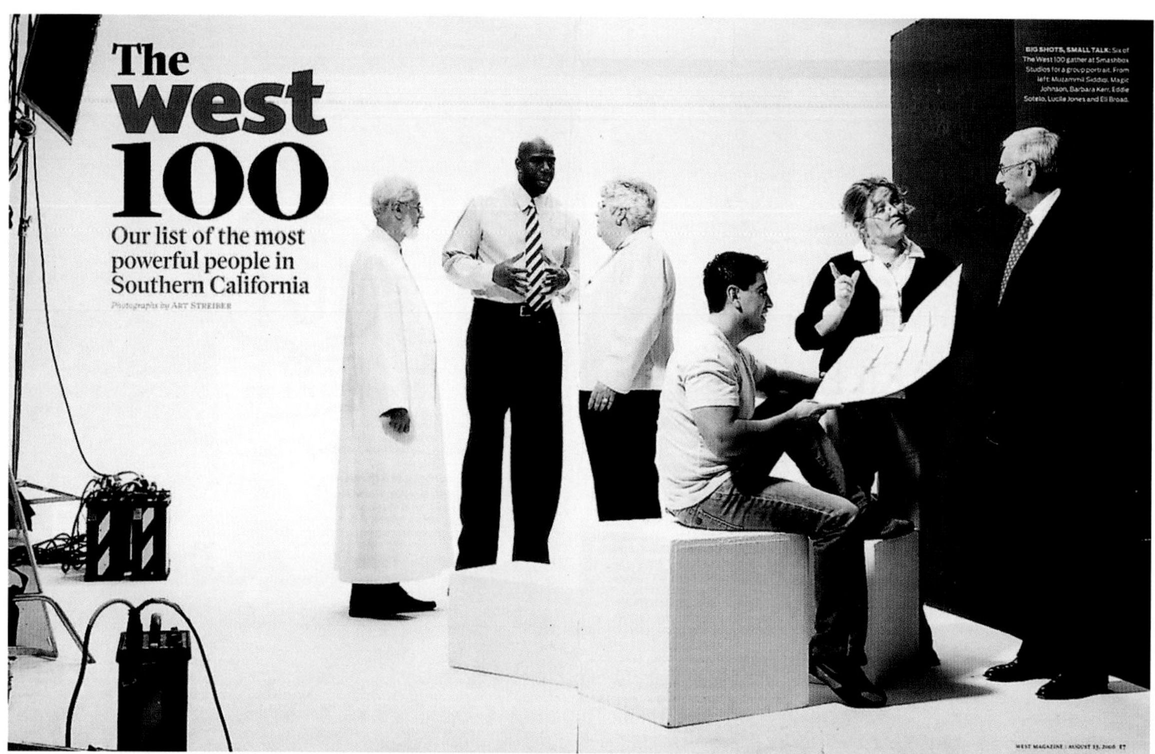


**LOS ANGELES TIMES WEST MAGAZINE**

Heidi Volpe, Joseph Hutchinson, Russell Devita, Carol Wakano, Art Streiber, Michelle Chang, Liz Hale

Magazine inside page

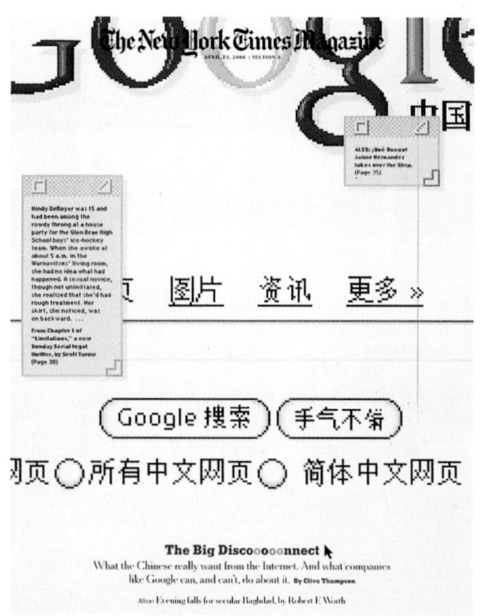


**THE NEW YORK TIMES MAGAZINE**

Janet Froelich, Arem Duplessis, Gail Bichler, Kathy Ryan, QuickHoney

Magazine cover design

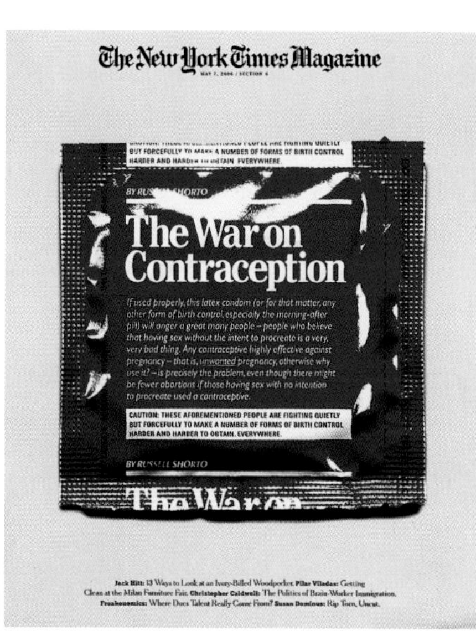


**THE NEW YORK TIMES MAGAZINE**

Janet Froelich, Arem Duplessis, Kathy Ryan, Tom Schierlitz

Magazine cover design

**DIÁRIO DE NOTÍCIAS,** Lisbon, Portugal

António José Teixeira, Ivone Ralha, Paulo Barata, Nuno Janela, Hugo Neves, Henriqúe Cayatte

Magazine cover design

Chapter Six

# VISUALS

Elementos visuales

**Illustration / Photography / Informational graphics / Miscellaneous**

Ilustración / Fotografía / Infográficos / Misceláneos

**EL MUNDO METROPOLI,** Madrid, Spain
Raul Arias
Single illustration

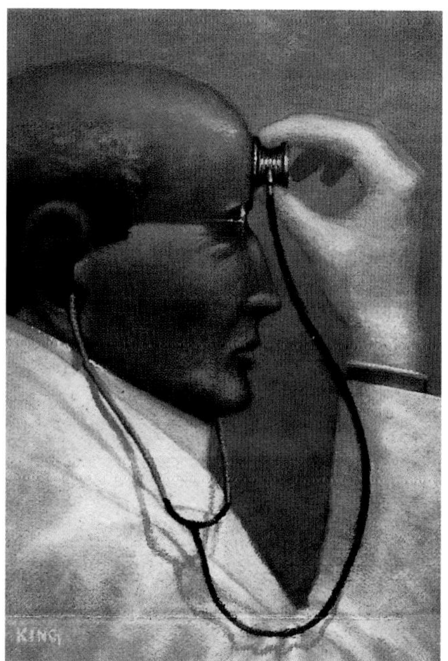

**THE PALM BEACH POST,** West Palm Beach, Fla.
Brennan King
Single illustration

**THE BOSTON GLOBE MAGAZINE**
Brendan Stephens, Pam Clifford, Melina Vanderpile, Doug Most, Dan Zedek
Single illustration

**EL MUNDO METROPOLI,** Madrid, Spain
Raul Arias
Single illustration

**CHICAGO TRIBUNE**
Elliott Golden, Tom Heinz, Denise Joyce
Single illustration

**EL COMERCIO,** Lima, Peru
Claudia Gastaldo
Single illustration

**ZAMAN,** Yenibosna, Turkey
Fevzi Yazici, Cem Kiziltug
Single illustration

# JUGUETES RABIOSOS

**ALARMA.** COREA DEL NORTE JUEGA CON FUEGO Y PONE EN RIESGO AL MUNDO CON DISPARATADA AVENTURA NUCLEAR.

Kim Jong Il desafió a la comunidad internacional probando su renovado arsenal nuclear al lanzar un total de siete misiles de mediano y largo alcance hacia el mar del Japón y supuestamente hacia las costas de EE.UU. El ejercicio militar provocó un verdadero remezón entre los países de la cuenca del Pacífico, y desató una serie de especulaciones en torno a los motivos que se ocultan detrás de su maquiavélica intención. George W. Bush activa una ofensiva diplomática mientras que Rusia y China se muestran aún reticentes a sancionar a su socio.

ESCRIBE LUIS JAIME CISNEROS H. ILUSTRA GOSTER

**THE SOMOS MAGAZINE,** Lima, Peru
Claudia Burga Cisneros, Jose Antonio Mesones
Single illustration

**ZAMAN,** Yenibosna, Turkey
Fevzi Yazici, Osman Turhan
Single illustration

**ZAMAN,** Yenibosna, Turkey
Fevzi Yazici, Cem Kiziltug
Single illustration

El Comercio

¡Viernes!

* NITZER EBB TOCARÁ EN LIMA PARA DELIRIO ABSOLUTO DE LOS FANÁTICOS DE LA MÚSICA INDUSTRIAL, GÓTICA Y DARK

Dark, wave, gothic, industrial, pospunk... Si te gusta alguno de esos géneros musicales, Lima es la ciudad perfecta para ti. Basta repasar en el calendario semanal de conciertos, en las visitas de artistas internacionales que no forman parte de las carteleras más comerciales o en la abundancia de discotecas y similares consagrados a las formas menos luminosas del rock & roll para entender rápidamente que el grisáceo clima de la capital del Perú parece ejercer una suerte de ascendiente en las preferencias musicales de los limeños. Así como antes recibimos las visitas de artistas foráneos como The Mission U.K., Red Flag, Mellotron, Clan of Xymox, Frozen Autumn y tantos otros, esta vez es el turno del que es, probablemente, el conjunto de rock industrial más legendario de todos los tiempos, Nitzer Ebb, que llega desde Inglaterra para ofrecer el próximo jueves un concierto que promete ser sencillamente inolvidable. Desde que corrió el rumor de la llegada de la banda a Lima por foros y páginas de Internet, la expectativa no dejó de crecer. Será una noche memorable. Que nadie lo dude. Tiempos oscuros [c4].

zona DARK

SILVER

**EL COMERCIO,** Lima, Peru
Claudia Gastaldo
Single illustration

The page is mysterious — and very strong. The contrast between the black and the red adds to the mystery and makes it very engaging. It's quite a strong composition.

Esta página es misteriosa y muy potente. El contraste entre el negro y el rojo hace mayor el misterio y lo vuelve muy llamativo. Es una composición muy potente.

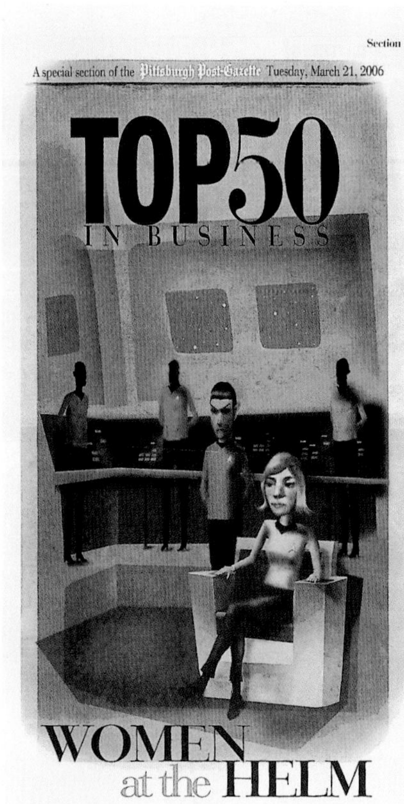

Section E

A special section of the Pittsburgh Post-Gazette Tuesday, March 21, 2006

TOP50 IN BUSINESS

WOMEN at the HELM

**PITTSBURGH POST-GAZETTE**
Stacy Innerst
Single illustration

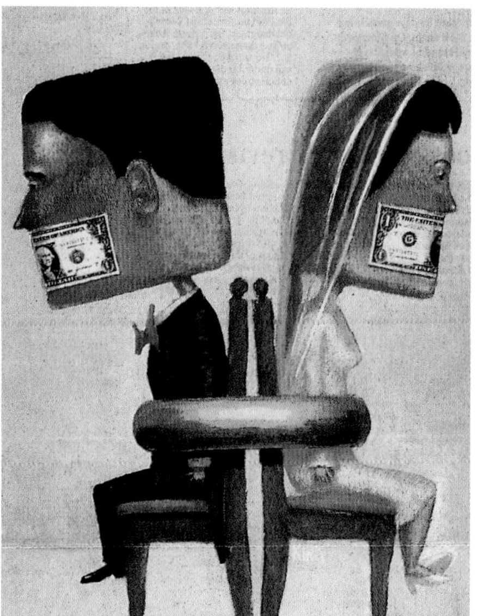

**THE PALM BEACH POST,** West Palm Beach, Fla.
Brennan King
Single illustration

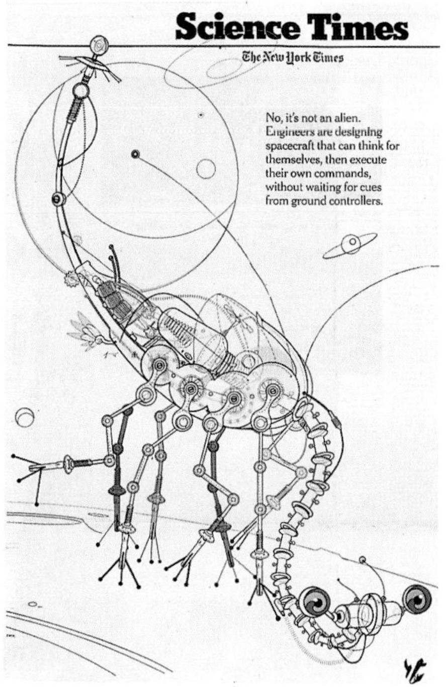

Science Times

The New York Times

No, it's not an alien. Engineers are designing spacecraft that can think for themselves, then execute their own commands, without waiting for cues from ground controllers.

**THE NEW YORK TIMES**
Tom Bodkin, Feric, Kelly Doe
Single illustration

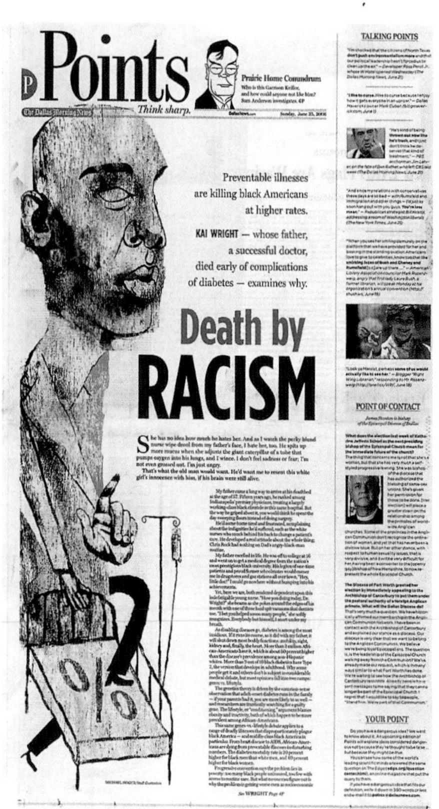

Points

Think sharp.

The Dallas Morning News

Prairie Home Conundrum

TALKING POINTS

Preventable illnesses are killing black Americans at higher rates.

KAI WRIGHT — whose father, a successful doctor, died early of complications of diabetes — examines why.

Death by RACISM

POINT OF CONTACT

YOUR POINT

**THE DALLAS MORNING NEWS**
G. Noel Gross, Michael Hogue
Single illustration

FORUM

GARRISON KEILLOR

INSIDE F

Smoke and mirrors?

As others cut back on emissions, U.S. looks to uncertain technology, volunteer efforts to rein in warming gases

Boys and girls can learn together

U.S. greenhouse emissions climb

**CAPE COD TIMES,** Hyannis, Mass.
James Warren
Single illustration

Pittsburgh Post-Gazette

WEEKEND MAG

05.04.06

THE PILLOWMAN

page20

INSIDE GREG JOSEPH page13 NEW PEARL JAM page14 MARY CLEERE HARAN page17 MAY DVDS page38

**PITTSBURGH POST-GAZETTE**
Stacy Innerst, Daniel Marsula
Single illustration

LA LUNA DE

METROPOLI

LA REVISTA DE OCIO PARA EL FIN DE SEMANA DE EL MUNDO. Nº 96. DEL 3 AL 9 DE MARZO DE 2006

BIENVENIDOS A LA FIESTA DEL CHIVO

LA PELÍCULA BASADA EN EL BEST-SELLER DE MARIO VARGAS LLOSA MUESTRA EN TODA SU CRUDEZA EL RÉGIMEN SANGUINARIO DEL DICTADOR DOMINICANO TRUJILLO

**EL MUNDO METROPOLI,** Madrid, Spain
Raul Arias
Single illustration

THE SEVEN WONDERS

OF THE CAROLINAS

**THE CHARLOTTE OBSERVER** (N.C.)

James Denk

Single illustration

NORTH KOREA:
unraveling the puzzle
RICHARD SACCONE says it's time to change strategy — and for once the United States can give a little and actually gain something in return
Stacy Innerst/ Post-Gazette


**PITTSBURGH POST-GAZETTE**

Stacy Innerst, Steve Urbanski

Single illustration

★ THE HOTTEST DOGS ★ THE COOLEST CONCERTS ★
Chicago Tribune Magazine
SUMMER
PLEASURES
★ THE JUICIEST BOOKS ★ AND A NON-STOP CALENDAR ★


**THE CHICAGO TRIBUNE MAGAZINE**

David Syrek, Joseph Darrow, Noah Woods

Single illustration

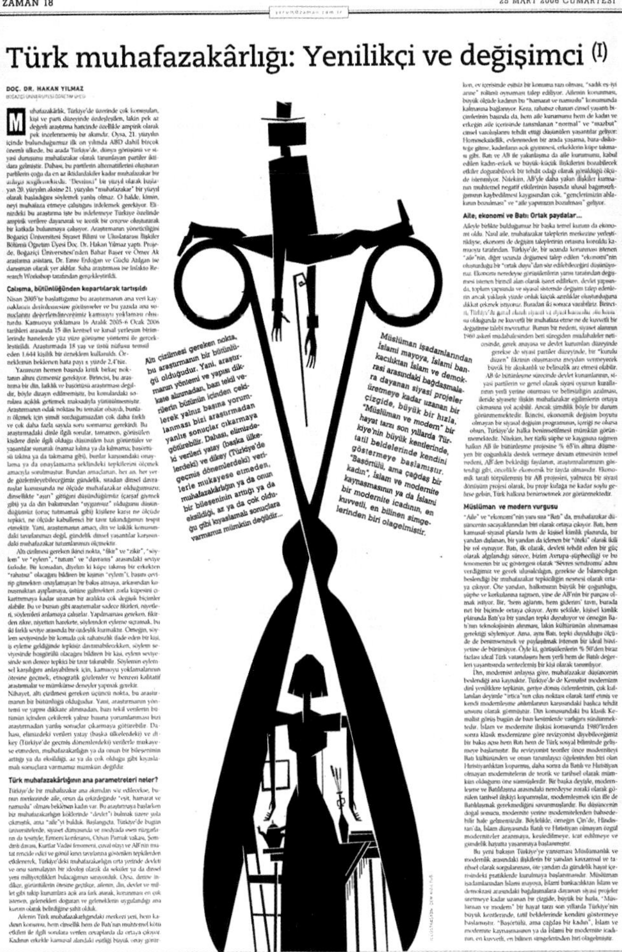

ZAMAN 18 YORUM 25 MART 2006 CUMARTESİ

yorum@zaman.com.tr

# Türk muhafazakârlığı: Yenilikçi ve değişimci (I)

DOÇ. DR. HAKAN YILMAZ

Muhafazakârlık, Türkiye'de üzerinde çok konuşulan, kişi ve parti düzeyinde özdeşleşilen, lakin pek az değerli araştırma hanında özellikle ampirik olarak pek incelenmemiş bir akımdır. Oysa, 21. yüzyılın içinde bulunduğumuz ilk on yılında ABD dahil birçok önemli ülkede, bu arada Türkiye'de, dünya görüşünü ve siyasi duruşunu muhafazakar olarak tanımlayan partiler iktidara gelmiştir. Dahası, bu partilerin alternatiflerini oluşturan partilerin çoğu da en az iktidardakiler kadar muhafazakar bir anlayışa sahiptir. "Devrimci" bir yüzyıl olarak başlayan 20. yüzyılın aksine 21. yüzyılın "muhafazakar" bir yüzyıl olarak başladığını söylemek yanlış olmaz. O halde, kimin, neyi muhafaza etmeye çalıştığını incelemek gerekiyor.

Altı çizilmesi gereken nokta, bu araştırmanın bir bütünlüğü olduğudur. Yani, araştırmanın yöntemi ve yapısı dikkate alınmadan, bazı tekil verilerin bütünün içinden çekilerek yalnız başına yorumlanması bizi araştırmadan yanlış sonuçlar çıkarmaya götürebilir. Dahası, elimizdeki verileri yatay (başka ülkelerdeki) ve dikey (Türkiye'de geçmiş dönemlerdeki) verilerle mukayese etmeden, muhafazakârlığın ya da onun bir bileşeninin arttığı ya da eksildiği, az ya da çok olduğu gibi kıyaslamalı sonuçlara varmamız mümkün değildir...

Müslüman işadamlarından İslami mayoya, İslami bankacılıktan İslam ve demokrasi arasındaki bağdaşmalara dayanan siyasi projeler üretmeye kadar uzanan bir çizgide, büyük bir hızla, "Müslüman ve modern" bir hayat tarzı son yıllarda Türkiye'nin büyük kentlerinde, tatil beldelerinde kendini göstermeye başlamıştır. "Başörtülü, ama çağdaş bir kadın", İslam ve modernite kaynaşmasının ya da İslami bir modernite icadının, en kuvvetli, en bilinen simgelerinden biri olagelmiştir.

**Aile, ekonomi ve Batı: Ortak paydalar...**

**Müslüman ve modern vurgusu**

**Türk muhafazakârlığının ana parametreleri neler?**

SILVER

**ZAMAN,** Yenibosna, Turkey

Fevzi Yazici, Cem Kiziltug

Single illustration

The contrast between the black and white — we really love the style. The illustrations are integrated with the type, and by using only black with the one shade of gray, it's very nice.

Nos encanta este estilo de contraste entre blanco y negro. Las ilustraciones están integradas con la tipografía, y el uso de negro y un tono de gris solamente es muy agradable.

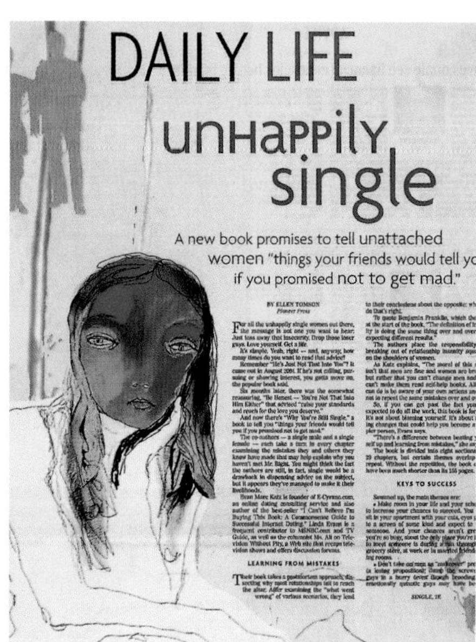

DAILY LIFE

unHaPPily single

A new book promises to tell unattached women "things your friends would tell you if you promised not to get mad."

**ST. PAUL PIONEER PRESS** (Minn.)
Ellen Thomson
Single illustration

focus S

Verano sin deberes

Tras las huellas de Tintín

Partimos con 12

CARNET POR PUNTOS. La implantación del nuevo sistema sancionador se fija la meta de modificar los hábitos al volante para reducir las tasa de siniestralidad P6

Un ojo en la carretera

EL CORREO

**EL CORREO,** Bilbao, Spain
Diego Zúñiga, María del Carmen Navarro, Mikel García Macías, Aurelio Garrote, Ana Espligares, Noelia Martínez, Juan Antonio Salazar, Laura Piedra, Pacho Igartua
Single illustration

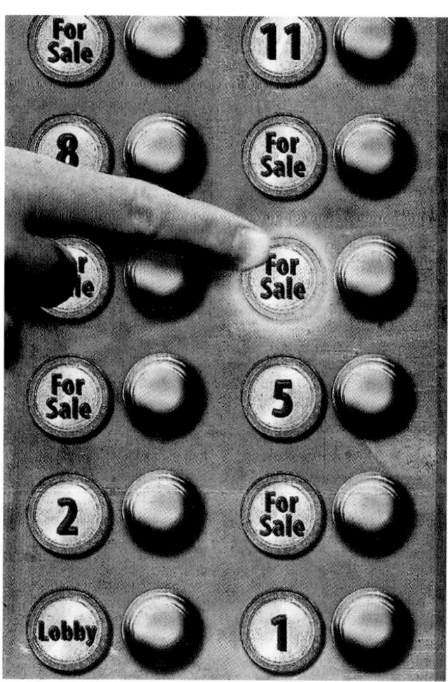


**CHICAGO TRIBUNE**
Dennis Odom
Single illustration

**THE NEW YORK TIMES**
Tom Bodkin, Yuko Shimizu, Nicki Kalish
Single illustration

Loose ends tied up

Waves of wireless replace tangle of wires

**MILWAUKEE JOURNAL SENTINEL** (Wis.)
Bob Helf
Single illustration

Swingshift

A do-it-yourself dad decides to build his kids a backyard playground and lives to tell the tale. Barely.

By JOHN NAYLOR

As a child

**FORT WORTH STAR-TELEGRAM** (Texas)
Mark Hoffer
Single illustration

Cape Cod Times
LIFESTYLE&ARTS
Learning from the techno gap
FASHION forward
Rhapsodies in blue
We just plain love denim

**CAPE COD TIMES,** Hyannis, Mass.
James Warren
Single illustration

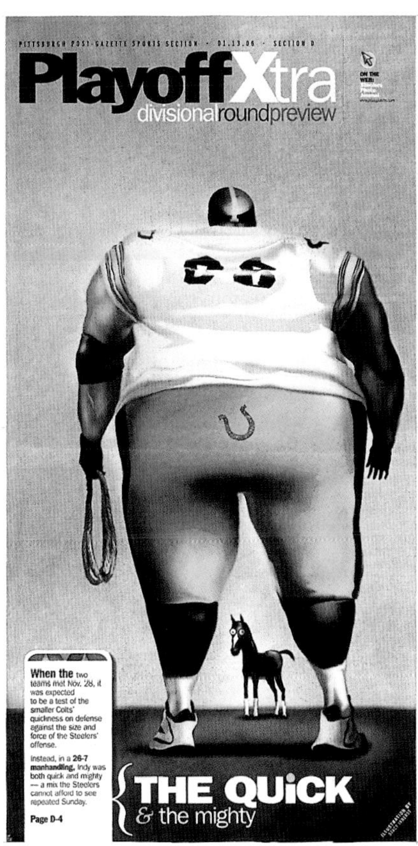
PlayoffXtra
divisionalroundpreview
When the two teams met Nov. 28, it was expected to be a test of the smaller Colts' quickness on defense against the size and force of the Steelers' offense.
Instead, in a 26-7 manhandling, Indy was both quick and mighty — a mix the Steelers cannot afford to see repeated Sunday.
Page D-4
THE QUiCK & the mighty

**PITTSBURGH POST-GAZETTE**
Stacy Innerst, Bill Pliske
Single illustration

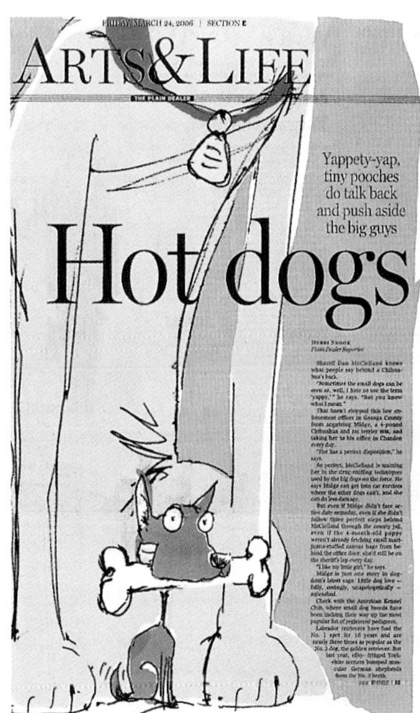
ARTS&LIFE
Yappety-yap, tiny pooches do talk back and push aside the big guys
Hot dogs

**THE PLAIN DEALER,** Cleveland
David Kordalski
Single illustration

KÜRSÜ
'Herkes yaptı yapacağını, şimdi sıra bende'
Zübeyde Hatun'u kurtaran küçük amel
Her şey Sen'den

**ZAMAN,** Yenibosna, Turkey
Fevzi Yazici, Osman Turhan
Single illustration

THE BOSTON GLOBE
FALL FOLIAGE
GOOD TO THE LAST DROP

**THE BOSTON GLOBE**
Chin Wang, Marc Boutavant, Ann Scales, Dan Zedek
Single illustration

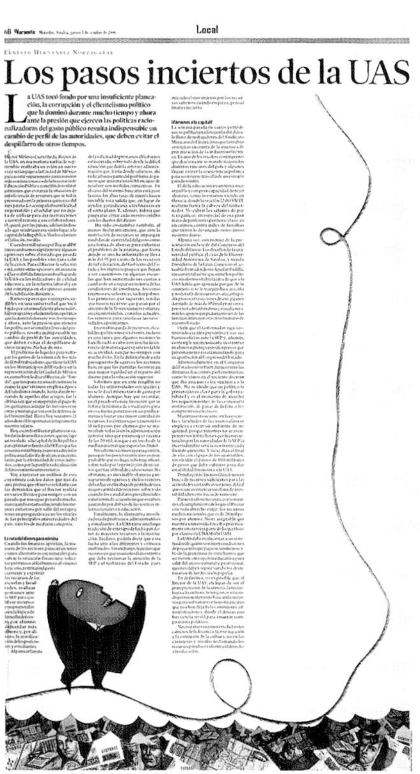
Local
Los pasos inciertos de la UAS

**NOROESTE,** Mazatlán, México
Jorge Luis López Sánchez, Alexander Probst, Wilfredo Camarena, Joel Díaz, Guillermina García
Single illustration

Travel
2006 SKI GUIDE
Powder tripping

**THE DENVER POST**
Jeff Neumann
Single illustration

KÜRSÜ

'Ben bunun için Müslüman olmamıştım'

İnsan, zaaflarını merdiven gibi kullanmalıdır

HEY GİDİ GÜNLER

İlk kahve sohbetini asla unutamam

**ZAMAN,** Yenibosna, Turkey
Fevzi Yazici, Osman Turhan
Single illustration

**THE GLOBE AND MAIL,** Toronto
Rachel Ann Lindsay, Cinders McLeod, David Pratt, Cathrin Bradbury, Sheree-Lee Olson
Single illustration

YORUM

ÇETELER
VATANSEVERLİK
KAHRAMANLAR
[1]

M. ŞÜKRÜ HANİOĞLU

İttihad ve Terakki Cemiyeti iktidara geldiğinde kendisine iktidar yolunu açan değişik nitelikteki çetelere işbirliğini sürdürmenin ne denli zor olduğunu anlamakta gecikmedi. Siyasîleştirilen

**ZAMAN,** Yenibosna, Turkey
Fevzi Yazici, Cem Kiziltug
Single illustration

**EL ECONOMISTA,** Madrid, Spain
Miguel Buckenmeyer, Elisabeth Nogales, Toño Benavides
Single illustration

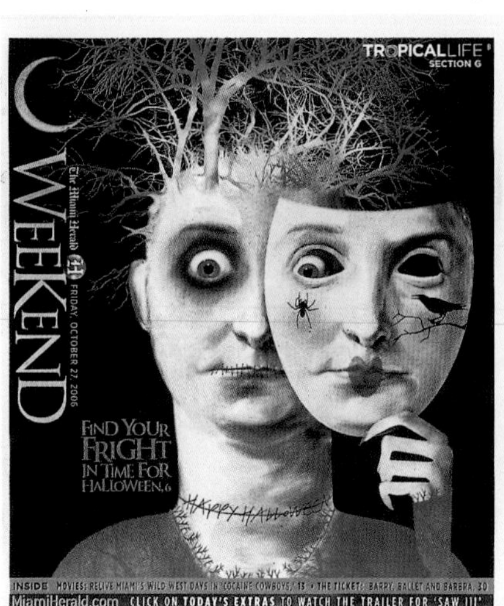


**THE MIAMI HERALD**
Eddie Alvarez, Paul Cheung, Ana Larrauri
Single illustration

**THE BUFFALO NEWS** (N.Y.)
Daniel Zakroczemski
Single illustration

**ZAMAN,** Yenibosna, Turkey
Fevzi Yazici, Cem Kiziltug
Single illustration

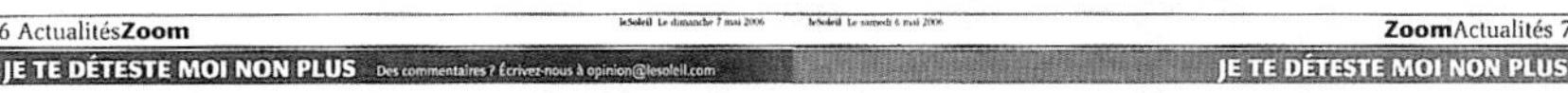
6 ActualitésZoom — leSoleil Le dimanche 7 mai 2006 — leSoleil Le samedi 6 mai 2006 — ZoomActualités 7

JE TE DÉTESTE MOI NON PLUS — Des commentaires ? Écrivez-nous à opinion@lesoleil.com — JE TE DÉTESTE MOI NON PLUS

Anne-Marie Voisard

Un couple sur deux, marié ou non, éclate. La plupart règlent sans s'entre-déchirer. Restent les autres qui ne parviennent pas à s'entendre. Les enfants sont au cœur du conflit. Comment dénouer la question de la garde, de la pension alimentaire ? C'est un juge de la Cour supérieure qui doit trancher, au risque de voir les Fathers 4 Justice grimper sur les ponts. Il le fait dans le meilleur intérêt de ceux qui ne sont que les victimes de ces chicanes d'adultes. *Le Soleil* a pu le constater. Pendant cinq jours, en avril, la Chambre de la famille nous a exceptionnellement ouvert ses portes et permis d'entendre les histoires de tous et chacun.

# S'offrir le luxe de divorcer

**Les conflits sont parfois si virulents qu'on s'engage dans les procédures. Le prix est élevé. Un avocat demande entre 100 $ et 150 $ l'heure, parfois plus**

« La justice des années 50 n'existe plus »

« Entre 15 et 20 % de ceux pour qui on ouvre un dossier vont pousser les procédures »

CHICANE DE PENSION



MÈRE DANS LE COMA — UN EX DE LA DAVIE — UNE MÈRE REPENTANTE — PAPA EST TRISTE — UN EX RÉCALCITRANT

**LE SOLEIL,** Québec City
Pascale Chayer, Linda Larouche, Yves Bellefleur, Myléne Moisan, Gilbert Lavoie, Anne-Marie Voisart
Multiple illustrations

Magazine
Pittsburgh Post-Gazette

# The Queen of Mean

A short history of meanies

Ann Coulter's sharp attacks on liberals bring political discourse to a whole new level

**PITTSBURGH POST-GAZETTE**
Stacy Innerst, Steve Urbanski
Single illustration

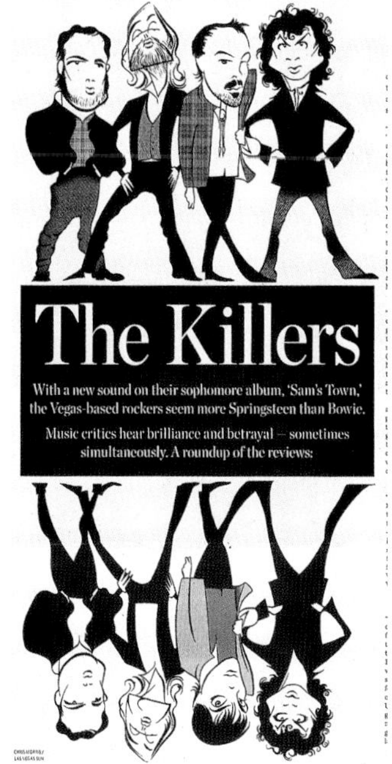
# The Killers

With a new sound on their sophomore album, 'Sam's Town,' the Vegas-based rockers seem more Springsteen than Bowie. Music critics hear brilliance and betrayal — sometimes simultaneously. A roundup of the reviews:

**THE LAS VEGAS SUN,** Henderson, Nev.
Chris Morris, Tyson Evans
Single illustration

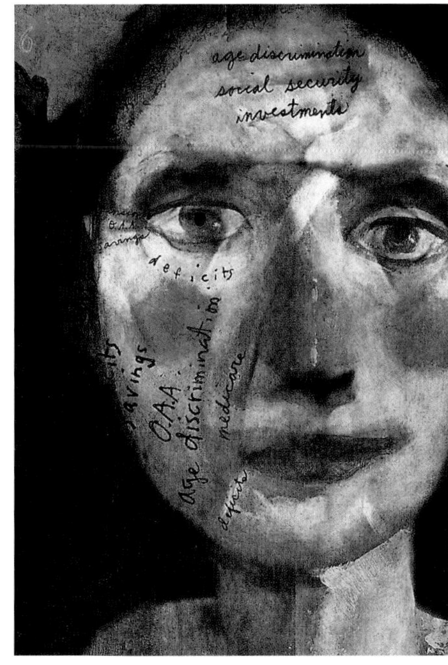


**PITTSBURGH POST-GAZETTE**
Stacy Innerst, Steve Urbanski
Single illustration

# Onde øjne

PORTRÆT

Tegning: Mette Dreyer

**POLITIKEN,** Copenhagen, Denmark
Mette Dreyer
Single illustration

**LA PRESSE,** Montréal
Francis Leveillee, Benoit Giguere, Genevieve Dinel, Isabelle Hachey, Alexandre Sirois, Michele Ouimet
Multiple illustrations

# Chicago Tribune Magazine

FEBRUARY 5, 2006

THE URBAN RENAISSANCE

CITY LIVING IS GLAMOROUS AGAIN AS NEIGHBORHOODS ONCE ON LIFE SUPPORT COME STORMING BACK

SPRING FASHION THAT'S NOT SHY

**THE CHICAGO TRIBUNE MAGAZINE**
David Syrek, Joseph Darrow, Jeffrey Decoster
Single illustration

DOSSIER SPECIAL > EN BAS DE LA CEINTURE

# UN MONDE SANS SERVIETTE

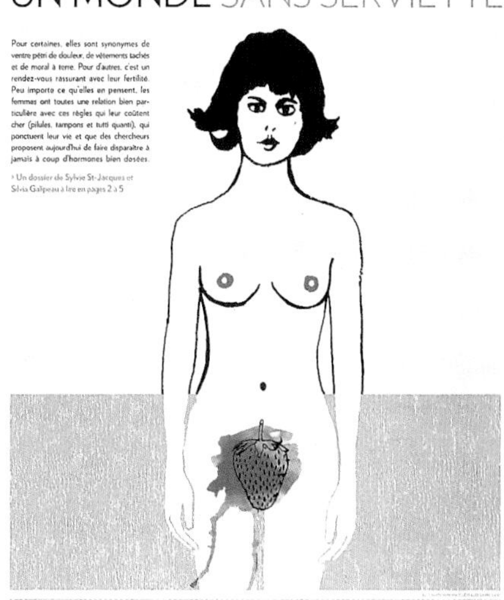
Pour certaines, elles sont synonymes de ventre pété de douleur, de vêtements tachés et de moral à terre. Pour d'autres, c'est un rendez-vous rassurant avec leur fertilité. Peu importe ce qu'elles en pensent, les femmes ont toutes une relation bien particulière avec ces règles qui leur coûtent cher (pilules, tampons et tutti quanti), qui ponctuent leur vie et que des chercheurs proposent aujourd'hui de faire disparaître à jamais à coup d'hormones bien dosées.

> Un dossier de Sylvie St-Jacques et Silvia Galipeau à lire en pages 2 à 5

**LA PRESSE,** Montréal
Francis Leveillee, Benoit Giguere, Genevieve Dinel, Michele Ouimet, Marie-Claude Lortie, Silvia Galipeau, Mario Girard, Sylvie St-Jacques
Multiple illustrations

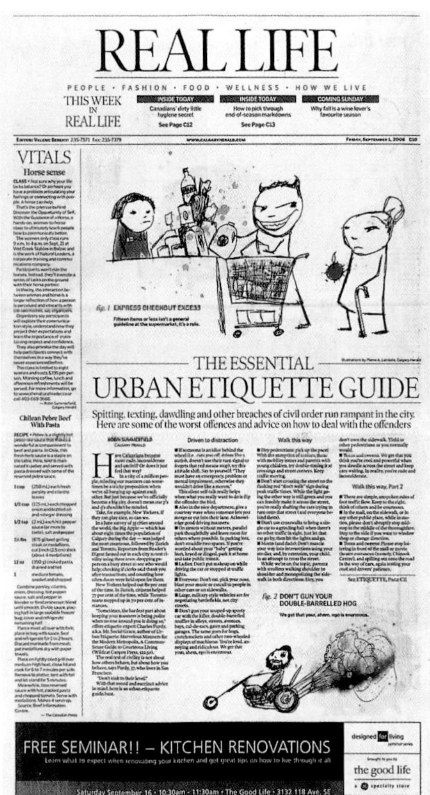

# REAL LIFE

PEOPLE • FASHION • FOOD • WELLNESS • HOW WE LIVE

THIS WEEK IN REAL LIFE

VITALS

Horse sense

THE ESSENTIAL

URBAN ETIQUETTE GUIDE

Spitting, texting, dawdling and other breaches of civil order run rampant in the city. Here are some of the worst offences and advice on how to deal with the offenders

Driven to distraction

Walk this way

Fig. 2 DON'T GUN YOUR DOUBLE-BARRELLED HOG

FREE SEMINAR!! – KITCHEN RENOVATIONS

the good life

**CALGARY HERALD** (Alberta, Canada)

Pierre Lamielle, Robin Summerfield, Valerie Berenyi, Janet Matiisen, Lorne Motley, Monica Zurowski

Multiple illustrations

Calcio

odio e amore

*In bilico tra la vergogna per gli scandali e lo show mondiale, due grandi scrittori ci raccontano lo sport che continua a regalare più emozioni*

**LA REPUBBLICA,** Rome

Angelo Rinaldi, Silvia Rossi, Stefano Cipolla, Isabella Maoloni, Gipi

Multiple illustrations

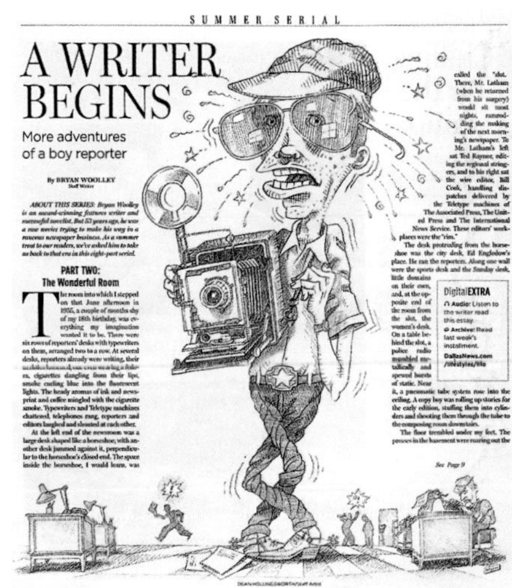

SUMMER SERIAL

A WRITER BEGINS

More adventures of a boy reporter

PART TWO: The Wonderful Room

**THE DALLAS MORNING NEWS**

Dean Hollingsworth

Multiple illustrations

**PLAY, THE NEW YORK TIMES SPORTS MAGAZINE**

Janet Froelich, Dirk Barnett, Marc Bell

Multiple illustrations

**THE NEWS JOURNAL,** Wilmington, Del.

Dan Garrow

Multiple illustrations

LA PRESSE MONTRÉAL SAMEDI 21 OCTOBRE 2006

PLUS

///SAMEDI

FORUM

UN HOMME ET SON AVENUE LA CHRONIQUE DE LYSIANE GAGNON PAGE 7

BYE-BYE KYOTO! L'ÉDITORIAL DE NATHALIE COLLARD PAGE 8

SÉRIE / FILLES DE GANG

UNE FILLE DANS LES GANGS DE RUE

CAROLINE TOUZIN

**LA PRESSE,** Montréal

Francis Leveillee, Benoit Giguere, Genevieve Dinel, Marie-Claude Mongrain, Caroline Touzin

Multiple illustrations

**LOS ANGELES TIMES WEST MAGAZINE**

Liz Hale, Joseph Hutchinson

Multiple illustrations

NATIONAL POST TORONTO

FILM FESTIVAL SPECIAL · SHINAN · STARS · SPAS · SHOPS · SEATS · STYLE · SUDOKU

**NATIONAL POST,** Toronto
Doug Kelly, Gayle Grin, Kagan McLeod
Multiple illustrations

school names pop quiz

Thought Experiment I

Pop Quiz I: Lives of the Saints

**SWERVE,** Calgary, Alberta, Canada
Mike Kerr, Nicole Salzano
Multiple illustrations

**Das Budget der Studenten.** Jetzt geht das Semester los. Viele Studenten stehen zum ersten Mal a zahlen Miete und haben hohe Fahrtkosten. Wir erklären, wie sie Geld verdienen, ausgeben und s

# Richtig jobben

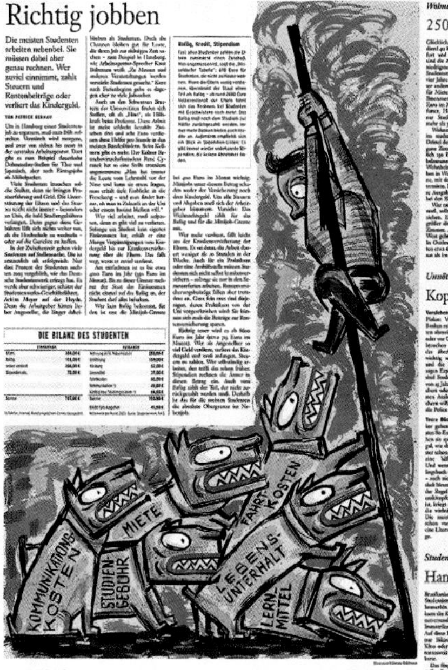


DIE BILANZ DES STUDENTEN

Auf Stellensuche · Viel unterwegs · Ohne Computer · Teure Großstadt

**FRANKFURTER ALLGEMEINE SONNTAGSZEITUNG**
Frankfurt am Main, Germany
Staff
Use of illustrations

Richmond Times-Dispatch • Sunday, December 17, 2006

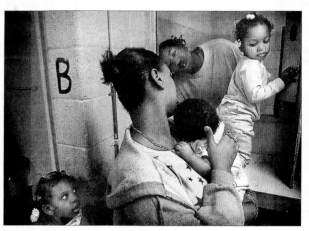

**MAINTAINING CONNECTIONS** With more than 20,000 people going to jail in Richmond every year — some are counted more than once because they are sent multiple times — the visitor booths in the Fairfield Way building stay busy. Jacquetta Jones visits boyfriend Shaine Johnson once a week. Her daughters (from left) Quedesha Jones, My'Angel Johnson and Amya Jones come, too.

**GAMBLING** They gamble on the street, betting they'll get away with breaking another law. They gamble in jail, though it is not allowed. Here, F-1 inmates shoot craps. The stakes are the snacks they buy from the jail canteen. Settling debts before and after deliveries make Thursdays and Fridays the most tense, violent days in jail.

SILVER
**RICHMOND TIMES-DISPATCH** (Va.)
Eva Russo
General news photo

It's a story that everyone knows, but the photo brings it home. The broken family is the social issue of our time, and this picture captures it. The children's faces — that connection. It portrays emotion as it defines the state of documentary photography.

Ésta es una historia conocida por todos, pero la foto la trae a casa. La familia fracturada es un asunto social de nuestro tiempo, y esta foto lo captura. Las caras de los niños; esa conexión. Retrata la emoción al tiempo que define la actual fotografía documental.

**PITTSBURGH POST-GAZETTE**
Robin Rombach
General news photo

**THE SAN DIEGO UNION-TRIBUNE**
Peggy Peattie
Feature photo

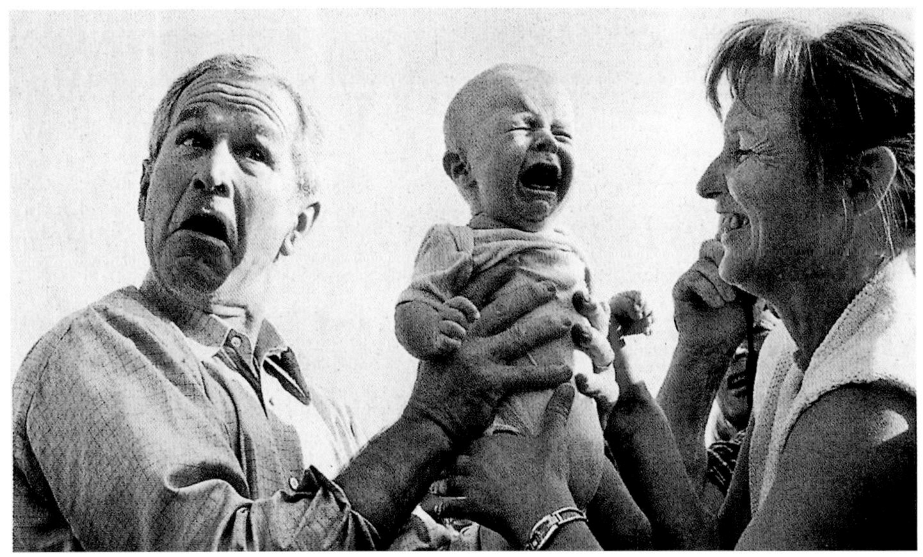

**FINANCIAL TIMES DEUTSCHLAND,** Hamburg, Germany
General news photo

**THE DENVER POST**
Craig F. Walker
Feature photo

**THE NEWS TRIBUNE,** Tacoma, Wash.
Dustin Snipes
Feature photo

**ROCKY MOUNTAIN NEWS,** Denver
Chris Schneider
General news photo

**RICHMOND TIMES-DISPATCH** (Va.)
Mark Gormus
General news photo

**PROVINCIA,** Morelra, México
Manuel Baeza, Gustavo Vega, Alfredo Desgarennes
General news photo

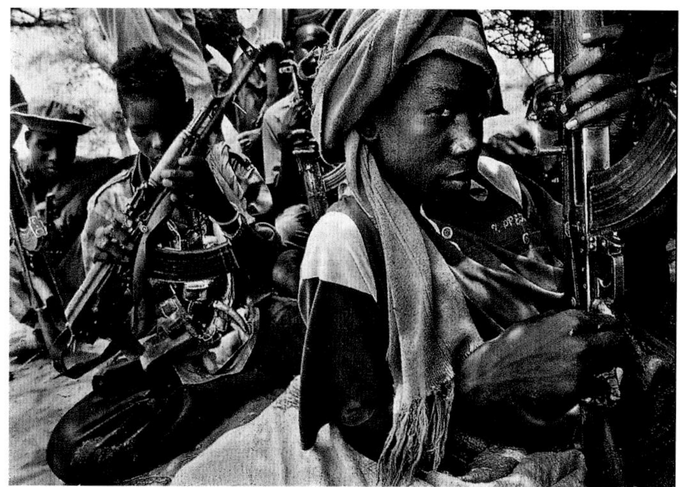

**LOS ANGELES TIMES**
Carolyn Cole, Steve Stroud, Alex Brown, Michael Whitley
General news photo

**THE DENVER POST**
Craig F. Walker
General news photo

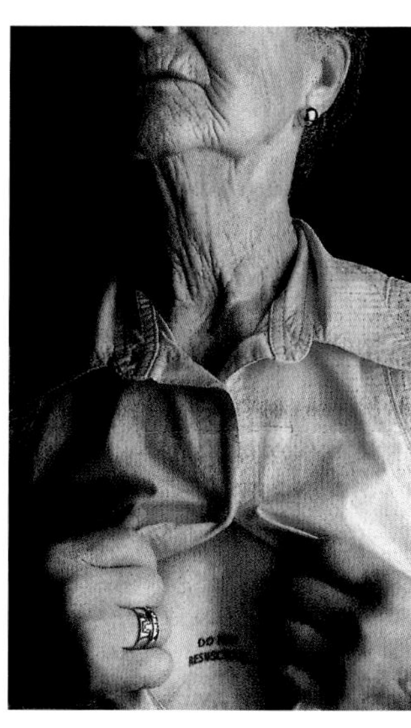

**TELEGRAPH HERALD,** Dubuque, Iowa
Jeremy Portje
General news photo

**QUAD-CITY TIMES,** Davenport, Iowa
Jeff Cook
General news photo

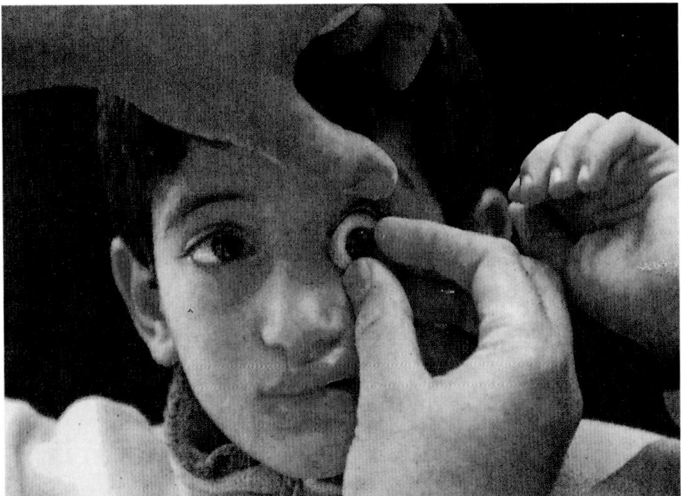

**PITTSBURGH POST-GAZETTE**
John Beale
General news photo

**ROCKY MOUNTAIN NEWS,** Denver
Evan Semon
General news photo

**ARKANSAS DEMOCRAT-GAZETTE,** Little Rock
Benjamin Krain
General news photo

**SOUTH FLORIDA SUN-SENTINEL,** Fort Lauderdale
Robert Mayer, Meghan Lyden
General news photo

**THE STAR-LEDGER,** Newark, N.J.
John Munson, Rachel French, Pim Van Hemmen, Mark Morrisey, Mark Miller, Chris D'Amico
General news photo

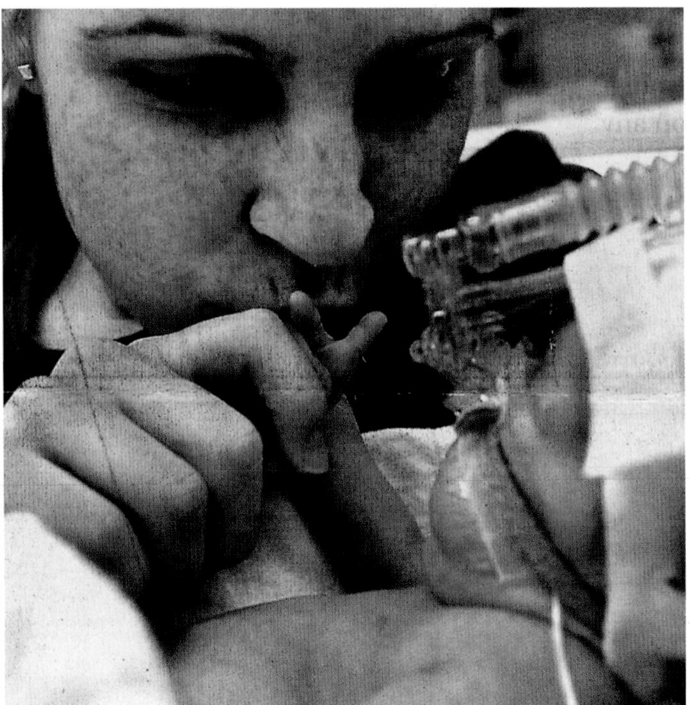

**NATIONAL POST,** Toronto
Doug Kelly, Gayle Grin, Stephen Meurice, Tom Philip, Kelly McParland, Jeff Wasserman, Laura Koot, Brent Foster
General news photo

**EL UNIVERSAL,** México City

Roberto Rock L., Francisco Santiago, Oscar Santiago Méndez, Rubén Álvarez, Francisco Vega, Fernando Villa del Ángel, Saúl Navarri, Carlos Morales, Esteban Román

General news photo

**THE NEW YORK TIMES**

James Estrin

Spot news photo

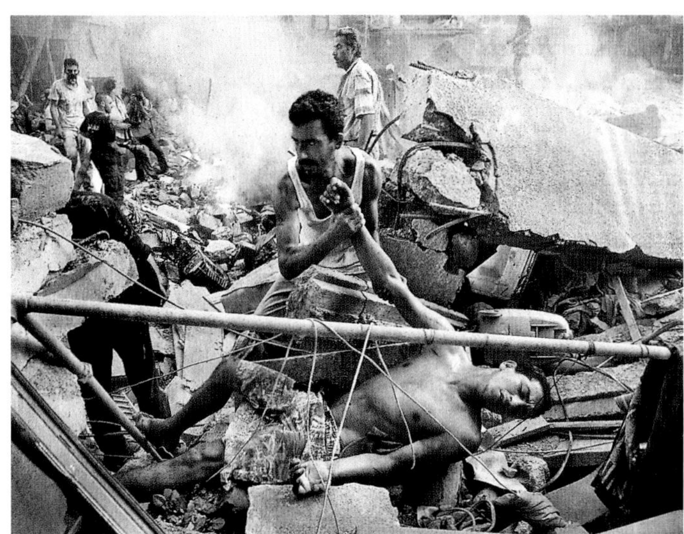

**THE NEW YORK TIMES**

Tyler Hicks

Spot news photo

**TORONTO STAR**

Lucas Oleniuk

General news photo

**THE LAS VEGAS SUN**

Sam Morris, Karin Anderson

Sports photo

**SEATTLE POST-INTELLIGENCER**

Meryl Schenker

General news photo

**LEXINGTON HERALD-LEADER** (Ky.)
Matt Goins
Sports photo

**THE NEWS & OBSERVER,** Raleigh, N.C.
Joshua Lott, Kevin Keister, Jessaca Giglio, Jennifer Bowles
Sports photo

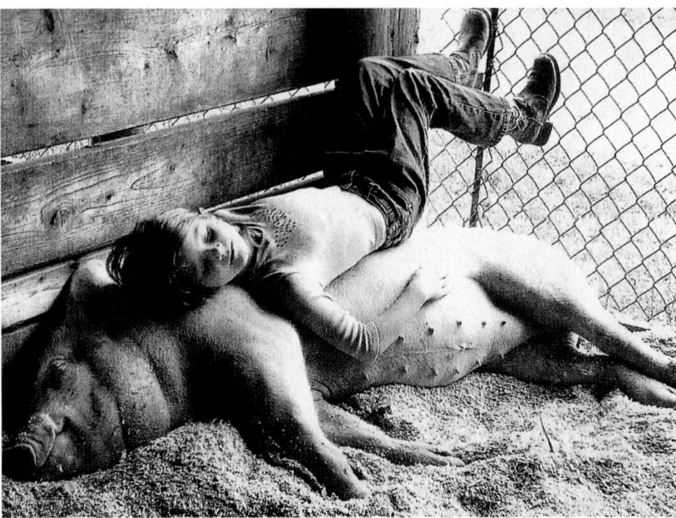

**SUN JOURNAL,** Lewiston, Maine
Russ Dillingham, Nick Masuda, Douglas Van Reeth
Feature photo

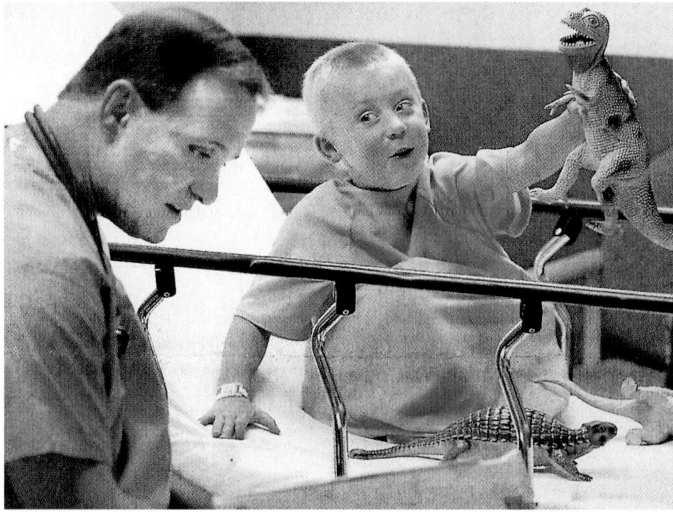

**ST. PAUL PIONEER PRESS** (Minn.)
Sherri LaRose-Chiglo, Hillery Shay
Feature photo

**LOS ANGELES TIMES**
Damon Winter, Gail Fisher, Lorraine Wang, Kelli Sullivan
Portrait photo

**THE DALLAS MORNING NEWS**
John F. Rhodes
Sports photo

**THE HARTFORD COURANT** (Conn.)
Beth Bristow, John Woike, Nicole Dudka
Photo illustration

**THE PLAIN DEALER,** Cleveland
Andrea Levy
Photo illustration

**THE SEATTLE POST-INTELLIGENCER**
Andy Rogers, Jim Woolace
Photo illustration

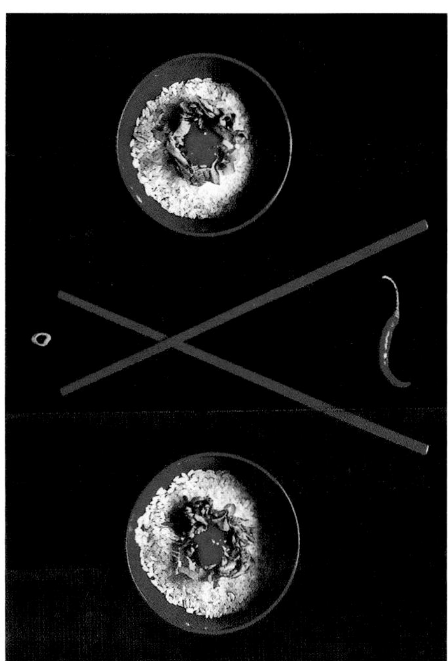

**THE HARTFORD COURANT** (Conn.)
Beth Bristow, Ross Taylor, Timothy Reck
Photo illustration

**THE BOSTON GLOBE MAGAZINE**
Emily Reid Kehe, Dina Rudick, Doug Most, Brendan Stephens
Portrait photo

**THE SEATTLE POST-INTELLIGENCER**
Andy Rogers
Portrait photo

**LOS ANGELES TIMES**
Mel Melcon, Cindy Hively, Kirk McKoy, Paul Gonzales
Portrait photo

THEATER

Who rules the musical?

Daring storytelling that integrates song and dance is rare. But a few auteurs strive for the elusive formula.

**SOUTH FLORIDA SUN-SENTINEL,** Fort Lauderdale
Tim Rasmussen, Mary Vignoles, Rebekah Monson, Chris Mihal, Joe Amon, Tim Frank
Photo project

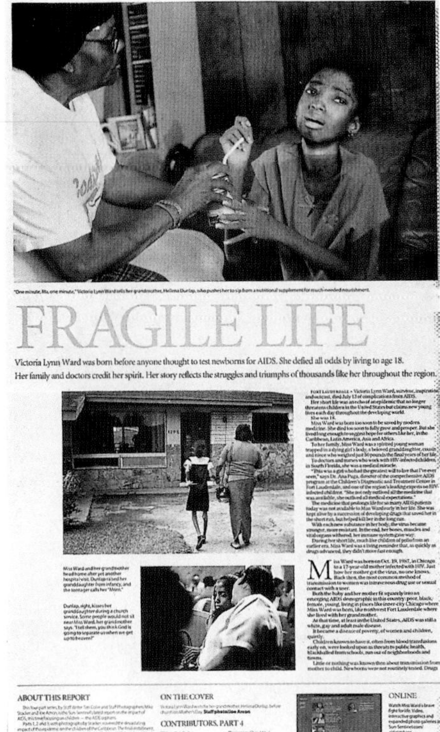
FRAGILE LIFE

Victoria Lynn Ward was born before anyone thought to test newborns for AIDS. She defied all odds by living to age 18. Her family and doctors credit her spirit. Her story reflects the struggles and triumphs of thousands like her throughout the region.

ABOUT THIS REPORT

ON THE COVER

CONTRIBUTORS, PART 4

ONLINE

CONTACT US

**THE SEATTLE TIMES**
Alan Berner, Nick Perry, Fred Nelson, Ted Basladynski
Photo project

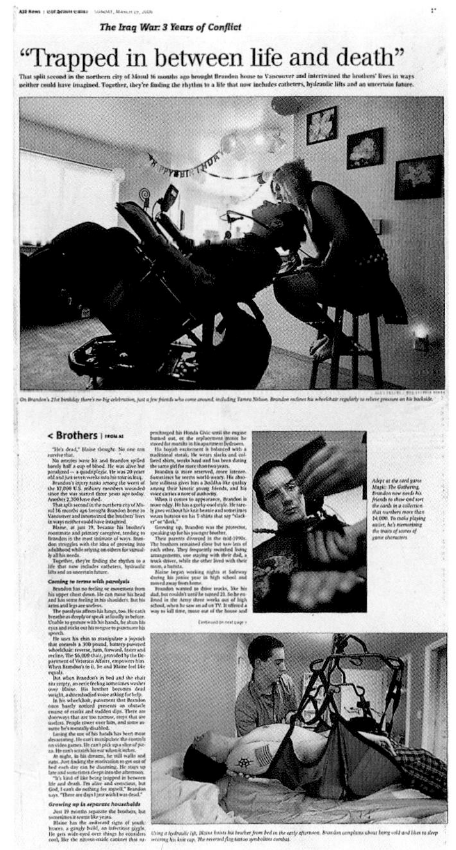
The Iraq War: 3 Years of Conflict

"Trapped in between life and death"

That split second in the northern city of Mosul 16 months ago brought Brandon home to Vancouver and intertwined the brothers' lives in ways neither could have imagined. Together, they're finding the rhythm to a life that now includes catheters, hydraulic lifts and an uncertain future.

< Brothers

**THE ATLANTA JOURNAL-CONSTITUTION**
Rich Addicks
Photo series

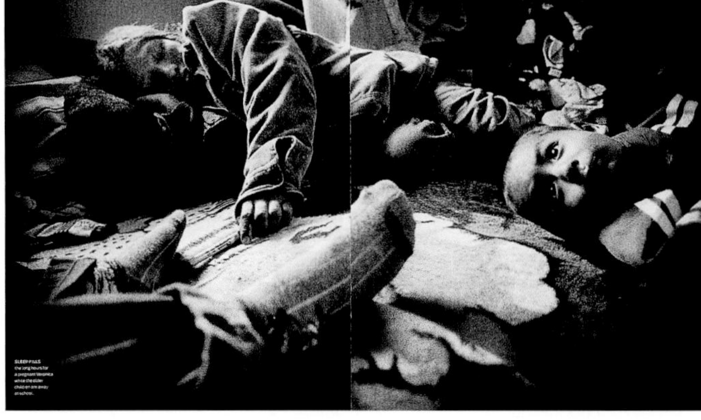

**LOS ANGELES TIMES WEST MAGAZINE**
Heidi Volpe, Joseph Hutchinson, Russell Devita, Matt Black
Photo project

AVENUE

Arts, Culture & Society

Uganda

nationalpost.com

**NATIONAL POST,** Toronto
Doug Kelly, Gayle Grin, Jeff Wasserman, Laura Koot, Colin O'Connor
Photo project

The water. Why we are here, and who we are.

We draw from it, and we are drawn to it.

SILVER

**THE VIRGINIAN-PILOT,** Norfolk

Photo Staff, Alex Burrows, Deborah Withey

Photo series

The series "Of Time and Tides" conveys how the coastal community is tied to the water. It's looking at something you see every day: "How can we do a story on this? How can we make our community understand what we all take for granted?" The ideas are so smart, from the propeller on the boat to the baptism, and they capture the human relationship with water.

La serie "Sobre el tiempo y las mareas" enseña la forma en que la comunidad costera está unida al agua. Es como ver algo que se ve cotidianamente: "¿De qué forma podemos hacer un relato sobre esto?" ¿De que forma podemos hacer que nuestra comunidad comprenda lo que damos por hecho?" Las ideas son muy inteligentes, desde la hélice en el bote hasta el bautismo, y captan la relación entre los seres humanos y el agua.

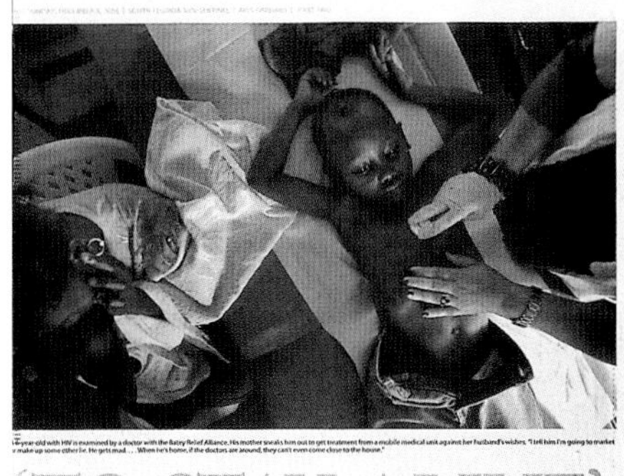

'TO STAY ALIVE'

Bateyes, labor camps for old sugar plantations in the Dominican Republic, have the highest HIV infection rate in the Caribbean. Some men deny the disease exists. But some women overcome fear to get treatment for themselves and their children.

**SOUTH FLORIDA SUN-SENTINEL,** Fort Lauderdale

Tim Rasmussen, Mary Vignoles, Rebekah Monson, Chris Mihal, Mike Stocker, Tim Frank

Photo project

The Birmingham News

DESEGREGATING THE SCHOOLS | 1962-1963

DIFFICULT LESSONS

Black students' attempts to enroll at the University of Alabama and the University of Mississippi were thwarted and sparked legal battles. Integration of Birmingham public schools in 1963 brought violence. Lawyer Arthur D. Shores' home was bombed Aug. 20. On Sept. 5, after James Armstrong registered his sons at Graymont Elementary, a phone caller warned, "How would you like to see all your kids lying in a casket?" That night another bomb hit the Shores home and gunfire erupted nearby. Schools closed, then reopened a week later with 24 black children joining 5,500 white children in nine schools. Five days later, a bomb killed four girls at Sixteenth Street Baptist Church.

Sept. 15, 1963

Birmingham Mayor Albert Boutwell after news circulates that the Sixteenth Street Baptist Church was bombed. "All of us are victims. Most of us are innocent victims," Boutwell told a stunned city that evening. Birmingham News columnist Walling Keith is at right.

The reaction

West End students boycott class to protest the enrollment of Marcus and Josephine Powell.

**THE BIRMINGHAM NEWS** (Ala.)

Scott Walker, Walt Stricklin , Alexander Cohn, Napo Monasterio, Rick Frennea, Barnett Wright

Photo project

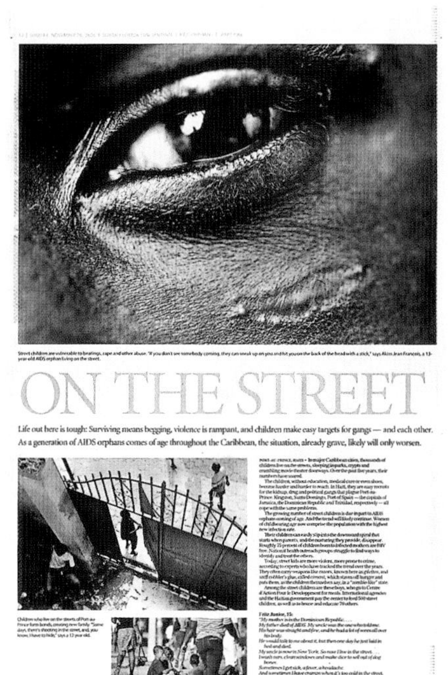

ON THE STREET

Life out here is tough: Surviving means begging, violence is rampant, and children make easy targets for gangs — and each other. As a generation of AIDS orphans comes of age throughout the Caribbean, the situation, already grave, likely will only worsen.

**LOS ANGELES TIMES WEST MAGAZINE**

Joseph Hutchinson, Carol Wakano, José Picayo

Magazine inside page

**THE SPOKESMAN-REVIEW,** Spokane, Wash.
Brian Plonka
Special news topics, local

**SACRAMENTO BEE** (Calif.)
Renee C. Byer, Sue Morrow, Mark Morris, Robert Casey
Photo series

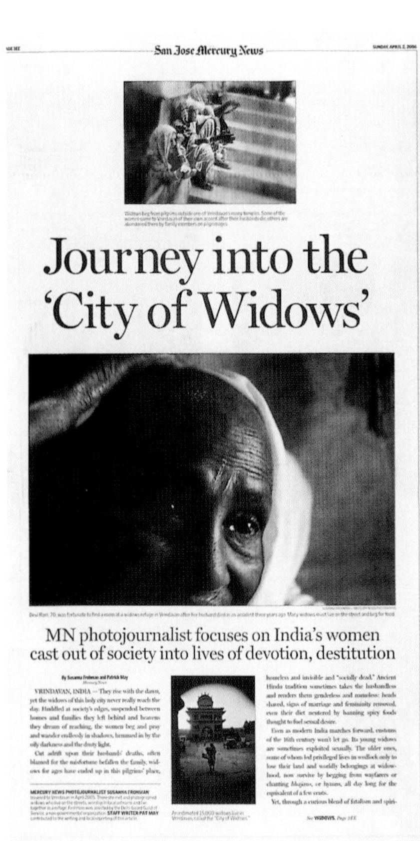

San Jose Mercury News

# Journey into the 'City of Widows'

## MN photojournalist focuses on India's women cast out of society into lives of devotion, destitution

**SAN JOSE MERCURY NEWS** (Calif.)
Susanna Frohman, Geri Migielicz, Mark Damon, Jami C. Smith, Michael Tribble
Photo project

SPRING 2006 BASEBALL ALL-AREA

# JOHN TOLISANO

JUNIOR – SHORTSTOP – ESTERO

Q&A

ALL-AREA FIRST TEAM

John Tolisano, Bo Greenwell, Marcus Rodriguez, Taylor Hashman, Todd Waller, Zach See, Robert Greene, Rey Delesus, Jeff Schaus, Aaron Crittenden, Brett Eckler, Ian Parry

SECOND TEAM

HONORABLE MENTION

THIRD TEAM

THE NEWS-PRESS COACH OF THE YEAR

Ted Parsons

**THE NEWS-PRESS,** Fort Myers, Fla.
Todd Stubing, Ricardo Rolon, Kinfe Moroti, Javier Torres
Photo series

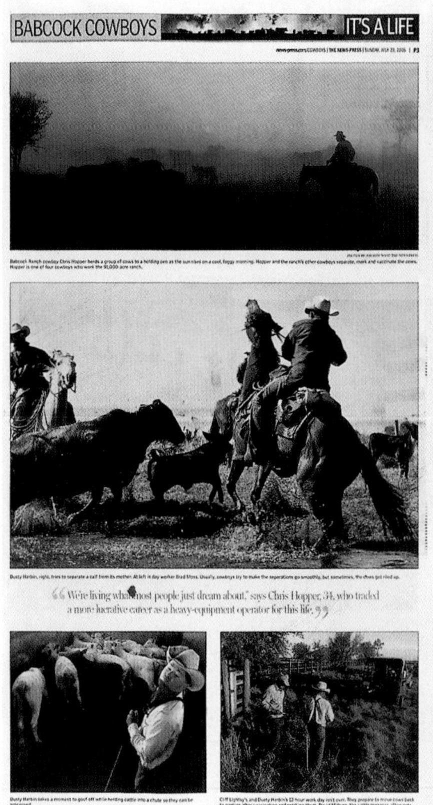

BABCOCK COWBOYS IT'S A LIFE

"We're living what most people just dream about," says Chris Hopper, 34, who traded a more lucrative career as a heavy-equipment operator for this life.

**THE NEWS-PRESS,** Fort Myers, Fla.
Andrew West, Javier Torres, Kinfe Moroti, Amy Williams
Photo series

THE BRIDE PRICE

IN AFGHANISTAN, SOME DAUGHTERS SENT OFF TO BE MARRIED ARE JUST CHILDREN.

**THE NEW YORK TIMES MAGAZINE**
Janet Froelich, Arem Duplessis, Jeff Docherty, Kathy Ryan, Stephanie Sinclair
Photo series

Studies in athletic eloquence.
Photographs by ANDRES SERRANO

**PLAY, THE NEW YORK TIMES SPORTS MAGAZINE**
Janet Froelich, Dirk Barnett, Andres Serrano
Photo series

Lifestyle

9-11: FIVE YEARS AFTER

I remember

Staff photos by Michael Laughlin Text by Staff Writer John Tanasychuk

We asked people across South Florida to take us back to Sept. 11, 2001. Where they were. What they were doing. What they felt. After taking a portrait, we gave each a copy of the image and a pen.

**SOUTH FLORIDA SUN-SENTINEL,** Fort Lauderdale
Michael Laughlin, Mary Vignoles, Susana Sanchez
Photo page design

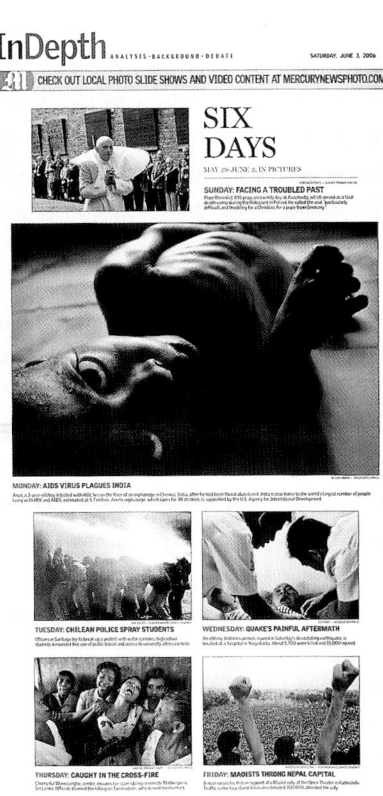

InDepth ANALYSES · BACKGROUND · DEBATE SATURDAY, JUNE 3, 2006 3A

CHECK OUT LOCAL PHOTO SLIDE SHOWS AND VIDEO CONTENT AT MERCURYNEWSPHOTO.COM

SIX DAYS

MAY 29–JUNE 2, IN PICTURES

SUNDAY: FACING A TROUBLED PAST

MONDAY: AIDS VIRUS PLAGUES INDIA

TUESDAY: CHILEAN POLICE SPRAY STUDENTS

WEDNESDAY: QUAKE'S PAINFUL AFTERMATH

THURSDAY: CAUGHT IN THE CROSS-FIRE

FRIDAY: MAOISTS THRONG NEPAL CAPITAL

**SAN JOSE MERCURY NEWS** (Calif.)
Staff
Photo page design

ARTS & ENTERTAINMENT

PHOTOGRAPHY

1912–2006

Gordon Parks

This renaissance man's real claim to fame was as a brilliant photographer, who delivered multitudes of memorable images.

**CHICAGO TRIBUNE**
Robin Daughtridge, Joan Cainey
Photo page design

Everything hurts — her back, her belly, her incision. It'll be days before she gets her pain medication.

**RICHMOND TIMES-DISPATCH** (Va.)
Eva Russo
Photo series

5 STORIES TO TALK ABOUT TODAY

**CARDS SOAR!**
St. Louis tames Tigers in Series opener | C1

**TARGETED:** Will Davis voters ban big boxes? | B1

**DAD'S VIEW:** Coping with MySpace fallout | E1

**PET PLANS:** Should you get insurance? | L1

**UNLEASHED:** Carmel is heaven for dogs | M1

FOUNDED 1857

# The Sacramento Bee

SUNDAY, OCTOBER 22, 2006 •• www.sacbee.com •••• FINAL EDITION $1.50

A SACRAMENTO BEE SPECIAL REPORT ■ A FOUR-DAY SERIES

## THE WEIGHT

CHAPTER ONE
HEAVY BEGINNINGS

The burdens they carry are enormous – not just on their oversized frames, but in so many other facets of their lives. Meet Ricci, Annya and Jahcobie, three teens struggling with obesity and all its complications. They arrive at the Academy of the Sierras not only to shed pounds, but to forever transform themselves.

RICCI AMORUSO, 16, Folsom
Fall 2005: 304 pounds

ANNYA MAGALLANES, 13, Orosi, Calif.
Fall 2005: 407 pounds

JAHCOBIE COSUM, 15, Boston
Fall 2005: 483 pounds

■ STORIES AND PHOTOGRAPHS BY MANNY CRISOSTOMO SACRAMENTO BEE STAFF PHOTOGRAPHER

For a multimedia presentation of this story, including the students' experiences told in their own words, please go to: www.sacbee.com/theweight

## Kings' new coach busted

Musselman is arrested in Sacramento on suspicion of driving while drunk.

By Ryan Lillis and Sam Amick

First-year Kings coach Eric Musselman was arrested early Saturday on suspicion of drunken driving, authorities said.

Eric Musselman

▶ MUSSELMAN, back page, A22

CAMPAIGN 2006
Bonds on the ballot

## Rebuilding tab is slow to set in

Many voters draw a blank on $37.3 billion impact.

By Andy Furillo

▶ BONDS, Page A19

INSIDE

▶ Page A3

## Tribunals law divides experts

With a high court test likely, analysts are split over whether the measure will pass muster.

By James Rosen
McCLATCHY WASHINGTON BUREAU

▶ TRIBUNALS, Page A18

Sen. Lindsey Graham, R-S.C., says he expects the Supreme Court to rule in favor of a compromise military tribunal law he helped work out with the White House.

INDEX

METRO
**Giving the gift of life**

SPORTS
**Cal wins in OT**

BUSINESS
**CalPERS rethinks game plan**

TICKET +
**Ballet and the beasts**

WEATHER
Mostly sunny
83|49

**SACRAMENTO BEE** (Calif.)
Manny Cristosomo, Sue Morrow, Mark Morris, Robert Casey
Photo series

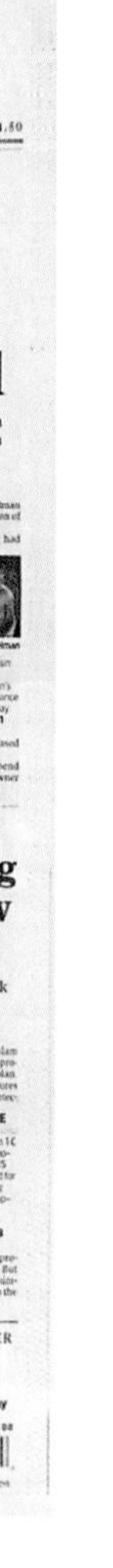

**THE NEW YORK TIMES STYLE MAGAZINE**
Janet Froelich, David Sebbah, Chris Martinez, Robert Maxwell
Photo series

Eyewitness International Space Station, Atlantis and the sun

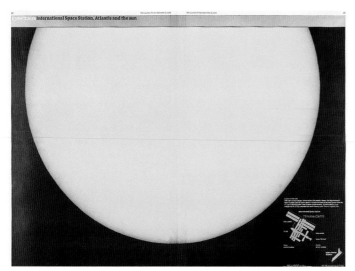

**THE GUARDIAN,** London
Thierry Legault, Roger Tooth
Photo page design

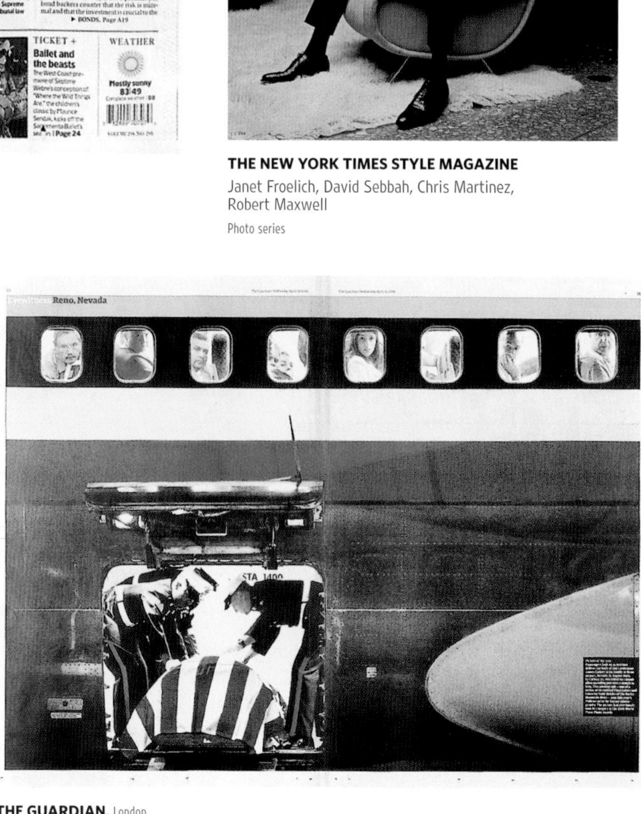

Eyewitness Reno, Nevada

**THE GUARDIAN,** London
Todd Heisler, Roger Tooth
Photo page design

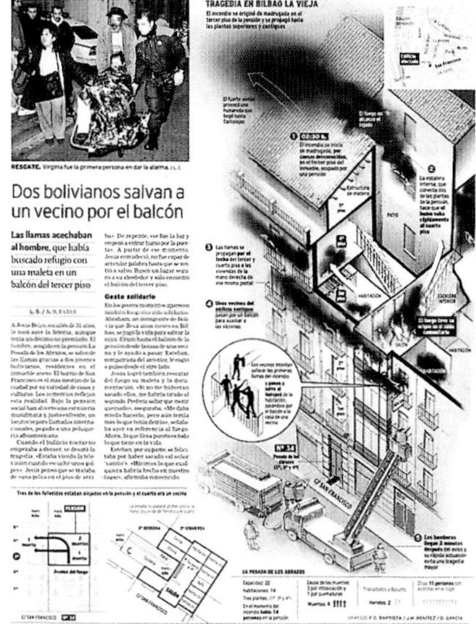


**EL CORREO,** Bilbao, Spain
Fernando G. Baptista, José Miguel Benítez, Daniel Garcia
Information graphics, breaking news, 50,000-174,999

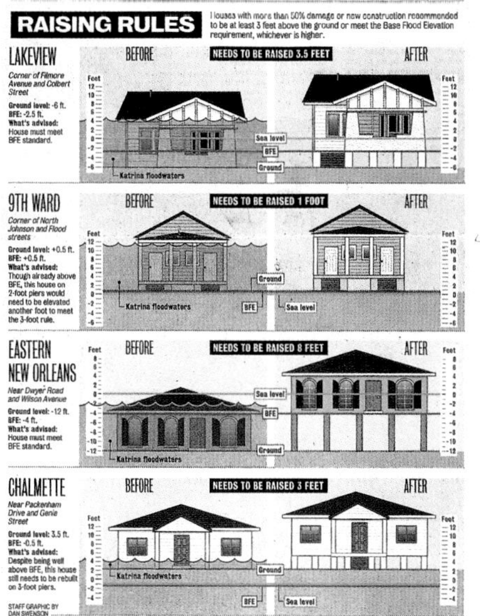


**THE TIMES-PICAYUNE,** New Orleans
Dan Swenson
Information graphics, breaking news, 175,000+

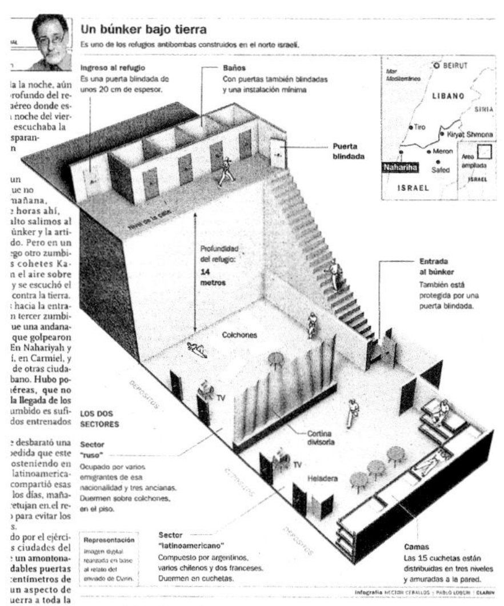


**CLARÍN,** Buenos Aires, Argentina
Alejandro Tumas, Pablo Loscri, Héctor Ceballos
Information graphics, breaking news, 175,000+

**EL MUNDO DEL SIGLO XXI,** Madrid, Spain
Juantxo Cruz, Emilio Amade, Modesto J. Carrasco, Rafa Estrada, Daniel Izeddin
Information graphics, breaking news, 175,000+

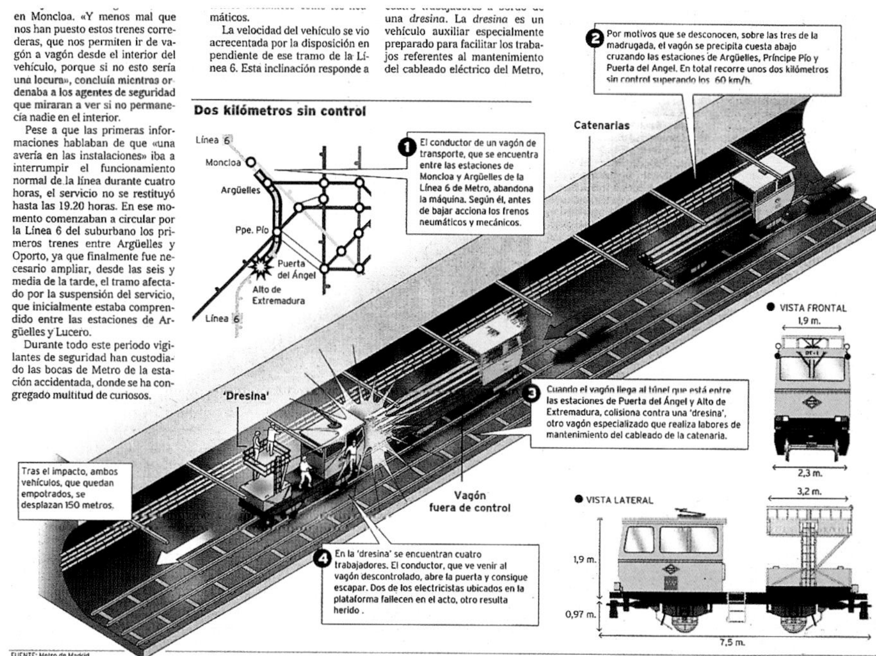

en Moncloa. «Y menos mal que nos han puesto estos trenes correderas, que nos permiten ir de vagón a vagón desde el interior del vehículo, porque si no esto sería una locura», concluía mientras ordenaba a los agentes de seguridad que miraran a ver si no permanecía nadie en el interior.

Pese a que las primeras informaciones hablaban de que «una avería en las instalaciones» iba a interrumpir el funcionamiento normal de la línea durante cuatro horas, el servicio no se restituyó hasta las 19.20 horas. En ese momento comenzaban a circular por la Línea 6 del suburbano los primeros trenes entre Argüelles y Oporto, ya que finalmente fue necesario ampliar, desde las seis y media de la tarde, el tramo afectado por la suspensión del servicio, que inicialmente estaba comprendido entre las estaciones de Argüelles y Lucero.

Durante todo este periodo vigilantes de seguridad han custodiado las bocas de Metro de la estación accidentada, donde se ha congregado multitud de curiosos.

máticos.

La velocidad del vehículo se vio acrecentada por la disposición en pendiente de ese tramo de la Línea 6. Esta inclinación responde a

una *dresina*. La *dresina* es un vehículo auxiliar especialmente preparado para facilitar los trabajos referentes al mantenimiento del cableado eléctrico del Metro,

**CLARÍN,** Buenos Aires, Argentina
Alejandro Tumas, Pablo Loscri, Jorge Portaz, Gerardo Morel, Guillermo Milla
Information graphics, breaking news, 175,000+

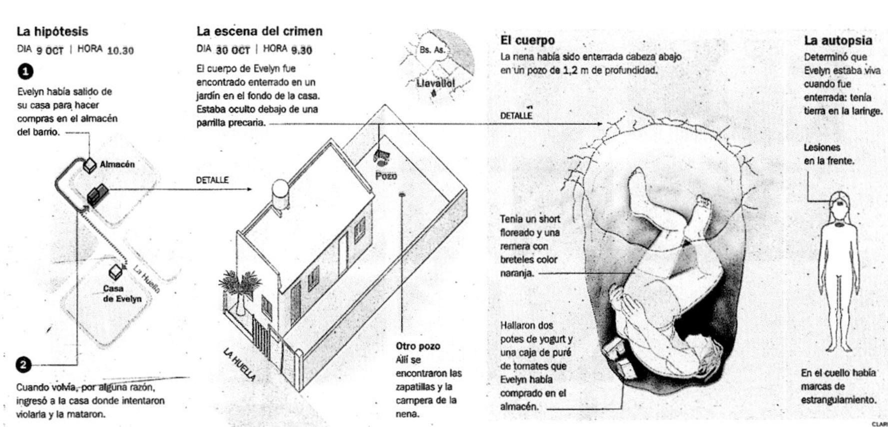


**CLARÍN,** Buenos Aires, Argentina
Alejandro Tumas, Pablo Loscri, Jorge Portaz
Information graphics, breaking news, 175,000+

**THE NEW YORK TIMES**
Staff
Information graphics, breaking news, 175,000+

Sequence of Events

A single-engine plane registered to New York Yankees pitcher Cory Lidle crashed into a residential building on East 72nd Street. Mr. Lidle and his flight instructor were both killed, but there were no other serious injuries.

**THE WASHINGTON POST**
Laura Stanton, Dita Smith, Laris Karklis, Larry Nista
Information graphics, breaking news, 175,000+

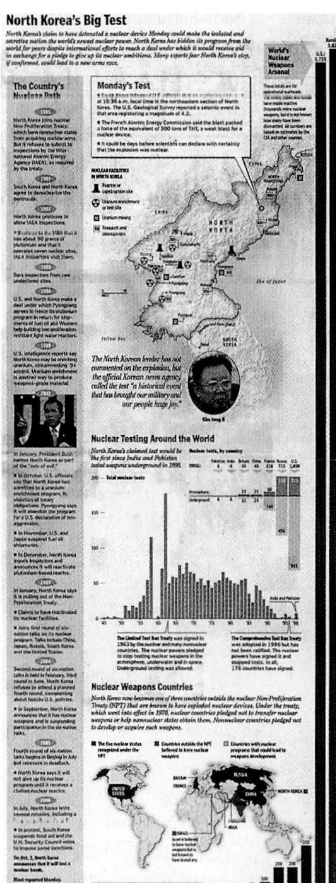
North Korea's Big Test

The Country's Nuclear Path

Monday's Test

World's Nuclear Weapons Arsenal

Nuclear Testing Around the World

Nuclear Weapons Countries

**EL CORREO,** Bilbao, Spain
Fernando G. Baptista, José Miguel Benítez
Information graphics, breaking news, 50,000-174,999

Vivir

La mujer a la que extirparon 60 kilos de grasa en Cruces aprende a andar y respirar de nuevo

El faldón abdominal retirado a la paciente es el más grande que recogen los anales de la medicina

«¡Vaya, ahora me veo los pies!», exclamó la enferma al despertar de los efectos de la anestesia

Problemas respiratorios

Fue necesario diseñar un sistema de grúas y una camilla especial

TERROR FRENTE A CIUDAD UNIVERSITARIA

SAN SALVADOR

**LA PRENSA GRÁFICA,** Antiguo Cuscatlán, El Salvador
Enrique Contreras, Héctor Ramírez, Óscar Rivas Corvera, Ricardo Orellana, Jorge Luis Contreras
Information graphics, breaking news, 50,000-174,999

The shuttle roars back

The Virginian-Pilot

Defiant N. Korea tests missiles

LifeNet files suit against claims of competitor

"PROVOCATIVE" LAUNCHES QUICKLY DRAW CRITICISM

Take-charge style, once an asset, may cost Suffolk manager his job

Celebrating the Fourth

**THE VIRGINIAN-PILOT,** Norfolk
Staff
Use of photography

InDepth ANALYSIS · BACKGROUND · DEBATE

CHECK OUT LOCAL PHOTO SLIDE SHOWS AND VIDEO CONTENT AT MERCURYNEWSPHOTO.COM

SIX DAYS

FEB. 19-24, IN PICTURES

SUNDAY: CARTOONS STILL DISTRESSING

MONDAY: UGANDAN ELECTION FACE-OFF

WEDNESDAY: MINING FAMILIES' ANGUISH

THURSDAY: IDENTIFYING MUSLIDE VICTIMS

FRIDAY: AMERICAN HOSTAGE IN NIGERIA

TUESDAY: LONELY PLACE TO BE DISABLED CHINESE ORPHAN

**SAN JOSE MERCURY NEWS** (Calif.)
Staff
Photo page design

LOOK INSIDE FOR SATURDAY'S PUZZLES — PAGE E4

ARTS&LIFE

'Mystic River' author's winding road

MUST LOVE DOGS

**THE PLAIN DEALER,** Cleveland
David Kordalski, Emmet Smith, Joshua Gunter, Bill Gugliotta, Bill Kennedy
Photo page design

**THE GLOBE AND MAIL,** Toronto
Cinders McLeod, Brian Kerrigan, Erin Elder, Cathrin Bradbury, Jerry Johnson
Photo page design

**THE PALM BEACH POST,** West Palm Beach, Fla.
Mark Edelson, Amy Royster, Cheryl Blackerby
Photo page design

**THE GUARDIAN,** London
Saurabh Das, Roger Tooth
Photo page design

# LOCAL & STATE

B
AUGUST 13, 2006
SUNDAY MONITOR
concordmonitor.com

PENACOOK

## Never fear: MVHS to open on time

Work will continue as school year begins

By LISA ARSENAULT
Monitor staff

A walk through Merrimack Valley High School with less than three weeks left until the start of school reveals classrooms with missing windows and hallways with pipes and wires hanging loose. But school officials say students need to give up those wishful thoughts of an extended summer vacation; the building will be ready for opening day Aug. 30, and it will be business as usual.

"It's amazing what a work crew can do," said Principal Michael Jette. "Eighty people can get a lot accomplished in a short amount of time."

Voters approved a $20.6 million package of districtwide renovations and additions in 2005. Construction started this spring. The high school, which was built in 1967, will become a new, larger school built on the frame of the old model; it will look different from the outside and have new ceilings, windows and floors.

This summer, crews began redoing the outer shell of the building and renovating classrooms. The rooms have all-new fixtures – including cable jacks, outlets and an improved intercom system. A firewall has been added down the center of the building, and a new heating system with a wood-burning boiler has been installed.

Students and teachers are asked to remain patient with the sights and

See HIGH SCHOOL – B6

HIGH SCHOOL MATH
28,000: New square feet being built
225,000: bricks for the new façade
120: new windows
2007: year project will be completed
20.6 MILLION: cost of the districtwide construction project
10: classrooms will be renovated by the start of school
985: Students and teachers showing up Aug. 30
80: people on the construction crew
Source: Merrimack Valley High School Principal Michael Jette and District Facilities Director Fred Reagan

SPECIAL GUESTS

BEST PET EVER

5 QUESTIONS

LUCKY NUMBERS

THE TIME OF THEIR LIVES

*Top:* Rhett Courser, 9, works to get his Red Dutch Belts back into line during steer judging at the 63rd annual Belknap County 4-H Fair in Belmont yesterday. The only nonprofit 4-H fair in the state, the event features animal shows, vendors, music, entertainment, exhibits, a chicken barbecue and the annual garden tractor pull. The fair continues today.

*Above:* Christy Stover, 17, of Northfield, waits after the handiness class competition at the fair. During the event, Stover and her horse performed choreography to the song "I've Had the Time of My Life," from the *Dirty Dancing* soundtrack.

*Left:* Marin Randall, 4, checks out the horses with her mother, Stephanie Randall of Laconia. The duo has visited fairs before, so they were prepared with their flowered boots.

Photos by Lori Duff
Monitor staff

SILVER

**CONCORD MONITOR** (N.H.)
Staff
Use of photography

This is a small publication among large competition, but it shows how a small newsroom can rise above larger papers. Real images of everyday life replace portraits, making a connection with the town that you don't see often. So much of the strong work is from routine assignments — town meetings and community events. That approach becomes the strength. They're alive, and they're close.

Éste es un periódico de baja circulación en un mercado de alta competitividad, pero demuestra cómo una pequeña sala de noticias puede alzarse por sobre los grandes diarios. Imágenes reales de la vida cotidiana reemplazan los retratos, conectándose con el pueblo de una forma rara vez vista. Buena parte del potente trabajo proviene de encargos rutinarios; reuniones de alcaldía y eventos de la comunidad. Ese enfoque se vuelve una fortaleza. Están vivos y están por llegar.

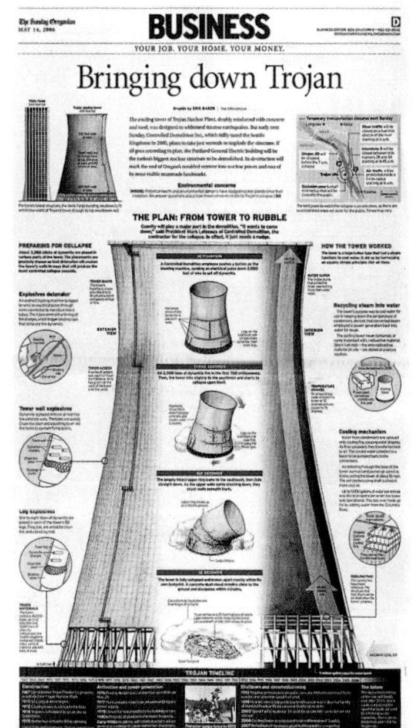


**THE OREGONIAN**
Portland
Steve McKinstry, Eric Baker
Information graphics, non-breaking news & features, 175,000+

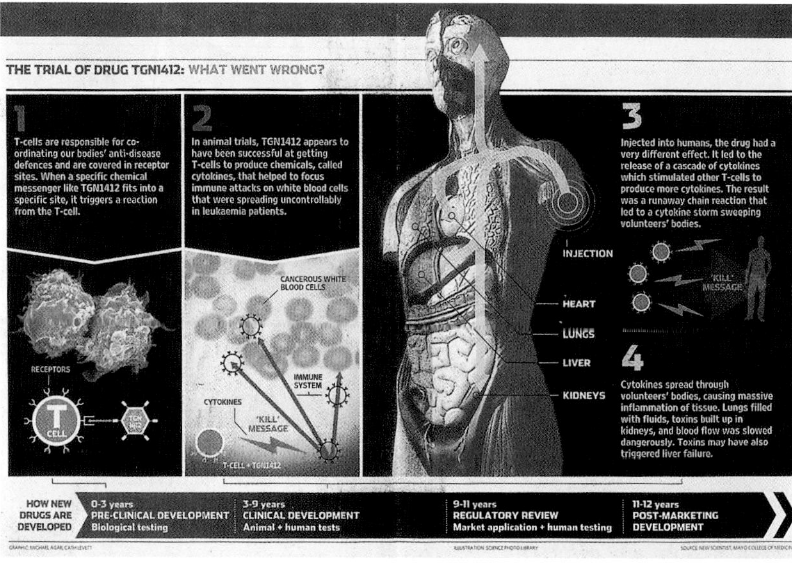


**THE OBSERVER,** London
Michael Agar, Catherine Levett
Information graphics, breaking news, 175,000+

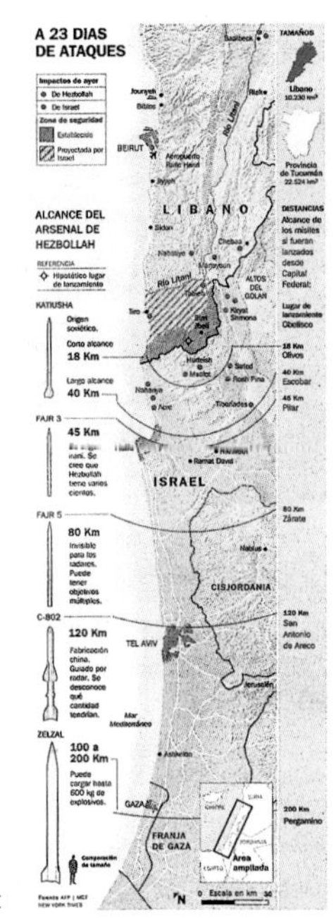


**CLARÍN,** Buenos Aires, Argentina
Alejandro Tumas, Pablo Loscri, Staff Artist
Information graphics, breaking news, 175,000+

**EL CORREO,** Bilbao, Spain
Fernando G. Baptista, Gonzalo de las Heras, Isabel Toledo
Information graphics, breaking news, 50,000-174,999

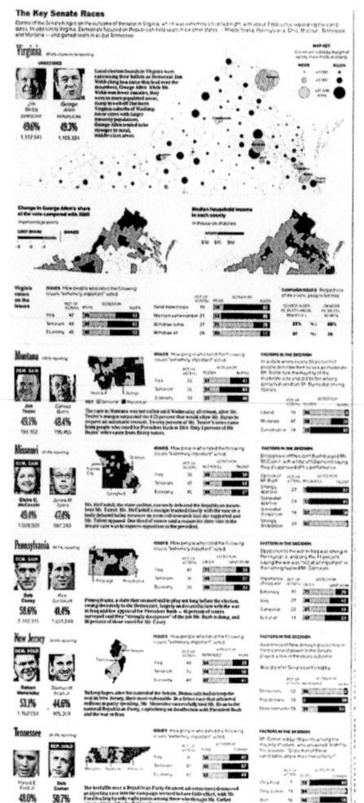
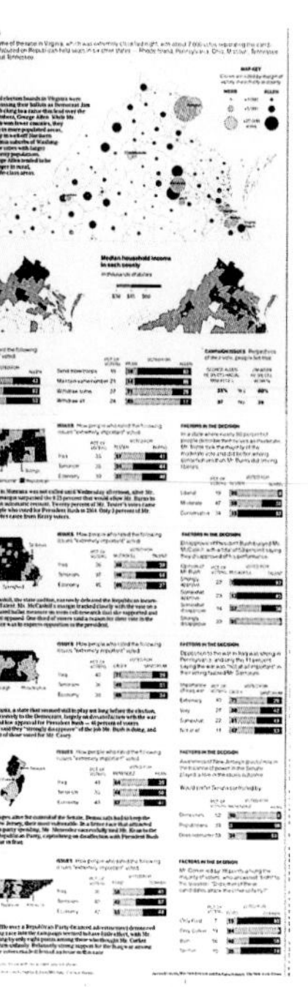

**THE NEW YORK TIMES**
James Bronzan, Matthew Ericson, Farhana Hossain
Information graphics, breaking news, 175,000+

Una explosión de gas lleva el horror al verano de Laredo

Tres miembros de una familia de Bilbao y dos vecinas de Getxo mueren intoxicados por el humo

Unos cuarenta inquilinos fueron desalojados tras permanecer una hora atrapados por las llamas

Un niño de 4 años, con graves quemaduras

**EL CORREO,** Bilbao, Spain
Fernando G. Baptista, Gonzalo de las Heras, Isabel Toledo, María Almela
Information graphics, breaking news, 50,000-174,999

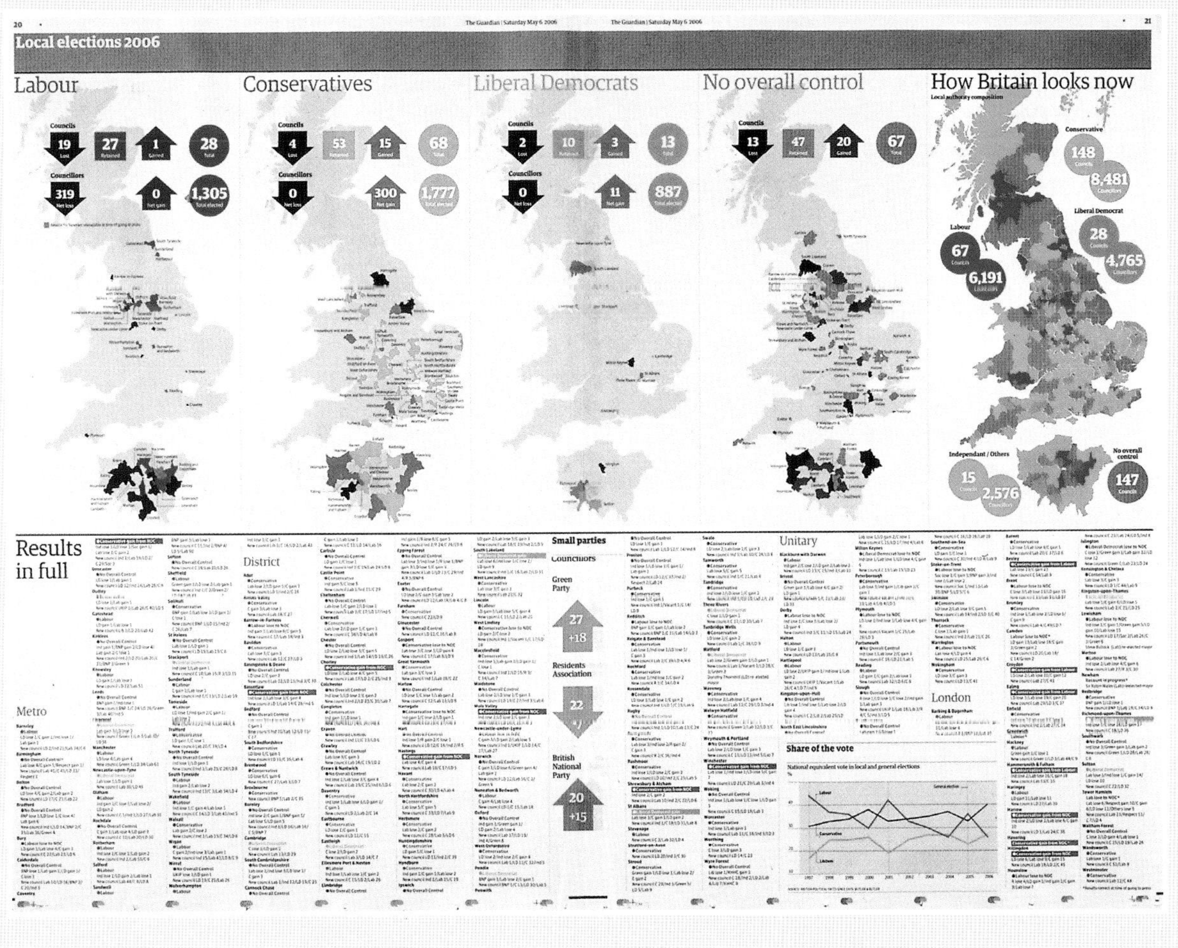


SILVER

**THE GUARDIAN,** London

Paul Scruton, Michael Robinson, Simon Rogers

Information graphics, breaking news, 175,000+

This graphic on British local elections builds like a beautifully layered painting. We love its openness and the colors tied to geographic locations. Very good use of color throughout.

Este gráfico sobre las elecciones locales británicas está construido como una bella pintura de capas. Nos encantan su apertura y los colores unidos a las localidades geográficas. Muy buen uso del color a lo largo de todo el gráfico.

**THE NEW YORK TIMES**

Archie Tse

Information graphics, breaking news, 175,000+

**LA PRENSA GRÁFICA**

Antiguo Cuscatlán, El Salvador

Enrique Contreras, Héctor Ramírez, Jorge Luis Contreras, Óscar Corvera, Efren Lemus

Information graphics, non-breaking news & features, 50,000-174,999

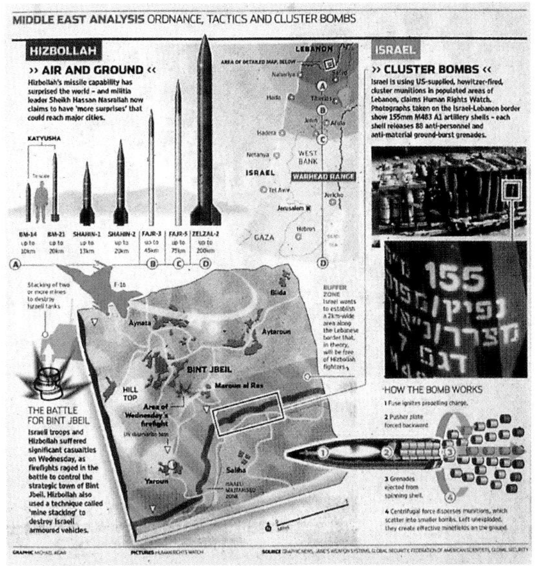


**THE OBSERVER,** London

Michael Agar, Catherine Levett

Information graphics, breaking news, 175,000+

PEINADOS Y SOMBREROS

ROPA INTERIOR

M

O

## GOLD

**EL MUNDO DEL SIGLO XXI,** Madrid, Spain

Juantxo Cruz, Emilio Amade, Isabel Gonzalez, Enrique Muñoz, Infographics Staff

Information graphics, non-breaking news & features, 175,000+

This isn't just big. It's clean and organized. A very strong grid and harmonizing color seamlessly blend one fashion into another. Instead of overpowering, it's fun and quite interactive. The formality of the background grid emphasizes the center image. Even if you're not fashion-minded, you'll be drawn to the crazy skirts and wacky shoes.

Este gráfico no es simplemente grande; es limpio y organizado. Una grilla muy potente y un color armónico combinan una moda con otra. En vez de agobiar, es divertido y bastante interactivo. La formalidad de la grilla del fondo enfatiza la imagen central. Incluso a quienes no se interesan por la moda les llamarán la atención las locas faldas y los excéntricos zapatos.

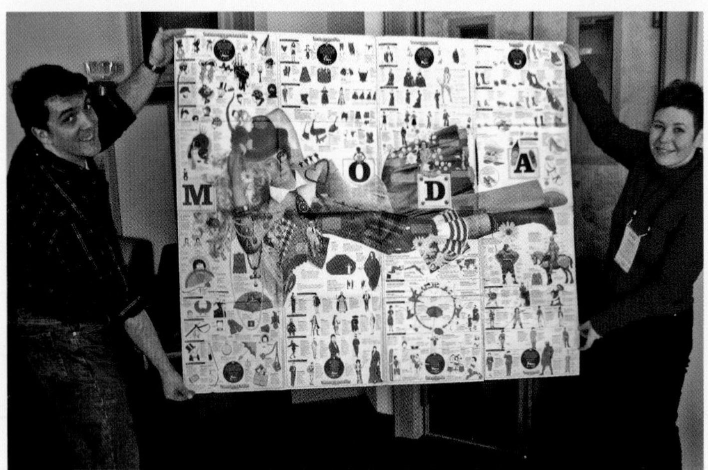


**Sean McNaughton, Syracuse University, and Anna Östlund, SND/Scandinavia, display the gold-winning El Mundo graphic on the history of fashion during the 28th-annual judging.**

PHOTO BY STEVE DORSEY, DETROIT FREE PRESS

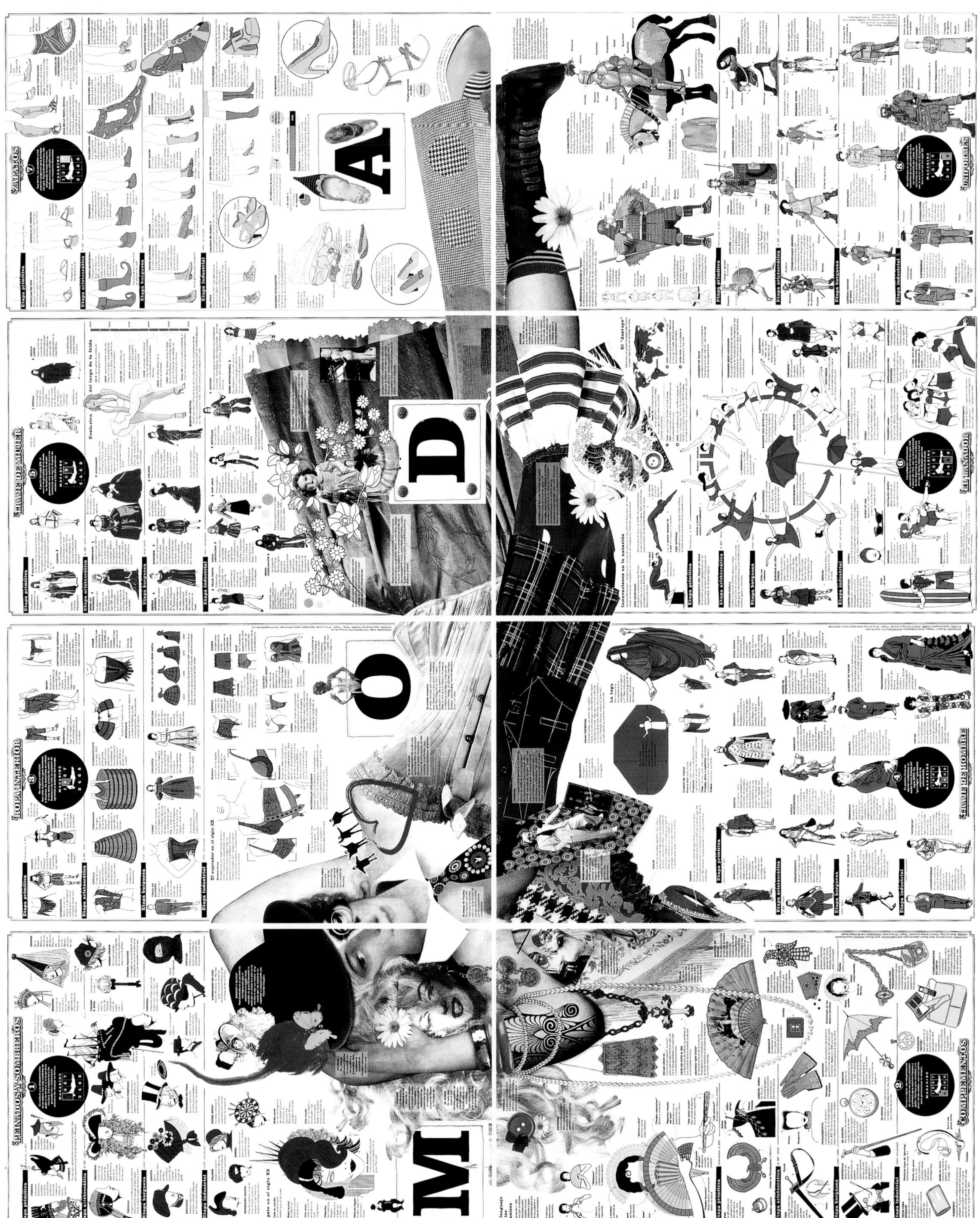

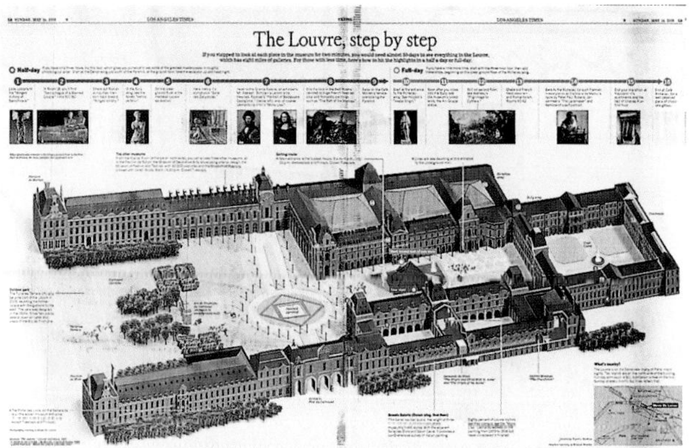

The Louvre, step by step

**LOS ANGELES TIMES**

Raoul Rañoa, Susan Spano, Les Dunseith

Information graphics, non-breaking news & features, 175,000+

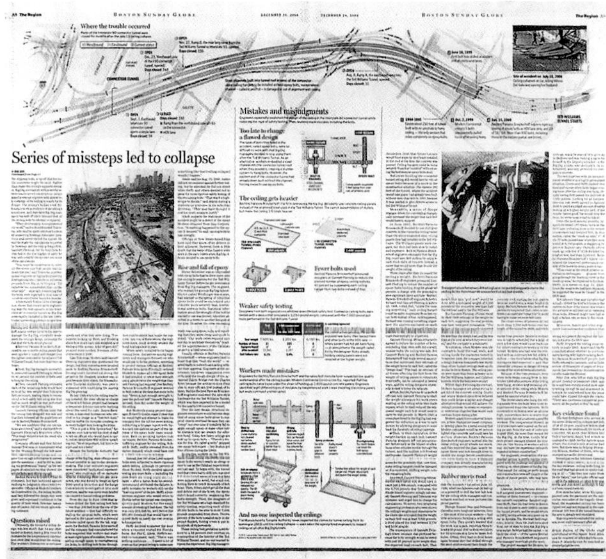

Series of missteps led to collapse

Mistakes and misjudgments

**THE BOSTON GLOBE**

Aaron Atencio, David Butler, Scott Allen

Information graphics, non-breaking news & features, 175,000+

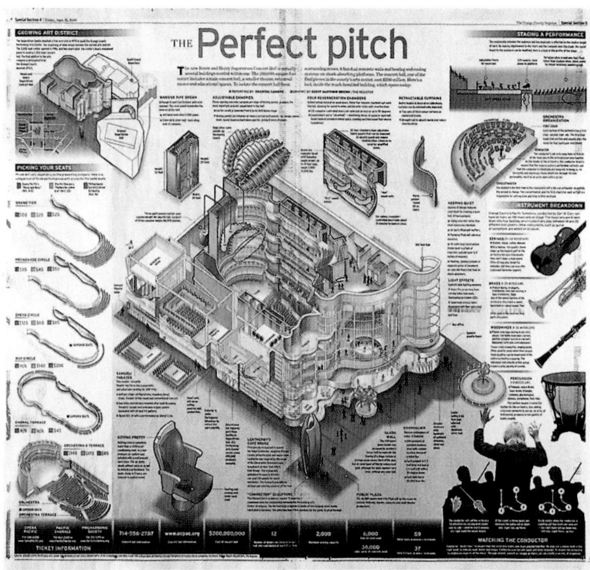

THE Perfect pitch

**THE ORANGE COUNTY REGISTER,** Santa Ana, Calif.

Scott Brown, Chantal Lamers

Information graphics, non-breaking news & features, 175,000+

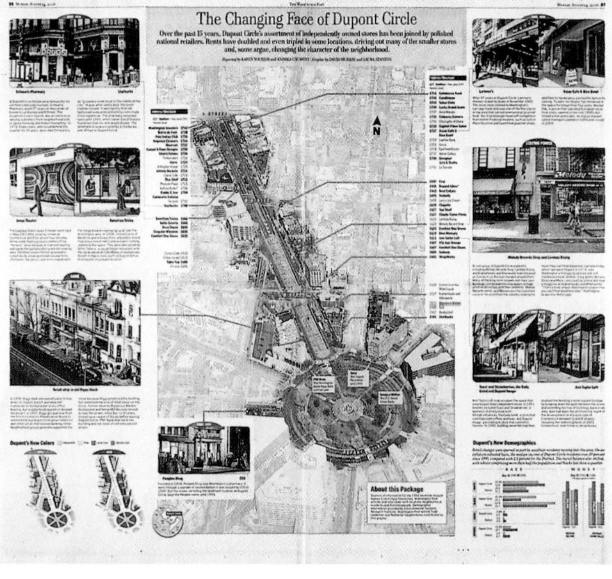

The Changing Face of Dupont Circle

**THE WASHINGTON POST**

Laura Stanton, David Murray, Karen Yourish, Andrea Caumont

Information graphics, non-breaking news & features, 175,000+

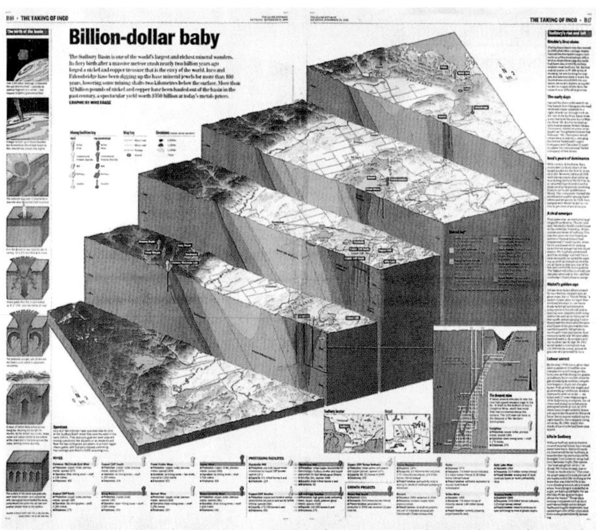

Billion-dollar baby

**THE GLOBE AND MAIL,** Toronto

Mike Faille, David Pratt, John Stackhouse, Mike Bird

Information graphics, non-breaking news & features, 175,000+

Outlook

A push to drill

Unless Congress acts, the Bush administration will allow oil and gas exploration as close as 100 miles to Florida's coast in July 2007.

CRUDE OIL

NATURAL GAS

**SOUTH FLORIDA SUN-SENTINEL,** Fort Lauderdale

Hiram Henriquez, Karsten Ivey, R. Scott Horner, Len De Groot, Tim Frank

Information graphics, non-breaking news & features, 175,000+

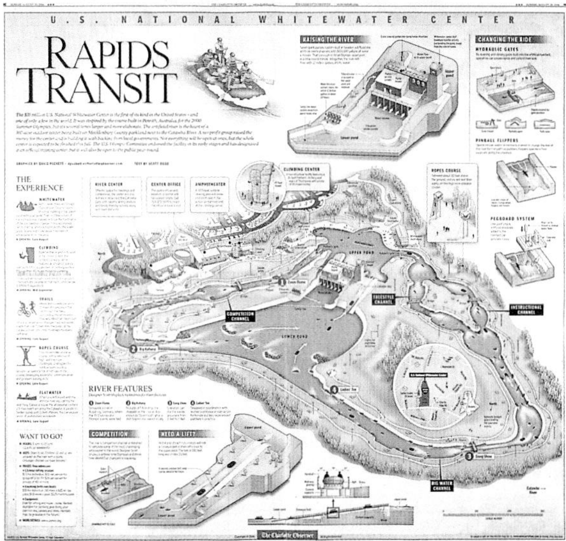


**THE CHARLOTTE OBSERVER** (N.C.)
David Puckett, Scott Dodd, Joanne Miller Long, Sarah Franquet, Tom Tozer, Rogelio Aranda
Information graphics, non-breaking news & features, 175,000+

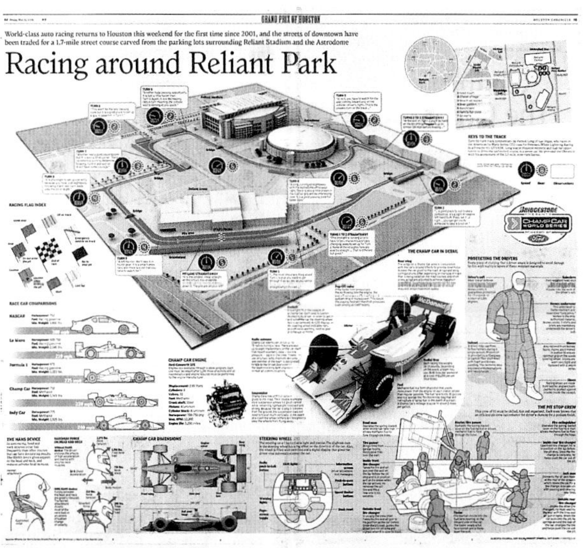


**HOUSTON CHRONICLE**
Jay Carr, Alberto Cuadra, Robert Dibrell, Ken Ellis
Information graphics, non-breaking news & features, 175,000+

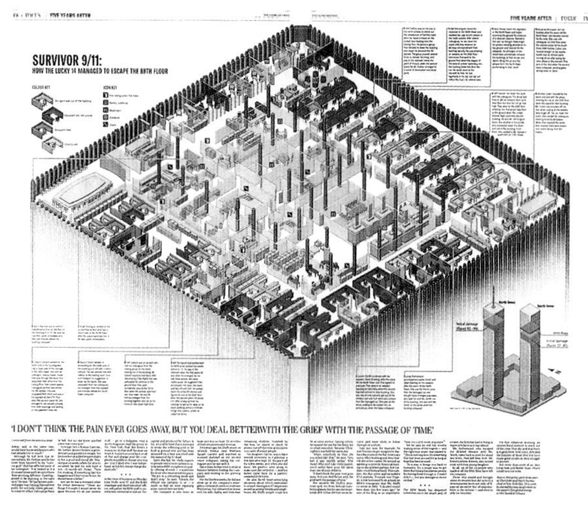


**THE GLOBE AND MAIL,** Toronto
Mike Faille, David Pratt, Cathrin Bradbury, Jerry Johnson
Information graphics, non-breaking news & features, 175,000+

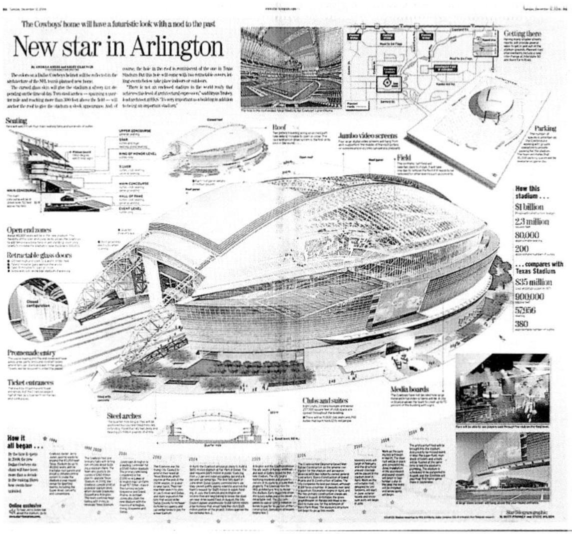


**FORT WORTH STAR-TELEGRAM** (Texas)
Steve Wilson, W. Matt Pinkney
Information graphics, non-breaking news & features, 175,000+

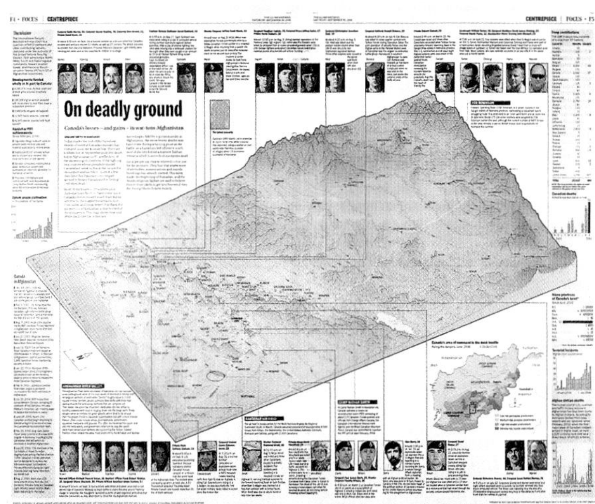


**THE GLOBE AND MAIL,** Toronto
Richard Johnson, David Pratt, Cathrin Bradbury, Jerry Johnson
Information graphics, non-breaking news & features, 175,000+

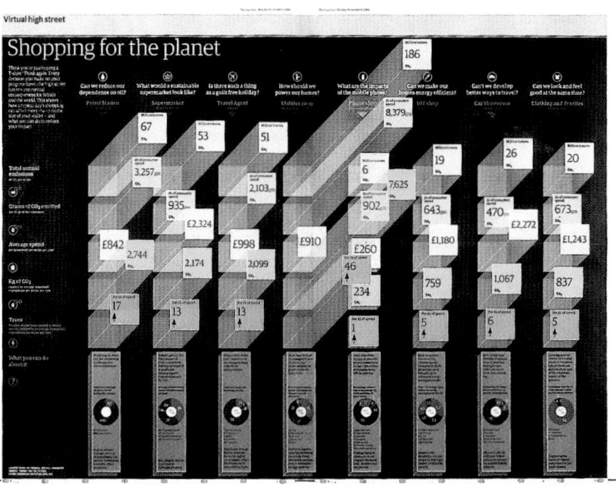


**THE GUARDIAN,** London
Mark McCormick, Michael Robinson
Information graphics, non-breaking news & features, 175,000+

**THE COLUMBUS DISPATCH** (Ohio)
Steve Spencer, Todd Bayha
Information graphics, non-breaking news & features, 175,000+

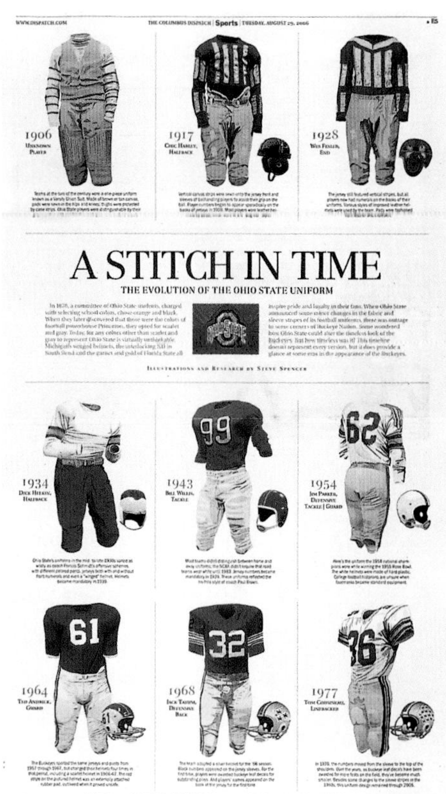
A STITCH IN TIME
THE EVOLUTION OF THE OHIO STATE UNIFORM

**THE NEW YORK TIMES**
Dill Marsh
Information graphics, non-breaking news & features, 175,000+

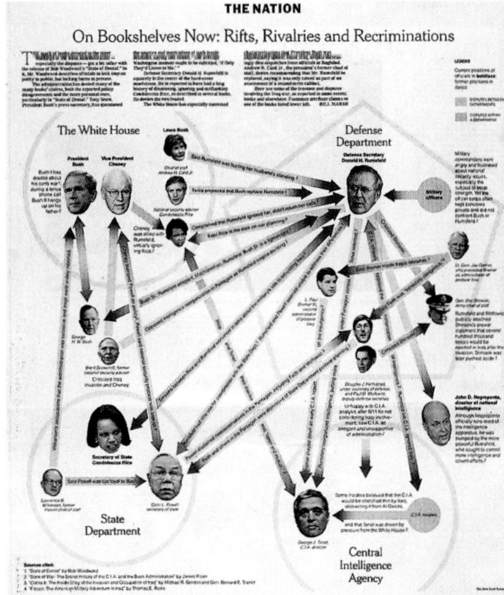
THE NATION
On Bookshelves Now: Rifts, Rivalries and Recriminations

**THE NEW YORK TIMES**
Frank O'Connell
Information graphics, non-breaking news & features, 175,000+

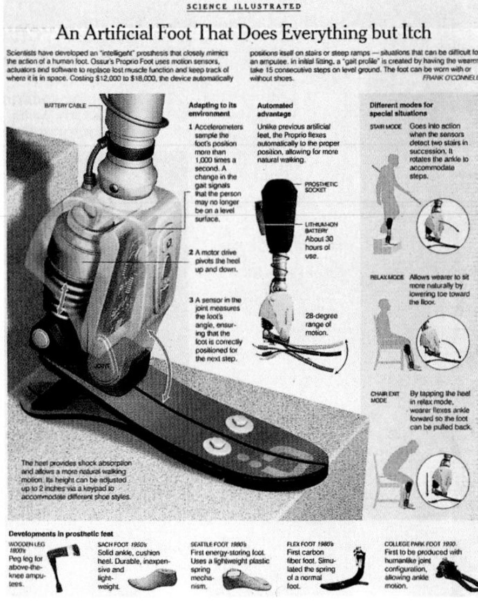
SCIENCE ILLUSTRATED
An Artificial Foot That Does Everything but Itch

**EL CORREO,** Bilbao, Spain
Fernando G. Baptista, José Miguel Benítez, Gonzalo de las Heras
Information graphics, non-breaking news & features, 50,000-174,999

22.000 kilómetros separan a los seis patrones que zarpan hoy de Bilbao de su puerto de arribada, Fremantle, en Australia, al otro lado del mundo
Comienza la aventura

Vivir
Un astillero bermeano construirá la réplica del buque insignia español en Trafalgar

**EL CORREO,** Bilbao, Spain
Fernando G. Baptista, José Miguel Benítez, Gonzalo de las Heras
Information graphics, non-breaking news & features, 50,000-174,999

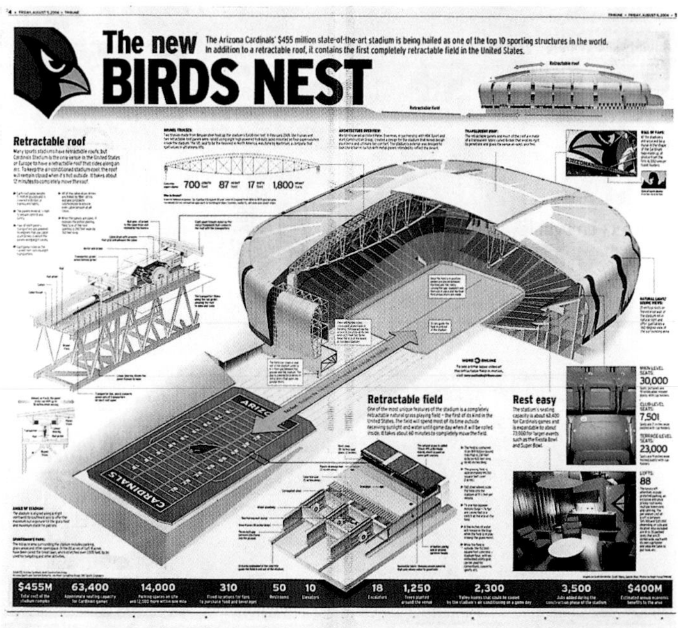
The new BIRDS NEST
Retractable roof
Retractable field
Rest easy

**THE EAST VALLEY TRIBUNE,** Mesa, Ariz.
Scott Kirchhofer, Scott Sheils, Gabriel Utasi, Ralph Freso, Amanda Rohrer
Information graphics, non-breaking news & features, 50,000-174,999

**EL CORREO,** Bilbao, Spain
Fernando G. Baptista
Information graphics, non-breaking news & features, 50,000-174,999

Ciudadanos

**Una rozadora gigante excavará desde este mes el túnel para soterrar Feve en Basurto**

La roca extraída de la perforación de la galería, de 720 metros, se reutilizará a posteriori como relleno en las obras de Abandoibarra

La máquina supera los 13 metros de largo y pesa 150 toneladas

Los trenes pasarán a 15 metros de los portales

SÍ, QUIERO

Vivir

**El enigma neandertal**

La identificación de esta especie, hace 150 años, abrió un interrogante que sigue sin respuesta: la causa de su extinción

Retrato de otro humano

**EL CORREO,** Bilbao, Spain
Fernando G. Baptista
Information graphics, non-breaking news & features, 50,000-174,999

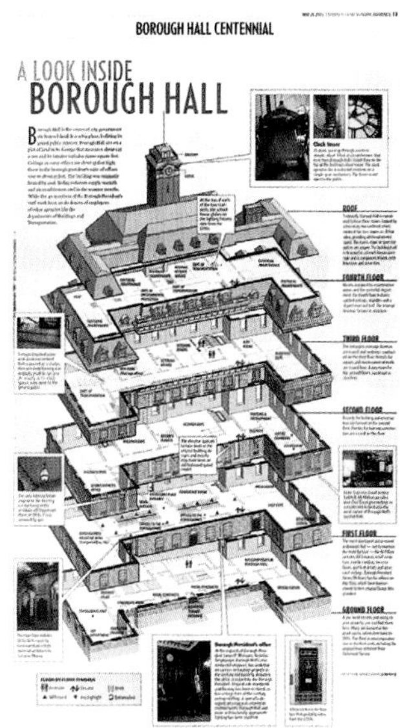
BOROUGH HALL CENTENNIAL

A LOOK INSIDE BOROUGH HALL

**STATEN ISLAND ADVANCE** (N.Y.)
Sean Noyce
Information graphics, non-breaking news & features, 50,000-174,999

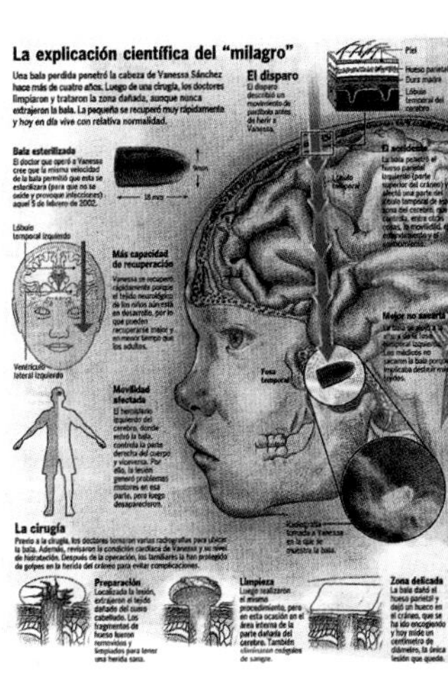
**La explicación científica del "milagro"**

**LA PRENSA GRÁFICA,** Antiguo Cuscatlán, El Salvador
Enrique Contreras, Héctor Ramírez,
Jorge Luis Contreras, Óscar Corvera,
Evelyn Susana Machuca
Information graphics, non-breaking news & features, 50,000-174,999

**SOUTH FLORIDA SUN-SENTINEL,** Fort Lauderdale
Hiram Henriquez, Karsten Ivey, Len De Groot, Tim Frank
Information graphics, non-breaking news & features, 175,000+

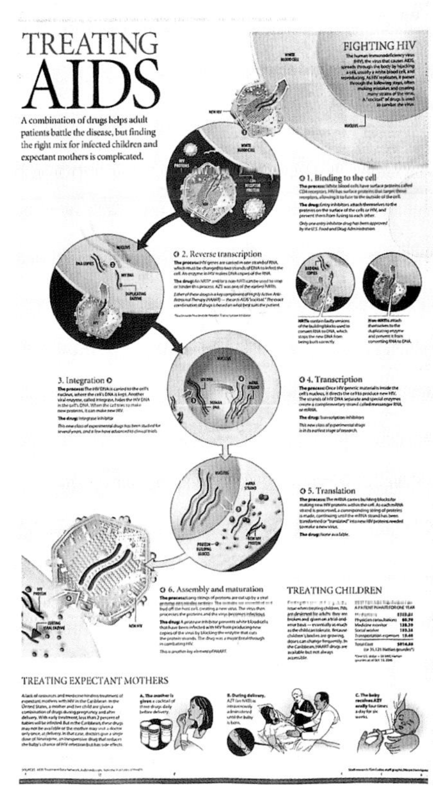
TREATING AIDS

A combination of drugs helps adult patients battle the disease, but finding the right mix for infected children and expectant mothers is complicated.

FIGHTING HIV

1. Binding to the cell

2. Reverse transcription

3. Integration

4. Transcription

5. Translation

6. Assembly and maturation

TREATING CHILDREN

TREATING EXPECTANT MOTHERS

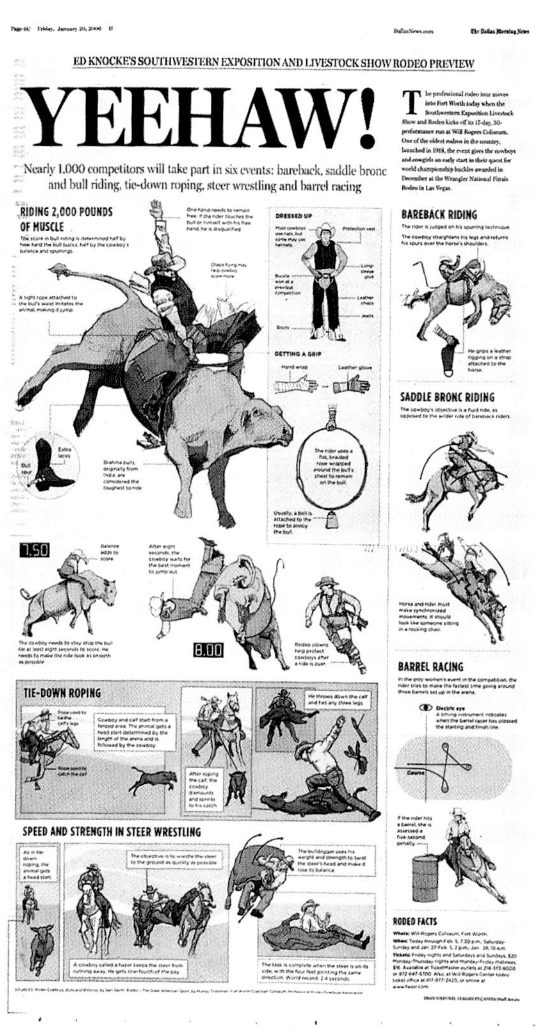
ED KNOCKE'S SOUTHWESTERN EXPOSITION AND LIVESTOCK SHOW RODEO PREVIEW

YEEHAW!

Nearly 1,000 competitors will take part in six events: bareback, saddle bronc and bull riding, tie-down roping, steer wrestling and barrel racing

RIDING 2,000 POUNDS OF MUSCLE

BAREBACK RIDING

SADDLE BRONC RIDING

TIE-DOWN ROPING

BARREL RACING

SPEED AND STRENGTH IN STEER WRESTLING

RODEO FACTS

**THE DALLAS MORNING NEWS**
Sergio Pecanha, Troy Oxford
Information graphics, non-breaking news & features, 175,000+

**THE GUARDIAN,** London

Paul Scruton, Jenny Ridley, Michael Robinson, Simon Rogers

Charting, 175,000+

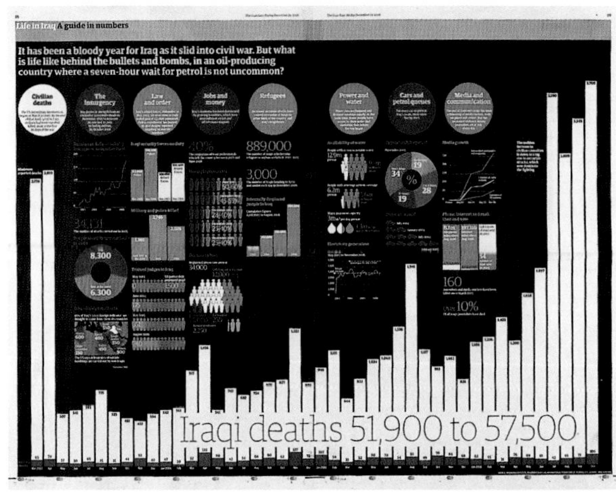


**THE SAN DIEGO UNION-TRIBUNE**

Matt Perry, Brian Cragin, Michael Price

Charting, 175,000+

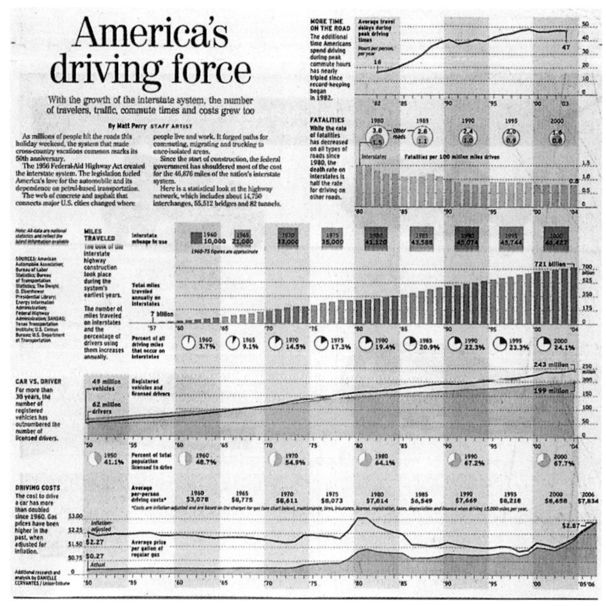


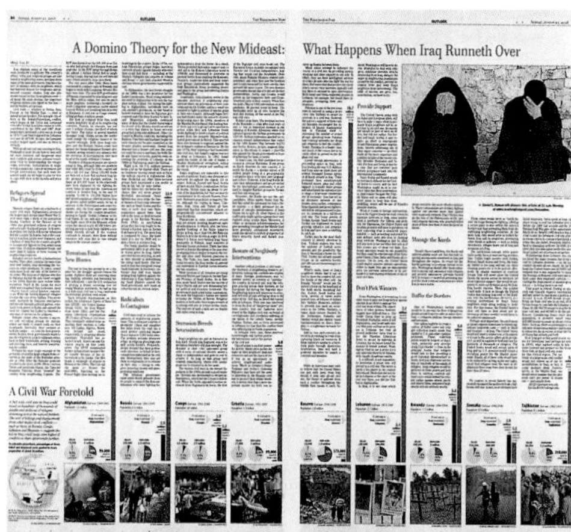


**THE WASHINGTON POST**

Laura Stanton, Justin Ferrell

Charting, 175,000+

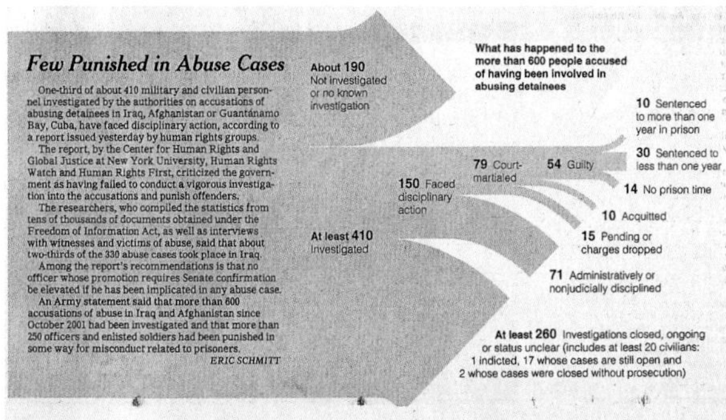

*Few Punished in Abuse Cases*

One-third of about 410 military and civilian personnel investigated by the authorities on accusations of abusing detainees in Iraq, Afghanistan or Guantánamo Bay, Cuba, have faced disciplinary action, according to a report issued yesterday by human rights groups.

The report, by the Center for Human Rights and Global Justice at New York University, Human Rights Watch and Human Rights First, criticized the government as having failed to conduct a vigorous investigation into the accusations and punish offenders.

The researchers, who compiled the statistics from tens of thousands of documents obtained under the Freedom of Information Act, as well as interviews with witnesses and victims of abuse, said that about two-thirds of the 330 abuse cases took place in Iraq.

Among the report's recommendations is that no officer whose promotion requires Senate confirmation be elevated if he has been implicated in any abuse case.

An Army statement said that more than 600 accusations of abuse in Iraq and Afghanistan since October 2001 had been investigated and that more than 250 officers and enlisted soldiers had been punished in some way for misconduct related to prisoners.

ERIC SCHMITT



**THE NEW YORK TIMES**

Archie Tse

Charting, 175,000+

**CLARÍN,** Buenos Aires, Argentina

Alejandro Tumas, Pablo Loscri

Charting, 175,000+

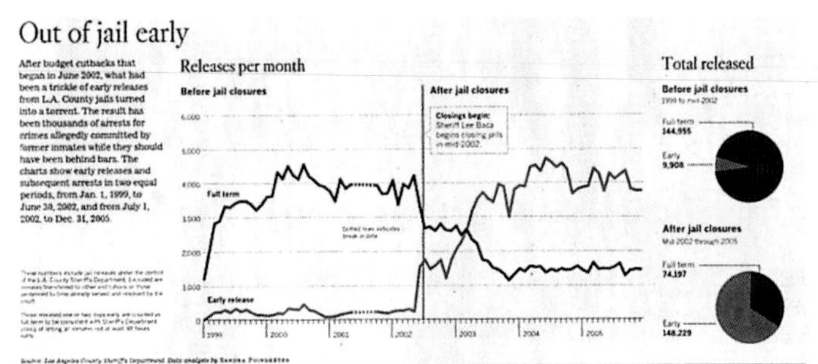

Out of jail early

After budget cutbacks that began in June 2002, what had been a trickle of early releases from L.A. County jails turned into a torrent. The result has been thousands of arrests for crimes allegedly committed by former inmates while they should have been behind bars. The charts show early releases and subsequent arrests in two equal periods, from Jan. 1, 1999, to June 30, 2002, and from July 1, 2002, to Dec. 31, 2005.



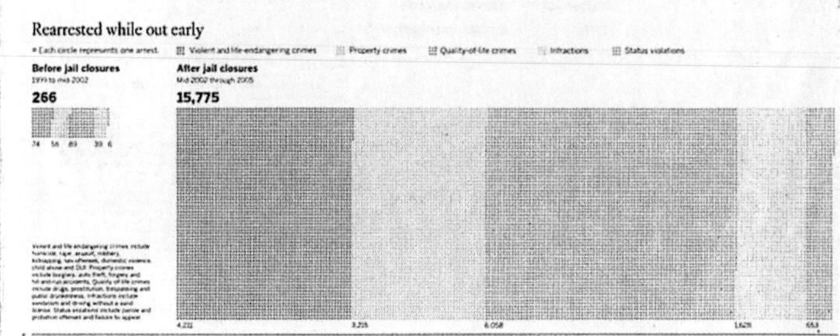


**LOS ANGELES TIMES**

Thomas Suh Lauder, Sandra Poindexter, Les Dunseith

Charting, 175,000+

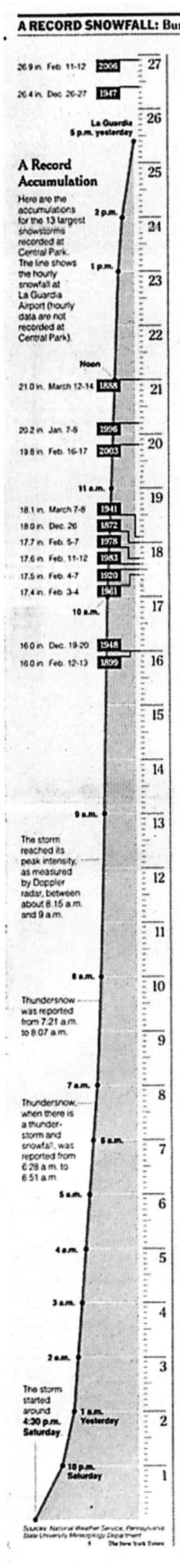


THE NEW YORK TIMES
Archie Tse
Charting, 175,000+

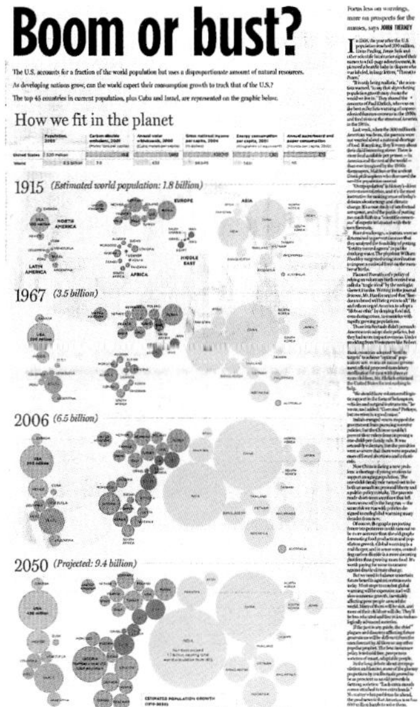


THE DALLAS MORNING NEWS
Michael Hogue, Sergio Pecanha, Darby Tober
Charting, 175,000+

EXECUTIVE PAY: A SPECIAL REPORT
Off to the Races Again, Leaving Many Behind
The Wide Divide


THE NEW YORK TIMES
Amanda Cox
Charting, 175,000+

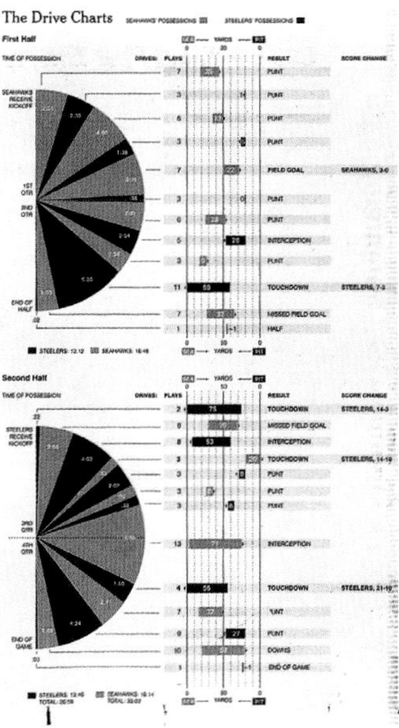


THE NEW YORK TIMES
Joe Ward, Amanda Cox
Charting, 175,000+

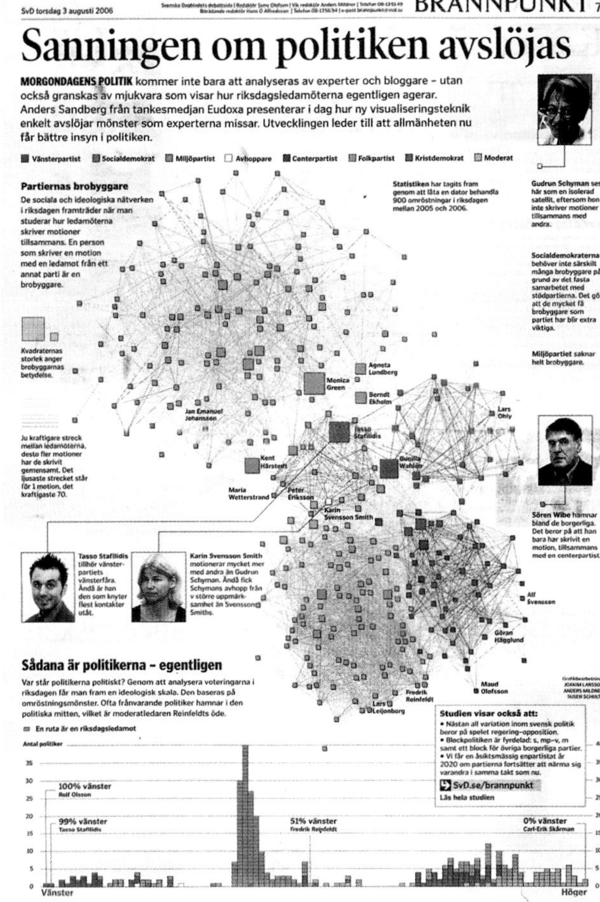

SvD torsdag 3 augusti 2006

BRÄNNPUNKT 7

# Sanningen om politiken avslöjas

**MORGONDAGENS POLITIK** kommer inte bara att analyseras av experter och bloggare – utan också granskas av mjukvara som visar hur riksdagsledamöterna egentligen agerar. Anders Sandberg från tankesmedjan Eudoxa presenterar i dag hur ny visualiseringsteknik enkelt avslöjar mönster som experterna missar. Utvecklingen leder till att allmänheten nu får bättre insyn i politiken.

Vänsterpartist | Socialdemokrat | Miljöpartist | Avhoppare | Centerpartist | Folkpartist | Kristdemokrat | Moderat

**Partiernas brobyggare**

De sociala och ideologiska nätverken i riksdagen framträder när man studerar hur ledamöterna skriver motioner tillsammans. En person som skriver en motion med en ledamot från ett annat parti är en brobyggare.

Statistiken har tagits fram genom att låta en dator behandla 900 omröstningar i riksdagen mellan 2005 och 2006.

Gudrun Schyman ses här som en isolerad satellit, eftersom hon inte skriver motioner tillsammans med andra.

Socialdemokraterna behöver inte särskilt många brobyggare på grund av det fasta samarbetet med stödpartierna. Det gör att de mycket få brobyggare som partiet har blir extra viktiga.

Miljöpartiet saknar helt brobyggare.

Kvadraternas storlek anger brobyggarnas betydelse.

Ju kraftigare streck mellan ledamöterna, desto fler motioner har de skrivit gemensamt. Det ljusaste strecket står för 1 motion, det kraftigaste 70.

Agneta Lundberg
Monica Green
Berndt Ekholm
Jan Emanuel Johansson
Lars Ohly
Tasso Stafilidis
Kent Härstedt
Gunilla Wahlén
Maria Wetterstrand
Peter Eriksson
Karin Svensson Smith
Alf Svensson
Göran Hägglund
Maud Olofsson
Fredrik Reinfeldt
Lars Leijonborg

Sören Wibe hamnar bland de borgerliga. Det beror på att han bara har skrivit en motion, tillsammans med en centerpartist.

**Tasso Stafilidis** tillhör vänsterpartiets vänsterfåra. Ändå är han den som knyter flest kontakter utåt.

**Karin Svensson Smith** motionerar mycket mer med andra än Gudrun Schyman. Ändå fick Schymans avhopp från v större uppmärksamhet än Svensson Smiths.

Grafikbearbetning: JOAKIM LARSSON ANDERS MILDNER SUSEN SCHULTZ

**Sådana är politikerna – egentligen**

Var står politikerna politiskt? Genom att analysera voteringarna i riksdagen får man fram en ideologisk skala. Den baseras på omröstningsmönster. Ofta frånvarande politiker hamnar i den politiska mitten, vilket är moderatledaren Reinfeldts öde.

En ruta är en riksdagsledamot

Antal politiker

100% vänster Rolf Olsson
99% vänster Tasso Stafilidis
51% vänster Fredrik Reinfeldt
0% vänster Carl-Erik Skårman

Vänster — Höger

**Studien visar också att:**

- Nästan all variation inom svensk politik beror på spelet regering-opposition.
- Blockpolitiken är fyrdelad: s, mp–v, m samt ett block för övriga borgerliga partier.
- Vi får en åsiktsmässig enpartistat år 2020 om partierna fortsätter att närma sig varandra i samma takt som nu.

SvD.se/brannpunkt
Läs hela studien

SILVER

**SVENSKA DAGBLADET,** Stockholm, Sweden
Joakim Larsson, Anders Mildner, Susen Schultz
Charting, 175,000+

People vote on what politicians say, but here their records are quantified. That's what we like about this entry. The connections link written proposals to politicians, and the density of the lines shows how they interact behind closed doors. The interior content is brilliant. The sheer volume of information is clear. People need to get used to seeing data like this — it's a new way of looking at information.

La gente vota según lo que dicen los políticos, pero aquí se cuantifica lo que anunciaron en sus registros. Eso es lo que nos gusta de esta pieza. Las conexiones unen las propuestas escritas con los políticos, y el grosor de las líneas muestra la forma en que interactuaron a puertas cerradas. El contenido interior es excelente. El enorme volumen de información es claro. La gente debe acostumbrarse a ver información como ésta; es una nueva forma de ver información.

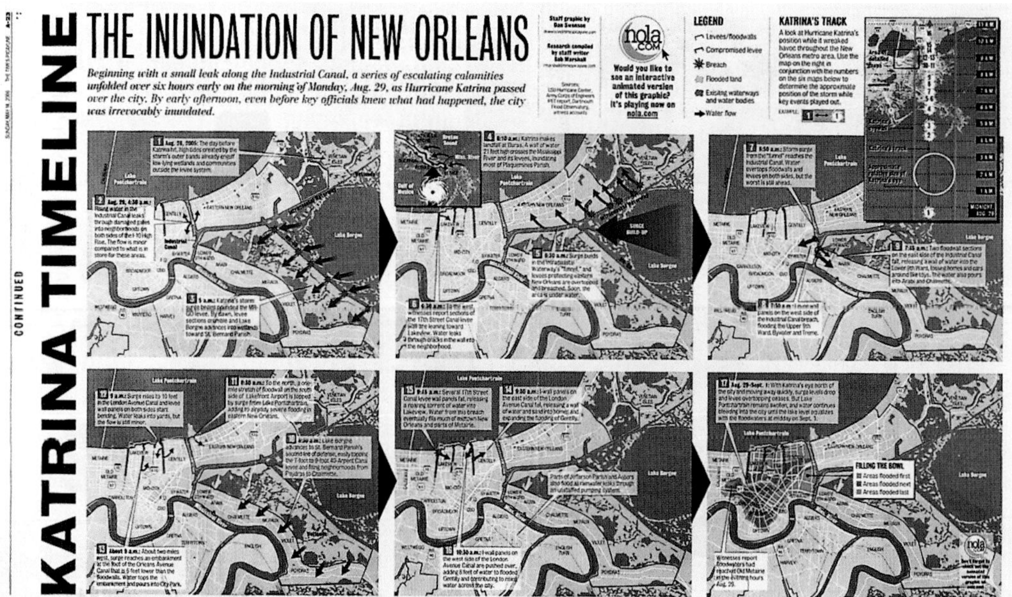

KATRINA TIMELINE

# THE INUNDATION OF NEW ORLEANS

*Beginning with a small leak along the Industrial Canal, a series of escalating calamities unfolded over six hours early on the morning of Monday, Aug. 29, as Hurricane Katrina passed over the city. By early afternoon, even before key officials knew what had happened, the city was irrevocably inundated.*



**THE TIMES-PICAYUNE,** New Orleans
Dan Swenson, Bob Marshall
Mapping, 175,000+

STATE OF OUR LEVEES

# HOW WE'RE LOOKING THIS HURRICANE SEASON

*More than 60 hurricane protection projects throughout the New Orleans metro area are either under way or have been completed. A look at the status of the more crucial projects:*

**THE TIMES-PICAYUNE,** New Orleans
Dan Swenson, Mark Schleifstein, Sheila Grissett
Mapping, 175,000+

**EL MUNDO DEL SIGLO XXI,** Madrid, Spain
Juantxo Cruz, Emilio Amade, Modesto J. Carrasco, Beatriz Santacruz, Daniel Izeddin
Mapping, 175,000+

# REBUILDING NEW ORLEANS: A POST-KATRINA ACTIVITY REPORT

Tearing it down

DEMOLITION PERMITS

Turning on the power

ELECTRICAL PERMITS

Permission to work

ALL PERMITS

Changing hands

HOME SALES

**THE TIMES-PICAYUNE,** New Orleans
Dan Swenson, Richard Russell
Mapping, 175,000+

**THE OREGONIAN,** Portland

Steve McKinstry, Steve Cowden, Terry Richard

Mapping, 175,000+

The Sunday Oregonian
AUGUST 6, 2006

# DESTINATIONS

TRAVELING IN THE NORTHWEST, THE NATION AND THE WORLD

THE OREGONIAN'S

HIGH FIVE

## Terry Richard picks Oregon's best mountain hikes

WIZARD ISLAND



INSIDE

ONLINE

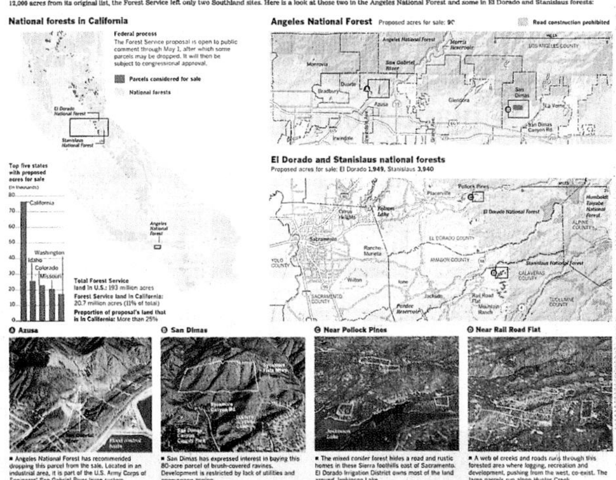

PROPOSED FOREST LAND SALE

## Part 1: Parcels nearest Los Angeles

National forests in California

Angeles National Forest

El Dorado and Stanislaus national forests



**LOS ANGELES TIMES**

Lorena Iñiguez, Cheryl Brownstein-Santiago, Doug Smith, Thomas Suh Lauder, Les Dunseith

Mapping, 175,000+

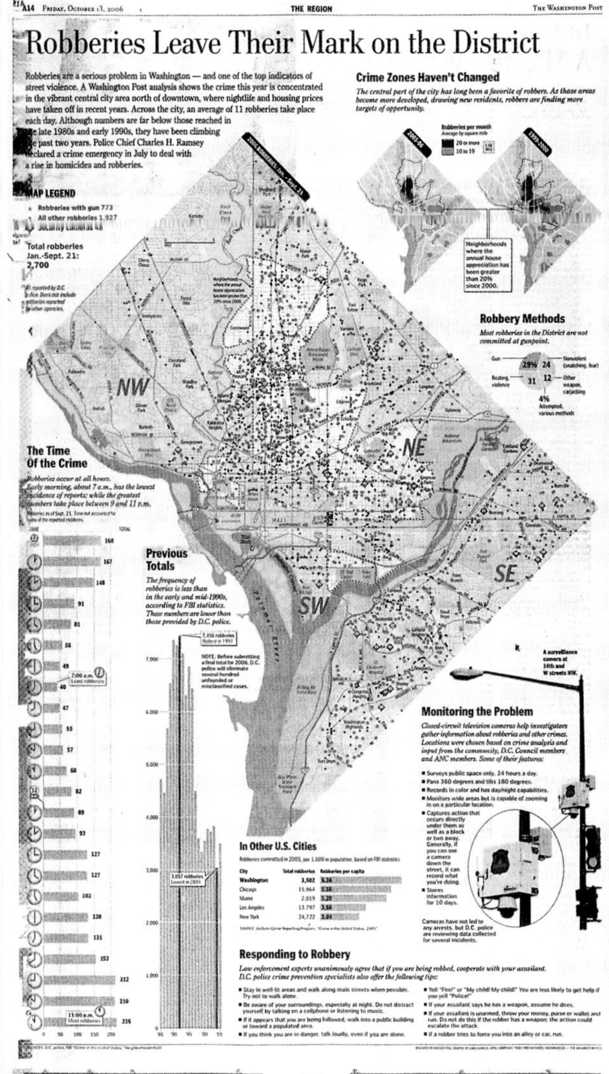

A14 Friday, October 13, 2006 THE REGION The Washington Post

# Robberies Leave Their Mark on the District



SILVER

**THE WASHINGTON POST**

Laris Karklis, Nathaniel Vaughn Kelso, Pam Tobey, Dan Keating, April Umminger, Larry Nista

Mapping, 175,000+

This graphic on robberies in the Washington, D.C., area is just gorgeous. In a mapping context, you can't fault it, and the big map offers a great way to see the information. We appreciate the charts showing the times of day, as well as the nice, easy comparisons among the large and small maps. All you want to know is right there.

Este gráfico sobre robos en el área metropolitana de Washington DC es simplemente hermoso. En un contexto de mapas, no se le puede culpar, y el gran mapa ofrece una gran forma de ver la información. Valoramos las tablas que muestran las horas del día y también las agradables y fáciles comparaciones entre los mapas grandes y pequeños. Todo lo que se quiere saber está contenido aquí mismo.

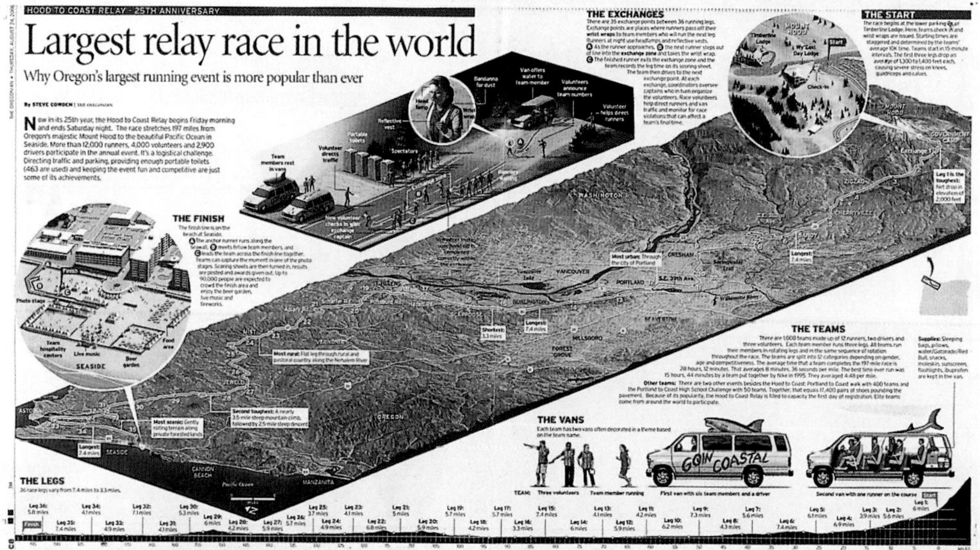


**THE OREGONIAN,** Portland

Steve McKinstry,
Steve Cowden

Mapping, 175,000+

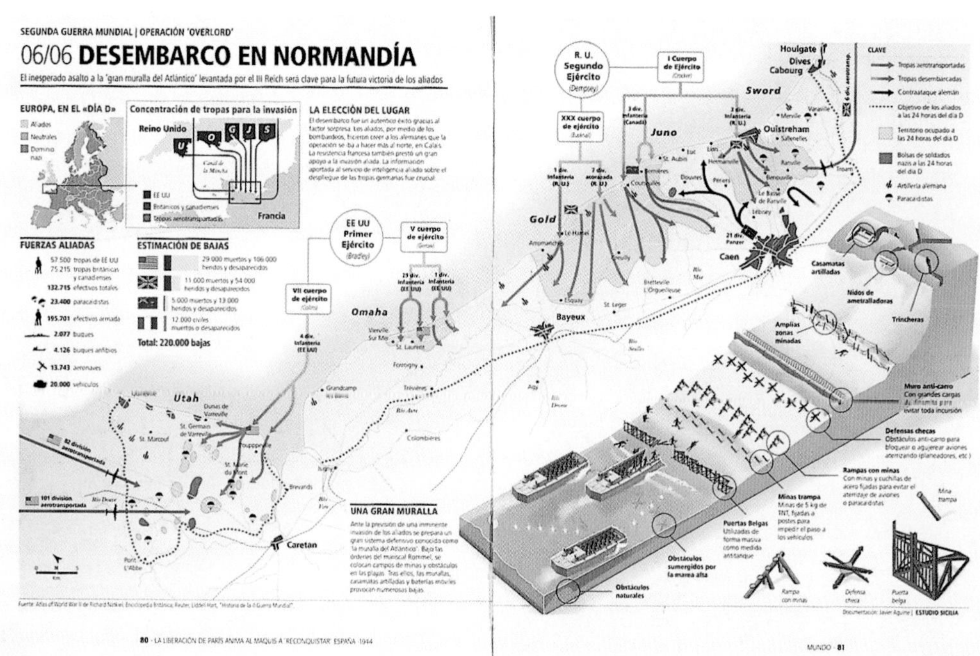


**EL MUNDO DEL SIGLO XXI**
Madrid, Spain

Juantxo Cruz,
Alfonso Everlet,
Carlos Martínez,
Estudio Sicilia,
Javier Aguierre Redondo

Mapping, 175,000+

**EL MUNDO DEL SIGLO XXI**
Madrid, Spain

Juantxo Cruz, Emilio Amade,
Modesto J. Carrasco,
Mario Chimeno,
Jorge B. Montañes

Mapping, 175,000+

**THE PRESS DEMOCRAT,** Santa Rosa, Calif.
Dennis Bolt
Mapping, 50,000-174,999

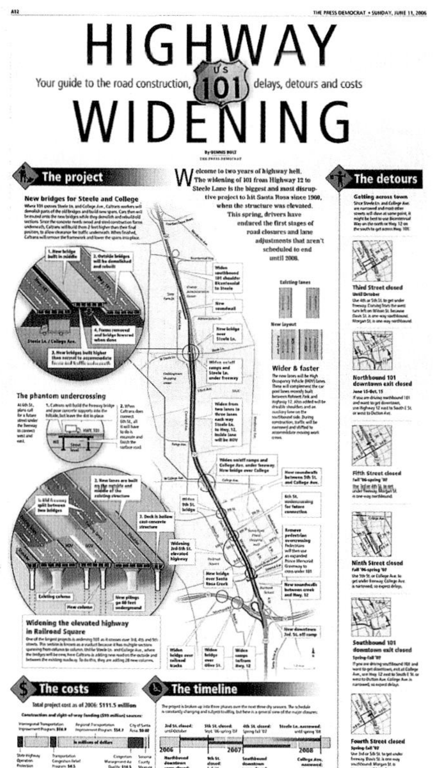
HIGHWAY 101 WIDENING
Your guide to the road construction, delays, detours and costs
The project
The detours
The phantom undercrossing
Widening the elevated highway in Railroad Square
The costs
The timeline

**THE ATLANTA JOURNAL-CONSTITUTION**
Jerome Thompson
Mapping, 175,000+

Living
Centennial Olympic Park
Where Atlanta comes together
DOWNTOWN DEVELOPMENT BOOM

**THE NEW YORK TIMES**
Staff
Use of information graphics

Science Times
The New York Times
His Subject: Highly Evolved And Exquisitely Thirsty
In the Execution Chamber, The Moral Compass Wavers
A Lesson for the Birds: Those People Aren't So Bad After All

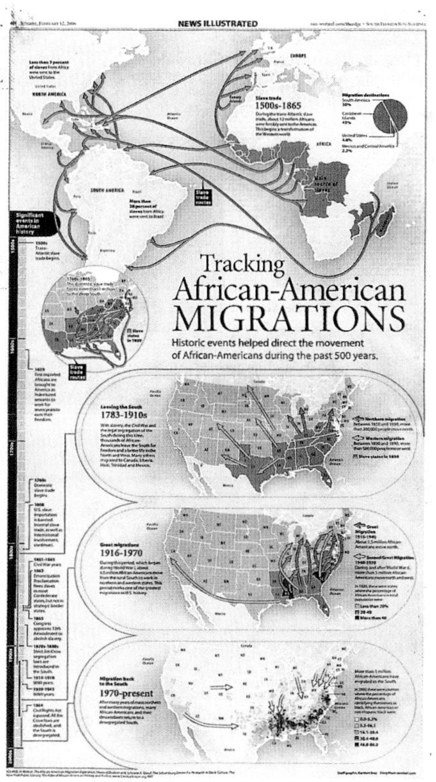
NEWS ILLUSTRATED
Tracking African-American MIGRATIONS
Historic events helped direct the movement of African-Americans during the past 500 years.

**SOUTH FLORIDA SUN-SENTINEL,** Fort Lauderdale
Karsten Ivey, R. Scott Horner, Len De Groot, Tim Frank
Mapping, 175,000+

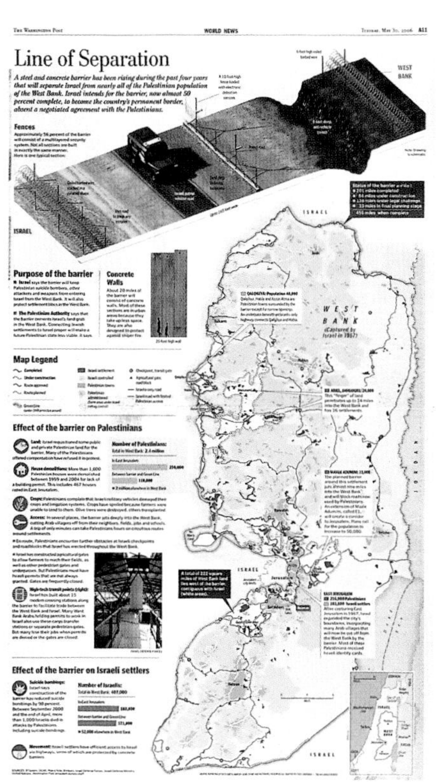
Line of Separation
Purpose of the barrier
Map Legend
Effect of the barrier on Palestinians
Effect of the barrier on Israeli settlers

**THE WASHINGTON POST**
Gene Thorp, Nathaniel Vaughn Kelso, Todd Lindeman, Dita Smith, Laris Karklis, Larry Nista
Mapping, 175,000+

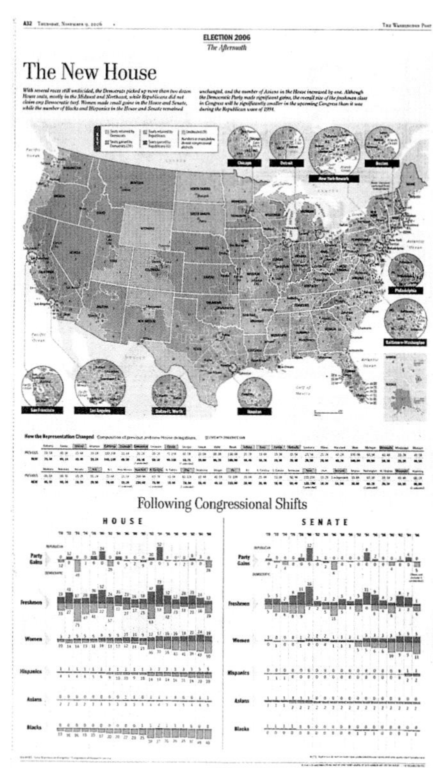
ELECTION 2006
The New House
Following Congressional Shifts
HOUSE
SENATE

**THE WASHINGTON POST**
Staff
Use of information graphics

**FRANKFURTER ALLGEMEINE SONNTAGSZEITUNG,** Frankfurt am Main, Germany

Staff

Use of information graphics

66 WISSENSCHAFT

67

**Astronomie** In unserer Milchstraße dreht sich alles um ein Schwarzes Loch. Es ist riesengroß, doch zum Glück vergleichsweise friedlich. Fast schon zu friedlich, finden die Astrophysiker.

# *Im* NABEL *der Milchstraße*

**Die Elsheimer-Galaxis**

**Sie befinden sich hier**

**Das All steckt voller Ungeheuer**

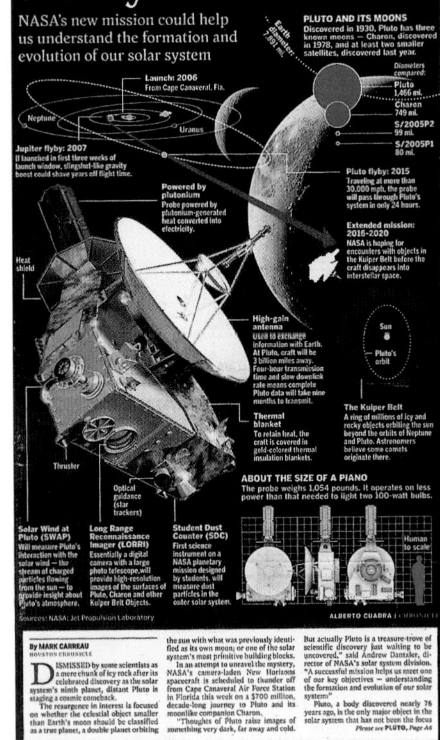

# Taking a long look at the mysteries of Pluto

NASA's new mission could help us understand the formation and evolution of our solar system

PLUTO AND ITS MOONS
Discovered in 1930, Pluto has three known moons — Charon, discovered in 1978, and at least two smaller satellites, discovered last year.
Earth diameter: 7,891 mi.
Diameters compared:
Pluto 1,466 mi.
Charon 749 mi.
S/2005P2 99 mi.
S/2005P1 80 mi.
Launch: 2006
From Cape Canaveral, Fla.
Neptune
Uranus
Jupiter flyby: 2007
If launched in first three weeks of launch window, slingshot-like gravity boost could shave years off flight time.
Pluto flyby: 2015
Traveling at more than 30,000 mph, the probe will pass through Pluto's system in only 24 hours.
Extended mission: 2016-2020
NASA is hoping for encounters with objects in the Kuiper Belt before the craft disappears into interstellar space.
Powered by plutonium
Probe powered by plutonium-generated heat converted into electricity.
Heat shield
High-gain antenna
Used to exchange information with Earth. At Pluto, craft will be 3 billion miles away. Four-hour transmission time and slow downlink rate means complete Pluto data will take nine months to transmit.
Sun
Pluto's orbit
The Kuiper Belt
A ring of millions of icy and rocky objects orbiting the sun beyond the orbits of Neptune and Pluto. Astronomers believe some comets originate there.
Thermal blanket
To retain heat, the craft is covered in gold-colored thermal insulation blankets.
Thruster
Optical guidance (star trackers)
ABOUT THE SIZE OF A PIANO
The probe weighs 1,054 pounds. It operates on less power than that needed to light two 100-watt bulbs.
Human to scale
Solar Wind at Pluto (SWAP)
Will measure Pluto's interaction with the solar wind — the stream of charged particles flowing from the sun — to provide insight about Pluto's atmosphere.
Long Range Reconnaissance Imager (LORRI)
Essentially a digital camera with a large photo telescope, will provide high-resolution images of the surfaces of Pluto, Charon and other Kuiper Belt Objects.
Student Dust Counter (SDC)
First science instrument on a NASA planetary mission designed by students, will measure dust particles in the outer solar system.
Sources: NASA; Jet Propulsion Laboratory
ALBERTO CUADRA : CHRONICLE

By MARK CARREAU
HOUSTON CHRONICLE

DISMISSED by some scientists as a mere chunk of icy rock after its celebrated discovery as the solar system's ninth planet, distant Pluto is staging a cosmic comeback.

The resurgence in interest is focused on whether the celestial object smaller than Earth's moon should be classified as a true planet, a double planet orbiting the sun with what was previously identified as its own moon; or one of the solar system's most primitive building blocks.

In an attempt to unravel the mystery, NASA's camera-laden New Horizons spacecraft is scheduled to thunder off from Cape Canaveral Air Force Station in Florida this week on a $700 million, decade-long journey to Pluto and its moonlike companion Charon.

"Thoughts of Pluto raise images of something very dark, far away and cold. But actually Pluto is a treasure-trove of scientific discovery just waiting to be uncovered," said Andrew Dantzler, director of NASA's solar system division. "A successful mission helps us meet one of our key objectives — understanding the formation and evolution of our solar system."

Pluto, a body discovered nearly 76 years ago, is the only major object in the solar system that has not been the focus

*Please see* **PLUTO,** *Page A6*

**HOUSTON CHRONICLE**

Staff

Use of information graphics

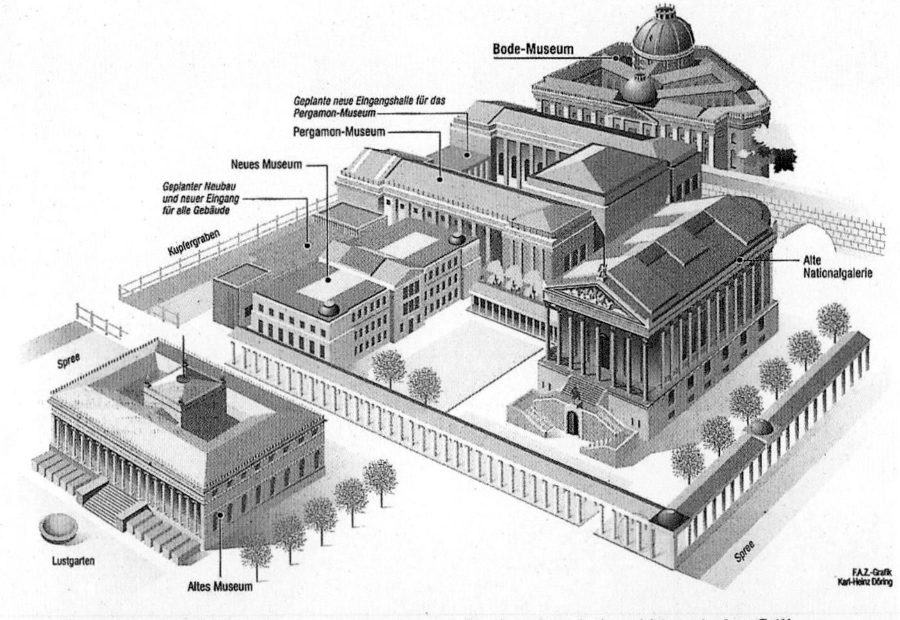

Bode-Museum
Geplante neue Eingangshalle für das Pergamon-Museum
Pergamon-Museum
Neues Museum
Geplanter Neubau und neuer Eingang für alle Gebäude
Kupfergraben
Alte Nationalgalerie
Spree
Lustgarten
Altes Museum
Spree
F.A.Z.-Grafik Karl-Heinz Döring

**Wo das Bode-Museum liegt: zwischen neuem Großstadttrubel und historischer Stille**

Beginnend mit Schinkels Altem Museum (vorn links) von 1830 entwickelte sich in hundert Jahren das Ensemble der Museumsinsel. Das auf einem zwickelförmigen Grundriß erbaute Bode-Museum (rechts oben) wurde 1904 als vorletzter Bau eröffnet, gefolgt 1930 vom Pergamon-Museum. Mit seiner halbrunden Schaufront wendet sich das Bode-Museum der Weidendammer Brücke samt der turbulenten Friedrichstraße zu – und damit von der stillen historischen Mitte ab. (F.A.Z.)

**FRANKFURTER ALLGEMEINE ZEITUNG,** Frankfurt am Main, Germany

Staff

Use of information graphics

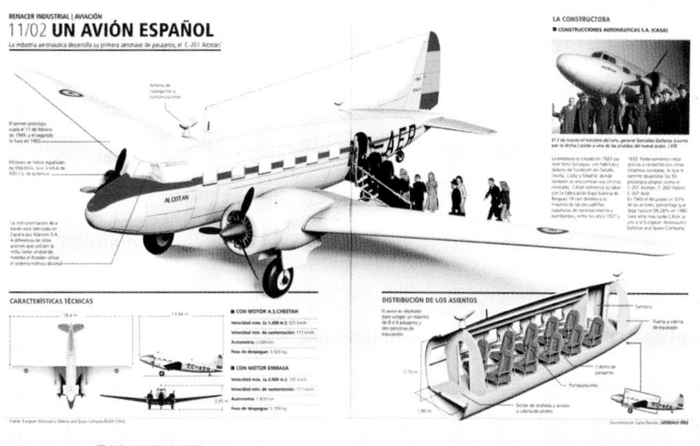


## GOLD

**EL MUNDO DEL SIGLO XXI,** Madrid, Spain

Staff

Miscellaneous

To increase subscriptions, El Mundo created and mailed these individual graphics to subscribers to create a book about Francisco Franco. This shows exceptional thinking outside the normal avenues of a newspaper's reach. The paper is exploring new ways of conveying information. Each is different, with no template, and the drawings are clear and beautifully presented. Any artist would be thrilled to have just one of these in a portfolio.

Con el fin de aumentar las suscripciones, El Mundo creó y envió por correo estos gráficos individuales a los suscriptores para formar un libro sobre Francisco Franco. Esto demuestra una forma excepcional, fuera de las vías normales del alcance de un periódico. El diario está explorando nuevas formas de entrega informativa. Cada uno es diferente, sin pro forma, y los dibujos son claros y están presentados de forma muy bella. Cualquier artista estaría emocionado de poder incluir uno de éstos en su portafolio.

**COMERCIO,** Quito, Ecuador
Jorge Mantilla, Armando Prado, Pavel Calahorrano, Staff Photographer
Miscellaneous

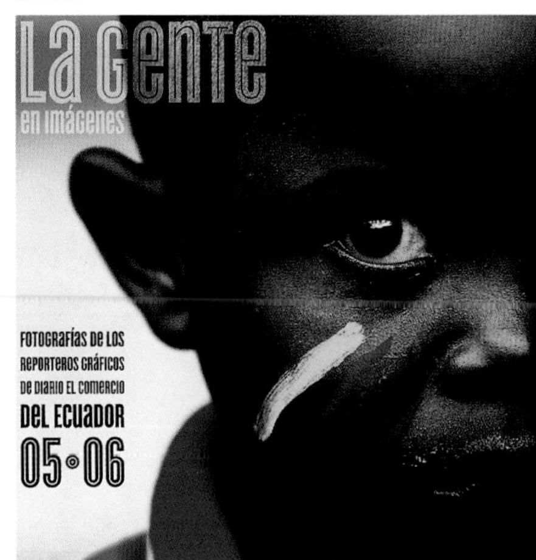


**THE FLORIDA TIMES-UNION,** Jacksonville
Robert Davis, Jennifer Merritt, Denise M. Reagan, Brandon Stuck, Kelly Jordan, Jon M. Fletcher
Miscellaneous

Business

MONDAY: How do films affect the area's tourism industry? IN FIRST BUSINESS

PERSONAL TECHNOLOGY
Mild-mannered man becomes butt-kicking chick online PAGE G-3

PERSONAL FINANCE
Think you've saved too much for retirement? Think again. PAGE G-4

SUNDAY

LIVE. WORK. GATHER.
Show us your dream downtown.

Send us your vision

Signature skyline

Main Street east

The rules

Sports central

Where to send your drawings

The deadline

Look for the results

The Southbank

what's your vision for downtown?

**NATIONAL POST,** Toronto
Doug Kelly, Gayle Grin, Jonathan Kay, John Turley-Ewart, Paul Russell, Laura Koot, Gary Clement
Miscellaneous

**DETROIT FREE PRESS**
Ryan Ford, Diane Weiss, Gene Myers, Steve Dorsey, Dave Robinson
Miscellaneous

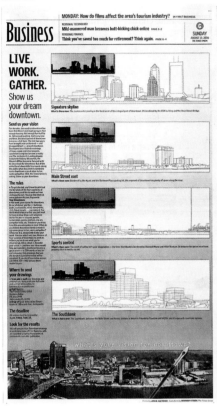

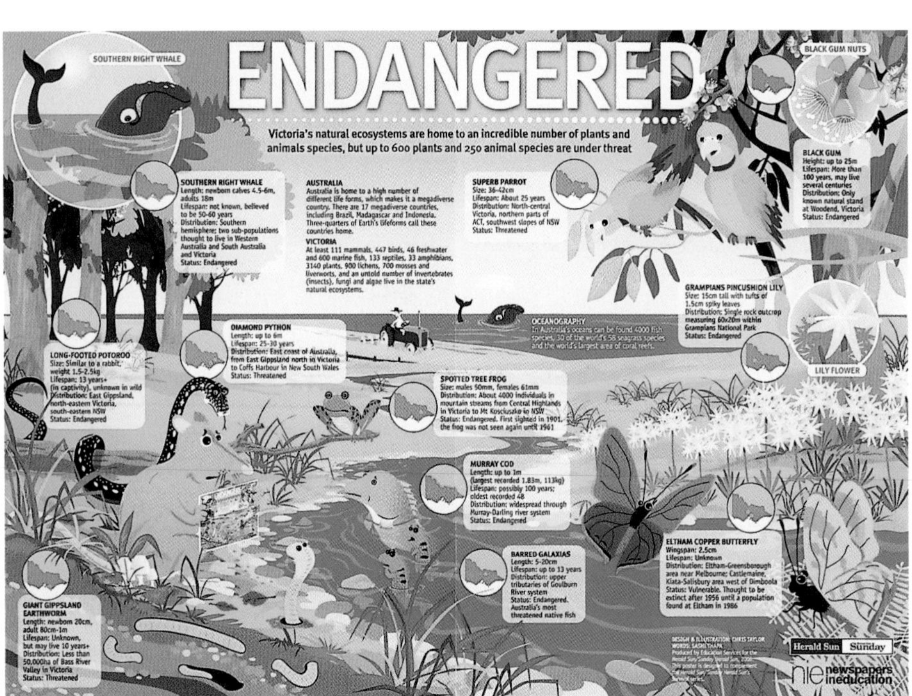


**HERALD SUN,** Melbourne, Australia
Chris Taylor, Sashi Thapa
Miscellaneous

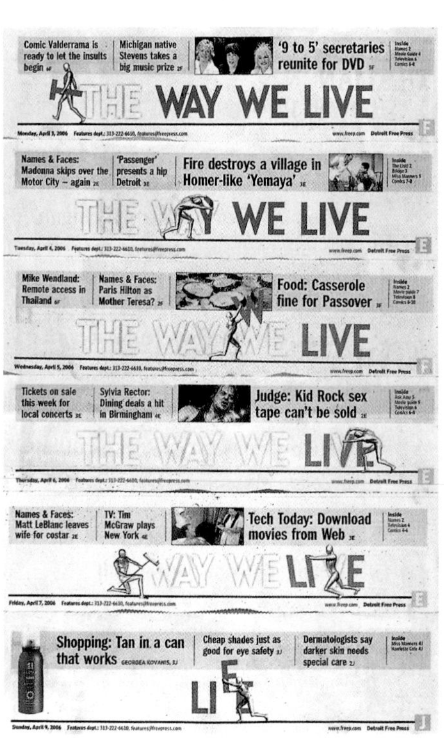

Comic Valderrama is ready to let the insults begin | Michigan native Stevens takes a big music prize | '9 to 5' secretaries reunite for DVD

THE WAY WE LIVE

Names & Faces: Madonna skips over the Motor City – again | 'Passenger' presents a hip Detroit | Fire destroys a village in Homer-like 'Yemaya'

THE WAY WE LIVE

Mike Wendland: Remote access in Thailand | Names & Faces: Paris Hilton as Mother Teresa? | Food: Casserole fine for Passover

THE WAY WE LIVE

Tickets on sale this week for local concerts | Sylvia Rector: Dining deals a hit in Birmingham | Judge: Kid Rock sex tape can't be sold

THE WAY WE LIVE

Names & Faces: Matt LeBlanc leaves wife for costar | TV: Tim McGraw plays New York | Tech Today: Download movies from Web

WAY WE LIVE

Shopping: Tan in a can that works | Cheap shades just as good for eye safety | Dermatologists say darker skin needs special care

LIFE

Detroit Free Press

**DETROIT FREE PRESS**
Rick Nease, Mauricio Gutierrez, Steve Dorsey
Miscellaneous

**THE VIRGINIAN-PILOT,** Norfolk
Lori Kelley, Sam Hundley, Erica Smith, Bill Bartel, Paul Nelson, Deborah Withey
Miscellaneous

**GULF NEWS,** Dubai, United Arab Emirates
Douglas Okasaki, Ramachandra Babu, Robin Chatterjee, Miguel Angel Gomez, Abdul Hamid Ahmad
Miscellaneous

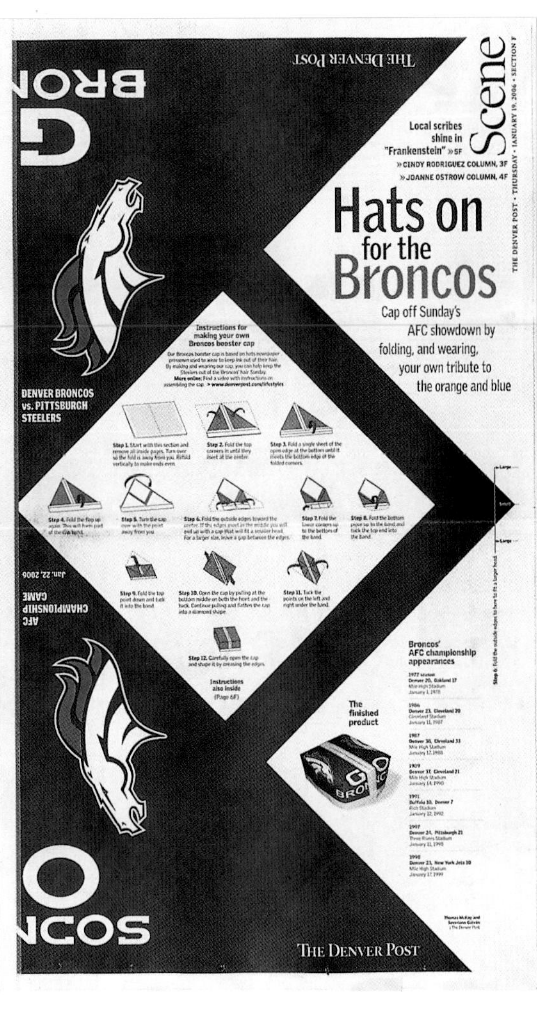

THE DENVER POST

Scene

Local scribes shine in "Frankenstein" »5F

»CINDY RODRIGUEZ COLUMN, 3F

»JOANNE OSTROW COLUMN, 4F

# Hats on for the Broncos

Cap off Sunday's AFC showdown by folding, and wearing, your own tribute to the orange and blue

DENVER BRONCOS vs. PITTSBURGH STEELERS

AFC CHAMPIONSHIP GAME

Jan. 22, 2006

Instructions for making your own Broncos booster cap

The finished product

Broncos' AFC championship appearances

THE DENVER POST

**THE DENVER POST**

Thomas McKay, Severiano Galván, Jeff Goertzen

Miscellaneous

Detroit Free Press

BROUGHT TO YOU BY freep.com

# BE YOUR FAVORITE TIGER

**1. Trim** on the dotted orange line. Trim eye holes so you won't miss a single moment of the game.

**2. Tape . . .** a paint stir or ruler to the back of trimmed mask. Do the wave with your favorite Tiger.

**3. . . . or Tie** by punching small holes as shown and stringing yarn through holes to wear your mask.

Yarn

Holes

| | |
|---|---|
| Uniform number: | 37 |
| Position: | Pitcher |
| Bats: | Left |
| Throws: | Left |
| ERA: | 3.84 |
| Wins-Losses: | 17-8 |
| Saves: | 0 |
| Strikeouts: | 99 |
| Born: | Nov. 10, 1964 Savannah, Ga. |

Kenny **Rogers**

**DETROIT FREE PRESS**

Martha Thierry, John W. Fleming

Miscellaneous

Chapter Seven

# SMALL NEWSPAPERS

Periódicos pequeños

**Circulation 49,999 and below**

Circulación de 49.999 y menos

**THE TRIBUNE,** San Luis Obispo, Calif.
Joe Tarica, Beth Anderson, Jessica Fearnow, Rex Chekal, Andy Castagnola, Chrissy Janocko, Jennifer Robillard, Adrienne Lynett, Richard Atkinson, Don Chapman
News, A-Section

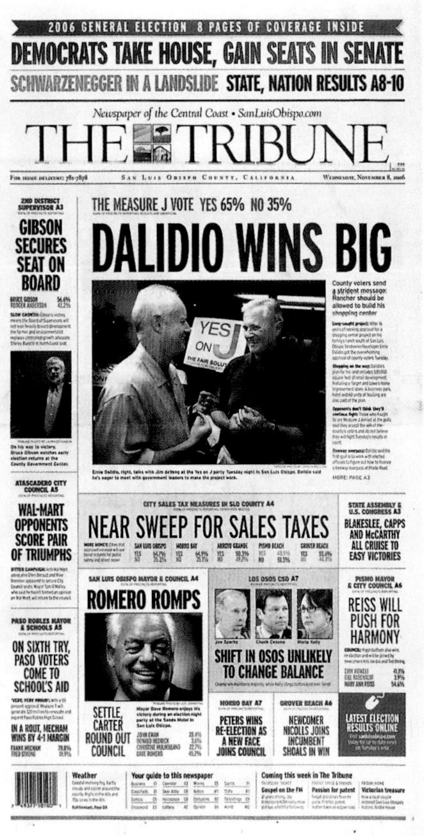
2006 GENERAL ELECTION 8 PAGES OF COVERAGE INSIDE
DEMOCRATS TAKE HOUSE, GAIN SEATS IN SENATE
SCHWARZENEGGER IN A LANDSLIDE STATE, NATION RESULTS A8-10
Newspaper of the Central Coast • SanLuisObispo.com
THE TRIBUNE
GIBSON SECURES SEAT ON BOARD
THE MEASURE J VOTE YES 65% NO 35%
DALIDIO WINS BIG
WAL-MART OPPONENTS SCORE PAIR OF TRIUMPHS
NEAR SWEEP FOR SALES TAXES
ROMERO ROMPS
SHIFT IN OSOS UNLIKELY TO CHANGE BALANCE
REISS WILL PUSH FOR HARMONY
ON SIXTH TRY, PASO VOTERS COME TO SCHOOL'S AID
SETTLE, CARTER ROUND OUT COUNCIL
PETERS WINS RE-ELECTION AS A NEW FACE JOINS COUNCIL
NEWCOMER NICOLLS JOINS INCUMBENT SHOALS IN WIN
LATEST ELECTION RESULTS ONLINE

**THE TRIBUNE,** San Luis Obispo, Calif.
Heather Foran, Melissa Geisler, Ashley Conklin
Sports section

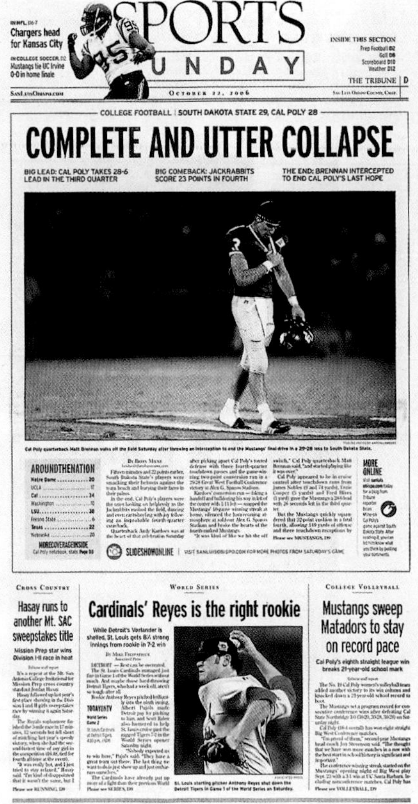
SPORTS SUNDAY
Chargers head for Kansas City
COMPLETE AND UTTER COLLAPSE
Hasay runs to another Mt. SAC sweepstakes title
Cardinals' Reyes is the right rookie
Mustangs sweep Matadors to stay on record pace

**SUN JOURNAL,** Lewiston, Maine
Corey LaFlamme, Nick Masuda, Douglas Van Reeth, Mark Morgensen, Carol Coultas
Business section

GENDER EQUALITY: The number of female gamers is rising rapidly: F2
BUSINESS
25 years and growing
Lewiston-Auburn Economic Growth Council has been a player in nearly every deal that's brought significant investment and jobs to the Twin Cities. See story on F3.

JOURNAL COURIER
AFTER THE STORM
DAMAGED
South of Jacksonville, violent weather leaves homes, nerves torn
14,500 area homes and businesses wait for electricity to return
➤ A scary night in Greene County.
➤ Taking shelter in a dairy cooler.
➤ Photographers collect stories.

**JOURNAL-COURIER,** Jacksonville, Ill.
Larry Rowe
News, A-Section page, broadsheet

YANKS SHUT DOWN RAYS AGAIN
SUNDAY
Which top dogs will move on?
BRADENTON THE HERALD
ART of HANDWRITING
In computer age, who will carry on manuscript tradition?
Gripping a Pencil
6-year-old Soumya Kona
sat at a table in her kindergarten classroom,
carefully positioned a sheet of paper before her
and started to write: "If I lived in a rainforest,
Cargo industry fatally flawed, mostly ignored
Human smuggling turns deadly at sea

**THE BRADENTON HERALD** (Fla.)
Brent Conklin, Jennifer Conklin
News, A-Section page, broadsheet

www.provincia.com.mx
PROVINCIA
EL DIARIO GRANDE DE MICHOACÁN
¡CON TODOS!
Atenco: juez va por 23 policías
Prohíbe el alcalde viajes internacionales
JACKSON, OTRA VEZ DEMANDADO
PARA LEER HOY

**PROVINCIA,** Morelia, México
Manuel Baeza, Juan Carlos Ortega Prado, Gustavo Vega, Helena Vari Ortega Prado, Erik Knobl
News, A-Section page, broadsheet

**THE SALEM NEWS** (Mass.)
Dan Ryan
News, A-Section page, broadsheet

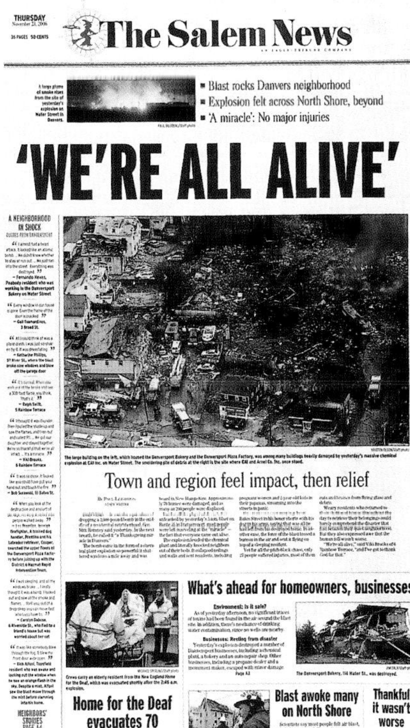

The Salem News

■ Blast rocks Danvers neighborhood
■ Explosion felt across North Shore, beyond
■ 'A miracle': No major injuries

# 'WE'RE ALL ALIVE'

Town and region feel impact, then relief

What's ahead for homeowners, businesses

Home for the Deaf evacuates 70

Blast awoke many on North Shore

Thankful it wasn't worse

**THE TRIBUNE,** San Luis Obispo, Calif.
Rex Chekal, Joe Tarica
News, A-Section page, broadsheet

Newspaper of the Central Coast • SanLuisObispo.com

THE TRIBUNE SUNDAY

LATE RALLY LIFTS POLY TO VICTORY

Fishing industry in a fight for its life

Stories on surviving cancer

ARE YOUR CHILDREN SAFE ONLINE?

Medi-Cal is moving to managed care here

**KITSAP SUN,** Bremerton, Wash.
Jessica Randklev
News, A-Section page, broadsheet

DEMOCRATS TAKE HOUSE

Kitsap Sun

Dems Sweep Kitsap

Cantwell, Dicks, Inslee Return to a New D.C.

Kilmer to Senate

Rolfes In Upset

SÚPER DOMINGO

DETROIT

¡Arrancan sus motores!

**FRONTERA,** Tijuana, México
Lorena Soria, Allan de la Rosa, Daniel Acuña, José Madrigal
News, A-Section page, broadsheet

www.provincia.com.mx

PROVINCIA

EL DIARIO GRANDE DE MICHOACÁN

# La batalla de San Lázaro

UNA ESTAMPA DE LA VIDA LEGISLATIVA

Calderón designa a Ramírez Acuña para Gobernación

Seguridad, deuda de Fox: Lázaro

**PROVINCIA,** Morelia, México
Manuel Baeza, Juan Carlos Ortega Prado, Gustavo Vega, Erik Knobl, Helena Vari Ortega Prado
News, A-Section page, broadsheet

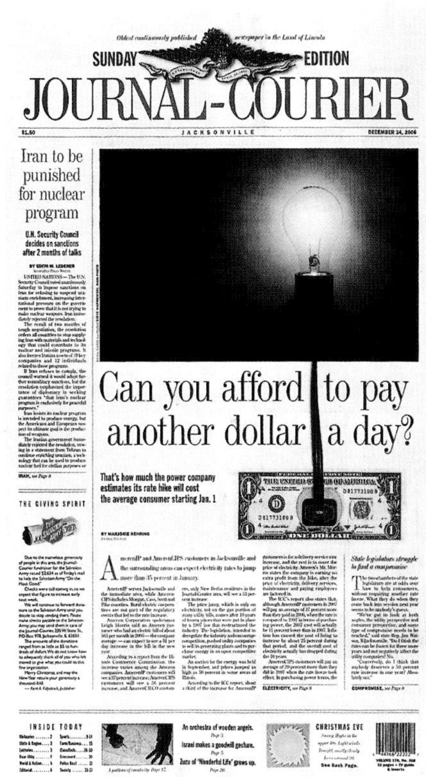

SUNDAY EDITION

JOURNAL-COURIER

Iran to be punished for nuclear program

Can you afford to pay another dollar a day?

**JOURNAL-COURIER,** Jacksonville, Ill.
Larry Rowe
News, A-Section page, broadsheet

**SOUTHWEST JOURNAL,** Minneapolis
Bryan Nanista, Sarah McKenzie
News, A-Section page, tabloid

27 BANZAI!
28 Russian Lacquer Art

southwestjournal

2006 VOTER'S GUIDE

COUNTYWIDE SALES TAX FUNDS NEW STADIUM

HOUSE OF REPRESENTATIVES

SECRETARY OF STATE

MINNESOTA'S TRANSPORTATION AMENDMENT

CUT THROUGH THE CLUTTER

MINNEAPOLIS BOARD OF EDUCATION

GET READY FOR ELECTION DAY

Uptown's Mozaic project will feature luxury hotel

Development will have fewer condos

Civilian Police Review Authority set for changes

Community leaders push to make MPD more accountable

**DIÁRIO DE NOTÍCIAS,** Lisbon, Portugal
António José Teixeira, Ivone Ralha, Paulo Barata, André Carrillo, Henriqúe Cayatte
News, A-Section page, tabloid

Diário de Notícias

Solteiros vão pagar mais IRS em 2007

Governo apresentou ontem o Orçamento do Estado para o próximo ano. Cortes de 5,1% na função pública serão decisivos para controlar o défice público

- Fisco preenche declaração de IRS dos faltosos
- Deficientes perdem benefícios fiscais
- Estado reduz comparticipação nos medicamentos

A Saúde Sexual

César recusa aplicar taxas de internamento hospitalar

Apelo aos médicos para a revisão do código deontológico

Mês da Poupança BPN

30 dias únicos para as suas poupanças.

**BEAVER COUNTY TIMES,** Beaver, Pa.
Clif Page
News, A-Section page, tabloid

FEBRUARY 11, 2006

Saturday Times

SMALL SPACE, BIG TROUBLE

A HOLE THIS SIZE ALLOWED SOMEONE TO VIDEOTAPE INSIDE A BATHROOM STALL AT CENTER AREA MIDDLE SCHOOL

PAGE A4

'WE WERE REALIZING OUR WORST NIGHTMARE'

FORMER FEMA DIRECTOR TESTIFIES TO SENATE PANEL INVESTIGATING HURRICANE RESPONSE | A10

Local

Noroeste

GUSTA AL MUNDO POR SU SABOR

Los camarones sinaloenses compiten a nivel internacional por su calidad

RADIOGRAFÍA DE UN CAMARÓN

CÓMO SE PESCA

LAS TALLAS

GUÍA DE TALLAS DE CAMARÓN

Diferencia de clases

51/60

41/50

31/40

26/30

16/20

U/15

U/12

**NOROESTE,** Mazatlán, México
Martha García, Alexander Probst, Wilfredo Camarena, Joel Díaz, Guillermina García, Ariel Noriega, Daniel Santana
Local page, broadsheet

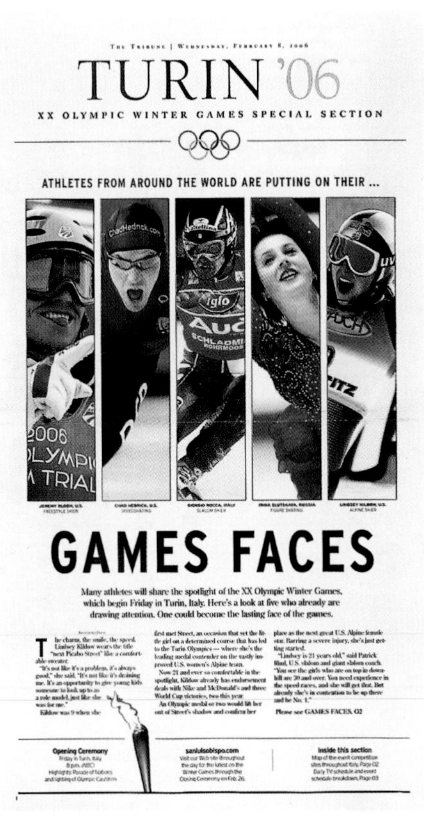

TURIN '06

XX OLYMPIC WINTER GAMES SPECIAL SECTION

ATHLETES FROM AROUND THE WORLD ARE PUTTING ON THEIR ...

GAMES FACES

Many athletes will share the spotlight of the XX Olympic Winter Games, which begin Friday in Turin, Italy. Here's a look at five who already are drawing attention. One could become the lasting face of the games.

**THE TRIBUNE,** San Luis Obispo, Calif.
Heather Foran, Melissa Geisler
Sports page, broadsheet

THURSDAY SPORTS

BASEBALL AT THE BREAK

Braves in a new world at midpoint of season

Recent surge keeps playoff hopes alive

THE MOST BORING DAY IN SPORTS

**ATHENS BANNER-HERALD** (Ga.)
Nick Mathews
Sports page, broadsheet

**EL IMPARCIAL,** Hermosillo, Sonora, México
Alfredo Zazueta, Carlos René Gutiérrez, Manuel Lizárraga, Miyoshi Katsuda
Sports page, broadsheet

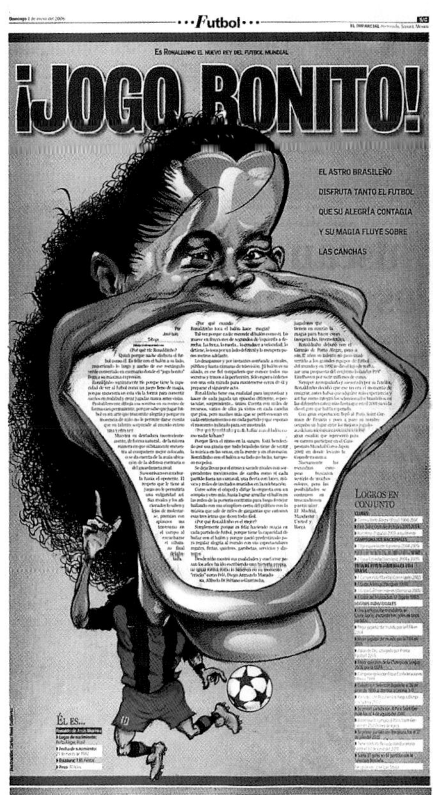
Futbol

Es Ronaldinho el nuevo rey del futbol mundial

¡JOGO BONITO!

El astro brasileño disfruta tanto el futbol que su alegría contagia y su magia fluye sobre las canchas

Logros en conjunto

Él es...

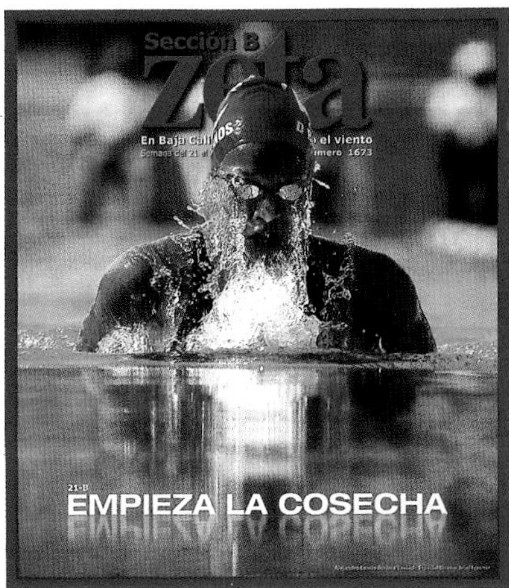
Sección B

Zeta

EMPIEZA LA COSECHA

**ZETA WEEKLY,** Tijuana, México
Ariel Freaner, Alejandro Cossio
Sports page, tabloid

THE EDGE

Travis Pastrana es el hombre más valiente en dos ruedas. En su moto es capaz de hacer cualquier cosa y sin miedo a nada.

SEÑOR X

TEXTO › EL GRÁFICO

FICHA



**EL GRÁFICO,** Antiquo Cuscatlan, El Salvador
Agustín A. Palacios, Oscar Guerra
Sports page, tabloid

THE EDGE

El windsurfista Jason Polakow explica si encontrar las olas correctas es una cuestión de suerte o se trata de un riesgo calculado.

WIND SURFING

TEXTO › JASON POLAKOW

FICHA

**EL GRÁFICO,** Antiquo Cuscatlan, El Salvador
Agustín A. Palacios, Oscar Guerra
Sports page, tabloid

Economía

El día que cambió nuestras vidas Los aeropuertos extreman la vigilancia

FORTINES QUE VELAN POR SU SEGURIDAD

La lucha contra el terrorismo se desplaza a la terminal

11.09.2001

El largo camino hasta el avión

Las empresas también quieren estar protegidas

Pagan 35.000 euros para ser seguras

**EL ECONOMISTA,** Madrid, Spain
Gorka Sampedro, Raquel Nieto, Amaya Verde
Information graphics, non-breaking news & features

**ATLANTA BUSINESS CHRONICLE**
James C. Watts, Jeff Mahurin
Business page, tabloid

Page 34A · September 8-14, 2006 · www.atlantabusinesschronicle.com · ATLANTA BUSINESS CHRONICLE

HUMAN RESOURCES & EMPLOYMENT
SPECIAL SECTION

DROP OFF

'Gray ceiling,' lack of younger employees force companies to adjust

HR Sound Off 36A · Promoting pensions 37A · Internet changing recruiting 38A
Alston & Bird exec brings new thinking to HR 39A · Executive Recruiters 40A · Retained Executive Search Firms 41A

**KRISTIANSTADSBLADET,** Koping, Sweden
Maria Nilson, My Ericson, Jacob Nortstrom
Lifestyle section

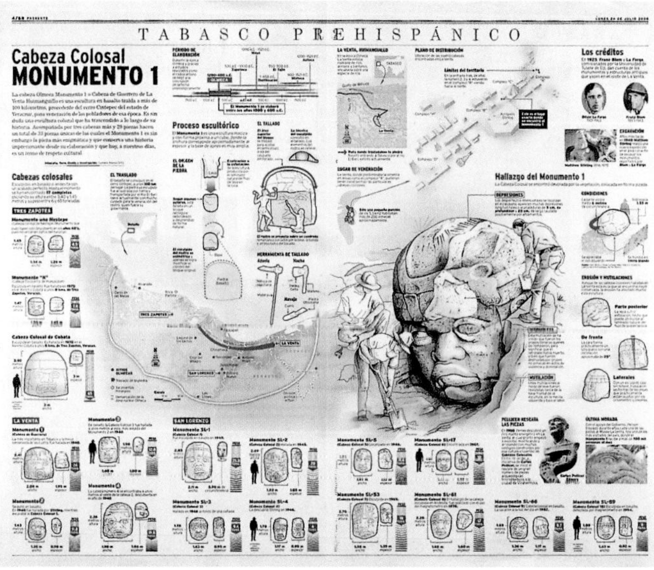


**PRESENTE,** Villahermosa, México
Gustavo Alonso Ortiz
Information graphics, non-breaking news & features

**KRISTIANSTADSBLADET,** Koping, Sweden
Maria Nilson
Lifestyle section

**SUNNMØRSPOSTEN,** Alesund, Norway
Maj Ribergaard, Ole Munk, Janne Barstad Ose, Sissel Bigset Leira
Other feature section

**SUN JOURNAL,** Lewiston, Maine

Ursula Albert, Nick Masuda, Pete Gorski, Lindsay Tice, Mark Morgensen, Judy Meyer, Rex Rhoades

Lifestyle page, broadsheet

FAMILY FUN: GET CREATIVE AND MAKE HOLIDAY DECORATIONS: E5-6

LIVING

SUNDAY, DECEMBER 17, 2006

# Merry Christmas
*now get out of my way!*

It's Christmas Eve and you're shopping (frantically) for last-minute gifts. You've circled the parking lot several times to no avail. Suddenly, you spot the perfect space. But you and another driver arrive there at the same time. Who gets it?

**STYLE WEEKLY,** Richmond, Va.

Jeffrey Bland

Entertainment page, tabloid

CIVIL RIGHTS MEMORIAL CAPTURING THE CLUB SCENE BEING A BOOMER

New! STYLE WEEKLY

VARIETY PACK

97 flavors of summer fun!

OPEN HERE

**THE TRIBUNE,** San Luis Obispo, Calif.

Jessica Fearnow

Entertainment page, tabloid

ticket

THE TRIBUNE GUIDE TO MOVIES, MUSIC AND MORE

DINING OUT: Rancho Nipomo mixes Mexican cuisine with barbecued meats, 16

THE ROAD TO COMEDY STARDOM

BOB & TOM RADIO SHOW

THE BOB & TOM EFFECT

How SLO morning radio's most popular show became a launch pad for young comics making a name for themselves (their tour stops at the PAC this weekend), 3

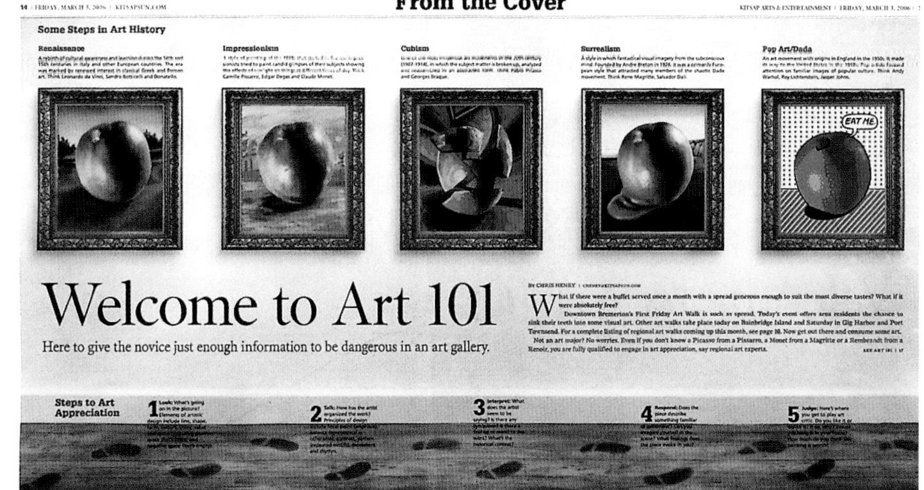
From the Cover

Some Steps in Art History

Renaissance · Impressionism · Cubism · Surrealism · Pop Art/Dada

# Welcome to Art 101

Here to give the novice just enough information to be dangerous in an art gallery.

Steps to Art Appreciation

**KITSAP SUN,** Bremerton, Wash.

Jessica Randklev

Entertainment page, tabloid

FOOD • HOME • GARDEN

TUESDAY

AT HOME

F

GARDENING

Pruning apple and pear trees now leads to great fruit later

grape to glass

Science and a bit of magic combine to make a great bottle of wine

HOME

Let the sunshine into your home

TODAY'S RECIPES

Cooking school at fairgrounds

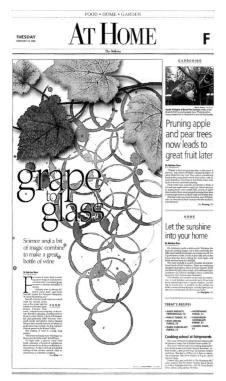

**THE BULLETIN,** Bend, Ore.

Renee Fullerton, Julie Johnson, Anders Ramberg

Food page, broadsheet

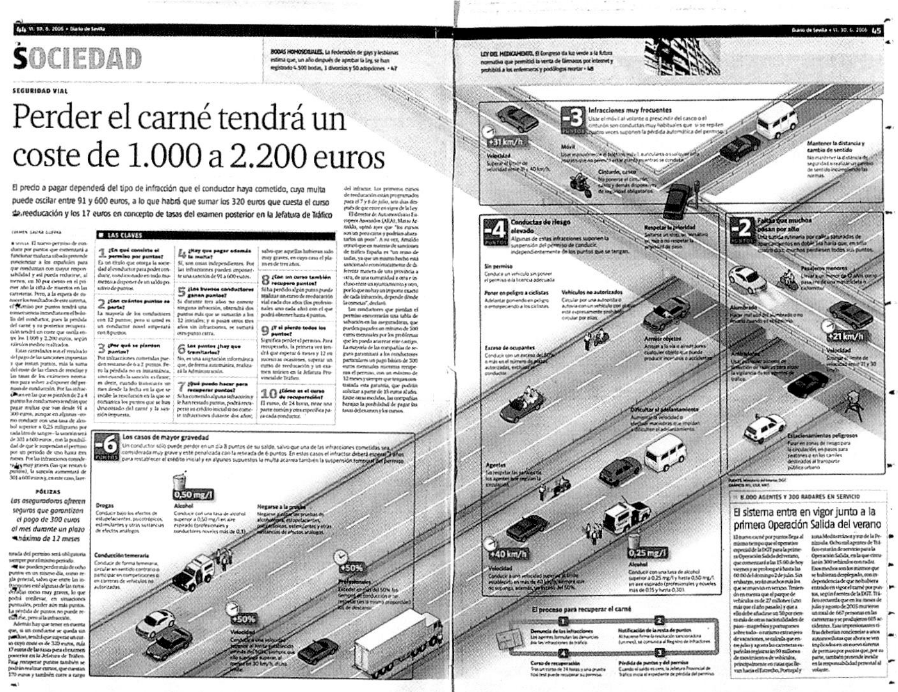
SOCIEDAD

SEGURIDAD VIAL

# Perder el carné tendrá un coste de 1.000 a 2.200 euros

El precio a pagar dependerá del tipo de infracción que el conductor haya cometido, cuya multa puede oscilar entre 91 y 600 euros, a lo que habrá que sumar los 320 euros que cuesta el curso de reeducación y los 17 euros en concepto de tasas del examen posterior en la Jefatura de Tráfico

LAS CLAVES

Infracciones muy frecuentes

Conductas de riesgo elevado

Faltas que muchos pasan por alto

Las conductas de mayor gravedad

El proceso para recuperar el carné

6.000 AGENTES Y 300 RADARES EN SERVICIO

El sistema entra en vigor junto a la primera Operación Salida del verano

**DIARIO DE SEVILLA** (Spain)

Manuel Romero, Cristina G. Rivera, Raquel Feria, Francisco Barquilla

Information graphics, non-breaking news & features

**LEVANTE-EMV,** Valencia, Spain
Javier Pérez Belmonte
Fashion page, broadsheet

34 TEMPORADA CROMÁTICA

Hay un lenguaje no verbal, un código semiótico en cada color y una convención que asigna una emoción a cada uno. Pero sin olvidar nunca que a veces un tono puede tener dos o más significados distintos, u opuestos, que cada cultura, época, religión o persona hace su propia lectura y que todo puede variar en función de la combinación. Vestir colores es sentir y hacer sentir.

SENTIR el COLOR

Vestido para...

LA PALETA DEL FONDO DE ARMARIO

TEMPORADA CROMÁTICA 35

FOOD • HOME • GARDEN

TUESDAY

AT HOME

F

Paint it nude

Skin-toned neutrals are among the hottest colors of the year

TODAY'S RECIPES

GARDENING

Give aching muscles a rest with lasagna gardening

FOOD

Bacon's not health food, but darn it's good!

**THE BULLETIN,** Bend, Ore.
Renee Fullerton, Julie Johnson, Anders Ramberg, Melissa Jansson
Home/real estate page, broadsheet

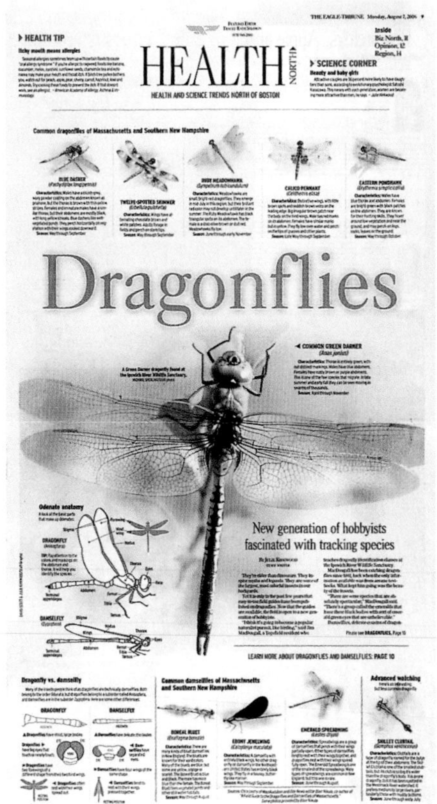
THE EAGLE-TRIBUNE Monday, August 7, 2006

HEALTH TIP

HEALTH NORTH

HEALTH AND SCIENCE TRENDS NORTH OF BOSTON

SCIENCE CORNER

Common dragonflies of Massachusetts and Southern New Hampshire

Dragonflies

COMMON GREEN DARNER

New generation of hobbyists fascinated with tracking species

Odonate anatomy

DRAGONFLY

DAMSELFLY

LEARN MORE ABOUT DRAGONFLIES AND DAMSELFLIES: PAGE 10

Dragonfly vs. damselfly

Common damselflies of Massachusetts and Southern New Hampshire

Advanced watching

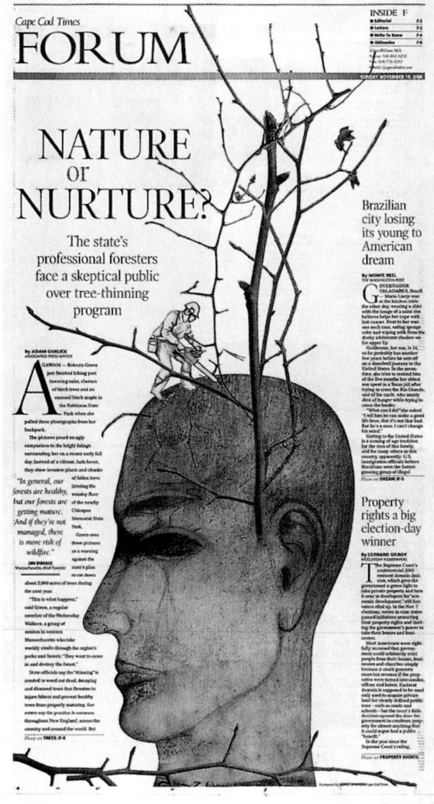
Cape Cod Times

FORUM

INSIDE F

NATURE or NURTURE?

The state's professional foresters face a skeptical public over tree-thinning program

Brazilian city losing its young to American dream

Property rights a big election-day winner

**THE EAGLE-TRIBUNE,** North Andover, Mass.
David Scott
Science/technology page, broadsheet

**CAPE COD TIMES,** Hyannis, Mass.
James Warren
Other feature page, broadsheet

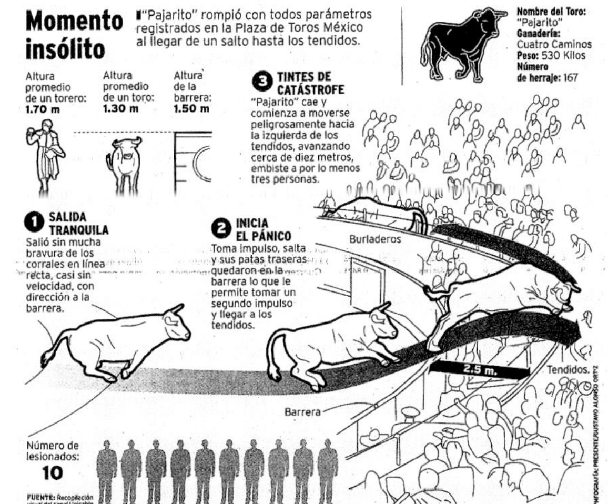

Momento insólito
"Pajarito" rompió con todos parámetros registrados en la Plaza de Toros México al llegar de un salto hasta los tendidos.
Altura promedio de un torero: 1.70 m
Altura promedio de un toro: 1.30 m
Altura de la barrera: 1.50 m
Nombre del Toro: "Pajarito"
Ganadería: Cuatro Caminos
Peso: 530 Kilos
Número de herraje: 167
1 SALIDA TRANQUILA
Salió sin mucha bravura de los corrales en línea recta, casi sin velocidad, con dirección a la barrera.
2 INICIA EL PÁNICO
Toma impulso, salta y sus patas traseras quedaron en la barrera lo que le permite tomar un segundo impulso y llegar a los tendidos.
3 TINTES DE CATÁSTROFE
"Pajarito" cae y comienza a moverse peligrosamente hacia la izquierda de los tendidos, avanzando cerca de diez metros, embiste a por lo menos tres personas.
Burladeros
2.5 m.
Tendidos
Barrera
Número de lesionados: 10


**PRESENTE,** Villahermosa, México
Juan Luis Arteaga, Gustavo Alonso Ortiz
Information graphics, breaking news

Mercados
BBVA desconcierta a los inversores con su ampliación de capital por sorpresa P4

Entrevista
Victoriano Muñoz: "Con la mitad de plantilla, en EEUU producimos más que en España" P7

Motor
Su silencioso motor y sus dimensiones hacen del Passat Variant el mejor familiar de su tipo P14

Estilo
Se abren en España las dos primeras tiendas de 'lifestyle': marcan tendencias P20

elEspecial

may
?
dic
¿Otro tropiezo como el de mayo?
Valores para evitar las pérdidas


**EL ECONOMISTA,** Madrid, Spain
Miguel Buckenmeyer
Other feature page, tabloid

Paper Trail

Amid an industry upheaval, Richmond's daily newspaper is trying to figure out its next move. But why is its newsroom under a gag order?

by Greg Weatherford

This isn't the story I had in mind.

**STYLE WEEKLY,** Richmond, Va.
Jeffrey Bland
Other feature page, tabloid

Mercado
Endesa será alemana siempre que E.ON eleve su oferta en torno a los 30 euros P5

Fondos
Los partícipes se olvidan de invertir, hacen caja y se van de vacaciones P7

Reportaje
Antes de la aviación, la ruta del Atlántico Norte vivió la edad dorada de los transatlánticos P8

Motor
El majestuoso Lexus LS 460, el primer vehículo que incorpora ocho marchas P10

elEspecial

13.500
13.000
12.500
30 expertos opinan
¿Alcanzará la bolsa su techo histórico?
Pags. 2, 3 y 4


**EL ECONOMISTA,** Madrid, Spain
Miguel Buckenmeyer, Jorge Arévalo, Lola Gallego
Other feature page, tabloid

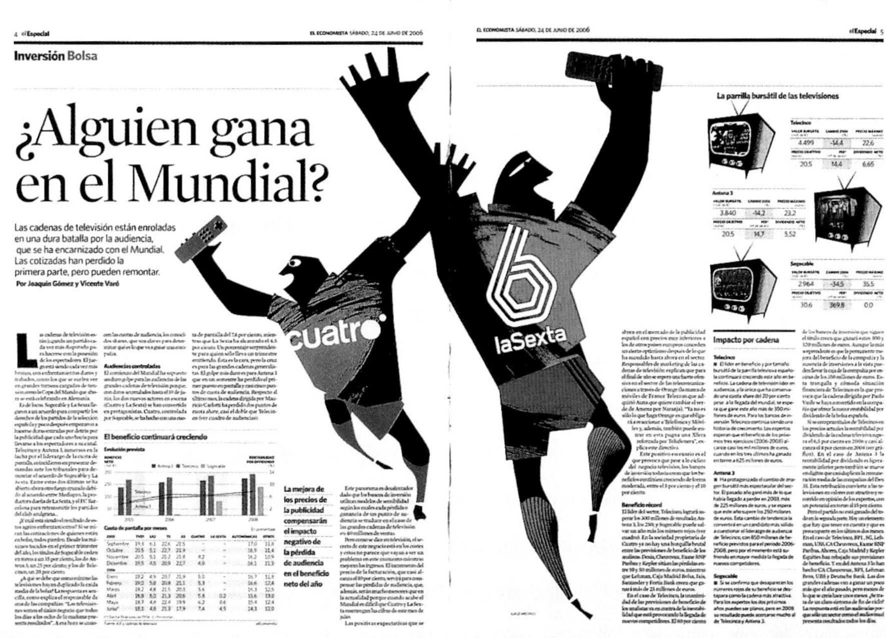

Inversión Bolsa
¿Alguien gana en el Mundial?
Las cadenas de televisión están enroladas en una dura batalla por la audiencia, que se ha encarnizado con el Mundial. Las cotizadas han perdido la primera parte, pero pueden remontar.
Por Joaquín Gómez y Vicente Varó
cuatro
laSexta
La parrilla bursátil de las televisiones
El beneficio continuará creciendo
Impacto por cadena
La mejora de los precios de la publicidad compensarán el impacto negativo de la pérdida de audiencia en el beneficio neto del año


**EL ECONOMISTA,** Madrid, Spain
Miguel Buckenmeyer, Jorge Arévalo, Lola Gallego, Gorka Sampedro
Other feature page, tabloid

**SOUTHWEST JOURNAL,** Minneapolis
Bryan Nanista
Other feature page, tabloid

2006

year in review

people 2
Southwest is alive with strange characters, everyday heroes and hard-working folks who make the city a good place to live.

photographs 6

headlines 8

southwest journal

**UN PASQUÍN,** Bogotá, Colombia
Vladimir "Vladdo" Flórez
News page design portfolio

EL PERIÓDICO DE LA O

OPOSICIÓN EN BLANCO Y NEGRO

UN PASQUÍN

POLÍTICAMENTE INCORRECTO

¡Sálvese quien pueda!

Con la Seguridad Democrática en su peor momento, el gobierno se opone al desarme de los particulares y les ofrece armas subsidiadas a los concejales amenazados.

**STYLE WEEKLY,** Richmond, Va.
Jeffrey Bland
Feature page design portfolio

VCU DUMPS CRITIC WILDER'S NEXT ELECTION VCR DEFIES EXPECTATIONS

Inside: home style.

STYLE WEEKLY

Death of a Salesman

How CarMax attacked the used-car industry — and won.

by Scott Bass

elEconomista

AGUIRRE AHORRA Y GALLARDON DERROCHA

EL DINERO, EN LA BIOGRAFÍA DE LA DISCORDIA

EN MADRID Y BARCELONA SE DUERME MAL

Sumario

Montilla se confiesa

"Apoyaremos las fusiones lideradas por empresas catalanas"

Los clientes de Arte y Naturaleza se querellarán contra el Estado

Consideran que puede haber negligencias como las cometidas con Fórum y Afinsa

"La solución a todos los problemas es el fin de los gobiernos"

Aviso a las cajas: cuidado al crear holdings bursátiles como La Caixa

La bolsa negocia en un minuto tanto dinero como gana Raúl en un año

**EL ECONOMISTA,** Madrid, Spain
Miguel Buckenmeyer
Combination page design portfolio

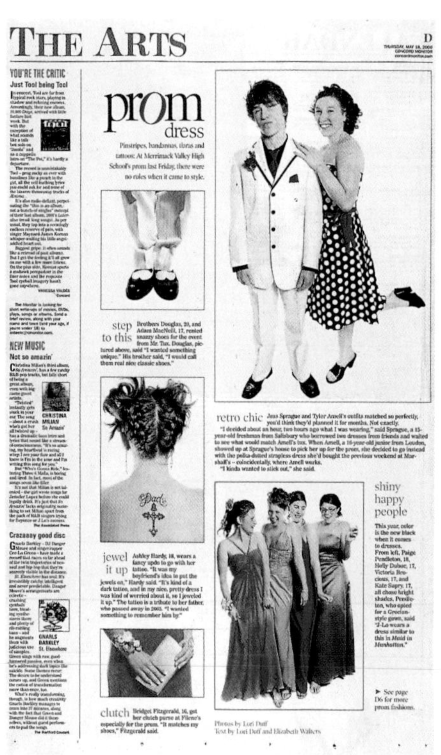
THE ARTS

D

prom dress

step to this

retro chic

shiny happy people

jewel it up

clutch

**CONCORD MONITOR** (N.H.)
Vanessa Valdes
Feature page design portfolio

here

Section E: The Mercury's Weekend Read

Saturday, October 14, 2006

It's not Spain. It's not France. It's not the Niagara region. But still, Guelphites are

Getting corked

brother

fall showcase OF SAVINGS

**GUELPH MERCURY** (Ontario, Canada)
Brad Needham
Feature page design portfolio

SILVER

**EL ECONOMISTA,**

Madrid, Spain

Miguel Buckenmeyer,
Augusto Costanzo,
Lola Gallego,
Gorka Sampedro

Other feature page, tabloid

Imagery from "War of the Worlds" tells the story of ratings for competing TV networks. The lone alien robot on the cover sets the stage for the battle inside. Business stories can be so boring, but this page uses a fun metaphor. The balanced color and type, plus the graphic simplicity, advance this attractive package.

Las imágenes de "La guerra de los mundos" cuentan la historia de los ratings de las estaciones televisivas competidoras. El solitario robot extraterrestre en la portada anuncia la batalla que se da en el interior. Los artículos sobre negocios pueden ser muy aburridos, pero esta página usa una metáfora entretenida. El equilibrio en el color y la tipografía, junto con la simplicidad del gráfico, hacen resaltar este atractivo paquete informativo.

**EL ECONOMISTA,** Madrid, Spain

Miguel Buckenmeyer

Combination page design portfolio

**CONCORD MONITOR** (N.H.)

Dan Habib

Combination page design portfolio

**THE FREE LANCE-STAR,** Fredericksburg, Va.

Meredith Sheffer

Combination page design portfolio

Un gran desfile pone hoy fin a la festividad de las Fuerzas Armadas

**DIARIO DE SEVILLA** (Spain)
Manuel Romero, Raquel Feria, Francisco Barquilla
Information graphics, non-breaking news & features

**EL ECONOMISTA,** Madrid, Spain
Amaya Verde, Gorka Sampedro
Information graphics, non-breaking news & features

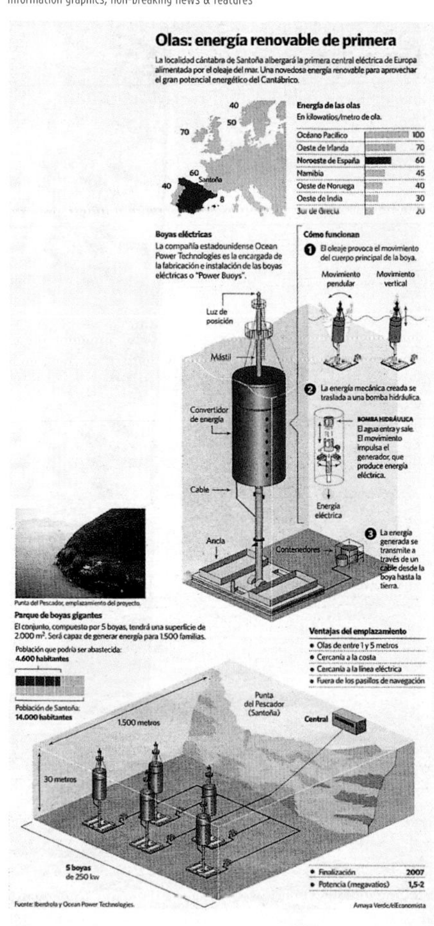

Olas: energía renovable de primera

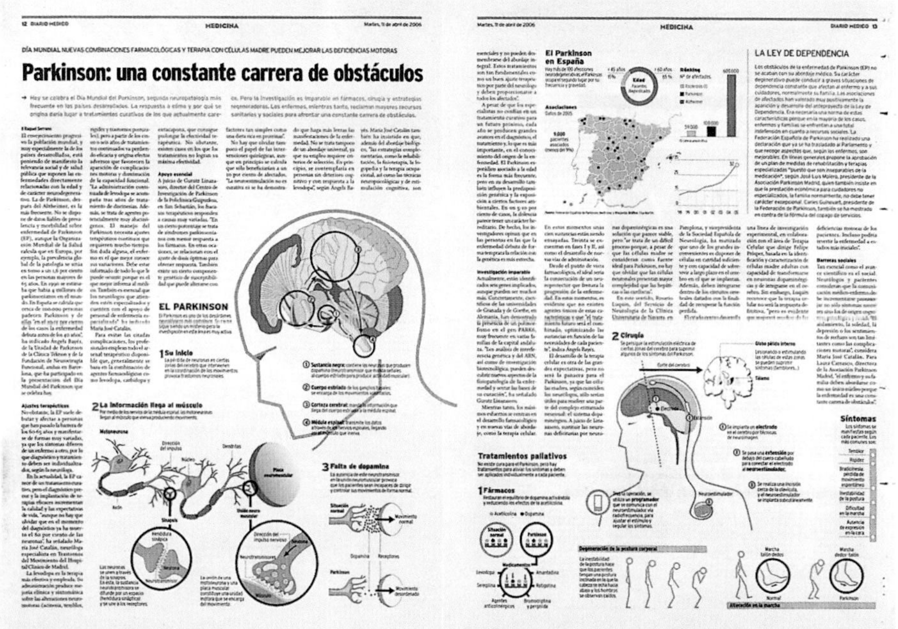

Parkinson: una constante carrera de obstáculos

**DIARIO MEDICO,** Madrid, Spain
José Juan Gámez, Elsa Martín
Information graphics, non-breaking news & features

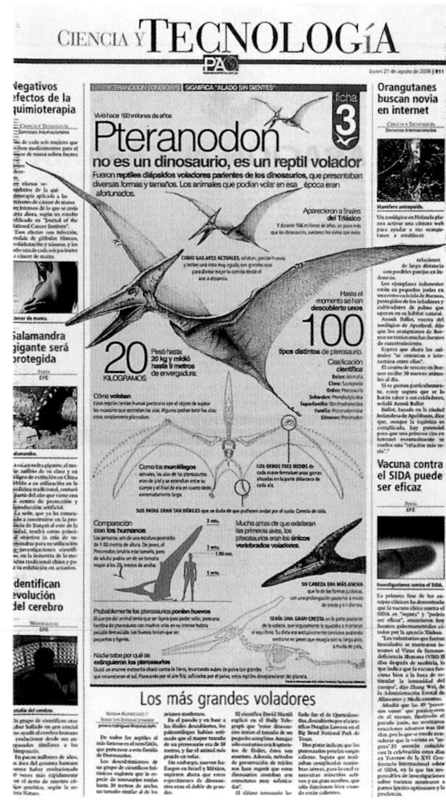

Ciencia y Tecnología

Pteranodon no es un dinosaurio, es un reptil volador

Los más grandes voladores

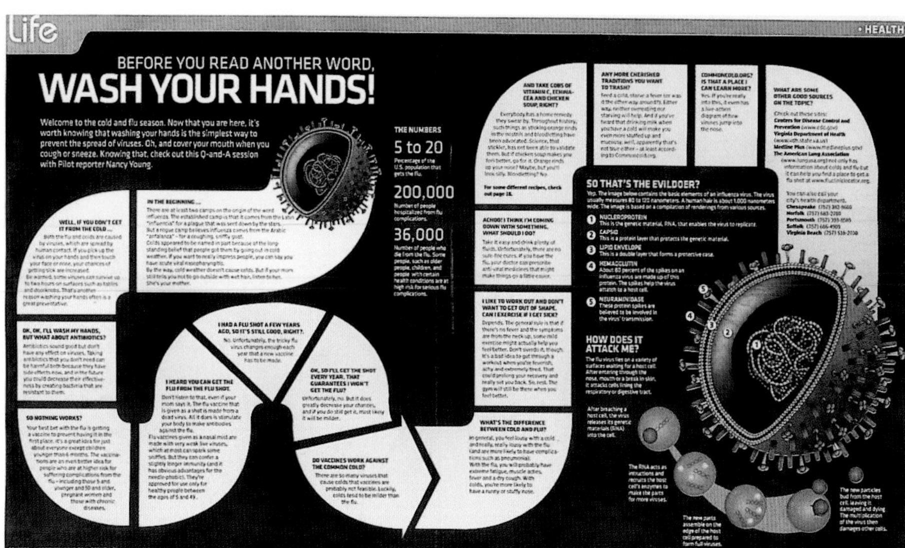

BEFORE YOU READ ANOTHER WORD, WASH YOUR HANDS!

**PANAMÁ AMÉRICA,** Panama City, Panama
Nelson Fernández, Roy Hernández, Yelena Rodríguez, Alejandro Ortiz
Information graphics portfolio, staff, non-breaking news & features

**LINK,** Norfolk, Va.
Brandon Stuck
Combination page design portfolio

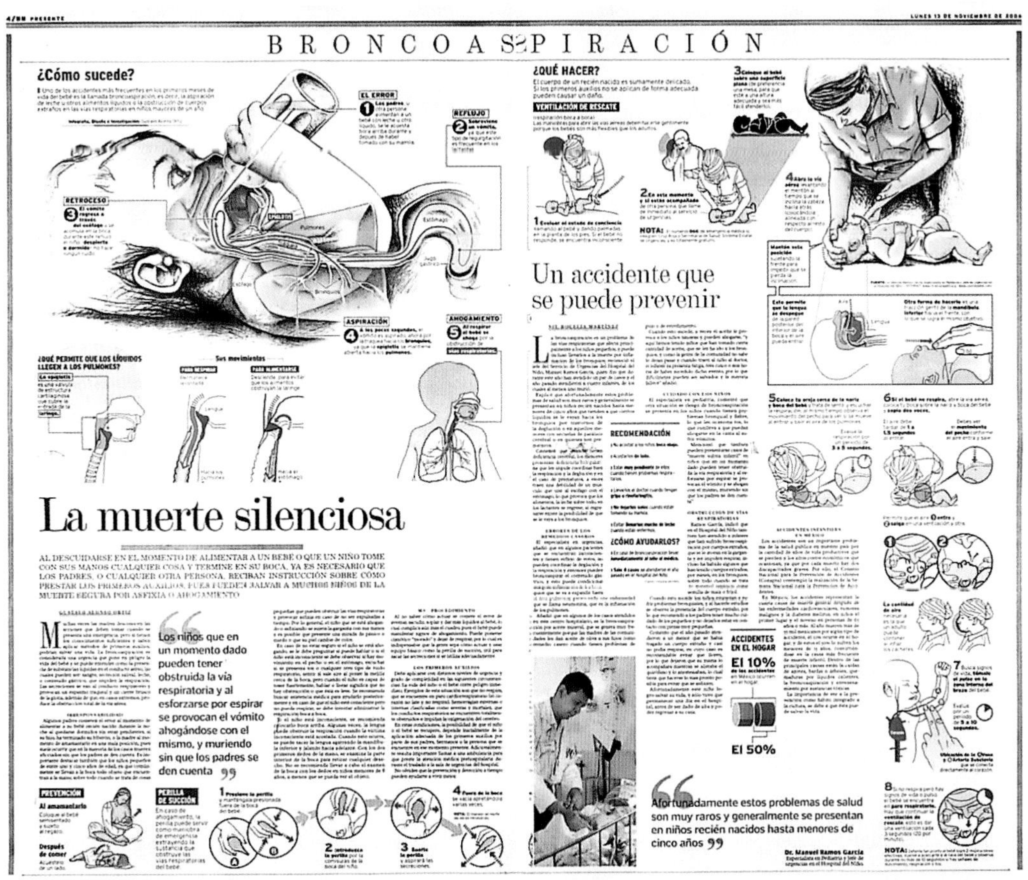

**PRESENTE, DIARIO DEL SURESTE,**
Villahermosa, México
Gustavo Alonso Ortiz
Information graphics, non-breaking news & features

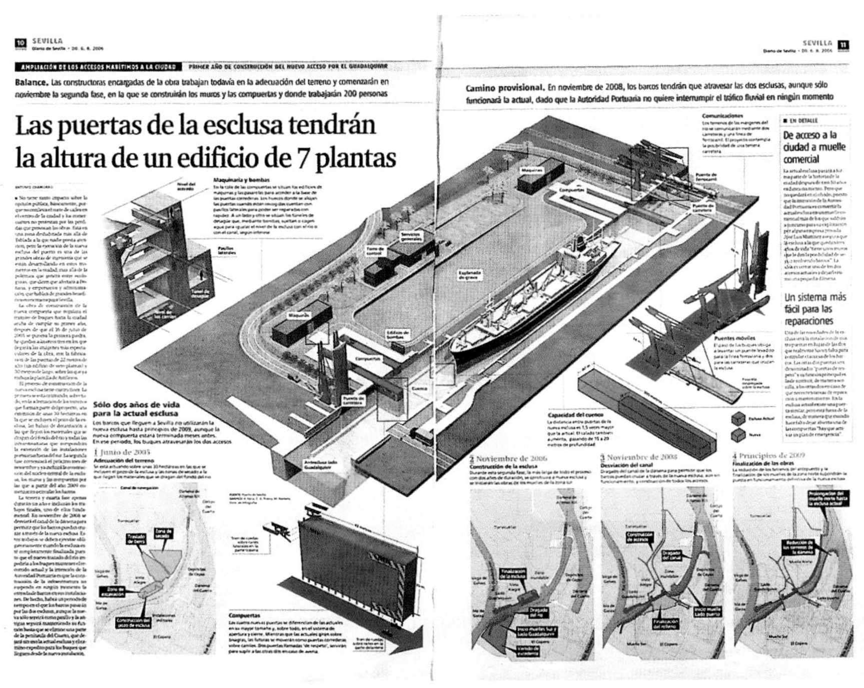

**DIARIO DE SEVILLA** (Spain)
Manuel Romero, Cristina G. Rivera
Information graphics, non-breaking news & features

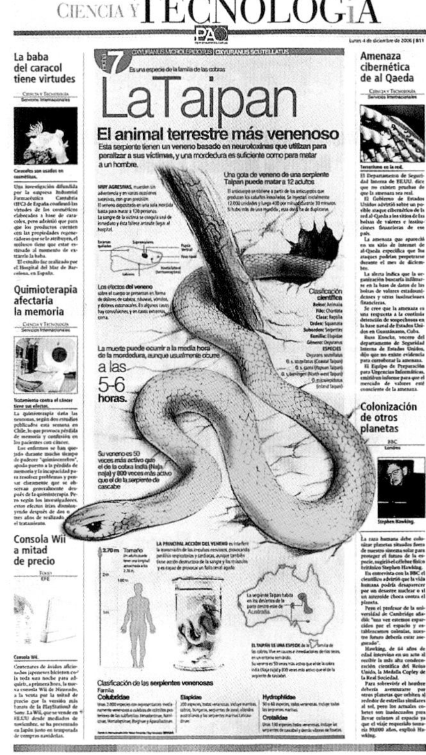

**PANAMÁ AMÉRICA,** Panama City
Nelson Fernández, Roy Hernández, Yelena Rodríguez, Alejandro Ortiz
Information graphics portfolio, staff, non-breaking news & features

**TABASCO HOY,** Villahermosa, México
Gonzalo Hernandez
Information graphics portfolio, individual, non-breaking news & features

**PRESENTE, DIARIO DEL SURESTE,** Villahermosa, México
Gustavo Alonso Ortiz
Information graphics, non-breaking news & features

**EL COMERCIO,** Gijon, Spain
Susana García Coya
Information graphics portfolio, individual, non-breaking news & features

**PRESENTE, DIARIO DEL SURESTE,** Villahermosa, México
Gustavo Alonso Ortiz
Information graphics portfolio, staff, breaking news

Chapter Eight

# SPECIAL COVERAGE

Cobertura especial

**Single Subjects / Sections**
**Cover Pages / Inside Pages / Reprints**

Temas Únicos / Secciones
Páginas de Portada / Páginas de Crónica / Reimpresiones

**MORGENAVISEN JYLLANDS-POSTEN,** Viby, Denmark
Rina Kjeldgaard, Ove Hougaard, Orla Borg, Henrik Vinther Olesen
Single-subject special coverage

MORGENAVISEN Jyllands-Posten STORE BEDEDAG
2.sektion
MUSLIM
med måde

**THE WASHINGTON POST**
Kevin Merida, Beth Broadwater, Dwuan June, Jon Wile, Dennis Brack, Keith Jenkins, Michel du Cille, Jahi Chikwendiu, Phil Bennett, Laura Stanton
Single-subject special coverage

The Best of the Summer's Shows Weekend Section
The Washington Post
DISTRICT HOME EDITION
BEING A BLACK MAN
AT THE CORNER OF PROGRESS AND PERIL
Six Powers Reach Accord On Iran Plan
U.S. Supports Combination Of Incentives, 'Disincentives'
D.C. at Low Risk Of Attack, Says Federal Agency
What does it mean to be a black man?
IRS Ruling Imperils 'Gift Fund' Charities For Home Buyers
INSIDE
From Way Out in Right Field
Yankees Fan Who Beat O's in Stands Could Join Them in Dugout

**THE COMMERCIAL APPEAL,** Memphis, Tenn.
John Nelson, John Sale, Alan Spearman
Single-subject special coverage

THE COMMERCIAL APPEAL SPECIAL SECTION SUNDAY, DECEMBER 24, 2006
MYSTERY MISSISSIPPI
THE RIVER YOU DON'T KNOW
Discovery
Our next-door river, America's greatest, is also our great unknown
IN THIS SERIES
VIEWPOINTS INSIDE
In all its sinuous, sun-spangled majesty, it's the Mississippi.

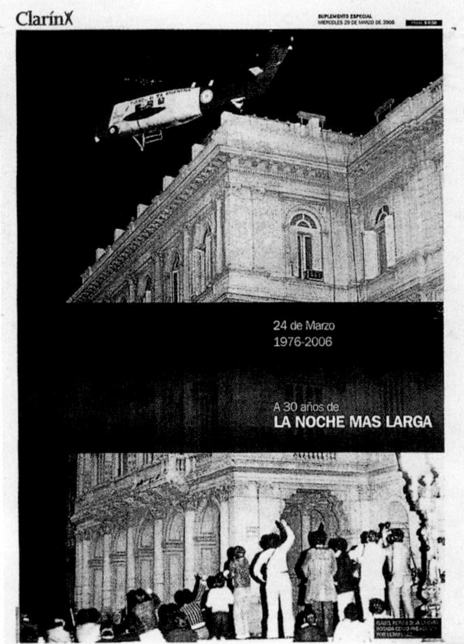
Clarín
SUPLEMENTO ESPECIAL
24 de Marzo
1976-2006
A 30 años de
LA NOCHE MAS LARGA

**CLARÍN,** Buenos Aires, Argentina
Gustavo Lo Valvo, Juan Elissetche
Special coverage, section, no ads

WEB SITES EASE TRAVELERS' GUILT | SHARKS FINISH STRONG, EDGE DUCKS 4-3
San Jose Mercury News
MERCURYNEWS.COM
Coming home
A MERCURY NEWS SPECIAL REPORT | Frank and Michelle leave the hospital and try to pick up their lives together. Their future happiness will depend on their own strengths.
FOLLOW THE STORY ONLINE
ABOUT THIS SERIES
LAST OF FIVE PARTS
MONDAY
Records reveal years of 49ers' stadium gripes
Iraq forcing Bush to decide if determination has its limits
PALESTINIAN VOTE DEMANDED
MEXICO'S TOP POP ACT HEADS FOR U.S.
P.A. HIGH LOSES STATE TITLE GAME
OPTIONS SCANDAL: SO WHAT?

**SAN JOSE MERCURY NEWS** (Calif.)
Michael Tribble, Pauline Lubens, Geri Migielicz, Jonathon Berlin, Matt Mansfield
Single-subject special coverage

LA PRESSE MONTRÉAL SAMEDI 14 OCTOBRE 2006
LA PRESSE AFFAIRES
LE DÉFI
MAÎTRISEZ VOS DETTES

**LA PRESSE,** Montréal
Philippe Tardif, Benoit Giguere, Genevieve Dinel, Michel Marois, Stephane Lavallee, Marc Tison, Stephanie Grammond
Special coverage, section, no ads

**SUN JOURNAL,** Lewiston, Maine

Nick Masuda, Pete Gorski, Amber Waterman, Carol Coultas, Rex Rhoades, Judy Meyer, Keith Hagel, Douglas Van Reeth

Special coverage, section, no ads

SEEING GREEN: Fiber, forests, futures

Brazil's paper chase, mounting rewards

The Brazil project

**LA PRENSA GRÁFICA**

Antiguo Cuscatlán, El Salvador

Enrique Contreras, Héctor Ramírez, Ricardo Orellana

Special coverage, section, no ads

LA CAÍDA DEL VUELO 901

Cuando escuchó el "jup jup" de la alarma del avión, el piloto Axel Miranda no supo qué hacer. Pidió al segundo al mando del avión, Víctor Sandoval, que se comunicara con la torre de control en Comalapa. No le alcanzó el tiempo. Cuatro segundos antes de las 8:14 de la noche del 9 de agosto de 1995, el Aviateca 901 chocó contra el volcán Chichontepec en el peor accidente aéreo de la historia de El Salvador. Por primera vez en 11 años, se hace una reconstrucción detallada de los últimos 15 minutos de vuelo, señalando las decisiones erradas de controlador y piloto. Murieron 65 personas, 58 pasajeros y siete tripulantes, ninguno de ellos salvadoreño. Se revela las últimas palabras que intercambiaron piloto y copiloto, apenas un segundo antes de la colisión. Esta es la historia de uno de los pocos accidentes aéreos en el mundo en que la caja negra, crucial para saber si hubo fallas técnicas, nunca apareció.

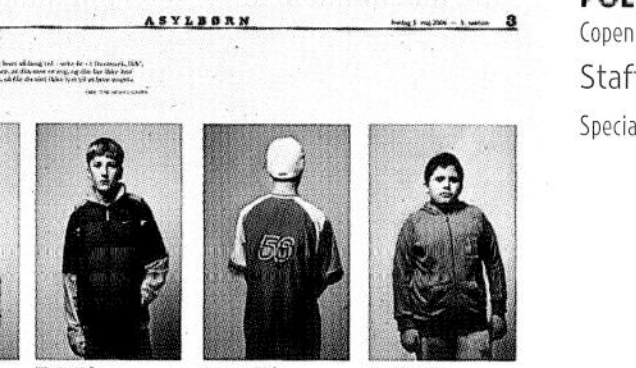

**POLITIKEN**

Copenhagen, Denmark

Staff

Special coverage, section, no ads

**FRANKFURTER ALLGEMEINE SONNTAGSZEITUNG,**

Frankfurt am Main, Germany

Peter Breul, Kat Menschik, Thomas Schmid, Bertram Eisenhauer, Andreas Kuther

Special coverage, section, no ads

B6 NINE/ELEVEN

Am Ende lohnt sich Terror nicht

Seine Bekämpfung ist zwar teuer. Aber er bringt die Weltwirtschaft nicht in Schwierigkeiten. *Von Gerald Braunberger*

Der Tourismus hält dagegen

**THE GLOBE AND MAIL,** Toronto

Cinders McLeod, David Pratt, Cathrin Bradbury, Jerry Johnson, Brian Kerrigan, Richard Johnson

Special coverage, section, with ads

60 50 40

talkin' 'bout their generation

It's often thought of as one overwhelming mass of humanity, but the baby boom divides into distinct age groups, each with its own particular profile. JILL MAHONEY sounds out three representatives

**LOS ANGELES TIMES**

Kelli Sullivan, Joseph Hutchinson, Michael Whitley, Steven R. Hawkins, Nick Cuccia, Mary Cooney, Calvin Hom, Richard Derk

Special coverage, section, with ads

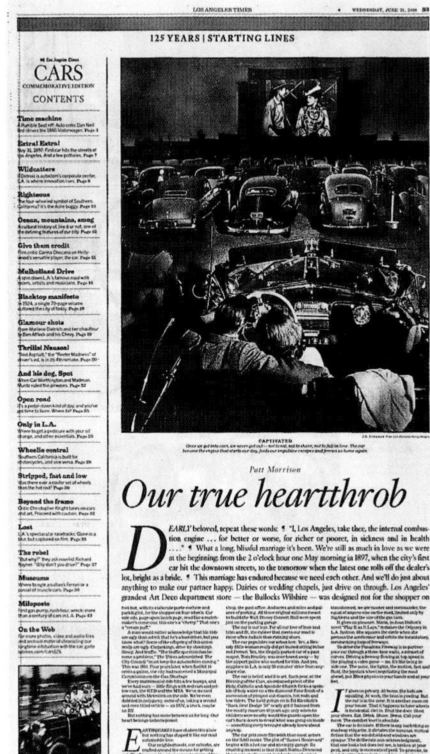

LOS ANGELES TIMES

125 YEARS | STARTING LINES

CARS

COMMEMORATIVE EDITION

CONTENTS

Time machine

Extra! Extra!

Wildcatters

Righteous

Ocean, mountains, smog

Give them credit

Mulholland Drive

Blacktop manifesto

Glamour shots

Thrills! Nausea!

Open road

Only in L.A.

Wheelie central

Stripped, fast and low

Beyond the frame

Lost

The rebel

Museums

Mileposts

On the Web

CAPTIVATED

Patt Morrison

*Our true heartthrob*

DEARLY beloved, repeat these words: ¶ "I, Los Angeles, take thee, the internal combustion engine . . . for better or worse, for richer or poorer, in sickness and in health . . . ." ¶ What a long, blissful marriage it's been. We're still as much in love as we were at the beginning: from the 2 o'clock hour one May morning in 1897, when the city's first car hit the downtown streets, to the tomorrow when the latest one rolls off the dealer's lot, bright as a bride. ¶ This marriage has endured because we need each other. And we'll do just about anything to make our partner happy. Dairies or wedding chapels, just drive on through. Los Angeles' grandest Art Deco department store — the Bullocks Wilshire — was designed not for the shopper on

**THE GLOBE AND MAIL,** Toronto

Cinders McLeod, David Pratt, Cathrin Bradbury, Jerry Johnson, Brian Kerrigan

Special coverage, section, with ads

CANCER: A DAY IN THE LIFE | FOCUS · F15

**HERALDO DE ARAGÓN,** Zaragoza, Spain

Kristina Urresti, Irán Santos, Pilar Ostalé, Jorge Luis Mora, Pedro Zapater, Luis Grañena, Alberto Aragón, Isidro Gil, Paula R. Español

Special coverage, section, with ads

HERALDO DE ARAGÓN DOMINGO, 23 DE ABRIL DE 2006 ESPECIAL SAN JORGE

De vuelta a casa

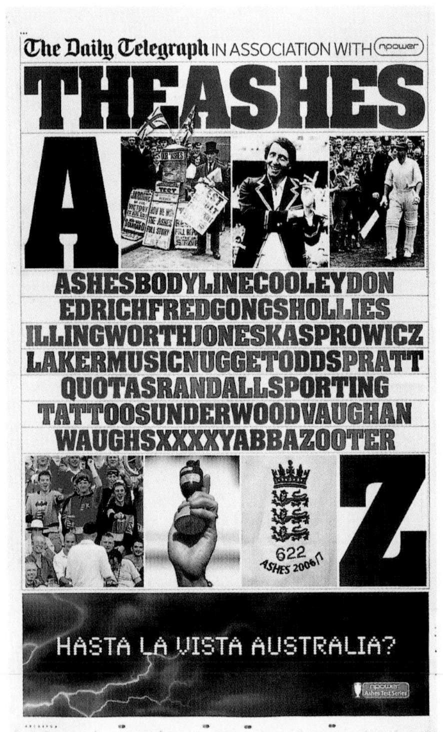

The Daily Telegraph IN ASSOCIATION WITH npower

THE ASHES

A

ASHESBODYLINECOOLEYDON
EDRICHFREDGONGSHOLLIES
ILLINGWORTHJONESKASPROWICZ
LAKERMUSICNUGGETODDSPRATT
QUOTASRANDALLSPORTING
TATTOOSUNDERWOODVAUGHAN
WAUGHSXXXXYABBAZOOTER

Z

622 ASHES 2006/7

HASTA LA VISTA AUSTRALIA?

**THE DAILY TELEGRAPH,** London

Staff

Special coverage, section, with ads

# Manchester United

## The club

**Years since a trophy**
0 (Carling Cup, 2006). But three since they last won "their" Premiership trophy.
**The bottom line**
The ever-popular Glazer family, headed by Malcolm, who made his money by investing in mobile-home parks. Bought the Tampa Bay Buccaneers in 1995. Debts currently stand at a trifling £660m.
**An optimist speaks**
If United finished second without a midfield last season, what will they do with Michael Carrick and Paul Scholes? And attacks will be much more liquid without the constipated presence of Ruud van Nistelrooy.
**A pessimist speaks**
The midfield has less bite than Shane McGowan, Cristiano Ronaldo's heart isn't in it, the fragile Louis Saha makes Darren Anderton seem like Geoff Capes and referees will have it in for Wayne Rooney.
**Fans chant**
"La la la la la la la la, Keano!" (as Darren Fletcher loses his 34th fifty-fifty ball).
**Manchester United: the movie**
It began with some railway workers in Newton Heath having a post-work kickaround. Gold Trafford takes in tragedy (the Munich air crash), triumph (the unique treble of 1999) and disaster (Ralph Milne). Starring John McCririck as Malcolm Glazer, Marshall Mathers as Alan Smith and Peter Kay (who put on two stone for the role) as John O'Shea.
**Remaindered by Christmas**
You've Been Merked: Rio Ferdinand's Alternative Dictionary. How To Get A Six Pack In Just 40 Years, by John O'Shea.

## If they were a sweet...
Ferrero Rocher

A high-class confection traditionally offered to guests at major occasions. Huge international popularity but is all as it seems? The gold wrapping is not even made of foil, there's a distinctly soft and insubstantial centre and the whole thing is presided over by an ageing ambassadorial figure who some suggest is spoiling everything.

## Fixtures

**August**
20 Fulham H PPV
23 Charlton A
26 Watford A
**September**
9 Tottenham H PPV
17 Arsenal H TV
23 Reading A PPV
30 Newcastle H
**October**
14 Wigan A TV
22 Liverpool H TV
28 Bolton A
**November**
4 Portsmouth H
11 Blackburn A PPV
18 Sheff Utd A
26 Chelsea H TV
29 Everton H
**December**
2 Middlesbrough A PPV
9 Man City H PPV
17 West Ham A TV
23 Aston Villa A
26 Wigan H
30 Reading H
**January**
1 Newcastle A
13 Aston Villa H
20 Arsenal A
31 Watford H
**February**
3 Tottenham A
10 Charlton H
24 Fulham A
**March**
3 Liverpool A
17 Bolton H
31 Blackburn H
**April**
7 Portsmouth A
10 Sheff Utd H
14 Chelsea A
21 Middlesbrough H
28 Everton A
**May**
5 Man City A
13 West Ham H

## The facts

**Ground**
Old Trafford, Sir Matt Busby Way, Manchester M16 0RA
**Switchboard**
0870 442 1994
**Capacity** 76,000
**Away allocation** 2,000-6,000
**Ticket prices**
£23-£37
**Ticket office**
0870 442 1999
**Disabled facilities**
0845 230 1989
**Club shop**
0870 111 8107
**Official website**
www.manutd.com

## The manager Sir Alex Ferguson

**Touchline type**
Chews more gum than a bad kisser; plays his own interactive game that involves Glasgow kissing fresh air every time someone heads for goal; looks at his watch about 474 times per minute.
**Fans hate**
The persistence with The Scottish Player, Darren Fletcher; tactical tinkering; increasingly peculiar babbling; the ceding of significant responsibility to serial failure Carlos Queiroz.
**Will say**
"Youse are all a bunch of idiots"

## The players

**World Cup report**
Ronaldo and Rooney played text tennis; Rio Ferdinand was quietly excellent on the pitch and gobbily useless off it; Gabriel Heinze took defeat with admirable dignity; Louis Saha also went to Germany.
**Line into McClaren?**
Like t'new England manager, Alan Smith is of proper Yorkshire stock and can properly enunciate t'word 'booger'.
**New boy**
The acquisition of Carrick shows that, just five years after Juan Sebastián Verón, United's brief flirtation with galacticism is over and that Lord Ferg hasn't lost his rare ability to pay ridiculously inflated prices or got over his obsession with Verón-style schemers.
**Poll could show three yellows to**
Alan Smith, whose reversion to centre-forward shouldn't stop up him blundering into tackles with all the subtlety and forensic precision of Leslie Nielsen in Police Squad.
**Their Theo**
Giuseppe Rossi, 19, an American-born Italian forward with the touch of a Dalglish and the finish of a Rush – when he plays for the reserves.
**Key Wag**
Colleen McLoughlin, the future Mrs Rooney, is even more bankable than Posh: she shops, presents TV shows, shops, writes a column, shops, shops, models for Asda, shops.

Past 10 seasons

Michael Carrick Henry Browne/Action Images

## The tactics

**Plan A**
After an ill-fated dalliance with 4-5-1, to protect Roy Keane and pander to Queiroz, Ferguson switched to his tried-and-trusted 4-4-1-1 last season. Rooney will buzz off the perpetual motion Saha, while Carrick and Scholes should ensure a higher class of ball retention than towards the end of last season. But don't be surprised by a cunning switch to 4-5-1, with Rooney on the wing.
**Plan B**
OK, Teddy, get stripped off. Those were the days, eh Fergie?

## Last season

2nd

Champ Lg Group stage
FA Cup 5th round
League Cup Winners
League discipline Y60 R2
Top scorer V Nist'rooy 21

## The ground

**Getting there**
Train and Metrolink services go to Old Trafford from Manchester Piccadilly. Or park in Altrincham and get the Metrolink.
**Being there**
The Pamela Anderson of Premiership stadia: vacuous, strikingly attractive and relentlessly in-your-face. Commercialism hits you at every corner. Has an atmosphere that could be cut with the handle of a butter knife. Red Café diners are advised to "Be sure to keep glancing at the door. You never know who might walk in." Les the builder from Chorlton?
**Title odds** 6-1

42 The Season

The Season 43

**THE GUARDIAN,** London

Barry Ainslie

Special coverage, section, with ads

# Extreme makeovers

Children with terrible facial disfigurements from some of the poorest countries in the world are coming to Britain to have their faces rebuilt. **Aida Edemariam** reports on the British medical team who are transforming their lives

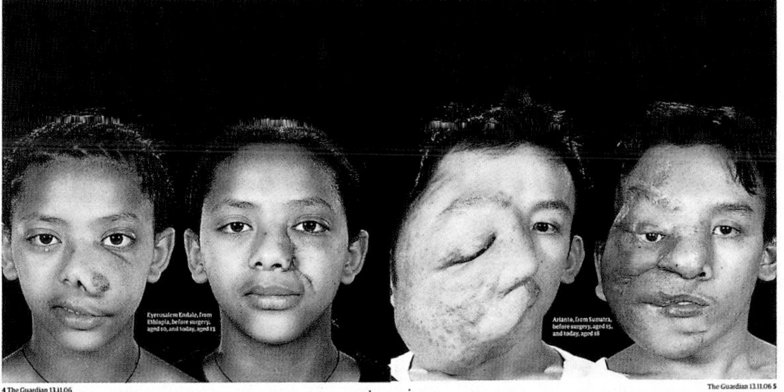

4 The Guardian 13.11.06 The Guardian 13.11.06 5

**THE GUARDIAN,** London
Richard Turley
Special coverage, section, with ads

**EL GRÁFICO,** Antiquo Cuscatlan, El Salvador
Agustín A. Palacios, Cristian Villalta, Juan José, Edgar Martínez
Special coverage, section, with ads

anuario06 | especial **última hora** especial **última hora** | anuario06

/30
**ETA sella con un coche bomba el final de la tregua**

**SUR, MALAGA,** Spain
Mª Dolores de la Vega, Rafael Ruiz, Baldomero Villanueva, Javier Romero, Fernando González, Francisco Sánchez Ruano, Alberto Torregrosa
Special coverage, section, with ads

**FRANKFURTER ALLGEMEINE ZEITUNG,** Frankfurt am Main, Germany
Peter Breul, Frank Schirrmacher, Hubert Spiegel
Special coverage, section, with ads

Frankfurter Allgemeine

# Günter Grass Beim Häuten der Zwiebel

Das Drama einer Selbsterfindung: Der Nobelpreisträger erinnert sich an seine Kindheit, die Kriegserlebnisse an der Front und in Gefangenschaft sowie an seine Anfänge als Künstler. Wie wurde einer zu dem, der er geworden ist? Ein exklusiver Vorabdruck in der Frankfurter Allgemeinen Zeitung.

Die Häute unter der Haut

LÖRDAG 23 DECEMBER 2006

familjefriden
tv-ankan
skinkan
resorna
jesusbarnet
persisk jul
tomten
spriten
trädet
klappen

Vad vore julen utan alla sina ingredienser? Här är tio julord som tillsammans rymmer en riktigt god jul. I bästa fall.

**UPSALA NYA TIDNING,** Uppsala, Sweden
Mats Hagberg, Lotta Frithiof
Special coverage, section, with ads

**FOLHA DE SÃO PAULO** (Brazil)
Massimo Gentile, Fabio Marra, Jair de Oliveira, Marcio Freitas, Kleber Bonjoan, Clauton Danelli de Souza, Mario Kanno
Special coverage, section, with ads

**THE NEWS-PRESS,** Fort Myers, Fla.
Valerie Roche, Ricardo Rolon, Kinfe Moroti, Javier Torres, Matt Tarr
Special coverage, section, with ads

**LA PRESSE,** Montréal
Catherine Bernard, Alain Roberge, Stephanie Berube, Benoit Giguere, Genevieve Dinel, Michel Marois, Alain-Pierre Hovasse, Marie-Claude Girard
Special coverage, section, with ads

**EL CORREO,** Bilbao, Spain
Diego Zúñiga, María del Carmen Navarro, Mikel García Macías, Aurelio Garrote, Ana Espligares, Noelia Martínez, Juan Antonio Salazar, Laura Piedra, Pacho Igartua
Special coverage, section, with ads

Los Angeles Times
EDUCATION
COMMEMORATIVE EDITION
The path to learning
The California college experience started with small, religious-based schools, expanded to include "teachers colleges" — and evolved into an ecumenical movement studied worldwide. MASTER PLAN: It's a state where anyone can enroll, Page 4. PROTESTS: A new kind of education, and arrests by the hundreds, Page 6. DREAM MACHINES: A college whose graduates rule the four-wheel world, Page 20. PLUS: Inventions bring cachet — and cash. Hollywood goes to college. Fashion. Fun with mascots. Pranks. Classrooms of tomorrow.


**LOS ANGELES TIMES**
Kelli Sullivan, Joseph Hutchinson, Michael Whitley, Steven Sedam, Mary Cooney, Robert St. John
Special coverage, section, with ads

**HERALDO DE ARAGÓN**
Zaragoza, Spain
Kristina Urresti, Irán Santos, Pilar Ostalé, Jorge Luis Mora, Pedro Zapater, Luis Grañena, Alberto Aragón, Isidro Gil, Paula R. Español
Special coverage, section, with ads

## SILVER

**WELT AM SONNTAG,** Berlin

Jördis Guzmán Bulla, Karin Sturm

Single-subject special coverage

The editors describe the world of the senses with a unit of graphics and photographs. The layers are impressive — they could easily have done one or the other, but they did both. The photo editing lets you see things in a new way. The package doesn't overwhelm.

Los editores describen el mundo de los sentidos con una unidad de gráficos y fotografías. Los niveles de información son impresionantes; fácilmente podrían haber hecho sólo uno u otro, pero hicieron los dos. La edición fotográfica permite ver las cosas de una forma novedosa. El paquete informativo no está sobrecargado.

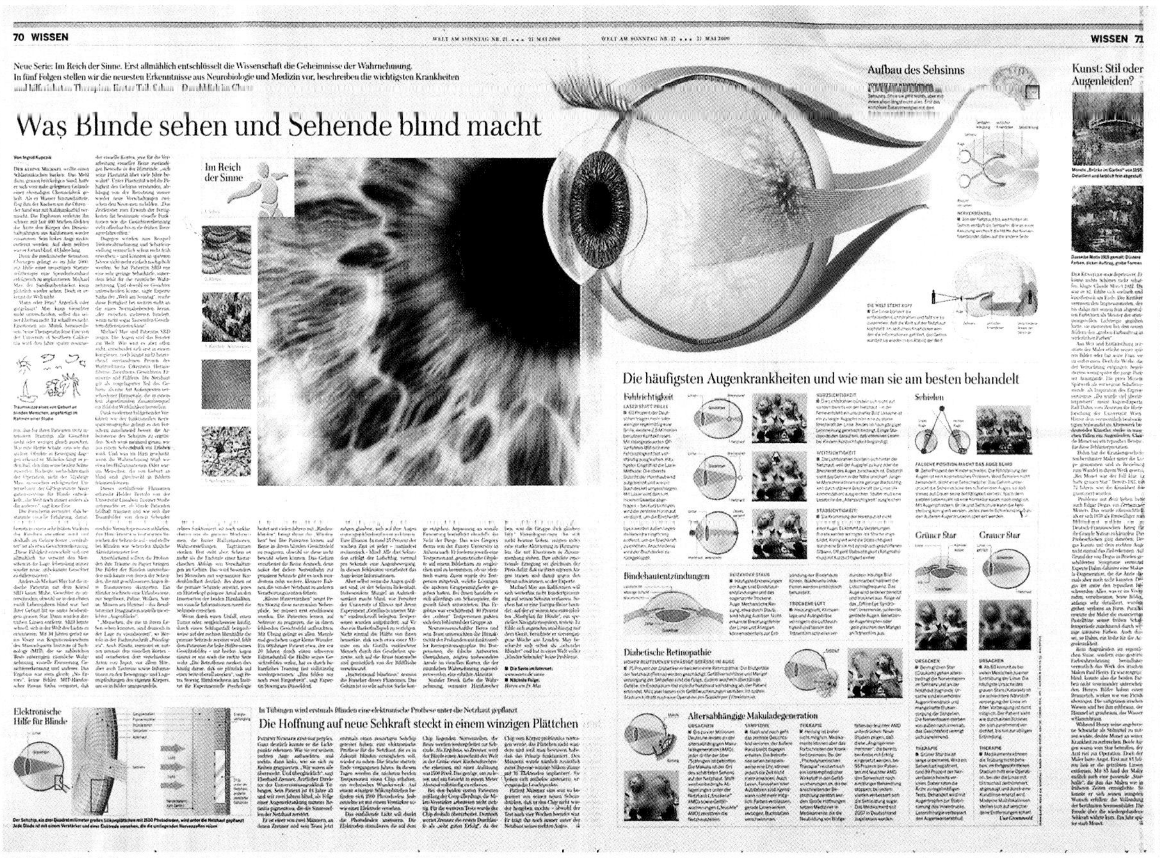

70 WISSEN — WISSEN 71

Neue Serie: Im Reich der Sinne. Erst allmählich entschlüsselt die Wissenschaft die Geheimnisse der Wahrnehmung. In fünf Folgen stellen wir die neuesten Erkenntnisse aus Neurobiologie und Medizin vor, beschreiben die wichtigsten Krankheiten

# Was Blinde sehen und Sehende blind macht

Im Reich der Sinne

Aufbau des Sehsinns

Kunst: Stil oder Augenleiden?

Die häufigsten Augenkrankheiten und wie man sie am besten behandelt

Fehlsichtigkeit

Schielen

Grüner Star

Grauer Star

Bindehautentzündungen

Diabetische Retinopathie

Altersabhängige Makuladegeneration

Elektronische Hilfe für Blinde

In Tübingen wird erstmals Blinden eine elektronische Prothese unter die Netzhaut gepflanzt

## Die Hoffnung auf neue Sehkraft steckt in einem winzigen Plättchen

Group D

# Portugal

Group fixtures
**Angola** June 11, Cologne 8pm
**Iran** June 17, Frankfurt 2pm
**Mexico** June 21, Gelsenkirchen 3pm

### The team

**The cliché**
The final chance for the Golden Generation to win something.
**The reality**
Most of the Golden Generation have, of course, died of old age. But this is surely the last hurrah for Luis Figo. Portugal finally proved they have what it takes in tournament play at Euro 2004, although in the end they still blew their best chance to win a major honour. Still, with Maniche, Deco, Cristiano Ronaldo and Simao to call on, the Seleçao will hope to match their qualifying form, in which they tonked Russia 7-1.
**Where they're staying**
The Sporthotel Klosterpforte in Marienfeld looks like a conference centre with an abnormally large World War II helmet wedged on the roof. It is more charming than we make it sound, though: it has been family-run since 1953.
**Grudge match**
Beating Spain would get rid of a shoulder chip as big as Scotland, Canada and New Zealand put together but they'll have to concentrate on fending off their former colonial outpost Angola, who are waiting to give them a whack up the bracket in their opening game.

**If they were shoes . . .**
**Floral wellies**
Two years ago they were THE thing. But in the blink of an eye 2004 has become 2006 and we're already looking back and asking ourselves: what the hell was that all about? Not likely to take the world by storm for a while yet

**The politics**
Ricardo and the frankly amusingly monickered Quim are involved in a tug-of-war for the goalkeeping shirt. As it's rumoured some of the players wanted it to go to Vitor Baia, who's not even in the squad, whoever wins had better keep hold of every cross.
**Supported by**
The usual Mediterranean mix of men in face paint and women with charms that cause television directors to forget to show any of the game.
**Slogan on team coach**
"With a flag in the window and a nation on the pitch. Força Portugal!"

### The coach Luiz Felipe Scolari

**On his chalkboard**
Ever security-conscious, he details Maniche and Costinha to sit in front of his back four. It will be up to the trio of Ronaldo, Deco and Figo to feed the lonesome (and often hapless) Pauleta.
**In his closet**
One meeting with Brian Barwick launched a thousand investigations into his every utterance. Gold was found in an El Grafico interview in which he offered a Thatcheresque critique of General Pinochet: "[He] tortured a lot but there is no illiteracy in Chile."

### The players

**Most likely to move to Bolton**
Nuno Gomes is getting on a bit now and has never realised his potential, so a kick up the hole from Big Sam is probably what he needs. And of course Figo, 83, fits the Reebok demographic perfectly.
**Oscar nominee**
There's only one Ronaldo when it comes to falling over when there's no one near him: Manchester United's winger Cristiano. The cockatiel-coiffed, Hale-based hot-stepper may have an inner-ear problem or, as Sir Alex prefers, is a fine exponent of the new art of foul anticipation.
**King of the endorsements**
Figo pockets a cool £1.45m a year from Nike, making him the not-so-unlucky 13th best-sponsored player in the world.
**You'll be copying . . .**
Should Ronaldo finally manage to achieve something with one of his manic stepover routines, expect kids worldwide to be running around like Michael Flatley with rickets.
**Nation sweating on**
Maniche and Costinha make up Portugal's midfield and each played so little for his club, Chelsea and Dynamo Moscow, since Christmas that they are no longer there. They may be fresh, they may have gone stale. Who knows?
**Rooney to have a grand on**
Big Phil Scolari to become next England manager. Ronaldo not crying hysterically when they get knocked out.

Cristiano Ronaldo

### The stats

**Fifa ranking** =8th
**Odds to win** 20-1
**World Cup finals record** P12 W7 D0 L5 F25 A16
**World Cup best** Third place 1966
**Record in qualifying**
D3 W9

### The country

**On the psychiatrist's couch**
"I've always been a bit of a wanderer, though I don't get out as much as I used to. In my younger days I wasn't always the most respectful of visitors, which is why a few people who put me up back in the day are still narked, but what can you do? I've said I'm sorry. Anyway, whatever I've done, I'm not as bad as them next door."
**What they eat**
The Portuguese are as guilty as anyone of depleting the world's resource of cod; they famously have 365 different ways of cooking it, a dish for every day.
**What they watch**
One of the most popular shows in the country is O Preço Certo Em Euros, a version of The Price Is Right. Unlike ours, it is shown in prime time. We assume it's better. Actually, it isn't presented by Joe Pasquale, so we know it's better.
**Anthem in brief** A Portuguesa
The Portuguese are a splendid and indomitable people. Their country offers a range of attractive features and a pleasant climate. And they would like to take this opportunity to remind us who discovered most of America.
**Well I never**
Portugal's first-ever flag was exactly the same as Finland's.

### The squad

Goalkeepers
**Ricardo** 1 — Sporting Lisbon, Age 30, 48 caps
**Quim** 12 — Benfica, 30, 24 caps
**Bruno Vale** 22 — Estrela Amadora, 23, 1 cap

Defenders
**Paulo Ferreira** 2 — Chelsea, England, 27, 30 caps
**Marco Caneira** 3 — Sporting Lisbon, 27, 14 caps
**Ricardo Costa** 4 — Porto, 25, 2 caps
**Fernando Meira** 5 — VfB Stuttgart, Germany, 28, 6 caps
**Miguel** 13 — Valencia, Spain, 26, 27 caps
**Nuno Valente** 14 — Everton, England, 31, 22 caps
**Ricardo Carvalho** 16 — Chelsea, England, 28, 21 caps

Midfielders
**Costinha** 6 — unattached, 31, 43 caps
**Armando Petit** 8 — Benfica, 29, 35 caps
**Hugo Viana** 10 — Valencia, Spain, 23, 20 caps
**Simao Sabrosa** 11 — Benfica, 26, 42 caps
**Cristiano Ronaldo** 17 — Manchester United, Eng, 21, 31 caps
**Maniche** 18 — Dynamo Moscow, Rus, 28, 30 caps
**Tiago** 19 — Lyon, France, 25, 21 caps
**Deco** 20 — Barcelona, Spain, 28, 34 caps

Forwards
**Luis Figo** 7 — Internazionale, Italy, 33, 119 caps
**Pauleta** 9 — Paris St-Germain, France, 33, 81 caps
**Luis Boa Morte** 15 — Fulham, England, 28, 24 caps
**Nuno Gomes** 21 — Benfica, 29, 53 caps
**Helder Postiga** 23 — St Etienne, France, 23, 21 caps

**THE GUARDIAN,** London

Barry Ainslie

Special coverage, section, with ads

"Buildings swayed, tottered, fell and people were hurled from their beds, chimneys crushed through roofs, beams were twisted and bent. There were two distinct shocks and the second finished the work of destruction, undoing in the brief lyric space of fifty-eight seconds the work of man for half a century."

HERBERT SLATER, future state legislator from Santa Rosa

# 1906

APRIL 18 AT 5:12 A.M.

## OUR DEFINING MOMENT

The Survivor

**THE PRESS DEMOCRAT,** Santa Rosa, Calif.

Staff

Special coverage, section, with ads

**THE WASHINGTON POST**

Greg Manifold, Tracee Hamilton, Courtney A. Crowley, Bonnie Berkowitz, Nathaniel Vaughn Kelso, Steve McCracken, Liz Clarke, Amy Shipley

Special coverage, section, with ads

The Washington Post

WINTER OLYMPICS

TURIN

A GUIDE TO THE GAMES

FEBRUARY 10-26

**FOLHA DE SÃO PAULO** (Brazil)

Massimo Gentile, Fabio Marra, Jair de Oliveira, Marcio Freitas, Kleber Bonjoan, Clauton Danelli de Souza, Mario Kanno

Special coverage, section, with ads

eleições2006

FOLHA DE S.PAULO

>> ACOMPANHE A COBERTURA DA VOTAÇÃO E A APURAÇÃO NA FOLHA ONLINE www.folha.com.br/eleicoes2006

# Lula deve ser reeleito hoje, indica Datafolha

Pesquisa concluída ontem mostra atual presidente 22 pontos percentuais à frente de Alckmin; petista já canta vitória e pede trégua, enquanto tucano ainda fala em virada



O PRESIDENTE Luiz Inácio Lula da Silva, 61 completados na sexta, deve ser reeleito hoje para governar o Brasil até 31 de dezembro de 2010. Pesquisa Datafolha realizada ontem e anteontem dá a Lula 61% dos votos válidos, 22 pontos percentuais à frente de seu adversário do PSDB, o ex-governador de São Paulo Geraldo Alckmin, 53. Confirmado o resultado, será a segunda vez que um presidente brasileiro é eleito por voto popular para dois mandatos consecutivos — o outro foi Fernando Henrique Cardoso (1995-98 e 99-02). Antes dele, só Getúlio Vargas comandou o país por dois períodos (1930-45 e 50-54). Se eleito, Lula, ex-torneiro mecânico e líder sindical, será novamente o 39º presidente do Brasil. Estão registrados para ir às urnas 125.913.479 eleitores. Eles podem dar a Lula votação recorde em números absolutos. Em 2002, o petista teve 52.793.364 votos no segundo turno. Caso se confirme sua reeleição, Lula terá que lidar com a sombra da tentativa da compra de um dossiê contra tucanos por membros de sua campanha. O Tribunal Superior Eleitoral investiga a responsabilidade do presidente, e a Polícia Federal tenta descobrir a origem do R$ 1,75 milhão envolvido na negociação. Dez Estados também elegem hoje seus governadores. No Rio, Sérgio Cabral deve manter o PMDB no poder. Será mais um entre os governadores a reforçar a base de aliados de Lula, que deve se expandir em relação à de 2002. A votação acontece em todo o país de 8h a 17h. O TSE estima que, até as 23h, 99% das urnas estejam apuradas.

RIO GRANDE DO SUL

Ibope dá dez pontos de vantagem a Yeda Crusius (PSDB) sobre o petista Olívio Dutra na reta final

MARANHÃO

Roseana veste vermelho do PT para evitar que os Sarney sejam batidos no Estado depois de 40 anos

PARANÁ

Requião (PMDB) tem 53% dos votos válidos contra 47% de Osmar (PDT), segundo pesquisa Datafolha

**THE NEWS & OBSERVER,** Raleigh, N.C.

Andrea Jones, Corey Lowenstein, John Hansen, Suzanne Brown

Special coverage, section, with ads

Monet.

Paul Cézanne had Provence, Vincent van Gogh had Arles, and Georgia O'Keeffe the American Southwest. Claude Monet found endless fascination in the seaside towns and rural fields of Normandy.

From the coastal village of Honfleur to the cliffs at Etretat, Normandy inspired Monet's bold experiments with atmosphere and light. He rendered grain stacks and poplars and the Gothic cathedral at Rouen. He cultivated gardens at Giverny that became a working laboratory for color. In Normandy, he created works that made him the leading light of impressionism, the 19th-century art revolution that changed the way painters reflected the world.

The region defined Monet's career. In turn, his body of work defines Normandy in ways that survive wars and eight decades of progress. This special section reflects his domain through the lens of a camera and the prism of time.

"MONET IN NORMANDY" | N.C. MUSEUM OF ART | OCT. 15, 2006 – JAN. 14, 2007

**HERALDO DE ARAGÓN,** Zaragoza, Spain

Kristina Urresti, Irán Santos, Pilar Ostalé, Jorge Luis Mora, Pedro Zapater, Luis Grañena, Alberto Aragón, Isidro Gil, Paula R. Español

Special coverage, section, with ads

THE QUEEN AT 80

*Snapshots of memorable moments over the past eight decades show a woman whose dedication to duty cannot hide her warmth, sense of humour and love of life*

**THE DAILY TELEGRAPH,** London

Staff

Special coverage, section, with ads

SILVER

**EL GRÁFICO,** Antiguo Cuscatlan, El Salvador

Agustín A. Palacios, Alexander Rivera, Redacción Staff

Special coverage, multiple sections, with ads

This work shows you can stretch outside your usual format. The reader utility stands out — it's a great explainer with everything you want to know. It's Wikipedia in print. Editors clearly wanted people to collect these, so they presented them in an easy format. It's a fantastic reference for watching the World Cup at home.

Este trabajo demuestra que se puede salir del formato común. Se destacan los datos útiles para el lector, un excelente recuadro explicativo con todo lo que se quiere saber. Es Wikipedia impreso. Queda claro que los editores querían que la gente los coleccionara, por lo que los presentaron en un formato práctico. Es una fantástica referencia para ver el Mundial de Fútbol en casa.

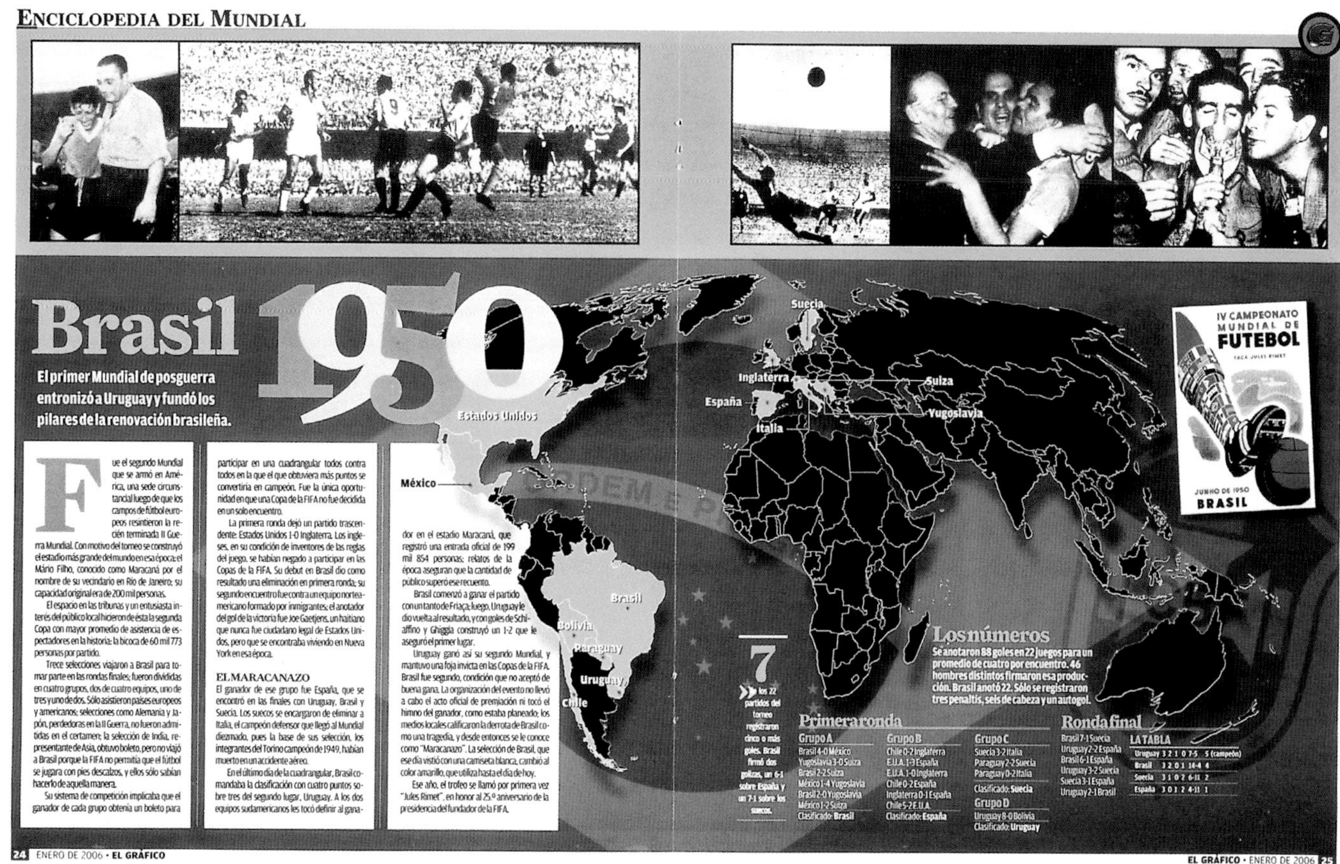

ENCICLOPEDIA DEL MUNDIAL

# Brasil 1950

**El primer Mundial de posguerra entronizó a Uruguay y fundó los pilares de la renovación brasileña.**

Fue el segundo Mundial que se armó en América, una sede circunstancial luego de que los campos de fútbol europeos resintieron la recién terminada II Guerra Mundial. Con motivo del torneo se construyó el estadio más grande del mundo en esa época: el Mário Filho, conocido como Maracaná por el nombre de su vecindario en Río de Janeiro; su capacidad original era de 200 mil personas.

El espacio en las tribunas y un entusiasta interés del público local hicieron de ésta la segunda Copa con mayor promedio de asistencia de espectadores en la historia: la bicoca de 60 mil 773 personas por partido.

Trece selecciones viajaron a Brasil para tomar parte en las rondas finales; fueron divididas en cuatro grupos, dos de cuatro equipos, uno de tres y uno de dos. Sólo asistieron países europeos y americanos; selecciones como Alemania y Japón, perdedoras en la II Guerra, no fueron admitidas en el certamen; la selección de India, representante de Asia, obtuvo boleto, pero no viajó a Brasil porque la FIFA no permitía que el fútbol se jugara con pies descalzos, y ellos sólo sabían hacerlo de aquella manera.

Su sistema de competición implicaba que el ganador de cada grupo obtenía un boleto para participar en una cuadrangular todos contra todos en la que el que obtuviera más puntos se convertiría en campeón. Fue la única oportunidad en que una Copa de la FIFA no fue decidida en un solo encuentro.

La primera ronda dejó un partido trascendente: Estados Unidos 1-0 Inglaterra. Los ingleses, en su condición de inventores de las reglas del juego, se habían negado a participar en las Copas de la FIFA. Su debut en Brasil dio como resultado una eliminación en primera ronda; su segundo encuentro fue contra un equipo norteamericano formado por inmigrantes; el anotador del gol de la victoria fue Joe Gaetjens, un haitiano que nunca fue ciudadano legal de Estados Unidos, pero que se encontraba viviendo en Nueva York en esa época.

## EL MARACANAZO

El ganador de ese grupo fue España, que se encontró en las finales con Uruguay, Brasil y Suecia. Los suecos se encargaron de eliminar a Italia, el campeón defensor que llegó al Mundial diezmado, pues la base de sus selección, los integrantes del Torino campeón de 1949, habían muerto en un accidente aéreo.

En el último día de la cuadrangular, Brasil comandaba la clasificación con cuatro puntos sobre tres del segundo lugar, Uruguay. A los dos equipos sudamericanos les tocó definir al ganador en el estadio Maracaná, que registró una entrada oficial de 199 mil 854 personas; relatos de la época aseguran que la cantidad de público superó ese recuento.

Brasil comenzó a ganar el partido con un tanto de Friaça; luego, Uruguay le dio vuelta al resultado, y con goles de Schiaffino y Ghiggia construyó un 1-2 que le aseguró el primer lugar.

Uruguay ganó así su segundo Mundial, y mantuvo una foja invicta en las Copas de la FIFA. Brasil fue segundo, condición que no aceptó de buena gana. La organización del evento no llevó a cabo el acto oficial de premiación ni tocó el himno del ganador, como estaba planeado; los medios locales calificaron la derrota de Brasil como una tragedia, y desde entonces se le conoce como "Maracanazo". La selección de Brasil, que ese día vistió con una camiseta blanca, cambió al color amarillo, que utiliza hasta el día de hoy.

Ese año, el trofeo se llamó por primera vez "Jules Rimet", en honor al 25.º aniversario de la presidencia del fundador de la FIFA.



**7** De los 22 partidos del torneo registraron cinco o más goles. Brasil firmó dos golizas, un 6-1 sobre España y un 7-1 sobre los suecos.

### Los números

Se anotaron 88 goles en 22 juegos para un promedio de cuatro por encuentro. 46 hombres distintos firmaron esa producción. Brasil anotó 22. Sólo se registraron tres penaltis, seis de cabeza y un autogol.

### Primera ronda

**Grupo A**
Brasil 4-0 México
Yugoslavia 3-0 Suiza
Brasil 2-2 Suiza
México 1-4 Yugoslavia
Brasil 2-0 Yugoslavia
México 1-2 Suiza
Clasificado: **Brasil**

**Grupo B**
Chile 0-2 Inglaterra
E.U.A. 1-3 España
E.U.A. 1-0 Inglaterra
Chile 0-2 España
Inglaterra 0-1 España
Chile 5-2 E.U.A.
Clasificado: **España**

**Grupo C**
Suecia 3-2 Italia
Paraguay 2-2 Suecia
Paraguay 0-2 Italia
Clasificado: **Suecia**

**Grupo D**
Uruguay 8-0 Bolivia
Clasificado: **Uruguay**

### Ronda final

Brasil 7-1 Suecia
Uruguay 2-2 España
Brasil 6-1 España
Uruguay 3-2 Suecia
Suecia 3-1 España
Uruguay 2-1 Brasil

**LA TABLA**

| | | | | | | |
|---|---|---|---|---|---|---|
| Uruguay | 3 | 2 | 1 | 0 | 7-5 | 5 (campeón) |
| Brasil | 3 | 2 | 0 | 1 | 14-4 | 4 |
| Suecia | 3 | 1 | 0 | 2 | 6-11 | 2 |
| España | 3 | 0 | 1 | 2 | 4-11 | 1 |

24 ENERO DE 2006 • EL GRÁFICO

EL GRÁFICO • ENERO DE 2006 25

GRUPO H

1 UCRANIA

0 TÚNEZ

ARBITRO FAVORECIÓ A UCRANIA

DIRECTO A OCTAVOS

EL ÁRBITRO NO PITÓ UN PENALTI A FAVOR DE TÚNEZ Y EN LA SIGUIENTE JUGADA SE SACÓ UN INEXISTENTE QUE BENEFICIÓ A UCRANIA.

IMPORTA EL RESULTADO

53

**LA PRENSA GRÁFICA,** Antiguo Cuscatlán, El Salvador

Enrique Contreras, Héctor Ramírez, Erick Cortez, Denis García Márquez, Giovanni Paniagua

Special coverage, section, with ads

JUEVES 29 JUNIO DE 2006

laTribuna Mundial

LA PRENSA GRÁFICA

A EXCEPCIÓN DE UCRANIA Y PORTUGAL, LOS CUARTOS DE FINAL ENFRENTARÁN A SEIS SELECCIONES QUE HAN SIDO CAMPEONAS DEL MUNDO. UNA FIESTA DE REYES.

DUELO DE MONARCAS

**LA PRENSA GRÁFICA,** Antiguo Cuscatlán, El Salvador

Enrique Contreras, Héctor Ramírez, Erick Cortez, Denis García Márquez, Giovanni Paniagua, Mauricio Duarte

Special coverage, section, with ads

MIÉRCOLES 21 JUNIO DE 2006

laTribuna Mundial

LA PRENSA GRÁFICA

1974, 1978, 1998... LOS DUELOS ENTRE HOLANDA Y ARGENTINA HAN TEÑIDO DE GLORIA Y TRAGEDIA DEPORTIVA LA HISTORIA DE LOS MUNDIALES. HOY A LA 1 P.M. SE DISPUTAN EL LIDERAZGO DEL GRUPO C Y SIRVEN EL PRIMER PLATO FUERTE DE ALEMANIA 2006.

DUELO DE GIGANTES

YA HAY OCTAVOS

**LA PRENSA GRÁFICA,** Antiguo Cuscatlán, El Salvador

Enrique Contreras, Héctor Ramírez, Erick Cortez, Denis García Márquez, Giovanni Paniagua

Special coverage, section, with ads

**THE NEW YORK TIMES**

Tom Bodkin, Mika Grondahl, Wayne Kamidoi, Bedel Saget, Tim O'Brien, Sports Staff

Special coverage, section, with ads

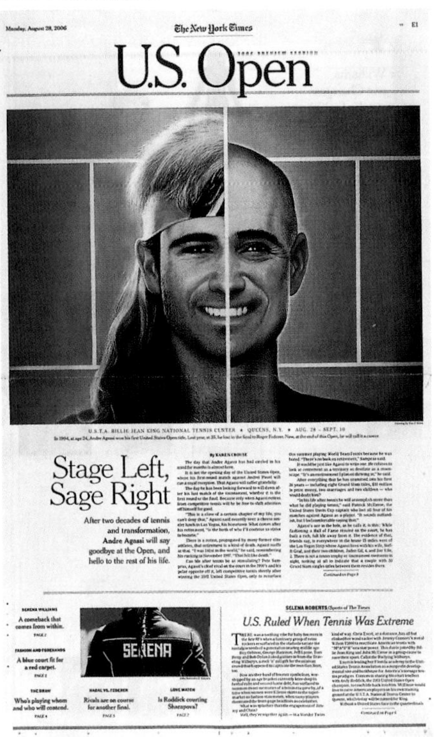
The New York Times

U.S. Open

Stage Left, Sage Right

After two decades of tennis and transformation, Andre Agassi will say goodbye at the Open, and hello to the rest of his life.

U.S. Ruled When Tennis Was Extreme

**LA PRESSE,** Montréal

Genevieve Dinel, Benoit Giguere, Michel Marois, Alain de Repentigny, Marie-Claude Lortie

Special coverage, section, with ads

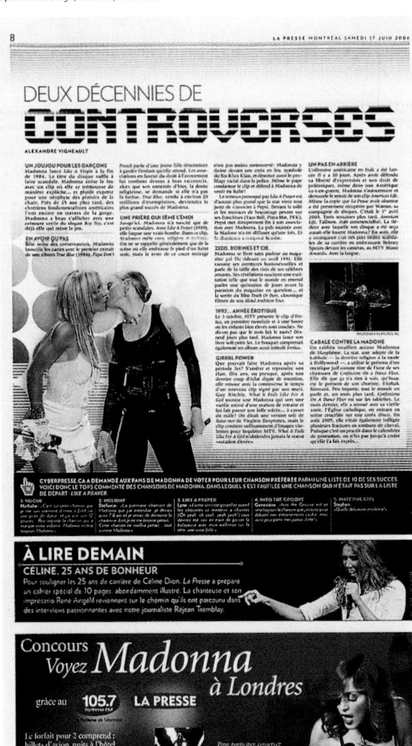
DEUX DÉCENNIES DE

CONTROVERSES

À LIRE DEMAIN

CÉLINE, 25 ANS DE BONHEUR

Pour souligner les 25 ans de carrière de Céline Dion, *La Presse* a préparé un cahier spécial de 10 pages abondamment illustré. La chanteuse et son impresario René Angélil reviennent sur le chemin qu'ils ont parcouru dans des entrevues passionnantes avec notre journaliste Réjean Tremblay.

Concours Voyez *Madonna* à Londres grâce au 105.7 LA PRESSE

Le forfait pour 2 comprend : billets d'avion, nuits à l'hôtel et billets pour Madonna à Londres. Une valeur de 3 000 $.

**LOS ANGELES TIMES**

Kelli Sullivan, Joseph Hutchinson, Michael Whitley, Steven Sedam, Mary Cooney, Robert St. John, Calvin Hom

Special coverage, section, with ads

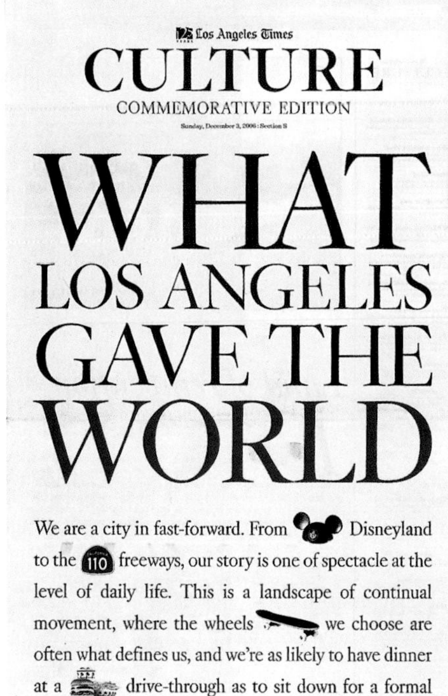
Los Angeles Times

CULTURE

COMMEMORATIVE EDITION

WHAT LOS ANGELES GAVE THE WORLD

We are a city in fast-forward. From Disneyland to the freeways, our story is one of spectacle at the level of daily life. This is a landscape of continual movement, where the wheels we choose are often what defines us, and we're as likely to have dinner at a drive-through as to sit down for a formal meal. We perfected casual yet have grand designs: Take a look at Hollywood. Mostly, we are a city of reinvention that exports the promise of possibility.

LEAVING HIS MARK

Senior Lorenzo Booker wants to fulfill his high expectations. By Staff Writer Dave Joseph.

"THE ONLY WAY TO BE REMEMBERED IS TO DO SOMETHING NO ONE HAS EVER DONE OR DO IT IN A WAY NO ONE EVER DID."

**SOUTH FLORIDA SUN-SENTINEL,** Fort Lauderdale

Andrea Vigil, Christian Font, Jonathan Boho, Amy Beth Bennett, Tom Peyton, Tim Rasmussen, Tim Frank

Special coverage, multiple sections, with ads

Los gigantes de la música quieren descolar al iPod del mundo MP3

Los diseños de Sony, Samsung, Phillips pelean el mercado. Una guerra entre 'goliats'.

JORGE RIBADENEIRA

Así fue el comienzo...

EL COMERCIO nació con la crisis

DIARIO INDEPENDIENTE • FUNDADO EN 1906

EL COMERCIO

Un siglo de periodismo

10 firmas rompen la barrera de los 100 años en el Ecuador

La fiebre del voto se riega por el país y por la región

Drogas: el vicio visto desde las entrañas

La capital con cuatro tareas pendientes...

Mañana El emigrante trae referentes culturales. Es un fenómeno que cambia al país.

**COMERCIO,** Quito, Ecuador

Ponto Moreno, Jorge Mantilla, Guillermo Corral, Francisco Cajas, Samuel Fernandez, Staff

Special coverage, multiple sections, with ads

SOUVENIR EDITION | PITTSBURGH TRIBUNE-REVIEW

50¢

SUPER SEASON

SEASON RECAP: A GAME-BY-GAME REVIEW OF THE STEELERS' 2005 CHAMPIONSHIP RUN

**PITTSBURGH TRIBUNE-REVIEW**

Staff

Special coverage, multiple sections, with ads

**THE GUARDIAN,** London

Barry Ainslie

Special coverage, multiple sections, with ads

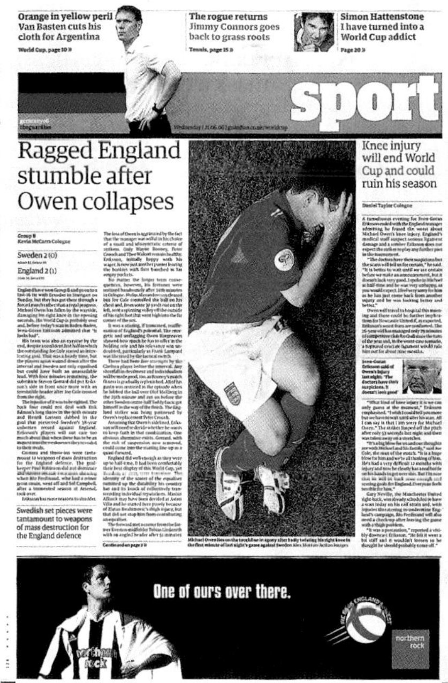

Orange in yellow peril
Van Basten cuts his cloth for Argentina

The rogue returns
Jimmy Connors goes back to grass roots

Simon Hattenstone
I have turned into a World Cup addict

sport

Ragged England stumble after Owen collapses

Knee injury will end World Cup and could ruin his season

Swedish set pieces were tantamount to weapons of mass destruction for the England defence



**WELT AM SONNTAG,** Berlin

Jördis Guzmán Bulla, Reto Klar, Claudia Bernhardt

Special coverage, multiple sections, with ads

Familie 2006

WELT am SONNTAG | 91

SERIE
DRITTE VON VIER FOLGEN

Verliebt, verlobt, verarmt

**EL UNIVERSAL,** México City

Roberto Rock L., Francisco Santiago, Oscar Santiago Méndez, Rubén Álvarez, Felipe de Jesús González, Ágeles Gutierrez Castro, Nilton Torres Pérez, Staff Designers

Special coverage, multiple sections, no ads

MÉXICO SIP/06

THE WALL STREET JOURNAL SE REINVENTA/4 LOS BLOGS AVANZAN COMO NUEVO GÉNERO/4

EL UNIVERSAL, 90 AÑOS

DISEÑOS MUY MEXICANOS

ASOMBRO POR ARTE MEXICANO

HAY QUE APOSTAR A BUENAS HISTORIAS: MONSIVAIS

LOS PERIÓDICOS DEBEN PRESERVAR EL ESPAÑOL/3
LA ERA DIGITAL CREA UN PERIODISMO CIUDADANO/4

**THE CHARLOTTE OBSERVER** (N.C.)

Tiffany Pease, Mary Ann Lawrence, Wendy Yang

Special coverage, section cover

HOW TO BUILD A WINNING BRACKET

SOME ASSEMBLY REQUIRED

NCAA TOURNAMENT 2006

TEAM-BY-TEAM | A look at each of the teams in the tournament, 4X, 6-9X.

SORENSEN | Having trouble with your bracket? Here, just copy Tom's. 2X.

REGION-BY-REGION | David Scott tells you what you need to know. 5X.

The Charlotte Observer

**THE COLUMBUS DISPATCH** (Ohio)

Patrick Kastner, Scott Minister

Special coverage, section cover

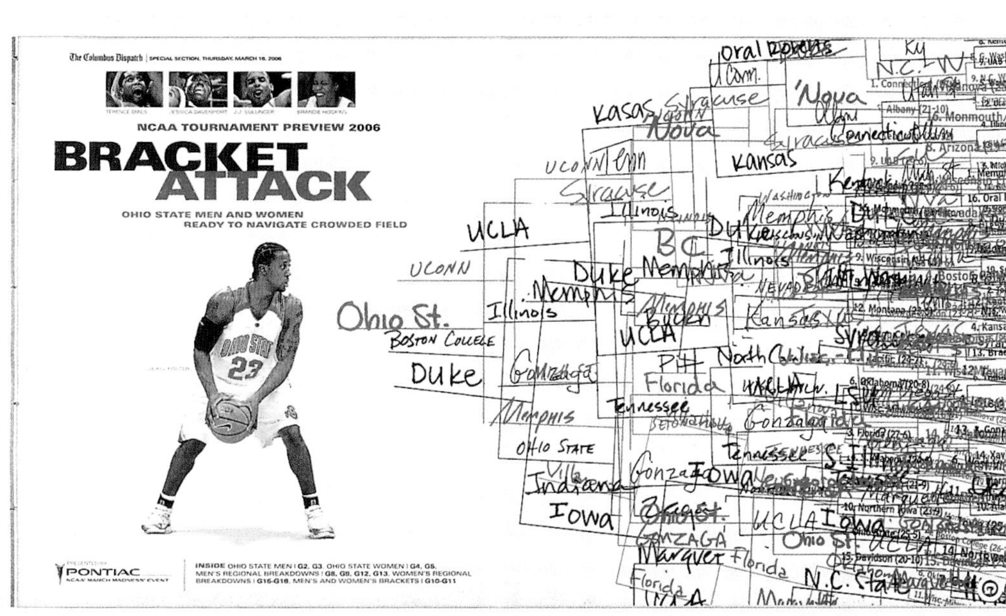

The Columbus Dispatch | SPECIAL SECTION, THURSDAY, MARCH 16, 2006

NCAA TOURNAMENT PREVIEW 2006

BRACKET ATTACK

OHIO STATE MEN AND WOMEN READY TO NAVIGATE CROWDED FIELD

PONTIAC

INSIDE OHIO STATE MEN | G2, G3 OHIO STATE WOMEN | G4, G5. MEN'S REGIONAL BREAKDOWNS | G8, G9, G12, G13. WOMEN'S REGIONAL BREAKDOWNS | G16-G18. MEN'S AND WOMEN'S BRACKETS | G10-G11

**SOUTH FLORIDA SUN-SENTINEL,** Fort Lauderdale

Chris Mihal, Rebekah Monson, Mike Stocker, Joe Amon, Mary Vignoles, Tim Rasmussen, Tim Frank

Special coverage, section cover

OUTLOOK

AIDS ORPHANS

This generation of children comes of age at a critical time. Stigma and fear could prevail. So could science and hope. The world extends a hand to help — and waits.

Third of four parts

**THE WALL STREET JOURNAL,** New York

Orlie Kraus, Craig Frazier

Special coverage, section cover

Encore: A Guide to Retirement Planning & Living

THE JOURNAL REPORT

THE WALL STREET JOURNAL.

Avoiding the Volunteer Trap

Too many retirees, when donating their time and energies, are falling into dead-end jobs. Here's how to do good—for others and yourself.

INSIDE

To Drive, or Not to Drive

A Family Affair

Alphabet Soup

Sights and Sounds

Fountain of Youth

Ask Encore

Missing Links

Go Down to the Sea

**SOUTH FLORIDA SUN-SENTINEL,** Fort Lauderdale

Jonathan Boho, Angel Valentin

Special coverage, section cover

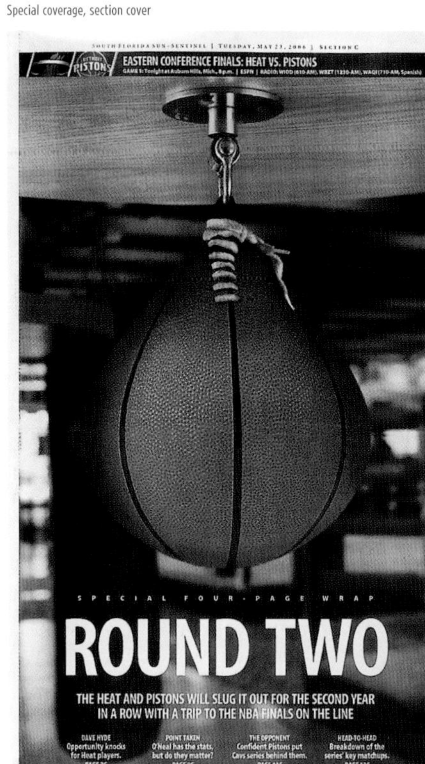

EASTERN CONFERENCE FINALS: HEAT VS. PISTONS

SPECIAL FOUR-PAGE WRAP

ROUND TWO

THE HEAT AND PISTONS WILL SLUG IT OUT FOR THE SECOND YEAR IN A ROW WITH A TRIP TO THE NBA FINALS ON THE LINE

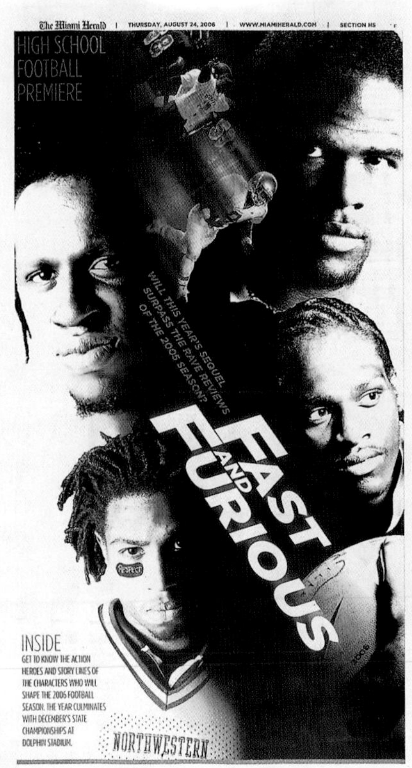

The Miami Herald | THURSDAY, AUGUST 24, 2006 | WWW.MIAMIHERALD.COM | SECTION HS

HIGH SCHOOL FOOTBALL PREMIERE

WILL THIS YEAR'S SEQUEL SURPASS THE RAVE REVIEWS OF THE 2005 SEASON?

FAST AND FURIOUS

INSIDE

GET TO KNOW THE ACTION HEROES AND STORY LINES OF THE CHARACTERS WHO WILL SHAPE THE 2006 FOOTBALL SEASON. THE YEAR CULMINATES WITH DECEMBER'S STATE CHAMPIONSHIPS AT DOLPHIN STADIUM.

**THE MIAMI HERALD**

Eddie Alvarez, Paul Cheung, Zach Folzenlogen

Special coverage, section cover

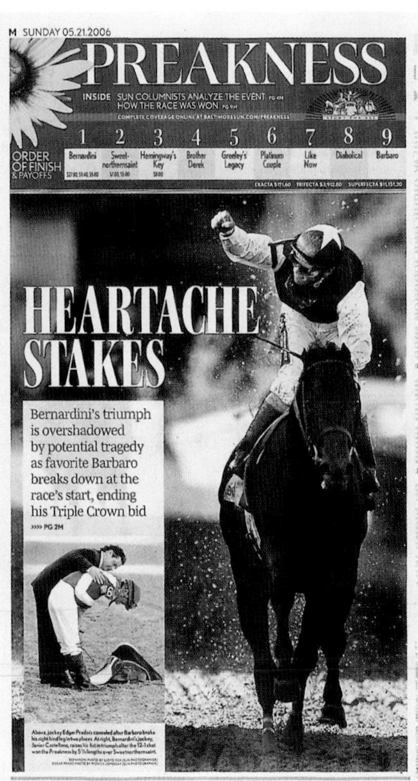

M SUNDAY 05.21.2006

PREAKNESS

ORDER OF FINISH & PAYOFFS

1 Bernardini 2 Sweetnorthernsaint 3 Hemingway's Key 4 Brother Derek 5 Greeley's Legacy 6 Platinum Couple 7 Like Now 8 Diabolical 9 Barbaro

HEARTACHE STAKES

Bernardini's triumph is overshadowed by potential tragedy as favorite Barbaro breaks down at the race's start, ending his Triple Crown bid

**THE BALTIMORE SUN**

Derrick Barker, Lloyd Fox, Monica Lopossay, Jay Judge, Tim Wheatley, Monty Cook

Special coverage, section cover

WEDNESDAY, NOVEMBER 1, 2006 | CAVS/NBA PREVIEW | SECTION S

LeBron James has been known as King James since he was in high school. In the NBA, however, basketball royalty is a much more exclusive club. To join this elite group, the King will need to win a crown. S2

RANKINGS S4-5 | INSIDE THE LOCKER ROOM S8 | NEW AT THE Q S9

**THE PLAIN DEALER,** Cleveland

David Kordalski, Ted Crow, Ryan Powell, Roy Hewitt, Mike Starkey

Special coverage, section cover

**THE SEATTLE TIMES**
Mark McTyre, Rod Mar
Special coverage, section cover

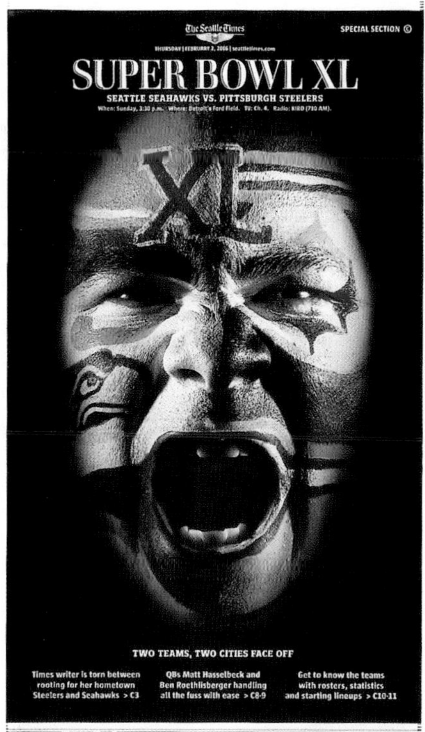
The Seattle Times
SPECIAL SECTION C
SUPER BOWL XL
SEATTLE SEAHAWKS VS. PITTSBURGH STEELERS
TWO TEAMS, TWO CITIES FACE OFF
Times writer is torn between rooting for her hometown Steelers and Seahawks > C3
QBs Matt Hasselbeck and Ben Roethlisberger handling all the fuss with ease > C8-9
Get to know the teams with rosters, statistics and starting lineups > C10-11


**THE DENVER POST**
Jeff Neumann
Special coverage, section cover

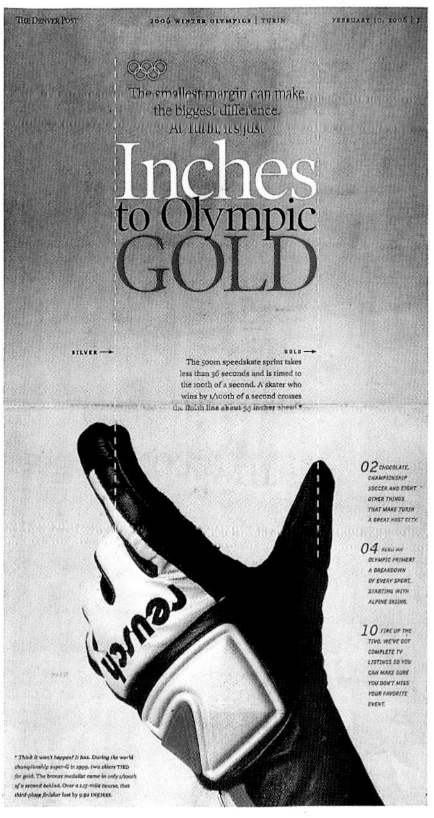
The Denver Post
2006 WINTER OLYMPICS | TURIN
The smallest margin can make the biggest difference. At Turin, it's just
Inches to Olympic GOLD
SILVER →
GOLD →
The 500m speedskate sprint takes less than 36 seconds and is timed to the 100th of a second. A skater who wins by 1/100th of a second crosses the finish line about 5.5 inches ahead.*
02 CHOCOLATE, CHAMPIONSHIP SOCCER AND EIGHT OTHER THINGS THAT MAKE TURIN A GREAT HOST CITY.
04 NEED AN OLYMPIC PRIMER? A BREAKDOWN OF EVERY SPORT, STARTING WITH ALPINE SKIING.
10 FIRE UP THE TIVO. WE'VE GOT COMPLETE TV LISTINGS SO YOU CAN MAKE SURE YOU DON'T MISS YOUR FAVORITE EVENT.

**SAN FRANCISCO CHRONICLE**
Tracy Cox, Douglas Fraser, Frank Mina, Nanette Bisher
Special coverage, section cover

San Francisco Chronicle
SECTION
NFL 2006
THE DARK AGES
struggle to build for a brighter future
RAIDERS
13
8
2
19
23
38
Local teams must get a lot smarter to get better
Nancy Gay
On the NFL
TV SCENE
RAY RATTO
49ERS
RAIDERS
PREVIEWS
NUMBERS

SECTION F CANADA'S NATIONAL NEWSPAPER • FOUNDED 1844 • GLOBEANDMAIL.COM • TUESDAY, MAY 2, 2006
A special report on the 11th annual awards honouring young people of influence
top40under40 2005
Whether they founded a business, run major companies, work in medical research or head up charities, these Canadians have one thing in common: They are among our brightest young leaders. These pages celebrate their achievements and their promise
DOV BERCOVICI
CRAIG KIELBURGER
DAVID COOLIN

**THE GLOBE AND MAIL,** Toronto
Jayson Taylor, David Pratt, Simon Beck
Special coverage, section cover

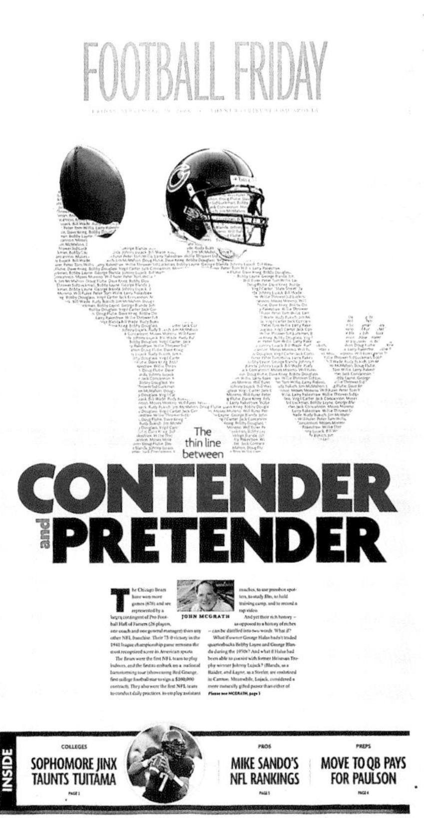
FOOTBALL FRIDAY
The thin line between
CONTENDER and PRETENDER
JOHN MCGRATH
INSIDE
SOPHOMORE JINX TAUNTS TUITAMA
MIKE SANDO'S NFL RANKINGS
MOVE TO QB PAYS FOR PAULSON

**THE NEWS TRIBUNE,** Tacoma, Wash.
David Montesino
Special coverage, section cover

WWW.KANSASCITY.COM
THE KANSAS CITY STAR
SUNDAY, JUNE 25, 2006
Greater Kansas City Golf Classic
CHAMPIONS TOUR
STRIKING WHILE THE IRONS ARE HOT
The 50-and-over circuit gives golfers a second chance, but not for long. | 1-2

**THE KANSAS CITY STAR** (Mo.)
Lynn Nguyen, Mike Ransdell, Greg Branson, Tom Dolphens, Mike Fannin, Holly Lawton
Special coverage, section cover

FUTBOL
ALEMANIA 2006
MINUTO A MINUTO
PRIMER TIEMPO
SEGUNDO TIEMPO
TIEMPO EXTRA
LA MURALLA ITALIANA
FABIO CANNAVARO
DE RECOGE BALONES A CAMPEÓN DEL MUNDO
Escolta Italia a brasileños
ZONAFANÁTICA

**NOROESTE,** Mazatlán, México
Alexander Probst, Wilfredo Camarena, Joel Díaz, Guillermina García, José Manuel García
Special coverage, inside page

A CUARTOS
Alemania contó con dos goles tempraneros de Lucas Podolski y eliminó a Suecia. (7)
Noroeste
GOLES: 122
DOMINGO 25 DE JUNIO 2006
FUTBOL
ALEMANIA 2006
CON LA CARA AL SOL
1 2
MÉXICO ARGENTINA
OCTAVOS DE FINAL

NOROESTE / REDACCIÓN

México hizo uno de sus mejores juegos en muchos mundiales, pero un soberbio gol de Maxi Rodríguez, en tiempo extra, lo mandó de regreso a casa, al ganar Argentina 2-1.

Los mexicanos dominaron casi todo el partido, pero un gol fortuito de Hernán Crespo y una joya de Rodríguez los despertaron de su sueño.

Nada que ver con los juegos ante Angola y Portugal. Ayer el Tri se plantó y puso en aprietos a los argentinos, que no podían descifrar la táctica sorpresiva de Ricardo La Volpe.

Al final, México volvió a perder con la cara al sol, pero con el mismo final de varias películas mundialistas. A ver si para la otra.

Un golazo los mata (4, 5 y 8)

HOY
INGLATERRA VS ECUADOR
PORTUGAL VS HOLANDA
MAÑANA
OCTAVOS DE FINAL
ITALIA VS. AUSTRALIA
SUIZA VS. UCRANIA
Porto Cervo

**NOROESTE,** Mazatlán, México
Alexander Probst, Wilfredo Camarena, Joel Díaz, Guillermina García, José Manuel García
Special coverage, section cover

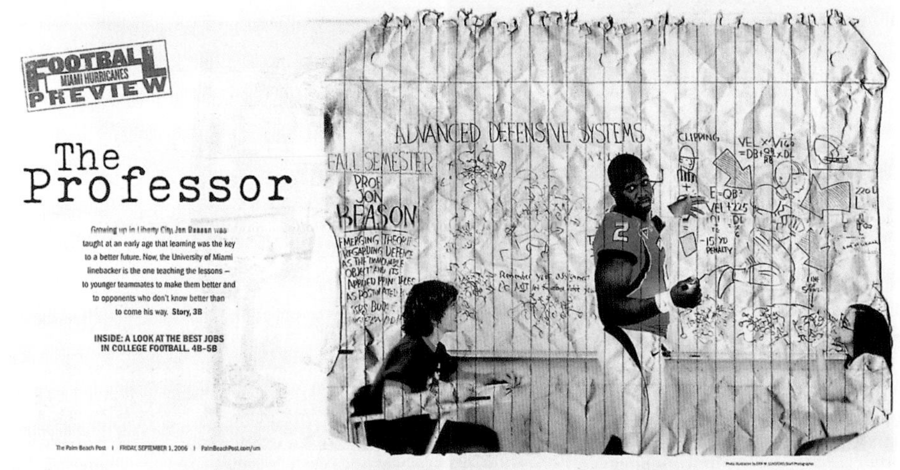
FOOTBALL
MIAMI HURRICANES
PREVIEW

The Professor

Growing up in Liberty City, Jon Beason was taught at an early age that learning was the key to a better future. Now, the University of Miami linebacker is the one teaching the lessons – to younger teammates to make them better and to opponents who don't know better than to come his way. Story, 3B

INSIDE: A LOOK AT THE BEST JOBS IN COLLEGE FOOTBALL. 4B-5B

The Palm Beach Post | FRIDAY, SEPTEMBER 1, 2006 | PalmBeachPost.com/um



**THE PALM BEACH POST** West Palm Beach, Fla.
Erik Lunsford, Chris Rukan, Nick Moschella, Dave Tepps, Mark Edelson, John J. Lopinot, Pat Crowley, Tim Stepien
Special coverage, section cover

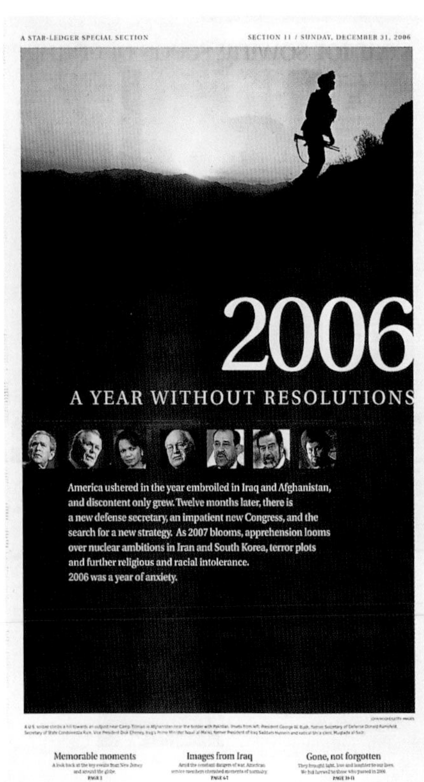
A STAR-LEDGER SPECIAL SECTION
SECTION 11 / SUNDAY, DECEMBER 31, 2006

2006
A YEAR WITHOUT RESOLUTIONS

America ushered in the year embroiled in Iraq and Afghanistan, and discontent only grew. Twelve months later, there is a new defense secretary, an impatient new Congress, and the search for a new strategy. As 2007 blooms, apprehension looms over nuclear ambitions in Iran and South Korea, terror plots and further religious and racial intolerance.
2006 was a year of anxiety.

Memorable moments
Images from Iraq
Gone, not forgotten

**THE STAR-LEDGER,** Newark, N.J.
Linda Grinbergs, Rachel French, Mark Miller, Joel Pisitzner, Steve Crabill
Special coverage, section cover

FUTBOL
ALEMANIA 2006
ALEMANIA
INGLATERRA
ARGENTINA
PORTUGAL
ITALIA
BRASIL
UCRANIA
FRANCIA
CUARTOS DE FINAL
SEMIFINALES
FINAL
ESTÁN LOS 8 MEJORES

**NOROESTE,** Mazatlán, México
Alexander Probst, Wilfredo Camarena, Joel Díaz, Guillermina García, José Manuel García
Special coverage, inside page

**LOS ANGELES TIMES**

Kelli Sullivan, Joseph Hutchinson, Michael Whitley, Mary Cooney, Cindy Hively

Special coverage, inside page

125 YEARS | GLAMOUR INC.

The allure of illusion

**NOROESTE,** Mazatlán, México

Alexander Probst, Wilfredo Camarena, Joel Díaz, Guillermina García, José Manuel García

Special coverage, inside page

FUTBOL

ZONAFANÁTICA

BRASIL VS GHANA

LETALES

Tuvimos suerte: Parreira

FROM 1D

'VELVET' TRIVIA

'BLUE VELVET' PREMIERED ON SEPT. 19, 1986. TWENTY YEARS LATER, WILMINGTON'S WEIRDEST MOVIE LIVES ON AS A CULT CLASSIC. RETURN WITH US NOW TO THOSE BIZARRO DAYS OF YESTERYEAR FOR A CLOSER LOOK AT THE DAVID LYNCH MASTERPIECE.

'BLUE VELVET' @20

WHO'S WHO

POP-QUIZ

WHAT THE CRITICS SAID AT THE TIME

'BLUE VELVET' JUKEBOX

FAMOUS LOCATIONS

**STAR-NEWS,** Wilmington, N.C.

Nicole Neuman, Ben Steelman, Amanda Kingsbury, Jeff Hidek

Special coverage, inside page

NASCAR VS. NFL

Tynes, Colquitt talk racin'

They played other games

**THE KANSAS CITY STAR** (Mo.)

Lynn Nguyen, Mike Ransdell, Dave Eames, Tom Dolphens, Mike Fannin, Holly Lawton

Special coverage, inside page

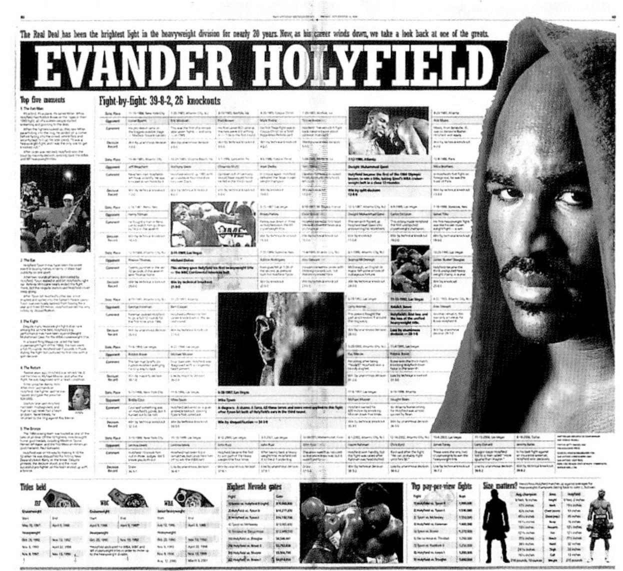

The Real Deal has been the brightest light in the heavyweight division for nearly 20 years. Now, as his career winds down, we take a look back at one of the greats.

EVANDER HOLYFIELD

Top five moments

Fight-by-fight: 39-8-2, 26 knockouts

Titles held

Highest Nevada gates

Top pay-per-view fights

Size matters?

**SAN ANTONIO EXPRESS-NEWS**

Joshua Trudell

Special coverage, inside page

**SOUTH FLORIDA SUN-SENTINEL,** Fort Lauderdale
Andrea Vigil, Jonathan Boho, Amy Beth Bennett, Christian Font, Andrew Innerarity
Special coverage, inside page

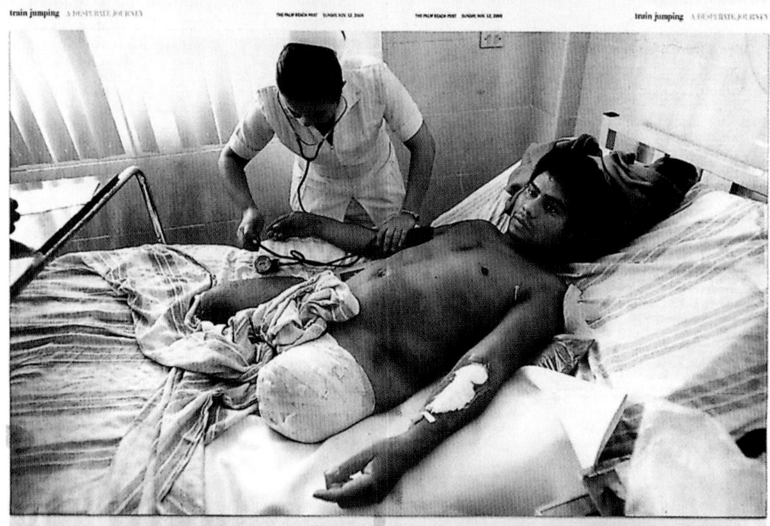

**THE PALM BEACH POST,** West Palm Beach, Fla.
Nicole Bogdas, Gary Coronado, Mark Edelson
Special coverage, inside page

**NOROESTE,** Mazatlán, México
Alexander Probst, Wilfredo Camarena, Joel Díaz, Guillermina García, José Manuel García
Special coverage, inside page

**THE SEATTLE TIMES**
Denise Clifton, Fred Nelson, Aldo Chan
Special coverage, inside page

**THE DALLAS MORNING NEWS**
Rob Schneider, Troy Oxford, Noel Nash, Bill Nicholls
Special coverage, inside page

**SOUTH FLORIDA SUN-SENTINEL,** Fort Lauderdale
Andrea Vigil, Jonathan Boho, Amy Beth Bennett, Christian Font, John L. White
Special coverage, inside page

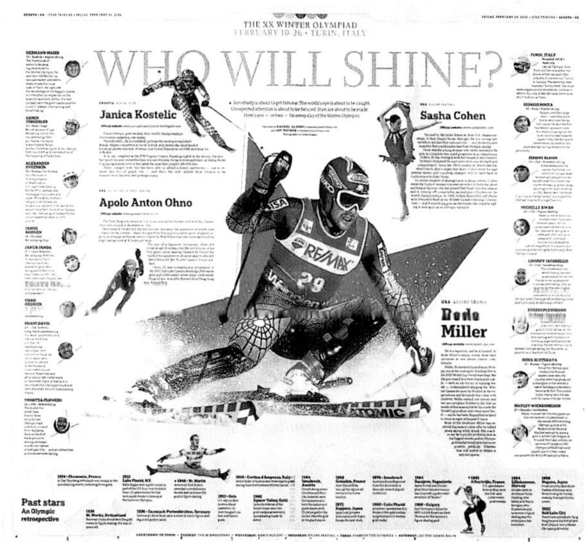

**STAR TRIBUNE,** Minneapolis
Phill Spiker, Mark Wollemann, Glen Crevier, Kevin Bertels
Special coverage, inside page

**SOUTH FLORIDA SUN-SENTINEL,** Fort Lauderdale
Andrea Vigil, Jonathan Boho, Amy Beth Bennett, Christian Font, Andrew Innerarity
Special coverage, inside page

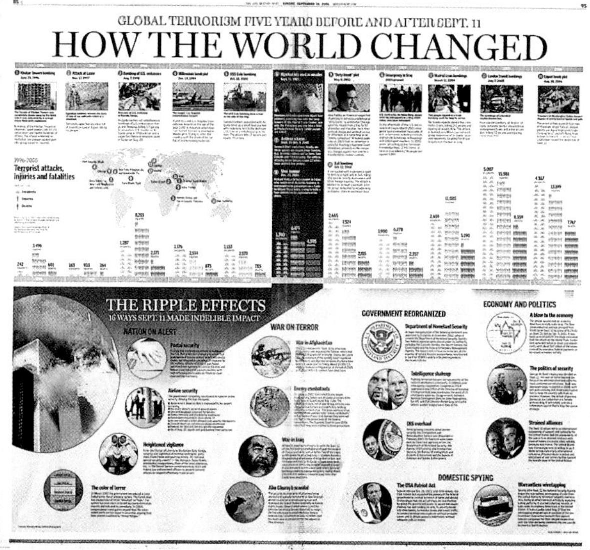

**EL ECONOMISTA,** Madrid, Spain
Miguel Buckenmeyer, Jorge Arévalo, Lola Gallego
Other feature page, tabloid

**SOUTH FLORIDA SUN-SENTINEL,** Fort Lauderdale
Andrea Vigil, Jonathan Boho, Amy Beth Bennett, Christian Font, Andrew Innerarity
Special coverage, inside page

**THE INDIANAPOLIS STAR**
Greg Nichols, Curt Cavin, Jennifer Imes, Scott Goldman
Special coverage, inside page

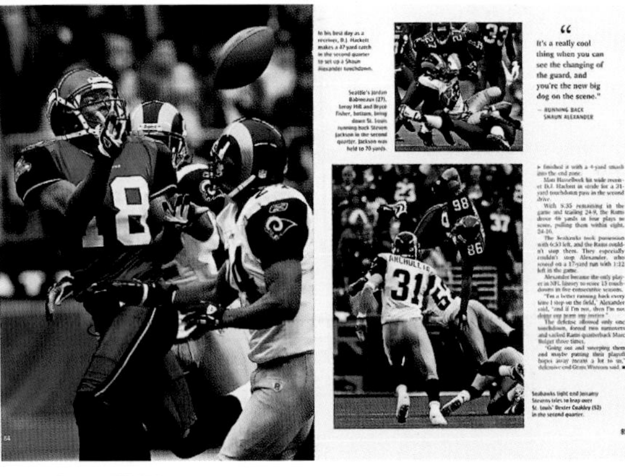
It's a really cool thing when you can see the changing of the guard, and you're the new big dog on the scene.

**THE SEATTLE TIMES**
David Miller, Cathy Henkel, Angela Gottschalk, Evelyn Edens
Reprints

**SAN FRANCISCO CHRONICLE**
Nanette Bisher, Frank Mina, Matt Petty, Rick Nobles, Elizabeth Burr, Todd Trumbull, Joe Shoulak, Gus D'Angelo, Kathleen Hennessy, Kat Wade
Reprints

THE GREAT QUAKE: 1906–2006

THEN & NOW

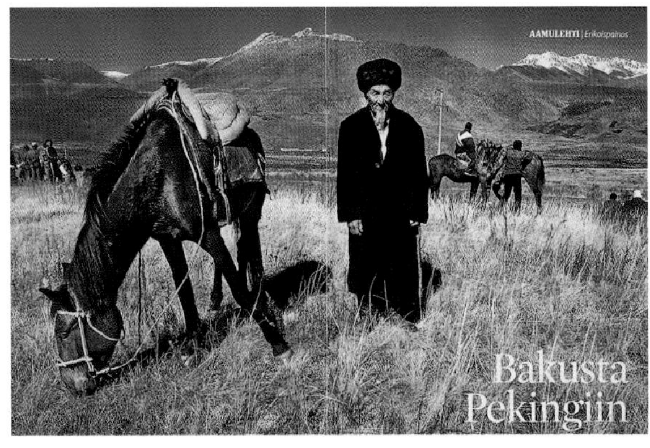
AAMULEHTI | Erikoispainos

Bakusta Pekingiin

**AAMULEHTI, TAMPERE,** Finland
Raino Lehtoranta, Ari Kinnari
Reprints

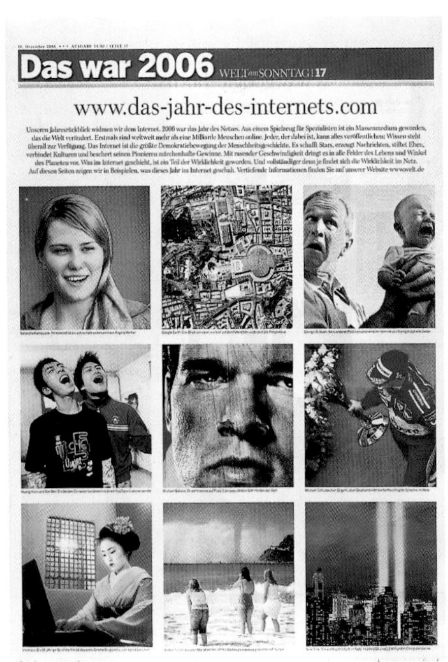
Das war 2006 WELT am SONNTAG | 17

www.das-jahr-des-internets.com

**WELT AM SONNTAG,** Berlin
Jördis Guzmán Bulla, Tobias Schönpflug
Reprints

Kevin Chapple

Brooks Neal

BEING A BLACK MAN

Decades of societal changes play a role

**THE WASHINGTON POST**
Beth Broadwater, Dennis Brack
Reprints

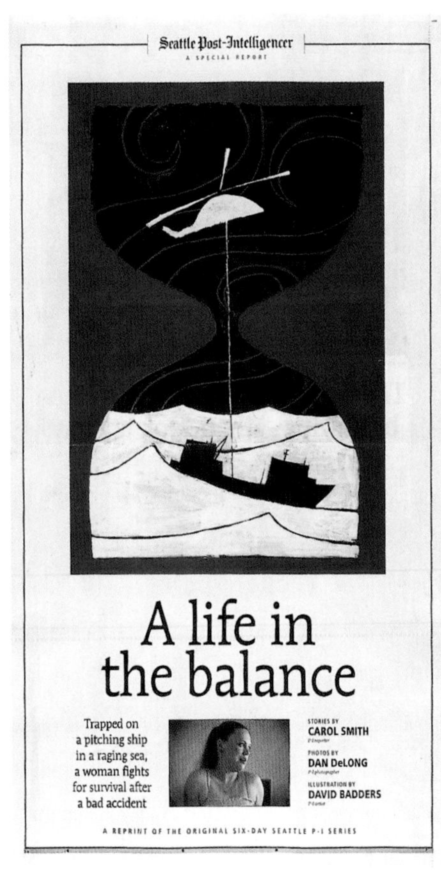
Seattle Post-Intelligencer

A SPECIAL REPORT

A life in the balance

Trapped on a pitching ship in a raging sea, a woman fights for survival after a bad accident

STORIES BY CAROL SMITH

PHOTOS BY DAN DeLONG

ILLUSTRATION BY DAVID BADDERS

A REPRINT OF THE ORIGINAL SIX-DAY SEATTLE P-I SERIES

**SEATTLE POST-INTELLIGENCER**
Scott Stoddard
Reprints

Chapter Nine

# PORTFOLIOS

Portafolios

**News / Sports / Features / Magazines**
**Photography / Illustration / Information Graphics / Combination**

Noticias / Deportes / Reportajes / Revistas
Fotografía / Ilustración / Infográficos / Combinados

**LOS ANGELES TIMES**
Joseph Hutchinson
News page design, 175,000+

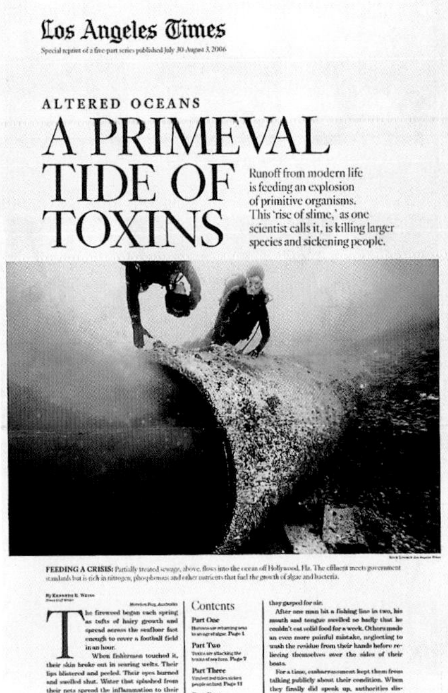
Los Angeles Times

ALTERED OCEANS

# A PRIMEVAL TIDE OF TOXINS

Runoff from modern life is feeding an explosion of primitive organisms. This 'rise of slime,' as one scientist calls it, is killing larger species and sickening people.

FEEDING A CRISIS:

Contents
Part One
Part Two
Part Three
Part Four
Part Five
The Journalists
Response

**THE WALL STREET JOURNAL,** New York
Orlie Kraus
News page design, 175,000+

Energy
THE JOURNAL REPORT
THE WALL STREET JOURNAL.

# Less Power TO THE People

TEN INNOVATIONS THAT WILL REDUCE THE AMOUNT OF ENERGY WE CONSUME

INSIDE
How to Save Gas
Fanning the Flames
Where the Money Is
Power Plays
Think Globally, Act Locally
Going Deep
Back in the Spotlight
Refined Reasons

**THE PHILADELPHIA DAILY NEWS**
John Sherlock
News page design, 50,000-174,999

FRIDAY, JUNE 16, 2006
PHILADELPHIA DAILY NEWS
THE PEOPLE PAPER
FATHER'S DAY
A GRIEVING DAD REACHES OUT TO TEENS
RACING TO CALIFORNIA
DEAD FISH IN WISSAHICKON

# SPIKED!

CITY COUNCIL PASSES SMOKING BAN: PAGE 3
CARE TO COMMENT? GO.PHILLY.COM/NOSMOKING

City Weekly
Boston Sunday Globe September 3, 2006

BOSTON

While far-flung tourists still stream in, many neighbors don't venture our way if they can help it. So the powers that be have launched a plan to bring them back.

# Snub hubbub

9.6%

It doesn't get any fresher than this

Software may let boss spot your e-mail abuse

**THE BOSTON GLOBE**
Lesley Becker
News page design, 175,000+

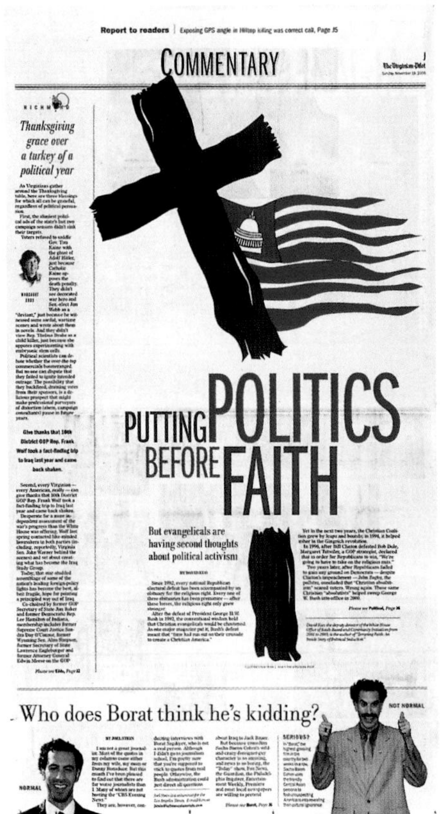
COMMENTARY

Thanksgiving grace over a turkey of a political year

PUTTING POLITICS BEFORE FAITH

But evangelicals are having second thoughts about political activism

Who does Borat think he's kidding?

**THE VIRGINIAN-PILOT,** Norfolk
Ryan Healy
News page design, 175,000+

Boston Sunday Globe
Ideas
& Books

Democracy in America, part deux
Imagine no Supreme Court hearings
The final exam

STATE OF INDEPENDENTS

Everyone knows Massachusetts isn't a Republican state. But if you think it's a Democratic state, think again.

Under the microscope

Recent revelations of fraud have caused some editors of scientific journals to rethink their responsibilities. But can journal editors be muckrakers?

**THE BOSTON GLOBE**
Gregory Klee
News page design, 175,000+

**STAR TRIBUNE,** Minneapolis
Chris Carr
Sports page design, 175,000+

WOLVES PREVIEW

Stay or go? That's the question facing Wolves superstar Kevin Garnett and many others in the organization. How this season, framed by uncertainty and big questions, unfolds will likely provide most of the answers. Stories: S4-7

CURTAINS?

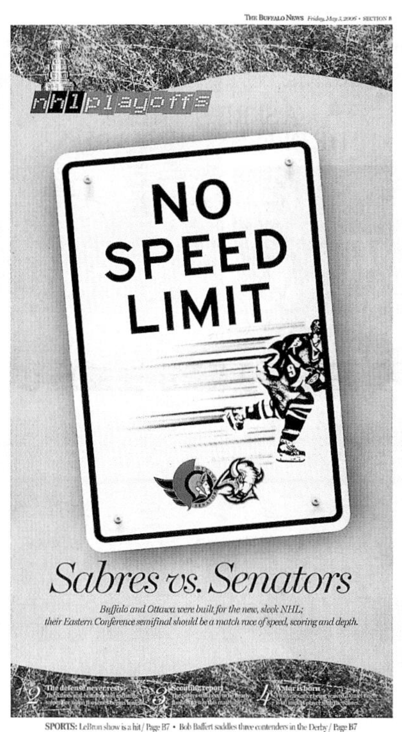
nhl playoffs



Sabres vs. Senators

Buffalo and Ottawa were built for the new, sleek NHL; their Eastern Conference semifinal should be a match race of speed, scoring and depth.

**THE BUFFALO NEWS** (N.Y.)
Vincent J. Chiaramonte
Sports page design, 175,000+

The New York Times

Week in Review

Opinion Pages 11-13
Education Advertising
Careers in Education and Health Care Employment

Sunday, March 19, 2006

Section 4

IMAGINE

Suppose We Just Let Iran Have The Bomb

By DAVID E. SANGER

*The big unknown is if deterrence works in a time of terror and smugglers.*

But Will They Love Him Tomorrow?

By ANNE E. KORNBLUT

*Barack Obama, and the perfection problem.*

WHERE THE BARS ARE | 3
The birth of the spring bacchanal: First came the swim team. The rest is a blur.
By Bill Marsh

A CATHOLIC SPLIT | 4
Republicans fighting illegal immigration aren't happy with the church.
By Rachel L. Swarns

CUBABALL | 14
A photographic essay on the nacional pastime.
By Fred R. Conrad

OPINION PAGES | 11-13
David Brooks on manliness; Michael Crichton on patents.

The New York Times

Week in Review

Sunday, May 7, 2006

Section 4

GO FIGURE

31%
Percentage who approve of the way President Bush is handling the economy.

57%
Percentage of those who say the national economy is very good or fairly good.

For Bush, the Economy Is a Glass Half Empty

*The Republican problem: money wallets are thick, but the party can't cash in.*

DESIGNED AT THE PUMP | 4
The rest of the world just isn't as exercised as the U.S. by those petrol prices.
By Mark Landler

RANDY BRITAIN | 14
In the halls of Westminster, a bench is as good as a bed.
By Sarah Lyall

OPINION PAGES | 11-13
Nicholas D. Kristof on speaking out and staying silent on Sudan; Frank Rich on the meaning of the Moussaoui verdict.

Between Addiction and Abstinence

*Patrick Kennedy's relapse begs the question: can there be a middle ground?*

SILVER

**THE NEW YORK TIMES**
Nicholas Blechman
News page design, 175,000+

This conceptual material is at a higher level than many of the portfolios we saw.
It fits the mold of The New York Times, but it is surprising.
Each story is well told.
You don't need to read the headlines to know what the stories are about.

Este diseñador usa bien muchas herramientas. Gracias a los niveles en todas las páginas, este portafolio demuestra una gran variedad: avances, noticias de último minuto, temas propios, ilustración, fotoperiodismo, tipografía y gráficos.

**NATIONAL POST,** Toronto
Geneviève Biloski
Feature page design, 175,000+

AVENUE

VAVAVAVOOM!

nationalpost.com

**SOUTH FLORIDA SUN-SENTINEL,** Fort Lauderdale
Jonathan Boho
Sports page design, 175,000+

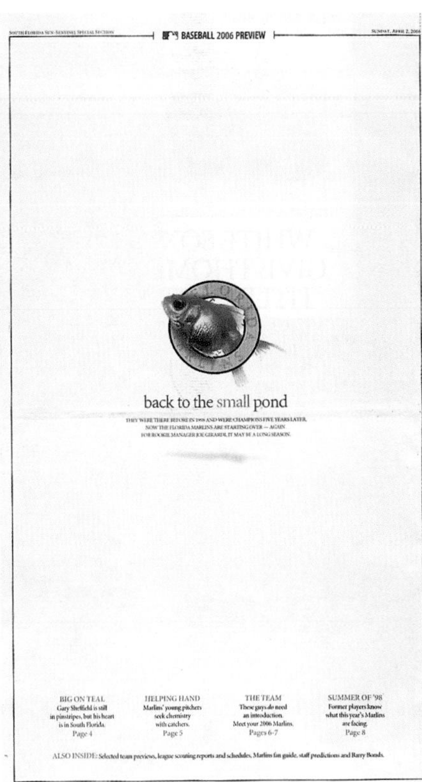
BASEBALL 2006 PREVIEW

back to the small pond

THEY WERE THERE BEFORE IN 1998 AND WERE CHAMPIONS FIVE YEARS LATER. NOW THE FLORIDA MARLINS ARE STARTING OVER — AGAIN. FOR ROOKIE MANAGER JOE GIRARDI, IT MAY BE A LONG SEASON.

BIG ON TEAL
Gary Sheffield is still in pinstripes, but his heart is in South Florida.
Page 4

HELPING HAND
Marlins' young pitchers seek chemistry with catchers.
Page 5

THE TEAM
These guys *do* need an introduction. Meet your 2006 Marlins.
Pages 6-7

SUMMER OF '98
Former players know what this year's Marlins are facing.
Page 8

ALSO INSIDE: Selected team previews, league scouting reports and schedules, Marlins fan guide, staff predictions and Barry Bonds.

**SAN FRANCISCO CHRONICLE**
Erick Wong
Feature page design, 175,000+

San Francisco Chronicle | Saturday | 8.19.2006

DATEBOOK

'Super Vision' scores an all-too-familiar point

REVIEW

Hilary Duff and Haylie Duff in "Material Girls."

Like, who wants to see two icky girls rewarded?

Peter Hartlaub

REVIEW

Ms. Gonick
*Failing at Living*

'H' is for heinousness of Mack's childhood

Great 'Snakes'!

Had it with this %$#!*@* hype? Well, the movie is finally here, and it lives up to its promise. Fasten your seat belts and enjoy the ride.

By Mick LaSalle

Samuel L. Jackson plays an FBI agent whose patience has been taxed on a flight from Honolulu to Los Angeles in "Snakes on a Plane."

REVIEW

**THE GUARDIAN**
London
Richard Turley
Feature page design, 175,000+

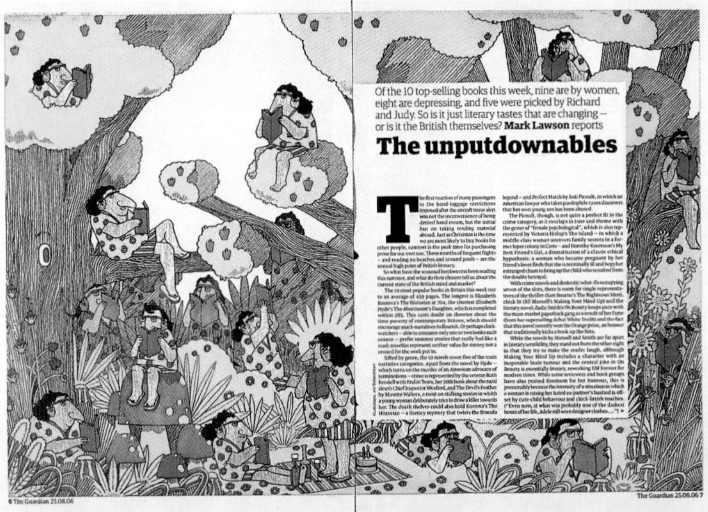
Of the 10 top-selling books this week, nine are by women, eight are depressing, and five were picked by Richard and Judy. So is it just literary tastes that are changing – or is it the British themselves? **Mark Lawson** reports

**The unputdownables**

The first reaction of many passengers to the hand-luggage restrictions imposed after the aircraft terror alert was not the inconvenience of being denied hand cream, but the initial ban on taking reading material aboard. Just as Christmas is the time we are most likely to buy books for other people, summer is the peak time for purchasing prose for our own use. These months of frequent flights – and reading on beaches and around pools – are the annual high point of British literacy.

6 The Guardian 25.08.06

The Guardian 25.08.06 7

**PITTSBURGH POST-GAZETTE**
Ben Howard
Sports page design, 175,000+

84 LUMBER CLASSIC

WEDNESDAY, SEPTEMBER 13, 2006 • SECTION G

*lei it on the line*

At an early age in Hawaii, Michelle Wie disdained most activities little girls enjoy, such as ballet class. Instead, she insisted on playing baseball or basketball with the boys. Now, at 16, her persistence is even greater — to compete against the men of the PGA Tour. PAGE G-4

INSIDE
Just when it seemed as if the 84 Lumber Classic was about to come of age came the announcement of its demise. The Post-Gazette looks at its rise and sudden fall.

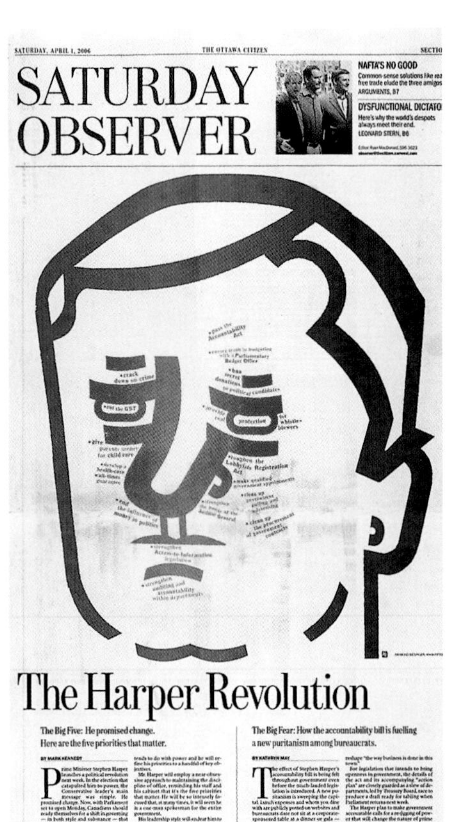
SATURDAY, APRIL 1, 2006 — THE OTTAWA CITIZEN

SATURDAY OBSERVER

NAFTA'S NO GOOD
Common-sense solutions like real free trade elude the three amigos
ARGUMENTS, B7

DYSFUNCTIONAL DICTATORS
Here's why the world's despots always meet their end.
LEONARD STERN, B6

The Harper Revolution

The Big Five: He promised change. Here are the five priorities that matter.

BY MARK KENNEDY

The Big Fear: How the accountability bill is fuelling a new puritanism among bureaucrats.

BY KATHRYN MAY

**THE OTTAWA CITIZEN**
Susan McDonough
Feature page design, 50,000-174,999

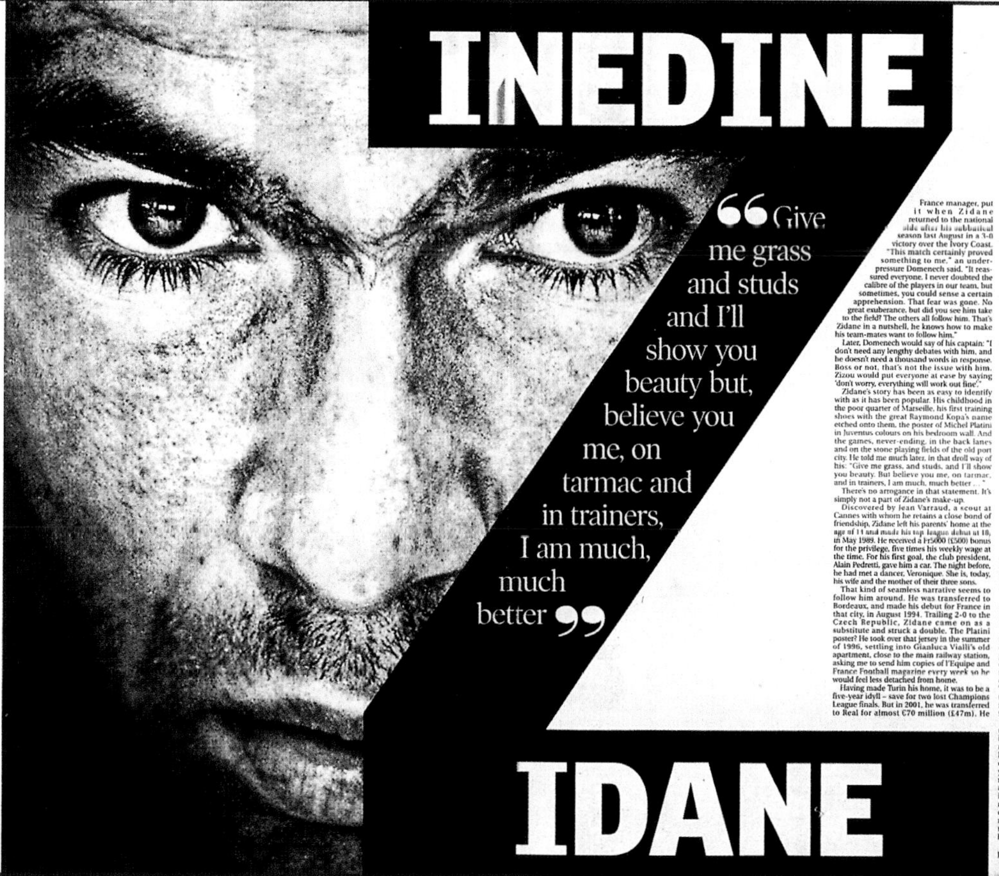

18 FOOTBALL sundayherald 30 April 2006 | sundayherald 30 April 2006 FOOTBALL 19

# ZINEDINE ZIDANE

It could be our last chance to see the game at its most beautiful, for after this World Cup 'Zizou' will leave football behind forever. Vincent Duluc, chief football writer at l'Equipe, looks back at the amazing career of France's favourite star, from his humble origins in Marseille to feats of brilliance on the world stage

IT'S a strange feeling having to remind yourself that Zinedine Zidane's talent is not everlasting, and that he will no longer play football beyond this summer. It seems awfully soon to be thinking about savouring his last few matches, and even odder to be missing him before he has even got to Germany and his World Cup swansong. In making the announcement, on Tuesday, that he is to retire completely at the end of France's tournament bid, a year before his contract expires at Real Madrid, Zidane brought forth a wave of nostalgia over his gifts – even before he has taken them off the game's greatest stage. His exit lends drama, and no little intensity, to Les Bleus, who have long taken his genius for granted.

At the very most, he will have 13 games left to play – although that would mean France reaching the final in Berlin. Having gone public with his decision some six weeks short of the opening tie against Switzerland on June 13, Zidane has put to bed any professional dilemmas and can at least travel with an inner peace. In an improvement from Euro 2004 (at the end of which he briefly quit the international game, only to return halfway through qualifying for Germany), the question of his future won't pollute the France camp either, since the answer is already known.

However, amid an ocean of tributes this week, Arsene Wenger emerged as one of the few to question the timing. After paying his own homage, the Arsenal manager and Champions League finalist said: "I saw him make his debut for Cannes, and it's always sad to see the departure of a great player who has given so much pleasure for so many years. But I would have chosen a different way to break the news. I can't help feeling it would have been better to do it after the World Cup."

His sixth successive tournament finals with France will have the bittersweet taste of his last. The others all had their own individual flavour: a frustrating Euro 96, immediately following a car accident which left him decidedly shaky and in pain, where he was even forced to apply make-up to his face for the official team photograph to cover up the cuts and bruises; a home World Cup in 1998 which began with his being sent off and ended with his scoring twice in the 3-0 final triumph over Brazil; his finest hours in a simply magnificent Euro 2000; a 2002 World Cup ruined by injury, and with Euro 2004, the end of "la belle epoque" and the break-up of a team of friends.

Can he really be reborn, just before he hangs up his boots, in the space of a month and a half? The genius of Zidane, perhaps, lies in the ability to make people continue believing anything is possible.

That's how Raymond Domenech, the current France manager, put it when Zidane returned to the national side after his sabbatical season last August in a 3-0 victory over the Ivory Coast. "This match certainly proved something to me," an under-pressure Domenech said. "It reassured everyone. I never doubted the calibre of the players in our team, but sometimes, you could sense a certain apprehension. That fear was gone. No great exuberance, but did you see him take to the field? The others all follow him. That's Zidane in a nutshell, he knows how to make his team-mates want to follow him."

> "Give me grass and studs and I'll show you beauty but, believe you me, on tarmac and in trainers, I am much, much better"

Later, Domenech would say of his captain: "I don't need any lengthy debates with him, and he doesn't need a thousand words in response. Boss or not, that's not the issue with him. Zizou would put everyone at ease by saying 'don't worry, everything will work out fine'."

Zidane's story has been as easy to identify with as it has been popular. His childhood in the poor quarter of Marseille, his first training shoes with the great Raymond Kopa's name etched onto them, the poster of Michel Platini in Juventus colours on his bedroom wall. And the games, never-ending, in the back lanes and on the stone playing fields of the old port city. He told me much later, in that droll way of his: "Give me grass, and studs, and I'll show you beauty. But believe you me, on tarmac, and in trainers, I am much, much better ..."

There's no arrogance in that statement. It's simply not a part of Zidane's make-up.

Discovered by Jean Varraud, a scout at Cannes with whom he retains a close bond of friendship, Zidane left his parents' home at the age of 14 and made his top league debut at 18, in May 1989. He received a Fr5000 (£500) bonus for the privilege, five times his weekly wage at the time. For his first goal, the club president, Alain Pedretti, gave him a car. The night before, he had met a dancer, Veronique. She is, today, his wife and the mother of their three sons.

That kind of seamless narrative seems to follow him around. He was transferred to Bordeaux, and made his debut for France in that city, in August 1994. Trailing 2-0 to the Czech Republic, Zidane came on as a substitute and struck a double. The Platini poster? He took over that jersey in the summer of 1996, settling into Gianluca Vialli's old apartment, close to the main railway station, asking me to send him copies of l'Equipe and France Football magazine every week so he would feel less detached from home.

Having made Turin his home, it was to be a five-year idyll – save for two lost Champions League finals. But in 2001, he was transferred to Real for almost €70 million (£47m). He emerged from his innate shyness but not from his honest education, nor from his natural sense of values. The sum involved scandalised him, but he escaped from the madness surrounding him at the time and reached the pinnacle of a club footballer's career one summer night in 2002, at Hampden Park.

After a volley with his left foot which defeated Bayer Leverkusen in the Glasgow rain and brought gasps from a crowd reared on the great Real victory of 1963, Zidane admitted: "Now, I feel satisfied."

That night, David Beckham compared him to a ballerina for the sheer grace of his movement, control and passing. Unfortunately, the last dance approaches. And you would have to be blind not to notice that those fleet-footed steps are getting heavier. At the start of a World Cup, where you are expected to peak every few days, it is natural to question the physical resources of a player who may go down as exceptional, but who is almost 34. And yet, how do you extinguish his threat, not only out of respect for his sublime skills and status as France captain, but given these will be his last hours in football?

The tributes from the footballing family these last few days give you an idea of the anticipation building. Marcello Lippi, his manager at Juventus, stated: "I think Zidane is the greatest talent we've known in football these last 20 years, yet he never played the prima donna. I am honoured to have been his manager."

Long-term accomplice, Bixente Lizarazu, underlined: "Unlike certain big-name players, he was incredibly selfless. He has this knack for making his team-mates tick, getting the best out of them – I am living proof of that."

Oddly enough, that has yet to apply in the case of Thierry Henry. Somehow the pair never quite gelled on the pitch for France, and I can't recall a single decisive pass Zizou made for the Gunner. But Henry's respect remains total. He said: "Now we are going to try and ensure Zizou goes out on a high. It's the least we can do for a player like him. To think he'll no longer be there for us to enjoy is such a shame, in fact it's very sad."

Paul Le Guen agrees, saying: "It's always a shame when a really great player decides to call it a day. But he does seem quite relieved to have made it public."

Zidane even answered the phone last week to find France president Jacques Chirac on the end of the line. Last September, a radio DJ prankster successfully imitated Chirac on the eve of the 1-0 defeat to Ireland in Dublin. He told Zidane and Domenech to put their hands on their hearts during the national anthem. They did as they were told. But this time, it was the real Chirac, who told him of his "admiration, as with all of France, for your career as a footballer, and for the values you embody".

Any politician knows that, even in retirement, Zidane will remain a forceful personality, whose status goes well beyond that of a mere player. Opinion polls continue to place him as France's favourite star. One who offered, in the space of a balmy summer eight years ago, the perfect illusion of a rainbow nation ready to integrate amid joy shared across generations of immigrant groupings. But as recent events underline, the illusion remains a long way from reality. Zidane's father doesn't even have the right to vote. Zidane never got embroiled in such disputes. Through timidity, a little; through fear of losing what he had gained, a bit more.

He was just always more comfortable on the pitch. The one he is about to leave behind.

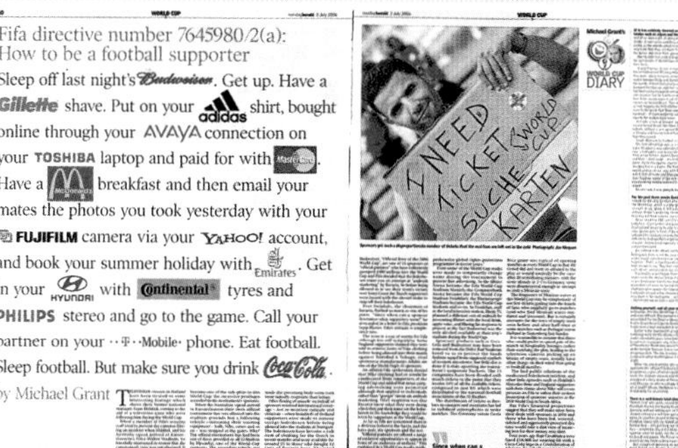

Fifa directive number 7645980/2(a): How to be a football supporter

Sleep off last night's Budweiser. Get up. Have a Gillette shave. Put on your adidas shirt, bought online through your AVAYA connection on your TOSHIBA laptop and paid for with MasterCard. Have a McDonald's breakfast and then email your mates the photos you took yesterday with your FUJIFILM camera via your YAHOO! account, and book your summer holiday with Emirates. Get in your HYUNDAI with Continental tyres and PHILIPS stereo and go to the game. Call your partner on your T-Mobile phone. Eat football. Sleep football. But make sure you drink Coca-Cola.

by Michael Grant



SILVER

**SUNDAY HERALD,** Glasgow, Scotland

Stephen Penman

Sports page design, 50,000-174,999

These pages show a great designer at work. They offer simplicity and restraint, but also power and energy. These are very strong pages, even in black and white. The designer doesn't use the same gimmick on each page — this portfolio has range.

Estas páginas muestran el desempeño de un gran diseñador. Ofrecen simplicidad y control, pero también poder y energía. Estas páginas son potentes, incluso en blanco y negro. El diseñador no emplea el mismo truco en cada una; este portafolio tiene variedad.

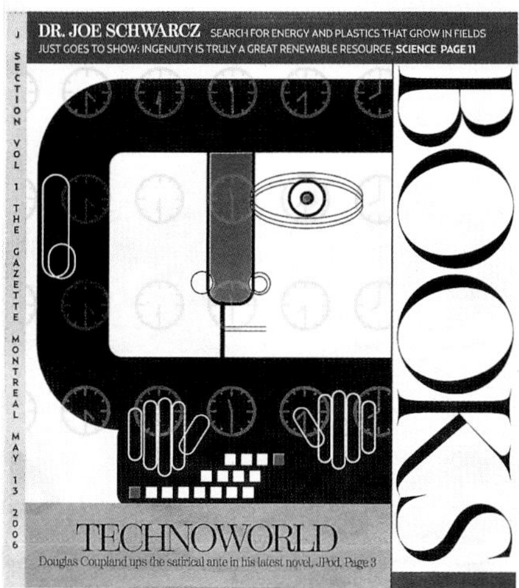


**THE GAZETTE,** Montreal

Nuri Ducassi

Feature page design, 50,000-174,999

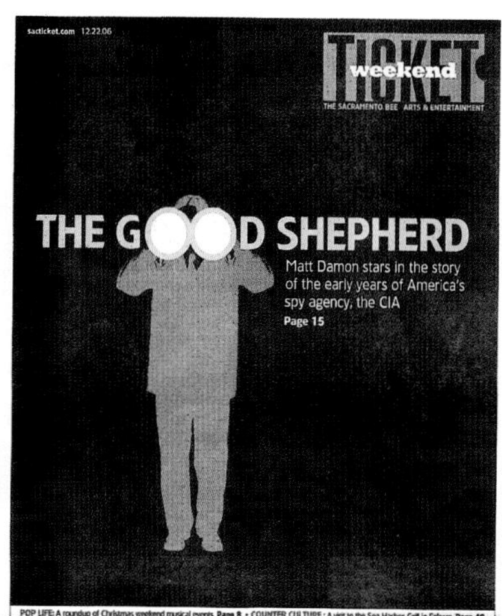


**THE SACRAMENTO BEE** (Calif.)

Margaret Spengler

Feature page design, 175,000+

**THE SEATTLE TIMES**

Erin Jang

Feature page design, 175,000+

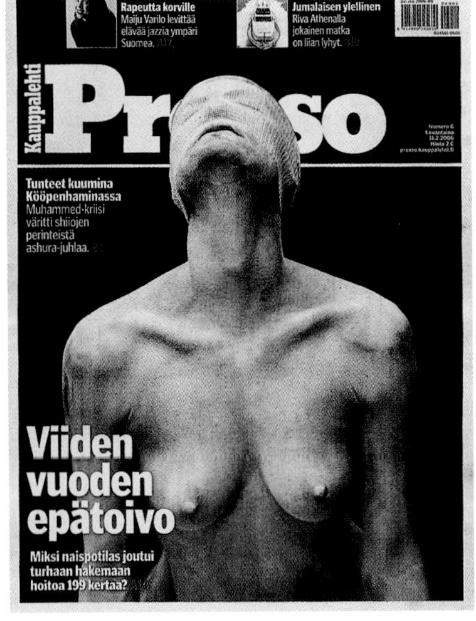

Bulevardi

Rapeutta korville
Maiju Varilo levittää eloaa jazzia ympäri Suomea.

Jumalaisen ylellinen
Riva Athenalla jokainen matka on liian lyhyt.

Kauppalehti Presso

Tunteet kuumina Kööpenhaminassa
Muhammed-kriisi väritti shiiojen perinteistä ashura-juhlaa.

Viiden vuoden epätoivo
Miksi naispotilas joutui turhaan hakemaan hoitoa 199 kertaa?

**KAUPPALEHTI PRESSO,** Helsinki, Finland
Markus Frey
Feature page design, 50,000-174,999

**SAN FRANCISCO CHRONICLE**
Matt Petty
Feature page design, 175,000+

SAN FRANCISCO CHRONICLE | 3.19.06 | BOUQUETS TO ART | VIN DIESEL | MIMI FOX | 'ZORRO'

**SAN JOSE MERCURY NEWS** (Calif.)
Stephanie Grace Lim
Feature page design, 175,000+

ENTERTAINMENT GUIDE www.mercurynews.com/entertainment | San Jose Mercury News | July 13-19, 2006

eye

OLD-FASHIONED FUN

BRAVE THE HURRICANE

RIDE THE GIANT DIPPER

PLAY IN THE SAND

STROLL THE BOARDWALK

SOAR WITH SKY GLIDER

FOR FANS OF CLASSIC AMUSEMENT PARKS, THE SANTA CRUZ BEACH BOARDWALK IS A TRIP BACK IN TIME
PAGES 26-27

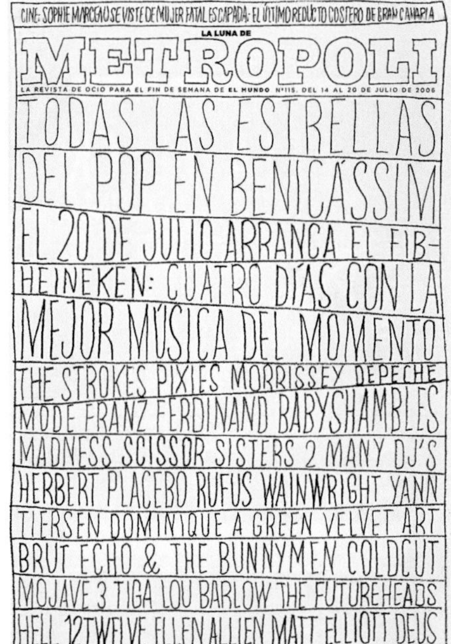

CINE: SOPHIE MARCEAU SE VISTE DE MUJER FATAL ESCAPADA: EL ÚLTIMO REDUCTO COSTERO DE GRAN CANARIA

LA LUNA DE METROPOLI

LA REVISTA DE OCIO PARA EL FIN DE SEMANA DE EL MUNDO Nº115. DEL 14 AL 20 DE JULIO DE 2006

TODAS LAS ESTRELLAS DEL POP EN BENICÁSSIM
EL 20 DE JULIO ARRANCA EL FIB-HEINEKEN: CUATRO DÍAS CON LA MEJOR MÚSICA DEL MOMENTO
THE STROKES PIXIES MORRISSEY DEPECHE MODE FRANZ FERDINAND BABYSHAMBLES MADNESS SCISSOR SISTERS 2 MANY DJ'S HERBERT PLACEBO RUFUS WAINWRIGHT YANN TIERSEN DOMINIQUE A GREEN VELVET ART BRUT ECHO & THE BUNNYMEN COLDCUT MOJAVE 3 TIGA LOU BARLOW THE FUTUREHEADS HELL 12TWELVE ELLEN ALLIEN MATT ELLIOTT DEUS

**EL MUNDO METROPOLI,** Madrid, Spain
Rodrigo Sanchez
Magazine page design, 175,000+

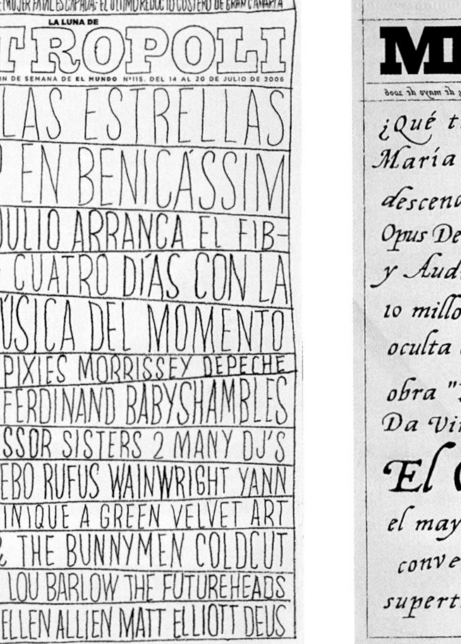

La Luna de

METROPOLI

¿Qué tienen que ver Jesucristo, María Magdalena, sus posibles descendientes, los Templarios y el Opus Dei con Ron Howard, Tom Hanks y Audrey Tautou? La clave, como 10 millones de lectores saben, se halla oculta en el Museo del Louvre y en la obra "La Última Cena". Ni siquiera Da Vinci lo hubiera imaginado...

El Código Da Vinci
el mayor best-seller de la Historia convertido en una película supertaquillera y polémica

**EL MUNDO METROPOLI,** Madrid, Spain
Rodrigo Sanchez
Magazine page design, 175,000+

**SUNDAY HERALD,** Glasgow, Scotland

Roxanne Sorooshian

Combination page design, 50,000-174,999

you rocked

MONDAY

The Virginian-Pilot

The story of Virginia's first slaves, finally told

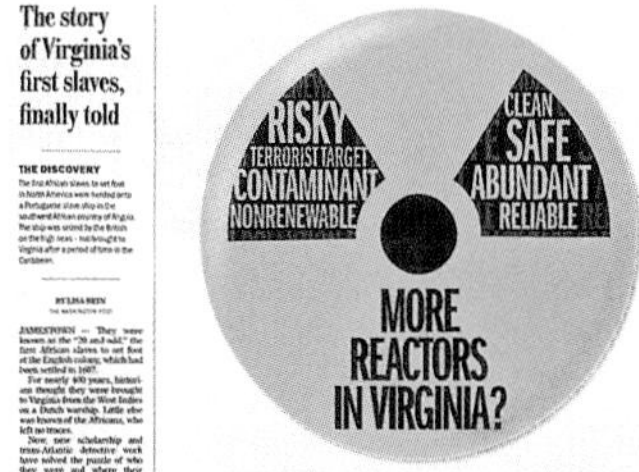


A top leader of al-Qaida in Iraq is captured

Wealth hasn't brought security to 9/11 spouses in U.S. illegally

COMMUNITY FEELS SQUEEZE OF EXPANSION

A goodbye full of tears

The jobs they'd rather forget

**THE VIRGINIAN-PILOT,** Norfolk

Luis Viches

Combination page design, 175,000+

P SUNDAY JULY 2, 2006

# Perspective

www.mercurynews.com

NEWS ANALYSIS AND COMMENTARY FROM THE NEWSPAPER OF SILICON VALLEY

In the Opinion section

**San Jose leaders**

A strong city manager is especially important now **EDITORIAL | 4P**

NEW YORK TIMES / MERCURY NEWS PHOTO ILLUSTRATION

## political taunting

By Geoffrey Nunberg

It may be hard to believe when you listen to the ambient chatter, but contemporary public discourse is actually no more rancorous than it was in ages past. As Eric Burns shows in his new book "Infamous Scribblers," the American press was malicious and mendacious from the outset, and by most historical standards the tone of our present dialogue is positively genteel.

TODAY'S POLITICAL DISCOURSE LACKS THINKERS; RATHER, PUNDITS BENT ON MALICE AND SUPREMELY GIFTED IN THEATRICS THAT MASQUERADES AS SATIRE GET THE INVITATIONS TO JAY LENO AND OTHER SHOWS

## ON THE NIGHT I KILLED MEL

By Anne Lamott

Inside this section

WILL MEXICO TURN TO LEFT?

If Mexicans elect Andrés Manuel López Obrador president today, reforms may be changed. **6P**

E MONDAY

# Tech Monday

Insider trading

Tech traffic sensors

Microsoft aims for easy

BROWSE, CLICK, TALK!

MORE COMPANIES USING INSTANT-CONNECT TOOLS TO ANSWER QUESTIONS FROM SHOPPERS ONLINE

TECHFILE

Flurry offers free e-mail for cell phones

*Security report: Cybercrooks turn attention to home PCs*

SILVER

**SAN JOSE MERCURY NEWS** (Calif.)

Martin Gee

Combination page design, 175,000+

This is the most consistent range of pages we saw. The portfolio shows huge range — fun and serious, multiple illustration styles and multiple sections. After using personal illustrations, this winner can make the most of very little.

Ésta es la muestra de páginas más consistente que vimos. El portafolio exhibe un amplio rango; divertido y serio, variados estilos de ilustración y secciones múltiples. Tras usar ilustraciones personales, esta pieza ganadora demuestra que puede sacarle gran partido a algo muy pequeño.

**SEATTLE POST-INTELLIGENCER**
David Badders
Illustration, individual

**EL ECONOMISTA,** Madrid, Spain
Javier Olivares
Illustration, individual

**EL ECONOMISTA,** Madrid, Spain
Elisabeth Nogales
Illustration, individual

**THE SEATTLE TIMES**
Susan Jouflas
Illustration, individual

**EL ECONOMISTA,** Madrid, Spain
David De Ramón
Illustration, individual

**DIÁRIO DE NOTÍCIAS,** Lisbon, Portugal
André Carrillo
Illustration, individual

**THE COLUMBUS DISPATCH** (Ohio)
Scott Minister
Combination page design, 175,000+

**COMERCIO,** Quito, Ecuador
Francisco Cajas
Illustration, individual

La cinta *Hostal* se convirtió en una de las sangrientas y atractivas opciones entre los asiduos al cine, durante el puente

FUNCIÓN

Sólo diego sabe

EN CINE ES GOLEADOR Y EN POLÍTICA PIDE JUEGO LIMPIO

Se rolan a Pam

Marcha en Nueva York

FUERA ROPA

MEXICANOS A CANNES

**EXCELSIOR,** México City
Nancy Araiza
Combination page design, 50,000-174,999

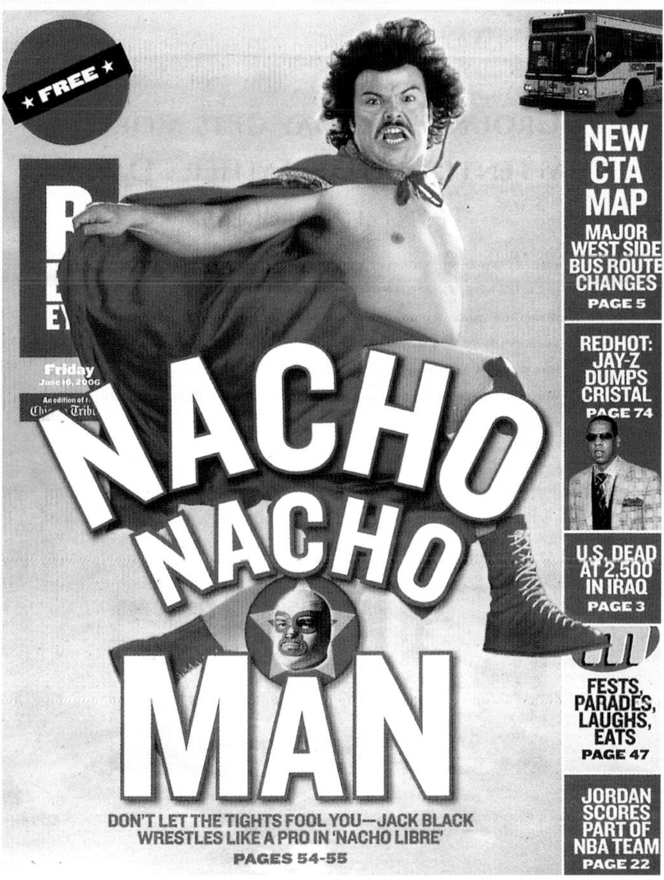
★ FREE ★

Friday June 16, 2006

NACHO NACHO MAN

DON'T LET THE TIGHTS FOOL YOU—JACK BLACK WRESTLES LIKE A PRO IN 'NACHO LIBRE'
PAGES 54-55

NEW CTA MAP
MAJOR WEST SIDE BUS ROUTE CHANGES
PAGE 5

REDHOT: JAY-Z DUMPS CRISTAL
PAGE 74

U.S. DEAD AT 2,500 IN IRAQ
PAGE 3

FESTS, PARADES, LAUGHS, EATS
PAGE 47

JORDAN SCORES PART OF NBA TEAM
PAGE 22

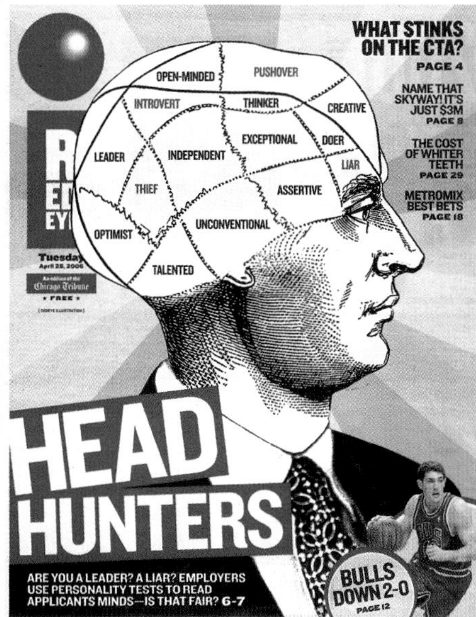
WHAT STINKS ON THE CTA?
PAGE 4

NAME THAT SKYWAY! IT'S JUST $3M
PAGE 8

THE COST OF WHITER TEETH
PAGE 29

METROMIX BEST BETS
PAGE 18

Tuesday April 25, 2006

HEAD HUNTERS

ARE YOU A LEADER? A LIAR? EMPLOYERS USE PERSONALITY TESTS TO READ APPLICANTS MINDS—IS THAT FAIR? 6-7

BULLS DOWN 2-0
PAGE 12

SILVER

**REDEYE,** Chicago
Mike Rich
Combination page design, 50,000-174,999

This designer is really working hard. These pages are bold and creative without having much more than handout art to work with. The consistent use of color and typographic styles reinforce the publication's identity. The pages have a playful sense of humor that speaks with an edgy appeal. This publication knows its market.

En verdad, este diseñador está trabajando duro. Estas páginas son audaces y creativas pese a que no cuentan con mucho más que imágenes prediseñadas. El consistente uso del color y de los estilos tipográficos refuerzan la identidad del periódico. Las páginas tienen un sentido del humor juguetón que se expresa con un tenso atractivo. Este periódico conoce bien su mercado.

**SAN FRANCISCO CHRONICLE**
Rico Mendez, Hulda Nelson, Matt Petty, Nanette Bisher, Oscar Villalon
Illustration, staff

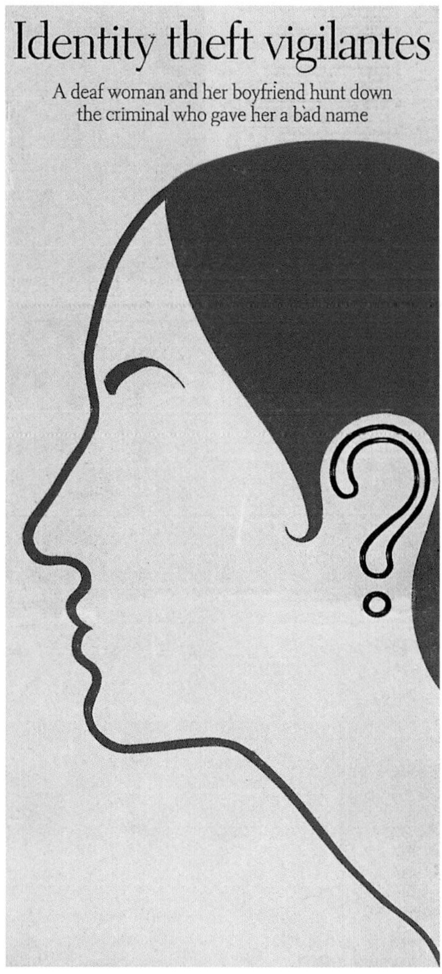

Identity theft vigilantes
A deaf woman and her boyfriend hunt down the criminal who gave her a bad name


**SOUTH FLORIDA SUN-SENTINEL,** Fort Lauderdale
Mike Stocker
Individual photo

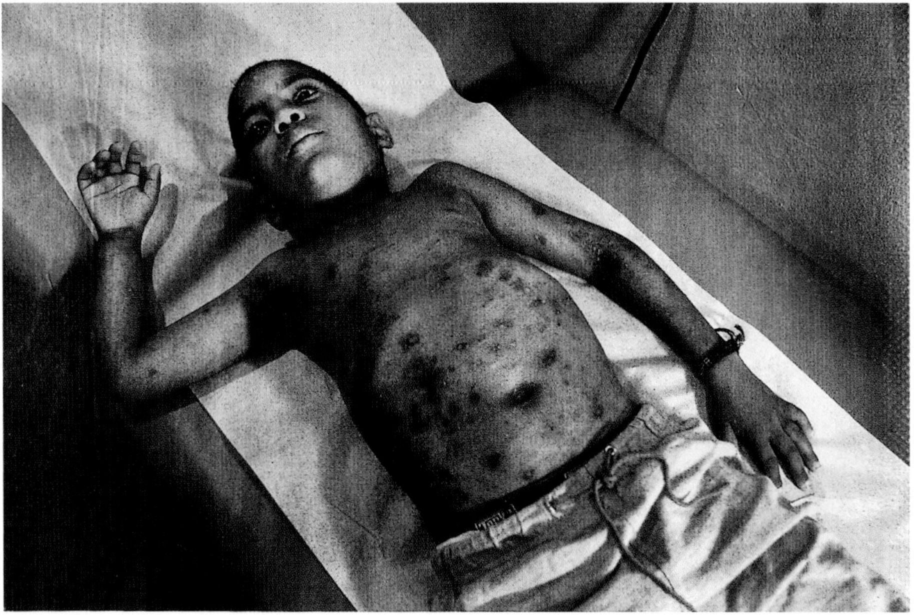

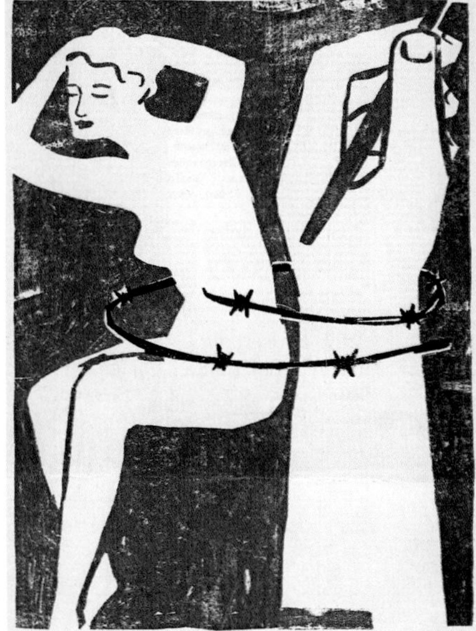

**SAN FRANCISCO CHRONICLE**
Rico Mendez, Hulda Nelson, Matt Petty, Nanette Bisher, Oscar Villalon
Illustration, staff

6TH ANNUAL
BEST
OF THE
UNDERGROUND

Munly takes No. 1 in Post music poll

Munly & the Lee Lewis Harlots were voted No. 1 in Post's poll.

By Ricardo Baca
Denver Post Pop Music Critic

THE LIST: HOW THE BANDS RANKED IN OUR POLL > 4F

THE BEST OF THE BEST: PLENTY OF TALENT BEYOND THE TOP 10 > 5F

Sixth annual Denver Post Underground Music Showcase

**THE DENVER POST**
Jeff Neumann
Illustration, individual

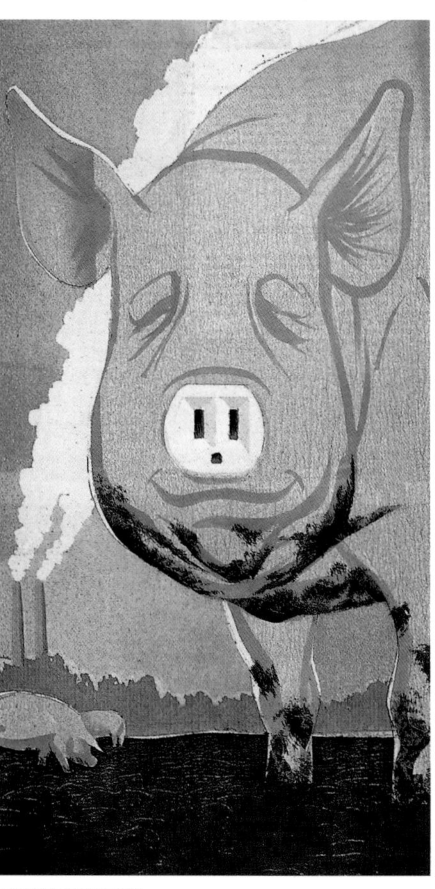

**LOS ANGELES TIMES**
Kelli Sullivan, Michael Whitley, Shout, Steve Sedam, Alex Nabaum, Edel Rodriguez, Ken Orvidas
Illustration, staff

**SOUTH FLORIDA SUN-SENTINEL,** Fort Lauderdale
Joe Amon
Individual photo

**BERLINER MORGENPOST,** Berlin
André Rival
Individual photo

Berlinerin von André Rival

Eva Sichelschmidt , Unternehmerin
„Ängste verpflichten."

**THE NEW YORK TIMES**
Tyler Hicks
Individual photo

A Drive to Root Out the Resurgent Taliban

**THE COLUMBUS DISPATCH** (Ohio)
Neal C. Lauron
Individual photo

Cold wind hot water

In southeastern Oregon's lonely landscapes, pools of warm water can soak all the way into your soul

**THE OREGONIAN,** Portland
Jamie Francis
Individual photo

**SAN JOSE MERCURY NEWS** (Calif.)

Pai, Karl Kahler, Andrea Maschietto, Rob Hernandez, Doug Griswold, Wes Killingbeck

Information graphics, staff, extended coverage, 175,000+

THE MCCLATCHY-KNIGHT RIDDER DEAL

# Are still viable?

Sale of chain sends mixed message on health of an industry under pressure

Online newspapers gaining readership

## MCCLATCHY PLANS TO SELL 12 KNIGHT RIDDER PAPERS

Papers for sale

With sale, key markets in play

**THE OREGONIAN,** Portland

Steve McKinstry, Derrik Quenzer, Steve Cowden, Michael Mode, Lisa Cowan

Information graphics, staff, extended coverage, 175,000+

Northwest passage to the Winter Olympics

# Leslee Olson takes her shot

Snowboardcross

Who to watch

2006 Winter Olympics, Feb. 10-26

**THE SAN DIEGO UNION-TRIBUNE**

Staff

Illustration, staff

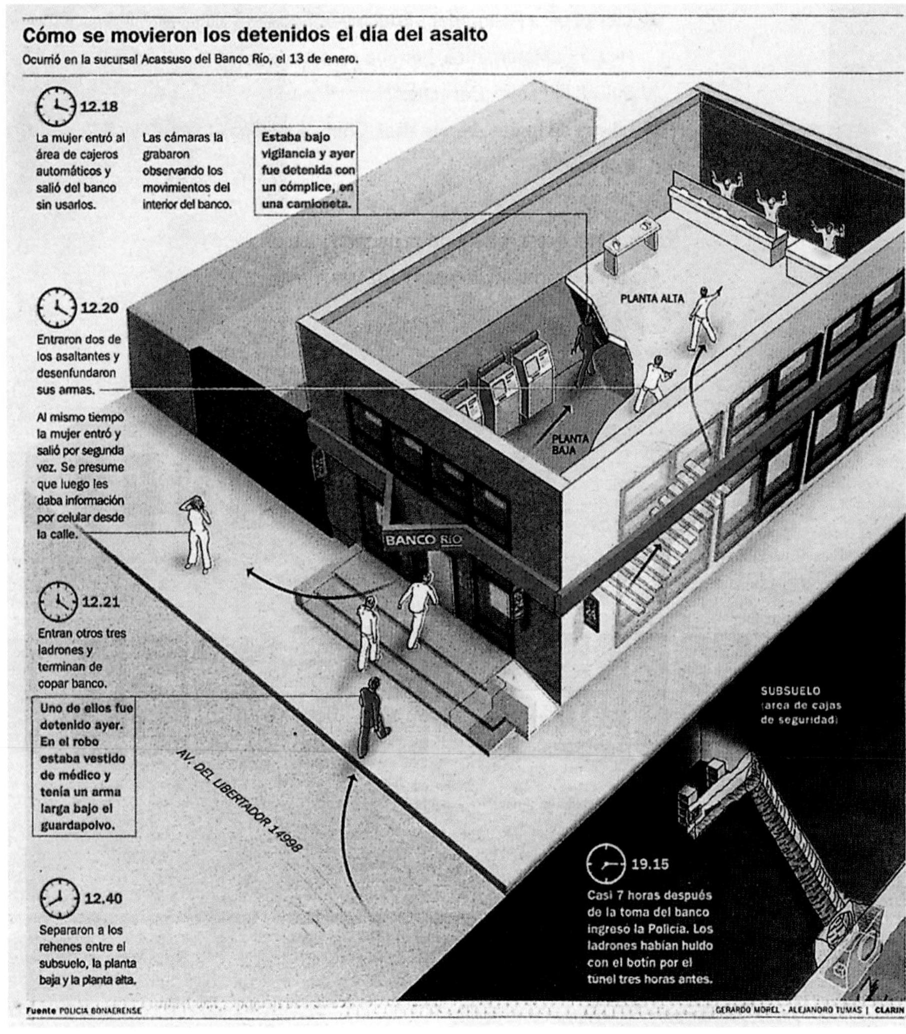

Cómo se movieron los detenidos el día del asalto
Ocurrió en la sucursal Acassuso del Banco Río, el 13 de enero.
12.18
La mujer entró al área de cajeros automáticos y salió del banco sin usarlos.
Las cámaras la grabaron observando los movimientos del interior del banco.
Estaba bajo vigilancia y ayer fue detenida con un cómplice, en una camioneta.
12.20
Entraron dos de los asaltantes y desenfundaron sus armas.
Al mismo tiempo la mujer entró y salió por segunda vez. Se presume que luego les daba información por celular desde la calle.
12.21
Entran otros tres ladrones y terminan de copar banco.
Uno de ellos fue detenido ayer. En el robo estaba vestido de médico y tenía un arma larga bajo el guardapolvo.
12.40
Separaron a los rehenes entre el subsuelo, la planta baja y la planta alta.
PLANTA ALTA
PLANTA BAJA
BANCO RÍO
AV. DEL LIBERTADOR 14998
SUBSUELO (área de cajas de seguridad)
19.15
Casi 7 horas después de la toma del banco ingresó la Policía. Los ladrones habían huido con el botín por el túnel tres horas antes.
Fuente POLICÍA BONAERENSE
GERARDO MOREL - ALEJANDRO TUMAS | CLARÍN

# METRO

NEWS FROM THE PORTLAND AREA AND THE NORTHWEST

Prison stretch will keep roads safer for 5 years

## Prepare to soar

## Candy Lane Elementary may want a new name

Soldier upheld peace amid Afghan war

## 27-foot 'setback' moves Portland high-rise forward

**THE OREGONIAN,** Portland

Steve McKinstry, Steve Cowden, Michael Mode

Information graphics, staff, extended coverage, 175,000+

**CLARÍN,** Buenos Aires, Argentina

Alejandro Tumas, Pablo Loscri, Staff

Information graphics, staff, extended coverage, 175,000+

**THE NEW YORK TIMES**
Staff
Information graphics, staff, extended coverage, 175,000+

THE NEW YORK TIMES INTERNATIONAL FRIDAY, AUGUST 4, 2006 A9

HOSTILITIES IN THE MIDEAST: A Threat, and a Search

*Israel Hunts For Tunnels In Gaza Strip*

*Boy, 12, Is Among 8 Palestinians Killed*

Pummeling the Heart of Hezbollah

*An Israeli operation aimed at thwarting*

*12 Israelis Die; Hezbollah Leader Threatens Tel Aviv With Rockets*

COOKING By Sheryl Julian and Julie Riven /// Photograph by Jim Scherer

Time to Loaf

A touch of citrus is all these old-fashioned cakes need to brighten a winter table.

LEMON POUNDCAKE has the fine texture of an old-fashioned confection.

**THE BOSTON GLOBE**
Jim Scherer
Individual photo

12 [MARTES DE PASIÓN]

RESPONSABLE: MOISÉS RAMÍREZ SEGUNDO

# 'LAVI', EL PAYASO DEL TOREO

Manuel Díaz fue un matador de toros que muchos consideraron un bufón de la profesión, por salirse de los lineamientos clásicos en el arte de la lidia de reses bravas. Murió por un aneurisma

TEXTO: GUILLERMO SALAS ALONSO
ILUSTRACIÓN: BOLIGÁN

Una amplia gama de escuelas, estilos y cortes existe en el medio taurino. Es precisamente lo que hace de la profesión ser tan pasional.

En efecto, el trazo del toreo está basado en unas normas muy estrictas de la técnica; sin embargo, siendo las suertes las mismas para todos los toreros, cada quien las ejecuta en su sentimiento particular y con ello se impone un sello.

Se habla de escuelas, como la sevillana, la rondeña y la mexicana. En el medio taurino, entre los eruditos en la materia, se considera que más que escuelas, son estilos, es el adjetivo más exacto para calibrarlas en su realidad.

Siempre ha habido toreros que se les califica de charlots, bufones o cómicos, sin serlo realmente, aunque en defensa de estas figuras, cabe señalar que deben tener una técnica muy depurada y ser diestros que dominan el oficio de manera excelsa, pues de lo contrario no podrían hacerle a los bureles la infinidad de suertes que reúne un incalculable mérito, para estar en el terreno, la distancia justa y darle su tiempo al "enemigo". En ocasiones resulta más complicado hacer las cosas de guasa que las que llevan la pureza de las normas.

Manuel Díaz *Lavi*, siendo un torero de indudable valía, los aficionados de la romántica época de cuando se empezó a escribir la historia de la fiesta brava, lo catalogaban de ser un payaso de la profesión, pues en ocasiones se salía de los lineamientos clásicos en el arte de la lidia de reses bravas.

Al salirse de esos moldes, por sentirlo así en su estilo y corte, a muchos no les agradaba, a otros sí. Lo de siempre en el espectáculo, en gustos se rompen muchos géneros, según el adagio.

**De origen gitano**

Manuel Díaz *Lavi* nació en Cádiz en 1812. De origen gitano, no negaba por su actitud y comportamiento su modo de expresarse.

Ahí mismo, en Cádiz, se inició como torero y el 8 de agosto de 1841 figuró como sobresaliente en la corrida en que actuaron nada menos que Francisco Montes *Paquiro* y Gaspar Díaz. Sí, éste era su hermano. En septiembre actuó otra vez con *Paquiro*, que era una figura de la fiesta, en la plaza de Jerez de la Frontera. Y al año siguiente sumó fechas en esa región de Andalucía al lado de su consanguíneo y el maestro Montes, al que le aprende muchísimo. Tanto que, en 1843, se presenta en Madrid, el 17 de abril, y eso le abre las puertas y extiende su radio de acción en las regiones toreras de Castilla y Aragón.

En la capital de España hace campañas hasta 1858. Obeso y sin facultades se obstinaba en pelearle las palmas y rivalizar con el garboso *Chiclanero*, torero elegante y fino por excelencia... Sí, también al grupo de excelentes exponentes de la profesión que deambulaba, en esos principios de la romántica época.

Realizaba *Lavi* en el ruedo algunas extravagancias a las que los "conocedores" de esa época, les parecía fuera de las normas puras y clásicas en el arte del toreo.

Manuel Díaz tuvo una obesidad prematura y desde 1852 se le empezó a manifestar. Esos kilos que el cuerpo recibía y sin poderlos eliminar, restaba al diestro movilidad y sufrió varios percances por esa razón.

Inclusive, pese a ello, además de la natural simpatía que le salía a flor de piel, por ese tiempo estuvo en La Habana, Cuba, y también actuó en México. Casi no hay noticias de ello, pero en ese entonces el que partía la rebanada grande del pastel era Bernardo Gaviño, capitán de cuadrilla que dominó el mercado mexicano por algunas décadas, sin que nadie le hiciese sombra, no obstante las cuadrillas de gran cartel que llegaban de España.

Y cuando retornó a su patria, contaba sus hazañas y con su proverbial gracejo exponía: "Si no me voy de aquella tierra me "jacen emperaor".

**Muy lejos de Cádiz**

Un tanto obeso, ya en el tobogán de la decadencia, en 1858 fue contratado para actuar en Lima, Perú. Llegó a la capital inca lleno de entusiasmo e ilusiones.

Como suelen hacerlo siempre los matadores, desde aquel tiempo hasta el actual, Manuel Díaz *Lavi*, lo primero que realizó, a medianos de noviembre, fue visitar las ganaderías donde pastaban los astados que iba a lidiar. Por tanto, visitó diversas dehesas cerca de Lima. Los toreros señalan que tiene que ver al enemigo.

A su regreso, se sintió indispuesto con un malestar que lo obligó a guardar cama y fue preciso aplazar el festejo de su presentación. Ya en el periodo de convalecencia, se sintió muy fatigado. No reaccionó favorablemente, la fatiga se acentuó y fue en ascenso.

Y llegó el fatal día, 9 de diciembre. El artista solicitó un vaso de agua de goma, que bebió sin cesar. De pronto, cayó exánime y más tarde murió a consecuencia de un aneurisma.

Ilógico y triste final de este matador de toros, al que el tratadista Sánchez de Neira, en la obra "La Historia del Toreo" de Daniel Tapia, lo dibuja íntegro:

*Es más difícil de lo que a primera vista parece calificar acertadamente el mérito que pudo tener este celebrado matador de toros; porque "Lavi" fue el payaso del toreo y en este caso no merecía figurar al lado de los grandes maestro y de los matadores que hoy están más en boga; pero también hizo cosas toreando que muchos envidiarían...".*

*Todos recuerdan su nombre y ninguno lo desprecia. Ser inconsciente, que por instinto, [illegible] torero y otras de menos valer, las rehuía y esquivaba hasta el miedo.*

*Hombre incomprensible, que en la arena tanto tenía de malo como de bueno y que lo mismo recibía con alegría infantil los aplausos de los espectadores que con lágrimas y cara compungida las más ruidosas y ostensibles muestras de desagrado. En la hora de la muerte no es tan mal diestro como algunos le suponen; sabe pararse en jurisdicción, mejorar el terreno, dar los pasos en corto, cambiarse en la cabeza y otras cosas que algunos que se las echan de maestro no las hacen, aunque las comprendan.*

Está dicho todo.

SILVER

**EL UNIVERSAL**
México City
Ángel Boligán
Illustration, individual

We love how bold these illustrations are. They excel with volume and texture. Each illustration implies that it's a photograph from a different angle.

Nos encanta cuán audaces son estas ilustraciones. Se lucen con volumen y textura. Cada ilustración implica que es una fotografía desde un ángulo diferente.

**CLARÍN,** Buenos Aires, Argentina
Alejandro Tumas, Pablo Loscri, Staff
Information graphics, staff, breaking news, 175,000+

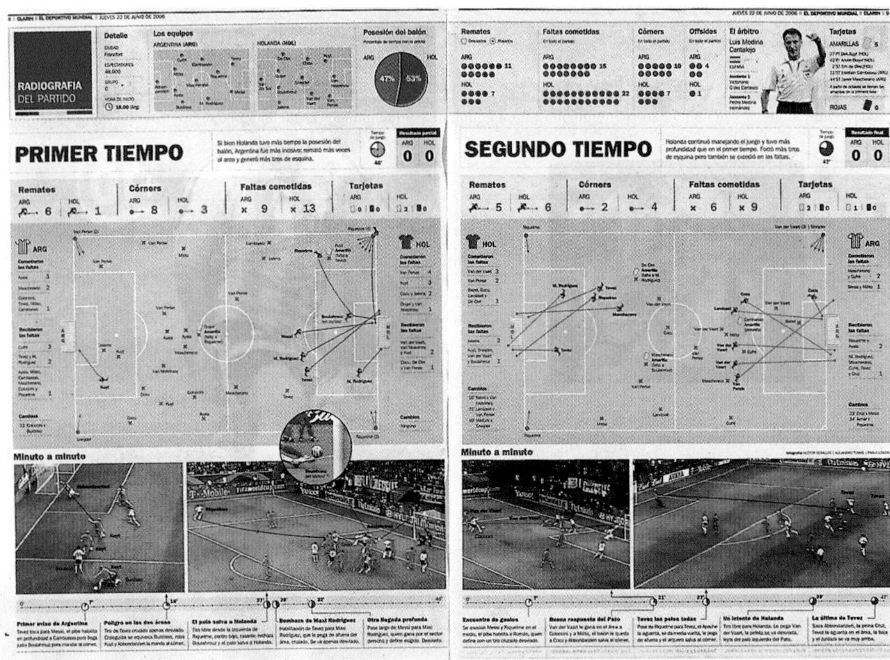


**THE BOSTON GLOBE**
Staff
Information graphics, staff, breaking news, 175,000+

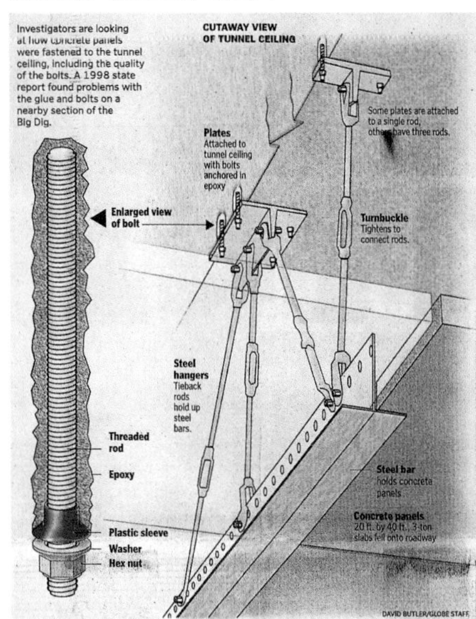


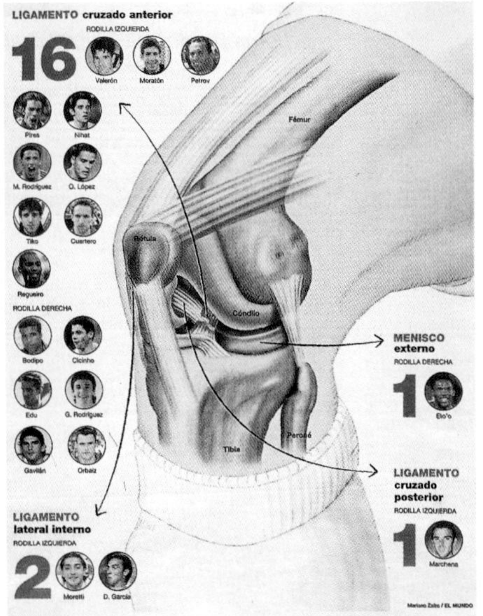


**EL MUNDO DEL SIGLO XXI,** Madrid, Spain
Mariano Zafra
Information graphics, individual, non-breaking news & features, 175,000+

How the shooting unfolded
When police arrived at the Glenn home Sept. 16, it was dark and the side door was only about 10 feet from the garage where Lukus Glenn, already bloodied from smashing car windows, stood. Experts say such close proximity contributed to the incident. Police are trained to keep at least 20 to 25 feet between themselves and an armed person.
Hope Glenn called police at 3:05 a.m. requesting help calming her drunken 18-year-old son, Lukus, who she told dispatchers was "out of control." About 10 minutes elapsed between her call to police and the shooting. Based on the police, 9-1-1 tapes and witness accounts, here's what happened in the last eight minutes:
1 3:07 A.M. Hope Glenn, who's looking out a door window, tells the dispatcher her son is "bleeding pretty bad" after smashing windows with his hands. She says his two friends, David Lucas and Tony Morales, are trying to calm him.
3:10 A.M. Hope Glenn says her son, holding a knife to his throat, says he's not going down without killing someone.
2 3:11 A.M. Two deputies from the Washington County Sheriff's Office, Mikhail Gerba and Timothy Mateski, arrive at the home and take up positions in the yard. Tigard Officer Andrew Pastore arrives, equipped with a nonlethal beanbag weapon.
Hope Glenn
Bullet holes
Lukus Glenn
Knife
Deputies Gerba and Mateski
Officer Pastore
S.W. Oleson Rd
S.W. Hall Blvd.
S.W. 80th Ave.
Shooting
TIGARD
Portland
3:13 A.M. Lukus Glenn stands at the corner of the garage. Hope Glenn says "They're telling him to drop the knife or they're going to shoot him."
3 3:15 A.M. Pastore fires several beanbag rounds at Lukus Glenn, who slumps against the garage but otherwise appears unaffected.
4 Lukus Glenn moves toward the door of the home, 10 feet away, where the family is inside.
5 Gerba and Mateski fire their guns, and Lukus Glenn collapses at the doorstep. Hope Glenn tells the dispatcher, "They shot him." The dispatcher calls Hope Glenn's name over and over, but there is no answer.
Hope Glenn re-enacts her son's final moments
5
4
3


**THE OREGONIAN,** Portland
Steve Cowden
Information graphics, individual, non-breaking news & features, 175,000+

**EL MUNDO DEL SIGLO XXI,** Madrid, Spain

Juantxo Cruz, Emilio Amade, Modesto J. Carrasco, Rafa Estrada, Daniel Izeddin, Raul Camañas

Information graphics, staff, breaking news, 175,000+

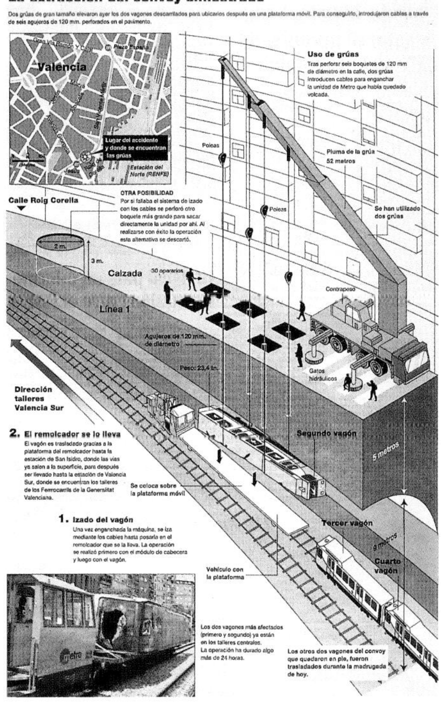

THE NEW YORK TIMES, TUESDAY, OCTOBER 3, 2006

VITAL SIGNS

When Young People Use, Parents Seldom Know

A Link Between Poverty and a Telltale Protein

Hormone May Help Heal Brain Injuries

Doctors Prescribe More Than They Explain

Out-of-Body Experience? Your Brain Is to Blame

One Body When the Brain Says Two

What some attribute to paranormal forces can be induced.

SCIENCE ILLUSTRATED

An Artificial Foot That Does Everything but Itch

**THE NEW YORK TIMES**

Frank O'Connell

Information graphics, individual, non-breaking news & features, 175,000+

SILVER

**HERALDO DE ARAGÓN,**

Zaragoza, Spain

Kristina Urresti, Irán Santos, Pilar Ostalé, Jorge Luis Mora, Pedro Zapater, Luis Grañena, Alberto Aragón, Isidro Gil

Illustration, staff

The portfolio shows the art director's good judgment in choices and play. Though it's limited in the range, it is specific in purpose. It shows consistency and gives a distinctive style to the publication.

El portafolio muestra el buen juicio del director de arte en la selección de las imágenes y el rol que cumplen. Aunque su variedad es limitada, su propósito es específico. Muestra consistencia y le da un estilo distintivo al periódico.

**EL CORREO,** Bilbao, Spain

Fernando G. Baptista

Information graphics, individual, non-breaking news & features, 50,000-174,999

Se cumplen 160 años del aniquilamiento de un destacamento del Séptimo de Caballería a las órdenes del legendario general Custer en Little Bighorn

Sansón y los pieles rojas

**THE NEWS-PRESS,** Fort Myers, Fla.

Michael Donian, Karen Bellville, Megan Kissinger, Ray Sarracino, Javier Torres

Information graphics, staff, non-breaking news & features, 50,000-174,999

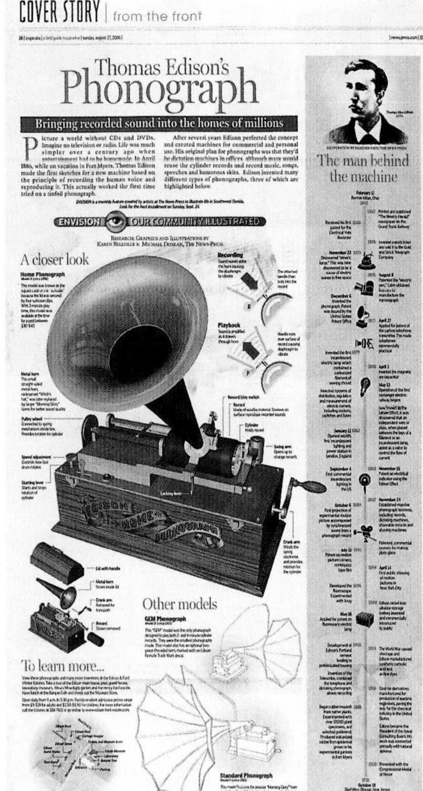

COVER STORY | from the front

Thomas Edison's Phonograph

Bringing recorded sound into the homes of millions

The man behind the machine

A closer look

Other models

To learn more...

**THE NEW YORK TIMES**

Staff

Information graphics, staff, non-breaking news & features, 175,000+

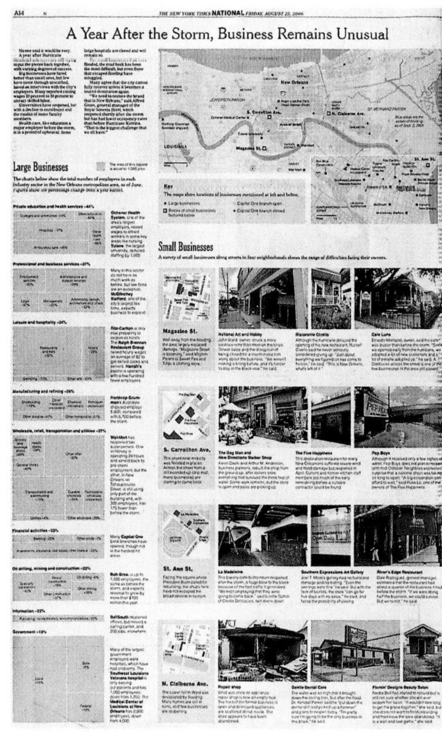

A Year After the Storm, Business Remains Unusual

Large Businesses

Small Businesses

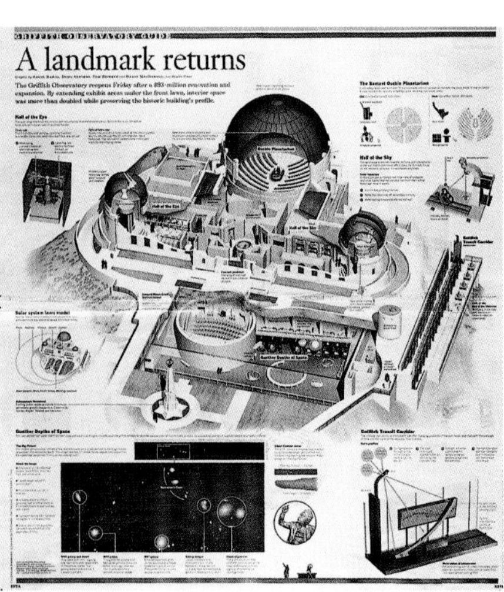

A landmark returns

**LOS ANGELES TIMES**

Raoul Rañoa, Lorena Iñiguez, Doug Stevens, Leslie Carlson, Cheryl Brownstein-Santiago, Tom Reinken, Brady MacDonald, Sandra Poindexter, Thomas Suh Lauder, Les Dunseith

Information graphics, staff, non-breaking news & features, 175,000+

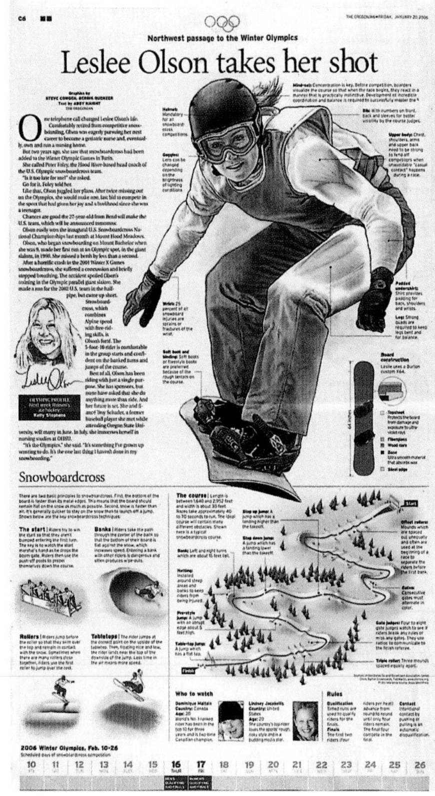

Northwest passage to the Winter Olympics

Leslee Olson takes her shot

Snowboardcross

**THE OREGONIAN,** Portland

Steve McKinstry, Derrik Quenzer, Steve Cowden, Eric Baker

Information graphics, staff, non-breaking news & features, 175,000+

ANATOMY OF A BREAKDOWN

STEP 1: HOW THE BUILDING MIGHT HAVE BEEN BREACHED

STEP 2: AFTER THE BREACH, THE DAMAGE CASCADED

DAMAGE TO THE BUILDING

**THE INDIANAPOLIS STAR**

Chris Johnson, Theodore Kim, Jennifer Imes, James G. Nichols, Michael Campbell, Angela Edwards, Emily Kuzniar, Ryan Hildebrandt, Scott Goldman

Information graphics, staff, non-breaking news & features, 175,000+

**HOUSTON CHRONICLE**

Jay Carr, Alberto Cuadra, Robert Dibrell, Ken Ellis, John T. Valles

Information graphics, staff, non-breaking news & features, 175,000+

COMMISSIONING THE USS TEXAS

The Navy's newest fast-attack submarine will be put in service today in Galveston with first lady Laura Bush doing the honors

THIS IS WHAT $2.7 BILLION LOOKS LIKE

# This Texas lady is a high-tech killer

CARLOS ANTONIO RIOS : CHRONICLE

**BOSS:** Capt. John Litherland will command the Texas until it is deployed next year.

By MIKE TOLSON
HOUSTON CHRONICLE

GALVESTON — The long, black cylinder sits baking at water's edge in the oppressive coastal heat, its upwardly protruding wedge making it instantly recognizable as a machine not to be trifled with.

A raft of images comes to mind: tense moments of confrontation with the enemy inspired by a score of old movies and television shows. The sonar operator makes contact. The captain orders the ship to periscope depth.

Everyone in the crowded command center watches the depth gauge. Finally, he climbs a few steps up to the conning tower, pushes a button and a sleek metal pole rises toward the surface.

Wait a minute . . . wrong sub. That's your father's submarine, the USS Cavalla, permanently berthed a few miles away at Galveston's Seawolf Park.

This dark tube is the latest and greatest the U.S. Navy has to offer: a $2.7 billion, state-of-the-art, fast-attack sub bearing a nuclear power plant, a formidable array of weapons and every electronic bell and whistle imaginable.

But no periscope. That has been replaced by a "photonic mast," essentially a fancy digital camera that displays what it sees on a large screen. An operator moves the camera with a joystick. Submarine movies will never be the same.

The 377-foot SSN 775, to be formally commissioned as the USS Texas in a dockside ceremony this morning, is to the diesel electric subs of yore as today's F-16 is to the P-51 Mustang that battled over the skies of Europe. Both have lethal potential, but . . .

*Please see* TEXAS, *Page A23*

FOR A PHOTO GALLERY OF THE USS TEXAS, SEE PAGE A23

THE SCIENCE OF

# PLASTINATION

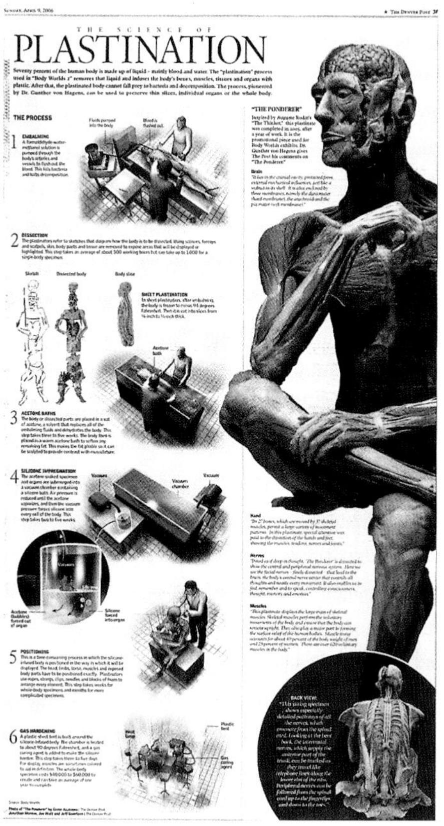


**THE DENVER POST**

Staff

Information graphics, staff, non-breaking news & features, 175,000+

# SUNDAY PUNCHES

OBSERVANCES

## Dylan Suits Us Just Fine

Wednesday is National Tailors Day. Elias Harb, who has owned Elias Custom Tailoring in Santa Monica for more than 30 years, has heard that one before. "Every damn day is tailor's day around here." In that case, we'll watch Pierce Brosnan in "The Tailor of Panama" or Alec Guinness in "Tinker, Tailor, Soldier, Spy." Better yet, we'll listen to "House of the Rising Sun" by Bob Dylan, at right. The folk ballad was originally recorded in the early 20th century and later made popular, or not, by a number of artists, including Dolly Parton, Bachman-Turner Overdrive and Eric Burdon and the Animals. Dylan put it on his first album in 1962. Our excuse for connecting it to the holiday? One lyric: "My mother was a tailor/She sewed these new blue jeans. . . ."

**STAPLES:** Clippers rule

THE RIDE

## Buckle Up, It's Bumpy

Just in time for summer, Cedar Fair, the outfit that owns Knott's Berry Farm in Buena Park, scrounged up $1.24 billion to add five parks to its arsenal, including Great America in Santa Clara. What if theme park companies stepped out of the suburbs and bought properties in Los Angeles proper, which some wags think of as one big amusement park anyway? We have some suggestions:

| SITE | DREAM RIDE |
|---|---|
| **Rocky Delgadillo Campaign Headquarters** | Delusions of Gridiron Grandeur |
| **L.A. School Board Headquarters** | Public Servants Under Siege |
| **Staples Center** | Clippers Kingdom (formerly Lakers Land) |
| **Standard Oil Building** | The Tower of Gouge |

TWO-WORD TALE

## Tom Cruise's Publicist Works Overtime to Make Him Seem Normal

Mission impossible.

THE DISCOUNT BIN [By Riley Ray Chiorando]

## Between a Rock and a Car Chase

Spotted recently at 99 Cents Only Stores and Big Lots locations:

Jessica Simpson "The Dukes of Hazzard" poster · Hayden Christensen "Star Wars: Episode III" fruit snack · Interactive CD-ROM guide to grilling by star George Foreman · "Madagascar" dog toy (Gloria, aka Jada Pinkett Smith) · WWF paper party plates featuring The Rock

ILLUSTRATION BY TIM BOWER; PHOTOGRAPHS COURTESY STAPLES CENTER/REUTERS (TOP) AND BY KEVIN WINTER/GETTY IMAGES (BOTTOM) WEST MAGAZINE : JUNE 4, 2006 11

# SUNDAY PUNCHES

OBSERVANCES

## Listen to Lucinda

Tuesday is Dump Your Significant Jerk Day. We suggest you take the advice of the holiday's inventor, Marcus P. Meleton Jr. of Orange County, and discard the louse in your life. Then head for the 4100 Bar in Silver Lake, where Jennifer Hubl will make you a Flaming la Cucaracha. "This," she says, "is how to celebrate getting rid of a cockroach." After you've downed the blend of Kahlúa, Bacardi and Baileys, you'll be ready to kick back and listen to one of the great good-riddance songs. Sure, Ray Charles' "Hit the Road Jack" is one of them, but our favorite is "Greenville," by Lucinda Williams, left:

Don't wanna see you again
or hold your hand
Cause you don't really love me
you're not my man. . . .

THE RANT

## G'Day? No Way

California vintners have been in a funk since Merrill Lynch reported a few weeks ago that their rivals Down Under have been stealing market share. We asked Randall Grahm, president of Bonny Doon Vineyard in Santa Cruz, to offer up the five other things that annoy him about the Aussies:

**1. Rupert Murdoch** and the Fox network in general ("24" isn't enough to redeem either of them).

**2. Statements** prefaced with the assurance: "I'm descended from free men y'know, mate."

**3. "Jammy" as a** word to describe a wine rather than a garment you retire in.

**4. The exploitation** of wombats, koalas, cockatoos and other wildlife on wine labels.

**5. Grown men** biting one another's ears, even if only during rugby scrums.

SO SUE ME [By Milt Policzer]

## I'm OK, You're OK

**From Kehyan vs. Sarkissian, a dental malpractice complaint, in Los Angeles County Superior Court:**

"In the process of removing one of Plaintiff's wisdom teeth, Defendant Sarkissian severed Plaintiff's right lingual nerve. Rather than admit to his mistake, Defendant Sarkissian advised Plaintiff that the pain, lack of taste, and lack of sensation were normal."

TWO-WORD TALE
[By M. Stanley Bubien]

## Why There Could Be a Rush on Nausea Medication When the Rolling Stones Perform at Today's Halftime Show

Wardrobe malfunction.

ILLUSTRATION BY PHILIP BURKE; PHOTOGRAPH BY STEVEN SENNE/ASSOCIATED PRESS WEST MAGAZINE : FEBRUARY 5, 2006 11

SILVER

**LOS ANGELES TIMES**

Staff

Illustration, staff

These illustrations are quite lively, and there's consistency in the differences. You never know what style will be used. The quality of each single illustration is phenomenal. There are many styles, and that variety makes this entry succeed. The illustrations are tasteful and polished.

Estas ilustraciones son muy vivaces y hay consistencia en las diferencias. Nunca se sabe qué estilo se va a usar. La calidad de cada una de las ilustraciones es fenomenal. Hay muchos estilos y esa variedad hace que esta pieza tenga éxito. Las ilustraciones tienen buen gusto y están bien pulidas.

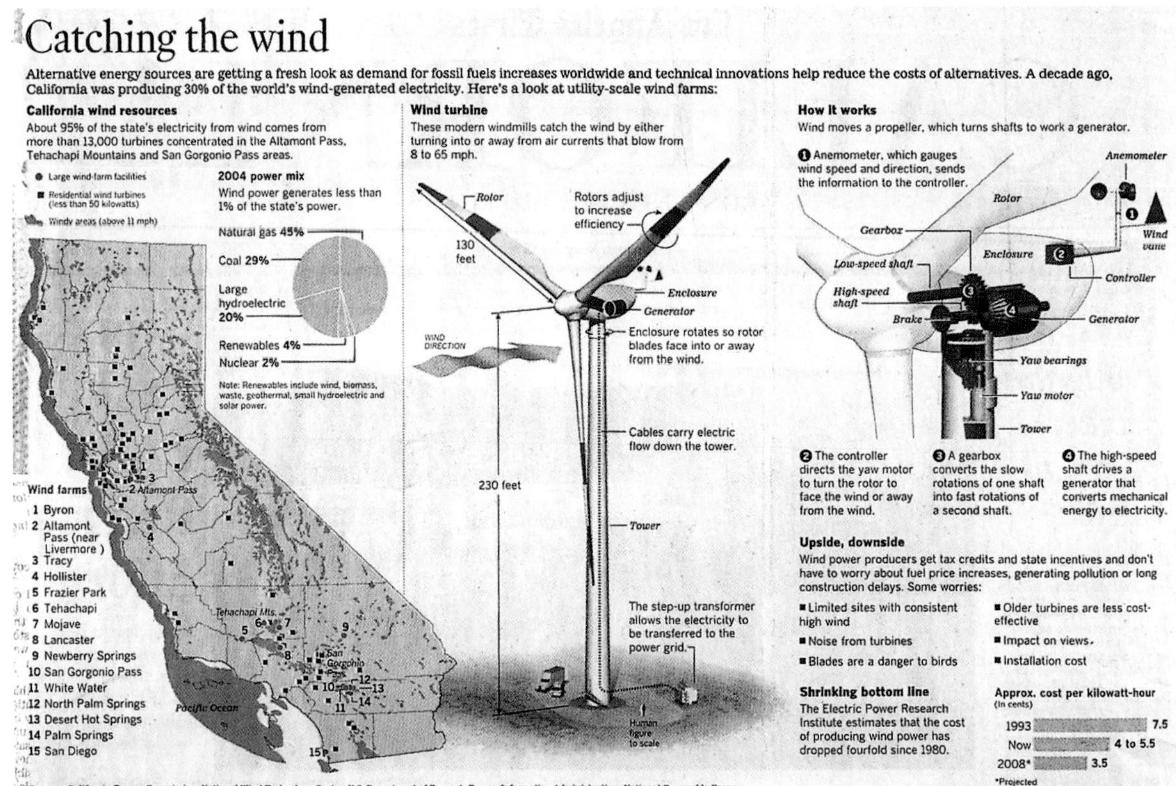

Catching the wind
Alternative energy sources are getting a fresh look as demand for fossil fuels increases worldwide and technical innovations help reduce the costs of alternatives. A decade ago, California was producing 30% of the world's wind-generated electricity. Here's a look at utility-scale wind farms:
California wind resources
About 95% of the state's electricity from wind comes from more than 13,000 turbines concentrated in the Altamont Pass, Tehachapi Mountains and San Gorgonio Pass areas.
Large wind-farm facilities
Residential wind turbines (less than 50 kilowatts)
Windy areas (above 11 mph)
2004 power mix
Wind power generates less than 1% of the state's power.
Natural gas 45%
Coal 29%
Large hydroelectric 20%
Renewables 4%
Nuclear 2%
Note: Renewables include wind, biomass, waste, geothermal, small hydroelectric and solar power.
Wind farms
1 Byron
2 Altamont Pass (near Livermore )
3 Tracy
4 Hollister
5 Frazier Park
6 Tehachapi
7 Mojave
8 Lancaster
9 Newberry Springs
10 San Gorgonio Pass
11 White Water
12 North Palm Springs
13 Desert Hot Springs
14 Palm Springs
15 San Diego
Altamont Pass
Tehachapi Mts.
San Gorgonio
Pacific Ocean
Wind turbine
These modern windmills catch the wind by either turning into or away from air currents that blow from 8 to 65 mph.
Rotor
Rotors adjust to increase efficiency
130 feet
Enclosure
Generator
WIND DIRECTION
Enclosure rotates so rotor blades face into or away from the wind.
Cables carry electric flow down the tower.
230 feet
Tower
The step-up transformer allows the electricity to be transferred to the power grid.
Human figure to scale
How it works
Wind moves a propeller, which turns shafts to work a generator.
1 Anemometer, which gauges wind speed and direction, sends the information to the controller.
Anemometer
Rotor
Wind vane
Gearbox
Enclosure
Low-speed shaft
Controller
High-speed shaft
Brake
Generator
Yaw bearings
Yaw motor
Tower
2 The controller directs the yaw motor to turn the rotor to face the wind or away from the wind.
3 A gearbox converts the slow rotations of one shaft into fast rotations of a second shaft.
4 The high-speed shaft drives a generator that converts mechanical energy to electricity.
Upside, downside
Wind power producers get tax credits and state incentives and don't have to worry about fuel price increases, generating pollution or long construction delays. Some worries:
Limited sites with consistent high wind
Noise from turbines
Blades are a danger to birds
Older turbines are less cost-effective
Impact on views
Installation cost
Shrinking bottom line
The Electric Power Research Institute estimates that the cost of producing wind power has dropped fourfold since 1980.
Approx. cost per kilowatt-hour (In cents)
1993 7.5
Now 4 to 5.5
2008* 3.5
*Projected
Sources: California Energy Commission, National Wind Technology Center, U.S. Department of Energy's Energy Information Administration, National Renewable Energy Laboratory, UC Berkeley Geoimages, L.A. Department of Water and Power, Southern California Edison. Graphics reporting by Cheryl Brownstein-Santiago
Recent regional explainer graphics are available at latimes.com/localgraphics


**LOS ANGELES TIMES**

Raoul Rañoa, Lorena Iñiguez, Doug Stevens, Perry Perez, Leslie Carlson, Cheryl Brownstein-Santiago, Tom Reinken, Thomas Suh Lauder, Doug Smith, Les Dunseith

Information graphics, staff, extended coverage, 175,000+

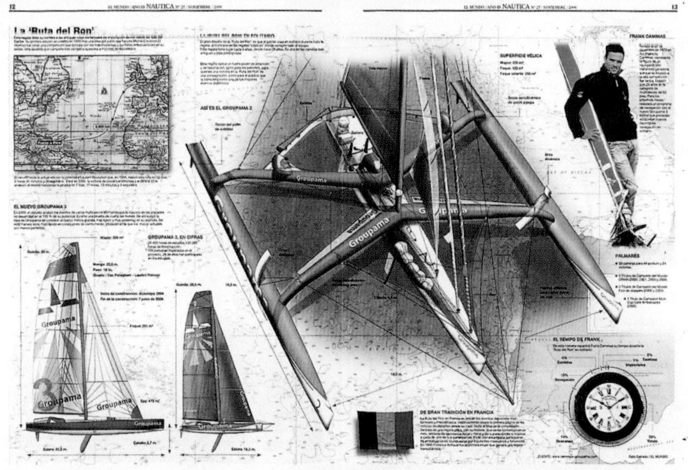
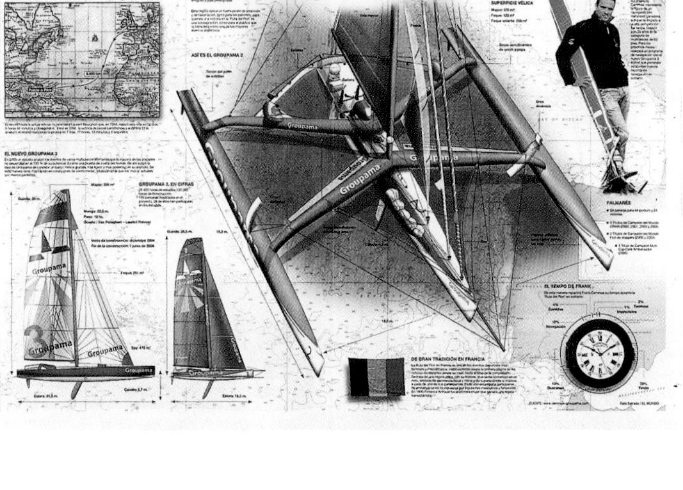


**EL MUNDO DEL SIGLO XXI**
Madrid, Spain

Rafa Estrada

Information graphics, individual, non-breaking news & features, 175,000+

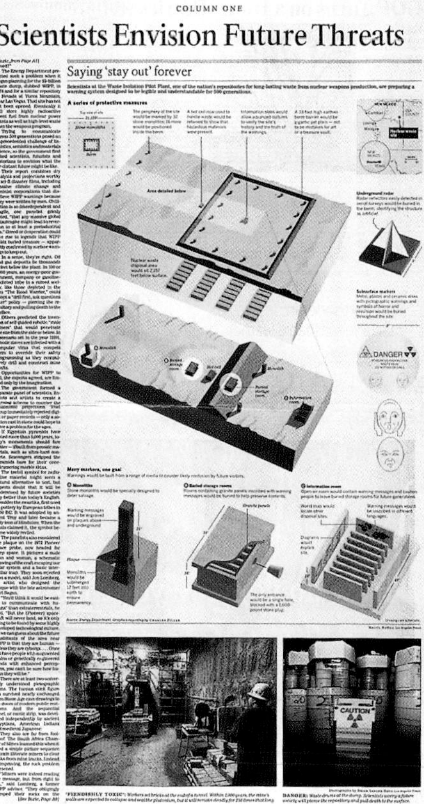

COLUMN ONE
Scientists Envision Future Threats
Saying 'stay out' forever
DANGER


**LOS ANGELES TIMES**

Raoul Rañoa

Information graphics, individual, non-breaking news & features, 175,000+

Una explosión de gas lleva el horror al verano de Laredo
Tres miembros de una familia de Bilbao y dos vecinas de Getxo mueren intoxicados por el humo
Unos cuarenta inquilinos fueron desalojados tras permanecer una hora atrapados por las llamas
Un niño de 4 años, con graves quemaduras


**EL CORREO,** Bilbao, Spain

Fernando G. Baptista, José Miguel Benítez, Gonzalo de las Heras, Daniel Garcia, Isabel Toledo, María Almela, Saioa Exteazarra, Bárbara Sarrionainda, Jorge Dragonetti

Information graphics, staff, breaking news, 50,000-174,999

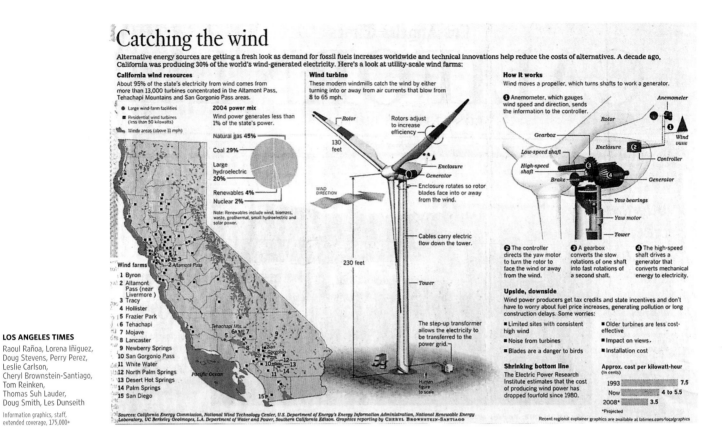

Chapter Ten

# REDESIGNS

Rediseños

**Overall Newspaper / Sections / Pages**

Periódico total / Secciones / Páginas

**EXPRESSO,** Lisbon, Portugal

Marco Grieco, Pedro Figueiral, Jorge Barbosa, Teresa Hasse e Silva, João Paulo Galacho, Jaime Figueiredo, Luiz Carvalho, Javier Errea

Overall newspaper

UMA AGENDA DIFERENTE
Livro Banif/Expresso 52 Ideias GRÁTIS no próximo sábado
Expresso
24h
Hezbollah suspeita de Luís Amado
"É uma questão absurda", considera o MNE. Mas em causa pode estar a segurança dos militares portugueses
27 nomes de que vamos ouvir falar
Durão e Sócrates disputam palco europeu
Uma antevisão original do Ano Novo
Liga e Federação não têm colaborado
Rali em três áreas protegidas
SÓ AQUI GANHA DUAS VEZES

After

GRÁTIS
CONFIE EM QUEM LHE QUER BEM
Expresso
24 HORAS
10 mil professores pedem para não dar aulas
Ramos-Horta vai explicar-se na ONU
40 mil milhões
30 DIAS que param o mundo
500 milhões
1 casa
40 mil
36 milhões
Alemanha pede foto de 'skin' português
«Ainda vão fazer dos ricos Madres Teresas»
«Progressões automáticas acabam»
«Nove milhões em subsídios têm uso indevido»
Dividendos dividem Galp
Borges
Vencer o deserto
CORREIO EXPRESSO
808 30 40 20

Before

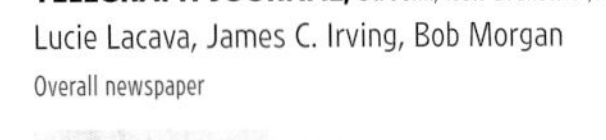

**TELEGRAPH-JOURNAL,** St. John, New Brunswick, Canada

Lucie Lacava, James C. Irving, Bob Morgan

Overall newspaper

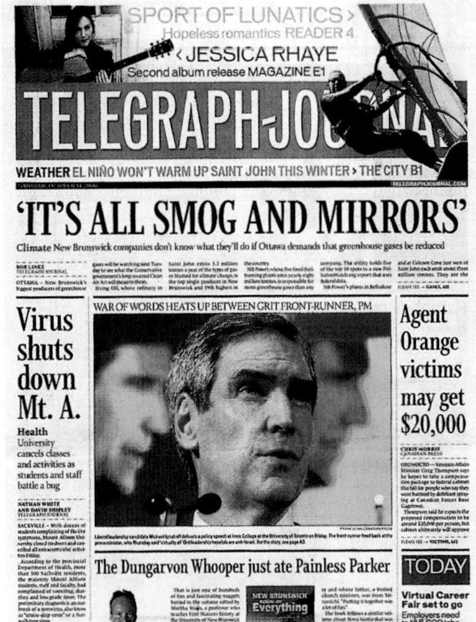
SPORT OF LUNATICS › Hopeless romantics READER 4
‹ JESSICA RHAYE Second album release MAGAZINE E1
TELEGRAPH-JOURNAL
WEATHER EL NIÑO WON'T WARM UP SAINT JOHN THIS WINTER › THE CITY B1
'IT'S ALL SMOG AND MIRRORS'
Climate New Brunswick companies don't know what they'll do if Ottawa demands that greenhouse gases be reduced
WAR OF WORDS HEATS UP BETWEEN GRIT FRONT-RUNNER, PM
Virus shuts down Mt. A.
Health University cancels classes and activities as students and staff battle a bug
Agent Orange victims may get $20,000
The Dungarvon Whooper just ate Painless Parker
TODAY
Virtual Career Fair set to go
Goldsmith Studio at SEARS
One of the Largest Selections of Set & Loose Diamonds in Eastern Canada

After

TELEGRAPH-JOURNAL
Torrential rain compounds quake misery
Moncton falls short of Cup quest
Report pans expensive Liberal Kyoto strategy
Passports would devastate tourism south of the border, poll indicates
Giant sponge could sop up emissions

Before

**EL PAIS,** Madrid, Spain

Carlos Perez-Díaz, Montse Ortiz Roca, Staff

Overall newspaper

HOY, REVISTA PAULA Y LA SERIE "19 DEPARTAMENTOS"
EL PAIS
Fiesta de luces en la costa
La rambla se prepara para los fuegos artificiales
Dos directores camino al Oscar
Clint Eastwood y Pedro Almodóvar reciben premios en Nueva York
URUGUAY MÁS DURO CON MERCOSUR
Reclamo. Volverá a exigir en Brasilia poder firmar acuerdos de comercio bilaterales
Alertan sobre riesgo de una posible crisis de la energía
Juez duda que al fin se otorgue extradición
Severos controles en la rambla
Inauguran Instituto Pasteur que apunta a ser el parque biotecnológico regional
HOY RECLAMÁ CON PAULA TU H2Oh!

After

VUELVE MONTEVIDEO MIAMI SIN ESCALAS
EL PAIS
Ley busca reabrir juicios cerrados por la caducidad
Astori se opone a aplicar deducción
Gremiales piden más intervención
Hay 4.500 autos en depósitos
Primer gran incendio en la costa obligó a cortar la ruta
hoy y todos los martes gratis
CRONOLOGIA

Before

**DIÁRIO DE NOTÍCIAS,** Lisbon, Portugal
Henriqúe Cayatte
Overall newspaper

# Diário de Notícias

Domingo | 19 de Março de 2006 | Ano 142.º | N.º 50 027 | 1,30€ www.dn.pt
Director António José Teixeira | Directores adjuntos João Morgado Fernandes | Eduardo Dâmaso | Helena Garrido

Revista
**Notícias Magazine**
Filhos que seguiram as pisadas dos pais no futebol, na música, ou na política
As surpresas dos mais pequenos na "Terra do Nunca"

Justiça 20 e 21
**Como se forma um juiz de direito?**

Porto 30
**Reformados e estudantes com desconto no metro**

Entrevista 34 e 35
**Maria Filomena Mónica contra controleiros da herança de Eça de Queirós**

Media 40
**Blogues também estão sujeitos às leis civis e criminais**

## Irregularidades crescem nas escolas de condução

**Relatórios da Direcção-Geral de Viação revelam um "acréscimo de processos-crimes" nos últimos anos** 2 a 4

## Cidades francesas contestam Governo na rua

**Contrato de Primeiro Emprego gera protesto de estudantes, sindicatos e partidos de esquerda** Fernando de Sousa, em Paris 12

Iraque

Especial
## Memória de três anos de terror sem Saddam

**Balanço de uma guerra num suplemento de oito páginas**
**Entrevista com Tarik Ali, historiador anglo-paquistanês, e Editorial**

CONGRESSO
## PSD escolhe directas e Mendes candidata-se
5 e 6



*After*

dn domingo
As células estaminais que causam polémica mas salvam vidas
Baianos desavindos
Caetano Veloso publica carta aberta em que critica a política do ministro Gilberto Gil
Página 37
CIÊNCIA. Pág. 48
Revelado o mistério do crânio de Mozart
Peterhansel já é líder

Diário de Notícias

A partir de amanhã, um novo DN. O diário de Portugal.

Cavaco aponta erros à esquerda e Soares garante que vai à 2.ª volta

PS mobiliza-se para apoiar o seu candidato. Líderes do PSD e do CDS entram na campanha. Faltam duas semanas para as eleições

Reportagem nos bastiões rosa e laranja de Leiria

FRANÇOIS MITTERRAND 1916 - 1996
Le promeneur Paris

HOMENAGEM. Mazarine, ontem, em Paris, na inauguração de uma exposição sobre o pai

Dez anos sem Mitterrand
"Entre os presidentes da V República, há De Gaulle e o meu pai."
ENTREVISTA COM MAZARINE PINGEOT

Imigrantes PÁGS. 22 E 23
Religiões unidas sob o mesmo tecto às portas de Lisboa
Católicos, adventistas, muçulmanos. Todas as religiões são bem-vindas ao Espaço de Culto da Quinta do Mocho

SOCIEDADE. Pág. 26
Cuidados paliativos esquecem crianças

INTERNACIONAL. Pág. 15
Chefe do exército detido em Espanha

DESPORTO. Pág. 30
Sporting derrotado num jogo de nervos em Braga



*Before*

**LA TRIBUNE,** Paris
Mario Garcia, Christian Fontanet, Henri Houssay, Anne Debray
Overall newspaper

**BUSINESS MANAGERS** / P. 14
Pourquoi externaliser la logistique des ventes.

**ANALYSES** / P. 22
Vers un marché des dirigeants d'entreprise.

**TRIBUNES** / P. 30
Chronique internationale : L'Union fait-elle la vertu ?

**RENDEZ-VOUS PERSO** / P. 35
Bientôt, la voiture anti-accident.

# La Tribune

www.latribune.fr

Mercredi 20 décembre 2006 - N° 3.564 - 1,20 € - France métropolitaine

## Patrick Ricard lève le voile sur sa succession

■ Le PDG de Pernod-Ricard a tout réglé pour son départ en 2008.
■ Dans un entretien à « La Tribune », il laisse entendre qu'un membre de la famille lui succédera… mais pas dans l'immédiat.

*L'idéal pour moi, ce serait naturellement qu'un Ricard me succède un jour »* : Patrick Ricard, qui cédera les rênes du numéro deux mondial des spiritueux en 2008, a déjà préparé sa succession. Pour lui, ses deux neveux César Giron, 42 ans, et Alexandre Ricard, 33 ans, seront tous deux à même de diriger le groupe dans quelques années. Dans l'intervalle, c'est Pierre Pringuet, 56 ans, actuel directeur général délégué de Pernod-Ricard, qui semble le mieux placé pour prendre la relève.

En attendant, après le rachat de Seagram et d'Allied Domecq, le challenger français va poursuivre ses acquisitions ciblées pour se rapprocher du leader mondial Diageo. Le rachat de la vodka Stolichnaya semble bien engagé.

P. 32 et 33

M 00160 - 1220 - F: 1,20 €

**360°**
L'ESSENTIEL DE L'ACTUALITÉ EN PAGES 2 ET 3

■ **ENTREPRISES**
**GAZ DE FRANCE-SUEZ**
Un nouveau calendrier devrait être évoqué aujourd'hui. Il pourrait remettre en cause le mariage. P. 6

## Euronext-Nyse : la fusion plébiscitée

À 98,2 %, les actionnaires d'Euronext présents ou représentés (soit 65 % au total) hier à Amsterdam à l'assemblée générale de la Bourse paneuropéenne ont donné leur bénédiction à sa fusion avec la Bourse de New York. Les actionnaires de cette dernière se prononcent aujourd'hui sur le sujet. Le New York Stock Exchange n'aura alors plus qu'à attendre le feu vert définitif des régulateurs d'Euronext et du ministre des Finances néerlandais pour déposer formellement son offre sur Euronext. Plus rien ne saurait donc empêcher la naissance de la première Bourse transatlantique libellée en euros qui deviendrait du même coup un *« partenaire de choix »* pour des Bourses comme Milan ou Madrid, voire asiatiques.

P. 18 et éditorial P. 50

## L'hôpital va faire plus d'heures supplémentaires

Serait-ce un premier coup de canif porté aux 35 heures à l'hôpital ? Le gouvernement prépare un décret afin d'augmenter le recours aux heures supplémentaires dans les établissements publics de santé. Le quota passera de 120 à 220 heures sup annuelles pour les personnels soignants spécialisés. L'objectif est de faire face à la pénurie de personnel. P. 26

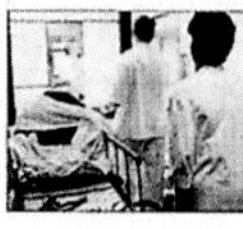

## L' Allemagne pleine de confiance en l'avenir

L'indice IFO du climat des affaires en novembre a enregistré un gain plus fort qu'attendu, les chefs d'entreprise étant désormais optimistes pour la mi-2007. Cela signifie que la baisse de la consommation prévisible cet hiver du fait de la hausse de la TVA ne serait qu'une brève pause. Surtout, les patrons continuent de tabler sur de belles perspectives à l'export. Car le pays est bien placé pour tirer parti des achats d'équipement des pays émergents en forte croissance.

P. 27

*After*

Aérien. Ryanair part à l'assaut d'Aer Lingus P. 15

La Tribune

Vendredi 6 et samedi 7 octobre 2006 - 1,20 € LE QUOTIDIEN ÉCONOMIQUE ET FINANCIER www.latribune.fr

LA MARQUE FÊTE SES 40 ANS
Benetton cherche des habits neufs
Le groupe, qui a construit sa renommée sur ses pulls, peine à retrouver sa place sur un marché de l'habillement très encombré. P. 38 ET 39

▶ ÉCONOMIE
TABAC. De nouvelles aides pour les buralistes. P. 5

▶ ENTREPRISES
PSA. Philippe Varin, candidat favori de Folz pour lui succéder. P. 14
TECHNOLOGIES. Les Chinois à la peine sur la high-tech occidentale. P. 17

▶ FINANCE
ASSURANCE. Les courtiers s'unissent pour défendre leur profession. P. 21

▶ MARCHÉS
AUTOMOBILE. Le divorce entre Renault et GM rassure la Bourse. P. 26
SPIRITUEUX. Pernod-Ricard se dote d'un dispositif anti-OPA. P. 26

EXPERTISES
La responsabilité élargie des commissaires aux comptes devant l'AMF. P. 35

DOSSIER PLACEMENTS
OPCVM : les belles promesses de la multigestion. P. 40 À 43

M 00160 - 1006 - F: 1,20 €

La crise s'amplifie chez Airbus et EADS

■ Après le retard de deux ans de l'A380, des incertitudes pesent sur les programmes A350 et A400M. ■ Un petit actionnaire allemand attaque EADS, estimant que le groupe a dissimulé ses difficultés industrielles. P. 12, 13 ET ÉDITORIAL P. 44

MSN007

LE TAUX DIRECTEUR EST PORTÉ À 3,25 %
Cinquième tour de vis monétaire de la BCE
Réunie à Paris pour son second conseil annuel décentralisé, la Banque centrale européenne a procédé à la cinquième hausse de son taux directeur depuis l'enclenchement du cycle en décembre dernier, pour le porter à 3,25 %. Lors de sa traditionnelle conférence de presse, son président, Jean-Claude Trichet, jugeant la politique monétaire de la zone euro toujours accommodante, a laissé anticiper un nouveau tour de vis cette année. Il devrait intervenir lors de la réunion de la BCE du 7 décembre. P. 2 ET 3

CONSOLIDATION BOURSIÈRE
Lachmann s'oppose à la fusion Euronext-Nyse
Très attendues, les conclusions de son rapport de place renvoient les Bourses américaine et allemande dos à dos. P. 23

BANQUE
Le Crédit Agricole veut se déployer en Italie
Il négocie ferme avec Banca Intesa sur la gestion d'actifs et s'apprête à acquérir un réseau de banques de détail. P. 21

*Before*

**PARI DAILY,** Sofia, Bulgaria

Valentin Panayotov, Zdravko Spassov, Stefan Nedelchev, Zdravka Simeonova, Darina Dimova, Evgeni Gavrilov, Dimitar Djenev, Rosen Todorovsky

Overall newspaper

Бюджет 2007

Спор за размера на осигуровките

Пари

www.pari.bg

Сряда

1.01.2007 г. Влизаме в европейското семейство

Три години под лупа в Европа

Плашат ни с предрязни клаузи и орязване на субсидиите в случай на изоставане

Инвеститор

Днес пліос

2856

www.pari.bg Бизнесът призова да станем данъчен шампион на общността

*After*

ПАРИ

ПАРИ + weekend

Индустрията на колене пред газа

Държавен монополизъм в пристанищата

Как се налага българско мляко в Европа

Годината на трилобия съюз

Хората ще продължат да вярват в мен

КОЛЕДНА ПРОМОЦИЯ!

*Before*

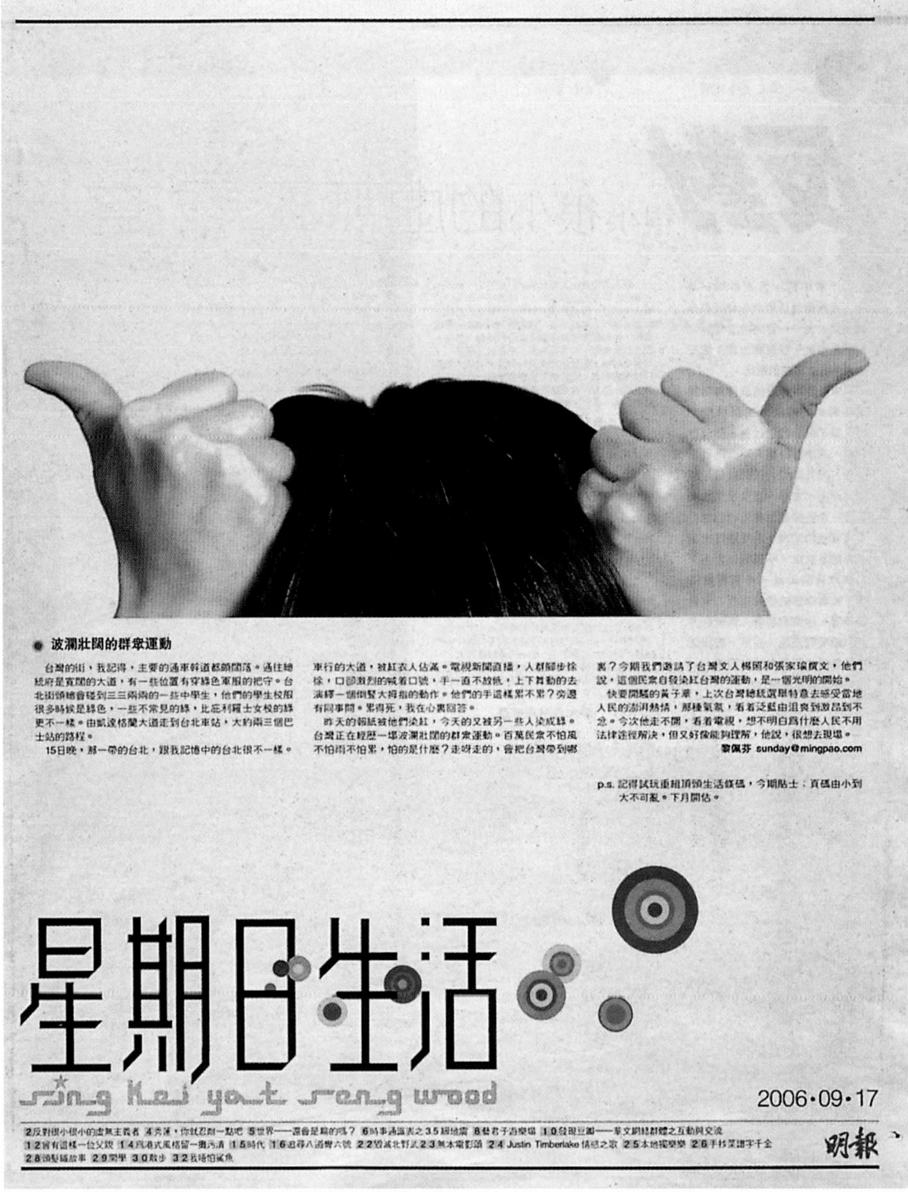

● 波瀾壯闊的群衆運動

p.s. 記得試玩重組頂頭生活媒碼，今期貼士：頁碼由小到大不可亂。下月開估。

黎佩芬 sunday@mingpao.com

星期日生活

sing kei yat sang wood

2006•09•17

明報

*After*

**MING PAO,** Hong Kong

Chun Wong Wu, Ping Hsian Wang, Li Chau

Section

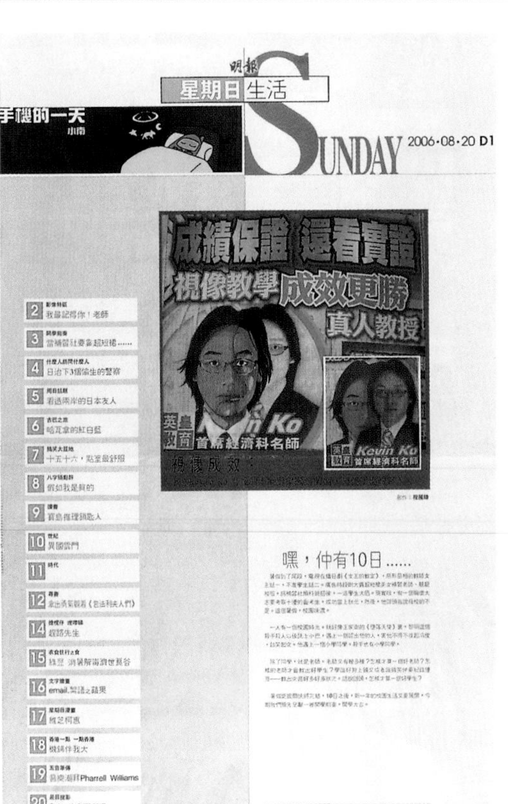

明報

星期日生活

SUNDAY 2006•08•20 D1

手機的一天

成績保證 還看實證

視像教學 成效更勝

真人教授

Kevin Ko

嘿，仲有10日……

*Before*

**MING PAO,** Hong Kong
Ming Chit Yeung, Ping Hsian Wang
Section

TRENDY

Converse★

香港第一店

南韓別注版秋冬裝

All Star籃球鞋起家

F-N-E-W-S

穿金戴銀起步點

Converse概念店

電話：2627 5630

12

13

*After*

teens Focus

涼茶文化

世代相傳

百年老牌「草眼佬涼茶」

飲涼茶也是生活習慣

涼茶Q & A

涼茶舖各具秘方

廿四味

五花茶

直擊製作過程

6

7

*Before*

**EL ECONOMISTA,** Madrid, Spain

Miguel Buckenmeyer, Victor Arias

Section

Así van los mercados

Ibex 35

Mercado continuo

After

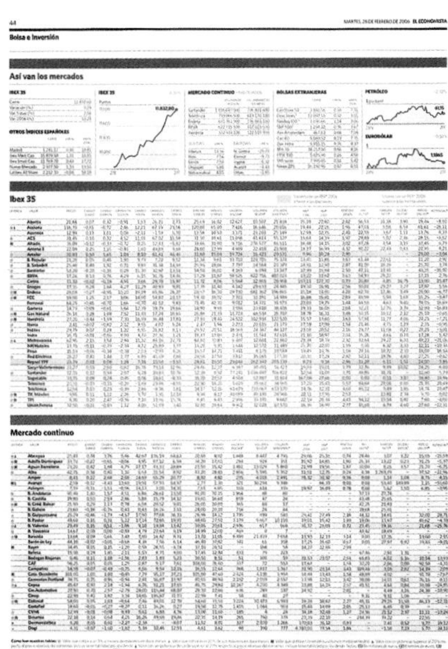

Así van los mercados

Ibex 35

Mercado continuo

Before

18 / LaTribune MARDI 12 DÉCEMBRE 2006 www.latribune.fr

# MARCHÉS & FINANCE

*Les Places, l'Industrie financière*

**PLACES.** WALL STREET VISE 10 % DE HAUSSE POUR LE S&P 500 EN 2007 P. 19

**INDUSTRIE FINANCIÈRE.** UN MARIAGE ENTRE BANK OF AMERICA ET BARCLAYS NE FAIT PAS L'UNANIMITÉ P. 22

**ANALYSES.** LES STRATÉGIES POUR CONTRER L'APPÉTIT DES FONDS P. 24

## Ils bougent

**SGSS ESPAGNE**

**Paloma Pedrola**

Directeur des services aux investisseurs de Société Générale Securities Services en Espagne, elle succède à Jean-Louis Vayne, appelé à la direction des opérations internationales au sein des services aux investisseurs. Paloma Pedrola était responsable du contrôle du département Global Securities Services chez Citibank International Plc.

**MIG**

**Dr Thierry Chignon**

Précédemment directeur de la BU européenne Medtech de Quintiles Consulting, il devient le troisième associé responsable de la gestion des fonds Matignon Technologies chez Matignon Investissement et Gestion.

**CRÉDIT AGRICOLE SA**

**Marc Carlos**

Jusqu'ici président du directoire d'Eurofactor, il a été nommé directeur des banques de détail à l'international de Crédit Agricole SA. 47 ans, X-Mines, Marc Carlos a débuté au ministère de l'Industrie et de la Recherche, puis il a occupé successivement les postes d'ingénieur d'affaires chez Borie SAE, directeur de projet chez SAE, DG du groupe Lacroix (1992-1997) et de sa filiale Duarib, puis président du directoire de Sofrel (1998-2001).

**EULER HERMES SFAC**

**Nicolas Delzant**

54 ans, Essec, il devient membre du directoire, responsable des directions de l'arbitrage, du réseau risques ainsi que du recouvrement et de l'indemnisation, en France, Espagne, Grèce, Maroc, Portugal et Turquie. Philippe Bastié, 46 ans, docteur ès sciences économiques, DESS IAE, son adjoint depuis 2004 après cinq ans chez Euler Hermes aux États-Unis, le remplace comme directeur des risques groupe.

*fdegan@latribune.fr*

## Rothschild amarre l'Afrique et l'Asie à son royaume financier

**BANQUE**

La banque donne aujourd'hui le coup d'envoi à ses activités de conseil en fusions au Moyen-Orient. Pour David de Rothschild le modèle économique de sa banque est adapté à la région.

Pour les métiers de la banque d'affaires et d'investissement, les pays émergents apparaissent chaque jour un peu plus comme un véritable relais de croissance. Rothschild & Cie n'a pas attendu qu'ils soient à la mode. Fort de l'expertise de ses maisons londonienne et parisienne le groupe sur lequel règne en maître depuis 2003 David de Rothschild n'a, de l'Amérique du Sud à l'Asie en passant par l'Afrique, eu de cesse de développer un solide réseau de bureaux locaux.

Plus récemment, les projections faites de Londres comme de Paris sur *« ce théâtre des opérations extérieures de la banque »* ont rapidement fait prendre conscience au baron que le Moyen-Orient serait rapidement appelé à devenir un quartier général. Aussi David de Rothschild a-t-il placé au début de cette année la région au rang des priorités de son groupe. Ce cheval de bataille, Lionel Zinsou, associé gérant de la banque auquel le baron a confié la responsabilité de Rothschild Middle East and Africa s'en est promptement emparé.

**DOUBLE ENJEU**

Chez Rothschild efficacité fait loi : le groupe a obtenu hier du Dubai Financial Services Authority (DFSA), équivalent aux Émirats arabes unis du FSA britannique ou de notre Commission bancaire française, sa licence de banque pour opérer et rayonner sur la région voire au-delà au sein du Dubai International Financial Center (DIFC). Les ambitions régionales de cette Bourse tout récemment démutualisée et cotée depuis peu ont séduit Rothschild. La banque donne officiellement aujourd'hui le coup d'envoi à ses activités de conseil en fusions-acquisitions, financement de la dette au Moyen-Orient.

LE BARON A PRIS CONSCIENCE QUE LE MOYEN-ORIENT SERAIT RAPIDEMENT APPELÉ À DEVENIR UN QUARTIER GÉNÉRAL.

Pour David de Rothschild le *« modèle économique »* de sa banque qui repose exclusivement sur le conseil, ou *advisory* dans le jargon anglo-saxon, et a fait son succès ces dernières années en le hissant dans les premiers rangs des classements officiels. Il lui *« parait parfaitement adapté à la région »*. Aussi pour lui comme pour Lionel Zinsou, qui s'est vu confier la présidence de cette activité bancaire dans le Golfe, l'enjeu est double.

Dans un premier temps, il s'agit de faire de Dubaï, où de grands groupes internationaux ne cessent d'implanter leur siège pour le Moyen-Orient d'abord et ensuite pour l'Asie, une tête de pont sur l'Europe. Ces grands groupes internationaux comme les acteurs locaux ont déjà fait montre d'un réel courant de sympathie à l'égard du groupe Rothschild. D'autant que ce dernier, en conseillant dernièrement Dubai Ports World d'un côté dans son opération de rachat de Peninsular and Oriental, plus connu sous le nom de P&O, et de l'autre le consortium gouvernemental de Dubaï et Abou Dhabi pour le rachat de SR Technic's, finit par étayer sa réputation déjà solide dans la région.

Et Rothschild n'entend pas en rester là dans le golfe Persique. Alors que son QG à Dubaï placé sous la direction de Michael Helou attendra la visite de David fin décembre pour voir débarquer de Londres et de Paris les renforts nécessaires à la constitution d'une véritable force de frappe opérationnelle à partir du DIFC, il est d'ores et déjà question d'ouvrir très vite des bureaux à Abou Dhabi, autre place forte à l'ouest des Émirats arabes unis et au Qatar.

Dans un second temps, son rôle de tête de pont, Dubaï le jouera à plus fortes raisons en direction de l'Asie. Car *« si d'un point de vue européen, notre présence à Dubaï et dans le Golfe fait réellement du sens, d'un point de vue asiatique elle est devenue une impérieuse nécessité »*, confie Lionel Zinsou.

**CENTRE DE GRAVITÉ**

Et David de lui rappeler que c'est des bureaux de Bombay, de Shanghai, de Hong Kong et de Singapour que *« la création d'une plateforme pour ne pas dire d'un hub au Moyen-Orient est apparue comme un impératif pour le groupe »*. La région, et Dubaï en particulier, constitue ni plus ni moins le centre de gravité pour asseoir définitivement le développement des activités de banques d'affaires et d'investissement sur le continent indien, l'Asie du Sud-Est mais aussi pour l'Asie centrale et notamment le Kazakhstan. C'est d'ailleurs la raison pour laquelle d'autres « majors » de la banque d'affaires et d'investissement comme Morgan Stanley, Crédit Suisse, Merrill Lynch, JP Morgan Chase et Goldman Sachs ont au cours des dix-huit derniers mois délocalisé une partie de leurs équipes à Dubaï. ■

BRUNO SEGRÉ

**› À l'affiche**

**DAVID DE ROTHSCHILD**

*Président du groupe Rothschild*

Dans trois jours le baron fêtera ses **64 ans.** Un anniversaire qu'il ne célébrera probablement pas à New York, sa ville de naissance : il s'apprête en effet en cette fin d'année à faire une tournée dans les pays du Golfe. Le business passe avant tout pour David de Rothschild. À plus forte raison depuis qu'en 2003 sir Evelyn, son cousin, lui a passé le témoin pour **présider** les banques **Rothschild & Cie** et **NM Rothschild & Sons** réunies la même année.

After

**LA TRIBUNE,** Paris

Mario Garcia, Christian Fontanet, Henri Houssay, Anne Debray

Section

La Tribune DES MARCHÉS

La société présentait ses résultats semestriels hier

Vinci multiplie les gestes envers ses actionnaires

LVMH améliore fortement sa rentabilité

Before

UDLAND
**Ford helede USA's dybe sår**

ERHVERV
**Fart på bagmandspolitiet**

LEDER
**Forskning på is**

# MORGENAVISEN Jyllands-Posten

MADANMELDELSE
**Restaurant Piaf i Silkeborg**

# Udlændinge åbner fem nye firmaer i Danmark om dagen

**Arbejdsmarked:** Antallet af udenlandske virksomheder i Danmark er eksploderet. Hver dag kommer fem nye til. Tyskere og polakker er de mest aktive i Danmark. Dansk Byggeri er begejstret over udviklingen.

De nye gæstearbejdere

## Gæmelke: Stop lange transporter af smågrise

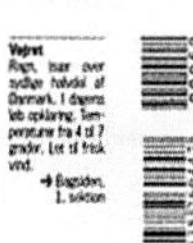

JP'S NYTÅRSSPIL

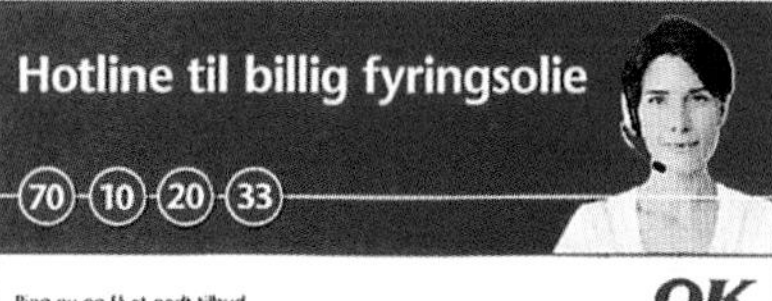

*After*

**MORGENAVISEN JYLLANDS-POSTEN,** Viby, Denmark
Lars Pryds
Section

*Before*

**THE KANSAS CITY STAR** (Mo.)
Randy Wyrick, Tom Dolphens, Barbara Hill-Meyer, Jill Silva
Section

SCHOOL LUNCH | Boosting the nutrition

# REAP IT AND EAT

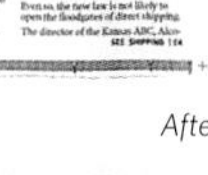

## HUBRIS DOESN'T CHANGE FLAWED LAW

*After*

# food

The label says it all

# WOK OF AGES

Ancient pan proves its mettle in modern kitchens

## Banana's Caribbean cousin has a bunch to offer

*Before*

**THE GAZETTE,** Montreal

Nuri Ducassi, Dawn Lemieux, Marie Cuffaro, Peter Cooney, Catherine Wallace

Section

INSIGHT

LIVING DOWN THE PAST

GOLDEN SPICE

PRESSURE'S ON: HARPER AND CHAREST MUST DELIVER GOODS

Brrrrr!

IS THIS THE FUTURE OF CONSERVATION?

THEY SAID IT

Before

A12 THE GAZETTE | MONTREAL | SUNDAY, JUNE 18, 2006

# INSIGHT

## 'THE URBANIZATION OF POVERTY'

WHAT THAT HEADLINE MEANS IS THAT MORE THAN A BILLION PEOPLE NOW LIVE IN BLEAK, HOPELESS SLUMS

BUSTEES . SLUMS . FAVELAS . CIUDADES PERDIDAS . VILLAS MISERIAS . BUSTEES . BIDONVILLES . SLUM

THE GAZETTE | MONTREAL | SUNDAY, JUNE 18, 2006 A13

QUOTE OF THE WEEK

*"The treatment of mental health is exceedingly complex. If there wasn't such a stigma about mental illness, we'd have even better treatment."*

Jacques Hendlisz, director-general of the Douglas Hospital

## Angola's oil wealth hasn't trickled down to the thirsty people

GOVERNMENT IS AWASH WITH CASH BUT THERE'S A HUGE WATER SHORTAGE AND CHOLERA HAS MADE A COMEBACK

After

Detroit News: Nolan Finley on Granholm's betrayal

Letters: Donald Rumsfeld insults Americans

Ron Dzwonkowski: Young people on the move

ON POINT

Detroit Free Press

Liberals remake Barry Goldwater

YES! NO!

FREE PRESS EDITORIAL

Erase Petition Deception

State should outlaw any future signature-gathering trickery

"We have to go back to 1974 (during Watergate) to find such a favorable environment. If we can't win in this environment, we have to question the whole premise of the party."

After

The Detroit News

Commentary

Privacy ends at office door

Rap draws its toughest critics yet

Bigger families aid the elderly

Watchdog

Thomas Sowell says the art of disagreeing is quickly disappearing in America. Page 14A

Before

**DETROIT FREE PRESS**

Amy Martin, Mauricio Gutierrez, Gerry Skora, Steve Dorsey

Section

la Tribuna

Apuestas del mañana

LA NUEVA GENERACIÓN DE ATLETAS SALVADOREÑOS VIENE LIDERADA POR MUJERES. LAS CHICAS PROMETEN Y DEMANDAN UNA APUESTA CONCRETA PARA SU DESARROLLO.

After

LA PRENSA GRÁFICA

la Tribuna

Historia de grandes

Before

**LA PRENSA GRÁFICA,** Antiguo Cuscatlán, El Salvador

Enrique Contreras, Héctor Ramírez, Erick Cortez, Denis García Márquez

Section

**THE KANSAS CITY STAR** (Mo.)
Tom Dolphens, Greg Branson, Gentry Mullen, Dave Olson
Section

After

Before

St. Petersburg Times | Published Sundays and Wednesdays for Pinellas Park, Kenneth City and Lealman

# Neighborhood Times

tampabay.com

Sunday, November 5, 2006 | NWE

Special report

## Streets of change

We drive them every day, whizzing along on our way to work, an afternoon matinee, the kids' soccer practice or a rendezvous with friends. But seldom do we stop to really see the changes surrounding these roads that define our communities. Today, *Neighborhood Times* examines six thoroughfares and how they've developed in five years.

**Fourth Street, 12 • Park Boulevard, 13 • 34th Street S, 14 • Tyrone Boulevard, 16 • Gandy Boulevard, 17 • Gulf Boulevard, 19**

After

**ST. PETERSBURG TIMES** (Fla.)
Nikki Life, Deborah Block, Holly Braford, Patty Cox
Section

ALLENDALE, CRESCENT LAKE, EUCLID/ST. PAUL, FEATHER SOUND, FOSSIL PARK, KENWOOD, OLD NORTHEAST, ROSER PARK, SHORE ACRES, SNELL ISLE, UPTOWN AND WOODLAWN

# NEIGHBORHOOD TIMES

SUNDAY, FEBRUARY 26, 2006 ■ A TWICE WEEKLY SECTION OF THE TIMES

## Bayway Lofts' new look

Having acquired an entire half-block for Bayway Lofts, Grady Pridgen now plans two 371-foot towers and two lower buildings with a total of 350 units. The design is described as "the idea of an undulating glass sail."

Grady Pridgen Inc.

Instead of one tower, four buildings of glass are now planned in the heart of downtown.

By SHARON L. BOND
Neighborhood Times Business Editor

ST. PETERSBURG — Developer Grady Pridgen said his ability to buy more land at the Bayway Lofts site prompted the complete overhaul of the project's design.

Bayway Lofts has morphed from the tallest building in the city, with points of interest like a rooftop restaurant and an exterior elevator, to four lower buildings of glass that look like a moving sail.

The latest design will get its first review before city development officials in April. It actually is the third look at the project.

Initial plans from 2003 called for a 510-foot tower with 42 stories that drew concern from city officials and complaints from neighbors. The project is on Third Avenue N between Second and Third streets and will replace several older houses. One of its closest neighbors is the Huntington Townhomes, which are three stories high.

The second design, introduced in 2004, included a lower tower, 371 feet with 29 stories. It had 350 units instead of the original 277. During this time, Pridgen was trying to amass a complete half-block for Bayway Lofts.

"We finally have done that," Pridgen said Friday. "That gave us the flexibility to be more creative. We

Please see BAYWAY Page 8

## Buses to continue stopping at park

■ But officials agree they shouldn't linger there, blocking the view and emitting diesel fumes.

By JON WILSON
Times Staff Writer

ST. PETERSBURG — Heart-of-downtown Williams Park, a makeover target as offices and luxury living sites go up around it, is bound for eventual change.

Exactly what will take place is not certain.

But officials and other city leaders are looking closest at homeless people who use the park and the buses that stop around its perimeter.

The homeless issue is being addressed by the county's 10-year plan and perhaps further by Mayor Rick Baker's proposal to create a city outreach function, officials say.

As for buses, chatter among riders sometimes says the vehicles are going to be sent elsewhere and Williams Park is going to be eliminated as a stop.

Officials say no.

They point out that the park is the most heavily used terminal in Pinellas County.

They cite statistics showing 68 percent of the riders who board buses there have not transferred from a bus coming in from another part of the city, but have walked from somewhere downtown.

Likewise, 56 percent of those getting off are within walking distance of their destination and do not have to transfer to another bus, statistics show.

St. Petersburg College has a downtown center. About 1,300 students use it, 35 percent coming from Midtown on a bus, said Don Shea, Downtown Partnership president.

"That's a constituency we want to encourage," Shea said.

Given all that, the upshot is: Buses won't be banned from Williams Park, but the way they come and go may be different.

Joe Kubicki is director of the city's transportation planning department.

He said reducing the amount of time the buses wait at

Please see WILLIAMS PARK Page 8

**A 'TOWN' FORMING NORTH OF GANDY:** Off Interstate 275 in St. Petersburg, La Entrada is beginning to take shape. It's a sprawling, truly mixed-use model that may take 20 years to complete. Story, **PAGE 3**

**CIVIL RIGHTS GROUP LOOKS AHEAD AND BACK:** The African-American Voters Research and Education Committee recognized efforts of the past and the challenges of the future. Story, **PAGE 4**

**FREE SCHOOL SUPPLY STORE IS NO MORE:** A Gift for Teaching of Pinellas can't keep going without operating funds, despite plenty of volunteers and donations of supplies. Story, **PAGE 5**

**OUT OF AFRICA, ART AND DIALOGUE:** An artist from Nigeria wants to share his Yoruba culture with those who like to think outside the geographic box. What's Yoruba culture, you say? Story, **PAGE 6**

**HISTORY OF MIDTOWN PUT DOWN ON PAPER:** A shared love of St. Petersburg — and history — leads to a collaboration on a book full of stories about 22nd Street S. Story, **PAGE 9**

NEA

Before

**TELEGRAPH-JOURNAL,** St. John, New Brunswick, Canada
Lucie Lacava, James C. Irving, Bob Morgan, Sue Johnson, David Stonehouse
Section

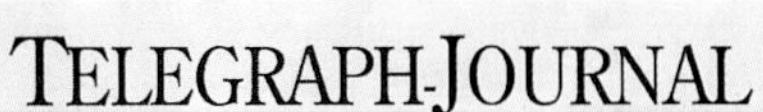

TELEGRAPH-JOURNAL

MONDAY, FEBRUARY 27, 2006 — NEW BRUNSWICK'S NEWSPAPER. EST. 1862

**Countdown to Canadian Olympics in 2010 begins**

It's time to pay for Tory campaign promises

Extreme makeover helps sell Olympics

LNG foes give PM a 'step in' deadline

Mother Ship Corp. all set to bleep Bubbles

*After*

**EL PAIS,** Madrid, Spain
Carlos Perez-Díaz, Montse Ortiz Roca, Staff
Section

**Al poder.** Las mujeres suben posiciones en la política estadounidense. **Podrida.** 1.100 millones de personas carecen de agua limpia. **Cool-hunters.** La caza de tendencias es profesión rentable en el mundo

DOMINGO

EL PAIS

EL ARTE ROBADO POR LOS NAZIS

Tesoros perdidos... y encontrados

Austria devolvió un nuevo cuadro a sus legítimos dueños judíos y la "ola de reclamos" continúa. En Alemania se lenema fijar un plazo de prescripción, pero aún prima el "deber moral"

*After*

**ST. PETERSBURG TIMES** (Fla.)
Joshua Engleman, Nikki Life, Patty Cox
Section

»literature »arts »travel

latitudes

the ultimate road trip

California's Highway 1 twists and turns through some of America's most dramatic coastal scenery. Put the top down and go.

»travel Globespotting: Readers share their vacation photos. First stop, the dunes of Namibia.

»arts Perfectly polished: How a silver pitcher inspired an obsession – and a gorgeous exhibit in St. Petersburg.

Listen to this: The latest from British rock icons Sting, Eric Clapton, Elton John and the Who.

»literature

A painful memory: An author recalls his 65-mile trudge toward inhumanity

*After*

DECISION 2006 COMPLETE PROVINCIAL ELECTION COVERAGE› INSIDE A SECTION

TELEGRAPH-JOURNAL

DECISION 2006 RIDING BY RIDING RESULTS IN SOUTHERN N.B.› INSIDE THE CITY

LIBERALS WIN

Slim majority **Shawn Graham becomes the 30th premier of New Brunswick after guiding the Grits** to a three-seat victory over Bernard Lord's Conservatives in Monday's provincial election

"TODAY NEW BRUNSWICKERS HAVE SPOKEN AND THEY HAVE DARED TO HAVE BIGGER DREAMS."

*Before*

Domingos Suplemento

Ds

EL PAIS

CARLOS OTT

*El arquitecto y los proyectos del futuro*

Pág. 9

MAMÁ, ¿PUEDO IR?

Adolescentes de vacaciones

CADA VEZ MÁS JÓVENES PREFIEREN PASAR EL VERANO SIN SUS PADRES. VAN EN GRUPOS A CAMPINGS O ALQUILAN CASAS, PESE A QUE LAS INMOBILIARIAS NO LOS QUIEREN. ELIGEN PUNTA DEL ESTE Y LOS BALNEARIOS DE ROCHA. EL ALCOHOL, LAS DROGAS Y EL SEXO SON LOS RIESGOS CONTRA LA VENTAJA DE UNA INDEPENDENCIA QUE LOS AYUDARÁ A PREPARARSE PARA LA ADULTEZ

Esta es la clave para El País Digital

*Before*

SIDE TRIP: A VACATION ON THE RUN. 6T

TRAVEL

My own private Mexico

On a vessel with just 22 passengers traveling through the Sea of Cortez, personal attention is eclipsed only by the rich variety of sea life, literally at cruisers' fingertips.

Beauty from behind the wheel

*Before*

*After*

**SVENSKA DAGBLADET,** Stockholm, Sweden
Lena K. Samuelsson, Mats-Eric Nilsson, Anna W. Thurfjell, Staff
Section

NÄRINGSLIV
Söndag 5 februari 2006 SVERIGES STÖRSTA AFFÄRSTIDNING SVENSKA DAGBLADET

+0,6 -1,0 -2,7 ↑ 1,90 ↑ 3,25 $ 7,70 € 9,30

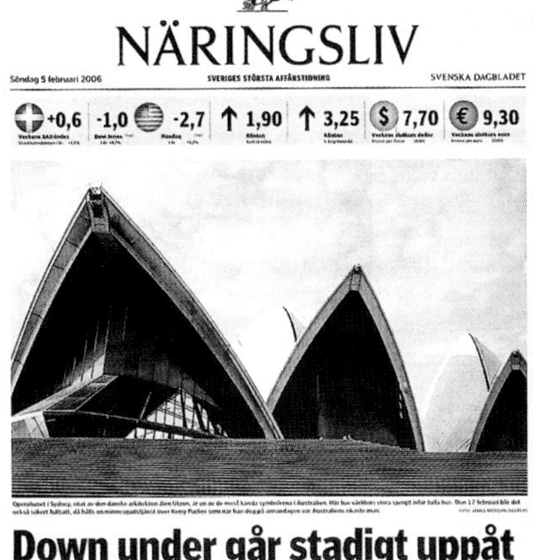

Down under går stadigt uppåt

*Before*

**KITSAP SUN,** Bremerton, Wash.
David Frazier
Page

INSIDE > IOWA CAUCUS: STILL FIRST | A12 OPINION > HELP OUT YOUR NEIGHBORS | A13

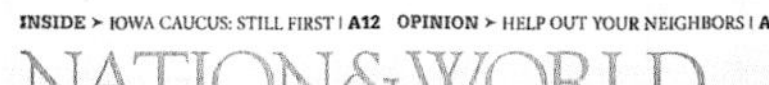


SATURDAY IN REVIEW

THE WAR IN IRAQ | WHAT'S NEXT?

The boldest suggestions by the Iraq Study Group have largely been dismissed. So where does the president have to go from here?

Weighing His No-Exit Options

As Third Tour Approaches, Deployment Taken in Stride

Been Online This Year?

If so, you've just been honored as Time Magazine's "Person of the Year."

*After*

A2 | MONDAY, FEBRUARY 20, 2006 KITSAP SUN KITSAPSUN.COM

WORLD

MORE ON OUR WEB SITE
> Russia to host crucial talks on Iran nuclear program.
> India begins mass slaughter of birds.

IN THE HEADLINES

Bin Laden Vows Never to Be Captured Alive

Explosion Traps Miners in Mexico

Capital Sealed Off to Stop Protests

Little Hope As Workers Bury Slide Victims

PHILIPPINES | U.S. Marines arrived Sunday to aid in the rescue and recovery effort.

Israel Halts Tax Money to Pakistan

Iraqi Government Talks Hit Major Snag

*Before*

**THE SALT LAKE TRIBUNE,** Salt Lake City
Josh Awtry, Colin Smith, Keira Dirmyer, Michael Limon
Page

MONEY

Settlement, 2E: GLAXOSMITHKLINE TO PAY OUT $3.4B

'PRETEXTING,' 6E: FEDS NOW IN ON HP PROBE

E

The Salt Lake Tribune

Market Summary

In Utah

Inside

Home automation

Control4 promotes its marketing boss to president-COO

Utah's economy

## Study: Beer serves state's coffers well

$754 MILLION

$67.5 MILLION

$497 MILLION

14 & 12

28,000

Supercomputers

Linux Networx raises $37 million from investors

## $16B deal rumored for chip maker

Freescale Semiconductor sale would be record leveraged buy

Banking industry

## Zions buys Stockmen's, a small Arizona bank

MARKET REVIEW: 2E ■ DILBERT: 3E ■ NON SEQUITUR: 4E ■ WEATHER: 8E ■ WWW.SLTRIB.COM

After

INSIDE O&A
CLUBS: After Dark, Page 32; Laugh Track, Page 33
DINING: Review, Page 38; Small Bites, Pages 40-46
RESTAURANTS ONLINE: www.cleveland.com/smallbites

T31 EA | THE PLAIN DEALER | Friday, November 24, 2006

OUT & ABOUT ON THE TENS

## If you want to spend...

**<$10** I chose the Hillbilly Dog, regular size ($1.74), at Hot Dog Diner (4407 Brookpark Road, Parma; 216-335-9060). I added an order of fries ($1.99). The order came up fast, and I headed back to the office with lunch. The Hillbilly Dog came covered in chili sauce, coleslaw, ketchup and mustard. The chili's taste was rather bland. It did not rock my taste buds as I had hoped. But the coleslaw was crunchy, snappy and fresh. The dog was not overloaded with condiments, which made eating it at my desk easy and not a messy affair. The bun was supersoft, which I liked. — **John Kuehner**

**<$10** My to-go order at B# Sharp Cafe (inside Rainbow Family Book Center, 5398 Northfield Road, Maple Heights; 216-662-2233) consisted of the Classical Panini Grill ($4.95), which had ciabatta bread loaded with smoked turkey, ham, bacon and cheese. It may be a little high on the sodium count, but it's a filling and tasty lunch. The moist and tender red velvet cake ($2.95) is worth every granule of refined sugar it contains. It's frosted with a smooth cream-cheese frosting with crushed walnuts. — **Greg Burnett**

**<$20** At Machu Picchu (850 Euclid Ave., City Club building, Cleveland; 216-664-9712), two items were knockouts. The Jalea ($14), a kind of Peruvian tempura done with shrimp and tilapia the night I was there, had a wispy, crisp breading, perfectly counterpointed by the salsa criolla, or lime-marinated red onions. And you'll want to order chicken when faced with the rotisserie chicken here ($8, $10, $16). Cooked until the skin is mahogany and the grain of the meat surrenders to a fork, it is served with a delicate herb dipping sauce and one that blends sweet and hot yellow peppers. — **Debbi Snook**

PICK3

Eat

**Angelo's Pizza, 13715 Madison Ave., Lakewood 216-221-0440**

Angelo's is known for its pizza. It's one of my favorites. Unfortunately, I cannot live by pizza alone, try as I might. So occasionally I venture off the well-traveled path and actually eat — gasp — a salad. Luckily, Angelo's menu has a few delicious salad options. My favorite is the pecan chicken salad ($6.95). The chicken strips are moist and tender. They are not breaded chunks, but lightly grilled. The mixed greens are dark, fresh and snappy. Tomatoes, croutons and red onion rings are scattered among the greens. But what makes this salad irresistible to me is the ample quantity of sweet and crunchy pecan pieces. You'll find enough to load your fork with a few in every bite. If you don't think the salad will be enough to satisfy your hunger, consider adding an order of chicken strips, which are breaded ($6.50). They come with your choice of dipping sauces. I like the honey mustard. — **John Kuehner**

PLAIN DEALER FILE PHOTOGRAPH

RESTAURANT NEWS

## Tequila and dinner

Momocho Mod Mex Cuisine will host a five-course tequila dinner at 7:30 p.m. Wednesday, Dec. 20, and Wednesday, Feb. 28. Tequilas being served are ginger-spiked Patron Silver, Corazon Blanco, Herradura Anejo, Don Julio Anejo and Milagro Reposado. Price is $40 (plus tax/gratuity) per person. Momocho is at 1835 Fulton Road, Cleveland. Call 216-694-2122 for reservations. — **Merlene Santiago**

Party

**Smedley's, 17004 Lorain Ave., Cleveland 216-941-0124**

You don't have to be a biker to enjoy Smedley's, but it might help you fit in. From the Sturgis motorcycle rally banners and Harley-Davidson signs on the wall to the classic rock in heavy rotation on the jukebox to the leather and denim on the patrons, this Kamm's Corners bar is blue collar to the core. It's also a great place to catch blues bands and the occasional rock act.

Drink

**Houma Houma Battiste & Dupree 1992 Warrensville Center Road, South Euclid 216-381-5338**

Mardi Gras is a few months away. But you can get in the mood now with a New Orleans drink called the Houma Houma. The mellow mix includes amaretto, pineapple and bourbon. Caution: One sip at a time, please. This drink will have you donning beads and dancing in the street long before the celebration. A perfect time to check one out is during Friday night happy hour. All drinks are $1 off. And you get a chance to try Junior Dupree's Cajun wings and jambalaya on the house. — **Greg Burnett**

After

**THE PLAIN DEALER,** Cleveland
David Kordalski, Scott Sheldon, Michael Norman, John Kappes, Staci Andrews
Page

DINING

www.cleveland.com/friday | Small Bites 18 | Tasty Twenty 19

17 | THE PLAIN DEALER | Friday, March 4, 2005

# Pie to die for

## Great pizza in Cleveland? For 26 years at Vincenza's

Nick Turchi stretches dough into a perfect circle. At Vincenza's Pizza and Pasta downtown, tossing is a rarity.

TASTE BITES

**Vincenza's Pizza and Pasta**

Before

The Salt Lake Tribune

D10 BUSINESS

MARKET Indicators

# Delta pilots seek solidarity

They will ask other airlines' aviators to refuse extra flights in case of strike

Northwest pilots tentatively agree to pay cut that may save company

## Two shopping centers will cater to Utah's Latino market

BUSINESS SURVIVAL

Maintain and promote your business during road construction

UDOT

## Dealing with reality

## Huntsman Corp. revamps its strategy

Before

**DETROIT FREE PRESS**

Mauricio Gutierrez, Rosa E. Castellanos, Patrick Sedlar, Steve Dorsey

Page

EVERY DAY: LIFE

SHOPPING

GIFTS THAT GIVE

twice

CHARITY GIVES THE RECIPIENT A HAND AND THE HONOREE A WARM FEELING

READY TO RECEIVE

WHAT'S HOT FOR SPRING

Miss Kitty says

STEPHANIE ORAM: BLOOMFIELD HILLS

*After*

THE WAY WE LIVE

SUICIDE | Groups try to erase taboo, help families deal with their anguish

LOVE LIFE | REAL PEOPLE, REAL STORIES

HOROSCOPE

Start your lawn work now

Preventing suicide

HAIR | Garden to celebrate anniversary

Weight talk offends reader

*Before*

6 | THE PLAIN DEALER | Friday, February 10, 2006

FRIDAY | ARTS&ENTERTAINMENT

**ENTERTAINMENT ON THE TENS**

## If you want to spend...

**<$10:** Laughter, they say, is the best medicine. Money for vital research doesn't hurt either, especially when it's research to fight cancer. The two meld at 3 p.m. Sunday for a performance of **Peter Cook** and **Dudley Moore's "Good Evening"** to benefit the Lance Armstrong Foundation. Dan Dean, a 25-year-old cancer survivor and Cleveland-based actor, stars along with Richard Figge at Hilarities 4th Street Theatre inside Pickwick & Frolic. Tickets are $10 general admission, $15 for preferred seating and $46 for a brunch (11 a.m. to 2 p.m.) followed by the show. Call 216-241-7425. Pickwick & Frolic is at 2035 East Fourth St., Cleveland.

**<$20:** It's so hard to decide. Should you see the wonderful Michelangelo Antonioni film "The Passenger," starring Jack Nicholson? Or catch the gripping film that was just nominated for an Academy Award as best documentary, "Darwin's Nightmare"? Why not see both? **The Cleveland Institute of Art Cinematheque** is screening both films (special $13 price to see both, or $8 to see one film). Tonight: "Darwin's Nightmare," 7:30; "The Passenger," 9:40. Saturday: "The Passenger," 7 p.m.; "Darwin's Nightmare," 9:30 p.m. Sunday: "The Passenger" only, 3:45 p.m. The Cinematheque is at 11141 East Blvd.

**Free:** The **Musical Spirit of Hungary** will be on display at the Cleveland Institute of Music tonight as faculty members perform an evening of music. There is no charge, but the box office reports a lot of calls, so they suggest patrons arrive early for the 8 p.m. show. Debunking Shaw's axiom "Those who can do; those who can't teach" are: Marla Berg, soprano; Jeffrey Irvine, viola; Linda Jones, piano; Paul Kanto, violin; Peter Salaff, violin; Virginia Weckstrom, piano; and Alison Wells, cello. The music institute is at 11021 East Blvd. — **Michael K. McIntyre**

**HOT LIST**

The top stuff in America last week, for better or worse.

**MOVIE: "When a Stranger Calls."** Because nothing goes over in the dead of winter like a horror story.

**TV SHOW: The Super Bowl.** Ditto.

**ALBUM: Barry Manilow, "Greatest Songs of the Fifties."** Because kitsch almost rhymes with cash.

**NOVEL: Dan Brown, "The Da Vinci Code."** Ditto.

**ARTS EVENT: Steelers win ugly in the Super Bowl.** Which, as Sylvia Plath said of dying, is an art, like everything else.

**DVD: "Lord of War."** Not a biography of Donald "Rummy" Rumsfeld, though Nicolas Cage does have the jowls. Maybe for the sequel.

Compiled by John Kappes from wire reports

## PICK3

### Arts

**Dayton Contemporary Dance Company** celebrates the rich heritage of black modern dance with a program featuring the premiere of William B. McClellan Jr.'s "Sagas de Salvador" and revivals of Asadata Dafora's "Ostrich" (below), Donald McKayle's "Rainbow 'Round My Shoulder" and artistic director Kevin Ward's "Sets and Chasers." Performances are at 8 p.m. Friday and Saturday at the Cuyahoga Community College Metro Campus Theatre, 2900 Community College Ave., Cleveland. Tickets are $20. Call 216-987-4400. — **Wilma Salisbury**

ANDY SNOW

### Music

**Ex-Animals singer Eric Burdon** used to run with the late, great likes of Jimi Hendrix and Jim Morrison in rock 'n' roll's drug-fueled fast lane. "In today's world, both Jimi and Jim probably would've gotten help," Burdon said when I interviewed him a few years ago. "Back then, we didn't give a damn." He's sure to share some ripping yarns when he discusses his career and performs at 7 p.m. Monday at the Rock and Roll Hall of Fame and Museum, 1 Key Plaza, Cleveland. Tickets are $10 at the Rock Hall and Ticketmaster outlets, or charge by phone, 216-241-5555 (Cleveland) or 330-945-9400 (Akron). — **John Soeder**

SPV

### Movies

**"Capote"**

**Rated R for some violent images and brief strong language. 98 minutes. Grade: A-**

The Oscars can be an overblown drag. But Oscar nominations are gold for small-budget films such as "Capote." Now with five Oscar nods, including a best-picture nomination, Bennett Miller's look at author Truman Capote (Philip Seymour Hoffman) and his reporting and writing of "In Cold Blood" has expanded to many theaters in Greater Cleveland. It's a fine film about duplicity, deception, betrayal and meticulously milking sources. Journalism 101. — **Clint O'Connor**

*After*

**THE PLAIN DEALER,** Cleveland

David Kordalski, Scott Sheldon, Michael Norman, John Kappes, Lori DeMarco, Staci Andrews

Page

34 EA | THE PLAIN DEALER | Friday, January 21, 2005

# FINE ARTS



## *A timeless treat*

### *Early-music group offers a feast of medieval melodies*

WILMA SALISBURY
*Plain Dealer Music Critic*

"Dukes & Angels," the exquisite exhibition of Burgundian art at the Cleveland Museum of Art, has ended. But the medieval melodies linger on.

"Music of the Valois," the last in a series of early-music concerts presented in conjunction with the exhibition, will be performed by Fortune's Wheel Saturday night at Case Western Reserve University's Harkness Chapel.

Robert Mealy, the ensemble's co-founder, likens the repertoire to a feast for the ear, seasoned with the tasty flavors of Old French texts and the lean sonorities of medieval instruments.

"It's a kind of banquet for the audience," he said by phone last week from his home in New York City's East Village. "It was inspired by the exhibition."

One of the courtly love songs on the program was performed at the historic *Banquet du Voeu* (Feast of the Pheasant) at Lille in 1454.

"Constantinople had recently fallen to the Turks, and Philip the Good [the second-to-the-last Duke of Burgundy] was trying to launch a crusade by inviting all his Knights of the Golden Fleece to this sumptuous feast," Mealy writes in a program note. "One witness describes 18 different entertainments between courses."

One of the delectable interludes, *Je ne vis onques la pareille* ("I never saw a woman like you"), was sung by a 12-year-old boy who entered the banquet hall on the back of a man disguised as a stag. The music is attributed to Guillaume Dufay or Gilles Binchois, court composers whose names, like those of Bach and Handel or Haydn and Mozart, are eternally linked in music history.

"Binchois' music was smooth and courtly. He was the last master of courtly love," Mealy said. "Dufay was thought of at the time as a composer of sacred music. We are performing his secular music."

The two composers are pictured in a famous illumination showing Binchois with a harp and Dufay with a portative organ. At Harkness Chapel, Mealy will play the medieval harp and vielle (a late medieval fiddle). His colleagues will play vielle, viola da gamba and tambourine. All sing, and they also might dance.

"Machaut [the great 14th-century French composer] said music is a science, a science that makes you laugh and sing and dance," Mealy said. "I'm not sure we will have dancing. But we will play music from a collection of basse dances that Binchois performed at court."

Fortune's Wheel was formed nine years ago, when Mealy and mezzo-soprano Lydia Heather Knutson were invited to perform with a group that fell apart shortly before its scheduled appearance at the International Festival of Early Music in Mexico City.

"We were left with two programs to fill," he said. "We called up early-music performers at the last minute. We had to have a name. We called the group Fortune's Wheel because it was formed by a stroke of fate, and because Fortuna was an important medieval figure, a powerful goddess."

The ensemble originally included Shira Kammen, vielle, and the late John Fleagle, tenor.

SEE | 35

CONCERT PREVIEW

**Fortune's Wheel**

**What:** The early-music group performs "Music of the Valois" as part of the series Chapel, Court & Countryside: Early Music at Harkness.
**When:** 7:30 p.m. Saturday.
**Where:** Harkness Chapel, 11200 Bellflower Road, Cleveland.
**Tickets:** $10-$20. Call 216-368-2402.
**Also:** The musicians will teach a free master class at 12:30 p.m. today at Harkness Chapel.

FORTUNE'S WHEEL

**Members of Fortune's Wheel are, seated, vielle players Shira Kammen and Robert Mealy, and standing, mezzo-soprano Lydia Heather Knutson. Tenor Paul Cummings, top, recently was replaced by tenor Aaron Sheehan.**

*Before*

**THE NEWS-PRESS,** Fort Myers, Fla.
Erin Berry, Marck Bickel, Ed Reed, Dan DeLuca, Annabelle Tometich, Javier Torres
Page

HS ZONE

ZONE POLL

STANDINGS

ZONE BLOG

PARTY OF ONE

Dunbar's Doerr is making waves as only girls swimmer for the Tigers

ZONE CHAT

ZONE BUZZ

ZONE SNAPSHOT

ZONE IN

HOT DATES OCT 17 19 21

*After*

HIGH SCHOOLS

BASKETBALL

WRESTLING: LCAC RANKINGS

Bevy of hoops on the horizon

Several holiday events take place in next 2 weeks

AREA HOLIDAY BASKETBALL TOURNAMENT SCHEDULE

*Before*

**ST. PETERSBURG TIMES** (Fla.)
Patty Cox, Amy Hollyfield, Dan Hieb
Page

THE METRO REPORT

With these three, Big Easy has promise

Vandals deface church mural

'Make it the first priority'

Crime journal

*After*

LOCAL NEWS

Next lesson from prison: the new feel of freedom

Meeting turns into homeless debate

School Board District 7 draws its 4th candidate

NAACP forum reaches out to black parents

Dog that bit commissioner's father to be euthanized; owner to appeal

*Before*

**THE STATE NEWS,** Michigan State University, East Lansing, Mich.
Staff
Page

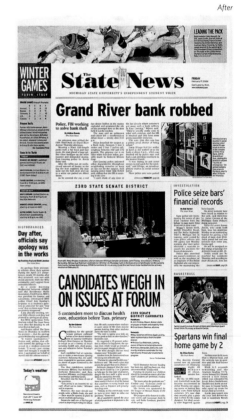

**FIRING FALLOUT.** Players confused. Recruits reconsidering. Oh yeah, and there's still a game on Saturday. Keep track of it all in Sidelines.

**SICK OF FOOTBALL?** Go to www.statenews.com for full coverage of the women's basketball team's 64-55 exhibition win.

The State News Weekend Edition

What the party animals do outside the election circus

PEOPLE BEHIND THE PODIUM

If you're sick of attack ads and campaign rhetoric, take a minute to get to know the lighter side of election season. At least two candidates **RIDE HOGS**. Somebody has the **BLACK EYED PEAS** on heavy rotation. One challenger **WAKES UP AT NOON**. There's an incumbent who **EATS PRETZELS AND CHEESE** at midnight. A certain senator lived in **HUBBARD HALL** (a few decades ago). And there's even an **ALEC BALDWIN** look-alike.

TURN THE PAGE TO MATCH THE CANDIDATES WITH THEIR QUIRKS.

*After*

WINTER GAMES

The State News

LEADING THE PACK

Grand River bank robbed

23RD STATE SENATE DISTRICT

Police seize bars' financial records

Day after, officials say apology was in the works

CANDIDATES WEIGH IN ON ISSUES AT FORUM

5 contenders meet to discuss health care, education before Tues. primary

Spartans win final home game by 2

Today's weather

*Before*

**OMAHA WORLD-HERALD** (Neb.)

Josh Crutchmer, Dave Elsesser, Thad Livingston, Tim Parks

Page

nflpreview WEEK 7

Vikings receivers must get on the ball

*After*

NFL

Giants' Barber cuts up Chiefs

Smith helps Broncos bust Bills

No rolling stone, owner Irsay is Colts' anchor

*Before*

**THE PLAIN DEALER,** Cleveland

David Kordalski, Debbie Van Tassel, Bill Lammers, Ken Marshall, William Neff, Kathryn Kroll

Page

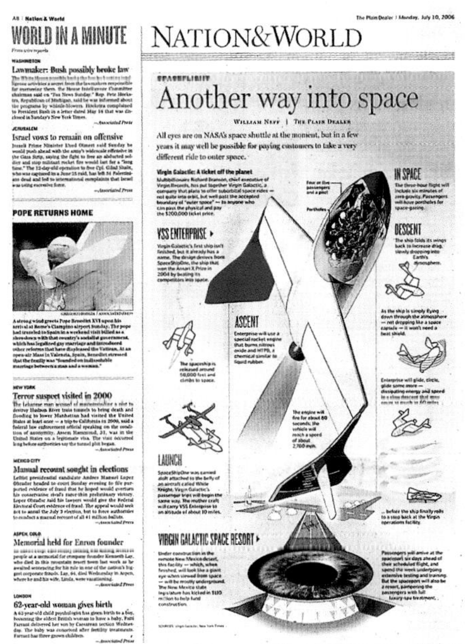

WORLD IN A MINUTE

NATION&WORLD

Another way into space

Slavery reparations movement gains political traction

*After*

BRIEFS

Captain's reluctance complicates crew's rescue

*Before*

**ROCKFORD REGISTER STAR** (Ill.)

Chris Soprych, Margo Pearson

Page

TUESDAY MARKET REPORT

*After*

*Before*

**THE PLAIN DEALER,** Cleveland

David Kordalski, Keith Bracken, Mike Starkey, Roy Hewitt, Emmet Smith

Page

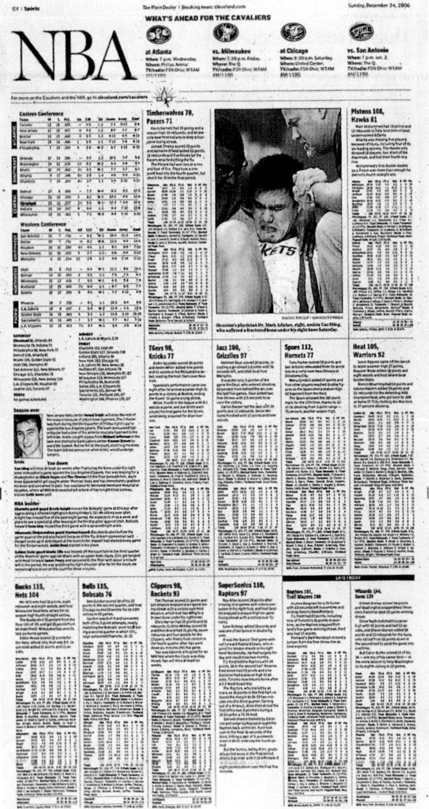
NBA

WHAT'S AHEAD FOR THE CAVALIERS

After

**THE PLAIN DEALER,** Cleveland

David Kordalski, Emmet Smith, Mike Starkey, Roy Hewitt, Keith Bracken

Page

MLB

After

**THE KANSAS CITY STAR** (Mo.)

Tom Dolphens, Kelly Frankeny

Page

Opinion

THE STAR'S EDITORIALS

KC should make sincere effort to explore light-rail plan

Cooperation must replace divisive approach

WHAT OTHERS ARE SAYING

STEALING CAMPAIGN SIGNS CAN BE A STICKY SITUATION

After

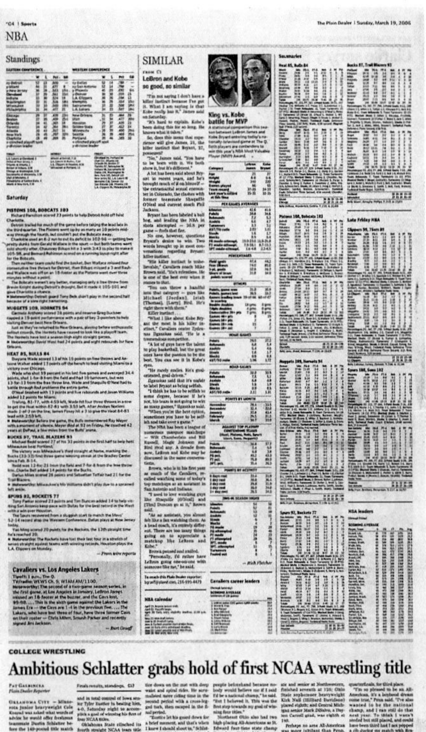
NBA

SIMILAR

Ambitious Schlatter grabs hold of first NCAA wrestling title

Before

BASEBALL REPORT

American League standings

NEWSWATCH

Dempster agrees to three-year extension

MLB TEAM AVERAGES

Before

OPINION

EDITORIALS

Chiefs' inflexibility threatens roof plan

No reason to reject Wal-Mart proposal

Minorities left isolated at UMKC

LETTERS

Before

Chapter Eleven

# DETAILS, DETAILS

Detalles, detalles

**Judges' bios, indices, credits & colophon**

Biografía de los jueces, índices, créditos y colofón

# Meet the judges

*WB = World's Best Designed™*
*F = features team*  *N = news team*
*P = photo and small papers team*
*G = graphics team*
*L = long form team*
*C = conflict of interest judges*

**EDDIE ÁLVAREZ** is presentation editor at The Miami Herald (Fla.), his position since July 2004. He oversees the design of news and features sections, as well as information graphics and illustrations. He manages 35 designers, graphic artists and illustrators. Alvarez joined the Herald in 1988 as a sports clerk and went full time as a sports copy editor in 1992 before working his way to assistant sports editor. *(N)*

Eddie Álvarez es el editor de presentación del periódico norteamericano The Miami Herald desde julio de 2004. Se ocupa tanto del diseño de las secciones de noticias y reportajes como de las infografías y las ilustraciones, y dirige un grupo de 35 diseñadores, artistas gráficos e ilustradores. Álvarez comenzó a trabajar en el Herald en 1988, en la sección de deportes. En 1992 se convirtió en editor de textos de jornada de tiempo completo de la sección y luego fue editor asistente de deportes. *(N)*

**CHARLES APPLE** is graphics director of The Virginian-Pilot, Norfolk. Previously, he worked for papers in Raleigh, N.C., and Des Moines, Iowa, and for the Chicago Tribune. The winner of several SND awards for graphics and graphics reporting, Apple has taught numerous workshops and contributes to SND's Design magazine and various online forums. *(G)*

Charles Apple es el director de gráficos del diario The Virginian-Pilot, de Norfolk, Virginia, Estados Unidos. Anteriormente trabajó en el Chicago Tribune y en periódicos de Raleigh, Carolina del Norte, y Des Moines, Iowa. Ha ganado varios premios de la SND por diseño y reporteo de gráficos. Apple ha dirigido muchos talleres, y ha colaborado con la revista Design de la SND y en varios foros online. *(G)*

**NATHALIE BAYLAUCQ** is artistic director of Baylaucq & Co., a Paris design studio where she began to specialize in newspaper and magazine design. She has been designing newspapers for the past 15 years. She studied at the Parsons School of Design in New York City and has won many awards. *(F)*

Nathalie Baylaucq es la directora de arte de Baylaucq & Co., un estudio especializado en diseño de periódicos y revistas que ella fundó en París. Se ha dedicado al diseño de publicaciones durante los últimos 15 años. Estudió en la escuela de diseño de Parsons, en Nueva York, y ha ganado mucho premios. *(F)*

**PÄL A. BERG** is editor for development and digital media at Haugesunds Avis, in Norway. Prior to that, he worked eight years with design and news graphics at Verdens Gang, Oslo. Berg was president of SND/Scandinavia from 1999 to 2003. He was a 2000-2002 judge of the Scandinavian Best of Newspapers competition jury and a 2005-2007 judge for the Norwegian competition jury. *(WB)*

Päl A. Berg es editor de desarrollo y medios digitales del Haugesunds Avis, de Noruega. Anteriormente, trabajó durante ocho años en la sección de diseño e infográficos de Verdens Gang, Oslo. Berg fue presidente de la SND/Scandinavia entre 1999 y 2003. Además, del 2000 al 2002 fue juez de la competencia "Lo mejor del diseño de periódicos escandinavos" y entre el 2005 y el 2007 integró el jurado noruego de la competición. *(WB)*

<P.10 What did judges think of their categories?
**JUDGING TEAM STATEMENTS**

**KATHY BOGAN** is design director at the Rocky Mountain News, Denver, where she has worked since 1995. She began her newspaper career at the High Country News, a biweekly environmental tabloid, starting her visual-journalism career in 1980. She worked at the Casper Star-Tribune (Wyo.) before the News. *(N)*

Kathy Bogan es directora de diseño del diario Rocky Mountain News, de Denver, en el cual ha trabajado desde 1995. Comenzó su carrera en periodismo visual en 1980 en el High Country News, un tabloide bisemanal sobre el medio ambiente. También trabajó en el Casper Star-Tribune, del estado norteamericano de Wyoming. *(N)*

**BETH BROADWATER** is an art director at The Washington Post, which she joined in 2001. After more than a decade on various news desks, most recently as deputy editor in charge of projects, she made the leap into features in September. Included in Beth's SND awards are the coverage of President Reagan's funeral and the revelation of Deep Throat's identity. *(L)*

Beth Broadwater es directora de arte de The Washington Post, en el cual comenzó a trabajar en el 2001. Desempeñó labores en varias secciones de noticias durante más de una década, incluyendo la subedición de proyectos especiales, antes de pasar a los reportajes en septiembre pasado. Entre los premios de la SND que Beth ha recibido figuran la cobertura del funeral del ex presidente Reagan y la revelación de la identidad de "Garganta Profunda". *(L)*

**TIM BROEKEMA** is an assistant professor of photojournalism/new media at Western Kentucky University. He has worked as a picture editor for The Courier-Journal, Louisville, Ky.; The Providence Journal (R.I.); and the Chicago Tribune. Broekema was director of photography for the Kalamazoo Gazette (Mich.) before joining academia in 2001. *(P)*

Tim Broekema es profesor asistente de fotoperiodismo y nuevos medios en Western Kentucky University. Ha trabajado como editor de fotografía en los periódicos norteamericanos The Courier-Journal, de Louisville, Kentucky; Providence Journal, de Providence, Rhode Island; y Chicago Tribune. Broekema fue director de fotografía del diario Kalamazoo Gazette, del estado de Michigan, antes de dedicarse a la educación universitaria en el 2001. *(P)*

**STEVE CAVENDISH** is the graphics editor of the Chicago Tribune. A native Tennessean, he got his start at the now-defunct Nashville Banner. He has been recognized by SND and other organizations for outstanding work while he was a designer at the Asbury Park Press (N.J.), San Jose Mercury News (Calif.) and The Washington Post. *(N)*

Steve Cavendish es el editor de gráficos del diario Chicago Tribune. Originario del estado norteamericano de Tennessee, comenzó su carrera en el desaparecido periódico Nashville Banner. Ha sido premiado por la SND y otras organizaciones por su sobresaliente trabajo mientras fue diseñador en los diarios Asbury Park Press, de Nueva Jersey; San Jose Mercury News, de California; y The Washington Post. *(N)*

**CAROLYN "CARRIE" COCKBURN** is a graphic artist in the news section of The Globe and Mail, Toronto. She has won two awards from SND for graphics at the newspaper. Previously, she ran a photography business, as well as working for the Financial Post in Toronto as assistant photo editor and then graphic artist. *(G)*

Carolyn "Carrie" Cockburn es artista gráfica de la sección de noticias del diario Globe and Mail de Toronto. Ha sido ganadora de dos premios de la SND por sus gráficos. Anteriormente tuvo una empresa fotográfica y trabajó en el Financial Post de Toronto como editora asistente de fotografía y luego artista gráfica. *(G)*

**NURI J. DUCASSI** is design director at The Gazette, the only English-language daily in Montreal, where she led a redesign. The Gazette received several SND awards in the last competition. She began her career at El Nuevo Herald, in Miami. Ducassi worked as design director at the Hartford Courant (Conn.) before moving to the San Jose Mercury News (Calif.) as features design director. She was design director at The Miami Herald, where she led an award-winning redesign. *(WB)*

Nuri J. Ducassi es directora de diseño de The Gazette, el único diario en inglés de la ciudad canadiense de Montreal. Ella estuvo a cargo del rediseño de ese periódico, que obtuvo varios premios en la última versión de la competencia de la SND. Comenzó su carrera en El Nuevo Herald, de Miami, Florida, EE.UU. Ducassi se ha desempeñado como directora de diseño del Hartford Courant (del estado nortamericano de Connecticut) antes de mudarse al San Jose Mercury News (de California) como directora de diseño de reportajes. Fue directora de diseño de The Miami Herald, en el cual lideró un premiado rediseño. *(WB)*

**ARIEL FREANER** is president of Freaner & Associates, in San Diego. As a designer, illustrator and photographer, he may be best known for his ZETA covers. He has won numerous awards from SND and was honored by Print magazine. His work has been published in the San Diego Union-Tribune and Reforma. His clients include Motorola, Fujitsu, the U.S. Navy and Uniradio, among others. *(P)*

Ariel Freaner es el presidente de Freaner & Associates, de San Diego, Estados Unidos. Como diseñador, ilustrador y fotógrafo, es más bien conocido por sus tapas de ZETA. Ha ganado muchos premios de la SND y fue reconocido por la revista Print. Su trabajo ha aparecido en los diarios San Diego Union-Tribune y Reforma. Entre sus clientes figuran Motorola, Fujitsu, la Armada norteamericana y Uniradio. *(P)*

**KARL GUDE** left a 27-year news career to teach information graphics at Michigan State University's School of Journalism. For the past decade, he has worked at Newsweek magazine. He was director of information graphics for most of that time. During the 17 years prior, he worked in a similar capacity at United Press International and the Associated Press, and at the Daily News, in New York, and the now-defunct National Sports Daily. *(G)*

Karl Gude dejó una carrera de 27 años dedicado a las noticias para dedicarse a enseñar infografía en la escuela de periodismo de Michigan State University. En la última década, trabajó en la revista Newsweek, principalmente como director de infografía. Anteriormente, pasó 17 años a cargo de los gráficos de las agencias informativas United Press International y Associated Press, y los diarios Daily News, de Nueva York, y el desaparecido National Sports Daily. *(G)*

**MAURICIO GUTIÉRREZ** has designed newspapers and magazines in Mexico, Spain and the United States. He is now deputy design director at the Detroit Free Press and a design consultant. In Detroit, he supervises features designers, has worked on the paper's redesign and created new sections and special projects. *(F)*

Mauricio Gutiérrez ha diseñado periódicos y revistas en España, Estados Unidos y México. Actualmente, es subdirector de diseño del diario Detroit Free Press, donde supervisa a los diseñadores de reportajes, y también es consultor de diseno. Ha trabajado en el rediseño del Free Press y ha creado secciones y proyectos especiales. *(F)*

**SARAH HABERSHON** is an art director at The Guardian, London, and is responsible for the Travel, Family, Money and Work sections of the Saturday paper. She was part of the design team for the Berliner-tab launch of the paper in 2005, and for five years she was art director of the Guide, The Guardian's weekly entertainment magazine. Previously she worked on consumer magazines. *(F)*

Sarah Habershon es directora de arte del periódico londinense The Guardian y está encargada de las secciones de viajes, familia, dinero y mercado laboral de la edición del sábado. Integró el equipo de diseño del lanzamiento del tamaño berlinés del diario en 2005 y durante cinco años fue directora de arte de Guide, la revista de entretención semanal del periódico. Anteriormente trabajó en revistas de consumo. *(F)*

**ANITA HAGIN** is the assistant managing editor for features and presentation at the Savannah Morning News (Ga.). During her six years at the Morning News, she has designed Bluffton Today (S.C.) and more recently redesigned the Morning News. She has worked as a features designer at the Anderson Independent-Mail (S.C.) and as a production and design editor for MidAmerica Farm Publications (Mo.). She has won several design awards from SND, the South Carolina Press Association and the Georgia Press Association. *(L)*

Anita Hagin es la editora ejecutiva asistente de reportajes y presentación del Savannah Morning News, del estado norteamericano de Carolina del Sur. Durante sus seis años en ese diario, ha diseñado Bluffton Today y más recientemente ha rediseñado el propio Morning News. Trabajó como diseñadora de reportajes del Anderson Independent-Mail, de Carolina del Sur, y como editora de producción y diseño de MidAmerica Farm Publications, del estado de Missouri. Ha recibido varios premios de diseño de la SND, la South Carolina Press Association y la Georgia Press Association. *(L)*

**JOSEPH HUTCHINSON** is creative director of the Los Angeles Times, where he oversees design and information graphics for the newspaper and its Sunday magazine. He has redesigned the paper and incorporated visual journalism into its culture. Under his leadership, the paper won 239 SND

# Meet the judges

*WB = World's Best Designed™*
*F = features team*  *N = news team*
*P = photo and small papers team*
*G = graphics team*
*L = long form team*
*C = conflict of interest judges*

awards in five years, including Gold and Silver medals, as well as Judges' Special Recognition awards. *(C)*

Joseph Hutchinson es director creativo de Los Angeles Times, donde está a cargo del diseño y los infográficos del diario y la revista dominical. Ha rediseñado el periódico y desarrollado el periodismo visual en la redacción. Bajo su liderazgo, el diario ha obtenido 239 premios de la SND durante cinco años, incluyendo tanto medallas de oro y plata, como premios de reconocimiento especial de los jueces. *(C)*

**JAY JUDGE** is the assistant managing editor for design and graphics at The Baltimore Sun. Since joining the paper in 1997, he has designed news and sports pages, managed the news design desk and helped coordinate the 2005 redesign project. Previously he worked at The Times of Northwest Indiana. *(N)*

Jay Judge es editor ejecutivo asistente de diseño y gráficos en The Baltimore Sun. Desde que comenzó a trabajar en ese diario en 1997, ha diseñado páginas de crónica y deportes, dirigido la sección de diseño de noticias y ayudado a coordinar el proyecto de rediseño de 2005. Anteriomente trabajó en The Times, del noroeste del estado norteamericano de Indiana. *(N)*

**VIVIAN KENT**, a freelance graphic artist for the Daily Mail in London, is a qualified cartographer. She joined the Economist in 1969, later becoming department head. Kent was elected a Fellow of the Royal Geographical Society in 1987. Following a year at the Sunday Correspondent, she joined The Daily Telegraph in 1990, subsequently becoming deputy graphics editor. She is the winner of many awards for animated news graphics. *(G)*

Vivian Kent es artista gráfica freelance del periódico londinense Daily Mail y una cartógrafa calificada. Fue contratada por la revista The Economist en 1969 y luego llegó a dirigir una sección. Kent fue elegida miembro de la Royal Geographical Society en 1987. Luego de un año en el Sunday Corespondent, se integró al periódico The Daily Telegraph en 1990, donde llegó a ser subeditora de gráficos. Ha sido ganadora de muchos premios por sus infográficos animados. *(G)*

**LENA GRAPE LILLIEHORN** is design and features editor at Östgöta Correspondenten, one of Sweden's largest regional daily papers. She has been working with all aspects of editorial design since 1979. She was a board member for the Society for News Design/Scandinavia for five years and a member of the Scandinavian design jury for four years. She leads yearly seminars in typography, design and creativity at the Institute for Further Education of Journalists in Sweden. *(P)*

Lena Grape Lilliehorn es editora de diseño y reportajes de Östgöta Correspondenten, uno de los diarios regionales más grandes de Suecia. Ha trabajado en todos los aspectos del diseño editorial desde 1979. Integró el directorio del capítulo escandinavo de la SND durante cinco años y fue parte del jurado de la competencia de diseño escandinavo durante cuatro. Dirige seminarios anuales de tipografía, diseño y creatividad en el instituto de educación continua para periodistas de Suecia. *(P)*

<P.10 What did judges think of their categories? **JUDGING TEAM STATEMENTS**

**STEPHANIE GRACE LIM** is now principal creative designer at eBay's PayPal division. She was features design director at the San Jose Mercury News (Calif.). Lim has won awards from almost every professional organization in her field, including a Pulitzer nomination. Her work has been featured in Life, People, Photographer's Forum and Print magazine. *(F)*

Stephanie Grace Lim es actualmente la diseñadora creativa principal de la división PayPal de eBay. Fue directora de diseño de reportajes del diario californiano San Jose Mercury News. Lim ha ganado premios de casi todas las organizaciones profesionales de su campo, incluyendo una nominación al Pulitzer. Su trabajo ha sido publicado en las revistas Life, People, Photographer's Forum y Print. *(F)*

**SUSAN McDONOUGH**, design director at the Ottawa Citizen (Ontario, Canada), leads a group of designers and artists who produce graphics, print and Web content. A native of Montreal, she started her career in advertising before making the switch and joining the Toronto Star as an editorial designer. At the Star, she worked on editorial projects, participated in a redesign and helped implement a new production system. *(N)*

Susan McDonough, directora de diseño del diario canadiense Ottawa Citizen, dirige a un grupo de diseñadores y artistas que producen gráficos y contenido impreso y online. Originaria de Montreal, comenzó su carrera en publicidad antes de cambir de carrera e integrarse al Toronto Star como diseñadora editorial. En ese diario, ha trabajado en proyectos editoriales, ha participado en un rediseño y ha ayudado a implementar un nuevo sistema de producción. *(N)*

**BONNIE JO MOUNT** teaches visual journalism at Hampton University (Va.). Previously she was deputy managing editor for visuals and interactive media at The News & Observer, Raleigh, N.C. Mount has worked as a director of photography and photojournalist in newsrooms across the country. She has judged a variety of photography contests and taught at several national workshops. In 2002 she spent an academic year at Stanford University as a John S. Knight Fellow. *(WB)*

Bonnie Jo Mount enseña periodismo visual en Hampton University (Virginia, EE.UU.). Anteriormente, fue subeditora ejecutiva de elementos visuales y medios interactivos de The News & Observer, de Raleigh, Carolina del Norte, EE.UU. Mount se ha desempeñado como directora de fotografía y fotoperiodismo en salas de noticias en todo Estados Unidos. Ha sido jueza en una serie de competencias de fotografía y ha enseñado en varios talleres de convocatoria nacional. En 2002 pasó un año académico en Stanford University como becaria del programa John S. Knight. *(WB)*

**PETER ONG** is a newspaper consultant in Sydney, Australia. He has consulted for or worked with newspapers in more than 10 countries in the Pacific Rim. Ong's latest projects are revamping newspapers in Saudi Arabia and India. A journalist with more than 30 years' experience, he is also a long-time regional director for SND. *(L)*

Peter Ong es un consultor de periódicos de Sydney, Australia. Ha trabajado para diarios de más de 10 países de la región Asia-Pacífico. Sus más recientes proyectos incluyen el rediseño de diarios en Arabia Saudita e India. Ong es un periodista con más de 30 años de carrera y ha sido director regional de la SND durante mucho tiempo. *(L)*

**PILAR OSTALE** is a journalist and designer at Heraldo De Aragón, Zaragoza, Spain. Her career at the journal began in 1990. She was graphics and design editor from 2002-05. Ostale took part in the core team that redesigned the newspaper in 2001, receiving several international awards. She is studying the history of visual journalism at the University of Zaragoza. *(F)*

Pilar Ostale es una periodista y diseñadora del Heraldo de Aragón, de Zaragoza, España. Su carrera en el diario comenzó en 1990, y entre 2002 y 2005 fue editora de gráficos y diseño. Ostale fue parte del equipo central que rediseñó el periódico en el 2001, por lo cual recibió varios premios internacionales. Actualmente está estudiando la historia del periodismo visual en la Universidad de Zaragoza. *(F)*

**ALLY PALMER** is founding director of UK-based Palmer Watson, Edinburgh, Scotland. Palmer has been a consultant since 1998 and has a record of creating internationally acclaimed designs for newspapers across the world. Before becoming a consultant, he was group art director for Scotsman Publications, whose titles included The Scotsman and The European. *(WB)*

Ally Palmer es director y fundador de la agencia de diseño de medios impresos Palmer Watson, de Edinburgo, Escocia. Palmer ha sido consultor desde 1998 y ostenta un récord en la creación de diseños de periódico celebrados en todo el mundo. Antes de convertirse en consultor, fue el director de arte grupal de Scotsman Publications, entre cuyos periódicos figuran The Scotsman y The European. *(WB)*

**KIM PARSON**, managing editor in the Integrated Consumer Experience area of Humana's Innovation Center, has worked in publication design for 20 years. As assistant managing editor at the Lexington Herald-Leader (Ky.), she led the presentation staff through a redesign and numerous Kentucky Derbies. She is a former design director for the Orlando Sentinel and has won several SND awards. *(L)*

Kim Parson, editora ejecutiva del área de experiencia integral del consumidor del centro de innovación de Humana, ha trabajado en el diseño de publicaciones durante 20 años. Como asistente editorial ejecutiva en el Lexington Herald-Leader, de Kentucky, EE.UU., encabezó el grupo de presentación en el rediseño del diario y la cobertura de muchas competencias ecuestres del Derby de Kentucky. Anteriormente fue directora de diseño del Orlando Sentinel. Ha ganado varios premios de la SND. *(L)*

**JAMILA ROBINSON** is the home editor for the St. Louis Post-Dispatch. After 11 years as an award-winning features designer — with stints at the Detroit Free Press and The Washington Post — Robinson now uses her art direction and editing experience as a foundation for alternative and creative approaches to storytelling. *(C)*

Jamila Robinson es la editora de la sección de hogar del diario St. Louis Post-Disptach. Luego de 11 años de una premiada carrera en el diseño de reportajes, con trabajos en los diarios Detroit Free Press y The Washington Post, Robinson ha dedicado su experiencia en dirección de arte y edición como base para desarrollar enfoques alternativos y creativos de narración. *(C)*

**LÉO TAVEJNHANSKY**, art director for O Globo, Rio de Janeiro, Brazil, has designed and redesigned many newspapers across Brazil. He has been working as an art director and designer since 1970. He has received SND awards, and he has spoken at two SND Annual Workshops. He is the subcommittee coordinator on design/photography at Brazil's Association of Newspapers. *(G)*

Léo Tavejnhansky, director de arte de O Globo, de Río de Janeiro, ha diseñado y rediseñado muchos periódicos en Brasil. Se ha dedicado a la dirección de arte y el diseño desde 1970. Ha sido reconocido con premios de la SND y ha dado presentaciones en dos talleres anuales de la Sociedad. Es el coordinador del subcomité de diseño y fotografía de la Asociación de Periódicos de Brasil. *(G)*

**HARRY E. WALKER**, director of McClatchy-Tribune Photo Service (MCT) and Photographer's Showcase, joined KRT, now MCT, in 1995 as deputy director. MCT is the second largest wire-photo service in the United States. Prior to joining MCT, Walker worked at the Kansas City Star (Mo.) and The Columbus Dispatch (Ohio). *(P)*

Harry E. Walker, director del servicio fotográfico de McClatchy-Tribune (MCT) y Photographer's Showcase, se integró a KRT, actualmente MCT, como subdirector en 1995. MCT es la segunda mayor agencia fotográfica de Estados Unidos. Anteriormente, Walker trabajó en los diarios norteamericanos Kansas City Star y The Columbus Dispatch. *(P)*

**PAUL WALLEN** is a sports designer at The San Diego Union-Tribune. Wallen was previously the managing editor for visuals at the Sun Journal, Lewiston, Maine, and a design editor at The Baltimore Sun. He began his career as a journalist in the U.S. Navy and has worked as a writer, editor, graphic artist and designer at a variety of small and mid-size newspapers. *(P)*

Paul Wallen es diseñador de deportes en el diario The San Diego Union-Tribune. Anteriormente Wallen fue editor ejecutivo de arte del periódico Sun Journal, de Lewiston, Maine, y editor de diseño de The Baltimore Sun. Inició su carrera como periodista en la armada norteamericana y se desempeñó como redactor, editor, artista gráfico y diseñador en varios periódicos de circulación pequeña y mediana. *(P)*

**ERIC WHITE** is the design director at the Chicago Sun-Times, supervising layout, graphics and illustration. He helped lead the team that redesigned the paper in 2003. His work has been honored by SND, the Associated Press and the Chicago Headline Club. *(L)*

Eric White es director de diseño del diario Chicago Sun-Times y supervisa la maquetación de página, los gráficos y la ilustración. Ayudó a dirigir el equipo que rediseñó el diario en el 2003. Su trabajo ha sido reconocido por la SND, la Associated Press y el Chicago Headline Club. *(L)*

# Facilitators

*The faces behind the scenes*

## THE COMPETITION

Competition committee director & judging director
**MARSHALL MATLOCK**
Syracuse University (N.Y.)

28th edition coordinator
**KRIS KINKADE**
Design editor, Kalamazoo Gazette (Mich.)

## CO-SPONSOR

S.I. Newhouse School of Public Communications
Syracuse University (N.Y.)

## JUDGING FACILITATORS

**MELISSA ANGLE**, senior designer, Orlando Sentinel (Fla.)

**STANLEY BONDY**, Syracuse University (N.Y.)

**BILL BOOTZ**, presentation editor, The Oklahoman, Oklahoma City

**RICH BOUDET**, sports designer, The Seattle Times

**ANDREW BRAFORD**, designer, The St. Petersburg Times (Fla.)

**REAGAN BRANHAM**, features designer, St. Louis Post-Dispatch

**AUDREY BURIAN**, Syracuse University (N.Y.)

**ELISE BURROUGHS**, SND executive director, North Kingstown, R.I.

**ALBERTO CAIRO**, assistant professor of graphic design and infographics, University of North Carolina, Chapel Hill

**WANDA DAMIAN**, SND office assistant, North Kingstown, R.I.

**STEVE DORSEY**, assistant managing editor for presentation, Detroit Free Press, and SND publications director

**MATT ERICKSON**, design director, The Times of Northwest Indiana, Munster, and SND Region 4 director

**JUSTIN FERRELL**, Outlook art director, The Washington Post

**RYAN FORD**, lead sports designer, Detroit Free Press

**RENEE FULLERTON**, assistant presentation editor, The Bulletin, Bend, Ore.

**BILL GASPARD**, deputy managing editor, Las Vegas Sun, and SND Foundation president

**GAYLE GRIN**, managing editor for design and graphics, National Post, Toronto, and SND vice president

**SCOTT GOLDMAN**, assistant managing editor for visuals, The Indianapolis Star, and SND president

**EMILY GORMAN**, designer, Press of Atlantic City (N.J.)

**RON JOHNSON**, editor, The Best of Newspaper Design™, Kansas State University

**KRIS KINKADE**, design editor, Kalamazoo Gazette (Mich.), and 28th edition coordinator

**LUKE KNOX**, sports designer, The Arizona Republic, Phoenix

**MEGAN LAVEY**, news designer, Arizona Daily Star, Tucson

**MATT MANSFIELD**, deputy managing editor, San Jose Mercury News (Calif.), and SND treasurer/secretary

**KENNEY MARLATT**, designer, The Indianapolis Star, and SND Web editor

**MARSHALL MATLOCK**, competition committee and judging director, Syracuse University (N.Y.)

**SEAN McNAUGHTON**, assistant professor, Syracuse University (N.Y.)

**GORDON MURRAY**, designer, The San Diego Union-Tribune

**TERENCE OLIVER**, associate professor, Ohio University, Athens

**ANNA ÖSTLUND**, project manager, Confetti, Borlange, Sweden, and president of SND/Scandinavia

**ERIC PALM**, news designer, Orlando Sentinel (Fla.)

**TIFFANY PEASE**, news designer, San Jose Mercury News (Calif.)

**BECKY PENDERGAST**, assistant managing editor for art, The Chronicle of Higher Education, Washington

**KEELI POINTER**, sports designer, Fort Worth Star-Telegram (Texas)

**BEN RAMSDEN**, Sunday front and special projects designer, Pioneer Press, St. Paul, Minn.

Collage photos by Steve Wolgast/ The New York Times. Assembly by Phill Spiker/Star Tribune & Steve Dorsey/Detroit Free Press.

**EVERYTHING'S ON THE TABLE**

**Just one of the dozens of tables of entries at the 28th Best of Newspaper Design™ competition at Syracuse University's Drumlins complex in February 2007. Above, the news team goes to work on a category of entries. From left, Susan McDonough, Joseph Hutchinson, Jay Judge and Kathy Bogen work the table.**

2,896

**The number of feet of table space needed to judge the 28th competition.**

362

**Number of 8-foot tables at the judging site.**

**DENISE M. REAGAN**, assistant managing editor for visual journalism, The Florida Times-Union, Jacksonville, and SND education and training director

**MIKE RICE**, visual team leader for design and graphics, Arizona Daily Star, Tucson

**CHRIS ROSS**, news design editor, The San Diego Union-Tribune

**CHRIS RUKAN**, sports layout editor, The Washington Post

**SUSAN SANTORO**, SND membership manager, North Kingstown, R.I.

**GREG SWANSON**, assistant managing editor for presentation, Quad-City Times, Davenport, Iowa, and SND design Quick Course director

**SHRADDHA SWAROOP**, news designer, San Jose Mercury News (Calif.)

**DENNIS VARNEY**, sports designer and copy editor, Lexington Herald-Leader (Ky.)

**SHAMUS WALKER**, SND audit and entry director, Syracuse University (N.Y.)

**MICHAEL WHITLEY**, news design director, Los Angeles Times, and SND long-range workshops director

**STEVE WOLGAST**, staff editor for news design, The New York Times

### SYRACUSE UNIVERSITY STUDENTS

Leah Copertino, Jessica Donovan, Hannah Fessler, Brittany Henning, Susie Hume, Kellyann Kanaley, Alisa Lopano, Angela Madonia, Melissa Manikowski, Carly Miglior, Jenna McKnight and Dana Moran

### OHIO UNIVERSITY STUDENTS

Allison Achberger, Rachel Conn, Nikki Davis, Alyce Jones, Brian Kennedy, Lauren Kuntz, Maggie Lyon and Elizabeth Zuhl

## THE BOOK

Editor
**RON JOHNSON**
Kansas State University

**STEVE WOLGAST**, The New York Times

**STEVE DORSEY**, Detroit Free Press

**CRISTOBAL EDWARDS**, Universidad Catolica, Santiago, Chile

**JOE JAYJACK**, The Topeka Capital-Journal (Kan.)

**LONI WOOLERY**, Wichita Magazine (Kan.)

**AMY DeVAULT**, Wichita State University

**TIM PARKS**, Omaha World Herald (Neb.)

**SARAH RICE**, Associated Collegiate Press, Minneapolis

**PAUL RESTIVO**, Olathe Northwest High School (Kan.)

**PHILL SPIKER**, Star Tribune, Minneapolis

**STEPHANIE GORGES**, Kansas State University

**MIRANDA KENNEDY**, The Kansas City Star (Mo.)

### KANSAS STATE UNIVERSITY ADVANCED-EDITING STUDENTS

Chesney Allen, Jessica Barnard, Mary Bershenyi, Eric Brown, Adrianne Deweese, Jessica Durham, Chelsea Good, Katelynn Hasler, Wendy Haun, Kristin Hodges, Leah Killebrew, Annette Lawless, Joe Moore, Elise Nimtz, Maya Ristic, Annie Shultz, Holly Smith and Ben Spicer

## THE SOCIETY

President
**SCOTT GOLDMAN**
The Indianapolis Star

Vice president
**GAYLE GRIN**
National Post, Toronto

Treasurer/Secretary
**MATT MANSFIELD**
San Jose Mercury News (Calif.)

Immediate past president
**CHRISTINE McNEAL**
Milwaukee Journal Sentinel (Wis.)

Executive director
**ELISE BURROUGHS**
North Kingstown, R.I.

President / SND Foundation
**BILL GASPARD**
Las Vegas Sun

# Index: People

# Index: People

# M



# N



# O



# P

# Index: People



## Q



## R



## S

# T

# W

# Z

# Index: Publications

# Colophon

*A note about the type*

Professional and student designers produced the 28th edition of The Best of Newspaper Design™ using InDesign CS2 on Apple Power Macs on the campus of Kansas State University, Manhattan.

Fonts used in the book:
▮ **UTOPIA** is a versatile font family created by Robert Slimbach in the late 1980s. It was intended to solve a number of typographic problems related to office correspondence. Its forms and aesthetics make it a balanced, elegant font for any use. It was influenced by the fonts Baskerville and Walbaum.
▮ **RETINA** was initially created for The Wall Street Journal redesign of April 2002. It is specifically engineered to succeed in small sizes.
▮ **WHITNEY** was developed when Tobias Frere-Jones was asked to develop an institutional typeface for New York's Whitney Museum. He had created it for both editorial typography and museum signage.

Special thanks to Jonathan Hoefler and Tobias Frere-Jones, of Hoefler & Frere-Jones, *www.typography.com*, for use of various weights and styles of Retina and Whitney.

The book was printed in a softcover format and a hardcover format by Rockport Publishers. Public copies are available through booksellers, and copies for news professionals are available through the Society for News Design, *www.snd.org*.

Also telling the story of the competition were the Society's publications — the quarterly Design Journal, Update newsletter and the Society's blog, *www.snd.org/update*. ▮

# Colofón

*Una nota sobre la tipografía*

Diseñadores profesionales y estudiantes de diseño produjeron la 28ª versión de "Lo mejor del Diseño de Periódicos"™ con el programa InDesign CS2 en computadores Power Mac de Apple, en el campus de Kansas State University, ubicado en Manhattan, Kansas, EE.UU.

Las fuentes utilizadas en el libro son las siguientes:
▮ **UTOPIA** es una versátil familia de fuentes creada por Robert Slimbach a fines de los años 80. El propósito era solucionar una serie de problemas tipográficos relacionados con la correspondencia en el trabajo. Su forma y valor estético la convierten en una fuente equilibrada y elegante para cualquier uso. Fue influenciada por las fuentes Baskerville y Walbaum.
▮ **RETINA** fue originalmente creada para el rediseño de The Wall Street Journal, en abril de 2002. Fue diseñada específicamente para funcionar con éxito en cuerpos o tamaños pequeños.
▮ **WHITNEY** fue desarrollada cuando a Tobias Frere-Jones se le encargó que creara una tipografía institucional para el museo de arte Whitney de Nueva York. La desarrolló tanto como fuente editorial como para la señalética del museo.

Un agradecimiento especial a Jonathan Hoefler y Tobias Frere-Jones, de Hoefler & Frere-Jones, *www.typography.com*, por el uso de Retina y Whitney en varios estilos y pesos o grosores.

Este libro fue impreso en un formato de tapa blanda y de tapa dura por Rockport Publishing. Los ejemplares del libro para el público general están a la venta en las liberías, y los para profesionales están disponibles a través del sitio web de la Society for News Design, *www.snd.org*.

El relato de la competencia también se encuentra en las demás publicaciones de la SND; la revista trimestral Design Journal y el boletín Update, además del blog de la SND, *www.snd.org/update*. ▮